Baseball America

2024

PROSPECT
HANDBOOK

BASEBALL AMERICA INC. DURHAM, N.C.

Baseball America
2024
PROSPECT HANDBOOK

Editors
CARLOS COLLAZO, J.J. COOPER,
MATT EDDY AND JOSH NORRIS

Assistant Editors
BEN BADLER, TEDDY CAHILL,
MARK CHIARELLI, PETER FLAHERTY,
KYLE GLASER, KAYLA LOMBARDO,
SAVANNAH MCCANN AND GEOFF PONTES

Database and Application Development
MARK TAYLOR

Contributing Writers
JON MEOLI, BILL MITCHELL,
NICK PIECORO, JEFF SANDERS,
ALEX SPEIER AND
TAYLOR BLAKE WARD

Design & Production
SETH MATES

Cover Photo
JACKSON HOLLIDAY BY
MIKE JANES/FOUR SEAM IMAGES

NO PORTION OF THIS BOOK MAY BE
REPRINTED OR REPRODUCED WITHOUT
THE WRITTEN CONSENT OF THE PUBLISHER.

FOR ADDITIONAL COPIES
VISIT OUR WEBSITE AT BASEBALLAMERICA.COM
OR CALL 1-800-845-2726 TO ORDER.

US $39.95, PLUS SHIPPING AND HANDLING PER ORDER.
EXPEDITED SHIPPING AVAILABLE.

DISTRIBUTED BY SIMON & SCHUSTER
ISBN: 979-8-9869573-3-3

STATISTICS PROVIDED BY MAJOR LEAGUE BASEBALL
ADVANCED MEDIA AND COMPILED BY
BASEBALL AMERICA

Baseball America

ESTABLISHED 1981
P.O. BOX 12877, DURHAM, NC 27709 • PHONE (800) 845-2726

EDITOR IN CHIEF J.J. Cooper *@jjcoop36*
EXECUTIVE EDITOR Matt Eddy *@MattEddyBA*
CHIEF INNOVATION OFFICER Ben Badler *@benbadler*
VICE PRESIDENT, DESIGN & STRATEGY Seth Mates *@sethmates*
HEAD OF AUDIENCE DEVELOPMENT Mark Chiarelli *@Mark_Chiarelli*
DIRECTOR OF FINANCE AND REVENUE Mike Stewart

EDITORIAL
SENIOR EDITOR Josh Norris *@jnorris427*
SENIOR WRITER Kyle Glaser *@KyleAGlaser*
NATIONAL WRITERS Teddy Cahill *@tedcahill*
Carlos Collazo *@CarlosACollazo*
Peter Flaherty *@PeterGFlaherty*
PROSPECT WRITER Geoff Pontes *@GeoffPontesBA*
SENIOR EDITOR, DIGITAL & SOCIAL Kayla Lombardo *@KaylaLombardo11*
CONTENT PRODUCER Savannah McCann *@savjaye*
SPECIAL CONTRIBUTOR Tim Newcomb *@tdnewcomb*

BUSINESS
MARKETING/OPERATIONS COORDINATOR Angela Lewis
CUSTOMER SERVICE Melissa Sunderman

STATISTICAL SERVICE
MAJOR LEAGUE BASEBALL ADVANCED MEDIA

BASEBALL AMERICA ENTERPRISES

CHAIRMAN & CEO Gary Green
PRESIDENT Larry Botel
GENERAL COUNSEL Matthew Pace
DIRECTOR OF OPERATIONS Joan Disalvo
PARTNERS Stephen Alepa
Jon Ashley
Martie Cordaro
David Geaslen
Glenn Isaacson
Sonny Kalsi
Peter R. Riguardi
Ian Ritchie
Brian Rothschild
Beryl Snyder
Tom Steiglehner

PJL MEDIA
PRESIDENT Jonathan Segal
VICE PRESIDENT, OPERATIONS B.J. Schecter

BASEBALL AMERICA is published monthly, 12 issues per year, by Baseball America
Enterprises, LLC, 650 Fifth Avenue, Suite 2400, New York, NY 10019. Subscription rate is
$109.99 for one year; Canada $112.99 (U.S. funds); all other foreign $125.99 per year (U.S.
funds). Periodicals postage paid at New York NY, & additional mailing offices. Occasionally
our subscriber list is made available to reputable firms offering goods and services we
believe would be of interest to our readers. If you prefer to be excluded, please send
your current address label and a note requesting to be excluded from these promotions
to Baseball America Enterprises, LLC, PO Box 12877, Durham, NC 27709, Attn:
Privacy Coordinator. POSTMASTER: Send all UAA to CFS (See DMM 707.4.12.5); NONPOSTAL
& MILITARY FACILITIES: send address corrections to Baseball America, P.O. Box
420235, Palm Coast, FL 32142-0235. CANADA POST: Return undeliverable Canadian
addresses to IMEX Global Solutions, P.O. Box 25542, London, ON N6C 6B2. Please contact
1-800-381-1288 to start carrying Baseball America in your store.

© 2023 by Baseball America Enterprises, LLC. All Rights Reserved. Printed in the USA.

FOREWORD

If only there were a little more time.

The Prospect Handbook is the book that devours time, because we always wish we had just a little longer to perfect a book for which perfection is an impossible goal.

If we only had an extra week to spend talking to more scouts, coaches and front office executives. If only we had more time to watch video of that intriguing teenage pitcher who popped up last year, or to compare the two infielders who both have cases to rank 30th on that other team's list.

The deadline is the deadline, and we're going to make sure we never miss it. So come mid December, time is called, and we finalize the best book we can produce in the time allotted.

To make this book as timely as possible, we always race to finish it before we break for the holidays. Doing so ensures the print edition will be in readers' hands for spring training or Opening Day. And anyone who orders the print or digital edition directly from us at Baseball America now gets a digital copy in January.

That means that even before the final out is recorded at the World Series, we're busy at work gathering reporting, stats and insights for our prospect preview of the upcoming season and beyond. While we wish we had more time, we are quite proud of the book we can produce in the time allotted. Every year we try to take last year's book and one-up it. We hope we have succeeded again.

So enjoy the 24th edition of the Baseball America Prospect Handbook. We hope you enjoy reading it as much as we enjoyed producing it. And if you have any thoughts about the book and how we can make the 2025 edition even better, feel free to email me at jj.cooper@baseballamerica.com.

J.J. Cooper
Editor in chief, Baseball America

ABOUT THIS EDITION

All BA Grades and scouting grades are projected to players' peak seasons and are assessed on the 20-80 scouting scale, where 50 is average.

Position players are graded on the five scouting tools:

HIT: hitting ability
POW: game power
RUN: speed
FLD: fielding ability
ARM: throwing arm

Pitchers are graded on pitch types they throw and their control:

FB: fastball
CB: curveball
SL: slider
CHG: changeup
CUT: cutter
SPLT: splitter
CTL: control

This year we rank two pitchers who throw knuckleballs (KNUCKLE).

Statistics generated in the affiliated minor leagues and major leagues in 2023 are presented for all players, along with their career minor league totals and career MLB totals, where applicable.

Age listed for players is their "baseball age" in 2023, i.e. their age as of June 30, 2023.

EDITOR'S NOTE: The transaction deadline for this book was Dec. 8, 2023. You can find players who changed organizations by using the index in the back.

>> For the purposes of Baseball America rankings, a prospect is any player who is signed with a major league organization and who has not exceeded 130 at-bats, 50 innings or 30 relief appearances in the major leagues, regardless of major league service time. This leads to rare instances in which a player is prospect-eligible for BA but *not* eligible for the 2024 American or National league Rookie of the Year awards because he has exceeded the MLB service time threshold of 45 days. Notable examples of prospects who are no longer ROY eligible in this year's book include Shane Baz, DL Hall, Mason Miller, Garrett Mitchell and Tyler Soderstrom.

TABLE OF CONTENTS

ARIZONA DIAMONDBACKS — STARTS ON PAGE 18

No. Player, Pos.	BA Grade/Risk	No. Player, Pos.	BA Grade/Risk	No. Player, Pos.	BA Grade/Risk
1. Jordan Lawlar, SS	60/M	11. Blake Walston, LHP	45/M	21. Dominic Fletcher, OF	40/M
2. Druw Jones, OF	60/X	12. Blaze Alexander, SS	45/M	22. Jorge Barrosa, OF	45/H
3. Tommy Troy, SS	55/H	13. Yilber Diaz, RHP	50/H	23. Caleb Roberts, OF/C	45/H
4. Ivan Melendez, 1B/3B	50/H	14. Caden Grice, LHP	50/H	24. Pedro Catuy, OF	50/X
5. Gino Groover, 3B	50/H	15. Slade Cecconi, RHP	45/M	25. Bryce Jarvis, RHP	40/M
6. Jansel Luis, 2B/SS	55/X	16. Cristofer Torin, SS	45/H	26. Christian Cerda, C	45/H
7. Yu-Min Lin, LHP	50/H	17. AJ Vukovich, OF	45/H	27. Gian Zapata, OF	50/X
8. Dylan Ray, RHP	50/H	18. Yassel Soler, 3B	50/X	28. Adrian Del Castillo, C	45/H
9. Ruben Santana, 3B	55/X	19. Grayson Hitt, LHP	50/X	29. Kristian Robinson, OF	50/X
10. Jack Hurley, OF	50/H	20. Landon Sims, RHP	50/X	30. Andrew Saalfrank, LHP	40/M

ATLANTA BRAVES — STARTS ON PAGE 34

No. Player, Pos.	BA Grade/Risk	No. Player, Pos.	BA Grade/Risk	No. Player, Pos.	BA Grade/Risk
1. AJ Smith-Shawver, RHP	55/H	11. Dylan Dodd, LHP	40/M	21. Hayden Harris, LHP	40/H
2. Hurston Waldrep, RHP	55/H	12. Darius Vines, RHP	40/M	22. Sabin Ceballos, 3B	45/X
3. JR Ritchie, RHP	55/X	13. Jhancarlos Lara, RHP	50/V	23. Luis De Avila, LHP	35/M
4. Owen Murphy, RHP	50/H	14. Lucas Braun, RHP	45/H	24. Blake Burkhalter, RHP	45/X
5. Spencer Schwellenbach, RHP	50/H	15. Jesse Franklin, OF	45/H	25. Diego Benitez, SS	45/X
6. David McCabe, 3B	45/H	16. Allan Winans, RHP	40/M	26. Cody Milligan, OF/2B	40/H
7. Drake Baldwin, C	45/H	17. Luis Guanipa, OF	50/X	27. Ian Mejia, RHP	40/H
8. Ignacio Alvarez, 3B/SS	45/H	18. Garrett Baumann, RHP	45/X	28. Douglas Glod, OF	45/X
9. Drue Hackenberg, RHP	45/H	19. Isaiah Drake, OF	45/X	29. Keshawn Ogans, 2B	40/H
10. Cade Kuehler, RHP	45/H	20. Tyler Owens, RHP	40/H	30. Ambioris Tavarez, SS	45/X

BALTIMORE ORIOLES — STARTS ON PAGE 50

No. Player, Pos.	BA Grade/Risk	No. Player, Pos.	BA Grade/Risk	No. Player, Pos.	BA Grade/Risk
1. Jackson Holliday, SS	70/M	11. Cade Povich, LHP	50/H	21. Luis Almeyda, SS	50/X
2. Samuel Basallo, C	65/H	12. Seth Johnson, RHP	50/H	22. Juan Nuñez, RHP	50/X
3. Coby Mayo, 3B	60/H	13. Dylan Beavers, OF	50/H	23. Trace Bright, RHP	45/H
4. Colton Cowser, OF	50/M	14. Jackson Baumeister, RHP	50/V	24. Justin Armbruester, RHP	45/H
5. Heston Kjerstad, OF	50/M	15. Jud Fabian, OF	50/V	25. Hudson Haskin, OF	45/H
6. DL Hall, LHP	50/M	16. Luis De Leon, LHP	50/X	26. John Rhodes, OF	45/H
7. Joey Ortiz, SS	50/M	17. Max Wagner, 3B	45/H	27. Alex Pham, RHP	45/H
8. Connor Norby, 2B/OF	50/M	18. Kyle Stowers, OF	45/H	28. Frederick Bencosme, SS	45/H
9. Enrique Bradfield Jr., OF	50/H	19. Mac Horvath, 3B	50/X	29. Kiefer Lord, RHP	45/H
10. Chayce McDermott, RHP	50/H	20. Braylin Tavera, OF	50/X	30. Keagan Gillies, RHP	45/H

BOSTON RED SOX — STARTS ON PAGE 66

No. Player, Pos.	BA Grade/Risk	No. Player, Pos.	BA Grade/Risk	No. Player, Pos.	BA Grade/Risk
1. Marcelo Mayer, SS	60/H	11. Richard Fitts, RHP	50/H	21. Blaze Jordan, 1B/3B	45/H
2. Roman Anthony, OF	60/H	12. Nazzan Zanetello, SS/OF	50/X	22. Antonio Anderson, 3B	50/X
3. Kyle Teel, C	55/H	13. Chase Meidroth, 2B/3B	45/H	23. Franklin Arias, SS	50/X
4. Ceddanne Rafaela, OF/SS	50/M	14. Johanfran Garcia, C	50/X	24. Chris Murphy, LHP	40/M
5. Miguel Bleis, OF	55/X	15. Nathan Hickey, C	45/H	25. Hunter Dobbins, RHP	45/H
6. Wilyer Abreu, OF	45/M	16. Mikey Romero, 2B/SS	50/X	26. Angel Bastardo, RHP	45/H
7. Wikelman Gonzalez, RHP	50/H	17. Allan Castro, OF	45/H	27. Justin Slaten, RHP	40/M
8. Nick Yorke, 2B	50/H	18. Yordanny Monegro, RHP	45/H	28. Brooks Brannon, C	45/X
9. Luis Perales, RHP	50/V	19. Eddinson Paulino, SS/3B	45/H	29. Elmer Rodriguez-Cruz, RHP	45/X
10. Yoeilin Cespedes, SS	55/X	20. David Hamilton, 2B/SS/OF	40/M	30. Bryan Mata, RHP	45/X

CHICAGO CUBS — STARTS ON PAGE 82

No. Player, Pos.	BA Grade/Risk	No. Player, Pos.	BA Grade/Risk	No. Player, Pos.	BA Grade/Risk
1. Pete Crow-Armstrong, OF	55/M	11. Alexander Canario, OF	45/M	21. Porter Hodge, RHP	45/H
2. Cade Horton, RHP	60/H	12. James Triantos, 3B	50/H	22. Jaxon Wiggins, RHP	50/X
3. Matt Shaw, SS	55/H	13. Matt Mervis, 1B	45/M	23. Cristian Hernandez, SS	50/X
4. Owen Caissie, OF	55/H	14. Luke Little, LHP	45/H	24. Brandon Birdsell, RHP	45/H
5. Moises Ballesteros, C	55/H	15. Luis Vazquez, SS	45/M	25. Caleb Kilian, RHP	40/M
6. Jordan Wicks, LHP	50/M	16. Daniel Palencia, RHP	45/M	26. Haydn McGeary, 1B	45/H
7. Kevin Alcantara, OF	55/V	17. B.J. Murray, 3B	45/H	27. Bailey Horn, LHP	40/M
8. Ben Brown, RHP	50/H	18. Michael Arias, RHP	50/X	28. Brody McCullough, RHP	45/H
9. Jefferson Rojas, SS	55/X	19. Pablo Aliendo, C	45/H	29. Pedro Ramirez, 2B	45/V
10. Jackson Ferris, LHP	55/X	20. Drew Gray, LHP	50/X	30. Brennen Davis, OF	45/X

CHICAGO WHITE SOX

STARTS ON PAGE 98

No.Player, Pos.	BA Grade/Risk	No.Player, Pos.	BA Grade/Risk	No.Player, Pos.	BA Grade/Risk
1. Colson Montgomery, SS	60/H	11. Ky Bush, LHP	45/M	21. Terrell Tatum, OF	45/H
2. Noah Schultz, LHP	60/V	12. George Wolkow, OF	50/X	22. Javier Mogollon, 2B	50/X
3. Nick Nastrini, RHP	55/H	13. Sean Burke, RHP	50/X	23. Jose Rodriguez, SS	45/H
4. Bryan Ramos, 3B	55/H	14. Jordan Leasure, RHP	45/H	24. Mathias LaCombe, RHP	50/X
5. Edgar Quero, C	55/H	15. Tanner McDougal, RHP	45/H	25. Shane Drohan, LHP	40/M
6. Jacob Gonzalez, SS	55/H	16. Wilfred Veras, OF	45/H	26. Braden Shewmake, SS	40/M
7. Jake Eder, LHP	50/H	17. Grant Taylor, RHP	50/X	27. Matthew Thompson, RHP	45/H
8. Cristian Mena, RHP	50/H	18. Seth Keener, RHP	45/H	28. Christian Oppor, LHP	45/H
9. Jonathan Cannon, RHP	50/H	19. Ryan Burrowes, SS	45/H	29. Juan Carela, RHP	40/H
10. Peyton Pallette, RHP	50/H	20. Jacob Burke, OF	45/H	30. Tyler Schweitzer, LHP	45/H

CINCINNATI REDS

STARTS ON PAGE 114

No.Player, Pos.	BA Grade/Risk	No.Player, Pos.	BA Grade/Risk	No.Player, Pos.	BA Grade/Risk
1. Noelvi Marte, 3B	55/M	11. Ty Floyd, RHP	50/H	21. Cole Schoenwetter, RHP	50/X
2. Rhett Lowder, RHP	55/H	12. Ricardo Cabrera, SS	50/H	22. Jacob Hurtubise, OF	40/M
3. Connor Phillips, RHP	55/H	13. Blake Dunn, OF	50/H	23. Christian Roa, RHP	45/H
4. Edwin Arroyo, SS	50/M	14. Julian Aguiar, RHP	50/H	24. Adam Serwinowski, LHP	45/H
5. Chase Petty, RHP	55/H	15. Sammy Stafura, SS	55/X	25. Ariel Almonte, OF	50/X
6. Carlos Jorge, 2B/OF	55/H	16. Lyon Richardson, RHP	50/H	26. Zach Maxwell, RHP	50/X
7. Sal Stewart, 3B	50/H	17. Carson Spiers, RHP	45/H	27. Sheng-En Lin, SS/OF	50/X
8. Leo Balcazar, SS	50/H	18. Victor Acosta, SS	45/H	28. Hunter Hollan, LHP	45/X
9. Alfredo Duno, C	55/X	19. Hector Rodriguez, OF	45/H	29. Tyler Callihan, 2B	40/M
10. Cam Collier, 3B	50/H	20. Rece Hinds, OF	50/X	30. Connor Burns, C	45/X

CLEVELAND GUARDIANS

STARTS ON PAGE 130

No.Player, Pos.	BA Grade/Risk	No.Player, Pos.	BA Grade/Risk	No.Player, Pos.	BA Grade/Risk
1. Chase DeLauter, OF	60/H	11. Joey Cantillo, LHP	50/H	21. Kahlil Watson, SS	50/X
2. Brayan Rocchio, SS	55/H	12. Welbyn Francisca, SS	55/X	22. Jose Tena, SS	45/H
3. Daniel Espino, RHP	60/X	13. Deyvison De Los Santos, 3B/1B	50/V	23. Jake Fox, OF	45/H
4. Kyle Manzardo, 1B	55/H	14. Petey Halpin, OF	45/H	24. Johnathan Rodriguez, OF	45/H
5. Juan Brito, 2B	50/H	15. Angel Genao, SS/3B	45/H	25. Cade Smith, RHP	45/H
6. Angel Martinez, 2B	50/H	16. Jackson Humphries, LHP	50/X	26. Parker Messick, LHP	45/H
7. George Valera, OF	50/H	17. Rafael Ramirez Jr., SS	50/X	27. Justin Campbell, RHP	45/V
8. Jaison Chourio, OF	50/H	18. Andrew Walters, RHP	45/H	28. Jhonkensy Noel, OF	45/V
9. Ralphy Velazquez, C	55/X	19. Dayan Frias, 3B	45/H	29. Cody Morris, RHP	45/V
10. Alex Clemmey, LHP	55/X	20. Jose Devers, SS	45/H	30. Tim Herrin, LHP	40/M

COLORADO ROCKIES

STARTS ON PAGE 146

No.Player, Pos.	BA Grade/Risk	No.Player, Pos.	BA Grade/Risk	No.Player, Pos.	BA Grade/Risk
1. Adael Amador, SS	60/H	11. Benny Montgomery, OF	55/X	21. Julio Carreras, SS	40/M
2. Chase Dollander, RHP	55/H	12. Cole Carrigg, C/SS/OF	50/H	22. Angel Chivilli, RHP	45/H
3. Yanquiel Fernandez, OF	55/H	13. Hunter Goodman, 1B/C	45/M	23. Anthony Molina, RHP	40/H
4. Jordan Beck, OF	50/H	14. Carson Palmquist, LHP	45/H	24. Juan Mejia, RHP	40/H
5. Sterlin Thompson, 2B/OF	50/H	15. Gabriel Hughes, RHP	50/X	25. Joe Rock, LHP	40/H
6. Zac Veen, OF	50/H	16. Sean Sullivan, LHP	45/H	26. Warming Bernabel, 3B	45/X
7. Dyan Jorge, SS	50/H	17. Jackson Cox, RHP	50/X	27. Victor Juarez, RHP	40/H
8. Jordy Vargas, RHP	50/H	18. Ryan Ritter, SS	45/H	28. Derek Bernard, 2B/OF	45/X
9. Drew Romo, C	50/H	19. Sean Bouchard, OF	40/H	29. Mason Albright, LHP	40/H
10. Robert Calaz, OF	55/X	20. Michael Prosecky, LHP	45/H	30. Bladimir Restituyo, OF	40/H

DETROIT TIGERS

STARTS ON PAGE 162

No.Player, Pos.	BA Grade/Risk	No.Player, Pos.	BA Grade/Risk	No.Player, Pos.	BA Grade/Risk
1. Max Clark, OF	60/H	11. Justice Bigbie, OF	50/H	21. Dylan Smith, RHP	50/X
2. Jackson Jobe, RHP	60/H	12. Hao-Yu Lee, 2B	50/H	22. Carson Rucker, 3B/SS	50/X
3. Colt Keith, 3B	55/M	13. Keider Montero, RHP	50/H	23. Izaac Pacheco, 3B	45/H
4. Jace Jung, 2B	50/M	14. Brant Hurter, LHP	45/M	24. Tyler Mattison, RHP	45/H
5. Ty Madden, RHP	50/H	15. Wilmer Flores, RHP	50/H	25. Peyton Graham, SS	50/X
6. Justyn-Henry Malloy, 3B/OF	50/M	16. Paul Wilson, LHP	55/X	26. Enrique Jimenez, C	50/X
7. Parker Meadows, OF	45/M	17. Max Anderson, 2B	45/H	27. Samuel Gil, 2B/SS	45/H
8. Kevin McGonigle, SS	50/H	18. Josue Briceño, C	50/X	28. Eddys Leonard, INF/OF	40/M
9. Dillon Dingler, C	45/M	19. Sawyer Gipson-Long, RHP	40/H	29. Cristian Santana, SS	50/X
10. Troy Melton, RHP	50/H	20. Wenceel Perez, OF/2B	45/H	30. Andre Lipcius, 3B/1B	40/M

TABLE OF CONTENTS

HOUSTON ASTROS

STARTS ON PAGE 178

No. Player, Pos.	BA Grade/Risk	No. Player, Pos.	BA Grade/Risk	No. Player, Pos.	BA Grade/Risk
1. Jacob Melton, OF	50/H	11. Jake Bloss, RHP	45/H	21. Grae Kessinger, SS	40/M
2. Luis Baez, OF	55/X	12. AJ Blubaugh, RHP	45/H	22. Shay Whitcomb, SS	40/H
3. Spencer Arrighetti, RHP	50/H	13. Miguel Ullola, RHP	50/X	23. Cam Fisher, OF	40/H
4. Brice Matthews, SS	50/H	14. MIchael Knorr, RHP	45/H	24. Nehomar Ochoa Jr., OF	45/X
5. Zach Dezenzo, 3B	50/H	15. Jose Fleury, RHP	45/H	25. Camilo Diaz, SS	45/X
6. Joey Loperfido, OF	50/H	16. Will Wagner, 3B	45/H	26. Colin Barber, OF	40/H
7. Zachary Cole, OF	50/X	17. Rhett Kouba, RHP	40/H	27. Forrest Whitley, RHP	45/X
8. Alonzo Tredwell, RHP	50/X	18. Colton Gordon, LHP	40/M	28. Alimber Santa, RHP	45/X
9. Kenedy Corona, OF	45/H	19. Nolan DeVos, RHP	45/H	29. Justin Dirden, OF	40/H
10. Andrew Taylor, RHP	45/H	20. Trey Dombroski, LHP	45/H	30. Alberto Hernandez, SS	45/X

KANSAS CITY ROYALS

STARTS ON PAGE 194

No. Player, Pos.	BA Grade/Risk	No. Player, Pos.	BA Grade/Risk	No. Player, Pos.	BA Grade/Risk
1. Blake Mitchell, C	55/X	11. Carter Jensen, C	45/H	21. Ramon Ramirez, C	50/X
2. Frank Mozzicato, LHP	50/H	12. Tyler Gentry, OF	45/H	22. Noah Cameron, LHP	45/H
3. Nick Loftin, 3B/OF	45/M	13. Austin Charles, SS	50/X	23. Matt Sauer, RHP	40/M
4. Cayden Wallace, 3B	50/H	14. Carson Roccaforte, OF	45/H	24. Hiro Wyatt, RHP	45/X
5. Anthony Veneziano, LHP	45/M	15. Javier Vaz, 2B/OF	45/H	25. Peyton Wilson, 2B/OF	40/H
6. Mason Barnett, RHP	45/H	16. John McMillon, RHP	45/H	26. Steven Zobac, RHP	40/H
7. Chandler Champlain, RHP	45/H	17. Will Klein, RHP	45/H	27. Henry Williams, RHP	40/H
8. Blake Wolters, RHP	50/X	18. Jonathan Bowlan, RHP	45/H	28. Tyson Guerrero, RHP	40/H
9. Gavin Cross, OF	45/H	19. David Sandlin, RHP	45/H	29. Eric Cerantola, RHP	40/H
10. Ben Kudrna, RHP	45/H	20. Daniel Vazquez, SS	45/H	30. Trevor Werner, 3B	45/X

LOS ANGELES ANGELS

STARTS ON PAGE 210

No. Player, Pos.	BA Grade/Risk	No. Player, Pos.	BA Grade/Risk	No. Player, Pos.	BA Grade/Risk
1. Nolan Schanuel, 1B	50/M	11. Alberto Rios, OF/C	45/H	21. Camden Minacci, RHP	40/M
2. Nelson Rada, OF	50/H	12. Dario Laverde, C	45/H	22. Jordyn Adams, OF	40/M
3. Caden Dana, RHP	50/H	13. Adrian Placencia, 2B	45/H	23. Jorge Ruiz, OF	40/H
4. Kyren Paris, SS	45/M	14. Walbert Urena, RHP	45/H	24. Werner Blakely, 3B	40/H
5. Sam Bachman, RHP	45/M	15. Felix Morrobel, SS	45/H	25. Anthony Scull, OF	40/H
6. Ben Joyce, RHP	45/H	16. Juan Flores, C	40/M	26. Adrian Acosta, RHP	40/V
7. Barrett Kent, RHP	50/X	17. Ryan Costeiu, RHP	40/M	27. Capri Ortiz, SS	40/V
8. Jack Kochanowicz, RHP	45/H	18. Kelvin Caceres, RHP	40/M	28. David Calabrese, OF	40/V
9. Denzer Guzman, SS	45/H	19. Jadiel Sanchez, OF	40/M	29. Joe Redfield Jr., OF	40/V
10. Victor Mederos, RHP	45/H	20. Joel Hurtado, RHP	40/M	30. Jorge Marcheco, RHP	40/V

LOS ANGELES DODGERS

STARTS ON PAGE 226

No. Player, Pos.	BA Grade/Risk	No. Player, Pos.	BA Grade/Risk	No. Player, Pos.	BA Grade/Risk
1. Michael Busch, 3B/2B	55/H	11. Landon Knack, RHP	45/M	21. Yeiner Fernandez, C/2B	45/H
2. Dalton Rushing, C	55/H	12. Thayron Liranzo, C	50/H	22. Gus Varland, RHP	40/M
3. Gavin Stone, RHP	50/H	13. Jonny Deluca, OF	45/M	23. Ben Casparius, RHP	45/H
4. Andy Pages, OF	55/H	14. Justin Wrobleski, LHP	45/H	24. Jose Ramos, OF	45/H
5. Nick Frasso, RHP	55/H	15. Kendall George, OF	50/X	25. Alex Freeland, SS	45/H
6. Josue De Paula, OF	55/H	16. Ronan Kopp, LHP	45/H	26. Jake Gelof, 3B	45/H
7. Kyle Hurt, RHP	50/M	17. Jorbit Vivas, 2B	45/H	27. Peter Heubeck, RHP	50/X
8. River Ryan, RHP	50/M	18. Payton Martin, RHP	50/X	28. Samuel Muñoz, OF	50/X
9. Diego Cartaya, C	50/H	19. Joendry Vargas, SS	50/X	29. John Rooney, LHP	40/M
10. Maddux Bruns, LHP	50/H	20. Austin Gauthier, 3B/SS	45/H	30. Chris Newell, OF	40/H

MIAMI MARLINS

STARTS ON PAGE 242

No. Player, Pos.	BA Grade/Risk	No. Player, Pos.	BA Grade/Risk	No. Player, Pos.	BA Grade/Risk
1. Noble Meyer, RHP	60/X	11. Jacob Miller, RHP	50/X	21. Anthony Maldonado, RHP	40/H
2. Max Meyer, RHP	55/H	12. Andres Valor, OF	50/X	22. Joe Mack, C	45/H
3. Thomas White, LHP	55/X	13. Fabian Lopez, SS	50/X	23. Patrick Monteverde, LHP	40/H
4. Xavier Edwards, 2B/OF	45/M	14. Dane Myers, OF	40/M	24. Juan De La Cruz, RHP	45/X
5. Victor Mesa Jr., OF	50/H	15. Will Banfield, C	45/H	25. Ike Buxton, RHP	40/H
6. Yiddi Cappe, 2B/SS	50/H	16. Javier Sanoja, OF/2B	45/H	26. Mark Coley, OF	40/H
7. Karson Milbrandt, RHP	50/X	17. Troy Johnston, 1B	45/H	27. Nigel Belgrave, RHP	45/X
8. Dax Fulton, LHP	50/X	18. Brock Vradenburg, 1B	45/H	28. Xavier Meachem, RHP	45/X
9. Jacob Berry, 3B	45/H	19. Kemp Alderman, OF	40/H	29. Emmett Olson, LHP	40/H
10. Jacob Amaya, SS	40/M	20. Jose Gerardo, OF	45/X	30. Torin Montgomery, 1B	40/H

MILWAUKEE BREWERS
STARTS ON PAGE 258

No. Player, Pos.	BA Grade/Risk	No. Player, Pos.	BA Grade/Risk	No. Player, Pos.	BA Grade/Risk
1. Jackson Chourio, OF	70/H	11. Yophery Rodriguez, OF	55/X	21. Jadher Areinamo, 2B/3B/SS	45/H
2. Jacob Misiorowski, RHP	60/H	12. Eric Bitonti, 3B/SS	55/X	22. Daniel Guilarte, SS	45/H
3. Jeferson Quero, C	55/H	13. Luke Adams, 3B	45/H	23. Juan Baez, SS/3B	50/X
4. Tyler Black, 3B	50/M	14. Cooper Pratt, SS	50/X	24. Eric Brown Jr., SS	45/H
5. Robert Gasser, LHP	50/M	15. Mike Boeve, 2B	45/H	25. Pedro Ibarguen, 2B/3B/OF	45/X
6. Garrett Mitchell, OF	50/H	16. Wes Clarke, 1B/C	45/H	26. Ryan Birchard, RHP	40/H
7. Luis Lara, OF	50/H	17. Bradley Blalock, RHP	45/H	27. Bishop Letson, RHP	45/X
8. Brock Wilken, 3B	50/H	18. Logan Henderson, RHP	45/H	28. Matt Wood, C	40/H
9. Carlos Rodriguez, RHP	45/M	19. Oliver Dunn, 2B	40/M	29. Filippo Di Turi, SS	45/X
10. Josh Knoth, RHP	55/X	20. Dylan O'Rae, 2B/OF/SS	45/H	30. Gregory Barrios, SS	40/H

MINNESOTA TWINS
STARTS ON PAGE 274

No. Player, Pos.	BA Grade/Risk	No. Player, Pos.	BA Grade/Risk	No. Player, Pos.	BA Grade/Risk
1. Walker Jenkins, OF	60/H	11. Luke Keaschall, 2B	50/H	21. DaShawn Keirsey Jr., OF	40/M
2. Brooks Lee, SS	55/M	12. Danny De Andrade, SS	50/H	22. Noah Miller, SS	45/H
3. Emmanuel Rodriguez, OF	55/H	13. Kala'i Rosario, OF	50/H	23. Kody Funderburk, LHP	40/M
4. David Festa, RHP	50/H	14. Zebby Matthews, RHP	50/H	24. Jordan Balazovic, RHP	40/M
5. Marco Raya, RHP	55/X	15. Brandon Winokur, OF	50/X	25. Jair Camargo, C	40/M
6. Matt Canterino, RHP	50/H	16. Connor Prielipp, LHP	50/X	26. Andrew Cossetti, C	45/H
7. Tanner Schobel, 3B	50/H	17. Cory Lewis, RHP	45/H	27. Dameury Pena, 2B	50/X
8. CJ Culpepper, RHP	50/H	18. Yasser Mercedes, OF	50/X	28. Simeon Woods Richardson, RHP	40/M
9. Austin Martin, 2B/OF	45/M	19. Yunior Severino, 1B/3B	40/M	29. Brent Headrick, LHP	40/M
10. Charlee Soto, RHP	55/X	20. Jose Rodriguez, OF	50/X	30. Michael Helman, OF/2B	40/M

NEW YORK METS
STARTS ON PAGE 290

No. Player, Pos.	BA Grade/Risk	No. Player, Pos.	BA Grade/Risk	No. Player, Pos.	BA Grade/Risk
1. Jett Williams, SS/OF	55/H	11. Brandon Sproat, RHP	50/H	21. Tyler Stuart, RHP	45/H
2. Ronny Mauricio, 2B/SS	50/M	12. Dominic Hamel, RHP	45/M	22. Boston Baro, SS/2B	50/X
3. Drew Gilbert, OF	50/M	13. Alex Ramirez, OF	50/H	23. Branny De Oleo, SS	50/X
4. Luisangel Acuña, SS/2B	50/M	14. Nolan McLean, RHP/DH	55/X	24. Ronald Hernandez, C	45/H
5. Ryan Clifford, OF/1B	55/H	15. Jacob Reimer, 3B	50/H	25. Matt Rudick, OF	45/H
6. Christian Scott, RHP	55/H	16. Jesus Baez, SS	50/H	26. Raimon Gomez, RHP	50/X
7. Blade Tidwell, RHP	50/H	17. Jeremy Rodriguez, SS	55/X	27. Calvin Ziegler, RHP	50/X
8. Colin Houck, SS	55/X	18. Marco Vargas, SS/2B	50/H	28. Joel Diaz, RHP	50/X
9. Mike Vasil, RHP	50/H	19. Jose Butto, RHP	45/M	29. Rowdey Jordan, OF	40/H
10. Kevin Parada, C	50/H	20. Kade Morris, RHP	45/H	30. Saul Garcia, RHP	40/H

NEW YORK YANKEES
STARTS ON PAGE 306

No. Player, Pos.	BA Grade/Risk	No. Player, Pos.	BA Grade/Risk	No. Player, Pos.	BA Grade/Risk
1. Jasson Dominguez, OF	60/H	11. Brando Mayea, OF	55/X	21. Keiner Delgado, SS	50/X
2. Spencer Jones, OF	60/V	12. Ben Rice, C	50/H	22. Engelth Ureña, C	50/X
3. Everson Pereira, OF	55/H	13. Carlos Lagrange, RHP	55/X	23. Jordarlin Mendoza, RHP	50/X
4. Roderick Arias, SS	60/X	14. Brock Selvidge, LHP	50/H	24. John Cruz, OF	50/X
5. Austin Wells, C	55/H	15. Trey Sweeney, SS	45/H	25. Jerson Alejandro, RHP	50/X
6. Chase Hampton, RHP	55/H	16. Clayton Beeter, RHP	45/H	26. Enmanuel Tejeda, 2B/3B	45/X
7. Henry Lalane, LHP	55/X	17. Yoendrys Gomez, RHP	40/M	27. Roc Riggio, 2B	40/H
8. George Lombard Jr., RHP	55/X	18. Luis Gil, RHP	40/M	28. TJ Rumfield, 1B	40/H
9. Will Warren, RHP	50/H	19. Agustin Ramirez, C	45/H	29. Jack Neely, RHP	40/H
10. Kyle Carr, LHP	55/X	20. Jared Serna, 2B	45/H	30. Rafael Flores, C/1B	40/H

OAKLAND ATHLETICS
STARTS ON PAGE 322

No. Player, Pos.	BA Grade/Risk	No. Player, Pos.	BA Grade/Risk	No. Player, Pos.	BA Grade/Risk
1. Mason Miller, RHP	55/H	11. Daniel Susac, C	45/H	21. Cooper Bowman, 2B	45/H
2. Tyler Soderstrom, C/1B	55/H	12. Myles Naylor, SS/3B	50/X	22. Brady Basso, LHP	45/H
3. Jacob Wilson, SS	55/H	13. Henry Bolte, OF	50/X	23. Nathan Dettmer, RHP	45/H
4. Luis Morales, RHP	60/X	14. Royber Salinas, RHP	50/X	24. Freddy Tarnok, RHP	40/M
5. Denzel Clarke, OF	55/V	15. Jack Perkins, RHP	45/H	25. Ryan Cusick, RHP	45/V
6. Lawrence Butler, OF	50/H	16. Joey Estes, RHP	45/H	26. Cesar Gonzalez, C	45/X
7. Darell Hernaiz, SS	50/H	17. Brett Harris, 3B	45/H	27. Mitch Spence, RHP	40/H
8. Joe Boyle, RHP	55/X	18. Ryan Lasko, OF	45/H	28. Jonah Cox, OF	40/H
9. Max Muncy, SS	50/H	19. Cole Miller, RHP	50/X	29. Will Simpson, 1B	40/H
10. Steven Echavarria, RHP	50/X	20. Colby Thomas, OF	50/X	30. Jacob Watters, RHP	45/X

L = Low.   M = Medium.   H = High.   V = Very High.   X= Extreme.

TABLE OF CONTENTS

PHILADELPHIA PHILLIES
STARTS ON PAGE 338

No. Player, Pos.	BA Grade/Risk	No. Player, Pos.	BA Grade/Risk	No. Player, Pos.	BA Grade/Risk
1. Andrew Painter, RHP	70/X	11. Griff McGarry, RHP	50/X	21. Kehden Hettiger, C	50/X
2. Justin Crawford, OF	55/H	12. Devin Saltiban, SS	50/X	22. Simon Muzziotti, OF	40/M
3. Mick Abel, RHP	55/H	13. TJayy Walton, OF	50/X	23. Emaarion Boyd, OF	45/X
4. Aidan Miller, 3B	55/X	14. Carlos De La Cruz, OF	45/X	24. Hendry Mendez, OF	45/X
5. Starlyn Caba, SS	55/X	15. Samuel Aldegheri, LHP	45/H	25. Andrew Baker, RHP	40/H
6. Orion Kerkering, RHP	45/M	16. Christian McGowan, RHP	45/H	26. George Klassen, RHP	40/H
7. Bryan Rincon, SS	50/H	17. Alex McFarlane, RHP	50/X	27. Tommy McCollum, RHP	40/H
8. William Bergolla Jr., SS	50/H	18. Wen Hui Pan, RHP	45/H	28. Jacob Eddington, RHP	40/H
9. Eduardo Tait, C	55/X	19. Caleb Ricketts, C	45/H	29. Cam Brown, RHP	40/H
10. Gabriel Rincones Jr., OF	45/H	20. Raylin Heredia, OF	50/X	30. Enrique Segura, RHP	45/X

PITTSBURGH PIRATES
STARTS ON PAGE 354

No. Player, Pos.	BA Grade/Risk	No. Player, Pos.	BA Grade/Risk	No. Player, Pos.	BA Grade/Risk
1. Paul Skenes, RHP	65/H	11. Mitch Jebb, SS	45/H	21. Jackson Wolf, LHP	40/M
2. Bubba Chandler, RHP	55/H	12. Jack Brannigan, SS/3B	45/H	22. Alika Williams, SS	40/M
3. Jared Jones, RHP	55/H	13. Kyle Nicolas, RHP	40/M	23. Estuar Suero, OF	50/X
4. Termarr Johnson, 2B	55/H	14. Michael Burrows, RHP	40/M	24. Garret Forrester, 3B	40/H
5. Anthony Solometo, LHP	55/H	15. Matt Gorski, OF	40/M	25. Carlson Reed, RHP	40/H
6. Thomas Harrington, RHP	50/H	16. Zander Mueth, RHP	50/X	26. Jase Bowen, OF	40/H
7. Tsung-Che Cheng, SS	50/H	17. Lonnie White Jr., OF	50/X	27. Tres Gonzalez, OF	40/H
8. Quinn Priester, RHP	45/M	18. Hunter Barco, LHP	50/X	28. Brandan Bidois, RHP	45/X
9. Nick Gonzales, 2B	45/M	19. Jun-Seok Shim, RHP	50/X	29. Colin Selby, RHP	40/H
10. Braxton Ashcraft, RHP	50/H	20. Michael Kennedy, LHP	45/H	30. Tony Blanco Jr., OF	45/X

ST. LOUIS CARDINALS
STARTS ON PAGE 370

No. Player, Pos.	BA Grade/Risk	No. Player, Pos.	BA Grade/Risk	No. Player, Pos.	BA Grade/Risk
1. Masyn Winn, SS	55/M	11. Sam Robberse, RHP	45/H	21. Edwin Nuñez, RHP	45/H
2. Tekoah Roby, RHP	60/X	12. Max Rajcic, RHP	45/H	22. Zack Showalter, RHP	50/X
3. Victor Scott II, OF	55/H	13. Won-Bin Cho, OF	50/X	23. Quinn Mathews, LHP	45/H
4. Tink Hence, RHP	55/H	14. Michael McGreevy, RHP	40/M	24. Nick Robertson, RHP	40/M
5. Thomas Saggese, 2B	50/M	15. Jimmy Crooks, C	45/H	25. Drew Rom, LHP	40/M
6. Ivan Herrera, C	45/M	16. Travis Honeyman, OF	50/X	26. Luken Baker, 1B	40/M
7. Chase Davis, OF	55/X	17. Cesar Prieto, 2B	45/H	27. Pete Hansen, LHP	40/H
8. Cooper Hjerpe, LHP	50/H	18. Zach Levenson, OF	45/H	28. Adam Kloffenstein, RHP	40/H
9. Gordon Graceffo, RHP	50/H	19. Pedro Pages, C	45/H	29. Ryan Fernandez, RHP	40/H
10. Leonardo Bernal, C	50/X	20. Brycen Mautz, LHP	45/H	30. Joshua Baez, OF	45/X

SAN DIEGO PADRES
STARTS ON PAGE 386

No. Player, Pos.	BA Grade/Risk	No. Player, Pos.	BA Grade/Risk	No. Player, Pos.	BA Grade/Risk
1. Ethan Salas, C	70/V	11. Jakob Marsee, OF	45/M	21. Blake Dickerson, LHP	50/X
2. Jackson Merrill, SS	60/H	12. Randy Vasquez, RHP	45/M	22. Kannon Kemp, RHP	50/X
3. Robby Snelling, LHP	60/H	13. Ryan Bergert, RHP	50/X	23. Ray Kerr, LHP	40/M
4. Dylan Lesko, RHP	60/X	14. J.D. Gonzalez, C	50/X	24. Matt Waldron, RHP	40/M
5. Drew Thorpe, RHP	55/H	15. Homer Bush Jr., OF	45/H	25. Alek Jacob, RHP	40/M
6. Samuel Zavala, OF	55/V	16. Eguy Rosario, 2B/3B	40/M	26. Marcos Castañon, 3B/2B	40/H
7. Dillon Head, OF	55/X	17. Nathan Martorella, 1B	45/H	27. Jagger Haynes, LHP	45/X
8. Jairo Iriarte, RHP	50/H	18. Victor Lizarraga, RHP	45/H	28. Brandon Valenzuela, C	40/H
9. Adam Mazur, RHP	50/H	19. Braden Nett, RHP	50/X	29. Garrett Hawkins, RHP	45/X
10. Graham Pauley, 3B	50/X	20. Isaiah Lowe, RHP	50/X	30. Austin Krob, LHP	40/H

SAN FRANCISCO GIANTS
STARTS ON PAGE 402

No. Player, Pos.	BA Grade/Risk	No. Player, Pos.	BA Grade/Risk	No. Player, Pos.	BA Grade/Risk
1. Kyle Harrison, LHP	60/H	11. Vaun Brown, OF	50/H	21. Eric Silva, RHP	45/X
2. Marco Luciano, SS	55/H	12. Keaton Winn, RHP	45/H	22. Cole Foster, SS	40/H
3. Bryce Eldridge, OF/RHP	60/X	13. Joe Whitman, LHP	50/H	23. Diego Velasquez, SS/2B	40/H
4. Carson Whisenhunt, LHP	50/H	14. Landen Roupp, RHP	45/H	24. Adrian Sugastey, C	40/H
5. Walker Martin, SS	55/X	15. Wade Meckler, OF	40/H	25. Heliot Ramos, OF	40/H
6. Hayden Birdsong, RHP	50/H	16. Aeverson Arteaga, SS	45/H	26. Ryan Murphy, RHP	40/H
7. Rayner Arias, OF	55/X	17. Onil Perez, C	45/H	27. William Kempner, RHP	40/H
8. Mason Black, RHP	50/H	18. Maui Ahuna, SS	50/X	28. Jose Cruz, RHP	40/H
9. Reggie Crawford, LHP/1B	55/X	19. Trevor McDonald, RHP	40/H	29. Gerelmi Maldonado, RHP	45/X
10. Grant McCray, OF	50/H	20. Carson Seymour, RHP	40/H	30. Liam Simon, RHP	45/X

SEATTLE MARINERS

STARTS ON PAGE 418

No. Player, Pos.	BA Grade/Risk	No. Player, Pos.	BA Grade/Risk	No. Player, Pos.	BA Grade/Risk
1. Cole Young, SS	55/H	11. Jonatan Clase, OF	50/H	21. Walter Ford, RHP	50/X
2. Harry Ford, C	55/H	12. Prelander Berroa, RHP	50/H	22. Spencer Packard, OF	40/M
3. Colt Emerson, SS	55/H	13. Tai Peete, SS/OF	55/X	23. Michael Morales, RHP	45/H
4. Lazaro Montes, OF	55/V	14. Zach DeLoach, OF	45/M	24. Darren Bowen, RHP	45/V
5. Gabriel Gonzalez, OF	55/V	15. Taylor Dollard, RHP	45/M	25. Brock Rodden, 2B/3B	40/H
6. Tyler Locklear, 1B	50/H	16. Ben Williamson, 3B	40/H	26. Jimmy Joyce, RHP	40/H
7. Felnin Celesten, SS	55/X	17. Ryan Bliss, 2B/SS	45/M	27. Hogan Windish, 1B	40/H
8. Jonny Farmelo, OF	55/X	18. Teddy McGraw, RHP	50/X	28. Troy Taylor, RHP	40/H
9. Michael Arroyo, 2B	55/X	19. Aidan Smith, OF	50/X	29. Reid VanScoter, LHP	40/H
10. Emerson Hancock, RHP	45/M	20. Alberto Rodriguez, OF	45/H	30. Jeter Martinez, RHP	45/X

TAMPA BAY RAYS

STARTS ON PAGE 434

No. Player, Pos.	BA Grade/Risk	No. Player, Pos.	BA Grade/Risk	No. Player, Pos.	BA Grade/Risk
1. Junior Caminero, 3B/SS	70/H	11. Colton Ledbetter, OF	50/H	21. Brailer Guerrero, OF	50/X
2. Carson Williams, SS	60/H	12. Santiago Suarez, RHP	50/H	22. Tre' Morgan, 1B	45/H
3. Curtis Mead, 3B	50/M	13. Marcus Johnson, RHP	50/H	23. Willy Vasquez, 3B	50/X
4. Shane Baz, RHP	60/X	14. Jose Urbina, RHP	50/X	24. Mason Auer, OF	50/X
5. Xavier Isaac, 1B	55/H	15. Mason Montgomery, LHP	45/H	25. Kameron Misner, OF	45/H
6. Brayden Taylor, 3B	55/H	16. Ian Seymour, LHP	45/H	26. Jacob Lopez, LHP	40/M
7. Osleivis Basabe, SS	45/M	17. Austin Shenton, 1B/3B	40/M	27. Ben Peoples, RHP	45/H
8. Adrian Santana, SS	55/X	18. Chandler Simpson, OF	45/H	28. Dru Baker, OF	45/H
9. Dominic Keegan, C	50/H	19. Cole Wilcox, RHP	45/H	29. Cooper Kinney, 2B	50/X
10. Yoniel Curet, RHP	55/X	20. Shane Sasaki, OF	45/H	30. Erick Lara, SS/3B	50/X

TEXAS RANGERS

STARTS ON PAGE 450

No. Player, Pos.	BA Grade/Risk	No. Player, Pos.	BA Grade/Risk	No. Player, Pos.	BA Grade/Risk
1. Evan Carter, OF	65/M	11. Aaron Zavala, OF	50/H	21. Yeison Morrobel, OF	45/X
2. Wyatt Langford, OF	70/H	12. Jack Leiter, RHP	50/H	22. Liam Hicks, C	40/H
3. Sebastian Walcott, SS	60/X	13. Aidan Curry, RHP	50/H	23. Alejandro Rosario, RHP	40/H
4. Justin Foscue, 2B	50/M	14. Emiliano Teodo, RHP	50/H	24. Josh Stephan, RHP	40/H
5. Owen White, RHP	45/L	15. Abimelec Ortiz, 1B	45/H	25. Skylar Hales, RHP	40/H
6. Dustin Harris, OF	50/H	16. Echedry Vargas, SS/2B	50/X	26. Zak Kent, RHP	40/H
7. Brock Porter, RHP	55/X	17. Jose Corniell, RHP	45/H	27. Caden Scarborough, RHP	45/X
8. Cameron Cauley, SS	50/H	18. Braylin Morel, OF	50/X	28. Mitchell Bratt, LHP	40/H
9. Kumar Rocker, RHP	55/X	19. Gleider Figuereo, 3B	50/X	29. Joseph Montalvo, RHP	40/H
10. Anthony Gutierrez, OF	55/X	20. Izack Tiger, RHP	50/X	30. Jonathan Ornelas, SS/OF	40/H

TORONTO BLUE JAYS

STARTS ON PAGE 466

No. Player, Pos.	BA Grade/Risk	No. Player, Pos.	BA Grade/Risk	No. Player, Pos.	BA Grade/Risk
1. Ricky Tiedemann, LHP	65/V	11. Enmanuel Bonilla, OF	50/X	21. Spencer Horwitz, 1B	40/M
2. Orelvis Martinez, SS	55/H	12. Yosver Zulueta, RHP	50/X	22. Hagen Danner, RHP	40/M
3. Arjun Nimmala, SS	55/X	13. Landen Maroudis, RHP	50/X	23. Fernando Perez, RHP	45/X
4. Brandon Barriera, LHP	55/X	14. Chad Dallas, RHP	45/H	24. T.J. Brock, RHP	40/H
5. Addison Barger, SS	50/H	15. Josh Kasevich, SS	45/H	25. Nolan Perry, RHP	45/X
6. Kendry Rojas, LHP	55/X	16. Adam Macko, LHP	45/H	26. Mason Fluharty, LHP	40/H
7. Leo Jimenez, SS	45/H	17. Juaron Watts-Brown, RHP	45/H	27. Hayden Juenger, RHP	40/H
8. Davis Schneider, 2B	40/M	18. Dahian Santos, RHP	50/X	28. Sam Shaw, 2B	45/X
9. Alan Roden, OF	45/H	19. Damiano Palmegiani, 3B	45/H	29. Tucker Toman, 3B	45/X
10. Connor Cooke, RHP	45/H	20. Jace Bohrofen, OF	45/H	30. Cade Doughty, 2B	40/H

WASHINGTON NATIONALS

STARTS ON PAGE 482

No. Player, Pos.	BA Grade/Risk	No. Player, Pos.	BA Grade/Risk	No. Player, Pos.	BA Grade/Risk
1. Dylan Crews, OF	70/H	11. Daylen Lile, OF	45/H	21. Drew Millas, C	40/H
2. James Wood, OF	65/H	12. Jake Bennett, LHP	45/H	22. Cole Henry, RHP	45/X
3. Brady House, 3B	55/H	13. Travis Sykora, RHP	50/X	23. Kevin Made, SS	40/H
4. Cade Cavalli, RHP	55/V	14. DJ Herz, LHP	45/H	24. Jeremy De La Rosa, OF	45/X
5. Yohandy Morales, 3B	55/V	15. Trey Lipscomb, 3B	40/M	25. Armando Cruz, SS	45/X
6. Jackson Rutledge, RHP	50/H	16. Nasim Nunez, SS	45/H	26. Darren Baker, 2B	40/H
7. Robert Hassell III, OF	50/V	17. Jacob Young, OF	40/M	27. TJ White, 1B	45/X
8. Cristhian Vaquero, OF	55/X	18. Andrew Pinckney, OF	45/H	28. Mitchell Parker, LHP	40/V
9. Elijah Green, OF	50/X	19. Zach Brzykcy, RHP	45/V	29. Andrew Alvarez, LHP	40/V
10. Jarlin Susana, RHP	50/X	20. Israel Pineda, C	40/H	30. Andry Lara, RHP	40/X

BA GRADES

For the 13th year, Baseball America has assigned Grades and Risk Factors for each of the 900 prospects in the Prospect Handbook. For the BA Grade, we used a 20-to-80 scale, similar to the scale scouts use, to keep it familiar. However, most major league clubs put an overall numerical grade on players, called Overall Future Potential or OFP. Often, the OFP is merely an average of the player's tools.

The BA Grade is not an OFP. It's a measure of a prospect's value, and it attempts to gauge the player's realistic ceiling. We've continued to adjust our grades to try to be more realistic, and less optimistic, and keep refining the grade-vetting process. The majority of the players in this book rest in the 50 High/45 Medium range, because the vast majority of worthwhile prospects in the minors are players who either have a chance to be everyday regulars but are far from that possibility, or players who are closer to

BA GRADE
50 Risk: High

the majors but who are likely to be role players and useful contributors. Few future franchise players or perennial all-stars graduate from the minors in any given year. The goal of the Grade/Risk system is to allow readers to take a quick look at how strong their team's farm system is, and how much immediate help the big league club can expect from its prospects. Got a minor leaguer who was traded from one organization to the other after the book went to press? Use the player's Grade/Risk and see where he would rank in his new system.

It also helps with our Organization Rankings, but those will not simply flow, in formulaic fashion, from the Grade/Risk results because we incorporate a lot of factors into our talent rankings, including the differences in risk between pitchers and hitters. Hitters have a lower injury risk and therefore are safer bets.

BA Grade Scale

GRADE	HITTER ROLE	PITCHER ROLE	EXAMPLES
75-80	Franchise Player	No. 1 starter	Shohei Ohtani, Ronald Acuña Jr., Gerrit Cole
65-70	Perennial All-Star	No. 2 starter	Freddie Freeman, Nolan Arenado, Aaron Nola
60	Occasional All-Star	No. 3 starter, Game's best reliever	Kyle Tucker, Luis Robert, Josh Hader
55	First-Division Regular	No. 3/No. 4 starter, Elite closer	Nick Castellanos, Ian Happ, Logan Gilbert
50	Solid-Average Regular	No. 4 starter, Elite set-up reliever	Alex Verdugo, Brandon Drury, Alex Cobb
45	Second-Division Regular/Platoon	No. 5 starter, Middle reliever	J.D. Davis, Maikel Garcia, Kyle Gibson
40	Reserve	Fill-in starter, Low-leverage reliever	Rodolfo Castro, Dominic Leone, Ty Blach

RISK FACTORS

LOW: Likely to reach realistic ceiling, certain big league career barring injury.

MEDIUM: Some work left to refine their tools, but a polished player.

HIGH: Most top draft picks in their first seasons, players with plenty of projection left, players with a significant flaw left to correct or players whose injury history is worrisome.

VERY HIGH: Recent draft picks with a limited track record of success or injury issues.

EXTREME: Teenagers in Rookie ball, players with significant injury histories or players who struggle with a key skill (especially control for pitchers or strikeout rate for hitters).

Explaining The 20-80 Scouting Scale

None of the authors of the Prospect Handbook is a scout, but we all have spoken to plenty of scouts to report on the prospects and scouting reports enclosed. So we use their lingo, including the 20-80 scouting scale. Many of these grades are measurable data, such as fastball velocity and speed (usually timed from home to first or in workouts over 60 yards). A fastball grade doesn't stem solely from its velocity—command and life are crucial elements as well. A 100 mph fastball with poor movement characteristics may grade below a 97 mph fastball with elite movement. Secondary pitches are graded in a similar fashion. The more swings and misses a pitch induces from hitters and the sharper the bite of the movement, the better the grade.

Velocity steadily has increased over the past decade. Not all that long ago an 88-91 mph fastball was considered major league average, but current data show it is now below-average. Big league starting pitchers now sit 93 mph on average. You can reduce the scale by 1 mph for lefthanders, whose velocities are usually slightly lower. Fastballs earn their grades based on the average range of the pitch over the course of a typical outing, not their peak velocity.

A move to the bullpen complicates in another direction. Pitchers airing it out for one inning should throw harder than someone trying to last six or seven innings, so add 1-2 mph for relievers.

Hitting ability is as much a skill as it is a tool, but the physical elements—hand-eye coordination, swing mechanics, bat speed—are key factors in how it is graded. Raw power generally is measured by how far a player can hit the ball, but game power is graded by how many home runs the hitter projects to hit in the majors, preferably an average over the course of a career. We have tweaked our power grades based on the recent rise in home run rates.

Arm strength can be evaluated by observing the velocity and carry of throws, measured in workouts with radar guns or measured in games for catchers with pop times—the time it takes from the pop of the ball in the catcher's mitt to the pop of the ball in the fielder's glove at second base. Defense takes different factors into account by position but starts with proper footwork and technique, incorporates physical attributes such as hands, short-area quickness and fluid actions, then adds subtle skills such as instincts and anticipation.

Not every team uses the wording below. Some use a 2-to-8 scale without half-grades, and others use above-average and plus synonymously. For the Handbook, consider this BA's 20-80 scale.

20: As bad as it gets for a big leaguer. Think Myles Straw's power or Daniel Vogelbach's speed.

30: Poor, but not unplayable, such as Kyle Hendricks' fastball.

40: Below-average, such as Rafael Devers' defense or Dylan Cease's control.

45: Fringe-average. Matt Chapman's hitting ability and Mike Zunino's arm qualify.

50: Major league average. Jeff McNeil's speed.

55: Above-average. Randy Arozarena's power.

60: Plus. Marcus Semien's defense or Zac Gallen's control.

70: Plus-Plus. Among the best tools in the game, such as Freddie Freeman's hitting ability, Blake Snell's curveball and Ronald Acuña Jr.'s arm.

80: Top of the scale. Some scouts consider only one player's tool in all of the major leagues to be 80. Think of Shohei Ohtani's power, Corbin Carroll's speed or Devin Williams' changeup.

20-80 Measurables

HIT	POWER	SPEED		FASTBALL	ARM STRENGTH
Grade Batting Avg	Grade Home Runs	Home-First (In Secs.)		Velocity (Starters)	Catcher: Pop
		RHH—LHH		Grade Velocity	Times To Second
80 . . . . .315+	80 . . . . .40+	80 . . .4.00—3.90		80 . . . . .98+ mph	Base (In Seconds)
70 . . . . . .295-.314	70 34-39	70 . . . .4.10—4.00		70 97	80 . . . . < 1.90
60 . . . . .275-.294	60 28-33	65 . . . .4.15—4.05		65 96	70 . . . . . .1.90-1.94
55 . . . . .265-.274	55 23-27	60 . . . .4.20—4.10		60 95	60 . . . . . .1.95-1.99
50 . . . . .255-.264	50 19-22	55 . . . .4.25—4.15		55 94	50 . . . . . .2.00-2.04
45 . . . . .245-.254	45 14-18	50 . . . .4.30—4.20		50 93	40 . . . . . .2.05-2.09
40 . . . . .235-.244	40 10-13	45 . . . .4.35—4.25		45 92	30 . . . . . .2.10-2.14
30 . . . . .215-.234	30 5-9	40 . . . .4.40—4.30		40 90-91	20 . . . . > 2.15
20 . . . . <.215	20 0-4	30 . . . .4.50—4.40		30 88-89	
		20 . . . .4.60—4.50		20 . . . . .87 or less	

AN OVERVIEW

Another feature of the Prospect Handbook is a depth chart of every organization's minor league talent. This shows you at a glance what kind of talent a system has and provides even more prospects beyond the Top 30.

Players are usually listed on the depth charts where we think they'll ultimately end up. To help you better understand why players are slotted at particular positions, we show you here what scouts look for in the ideal candidate at each spot, with individual tools ranked in descending order.

LF
- Power
- Hitting
- Fielding
- Arm Strength
- Speed

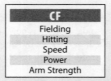

CF
- Fielding
- Hitting
- Speed
- Power
- Arm Strength

RF
- Power
- Hitting
- Arm Strength
- Fielding
- Speed

3B
- Power
- Hitting
- Fielding
- Arm Strength
- Speed

SS
- Fielding
- Arm Strength
- Hitting
- Power
- Speed

2B
- Hitting
- Fielding
- Power
- Speed
- Arm Strength

1B
- Power
- Hitting
- Fielding
- Arm Strength
- Speed

C
- Fielding
- Hitting
- Arm Strength
- Power
- Speed

STARTING PITCHERS

No. 1 starter	No. 2 starter	No. 3 starter	No. 4-5 starters
• Two plus pitches	• Two plus pitches	• One plus pitch	• Command of two major league pitches
• Average third pitch	• Average third pitch	• Two average pitches	• Average velocity
• Plus-plus command	• Average command	• Average command	• Consistent breaking ball
• Plus makeup	• Average makeup	• Average makeup	• Decent changeup

CLOSER
- One dominant pitch
- Second plus pitch
- Plus command
- Plus-plus makeup

SETUP MAN
- Plus fastball
- Second above-average pitch
- Average command

POSITION RANKINGS

Context is crucial to prospect evaluations. So, to provide yet another layer of context, we rank prospects at all eight field positions plus righthanded and lefthanded starting pitchers. The rankings go deeper at the glamour positions, i.e. shortstop, center field and righthanded starter.

We grade players' tools on the 20-80 scouting scale, where 50 is average. The tools listed for position players are ability to hit for average (HIT), hit for power (POW), speed (SPD), fielding ability (FLD) and throwing arm (ARM). The tools listed for pitchers are fastball (FB), curveball (CB), slider (SL), changeup (CHG), other (OTH) and control (CTL). The "other" category can be a splitter, cutter or screwball.

Included as the final categories are BA Grades and Risk levels on a scale ranging from low to extreme.

CATCHER

No	Player	Org	HIT	POW	RUN	FLD	ARM	BA Grade	Risk
1.	Ethan Salas	Padres	60	60	45	70	60	70	Very High
2.	Samuel Basallo	Orioles	55	70	40	45	70	65	High
3.	Jeferson Quero	Brewers	50	50	40	70	60	55	High
4.	Tyler Soderstrom	Athletics	50	60	40	45	55	55	High
5.	Dalton Rushing	Dodgers	45	65	45	45	55	55	High
6.	Harry Ford	Mariners	50	50	60	45	55	55	High
7.	Kyle Teel	Red Sox	55	45	50	55	55	55	High
8.	Edgar Quero	White Sox	55	45	30	45	50	55	High
9.	Moises Ballesteros	Cubs	60	50	20	40	55	55	High
10.	Austin Wells	Yankees	45	55	30	40	40	55	High

FIRST BASE

No	Player	Org	HIT	POW	RUN	FLD	ARM	BA Grade	Risk
1.	Kyle Manzardo	Guardians	50	55	20	50	50	55	High
2.	Xavier Isaac	Rays	55	65	40	50	50	55	High
3.	Nolan Schanuel	Angels	60	50	40	50	50	50	Medium
4.	Ryan Clifford	Mets	55	55	30	50	70	55	High
5.	Tyler Locklear	Mariners	45	65	40	45	50	50	High
6.	Ivan Melendez	D-backs	40	60	35	50	55	50	High
7.	Deyvison De Los Santos	Guardians	40	60	50	40	50	50	Very High
8.	Blaze Jordan	Red Sox	45	55	40	40	60	45	High
9.	Abimelec Ortiz	Rangers	40	55	30	40	40	45	High
10.	Troy Johnston	Marlins	45	60	30	50	45	45	High

SECOND BASE

No	Player	Org	HIT	POW	RUN	FLD	ARM	BA Grade	Risk
1.	Termarr Johnson	Pirates	55	50	50	50	50	55	High
2.	Thomas Saggese	Cardinals	55	50	45	45	45	50	Medium
3.	Ronny Mauricio	Mets	40	55	55	50	60	50	Medium
4.	Justin Foscue	Rangers	60	50	30	40	40	50	Medium
5.	Connor Norby	Orioles	55	50	50	45	40	50	Medium
6.	Luisangel Acuña	Mets	50	40	60	60	60	50	Medium
7.	Jace Jung	Tigers	45	60	40	45	50	50	Medium
8.	Carlos Jorge	Reds	60	40	60	50	50	55	High
9.	Nick Yorke	Red Sox	55	45	40	50	45	50	High
10.	Michael Arroyo	Mariners	55	45	40	45	55	55	Extreme

THIRD BASE

No	Player	Org	HIT	POW	RUN	FLD	ARM	BA Grade	Risk
1.	Junior Caminero	Rays	55	80	55	50	60	70	High
2.	Noelvi Marte	Reds	55	60	45	55	60	55	Medium
3.	Colt Keith	Tigers	60	60	45	40	50	55	Medium
4.	Coby Mayo	Orioles	50	70	45	50	70	60	High
5.	Michael Busch	Dodgers	55	60	45	40	40	55	High
6.	Brady House	Nationals	50	60	50	55	60	55	High
7.	Tyler Black	Brewers	60	45	60	40	45	50	Medium
8.	Brayden Taylor	Rays	60	50	50	50	50	55	High
9.	Bryan Ramos	White Sox	55	55	45	50	55	55	High
10.	Tanner Schobel	Twins	55	40	50	55	50	50	High

POSITION RANKINGS

SHORTSTOP

No	Player	Org	HIT	POW	RUN	FLD	ARM	BA Grade	Risk
1.	Jackson Holliday	Orioles	70	55	60	55	50	70	Medium
2.	Jordan Lawlar	D-backs	60	55	70	55	60	60	Medium
3.	Jackson Merrill	Padres	60	55	50	55	55	60	High
4.	Marcelo Mayer	Red Sox	55	60	40	60	60	60	High
5.	Colson Montgomery	White Sox	55	60	45	55	55	60	High
6.	Carson Williams	Rays	40	60	55	65	70	60	High
7.	Brooks Lee	Twins	60	50	50	50	50	55	Medium
8.	Masyn Winn	Cardinals	55	45	60	55	80	55	Medium
9.	Adael Amador	Rockies	70	50	55	50	45	60	High
10.	Marco Luciano	Giants	50	60	40	50	60	55	High
11.	Brayan Rocchio	Guardians	50	50	55	60	50	55	High
12.	Cole Young	Mariners	60	45	50	55	50	55	High
13.	Joey Ortiz	Orioles	50	45	50	70	55	50	Medium
14.	Matt Shaw	Cubs	55	55	50	45	45	55	High
15.	Jacob Wilson	Athletics	60	40	50	55	55	55	High
16.	Tommy Troy	D-backs	55	55	50	50	50	55	High
17.	Roderick Arias	Yankees	55	60	55	60	70	60	Extreme
18.	Sebastian Walcott	Rangers	50	60	55	45	60	60	Extreme
19.	Colt Emerson	Mariners	60	50	45	50	55	55	High
20.	Orelvis Martinez	Blue Jays	45	60	45	45	60	55	High
21.	Jacob Gonzalez	White Sox	55	50	30	50	55	55	High
22.	Jefferson Rojas	Cubs	55	55	50	50	55	55	Extreme
23.	Starlyn Caba	Phillies	60	40	60	60	55	55	Extreme
24.	Colin Houck	Mets	55	55	55	55	55	55	Extreme
25.	Felnin Celesten	Mariners	50	60	60	55	60	55	Extreme

CENTER FIELD

No	Player	Org	HIT	POW	RUN	FLD	ARM	BA Grade	Risk
1.	Jackson Chourio	Brewers	60	70	70	60	45	70	High
2.	Evan Carter	Rangers	65	50	80	60	50	65	Medium
3.	Dylan Crews	Nationals	65	65	55	55	60	70	High
4.	Pete Crow-Armstrong	Cubs	55	45	60	80	55	55	Medium
5.	Jasson Dominguez	Yankees	55	60	60	50	60	60	High
6.	Max Clark	Tigers	60	50	70	60	70	60	High
7.	Roman Anthony	Red Sox	50	60	50	55	55	60	High
8.	Jett Williams	Mets	60	50	60	50	55	55	High
9.	Justin Crawford	Phillies	50	40	70	55	50	55	High
10.	Victor Scott II	Cardinals	55	40	80	70	50	55	High

CORNER OUTFIELD

No	Player	Org	HIT	POW	RUN	FLD	ARM	BA Grade	Risk
1.	Wyatt Langford	Rangers	60	70	50	45	45	70	High
2.	James Wood	Nationals	50	65	55	50	55	65	High
3.	Walker Jenkins	Twins	60	65	55	55	60	60	High
4.	Chase DeLauter	Guardians	50	60	55	50	60	60	High
5.	Spencer Jones	Yankees	40	60	55	50	50	60	Very High
6.	Owen Caissie	Cubs	40	60	55	55	60	55	High
7.	Andy Pages	Dodgers	40	60	45	50	70	55	High
8.	Heston Kjerstad	Orioles	50	60	45	45	55	50	Medium
9.	Josue De Paula	Dodgers	60	55	45	30	55	55	High
10.	Bryce Eldridge	Giants	50	60	30	50	55	60	Extreme

RIGHTHANDER

No	Pitcher	Team	FB	CB	SL	CHG	OTH	CTL	BA Grade	Risk
1.	Paul Skenes	Pirates	70	—	70	60	—	60	65	High
2.	Andrew Painter	Phillies	70	50	60	55	—	70	70	Extreme
3.	Cade Horton	Cubs	60	50	65	50	—	55	60	High
4.	Jackson Jobe	Tigers	60	—	70	60	50†	60	60	High
7.	Jacob Misiorowski	Brewers	80	60	70	40	—	40	60	High
5.	Dylan Lesko	Padres	70	55	—	70	—	60	60	Extreme
6.	AJ Smith-Shawver	Braves	65	55	60	50	—	55	55	High
8.	Noble Meyer	Marlins	60	—	70	50	—	55	60	Extreme
9.	Shane Baz	Rays	70	45	60	50	—	55	60	Extreme
10.	Mick Abel	Phillies	70	60	55	60	—	40	55	High
11.	Chase Hampton	Yankees	60	55	55	45	50†	45	55	High
12.	Mason Miller	Athletics	70	—	60	50	60†	50	55	High
13.	Chase Dollander	Rockies	60	50	60	55	—	55	55	High
14.	Hurston Waldrep	Braves	60	—	60	65	—	40	55	High
15.	Tekoah Roby	Cardinals	55	60	50	50	—	60	60	Extreme
16.	Drew Thorpe	Padres	50	40	55	60	—	60	55	High
17.	Daniel Espino	Guardians	80	55	70	50	—	55	60	Extreme
18.	Rhett Lowder	Reds	55	—	55	60	—	60	55	High
19.	Max Meyer	Marlins	55	—	70	55	—	55	55	High
20.	Connor Phillips	Reds	60	50	60	30	—	45	55	High
21.	Gavin Stone	Dodgers	55	—	50	65	—	55	50	Medium
22.	Tink Hence	Cardinals	55	45	50	55	—	45	55	High
23.	Nick Frasso	Dodgers	70	—	60	50	—	50	55	High
24.	Luis Morales	Athletics	70	55	60	45	—	50	60	Extreme
25.	Bubba Chandler	Pirates	60	—	55	55	—	50	55	High
26.	Christian Scott	Mets	60	40	55	50	—	60	55	High
27.	Kyle Hurt	Dodgers	60	50	55	60	—	45	50	Medium
28.	River Ryan	Dodgers	65	55	60	55	—	45	50	Medium
29.	Chase Petty	Reds	50	—	60	55	—	60	55	High
30.	Nick Nastrini	White Sox	65	55	55	50	—	45	55	High
31.	Jared Jones	Pirates	70	50	60	45	—	45	55	High
32.	Owen White	Rangers	50	55	55	50	—	45	45	Low
33.	Cade Cavalli	Nationals	70	65	55	55	—	50	55	Very High
34.	Brock Porter	Rangers	60	—	55	60	—	40	55	Extreme
35.	JR Ritchie	Braves	55	—	60	50	—	60	55	Extreme

LEFTHANDER

No	Pitcher	Team	FB	CB	SL	CHG	OTH	CTL	BA Grade	Risk
1.	Ricky Tiedemann	Blue Jays	65	—	60	60	—	55	65	Very High
2.	Robby Snelling	Padres	55	60	—	50	—	60	60	High
3.	Kyle Harrison	Giants	60	—	60	40	50†	45	60	High
4.	Noah Schultz	White Sox	65	—	60	55	—	60	60	Very High
5.	Anthony Solometo	Pirates	60	—	60	55	—	50	55	High
6.	Jordan Wicks	Cubs	50	40	50	60	40†	55	50	Medium
7.	Robert Gasser	Brewers	50	—	55	45	50†	50	50	Medium
8.	DL Hall	Orioles	80	60	70	60	—	30	50	Medium
9.	Carson Whisenhunt	Giants	60	40	—	70	—	55	50	High
10.	Jackson Ferris	Cubs	60	60	55	50	—	40	55	Extreme
11.	Thomas White	Marlins	60	60	—	55	—	45	55	Extreme
12.	Henry Lalane	Yankees	60	—	65	60	—	60	55	Extreme
13.	Brandon Barriera	Blue Jays	55	45	65	45	—	50	55	Extreme
14.	Cooper Hjerpe	Cardinals	55	40	50	55	40†	50	50	High
15.	Yu-Min Lin	D-backs	45	55	50	60	—	60	50	High

* Splitter. † Cutter

Organization	2023	2022	2021	2020	2019
1. Baltimore Orioles	1	4	7	12	22

Until 2023, the Orioles had never topped Organization Talent Rankings. Now, they've ranked No. 1 in back-to-back years, and in our estimation, there's a significant gap between the Orioles and the other 29 organizations. Jackson Holliday leads the way, but the Orioles are deep in close-to-the-majors prospects.

2. Milwaukee Brewers	13	25	28	30	26

There's a significant gap between No. 1 and No. 2 on this list, but a system led by the high-impact pair of OF Jackson Chourio and RHP Jacob Misiorowski is off to a great start. The Brewers also have a solid second tier of prospects led by C Jeferson Quero, 2B Tyler Black and LHP Robert Gasser.

3. Texas Rangers	12	9	24	20	24

Not everything has gone right for the Rangers. RHPs Kumar Rocker and Jack Leiter have struggled to live up to lofty expectations, but that blip pales in comparison with the scouting success story of OF Evan Carter and the pro debut of 2023 top pick OF Wyatt Langford.

4. Chicago Cubs	17	15	22	21	29

This system has improved dramatically over the past few years. Chicago is showing that it can develop pitching for the first time in quite a while, but it's the mix of upside and steady potential regulars like OFs Pete Crow-Armstrong and Owen Caissie, SS Matt Shaw and C Moises Ballesteros that has the Cubs in the top five.

5. Detroit Tigers	26	6	5	11	14

The Tigers have ranked this high only once before in 40-plus years of talent rankings. That happened in 2021, when Detroit had LHP Tairk Skubal, 1B Spencer Torkelson and OF Riley Greene in their system. The Tigers have loaded up on hitters, but they also have one of the best pitching prospects in baseball in RHP Jackson Jobe.

6. San Diego Padres	23	21	3	2	1

San Diego has a remarkable ability to regenerate top prospects despite trading away so much future value in the past few years in a so-far-unsuccessful attempt to catch the Dodgers. If RHP Dylan Lesko can regain his high school form, the combination of him and LHP Robby Snelling could be the best pitching duo in the minors.

7. Tampa Bay Rays	6	2	1	1	2

The Rays' system keeps getting thinner, but the club's ability to continue producing top prospects keeps it in the top 10. 3B Junior Caminero, SS Carson Williams, 2B Curtis Mead and 1B Xavier Isaac gives Tampa Bay a complete infield of elite prospects, but the organization's pitching depth has disappeared.

8. New York Mets	5	16	19	25	19

While the 2023 MLB season was a disaster, the silver lining is that the Mets' farm system got a boost from trade deadline deals, which yielded five of the organization's top 20 prospects. Keep an eye on SS/OF Jett Williams. His ability to play up the middle and get on base could make him a productive addition to the lineup.

9. Los Angeles Dodgers	3	8	9	3	10

The Dodgers' exceptionally productive player development system rolls on, even after graduations and trades have thinned the team's top-end talent. While the Dodgers don't have any top 25 prospects in baseball, they have more near-proximity than almost anyone, led by RHP Gavin Stone.

10. New York Yankees	16	13	16	17	20

The Yankees' struggles to meet expectations in the major leagues has led to incriminations about the organization's player development system, some of which seems a tad overblown. New York churns out useful pitchers, while the team's lower levels are filled with high-ceiling, high-risk prospects.

11. Cincinnati Reds	8	7	18	29	7

The Reds graduated eight rookies in 2023, but they still have a relatively deep farm system thanks to a productive international department, a large bonus pool in the 2023 draft and astute pro prospect pickups in trades of veterans in 2021 and 2022. The system should get yet another boost by picking second in the 2024 draft.

12. Pittsburgh Pirates	11	3	15	24	18

Picking RHP Paul Skenes first overall is going to boost any system, but graduations and the struggles of some recent top picks have pushed Pittsburgh toward the middle of the pack. The Pirates are somewhat pitching-heavy at the top, which is both an opportunity but also a risk because of pitchers' volatility.

13. Boston Red Sox	10	11	21	22	30

The Red Sox have developed a nice mix of top prospects, led by top recent draft picks SS Marcelo Mayer, OF Roman Anthony and C Kyle Teel, as well as likely solid MLB contributors, such as OFs Ceddanne Rafaela and Wilyer Abreu. Boston's system is a little hitter-heavy.

14. Minnesota Twins	21	14	8	7	8

The Twins have been quite productive in recent years in producing big leaguers, but trades have meant that Spencer Steer, Yennier Cano and Christian Encarnacion-Strand graduated elsewhere. Getting the gift of the fifth pick in the 2023 draft bestowed OF Walker Jenkins and gave the organization another elite prospect.

15. Washington Nationals	7	26	30	23	16

A system led by outfielders Dylan Crews and James Wood is going to be in better shape than a lot of organizations, and third baseman Brady House had an encouragingly healthy 2023. Now, the Nationals need Elijah Green and/or Robert Hassell III to have bounceback seasons in 2024, like House had in 2023.

Organization	2022	2021	2020	2019	2018
16. Seattle Mariners	22	1	2	5	17

The Mariners' system may be setting up nicely to complement the big league club. Hitting on pitchers like George Kirby, Logan Gilbert, Bryce Miller and Bryan Woo has given Seattle a core of young starters. Now the system is heavy in position players, led by SSs Cole Young and Colt Emerson and C Harry Ford.

Organization	2022	2021	2020	2019	2018
17. Arizona Diamondbacks	2	10	17	10	21

Graduating Rookie of the Year Corbin Carroll and C Gabriel Moreno along with numerous pitchers, including Brandon Pfaadt and Ryne Nelson, is a great reason to plummet to the middle of the pack, especially when those young stars helped Arizona win a pennant. SS Jordan Lawlar's presence means the cupboard is not bare.

Organization	2022	2021	2020	2019	2018
18. Chicago White Sox	28	30	20	8	6

Chicago's system is much improved from where it was a couple of years ago. It still has a ways to go, but SS Colson Montgomery and high-ceiling LHP Noah Schultz help drive the organization to a mid-tier ranking. While trades have helped, the White Sox need to develop more homegrown depth.

Organization	2022	2021	2020	2019	2018
19. Cleveland Guardians	4	12	11	19	15

The Guardians' ability to develop and produce starting pitchers remains impressive, as RHPs Tanner Bibee and Gavin Williams and LHP Logan Allen demonstrated in 2023. But Cleveland's postseason hopes will be helped if OF Chase DeLauter or 1B Kyle Manzardo can bring needed power to Cleveland.

Organization	2022	2021	2020	2019	2018
20. St. Louis Cardinals	9	18	12	14	11

Jordan Walker's successful graduation to the majors has dropped the Cardinals' farm system back, though exciting up-the-middle hitters like SS Masyn Winn and OF Victor Scott II are ready to follow in Walker's footsteps. Getting the most out of arms like RHPs Tekoah Roby and Tink Hence is crucial.

Organization	2022	2021	2020	2019	2018
21. Philadelphia Phillies	19	23	27	26	12

Philadelphia's system remains more top-heavy than deep and falls off after Andrew Painter, Justin Crawford, Mick Abel and newly acquired Aidan Miller. Still, the organization regularly infuses big tools and stuff with an aggressive scouting philosophy that could easily lead to a few more Orion Kerkering types.

Organization	2022	2021	2020	2019	2018
22. San Francisco Giants	18	17	14	13	28

The Giants have been in the difficult middle-ground limbo. They haven't consistently been a top big league team, nor have they picked at the top of the draft. That's led to a fairly lukewarm farm system, though Kyle Harrison and Marco Luciano are MLB ready, and Bryce Eldridge and Walker Martin provide tools and athleticism.

Organization	2022	2021	2020	2019	2018
23. Colorado Rockies	14	24	25	28	23

It was an up-and-down year for the Rockies' system. There were bright spots with strong offensive years by Jordan Beck and Sterlin Thompson, as well as key international names like Adael Amador and Yanquiel Fernandez, but also a slew of injuries, including Zac Veen, Gabriel Hughes, Jordy Vargas and Jackson Cox.

Organization	2022	2021	2020	2019	2018
24. Toronto Blue Jays	15	19	4	6	3

The 2023 season was a step back for Toronto's farm because many 2022 draft picks struggled. Dominican slugger Orelvis Martinez was a rare bright spot, but much of the system's strength is reliant on top prospect LHP Ricky Tiedemann—who possesses elite upside and pure stuff but also has significant health and durability questions.

Organization	2022	2021	2020	2019	2018
25. Oakland Athletics	27	27	29	15	9

Oakland's farm system took a slight step forward in 2023 thanks to additions that included SS Jacob Wilson and Darell Hernaiz, but there's not nearly enough impact talent here to inspire hope for an organization that has been dreadful on and off the field. Worse, the A's are locked out of a top six pick in 2025 by draft lottery rules.

Organization	2022	2021	2020	2019	2018
26. Atlanta Braves	30	22	6	4	4

It's now been three straight years with the Braves sitting in the back third of farm system rankings. The organization could sorely use more reinforcements on the hitting side. Renewed activity in the international market helps build depth. Through it all, Atlanta continues to find ways to annually pump out pitching reinforcements.

Organization	2022	2021	2020	2019	2018
27. Miami Marlins	20	20	10	9	25

No one doubts Miami's ability to scout, develop and graduate pitchers, and new additions like Noble Meyer and Thomas White add more firepower. The system falls off quickly afterward, though, and has very little offensive impact talent, especially considering 2022 No. 6 pick Jacob Berry's rough start to pro ball.

Organization	2022	2021	2020	2019	2018
28. Los Angeles Angels	25	29	23	16	13

The Angels have seemingly scrapped a high-upside, athlete-oriented approach that led to first-round misses in previous years. Instead, they have opted for safer profiles like Zach Neto and 2023 first-rounder Nolan Schanuel. Not missing isn't the same as hitting big, and the Angels still lack quality impact talent in all phases.

Organization	2022	2021	2020	2019	2018
29. Houston Astros	24	28	26	27	5

Lost draft picks and trades for win-now moves have thinned Houston's system in recent years, which will soon need to help reinforce a championship core that is aging or nearing free agency. The farm system is weak on paper, but the Astros have a solid track record of getting the most out of their players.

Organization	2022	2021	2020	2019	2018
30. Kansas City Royals	29	5	13	18	27

When the Royals plummeted in the rankings last year, it was because of a bundle of graduations of prospects. They fell even further back this year because they have struggled to hit on their top picks. The Royals have little to show at the moment for top 10 overall picks such as Asa Lacy, Frank Mozzicato and Gavin Cross.

Arizona Diamondbacks

BY NICK PIECORO

More than a half-decade's worth of labor began to bear fruit in 2023 for the Diamondbacks.

A young core of players not only got Arizona back to the postseason for the first time in six years but led an improbable run through October that ended in the second World Series appearance in franchise history.

It was, in many ways, a run fueled by player development.

Whether it was homegrown players like Corbin Carroll, Brandon Pfaadt, Alek Thomas or other young or prime-age players like Zac Gallen and Gabriel Moreno—players acquired in exchange for other products of the farm system—the club's postseason success felt like an organizational victory.

Carroll in particular stood out. The outfielder was the unanimous National League Rookie of the Year after hitting .285/.362/.506 with 25 home runs and 54 stolen bases. He led the team with 5.4 bWAR.

The farm system doesn't look the same as it did a year ago. Some of that is due to the graduation of prospects. But some of it can change quickly, and it makes 2024 a sort of "TBD" year in terms of finding out whether the D-backs system can keep churning out talent at the same rate it has in years past.

There are clear paths for that to become reality. One is if Druw Jones—the No. 2 overall pick from 2022—stays healthy, cleans up his swing and starts to look more like the top-of-the-draft candidate he was only a couple of years ago. Elsewhere, Tommy Troy and Gino Groover could mash. Landon Sims might recover his velocity, and Ivan Melendez could make a little more contact.

The D-backs, who tend to operate with a modest payroll, will need their system to continue to lead the way forward. With Gallen and fellow righthander Merrill Kelly two years from free agency, the club likely will need to backfill from within or generate enough prospect inventory to find replacements via trade.

It is also likely the organization has enough talent to get by for the time being. Carroll is already a star. Moreno and Pfaadt appeared to take big steps forward in October. Shortstop Jordan Lawlar is knocking on the door, and he too might have stardom in his future. It is not far-fetched to think another of their young starters—one of, say, Tommy Henry, Ryne Nelson, Blake Walston, Slade Cecconi or Bryce Jarvis—can establish himself in 2024.

The D-backs do have another route available to beef up the system. They will have not just their

Corbin Carroll had one of just six 6 WAR seasons by rookie position players this century.

ROB TRINGALI/MLB PHOTOS VIA GETTY IMAGES

PROJECTED 2027 LINEUP

Position	Player	Age
Catcher	Gabriel Moreno	27
First Base	Gino Groover	25
Second Base	Ketel Marte	33
Third Base	Tommy Troy	24
Shortstop	Jordan Lawlar	24
Left Field	Alek Thomas	27
Center Field	Druw Jones	23
Right Field	Corbin Carroll	26
Designated Hitter	Ivan Melendez	27
No. 1 Starter	Zac Gallen	31
No. 2 Starter	Eduardo Rodriguez	34
No. 3 Starter	Brandon Pfaadt	28
No. 4 Starter	Tommy Henry	29
No. 5 Starter	Ryne Nelson	29
Closer	Kevin Ginkel	33

usual first-round pick and a competitive balance pick, but also a Prospect Promotion Incentive pick after the first round, thanks to Carroll winning the ROY award. That will mean the organization has three picks in the top 40 or so, a big opportunity to replenish the system.

The D-backs are headed in the right direction. They have a talented young core. They will soon be devoid of onerous long-term contracts. They have general manager Mike Hazen and manager Torey Lovullo locked in.

And they have fans excited about potentially having a sustainable winner in place for the first time since the early days of the franchise. It is up to them to make that possibility a reality. ∎

ARIZONA DIAMONDBACKS

TOP 2024 CONTRIBUTORS	RANK
1. Jordan Lawlar, SS	1
2. Slade Cecconi, RHP	15
3. Dominic Fletcher, OF	21

BREAKOUT PROSPECTS	RANK
1. Caden Grice, LHP	14
2. Yassel Soler, 3B	18
3. Gian Zapata, OF	27

SOURCE OF TOP 30 TALENT

Homegrown	29	Acquired	1
College	14	Trade	1
Junior college	0	Rule 5 draft	0
High school	5	Independent league	0
Nondrafted free agent	0	Free agent/waivers	0
International	10		

LF
Caleb Roberts (23)
Kristian Robinson (29)
Anderdson Rojas
Jakey Josepha

CF
Druw Jones (2)
Jack Hurley (10)
Dominic Fletcher (21)
Jorge Barrosa (22)
Pedro Catuy (24)
Jose Alpuria

RF
A.J. Vukovich (17)
Gian Zapata (27)
Wilderd Patiño

3B
Gino Groover (5)
Ruben Santana (9)
Yassel Soler (18)
Kevin Sim
Riquelmin Cabral

SS
Jordan Lawlar (1)
Tommy Troy (3)
Jansel Luis (6)
Blaze Alexander (12)
Cristofer Torin (16)
Jose Fernandez

2B
Andrew Pintar
Tim Tawa
Manuel Pena

1B
Ivan Melendez (4)

C
Christian Cerda (26)
Adrian Del Castillo (28)
J.J. D'Orazio
Carlos Virahonda
Adrian De Leon
Alberto Barriga

LHP

LHSP	LHRP
Yu-Min Lin (7)	Andrew Saalfrank (30)
Blake Walston (11)	Ryan Bruno
Caden Grice (14)	Carlos Meza
Grayson Hitt (19)	
Spencer Giesting	
Wilkin Paredes	

RHP

RHSP	RHRP
Dylan Ray (8)	Justin Martinez
Yilber Diaz (13)	Ricardo Yan
Slade Cecconi (15)	Austin Pope
Landon Sims (20)	Christian Montes De Oca
Bryce Jarvis (25)	Conor Grammes
Joe Elbis	Zane Russell
Anderson Cardenas	Eli Saul

1 JORDAN LAWLAR, SS

Born: July 17, 2002. **B-T:** R-R. **HT:** 6-1. **WT:** 190.
Drafted: HS—Dallas (1st round).
Signed by: J.R. Salinas.

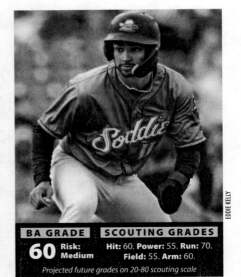

EDDIE KELLY

TRACK RECORD: Lawlar was a well-regarded prep player who won the Gatorade Texas player of the year honors and performed well on the showcase circuit. His well-rounded skill set had him in the mix to go No. 1 overall in 2021, but he slid to sixth, where the D-backs swooped in and signed him away from a Vanderbilt commitment for $6.7 million, the third-highest bonus in the draft and 17% over slot value. Lawlar needed surgery to repair a labrum tear in his left shoulder shortly after signing and dealt with a variety of relatively minor injuries in his first year as a pro. But he put together a strong season in 2022, finishing in the Arizona Fall League. He started 2023 at Double-A Amarillo and finished in the majors after a late-season callup in the middle of a pennant race. He struggled facing big league pitching but was dependable at shortstop and made the postseason roster.

SCOUTING REPORT: Lawlar has a well-roundedness to his game that stands out at the plate. He has plus bat speed and above-average to plus raw power, he controls the zone and draws walks, he uses all fields and he has the ability to hit a variety of pitches. His path keeps his barrel in the zone, making it adaptable to a variety of pitches and locations. He made strides in 2023 with some of his underlying data, decreasing his groundball rate, hitting more fly balls and line drives and seeing a jump in the number of balls he hit with an exit velocity of at least 95 mph. He had a stretch early in the season in which he appeared to get too pull happy, sending him into a five-week funk, but showed the ability to adjust and posted a .970 OPS from June 1 until his callup. He has pronounced splits and could stand to improve against righthanded pitchers, in particular against breaking balls. Lawlar is a tremendous baserunner who combines plus speed with basestealing prowess and has the instincts to routinely take the extra base. His biggest strides came on defense, where he quieted concerns about a potential shift off the position by turning in a strong and consistent performance. He started getting rid of his throws more quickly and dropped down to a three-quarters arm slot, and his overall comfort at shortstop seemed much improved after more reps.

BA GRADE	SCOUTING GRADES
60 Risk: Medium	Hit: 60. Power: 55. Run: 70. Field: 55. Arm: 60.

Projected future grades on 20-80 scouting scale

BEST TOOLS

BATTING

Best Hitter for Average	Jordan Lawlar
Best Power Hitter	Ivan Melendez
Best Strike-Zone Discipline	Christian Cerda
Fastest Baserunner	Jordan Lawlar
Best Athlete	Tommy Troy

PITCHING

Best Fastball	Yilber Diaz
Best Curveball	Yilber Diaz
Best Slider	Conor Grammes
Best Changeup	Yu-Min Lin
Best Control	Dylan Ray

FIELDING

Best Defensive Catcher	Christian Cerda
Best Defensive Infielder	Jordan Lawlar
Best Infield Arm	Blaze Alexander
Best Defensive Outfielder	Druw Jones
Best Outfield Arm	Druw Jones

THE FUTURE: As a player who profiles to hit for average and power, steal bases and hold down shortstop, Lawlar has the potential to join outfielder Corbin Carroll as a franchise cornerstone for years to come. It is unclear how the club will clear a path for him given the presence of shortstop Geraldo Perdomo, a 2023 all-star. But Perdomo can play third base, and Lawlar started working there as well at Triple-A prior to his callup. Lawlar figures to at least have a chance to win a role in spring training and could follow Carroll's path as National League Rookie of the Year should he crack the Opening Day roster. ∎

Year	Age	Club (League)	Level	AVG	G	AB	R	H	2B	3B	HR	RBI	BB	SO	SB	OBP	SLG
2023	20	Amarillo (TL)	AA	.263	89	350	77	92	23	3	15	48	47	89	33	.366	.474
2023	20	Reno (PCL)	AAA	.358	16	67	18	24	0	1	5	19	9	12	3	.438	.612
2023	20	Arizona (NL)	MLB	.129	14	31	2	4	0	0	0	0	2	11	1	.206	.129
Minor League Totals				.291	207	811	193	236	42	11	36	130	114	217	76	.390	.503
Major League Totals				.129	14	31	2	4	0	0	0	0	2	11	1	.206	.129

2 DRUW JONES, OF

HIT: 45. **POW:** 55. **RUN:** 65. **FLD:** 70. **ARM:** 60. **BA Grade:** 60. **Risk:** Extreme.

Born: November 28, 2003. **B-T:** R-R. **HT:** 6-4. **WT:** 180.
Drafted: HS—Peachtree Corners, GA, 2022 (1st round). **Signed by:** Hudson Belinsky.
TRACK RECORD: Jones, the son of 10-time Gold Glove center fielder Andruw Jones, has long reminded onlookers of his father. He had an impressive run on the prep showcase circuit before winning Gatorade's player of the year award in Georgia in 2022. He was drafted by the D-backs, who had him ranked atop their draft board, with the second overall pick and signed for full slot value of just shy of $8.2 million. His professional career has thus far been clouded by injuries. Jones needed surgery for a left labrum tear almost immediately after signing, then missed significant time in 2023 with right quadriceps and hamstring issues. He enters 2024, his third pro season, having played just 41 games.
SCOUTING REPORT: Jones still has all the raw tools that made him a top-of-the-draft talent, but far more questions were introduced in 2023 in terms of his ability to tap into them, starting with his direction at the plate. He has plus bat speed, plus raw power, recognizes pitches well and makes good swing decisions. Yet he tapped into his offensive upside infrequently because he routinely bailed out on swings, giving the impression he was afraid of the ball. Stepping in the bucket left him off-balance, which led to a high groundball rate. Cleaning up his direction—or at least ensuring he is in a better launch position—will be a focus for Jones and the D-backs. He came mostly as advertised on defense, showing plus range and a plus arm in center field and looking like a future double-plus defender at the position. When healthy, he is at least a plus runner.
THE FUTURE: If Jones can stay healthy and get his swing ironed out, he might still have the same massive upside as before. If the swing issues persist, he could still end up a plus defender with occasional power.

Year	Age	Club (League)	Level	AVG	G	AB	R	H	2B	3B	HR	RBI	BB	SO	SB	OBP	SLG
2023	19	ACL D-backs Black	Rk	.111	3	9	1	1	0	1	0	1	1	4	0	.200	.333
2023	19	ACL D-backs Red	Rk	.222	9	27	8	6	0	0	0	2	5	7	3	.344	.222
2023	19	Visalia (CAL)	A	.252	29	111	19	28	3	1	2	9	20	34	6	.366	.351
Minor League Totals				.238	41	147	28	35	3	2	2	12	26	45	9	.353	.327

3 TOMMY TROY, SS

HIT: 55. **POW:** 55. **RUN:** 50. **FLD:** 50. **ARM:** 50. **BA Grade:** 55. **Risk:** High.

Born: January 17, 2002. **B-T:** R-R. **HT:** 5-10. **WT:** 197.
Drafted: Stanford, 2023 (1st round). **Signed by:** Andrew Allen.
TRACK RECORD: Troy went undrafted in 2020 out of Los Gatos (Calif.) High due to some combination of his commitment to Stanford, the pandemic cutting short his senior season and that year's shortened draft. A three-year starter at Stanford, Troy had a big sophomore year, followed that with a strong showing in the Cape Cod League, then capped his college career by hitting .394/.478/.699 with 17 homers in 2023. The D-backs, enamored of his bat and well-rounded skill set, selected him at No. 12 overall and signed him for a below-slot $4.4 million.
SCOUTING REPORT: Troy has a compact and powerful righthanded swing, employing a leg lift at the start and scissoring his back leg after contact. He has a stout, 5-foot-10, muscular build that helps him generate impressive exit velocities. He improved his approach throughout his collegiate career and posted above-average walk and chase rates in his pro debut. Drafted as a shortstop, Troy might profile best at second base, but he also needed surgery after the year to remove bone fragments from his left foot. That injury could partly explain the limited range and inconsistent throwing he displayed as a pro. He is an average to perhaps slightly above-average runner, and he will need to maintain his body—namely his thick lower half—to retain his speed and quickness. He drew raves from Arizona player development for his work ethic and makeup and showed significant improvement in a number of areas from when he signed through the end of the season. He has good baseball acumen and asks good questions.
THE FUTURE: Troy has the tools and attributes to be a well-rounded, above-average everyday player at second base or perhaps third. He should spend the bulk of 2024 at Double-A Amarillo, with a promotion to Triple-A in the cards.

Year	Age	Club (League)	Level	AVG	G	AB	R	H	2B	3B	HR	RBI	BB	SO	SB	OBP	SLG
2023	21	ACL D-backs Red	Rk	.455	4	11	4	5	0	1	0	5	4	2	1	.563	.636
2023	21	Hillsboro (NWL)	A+	.247	23	85	13	21	5	0	4	16	12	26	8	.343	.447
Minor League Totals				.271	27	96	17	26	5	1	4	21	16	28	9	.374	.469

4 IVAN MELENDEZ, 1B/3B

HIT: 40. **POW:** 60. **RUN:** 35. **FLD:** 50. **ARM:** 55. **BA Grade:** 50. **Risk:** High.

Born: January 24, 2000. **B-T:** R-R. **HT:** 6-3. **WT:** 225.
Drafted: Texas, 2022 (2nd round). **Signed by:** J.R. Salinas.
TRACK RECORD: Melendez transferred to Texas after two seasons at Odessa Junior College and quickly became one of the better hitters in the Big 12 Conference. A DH only his first year with the Longhorns in 2021, he was drafted by the Marlins in the 16th round but did not sign. Melendez returned to Texas and had a monster 2022 season, becoming the first Golden Spikes Award winner in program history. He popped 32 home runs to set a since-broken BBCOR record to earn BA College Player of the Year honors, a rare feat for a 22-year-old senior first baseman. Melendez's pro debut was unimpressive and he started slowly in 2023, but he eventually found his swing and led the organization with 30 homers while showing better than expected defense at third base.
SCOUTING REPORT: Melendez's calling card is his massive power. He generates top-end exit velocities in the 114 mph range and can hit the ball out to all fields. The righthanded batter does not hit many ground balls, but his swing can get steep and he can get beat by fastballs, particularly versus righthanders at the top of the zone. It led to a highly alarming 34% strikeout rate, but he is harder to write off because he also hit for a decent .272 average, suggesting there is more feel to hit than most all-or-nothing sluggers. Melendez has a strong arm and surprisingly good hands at third base, and while his instincts and game clock are fine, his range and quickness limit him to being average at best there. He has a chance to be above-average at first base.
THE FUTURE: If Melendez can find a way to make more contact, especially versus righthanders, perhaps he could be something in the Jake Burger mold. But for now he looks, at the least, like a mistake-hitting lefty masher.

Year	Age	Club (League)	Level	AVG	G	AB	R	H	2B	3B	HR	RBI	BB	SO	SB	OBP	SLG
2023	23	Hillsboro (NWL)	A+	.270	58	226	36	61	17	1	18	43	21	86	4	.352	.593
2023	23	Amarillo (TL)	AA	.275	38	153	29	42	5	1	12	33	10	60	0	.335	.556
Minor League Totals				.258	125	476	78	123	25	3	33	84	44	171	4	.348	.532

5 GINO GROOVER, 3B

HIT: 55. **POW:** 50. **RUN:** 40. **FLD:** 45. **ARM:** 50. **BA Grade:** 50. **Risk:** High.

Born: April 16, 2002. **B-T:** R-R. **HT:** 6-2. **WT:** 212.
Drafted: North Carolina State, 2023 (2nd round). **Signed by:** George Swain.
TRACK RECORD: Groover might have had a chance to be drafted in the top five rounds out of his suburban Atlanta high school had the pandemic not cut short his senior season in 2020. He wound up at UNC Charlotte for a year before transferring to North Carolina State in 2022. He hit .332/.430/.546 with a team-leading 13 homers as a junior in 2023. Questions about his future defensive home and ultimate power potential might have kept Groover from going higher, but the D-backs grabbed him with the 48th overall pick and signed him for slot value of $1.78 million.
SCOUTING REPORT: Groover has a simple, low-maintenance righthanded swing and has a knack for finding the barrel, using his fast hands and quick bat to make consistent, solid contact. He could benefit from hitting fewer balls on the ground but has enough raw juice to project as a 15-20 homer threat. Groover had an appealing combination of a low in-zone whiff rate and high exit velocities in college, though the latter did not translate to the same degree in his 100 plate appearance sample with High-A Hillsboro. He chased at a roughly average rate. Many envisioned Groover moving off third base based on college looks, but upon signing he made adjustments to his throwing motion, started using his legs more and impressed with his athleticism to the point that he could have a chance to stick. He is a below-average, heavy-footed runner who could slow down as he matures.
THE FUTURE: The D-backs see Groover as one of the top pure hitters in their system, and whether he sticks at third base or ends up shifting to second, first or an outfield corner, they see someone who can hit for average and occasional power, perhaps in the mold of Wilmer Flores.

Year	Age	Club (League)	Level	AVG	G	AB	R	H	2B	3B	HR	RBI	BB	SO	SB	OBP	SLG
2023	21	ACL D-backs Black	Rk	.500	1	2	0	1	0	0	0	0	0	1	0	.500	.500
2023	21	ACL D-backs Red	Rk	.400	3	10	2	4	1	0	0	2	0	0	0	.400	.500
2023	21	Hillsboro (NWL)	A+	.264	23	87	13	23	5	1	1	14	8	9	1	.340	.379
Minor League Totals				.283	27	99	15	28	6	1	1	16	8	10	1	.348	.394

6 JANSEL LUIS, 2B/SS

HIT: 55. **POW:** 45. **RUN:** 55. **FLD:** 50. **ARM:** 50. **BA Grade:** 55. **Risk:** Extreme.

Born: March 6, 2005. **B-T:** B-R. **HT:** 6-0. **WT:** 170.
Signed: Dominican Republic, 2022. **Signed by:** Cesar Geronimo Jr./Pedro Meyer.
TRACK RECORD: The D-backs were drawn to Luis by his quick-twitch athleticism and his feel for finding the barrel from both sides of the plate. They signed him for $525,000 in January 2022. After a strong debut year in the Dominican Summer League, Luis opened eyes after moving stateside in 2023, when he excelled in the Arizona Complex League and more than holding his own at Low-A Visalia following a mid-July promotion. Luis is the cousin of former big league infielder Pedro Ciriaco and younger brother of former minor league infielder Audy Ciriaco, who topped out at Triple-A in 2015.
SCOUTING REPORT: Luis has a simple, repeatable and quick swing from both sides of the plate. He gets on plane well and remains in the zone for a long time, and he has the ability to spray line drives to all fields. His bat-to-ball skills, ability to find the barrel and strong frame make average future power within reach. His lefthanded swing looks cleaner, and he has been more productive from that side of the plate, hitting .274/.333/.457 versus righthanders in 2023. He has the makings of a decent approach but showed extreme chase tendencies following a promotion to Low-A. He might end up shifting to second base, but if he can improve his first-step reactions and add a tick of arm strength, he could grow into an average defender at shortstop. He has a good baseball IQ and is at least an above-average runner.
THE FUTURE: Given his age—he played all of the 2023 season at age 18—Luis offers plenty of projection, both in terms of skills and strength. He could develop into an everyday player in the mold of Andres Gimenez. A return to the California League is probable in 2024, where he can build success and confidence while also avoiding the coldest portion of the Northwest League schedule.

Year	Age	Club (League)	Level	AVG	G	AB	R	H	2B	3B	HR	RBI	BB	SO	SB	OBP	SLG
2023	18	ACL D-backs Black	Rk	.297	25	91	18	27	7	1	3	12	9	15	9	.381	.495
2023	18	ACL D-backs Red	Rk	.000	1	3	0	0	0	0	0	0	0	1	0	.000	.000
2023	18	Visalia (CAL)	A	.257	36	144	19	37	5	3	4	15	8	35	7	.310	.417
Minor League Totals				.301	109	412	72	124	19	5	8	45	29	74	25	.362	.430

7 YU-MIN LIN, LHP

FB: 45. **CB:** 55. **SL:** 50. **CHG:** 60. **CTL:** 60. **BA Grade:** 50. **Risk:** High.

Born: July 12, 2003. **B-T:** L-L. **HT:** 5-11. **WT:** 160.
Signed: Taiwan, 2021. **Signed by:** Tzu-Yao Wei/Peter Wardell.
TRACK RECORD: The D-backs watched Lin carve through hitters several years older than him at an international tournament in late 2021, an outing that served as the impetus for the $525,000 bonus they gave the Taiwanese lefthander that December. He has done much of the same in two full seasons as a pro, eliciting swings-and-misses at a high rate thanks to his deep repertoire and an understanding of how to use it—and doing it without elite velocity. Lin led all teenagers in 2023 with 121.1 innings.
SCOUTING REPORT: Lin can touch 93-94 mph with his four-seam fastball but averages just 90, sometimes pitching in the 88-89 mph range, and doesn't get great ride on the pitch. His best offering is a changeup that gets good separation off his fastball and falls off the table late. Lin's curveball can be wicked, with excellent spin and no hump, but his command of it is inconsistent. He also throws a slider, cutter and was tinkering with a sinker. None of his pitches are elite but everything plays up thanks to his plus command and good feel for pitching. Lin's command has to be on point; he gets hit around on days it isn't. Questions remain about his upside. His velocity is pedestrian at best and his slightly-built, 5-foot-11 frame makes projecting gains there difficult. It also raises questions about his ability to maintain his stuff while logging a starter's workload. Moreover, there have not been many sub-6-foot lefthanded starters in recent years.
THE FUTURE: Lin's ability to command pitches and miss bats should give him a chance at the highest level, but given the scarcity of midrotation pitchability starters in today's game, it is hard to project him as any more than a No. 4 or 5 type.

Year	Age	Club (League)	Level	W	L	ERA	G	GS	IP	H	HR	BB	SO	BB%	SO%	WHIP	AVG
2023	19	Hillsboro (NWL)	A+	1	3	3.43	13	13	60	47	3	22	76	9.3	32.1	1.14	.223
2023	19	Amarillo (TL)	AA	5	2	4.28	11	11	61	49	7	26	64	10.0	24.7	1.23	.221
Minor League Totals				8	7	3.51	38	38	178	136	12	70	231	9.7	32.0	1.16	.216

8 DYLAN RAY, RHP

FB: 60. **CB:** 45. **SL:** 55. **CHG:** 50. **CTL:** 50. **BA Grade:** 50. **Risk:** High.

Born: May 9, 2001. **B-T:** R-R. **HT:** 6-3. **WT:** 230.
Drafted: Alabama, 2022 (4th round). **Signed by:** Stephen Baker.
TRACK RECORD: Ray's progression was slowed by a pair of major injuries—he tore the anterior cruciate ligament in his knee in a high school football injury, then needed Tommy John surgery shortly after arriving at Alabama—but the D-backs saw enough upside to gamble on his athleticism. They drafted him in the fourth round in 2022. That bet started to pay off in 2023 as Ray showed he had the makings of a potential big league starter at High-A Hillsboro, though he still lacks refinement in a number of areas. His 22.5 K-BB% ranked first among Northwest League pitchers with at least 80 innings.
SCOUTING REPORT: Ray's fastball fluctuated throughout the season. It's a four-seamer that sometimes sat in the mid 90s and touched 98 mph and other times averaged closer to 92 mph. The pitch gets on hitters thanks to good carry and deception. Similarly, his slider could be inconsistent, but at its best it is hard—around 91 mph—and tight with tilt. Ray's changeup had been viewed as his fourth pitch but was surprisingly solid with good depth. He also throws a snappy curveball with depth in the high 70s but the pitch is inconsistent. Ray has good pitchability, showing acumen for reading swings, mixing pitches and adding and subtracting. He has a prototype starter's frame that ought to allow him to be a durable innings-eater.
THE FUTURE: Ray has all the ingredients to be at least a No. 4 or 5 starter. He might have more upside than that given his injury history and his relative inexperience on the mound. The hope is that he will be better equipped in his second full season for the physical demands of starting and can maintain his best stuff for more of the year. He is likely to open the 2024 season back at Double-A Amarillo.

Year	Age	Club (League)	Level	W	L	ERA	G	GS	IP	H	HR	BB	SO	BB%	SO%	WHIP	AVG
2023	22	Hillsboro (NWL)	A+	7	6	3.81	22	22	99	84	8	32	123	7.9	30.4	1.17	.229
2023	22	Amarillo (TL)	AA	1	2	8.36	3	3	14	17	3	8	15	11.9	22.4	1.79	.309
Minor League Totals				8	11	4.61	33	33	127	117	16	44	155	8.3	29.1	1.27	.244

9 RUBEN SANTANA, 3B

HIT: 50. **POW:** 55. **RUN:** 50. **FLD:** 50. **ARM:** 60. **BA Grade:** 50. **Risk:** Extreme.

Born: February 16, 2005. **B-T:** R-R. **HT:** 6-0. **WT:** 190.
Signed: Dominican Republic, 2022. **Signed by:** Cesar Geronimo Jr./Pedro Meyer.
TRACK RECORD: Santana's combination of physicality, tools and feel for the game spurred the D-backs to sign him for $750,000 in January 2022. He followed up his strong debut in the Dominican Summer League with a good showing in the Arizona Complex League in 2023. That showed he has the ingredients, including a rocket arm and the ability to hit balls hard, to develop into an impact third baseman.
SCOUTING REPORT: Santana has a loose, quick and powerful righthanded swing that generates hard contact with massive pull-side power. He shows an ability to drive all types of pitches, including breaking balls. While his approach is aggressive, he does not have major red flags with his strikeout or in-zone contact rates, but he does chase from time to time. His posture at the plate can cause him to get stuck on his back side. The D-backs hope to clean that up and get him moving more freely and naturally through the zone. Santana has a cannon for an arm and can show good actions in the field but has room to improve when it comes to the consistency of his footwork and glovework. Santana has a strong, physical, 6-foot, 190-pound frame that would fit well on a football field, but while he is an above-average runner now he looks like he could slow down a bit as he matures.
THE FUTURE: Santana's propensity for loud contact got the attention of rival clubs, who inquired about him often at the 2023 trade deadline. He still has work to do in terms of his approach, but he has a chance to develop into an impact player on both sides of the ball. In many ways, Santana is reminiscent of Deyvison De Los Santos in terms of skills and upside. An assignment to Low-A Visalia is on tap for 2024.

Year	Age	Club (League)	Level	AVG	G	AB	R	H	2B	3B	HR	RBI	BB	SO	SB	OBP	SLG
2023	18	ACL D-backs Black	Rk	.316	52	187	33	59	12	4	4	35	17	50	7	.389	.487
Minor League Totals				.316	95	320	68	101	17	8	5	52	42	83	22	.409	.466

10 JACK HURLEY, OF

HIT: 45. **POW:** 50. **RUN:** 60. **FLD:** 50. **ARM:** 50. **BA Grade:** 50. **Risk:** High.

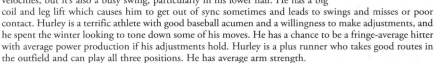

Born: March 13, 2002. **B-T:** L-R. **HT:** 6-0. **WT:** 185.
Drafted: Virginia Tech, 2023 (3rd round). **Signed by:** Rick Matsko.
TRACK RECORD: Small and physically underdeveloped in high school, Hurley landed at Virginia Tech and gained size and strength to develop into one of the best hitters in the Atlantic Coast Conference. He became a two-time all-ACC selection and hit .320 with 17 home runs as a junior, leading the D-backs to draft him in the third round, No. 80 overall, and sign him for $887,000.
SCOUTING REPORT: Hurley has a powerful swing that generates loud exit velocities, but it's also a busy swing, particularly in his lower half. He has a big coil and leg lift which causes him to get out of sync sometimes and leads to swings and misses or poor contact. Hurley is a terrific athlete with good baseball acumen and a willingness to make adjustments, and he spent the winter looking to tone down some of his moves. He has a chance to be a fringe-average hitter with average power production if his adjustments hold. Hurley is a plus runner who takes good routes in the outfield and can play all three positions. He has average arm strength.
THE FUTURE: Hurley will need to tone down his swing and dial in his approach, but his track record suggests he has a chance to hit enough to develop into an everyday player.

Year	Age	Club (League)	Level	AVG	G	AB	R	H	2B	3B	HR	RBI	BB	SO	SB	OBP	SLG
2023	21	ACL D-backs Red	Rk	.182	4	11	6	2	0	0	0	0	4	6	1	.471	.182
2023	21	Visalia (CAL)	A	.265	9	34	3	9	4	0	1	5	7	13	3	.405	.471
2023	21	Hillsboro (NWL)	A+	.293	20	82	12	24	5	1	1	6	5	25	6	.341	.415
Minor League Totals				.276	33	127	21	35	9	1	2	11	16	44	10	.374	.409

11 BLAKE WALSTON, LHP

FB: 45. **CB:** 50. **SL:** 55. **CHG:** 60. **CTL:** 50. **BA Grade:** 45. **Risk:** Medium.

Born: June 28, 2001. **B-T:** L-L. **HT:** 6-5. **WT:** 195. **Drafted:** HS—Wilmington, NC, 2019 (1st round). **Signed by:** George Swain.
TRACK RECORD: Walston was a standout prep quarterback who led all North Carolina high schoolers in passing yards while taking New Hanover High to a state championship his junior year. The D-backs bet on his athleticism when they drafted him 26th overall in 2019 and bought him out of a North Carolina commitment. Walston rose quickly through the low minors, but his progress hit a speedbump in 2023 at Triple-A Reno. His stuff and control backed up pitching in a difficult environment, raising questions about his ceiling.
SCOUTING REPORT: Walston is a lanky, 6-foot-5 lefthander who has to grow into his velocity. His fastball averages 91 mph and was flatter than before in 2023, making it a less effective pitch with little margin for error. He lost feel for what had been a plus changeup, his above-average slider essentially turned into a cutter and his once-dominant curveball became less consistent. The result was nearly as many walks (93) as strikeouts (104) in 149.1 innings and the lowest strikeout rate of his career. Walston showed impressive toughness despite the loss of stuff and finished 12-6, 4.52, the second-lowest ERA among qualified starters in the Pacific Coast League, to earn a 40-man roster spot after the season.
THE FUTURE: The D-backs remain steadfast in their belief Walston has midrotation potential, but his stuff has to rebound for him to be more than a back-end starter. He'll enter spring training looking to establish himself in the starting pitching pecking order.

Year	Age	Club (League)	Level	W	L	ERA	G	GS	IP	H	HR	BB	SO	BB%	SO%	WHIP	AVG
2023	22	Reno (PCL)	AAA	12	6	4.52	30	30	149	142	9	93	104	14.0	15.6	1.57	.254
Career Minor League				24	14	4.36	80	79	380	364	41	174	375	10.6	22.8	1.42	.250

12 BLAZE ALEXANDER, SS

HIT: 45. **POW:** 55. **RUN:** 50. **FLD:** 55. **ARM:** 70. **BA Grade:** 45. **Risk:** Medium.

Born: June 11, 1999. **B-T:** R-R. **HT:** 6-0. **WT:** 175. **Drafted:** HS—Bradenton, FL, 2018 (11th round).
Signed by: Luke Wrenn.
TRACK RECORD: Alexander was an older high school senior with contact questions and a supposedly high price tag in the 2018 draft, but the D-backs took a flier on him in the 11th round and signed him for $500,000. After some early-career struggles, Alexander broke out at Double-A Amarillo in 2022 and was added to the 40-man roster after the season. He moved to Triple-A Reno in 2023 and hit .292/.408/.458 for the Aces despite missing two months with a broken right thumb.

SCOUTING REPORT: Alexander is a well-rounded athlete who does a little bit of everything. At the plate he uses a leg lift before unleashing a controlled, relatively simple swing. He generates plus raw power but can struggle to get to it due to occasional contact issues, including on pitches in the strike zone. He has steadily improved his contact skills and plate discipline over the years and projects to be a fringe-average hitter with above-average power production. He does most of his damage against lefthanded pitching. Alexander is a reliable defender at shortstop with smooth actions and a plus-plus arm that is his best tool. He has the athleticism to bounce around the infield and has seen time at second and third base.

THE FUTURE: Alexander projects to be a versatile infielder who produces against lefthanded pitching. He has a chance to be more if his hitting ability continues to improve.

Year	Age	Club (League)	Level	AVG	G	AB	R	H	2B	3B	HR	RBI	BB	SO	SB	OBP	SLG
2023	24	ACL D-backs Black	Rk	.364	3	11	2	4	1	0	1	3	0	2	0	.417	.727
2023	24	ACL D-backs Red	Rk	.182	3	11	2	2	1	0	1	3	0	3	0	.182	.545
2023	24	Reno (PCL)	AAA	.291	73	247	45	72	13	2	8	52	42	83	2	.408	.457
Minor League Totals				.276	421	1513	274	417	80	17	52	244	197	457	53	.371	.454

13 YILBER DIAZ, RHP

FB: 70. **CB:** 60. **SL:** 50. **CHG:** 40. **CTL:** 45. **BA Grade:** 50. **Risk:** High.

Born: August 19, 2000. **B-T:** R-R. **HT:** 6-0. **WT:** 190. **Signed:** Venezuela, 2021.
Signed by: Cesar Geronimo Jr./Ronald Salazar.

TRACK RECORD: After going unsigned at 16 out of Venezuela, Diaz quit baseball for a year or so before giving it another try. The D-backs saw him throwing 92 mph and brought him to work out at their facility in the Dominican Republic, where he got stranded due to the coronavirus pandemic. He continued to improve at the D-backs facility and eventually signed for $10,000 as a 20 year old. Diaz broke out in his first full season stateside and reached Double-A in 2023. He showed flashes of potential but went 3-10, 4.82 with an overly high walk rate to amplify lingering questions about his future role.

SCOUTING REPORT: Diaz has some of the most electric stuff in the system. His plus-plus fastball ranges from 95-100 mph with solid carry at the top of the strike zone to induce swings and misses. He backs up his heater with a plus, power curveball that gives him another swing-and-miss weapon. He also throws an average slider that flashes higher and a below-average changeup he rarely uses but is being emphasized by player development staff. Diaz has plenty of stuff, but his delivery remains a work in progress and his control is inconsistent.

THE FUTURE: Diaz projects to be a hard-throwing reliever. He has a chance to remain a starter if he refines his control and a third pitch.

Year	Age	Club (League)	Level	W	L	ERA	G	GS	IP	H	HR	BB	SO	BB%	SO%	WHIP	AVG
2023	22	Hillsboro (NWL)	A+	2	10	5.03	22	22	88	68	13	49	124	13.0	33.0	1.33	.215
2023	22	Amarillo (TL)	AA	1	0	3.60	3	3	15	12	1	9	16	14.1	25.0	1.40	.222
Minor League Totals				9	16	4.59	63	43	207	160	20	114	256	12.8	28.8	1.33	.216

14 CADEN GRICE, LHP

FB: 55. **SL:** 55. **CHG:** 55. **CTL:** 50. **BA Grade:** 50. **Risk:** High.

Born: June 15, 2002. **B-T:** L-L. **HT:** 6-6. **WT:** 250. **Drafted:** Clemson, 2023 (2nd round supp). **Signed by:** George Swain.

TRACK RECORD: Grice has been an intriguing two-way prospect since his high school days and played both ways at Clemson as a lefthanded pitcher and power-hitting first baseman. He hit .307 with 18 home runs for the Tigers as a junior while going 8-1, 3.35 on the mound in his first year as a starter. Arizona drafted him as a pitcher in the supplemental second round and signed him for $1.25 million.

SCOUTING REPORT: Grice may have a higher ceiling at the plate due to his plus-plus raw power, but his propensity for striking out led the Diamondbacks to believe he offered more certainty on the mound. His fastball sits in the low 90s and touches 95 with good angle and ride to play as an above-average pitch. His breaking ball is another above-average pitch that alternates between a slider with tight break and a power curveball. Grice also throws an average changeup that has flashed better in the past. The D-backs were encouraged given his relative inexperience on the mound—just 94 innings in three years at Clemson—by the quality of both his strikes and pitch mix. He has surprising athleticism given his husky frame and his arm works well out of a sound delivery.

THE FUTURE: Grice may still get some opportunities to hit, but pitching will be his focus. He still has upside in development and projects to be a back-of-the-rotation starter.

Year	Age	Club (League)	Level	W	L	ERA	G	GS	IP	H	HR	BB	SO	BB%	SO%	WHIP	AVG
2023	21	Did not pitch															

15 SLADE CECCONI, RHP

FB: 50. **CB:** 45. **SL:** 60. **CHG:** 40. **CTL:** 55. **BA Grade:** 45. **Risk:** Medium.

Born: June 24, 1999. **B-T:** R-R. **HT:** 6-4. **WT:** 219. **Drafted:** Miami, 2020 (1st round supp). **Signed by:** Eric Cruz.

TRACK RECORD: Cecconi looked like a possible first-rounder entering his senior year of high school, but a triceps injury slowed him in the spring. He reached campus at Miami and pitched parts of two seasons in the Hurricanes rotation before the D-backs drafted him 33rd overall in 2020. Cecconi gradually worked his way through the system and made his major league debut last August. He posted a 4.33 ERA over 27 innings alternating as a starter and reliever and was included on the D-backs' NLCS roster.

SCOUTING REPORT: Cecconi is a big righthander with plenty of arm strength. His fastball sits 94-95 and touches 98 mph, but it doesn't miss many bats and tends to get hit hard. His best secondary pitch is a plus slider that has sharp, two-plane action at its best. Cecconi rounds out his arsenal with a fringy curveball that gets loopy at times and a below-average, rarely used changeup, though he tinkered with an adjustment he picked up from teammate Merrill Kelly. Cecconi flashes plus stuff in spurts but loses it within outings. He has above-average control but needs to mix his pitches more strategically.

THE FUTURE: Cecconi needs continued innings and experience to reach his potential as a back-end starter. He could be a bullpen option should the need arise.

Year	Age	Club (League)	Level	W	L	ERA	G	GS	IP	H	HR	BB	SO	BB%	SO%	WHIP	AVG
2023	24	Reno (PCL)	AAA	5	9	6.11	23	23	116	124	24	36	118	7.1	23.3	1.38	.268
2023	24	Arizona (NL)	MLB	0	1	4.33	7	4	27	27	4	4	20	3.6	18.0	1.15	.260
Career Minor League				16	17	4.99	61	60	305	316	51	88	308	6.7	23.3	1.32	.261
Major League Totals				0	1	4.33	7	4	27	27	4	4	20	3.6	18.0	1.15	.260

16 CRISTOFER TORIN, SS

HIT: 45. **POW:** 30. **RUN:** 50. **FLD:** 60. **ARM:** 60. **BA Grade:** 45. **Risk:** High.

Born: May 26, 2005. **B-T:** R-R. **HT:** 5-10. **WT:** 175. **Signed:** Venezuela, 2022.
Signed by: Cesar Geronimo Jr./Didimo Bracho.

TRACK RECORD: Torin stood out as one of the best defensive shortstops in the 2022 international class and signed with the D-backs for $240,000 out of Venezuela. He showed a better approach and contact skills than anticipated in his stateside debut and had a standout spring training at age 17, routinely being brought over to big league camp to be a reserve in Cactus League games. He continued to star in the Arizona Complex League, batting .320/.437/.427, and finished the year at Low-A Visalia.

SCOUTING REPORT: Torin has a short, repeatable swing and a discerning eye, a combination that leads to lots of contact and few chases. He has subpar bat speed and doesn't hit the ball hard, however, limiting his power projection. He may benefit from being more aggressive on pitches he can drive, but he projects to be a pesky, contact-oriented hitter who gets on base. He is an average runner with good instincts on the basepaths. Torin is a polished defender with plus actions and a plus arm at shortstop, though he runs into some consistency issues. His lower half has gotten thicker and he'll need to maintain his body to ensure he doesn't lose range and have to move off the position.

THE FUTURE: Torin projects to be an up-the-middle defender who puts together tough at-bats and finds his way on base despite limited impact. It will be key for him to remain a shortstop.

Year	Age	Club (League)	Level	AVG	G	AB	R	H	2B	3B	HR	RBI	BB	SO	SB	OBP	SLG
2023	18	ACL D-backs Red	Rk	.320	26	103	31	33	3	1	2	13	21	9	15	.437	.427
2023	18	Visalia (CAL)	A	.236	39	140	16	33	1	1	2	11	14	30	6	.314	.300
Minor League Totals				.296	115	402	92	119	16	4	4	50	72	59	42	.409	.386

17 A.J. VUKOVICH, OF

HIT: 40. **POW:** 50. **RUN:** 55. **FLD:** 45. **ARM:** 50. **BA Grade:** 45. **Risk:** High.

Born: July 20, 2001. **B-T:** R-R. **HT:** 6-5. **WT:** 230. **Drafted:** HS—East Troy, WI, 2020 (4th round). **Signed by:** Nate Birtwell.

TRACK RECORD: Vukovich was a multisport standout in high school and a finalist for Wisconsin's Mr. Basketball award. The D-backs drafted him in the fourth round of the shortened 2020 draft and bought him out of a Louisville commitment for a $1.25 million bonus. A raw player entering the system, Vukovich made strides every year and had his best season in 2023. He set career highs with 24 home runs and an .818 OPS at Double-A Amarillo and finished the year in the Arizona Fall League.

SCOUTING REPORT: Vukovich is a big, physical athlete who has taken time to find what works best for him. After years of starting with a closed batting stance and striding neutral, he started neutral before striding open last year and broke out. He has a relatively clean swing with average bat speed and is beginning to tap into his above-average raw power more often. Vukovich's swing decisions are improving, but he still has too many weakly hit balls and swings and misses. He projects to be a below-average hitter whose power plays down in games. Drafted as a third baseman, Vukovich moved to the outfield in 2023 and showed the athleticism to play all three positions. He has above-average speed and average arm strength and is most natural in right field.

THE FUTURE: Vukovich is moving in the right direction and is still only 22 with lots of room for growth. He has a chance to be a part-time outfielder who hits for occasional power if he continues to make strides.

Year	Age	Club (League)	Level	AVG	G	AB	R	H	2B	3B	HR	RBI	BB	SO	SB	OBP	SLG
2023	21	Amarillo (TL)	AA	.263	115	456	84	120	19	5	24	96	46	144	20	.333	.485
Minor League Totals				.270	324	1292	200	349	64	10	54	236	87	367	72	.321	.461

18 YASSEL SOLER, 3B

HIT: 60. **POW:** 45. **RUN:** 40. **FLD:** 60. **ARM:** 55. **BA Grade:** 50. **Risk:** Extreme.

Born: January 26, 2006. **B-T:** R-R. **HT:** 5-11. **WT:** 185. **Signed:** Dominican Republic, 2023.
Signed by: Cesar Geronimo Jr./Peter Wardell/David Felida.

TRACK RECORD: The son of former Rays minor leaguer Ramon Soler, Yassel won over D-backs scouts with his consistent offensive performance and solid defense at third base as an amateur in the Dominican Republic. He signed with the club for $425,000 and made his debut in the Dominican Summer League a few months later. Soler hit .252/.363/.358 in the DSL while showing promising underlying traits, overcoming concerns he didn't have the elite athleticism the D-backs tend to prefer on the international market.

SCOUTING REPORT: Soler is a polished hitter who has a clean, balanced swing and makes consistent hard contact. He still needs to learn to drive the ball in the air, but he posts solid exit velocities for his age and level. He has an impressive ability to put the bat on the ball and rarely swings and misses in the strike zone. He is a potentially plus hitter with double-digit home run potential. Soler is an excellent defender who projects as a plus third baseman. He has plus hands and feet and an above-average, accurate arm. He earns high praise for his makeup, worth ethic and insightful questions.

THE FUTURE: Soler is a strong defender with a chance to hit enough to profile at third base. He'll make his stateside debut in 2024.

Year	Age	Club (League)	Level	AVG	G	AB	R	H	2B	3B	HR	RBI	BB	SO	SB	OBP	SLG
2023	17	DSL D-backs Black	Rk	.252	37	123	23	31	7	0	2	16	14	18	1	.363	.358
Minor League Totals				.252	37	123	23	31	7	0	2	16	14	18	1	.363	.358

19 GRAYSON HITT, LHP

FB: 60. **CB:** 55. **SL:** 50. **CUT:** 60. **CTL:** 45. **BA Grade:** 50. **Risk:** Extreme.

Born: December 11, 2001. **B-T:** R-L. **HT:** 6-3. **WT:** 210. **Drafted:** Alabama, 2023 (4th round). **Signed by:** Steven Baker.

TRACK RECORD: An intriguing pitching prospect and standout wide receiver in high school, Hitt's draft stock was on the rise before the coronavirus pandemic shut down the 2020 season. He landed at Alabama and turned in a pair of inconsistent seasons before appearing on the verge of a breakout junior year. That promise was cut short when he suffered an elbow injury after eight starts and had season-ending Tommy John surgery. The D-backs remained intrigued with his potential despite the injury and drafted him in the fourth round. He signed for $1.2 million, more than double the recommended slot amount.

SCOUTING REPORT: Hitt is an athletic, 6-foot-3 lefthander with power stuff. His fastball sat in the mid 90s and touched 98 before his injury. He also features a potentially plus low-90s cutter and a pair of solid breaking balls. His low-80s slider projects to be an average pitch while his mid-to-upper 70s curveball is a potentially above-average offering that has flashed higher. Hitt has long battled fringe-average command and control, but he has the stuff to overpower hitters even when he misses his spots. He has an athletic, lean build with an easy arm action. Hitt struggled with wildly inconsistent outings in college, but the D-backs are optimistic his athleticism will allow him to flourish with more development.

THE FUTURE: Hitt's surgery will keep him out until at least the middle of the 2024 season. He projects to be a hard-throwing No. 4 starter if he returns with his stuff intact.

Year	Age	Club (League)	Level	W	L	ERA	G	GS	IP	H	HR	BB	SO	BB%	SO%	WHIP	AVG
2023	21	Did not play															

20 LANDON SIMS, RHP

FB: 60. **SL:** 60. **CHG:** 45. **CTL:** 50. **BA Grade:** 50. **Risk:** Extreme.

Born: January 3, 2001. **B-T:** R-R. **HT:** 6-2. **WT:** 227. **Drafted:** Mississippi State, 2022 (1st round supplemental).
Signed by: Stephen Baker.
TRACK RECORD: Sims was a well-known prep pitcher, but questions about his future role helped push him to Mississippi State. He was arguably the top closer in the country as a sophomore and helped the Bulldogs win their first national title. He transitioned into a starting role as a junior and impressed in three starts before blowing out his elbow and needing Tommy John surgery. The D-backs rolled the dice on his upside, taking him 34th overall and giving him $2.35 million. Sims returned to make his pro debut in 2023 and struggled to a 5.47 ERA over 24.2 innings across the lower levels.
SCOUTING REPORT: Sims had two electric, swing-and-miss pitches before his surgery. His fastball touched 97-98 mph with exceptional carry and he backed it up with a tight, mid-80s power slider with late tilt. Unfortunately, his stuff did not return in his pro debut. His fastball instead sat in the low 90s and he surrendered nearly a hit per inning. The D-backs believe his velocity will tick back up as he gets further removed from surgery. He has a fringy changeup as well but threw it only a handful of times last year. Sims has a crossfire delivery that helps add deception to his pitches, although it also results in inconsistent control. He has shown average control at his best.
THE FUTURE: The D-backs believe Sims' stuff will bounce back and still see him as a potential starter. His fastball and slider should play in relief as a fallback.

Year	Age	Club (League)	Level	W	L	ERA	G	GS	IP	H	HR	BB	SO	BB%	SO%	WHIP	AVG
2023	22	ACL D-backs Black	Rk	0	1	4.50	5	4	6	5	0	3	5	12.5	20.8	1.33	.238
2023	22	ACL D-backs Red	Rk	0	0	0.00	3	2	3	2	0	1	4	8.3	33.3	1.00	.182
2023	22	Visalia (CAL)	A	0	3	6.89	7	7	16	16	3	8	19	11.0	26.0	1.53	.262
Minor League Totals				0	4	5.63	15	13	25	23	3	12	28	11.0	25.7	1.46	.247

21 DOMINIC FLETCHER, OF

HIT: 50. **POW:** 45. **RUN:** 45. **FLD:** 60. **ARM:** 55. **BA Grade:** 40. **Risk:** Medium.

Born: September 2, 1997. **B-T:** L-L. **HT:** 5-6. **WT:** 185. **Drafted:** Arkansas, 2019 (2nd round supplemental).
Signed by: Nate Birtwell.
TRACK RECORD: The younger brother of Angels infielder David Fletcher, Dominic spent three years at Arkansas developing a reputation for highlight-reel catches in center field and delivering more power than expected given his undersized frame. He had an uneven start to his pro career after the D-backs drafted him in the supplemental second round in 2019, but he progressively improved and had his best seasons at the upper levels. He reached the majors for the first time in 2023 and performed well in limited action before his season was cut short by a fractured left index finger.
SCOUTING REPORT: Undersized at 5-foot-6, Fletcher peppers all fields with a line-drive swing. He's primarily a contact hitter and can occasionally get into a ball to his pull side for over-the-fence power. He continues to make progress in terms of his approach, increasing his walk rate the last two years while limiting his strikeouts. He struggles somewhat against lefties, suggesting he might fit best on the strong side of a platoon. Fletcher makes up for fringe-average speed with great reads and above-average routes in the outfield, making him a plus defender at all three positions. He has above-average arm strength.
THE FUTURE: Fletcher will enter spring training looking to earn a bench spot in 2024.

Year	Age	Club (League)	Level	AVG	G	AB	R	H	2B	3B	HR	RBI	BB	SO	SB	OBP	SLG
2023	25	Reno (PCL)	AAA	.291	66	278	71	81	18	5	10	45	62	62	5	.399	.500
2023	25	Arizona (NL)	MLB	.301	28	93	10	28	5	1	2	14	7	22	0	.350	.441
Minor League Totals				.295	356	1417	262	418	85	21	42	201	144	334	18	.366	.474
Major League Totals				.301	28	93	10	28	5	1	2	14	7	22	0	.350	.441

22 JORGE BARROSA, OF

HIT: 50. **POW:** 40. **RUN:** 55. **FLD:** 65. **ARM:** 45. **BA Grade:** 45. **Risk:** High.

Born: February 17, 2001. **B-T:** B-L. **HT:** 5-5. **WT:** 165. **Signed:** Venezuela, 2017.
Signed by: Alfonso Mora/Cesar Geronimo Jr.
TRACK RECORD: Barrosa managed to overcome his small size and lack of physical projection to win over D-backs scouts—namely Alfonso Mora—by consistently performing well in games against older competition as an amateur in Venezuela. The D-backs signed him for $415,000 and he has since steadily climbed their system. Barrosa earned a spot on the 40-man roster prior to 2023 and spent the year at Triple-A Reno, batting .274/.394/.456 with 13 homers, 65 RBIs and 15 steals.

SCOUTING REPORT: A switch hitter, Barrosa has a simple, repeatable swing from the right side and more moving parts as a lefty, including a lengthy stride and more movement in his load. Either way, he has put up relatively even splits in the upper minors, demonstrating a consistent, sound approach and the ability to make lots of contact. His power is still somewhat limited, but he hits the ball hard for his size. Barrosa is a plus defender at all three outfield positions whose excellent jumps and reads give the impression he knows where a ball is about to be hit. He is an above-average runner who still has room to refine his basestealing skills.

THE FUTURE: Barrosa looks every bit like a future big leaguer. Whether he starts or is more of a reserve will be determined by how much extra-base impact he can generate.

Year	Age	Club (League)	Level	AVG	G	AB	R	H	2B	3B	HR	RBI	BB	SO	SB	OBP	SLG
2023	22	Reno (PCL)	AAA	.274	120	412	91	113	20	8	13	65	80	82	15	.394	.456
Minor League Totals				.276	461	1763	341	486	99	21	37	208	226	323	117	.369	.419

23 CALEB ROBERTS, OF/C

HIT: 45. **POW:** 50. **RUN:** 45. **FLD:** 45. **ARM:** 60. **BA Grade:** 45. **Risk:** High.

Born: February 9, 2000. **B-T:** L-R. **HT:** 5-11. **WT:** 195. **Drafted:** North Carolina, 2021 (5th round).
Signed by: George Swain.

TRACK RECORD: Recruited out of high school as a catcher, Roberts wound up mostly playing the outfield at North Carolina and developed into one of the Tar Heels' best hitters. He led the team with 10 home runs his junior year and was drafted by the D-backs in the fifth round. Roberts made clear he wanted to catch during the draft process and has split time between catcher, first base and the outfield as a pro. He reached Double-A Amarillo in 2023 and hit .278/.383/.523 with 17 home runs.

SCOUTING REPORT: Roberts is a short, strong lefthanded hitter who employs a quick, level swing that he uses to spray balls to all fields. He has a knack for producing backspin and good carry, especially to the opposite-field gap, and projects to be a fringe-average hitter with average power. He has a patient approach that produces walks at roughly a 13% clip, but he is prone to swinging and missing in the strike zone and has trouble against lefthanded pitching. Roberts has work to do behind the plate in terms of receiving premium stuff. He has plus arm strength and is adept at blocking pitches in the dirt.

THE FUTURE: Roberts might never be a frontline catcher, but if he develops into a passable option he could carve out a role as an outfielder/third catcher who logs at-bats against righthanded pitching.

Year	Age	Club (League)	Level	AVG	G	AB	R	H	2B	3B	HR	RBI	BB	SO	SB	OBP	SLG
2023	23	Amarillo (TL)	AA	.278	97	367	72	102	23	8	17	66	58	114	11	.382	.523
Minor League Totals				.252	252	902	155	227	53	14	27	141	138	285	31	.362	.431

24 PEDRO CATUY, OF

HIT: 55. **POW:** 45. **RUN:** 60. **FLD:** 60. **ARM:** 50. **BA Grade:** 50. **Risk:** Extreme.

Born: February 3, 2006. **B-T:** R-R. **HT:** 6-1. **WT:** 160. **Signed:** Panama, 2023.
Signed by: Cesar Geronimo Jr./Jose Luis Santos.

TRACK RECORD: A late-blooming prospect out of Panama, Catuy was physically immature when the D-backs first scouted him but continued to grow and improve with each subsequent look. Drawn to his loose, easy actions and elite athleticism, the D-backs signed him for $200,000 during the 2023 international signing period. He put together an impressive pro debut in the Dominican Summer League, posting an .803 OPS and 18 stolen bases.

SCOUTING REPORT: Catuy has a compact, quick righthanded swing with few moving parts that consistently generates line drives. He is aggressive early in counts but keeps his strikeout rate in check thanks to his ability to make contact with two strikes. He can get pull happy and needs to learn to use the whole field more often. Catuy is a plus runner who should be able to stick in center field, where his reads and routes are advanced for his age. He is thin with an athletic frame that has plenty of room for strength projection. Catuy is a confident, charismatic player whom players and staff gravitate to for his personality and work ethic.

THE FUTURE: Catuy has a chance to develop into a five-tool center fielder if his power develops. He still has a long development track ahead and will open 2024 in the Arizona Complex League.

Year	Age	Club (League)	Level	AVG	G	AB	R	H	2B	3B	HR	RBI	BB	SO	SB	OBP	SLG
2023	17	DSL D-backs Black	Rk	.288	48	170	30	49	10	2	4	24	15	33	18	.361	.441
Minor League Totals				.288	48	170	30	49	10	2	4	24	15	33	18	.361	.441

25 BRYCE JARVIS, RHP

FB: 45. **CB:** 50. **SL:** 60. **CHG:** 55. **CTL:** 45. **BA Grade:** 40. **Risk:** Medium.

Born: December 26, 1997. **B-T:** L-R. **HT:** 6-2. **WT:** 195. **Drafted:** Duke, 2020 (1st round). **Signed by:** George Swain.

TRACK RECORD: The son of 12-year major league pitcher Kevin Jarvis, Bryce had a dominant four-start run as a junior in the pandemic-shortened 2020 season, including a perfect game against Cornell, that prompted the D-backs to make him the highest-drafted player (18th overall) in Duke history. Jarvis struggled badly in his first few seasons but made adjustments that paid off in 2023. He climbed from Double-A to the majors and posted a 3.04 ERA in 11 outings with the D-backs.

SCOUTING REPORT: Jarvis averages 94-95 mph with his fastball and made changes to improve both his extension and deception in 2023. His fastball remains a fringy offering that plays down from its velocity, but it's more effective than it was before. Jarvis complements his fastball with a sharp, tight mid-80s slider that is a swing-and-miss offering at its best. He sells his changeup and gets late fade on it when he has a feel for it, but the pitch was not sharp in the majors, where hitters mostly let it go. His curveball has improved and has average potential, but he does not fully trust it. Jarvis' control and command are fringy and must improve if he hopes to remain a starter.

THE FUTURE: The D-backs are willing to remain patient with Jarvis as a starter and will give him time to further hone his command. If he doesn't he'll remain in the bullpen as a multi-inning option.

Year	Age	Club (League)	Level	W	L	ERA	G	GS	IP	H	HR	BB	SO	BB%	SO%	WHIP	AVG
2023	25	Amarillo (TL)	AA	2	1	3.86	3	3	14	8	0	7	17	12.7	30.9	1.07	.170
2023	25	Reno (PCL)	AAA	7	5	5.26	24	16	92	92	10	46	96	11.2	23.4	1.49	.256
2023	25	Arizona (NL)	MLB	2	1	3.04	11	1	24	14	3	9	12	9.8	13.0	0.97	.171
Minor League Totals				14	16	6.09	68	60	288	304	49	143	312	11.1	24.3	1.55	.271
Major League Totals				2	1	3.04	11	1	24	14	3	9	12	9.8	13.0	0.97	.171

26 CHRISTIAN CERDA, C

HIT: 45. **POW:** 45. **RUN:** 30. **FLD:** 55. **ARM:** 55. **BA Grade:** 45. **Risk:** High.

Born: December 27, 2002. **B-T:** R-R. **HT:** 6-0. **WT:** 190. **Signed:** Dominican Republic, 2019.
Signed by: Daniel Santana (Rays).

TRACK RECORD: Born in the Bronx, Cerda followed in the footsteps of his older brother, Allan, a Reds prospect, in moving to the Dominican Republic to train before signing professionally. Originally a third baseman, he moved to catcher, where his soft hands, quick feet and strong arm profiled well, and eventually signed with the Rays for $325,000. The D-backs acquired him for outfielder David Peralta at the 2022 trade deadline. Cerda played his first full season in the D-backs system in 2023 and hit .247/.402/.397 across the Class A levels.

SCOUTING REPORT: Cerda is a defense-first catcher with the attributes to be a backup. He has a simple, direct righthanded swing with few moving parts. He uses the whole field with occasional pull power. Cerda's best offensive attribute at the plate is his eye. He had nearly as many walks (93) as strikeouts (96) last season and is a consistent on-base threat. Cerda is at least an average receiver behind the plate. He blocks well and his above-average arm strength plays up with his accuracy and quick release. He has a thick, stocky build and is a slow runner. Cerda is bilingual and works well with pitchers. He is a good teammate who brings energy, positivity and toughness.

THE FUTURE: Cerda projects as a likely backup catcher. He could become more if he develops as a hitter.

Year	Age	Club (League)	Level	AVG	G	AB	R	H	2B	3B	HR	RBI	BB	SO	SB	OBP	SLG
2023	20	Visalia (CAL)	A	.252	68	238	35	60	14	1	5	32	55	61	1	.397	.382
2023	20	Hillsboro (NWL)	A+	.236	40	127	24	30	6	0	6	21	38	35	0	.411	.425
Minor League Totals				.244	185	586	97	143	37	3	14	84	141	140	11	.397	.389

27 GIAN ZAPATA, OF

HIT: 50. **POW:** 60. **RUN:** 55. **FLD:** 55. **ARM:** 60. **BA Grade:** 50. **Risk:** Extreme.

Born: September 13, 2005. **B-T:** L-L. **HT:** 6-4. **WT:** 195. **Signed:** Dominican Republic, 2023. **Signed by:** Cesar Geronimo/ Peter Wardell/Ronald Rivas.

TRACK RECORD: The D-backs followed Zapata closely for several years before signing him for $950,000 during the 2023 international signing period, their second-highest bonus in the class. Zapata flashed the ability to impact the game in several ways in his pro debut in the Dominican Summer League and hit .254/.364/.522 with nine home runs.

SCOUTING REPORT: Zapata has a classically smooth, strong swing from the left side. With a big 6-foot-4 frame that includes long levers, he has natural length to his swing that creates leverage and power but also holes, which he will need to cut down as he progresses. He doesn't chase much and hits the ball hard on contact. Tall, wiry and broad-shouldered, Zapata has tremendous physical projection and elite athleticism. He is a plus runner who chews up ground in the outfield and on the bases with graceful strides. He gets good reads and tracks balls well in center field, but his ultimate position could be in right field if he fills out and slows down as projected. He has plus arm strength.

THE FUTURE: Zapata's loud tools illustrate his massive upside, but he has to cut down on the holes in his swing. He is expected to arrive stateside in 2024.

Year	Age	Club (League)	Level	AVG	G	AB	R	H	2B	3B	HR	RBI	BB	SO	SB	OBP	SLG
2023	17	DSL D-backs Black	Rk	.118	7	17	3	2	1	0	0	1	6	6	2	.375	.176
2023	17	DSL D-backs Red	Rk	.274	37	117	23	32	8	0	9	30	13	42	3	.362	.573
Minor League Totals				.254	44	134	26	34	9	0	9	31	19	48	5	.364	.522

28 ADRIAN DEL CASTILLO, C

HIT: 50. **POW:** 45. **RUN:** 30. **FLD:** 40. **ARM:** 45. **BA Grade:** 45. **Risk:** High.

Born: September 27, 1999. **B-T:** L-R. **HT:** 5-11. **WT:** 208. **Drafted:** Miami, 2021 (2nd round supp). **Signed by:** Eric Cruz.

TRACK RECORD: Del Castillo has been an offensive-oriented catcher since his high school days and lived up to that reputation his first two years at Miami. He entered his junior year considered one of the top college hitters in the country and a likely first-round pick, but his production tailed off, making questions about his ability to catch more pronounced. He fell to the 67th overall pick, where the D-backs took him and signed him for a slightly above-slot $1 million

SCOUTING REPORT: Del Castillo has a flat, loose lefthanded swing that generates hard contact when he gets his foot down. He showed more power in 2023 than he had in the past, seeing his top-end exit velocity climb from 107 to 110 mph. He is a selective hitter who had a 14% walk rate last year, though he can have trouble with offspeed stuff. He holds his own against lefties and has a chance to be an average hitter with double-digit home run power. Del Castillo has improved as a blocker and receiver, but he's still a below-average defender who struggles to catch elite, lively stuff. He has fringe-average arm strength.

THE FUTURE: Del Castillo has work to do but could grow into an Alex Avila-type catcher. He finished last season at Triple-A and is in position to make his big league debut in 2024.

Year	Age	Club (League)	Level	AVG	G	AB	R	H	2B	3B	HR	RBI	BB	SO	SB	OBP	SLG
2023	23	Amarillo (TL)	AA	.273	63	220	36	60	13	1	12	45	40	67	2	.386	.505
2023	23	Reno (PCL)	AAA	.248	37	137	18	34	6	1	2	23	20	46	0	.340	.350
Minor League Totals				.241	210	755	99	182	45	6	22	113	106	222	7	.339	.404

29 KRISTIAN ROBINSON, OF

HIT: 40. **POW:** 60. **RUN:** 55. **FLD:** 50. **ARM:** 60. **BA Grade:** 50. **Risk:** Extreme.

Born: December 11, 2000. **B-T:** R-R. **HT:** 6-3. **WT:** 215. **Signed:** Bahamas, 2017.
Signed by: Cesar Geronimo Jr./Craig Shipley.

TRACK RECORD: The first big-dollar international signee of the Mike Hazen regime, Robinson rose quickly before legal issues stemming from an incident with a law-enforcement officer kept him off the field for three years. He returned to playing in May 2023 and showed flashes of the tremendous upside he once possessed. He hit .283/.352/.532 with 14 home runs in 65 games and rose to Double-A, but he also had a concerning 32% strikeout rate.

SCOUTING REPORT: Robinson strides forward with a leg kick ahead of a compact, powerful swing. He can drive balls to all fields with authority; his 90th percentile exit velocity of 105.8 mph ranked near the top of the system. He also controlled the zone well and carried a 10% walk rate, but his swing comes with big holes. He swung and missed at a 40% clip, including a highly alarming 34% in-zone whiff rate. Offspeed stuff gives him the most trouble. Once seen as a possible center fielder, he played primarily corner outfield in 2023, showing good range and athleticism. He remains an above-average runner with plus arm strength.

THE FUTURE: Robinson's future does not appear as bright as it once did, but with all the rust he had to knock off, he might deserve slack for the deficiencies he showed in 2023. Still just 23, the 2024 season will be a decisive year in his development.

Year	Age	Club (League)	Level	AVG	G	AB	R	H	2B	3B	HR	RBI	BB	SO	SB	OBP	SLG
2023	22	ACL D-backs Red	Rk	.296	7	27	3	8	1	1	1	4	0	8	1	.296	.519
2023	22	Visalia (CAL)	A	.288	43	156	29	45	6	3	9	26	24	58	20	.407	.538
2023	22	Hillsboro (NWL)	A+	.265	10	34	6	9	0	0	2	6	4	13	2	.359	.441
2023	22	Amarillo (TL)	AA	.250	5	16	4	4	1	0	2	6	1	7	0	.294	.688
Minor League Totals				.282	191	710	133	200	33	6	35	134	87	230	52	.371	.493

30 ANDREW SAALFRANK, LHP

FB: 50. **CB:** 60. **CTL:** 45. **BA Grade:** 40. **Risk:** Medium.

Born: August 18, 1997. **B-T:** L-L. **HT:** 6-3. **WT:** 220. **Drafted:** Indiana, 2019 (6th round). **Signed by:** Jeremy Kehrt.

TRACK RECORD: Saalfrank pitched mostly in relief his first two years at Indiana, but he shifted to the rotation his junior year and won Big Ten pitcher of the year. The D-backs drafted him in the sixth round and signed him for $225,000. Saalfrank missed consecutive seasons due to the coronavirus pandemic and Tommy John surgery, but he returned in 2022 and flourished in relief while reaching Double-A. He showed up to camp in excellent shape in 2023, earned his first callup in September and pitched in crucial spots throughout the postseason.

SCOUTING REPORT: Saalfrank operates with two pitches. His heavy sinker sits 92-93 mph and induces a high rate of grounders. His signature pitch is a hard, 83-84 mph curveball with depth and sweep that plays against both lefties and righties. Saalfrank's effectiveness simply depends on if he's throwing strikes. When he does, he is hard to hit. When he doesn't, which was the case when he walked seven of the 12 batters he faced in the National League Championship Series, he can be his own worst enemy.

THE FUTURE: Saalfrank figures to come to camp in 2024 with a leg up on a bullpen job. If he finds the strike zone, he's a safe bet to open the year in the majors.

Year	Age	Club (League)	Level	W	L	ERA	G	GS	IP	H	HR	BB	SO	BB%	SO%	WHIP	AVG
2023	25	Amarillo (TL)	AA	4	0	2.70	21	0	33	23	0	20	45	14.2	31.9	1.29	.195
2023	25	Reno (PCL)	AAA	4	2	2.35	23	0	31	22	2	15	48	11.7	37.5	1.21	.196
2023	25	Arizona (NL)	MLB	0	0	0.00	10	0	10	7	0	4	6	9.8	14.6	1.06	.189
Minor League Totals				12	6	3.05	90	5	130	95	9	66	185	11.8	33.2	1.24	.197
Major League Totals				0	0	0.00	10	0	10	7	0	4	6	9.8	14.6	1.06	.189

Jared Shuster made the Opening Day rotation but spent most of the second half at Triple-A.

DYLAN BUELL/GETTY IMAGES

Atlanta Braves

BY CARLOS COLLAZO

The Braves extended their National League East winning streak to six years in 2023, led all of baseball with 104 wins and entered the postseason as the presumptive favorites, thanks to a high-powered offense that was one of the best lineups in baseball history.

Led by face of the franchise Ronald Acuña Jr.—who won his first MVP award after a historic 41-homer, 73-stolen base season—the Braves led the majors in most offensive categories including runs, home runs, average, on-base percentage, slugging percentage and wRC+.

First baseman Matt Olson led MLB with 54 home runs and 139 RBIs. He finished fourth in NL MVP voting.

Beyond Acuña Jr. and Olson, the Braves' lineup was truly one without a hole the entire season. Each of the team's nine regulars finished the season with a wRC+ of 99 or better—with shortstop Orlando Arcia missing the league average 100 mark by a single point—and seven batters finished the year with 20 or more home runs.

The 2023 Braves slugged .501—the first team ever to finish at .500 or higher—and they were also the first team to hit 300 homers and steal 100 bases in the same season. While it might seem hyperbolic to compare the 2023 Braves to the vaunted 1927 Yankees, they became the first team to ever match the 125 wRC+ mark the Murderers' Row Yankees established nearly 100 years ago.

Yet for all that, the Braves were bounced from the postseason in the NL Division Series for the second straight year by the division-rival Phillies. Atlanta's vaunted offense went quiet at the wrong time, and injuries to the pitching staff meant the Braves were short-handed against a high-powered Phillies offense.

Spencer Strider pitched well in two postseason starts and once again looked like a reliable frontline arm throughout the regular season. He led the majors with 281 strikeouts and finished fourth in

PROJECTED 2027 LINEUP

Catcher	Sean Murphy	32
First Base	Matt Olson	33
Second Base	Ozzie Albies	30
Third Base	Austin Riley	30
Shortstop	Vaughn Grissom	26
Left Field	Jarred Kelenic	27
Center Field	Michael Harris II	26
Right Field	Ronald Acuña Jr.	29
Designated Hitter	David McCabe	27
No. 1 Starter	Spencer Strider	28
No. 2 Starter	Max Fried	33
No. 3 Starter	AJ Smith-Shawver	24
No. 4 Starter	Bryce Elder	28
No. 5 Starter	JR Ritchie	24
Closer	Hurston Waldrep	25

NL Cy Young Award voting.

While the Braves' young, team-controlled offensive core remains the envy of baseball, there are questions looming on the pitching front. Ace lefthander Max Fried will be a free agent after the 2024 season, and veteran stalwart Charlie Morton will pitch in his age-40 season.

While Atlanta's farm system remains thin on impact position players and overall depth, it is strong in the areas of need. Top prospect AJ Smith-Shawver and 2023 first-rounder Hurston Waldrep are MLB-ready righthanders with standout stuff. So too are a number of lower-upside, depth arms with proven success in the upper minors.

The Braves are solidly back in the mix on the international front, which should help supplement the lower levels of the system in the next few years. The team's scouting and player development groups continue to find hidden big league value.

Atlanta suffered a drain of front office and coaching talent. Former scouting director Dana Brown took the Astros' general manager job in January 2023. Third base coach Ron Washington left to manage the Angels after the season.

However, employees leaving the organization for roles that amount to promotions is typically a sign of a well-run organization, and that's exactly what the Braves have been for six years under general manager Alex Anthopoulos. ∎

DEPTH CHART

ATLANTA BRAVES

TOP 2024 CONTRIBUTORS	RANK
1. AJ Smith-Shawver, RHP	1
2. Hurston Waldrep, RHP	2
3. Dylan Dodd, LHP	11

BREAKOUT PROSPECTS	RANK
1. Jhancarlos Lara, RHP	13
2. Luis Guanipa, OF	17
3. Garrett Baumann, RHP	18

SOURCE OF TOP 30 TALENT

Homegrown	28	Acquired	2
College	14	Trade	0
Junior college	2	Rule 5 draft	2
High school	6	Independent league	0
Nondrafted free agent	1	Free agent/waivers	0
International	5		

LF
Jesse Franklin (15)
Ethan Workinger

CF
Luis Guanipa (17)
Isaiah Drake (19)
Cody Milligan (26)
Kevin Kilpatrick Jr.
Tyler Collins

RF
Douglas Glod (28)
Justin Dean

3B
David McCabe (6)
Sabin Ceballos (22)
John Gil

SS
Ignacio Alvarez (8)
Diego Benitez (25)
Ambioris Tavarez (30)
Mario Baez

2B
Keshawn Ogans (29)
Luke Waddell
Geraldo Quintero
Cal Conley

1B
Bryson Horne
Elian Cortorreal
Drew Compton

C
Drake Baldwin (7)
Tyler Tolve
Adam Zebrowski
Javier Valdes
Chadwick Tromp

LHP

LHSP	LHRP
Dylan Dodd (11)	Hayden Harris (21)
Luis De Avila (23)	Jake McSteen
Rolando Gutierrez	Samuel Strickland
Riley Frey	Adam Shoemaker
	Mitch Farris

RHP

RHSP	RHRP
AJ Smith-Shawver (1)	Tyler Owens (20)
Hurston Waldrep (2)	Blake Burkhalter (24)
JR Ritchie (3)	Jared Johnson
Owen Murphy (4)	Seth Keller
Spencer Schwellenbach (5)	Daysbel Hernandez
Drue Hackenberg (9)	Austin Smith
Cade Kuehler (10)	Trey Riley
Darius Vines (12)	
Jhancarlos Lara (13)	
Lucas Braun (14)	
Allan Winans (16)	
Garrett Baumann (18)	
Ian Mejia (27)	
Jorge Bautista	
Adam Maier	

1 AJ SMITH-SHAWVER, RHP

Born: November 20, 2002. **B-T:** R-R. **HT:** 6-3. **WT:** 205.
Drafted: HS—Colleyville, TX, 2021 (7th round).
Signed by: Trey McNickle.

TRACK RECORD: Smith-Shawver was a two-way player in high school, and he also had Division I offers as a three-star quarterback, but the Braves bought into his athleticism and arm talent on the mound. The team signed him to an over-slot deal of just under $1 million in the seventh round of the 2021 draft. Despite being fairly raw as a pitcher, Smith-Shawver advanced four levels in his second full professional season in 2023 and made his major league debut as a 20-year-old. He struck out three batters in a relief appearance on June 4, then made five more starts in the majors and posted a 4.26 ERA in 25.1 innings, with 20 strikeouts and 11 walks.

SCOUTING REPORT: Smith-Shawver has one of the best fastballs in the system. After topping out around 94-95 mph in high school, he now averages that speed with the pitch. He's been up to 100 mph at peak velocity and also generates plus carry on his fastball with around 19 inches of induced vertical break. The pitch is a definite plus offering and could be a 70-grade offering if he develops his command and is able to consistently attack hitters at the top of the zone. After focusing on a slider in previous years, Smith-Shawver now throws multiple breaking balls: a mid-80s slider with sweeping action and occasional hard tilt and an upper-70s curveball with 11-to-5 shape and more depth. Analytics prefer his slider, but scouts were impressed with the progress he made with his curveball this spring, and both pitches have a chance to be above-average or plus offerings. Smith-Shawver has reasonable feel for both pitches and throws them for strikes at a similar rate. His effectiveness would be improved on both breaking pitches with more refined command and consistency—sometimes his curveball will pop up out of his hand and he'll also yank the slider to his glove side with some regularity. Smith-Shawver has also developed a mid-80s split-changeup that has turned into a reliable fourth offering to attack lefthanded hitters. The pitch has decent tumbling action and fade to his arm side and generated a 53% whiff rate in the minors. Smith-Shawver's delivery has improved each year and he works

DAVID J. GRIFFIN/ICON SPORTSWIRE VIA GETTY IMAGES

BA GRADE		SCOUTING GRADES	
55	Risk: High	**FB:** 65. **CB:** 55. **SL:** 60.	
		CHG: 50. **CTL:** 55.	

Projected future grades on 20-80 scouting scale

BEST TOOLS

BATTING

Best Hitter for Average	Ignacio Alvarez
Best Power Hitter	Drake Baldwin
Best Strike-Zone Discipline	Ignacio Alvarez
Fastest Baserunner	Isaiah Drake
Best Athlete	AJ Smith-Shawver

PITCHING

Best Fastball	Owen Murphy
Best Curveball	AJ Smith-Shawver
Best Slider	JR Ritchie
Best Changeup	Hurston Waldrep
Best Control	Lucas Braun

FIELDING

Best Defensive Catcher	Tyler Tolve
Best Defensive Infielder	Ambioris Tavarez
Best Infield Arm	Sabin Ceballos
Best Defensive Outfielder	Kevin Kilpatrick Jr.
Best Outfield Arm	Douglas Glod

from the first-base side of the rubber and throws with great arm speed from a three-quarters slot before finishing with a closed-toe, crossfire landing. His balance has improved in his finish and he's now a fair strike-thrower, though he still needs to sharpen his command.

THE FUTURE: Smith-Shawver became the first prep pitcher from the 2021 class to make his MLB debut, and has consistently teased front-of-the-rotation upside. To fully realize that potential, he'll need to sharpen his command and consistency, though even if he doesn't he has the pure stuff, athleticism and strike-throwing to settle into a midrotation role. After making Atlanta's Division Series roster in 2023, he should get a chance to fully cement himself in 2024. ∎

Year	Age	Club (League)	Level	W	L	ERA	G	GS	IP	H	HR	BB	SO	BB%	SO%	WHIP	AVG
2023	20	Rome (SAL)	A+	1	0	0.00	3	3	14	6	0	4	23	7.7	44.2	0.71	.125
2023	20	Mississippi (SL)	AA	1	0	0.00	2	2	7	5	0	3	9	10.3	31.0	1.14	.192
2023	20	Gwinnett (IL)	AAA	2	2	4.17	10	10	41	26	4	26	47	15.2	27.5	1.27	.179
2023	20	Atlanta (NL)	MLB	1	0	4.26	6	5	25	17	7	11	20	10.5	19.0	1.11	.183
Minor League Totals				7	7	4.27	36	36	139	95	10	82	198	13.9	33.6	1.27	.191
Major League Totals				1	0	4.26	6	5	25	17	7	11	20	10.5	19.0	1.11	.183

2 HURSTON WALDREP, RHP

FB: 60. **SL:** 60. **CHG:** 65. **CTL:** 40. **BA Grade:** 55. **Risk:** High.

Born: March 1, 2002. **B-T:** R-R. **HT:** 6-2. **WT:** 210.
Drafted: Florida, 2023 (1st round). **Signed by:** Jon Bunnell.
TRACK RECORD: Waldrep started his career at Southern Mississippi, where he showcased some of the best pure stuff and arm speed in the country. After a stint with USA Baseball's Collegiate National Team, Waldrep spent his junior season at Florida, where he finished third in the country with 156 strikeouts in 2023. The Braves signed him to an under-slot deal just under $3 million with the 24th pick and he moved from Low-A Augusta all the way to Triple-A Gwinnett in his pro debut.
SCOUTING REPORT: Waldrep has a chance for three plus pitches, starting with a fastball that has easy plus velocity and averages 95-96 mph but has been up to 99 in the past. The pitch has just average life and carry and will primarily play thanks to its velocity and his quality secondaries. Waldrep threw both a slider and curveball in college, but the Braves had him scrap the curve and focus on his slider in his pro debut—a common theme of their pitching development. He throws the slider in the mid-to-upper 80s and the pitch features sharp, two-plane bite at its best. His most devastating pitch is an upper-80s splitter that completely falls off the table and generates ugly swings against hitters unable to hold back. Waldrep generated whiff rates north of 50% with both his slider and splitter in his pro debut. He has a violent delivery with a sharp head whack and below-average control.
THE FUTURE: The Braves worked with Waldrep to improve his rhythm and tempo in his pro debut, and continued refinement of his control and command will be crucial for him to profile as a midrotation starter. If not, he has the stuff to pitch in a high-leverage reliever role. Atlanta's fast-tracking of him indicates he could make his big league debut in 2024.

Year	Age	Club (League)	Level	W	L	ERA	G	GS	IP	H	HR	BB	SO	BB%	SO%	WHIP	AVG
2023	21	Augusta (CAR)	A	0	0	3.00	1	1	3	3	0	1	8	7.7	61.5	1.33	.250
2023	21	Rome (SAL)	A+	0	0	0.75	3	3	12	4	0	5	17	11.1	37.8	0.75	.100
2023	21	Mississippi (SL)	AA	0	1	2.70	3	3	10	8	1	7	11	15.6	24.4	1.50	.216
2023	21	Gwinnett (IL)	AAA	0	0	0.00	1	1	4	4	0	3	5	15.0	25.0	1.62	.235
Minor League Totals				0	1	1.55	8	8	29	19	1	16	41	13.0	33.3	1.21	.179

3 JR RITCHIE, RHP

FB: 55. **SL:** 60. **CHG:** 50. **CTL:** 60. **BA Grade:** 55 **Risk:** Extreme

Born: June 26, 2003. **B-T:** R-R. **HT:** 6-2. **WT:** 185.
Drafted: HS—Bainbridge Island, WA, 2022 (1st round supp). **Signed by:** Cody Martin.
TRACK RECORD: Ritchie stood out for his advanced feel for pitching out of high school, and after the Braves acquired the 35th overall pick in 2022 in a trade with the Royals, they selected and signed him to a $2.4 million bonus. Ritchie has been quietly excellent in his brief time in pro ball, though he was limited to just 14.1 innings in 2022 after signing, and then his 2023 season was cut short after just 13.1 innings in Low-A Augusta thanks to a UCL tear in his elbow that required Tommy John surgery.
SCOUTING REPORT: Ritchie has a lean pitcher's frame at 6-foot-2, 185 pounds and attacks hitters with a three-pitch mix. His fastball averaged 93.5 mph and touched 96, though he has gotten to 97-98 in the past. The pitch has just average life, but Ritchie has great feel to spot the pitch within the zone. His best offering in 2023 was a low-80s slider with high spin rates in the 2,500 rpm range. His slider has solid two-plane break that generated a 53% miss rate and an excellent 46% chase rate. Ritchie showed excellent feel to land his fastball and slider with precision and throw them for strikes. His mid-80s changeup is mostly used against lefthanders, and he frequently missed with the pitch down and to his arm side, though he got strong results with it in terms of misses and chases. Ritchie showed plus control prior to getting hurt and has a smooth, easy delivery. He repeats his release point consistently and lands balanced with minimal violence.
THE FUTURE: Ritchie will spend the offseason going through Tommy John rehab and should miss a portion of the 2024 season. The Braves could push him quickly if he returns fully healthy and continues to show advanced pitchability. He has midrotation starter upside.

Year	Age	Club (League)	Level	W	L	ERA	G	GS	IP	H	HR	BB	SO	BB%	SO%	WHIP	AVG
2023	20	Augusta (CAR)	A	0	1	5.40	4	4	13	11	0	3	25	5.7	47.2	1.05	.220
Minor League Totals				0	1	3.67	9	9	28	20	1	8	39	7.4	36.1	1.04	.202

4 OWEN MURPHY, RHP

FB: 60. **CB:** 55. **SL:** 55. **CTL:** 55. **BA Grade:** 50. **Risk:** High.

Born: September 27, 2003. **B-T:** R-R. **HT:** 6-1. **WT:** 190.
Drafted: HS—Riverside, IL, 2022 (1st round). **Signed by:** Jeremy Gordon.
TRACK RECORD: The Braves made Murphy one of the next in their long line of two-way players when they selected him 20th overall and signed him to a bonus just over $2.5 million in 2022. He also excelled on the football field and as a shortstop at Riverside-Brookfield High in suburban Chicago. After a limited pro debut in 2022, Murphy had a sound first full season in 2023 at Low-A Augusta, reaching High-A Rome for three starts. He was one of just 10 teenage pitchers to throw at least 80 innings, and of that group his 29.6% strikeout rate and 21.2 K-BB% were the highest.
SCOUTING REPORT: Murphy's fastball velocity backed up in 2023, but the pitch is still one of the better heaters in the organization given its spin characteristics and riding life. He averaged 90-91 mph and touched 94, but he averages more than 19 inches of induced vertical break from a lower attack angle and because of that generates lots of swings and misses at the top of the zone. He threw his fastball for strikes at a strong 68% clip. He throws a low-80s slider and a mid-70s curveball that both have above-average potential and impressive spin. The Braves were especially excited about the progress he made with his slider and noted that he threw it for strikes at a strong 71% clip. His curveball has more depth but is in the zone less frequently. Murphy took a step forward with his control and walked just 8.4% of batters and works with a relatively clean and athletic delivery.
THE FUTURE: With a strong full season under this belt, Murphy's next task will be to add more power to all of his pitches. He should get a chance at Double-A in 2024 with sustained performance, and he has No. 3 or No. 4 starter upside potential.

Year	Age	Club (League)	Level	W	L	ERA	G	GS	IP	H	HR	BB	SO	BB%	SO%	WHIP	AVG
2023	19	Augusta (CAR)	A	6	3	4.71	18	18	73	62	8	28	97	9.1	31.4	1.24	.227
2023	19	Rome (SAL)	A+	0	1	4.76	3	3	17	21	1	4	16	5.5	21.9	1.47	.313
Minor League Totals				6	5	4.72	26	26	102	90	9	38	130	8.8	30.2	1.27	.235

5 SPENCER SCHWELLENBACH, RHP

FB: 60. **CB:** 55. **SL:** 55. **CHG:** 50. **CTL:** 60. **BA Grade:** 50. **Risk:** High.

Born: May 31, 2000. **B-T:** R-R. **HT:** 6-1. **WT:** 200.
Drafted: Nebraska, 2021 (2nd round). **Signed by:** JD French.
TRACK RECORD: Schwellenbach was one of the best two-way players in the 2021 class, and the Braves loved his arm talent enough to sign him to a $1 million deal in the second round. He had Tommy John surgery after the draft and didn't pitch in 2021 or 2022. In his pro debut in 2023, Schwellenbach posted a 2.49 ERA in 65 innings with Low-A Augusta and High-A Rome, showed plus control and also represented the Braves in the Futures Game.
SCOUTING REPORT: The powerfully built, athletic righthander has a four-pitch mix led by a 94-96 mph fastball and was up to 98 post-surgery. While the pitch has always had big-time velocity, it can play down at times thanks to below-average riding life, though Schwellenbach does an excellent job throwing the pitch for strikes to get ahead in the count. He throws two breaking ball variants: the first a firm slider/cutter in the mid-to-upper 80s and the second a more slurve-like curve that has more depth and was a solid swing-and-miss offering at the lower levels. Schwellenbach showed good feel to throw both breaking balls for strikes at a high clip, and both feature high spin rates in the 2,400-2,500 rpm range. Against lefthanders, Schwellenbach will mix in an average mid-80s changeup, though his feel for the pitch is further behind his other three. Schwellenbach is a natural strike-thrower dating back to his college days and has a chance for plus control and plus pitchability.
THE FUTURE: Schwellenbach missed about a month in 2023 with right shoulder inflammation, so his medical history still raises questions. His control and athleticism should give him every opportunity to start, but there's a chance his stuff plays up in a bullpen role, which could be the route that leads him to the big leagues quickest.

Year	Age	Club (League)	Level	W	L	ERA	G	GS	IP	H	HR	BB	SO	BB%	SO%	WHIP	AVG
2023	23	Augusta (CAR)	A	4	2	2.63	13	13	51	44	3	15	41	7.2	19.6	1.15	.234
2023	23	Rome (SAL)	A+	1	0	1.98	3	3	14	4	0	1	14	2.2	30.4	0.37	.091
Minor League Totals				5	2	2.49	16	16	65	48	3	16	55	6.3	21.6	0.98	.207

6 DAVID McCABE, 3B/1B

HIT: 45. **POW:** 55. **RUN:** 30. **FLD:** 40. **ARM:** 55. **BA Grade:** 45 **Risk:** High

Born: March 25, 2000. **B-T:** B-R. **HT:** 6-3. **WT:** 230.
Drafted: UNC Charlotte, 2022 (4th round). **Signed by:** Billy Best.
TRACK RECORD: McCabe played high school ball outside Toronto then shined in three years at UNC Charlotte, hitting 30 home runs combined in his final two collegiate seasons. He ranked as the No. 315 prospect in the 2022 draft class, but he stood out for his excellent hitting ability, raw power and approach at the plate. The Braves signed him for $476,400 in the fourth round and in his first full season in 2023 he looked like one of the most well-rounded hitters in Atlanta's system. His 133 wRC+ trailed only Vaughn Grissom among Braves minor leaguers who batted at least 400 times, and he also hit 17 home runs and 23 doubles.
SCOUTING REPORT: McCabe has a large, physical frame with plus raw power from the left side and a great eye at the plate. His 15.3% walk rate was the highest of any player in the system with at least 500 plate appearances, and he consistently put together competitive at-bats and chased at just a 17.7% rate—one of the lowest marks in the system. A switch-hitter, McCabe is better from the left side of the plate and 16 of his 17 home runs came from the left side, in addition to 20 of his 23 doubles. He has an open setup at the plate and takes a sizable leg kick to get started before swinging in an uphill path. There are some questions about his ability to handle fastballs thrown 93 mph or faster, but his on-base skills and power could make him a productive offensive player even as a below-average pure hitter. McCabe is a below-average defender at third base and will need to move to either first base or a corner-outfield spot. He has below-average range and actions, and despite 10 stolen bases is heavy-footed and a well below-average runner. He has above-average arm strength.
THE FUTURE: McCabe was old for both levels in 2023, so he should be challenged at Double-A in 2024.

Year	Age	Club (League)	Level	AVG	G	AB	R	H	2B	3B	HR	RBI	BB	SO	SB	OBP	SLG
2023	23	Augusta (CAR)	A	.267	42	146	26	39	7	1	8	25	27	47	1	.381	.493
2023	23	Rome (SAL)	A+	.281	81	292	37	82	16	0	9	50	53	66	9	.388	.428
Minor League Totals				.270	152	544	78	147	29	1	18	98	96	140	10	.376	.427

7 DRAKE BALDWIN, C

HIT: 45. **POW:** 50. **RUN:** 30. **FLD:** 45. **ARM:** 50. **BA Grade:** 45. **Risk:** High.

Born: March 28, 2001. **B-T:** L-R. **HT:** 6-0. **WT:** 210.
Drafted: Missouri State, 2022 (3rd round). **Signed by:** JD French.
TRACK RECORD: Baldwin used a 19-homer platform draft year at Missouri State to catapult himself into early Day 2 draft range, and the Braves signed him for $633,300 in the third round in 2022. After a brief pro debut mostly with Low-A Augusta, Baldwin played mostly at High-A Rome in 2023 but saw time at both Double-A Mississippi and Triple-A Gwinnett. He was one of Atlanta's most productive minor league hitters with a 132 wRC+, 16 home runs and 26 doubles.
SCOUTING REPORT: Baldwin has a unique setup at the plate with an extremely high initial handset, before getting into a more typical launch position with a high leg lift as the pitcher drives toward the plate. While he's never had crazy bat speed, Baldwin does have solid raw power. He managed some of the best exit velocity numbers in Atlanta's system this year, with a 90.1 mph average and 105.1 mph 90th percentile EVs. He has solid plate discipline and managed a 14.1% walk rate, while hammering fastballs—including those at 93 mph plus—though he needs to cut down his swing-and-miss against secondaries. Baldwin is a fair defender behind the plate. He works from a one-knee setup and presents the ball reasonably well. He improved his ability to control the running game, though his arm strength is just average. He mostly clocks 2.00-second pop times to second, but will occasionally hit 1.90 on a clean release. Baldwin is a well below-average runner.
THE FUTURE: Baldwin's most likely outcome is a serviceable, lefthanded-hitting backup catcher who brings a solid combination of receiving ability, plate discipline and contact skills. He should spend 2024 in the upper minors. If he takes a step forward on either side of the ball he could profile more as a regular.

Year	Age	Club (League)	Level	AVG	G	AB	R	H	2B	3B	HR	RBI	BB	SO	SB	OBP	SLG
2023	22	Rome (SAL)	A+	.260	92	335	57	87	25	1	14	54	61	84	0	.385	.466
2023	22	Mississippi (SL)	AA	.321	14	53	4	17	1	0	1	5	6	11	0	.390	.396
2023	22	Gwinnett (IL)	AAA	.333	3	12	2	4	0	0	1	2	0	3	0	.333	.583
Minor League Totals				.268	133	489	78	131	31	1	16	70	86	123	1	.387	.434

8 IGNACIO ALVAREZ, 3B/SS

HIT: 50. **POW:** 40. **RUN:** 40. **FLD:** 45. **ARM:** 55. **BA Grade:** 45. **Risk:** High.

Born: April 11, 2003. **B-T:** R-R. **HT:** 5-11. **WT:** 190.
Drafted: Riverside (CA) JC, 2022 (5th round). **Signed by:** Ryan Dobson.
TRACK RECORD: Alvarez was a productive junior college hitter who helped lead his Riverside club to a California state championship, though scouts were mixed on his pro potential and upside. The Braves were high on his hitting and defensive ability and signed him to a $500,000 deal in the fifth round in 2022, and he's shown lots of contact and on-base skills in his first two seasons. As a 20-year-old in the South Atlantic League, Alvarez's .395 on-base percentage was ninth-best in the High-A circuit.
SCOUTING REPORT: Despite a swing with a lot of moving parts, Alvarez has arguably the best pure bat-to-ball skills in Atlanta's system. He has a high handset with lots of bat waggle, a toe tap that coincides with a hand push in his load before taking another step in his lower half and firing his hands with a level path through the zone. Alvarez chased a bit more against High-A pitching but still has a keen batting eye and strong swing decisions. He rarely misses within the strike zone, but is a hit-over-power offensive profile who might have more doubles power than home run juice. Alvarez has fine exit velocity data for his age—an 87.8 mph average and 102.2 mph 90th percentile mark—but he has limited physical projection with a filled-out frame. Alvarez turns in fringe-average run times, but his foot speed and range are his biggest defensive questions. He's sure-handed on the balls he gets to at shortstop with above-average arm strength, but most external scouts view him as a corner infielder.
THE FUTURE: Alvarez continues to showcase impressive contact ability that should get him to the big leagues, though his defensive role and power will ultimately determine his upside. He should keep playing every day at shortstop in 2024 in Double-A.

Year	Age	Club (League)	Level	AVG	G	AB	R	H	2B	3B	HR	RBI	BB	SO	SB	OBP	SLG
2023	20	Rome (SAL)	A+	.284	116	419	62	119	24	0	7	66	66	87	16	.395	.391
Minor League Totals				.285	146	513	87	146	27	2	8	77	92	102	24	.406	.392

9 DRUE HACKENBERG, RHP

FB: 50. **SL:** 50. **CHG:** 45. **CTL:** 55. **BA Grade:** 45. **Risk:** High.

Born: April 1, 2002. **B-T:** R-R. **HT:** 6-2. **WT:** 220.
Drafted: Virginia Tech, 2023 (2nd round). **Signed by:** Alan Sandberg.
TRACK RECORD: Hackenberg stepped into a full-time starting role from Day One with Virginia Tech. After posting a 4.50 ERA over two seasons and a stint with Team USA he ranked as the No. 148 prospect in the 2023 draft class. The Braves liked the draft-eligible sophomore better than that and selected him with the No. 59 overall pick and signed him to an over-slot bonus just under $2 million. Hackenberg made three starts after signing and looked too advanced for Low-A Augusta, but was uncharacteristically wild in his single outing with Double-A Mississippi.
SCOUTING REPORT: A Bryce Elder comparison isn't too far off with Hackenberg, who employs a similar sinker/slider pitch mix. Hackenberg's fastball sits in the 92-93 mph range and has been up to 96, with heavy armside running action that tends to keep contact on the ground. He generated a 55% groundball rate during his college career and was off to more of the same in his brief pro debut. Hackenberg pairs his sinker with a low-to-mid-80s breaking ball that mostly has slider shape, but he will occasionally blend into a slurvy curveball look. It's a solid-average pitch that took a step forward as a swing-and-miss offering in college and has spin rates in the 2,500 rpm range. Hackenberg also has a firm, upper-80s changeup that is almost exclusively used against lefthanded hitters. It's more of a fringe-average pitch without significant life or velocity separation from his fastball. But it could be useful in keeping lefty hitters off the barrel. Hackenberg historically is a strong strike-thrower, but his fastball was a bit more scattered than usual in his short pro debut.
THE FUTURE: Hackenberg has back-of-the-rotation upside. If he winds up being an Elder-esque arm with a better fastball, Atlanta will be quite happy. He should be challenged with a full season at Double-A.

Year	Age	Club (League)	Level	W	L	ERA	G	GS	IP	H	HR	BB	SO	BB%	SO%	WHIP	AVG
2023	21	Augusta (CAR)	A	0	0	0.00	2	2	6	3	0	2	12	8.7	52.2	0.88	.143
2023	21	Mississippi (SL)	AA	0	0	13.50	1	1	1	0	0	4	1	66.7	16.7	6.00	.000
Minor League Totals				0	0	1.50	3	3	6	3	0	6	13	20.7	44.8	1.50	.130

10 CADE KUEHLER, RHP

FB: 60. **CB:** 45. **SL:** 55. **CHG:** 45. **CTL:** 45. **BA Grade:** 45. **Risk:** High.

Born: May 24, 2002. **B-T:** R-R. **HT:** 6-0. **WT:** 215.
Drafted: Campbell, 2023 (2nd round supplemental). **Signed by:** Billy Best.
TRACK RECORD: Kuehler was a starter and reliever with Campbell early in his career before settling in as a full-time starter for his sophomore and junior seasons. He spent a summer with the USA Baseball Collegiate National Team in 2022, then had a career year with Campbell as a junior and ranked as the No. 53 prospect in the 2023 class. The Braves signed him for just over $1 million with the 70th overall pick and he made two starts with Low-A Augusta after signing.
SCOUTING REPORT: A filled-out, physical 6-foot righthander, Kuehler showed a diverse and deep pitch mix in college that was already pared down in his short pro debut. His calling card is a fastball that averaged 94 mph with Campbell and has been up to 98 with some of the best riding life in the 2023 draft class. The pitch averaged 20 inches of induced vertical break in college, and while it wasn't quite that high in the minors, he still has plus ride on the pitch. Kuehler has also thrown a slider, curveball, changeup and cutter, but with Augusta he primarily threw his mid-80s, short-breaking slider and worked on a low-to-mid-80s split-changeup. Kuehler's slider has gyro shape and sometimes looks more like a cutter, but it plays well off the fastball. Since shortening his slider, he's been able to land it for strikes more consistently. Kuehler has a below-average delivery with moving parts and a short, compact arm action, though the Braves had him work out of the stretch in Augusta to help him rotate on time and add consistency to his release point.
THE FUTURE: There's significant reliever risk with Kuehler based on his delivery, but he's got plenty of arm talent for an organization that has a strong track record developing college pitchers, ranging from Spencer Strider to Bryce Elder.

Year	Age	Club (League)	Level	W	L	ERA	G	GS	IP	H	HR	BB	SO	BB%	SO%	WHIP	AVG
2023	21	Augusta (CAR)	A	0	0	0.00	2	2	7	1	0	4	8	15.4	30.8	0.71	.045
Minor League Totals				0	0	0.00	2	2	7	1	0	4	8	15.4	30.8	0.71	.045

11 DYLAN DODD, LHP

FB: 45. **SL:** 50. **CHG:** 45. **CUT:** 45. **CTL:** 55. **BA Grade:** 40. **Risk:** Medium.

Born: June 6, 1998. **B-T:** L-L. **HT:** 6-2. **WT:** 210. **Drafted:** Southeast Missouri State, 2021 (3rd round).
Signed by: JD French.
TRACK RECORD: Dodd signed for an under-slot bonus of $125,000 in the third round of the 2021 draft and made his major league debut just two years after signing. He showed solid command and enough bat-missing traits in the lower minors, but in 2023 he got hit around more frequently in both Triple-A Gwinnett and in seven big league starts with the Braves. In seven big league starts, Dodd posted an 8.59 ERA, 7.76 FIP and allowed nine home runs.
SCOUTING REPORT: Dodd is a pitchability lefthander with fringe-average pure stuff, but above-average strike throwing that has pushed him to the big leagues. He throws a fastball that sits in the 90-94 mph range and has been up to 96. He can locate the fastball to both sides of the plate nicely, but its fringy velocity and mediocre life means it gets hit hard. Likewise, Dodd has feel to land a gradual, low-80s slider and soft, low-80s changeup, but neither pitch has ever shown above-average bat-missing traits. Dodd added a mid-80s cutter to his arsenal in 2023 to provide a different look, and it could be effective to avoid barrels and keep the ball on the ground more frequently but its usage was minimal.
THE FUTURE: Dodd has 40-man value as a depth starter or middle reliever, especially as a lefthanded pitcher, but he'll need to add something more—power, sharper secondaries—to establish himself as a regular on a contending team.

Year	Age	Club (League)	Level	W	L	ERA	G	GS	IP	H	HR	BB	SO	BB%	SO%	WHIP	AVG
2023	25	FCL Braves	Rk	0	0	0.00	1	1	3	0	0	0	4	0.0	40.0	0.00	.000
2023	25	Gwinnett (IL)	AAA	4	6	5.91	16	14	75	86	14	30	67	9.1	20.4	1.55	.291
2023	25	Atlanta (NL)	MLB	2	2	7.60	7	7	34	53	9	12	15	7.3	9.1	1.89	.351
Minor League Totals				16	17	4.46	47	45	234	241	28	64	244	6.5	24.7	1.30	.264
Major League Totals				2	2	7.60	7	7	34	53	9	12	15	7.3	9.1	1.89	.351

12 DARIUS VINES, RHP

FB: 40. **SL:** 45. **CHG:** 60. **CUT:** 45 **CTL:** 60. **BA Grade:** 40. **Risk:** Medium.

Born: April 30, 1998. **B-T:** R-R. **HT:** 6-1. **WT:** 190. **Drafted:** Cal State Bakersfield, 2019 (7th round).
Signed by: Kevin Martin.

TRACK RECORD: Vines signed for $130,000 as a seventh-round pick in the 2019 draft when he established himself as an advanced college strike thrower. He confirmed that reputation in pro ball, developed one of the system's best changeups and pushed through the minors despite below-average velocity to make his big league debut in 2023. Vines pitched as a starter and reliever in the majors and posted a 3.98 ERA in 20.1 innings.

SCOUTING REPORT: A solidly-built righthander with a clean and easy delivery, Vines attacks hitters from the third base side of the rubber and mixes and matches with four different pitches. He averages just 89-90 mph with his fastball and gets up to 93, but despite well below-average velocity Vines does have above-average riding life on the pitch. His low-80s changeup is his best offering, a plus pitch with tremendous tumbling action that he locates at will. He also locates a low-80s slider at a high clip, but the pitch has just mediocre power and shape. Vines added a mid-80s cutter to his arsenal in 2023 and in the majors used the pitch a third of the time. In isolation, none of Vines' pitches other than his changeup stands out, but he pitches on the edges at an above-average rate and might have just enough pitchability to keep hitters off-balance.

THE FUTURE: It's tough to find long-term success with a fastball as light as Vines', but he might have a deep enough pitch mix with enough command to add value as a swingman or long reliever.

Year	Age	Club (League)	Level	W	L	ERA	G	GS	IP	H	HR	BB	SO	BB%	SO%	WHIP	AVG
2023	25	FCL Braves	Rk	0	0	0.00	2	2	6	3	0	0	7	0.0	35.0	0.50	.150
2023	25	Rome (SAL)	A+	0	0	4.00	2	2	9	6	2	3	14	8.6	40.0	1.00	.188
2023	25	Gwinnett (IL)	AAA	3	2	2.36	6	5	34	29	5	13	28	9.4	20.1	1.22	.234
2023	25	Atlanta (NL)	MLB	1	0	3.98	5	2	20	15	3	7	14	8.3	16.7	1.08	.203
Minor League Totals				17	15	3.56	71	67	333	290	43	99	369	7.2	26.9	1.17	.229
Major League Totals				1	0	3.98	5	2	20	15	3	7	14	8.3	16.7	1.08	.203

13 JHANCARLOS LARA, RHP

FB: 55. **SL:** 60. **CHG:** 40. **CTL:** 50. **BA Grade:** 50. **Risk:** Very High.

Born: January 15, 2003. **B-T:** R-R. **HT:** 6-3. **WT:** 190. **Signed:** Dominican Republic, 2021.
Signed by: Carlos Sequera/Luis Santos.

TRACK RECORD: Lara signed with the Braves out of the Dominican Republic in 2021, and he pitched well as a 19-year-old in the Dominican Summer League in 2022. He made a strong domestic debut in 2023, where he posted a 4.09 ERA in 81.1 innings between Low-A Augusta and High-A Rome. His 33.1% strikeout rate was the second-best in Atlanta's system among pitchers who threw at least 30 innings.

SCOUTING REPORT: A powerfully built righthander with a well-developed frame and strong lower half, Lara attacks hitters from a fairly clean and simple delivery that includes a balanced finish. Lara averaged 95-96 mph and touched 99 with his fastball. While the pitch has above-average velocity, its life is just average and he also needs to sharpen its command, though he did improve his overall walk rate from 19% to 12.2% year-over-year. Lara's main weapon is a nasty, upper-80s slider that is among the better breaking balls in Atlanta's system. It's a hard and tight breaking ball that elicits chases out of the zone and misses bats within it at strong rates, and he throws it hard enough to get to 90-91 mph at top-end velocities. Lara has thrown an occasional mid-80s changeup, but his fastball/slider usage accounted for more than 90% of his pitches in 2023.

THE FUTURE: Lara's fastball/slider combination gives him exciting upside, and his 2023 performance was among the best in Atlanta's system. In 2024, he should get tested in the upper minors and continue to develop a starter's arsenal.

Year	Age	Club (League)	Level	W	L	ERA	G	GS	IP	H	HR	BB	SO	BB%	SO%	WHIP	AVG
2023	20	Augusta (CAR)	A	4	7	4.00	18	13	72	55	4	38	96	12.4	31.4	1.29	.210
2023	20	Rome (SAL)	A+	0	1	4.82	2	2	9	5	2	4	18	10.5	47.4	0.96	.156
Minor League Totals				5	9	3.49	30	24	112	80	6	68	152	14.1	31.6	1.33	.198

14 LUCAS BRAUN, RHP

FB: 50. **CB:** 50. **SL:** 50. **CHG:** 50. **CTL:** 60. **BA Grade:** 45. **Risk:** High.

Born: August 26, 2001. **B-T:** R-R. **HT:** 6-0. **WT:** 185. **Drafted:** Cal State Northridge, 2023 (6th round).
Signed by: Kevin Martin.
TRACK RECORD: Braun signed with the Braves in the sixth round of the 2023 draft for $347,500 after a strong season with Cal State Northridge, where he made a successful transition to a starting role. He then had one of the better pro debuts of any drafted 2023 pitcher, as his 27 innings and 32 strikeouts between Low-A Augusta and High-A Rome were second to only fellow Atlanta farmhand Hurston Waldrep.
SCOUTING REPORT: Braun immediately became one of the better command pitchers in the system, as evidenced by his 4.7% walk rate and 25.5% K-BB rate—both marks were second-best among Braves minor leaguers with at least 10 innings. A 6-foot, 185-pound righthander, who throws from a lower release height, Braun has four distinct pitches with an advanced ability to locate them. He throws an average fastball that sits around 92-93 and touches 94-95, but he landed it for strikes nearly 70% of the time and does a nice job establishing it at the top of the zone to help set up a trio of secondaries. Braun throws a low-80s slider and an upper-70s curveball that look like solid-average pitches in a vacuum, but his ability to execute them consistently and land them at the bottom of the zone allowed them to play up in the low minors. Braun also has a low-80s changeup that is mostly used to his arm side against lefthanded hitters.
THE FUTURE: Braun has perhaps the deepest pitch mix in Atlanta's system and might have the command to become a pitcher who is greater than the sum of his parts.

Year	Age	Club (League)	Level	W	L	ERA	G	GS	IP	H	HR	BB	SO	BB%	SO%	WHIP	AVG
2023	21	Augusta (CAR)	A	0	2	1.04	4	4	17	14	0	2	19	2.9	27.9	0.92	.212
2023	21	Rome (SAL)	A+	0	0	5.59	2	2	10	8	2	3	13	7.9	34.2	1.14	.229
Minor League Totals				0	2	2.67	6	6	27	22	2	5	32	4.7	30.2	1.00	.218

15 JESSE FRANKLIN, OF

HIT: 40. **POW:** 55. **RUN:** 50. **FLD:** 50. **ARM:** 40. **BA Grade:** 45. **Risk:** High.

Born: December 1, 1998. **B-T:** L-L. **HT:** 6-1. **WT:** 215. **Drafted:** Michigan, 2020 (3rd round). **Signed by:** Jeremy Gordon.
TRACK RECORD: Franklin signed with the Braves for $500,000 in the third round of the 2020 draft. As soon as Franklin makes his major league debut, Atlanta will be able to claim a 100% hit rate with their entire four-pick 2020 draft class, which also included lefthander Jared Shuster (1st) and righthanders Spencer Strider (4th) and Bryce Elder (5th). Injuries plagued Franklin in the past, and he dealt with a hamstring issue that sidelined him early in the 2023 season, but he homered 15 times and doubled 17 times in 94 games with Double-A Mississippi.
SCOUTING REPORT: Big power is the calling card with Franklin, and he possesses some of the biggest raw power and most consistently accessible in-game power in Atlanta's system. He gets to most of his power on the inner third and to the pull side, but he has enough juice to homer to the opposite field and both his average exit velocity and 90th percentile marks in 2023 were above average for 24-year-old hitters. Franklin is a power-over-hit profile, who is challenged on the outer third and at the top of the zone with swing-and-miss tendencies that are amplified vs. secondary pitches, though he has done a nice job against velocity. Franklin is an average runner and solid defender in the outfield. He can play all three positions but profiles best in left given below-average arm strength.
THE FUTURE: Franklin offers lefthanded power and his defensive ability could make him a solid bench piece, platoon bat or fourth outfielder if he's not able to hit enough for an everyday role.

Year	Age	Club (League)	Level	AVG	G	AB	R	H	2B	3B	HR	RBI	BB	SO	SB	OBP	SLG
2023	24	Mississippi (SL)	AA	.232	94	341	55	79	17	1	15	46	32	115	21	.315	.419
Minor League Totals				.238	210	756	116	180	42	4	41	116	72	248	42	.319	.467

16 ALLAN WINANS, RHP

FB: 40. **SL:** 45. **CHG:** 60. **CTL:** 55. **BA Grade:** 40. **Risk:** Medium.

Born: August 10, 1995. **B-T:** R-R. **HT:** 6-2. **WT:** 165. **Drafted:** Campbell, 2018 (17th round). **Signed by:** Billy Best.
TRACK RECORD: Never a top prospect, Winans signed for just $10,000 as a 17th rounder with the Mets in the 2018 draft, but has quietly put together excellent minor league performances for five years. The Braves took him in the third round of the 2021 Rule 5 draft and converted him to a starting role in 2022. He dominated Triple-A Gwinnett in 2023 and also made six big league starts.
SCOUTING REPORT: Winans has the dubious "pitchability righthander" tag that isn't a premium prospect phylum, but does adequately sum up his east-west game. He throws a four-seam and two-seam fastball with well below-average big league velocity in the 88-92 mph range, but both pitches have above-average

arm-side running life. His slow breaking ball checks in around 78-82 mph with slider shape but more typical curveball power and is most effective as a chase pitch that starts on the mid-to-outer third and then sweeps out of the zone. His top offering is a low-to-mid 80s tumbling changeup that he threw almost 30% of the time in the majors and generated a 31% whiff rate. He fills up the zone consistently and is a solidly above-average strike-thrower with a career 7.5% minor league walk rate.

THE FUTURE: Winans will be in his age-28 season in 2024, and he has little to no projection remaining, but he offers solid value as a depth starter/swingman type who can attack the zone with four pitches.

Year	Age	Club (League)	Level	W	L	ERA	G	GS	IP	H	HR	BB	SO	BB%	SO%	WHIP	AVG
2023	27	Gwinnett (IL)	AAA	9	4	2.85	23	17	126	101	11	36	113	7.1	22.3	1.08	.218
2023	27	Atlanta (NL)	MLB	1	2	5.29	6	6	32	37	5	8	34	5.7	24.1	1.39	.287
Minor League Totals				13	16	2.82	104	29	300	232	21	91	278	7.5	22.8	1.08	.210
Major League Totals				1	2	5.29	6	6	32	37	5	8	34	5.7	24.1	1.39	.287

17 LUIS GUANIPA, OF

HIT: 45. **POW:** 55. **RUN:** 70. **FLD:** 50. **ARM:** 45. **BA Grade:** 50. **Risk:** Extreme.

Born: December 15, 2005. **B-T:** R-R. **HT:** 5-11. **WT:** 188. **Signed:** Venezuela, 2023.
Signed by: Carlos Sequera/Junior Colatosti.
TRACK RECORD: Signing Guanipa was another sign of a return to normalcy in the international market for the Braves, whose penalties from international signing violations set back the lower levels of the system for several years. Atlanta signed Guanipa for $2.5 million as one of the toolsiest players in the 2023 class, and he had a respectable Dominican Summer League debut, where he slashed .238/.361/.384 with four home runs and 20 stolen bases.
SCOUTING REPORT: In terms of pure tools, Guanipa likely has the highest upside of any prospect in the Braves system. He's a double-plus runner, who explodes out of the box and can cover plenty of ground in center field, and he also has twitchy hands in the box that leads to great bat speed and plus raw power. Guanipa's exit velocity data for a 17-year-old is impressive, and he has significant home run potential as he continues to refine his offensive approach. In the DSL, he made a solid amount of contact with good swing decisions, though he might have to continue quieting some of the moving parts in his swing—which he's already done to an extent. Guanipa's arm strength is fringy now but could get to average.
THE FUTURE: Guanipa's talent is enticing, but he has a long way to go before scouts have conviction in his ultimate role or his pure hitting ability.

Year	Age	Club (League)	Level	AVG	G	AB	R	H	2B	3B	HR	RBI	BB	SO	SB	OBP	SLG
2023	17	DSL Braves	Rk	.238	46	172	34	41	11	1	4	17	23	42	20	.361	.384
Minor League Totals				.238	46	172	34	41	11	1	4	17	23	42	20	.361	.384

18 GARRETT BAUMANN, RHP

FB: 55. **SL:** 45. **CHG:** 55. **CTL:** 50. **BA Grade:** 45. **Risk:** Extreme.

Born: August 15, 2004. **B-T:** L-R. **HT:** 6-8. **WT:** 245. **Drafted:** HS—Oviedo, FL, 2023 (4th round).
Signed by: Jon Bunnell.
TRACK RECORD: Baumann was one of the most physically imposing players in the 2023 draft class as a high schooler, and ranked as the No. 263 prospect in the class. He signed an over-slot, $747,500 deal with the Braves in the fourth round and then threw one brief, two-inning outing with Low-A Augusta before the season ended. Baumann hails from the same Hagerty High program as current Brave Vaughn Grissom.
SCOUTING REPORT: Baumann stands out for his massive, 6-foot-8, 245-pound frame and the easy velocity that he's able to generate. In high school, he mostly pitched in the 91-93 mph range and touched 96, and he flashed that same velocity in his pro debut, but he still has room to add strength to his XL frame and could shortly be pitching regularly in the mid 90s. Baumann's fastball has more of a sinker profile than a high-riding pitch, and he also throws from a lower release point than you might expect given his size. His changeup is ahead of his slider currently, and it could become an above-average offering. Baumann's breaking ball has been slurvy and inconsistent in the past, but he showed some glimpses of adding more power to the pitch. It remains a work in progress for now.
THE FUTURE: The Braves are hoping to help Baumann improve the shape of his fastball and add more bite to his breaking ball, but they are excited about his raw talent, size and athleticism. He's far away, but has a chance to develop into a workhorse starter.

Year	Age	Club (League)	Level	W	L	ERA	G	GS	IP	H	HR	BB	SO	BB%	SO%	WHIP	AVG
2023	18	Augusta (CAR)	A	0	0	4.50	1	1	2	1	0	2	1	22.2	11.1	1.50	.143
Minor League Totals				0	0	4.50	1	1	2	1	0	2	1	22.2	11.1	1.50	.143

19 ISAIAH DRAKE, OF

HIT: 40. **POW:** 50. **RUN:** 80. **FLD:** 55. **ARM:** 50. **BA Grade:** 45. **Risk:** Extreme.

Born: July 15, 2005. **B-T:** L-R. **HT:** 6-0. **WT:** 180. **Drafted:** HS—Atlanta, 2023 (5th round). **Signed by:** Alan Butts.

TRACK RECORD: Drake ranked as the No. 215 prospect in the 2023 draft class and signed an over-slot deal with the Braves for $747,500 in the fifth round. Drake performed well in 11 games in the MLB Draft League and was also a standout at the pre-draft combine, but struggled in a brief 18-game pro debut after signing. He hit .221/.312/.279 with a 37.7% strikeout rate in the Florida Complex League.

SCOUTING REPORT: Drake is a lean, athletic outfielder who stands out for his raw tools more than his baseball polish presently. He has shown above-average raw power with fast hands through the zone, though his approach is rudimentary as he can get overly pull-happy and also has real swing-and-miss questions. He was one of the better runners in the 2023 draft class and has top-of-the-scale, 80-grade speed that should allow him to terrorize opposing batteries and give him a chance to be an impactful defender in center field. Like his offensive game, Drake needs to refine his defense and base running, as his jumps, reads and routes can all be inconsistent.

THE FUTURE: Drake was young for the class and will be in just his age-18 season in 2024 when he'll get his first extended taste of pro ball. His tools and natural athleticism give him upside, but the Braves might need to be patient as he develops.

Year	Age	Club (League)	Level	AVG	G	AB	R	H	2B	3B	HR	RBI	BB	SO	SB	OBP	SLG
2023	17	FCL Braves	Rk	.221	18	68	9	15	0	2	0	8	8	29	9	.312	.279
Minor League Totals				.221	18	68	9	15	0	2	0	8	8	29	9	.312	.279

20 TYLER OWENS, RHP

FB: 60. **SL:** 55. **CUT:** 50. **CTL:** 45. **BA Grade:** 40. **Risk:** High.

Born: January 9, 2001. **B-T:** R-R. **HT:** 5-10. **WT:** 185. **Drafted:** HS—Ocala, FL, 2019 (13th round). **Signed by:** Jon Bunnell.

TRACK RECORD: Owens ranked as the No. 182 prospect in the 2019 draft class and signed with the Braves for $547,500 in the 13th round. He had a reputation as a hard-throwing righthander with some reliever question marks and, after dealing with injuries and inconsistencies for three years, turned in perhaps the best season of his pro career. Owens posted a 3.03 ERA between High-A Rome and Double-A Mississippi and split time as a starter and reliever over 65.1 innings.

SCOUTING REPORT: A hard four-seam fastball is Owens' bread-and-butter. He averaged 95-96 mph on the pitch in 2023 and it gets up to 97-98 mph with cutting life that comes from a lower release angle that also helps the pitch play up. It's a plus offering that can overpower hitters when he's locating it well. Owens also has a mid-80s slider that has plus potential and is his primary breaking ball. It has solid spin in the mid-2,500 rpm range and flashes plus, though not consistently and not when he leaves it over the middle of the plate. In addition to the slider, Owens throws a cutter in the 89-91 mph range, though he doesn't have a distinct pitch that moves away from lefties or is a true change-of-pace offering.

THE FUTURE: Owens profiles as a hard-throwing reliever with a movement profile that might be best against righthanded hitters. He was unprotected and not selected in the Rule 5 draft.

Year	Age	Club (League)	Level	W	L	ERA	G	GS	IP	H	HR	BB	SO	BB%	SO%	WHIP	AVG
2023	22	Rome (SAL)	A+	0	5	2.27	15	11	40	35	3	9	42	5.5	25.6	1.11	.232
2023	22	Mississippi (SL)	AA	0	1	4.21	14	4	26	31	2	13	25	10.7	20.5	1.71	.290
Minor League Totals				5	15	4.37	77	32	169	173	15	68	183	9.0	24.2	1.43	.256

21 HAYDEN HARRIS, LHP

FB: 60. **SL:** 50. **CTL:** 50. **BA Grade:** 40. **Risk:** High.

Born: March 2, 1999. **B-T:** L-L. **HT:** 6-0. **WT:** 186. **Signed:** Georgia Southern, 2022 (NDFA). **Signed by:** Alan Butts.

TRACK RECORD: Harris went undrafted in 2022 after a four-year career with Georgia Southern, where he pitched out of the bullpen and finished his career with a 5.30 ERA. The Braves signed him as an undrafted free agent, and in his first full season he progressed three levels, from High-A Augusta to Double-A Mississippi, struck out 36.8% of batters and posted a 3.08 FIP—which was the lowest of any pitcher in the organization with at least 40 innings.

SCOUTING REPORT: Harris is a straight reliever with an average, 6-foot, 186-pound frame. He works from the stretch and throws from a lower, three-quarters arm slot, which paired with his drop-and-drive action creates a uniquely low attack angle for hitters to deal with. Harris averaged just 91-92 mph with his fastball and touched 93, but it's an extremely flat pitch with a shallow approach angle that played well above its velocity and generated a well above-average 39% miss rate. He showed great feel to land the pitch and threw it for strikes at a 70% clip, which helped him post a solid 9.7% walk rate. While Harris uses the fastball around 75% of the time, he also has an average, 82-85 mph slider with occasional hard-biting action.

THE FUTURE: Harris has perhaps already exceeded expectations as an NDFA, but he has a chance to provide big league value out of the bullpen thanks to his unique release traits and fastball command.

Year	Age	Club (League)	Level	W	L	ERA	G	GS	IP	H	HR	BB	SO	BB%	SO%	WHIP	AVG
2023	24	Augusta (CAR)	A	0	1	9.72	7	0	8	11	2	3	15	7.7	38.5	1.68	.314
2023	24	Rome (SAL)	A+	2	1	3.94	10	0	16	10	2	4	26	6.5	41.9	0.88	.182
2023	24	Mississippi (SL)	AA	3	2	2.83	23	0	35	27	1	17	50	11.6	34.2	1.26	.213
Minor League Totals				6	4	4.08	46	0	64	51	6	30	97	11.2	36.1	1.27	.219

22 SABIN CEBALLOS, 3B

HIT: 45. **POW:** 50. **RUN:** 30. **FLD:** 50. **ARM:** 60. **BA Grade:** 45. **Risk:** Extreme.

Born: August 17, 2002. **B-T:** R-R. **HT:** 6-3. **WT:** 225. **Drafted:** Oregon, 2023 (3rd round). **Signed by:** Cody Martin.

TRACK RECORD: Ceballos has been a notable prospect since his prep days, when he stood out for his bigtime arm strength. He developed a reputation as a solid hitter in college, first in two years with San Jacinto (Texas) JC and then during the 2023 season with Oregon. He signed an under-slot, $597,500 deal with the Braves in the third round, then had a solid pro debut in 14 games split between rookie ball and Low-A, where he slashed .300/.440/.375 with one home run.

SCOUTING REPORT: Ceballos is a large and physical third baseman with impressive raw power that mostly played to the pull side in college, though his lone home run in pro ball was an opposite-field blast. Ceballos generates impressive bat speed and torque in his swing and has a steep, uphill path that should create plenty of fly balls, but could also lead to swing-and-miss issues—which became more of a problem after Ceballos moved to Low-A Augusta and struck out at a 31.4% clip. Ceballos doesn't have great range at third base as a well below-average runner, but he has plus arm strength, makes the routine plays and was also named to the 2023 Rawlings Gold Glove team in college.

THE FUTURE: Ceballos has caught in the past and was a potential conversion candidate for some scouts, though the Braves view him as a third baseman.

Year	Age	Club (League)	Level	AVG	G	AB	R	H	2B	3B	HR	RBI	BB	SO	SB	OBP	SLG
2023	20	FCL Braves	Rk	.375	5	8	4	3	0	0	0	2	6	3	2	.667	.375
2023	20	Augusta (CAR)	A	.281	9	32	3	9	0	0	1	6	3	11	0	.343	.375
Minor League Totals				.300	14	40	7	12	0	0	1	8	9	14	2	.440	.375

23 LUIS DE AVILA, LHP

FB: 45. **CB:** 45. **CHG:** 45. **CTL:** 50. **BA Grade:** 35. **Risk:** Medium.

Born: May 29, 2001. **B-T:** L-L. **HT:** 5-9. **WT:** 215. **Signed:** Colombia, 2017. **Signed by:** Rafael Miranda (Royals).

TRACK RECORD: De Avila has put together back-to-back strong seasons for the Braves after being selected in the 2021 minor league Rule 5 draft. After spending all of 2022 with High-A Rome, De Avila spent the 2023 season primarily at Double-A Gwinnett, where he posted a 3.28 ERA in 123.1 innings with a 24% strikeout rate, 11.7% walk rate and 52.1% groundball rate that was good for 21st-best among minor league pitchers with at least 100 innings.

SCOUTING REPORT: De Avila has a short and filled out frame and attacks hitters with a stiffer delivery that features a heavy crossfire landing. He throws a two-seam fastball that sits around 90 mph and has been up to 93, though it's more of a ground ball pitch than a true bat-misser. De Avila was impacted by the baseball experiments in the Southern League, which could have been worse for sinker pitchers than riding four-seam arms, but he still managed to drive a strong ground ball rate. He throws a firm changeup in the mid-to-upper 80s that doesn't have much velo separation from his fastball, and will also throw a breaking ball around 80-82 mph that varies in shape between a slider and curve. None of his secondaries are above-average offerings, but he locates them effectively.

THE FUTURE: De Avila's pitch mix and physical profile aren't the most exciting, but he has outperformed his peripherals in back-to-back seasons and carries value as a depth starter or long-relief lefthander.

Year	Age	Club (League)	Level	W	L	ERA	G	GS	IP	H	HR	BB	SO	BB%	SO%	WHIP	AVG
2023	22	Mississippi (SL)	AA	6	10	3.28	25	25	123	99	8	61	125	11.7	24.0	1.30	.223
2023	22	Gwinnett (IL)	AAA	0	0	2.45	1	1	4	4	0	4	3	19.0	14.3	2.18	.250
Minor League Totals				19	24	3.90	85	57	342	322	25	146	348	9.9	23.5	1.37	.244

24 BLAKE BURKHALTER, RHP

FB: 60. **SL:** 60. **CHG:** 50. **CTL:** 50. **BA Grade:** 45. **Risk:** Extreme.

Born: September 19, 2000. **B-T:** R-R. **HT:** 6-0. **WT:** 204. **Drafted:** Auburn, 2022 (2nd round supplemental).
Signed by: Travis Coleman.
TRACK RECORD: Burkhalter signed a slightly under-slot $650,000 deal with the Braves as the 76th overall pick in the 2022 draft after turning in one of the better reliever seasons in college baseball with Auburn. He posted a career 3.01 ERA in 71.2 innings in college and produced a 34.9% strikeout rate and 8.7% walk rate. Burkhalter pitched briefly in spring training in 2023, but missed the season with an injury that required Tommy John surgery.
SCOUTING REPORT: Burkhalter has just 4.2 official pro innings under his belt, but when he's been healthy, he's shown loud pure stuff. His arsenal starts with a mid-90s fastball that has been up to 98, with the sort of riding life that should allow it to generate plenty of whiffs at the top of the zone. He throws a hard breaking ball that blends between a slider and a cutter in the upper 80s, though the Braves had planned to try and make that breaking ball a true slider. He also showed feel for a mid-80s changeup with solid arm-side fading life that gives him a complete three-pitch mix. Given his pitch mix and track record of throwing strikes, the Braves intended to try developing him in a starting role, though given his injury and missed 2023 season, going back to the bullpen is now more likely.
THE FUTURE: Burkhalter will play in his age-23 season in 2024, where he'll look to re-establish his prospect value and, if healthy, could be pushed aggressively.

Year	Age	Club (League)	Level	W	L	ERA	G	GS	IP	H	HR	BB	SO	BB%	SO%	WHIP	AVG
2023	22	Did not play—Injured															
Minor League Totals				1	0	3.86	3	1	5	4	0	1	7	5.3	36.8	1.97	.222

25 DIEGO BENITEZ, SS

HIT: 40. **POW:** 40. **RUN:** 50. **FLD:** 50. **ARM:** 55. **BA Grade:** 45. **Risk:** Extreme.

Born: November 19, 2004. **B-T:** R-R. **HT:** 6-0. **WT:** 180. **Signed:** Venezuela, 2022.
Signed by: Carlos Sequera/Richard Castillo.
TRACK RECORD: Benitez was the headliner of Atlanta's 2022 international signing class and stood out for his advanced offensive skills and well-rounded toolset at the time. He hit .196/.363/.283 in the Dominican Summer League in 2022, then traded some walks for power in the Florida Complex League in 2023, where he slashed .261/.332/.392 with two home runs, three triples and 11 doubles.
SCOUTING REPORT: While Benitez's overall line is just OK, the Braves were excited with the development he showed as the season wore on. He cut his strikeout rate slightly from 25% to 21% in the second half of the season compared to the first, and his .822 second-half OPS was much better than his .643 first-half OPS. He makes solid contact within the zone, but is overly aggressive with his swing decisions and gets himself into trouble at times, and also needs to learn to elevate to his pull side more frequently to tap into the solid raw power he has. Defensively, Benitez shows flashes and will make an occasional flashy, rangy play or show off above-average arm strength, but he needs to be more consistent on his routine chances.
THE FUTURE: The Braves have prioritized Benitez's reps at shortstop so far in his career, but if he has to move off the position, his profile could take a significant hit barring a step forward offensively.

Year	Age	Club (League)	Level	AVG	G	AB	R	H	2B	3B	HR	RBI	BB	SO	SB	OBP	SLG
2023	18	FCL Braves	Rk	.261	46	176	22	46	11	3	2	19	17	44	3	.332	.392
Minor League Totals				.232	89	314	47	73	17	3	4	46	46	81	6	.347	.344

26 CODY MILLIGAN, OF/2B

HIT: 40. **POW:** 30. **RUN:** 70. **FLD:** 55. **ARM:** 50. **BA Grade:** 40. **Risk:** High.

Born: December 23, 1998. **B-T:** L-R. **HT:** 5-9. **WT:** 170. **Drafted:** Cowley County (KS) JC, 2019 (9th round).
Signed by: JD French.
TRACK RECORD: Milligan began his college career at Oklahoma State but didn't play much. He transferred to Cowley County (Kan.) JC, where he hit .453, stole 30 bases and set a program record with nine triples before the Braves selected him in the ninth round. He signed for $197,500 and has developed into a speedy and versatile defender. He spent most of the 2023 season with Double-A Mississippi, where he hit .280/.377/.414 with 23 stolen bases.
SCOUTING REPORT: Milligan is a small and lean lefthanded hitter who doesn't project to have much offensive impact in the big leagues, but he can control the strike zone, make plenty of contact and consistently put together scrappy at-bats. His 78% overall contact rate and 87% in-zone contact rate were among the better marks in Atlanta's system, and while he has well below-average raw power, he should

be able to turn a few gapped singles into doubles and challenge opposing infielders with his speed out of the box. He's a double-plus runner and instinctual base stealer, and some scouts believe he could have big league value in a postseason pinch-running role. He's an above-average defender in center field and can play all three outfield positions and second base.

THE FUTURE: Milligan doesn't have the offensive chops to profile as a regular, but he does enough things well to potentially fit as a bench piece.

Year	Age	Club (League)	Level	AVG	G	AB	R	H	2B	3B	HR	RBI	BB	SO	SB	OBP	SLG
2023	24	FCL Braves	Rk	.429	2	7	2	3	0	0	1	1	0	1	1	.429	.857
2023	24	Mississippi (SL)	AA	.280	69	261	49	73	16	5	3	22	38	67	23	.377	.414
Minor League Totals				.269	349	1317	240	354	63	12	8	102	210	323	72	.373	.353

27 IAN MEJIA, RHP

FB: 40. **SL:** 50. **CHG:** 40. **CTL:** 60. **BA Grade:** 40. **Risk:** High.

Born: January 31, 2000. **B-T:** R-R. **HT:** 6-3. **WT:** 205. **Drafted:** New Mexico State, 2022 (11th round). **Signed by:** Anthony Flora.

TRACK RECORD: Mejia wasn't a prominent prospect coming out of college, but after cutting his ERA nearly in half while transitioning to a full-time starting role with New Mexico State in 2022, the Braves signed him for $100,000 in the 11th round. In his first full pro season spent entirely at High-A Rome, Mejia showed impressive control and command and posted a 4.69 ERA in 23 starts and 121 innings. His 5.6% walk rate was good for second-best in the system among pitchers with at least 50 innings.

SCOUTING REPORT: Mejia has a great pitcher's frame at 6-foot-3, 205 pounds and is an above-average strike-thrower thanks to a clean starter's delivery. He has a three-pitch mix headlined by a fastball that sits in the 90-92 mph range that will touch 93. The pitch has below-average velocity and generic riding life, but he does get solid arm-side run, and his ability to command the pitch is above-average or plus. Mejia also has great usability of a low-to-mid-80s slider that he threw nearly as frequently as his fastball in 2023. It has tight action and was a consistent swing-and-miss offering that he located nicely down and to his glove side. Mejia will also mix in a below-average, mid-80s changeup to lefthanded hitters.

THE FUTURE: Mejia has starter traits, but will need to add power to his fastball to project as more than a fill-in, depth starter at the big league level.

Year	Age	Club (League)	Level	W	L	ERA	G	GS	IP	H	HR	BB	SO	BB%	SO%	WHIP	AVG
2023	23	Rome (SAL)	A+	4	11	4.69	23	23	121	121	16	28	110	5.6	21.8	1.23	.260
Minor League Totals				4	12	4.60	29	29	138	137	17	33	123	5.7	21.4	1.24	.259

28 DOUGLAS GLOD, OF

HIT: 30. **POW:** 55. **RUN:** 45. **FLD:** 40. **ARM:** 50. **BA Grade:** 45. **Risk:** Extreme.

Born: January 20, 2005. **B-T:** R-R. **HT:** 5-9. **WT:** 185. **Signed:** Venezuela, 2022.
Signed by: Carlos Sequera/Junior Colatosti.

TRACK RECORD: Glod was the second biggest name in Atlanta's 2022 international signing class, behind shortstop Diego Benitez, and stood out at the time for his explosive righthanded bat speed and advanced physicality. He has flashed power and on-base skills in his first two years of affiliated ball, though in a 47-game stint in the Florida Complex League in 2023 he slashed .224/.387/.398 with five home runs and a 30.9% strikeout rate.

SCOUTING REPORT: Glod has a short, maxed out frame that doesn't provide much in the way of future projection, but he hits the ball harder than any teenager in Atlanta's system and absolutely crushes baseballs when he can find the barrel. That is the big question for Glod. Though his 104.4 mph 90th percentile exit velocity is a standout number for an 18-year-old, he struggled mightily with contact and missed at a 37.8% rate. To his credit, Glod's swing decisions were much better than his strikeout rate might suggest, but that only highlights concerns about his pure bat-to-ball skills. Previously a plus runner, Glod has slowed down quickly since signing and now turns in fringy running times and looks like a below-average defender in the outfield who will need to play in a corner.

THE FUTURE: Glod needs to find a way to make more contact, but he's an intriguing power option, who will still be just 19 years old in 2024.

Year	Age	Club (League)	Level	AVG	G	AB	R	H	2B	3B	HR	RBI	BB	SO	SB	OBP	SLG
2023	18	FCL Braves	Rk	.224	47	161	29	36	9	2	5	25	38	64	6	.386	.398
Minor League Totals				.215	79	265	52	57	15	4	7	38	60	100	9	.373	.381

29 KESHAWN OGANS, 2B

HIT: 40. **POW:** 40. **RUN:** 50. **FLD:** 45. **ARM:** 40. **BA Grade:** 40. **Risk:** High.

Born: August 26, 2001. **B-T:** R-R. **HT:** 5-8. **WT:** 180. **Drafted:** California, 2022 (20th round). **Signed by:** Al Skorupa.

TRACK RECORD: Ogans signed for $125,000 as a 20th-round pick in 2022 after a three-year career at California and had a modest pro debut that started in Rookie ball and finished in High-A Rome. Ogans spent the entirety of the 2023 season with Rome, where he was a pleasant offensive surprise for the club and hit .266/.360/.397 with nine home runs and 22 doubles. Following the season, he played in the Arizona Fall League and hit .299/.347/.403 in 17 games.

SCOUTING REPORT: Ogans is a shorter righthanded hitter with a frame that's close to maxed out without much physical projection to dream on. He has a simple, direct and fairly level swing at the plate with a pull-heavy approach. Ogans turns on the ball frequently and also gets the ball in the air often, but isn't able to fully take advantage of those angles thanks to below-average raw power. He makes contact at a solid clip and has posted 10% walk rates in High A in back-to-back seasons, but he can get exposed on the outer third and leaks out to the pull side too frequently. Ogans played all over the infield and has solid actions and hands, but his arm strength makes him best suited for second base. He's an average runner with short, choppy strides.

THE FUTURE: Ogans lacks a carrying tool and doesn't project to have much impact, but he could provide value as a utility infielder if he keeps hitting in the upper minors.

Year	Age	Club (League)	Level	AVG	G	AB	R	H	2B	3B	HR	RBI	BB	SO	SB	OBP	SLG
2023	21	Rome (SAL)	A+	.265	113	388	43	103	22	1	9	67	46	87	10	.360	.397
Minor League Totals				.262	142	496	61	130	25	1	10	77	55	110	19	.354	.377

30 AMBIORIS TAVAREZ, SS

HIT: 30. **POW:** 40. **RUN:** 55. **FLD:** 60. **ARM:** 60. **BA Grade:** 45. **Risk:** Extreme.

Born: November 12, 2003. **B-T:** R-R. **HT:** 5-11. **WT:** 168. **Signed:** Dominican Republic, 2021. **Signed by:** Jonathan Cruz/Luis Santos.

TRACK RECORD: Atlanta's first prominent international prospect since being sanctioned for rules violations in the market, Tavarez signed for $1.5 million in 2021. He was praised for his bat speed and power prior to signing, but has struggled mightily with the bat in the lower levels, and with Low-A Augusta in 2023 he slashed .216/.319/.337 with a 40.8% strikeout rate that was not only the worst in the Braves system, but one of the worst overall marks of any qualified minor league hitter.

SCOUTING REPORT: Tavarez remains interesting as a prospect almost entirely thanks to his athleticism and defensive ability at shortstop. He is the best defender in the Braves system with smooth actions, reliable hands and enough arm strength for the position. Tavarez does an excellent job throwing on the run and from difficult angles, and his quick exchange allows his plus arm to play up and make difficult plays deep in the hole to his arm side. As a hitter, Tavarez is simply overmatched presently. He does have solid bat speed and can hit the ball hard, but his contact skills against all pitch types are poor and he's particularly allergic to spin. He's an above-average runner but he also went 21-for-41 (51.2%) on stolen base attempts.

THE FUTURE: Tavarez has real tools and a glove that might keep him alive as a prospect to dream on, but he remains incredibly raw in many areas of the game.

Year	Age	Club (League)	Level	AVG	G	AB	R	H	2B	3B	HR	RBI	BB	SO	SB	OBP	SLG
2023	19	Augusta (CAR)	A	.216	108	416	61	90	19	5	7	34	44	196	21	.319	.337
Minor League Totals				.225	125	481	73	108	23	5	8	42	47	224	24	.317	.343

Baltimore Orioles

BY JON MEOLI

Just two years after a 110-loss season earned the No. 1 overall pick that landed shortstop Jackson Holliday, the Orioles won 101 games and their first American League East title since 2014.

Holliday is now the game's top prospect and sits atop one of the strongest farm systems in baseball.

That's the result of executive vice president and general manager Mike Elias' pledge to build an elite talent pipeline when he was hired following the 2018 season. Five years later, members of that pipeline have already helped the major league team—and more help is close at hand.

Catcher Adley Rutschman, the No. 1 pick in 2019, was an all-star for the first time in 2023. The Orioles' next pick in that draft, Gunnar Henderson, was the 2023 AL Rookie of the Year whose award win helps perpetuate the farm system via a Prospect Promotion Incentive draft pick after the first round in 2024.

Three other first-round picks debuted in 2023—righthander Grayson Rodriguez and outfielders Colton Cowser and Heston Kjerstad—while infielder Jordan Westburg, another top prospect, was a fixture at second and third base by the end of the season.

Holliday played at all four full-season minor league levels and finished his age-19 season at Triple-A, earning the BA Minor League Player of the Year award for Norfolk, the Minor League Team of the Year.

Catcher Samuel Basallo, the crown jewel of the organization's resurgent international program under Koby Perez, finished his age-18 season at Double-A Bowie with 20 home runs across three levels. Similarly, third baseman Coby Mayo swatted 29 home runs as a 21-year-old across Double-A and Triple-A to earn Eastern League MVP honors.

The Orioles' success is the result of a unique approach to developing talent. Baltimore's hitting program focuses on challenging pre-game work and unique drills that prepare prospects to thrive in games. It has produced one of the deepest groups of hitting prospects in the game.

All the high draft picks the Orioles used on hitters has helped, and at the same time dampened the progress on the pitching side. However, the success of Kyle Bradish and Rodriguez in the major league rotation showed the program can yield major league success.

The Orioles' emphasis on adding pitches that can miss bats has led to an intriguing mix of pitchers on the farm. Of the 36 pitchers who were 25 or younger and pitched at least 50 innings in the minors, 27 struck out a batter per inning or more.

Gunnar Henderson, the unanimous AL Rookie of the Year, hit .255/.325/.489 with 28 homers.

PROJECTED 2027 LINEUP

Catcher	Adley Rutschman	29
First Base	Ryan Mountcastle	30
Second Base	Jackson Holliday	23
Third Base	Coby Mayo	25
Shortstop	Gunnar Henderson	26
Left Field	Colton Cowser	27
Center Field	Enrique Bradfield Jr.	25
Right Field	Heston Kjerstad	28
Designated Hitter	Samuel Basallo	22
No. 1 Starter	Grayson Rodriguez	27
No. 2 Starter	Kyle Bradish	30
No. 3 Starter	DL Hall	28
No. 4 Starter	Dean Kremer	31
No. 5 Starter	Chayce McDermott	28
Closer	Felix Bautista	32

The emphasis on consistent and progressive development processes has created a strong talent base, with multiple paths to improvement. They can bet on their players being good enough to get them deeper in the playoffs than they made it in 2023—a Division Series loss to the eventual champion Rangers—or use their considerable prospect depth to add from the outside.

After largely keeping their powder dry in terms of payroll and trades in 2023, how the Orioles supplement this club and balance near-term needs with their long-term goals of a sustainable contender will be the most fascinating aspect of their offseason to monitor as they enter 2024 with high expectations. ∎

RON SCHWANE/GETTY IMAGES

DEPTH CHART

BALTIMORE ORIOLES

TOP 2024 CONTRIBUTORS — **RANK**
1. Jackson Holliday, SS — 1
2. Colton Cowser, OF — 4
3. DL Hall, LHP — 6

BREAKOUT PROSPECTS — **RANK**
1. Dylan Beavers, OF — 13
2. Jackson Baumeister, RHP — 14
3. Luis Almeyda, SS — 21

SOURCE OF TOP 30 TALENT

Homegrown	27	Acquired	3
College	19	Trade	3
Junior college	0	Rule 5 draft	0
High school	3	Independent league	0
Nondrafted free agent	0	Free agent/waivers	0
International	5		

LF
Dylan Beavers (13)
Hudson Haskin (25)
John Rhodes (26)
Shayne Fontana

CF
Colton Cowser (4)
Enrique Bradfield Jr. (9)
Jud Fabian (15)
Braylin Tavera (20)
Tavian Josenberger
Jake Cunningham

RF
Heston Kjerstad (5)
Kyle Stowers (18)
Billy Cook
Thomas Sosa

3B
Coby Mayo (3)
Max Wagner (17)
Mac Horvath (19)
Luis Almeyda (21)
Joshua Liranzo
Anderson De Los Santos

SS
Jackson Holliday (1)
Joey Ortiz (7)
Leandro Arias
Jalen Vazquez

2B
Connor Norby (8)
Frederick Bencosme (28)
Aron Estrada

1B
TT Bowens
Maxwell Costes

C
Samuel Basallo (2)
Silas Ardoin
Creed Willems
Maverick Handley

LHP

LHSP	LHRP
DL Hall (6)	Trey McGough
Cade Povich (11)	
Luis De Leon (16)	
Deivy Cruz	

RHP

RHSP	RHRP
Chayce McDermott (10)	Keagan Gillies (30)
Seth Johnson (12)	Teddy Sharkey
Jackson Baumeister (14)	Kade Strowd
Juan Nuñez (22)	Luis Sanchez
Trace Bright (23)	Juan De Los Santos
Justin Armbruester (24)	
Alex Pham (27)	
Kiefer Lord (29)	
Carter Baumler	
Ryan Long	
Cameron Weston	
Kyle Brnovich	
Brandon Young	
Zach Peek	
Peter Van Loon	
Daniel Lloyd	

1 JACKSON HOLLIDAY, SS

Born: December 4, 2003. **B-T:** L-R. **HT:** 6-1. **WT:** 175.
Drafted: HS—Stillwater, OK, 2022 (1st round).
Signed by: Ken Guthrie.

TRACK RECORD: The son of seven-time all-star Matt Holliday was a rapid riser from probable first-round pick to High School Player of the Year and No. 1 overall pick in 2022 thanks to some physical and swing gains. Since then, Holliday's trajectory hasn't flattened. He returned to Low-A Delmarva to begin 2023 and finished the season with Triple-A-champion Norfolk, excelling across all four full-season levels and earning Minor League Player of the Year honors. Holliday wasn't at a level long enough to qualify for any league awards, but his .323 average was only one point off the highest of any minor leaguer with at least 500 plate appearances, and no one at that threshold topped his .442 on-base percentage.

SCOUTING REPORT: Holliday's elite offensive skill set showed as he climbed to Triple-A as a 19-year-old, with a plus-plus hit tool and at least plus plate discipline. Those qualities allow him to control the strike zone and make consistent, high-quality contact. After a fair share of weak fly outs in his 2022 pro debut, Holliday sharpened his ball flight to more consistently hit crisp line drives to all fields in 2023. Holliday had a 45.5% hard-hit rate, up from 34.6% in his pro debut, while increasing his 90th percentile exit velocity from 99.4 mph to 102.5. His continued physical maturation could help him develop above-average power, but if not he will be a doubles machine because of the quality of his contact. He has demonstrated an ability to backspin the ball and give it extra carry. The Orioles were impressed with the way he tapped into his pull-side power as the season went on, and Holliday didn't sacrifice his all-fields approach to get to it. A gifted athlete who demonstrates the instincts of a baseball lifer both on and off the field, Holliday is loose and fluid at shortstop with the potential to be at least a plus shortstop and potentially a plus-plus second baseman, should the Orioles' infield situation call for such a move. He's a quick study defensively, can play one-handed, and has an advanced clock that means he doesn't rush throws and often delivers them on time and on target. Holliday is a plus runner who was successful on 24 of 33 stolen base attempts in 2023 and shows good instincts on the basepaths. He also has elite makeup, handling the pressures of his prospect status and expectations as well as anyone

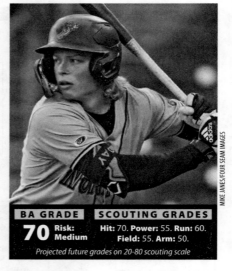

MIKE JANES/FOUR SEAM IMAGES

BA GRADE	SCOUTING GRADES
70 Risk: Medium	Hit: 70. Power: 55. Run: 60. Field: 55. Arm: 50.

Projected future grades on 20-80 scouting scale

BEST TOOLS

BATTING

Best Hitter for Average	Jackson Holliday
Best Power Hitter	Samuel Basallo
Best Strike-Zone Discipline	Jackson Holliday
Fastest Baserunner	Enrique Bradfield Jr.
Best Athlete	Jackson Holliday

PITCHING

Best Fastball	DL Hall
Best Curveball	Trace Bright
Best Slider	DL Hall
Best Changeup	DL Hall
Best Control	Alex Pham

FIELDING

Best Defensive Catcher	Silas Ardoin
Best Defensive Infielder	Joey Ortiz
Best Infield Arm	Coby Mayo
Best Defensive Outfielder	Enrique Bradfield Jr.
Best Outfield Arm	Jud Fabian

the Orioles have had in that position.

THE FUTURE: Holliday's month at Triple-A to end the season solidified the fact that he'll be in the majors in 2024. The Orioles expect he will more than hold his own when he arrives in Baltimore at age 20. Beyond that, the Orioles believe Holliday can be an all-star-caliber middle infielder who provides elite on-base presence at the top of the lineup. Holliday will be back in major league camp with a chance to break with the MLB club in spring training, and if he's not on the Orioles' Opening Day roster, he won't be with Norfolk for long. ■

Year	Age	Club (League)	Level	AVG	G	AB	R	H	2B	3B	HR	RBI	BB	SO	SB	OBP	SLG
2023	19	Delmarva (CAR)	A	.396	14	53	15	21	6	1	2	16	14	13	3	.522	.660
2023	19	Aberdeen (SAL)	A+	.314	57	207	52	65	11	5	5	35	50	54	17	.452	.488
2023	19	Bowie (EL)	AA	.338	36	142	28	48	9	3	3	15	21	34	3	.421	.507
2023	19	Norfolk (IL)	AAA	.267	18	75	18	20	4	0	2	9	16	17	1	.396	.400
Minor League Totals				.320	145	541	127	173	35	9	13	84	126	130	28	.449	.490

2 SAMUEL BASALLO, C

HIT: 55. **POW:** 70. **RUN:** 40. **FLD:** 45. **ARM:** 70. **BA Grade:** 65. **Risk:** High.

Born: August 13, 2004. **B-T:** L-R. **HT:** 6-3. **WT:** 180.
Signed: Dominican Republic, 2021. **Signed by:** Michael Cruz/Geraldo Cabrera.
TRACK RECORD: Basallo was an early, significant investment in the Orioles' return to the international scouting market. His $1.3 million bonus in January 2021 was a club record, and he has been at the forefront of their international program ever since. Basallo made his full-season debut in 2023 at Low-A Delmarva, hitting 12 home runs with an .887 OPS as an 18-year-old to earn Carolina League MVP honors. He destroyed the High-A South Atlantic League, hitting eight home runs with a 1.131 OPS in 27 games before ending the season with a week at Double-A Bowie.
SCOUTING REPORT: Recent Orioles international signees haven't fared well in transitioning to full-season ball, but Basallo was carried by improved plate discipline and advanced bat-to-ball skills for a slugger. He hits with a quiet but strong lower half and generates impressive bat speed, with his adjustability and pitch recognition giving him the potential to be at least an average hitter with double-plus power capabilities as he further adds strength and learns which pitches he can drive. Behind the plate, Basallo moves well for someone his size and is improving his actions and receiving as he climbs through the minors. His best trait behind the plate is a plus-plus arm with above-average accuracy, allowing him to control the running game. He may ultimately fall short of his fringe-average ceiling behind the plate, though he should be able to play there a few times a week, with his bat keeping him in the lineup elsewhere on days he's not catching.
THE FUTURE: Basallo has the skills to be a standout two-way catcher, with the potential to be an all-star for his bat in his peak offensive seasons. He'll be back at Double-A Bowie at age 19 to begin 2024, and will likely spend the season in the high minors before pushing for major league time in 2025.

Year	Age	Club (League)	Level	AVG	G	AB	R	H	2B	3B	HR	RBI	BB	SO	SB	OBP	SLG
2023	18	Delmarva (CAR)	A	.299	83	308	52	92	19	4	12	60	41	73	7	.384	.503
2023	18	Aberdeen (SAL)	A+	.333	27	96	21	32	6	2	8	24	19	20	5	.443	.688
2023	18	Bowie (EL)	AA	.467	4	15	2	7	1	1	0	2	1	1	0	.500	.667
Minor League Totals				.291	198	711	115	207	39	7	31	137	95	163	14	.378	.496

3 COBY MAYO, 3B

HIT: 50. **POW:** 70. **RUN:** 45. **FLD:** 50. **ARM:** 70. **BA Grade:** 60. **Risk:** High.

Born: December 10, 2001. **B-T:** R-R. **HT:** 6-5. **WT:** 215.
Drafted: HS—Parkland, FL, 2020 (4th round). **Signed by:** Brandon Verley.
TRACK RECORD: Signed for $1.75 million as one of the top raw power hitters in the 2020 draft, Mayo enjoyed his first full, healthy professional season in 2023 and made tremendous strides at age-advanced levels. He was named Eastern League MVP despite spending just half the season in the league, batting .307 with a 1.026 OPS and 17 home runs at the level. He excelled as his time at Triple-A Norfolk went on, ending the year with a system-high 29 home runs, 99 RBIs and a .974 OPS. Among 21-and-under hitters, only Junior Caminero and Abimelec Ortiz outpaced Mayo for homers.
SCOUTING REPORT: Mayo has always boasted plus-plus power, but continued refinement in his swing and plate discipline allowed him to better get to his raw power and dominate the high minors. He cut down on his strikeouts while increasing his walk rate from 9.1% to 15.1%, closing some holes on the outer half with his swing while maintaining his slug and making more consistent hard contact. Mayo cut his chase rate from 27% to 23%, while his hard-hit rate jumped from 31% to 46%. He's still at his best crushing mistakes and turning on inside pitches, but he showed improved adjustability in his swing and can be an average hitter at his peak. Mayo is athletic for someone his size, and while he boasts a plus-plus arm, he may never be better than average at third base and could move off of the position for first base or a corner outfield given the Orioles' infield depth.
THE FUTURE: Mayo represents one of the most improved Orioles' hitting prospects over the years, as well as one of their highest-upside young players. He can be a first-division regular on his bat alone, though there will be more pressure on it if he's not playing third base. Mayo seems set for more Triple-A time to begin 2024 before pushing for a major league debut around midseason.

Year	Age	Club (League)	Level	AVG	G	AB	R	H	2B	3B	HR	RBI	BB	SO	SB	OBP	SLG
2023	21	Bowie (EL)	AA	.307	78	287	48	88	30	2	17	44	51	86	4	.424	.603
2023	21	Norfolk (IL)	AAA	.267	62	217	36	58	15	1	12	55	42	62	1	.393	.512
Minor League Totals				.279	297	1074	202	300	79	6	57	209	162	302	21	.384	.523

4 COLTON COWSER, OF

HIT: 55. **POW:** 55. **RUN:** 55. **FLD:** 50. **ARM:** 55. **BA Grade:** 50. **Risk:** Medium.

Born: March 20, 2000. **B-T:** L-R. **HT:** 6-3. **WT:** 195.
Drafted: Sam Houston State, 2021 (1st round). **Signed by:** Thom Dreier.
TRACK RECORD: Another fast-moving Orioles prospect, Cowser signed for a below-slot $4.9 million as the fifth overall pick in 2021, ended his first full season at Triple-A Norfolk in 2022, then was in the majors by early July 2023 to help provide center field cover. He had a .996 OPS at the time of his promotion, but after being sent back to the minors to work on being more aggressive in the strike zone, he compiled a .777 OPS and his strikeout rate spiked.
SCOUTING REPORT: Cowser's tough major league debut didn't dim the Orioles' view of a player they believe still boasts one of the more attractive offensive profiles in their organization. Cowser has some of the most advanced plate discipline in the system, with good on-base ability and the capability to be an above-average hitter for average, even if there are some stark platoon splits on his résumé and there are swing-and-miss issues on non-fastballs. Cowser can have above-average power as he continues to learn which pitches he can best drive, and he improved his hard-hit rate substantially in 2023. Cowser's above-average speed and arm allow him to play all three outfield positions comfortably, though he'll probably be above-average in the corners and average to fringe-average in center.
THE FUTURE: Cowser has little left to prove in Triple-A, but it's unclear whether there's an opportunity with the Orioles for him to get the major league experience required for the next step in his development. He has the makings of a major league regular, potentially a first-division one, though there are aspects of his game that portend an even brighter future. He'll be in the mix to break camp with the Orioles in 2024.

Year	Age	Club (League)	Level	AVG	G	AB	R	H	2B	3B	HR	RBI	BB	SO	SB	OBP	SLG
2023	23	Norfolk (IL)	AAA	.300	87	323	72	97	18	1	17	62	64	107	9	.417	.520
2023	23	Baltimore (AL)	MLB	.115	26	61	15	7	2	0	0	4	13	22	1	.286	.148
Minor League Totals				.298	257	953	216	284	62	3	38	162	183	304	34	.420	.489
Major League Totals				.115	26	61	15	7	2	0	0	4	13	22	1	.286	.148

5 HESTON KJERSTAD, OF

HIT: 50. **POW:** 60. **RUN:** 45. **FLD:** 45. **ARM:** 55. **BA Grade:** 50. **Risk:** Medium.

Born: February 12, 1999. **B-T:** L-R. **HT:** 6-3. **Wt.:** 205.
Drafted: Arkansas, 2020 (1st round). **Signed by:** Ken Guthrie.
TRACK RECORD: The No. 2 overall pick in 2020 signed for a below-slot $5.2 million. Myocarditis (heart inflammation) and then a significant hamstring injury kept him off the field until the middle of 2022, but his first healthy pro season ended in the majors. Kjerstad had a .960 OPS at Double-A Bowie and added 10 home runs in 76 games at Triple-A Norfolk before joining the Orioles for their stretch run on Sept. 14.
SCOUTING REPORT: Kjerstad still has a unique swing with a high leg kick and a short stroke to the baseball, and he shows a knack for finding the barrel and hitting the ball hard at good angles. Kjerstad is advanced at formulating attack plans based on the pitcher he's facing and proved adept at making contact on pitches in the zone, but he's not a particularly stingy swinger, which could create challenges in the majors. However, his ability to put the bat on the ball could make him an average hitter with plus or better power. Kjerstad generates impressive carry off the bat and boasts power to all fields, often letting the location of the pitch determine where he drives it. While Kjerstad has worked some at first base to add versatility, his is a traditional corner outfield profile with a strong arm and decent athleticism but likely fringe-average overall defense.
THE FUTURE: After a long layoff, Kjerstad showed himself as a potential middle-of-the-order, everyday run producer that the Orioles drafted him to be during the pandemic. He could be poised for a significant role on the 2024 club as a bat-first corner outfielder who will continue to improve as he gains experience against high-level pitchers.

Year	Age	Club (League)	Level	AVG	G	AB	R	H	2B	3B	HR	RBI	BB	SO	SB	OBP	SLG
2023	24	Bowie (EL)	AA	.310	46	184	30	57	10	3	11	23	15	31	3	.383	.576
2023	24	Norfolk (IL)	AAA	.298	76	295	57	88	19	5	10	32	27	69	2	.371	.498
2023	24	Baltimore (AL)	MLB	.233	13	30	3	7	1	0	2	3	2	10	0	.281	.467
Minor League Totals				.305	187	722	132	220	46	10	26	92	71	164	6	.382	.504
Major League Totals				.233	13	30	3	7	1	0	2	3	2	10	0	.281	.467

6 DL HALL, LHP

FB: 80. **CB:** 60. **SL:** 70. **CHG:** 60. **CTL:** 30. **BA Grade:** 50. **Risk:** Medium.

Born: September 19, 1998. **B-T:** L-L. **HT:** 6-0. **WT:** 180.
Drafted: HS—Valdosta, GA, 2017 (1st round). **Signed by:** Arthur McConnehead.
TRACK RECORD: A $3 million signing as the 21st overall pick in 2017, Hall reached the majors in 2022 to help in the bullpen down the stretch. An off-season back injury hampered his ramp-up entering 2023, and he left Triple-A Norfolk in June to undergo a strength program and regain his velocity for the Orioles' playoff push. The plan worked, and Hall was a bright spot in relief after closer Felix Bautista's season-ending elbow injury.
SCOUTING REPORT: Hall pitches off an elite fastball from the left side. The pitch averaged 95.6 mph in the big leagues in 2023 and has routinely sat in the upper 90s over the last few years, with above-average hop and the ability to miss bats up in the zone. Hall pitched with diminished velocity at Triple-A earlier in the season, but he learned to better work with his secondary pitches and use them effectively in the zone. His mid-80s changeup has developed later in his career into a plus pitch and represents his best offering to righthanded hitters, while his slider in the mid-to-high 80s is a plus pitch at its best and is his primary way of attacking lefties. Hall reintroduced his curveball, his best pitch as an amateur, giving him a fourth pitch that could be above-average or better. Perhaps most importantly, he improved his command and threw more strikes in 2023 than in years past, giving hope that he'll be able to reach his upside and be able to have enough control to stay in the rotation.
THE FUTURE: In a brief sample down the stretch in 2023, Hall showed he can be a potentially elite reliever, but the Orioles still believe his electric four-pitch mix from the left side is that of a starter. He'll be in the majors in 2024 as long as he's healthy, though the team's offseason moves might determine his role.

Year	Age	Club (League)	Level	W	L	ERA	G	GS	IP	H	HR	BB	SO	BB%	SO%	WHIP	AVG
2023	24	FCL Orioles	Rk	1	0	0.00	2	1	3	1	0	2	8	16.7	66.7	1.00	.100
2023	24	Norfolk (IL)	AAA	1	2	4.22	17	11	49	38	7	30	70	13.8	32.3	1.39	.209
2023	24	Baltimore (AL)	MLB	3	0	3.26	18	0	19	18	2	5	23	6.2	28.4	1.19	.237
Minor League Totals				13	22	3.49	96	81	353	253	31	204	499	13.4	32.9	1.29	.196
Major League Totals				4	1	4.36	29	1	33	35	2	11	42	7.6	29.0	1.39	.263

7 JOEY ORTIZ, SS/2B

HIT: 50. **POW:** 45. **RUN:** 50. **FLD:** 70. **ARM:** 55. **BA Grade:** 50. **Risk:** Medium.

Born: July 14, 1998. **B-T:** R-R. **HT:** 5-11. **WT:** 175.
Drafted: New Mexico State, 2019 (4th round). **Signed by:** John Gillette
TRACK RECORD: Ortiz shed his all-glove, no-hit stigma with strength gains and swing changes coming out of the pandemic, and he broke out late in 2022 with a .991 second-half OPS that prompted the Orioles to add him to the 40-man roster that November to protect him from the Rule 5 draft. He made his major league debut in April 2023 for the first of three major league stints, though he spent the majority of the year proving last year's second half wasn't a fluke with an .850 OPS and 45 extra-base hits at Triple-A Norfolk.
SCOUTING REPORT: Ortiz has two true carrying tools to help him solidify his major league future: double-plus defensive traits and elite bat-to-ball skills. He's a true shortstop with plus range, play-making ability and above-average throwing at the position. He is equally strong at second base, giving him another position where his defense can thrive at the highest level. Ortiz has advanced contact ability and rarely swings and misses, though some regression in his swing decisions in 2023 meant he wasn't always swinging at pitches he could drive at good angles, even as he maintained consistent hard contact throughout the year. While he can be an average hitter with fringy power—or perhaps average at his peak—Ortiz's defense means he'll simply have to hit enough to justify a lineup spot and will still be plenty valuable to a team.
THE FUTURE: While he didn't get much of an opportunity on the Orioles in 2023, Ortiz still has an everyday major league ceiling, though on a championship-caliber team he may be more of a utility player. He'll be competing for a regular role in Baltimore in spring training.

Year	Age	Club (League)	Level	AVG	G	AB	R	H	2B	3B	HR	RBI	BB	SO	SB	OBP	SLG
2023	24	Norfolk (IL)	AAA	.321	88	349	66	112	30	4	9	58	32	69	11	.378	.507
2023	24	Baltimore (AL)	MLB	.212	15	33	4	7	1	0	0	4	0	9	0	.206	.242
Minor League Totals				.285	316	1219	205	348	76	12	33	177	128	236	25	.357	.449
Major League Totals				.212	15	33	4	7	1	0	0	4	0	9	0	.206	.242

8 CONNOR NORBY, 2B/OF

HIT: 55. **POW:** 50. **RUN:** 50. **FLD:** 45. **ARM:** 40. **BA Grade:** 50. **Risk:** High.

Born: June 8, 2000. **B-T:** R-R. **HT:** 5-10. **WT:** 190.
Drafted: East Carolina, 2021 (2nd round). **Signed by:** Quincy Boyd.
TRACK RECORD: Norby led Division I with 102 hits in an All-America junior season at East Carolina in 2021 and signed for a slightly below-slot $1.7 million as the 41st overall pick. He led the Orioles organization with 29 home runs in 2022. He spent all of 2023 at Triple-A Norfolk and surged in the second half, ending with an .847 OPS and 22 home runs. He also made 26 starts in left field to add versatility that might help work his righthanded bat into Baltimore's lefty-heavy lineup
SCOUTING REPORT: Norby's knack for hard contact showed as he continued to live up to the "pure hitter" description he had when he entered the organization. He hits the ball at good angles with a line-drive swing from the right side, showing a willingness to drive the ball the other way and an ability to tap into his pull-side power as the season progressed. He struggled to control the strike zone early in the season, particularly chasing fastballs up in the zone, but he was closer to the above-average hitter with average power he projects to be as he returned to a more disciplined approach over the course of the year. While not more than an average runner, Norby plays the game hard and runs the bases well. A below-average arm limits him to second base-only, and he'll likely be fringe-average there at best. He started once a week in left field at Triple-A to add that position to his repertoire.
THE FUTURE: Norby has a tricky profile as a bat-first second baseman, but the best of them enjoy fruitful careers, and he has the potential to do so for a second-division club. He might not have much left to prove at Triple-A, but considering the Orioles don't need to add him to the 40-man roster until after the 2024 season and don't have an obvious MLB role for him yet, he may return there in 2024.

Year	Age	Club (League)	Level	AVG	G	AB	R	H	2B	3B	HR	RBI	BB	SO	SB	OBP	SLG
2023	23	Norfolk (IL)	AAA	.290	138	565	104	164	40	3	21	92	57	137	10	.359	.483
Minor League Totals				.283	292	1163	216	329	69	8	53	184	134	286	32	.362	.493

9 ENRIQUE BRADFIELD JR., OF

HIT: 55. **POW:** 30. **RUN:** 80. **FLD:** 80. **ARM:** 40. **BA Grade:** 50. **Risk:** High.

Born: December 2, 2001. **B-T:** L-L. **HT:** 6-1. **WT:** 170.
Drafted: Vanderbilt, 2023 (1st round). **Signed by:** Trent Friedrich.
TRACK RECORD: Bradfield was in the mix for the top two rounds of the shortened 2020 draft, but bonus demands meant he went to Vanderbilt, where his elite speed made him one of college baseball's most dynamic players. He signed for a slot $4.17 million as the 17th overall pick in 2023 and performed largely as advertised. Bradfield had an .802 OPS over three levels with more walks (26) than strikeouts (16) and 25 steals in 27 tries.
SCOUTING REPORT: Bradfield has a pair of elite carrying tools in his 80-grade speed and center field defense, which together create a pretty high floor for his major league future. Advanced baserunning instincts could put him near the top of the league in stolen bases throughout his prime. He was drafted into an organization that has a track record for improving hitters with particular traits, and when it comes to the ability to manage the strike zone and make consistent contact without much whiff, Bradfield certainly qualifies. He had an astonishing 2% whiff rate in his pro debut, and walked nearly a quarter of the time. Another of those traits the Orioles work with is consistent hard contact, which isn't yet a part of Bradfield's game and may never manifest. The Orioles hope Bradfield's above-average hit tool can play up as he focuses on hitting the ball at good angles and producing line drives, which can make up for his well below-average power, even as he projects to add some strength in pro ball.
THE FUTURE: Provided he makes enough quality contact to let his speed and on-base capabilities shine through, Bradfield has the traits to be a high-level table-setter as an everyday center fielder with Gold Glove capabilities. He'll start 2024 at High-A Aberdeen, with the potential to move quickly through the Orioles' system.

Year	Age	Club (League)	Level	AVG	G	AB	R	H	2B	3B	HR	RBI	BB	SO	SB	OBP	SLG
2023	21	FCL Orioles	Rk	.556	3	9	4	5	1	0	0	0	3	3	1	.667	.667
2023	21	Delmarva (CAR)	A	.302	17	53	15	16	2	0	0	6	19	9	20	.494	.340
2023	21	Aberdeen (SAL)	A+	.118	5	17	3	2	0	0	0	0	4	4	4	.286	.118
Minor League Totals				.291	25	79	22	23	3	0	0	6	26	16	25	.473	.329

10 CHAYCE McDERMOTT, RHP

FB: 60. **CB:** 50. **SL:** 60. **SPLT:** 45. **CTL:** 45. **BA Grade:** 50. **Risk:** High.

Born: August 22, 1998. **B-T:** L-R. **HT:** 6-3. **WT:** 197.
Drafted: Ball State, 2021 (4th round). **Signed by:** Scott Oberhelman (Astros).
TRACK RECORD: Though he comes from a basketball family, McDermott has made a name for himself on the mound. The Ball State product was a senior sign by the Astros for $325,000 in 2022 and came to the Orioles a year later as part of a three-team trade that sent Trey Mancini to Houston, the eventual World Series champions. In his first full season with the Orioles, McDermott won the organization's minor league pitcher of the year honors and led all minor league pitchers with a .167 opponent average in 2023.
SCOUTING REPORT: Part of hitters' frustrations with McDermott stems from their inability to square up his fastball, which sits in the mid 90s and tops out at 97 mph with plus traits and the ability to miss bats at the top of the strike zone. His sweeper grades out as his best secondary pitch, though depending on the lineup, he'll also use a shorter, high-80s cutter to attack righties with as well. Against lefties, he uses an average curveball to help keep them off his fastball, and tunnels all of his breaking pitches extremely well off his heater. He swapped his changeup for a splitter in 2023, though it was a clear fourth pitch and has fringe-average potential. McDermott's command improved upon the jump to Triple-A, even though the walk rate was still on the high side. The level's automated ball-strike system brought McDermott more into the zone, where his stuff plays extremely well.
THE FUTURE: Continued refinement on the location front can keep McDermott on a starter's track, where he has the potential to be a No. 4 in a major league rotation. He'll start 2024 back at Triple-A Norfolk but could have a chance to make an impression in big league camp ahead of a potential midsummer debut.

Year	Age	Club (League)	Level	W	L	ERA	G	GS	IP	H	HR	BB	SO	BB%	SO%	WHIP	AVG
2023	24	Bowie (EL)	AA	5	6	3.56	16	14	68	42	6	44	88	15.3	30.7	1.26	.175
2023	24	Norfolk (IL)	AAA	3	2	2.49	10	8	51	27	3	24	64	11.7	31.2	1.01	.156
Minor League Totals				15	11	4.13	60	44	244	158	29	143	352	13.8	34.0	1.23	.181

11 CADE POVICH, LHP

FB: 55. **CB:** 55. **SL:** 55. **CUT:** 50. **CHG:** 50. **CTL:** 50. **BA Grade:** 50. **Risk:** High

Born: April 12, 2020. **B-T:** L-L. **HT:** 6-3. **WT:** 185. **Drafted:** Nebraska, 2021 (3rd round). **Signed by:** Joe Bisenius (Twins).
TRACK RECORD: Povich was enjoying a strong season at High-A in 2022 when the Orioles acquired him as a key piece in a four-player return from the Twins for all-star closer Jorge Lopez. He improved even more after the trade as he began to use a cutter, and then spent all of 2023 in the high minors. Povich struck out 31.1% of batters at Double-A and Triple-A—the sixth-highest rate among qualified full-season pitchers—but saw his results dip a bit at Triple-A Norfolk.
SCOUTING REPORT: Povich's best pitch is his tailing four-seam fastball, which averaged 92 mph and was up to 95 with the potential to be above-average for its ability to generate swinging strikes up in the zone as well as ground balls. He used his high-80s cutter more in 2023, especially as a swing-and-miss weapon to lefthanded hitters, and he deemphasized his sweeper to save it more for putaway situations. Both pitches have above-average potential, and his big 74-77 mph curveball is also a weapon to batters of both hands. Povich's changeup made strides in 2023, especially in Triple-A, and can be an average weapon to righties. The key will be commanding those pitches in the strike zone, where his stuff plays well.
THE FUTURE: Povich has a path to becoming a quality No. 4 starter in a major league rotation as he continues to refine his repertoire and maintain his ability to get outs in the zone with five pitches. He could push for a major league opportunity in 2024, though he'll start back at Triple-A Norfolk.

Year	Age	Club (League)	Level	W	L	ERA	G	GS	IP	H	HR	BB	SO	BB%	SO%	WHIP	AVG
2023	23	Bowie (EL)	AA	6	7	4.87	18	18	81	74	12	37	118	10.5	33.4	1.36	.240
2023	23	Norfolk (IL)	AAA	2	3	5.36	10	10	45	32	6	29	53	14.7	26.9	1.35	.194
Minor League Totals				18	20	4.64	56	54	251	209	32	107	338	10.0	31.5	1.26	.221

12 SETH JOHNSON, RHP

FB: 60. **CB:** 45. **SL:** 65. **CHG:** 45. **CTL:** 50. **BA Grade:** 50 **Risk:** High.

Born: September 19, 1998. **B-T:** R-R. **HT:** 6-1. **WT:** 200. **Drafted:** Campbell, 2019 (1st round supplemental).
Signed by: Joe Hastings (Rays).
TRACK RECORD: A converted pitcher at Campbell after spending two years as a shortstop at Louisburg (N.C.) JC, Johnson shot up draft boards in 2019 and was drafted 40th overall by the Rays. He was pitch-

ing well in 2021 before he suffered an elbow injury that ultimately required Tommy John surgery. Given the Rays' pending roster crunch, they made him available for what became a three-team trade that sent Trey Mancini from Baltimore to the Astros and Jose Siri from Houston to Tampa Bay. Johnson returned to the mound in August 2023 and ended the year at Double-A Bowie.

SCOUTING REPORT: Johnson's post-surgery delivery remains athletic and fluid. His fastball averaged 95 mph over his rehab stints with hoppy life at the top of the zone. While his slider was slow to return to form, it remains at least a plus future pitch in the mid 80s with late bite, and the Orioles believe targeting improvements and grip adjustments can help him regain its quality. Johnson used his mid-to-high-80s curveball, a fringe-average pitch, as his primary weapon to lefties upon his return, with his developing changeup a fourth pitch at this stage. Given Johnson's athleticism and relatively short track record as a pitcher, the Orioles expect he can approach average control.

THE FUTURE: Johnson maintains a midrotation ceiling based on his stuff and athleticism, though the impact of Tommy John surgery and the fact that he's already on the 40-man roster could push him to the major league bullpen in the near term. He'll likely start 2024 at Double-A Bowie.

Year	Age	Club (League)	Level	W	L	ERA	G	GS	IP	H	HR	BB	SO	BB%	SO%	WHIP	AVG
2023	24	FCL Orioles	Rk	0	0	0.00	1	1	1	1	0	0	2	0.0	50.0	1.00	.250
2023	24	Delmarva (CAR)	A	0	0	0.00	1	1	2	1	0	0	1	0.0	14.3	0.50	.143
2023	24	Aberdeen (SAL)	A+	0	1	8.31	2	2	4	4	0	3	7	15.0	35.0	1.62	.235
2023	24	Bowie (EL)	AA	0	0	3.00	1	1	3	3	1	2	4	14.3	28.6	1.67	.250
Minor League Totals				7	9	2.92	44	37	148	135	12	52	186	8.4	30.0	1.26	.239

13 DYLAN BEAVERS, OF

HIT: 50. **POW:** 55. **RUN:** 60. **FLD:** 50. **ARM:** 60. **BA Grade:** 50. **Risk:** High.

Born: August 11, 2001 **B-T:** L-R. **HT:** 6-4. **WT:** 205. **Drafted:** California, 2022 (1st round supp). **Signed by:** Scott Walter.

TRACK RECORD: A two-time all-Pacific-12 Conference star for California, Beavers was one of the college game's most consistent performers entering the 2022 draft, but he fell to the 33rd overall pick due to concerns about his swing. The Orioles signed him for a slightly below-slot $2.2 million, and began a collaborative effort to iron out some of those swing issues. After a period of extensive tweaking at High-A Aberdeen, Beavers settled back in for a strong finish to the 2023 season. He ended with a .971 OPS from June 13 onward and ended with 34 games at Double-A Bowie.

SCOUTING REPORT: The lefthanded-hitting Beavers' swing work helped him improve his timing and helped him get his swing more on a line and make higher quality contact as the season went on, but there were concerns about how solid he was hitting the ball at times. He can be an average hitter, given the unique bat-to-ball abilities for someone with his physical 6-foot-4 frame. He swung and missed just 8% of the time in 2023 and also had one of the lowest chase rates of any full-season minor league hitter in the organization. Beavers can have above-average power if he continues to optimize his swing, and is a plus runner who could be either above-average in a corner outfield spot or fringe-average in center.

THE FUTURE: Beavers has some of the highest upside in the organization, and the Orioles believe his aptitude and application can help him become an everyday outfielder. He'll be back at Double-A Bowie to build on how he ended 2023.

Year	Age	Club (League)	Level	AVG	G	AB	R	H	2B	3B	HR	RBI	BB	SO	SB	OBP	SLG
2023	21	Aberdeen (SAL)	A+	.273	85	311	46	85	26	3	9	48	50	84	22	.369	.463
2023	21	Bowie (EL)	AA	.321	34	134	29	43	9	3	2	12	20	32	5	.417	.478
Minor League Totals				.293	142	532	89	156	43	8	11	75	86	134	33	.392	.466

14 JACKSON BAUMEISTER, RHP

FB: 60. **SL:** 50. **CB:** 50. **CHG:** 40. **CTL:** 45. **BA Grade:** 50. **Risk:** Very High.

Born: July 10, 2002. **B-T:** R-R. **HT:** 6-4. **WT:** 225. **Drafted:** Florida State, 2023 (2nd round supplemental). **Signed by:** Eric Robinson.

TRACK RECORD: Baumeister was one of the highest-rated high school players eligible for the 2021 draft who made it to college, but he did so knowing he would be an eligible sophomore two years later. The Orioles drafted him 63rd overall out of Florida State in 2023 and signed him for an above-slot $1.605 million as the highest-drafted pitcher under Mike Elias. The Orioles appreciated his hoppy fastball and potential to further develop his arsenal, but they also valued his aptitude to make adjustments as his season went on and willingness to learn. Baumeister didn't pitch in game action after signing.

SCOUTING REPORT: Baumeister's fastball, which in college sat around 93 mph and touched 98, features above-averaged induced vertical break with elite extension and a flat approach angle that helps it play up in the zone. The club believes a focus on elevating it could lead to immediate improvements in results.

Baumesiter's curveball had at least average traits but was inconsistent, while the Orioles believe the slider he added during 2023 has the potential to grow into his best secondary pitch. Even if his changeup remains a fourth pitch, the Orioles believe his arm strength and ability to spin the ball can give him a starter's arsenal going forward.

THE FUTURE: Baumeister has the potential to be the best pitcher the Elias Orioles have drafted, with a midrotation upside and the chance for more if he can consistently throw his most effective breaking balls. He could move quickly through the system but likely will start at Low-A Delmarva in 2024.

Year	Age	Club (League)	Level	W	L	ERA	G	GS	IP	H	HR	BB	SO	BB%	SO%	WHIP	AVG
2023	20	Did not play															

15 JUD FABIAN, OF

HIT: 40. **POW:** 60. **RUN:** 60. **FLD:** 60. **ARM:** 55. **BA Grade:** 50. **Risk:** Very High.

Born: September 27, 2000. **B-T:** R-L. **HT:** 6-1. **WT:** 195. **Drafted:** Florida, 2022 (2nd round supplemental).
Signed by: Eric Robinson.
TRACK RECORD: The Red Sox drafted Fabian in the second round in 2021 but he returned to Florida for his senior year to team up with his younger brother Deric. Jud ended up signing with the Orioles—who were connected to him for an above-slot deal the year before—for $1.03 million as the 67th pick in the 2022 draft. Fabian fared well at High-A Aberdeen to begin 2023 before an all-or-nothing profile emerged at Double-A Bowie, where he struck out 108 times with 15 home runs in 288 plate appearances.
SCOUTING REPORT: Fabian kept his strikeout rate manageable at Aberdeen, but some of the hit tool issues he came out of Florida with resurfaced when he struck out nearly 38% of the time at Bowie. Much of that came as higher-level pitchers attacked him with high fastballs, which Fabian struggled to reach with his uphill swing. He could still have plus power in games, which would be a requirement if his hit tool is only fringe-avearge. Defensively, Fabian is a true plus center fielder with advanced instincts, range and playmaking ability and an above-average arm, giving him the potential to play the position every day in the big leagues.
THE FUTURE: Fabian's defense alone could make him a second-division regular or platoon player on a playoff team, and his contact ability is the only thing that is limiting him to that type of role. He'll likely be back at Bowie to attack those issues to begin 2024.

Year	Age	Club (League)	Level	AVG	G	AB	R	H	2B	3B	HR	RBI	BB	SO	SB	OBP	SLG
2023	22	Aberdeen (SAL)	A+	.281	56	192	35	54	13	0	9	43	37	61	19	.392	.490
2023	22	Bowie (EL)	AA	.176	64	238	36	42	6	1	15	31	44	108	12	.314	.399
Minor League Totals				.240	142	508	90	122	28	3	27	90	100	190	32	.366	.467

16 LUIS DE LEON, LHP

FB: 60. **SL:** 50. **CHG:** 50. **CTL:** 45. **BA Grade:** 50. **Risk:** Extreme.

Born: April 14, 2003. **B-T:** L-L. **HT:** 6-3. **WT:** 168. **Signed:** Dominican Republic, 2021.
Signed by: Michael Cruz/Gerardo Cabrera.
TRACK RECORD: De Leon was a late-developing prospect in the Dominican Republic who signed for $30,000 at age 18 in December 2021 after Orioles scouts followed him past his age group's signing year and noted his continued improvements. He made his U.S. debut in 2023 by dominating over six starts in the Florida Complex League before continuing his success at Low-A Delmarva. He struck out 11.2 batters per nine innings over the two levels.
SCOUTING REPORT: There's plenty of projection in De Leon's athletic 6-foot-3 frame, but his present-day stuff is hardly lacking. He averaged 95 mph on his fastball, giving it plus potential from the left side. He primarily attacks with his fastball and a high-80s changeup that can be an above-average pitch despite a small velocity difference from his fastball. That's because of its significant horizontal fade and his ability to command the pitch. De Leon made progress with a hard slider in 2023 that gives him both another movement profile for hitters to consider and another potentially above-average pitch. De Leon's ability to induce weak contact is an early strength, and opponents had a 69% groundball rate against him in 2023. Like many young power lefthanders, De Leon issued too many walks and will need to reduce free baserunners as he advances.
THE FUTURE: De Leon dominated light competition at the complex and during a late-season Low-A cameo, but he did so with the raw stuff and maturity that give indications he can be a midrotation starter at his peak. He's likely to return to Delmarva to begin 2024, but could be pushed quickly should the Orioles like what they see.

Year	Age	Club (League)	Level	W	L	ERA	G	GS	IP	H	HR	BB	SO	BB%	SO%	WHIP	AVG
2023	20	FCL Orioles	Rk	2	0	1.65	6	6	27	23	0	14	36	12.0	30.8	1.35	.230
2023	20	Delmarva (CAR)	A	3	1	2.39	9	5	26	17	0	16	31	14.2	27.4	1.25	.177
Minor League Totals				9	5	3.11	25	16	82	56	0	43	112	12.4	32.2	1.22	.191

17 MAX WAGNER, 3B

HIT: 50. **POW:** 50. **RUN:** 50. **FLD:** 55. **ARM:** 50. **BA Grade:** 45. **Risk:** High.

Born: August 19, 2001. **B-T:** R-R. **HT:** 6-0. **WT:** 215. **Drafted:** Clemson, 2022 (2nd round). **Signed by:** Quincy Boyd

TRACK RECORD: Wagner began his 2022 sophomore season at Clemson on the bench but ended it with 27 home runs and Atlantic Coast Conference player of the year honors. The Orioles capitalized on his draft-eligible status to sign him for $1.9 million in the second round. Wagner showed an ability to control the strike zone and make solid contact for most of the year at High-A Aberdeen in 2023 before a late-season promotion to Double-A Bowie. He had left hamate surgery after the season but should be ready for spring training.

SCOUTING REPORT: Wagner made significant gains in his top-end exit velocities in 2023, going from a 90th percentile EV of 101 mph in 2022 to 104 mph in 2023, but he did so with a slightly worse than expected contact rate and contact quality as he adjusted to higher-level pitching and spin. Wagner maintains a short, quick swing and can be an average hitter with a more consistent barrel path. He could have at least average power with those improvements, as his attractive EVs demonstrate. He is at least an above-average defender at third base with consistent movements and actions at the position, and he profiles well at second base as well. Wagner is also a heady basestealer despite average speed.

THE FUTURE: There was nothing remarkable about Wagner's full-season debut, though he remains a potential second-division regular or platoon player due to his steady offensive profile and defensive versatility. He'll start 2024 back at Double-A Bowie, with the potential to reach Triple-A at age 22.

Year	Age	Club (League)	Level	AVG	G	AB	R	H	2B	3B	HR	RBI	BB	SO	SB	OBP	SLG
2023	21	Aberdeen (SAL)	A+	.234	80	299	60	70	14	3	10	36	51	90	26	.356	.401
2023	21	Bowie (EL)	AA	.252	27	111	16	28	7	1	3	18	7	34	1	.303	.414
Minor League Totals				.240	126	480	88	115	24	6	14	65	67	142	29	.344	.402

18 KYLE STOWERS, OF

HIT: 30. **POW:** 65. **RUN:** 55. **FLD:** 50. **ARM:** 60. **BA Grade:** 45. **Risk:** High.

Born: January 2, 1998. **B-T:** L-L. **Ht.:** 6-3. **Wt.:** 200. **Drafted:** Stanford, 2019 (2nd round supp). **Signed by:** Scott Walter.

TRACK RECORD: The third pick in the Orioles' impressive 2019 draft behind Adley Rutschman and Gunnar Henderson, Stowers shared organizational player of the year honors with Rutschman in 2021 and made his major league debut in 2022. After making the Orioles out of spring training in 2023, Stowers struggled to make an impact in two stints before right shoulder inflammation shut him down for a month. Though he hit very well at Triple-A after his return, Stowers didn't return to the majors.

SCOUTING REPORT: In Triple-A, Stowers was largely the same player he had been in the past. While he might not ever be an average hitter due to elevated swing-and-miss that shows up against all pitch types, Stowers improved his swing decisions at Triple-A. Stowers remains at least a plus power hitter. He had a 55.7% hard-hit rate and an average exit velocity of 93.8 mph at Norfolk. While he boasts a plus arm that works in right field and above-average speed that gives him good range, Stowers' defense seemed to be viewed skeptically in the majors, further limiting his opportunities.

THE FUTURE: Stowers didn't show himself as a first-division regular in the majors this year, but his power and defense could still make him a second-division outfielder or platoon player for a playoff team. Whether he gets that opportunity with the Orioles remains to be seen, though he'll have an opportunity to compete for a job out of spring training.

Year	Age	Club (League)	Level	AVG	G	AB	R	H	2B	3B	HR	RBI	BB	SO	SB	OBP	SLG
2023	25	FCL Orioles	Rk	.714	3	7	2	5	0	0	1	1	1	2	0	.778	1.143
2023	25	Aberdeen (SAL)	A+	.500	4	18	7	9	1	0	3	8	2	2	0	.550	1.056
2023	25	Norfolk (IL)	AAA	.245	68	233	42	57	9	1	17	49	40	76	3	.364	.511
2023	25	Baltimore (AL)	MLB	.067	14	30	1	2	0	0	0	0	3	12	0	.152	.067
Minor League Totals				.263	349	1260	197	332	75	6	73	244	181	408	19	.362	.506
Major League Totals				.207	48	121	12	25	4	1	3	11	8	41	0	.267	.331

19 MAC HORVATH, 3B

HIT: 40. **POW:** 55. **RUN:** 60. **FLD:** 50. **ARM:** 60. **BA Grade:** 50. **Risk:** Extreme.

Born: January 28, 2002. **B-T:** R-R. **HT:** 6-1. **WT:** 195. **Drafted:** North Carolina, 2023 (2nd round).
Signed by: Quincy Boyd.
TRACK RECORD: The Orioles were interested in Horvath as a draft-eligible sophomore in 2022 but ended up signing him as the 53rd overall pick in 2023 for a slightly below-slot $1.4 million. He hit 47 home runs and stole 44 bases over three seasons at North Carolina, showing the kind of power-speed combo the Orioles have been attracted to atop recent drafts. His pro debut went well, with Horvath slugging five home runs with a 1.057 OPS and 14 steals in a stint centered on Low-A Delmarva and including two other levels.
SCOUTING REPORT: Horvath shows a power-speed tool set, with his hit tool the only thing potentially holding him back. He has a grooved swing path that can, at times, lead to swing-and-miss at the top of the zone as well as high ball flights that limit the impact of his high exit velocities. Still, Horvath controls the strike zone well—he had a 17% chase rate in his pro debut—and could have above-average power due to his strength and athleticism. Horvath is at least a plus runner with a plus arm, and while he's expected to primarily play third base, he could spend time at second base and in the outfield in his full-season debut.
THE FUTURE: Horvath has the profile to thrive in an Orioles hitting program that will attack his contact deficiencies and could help him reach a solid-average starter ceiling, potentially as a player who helps all over the field. He'll start his full-season debut at High-A Aberdeen.

Year	Age	Club (League)	Level	AVG	G	AB	R	H	2B	3B	HR	RBI	BB	SO	SB	OBP	SLG
2023	21	FCL Orioles	Rk	.556	3	9	6	5	2	0	1	3	3	3	0	.667	1.111
2023	21	Delmarva (CAR)	A	.308	14	52	11	16	4	0	2	5	10	17	9	.422	.500
2023	21	Aberdeen (SAL)	A+	.235	5	17	9	4	1	0	2	3	6	6	5	.435	.647
Minor League Totals				.321	22	78	26	25	7	0	5	11	19	26	14	.455	.603

20 BRAYLIN TAVERA, OF

HIT: 50. **POW:** 55. **RUN:** 55. **FLD:** 55. **ARM:** 50. **BA Grade:** 50. **Risk:** Extreme.

Born: February 19, 2005. **B-T:** R-R. **HT:** 6-2. **WT:** 175. **Signed:** Dominican Republic, 2022.
Signed by: Luis Noel/Gerardo Cabrera.
TRACK RECORD: Tavera's $1.7 million bonus when he signed at age 16 in January 2022 was, at the time, the Orioles' largest ever given to an international amateur free agent. He has proven to be an exciting player with five-tool potential since then, and demonstrated physical gains and maturity while walking nearly as many times (22) as he struck out (23) in the Rookie-level Florida Complex League in 2023.
SCOUTING REPORT: A lean, athletic player with a projectable frame, Tavera's swing decision improvements came amid an overall offensive jump in which his contact rates and exit velocities trended up from 2022. He walked at a plus rate in the Dominican Summer League in 2022, but the club was encouraged to see that sustain as he moved to a higher level. While Tavera didn't consistently hit the ball at the best angles, he showed traits of a future average hitter with potentially above-average power as he continues to get physically stronger, which will help him better solidify his movements. An above-average runner with an average arm, Tavera has the traits to play an above-average center field at his peak and make an impact as a defender wherever he plays in the outfield.
THE FUTURE: Tavera has significant projection, which in an Orioles system that has shown an ability to help get the most out of players, gives him everyday regular upside given his already intriguing tools. He'll face the challenging jump out of the Rookie complex league to Low-A Delmarva in 2023.

Year	Age	Club (League)	Level	AVG	G	AB	R	H	2B	3B	HR	RBI	BB	SO	SB	OBP	SLG
2023	18	FCL Orioles	Rk	.262	35	107	15	28	5	0	4	20	22	23	13	.391	.421
Minor League Totals				.251	82	251	39	63	10	0	6	34	58	70	20	.403	.363

21 LUIS ALMEYDA, SS

HIT: 45. **POW:** 60. **RUN:** 50. **FLD:** 55. **ARM:** 55. **BA Grade:** 50. **Risk:** Extreme.

Born: April 17, 2006. **B-T:** R-R. **HT:** 6-2. **WT:** 180. **Signed:** Dominican Republic, 2023.
Signed by: Michael Cruz/Gerardo Cabrera.
TRACK RECORD: Born in New Jersey, Almeyda was one of the top players in the 2025 high school class before moving to the Dominican Republic and signing for $2.3 million—a club record for an international amateur—when the 2023 period opened. He homered twice in his first six games in the Dominican Summer League but was limited to just 19 games due to a left ankle sprain, then had season-ending left shoulder surgery.

SCOUTING REPORT: Almeyda proved a quick study upon signing with the Orioles. He showed improvement in his ability to control the strike zone and with his bat-to-ball skills while demonstrating impressive top-end exit velocities. He may not be more than a fringe-average hitter, but his long limbs and developing strength give him the potential for plus power as he physically matures. He boasts smooth, controlled movements and the requisite footwork to play an above-average shortstop. His potential physical development may move him off the position to third base, where those traits and above-average arm would play. He has the power potential to support that move as well.

THE FUTURE: Almeyda's outstanding physical gifts give him the potential to be a bat-first everyday infielder on the left side, and being in the Orioles' system at such a young age can help that process along. He'll likely start 2024 at the Rookie complex level but could push to Low-A Delmarva by season's end.

Year	Age	Club (League)	Level	AVG	G	AB	R	H	2B	3B	HR	RBI	BB	SO	SB	OBP	SLG
2023	17	DSL Orioles Orange	Rk	.190	19	58	6	11	1	0	2	14	8	14	2	.290	.310
Minor League Totals				.190	19	58	6	11	1	0	2	14	8	14	2	.290	.310

22 JUAN NUÑEZ, RHP

FB: 55. **SL:** 60. **CB:** 55. **CHG:** 55. **CTL:** 45. **BA Grade:** 50. **Risk:** Extreme

Born: December 7, 2000. **B-T:** R-R. **HT:** 5-11. **WT:** 190. **Signed:** Dominican Republic, 2022.
Signed by: Luis Lajara (Twins).
TRACK RECORD: Nuñez was a late signing in the Twins' 2019 international class, but by the time he came to the U.S. to debut in the Florida Complex League, he showed plenty of promise. He had 47 strikeouts in 29.2 innings when the Orioles acquired him as part of a four-player return for closer Jorge Lopez at the 2022 trade deadline. Nuñez spent all of 2023 in full-season ball, and struck out 10.8 batters per nine innings with a 1.36 WHIP between Low-A Delmarva and High-A Aberdeen.
SCOUTING REPORT: Nuñez's success came primarily with two pitches: a fastball that averaged 94 mph and was up to 97 with ride, and a low-80s power curveball with sweeper traits and an upper-80s cutterish gyro-slider. Both will blend into each other at times, but when he's on them, both will flash above-average or plus. He met the challenge of throwing those pitches in the zone more often as the season progressed, though he might not have more than fringe-average command long term. He has added a potential above-average changeup to his arsenal to help round out his set of weapons. It has depth and separation to be effective. The Orioles are working with him to try to give him multiple ways to attack lefties and righties. It's a tough ask, but if he pulls it off, he could be a future solid starting pitcher.
THE FUTURE: Nuñez has a chance to be a player who rockets up these rankings in 2024, because he has the makings of an effective starter who can give hitters different looks in each at-bat. But he has yet to show the touch and feel expected of a starter who can do that. He's still young enough to get there, but he has an excellent fallback option as a power reliever.

Year	Age	Club (League)	Level	W	L	ERA	G	GS	IP	H	HR	BB	SO	BB%	SO%	WHIP	AVG
2023	22	Delmarva (CAR)	A	0	4	3.93	13	10	55	44	3	26	72	11.3	31.2	1.27	.218
2023	22	Aberdeen (SAL)	A+	0	2	3.99	13	9	50	40	5	32	53	14.7	24.4	1.45	.223
Minor League Totals				2	12	3.45	51	41	201	159	13	97	250	11.3	29.2	1.27	.215.

23 TRACE BRIGHT, RHP

FB: 55. **CB:** 60. **SL:** 45. **CHG:** 45. **CTL:** 45. **BA Grade:** 45. **Risk:** High.

Born: October 26, 2000. **B-T:** R-R. **HT:** 6-4. **WT:** 205. **Drafted:** Auburn, 2022 (5th round). **Signed by:** David Jennings.
TRACK RECORD: When the Orioles failed to sign third-rounder Nolan McLean in 2022, Bright became the highest-drafted pitcher they signed from that draft class. He signed for a below-slot $400,000 in the fifth round. Baltimore was drawn to his pitch shapes rather than his college performance. He spent most of 2023 at High-A Aberdeen and struck out 35% of batters before finishing well at Double-A Bowie.
SCOUTING REPORT: Bright spent his first full pro season expanding his pitch mix beyond his college repertoire. He throws an above-average 91-94 mph fastball that plays up at the top of the zone due to its plane. He tunnels a plus curveball in the mid 70s effectively off his heater. While he struggled with consistency on his slider and changeup early, both showed flashes of being at least average during the season. He ended the season with attractive swing-and-miss on his changeup, a pitch with depth and strong horizontal break. His hard, mid-80s gyro slider also progressed to be an effective pitch in the zone. Bright found success as the season went on due to improvements in those pitches as well as developing understanding of how to best use them. A high walk rate limits his upside.
THE FUTURE: Bright quietly had one of the more intriguing seasons on the Orioles farm, and the club believes further delivery refinements and strength gains can help his starter mix play up into a back-end rotation role. He'll begin 2024 at Double-A Bowie.

Year	Age	Club (League)	Level	W	L	ERA	G	GS	IP	H	HR	BB	SO	BB%	SO%	WHIP	AVG
2023	22	Aberdeen (SAL)	A+	2	6	4.35	22	18	83	62	8	48	127	13.2	35.0	1.33	.203
2023	22	Bowie (EL)	AA	1	0	2.12	4	3	17	13	1	8	20	11.3	28.2	1.24	.213
Minor League Totals				3	6	3.80	30	22	109	77	9	60	156	12.8	33.3	1.26	.195

24 JUSTIN ARMBRUESTER, RHP

FB: 50. **CUT:** 55. **SL:** 55. **CB:** 45. **CTL:** 55. **BA Grade:** 45. **Risk:** High.

Born: October 21, 1998. **B-T:** R-R. **HT:** 6-4. **WT:** 235. **Drafted:** New Mexico, 2021 (12th round). **Signed by:** Logan Schuemann.

TRACK RECORD: Armbruester was the 2019 Northwest Conference pitcher of the year at Division III Pacific Lutheran and the 2021 Mountain West Conference pitcher of the year at New Mexico. He nearly added that honor to his trophy chest for the Orioles organization in 2022. He followed that up by spending 2023 in the high minors, pitching to contact and missing barrels at Double-A Bowie before a more uneven stint at Triple-A Norfolk, where he ended up behind in counts more and was punished when he returned to the zone.

SCOUTING REPORT: Armbruester leaned heavily on his fastball and cutter in 2023—perhaps too much so—but those pitches grade among his best offerings. His low-90s heater works well at the top of the zone due to a deceptive arm action and good plane. His cutter in the 86-88 mph range is Armbruester's primary weapon to lefties. The pitch has above-average potential, as does his sweepier 81-83 mph slider. Armbruester added a curveball as his fourth pitch as the season progressed and was able to get swinging strikes and ground balls on the offering.

THE FUTURE: There's No. 5 starter potential with Armbruester given his ability to fill up the strike zone and carry his stuff deep into games, but the lack of an elite weapon against lefties may push him to the bullpen. He'll start 2024 at Triple-A Norfolk with a chance for a major league debut.

Year	Age	Club (League)	Level	W	L	ERA	G	GS	IP	H	HR	BB	SO	BB%	SO%	WHIP	AVG
2023	24	Bowie (EL)	AA	3	2	2.47	12	12	62	52	5	19	43	7.5	17.1	1.15	.228
2023	24	Norfolk (IL)	AAA	3	4	4.70	14	13	59	55	9	32	66	12.1	24.9	1.47	.238
Minor League Totals				12	8	3.64	60	48	248	202	36	91	251	8.8	24.4	1.19	.220

25 HUDSON HASKIN, OF

HIT: 50. **POW:** 45. **RUN:** 50. **FLD:** 50. **ARM:** 50. **BA Grade:** 45. **Risk:** High.

Born: December 31, 1998. **B-T:** R-R. **HT:** 6-2. **WT:** 200. **Drafted:** Tulane, 2020 (2nd round). **Signed by:** David Jennings.

TRACK RECORD: Haskin appeared poised for a breakout in 2020 at Tulane, but then the pandemic ended the season prematurely. The Orioles bet on that continued progress and selected him 39th overall and signed him for a $1.91 million bonus. Haskin came to spring training in 2023 stronger and with improvements in his lower half. He appeared to be on the cusp of a breakout with a 1.152 OPS in his first 13 games for Triple-A Norfolk before a hamstring injury cut that short. He played just 20 more games before surgery to repair a left hip impingement in June ended his season.

SCOUTING REPORT: Haskin's hot start came as he did a better job controlling his stride, which allowed him to have a better path to the ball and make harder contact. He hasn't shed the stigma of the unique, unorthodox swing that he had coming out of college, but he has potential to be an average hitter nonetheless. Haskin might grow into fringe-average power, but his ability to control the strike zone and get on base will likely define his offensive profile. He's decent in center field and may be more suited for a corner, but may not have the bat to support that move.

THE FUTURE: Haskin was left off the Orioles' 40-man roster and was not selected in the Rule 5 draft. He can work toward a major league future when he returns to Norfolk in 2024.

Year	Age	Club (League)	Level	AVG	G	AB	R	H	2B	3B	HR	RBI	BB	SO	SB	OBP	SLG
2023	24	Aberdeen (SAL)	A+	.333	5	12	3	4	1	0	0	5	4	4	2	.550	.417
2023	24	Bowie (EL)	AA	.333	5	21	3	7	1	0	0	2	0	6	1	.364	.381
2023	24	Norfolk (IL)	AAA	.268	23	82	14	22	5	1	3	13	6	34	5	.368	.463
Minor League Totals				.272	225	810	137	220	49	7	23	118	85	223	35	.376	.435

26 JOHN RHODES, OF

HIT: 50. **POW:** 45. **RUN:** 50. **FLD:** 45. **ARM:** 50. **BA Grade:** 45. **Risk:** High.

Born: August 15, 2000. **B-T:** R-R. **HT:** 6-0. **WT:** 200. **Drafted:** Kentucky, 2021 (3rd round). **Signed by:** Trent Friedrich.

TRACK RECORD: When MLB moved the 2021 draft from June to July, it made Rhodes an eligible sophomore. He signed with the Orioles for an above-slot $1.38 million as the 76th overall pick that summer. He reached Double-A Bowie in his first full season and took a step forward there in 2023, improving his chase rate and hitting 17 home runs with some improvements in his hard-hit rate.

SCOUTING REPORT: Rhodes led all minor leaguers in the increase of his 90th percentile exit velocity, up to 102.9 mph from 98.5 mph, as he added physicality to try to catch up in that department. Still, he will need to continue to add strength and improve the consistency of his contact quality to have anything more than fringe-average power. That's because his overall slugging production was underwhelming despite his home run total. He can be an average hitter, but that offensive profile will be challenged by the fact that Rhodes is a corner-only outfielder at this point. He is an average runner despite stealing just eight bases in 2023 and he has an average arm.

THE FUTURE: Considering he signed as a sophomore, Rhodes spending his entire age-22 season at Double-A and holding his own keeps a second-division regular profile alive. He may end up back in Double-A to master the level in 2024, given the Orioles' high-minors outfield depth.

Year	Age	Club (League)	Level	AVG	G	AB	R	H	2B	3B	HR	RBI	BB	SO	SB	OBP	SLG
2023	22	Bowie (EL)	AA	.228	108	408	60	93	22	3	17	69	53	123	8	.323	.422
Minor League Totals				.235	220	807	138	190	44	7	24	136	112	214	30	.340	.397

27 ALEX PHAM, RHP

FB: 50. **CB:** 50. **CUT:** 55. **SL:** 50. **CHG:** 50. **CTL:** 60. **BA Grade:** 45. **Risk:** High.

Born: October 10, 1999. **B-T:** R-R. **HT:** 5-11. **WT:** 165. **Drafted:** San Francisco, 2021 (19th round). **Signed by:** Scott Walter.

TRACK RECORD: Pham was primarily a reliever at San Francisco and signed for just $25,000 as a senior in 2021, but his ability to miss bats with a broad arsenal led the Orioles to stretch him out as a starter for 2023. With the help of a cutter he added for 2023, Pham missed bats at an elite level—13.3 strikeouts per nine innings and an 18% swinging-strike rate—at High-A Aberdeen. While his strikeout rate fell at Double-A Bowie, he still ended the year with a 2.57 ERA and 1.02 WHIP over two levels.

SCOUTING REPORT: Pham used a five-pitch mix and a consistently smart attack plan to his benefit in 2023. His low-90s fastball is just average, but it plays up at the top of the zone and is hard to barrel. When the pitch is in the 93-95 mph range, everything else plays up. Pham's above-average cutter in the mid 80s misses plenty of bats, while his slider, curveball and splitter all flashed at least average potential. His ability to mix, attack weaknesses and keep hitters off-balance is a separator. His plus control helps his repertoire play as well.

THE FUTURE: Pham's lack of elite velocity and stuff could create a challenging path to a No. 5 starter role, though his aptitude and arsenal give him a chance. He'll likely be back at Double-A Bowie to begin 2024.

Year	Age	Club (League)	Level	W	L	ERA	G	GS	IP	H	HR	BB	SO	BB%	SO%	WHIP	AVG
2023	23	Aberdeen (SAL)	A+	3	3	2.45	12	10	51	29	5	25	76	12.1	36.7	1.05	.163
2023	23	Bowie (EL)	AA	0	2	2.67	14	9	61	43	5	17	54	7.2	23.0	0.99	.197
Minor League Totals				11	8	3.06	52	19	157	113	12	63	188	10.0	29.7	1.13	.201

28 FREDERICK BENCOSME, SS

HIT: 50. **POW:** 40. **RUN:** 50. **FLD:** 45. **ARM:** 50. **BA Grade:** 45. **Risk:** High.

Born: December 25, 2002. **B-T:** L-R. **Ht.:** 6-0. **Wt.:** 160. **Signed:** Dominican Republic, 2020. **Signed by:** Francisco Rosario/Geraldo Cabrera.

TRACK RECORD: Bencosme wasn't high on the Orioles' shortstop depth chart when he signed for $10,000 late in the 2020 international signing period, but he shot through the low minors with a breakout in 2022 and spent all of 2023 at High-A Aberdeen for his age-20 season. He held his own at the level thanks to his athleticism and advanced bat-to-ball skills.

SCOUTING REPORT: Bencosme's ability to make contact has never been in question—he swung and missed just 8.1% of the time in 2023. Because of that, he could be an average hitter, and improved swing decisions and walk rates could enhance that ceiling. Despite a projectable frame upon which he is working to add strength, Bencosme's below-average exit speeds emphasize the need for him to hit the ball at line-drive angles to maximize his offensive production. Bencosme is a solid athlete who moves well on the infield but needs to refine his actions at shortstop. He has the arm to make all the throws required at the position. He could be average at second base.

THE FUTURE: Age is on Bencosme's side, and his profile is one that can develop into that of a second-division big leaguer as he climbs the minors and masters each level. He could end up back at Aberdeen to accomplish that to begin 2024.

Year	Age	Club (League)	Level	AVG	G	AB	R	H	2B	3B	HR	RBI	BB	SO	SB	OBP	SLG
2023	20	Aberdeen (SAL)	A+	.246	114	414	60	102	18	3	2	49	55	67	28	.338	.319
Minor League Totals				.278	231	823	114	229	34	11	7	96	95	125	46	.356	.372

29 KIEFER LORD, RHP

FB: 60. **SL:** 50. **CB:** 45. **CHG:** 30. **CTL:** 50. **BA Grade:** 45. **Risk:** High.

Born: June 22, 2002. **B-T:** R-R HT: 6-3. **WT:** 195. **Drafted:** Washington, 2023 (3rd round). **Signed by:** David Blume.

TRACK RECORD: Lord was one of the most fascinating stories in the 2023 draft as a self-taught pitcher who built his arm strength using online videos while at Division III Carleton (Minn.) before transferring to Washington for his junior year. The Orioles, enamored of his drive and aptitude to improve, signed him for slightly below-slot at $760,000 as a 2023 third-rounder. He made one appearance in the Florida Complex League before he was shut down for the season.

SCOUTING REPORT: Lord's riding fastball was his best pitch at Washington. It sits in the mid 90s and tops out at 99 mph. It was also his carrying pitch—he threw it more than 70% of the time. The Orioles believe he can be more effective as he mixes in his secondaries more often. His slider is the best of them as an average pitch that was 83-84 mph and up to 86 with good shape at Washington, followed by an upper-70s curveball that he showed the ability to spin.

THE FUTURE: Throwing that curveball and adding an effective changeup will be separators for Lord as he tries to stay in a rotation, though the fastball can help him move through the minors quickly. He'll likely begin at Low-A Delmarva with as he pursues a back-end rotation major league future.

Year	Age	Club (League)	Level	W	L	ERA	G	GS	IP	H	HR	BB	SO	BB%	SO%	WHIP	AVG
2023	21	FCL Orioles	Rk	0	0	0.00	1	0	2	0	0	1	1	14.3	14.3	0.50	.000
Minor League Totals				0	0	0.00	1	0	2	0	0	1	1	14.3	14.3	0.50	.000

30 KEAGAN GILLIES, RHP

FB: 60. **SL:** 55. **SPLT:** 55. **CTL:** 50. **BA Grade:** 45. **Risk:** High.

Born: January 27, 1998. **B-T:** R-R. **HT:** 6-8. **WT:** 255. **Drafted:** Tulane, 2021 (15th round). **Signed by:** David Jennings.

TRACK RECORD: Gillies' fifth season pitching out of the Tulane bullpen was his best, and the Orioles signed him as a 15th-round graduate student in 2021 for $50,000 based on that success. He missed most of 2022 with injury but was a revelation in 2023, striking out 61 in 40.2 innings with a 0.81 WHIP and a strikeout rate of 39.8% between High-A Aberdeen and Double-A Bowie.

SCOUTING REPORT: An imposing 6-foot-8 presence on the mound, Gillies works downhill with an over-the-top delivery and boasts an effective three-pitch mix he uses to work north-south. He averaged 93.5 mph on his fastball, but the pitch plays up with plus traits because of the extension he gets off the mound and the carry on the pitch. He tunnels his above-average mid-80s slider and above-average splitter off the pitch well, elevating the quality of his entire arsenal, meaning hitters have to quickly determine what they're seeing. The pair of secondaries means Gillies has weapons for both righthanded and lefthanded hitters.

THE FUTURE: Gillies is already a reliever and won't move off that path, but his quality pitch mix and ability to throw strikes could help him have a long career in a major league bullpen. He could return to Double-A Bowie in 2024, but may move quickly and could help the Orioles' bullpen at some point next year.

Year	Age	Club (League)	Level	W	L	ERA	G	GS	IP	H	HR	BB	SO	BB%	SO%	WHIP	AVG
2023	25	Aberdeen (SAL)	A+	3	0	0.54	15	0	17	2	1	4	27	7.1	48.2	0.36	.038
2023	25	Bowie (EL)	AA	2	1	3.75	18	0	24	17	2	10	34	9.9	33.7	1.13	.195
Minor League Totals				6	3	3.19	43	6	62	41	6	21	84	8.4	33.6	1.00	.182

Boston Red Sox

BY ALEX SPEIER

In 2019, the Red Sox fired Dave Dombrowski and hired Chaim Bloom to lead their baseball operations department with a renewed commitment to modernizing and replenishing a player development system that—despite a 2018 championship built largely around homegrown stars like Mookie Betts and Xander Bogaerts—seemingly had fallen behind other teams.

The Red Sox entrusted Bloom with building a sustainable winner, by marrying upper-tier big league payrolls with a renewable pipeline of standout prospects that could help the team end its boom-or-bust cycle of the 2010s.

In 2023, the Red Sox experienced the arrival of the team's largest wave of homegrown talent in years. First baseman Triston Casas emerged as a middle-of-the-order force while finishing third in AL Rookie of the Year voting; righthanders Brayan Bello and Kutter Crawford made cases to be part of the Red Sox rotation for years; and Jarren Duran enjoyed a breakout season in the outfield.

While all of those players had been acquired under Dombrowski, their development into mainstays seemingly pointed to philosophical and programmatic shifts that had occurred during Bloom's tenure. Yet the improvement of the system under Bloom was inadequate to save his job.

With the Red Sox on their way to a third last-place finish in four years in September 2023, and with almost all the gains in the farm system having occurred in the team's position playing core, the Red Sox fired Bloom. Less than two months later, they hired Craig Breslow—formerly a Red Sox pitcher and the assistant general manager of the Cubs—as their new chief baseball officer.

Breslow inherited what could be a very strong positional group. Casas and Rafael Devers are infield cornerstones; Ceddanne Rafaela and Wilyer Abreu—acquired in a 2022 deadline deal by Bloom—likewise are close to helping Duran in the outfield; and shortstop Marcelo Mayer, outfielder Roman Anthony and catcher Kyle Teel all should open 2024 together in Double-A Portland.

Yet the inability of the Red Sox to develop a steady flow of pitching not only led to an ongoing scramble to forge a big league rotation—they frequently turned to openers and bullpen games in 2023—but also cast a shadow over the future.

The Red Sox used few resources on pitchers under Bloom, never signing a free agent pitcher to a deal of more than two years and never drafting an arm in the first two rounds from 2020 to 2023.

The Red Sox do not have starters ready to graduate from the minors into the big league rotation at the start of 2024, and don't project to have one for 2025, either.

For the Red Sox, the appeal of Breslow went beyond his background as both a forward-thinking pitcher—he underwent a data-driven self-refashioning into a sidearmer at the end of his career—and front office member who had overhauled how the Cubs mold young arms.

Still, his hiring reflected in part the sense of urgency felt by Boston ownership to amplify the progress made in the team's pitching development in recent years and to start channeling more resources via both trades and free agency into building a staff that is capable of perennial contention, rather than an annual roll of the dice. ◾

PATRICK SMITH/GETTY IMAGES

Rookie Triston Casas' 1.034 second-half OPS ranked second among first basemen.

PROJECTED 2027 LINEUP

Catcher	Kyle Teel	25
First Base	Triston Casas	27
Second Base	Yoeilin Cespedes	21
Third Base	Marcelo Mayer	24
Shortstop	Trevor Story	34
Left Field	Jarren Duran	30
Center Field	Ceddanne Rafaela	26
Right Field	Roman Anthony	23
Designated Hitter	Rafael Devers	30
No. 1 Starter	Brayan Bello	28
No. 2 Starter	Kutter Crawford	31
No. 3 Starter	Wikelman Gonzalez	25
No. 4 Starter	Garrett Whitlock	31
No. 5 Starter	Nick Pivetta	34
Closer	Luis Perales	24

BOSTON RED SOX

TOP 2024 CONTRIBUTORS	RANK
1. Wilyer Abreu, OF	6
2. Ceddanne Rafaela, OF	4
3. Chris Murphy, LHP	24

BREAKOUT PROSPECTS	RANK
1. Allan Castro, OF	17
2. Yordanny Monegro, RHP	18
3. Franklin Arias, SS	23

SOURCE OF TOP 30 TALENT

Homegrown	27	Acquired	3
College	5	Trade	3
Junior college	0	Rule 5 draft	0
High school	9	Independent league	0
Nondrafted free agent	0	Free agent/waivers	0
International	13		

LF
Corey Rosier
Kristian Campbell

CF
Ceddanne Rafaela (4)
Miguel Bleis (5)
Caden Rose

RF
Roman Anthony (2)
Wilyer Abreu (6)
Allan Castro (17)
Natanael Yuten

3B
Yoeilin Cespedes (10)
Antonio Anderson (22)
Cutter Coffey

SS
Marcelo Mayer (1)
Nazzan Zanetello (12)
Franklin Arias (23)
Marvin Alcantara
Justin Riemer
Luis Ravelo

2B
Nick Yorke (8)
Chase Meidroth (13)
Mikey Romero (16)
Eddinson Paulino (19)
David Hamilton (20)
Brainer Bonaci

1B
Nathan Hickey (15)
Blaze Jordan (21)

C
Kyle Teel (3)
Johanfran Garcia (14)
Brooks Brannon (28)
Stephen Scott

LHP

LHSP	LHRP
Brandon Walter	Chris Murphy (24)
Dalton Rogers	Helcris Olivarez
	Zach Penrod

RHP

RHSP	RHRP
Wikelman Gonzalez (7)	Justin Slaten (27)
Luis Perales (9)	Bryan Mata (30)
Richard Fitts (11)	Greg Weissert
Yordanny Monegro (18)	Luis Guerrero
Hunter Dobbins (25)	Zack Kelly
Angel Bastardo (26)	Isaiah Campbell
Elmer Rodriguez-Cruz (29)	Nicholas Judice
Juan Daniel Encarnacion	Alex Hoppe
Gilberto Batista	Christopher Troye

1 MARCELO MAYER, SS

Born: December 12, 2002. **B-T:** L-R. **HT:** 6-3. **WT:** 205.
Drafted: HS—Chula Vista, CA, 2021 (1st round).
Signed by: J.J. Altobelli.

TOM PRIDDY/FOUR SEAM IMAGES

TRACK RECORD: After a standout career at Eastlake High outside San Diego, Mayer was a candidate to be drafted No. 1 overall by the Pirates in 2021. Pittsburgh and two others teams passed, leaving Mayer on the board for the Red Sox at No. 4 overall. Boston took advantage of its highest draft position since 1967 by selecting Mayer and signing him to a slot bonus of $6.64 million. He turned in a strong first full season at Low-A Salem and High-A Greenville in 2022, though he was limited to 91 games by a right wrist sprain. Mayer dominated at the start of 2023 in Greenville to earn a May 31 promotion to Double-A Portland at age 20. However, after some promising early adjustments, his performance unraveled as his strikeout rate soared in late July as he tried to play through a left shoulder impingement. The injury ultimately ended his season on Aug. 2 after 78 games and required a painkilling injection in September.

SCOUTING REPORT: Mayer is gifted with a balanced, adaptable lefthanded swing that permits him to get on plane with pitches in different parts of the zone and drive them from line to line. Though he showed a surprising amount of chase as well as swing-and-miss in 2023, that trait was at least partly attributable to his shoulder injury and his youth. Most evaluators project Mayer to develop at least an average future hit tool with some forecasting a plus attribute as he develops better control of the strike zone. The combination of a professional strength regimen—he barely lifted in high school—and weighted-bat program produced improvements in bat speed and exit velocities. He topped out at 112 mph in 2023, which points to above-average to plus power potential, especially because his swing naturally allows him to get the ball in the air with loft. At shortstop, Mayer's pure range is capped by a lack of foot speed, but even at 6-foot-3 he's a rhythmic, fluid defender who moves efficiently to the ball with quick hands to pick and transfer it cleanly. Most evaluators see him sticking at shortstop in the near term, with an average glove and plus arm. If he outgrows short—a possibility in his mid 20s—he has the attributes of an excellent third baseman. Though Mayer has below-average speed, he shows good instincts on the bases.

THE FUTURE: While Mayer likely will start 2024 at Double-A Portland, his combination of skills

and aptitude has given the Red Sox comfort in putting him on a fast track. If Mayer stays healthy for a full season, it wouldn't be shocking to see him in the big leagues by the end of the year. His offensive profile at a premium defensive position suggests a clear path to being an above-average regular with a chance he could emerge, in the words of one evaluator, as "a frickin' monster." ∎

BA GRADE

60 Risk: High

SCOUTING GRADES

Hit: 55. **Power:** 60. **Run:** 40.
Field: 60. **Arm:** 60.

Projected future grades on 20-80 scouting scale

BEST TOOLS

BATTING

Best Hitter for Average	Nick Yorke
Best Power Hitter	Marcelo Mayer
Best Strike-Zone Discipline	Roman Anthony
Fastest Baserunner	David Hamilton
Best Athlete	Miguel Bleis

PITCHING

Best Fastball	Luis Perales
Best Curveball	Wikelman Gonzalez
Best Slider	Alex Hoppe
Best Changeup	Chris Murphy
Best Control	Hunter Dobbins

FIELDING

Best Defensive Catcher	Kyle Teel
Best Defensive Infielder	Marcelo Mayer
Best Infield Arm	Brainer Bonaci
Best Defensive Outfielder	Ceddanne Rafaela
Best Outfield Arm	Wilyer Abreu

Year	Age	Club (League)	Level	AVG	G	AB	R	H	2B	3B	HR	RBI	BB	SO	SB	OBP	SLG
2023	20	Greenville (SAL)	A+	.290	35	145	23	42	11	1	7	34	17	37	5	.366	.524
2023	20	Portland (EL)	AA	.189	43	169	20	32	8	1	6	20	15	49	4	.254	.355
Minor League Totals				.261	195	755	129	197	53	5	29	124	115	220	33	.359	.460

2 ROMAN ANTHONY, OF

HIT: 50. **POW:** 60. **RUN:** 50. **FLD:** 55. **ARM:** 55. **BA Grade:** 60 **Risk:** High.

Born: May 13, 2004. **B-T:** L-R. **HT:** 6-3. **WT:** 200.
Drafted: HS—Parkland, FL, 2022 (2nd round supplemental). **Signed by:** Willie Romay.
TRACK RECORD: While Anthony's draft stock took a hit due to swing-and-miss issues on the showcase circuit, he rebounded with a fantastic senior season at Stoneman Douglas High. The Red Sox drafted him 79th overall in 2022 and signed him for $2.5 million, roughly triple slot value. Initially at Low-A Salem in 2023, Anthony earned raves for his swing decisions and exit velocities despite pedestrian surface stats. The Red Sox trusted the under-the-hood numbers and promoted him to High-A Greenville in June. There, his production caught up to his metrics in a startling power binge. Despite a late-summer strikeout surge, he moved to Double-A Portland to end the year.
SCOUTING REPORT: Anthony has the size, strength and body of a power hitter, and his disciplined approach amplifies the likelihood of him emerging as one. He's comfortable letting the ball travel deep, swinging at strikes and driving pitches to all fields. Though a level swing early in the year yielded a high groundball rate and little power in Salem, he proved increasingly adept at getting the ball in the air with impressive juice—110 mph max exit velocity—as the year progressed. Anthony whiffed a lot on breaking balls in the zone and will need to improve in that area to emerge as an average hitter. In 2023, he outplayed defensive expectations to earn a continued shot to stick in center field, though many evaluators see his future in right field, where he shows above-average potential. Anthony showed surprising speed, with times of 4.1 and 4.2 seconds from home to first base, but he likely will slow as he continues to grow.
THE FUTURE: Anthony looks like a potential middle-of-the-order force. He'll open 2024 back in Double-A, with a 2025 or even late-2024 big league arrival possible.

Year	Age	Club (League)	Level	AVG	G	AB	R	H	2B	3B	HR	RBI	BB	SO	SB	OBP	SLG
2023	19	Salem (CAR)	A	.228	42	158	27	36	9	1	1	18	38	38	11	.376	.316
2023	19	Greenville (SAL)	A+	.294	54	204	41	60	14	3	12	38	40	75	2	.412	.569
2023	19	Portland (EL)	AA	.343	10	35	10	12	4	0	1	8	8	6	3	.477	.543
Minor League Totals				.277	126	469	85	130	31	4	14	76	95	127	17	.399	.450

3 KYLE TEEL, C

HIT: 55. **POW:** 45. **RUN:** 50. **FLD:** 55. **ARM:** 55. **BA Grade:** 55. **Risk:** High.

Born: February 15, 2002. **B-T:** L-R. **HT:** 6-1. **WT:** 190.
Drafted: Virginia, 2023 (1st round). **Signed by:** Wallace Rios.
TRACK RECORD: Teel, whose father Garett was a minor league catcher, was an impressive high school prospect with rare athleticism for a catcher—he once played every defensive position in an East Coast Pro game—but withdrew from the 2020 draft to enroll at Virginia, where he was an everyday player for three years and spent two summers with USA Baseball's Collegiate National Team. His already-impressive all-fields offensive approach reached another level of consistency and impact as a junior, as the first-team All-American hit .407/.475/.655 with 13 homers. The Red Sox took him at No. 14 overall and signed him for $4 million, slightly below slot. He raced to Double-A in his pro debut.
SCOUTING REPORT: While Teel always displayed solid bat-to-ball skills and ability to hit for average, he added looseness to his lefthanded swing as a junior and became more comfortable taking chances in hitters' counts, tapping into power potential that had previously been theoretical. Still, his default setting is a flat bat path used to spray liners and gappers from line to line, suggesting at least an above-average hit tool with solid on-base ability. He currently projects to post mid-teens home run totals with loads of doubles, though there's room for strength gains that could yield more power, especially if he accepts an additional measure of swing-and-miss. That profile is already special for a catcher who shows excellent defensive traits—strong hands, twitch and fluidity—as well as an above-average arm and pop times in the range of 1.9 seconds on throws to second base. He runs well, period—not just for a catcher.
THE FUTURE: Teel's late-season promotion to Double-A was a likely preview of his opening spot in 2024. The Red Sox won't rush him out of Portland, given that he has just started to learn to call his own games, but Teel certainly has a chance to emerge as a frontline big league catcher by 2025.

Year	Age	Club (League)	Level	AVG	G	AB	R	H	2B	3B	HR	RBI	BB	SO	SB	OBP	SLG
2023	21	FCL Red Sox	Rk	.429	3	7	2	3	0	0	1	2	2	0	0	.556	.857
2023	21	Greenville (SAL)	A+	.377	14	53	10	20	4	0	0	9	11	11	1	.485	.453
2023	21	Portland (EL)	AA	.323	9	31	3	10	2	0	1	11	8	11	2	.462	.484
Minor League Totals				.363	26	91	15	33	6	0	2	22	21	22	3	.482	.495

4 CEDDANNE RAFAELA, OF/SS

HIT: 45. **POW:** 40. **RUN:** 60. **FLD:** 70. **ARM:** 60. **BA Grade:** 50. **Risk:** Medium.

Born: September 18, 2000. **B-T:** R-R. **HT:** 5-9. **WT:** 165.
Signed: Curacao, 2017. **Signed by:** Dennis Neuman/Rollie Pino/Todd Claus.
TRACK RECORD: Rafaela's diminutive stature made him easy to overlook as an amateur in Curacao, but Red Sox evaluators were captivated by his speed, defense, energy and bat-to-ball skills. He looked like a potential utility infielder until 2021, when he thrived with a move to center field and a swing adjustment. He eliminated a hitch with a higher hand load position which allowed him to start barreling balls in the air. Tasked with becoming a more disciplined hitter in 2023, the hyper-aggressive Rafaela lapsed at times into passivity at Double-A Portland but found a balance in mid May that fueled a long run at Triple-A Worcester and culminated in his Aug. 28 MLB debut.
SCOUTING REPORT: Rafaela's size and pre-swing setup—hands held high above his head, then lowered to shoulder height before whipping the barrel through the zone—invariably draws comparisons with Mookie Betts, but his offensive approach is the polar opposite of the superstar. Though he has the bat life to drive the ball with average raw power, Rafaela is a free-swinger who has posted sky-high chase rates in the minors, and big league pitchers readily exploited the trait in 2024. Red Sox officials believe he made progress focusing on areas where he could do damage over the 2023 season, when he posted his second straight 20-20 season. Rafaela's excellent first step in center field, plus speed, fearlessness and creativity offer elite defensive potential, and he also can play a solid shortstop.
THE FUTURE: As a potential Gold Glove center fielder, Rafaela must prove his offensive approach will offer enough consistency to play every day. He likely will open 2024 at Worcester to further hone his plate discipline, but he seems likely to spend considerable time in the big leagues.

Year	Age	Club (League)	Level	AVG	G	AB	R	H	2B	3B	HR	RBI	BB	SO	SB	OBP	SLG
2023	22	Portland (EL)	AA	.294	60	245	40	72	18	0	6	37	14	55	30	.332	.441
2023	22	Worcester (IL)	AAA	.312	48	199	40	62	13	3	14	42	12	48	6	.370	.618
2023	22	Boston (AL)	MLB	.241	28	83	11	20	6	0	2	5	4	28	3	.281	.386
Minor League Totals				.280	424	1686	296	472	93	28	60	264	105	365	115	.331	.475
Major League Totals				.241	28	83	11	20	6	0	2	5	4	28	3	.281	.386

5 MIGUEL BLEIS, OF

HIT: 40. **POW:** 60. **RUN:** 60. **FLD:** 60. **ARM:** 60. **BA Grade:** 55. **Risk:** Extreme.

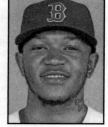

Born: March 1, 2004. **B-T:** R-R. **HT:** 6-2. **WT:** 180.
Signed: Dominican Republic, 2021. **Signed by:** Eddie Romero/Manny Nanita.
TRACK RECORD: Based on Bleis' electrifying bat speed and five-tool potential, the Red Sox signed him for $1.5 million in 2021—their biggest bonus for a Dominican amateur since Rafael Devers in 2013. Bleis' dynamic potential remained evident in two years of Rookie complex ball in 2021 and 2022, as well as at the start of the 2023 campaign in Low-A Salem. However, a subluxation in his left shoulder resulted in season-ending surgery in June. Bleis had resumed baseball activities—including swinging—by the fall and was expected to be healthy for spring training.
SCOUTING REPORT: Bleis has tools that give him franchise-changing upside, but with performance and injury risks that offer little floor. His bat speed creates the ability to launch fastballs of any velocity. He's one of the fastest runners in the Red Sox system, and his combination of speed and jumps creates a high defensive ceiling. However, he has the floor-crumbling traits of a typical teenager. He's a free-swinger who has a lot of work to do to improve against breaking balls. Moreover, while the Red Sox were optimistic about Bleis' recovery from a surgery that was similar to that of Fernando Tatis Jr., any shoulder surgery carries some risk of altering a player's swing and approach. Defensively, Bleis is a glider in center field who has been particularly adept at coming in on fly balls, while still working on routes on balls over his head. Still, his speed creates significant upside both in the outfield—particularly given his excellent arm strength—and on the bases.
THE FUTURE: Bleis carries a significant amount of bust risk in his profile but also a ceiling unrivaled in the system. After his lost 2023 campaign, assuming a return to health, he should open 2024 back in Salem but with a chance to reach High-A Greenville by the end of the year.

Year	Age	Club (League)	Level	AVG	G	AB	R	H	2B	3B	HR	RBI	BB	SO	SB	OBP	SLG
2023	19	Salem (CAR)	A	.230	31	126	18	29	3	3	1	16	10	38	11	.282	.325
Minor League Totals				.264	107	398	63	105	23	8	10	60	32	108	36	.324	.437

6 WILYER ABREU, OF

HIT: 50. **POW:** 50. **RUN:** 40. **FLD:** 50. **ARM:** 70. **BA Grade:** 45. **Risk:** Medium.

Born: June 24, 1999. **B-T:** L-L. **HT:** 6-0. **WT:** 217. **Signed:** Venezuela, 2017.
Signed by: Oz Ocampo/Roman Ocumarez/Tom Shafer (Astros).
TRACK RECORD: The Red Sox nearly signed Abreu in 2017, but when they were forbidden from signing players for two years as a penalty for circumventing international package signing rules, the Astros grabbed him for $300,000. After an unremarkable pro start, Abreu overhauled his approach during the 2020 shutdown, combining selectivity and damage on pitches in the zone. Boston acquired him for Christian Vazquez at the 2022 deadline. Abreu was limited at times in 2023 by hamstring injuries, but when healthy he torched the ball at Triple-A Worcester. The most notable example came during an August home run binge in which he hit nine in 17 games. His mature approach translated to an impressive big league debut to end 2023.
SCOUTING REPORT: Abreu is a fire hydrant, featuring a compact swing with barrel life on middle-in pitches, particularly those in the upper half of the zone. He struggled with his mechanics—particularly the balance in his weight transfer—early in 2023. Once he got healthy and locked in his timing, Abreu made consistently hard contact at Triple-A and in MLB, including a 49% hard-hit rate that ranked second among Red Sox big leaguers who batted least 50 times. He tended to whiff on pitches in the zone but rarely chased. In deference to a minor league platoon split, he faced few big league lefties. Abreu spent most of his big league time in center field and left field but may be best suited for right—despite below-average speed—thanks to good jumps and high-end arm strength.
THE FUTURE: Abreu should compete for a big league roster spot out of the gate in 2024. If he can remain healthy, he has a solid baseline as at least the strong side of a platoon and possibly an everyday player.

Year	Age	Club (League)	Level	AVG	G	AB	R	H	2B	3B	HR	RBI	BB	SO	SB	OBP	SLG
2023	24	Worcester (IL)	AAA	.274	86	299	67	82	11	1	22	65	59	74	8	.391	.538
2023	24	Boston (AL)	MLB	.316	28	76	10	24	6	0	2	14	9	23	3	.388	.474
Minor League Totals				.259	431	1493	289	386	82	5	59	233	262	432	70	.372	.439
Major League Totals				.316	28	76	10	24	6	0	2	14	9	23	3	.388	.474

7 WIKELMAN GONZALEZ, RHP

FB: 60. **CB:** 60. **CHG:** 50. **CUT:** 45. **CTL:** 40. **BA Grade:** 50 **Risk:** High.

Born: March 25, 2002. **B-T:** R-R. **HT:** 6-0. **WT:** 195.
Signed: Venezuela, 2018. **Signed by:** Wilder Lobo/Rollie Pino.
TRACK RECORD: The Red Sox signed Gonzalez for $250,000 in 2018 on the basis of his ability to shape three big league pitches anchored by a projectable low-90s fastball. His velocity took a jump during the 2020 shutdown, and he overwhelmed hitters in the Florida Complex League in 2021. After an up-and-down 2022, Gonzalez had an alarming start to 2023 at High-A Greenville, posting a 30% walk rate through four starts. In a heart-to-heart with coaches, he acknowledged that concern about his career had left him unable to eat and sleep properly. The Red Sox had him refocus his goals from game performance to his between-starts routines. From there, Gonzalez took off, with a 2.98 ERA and 13% walk rate in his final 21 starts at High-A and Double-A Portland. On the year, his 35.2% strikeout rate led all minor leaguers with at least 100 innings.
SCOUTING REPORT: Gonzalez possesses tremendous mobility in his hips to get far downhill on the mound and jump on hitters. He also features a low release point, yet works at the top of the zone. That creates the sort of upshoot angle of pitchers like Cristian Javier or Joe Ryan on a bat-missing, mid-90s four-seam fastball. He complements that with a potential plus curveball that has bat-missing spin, a changeup that is at least average and a cutter he added in 2023 for an in-zone weapon against lefties. Gonzalez can miss bats or limit hard contact in the zone, but it remains uncertain if he can work in the zone enough to start. Even with considerable progress in 2023, he still has well below-average control.
THE FUTURE: If diligent offseason and between-starts work allows Gonzalez to improve his control to at least average, he could develop into a No. 4 starter. If not, he's a bat-missing reliever. Gonzalez likely will open 2024 back in Double-A, with a chance to reach Boston as a member of the 40-man roster.

Year	Age	Club (League)	Level	W	L	ERA	G	GS	IP	H	HR	BB	SO	BB%	SO%	WHIP	AVG
2023	21	Greenville (SAL)	A+	6	3	5.14	15	15	63	49	5	42	105	15.1	37.6	1.44	.210
2023	21	Portland (EL)	AA	3	1	2.42	10	10	48	27	2	28	63	14.1	31.8	1.14	.162
Minor League Totals				17	12	3.77	76	75	309	228	14	164	399	12.5	30.4	1.27	.205

8 NICK YORKE, 2B

HIT: 55. **POW:** 45. **RUN:** 40. **FLD:** 50. **ARM:** 45. **BA Grade:** 50. **Risk:** High.

Born: April 2, 2002. **B-T:** R-R. **HT:** 6-0. **WT:** 210.
Drafted: HS—San Jose, CA, 2020 (1st round). **Signed by:** Josh Labandeira.

TRACK RECORD: The Red Sox stunned the industry when they selected Yorke with the 17th overall pick in the five-round 2020 draft and signed him for a below-slot $2.7 million. In 2021, he made the decision look brilliant with a .325/.412/.516 line at two Class A levels. Instead, he spent all of 2022 in High-A Greenville while struggling with injuries—turf toe, back and wrist—and his hitting mechanics. Yorke made adjustments to restore rhythm and timing to his swing, then had a streaky but ultimately solid year in Double-A Portland as a 21-year-old in 2023.

SCOUTING REPORT: After his timing struggles of 2022, Yorke made a striking adjustment, elevating his hands above his head as if wielding a battle ax before dropping them to shoulder height as the pitcher enters his delivery. Though unorthodox, the adjustment helped Yorke to a great start with improved plate discipline while producing hard liners from right-center field to left for two months. After midyear struggles in which he veered from passivity to hyper-aggressiveness, Yorke experimented late in the year with a more conventional pre-pitch setup—an adjustment some evaluators believe could limit his swing-and-miss and aid his development into a more consistent hitter who produces hard liners from gap to gap. Yorke's range at second base is limited by a lack of pure foot speed and arm strength that grades as slightly below-average, but he's a steady defender with good hands and an accurate arm. He turns balls in play into outs to the edge of his coverage area. He's a fringy but smart baserunner.

THE FUTURE: It's not out of the question Yorke that could open 2024 back at Double-A based on available playing time, but regardless of whether he's there or Triple-A, he could emerge as a potential major league depth option by midyear, and a bottom-of-the-order regular by 2025.

Year	Age	Club (League)	Level	AVG	G	AB	R	H	2B	3B	HR	RBI	BB	SO	SB	OBP	SLG
2023	21	Portland (EL)	AA	.268	110	444	74	119	25	5	13	61	51	122	18	.350	.435
Minor League Totals				.276	287	1159	198	320	55	11	38	168	136	285	39	.357	.441

9 LUIS PERALES, RHP

FB: 70. **SL:** 50. **CHG:** 40. **CTL:** 45. **BA Grade:** 50. **Risk:** Very High.

Born: April 14, 2003. **B-T:** R-R. **HT:** 6-1. **WT:** 160.
Signed: Venezuela, 2019. **Signed by:** Lenin Rodriguez/Ernesto Gomez/Rollie Pino.

TRACK RECORD: Perales showed the arm speed to suggest plenty of fastball projection as a $75,000 signee in 2019. He quickly generated buzz as his velocity ticked into the mid 90s shortly after he turned pro. Limited by the 2020 shutdown and injuries to two professional innings through 2021, Perales dominated in 2022 chiefly with an electrifying fastball in three-inning stints. He responded well to an increased workload in 2023, showing elite stuff—albeit with mixed results—and posting a 29% strikeout rate across two levels of Class A.

SCOUTING REPORT: Though his slight frame creates concerns about injury risk, Perales is a fast mover who generates plenty of power and whip with his arm. His fastball averages 95 mph and tops out at 99 with a ridiculous 21 inches of vertical ride and 6.7 feet of extension—elite traits that will miss bats. He throws both a high-80s slider that currently grades as average, given how it tunnels off his fastball, as well as a slower one in the low 80s that plays as a hard curveball. Perales also employs a changeup but may try to redirect his offspeed offering to a splitter. He struggled with both his walk rate (13%) and hard contact (2.0 home runs per nine innings) once promoted to the hitter-friendly environment of High-A Greenville. That left questions about whether he will have the command, control or durability to stick as a starter, but his stuff is that of an impact big leaguer regardless of role.

THE FUTURE: Despite never having pitched above High-A, Perales' fastball was good enough to force his way onto the 40-man roster in November. Though he'll most likely open 2024 at High-A Greenville, he'll get a chance to compete for a spot in Double-A. Perales will be given plenty of runway to develop as a starter, and has a likely big league ETA of 2025.

Year	Age	Club (League)	Level	W	L	ERA	G	GS	IP	H	HR	BB	SO	BB%	SO%	WHIP	AVG
2023	20	Salem (CAR)	A	4	4	3.21	13	13	53	38	2	28	71	12.4	31.4	1.24	.197
2023	20	Greenville (SAL)	A+	0	3	4.95	8	8	36	39	8	22	44	13.2	26.3	1.68	.275
Minor League Totals				4	9	3.33	35	33	127	98	11	71	168	13.0	30.7	1.33	.211

10 YOEILIN CESPEDES, SS

HIT: 55. **POW:** 55. **RUN:** 45. **FLD:** 45. **ARM:** 50. **BA Grade:** 55. **Risk:** Extreme.

Born: September 8, 2005. **B-T:** R-R. **HT:** 5-10. **WT:** 180.
Signed: Dominican Republic, 2023. **Signed by:** Eddie Romero/Manny Nanita.
TRACK RECORD: Cespedes was the most prominent Red Sox international addition in their 2023 signing class. Boston signed him for $1.4 million based on his compact swing that served as the basis both for atypical contact skills nd high exit velocities among the signing class. In his pro debut in the Dominican Summer League in 2023, Cespedes added to the high regard for his offensive potential, hitting .346/.392/.560 with six home runs and a modest 11% strikeout rate while showing defensive improvement at shortstop. He ranked sixth among qualifiers with a .346 average in the 50-team DSL.
SCOUTING REPORT: Cespedes holds little back in a violent swing that generates tremendous bat speed and yields impressive exit velocities. As a 17-year-old, he generated a max exit velocity of 107 mph and registered with a 90th percentile EV of 101 mph. Despite the aggressiveness of his hack, Cespedes showed relatively advanced pitch recognition for the level and made impressive swing decisions that accounted for his strengths. These qualities suggest significant offensive potential with average-to-plus abilities as both a hitter and power hitter and daydreams of an eventual contributor in the top half of a lineup. Cespedes spent the year at shortstop but most evaluators believe he'll eventually end up at either second base or third base because of the limits of his range and the likelihood that he'll get bigger.
THE FUTURE: Cespedes will be tested in the U.S. in 2024, likely opening in the Florida Complex League with a chance to spend part of the year in Low-A Salem. While the Red Sox will want to continue his near-term development at shortstop, he'll likely start to get greater exposure to other infield spots to ensure playing time.

Year	Age	Club (League)	Level	AVG	G	AB	R	H	2B	3B	HR	RBI	BB	SO	SB	OBP	SLG
2023	17	DSL Red Sox Blue	Rk	.346	46	191	37	66	15	4	6	38	14	24	1	.392	.560
Minor League Totals				.346	46	191	37	66	15	4	6	38	14	24	1	.392	.560

11 RICHARD FITTS, RHP

FB: 55. **SL:** 60. **CHG:** 45. **CUT:** 45. **CTL:** 55. **BA Grade:** 50. **Risk:** High.

Born: December 17, 1999. **B-T:** R-R. **HT:** 6-3. **WT:** 215. **Drafted:** Auburn, 2021 (6th round).
Signed by: Chuck Bartlett/Mike Wagner (Yankees).
TRACK RECORD: Fitts was taken out of Auburn in the sixth round of the 2021 draft by the Yankees when his stock dropped after a late-season injury affected his stuff. He was hit hard in his pro debut at Low-A before dominating at High-A for five starts. The righthander spent his entire 2023 season at Double-A Somerset, where his 163 strikeouts were third in the system and 10th in the minor leagues. The Red Sox acquired him from the Yankees as the centerpiece of the Alex Verdugo trade in December 2023.
SCOUTING REPORT: Fitts works primarily with two pitches: a four-seam fastball with ride that sits around 94 mph with which he attacks the zone and a sweeper around 84 mph. He threw the two pitches a combined 85% of the time in 2023. The Yankees tweaked the slider early in the season, and moved it away from a bullet shape. He also mixed in a changeup and cutter, each in the high 80s, but the Yankees wanted Fitts to focus most of his energy on finding a consistent slider shape. His changeup was unimpressive and will require development if he's to emerge as a starter.
THE FUTURE: If Fitts can find a reliable third pitch, he might fit toward the back of a rotation. If not, his fastball/slider combination could make him a useful reliever. He'll likely open 2024 in the Triple-A Worcester rotation.

Year	Age	Club (League)	Level	W	L	ERA	G	GS	IP	H	HR	BB	SO	BB%	SO%	WHIP	AVG
2023	23	Somerset (EL)	AA	11	5	3.48	27	27	153	131	22	43	163	6.8	25.9	1.14	.227
Minor League Totals				18	13	3.58	49	49	265	221	36	63	294	5.9	27.4	1.08	.222

12 NAZZAN ZANETELLO, SS/OF

HIT: 45. **POW:** 55. **RUN:** 55. **FLD:** 55. **ARM:** 55. **BA Grade:** 50. **Risk:** Extreme.

Born: May 25, 2005. **B-T:** R-R. **HT:** 6-2. **WT:** 180. **Drafted:** HS—St. Louis, 2023 (2nd round). **Signed by:** Alonzo Wright.
TRACK RECORD: Zanetello zoomed up 2023 draft boards as a high school senior thanks both to an excellent performance for Team USA in Mexico during the World Cup qualifiers and by standing out as an elite athlete with five-tool potential at showcase events, including the draft combine. The Red Sox drafted him 50th overall and nearly doubled slot value with a $3 million bonus to keep him away from Arkansas.

SCOUTING REPORT: Zanetello flashes the ability to do just about anything on a baseball field, with explosive athleticism suggesting a special ceiling. He possesses the super-quick hands and lean, athletic build to be a solid hitter with above-average to plus power. The catch is that his swing is still evolving after hitting .158 in his pro debut. His torso fires so quickly that it can get in front of his hands and cause his bat to flit in and out of the zone, an obvious area to tighten. Though raw defensively, Zanetello shows body control and actions that distinguish him from high school shortstops. He's currently a plus runner who may lose some speed as he fills out.

THE FUTURE: Zanetello should spend the bulk of 2024 in Low-A Salem. He may experience a significant adjustment to the advanced pitching of pro ball, but the Red Sox believe his combination of tools, athleticism and fearlessness in the face of failure could eventually yield a high-impact, middle-of-the-field player.

Year	Age	Club (League)	Level	AVG	G	AB	R	H	2B	3B	HR	RBI	BB	SO	SB	OBP	SLG
2023	18	FCL Red Sox	Rk	.139	12	36	6	5	3	0	0	1	9	15	5	.311	.222
2023	18	Salem (CAR)	A	.500	1	2	0	1	0	0	0	1	0	0	0	.500	.500
Minor League Totals				.158	13	38	6	6	3	0	0	2	9	15	5	.319	.237

13 CHASE MEIDROTH, 2B/3B

HIT: 50. POW: 45. RUN: 45. FLD: 50. ARM: 45. BA Grade: 45. Risk: High.

Born: July 23, 2001. **B-T:** R-R. **HT:** 5-10. **WT:** 170. **Drafted:** San Diego, 2022 (4th round). **Signed by:** J.J. Altobelli.
TRACK RECORD: Meidroth was limited to 19 games in his first two college seasons at San Diego as a result of the pandemic-compressed 2020 campaign and a shoulder injury in 2021. When he got on the field in 2022, his bat-to-ball skills, elite strike-zone judgment and feel for the game vaulted him from a potential Day 3 draftee to the Red Sox in the fourth round, where he signed a below-slot bonus for $272,500. He excelled at the start of 2023 in High-A Greenville, which resulted in a quick promotion to Double-A, where he appeared comfortable against the quality of competition.
SCOUTING REPORT: Though Meidroth's squat frame makes him easy to overlook, he tends to win over evaluators with his plate discipline, direct swing with a high-contact, all-fields approach and average defensive instincts at multiple spots. Power will never be his hallmark, but the Red Sox believe he has a chance to increase his bat speed to help more of his liners find the gaps with the potential for double-digit homer totals. Defensively, he's a sure-handed fielder with quick hands who shows adequate range and arm strength at both second and third base, suggesting a floor as a righthanded utility infielder with a chance to exceed that profile.
THE FUTURE: Meidroth could compete for a Triple-A spot out of spring training, and his well-rounded game could make him a big league infield depth option at some point in 2024. He could emerge as a bottom-of-the-order regular if he gains strength and bat speed.

Year	Age	Club (League)	Level	AVG	G	AB	R	H	2B	3B	HR	RBI	BB	SO	SB	OBP	SLG
2023	21	Greenville (SAL)	A+	.338	20	74	19	25	3	0	2	14	21	20	4	.495	.459
2023	21	Portland (EL)	AA	.255	91	325	59	83	16	1	7	43	59	78	9	.386	.375
Minor League Totals				.278	133	475	97	132	24	1	13	72	94	109	17	.413	.415

14 JOHANFRAN GARCIA, C

HIT: 40. POW: 55. RUN: 40. FLD: 50. ARM: 55. BA Grade: 50. Risk: Extreme.

Born: December 8, 2004. **B-T:** R-R. **HT:** 5-10. **WT:** 196. **Signed:** Venezuela, 2022. **Signed by:** Rollie Pino/Eddie Romero.
TRACK RECORD: The Red Sox have a long history with Garcia, whose older brother is outfielder Jhostynxon Garcia, who signed with the club in 2019. Johanfran stood out during the scouting process for his sound swing decisions, ability to hit the ball hard the other way and impressive exit velocities. He was a force in the Florida Complex League in 2023. His .904 OPS ranked fifth among 18-year-olds and he forced his way to Low-A Salem in August.
SCOUTING REPORT: Garcia has the strength and bat speed to drive the ball—particularly pitches down in the zone—with ease from his balanced, upright stance. He leaves little on the table when his bat syncs up with a powerful torso rotation. Garcia has all-fields power ability, but most of his righthanded power manifests to his pull side. His swing is long, which creates holes in the zone that suggest a below-average hit tool, but he limits his chases and shows plenty of potential impact when he makes contact. Garcia already has a powerful build and will have to work to avoid getting too big for catcher, but he moves well and shows average technical skills, including strike-stealing on the edges of the zone. He showed sub-2.0 -second pop times on throws to second base with solid accuracy, while he threw out 32% of basestealers in 2023. He also showed promise at first base as an amateur.
THE FUTURE: Garcia should open 2024 in Low-A Salem and has the potential to be an everyday catcher on the strength of his solid defense and above-average power.

Year	Age	Club (League)	Level	AVG	G	AB	R	H	2B	3B	HR	RBI	BB	SO	SB	OBP	SLG
2023	18	FCL Red Sox	Rk	.302	42	149	21	45	10	2	5	32	19	37	3	.408	.497
2023	18	Salem (CAR)	A	.203	15	59	8	12	3	0	1	5	5	24	3	.279	.305
Minor League Totals				.272	97	346	55	94	20	3	6	60	45	86	6	.370	.399

15 NATHAN HICKEY, C

HIT: 50. **POW:** 55. **RUN:** 40. **FLD:** 40. **ARM:** 50. **BA Grade:** 45. **Risk:** High.

Born: November 23, 1999. **B-T:** L-R. **HT:** 6-0. **WT:** 210. **Drafted:** Florida, 2021 (5th round). **Signed by:** Dante Ricciardi.

TRACK RECORD: Hickey was drafted out of Florida in the fifth round in 2021 and signed an over-slot bonus of $1 million as a bat-first catcher who would need to develop defensively in order to stay behind the plate. To date, that description has held true. The lefthanded-hitting Hickey crushed righthanders in 2023, hitting .277/.372/.530 with 18 homers against them at High-A Greenville and Double-A Portland. The downside is that he threw out 10 of 129 attempted basestealers, or just 7%.

SCOUTING REPORT: Hickey wields a sledgehammer, generating loud contact to his pull side by torquing powerfully and holding back little. While he swings with ill intent and will whiff—27% strikeout rate— he's disciplined enough with a 13% walk rate to force pitchers to work in the zone. His offensive profile is special for a catcher. But while Hickey continues to make gradual progress defensively, he remains stiff in his receiving and blocking, and his inability to control the running game raises questions about whether he will stay behind the plate. Hickey has taken grounders at first base but has played no position but catcher in pro ball.

THE FUTURE: After he spent almost all of 2023 in Double-A, Hickey may open 2024 back in Double-A to work on his defensive development. That said, his bat is nearly ready for the big leagues and will likely lead to both time in Triple-A and exposure to other positions in 2024.

Year	Age	Club (League)	Level	AVG	G	AB	R	H	2B	3B	HR	RBI	BB	SO	SB	OBP	SLG
2023	23	Greenville (SAL)	A+	.294	18	68	13	20	6	1	4	9	12	20	0	.402	.588
2023	23	Portland (EL)	AA	.258	80	291	49	75	18	0	15	56	40	91	3	.352	.474
Minor League Totals				.262	184	642	117	168	44	1	35	129	124	199	3	.386	.497

16 MIKEY ROMERO, 2B/SS

HIT: 50. **POW:** 40. **RUN:** 45. **FLD:** 50. **ARM:** 50. **BA Grade:** 50. **Risk:** Extreme.

Born: January 12, 2004. **B-T:** L-R. **HT:** 6-1. **WT:** 180. **Drafted:** HS—Orange, CA, 2022 (1st round). **Signed by:** J.J. Altobelli.

TRACK RECORD: Romero had a strong, steady amateur career as an advanced hitter and solid middle infielder both at Orange Lutheran High in Southern California and with USA Baseball's 12U and 15U national teams. Projected as a likely second-round pick in 2022, the Red Sox—fearful they wouldn't have another shot at him—snagged him in the first round at No. 34 overall and signed him to a below-slot $2.3 million bonus. Romero's first full pro season in 2023 was derailed by lower-back issues that kept him out of games until late June and ended his season in August.

SCOUTING REPORT: Romero's clean, direct swing path and adaptable barrel produced excellent contact rates and consistent gap-to-gap line drives both in high school and on the showcase circuit. The Red Sox were drawn to what they viewed as a potentially standout hit tool. As Romero's senior year progressed, the Red Sox saw an increased ability to drive the ball that suggested average power potential for a middle infielder. But in 2023 he showed below-average bat speed that likely will need to improve with strength gains for him to be an everyday player. Romero also showed solid but unspectacular range and quick, sure hands, suggesting average or better defensive potential at second base with a chance to competently back up shortstop. He's a slightly below-average runner.

THE FUTURE: If Romero gets healthy and starts making physical gains, he could reclaim his promise as one of the best pure hitters in the system, with a chance to be a solid two-way second baseman. He should open the year in High-A Greenville.

Year	Age	Club (League)	Level	AVG	G	AB	R	H	2B	3B	HR	RBI	BB	SO	SB	OBP	SLG
2023	19	FCL Red Sox	Rk	.250	8	24	4	6	1	0	0	4	5	4	0	.379	.292
2023	19	Salem (CAR)	A	.217	23	92	11	20	4	2	0	9	9	17	2	.288	.304
2023	19	Greenville (SAL)	A+	.100	3	10	0	1	0	0	0	0	0	4	0	.100	.100
Minor League Totals				.249	53	205	26	51	12	5	1	30	22	40	4	.322	.371

17 ALLAN CASTRO, OF

HIT: 50. **POW:** 40. **RUN:** 50. **FLD:** 50. **ARM:** 55. **BA Grade:** 45. **Risk:** High.

Born: May 24, 2003. **B-T:** B-R. **HT:** 6-0. **WT:** 170. **Signed:** Dominican Republic, 2019.
Signed by: Manny Nanita/Eddie Romero.

TRACK RECORD: The Red Sox signed Castro as a middle infielder in 2018, impressed with his athleticism and offensive potential in tryouts, with quick bat speed and the ability to manipulate the barrel from both sides of the plate. He proved a bit stiff to stay on the dirt in pro ball but quickly took to the outfield, where he could move more freely. After a solid 2022 season, Castro turned heads in spring training in 2023 with strength gains and increasingly loud contact. The strong first impression carried through a season when he hit .261/.368/.405 with a 14% walk rate and 18% strikeout rate at Low-A Salem and High-A Greenville.

SCOUTING REPORT: Though a natural righthanded hitter, Castro has made enough strides as a lefthanded hitter—with simple, clean stances—to project as a solid line-drive hitter against righthanders in the big leagues. He's currently more of a gap-to-gap hitter with solid plate discipline than a power hitter, though he does hit the ball hard enough to create more potential impact. That's a step that is necessary for him to emerge as an everyday player. Castro moves well enough in the outfield to handle both corners while also offering an option in center, and he possesses the arm to handle any outfield spot.

THE FUTURE: Castro likely will open 2024 in High-A, with a strong likelihood of moving to Double-A during the season. His solid, well-rounded skill set gives him a chance to be at least a fourth outfielder with a chance to improve that projection if he develops more power.

Year	Age	Club (League)	Level	AVG	G	AB	R	H	2B	3B	HR	RBI	BB	SO	SB	OBP	SLG
2023	20	Salem (CAR)	A	.247	69	251	39	62	20	2	3	29	51	54	15	.376	.378
2023	20	Greenville (SAL)	A+	.283	43	166	23	47	11	2	4	17	17	36	4	.355	.446
Minor League Totals				.254	207	735	112	187	44	17	13	86	108	176	30	.356	.414

18 YORDANNY MONEGRO, RHP

FB: 50. **CB:** 50. **CUT:** 50. **SPLT:** 35. **CTL:** 50. **BA Grade:** 45. **Risk:** High.

Born: October 14, 2002. **B-T:** R-R. **HT:** 6-4. **WT:** 180. **Signed:** Dominican Republic, 2020.
Signed by: Juan Carlos Calderon/Todd Claus.

TRACK RECORD: Monegro had the lanky build of a basketball player as an amateur when the Red Sox signed him for $35,000 shortly before the 2020 coronavirus shutdown. In pro ball, he has gained strength, power and shown the ability to develop pitches to attack different parts of the zone. After a poor Florida Complex League season in 2022, when he posted a 7.36 ERA and 12% walk rate, he made a major jump in stuff and command in 2023 and sprinted from the FCL to High-A Greenville.

SCOUTING REPORT: In 2023, Monegro attacked the strike zone with three pitches that project as average or better. His four-seamer has solid velocity, averaging just under 95 mph, and plays well at the top of the zone. His 12-to-6 curveball got plenty of swings-and-misses against Class A hitters, and his 88-90 mph cutter improved his ability to compete in the strike zone and keep hitters off his fastball. Monegro also has a two-seamer and splitter, though the latter is a work in progress. In order to stick as a starter, he'll likely need to either sharpen one of his pitches into a plus offering or develop the splitter into a solid offering.

THE FUTURE: After racing across three levels in 2023, Monegro should open 2024 in High-A Greenville and could reach the upper levels by the end of the year. He has a chance to be a back-of-the-rotation starter or middle-innings reliever.

Year	Age	Club (League)	Level	W	L	ERA	G	GS	IP	H	HR	BB	SO	BB%	SO%	WHIP	AVG
2023	20	FCL Red Sox	Rk	2	0	1.20	3	3	15	5	0	4	20	7.4	37.0	0.60	.102
2023	20	Salem (CAR)	A	3	2	2.43	9	9	41	33	0	17	60	9.8	34.5	1.23	.217
2023	20	Greenville (SAL)	A+	1	1	1.80	2	1	10	8	1	5	13	12.2	31.7	1.30	.222
Minor League Totals				7	6	3.57	36	32	131	114	8	65	158	11.5	28.1	1.37	.235

19 EDDINSON PAULINO, SS/3B

HIT: 50. **POW:** 40. **RUN:** 40. **FLD:** 50. **ARM:** 50. **BA Grade:** 45. **Risk:** High.

Born: July 2, 2002. **B-T:** L-R. **HT:** 5-9. **WT:** 170. **Signed:** Dominican Republic, 2018.
Signed by: Esau Medina/Eddie Romero.

TRACK RECORD: The Red Sox signed Paulino for $200,000 in 2018 based on his middle-infield defense with solid bat-to-ball skills and projectable strength. In pro ball, he's been a level-to-level mover, spending each season at one stop. Paulino had strong years in the Florida Complex League in 2021 and Low-A Salem in 2022, but he took a step back with High-A Greenville in 2023, when his strikeout rate ticked up from 19% to 23%.

SCOUTING REPORT: Paulino relies on quick hands to do the work in a direct-to-the-ball, lefthanded swing that features little involvement of his lower half. At his best, he lines the ball regularly from left-center field to the line in right. In 2023, Paulino's groundball rate jumped from 39% to 46%, offsetting improvements in his hard-hit rate. Still, despite a lack of physicality, he makes above-average swing decisions and produces enough hard contact to suggest an average hit tool with a lot of doubles. There's a chance for additional power with strength gains and greater use of his legs in his swing. That offensive profile would be valuable given Paulino's versatility. He has solid range and an accurate arm at second and third base. He plays below-average defense at shortstop and spent the 2023-24 offseason working to develop his outfield skills. He's an average runner.

THE FUTURE: Paulino could develop into a versatile reserve. An offensive bounceback in the upper levels in 2024 could put him back on a path to either a starting job or at least a regular role against righties.

Year	Age	Club (League)	Level	AVG	G	AB	R	H	2B	3B	HR	RBI	BB	SO	SB	OBP	SLG
2023	20	Greenville (SAL)	A+	.257	115	440	68	113	28	4	12	58	50	113	26	.338	.420
Minor League Totals				.271	300	1124	206	305	81	22	25	147	147	262	60	.362	.449

20 DAVID HAMILTON, 2B/SS/OF

HIT: 45. **POW:** 40. **RUN:** 70. **FLD:** 55. **ARM:** 45. **BA Grade:** 40. **Risk:** Medium.

Born: September 29, 1997. **B-T:** L-R. **HT:** 5-10. **WT:** 175. **Drafted:** Texas, 2019 (8th round).
Signed by: K.J. Hendricks (Brewers).

TRACK RECORD: Though Hamilton blew out his Achilles tendon in a scooter accident after an excellent sophomore year at Texas, the Brewers bet on the return of his athleticism by making him a Day 2 pick and signing him for $400,000 in 2019. After Hamilton had a solid season for the Brewers' High-A and Double-A affiliates in 2021, the Red Sox acquired him in a trade for Hunter Renfroe. In two years with the Red Sox, Hamilton has forged a reputation as one of the fastest players in the minors while improving his offense and defense. An excellent start to 2023 faded due to a left thumb injury that eventually required season-ending surgery.

SCOUTING REPORT: Previously a spray hitter with limited power, Hamilton showed improved bat speed after a weighted-bat program in 2023. He boosted his 90th percentile exit velocity to 102 mph—a mark that was suppressed by his thumb injury. While he generally makes contact when swinging at strikes and doesn't chase excessively, he lacks barrel control, alternating stretches where he drives the ball with authority with showers of infield popups. Defensively, Hamilton's explosive first step at both middle infield spots resulted in strong metrics despite an awkward throwing motion and light arm at short. Many evaluators believe he would thrive in center field thanks to elite speed, a trait that makes him a game-changer as a stolen base threat under MLB's new rules.

THE FUTURE: Hamilton's speed and defense ensure a big league role, and his bat now looks capable of making him at least a platoon option and potentially a bottom-of-the-order regular.

Year	Age	Club (League)	Level	AVG	G	AB	R	H	2B	3B	HR	RBI	BB	SO	SB	OBP	SLG
2023	25	Worcester (IL)	AAA	.247	103	393	74	97	16	4	17	54	71	109	57	.363	.438
2023	25	Boston (AL)	MLB	.121	15	33	2	4	2	0	0	0	6	10	2	.256	.182
Minor League Totals				.252	323	1259	221	317	51	24	37	139	177	318	179	.347	.419
Major League Totals				.121	15	33	2	4	2	0	0	0	6	10	2	.256	.182

21 BLAZE JORDAN, 1B/3B

HIT: 45. **POW:** 55. **RUN:** 40. **FLD:** 40. **ARM:** 60. **BA Grade:** 45. **Risk:** High.

Born: December 19, 2002. **B-T:** R-R. **HT:** 6-2. **WT:** 220. **Drafted:** HS—Southaven, MS, 2020 (3rd round).
Signed by: Danny Watkins.

TRACK RECORD: Jordan became a power-hitting sensation by hitting 500-foot homers as an eighth grader. The Red Sox were drawn to his power potential as a 17-year-old draftee and signed him to an over-slot bonus of $1.75 million in 2020. In pro ball, he's shown a hit-over-power profile, hitting .296/.351/.482 with 18 homers as a 20-year-old in High-A and Double-A in 2023. That performance included a .405/.452/.541 line against lefthanders for the righthanded hitter.

SCOUTING REPORT: Jordan's hallmark remains the ability to hit the ball hard. His 90th percentile exit velocity of just over 104 mph in 2023 is excellent for a 20-year-old. Still, most of his damage comes against offspeed pitches and lower-velocity fastballs, with sub-.700 OPS marks against pitches at 94 mph or faster. The best offensive version of Jordan likely involves swing adjustments that will result in more consistent fly balls, albeit with more strikeouts. Defensively, he's seen as a future first baseman or DH who will need to improve his agility and athleticism to contribute in the field. In recognition of that notion, Jordan dropped nearly 20 pounds in the first three months of the offseason.

THE FUTURE: Jordan will have to mash his way to a sustained place in MLB. He'll open 2024 at Double-A.

Year	Age	Club (League)	Level	AVG	G	AB	R	H	2B	3B	HR	RBI	BB	SO	SB	OBP	SLG
2023	20	Greenville (SAL)	A+	.324	73	287	48	93	22	1	12	55	28	47	2	.385	.533
2023	20	Portland (EL)	AA	.254	49	189	19	48	10	0	6	31	12	28	0	.296	.402
Minor League Totals				.296	270	1044	146	309	70	5	36	180	96	190	8	.358	.476

22 ANTONIO ANDERSON, 3B

HIT: 45. **POW:** 55. **RUN:** 45. **FLD:** 50. **ARM:** 55. **BA Grade:** 50. **Risk:** Extreme.

Born: June 28, 2005. **B-T:** B-R. **HT:** 6-3. **WT:** 205. **Drafted:** HS—Atlanta, 2023 (3rd round). **Signed by:** Kirk Fredricksson.

TRACK RECORD: Anderson, a longtime standout on the showcase circuit, was one of the top prep bats in the 2023 draft class thanks to significant power and excellent plate discipline. The Red Sox signed him for an over-slot bonus of $1.5 million as a third-round pick to keep him away from a Georgia Tech commitment. He appeared in 12 games across the Florida Complex League and Low-A Salem, hitting .167 with 15 strikeouts to four walks.

SCOUTING REPORT: Anderson has been switch-hitting since he was 10 years old and has developed balanced swings from both sides with more looseness and power potential batting lefthanded. He stands out in batting practice not only for his power but also for frequent takes that point to purposeful development of plate discipline. As he gets into a professional strengthening program, he could grow into plus power and a three true outcomes profile. While Anderson likely will move around the infield and play both middle infield spots as well as third base in 2024, the prospect of physical growth makes third base a likely destination. Given that he worked in the low 90s as a high school pitcher, he should have the arm for any infield spot.

THE FUTURE: Anderson will compete for a spot on the Low-A Salem roster to open 2024. He profiles as a potential power-hitting, everyday third baseman.

Year	Age	Club (League)	Level	AVG	G	AB	R	H	2B	3B	HR	RBI	BB	SO	SB	OBP	SLG
2023	18	FCL Red Sox	Rk	.133	5	15	0	2	1	0	0	3	3	6	1	.278	.200
2023	18	Salem (CAR)	A	.185	7	27	2	5	1	0	0	1	1	9	0	.214	.222
Minor League Totals				.167	12	42	2	7	2	0	0	4	4	15	1	.239	.214

23 FRANKLIN ARIAS, SS

HIT: 55. **POW:** 45. **RUN:** 50. **FLD:** 50. **ARM:** 55. **BA Grade:** 50. **Risk:** Extreme.

Born: November 19, 2005. **B-T:** R-R. **HT:** 5-11. **WT:** 170. **Signed:** Venezuela, 2023. **Signed by:** Rollie Pino.

TRACK RECORD: The Red Sox relied heavily on their area scouts in Venezuela amid pandemic-driven restrictions on travel early in the scouting process. The team was drawn to Arias' natural defensive actions, bat-to-ball skills and clearly projectable frame given that he weighed 145 pounds at the start of the scouting process. After Arias signed for $525,000 in 2023, he stood out for his advanced defense in the Dominican Summer League while making enough contact to rank 10th in average (.350) and draw more walks than strikeouts.

SCOUTING REPORT: Arias is raw offensively, but there's room to add strength to his frame and add some power to a high-contact, line-drive approach that points to an above-average or better hit tool. Even if Arias' power doesn't develop, his smooth defensive actions with good range in both directions, impressive body control and strong arm give him a chance at having big league value. He's an average runner with a chance to improve as he develops more burst.

THE FUTURE: Though years from the big leagues, Arias stands out for his multi-dimensional potential and chance to emerge as an everyday big league shortstop.

Year	Age	Club (League)	Level	AVG	G	AB	R	H	2B	3B	HR	RBI	BB	SO	SB	OBP	SLG
2023	17	DSL Red Sox Red	Rk	.350	37	137	32	48	9	1	1	15	19	14	3	.440	.453
Minor League Totals				.350	37	137	32	48	9	1	1	15	19	14	3	.440	.453

24 CHRIS MURPHY, LHP

FB: 45. **CB:** 50. **CHG:** 50. **CUT:** 45. **CTL:** 45. **BA Grade:** 40. **Risk:** Medium.

Born: June 5, 1998. **B-T:** L-L. **HT:** 6-1. **WT:** 175. **Drafted:** San Diego, 2019 (6th round). **Signed by:** J.J. Altobelli.

TRACK RECORD: When Murphy was in college, the Red Sox viewed him as a moldable pitcher whose results didn't match the potential of his stuff. He embraced data-driven adjustments to his pitch mix in pro ball and steadily improved as a starter each season. Viewed as potential rotation depth at the start of 2023, Murphy struggled to an 8.35 ERA through nine Triple-A starts. A late-May bullpen move freed him to attack more aggressively and resulted in a quick callup. He logged a 1.91 ERA through his first 28 big league innings before a late-season fade that saw him post a 9.78 ERA in his last 19.1 innings.

SCOUTING REPORT: Murphy attacks all quadrants with a diverse pitch mix. His four-seamer, which averages 94 mph and touches 97, is most effective setting up two solid-average secondary pitches. His two-plane curveball averages 62 inches of drop, while his firm changeup sneaks below the zone to his arm side. As the season progressed, Murphy reshaped his slider into a cutter in hopes of running a pitch onto the hands of righties. Though he has the pitch shapes to start, the Red Sox felt he was better suited to the bullpen due to strike-throwing inconsistencies—something that led him to pitch exclusively out of the stretch.

THE FUTURE: Though he'll be stretched out in spring training, Murphy likely will shuttle between Triple-A and the big leagues as a multi-inning bullpen contributor in 2024.

Year	Age	Club (League)	Level	W	L	ERA	G	GS	IP	H	HR	BB	SO	BB%	SO%	WHIP	AVG
2023	25	Worcester (IL)	AAA	2	3	6.32	15	9	53	63	7	31	61	12.3	24.2	1.78	.293
2023	25	Boston (AL)	MLB	1	2	4.91	20	0	48	50	5	17	49	8.0	23.1	1.41	.263
Minor League Totals				17	20	4.27	76	67	339	301	43	146	372	10.1	25.7	1.32	.236
Major League Totals				1	2	4.91	20	0	48	50	5	17	49	8.0	23.1	1.41	.263

25 HUNTER DOBBINS, RHP

FB: 50. **CB:** 45. **SL:** 55. **SPLT:** 50. **CTL:** 55. **BA Grade:** 45. **Risk:** High.

Born: August 30, 1999. **B-T:** R-R. **HT:** 6-2. **WT:** 185. **Drafted:** Texas Tech, 2021 (8th round). **Signed by:** Chris Reilly.

TRACK RECORD: Dobbins was a promising power arm at Texas Tech but blew out his elbow and required Tommy John surgery prior to his junior year. The Red Sox felt comfortable with their history with him and bet on his athleticism and work ethic to give him a strong chance of recovering. They drafted him in the eighth round in 2021. He had a decent pro debut in Low-A Salem in 2022, then asserted himself as a prospect in 2023. He posted an 8.8-to-1 strikeout-to-walk ratio with High-A Greenville that led the South Atlantic League and earned a quick promotion to Double-A Portland.

SCOUTING REPORT: Dobbins fills the strike zone with four pitches that project to be fringe-average or better. He has above-average command of a fastball that sits at 93-94 mph and tops out at 96. He also has a slider that showed potential to miss bats in the zone, a curveball, a splitter with good action that he's still learning to control, and a sweeper he developed in 2023. His control is above-average with average command.

THE FUTURE: Dobbins has enough tools to become a potential back-end starter if he can develop one pitch—likely his slider—into a plus offering, but he more likely fits as a multi-inning or bulk reliever.

Year	Age	Club (League)	Level	W	L	ERA	G	GS	IP	H	HR	BB	SO	BB%	SO%	WHIP	AVG
2023	23	Greenville (SAL)	A+	4	1	2.63	7	7	41	34	1	5	44	3.1	27.3	0.95	.222
2023	23	Portland (EL)	AA	5	5	4.27	13	12	72	69	8	26	78	8.5	25.4	1.33	.250
Minor League Totals				9	11	4.28	37	36	182	185	15	53	190	6.9	24.7	1.31	.264

26 ANGEL BASTARDO, RHP

FB: 45. **CB:** 45. **SL:** 50. **CHG:** 55. **CTL:** 40. **BA Grade:** 45. **Risk:** High.

Born: June 18, 2002. **B-T:** R-R. **HT:** 6-1. **WT:** 175. **Signed:** Venezuela, 2018. **Signed by:** Lenin Rodriguez/Eddie Romero.

TRACK RECORD: The Red Sox identified Bastardo as a pitcher who received little instruction but had fastball life and the solid changeup shape to suggest back-of-the-rotation potential as he added physicality. The team signed him for $35,000 in 2018 as a bet on his potential. After modest early-career performance, Bastardo impressed with a four-pitch mix and 32% strikeout rate at High-A Greenville in 2023, which was fourth-highest in the South Atlantic League among pitchers with at least 80 innings. He struggled to throw strikes or miss bats upon reaching Double-A at the end of the year.

SCOUTING REPORT: Bastardo generates good arm speed from his lean 6-foot-1 frame. It creates both solid velocity at 92-97 mph and three solid secondary pitches, headlined by an above-average changeup along with a viable slider and curveball. In the South Atlantic League, Bastardo's mix generated both swings-and-misses and solid groundball totals. He still looks like he has room to fill out and add strength that would lead to improved control and command.

THE FUTURE: Bastardo's mix of four pitches could allow him to emerge as a No. 5 starter if he improves his strike-throwing. At the least, he stands a solid chance of emerging as a multi-inning reliever.

Year	Age	Club (League)	Level	W	L	ERA	G	GS	IP	H	HR	BB	SO	BB%	SO%	WHIP	AVG
2023	21	Greenville (SAL)	A+	2	7	4.62	21	21	103	86	11	46	139	10.5	31.8	1.28	.223
2023	21	Portland (EL)	AA	0	1	5.06	3	3	16	12	3	9	10	13.0	14.5	1.31	.207
Minor League Totals				9	16	4.66	68	64	282	264	20	124	304	10.2	25.0	1.38	.246

27 JUSTIN SLATEN, RHP

FB: 60. **SL:** 60. **CUT:** 40. **CB:** 30. **CTL:** 45. **BA Grade:** 40. **Risk:** Medium.

Born: September 15, 1997. **B-T:** R-R. **HT:** 6-4. **WT:** 227. **Drafted:** New Mexico, 2019 (3rd round).
Signed by: Levi Lacey (Rangers).

TRACK RECORD: After three seasons at New Mexico, including the final two in the rotation, Slaten was drafted by the Rangers in the third round in 2019. He signed for $575,000, then spent his first pro season between the Rookie-level Arizona Complex League and short-season Spokane. Slaten dealt with elbow fatigue in 2022, then reached Triple-A in 2023. The Mets chose Slaten in the 2023 Rule 5 draft, then traded him to the Red Sox for lefthander Ryan Ammons and cash.

SCOUTING REPORT: Following an excellent stint in the Arizona Fall League, Slaten was one of the buzziest names leading up to the Rule 5 draft. After a command-plagued season in 2022, Slaten straightened out his strike-throwing in 2023. He cut his walk rate from 19.5% in 2022 to 8.5% in 2023. The improved control resulted in much better results at Double-A Frisco and earned him a late-season promotion to Triple-A. Slaten is a pure reliever who mixes four pitches with plenty of power across his arsenal. His four-seamer sits between 95-97 mph with ride and at times cut. He pairs his four-seam primarily with a mid-80s sweeping slider that generates heavy rates of swings-and-misses in and out of the zone. His cutter is his third pitch but is an effective weapon as a bridge between his fastball and slider. His cutter sits 89-91 mph. He'll also mix in a low-80s, two-plane curveball from time to time.

THE FUTURE: Slaten will get a chance in spring training to earn a spot the Red Sox's bullpen. He has a ceiling as a solid middle reliever.

Year	Age	Club (League)	Level	W	L	ERA	G	GS	IP	H	HR	BB	SO	BB%	SO%	WHIP	AVG
2023	25	Frisco (TL)	AA	4	3	3.16	35	1	51	41	9	16	76	7.9	37.4	1.11	.220
2023	25	Round Rock (PCL)	AAA	1	0	1.08	5	0	8	3	1	4	10	12.5	31.3	0.84	.107
Minor League Totals				10	19	5.31	97	35	210	207	35	106	284	11.5	30.7	1.49	.254

28 BROOKS BRANNON, C

HIT: 40. **POW:** 60. **RUN:** 30. **FLD:** 45. **ARM:** 60. **BA Grade:** 45. **Risk:** Extreme.

Born: May 4, 2004. **B-T:** R-R. **HT:** 6-0. **WT:** 210. **Drafted:** HS—Randleman, NC, 2022 (9th round).
Signed by: Kirk Fredriksson.

TRACK RECORD: As a high school senior, Brannon hit 20 homers, tying a North Carolina state record that had been set by his father Paul, who played in the Mariners system in the early 1990s. When Brooks remained on the board in the ninth round in 2022, the Red Sox pounced, signing him for a $712,500 bonus in line with a third-rounder. Brannon's first pro season featured an impressive power display at Low-A Salem, but a back strain limited him to 17 games.

SCOUTING REPORT: Brannon arrived in pro ball with the broad-shouldered, thick-legged physique of a big league catcher. He opens his hips early, using his powerful torso to generate some of the highest exit velocities in the system. He has plenty of pull power when he connects, but his 5% walk rate points to the need to control his aggressiveness and refine his swing decisions. Defensively, Brannon faces questions about whether he has the athleticism to stay behind the plate, but he has strong hands, plus arm strength and works relentlessly.

THE FUTURE: Brannon, who is expected to be healthy for spring training, has a chance to be an everyday catcher but requires significant development to get there. He'll open 2024 at Low-A Salem.

Year	Age	Club (League)	Level	AVG	G	AB	R	H	2B	3B	HR	RBI	BB	SO	SB	OBP	SLG
2023	19	FCL Red Sox	Rk	.250	11	48	8	12	3	1	3	14	3	12	0	.294	.542
2023	19	Salem (CAR)	A	.292	6	24	4	7	0	0	3	9	1	8	0	.320	.667
Minor League Totals				.294	22	85	18	25	4	3	6	28	6	25	0	.341	.624

29 ELMER RODRIGUEZ-CRUZ, RHP

FB: 50. **SL:** 50. **CHG:** 45. **CB:** 45. **CTL:** 55. **BA Grade:** 45. **Risk:** Extreme.

Born: August 18, 2003. **B-T:** L-R. **HT:** 6-3. **WT:** 160. **Drafted:** HS—Guaynabo, PR, 2021 (4th round).
Signed by: Edgar Perez.

TRACK RECORD: When the Red Sox made Rodriguez-Cruz their fourth-round pick in 2021, he was Boston's highest selection of a high school pitcher since Michael Kopech in 2014. They signed Rodriguez-Cruz, a projectable, rail-thin 17-year-old with some feel for four pitches, for an under-slot bonus of $497,500. He held his own as a 19-year-old in the Low-A Carolina League in 2023, but elbow inflammation limited him to two innings over the final two months.

SCOUTING REPORT: Rodriguez-Cruz attacks the strike zone aggressively with a mix of four pitches that mostly project as average. He averaged 92-93 mph on his fastball in 2023 and touched 95. The pitch lacks elite shape, but Rodriguez-Cruz's frame has room to add power and reach above-average velocity. He reshaped his changeup into a hybrid splitter in 2023 and altered his slider to create glove-side movement and get on the hands of lefties. Rodriguez-Cruz also has a strike-stealing slow curve. He has the feel to shape and reshape pitches, making Rodriguez-Cruz a work in progress who nonetheless has plenty of potential to make gains in both power and pitch quality as he develops.

THE FUTURE: Rodriguez-Cruz has back-of-the-rotation potential if he fills out and gains power. If that doesn't happen, his feel for pitching gives him a chance to be an up-and-down depth contributor.

Year	Age	Club (League)	Level	W	L	ERA	G	GS	IP	H	HR	BB	SO	BB%	SO%	WHIP	AVG
2023	19	Salem (CAR)	A	6	3	2.60	14	14	55	43	4	27	51	11.9	22.6	1.27	.219
Minor League Totals				6	6	2.32	27	24	94	74	4	42	93	10.9	24.0	1.25	.217

30 BRYAN MATA, RHP

FB: 60. **CUT:** 55. **SL:** 55. **CHG:** 45. **CB:** 40. **CTL:** 40. **BA Grade:** 45. **Risk:** Extreme.

Born: May 3, 1999. **B-T:** R-R. **Ht.:** 6-3. **Wt.:** 230. **Signed:** Venezuela, 2016. **Signed by:** Alex Requena/Eddie Romero.

TRACK RECORD: Mata emerged rapidly after signing for $25,000 in 2016 as one of the top Red Sox pitching prospects, but control problems and a torn ulnar collateral ligament that required Tommy John surgery sidelined him for all of 2021 and much of 2022. Mata turned heads by hitting triple digits in 2022 and the high 90s in big league camp 2023, but he couldn't throw strikes in Triple-A, where his work between starts was disappointing, then missed four months with a teres major strain.

SCOUTING REPORT: Mata has never managed to harness his standout raw stuff. He owns a 12% career walk rate and a 19% mark in Triple-A. His sinker sits at 97 mph and tops out at 99 while averaging 16 inches of armside run. It pairs well with a cutter that breaks to his glove side, a combination that can generate loads of grounders. As a starter, Mata has employed a four-seamer, mid-80s slider, curveball and changeup, though he scaled back those secondaries in a season-ending stint in the bullpen with both Triple-A Worcester and in the Arizona Fall League, where he walked just two of 42 batters.

THE FUTURE: Mata is out of minor league options in 2024, meaning that he can't be sent to the minors without first clearing waivers. This forces him to a bullpen role if he makes the big league team. Mata has the stuff to be an impact multi-inning contributor if he can throw enough strikes, and it's still possible to dream on his long-term development as a starter.

Year	Age	Club (League)	Level	W	L	ERA	G	GS	IP	H	HR	BB	SO	BB%	SO%	WHIP	AVG
2023	24	Worcester (IL)	AAA	0	3	6.33	9	7	27	29	1	30	28	21.3	19.9	2.19	.274
Minor League Totals				29	26	3.41	97	94	425	368	19	221	440	12.0	23.9	1.39	.233

Chicago Cubs

BY KYLE GLASER

When the Cubs traded Anthony Rizzo, Kris Bryant, Javier Baez and others at the 2021 trade deadline, it marked the end of the franchise's greatest run of success in recent history. In the aftermath, the question on everyone's mind was how long it would take for the Cubs to become competitive again.

The answer, as it turned out, was sooner than anyone expected.

The Cubs remained in the playoff hunt throughout the 2023 season before a late slide and finished 83-79. Through a combination of homegrown development successes and savvy free agent signings, the Cubs impressively struck the balance of competing in the major leagues while simultaneously bolstering their farm system.

Lefthander Justin Steele blossomed into a Cy Young Award contender and the franchise's greatest homegrown pitching success since Jeff Samardzija. Righthander Adbert Alzolay emerged as a dominant closer. Second baseman Nico Hoerner, utilityman Christopher Morel and Japanese import Seiya Suzuki all took major steps to become cornerstones of the lineup. Free agent additions Dansby Swanson and Cody Bellinger delivered immediate impact.

With the momentum of the season at their backs, the Cubs stunned the baseball world by hiring Craig Counsell away from the National League Central-rival Brewers in November to help them get back to the postseason. In the process, they discarded manager David Ross with little warning.

While the Cubs moved toward contention in the majors, their top prospects almost all progressed in the minors.

Center fielder Pete Crow-Armstrong made his major league debut, and 2021 first-round pick Jordan Wicks ascended to the Cubs' rotation to give the Wrigley faithful a preview of what's to come.

Most of the Cubs' remaining top prospects reached Double-A Tennessee by the end of the year to give the Smokies one of the most talented rosters in the minors. Led by righthander Cade Horton, catchers Moises Ballesteros and Pablo Aliendo, infielders Haydn McGeary, Matt Shaw and B.J. Murray and outfielders Owen Caissie and Kevin Alcantara, Tennessee went undefeated in the playoffs to win the Southern League title.

Eighteen-year-old Dominican shortstop Jefferson Rojas was a revelation in his U.S. debut in 2023, while teenage lefthander Jackson Ferris showed elite stuff at Low-A Myrtle Beach. Converted shortstop Michael Arias emerged as a flamethrowing righthander, while the return of projectable lefthander Drew Gray from Tommy

MATT DIRKSEN/GETTY IMAGES

Hayden Wesneski won a rotation spot but ran up a 5.33 ERA before moving to the bullpen.

PROJECTED 2027 LINEUP

Catcher	Miguel Amaya	28
First Base	Moises Ballesteros	23
Second Base	Nico Hoerner	30
Third Base	Matt Shaw	25
Shortstop	Dansby Swanson	33
Left Field	Owen Caissie	24
Center Field	Pete Crow-Armstrong	25
Right Field	Seiya Suzuki	32
Designated Hitter	Christopher Morel	28
No. 1 Starter	Justin Steele	31
No. 2 Starter	Cade Horton	25
No. 3 Starter	Jordan Wicks	27
No. 4 Starter	Ben Brown	28
No. 5 Starter	Jackson Ferris	23
Closer	Adbert Alzolay	32

John surgery gave the Cubs yet another promising arm at Low-A.

Players throughout the Cubs system got markedly better, a sign of the growing strength of their coaching and player development apparatus.

One of the architects of that success, assistant general manager and vice president of pitching Craig Breslow, was hired away to be chief baseball officer of the Red Sox in the offseason. Breslow oversaw the turnaround of the Cubs' pitching development program and his loss will be felt, but the processes he implemented remain in place.

As long as the Cubs maintain the track they're on, playoff baseball figures to return to Wrigley Field sooner rather than later. ∎

CHICAGO CUBS

TOP 2024 CONTRIBUTORS   **RANK**

1. Pete Crow-Armstrong, OF	1
2. Matt Shaw, SS	3
3. Jordan Wicks, LHP	6

BREAKOUT PROSPECTS   **RANK**

1. Michael Arias, RHP	19
2. Drew Gray, LHP	28

SOURCE OF TOP 30 TALENT

Homegrown	22	Acquired	8
College	9	Trade	7
Junior college	1	Rule 5 draft	0
High school	6	Independent league	0
Nondrafted free agent	1	Free agent/waivers	1
International	5		

LF
Cole Roederer
Yohendrick Pinango

CF
Pete Crow-Armstrong (1)
Kevin Alcantara (7)
Zyhir Hope
Christian Franklin
Darius Hill

RF
Owen Caissie (4)
Alexander Canario (11)
Brennen Davis (30)
Ezequiel Pagan

3B
B.J. Murray (17)
Jake Slaughter
Chase Strumpf

SS
Jefferson Rojas (9)
Luis Vazquez (15)
Cristian Hernandez (23)
Josh Rivera
Alexis Hernandez
Derniche Valdez

2B
Matt Shaw (3)
James Triantos (12)
Pedro Ramirez (29)
Reivaj Garcia

1B
Matt Mervis (13)
Haydn McGeary (26)
Felix Stevens
Brian Kalmer

C
Moises Ballesteros (5)
Pablo Aliendo (19)

LHP

LHSP	LHRP
Jordan Wicks (6)	Luke Little (14)
Jackson Ferris (10)	Bailey Horn (27)
Drew Gray (20)	Adam Laskey

RHP

RHSP	RHRP
Cade Horton (2)	Daniel Palencia (14)
Ben Brown (8)	Michael Arias (19)
Jaxon Wiggins (22)	Porter Hodge (21)
Brandon Birdsell (24)	Cam Sanders
Caleb Kilian (25)	Riley Martin
Brody McCullough (28)	Zac Leigh
Kohl Franklin	Eduarniel Nunez
Richard Gallardo	Tyler Santana
Will Sanders	Nick Hull
Koen Moreno	Chris Kachmar

1 PETE CROW-ARMSTRONG, OF

Born: March 25, 2002. **B-T:** L-L. **HT:** 5-11. **WT:** 184.
Drafted: HS—Los Angeles, 2020 (1st round).
Signed by: Rusty McNamara (Mets).

TRACK RECORD: Crow-Armstrong grew up in the spotlight as the son of actors Matthew Armstrong and Ashley Crow, the latter of whom played the mother of the lead character in the 1994 baseball move "Little Big League." Instead of following his parents into acting, Crow-Armstrong emerged early as a baseball prodigy and defensive savant in center field. He starred for USA Baseball's 12U, 15U and 18U national teams and set school records for hits and runs scored at Harvard-Westlake High, the alma mater of all-star pitchers Max Fried, Lucas Giolito and Jack Flaherty. The Mets drafted Crow-Armstrong 19th overall in 2020. He tore his right labrum a week into his pro career and missed the 2021 season, but that summer the Mets traded him to the Cubs for Javier Baez and Trevor Williams. Crow-Armstrong quickly made the Mets regret the move. He flew up to Double-A in his first season back from injury and followed with an even better year in 2023. He set career highs in doubles (26), home runs (20) and RBIs (82) across Double-A and Triple-A and received his first major league call-up in September.

SCOUTING REPORT: Crow-Armstrong is a future top-of-the-order hitter. He has a fast, balanced lefthanded swing geared for contact and the ability to manipulate the barrel to all parts of the strike zone. He tracks pitches and works counts, though he doesn't walk much, and makes solid contact from line to line. Crow-Armstrong is primarily a contact hitter, but he has grown into average raw power as he's gotten stronger, especially to his pull side. His swing gets too big at times, but he has the self-awareness to adjust his approach and emphasize contact in the right situations. Crow-Armstrong enhances his offensive game with his plus speed. He runs hard out of the box to rack up doubles and triples and puts constant pressure on opposing defenses. He's an aggressive runner and basestealer and stole more than 30 bases in each of the past two seasons. Crow-Armstrong shines brightest defensively in center field. He's a confident, graceful defender who gets elite jumps and runs pristine routes to catch anything hit in his area. He has exceptional range and closing speed in all directions, especially into the gaps, and is fearless going

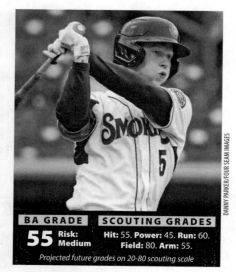

DANNY PARKER/FOUR SEAM IMAGES

BA GRADE	SCOUTING GRADES
55 Risk: Medium	Hit: 55. Power: 45. Run: 60. Field: 80. Arm: 55.

Projected future grades on 20-80 scouting scale

BEST TOOLS

BATTING

Best Hitter for Average	Moises Ballesteros
Best Power Hitter	Owen Caissie
Best Strike-Zone Discipline	B.J. Murray
Fastest Baserunner	Pete Crow-Armstrong
Best Athlete	Pete Crow-Armstrong

PITCHING

Best Fastball	Daniel Palencia
Best Curveball	Ben Brown
Best Slider	Cade Horton
Best Changeup	Jordan Wicks
Best Control	Jordan Wicks

FIELDING

Catcher	Pablo Aliendo
Best Defensive Infielder	Luis Vazquez
Best Infield Arm	Luis Vazquez
Best Defensive Outfielder	Pete Crow-Armstrong
Best Outfield Arm	Kevin Alcantara

back to the wall. He makes highlight-reel catches routinely and has an above-average, accurate arm that keeps runners from testing him. He is an intense competitor who always plays hard and is willing to do whatever his team needs.

THE FUTURE: Crow-Armstrong primarily served as a pinch-runner and defensive replacement in his MLB debut. With Cody Bellinger departing in free agency, he is set to take over as the Cubs' everyday center fielder in 2024. He projects to be a perennial Gold Glove winner who racks up hits and steals from leadoff or No. 2 spot on contending teams. ∎

Year	Age	Club (League)	Level	AVG	G	AB	R	H	2B	3B	HR	RBI	BB	SO	SB	OBP	SLG
2023	21	Tennessee (SL)	AA	.289	73	298	68	86	19	5	14	60	31	82	27	.371	.527
2023	21	Iowa (IL)	AAA	.271	34	140	30	38	7	2	6	22	15	47	10	.350	.479
2023	21	Chicago (NL)	MLB	.000	13	14	3	0	0	0	0	1	3	7	2	.176	.000
Minor League Totals				.301	214	885	193	266	48	17	36	147	89	237	71	.376	.515
Major League Totals				.000	13	14	3	0	0	0	0	1	3	7	2	.176	.000

2 CADE HORTON, RHP

FB: 60. **CB:** 50. **SL:** 65. **CHG:** 50. **CTL:** 50. **BA Grade:** 60. **Risk:** High.

Born: August 20, 2001. **B-T:** R-R. **HT:** 6-1. **WT:** 211.
Drafted: Oklahoma, 2022 (1st round). **Signed by:** Ty Nichols.
TRACK RECORD: A star quarterback and pitcher in high school, Horton committed to Oklahoma to play both football and baseball but dropped football after having Tommy John surgery as a freshman. He returned to the diamond as a draft-eligible sophomore and, after shaking off some early rust, led the Sooners to the College World Series finals as their top starter. He struck out a CWS finals-record 13 batters against Mississippi, leading the Cubs to draft him seventh overall and sign him for a below-slot $4.45 million. Horton didn't pitch after signing, but he debuted in style in 2023. He rose three levels to Double-A and dominated at every stop, finishing first in the Cubs system in ERA (2.65), WHIP (1.00) and opponent average (.190) and second in strikeouts (117).
SCOUTING REPORT: Horton is an athletic, physical righthander with power stuff. His plus fastball sits 94-96 mph and touches 98 with natural cut and ride out of an easy, repeatable delivery. His primary secondary is a plus, vertical slider at 84-86 mph with hard depth that gets swings and misses both in and out of the strike zone. Horton mostly dominates with his fastball and slider, but his low-80s curveball with good depth is an average third pitch and his sinking, mid-80s changeup progressed to average after he cut 4-5 mph off it. His delivery is a bit stiff at times, but he throws strikes with average control and has the strength to maintain his stuff and command. He has yet to fully stretch out after surgery and hasn't thrown more than 100 innings in a season.
THE FUTURE: Horton has the stuff to be a No. 2 or 3 starter but has to prove he can handle a heavier workload. He'll aim to build durability in 2024 and has a chance to make his major league debut before midseason 2024.

Year	Age	Club (League)	Level	W	L	ERA	G	GS	IP	H	HR	BB	SO	BB%	SO%	WHIP	AVG
2023	21	Myrtle Beach (CAR)	A	0	0	1.26	4	4	14	8	1	4	21	7.3	38.2	0.84	.157
2023	21	South Bend (MWL)	A+	3	3	3.83	11	11	47	35	6	12	65	6.5	35.1	1.00	.203
2023	21	Tennessee (SL)	AA	1	1	1.33	6	6	27	18	0	11	31	10.1	28.4	1.07	.188
Minor League Totals				4	4	2.66	21	21	88	61	7	27	117	7.7	33.5	1.00	.191

3 MATT SHAW, SS

HIT: 55. **POW:** 55. **RUN:** 55. **FLD:** 45. **ARM:** 45. **BA Grade:** 55. **Risk:** High.

Born: November 6, 2001. **B-T:** R-R. **HT:** 5-11. **WT:** 185.
Drafted: Maryland, 2023 (1st round). **Signed by:** Billy Swoope.
TRACK RECORD: Shaw had a storied three-year career at Maryland. He set the program's all-time home run record with 53, won the 2023 Big Ten Conference player of the year award and won the 2022 Cape Cod League MVP award after leading the league with a .360 batting average for Bourne. He became the highest-drafted player in Maryland history when the Cubs drafted him 13th overall in 2023 and signed for $4,848,500. Shaw continued to mash after signing, batting .357/.400/.618 with eight homers, 28 RBIs and 15 steals in 38 games while vaulting to Double-A in his pro debut.
SCOUTING REPORT: Shaw isn't particularly big at 5-foot-11, 185 pounds, but he's strong in his frame and packs a punch at the plate. His quick hands, strong forearms and exceptional barrel accuracy allow him to consistently drive balls hard to all fields. He regularly squares balls up and is particularly adept at driving the ball the other way to right-center field. Shaw is an aggressive hitter who doesn't walk much, but his natural feel for the barrel helps keep his strikeouts down. He projects to be an above-average hitter despite his aggressive approach and makes enough hard contact to envision above-average power with lots of doubles. He further enhances his offensive game as an above-average runner with elite basestealing instincts. Shaw primarily played shortstop at Maryland and is serviceable there, but his fringy arm strength plays better at second base. The Cubs experimented with him at third base and were encouraged by the early results. He plays extremely hard and is a polished, mature player for his age.
THE FUTURE: The Cubs internally see similarities between Shaw and Dustin Pedroia in both ability and playing style. Shaw is on the fast track and has a chance to make his major league debut in 2024.

Year	Age	Club (League)	Level	AVG	G	AB	R	H	2B	3B	HR	RBI	BB	SO	SB	OBP	SLG
2023	21	ACL Cubs	Rk	.500	3	8	3	4	1	0	1	1	2	1	2	.636	1.000
2023	21	South Bend (MWL)	A+	.393	20	84	14	33	4	3	4	18	4	12	7	.427	.655
2023	21	Tennessee (SL)	AA	.292	15	65	10	19	4	1	3	9	3	12	6	.329	.523
Minor League Totals				.357	38	157	27	56	9	4	8	28	9	25	15	.400	.618

4 OWEN CAISSIE, OF

HIT: 40. **POW:** 60. **RUN:** 55. **FLD:** 55. **ARM:** 60. **BA Grade:** 55. **Risk:** High.

Born: July 8, 2002. **B-T:** L-R. **HT:** 6-3. **WT:** 190.
Drafted: HS—Burlington, ON, 2020 (2nd round). **Signed by:** Chris Kemlo (Padres).
TRACK RECORD: Caissie stood out for his premium power on Canada's junior national team and was drafted 45th overall by the Padres in 2020. The Padres signed him for just over $1.2 million and traded him to the Cubs six months later as part of a five-player package for Yu Darvish. Caissie moved quickly through the low minors and opened 2023 as Canada's starting right fielder in the World Baseball Classic, where he hit a 427-foot home run off the batter's eye at Chase Field. He carried his success into the regular season at Double-A Tennessee and finished in the top five in the Southern League in hits (147), doubles (31), home runs (22), RBIs (84) and OPS (.917).
SCOUTING REPORT: Caissie is a tall, long-limbed lefthanded hitter who is starting to fill out his frame. He makes thunderous contact with his natural leverage and strength and sends towering drives out to all fields. He generates plus power with little effort and posts some of the highest exit velocities in professional baseball. Caissie's power is enormous, but he must make more contact to get to it. He struggles to be on time with his long limbs and goes through stretches where he strikes out prodigiously. His 164 strikeouts were third-most in the Southern League and he owns a 30% career strikeout rate. Caissie knows the strike zone and has flashed the ability to adjust in spurts, but must be more consistent to be even a fringy hitter. Caissie moves well for his size and is an above-average runner underway. He has improved to become an average defender in right field and has a plus arm that yielded 10 outfield assists in 2023.
THE FUTURE: Caissie has the power to be a middle-of-the-order force if he makes enough contact. Cutting his strikeouts will be a focus at Triple-A Iowa in 2024.

Year	Age	Club (League)	Level	AVG	G	AB	R	H	2B	3B	HR	RBI	BB	SO	SB	OBP	SLG
2023	20	Tennessee (SL)	AA	.289	120	439	77	127	31	2	22	84	76	164	7	.398	.519
Minor League Totals				.278	279	999	169	278	63	4	40	171	168	355	19	.387	.469

5 MOISES BALLESTEROS, C/1B

HIT: 60. **POW:** 50. **RUN:** 20. **FLD:** 40. **ARM:** 55. **BA Grade:** 55. **Risk:** High

Born: November 8, 2003. **B-T:** L-R. **HT:** 5-7. **WT:** 234.
Signed: Venezuela, 2021. **Signed by:** Louie Eljaua/Julio Figueroa/Hector Ortega.
TRACK RECORD: Ballesteros emerged on the international scene when he hit cleanup for Venezuela at the 2015 12U World Cup in Taiwan as the youngest player on the team. He continued to hit well throughout his amateur career and signed with the Cubs for $1.5 million on the first day of the 2021 international signing period. Ballesteros showed promising offensive attributes throughout his first two seasons before breaking out in 2023. He jumped three levels to Double-A as a 19-year-old and hit .285/.375/.449 with 14 home runs and 71 RBIs.
SCOUTING REPORT: Ballesteros hardly cuts an imposing figure with his short, rotund frame, but he's a gifted offensive player. He's a patient hitter who expertly controls the strike zone and has plus contact skills from the left side. He has a simple, fast swing and stings the ball to all fields when he gets a pitch over the plate. He hits lefties and righties, uses the whole field and stays within his approach. He demolishes fastballs in particular and shows average power potential, especially to right-center field. Ballesteros projects to hit for average and power, but his defensive outlook is cloudy. He has strong hands and is surprisingly flexible behind the plate, but his receiving is inconsistent and his framing is below-average. His thick lower half and chunky midsection limit his lateral agility and make him a liability in blocking. He has above-average arm strength and works hard for his pitchers, but he will have to improve his fitness to remain a catcher.
THE FUTURE: Ballesteros has the bat to hit in the middle of the order, regardless of where he ends up defensively. The Cubs will continue developing him behind the plate in the hope he can avoid a move to first base or DH.

Year	Age	Club (League)	Level	AVG	G	AB	R	H	2B	3B	HR	RBI	BB	SO	SB	OBP	SLG
2023	19	Myrtle Beach (CAR)	A	.274	56	197	28	54	12	0	8	32	40	30	5	.394	.457
2023	19	South Bend (MWL)	A+	.300	56	203	33	61	15	0	6	31	22	45	2	.364	.463
2023	19	Tennessee (SL)	AA	.238	5	21	3	5	0	0	0	1	1	3	0	.273	.238
Minor League Totals				.274	228	781	115	214	49	0	27	122	125	149	13	.373	.440

6 JORDAN WICKS, LHP

FB: 50. **CB:** 40. **SL:** 50. **CHG:** 60. **CUT:** 40. **CTL:** 55. **BA Grade:** 50. **Risk:** Medium.

Born: September 1, 1999. **B-T:** L-L. **HT:** 6-3. **WT:** 220.
Drafted: Kansas State, 2021 (1st round). **Signed by:** Ty Nichols.
TRACK RECORD: Wicks led the Big 12 Conference in strikeouts as a junior and set Kansas State records for strikeouts in a single season (118) and a career (230). The Cubs drafted him 21st overall in 2021, making him the highest Wildcats player ever drafted. Wicks quickly reached Double-A in his first full season and cruised through upper levels of the minors in 2023. He received his first major league callup in late August and went 4-1, 4.41 in seven starts down the stretch with the Cubs in the playoff race.
SCOUTING REPORT: Wicks is a sturdy, 6-foot-3, 220-pound lefthander who relies on command and changing speeds. His deep, six-pitch mix is topped by four-seam and two-seam fastballs that each sit 91-94 mph. Both are average pitches he commands to get ahead in counts and stay off of barrels. The jewel of Wicks' arsenal is a plus 80-83 mph changeup with late tumble and drop that gets awkward swings and misses. He sells his changeup with his arm speed and is comfortable throwing it in any count to both lefties and righties. Wicks' sweeping, 82-84 mph slider is an average pitch he throws to lefties, and he added a new 88-90 mph cutter in 2023 to give him another weapon for righties. His below-average, upper-70s curveball is a change-of-pace offering. Wicks' stuff isn't loud, but he is a smart, tough competitor who mixes his pitches effectively to keep hitters off-balance. His stuff plays up with his deceptive, crossfire delivery, which he is strong and athletic enough to maintain for average control.
THE FUTURE: Wicks projects to be a solid No. 4 starter who thrives on drawing weak contact. He is ready to fill that role now and should break camp in the Opening Day rotation.

Year	Age	Club (League)	Level	W	L	ERA	G	GS	IP	H	HR	BB	SO	BB%	SO%	WHIP	AVG
2023	23	Tennessee (SL)	AA	4	0	3.39	13	13	58	49	9	19	69	8.0	29.0	1.17	.227
2023	23	Iowa (IL)	AAA	3	0	3.82	7	7	33	26	3	13	30	9.6	22.2	1.18	.217
2023	23	Chicago (NL)	MLB	4	1	4.41	7	7	35	33	5	11	24	7.5	16.3	1.27	.252
Minor League Totals				11	6	3.73	48	48	193	172	22	63	225	7.8	27.9	1.22	.236
Major League Totals				4	1	4.41	7	7	35	33	5	11	24	7.5	16.3	1.27	.252

7 KEVIN ALCANTARA, OF

HIT: 45. **POW:** 55. **RUN:** 55. **FLD:** 60. **ARM:** 60. **BA Grade:** 55. **Risk:** V High.

Born: July 12, 2002. **B-T:** R-R. **HT:** 6-6. **WT:** 188.
Signed: Dominican Republic, 2018. **Signed by:** Edgar Mateo/Juan Piron (Yankees)
TRACK RECORD: Alcantara originally signed with the Yankees for $1 million out of the Dominican Republic. He starred as one of the top players in the complex leagues in his U.S. debut in 2021, leading the Cubs to acquire him with righthander Alexander Vizcaino for Anthony Rizzo at that summer's trade deadline. Alcantara had a solid full-season debut in the Cubs organization, but he got off to a slow start at High-A South Bend in 2023 and missed nearly a month with a leg injury. He rebounded to hit .336/.414/.548 over the final three months and earned a late promotion to Double-A Tennessee.
SCOUTING REPORT: Alcantara has a long, lean 6-foot-6 frame that wouldn't look out of place on a basketball court. He's a twitchy athlete who uses electric bat speed to impact the ball. He also has significantly toned down what used to be a sizable leg kick. He generates above-average power with his natural bat speed and leverage and could add more power as he gets stronger. Alcantara makes hard contact when he connects, but he struggles to keep his long limbs in sync and is prone to chasing breaking balls out of the zone. He falls into extended slumps where his timing and swing mechanics get out of whack and his swing decisions regress. He's extremely streaky and projects to be a fringy hitter who relies on getting to his power during hot stretches. Alcantara takes time to get up to full speed, but he's an above-average runner underway and covers plenty of ground in center field with his long strides. He's a plus defender with a plus arm and can stick in center even with his size.
THE FUTURE: Alcantara has tantalizing potential as a power-hitting center fielder, but he has to be more consistent with his swing and improve his pitch selection. He'll open 2024 back at Double-A.

Year	Age	Club (League)	Level	AVG	G	AB	R	H	2B	3B	HR	RBI	BB	SO	SB	OBP	SLG
2023	20	ACL Cubs	Rk	.250	2	4	2	1	0	0	0	1	2	1	0	.500	.250
2023	20	South Bend (MWL)	A+	.286	95	371	65	106	25	3	12	66	31	97	15	.341	.466
2023	20	Tennessee (SL)	AA	.250	5	16	4	4	1	0	1	4	3	7	0	.381	.500
Minor League Totals				.282	289	1099	205	310	57	17	34	199	116	300	39	.354	.458

8 BEN BROWN, RHP

FB: 60. **CB:** 60. **SL:** 55. **CHG:** 30. **CTL:** 40. **BA Grade:** 50. **Risk:** High

Born: September 9, 1999. **B-T:** R-R. **HT:** 6-6. **WT:** 210.
Drafted: HS—East Setauket, NY, 2017 (33rd round). **Signed by:** Alex Agostino (Phillies).

TRACK RECORD: Brown has impressed when he's been on the mound but struggled to stay healthy throughout his career. He fell to the Phillies in the 33rd round of the 2017 draft because of a burst appendix and pitched just 100 innings in his first four seasons due to Tommy John surgery, an elbow strain and a stint on the Covid-19 injured list. He finally stayed healthy in 2022 and had a breakout season, leading the Cubs to acquire him from the Phillies for David Robertson at the trade deadline. Brown climbed quickly to Triple-A Iowa in 2023 and was on the verge of a midseason callup, but he suffered a lat injury in late July and missed a month. He shifted to the bullpen when he returned and walked 10 batters in his final seven innings.
SCOUTING REPORT: Brown is a tall, 6-foot-6 righthander with formidable stuff. His fastball sits 94-97 mph with late run and gets swings and misses when located. His primary secondary pitch is a mid-80s power curveball with hard, downer action that gets swings and misses both in and out of the zone. Brown tweaked his slider to give it more sweep last year, and it has the potential to be an above-average pitch as he improves its usage. His firm, upper-80s changeup is well below-average and rarely thrown. Brown has flashed average control, but it regressed to below-average last season. He's inconsistent with his fastball command in particular. Brown has pitched more than 100 innings only once in six professional seasons and must prove he has the durability to start.
THE FUTURE: Brown has the stuff to be a No. 4 starter, but his injury history and inconsistent command point to a possible bullpen future. The Cubs remain hopeful he can start and plan to have him back in Triple-A Iowa's rotation when the 2024 season begins.

Year	Age	Club (League)	Level	W	L	ERA	G	GS	IP	H	HR	BB	SO	BB%	SO%	WHIP	AVG
2023	23	Tennessee (SL)	AA	2	0	0.45	4	4	20	13	1	6	30	7.8	39.0	0.95	.186
2023	23	Iowa (IL)	AAA	6	8	5.33	22	15	73	60	9	51	100	15.8	31.1	1.53	.226
Minor League Totals				19	17	3.67	82	56	297	250	25	130	391	10.3	31.1	1.28	.224

9 JEFFERSON ROJAS, SS

HIT: 55. **POW:** 55. **RUN:** 50. **FLD:** 50. **ARM:** 55. **BA Grade:** 55. **Risk:** Extreme.

Born: April 25, 2005. **B-T:** R-R. **HT:** 5-10. **WT:** 150.
Signed: Dominican Republic, 2022. **Signed by:** Gian Guzman/Miguel Diaz.

TRACK RECORD: Rojas put together a consistent track record of hitting throughout his amateur career in the Dominican Republic. He solidified himself as one of the top hitters in the 2021 international class and signed with the Cubs for $1 million on the first day the signing period opened. Rojas made his U.S. debut in 2023 and generated major buzz when he homered off veteran Zach Davies during a rehab start in extended spring training. He played only one game in the Arizona Complex League before the Cubs promoted him to Low-A Myrtle Beach, where took over as the Pelicans' starting shortstop and No. 3 hitter as an 18-year-old.
SCOUTING REPORT: Rojas is advanced beyond his years as a hitter. He has a fast, compact righthanded swing that is direct to the ball and makes loud contact off the barrel. He has few holes for pitchers to exploit and controls the strike zone with a mature, consistent approach. He projects to be an above-average hitter and has above-average raw power that could get better as he gets stronger. He's an average runner who makes tight turns on the bases and is an efficient basestealer. Rojas is a steady, smart defender at shortstop with good instincts and quick reactions. He isn't overly rangy, but he positions himself well and makes all the routine plays. He has an above-average, accurate arm and projects to stick at the position as an average defender.
THE FUTURE: Rojas was one of the most productive 18-year-old hitters in full-season ball in 2023. His numbers look even better in the context of the pitcher-friendly Carolina League and with half his games played at Myrtle Beach, a pitcher's park. Rojas is trending up and is a candidate to take another jump in 2024. He projects to be a bat-first shortstop who could be an all-around contributor.

Year	Age	Club (League)	Level	AVG	G	AB	R	H	2B	3B	HR	RBI	BB	SO	SB	OBP	SLG
2023	18	ACL Cubs	Rk	.000	1	3	0	0	0	0	0	0	0	1	0	.000	.000
2023	18	Myrtle Beach (CAR)	A	.268	70	272	48	73	14	1	7	31	23	61	13	.345	.404
Minor League Totals				.279	116	420	75	117	20	4	8	50	39	80	28	.359	.402

10 JACKSON FERRIS, LHP

FB: 60. **CB:** 60. **SL:** 55. **CHG:** 50. **CTL:** 40. **BA Grade:** 55. **Risk:** Extreme.

Born: January 15, 2004. **B-T:** L-L. **HT:** 6-4. **WT:** 195.
Drafted: HS—Bradenton, FL, 2022 (2nd round). **Signed by:** Tom Clark

TRACK RECORD: Ferris began his high school career at Mt. Airy (N.C.) High before transferring to IMG Academy in Florida, where went 16-0, 0.80 over two seasons facing top competition. The Cubs drafted him 47th overall in 2022 and signed him for $3 million, nearly double the slot value for that pick. Ferris made his pro debut with Low-A Myrtle Beach in 2023 and showed electric stuff in short stints. He went 2-3, 3.38 with 77 strikeouts in 56 innings for the Pelicans, but he averaged just three innings per start and struggled with walks (nearly 14% of batters) and pitch efficiency.

SCOUTING REPORT: Ferris is a tall, projectable lefthander with loud stuff. His fastball sits 93-95 mph with explosive late life that overwhelms hitters in the strike zone. His plus, 74-77 mph curveball is a hammer for which he shows has great touch and feel. He expertly manipulates the shape and velocity of his curveball and is able to neutralize righthanded hitters with it. Ferris added a 79-81 mph slider with power sweep in his first pro season and shows above-average potential with it, though his execution is inconsistent. He rarely throws his average 85-87 mph changeup. Ferris has plenty of stuff, but his complicated, contorted delivery yields below-average control. He has a deep stab in the back, his arm is late at foot strike and he finishes with a notable head whack. His arm action and command are below-average, but his stuff is good enough to beat hitters even when he misses his spot. He held opponents to a .179 average in the Carolina League and allowed only one home run all season.

THE FUTURE: Ferris has the stuff to be a midrotation starter, but he has to iron out his delivery to throw more strikes and last deeper into games. He'll head to High-A South Bend in 2024.

Year	Age	Club (League)	Level	W	L	ERA	G	GS	IP	H	HR	BB	SO	BB%	SO%	WHIP	AVG
2023	19	Myrtle Beach (CAR)	A	2	3	3.38	18	18	56	35	1	33	77	13.9	32.5	1.21	.179
Minor League Totals				2	3	3.38	18	18	56	35	1	33	77	13.9	32.5	1.21	.179

11 ALEXANDER CANARIO, OF

HIT: 40. **POW:** 60. **RUN:** 55. **FLD:** 55. **ARM:** 60. **BA Grade:** 45. **Risk:** Medium.

Born: May 7, 2000. **B-T:** R-R. **HT:** 5-11. **WT:** 212. **Signed:** Dominican Republic, 2016.
Signed by: Rudy Moretta (Giants).

TRACK RECORD: Canario signed with the Giants for $60,000 out of the Dominican Republic and began flashing huge power once he got to Low-A. The Cubs acquired him with righthander Caleb Kilian for Kris Bryant at the 2021 trade deadline. Canario finished second in the minors with 37 home runs in 2022, but he suffered a fractured ankle and dislocated shoulder in the Dominican Winter League. He missed the first two months of the 2023 season recovering, but he eventually returned. He received his first big league callup in September, when he hit a grand slam against the Pirates for his first career homer.

SCOUTING REPORT: Canario is a strong, physical righthanded hitter who can send balls a mile. His electric bat speed and torque generate plus power to all fields and allow him to drive balls even when he's off-balance. He crushes fastballs in particular and catches up to them at any velocity. Canario's power is massive, but he's an aggressive free swinger with a raw approach. He chases righthanded sliders and is a streaky hitter prone to alternating hot and cold. He projects to be a below-average hitter and has to improve his approach to fulfill his 30-homer potential. Canario has regained his above-average speed after his injuries and is an above-average right fielder with a plus arm.

THE FUTURE: Canario has a chance to be a slugging everyday right fielder if he tightens his approach. He should see the majors again in 2024.

Year	Age	Club (League)	Level	AVG	G	AB	R	H	2B	3B	HR	RBI	BB	SO	SB	OBP	SLG
2023	23	ACL Cubs	Rk	.286	7	21	6	6	2	1	1	5	4	5	0	.423	.619
2023	23	South Bend (MWL)	A+	.256	10	39	4	10	1	0	0	7	6	14	0	.370	.282
2023	23	Iowa (IL)	AAA	.276	36	145	23	40	12	0	8	35	15	45	2	.342	.524
2023	23	Chicago (NL)	MLB	.294	6	17	1	5	1	1	1	6	0	8	0	.294	.647
Minor League Totals				.264	455	1724	308	455	103	15	91	319	207	507	76	.348	.499
Major League Totals				.294	6	17	1	5	1	1	1	6	0	8	0	.294	.647

12 JAMES TRIANTOS, 3B

HIT: 55. **POW:** 45. **RUN:** 40. **FLD:** 45. **ARM:** 55. **BA Grade:** 50. **Risk:** High.

Born: January 29, 2003. **B-T:** R-T. **HT:** 6-1. **WT:** 195. **Drafted:** HS—Vienna, VA, 2021 (2nd round).
Signed by: Billy Swoope.

TRACK RECORD: Triantos was a standout two-way player in high school whose fastball touched 96 mph, but the Cubs saw greater upside as a hitter and drafted him as a third baseman. Triantos rewarded that belief when he led the Carolina League in hits in his first full season. He missed the first month of the 2023 season after having meniscus surgery on his right knee, but returned to hit .285/.363/.390 for High-A South Bend and found a defensive home after moving to second base. He finished the year with a late promotion to Double-A Tennessee.

SCOUTING REPORT: Triantos has a sharp eye for the strike zone and can hit almost any pitch. He has a fast, compact righthanded swing geared for contact and rarely chases or swings and misses. He has an innate feel for the barrel and projects to be an above-average hitter. Triantos makes lots of contact, but he is prone to swinging at pitches he can't drive and has struggled to hit for power. The Cubs want him to hone in on the middle third of the plate to fulfill his 15-20 home run power potential. After struggling defensively at third base, Triantos lost weight and improved his agility to handle a move to second base. He is a below-average runner with limited range, but he makes enough plays to be a fringy, albeit playable, second baseman with above-average arm strength.

THE FUTURE: Triantos projects to be a bat-first infielder and will go as far as his offense takes him. He'll begin 2024 back at Double-A.

Year	Age	Club (League)	Level	AVG	G	AB	R	H	2B	3B	HR	RBI	BB	SO	SB	OBP	SLG
2023	20	South Bend (MWL)	A+	.285	80	305	43	87	14	3	4	46	34	37	16	.363	.390
2023	20	Tennessee (SL)	AA	.333	3	12	2	4	1	0	0	2	1	2	0	.385	.417
Minor League Totals				.284	221	874	146	248	41	10	17	117	81	138	39	.350	.412

13 MATT MERVIS, 1B

HIT: 45. **POW:** 55. **RUN:** 30. **FLD:** 40. **ARM:** 70. **BA Grade:** 45. **Risk:** Medium.

Born: April 16, 1998. **B-T:** L-R. **HT:** 6-2. **WT:** 225. **Signed:** Duke, 2020 (NDFA). **Signed by:** Billy Swoope.

TRACK RECORD: An unsigned 39th-round pick of the Nationals out of high school, Mervis played both ways at Duke as a righthanded reliever and first baseman. He went unpicked as a senior in the shortened 2020 draft and signed with the Cubs as an undrafted free agent. Mervis made teams regret passing over him when he hit 36 home runs and led the minors with 310 total bases in 2022 as he climbed to Triple-A. He earned his first big league callup in 2023 when the Cubs needed help at first base, but he hit just .167 in 29 games and was sent back to Triple-A.

SCOUTING REPORT: Mervis is a large lefthanded hitter with average plate discipline and plus raw power. He has excellent bat speed and natural timing, which allows him to crush fastballs over the plate. Mervis' swing got overly rotational and he struggled to pick up lefthanders in his big league debut, but he rediscovered his previous form in his return to Triple-A. He still projects to be a fringe-average hitter as long keeps his approach geared toward the middle of the field, though he may need to sit against lefties. Mervis has to hit because he's a below-average runner and defender at first base who can't play any other position. He has plus-plus arm strength and touched 96 mph as a pitcher.

THE FUTURE: Mervis will get another shot at the majors in 2024. He turns 26 in April and needs to show he can stick in Chicago.

Year	Age	Club (League)	Level	AVG	G	AB	R	H	2B	3B	HR	RBI	BB	SO	SB	OBP	SLG
2023	25	Iowa (IL)	AAA	.282	100	362	77	102	23	1	22	78	67	100	2	.399	.533
2023	25	Chicago (NL)	MLB	.167	27	90	8	15	2	0	3	11	8	32	0	.242	.289
Minor League Totals				.277	309	1133	209	314	75	4	67	241	154	277	10	.370	.528
Major League Totals				.167	27	90	8	15	2	0	3	11	8	32	0	.242	.289

14 LUKE LITTLE, LHP

FB: 70. **SL:** 55. **CTL:** 40. **BA Grade:** 45. **Risk:** Medium.

Born: August 30, 2000. **B-T:** L-L. **HT:** 6-8. **WT:** 220. **Drafted:** San Jacinto (TX) JC, 2020 (4th round).
Signed by: Trey Forkerway.

TRACK RECORD: Little paired with 2019 Nationals first-rounder Jackson Rutledge to give San Jacinto (Texas) JC one of the best junior college rotations in the country as a freshman. He was limited to five appearances as a sophomore by a back injury and the coronavirus pandemic, but he went viral after he touched 104 mph in a workout video posted on Twitter. The Cubs drafted Little in the fourth round and signed him for $492,700. Little initially struggled with his conditioning and control, but he slimmed down and broke out in 2023. He rocketed from High-A to the majors and made seven scoreless relief appearances for the Cubs.

SCOUTING REPORT: Little is a jumbo-sized lefthander at 6-foot-8, 220 pounds. He hides the ball well behind his big body to generate deception and goes after hitters with an aggressive two-pitch mix. His plus-plus fastball is an explosive pitch that sits 96-98 mph, touches 100 and gets on hitters rapidly. He complements his fastball with an above-average, 80-82 mph slider that sweeps across the zone and plays well against both righties and lefties. His pitches play well off each other and frequently leave hitters caught in between. Little is difficult to hit and racks up strikeouts and ground balls, but his control is below-average. He struggles with walks and hit batters and often has to pitch his way out of trouble.

THE FUTURE: Little has a chance to be a lefthanded middle reliever if he keeps his walks under control. He should open 2024 in the Cubs bullpen.

Year	Age	Club (League)	Level	W	L	ERA	G	GS	IP	H	HR	BB	SO	BB%	SO%	WHIP	AVG
2023	22	South Bend (MWL)	A+	0	0	0.52	5	4	17	12	0	7	21	9.5	28.4	1.10	.194
2023	22	Tennessee (SL)	AA	3	2	3.12	23	0	35	20	1	28	63	18.2	40.9	1.38	.169
2023	22	Iowa (IL)	AAA	2	0	1.54	8	0	12	8	0	7	21	13.7	41.2	1.29	.186
2023	22	Chicago (NL)	MLB	0	0	0.00	7	0	7	5	0	4	12	13.3	40.0	1.35	.208
Minor League Totals				6	8	2.51	65	30	140	89	2	85	225	13.8	36.6	1.24	.178
Major League Totals				0	0	0.00	7	0	7	5	0	4	12	13.3	40.0	1.35	.208

15 LUIS VAZQUEZ, SS

HIT: 45. **POW:** 50. **RUN:** 50. **FLD:** 60. **ARM:** 60. **BA Grade:** 45. **Risk:** Medium.

Born: Oct 10, 1999. **B-T:** R-R. **HT:** 6-0. **WT:** 165. **Drafted:** HS—Orocovis, PR, 2017 (14th round).
Signed by: Edwards Guzman.

TRACK RECORD: The Cubs drafted Vazquez as a slick-fielding shortstop out of Puerto Rico in the 14th round in 2017 and signed him for $125,000. Vazquez shined defensively from the outset, but he failed to hit and went unprotected and unpicked in two consecutive Rule 5 drafts. He took an unexpected jump as a hitter in 2023 and surprised even Cubs officials with a breakout season. He hit .273 with 20 home runs, 80 RBIs and an .826 OPS, all career highs by a wide margin, and climbed to Triple-A Iowa.

SCOUTING REPORT: Vazquez is a smooth operator at shortstop and the best defensive infielder in the Cubs system. He positions himself well with elite anticipation and instincts, and cleanly fields every ball with his soft, reliable hands. He moves efficiently from side to side and is particularly adept at charging in and making barehanded plays. He has a plus, accurate arm and a quick release to get even the fastest runners. Vazquez long had bat speed, but he finally added strength to hit the ball harder and control his barrel through his swing. He now has the bat control to square up all types of pitches and generate power with ease, especially to right-center. Vazquez's balance and timing need to improve and he's an aggressive swinger, but he has the tools to be a fringy hitter with average power.

THE FUTURE: Vazquez's newfound offensive ability makes him a viable potential backup. He is in position to make his major league debut in 2024.

Year	Age	Club (League)	Level	AVG	G	AB	R	H	2B	3B	HR	RBI	BB	SO	SB	OBP	SLG
2023	23	Tennessee (SL)	AA	.284	58	232	38	66	13	0	11	40	16	65	4	.340	.483
2023	23	Iowa (IL)	AAA	.257	66	222	34	57	11	0	9	40	38	56	6	.381	.428
Minor League Totals				.236	465	1651	205	390	72	4	36	190	137	398	46	.304	.350

16 DANIEL PALENCIA, RHP

FB: 80. **SL:** 55. **CHG:** 50. **CB:** 40. **CTL:** 40. **BA Grade:** 45. **Risk:** Medium.

Born: February 5, 2000. **B-T:** R-R. **HT:** 5-11. **WT:** 195. **Signed:** Venezuela, 2020.
Signed by: Juan Carlos Villanueva/Argenis Paez (Athletics).

TRACK RECORD: Palencia signed with the A's for $10,000 when he was 20, four years older than most international signees, and was traded to the Cubs for Andrew Chafin at the 2021 trade deadline. Palencia broke out at High-A South Bend as a starter in his first full season with the Cubs and transitioned to relief in 2023 to help the team faster. He quickly rose through Double-A and Triple-A and made his big league debut on July 4, when he pitched two scoreless innings to earn the win. He remained in the Cubs bullpen the rest of the year and went 5-3, 4.45 in 27 appearances.

SCOUTING REPORT: Palencia's arm strength stands out in a big way. His fastball explodes out of his hand at 98-99 mph and regularly reaches 101 with hard ride and run. It's an 80-grade pitch he throws with little effort out of his strong, stocky build. Palencia's primary secondary pitch is a hard, short slider at 88-91 mph with late break that drops below barrels and flashes above-average. He also has an average, upper-80s changeup and usable low-80s curveball, but he effectively scrapped them with his move to the bullpen. Palencia is a good athlete, but he struggles to harness his power and has below-average control. His fastball command is inconsistent and his slider is primarily a chase pitch.

THE FUTURE: Palencia has the stuff to be a high-leverage reliever if he can fine-tune his control. He should open in the Cubs bullpen in 2024.

Year	Age	Club (League)	Level	W	L	ERA	G	GS	IP	H	HR	BB	SO	BB%	SO%	WHIP	AVG
2023	23	Tennessee (SL)	AA	0	0	5.87	5	5	15	11	3	9	18	13.6	27.3	1.30	.196
2023	23	Iowa (IL)	AAA	0	0	7.90	13	0	14	13	1	7	18	10.6	27.3	1.46	.232
2023	23	Chicago (NL)	MLB	5	3	4.45	27	0	28	22	3	14	33	11.8	27.7	1.27	.216
Minor League Totals				2	5	4.78	52	38	146	114	16	75	186	12.0	29.7	1.30	.213
Major League Totals				5	3	4.45	27	0	28	22	3	14	33	11.8	27.7	1.27	.216

17 B.J. MURRAY, 3B

HIT: 50. **POW:** 45. **RUN:** 55. **FLD:** 50. **ARM:** 50. **BA Grade:** 45. **Risk:** High.

Born: January 5, 2000. **B-T:** B-R. **HT:** 5-10. **WT:** 205. **Drafted:** Florida Atlantic, 2021 (15th round).
Signed by: Ralph Reyes.

TRACK RECORD: Murray was born and raised in the Bahamas before moving to Florida for high school. He earned a scholarship to Florida Atlantic and led the Owls with 14 home runs as a junior, which led the Cubs to draft him in the 15th round and sign him for $125,000. Murray broke out at Double-A Tennessee in 2023 and earned a Futures Game selection.

SCOUTING REPORT: Murray is a well-rounded player who does everything well, if nothing spectacular. He's a switch-hitter with a calm, patient approach and excellent strike-zone discipline from both sides of the plate. He doesn't have a ton of bat speed, but he manages counts and swings at the right pitches to do damage. His lefthanded swing is better and more powerful than his righthanded swing, though he's able to make contact with both and has roughly even career splits. His superb swing decisions give him a chance to be an average hitter with double-digit home run power. Murray is an above-average runner underway and is quick in small spaces defensively. He reads angles and hops well, has a good internal clock and projects to be an average third baseman with an average arm.

THE FUTURE: Murray's all-around game gives him a chance to carve out at least a part-time role in the majors. His debut could come in 2024.

Year	Age	Club (League)	Level	AVG	G	AB	R	H	2B	3B	HR	RBI	BB	SO	SB	OBP	SLG
2023	23	Tennessee (SL)	AA	.263	124	452	71	119	34	4	16	74	82	129	14	.382	.462
Minor League Totals				.273	235	823	136	225	56	6	26	135	149	220	24	.391	.451

18 MICHAEL ARIAS, RHP

FB: 70. **SL:** 55. **CHG:** 55. **CTL:** 40. **BA Grade:** 50. **Risk:** Extreme.

Born: November 15, 2021. **B-T:** R-R. **HT:** 6-0. **WT:** 155. **Signed:** Dominican Republic, 2018.
Signed by: Alexis De La Cruz (Blue Jays).

TRACK RECORD: The Blue Jays signed Arias as a shortstop for $10,000 out of the Dominican Republic in 2018, but they released him before he ever played a professional game. The Cubs signed him in 2021, converted him to pitching and watched him flourish. Arias played his first full season in 2023 across the Class A levels and logged a 4.09 ERA in 22 starts while flashing some of the best stuff in the organization. He struck out 110 batters in only 81.1 innings and started a combined no-hitter on July 6.

SCOUTING REPORT: Arias is a lean, athletic righthander with tremendous arm strength. His two-seam fastball sits 95-96 mph and touches 98 with heavy sink out of a low arm slot and release point. Hitters struggle to square his fastball up with its velocity and movement, and it has a chance to be a plus-plus pitch as Arias gets stronger and throws even harder. Arias complements his two-seamer with an above-average, 87-90 mph changeup with late dive that he sells well to get swings and misses. His third pitch is an 83-86 mph, short slider that plays against righthanded hitters and has above-average potential. Arias keeps the ball on the ground and overwhelms hitters when he's in the strike zone, but his control is below-average and his arm slot creates concern about the long-term health of his elbow.

THE FUTURE: Arias is still relatively new to pitching and could improve his control enough to remain a starter. If not, he has the stuff to be a high-leverage reliever.

Year	Age	Club (League)	Level	W	L	ERA	G	GS	IP	H	HR	BB	SO	BB%	SO%	WHIP	AVG
2023	21	Myrtle Beach (CAR)	A	1	4	2.55	11	11	42	24	1	25	64	14.5	37.2	1.16	.164
2023	21	South Bend (MWL)	A+	0	6	5.77	11	11	39	42	2	26	46	14.4	25.6	1.74	.278
Minor League Totals				5	15	4.02	48	32	122	91	7	87	155	16.3	29.0	1.47	.208

19 PABLO ALIENDO, C

HIT: 30. **POW:** 40. **RUN:** 50. **FLD:** 60. **ARM:** 60. **BA Grade:** 45. **Risk:** High.

Born: May 29, 2001. **B-T:** R-R. **HT:** 6-0. **WT:** 170. **Signed:** Venezuela, 2018. **Signed by:** Hector Ortega/Julio Figueroa.

TRACK RECORD: Aliendo signed with the Cubs for $200,000 out of Venezuela near the end of the 2017-18 international signing period. An advanced defender but raw hitter at the time, Aliendo progressively got stronger and blossomed offensively at Double-A Tennessee in 2023. He set new career highs with 23 doubles, 16 home runs, 147 total bases and a .790 OPS while ably guiding a high-octane pitching staff and helped lead the Smokies to the Southern League championship.

SCOUTING REPORT: Aliendo is the best defensive catcher in the Cubs system and one of the best in the minors overall. He is an excellent athlete with soft, quiet hands in receiving, above-average lateral agility in blocking and a plus, accurate arm. He receives high-velocity fastballs and quality breaking stuff without issue and has a calm, mature demeanor that keeps his pitchers steady. Beyond his physical skills, Aliendo is an exceptional game-caller who is highly intelligent and is nearly fluent in English. Aliendo spent the 2022 offseason working out at the Cubs complex in Arizona to get stronger and now possesses easy power. He's an aggressive free swinger and a well below-average hitter overall, but he gets to his power enough to project to hit double-digit home runs.

THE FUTURE: Aliendo's power, defense and intangibles give him a chance to be a second-division starter behind the plate. Even if he doesn't reach that, he should be a valuable backup catcher who plays in the majors for a long time.

Year	Age	Club (League)	Level	AVG	G	AB	R	H	2B	3B	HR	RBI	BB	SO	SB	OBP	SLG
2023	22	Tennessee (SL)	AA	.231	91	321	49	74	23	1	16	61	41	114	5	.332	.458
Minor League Totals				.234	335	1086	166	254	56	4	29	143	119	335	26	.329	.373

20 DREW GRAY, LHP

FB: 55. **CB:** 55. **SL:** 55. **CHG:** 40. **CTL:** 45. **BA Grade:** 50. **Risk:** Extreme.

Born: May 9, 2003. **B-T:** L-L. **HT:** 6-3. **WT:** 190. **Drafted:** HS—Bradenton, FL, 2021 (3rd round). **Signed by:** Tom Clark.

TRACK RECORD: Gray starred at Belleville East (Swansea, Ill.) High before transferring to IMG Academy, where his teammates included fellow Cubs pitching prospect Jackson Ferris. Gray excelled as both a hitter and pitcher at the premier program and was drafted by the Cubs in the third round as a pitcher, and signed for an over-slot bonus of $900,000. Gray's first full season was delayed when he had Tommy John surgery during 2022 spring training, but he returned midway through the 2023 season and showed loud stuff in short bursts at Low-A Myrtle Beach.

SCOUTING REPORT: Gray is a lean, athletic lefthander who oozes potential. His high-spin fastball sits 91-93 mph with late carry at the top of the strike zone and plays up with the angle he generates from his low, three-quarters arm slot. He has a natural feel to spin a 77-79 mph, downer curveball and a sweeping, low-80s slider that both flash above-average. He also has a below-average, 85-88 mph changeup he rarely throws. Gray has plenty of room to add weight and strength to his frame and should add velocity as he fills out. He repeats his delivery well but occasionally falls out of sync and loses his release point, leading to fringy control. He has yet to throw more than three innings in a start and must improve his durability.

THE FUTURE: Gray requires lots of projection, but he has a chance to be a mid-rotation starter if he makes the necessary strength gains. He's a breakout candidate in 2024.

Year	Age	Club (League)	Level	W	L	ERA	G	GS	IP	H	HR	BB	SO	BB%	SO%	WHIP	AVG
2023	20	ACL Cubs	Rk	0	0	5.68	3	3	6	3	0	6	11	20.7	37.9	1.42	.143
2023	20	Myrtle Beach (CAR)	A	0	3	4.23	11	11	28	19	0	23	45	18.4	36.0	1.52	.196
Minor League Totals				0	4	4.03	16	16	38	25	0	30	65	17.6	38.2	1.45	.188

21 PORTER HODGE, RHP

FB: 60. **CB:** 40. **SL:** 60. **CHG:** 40. **CTL:** 45. **BA Grade:** 45. **Risk:** High.

Born: February 21, 2001. **B-T:** R-R. **HT:** 6-4. **WT:** 230. **Drafted:** HS—Salt Lake City, 2019 (13th round). **Signed by:** Steve McFarland.

TRACK RECORD: Hodge led Cottonwood High to two Utah 5A state championships in three years and was drafted by the Cubs in the 13th round in 2019. Hodge was overweight when he was drafted, but he slimmed down and had a breakout season at the Class A levels in 2022. He rose to Double-A Tennessee in 2023 and tied for second in the Southern League with 11.5 strikeouts per nine innings, leading the Cubs to add him to the 40-man roster in November.

SCOUTING REPORT: Hodge is a big, 6-foot-4 righthander with power stuff. His fastball sits 93-96 mph with natural cut that makes it a plus pitch batters struggle to square up. His 83-85 mph slider is another plus pitch with late sweep and dive that gets swings and misses both in and out of the strike zone. Hodge mostly relies on those two pitches. His vertical 79-81 mph curveball and firm 86-89 mph changeup are below-average offerings that need development. Hodge has the size and athleticism of a starter, but his long arm action yields fringy control. He moved to the bullpen for the second half of the season at Tennessee and posted an ERA nearly a run lower than he had as a starter.

THE FUTURE: Hodge projects to be a solid middle reliever with his fastball and slider combination. His major league debut could come in 2024.

Year	Age	Club (League)	Level	W	L	ERA	G	GS	IP	H	HR	BB	SO	BB%	SO%	WHIP	AVG
2023	22	Tennessee (SL)	AA	6	7	5.13	35	12	81	64	3	49	103	13.6	28.5	1.40	.215
Minor League Totals				15	15	4.35	79	50	249	209	12	129	312	11.7	28.2	1.36	.225

22 JAXON WIGGINS, RHP

FB: 60. **CB:** 45. **SL:** 55. **CHG:** 50. **CTL:** 30. **BA Grade:** 50. **Risk:** Extreme.

Born: October 3, 2001. **B-T:** R-R. **HT:** 6-6. **WT:** 225. **Drafted:** Arkansas, 2023 (2nd round supp). **Signed by:** Ty Nichols.

TRACK RECORD: Wiggins tantalized as a 6-foot-6 righthander with an explosive fastball at Arkansas, but his results never quite matched his stuff. He logged a 6.17 ERA over two seasons while splitting time between the rotation and bullpen and missed his junior year after having Tommy John surgery. The Cubs decided to take a chance on his raw ability and drafted him No. 68 overall in the supplemental second round. He signed for an over-slot $1,401,500.

SCOUTING REPORT: Wiggins is a physically-imposing righthander with the stuff to match. His fastball sits 94-97 mph as a starter and ramps up to 98-100 in relief. His fastball gets on hitters quickly with the extension he generates from his large frame and is an overwhelming pitch when it's in the strike zone. Wiggins complements his fastball with an 84-88 mph slider with two-plane depth that gets swings and misses and has above-average potential. He also has a potentially average mid-80s changeup with late tumble and a downer, upper-70s curveball that is a fringy but usable pitch. Wiggns' stuff is loud, but he has well below-average control and is inconsistent in his execution. He is prone to overthrowing his fastball and frequently falls behind in counts.

THE FUTURE: Wiggins is set to return from surgery in 2024. He'll get a chance to start but projects to be a hard-throwing reliever.

Year	Age	Club (League)	Level	W	L	ERA	G	GS	IP	H	HR	BB	SO	BB%	SO%	WHIP	AVG
2023	21	Did not play															

23 CRISTIAN HERNANDEZ, SS

HIT: 40. **POW:** 30. **RUN:** 55. **FLD:** 50. **ARM:** 45. **BA Grade:** 50. **Risk:** Extreme.

Born: December 13, 2003. **B-T:** R-R. **HT:** 6-1. **WT:** 175. **Signed:** Dominican Republic, 2021. **Signed by:** Gian Guzman/Louie Eljaua/Alex Suarez.

TRACK RECORD: Hernandez signed with the Cubs for a franchise-record $3 million as one of the top prospects in the 2021 international class, but he's underwhelmed since arriving in the U.S. He had a 30% strikeout rate in the Arizona Complex League and continued to scuffle in his first full season at Low-A Myrtle Beach in 2023. He hit .233 with four home runs and a .603 OPS, fourth-lowest of any qualified player in the Carolina League, and lost the Pelicans' starting shortstop job to Jefferson Rojas at midseason.

SCOUTING REPORT: Hernandez has a long, lean frame and a smooth righthanded swing that covers the entire plate. While he flashes ability in practice settings, it doesn't translate in games. Hernandez has only average bat speed and lacks strength, which results in weak contact. He doesn't use his hands well in his swing and has limited ability to maneuver the barrel. He needs to get significantly stronger to even be a below-average hitter with 10-home run power. Hernandez is a smooth defensive shortstop with clean footwork and actions. He plays under control and handles the routine plays, but his fringy arm strength fits better at second base, where he played the second half of last season.

THE FUTURE: Hernandez has to get stronger to be even a utility middle infielder. Adding strength will be his primary goal in 2024.

Year	Age	Club (League)	Level	AVG	G	AB	R	H	2B	3B	HR	RBI	BB	SO	SB	OBP	SLG
2023	19	Myrtle Beach (CAR)	A	.223	106	385	46	86	12	3	4	40	39	118	27	.302	.301
Minor League Totals				.246	197	700	105	172	21	5	12	83	82	210	54	.329	.341

24 BRANDON BIRDSELL, RHP

FB: 55. **CB:** 45. **SL:** 45. **CHG:** 40. **CTL:** 55. **BA Grade:** 45. **Risk:** High.

Born: March 23, 2000. **B-T:** R-R. **HT:** 6-2. **WT:** 240. **Drafted:** Texas Tech, 2022 (5th round). **Signed by:** Todd George.

TRACK RECORD: An unsigned 39th-round pick of the Astros in high school, Birdsell began his college career at Texas A&M before transferring to San Jacinto (Texas) JC and eventually Texas Tech. The Twins drafted him in the 11th round as a draft-eligible sophomore, but he returned to school and won Big 12 Conference pitcher of the year. The Cubs drafted him in the fifth round and signed him for $385,000. Birdsell made his pro debut in 2023 and was one of the biggest breakouts in the Cubs system. He led the organization with a 2.77 ERA over 24 starts and rose to Double-A Tennessee.

SCOUTING REPORT: Birdsell is a confident, big-bodied righthander who fills up the strike zone. His fastball sits 92-95 mph and gets on batters faster than they expect with his short arm action and a slight pause in his delivery. His primary secondary is a fringy, 83-86 mph vertical slider with average depth that plays well against righthanded batters. He also has a fringy, 78-80 mph vertical curveball he throws to lefties and a below-average, 88-90 mph changeup he rarely uses. Birdsell throws strikes with above-average control and commands his fastball especially well. His command and aggressive mentality help his stuff play up.

THE FUTURE: Birdsell has a chance to be a back-end starter if he sharpens his secondaries. He'll begin 2024 back at Double-A.

Year	Age	Club (League)	Level	W	L	ERA	G	GS	IP	H	HR	BB	SO	BB%	SO%	WHIP	AVG
2023	23	South Bend (MWL)	A+	3	5	2.36	18	18	80	58	4	27	70	8.4	21.7	1.06	.201
2023	23	Tennessee (SL)	AA	1	3	3.95	6	6	27	32	5	5	27	4.1	22.3	1.35	.283
Minor League Totals				4	8	2.78	24	24	107	90	9	32	97	7.2	21.9	1.14	.224

25 CALEB KILIAN, RHP

FB: 55. **CB:** 55. **CHG:** 30. **CTL:** 45. **BA Grade:** 40. **Risk:** Medium.

Born: June 2, 1997. **B-T:** R-R. **HT:** 6-4. **WT:** 180. **Drafted:** Texas Tech, 2019 (8th round).
Signed by: Todd Thomas (Giants).

TRACK RECORD: Kilian pitched Texas Tech to back-to-back College World Series and was drafted in the eighth round by the Giants in 2019. The Cubs acquired him with outfielder Alexander Canario for Kris Bryant at the 2021 trade deadline. Kilian soared through the Cubs system and made his major league debut in 2022, but he's regressed since. He scuffled at Triple-A Iowa for a second straight year in 2023 and was hammered in his return to the majors, where he allowed 13 hits and 10 runs in 5.1 innings.

SCOUTING REPORT: Kilian is a physical, 6-foot-4 righthander with power stuff. He mixes a 94-97 mph four-seam fastball, 93-96 mph sinker and 90-92 mph cut fastball to keep opponents off-balance and guessing which way the ball will go out of his hand. Kilian mostly throws different variations of his fastball, but he also has an above-average 80-83 mph curveball with plus depth that draws swings and misses. His 85-88 mph changeup is a well below-average pitch he rarely throws, which has left him vulnerable against lefties (.389, 1.005 OPS) in the majors. Kilian relies on commanding his fastballs and moving them around the strike zone, but he's lost confidence during his struggles and no longer trusts his stuff.

THE FUTURE: Kilian flashes the stuff to be a back-end starter, but he has to overcome his mental hurdles. He'll try to get back to the majors in 2024.

Year	Age	Club (League)	Level	W	L	ERA	G	GS	IP	H	HR	BB	SO	BB%	SO%	WHIP	AVG
2023	26	Iowa (IL)	AAA	8	3	4.56	25	24	120	123	17	36	95	7.0	18.6	1.32	.266
2023	26	Chicago (NL)	MLB	0	1	16.88	3	1	5	13	0	2	5	6.1	15.2	2.81	.481
Minor League Totals				20	11	3.62	77	75	343	313	29	110	349	7.7	24.4	1.23	.240
Major League Totals				0	3	12.42	6	4	17	24	0	14	14	15.7	15.7	2.28	.348

26 HAYDN MCGEARY, 1B

HIT: 50. **POW:** 60. **RUN:** 30. **FLD:** 30. **ARM:** 50. **BA Grade:** 45. **Risk:** High.

Born: October 9, 1999. **B-T:** R-R. **HT:** 6-4. **WT:** 235. **Drafted:** Colorado Mesa, 2022 (15th round).
Signed by: Steve McFarland.

TRACK RECORD: McGeary set the all-time NCAA Division II record with 75 career home runs at Colorado Mesa and won back-to-back D-II national player of the year awards. He showed his skills translated with a wood bat during a standout showing in the Appalachian League, leading the Cubs to draft him in the 15th round and sign him for $125,000. McGeary continued to mash in his first full season in 2023. He finished among the organization leaders in hits (120), home runs (19), RBI (88), total bases (202) and OPS (.859) and rose to Double-A.

SCOUTING REPORT: McGeary is a massive 6-foot-4 slugger with immense strength. He has a simple, level righthanded swing that stays in the zone and pulverizes both fastballs and breaking balls. He has plenty of bat speed, stays balanced and has a keen eye for the strike zone. McGeary's swing is grooved and he hits the ball on the ground too often, but he swings at the right pitches and hits the ball harder than almost anyone. He uses the whole field and can clear any stadium when he gets the ball in the air. McGeary's bat will play, but he must find a position. He was primarily a DH in college and is still learning to play first base, where he is well below-average with slow reactions and poor hands.

THE FUTURE: McGeary's bat gives him a chance to keep rising. He should see Triple-A in 2024.

Year	Age	Club (League)	Level	AVG	G	AB	R	H	2B	3B	HR	RBI	BB	SO	SB	OBP	SLG
2023	23	South Bend (MWL)	A+	.368	20	76	9	28	8	0	3	13	13	16	3	.467	.592
2023	23	Tennessee (SL)	AA	.255	104	361	56	92	15	1	16	75	67	105	4	.382	.435
Minor League Totals				.274	142	503	71	138	29	1	20	99	87	139	7	.390	.455

27 BAILEY HORN, LHP

FB: 60. **CB:** 55. **SL:** 60. **CTL:** 30. **BA Grade:** 40. **Risk:** Medium.

Born: January 15, 1998. **B-T:** L-L. **HT:** 6-2. **WT:** 210. **Drafted:** Auburn, 2020 (5th round).
Signed by: Warren Hughes (White Sox).
TRACK RECORD: Horn had Tommy John surgery his sophomore year at McLennan (Texas) JC, but he transferred to Auburn and returned to lead the Tigers to the 2019 College World Series. He held opponents scoreless in three of his four starts during the pandemic-shortened 2020 season and was drafted by the White Sox in the fifth round. The Cubs acquired Horn for Ryan Tepera at the 2021 trade deadline and made him a reliever, which led to a breakout. Horn bounded up the Cubs system and went 7-3, 4.21 in 45 appearances across Double-A and Triple-A in 2023.
SCOUTING REPORT: Horn has power stuff but is not quite consistent with it. His fastball sits 94-96 mph, touches 98 and gets swings and misses when he throws it over the plate. His sharp, 84-86 mph slider flashes plus and is a wipeout offering at its best. His big-breaking, 75-79 mph curveball with sweep and depth is an above-average pitch that he can land on the backfoot of righties. Horn has plenty of stuff, but he struggles to repeat his delivery and has a violent arm action that yields well below-average control and significant injury risk.
THE FUTURE: Horn's power stuff makes him a potential low-leverage relief option. His major league debut should come in 2024. The Cubs added him to their 40-man roster after the season.

Year	Age	Club (League)	Level	W	L	ERA	G	GS	IP	H	HR	BB	SO	BB%	SO%	WHIP	AVG
2023	25	Tennessee (SL)	AA	0	1	2.00	6	0	9	3	0	5	19	14.3	54.3	0.89	.100
2023	25	Iowa (IL)	AAA	7	2	4.58	39	0	53	52	5	29	59	12.2	24.9	1.53	.265
Minor League Totals				11	9	4.20	99	14	174	149	17	95	221	12.5	29.0	1.40	.226

28 BRODY MCCULLOUGH, RHP

FB: 55. **CB:** 30. **SL:** 45. **CHG:** 40. **CTL:** 50. **BA Grade:** 45. **Risk:** High.

Born: June 30, 2000. **B-T:** R-R. **HT:** 6-4. **WT:** 205. **Drafted:** Wingate (NC), 2022 (10th round). **Signed by:** Billy Swoope.
TRACK RECORD: McCullough emerged as one of the nation's top Division II pitchers at Wingate (N.C.) and showed his stuff played against better competition with Hyannis in the Cape Cod League. The Cubs drafted him in the 10th round after his Cape showing and signed him for $125,000. McCullough made his full-season debut in 2023 and continued to shine. He posted a 3.44 ERA in 21 starts across the Class A levels and held opponents to a .192 batting average, second-lowest in the Cubs system, before a knee injury ended his season.
SCOUTING REPORT: McCullough is an intense competitor who confounds hitters with his high-spin fastball. His fastball sits 91-95 mph and plays up with significant cut and carry at the top of the strike zone. The pitch gets on hitters quickly with his above-average extension and evades their bat paths with its late movement. McCullough's 82-86 mph vertical slider is a fringy offering that plays up with his ability to command it and feel for when to throw it. His 84-87 mph changeup and 78-82 mph curveball are ineffective and will leave him vulnerable to lefties at higher levels. McCullough can be overly rotational in his delivery, but he has a clean arm action and throws strikes with average control.
THE FUTURE: McCullough projects to be a middle reliever who dominates with his fastball. He'll continue starting for now.

Year	Age	Club (League)	Level	W	L	ERA	G	GS	IP	H	HR	BB	SO	BB%	SO%	WHIP	AVG
2023	23	Myrtle Beach (CAR)	A	5	2	2.86	12	12	50	29	3	17	74	8.6	37.6	0.91	.166
2023	23	South Bend (MWL)	A+	0	3	4.25	9	9	36	32	3	14	34	9.1	22.1	1.28	.235
Minor League Totals				7	5	3.29	26	21	93	65	6	33	120	8.8	31.8	1.05	.194

29 PEDRO RAMIREZ, 2B

HIT: 55. **POW:** 40. **RUN:** 55. **FLD:** 50. **ARM:** 45. **BA Grade:** 45. **Risk:** Very High.

Born: April 1, 2004. **B-T:** B-R. **HT:** 5-8. **WT:** 165. **Signed:** Venezuela, 2021.
Signed by: Julio Figueroa/Carlos Figueroa/Cirilo Cumberbatch.
TRACK RECORD: Ramirez signed with the Cubs for $75,000 out of Venezuela and had immediate success as a top hitter in the DSL and Arizona Complex League. He hit his first speed bump in 2023 at Low-A Myrtle Beach and was demoted to extended spring training in mid-May, but he later returned to the Pelicans with renewed confidence and hit .288/.390/.460 the rest of the season.
SCOUTING REPORT: Ramirez is a polished switch-hitter with an advanced feel for hitting. He's a patient hitter with excellent strike-zone discipline and puts a short, fast swing on balls when he gets a pitch to hit. Ramirez is stronger batting lefthanded than righthanded, but he makes contact from both sides of the plate and has a chance to be an above-average hitter. He has started swinging harder to make more impactful contact and has a chance to reach 10-12 home runs. Ramirez is an above-average runner with average range and body control at second base and projects to be an average defender. He began playing third base but needs to improve his fringe-average arm strength to project there.
THE FUTURE: Ramirez's pure hitting ability gives him a path to the majors as a switch-hitting infielder. He'll head to High-A South Bend in 2024.

Year	Age	Club (League)	Level	AVG	G	AB	R	H	2B	3B	HR	RBI	BB	SO	SB	OBP	SLG
2023	19	Myrtle Beach (CAR)	A	.266	104	354	53	94	19	3	8	54	49	71	17	.358	.404
Minor League Totals				.303	207	736	123	223	39	15	13	99	81	123	41	.381	.450

30 BRENNEN DAVIS, OF

HIT: 30. **POW:** 30. **RUN:** 55. **FLD:** 50. **ARM:** 55. **BA Grade:** 45. **Risk:** Extreme.

Born: November 2, 1999. **B-T:** R-R. **HT:** 6-0. **WT:** 210. **Drafted:** HS—Chandler, AZ, 2018 (2nd round).
Signed by: Steve McFarland.
TRACK RECORD: The estranged son of former Chicago Bulls point guard Reggie Theus, Davis has flashed immense ability but struggled to stay healthy since the Cubs drafted him in the second round in 2018. He appeared on the verge of the major leagues after hitting two home runs at Coors Field to win the Futures Game MVP award in 2021, but he missed most of 2022 after having back surgery and battled injuries again in 2023. He missed two months after having core muscle surgery and hit just .187/.296/.279 in 62 games at Triple-A Iowa.
SCOUTING REPORT: Once a promising offensive prospect, Davis' injuries have taken a physical toll on his hitting ability. He is frequently late on pitches and has constantly tinkered with his swing trying to find answers. He is tentative in the box and has had his formerly above-average power sapped by his injuries, and now makes soft contact when he does connect. Davis is a long-limbed athlete who starred on the basketball court in high school. He's an above-average runner with above-average arm strength and has the athleticism and instincts to play all three outfield positions.
THE FUTURE: Davis is still young and has tools, but he has to stay healthy and regain his strength. He'll return to Triple-A for a fourth straight season in 2024.

Year	Age	Club (League)	Level	AVG	G	AB	R	H	2B	3B	HR	RBI	BB	SO	SB	OBP	SLG
2023	23	ACL Cubs	Rk	.455	4	11	0	5	2	0	0	1	1	3	0	.500	.636
2023	23	South Bend (MWL)	A+	.208	5	24	3	5	2	0	1	3	0	12	0	.208	.417
2023	23	Iowa (IL)	AAA	.187	62	219	27	41	8	0	4	26	22	58	9	.296	.279
Minor League Totals				.241	291	1016	156	245	54	3	37	133	126	306	27	.347	.409

Chicago White Sox

BY BILL MITCHELL

I t wasn't supposed to be like this for the White Sox in 2023.

Coming off a .500 season in 2022, Chicago expected to be back in the thick of the race in a weak American League Central. They had a new manager in Pedro Grifol, a solid pitching staff with the addition of veteran Mike Clevinger to support Dylan Cease, Lucas Giolito and Lance Lynn; and 25-year-old center fielder Luis Robert Jr. was about to break out with a monster healthy season.

Instead, the White Sox stumbled to a 61-101 record, third-worst in the AL and fourth-worst in all of MLB.

With one of the thinnest minor league systems in baseball, the outlook for the future of the White Sox looked bleak. They waved the white flag at the Aug. 1 trade deadline, dealing away veterans Giolito, Lynn, Reynaldo Lopez, Joe Kelly, Keynan Middleton and Kendall Graveman in five deals that went a long way in replenishing the farm system. Chicago also parted with 27-year-old Jake Burger, an emerging power source and 2017 first-round pick.

The returns were highlighted by four players now ranked among the organization's top 11 prospects: catcher Edgar Quero and pitchers Nick Nastrini, Jake Eder and Ky Bush.

The deadline deals weren't enough to prevent a sweep of the front office. President Kenny Williams and general manager Rick Hahn were fired just three weeks after the trade deadline.

Instead of going outside the organization for a new GM, the White Sox promoted farm director Chris Getz to the role. He quickly brought in Gene Watson from the Royals as director of player personnel, Josh Barfield from the D-backs as assistant GM and Brian Bannister from the Giants as director of pitching. Former major league shortstop Paul Janish later joined the staff as farm director.

Getz's first trade after the World Series was an interesting one that could pay dividends. He sent reliever Aaron Bummer to the Braves for five players, including big league reclamation projects Mike Soroka and Jared Shuster as well as middle infielders Nicky Lopez and Braden Shewmake and righthander Riley Gowens, a 2023 ninth-rounder out of Illinois.

In looking to get more upper-level depth in the system, the White Sox drafted only one high school player in 2023, outfielder George Wolkow, among its 20 picks.

Chicago's minor league affiliates combined to

Oscar Colas made the Opening Day roster but hit just .216/.257/.314 with five homers in 75 games.

PROJECTED 2027 LINEUP

Catcher	Edgar Quero	24
First Base	Andrew Vaughn	29
Second Base	Jacob Gonzalez	25
Third Base	Bryan Ramos	25
Shortstop	Colson Montgomery	25
Left Field	Andrew Benintendi	32
Center Field	Luis Robert Jr.	29
Right Field	Oscar Colas	28
Designated Hitter	Eloy Jimenez	30
No. 1 Starter	Dylan Cease	31
No. 2 Starter	Michael Kopech	31
No. 3 Starter	Noah Schultz	23
No. 4 Starter	Nick Nastrini	27
No. 5 Starter	Jake Eder	28
Closer	Gregory Santos	27

go 282-367 for a .435 winning percentage that ranked last among all 30 organizations. Top prospects Colson Montgomery and Bryan Ramos each missed a significant amount of time in 2023 but performed when healthy.

Montgomery, a 2021 first-round pick, retained his position as the organization's No. 1 prospect. He quickly got back into form by hitting .287/.455/.484 and reaching Double-A Birmingham. He is on track for his MLB debut in 2024.

Montgomery and Ramos both finished the year with strong performances in the Arizona Fall League, where they were joined by fellow prospects Jacob Burke and newly acquired pitchers Eder and Jordan Leasure. ∎

CHICAGO WHITE SOX

TOP 2024 CONTRIBUTORS	RANK
1. Colson Montgomery, SS	1
2. Nick Nastrini, RHP	3
3. Jordan Leasure, RHP	14

BREAKOUT PROSPECTS	RANK
1. George Wolkow, OF	12
2. Mathis LaCombe, RHP	24

SOURCE OF TOP 30 TALENT

Homegrown	23	Acquired	7
College	10	Trade	7
Junior college	2	Rule 5 draft	0
High school	5	Independent league	0
Nondrafted free agent	0	Free agent/waivers	0
International	6		

LF
Wilfred Veras (16)
DJ Gladney
Godwin Bennett

CF
Jacob Burke (20)
Terrell Tatum (21)
Eddie Park

RF
George Wolkow (12)
Abraham Nuñez Jr.

3B
Bryan Ramos (4)
Brooks Baldwin
Wes Kath
Mikey Kane
Ryan Galanie

SS
Colson Montgomery (1)
Jacob Gonzalez (7)
Ryan Burrowes (19)
Jose Rodriguez (23)
Braden Shewmake (26)

2B
Javier Mogollon (22)
Loidel Chapelli
Rikuu Nishida
Edrick Felix

1B
Tim Elko

C
Edgar Quero (5)
Korey Lee
Ronny Hernandez
Michael Turner
Calvin Harris
Stiven Flores
Adam Hackenberg

LHP

LHSP	LHRP
Noah Schultz (2)	Fraser Ellard
Jake Eder (6)	Sammy Peralta
Ky Bush (11)	
Shane Drohan (25)	
Christian Oppor (28)	
Tyler Schweitzer (30)	
Shane Murphy	
Lucas Gordon	

RHP

RHSP	RHRP
Nick Nastrini (3)	Jordan Leasure (14)
Cristian Mena (8)	Eric Adler
Jonathan Cannon (9)	Jared Kelley
Peyton Pallette (10)	Yohemy Nolasco
Sean Burke (13)	Riley Gowens
Tanner McDougal (15)	Lane Ramsey
Grant Taylor (17)	
Seth Keener (18)	
Mathias LaCombe (24)	
Matthew Thompson (27)	
Juan Carela (29)	
Mason Adams	
Maximo Martinez	
Aldrin Batista	
Luis Reyes	
Drew McDaniel	

1 COLSON MONTGOMERY, SS

Born: February 27, 2002. **B-T:** L-R. **HT:** 6-4. **WT:** 221.
Drafted: HS—Huntingburg, IN, 2021 (1st round).
Signed by: Justin Wechsler.

TRACK RECORD: A three-sport athlete in high school, Montgomery was recruited for basketball by in-state powerhouse Indiana, with the Hoosiers baseball program also wanting his services. In high school, he broke the Southridge basketball career scoring record and was also the quarterback for the football team, but he chose baseball as his profession. The White Sox drafted him 22nd overall in 2021 and signed him for a slot-value $3.027 million. Montgomery was on the fast track through the White Sox system before hitting a speed bump in 2023. He missed most of spring training and much of the first half of the season to a mid-back sprain, but after his return he looked just as good as ever. He hit a combined .287/.455/.484 with eight home runs, 56 walks and 56 strikeouts in 64 games across three levels, finishing the regular season with 37 games at Double-A Birmingham. His most impressive attribute is his outstanding plate discipline, as highlighted by a 15% walk rate at Double-A. Montgomery made up for lost time with a solid showing in the Arizona Fall League. His 20 RBIs tied for fourth in the AFL, while his .936 OPS placed 10th.

SCOUTING REPORT: Montgomery is a polished hitter who doesn't give away at-bats and consistently ranks as having the best strike-zone discipline in the organization. That is evident with his 56 walks in 64 games in 2023. His swing is simple and geared to use all fields, though he occasionally gets pull-oriented and looks to drive balls with authority. Montgomery is beginning to get more balls over the fence thanks to the 20 pounds of muscle he has added since starting his pro career, along with the torque generated by his long levers. He's a below-average runner down the line who gets to average speed underway. He can go from first to third on hits to the outfield but he rarely looks to steal bases. Scouts are divided on Montgomery's defense. Some see an above-average defender at shortstop who is athletic and has the good footwork and longer strides making up for the lack of pure speed. He is able to anticipate and read balls off the bat as well as position himself adeptly. Some see a player who might have to move to the outfield because of shaky hands and stiff actions on the infield. Those scouts also see a player with limited range who might fit best in an outfield corner, where his bat would certainly profile. Montgomery flashes an above-average arm and gets extra zip on his throws when necessary. He can also throw accurately without setting his feet.

THE FUTURE: With tastes of Double-A ball in the last two seasons, Montgomery is ready to advance to Triple-A Charlotte in 2024. Like other shortstop prospects his size, Montgomery has persistently faced the question of whether he can stay at the position, but he's passed every test so far. He is the organization's shortstop of the future, and that future could begin in 2024. ∎

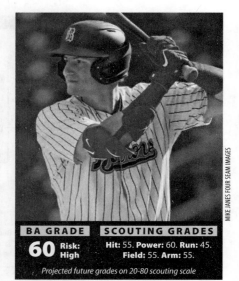

MIKE JANES FOUR SEAM IMAGES

BA GRADE	SCOUTING GRADES
60 Risk: High	Hit: 55. Power: 60. Run: 45. Field: 55. Arm: 55.

Projected future grades on 20-80 scouting scale

BEST TOOLS

BATTING

Best Hitter for Average	Jacob Gonzalez
Best Power Hitter	George Wolkow
Best Strike-Zone Discipline	Colson Montgomery
Fastest Baserunner	Terrell Tatum
Best Athlete	Colson Montgomery

PITCHING

Best Fastball	Jordan Leasure
Best Curveball	Peyton Pallette
Best Slider	Noah Schultz
Best Changeup	Nick Nastrini
Best Control	Mason Adams

FIELDING

Best Defensive Catcher	Adam Hackenberg
Best Defensive Infielder	Brooks Baldwin
Best Infield Arm	Wes Kath
Best Defensive Outfielder	Jacob Burke
Best Outfield Arm	George Wolkow

Year	Age	Club (League)	Level	AVG	G	AB	R	H	2B	3B	HR	RBI	BB	SO	SB	OBP	SLG
2023	21	ACL White Sox	Rk	.353	10	34	9	12	3	1	1	6	11	5	2	.511	.588
2023	21	Winston-Salem (SAL)	A+	.345	17	58	15	20	3	0	3	10	20	15	0	.537	.552
2023	21	Birmingham (SL)	AA	.244	37	131	27	32	8	2	4	21	25	36	0	.400	.427
Minor League Totals				.280	186	667	125	187	38	5	19	91	123	161	3	.409	.438

2 NOAH SCHULTZ, LHP

FB: 60. **SL:** 60. **CHG:** 55. **CTL:** 60. **BA Grade:** 60. **Risk:** Very High.

Born: August 5, 2003. **B-T:** L-L. **HT:** 6-9. **WT:** 220.
Drafted: HS—Oswego, IL, 2022 (1st round). **Signed by:** JJ Lally.
TRACK RECORD: The White Sox stayed close to home when they drafted Schultz 26th overall in 2022, signing the towering Chicago-area high school product for full slot value of $2.8 million. While his time on the mound has been limited to 27 innings since signing, Schultz has flashed tantalizing, mostly unhittable stuff. His 2023 pro debut was delayed until June 2 by a flexor strain. It wasn't until his seventh start a month and a half later that he finally gave up a run, the only game among his 10 starts in which he yielded an earned run. He spent the entire season at Low-A Kannapolis, striking out 38 batters while walking just six.
SCOUTING REPORT: Schultz's devastating mid-90s fastball touches the high 90s. It is difficult for hitters to square up because of the extreme deception provided by his low three-quarters arm slot and the way he hides the ball. It explodes on hitters with run and sink to generate whiffs up in the zone. Schultz's fastball has double-plus potential, as does his wipeout slider that averages 79-80 mph with late, hard movement and a high spin rate. He doesn't use his changeup much, but it's a potentially above-average pitch in the mid 80s with late movement and down action. He uses it to keep righthanded hitters from sitting on his slider. Using a modified windup, Schultz starts from what looks like a stretch position before going into a small side-rocker step, which helps keep his long levers in sync. He coordinates his tall frame and long levers well, throwing a lot of strikes and profiling as a starter.
THE FUTURE: Schultz has the components of a top-of-the rotation starter. He will continue to move through the system slowly, with his pitch counts being carefully controlled. He'll likely head to High-A Winston-Salem as a 20-year-old to start the 2024 season.

Year	Age	Club (League)	Level	W	L	ERA	G	GS	IP	H	HR	BB	SO	BB%	SO%	WHIP	AVG
2023	19	Kannapolis (CAR)	A	1	2	1.33	10	10	27	17	3	6	38	5.8	36.5	0.85	.175
Minor League Totals				1	2	1.33	10	10	27	17	3	6	38	5.8	36.5	0.85	.175

3 NICK NASTRINI, RHP

FB: 65. **CB:** 55. **SL:** 55. **CHG:** 45. **CTL:** 45. **BA Grade:** 55. **Risk:** High.

Born: February 18, 2000. **B-T:** R-R. **HT:** 6-3. **WT:** 215.
Drafted: UCLA, 2021 (4th round). **Signed by:** Dennis Moeller (Dodgers).
TRACK RECORD: The 2023 trade deadline deal that brought Nastrini and Double-A reliever Jordan Leasure from the Dodgers for veteran pitchers Lance Lynn and Joe Kelly may turn out to be Chicago's best trade of the year. Drafted in the fourth round in 2021, Nastrini pitched at Double-A for the Dodgers in 2023 and reached Triple-A Charlotte after the trade. That was an impressive feat for a pitcher who was dropped from the UCLA rotation late in 2021 with a case of the yips. The Dodgers got Nastrini back on track in pro ball, where he has flashed an outstanding fastball with a trio of average to above-average pitches. In his career he has compensated for elevated walk rates—11% for his career—with top-flight strikeout rates, including a mark near 28% in 2023.
SCOUTING REPORT: Nastrini has a four-pitch arsenal that he can throw for strikes and get swings-and-misses. His riding fastball sits 93-97 mph with tail and run, and he often uses it at the top of the zone. His heater is paired with an above-average 78-80 mph curveball down in the zone. The pitch has 12-to-6 break and some bite. Nastrini's 87 mph slider has tilt and depth, sometimes playing more like a cutter, and it gets chases from righthanded hitters. He pairs it with a mid-80s changeup that is effective against lefthanders. Nastrini has a polished, repeatable delivery but at times gets too upright and needs to stay consistent.
THE FUTURE: With the potential to be a No. 3 or 4 starter, Nastrini will likely reach Chicago at some point in 2024. He might have already made his MLB debut late in 2023 had he remained with the contending Dodgers, who suffered a rash of rotation injuries, but regardless he won't have to wait much longer.

Year	Age	Club (League)	Level	W	L	ERA	G	GS	IP	H	HR	BB	SO	BB%	SO%	WHIP	AVG
2023	23	Tulsa (TL)	AA	5	3	4.03	17	17	74	66	8	37	85	11.3	26.1	1.40	.232
2023	23	Birmingham (SL)	AA	3	0	4.22	4	4	21	20	1	7	31	7.4	33.0	1.27	.235
2023	23	Charlotte (IL)	AAA	1	2	4.12	4	4	20	10	2	10	23	12.7	29.1	1.02	.154
Minor League Totals				15	9	3.89	59	59	245	178	30	116	340	11.2	32.7	1.20	.198

4 BRYAN RAMOS, 3B

HIT: 55. **POW:** 55. **RUN:** 45. **FLD:** 50. **ARM:** 55. **BA Grade:** 55. **Risk:** High.

Born: March 12, 2002. **B-T:** R-R. **HT:** 6-3. **WT:** 225.
Signed: Cuba, 2018. **Signed by:** Ruddy Moreta/Doug Laumann/Marco Paddy.

TRACK RECORD: Ramos signed with the White Sox in 2018 after leaving his native Cuba and began his pro career in the Rookie-level Arizona League the next year at age 17, skipping over the customary assignment to the Dominican Summer League. He has consistently been young for each level, reaching Double-A Birmingham at 20 late in the 2022 season. He missed the early part of 2023 with a groin-related injury, not getting into an official game until May 23. Spending most of the rest of the season at Birmingham, Ramos put up solid numbers with a .271/.369/.457 batting line and 14 home runs in 77 games. His most notable stat at Birmingham was the 11% walk rate, the best of his career to date.

SCOUTING REPORT: Ramos has plenty of upside but faces development still ahead. He projects as an above-average hitter who hits for both average and power. He can destroy fastballs, using all fields, but he chases breaking balls down and away and gets busted inside. As he has gradually improved his body, Ramos' defense at third base has gotten better, projecting now to at least average. Ramos is adept at coming in on balls and making plays down the line, with an above-average arm. His speed has also ticked up, and he's now close to an average runner. Another difference-maker for Ramos is his makeup and work ethic, which have been described as being off the charts, and he has worked hard on firming his body since initially coming to the U.S.

THE FUTURE: Ramos is ready for the challenge of Triple-A as a 22-year-old in 2024. He has shown continual improvement from year to year, and he's just a year or two away from becoming the White Sox's regular third baseman.

Year	Age	Club (League)	Level	AVG	G	AB	R	H	2B	3B	HR	RBI	BB	SO	SB	OBP	SLG
2023	21	Kannapolis (CAR)	A	.125	4	16	3	2	0	0	1	2	0	4	0	.125	.313
2023	21	Birmingham (SL)	AA	.271	77	291	46	79	10	1	14	48	38	75	4	.369	.457
Minor League Totals				.260	367	1388	221	361	62	10	54	219	153	319	21	.347	.436

5 EDGAR QUERO, C

HIT: 55. **POW:** 45. **RUN:** 30. **FLD:** 45. **ARM:** 50. **BA Grade:** 55. **Risk:** High.

Born: April 6, 2003. **B-T:** B-R. **HT:** 5-11. **WT:** 204.
Signed: Cuba, 2021. **Signed by:** Brian Parker (Angels).

TRACK RECORD: Quero first popped on international scouts' radars in 2018 when starring for his native Cuba at the U-15 World Cup in Panama and signed with the Angels three years later. Making his full-season debut, he was Low-A California League MVP in 2022 when he hit .312/.435/.530 with 17 home runs. Quero was traded to the White Sox at the 2023 trade deadline, along with southpaw Ky Bush, in one of several deals made to replenish Chicago's farm system. He finished his first Double-A season with a combined .255/.380/.351 batting line. Quero was young for the level, having just turned 20 and skipping High-A completely.

SCOUTING REPORT: A switch-hitting catcher is a valuable commodity, and Quero has shown plenty of potential at the plate. He has good feel for the barrel and makes hard contact from both sides of the plate, smacking line drives to all fields. He shows more gap power from the right side and more pop from the left side, hitting five of six home runs in 2023 while batting lefthanded. A well below-average runner, Quero has slowed down as his lower half has gotten thicker. His defense is behind his offense, but he showed improvement in 2023, most notably in terms of his hands, framing and blocking. His throws were unleashed more quickly and were more accurate, and he recorded pop times as low as 1.92 seconds on throws to second base. Quero's English language fluency has improved and pitchers like throwing to him. His lower half has gotten thicker, so he'll need to focus on his conditioning to not get too big.

THE FUTURE: Quero was challenged with the jump to Double-A, but he continued to show promise, most notably with his improvements behind the plate. More time at the level might be best for him, but a strong spring training may get him to Triple-A right around the time of his 21st birthday.

Year	Age	Club (League)	Level	AVG	G	AB	R	H	2B	3B	HR	RBI	BB	SO	SB	OBP	SLG
2023	20	Rocket City (SL)	AA	.246	70	256	40	63	13	0	3	35	55	53	1	.386	.332
2023	20	Birmingham (SL)	AA	.277	31	112	12	31	4	0	3	22	17	23	0	.366	.393
Minor League Totals				.279	251	902	161	252	62	3	28	162	173	211	15	.409	.448

6 JACOB GONZALEZ, SS

HIT: 55. **POW:** 50. **RUN:** 30. **FLD:** 50. **ARM:** 55. **BA Grade:** 55. **Risk:** High.

Born: May 30, 2002. **B-T:** L-R. **HT:** 6-2. **WT:** 200.
Drafted: Mississippi, 2023 (1st round). **Signed by:** Warren Hughes.
TRACK RECORD: A top 300 draft prospect at his Los Angeles-area high school, Gonzalez went undrafted because of his strong commitment to Mississippi, where he was a three-year starter at shortstop. He helped the Rebels capture the 2022 College World Series championship. He was twice selected for Team USA's Collegiate National Team. The White Sox made Gonzalez the 15th overall pick in 2023, sealing the deal with a $3.9 million bonus that was roughly 13% under slot. In his pro debut he reached Low-A Kannapolis.
SCOUTING REPORT: Gonzalez is a patient and selective hitter who pairs a keen eye with solid pure bat-to-ball skills. He walked 15% of the time in his pro debut, which was in line with his career 14.3% rate in three years at Ole Miss. He struck out just 16% of the time in his pro debut. Gonzalez uses an unorthodox swing. He coils his upper half with his shoulders pointed toward first base, while his lower half is in an open stance, causing him to not always get back to an even position on contact. He hit for power in college, peaking at 18 homers as a sophomore, but in his pro debut he looked more like a hit-over-power type. Gonzalez is a well below-average runner, raising questions as to whether he can stay at shortstop despite good instincts and composure. He has solid hands and actions at the position but lacks quickness. He may be better suited for second or third base, where he projects to be an average defender.
THE FUTURE: Gonzalez is advanced enough to move to High-A Winston-Salem in 2024. Where he winds up on the field will be determined as he progresses, but with Colson Montgomery the likely long-term shortstop in Chicago he may find a role elsewhere in the infield.

Year	Age	Club (League)	Level	AVG	G	AB	R	H	2B	3B	HR	RBI	BB	SO	SB	OBP	SLG
2023	21	ACL White Sox	Rk	.250	4	12	2	3	0	0	0	4	3	2	0	.375	.250
2023	21	Kannapolis (CAR)	A	.207	30	111	16	23	3	0	1	13	20	23	1	.328	.261
Minor League Totals				.211	34	123	18	26	3	0	1	17	23	25	1	.333	.260

7 JAKE EDER, LHP

FB: 50. **SL:** 60. **CHG:** 50. **CTL:** 45. **BA Grade:** 50. **Risk:** High.

Born: October 9, 1998. **B-T:** L-L. **HT:** 6-4. **WT:** 215.
Drafted: Vanderbilt, 2020 (4th round). **Signed by:** J.T. Zink (Marlins).
TRACK RECORD: Eder was a well-regarded lefthander in high school before heading off to Vanderbilt, where he confounded scouts with his inconsistency. The Marlins drafted him in the fourth round in 2020 and opened his pro career at Double-A Pensacola in 2021. Eder was quickly hailed as one of the best southpaws in the minor leagues before an elbow injury required Tommy John surgery, putting him on the shelf until 2023. Sidelined in spring training with a hairline fracture in his left foot, Eder finally got back on the mound at High-A Jupiter for four starts before returning to Pensacola for another six outings. The White Sox acquired Eder at the trade deadline for third baseman Jake Burger, after which he made five starts at Double-A Birmingham. Eder got regular work in instructional league before finishing the year with six appearances in the Arizona Fall League.
SCOUTING REPORT: Eder steps to the mound with two plus pitches to go with control that could get to average as he gets further removed from surgery. In the fall, his four-seam fastball was sitting 93-94 mph and touching 97 with good angle and ride up in the zone. Eder's breaking ball is considered a slider, but it's more of a power slurve and sits 79-83 mph. It has depth when he's on top of it like a power curveball and is more of a slurvy slider when he works around it. His low-80s changeup has the potential to be an average pitch when he gets more consistent with his delivery. Eder was working on better use of his lower half in the AFL, and his stuff is best when his posture is straight up and he's consistent with his three-quarters arm slot.
THE FUTURE: Eder has the ceiling of a No. 3 starter, giving him the chance to have a long major league career if he stays healthy. With a wealth of Double-A experience behind him, he should start 2024 at Triple-A Charlotte and could make it to Chicago sometime during the summer.

Year	Age	Club (League)	Level	W	L	ERA	G	GS	IP	H	HR	BB	SO	BB%	SO%	WHIP	AVG
2023	24	Jupiter (FSL)	A	0	2	4.66	3	3	10	10	0	5	10	10.6	21.3	1.55	.250
2023	24	Pensacola (SL)	AA	2	1	3.94	6	6	30	22	4	16	38	12.9	30.6	1.28	.210
2023	24	Birmingham (SL)	AA	0	3	11.42	5	5	17	27	3	15	22	15.6	22.9	2.42	.360
Minor League Totals				5	11	3.80	29	29	128	102	10	63	169	11.4	30.5	1.29	.214

8 CRISTIAN MENA, RHP

FB: 50. CB: 60. SL: 50. CHG: 50. CTL: 50. BA Grade: 50. Risk: High.

Born: December 21, 2002. **B-T:** R-R. **HT:** 6-2. **WT:** 214.
Signed: Dominican Republic, 2019. **Signed by:** Marino De Leon.

TRACK RECORD: Mena signed with the White Sox in 2019 for $250,000, but because of the pandemic did not make his professional debut in the Rookie-level Arizona League until 2021. He has since moved rapidly through the system, spending most of his age-20 season at Double-A Birmingham in 2023 before moving up to Triple-A Charlotte for four starts. He has struck out more than a batter per inning at every assignment in his career, and his 136 strikeouts ranked fourth in the Southern League in 2023. Mena continued missing bats at Triple-A, indicating his bat-missing stuff was not solely a product of the pre-tacked ball used in the SL in the first half.

SCOUTING REPORT: Mena thrives with a combination of fastball, curveball and slider, with his heater sitting at 92 mph and touching 95 with riding life. He has feel for the pitch and gets swings-and-misses up in the zone. A plus 12-to-6 curveball with gloveside life has been his bread-and-butter pitch—and probably an overused one early in his career—but now complements it with a slider added to his repertoire in 2022. Mena's 80-85 mph curveball has 11-to-5 shape and more depth than his slider. He used his slider more than his curveball in 2023, with the pitch averaging 84 mph and touching 87 with more horizontal movement. He's gone back and forth between his slider being a sweeper and a smaller gyro shape. He needs to be more consistent with the pitch. Mena's average changeup is too hard at 88-90 mph, but he has good feel for it. Mena consistently shows confidence and good mound presence.

THE FUTURE: Mena will return to Triple-A Charlotte in 2024 and could make his major league debut while still just 21 years old. With a complete package of pitches and his desire for continual improvement, he should meet the projection of a No. 4 starter before long.

Year	Age	Club (League)	Level	W	L	ERA	G	GS	IP	H	HR	BB	SO	BB%	SO%	WHIP	AVG
2023	20	Birmingham (SL)	AA	7	6	4.66	23	23	114	99	17	55	136	11.3	27.9	1.35	.234
2023	20	Charlotte (IL)	AAA	1	1	5.95	4	4	20	26	1	9	20	9.8	21.7	1.78	.317
Minor League Totals				11	17	4.97	64	63	286	294	33	123	344	9.8	27.5	1.46	.266

9 JONATHAN CANNON, RHP

FB: 50. CB: 55. SL: 45. CHG: 50. CUT: 55. CTL: 60. BA Grade: 50. Risk: High.

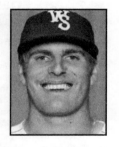

Born: July 19,2000 **B-T:** R-R. **HT:** 6-6. **WT:** 213.
Drafted: Georgia, 2022 (3rd round). **Signed by:** Kevin Burrell.

TRACK RECORD: Cannon generated first-round buzz early in 2021, when he was draft-eligible as a Georgia sophomore, but his stock dropped after he missed time with an illness. He went undrafted after announcing that he would return to school. The White Sox drafted him in the third round in 2022, signing him for $925,000. After throwing just 7.1 innings in his draft year, Cannon reached Double-A in his first full season, showing a full assortment of six pitches.

SCOUTING REPORT: Cannon is a polished pitcher with a high floor. He is a strike-thrower who pounds the zone with a fastball at 93-97 mph. His two-seamer has tail and sink to both sides of the plate, while his four-seamer has ride up in the zone. Cannon complements his fastball with a nasty, bat-breaking cutter right around 90 mph, and he holds his velocity deep into games. Cannon's best secondary offering is an above-average sweeping slider that averages 84 mph and gets up to 87. His average 80-82 mph curveball with 11-to-5 shape has more down action but also some horizontal movement. Cannon gets ground balls and soft contact from his 85-87 mph changeup with good down action. He's a control-over-command pitcher now, with the next step forward to consistently repeat his delivery and command his pitches better. He sometimes gets across his body and has a little stiffness on his front side, spinning off and losing his direction.

THE FUTURE: Cannon will head back to Double-A looking to refine his command and continue to develop his arsenal. He's a big-bodied, durable pitcher who should be a prototype No. 4 or 5 starter who burns innings, though it's not out of the question for Cannon to improve enough to slot into the middle of the rotation.

Year	Age	Club (League)	Level	W	L	ERA	G	GS	IP	H	HR	BB	SO	BB%	SO%	WHIP	AVG
2023	22	Winston-Salem (SAL)	A+	5	2	3.59	14	14	73	65	7	24	67	8.2	22.9	1.22	.246
2023	22	Birmingham (SL)	AA	1	4	5.77	11	11	48	61	8	15	39	6.7	17.3	1.57	.298
Minor League Totals				6	6	4.29	29	28	128	130	15	42	110	7.7	20.3	1.34	.264

10 PEYTON PALLETTE, RHP

FB: 60. **CB:** 50. **CHG:** 50. **CTL:** 45. **BA Grade:** 50. **Risk:** High.

Born: May 9, 2001. **B-T:** R-R. **HT:** 6-1. **WT:** 180.
Drafted: Arkansas, 2022 (2nd round). **Signed by:** Torreon Woods.
TRACK RECORD: Pallette was limited to just 19 games in his three-year college career at Arkansas, missing games first during the pandemic year. He moved to the Razorbacks' rotation in his sophomore year for 15 games before having Tommy John surgery just before the 2022 season. Originally projected as a first-round talent before the elbow injury, Pallette's three-pitch mix and pitch-data profile intrigued teams enough to keep him high on draft boards. The White Sox drafted him in the second round in 2022, signing him for an over-slot $1.5 million. After rehabbing for the entire 2022 season, Pallette got back on the mound in 2023 during spring training before getting a full slate of 22 starts at Low-A Kannapolis, where he posted a 4.13 ERA and struck out 78 in 72 innings.
SCOUTING REPORT: While size and durability concerns raise questions as to whether Pallette can stay in the rotation, he will continue to be developed as a starter because of the way his plus 93-95 mph fastball plays. His heater was up to 99 in college with impressive vertical break, and that velocity could come back the further he moves away from surgery. Pallette uses a four-seamer grip now and will look to add a two-seam sinker in time. He can really spin a 79-81 mph curveball with both 10-to-4 and 11-to-5 shape and a spin rate greater than 3,000 rpm. He's still regaining his feel and consistency for his breaking pitch, as he varies the shape and tends to cast it instead of getting out front and finishing it. Pallette's ultimate role may be determined by the development of a future average changeup that sits 86 mph and touches 88 when it's too firm.
THE FUTURE: Pallette's pair of plus pitches are a sign that he will have significant value either as a starter or reliever. With a strong spring, he could skip High-A and head right to Double-A Birmingham.

Year	Age	Club (League)	Level	W	L	ERA	G	GS	IP	H	HR	BB	SO	BB%	SO%	WHIP	AVG
2023	22	Kannapolis (CAR)	A	0	4	4.13	22	22	72	57	8	41	78	12.8	24.4	1.36	.213
Minor League Totals				0	4	4.13	22	22	72	57	8	41	78	12.8	24.4	1.36	.213

11 KY BUSH, LHP

FB: 50. **CB:** 50. **SL:** 50. **CHG:** 50. **CTL:** 50. **BA Grade:** 45. **Risk:** Medium.

Born: November 12,1999. **B-T:** L-L. **HT:** 6-6. **WT:** 240. **Drafted:** Saint Mary's, 2021 (2nd round).
Signed by: Scott Richardson (Angels).
TRACK RECORD: Bush spent three college seasons at three different schools before being drafted by the Angels in the second round in 2021 after his junior year at Saint Mary's. He signed for an over-slot bonus of $1,747,500. The big lefthander, who had significantly trimmed his body in college, spent just over two seasons in the Angels organization before moving again, this time to the White Sox as part of the return for Lucas Giolito and Reynaldo Lopez at the 2023 trade deadline. Bush was injured for much of the first half of 2023 with a lat strain, and his stuff was flat and inconsistent the rest of the year. He posted a combined 6.91 ERA and allowed a .288 opponent average.
SCOUTING REPORT: Bush delivers an average fastball at 91-96 mph and sits around 93-94 from a high, three-quarters arm slot with a wrist wrap in the back. His heater has tail and run, but he gets in trouble when he falls behind and leaves the ball over the plate. His best secondary pitch is a solid-average low-80s slider that's complemented by a mid-70s curveball that occasionally flashes above-average and an average mid-80s changeup. His stuff is better when he expands the plate, which will come with more consistency. Bush has solid pure stuff, so a season without injury issues may show a better version.
THE FUTURE: A good performance in spring training may allow Bush to break camp with Triple-A Charlotte, but he likely goes back to Double-A to get his feet back on the ground. He's got No. 4 starter potential and with good health he could move quickly in a White Sox system that is undergoing a serious overhaul.

Year	Age	Club (League)	Level	W	L	ERA	G	GS	IP	H	HR	BB	SO	BB%	SO%	WHIP	AVG
2023	23	ACL Angels	Rk	0	1	15.75	2	2	4	10	0	1	9	4.2	37.5	2.75	.435
2023	23	Rocket City (SL)	AA	1	3	5.88	6	6	26	23	6	14	33	12.6	29.7	1.42	.245
2023	23	Birmingham (SL)	AA	3	4	6.70	9	9	42	48	10	22	36	11.6	19.0	1.68	.293
Minor League Totals				11	14	4.98	43	43	187	188	30	71	199	8.8	24.7	1.39	.260

12 GEORGE WOLKOW, OF

HIT: 40. **POW:** 55. **RUN:** 50. **FLD:** 50. **ARM:** 60. **BA Grade:** 50. **Risk:** Extreme.

Born: January 11, 2006. **B-T:** L-R. **HT:** 6-7. **WT:** 239. **Drafted:** HS—Downers Grove, IL, 2023 (7th round). **Signed by:** JJ Lally.

TRACK RECORD: Wolkow ranked as the No. 6 player in the 2024 high school class before announcing in March 2022 that he was reclassifying for 2023. With his size, athleticism and raw power, he was impressive enough during the summer and fall showcase circuits that the White Sox took the local product in the seventh round, the only high school player they drafted in 2023. Wolkow signed for an over-slot bonus of $1 million. Primarily a corner infielder in his high school career, he played exclusively in the outfield during his pro debut in the Rookie-level Arizona Complex League and in the fall instructional league program.

SCOUTING REPORT: With his massive 6-foot-7, 240-pound frame, Wolkow already has plus raw power and could get to a double-plus grade as he matures and begins making more consistent contact. His lefthanded swing works well for his size, and he shows the ability to draw walks, but it comes with high strikeout totals. He struck out 33% of the time in a small pro sample. Wolkow moves surprisingly well for his size and took to the outfield quite well, splitting time between center and right field. He's an average runner now but covers plenty of ground with long, loping strides. He projects best in right field, where his plus arm will be more than enough for the position.

THE FUTURE: Wolkow was just 17 for the entirety of his first pro season, so there's still plenty to dream on. He's mature enough to handle a Low-A assignment in 2024, though a bit more time at the complex to further refine his swing might be best for his development. Because of Wolkow's age, the White Sox can afford to be patient.

Year	Age	Club (League)	Level	AVG	G	AB	R	H	2B	3B	HR	RBI	BB	SO	SB	OBP	SLG
2023	17	ACL White Sox	Rk	.225	13	40	6	9	1	0	1	3	9	17	2	.392	.325
Minor League Totals				.225	13	40	6	9	1	0	1	3	9	17	2	.392	.325

13 SEAN BURKE, RHP

FB: 60. **CB:** 60. **SL:** 50. **CHG:** 50. **CTL:** 40. **BA Grade:** 50. **Risk:** Extreme.

Born: December 18, 1999. **B-T:** R-R. **HT:** 6-6. **WT:** 236. **Drafted:** Maryland, 2021 (3rd round). **Signed by:** John Stott.

TRACK RECORD: The White Sox drafted Burke in the third round in 2021 after his college career at Maryland that was delayed a year due to Tommy John surgery his freshman year. He came off a strong first full season in 2022 during which he jumped three levels. After ending the year in Triple-A, he was considered on the fast track to the big leagues. Instead, his 2023 season was first delayed by shoulder soreness and then ended in mid June with a recurrence of the same problem. He started just nine games at Triple-A Charlotte and had mostly inconsistent results on the mound.

SCOUTING REPORT: When healthy, Burke has a solid four-pitch mix, with both his fastball and curveball as plus offerings. While his velocity on both pitches ticked down in 2023, the White Sox expect him to pitch between 91-98 mph and sit around 95-96 when healthy. He has solid ride up in the zone and gets late tailing life that is effective in all areas of the strike zone. His plus 77-80 mph curveball improved significantly prior to his shoulder issues, with 11-to-5 shape and tight downward break with depth. Burke's average slider is 84-88 mph with two-plane break, and his fading mid-80s changeup is delivered with good arm speed. Prior to 2023, Burke regularly walked around four batters per nine innings, so improved strike-throwing and consistently commanding his pitches will be a key in making the next step.

THE FUTURE: Burke has No. 4 starter upside, assuming he regains his health and previous stuff.

Year	Age	Club (League)	Level	W	L	ERA	G	GS	IP	H	HR	BB	SO	BB%	SO%	WHIP	AVG
2023	23	Charlotte (IL)	AAA	1	4	7.61	9	9	37	36	9	27	34	16.3	20.5	1.72	.265
Minor League Totals				5	15	5.20	43	42	162	154	24	86	196	12.2	27.8	1.49	.256

14 JORDAN LEASURE, RHP

FB: 70. **CB:** 55. **SL:** 55. **CTL:** 50. **BA Grade:** 45. **Risk:** High.

Born: August 15, 1998. **B-T:** R-R. **HT:** 6-3. **WT:** 215. **Drafted:** Tampa, 2021 (14th round). **Signed by:** Wes Sargent (Dodgers).

TRACK RECORD: Despite regularly throwing a mid-90s fastball, Leasure has consistently flown under the radar since being drafted by the Dodgers in the 14th round in 2021 after his five-year career at Division II Tampa. He lost one college season to Tommy John surgery but recovered with no lingering issues. Leasure sat in the low 90s in college, but the Dodgers' pitching development staff helped him add more velocity. Leasure was acquired by the White Sox in the deal that sent Lance Lynn and Joe Kelly to the Dodgers.

SCOUTING REPORT: Leasure now has a double-plus fastball that sits 95-98 mph and touches 100 and is the jewel of his arsenal. He elevates the pitch, and while it's relatively straight, it does have solid life up in the zone. He complements his heater with an above-average hard slider that's just a tick under 90 mph, and he lands it to both sides of the plate. What will help Leasure get to the next level is the recent addition of a curveball that has flashed plus potential and could be a weapon against lefthanded hitters. Leasure works out of the stretch on the third base side of the rubber and maintains rhythm with his three-quarters slot that offers good extension. He's more of a control-over-command profile, and he's shown enough improvement that he could be an above-average strike-thrower.

THE FUTURE: Leasure may get to Chicago at some point in 2024. He's been projected as a mid-leverage reliever, but with the potential for elite swing-and-miss stuff, it's not out of the question to see him closing games.

Year	Age	Club (League)	Level	W	L	ERA	G	GS	IP	H	HR	BB	SO	BB%	SO%	WHIP	AVG
2023	24	Tulsa (TL)	AA	2	2	3.09	29	0	35	21	6	16	56	11.3	39.7	1.06	.169
2023	24	Charlotte (IL)	AAA	0	2	6.08	15	0	13	16	3	8	23	12.3	35.4	1.80	.286
Minor League Totals				5	6	3.76	101	0	117	87	20	51	176	10.4	36.0	1.18	.200

15 TANNER McDOUGAL, RHP

FB: 60. **CB:** 60. **SL:** 50 **CHG:** 45. **CTL:** 45. **BA Grade:** 45. **Risk:** High.

Born: April 3, 2003. **B-T:** R-R. **HT:** 6-5. **WT:** 229. **Drafted:** HS—Las Vegas, 2021 (5th round). **Signed by:** Mike Baker.
TRACK RECORD: In his first year back from Tommy John surgery, McDougal began showing signs of why the White Sox signed the Nevada high school product in 2021 for an over-slot $850,000 bonus. After pitching in just six Rookie-level games in his draft season and then sitting out all of 2022 after surgery, McDougal was back on the mound at Low-A Kannapolis for a full slate of 21 starts in 2023. He struck out 80 batters in 69.1 innings while holding opposing hitters to a .218 average. He finished the year with an assignment to the Arizona Fall League.
SCOUTING REPORT: The arm and stuff are both there, but McDougal needs to become more consistent in all facets of pitching. His fastball averages 95 mph and touches 98-99. His curveball sits in the 79-82 mph range and has plus potential with two-plane break and significant depth and horizontal movement. McDougal's third pitch is a hard changeup in the 88-90 mph range. He started working with a slider late in the 2023 season and will continue developing that fourth pitch when spring training rolls around. The White Sox staff worked with him to smooth out his mechanics during his rehab period. His delivery became much quieter and his head held a better line. He still has some issues repeating his arm slot and release point, which could inhibit his control.
THE FUTURE: McDougal has worked hard since joining the organization, including adding more than 40 pounds. He's got a high ceiling but with plenty of development ahead. He'll move up one level to High-A Winston-Salem in 2024, where he could spend the entire season.

Year	Age	Club (League)	Level	W	L	ERA	G	GS	IP	H	HR	BB	SO	BB%	SO%	WHIP	AVG
2023	20	Kannapolis (CAR)	A	0	3	4.15	21	21	69	54	5	43	80	14.3	26.7	1.40	.218
Minor League Totals				1	5	4.78	27	25	79	64	7	48	97	14.0	28.4	1.42	.225

16 WILFRED VERAS, OF

HIT: 50. **POW:** 60. **RUN:** 40. **FLD:** 40. **ARM:** 50. **BA Grade:** 45. **Risk:** High.

Born: November 15, 2002. **B-T:** R-R. **HT:** 6-2. **WT:** 231. **Signed:** Dominican Republic, 2019. **Signed by:** Ruddy Moreta.
TRACK RECORD: Veras has baseball bloodlines as the son of former big leaguer Wilton Veras and nephew of Fernando Tatis Sr. He made it to Double-A Birmingham in 2023 while still just 20 years old and performed well there, with a batting line of .309/.346/.533. He combined for 17 home runs between High-A and Double-A. Veras has gotten considerably bigger since starting pro ball, with around 50 pounds of added weight since signing.
SCOUTING REPORT: It's all about the bat for Veras because he doesn't provide a lot of defensive value. With the hard work he's been putting into his game, he could become an above-average hitter with plus power at the absolute high end. Veras can hit to all fields with an aggressive approach. He handles breaking balls well but struggles at times with premium velocity. His plans at the plate need to improve because he chases balls out of the zone too frequently. Originally a corner infielder, Veras moved to the outfield during 2022 instructional league, and he primarily played right field in 2023. He's a below-average defender, and flashes an average arm when he is able to get through his throws. A below-average runner, Veras can get down the line well for his size and can go first to third well enough.
THE FUTURE: Improving his defense will be the key to Veras' ultimate role, whether it's left field, first base or DH, with his work ethic giving him a chance to stay in the outfield. He'll need to show that he

can consistently handle velocity to tap into his power at higher levels. Having just turned 21, a return to Double-A is the likely starting point in 2024.

Year	Age	Club (League)	Level	AVG	G	AB	R	H	2B	3B	HR	RBI	BB	SO	SB	OBP	SLG
2023	20	Winston-Salem (SAL)	A+	.277	92	372	52	103	25	1	11	63	20	101	18	.316	.438
2023	20	Birmingham (SL)	AA	.309	38	152	23	47	14	1	6	30	8	44	6	.346	.533
Minor League Totals				.283	289	1115	163	316	77	6	41	191	79	319	32	.335	.474

17 GRANT TAYLOR, RHP

FB: 60. **CB:** 55. **SL:** 50. **CUT:** 50. **CTL:** 40. **BA Grade:** 50. **Risk:** Extreme.

Born: May 20, 2002. **B-T:** R-R. **HT:** 6-3. **WT:** 230. **Drafted:** Louisiana State, 2023 (2nd round).
Signed by: Warren Hughes.

TRACK RECORD: Taylor began his college career at Louisiana State in 2022 as a 19-year-old freshman. He showed loud pure stuff but walked 6.1 batters per nine innings and posted a 5.81 ERA working mostly out of the bullpen. His stock went up in the 2022 Cape Cod League, where he was named the top pitching prospect in the league after fanning 30 batters in 21 innings while walking just two. Taylor continued to impress as a starter during LSU's fall ball season but didn't take the mound in 2023 because of an elbow injury that resulted in Tommy John surgery. The stuff that Taylor showed on the Cape and in the fall of his sophomore year was enough to get him ranked highly on draft boards, and the White Sox took him in the second round and signed him for $1,659,800. Taylor spent his first pro summer rehabbing at the White Sox's complex in Glendale, Ariz.

SCOUTING REPORT: Prior to his injury, Taylor threw a plus fastball in the 93-95 mph range and touched 98-99 with plus riding life. His go-to secondary is an upper-70s curveball with 12-to-6 shape and tons of spin in the 2,700-2,800 rpm range, but he'll also mix in a mid-80s slider and low-90s cutter. Taylor has high spin rates across the board with all pitches. He seldom threw a changeup, an area for development once he's back on the mound.

THE FUTURE: Taylor will start throwing early in 2024 and could get into games by midseason. He had reliever risk even before his injury but will be developed as a starter to begin his pro career.

Year	Age	Club (League)	Level	W	L	ERA	G	GS	IP	H	HR	BB	SO	BB%	SO%	WHIP	AVG
2023	21	Did not play—Injured															

18 SETH KEENER, RHP

FB: 55. **SL:** 55. **CHG:** 50. **CTL:** 50. **BA Grade:** 45. **Risk:** High.

Born: October 4, 2001. **B-T:** R-R. **HT:** 6-2. **WT:** 195. **Drafted:** Wake Forest, 2023 (3rd round). **Signed by:** John Stott.

TRACK RECORD: Keener spent three seasons at Wake Forest, where he pitched mostly out of the bullpen before breaking out in the 2022 Cape Cod League and then during his junior year in 2023. With the deep pitching staff at Wake Forest, Keener got just eight starts in 23 games in his final college season. He posted a 2.69 ERA with 94 strikeouts and 20 walks in 70.1 innings. The White Sox grabbed him in the third round in 2023, signing him for $800,000, and he began his pro career with four games at Rookie-level Arizona Complex League followed by three starts at Low-A Kannapolis.

SCOUTING REPORT: Keener has a three-pitch mix with a fastball that sits 93-94 mph and has been up to 97 with above-average life. His primary pitch is an above-average mid-80s slider that he used around 40% of the time in his final season at Wake Forest. His slider has sharp, two-plane break and gets lots of chases out of the zone, though he also can land it for strikes at a high clip. On top of the fastball/slider combination, Keener uses a firm, upper-80s changeup that also gets swings and misses.

THE FUTURE: Keener's athleticism, control, three-pitch mix and projectable frame indicate that he can make it as a starter. With his college experience, he could jump right to High-A Winston-Salem out of spring training in 2024. He'll continue his professional career as a starter, with a move to the bullpen always a possibility in the future.

Year	Age	Club (League)	Level	W	L	ERA	G	GS	IP	H	HR	BB	SO	BB%	SO%	WHIP	AVG
2023	21	ACL White Sox	Rk	1	0	1.50	4	2	6	2	0	2	7	9.1	31.8	0.67	.100
2023	21	Kannapolis (CAR)	A	0	1	7.11	3	3	6	9	1	2	7	6.7	23.3	1.74	.321
Minor League Totals				1	1	4.50	7	5	12	11	1	4	14	7.7	26.9	1.25	.229

19 RYAN BURROWES, SS

HIT: 45. **POW:** 40. **RUN:** 60. **FLD:** 50. **ARM:** 55. **BA Grade:** 45. **Risk:** High.

Born: August 17, 2004. **B-T:** R-R. **HT:** 6-3. **WT:** 170. **Signed:** Panama, 2022.
Signed by: Marco Paddy/Ricardo Ortiz/Ruddy Moreta.
TRACK RECORD: A native of Panama who signed with the White Sox for just $75,000 in 2022, Burrowes started his career that same year in the Dominican Summer League. He made his U.S. debut in 2023 in the Rookie-level Arizona Complex League with a batting line of .259/.330/.386. He brings natural athleticism and a complete kit of five tools to the field and projects to stick at shortstop.
SCOUTING REPORT: Burrowes has decent bat-to-ball skills and the ability to use all fields, with a blend of batting average and power as he adds strength to his wiry frame and gains more experience. He stays upright at the plate with a balanced swing and minimal movement and has both strong hands and solid bat speed. Using a leg kick, Burrowes stays through the ball and avoids over-swinging but needs to make more contact to cut down on strikeouts and put more balls in play. In 2023 he spent most of his time at shortstop where he's at least an average defender with strong actions and above-average arm strength. He has the ability to make throws on the move. He could easily handle both second and third base in a utility role. A plus runner, Burrowes has stolen 12 bases in each of his two short-season campaigns, with impressive instincts on the bases.
THE FUTURE: Even though he'll be just 19 for most of the next season, Burrowes could break camp with the Low-A Kannapolis squad. The fact that he's bilingual will help him settle in outside the Rookie complex environment.

Year	Age	Club (League)	Level	AVG	G	AB	R	H	2B	3B	HR	RBI	BB	SO	SB	OBP	SLG
2023	18	ACL White Sox	Rk	.259	43	158	24	41	8	3	2	15	12	51	12	.330	.386
Minor League Totals				.263	90	316	62	83	17	4	5	33	37	85	24	.363	.389

20 JACOB BURKE, OF

HIT: 45. **POW:** 40. **RUN:** 55. **FLD:** 55. **ARM:** 50. **BA Grade:** 45. **Risk:** High.

Born: February 26, 2001. **B-T:** R-R. **HT:** 6-1. **WT:** 208. **Drafted:** Miami, 2022 (11th round). **Signed by:** Abe Fernandez.
TRACK RECORD: Burke completed his college career in 2022 with one season at Miami after two years at Southeastern Louisiana. He had an outstanding season with the Hurricanes and hit .347/.425/.599 while earning second-team all-Atlantic Coast Conference honors. A football player in high school, Burke consistently plays hard and has drawn comparisons with former White Sox outfielder Adam Engel. Burke was drafted in the 11th round in 2022 and signed for $225,000. His 2023 season was delayed by lower back inflammation. He made it to Low-A Kannapolis on May 11, where he posted an outstanding batting line of .315/.416/.512 and continued to hit after a promotion to High-A Winston-Salem. He finished the year with an assignment to the Arizona Fall League.
SCOUTING REPORT: Burke has an aggressive approach at the plate, with a little wrap to his load, good timing and above-average bat speed. He grades as a tick below-average hitter with below-average power but is able to strike line drives to the gaps. But he has also shown a tendency to roll over on the ball when he doesn't get the bat head out in front. Burke is an above-average defender and has above-average speed and has mostly played center field. His average arm will allow him to play both left and right field. Burke plays the game hard and regularly demonstrates intentional pre-game work.
THE FUTURE: Double-A Birmingham is Burke's likely destination in 2024. He is the kind of player that every manager wants on his team, and could become a solid fourth outfielder.

Year	Age	Club (League)	Level	AVG	G	AB	R	H	2B	3B	HR	RBI	BB	SO	SB	OBP	SLG
2023	22	Kannapolis (CAR)	A	.315	35	127	23	40	11	1	4	22	15	33	9	.416	.512
2023	22	Winston-Salem (SAL)	A+	.281	50	203	40	57	13	2	2	18	21	52	10	.377	.394
Minor League Totals				.289	115	436	80	126	32	4	8	54	48	113	24	.394	.436

21 TERRELL TATUM, OF

HIT: 45. **POW:** 45. **RUN:** 60. **FLD:** 55. **ARM:** 45. **BA Grade:** 45. **Risk:** High.

Born: July 27, 1999. **B-T:** L-L. **HT:** 6-0. **WT:** 172. **Drafted:** North Carolina State, 2021 (16th round).
Signed by: John Stott.
TRACK RECORD: An unheralded prospect who wasn't a regular until his senior season at North Carolina State, Tatum had tools and athleticism that intrigued the White Sox. Chicago drafted the lefthanded-hitting outfielder in the 16th round in 2021. After a hot start at High-A Winston-Salem in 2023, Tatum cooled off after moving up to Double-A Birmingham.
SCOUTING REPORT: Tatum's speed and defense stand out most. He projects as a fringe-average hitter

with fringe-average raw power. Using a short stroke with above-average bat speed, Tatum does a nice job hitting the ball back up the middle, but he gets in trouble when he tries to sell out for power. A late bloomer who turned 24 one month after being promoted to Double-A, Tatum has added strength and shows good doubles power from a flatter hitting plane. He's a selective hitter—he drew 100 walks in 2023 to rank eighth among all minor league hitters—but he struck out too often at 27%. A plus runner, Tatum stole a combined 47 bases in 2023, and his on-base skills will continue to give him opportunities to swipe bags. In addition to using his wheels on the basepaths, Tatum is an above-average defender in center field with a fringe-average arm.

THE FUTURE: It's tempting to slap a fourth outfielder label on Tatum, but he could turn into more than that as a late bloomer with some exciting tools and somewhat limited baseball experience for his age. If he can make more consistent contact, he could be a starter on a second-division team.

Year	Age	Club (League)	Level	AVG	G	AB	R	H	2B	3B	HR	RBI	BB	SO	SB	OBP	SLG
2023	23	Winston-Salem (SAL)	A+	.268	60	209	54	56	14	3	4	29	58	69	32	.434	.421
2023	23	Birmingham (SL)	AA	.230	65	222	35	51	9	2	2	22	42	80	15	.361	.315
Minor League Totals				.253	193	644	132	163	40	6	10	84	156	232	70	.404	.380

22 JAVIER MOGOLLON, 2B
HIT: 55. **POW:** 50. **RUN:** 55. **FLD:** 50. **ARM:** 60. **BA Grade:** 50. **Risk:** Extreme.

Born: November 1, 2005. **B-T:** R-R. **HT:** 5-8. **WT:** 160. **Signed:** Venezuela, 2023.
Signed by: Reydel Hernandez/Amador Arias/Ruddy Moreta.
TRACK RECORD: Signed for $75,000 in January 2023, Mogollon quickly jumped to the head of the class among that year's White Sox international class. The native Venezuelan had an outstanding professional debut in the Dominican Summer League by hitting .315/.417/.582. His 10 home runs in 165 at-bats were tops in the league for 17-year-old players.
SCOUTING REPORT: Mogollon is a quick-twitch athlete with a short, muscular build. He gets low in the box with a wide stance and uses a simple, compact swing with no stride. He showed solid contact skills and above-average plate discipline. Despite his size, Mogollon has above-average raw power and registered above-average exit velocity numbers for his age group in his first season. He has a knack for optimizing his hard contact to his pull side at launch angles where they do the most damage. An average defender, Mogollon is better at second base and is more comfortable there, but he has the softness of hands and enough arm to play shortstop if his defense improves. He's a plus runner who stole 11 bases in 13 attempts, but he could slow down as his body continues to mature.
THE FUTURE: Mogollon will make his U.S. debut in 2024, first in extended spring training followed by a season in the Rookie-level Arizona Complex League. He will headline a potentially impressive crop of international newcomers on that team.

Year	Age	Club (League)	Level	AVG	G	AB	R	H	2B	3B	HR	RBI	BB	SO	SB	OBP	SLG
2023	17	DSL White Sox	Rk	.315	47	165	41	52	10	2	10	42	27	28	11	.417	.582
Minor League Totals				.315	47	165	41	52	10	2	10	42	27	28	11	.417	.582

23 JOSE RODRIGUEZ, SS
HIT: 40. **POW:** 45. **RUN:** 50. **FLD:** 45. **ARM:** 45. **BA Grade:** 45. **Risk:** High.

Born: May 13, 2001. **B-T:** R-R. **HT:** 5-11. **WT:** 196. **Signed:** Dominican Republic, 2018. **Signed by:** Ruddy Moreta.
TRACK RECORD: Rodriguez signed with the White Sox for $50,000 in 2018. He spent his second season at Double-A Birmingham in 2023 with nearly identical numbers to his 2022 output. He got into 19 games late in the season at Triple-A Charlotte and saw his first major league time in June as an emergency replacement when he appeared in one game as a pinch-runner and defensive replacement. The most notable development for Rodriguez was a significantly improved chase rate.
SCOUTING REPORT: Rodriguez has a contact-oriented swing but doesn't make a lot of impact with the bat. His lower chase rate was related more to his mentality and approach at the plate and was unrelated to any mechanical swing changes. Rodriguez's swing is simple and low maintenance, and he uses quick hands to drive the ball to all fields with fringe-average, gap-to-gap power. Defensively, Rodriguez should be able to stay on the middle infield. While not a burner, he has a quick first step, a good internal clock and average arm strength and range. With just average hands and arm, he profiles better at second base, and his defense could tick up if he's focusing on only one position. Rodriguez has been good for 30-40 stolen bases per year, supplementing his average speed with good baserunning instincts.
THE FUTURE: At this point in his career, Rodriguez looks more like a future utility infielder or a second-division regular at second base. He'll likely head back to Charlotte for the 2024 season.

Year	Age	Club (League)	Level	AVG	G	AB	R	H	2B	3B	HR	RBI	BB	SO	SB	OBP	SLG
2023	22	Birmingham (SL)	AA	.264	87	382	63	101	17	0	18	54	18	95	28	.297	.450
2023	22	Charlotte (IL)	AAA	.253	19	87	11	22	2	0	3	8	2	13	3	.270	.379
2023	22	Chicago (AL)	MLB	.000	1	0	1	0	0	0	0	0	0	0	0	.000	.000
Minor League Totals				.283	425	1793	287	508	87	17	57	235	102	320	124	.323	.446
Major League Totals				.000	1	0	1	0	0	0	0	0	0	0	0	.000	.000

24 MATHIAS LaCOMBE, RHP

FB: 60. **SL:** 50. **CHG:** 50. **CTL:** 50. **BA Grade:** 50/Extreme

Born: June 12, 2002. **B-T:** R-R. **HT:** 6-2. **WT:** 185. **Drafted:** Cochise (AZ) JC, 2023 (12th round).
Signed by: John Kazanas.
TRACK RECORD: Cochise (Ariz.) JC is located in southern Arizona, just 20 miles north of the border with Mexico. It's about the same distance from the Wild West town of Tombstone, an unlikely location for a group of French natives to show up to play junior college baseball. One of those transplants was LaCombe, who started to attract attention in his second season at Cochise when he posted a 1.74 ERA and a strikeout-to-walk ratio of 97-to-14 in 67.1 innings. A bullpen session for scouts who were in the Phoenix area for the Pacific-12 Conference Tournament generated interest. LaCombe was up to 96 mph that day, and the White Sox drafted him in the 12th round and signed him for $450,000. He didn't pitch in games during the summer but logged a couple brief one-inning starts at instructional league in the fall.
SCOUTING REPORT: LaCombe throws a plus sinker that sits 90-92 mph in longer outings, touches 97, and sits in the mid 90s in shorter stints. His fastball has more run than sink, with plus movement and plus velocity. He has average secondary pitches, including a slider in the low-to-mid 80s, and a split-changeup in the low 80s. Both could become above-average offerings with more development. More velocity could be coming with LaCombe's lean 6-foot-2 frame likely to add strength. Better utilization of his lower half in his delivery could also help.
THE FUTURE: LaCombe will turn 22 in June, and while it's likely he will start the 2024 season in extended spring training, it's not out of the question that he could hit Low-A Kannapolis by his birthday.

Year	Age	Club (League)	Level	W	L	ERA	G	GS	IP	H	HR	BB	SO	BB%	SO%	WHIP	AVG
2023	21	Did not play															

25 SHANE DROHAN, LHP

FB: 45. **CB:** 50. **CHG:** 55. **CUT:** 45. **CTL:** 45. **BA Grade:** 40. **Risk:** Medium.

Born: January 7, 1999. **B-T:** L-L. **HT:** 6-3. **WT:** 191. **Drafted:** Florida State, 2020 (4th round).
Signed by: Dante Ricciardi (Red Sox).
TRACK RECORD: Drohan entered Florida State relatively inexperienced thanks to a high school career that also included two seasons of football. He was athletic and had room to project more strength, leading the Red Sox to draft him in the fourth round in 2020. His stock jumped in 2023 after he added a cutter in the offseason, and he reached Triple-A Worcester early in the season. Drohan struggled with the automated ball-strike system in use in the International League, and his stuff ticked down as the season continued. The White Sox selected him in the Rule 5 draft.
SCOUTING REPORT: Drohan has steadily developed his repertoire in pro ball, starting as a fastball/curveball pitcher in 2021 before developing an above-average changeup in 2022 and adding a cutter in 2023 that helped him attack both sides of the plate. He also gained strength with the help of a diet that included two steaks per day, and the result was more velocity across the board and a more repeatable delivery. Faced with the ABS strike zone in Worcester, Drohan nibbled and saw his walk rate soar from 7% in Double-A to 15% in Triple-A, and International League hitters crushed him—especially his fastball and cutter—for 1.9 homers per nine innings.
THE FUTURE: Drohan will get a chance to stick on the White Sox's roster, perhaps as a swingman or a No. 5 starter.

Year	Age	Club (League)	Level	W	L	ERA	G	GS	IP	H	HR	BB	SO	BB%	SO%	WHIP	AVG
2023	24	Portland (EL)	AA	5	0	1.32	6	6	34	19	1	9	36	7.0	28.1	0.82	.161
2023	24	Worcester (IL)	AAA	5	7	6.47	21	19	89	103	19	63	93	14.9	21.9	1.87	.293
Minor League Totals				24	19	4.33	77	73	341	315	43	168	372	11.3	25.0	1.42	.243

26 BRADEN SHEWMAKE, SS

HIT: 40. **POW:** 40. **RUN:** 55. **FLD:** 50. **ARM:** 55. **BA Grade:** 40. **Risk:** Medium.

Born: November 19, 1997. **B-T:** L-R. **HT:** 6-3. **WT:** 190. **Drafted:** Texas A&M, 2019 (1st round).
Signed by: Darin Vaughan (Braves).

TRACK RECORD: Shewmake was a standout performer in his three years at Texas A&M. He signed a $3 million bonus as Atlanta's second first-round pick in 2019 and was moved aggressively by the Braves in pro ball. He made it to Double-A in his first pro season, but his bat has not developed. He played the last two seasons at Triple-A Gwinnett with almost identical results. He got his first taste of the big leagues when called up in May 2023 as an injury replacement and played in just two games. Shewmake was included with four other players in a November 2023 trade to the White Sox for lefty reliever Aaron Bummer.

SCOUTING REPORT: Shewmake flashes solid bat-to-ball skills but makes weak contact. He hasn't added strength to his lean body and struggles to do damage on higher-velocity pitches. He frequently expanded the zone and chased in 2023. His infield flyball rate has risen in each of the last three seasons, with a shockingly high 25% mark in 2023. That is the result of a flat bat path and a tendency to drop his hands in his load. Shewmake has been a solid-average defender at shortstop with good instincts and hands to go with an above-average arm. His defense has been inconsistent and he split time between shortstop and second base.

THE FUTURE: If the White Sox can coax just a marginal amount of improvement from Shewmake's bat, he'll have a career as at least a utility infielder capable of playing all non-first base positions.

Year	Age	Club (League)	Level	AVG	G	AB	R	H	2B	3B	HR	RBI	BB	SO	SB	OBP	SLG
2023	25	Gwinnett (IL)	AAA	.234	122	474	79	111	28	3	16	69	39	104	27	.298	.407
2023	25	Atlanta (NL)	MLB	.000	2	4	0	0	0	0	0	0	0	1	0	.000	.000
Minor League Totals				.250	346	1323	200	331	74	10	38	174	104	276	53	.309	.407
Major League Totals				.000	2	4	0	0	0	0	0	0	0	1	0	.000	.000

27 MATTHEW THOMPSON, RHP

FB: 55. **CB:** 55. **SL:** 45. **CHG:** 45. **CTL:** 45. **BA Grade:** 45. **Risk:** High.

Born: August 11, 2000. **B-T:** R-R. **HT:** 6-3. **WT:** 215. **Drafted:** HS—Cypress, TX, 2019 (2nd round).
Signed by: Chris Walker.

TRACK RECORD: The White Sox drafted Thompson in the second round in 2019 after a notable high school career, despite some struggles during his senior year, and signed the Texas product to an over-slot bonus of $2.1 million. Four years later, he remains an enigma who flashes the potential for plus stuff but with frustrating inconsistency. Thompson spent all of 2023 at Double-A Birmingham with mixed results, the most glaring being a jump in his walk rate from 3.3 per nine innings in 2022 to 6.15 in 2023.

SCOUTING REPORT: Thompson's above-average fastball flashes plus when he's on time and throwing the pitch for strikes. It's a 91-95 mph pitch and touches 97 with tailing life. His best secondary pitch is the power curveball with 1-to-7 shape. It could be above-average or plus with more consistency. He throws his curveball in the 78-81 mph range with good biting action. Thompson's hard slider/cutter is a relatively new addition. He throws it in the 84-87 mph range and in 2024 he'll look to make it a distinct slider or cutter. He used his 85-87 mph changeup more often in 2023 but needs to get more confidence in the pitch. Many of Thompson's issues stem from the effort in his delivery. He's a short strider and spins off in his finish.

THE FUTURE: Thompson was not added to the 40-man roster and was Rule 5 eligible. He went unselected and should spend more time in Double-A during a 2024 season in which he will still be 23 years old.

Year	Age	Club (League)	Level	W	L	ERA	G	GS	IP	H	HR	BB	SO	BB%	SO%	WHIP	AVG
2023	22	Birmingham (SL)	AA	6	15	4.85	27	27	124	110	15	85	136	15.0	23.9	1.57	.232
Minor League Totals				12	31	5.10	74	74	310	306	39	163	320	11.8	23.2	1.52	.258

28 CHRISTIAN OPPOR, LHP

FB: 55. **SL:** 55. **CHG:** 45. **CTL:** 50. **BA Grade:** 45. **Risk:** High.

Born: July 23, 2004. **B-T:** L-L. **HT:** 6-2. **WT:** 175. **Drafted:** Gulf Coast State (FL) JC, 2023 (5th round).
Signed by: Warren Hughes.

TRACK RECORD: Oppor was drafted from his Wisconsin high school by the Athletics in the 11th round in 2022, but the lanky southpaw instead headed south to Florida for a season of junior college ball at Gulf Coast State JC. He was offered $225,000 by the A's as a draft-and-follow but instead decided to go back into the 2023 draft. That proved to be a smart move when the White Sox took him in the fifth round and signed him for a $550,000 bonus. Oppor got into just five games in the Rookie-level Arizona Complex League before pitching in instructional league.

SCOUTING REPORT: With a high-waisted, loose athletic frame, Oppor throws an above-average fastball in the 90-94 mph range, but he has touched the upper 90s in bullpen sessions. His breaking ball is more of a hybrid and is thrown like a slider at 80-82 mph with good horizontal shape and sweep finish. He rarely uses his 81-84 mph changeup, but a key goal in his development moving forward is improving his feel of the offering to give him a complete three-pitch mix.

THE FUTURE: Oppor is still a work in progress with exciting projection remaining as he adds strength to what is currently an extremely lean frame. Whether he eventually becomes a bullpen arm is to be determined. He'll get to Low-A Kannapolis some time in 2024 but may begin in extended spring training.

Year	Age	Club (League)	Level	W	L	ERA	G	GS	IP	H	HR	BB	SO	BB%	SO%	WHIP	AVG
2023	18	ACL White Sox	Rk	0	0	1.17	5	1	8	6	0	2	9	6.7	30.0	1.04	.222
Minor League Totals				0	0	1.29	5	1	8	6	0	2	9	6.7	30.0	1.14	.222

29 JUAN CARELA, RHP

FB: 50. **CB:** 50. **SL:** 55. **CHG:** 55. **CUT:** 50. **CTL:** 55. **BA Grade:** 40. **Risk:** Medium.

Born: December 15, 2001. **B-T:** R-R. **HT:** 6-3. **WT:** 186. **Signed:** Dominican Republic, 2018.
Signed by: Jose Sabino (Yankees).

TRACK RECORD: Carela was acquired by the White Sox in the deal that sent reliever Keynan Middleton to the Yankees. Signed in 2018, he was one of the Yankees' intriguing young arms at the lower levels. He teased his potential in 2021 and looked excellent in the early portion of 2023 after the Yankees' pitching department tinkered with the grip on Carela's slider to help shape it into a shorter, tighter offering. He turned in a strong 2023 season at the High-A affiliates of both organizations, with a combined 3.58 ERA, .214 opponent average and a strong strikeout rate of 10.6 per nine innings.

SCOUTING REPORT: Carela has an array of pitches that all grade as average or better, starting with a 91-95 mph fastball with two-seam run. His slider flashes above-average potential at 82-85 mph with short break and tilt that he can land for strikes. Or he can add sweeping action to it for chases down away against righthanded hitters. Carela pairs the slider with a cutter at 88-90 mph with short, late action, and it's effective when he gets it in on the hands of lefthanded batters. He rounds out his arsenal with a potential above-average circle-changeup at 86-87 mph and an average curveball at 77-79 mph.

THE FUTURE: Carela projects as a bullpen arm, but with added strength he could fit into the back of a rotation. After his 2023 season at High-A, he'll head to Double-A Birmingham in 2024.

Year	Age	Club (League)	Level	W	L	ERA	G	GS	IP	H	HR	BB	SO	BB%	SO%	WHIP	AVG
2023	21	Hudson Valley (SAL)	A+	2	4	3.67	17	16	83	65	7	32	109	9.1	31.1	1.16	.214
2023	21	Winston-Salem (SAL)	A+	1	3	3.34	6	6	32	30	5	11	27	8.1	19.9	1.27	.244
Minor League Totals				13	23	4.64	70	62	297	250	25	147	346	11.2	26.3	1.34	.227

30 TYLER SCHWEITZER, LHP

FB: 50. **CB:** 50. **SL:** 50. **CHG:** 50. **CTL:** 55. **BA Grade:** 45. **Risk:** High.

Born: September 19, 2000. **B-T:** L-L. **HT:** 6-0. **WT:** 185. **Drafted:** Ball State, 2022 (5th round).
Signed by: Justin Wechsler.

TRACK RECORD: Schweitzer was the Mid-American Conference pitcher of the year in his final season at Ball State. The White Sox drafted him in the fifth round in 2022 and signed him for $325,000. Working strictly on his throwing program after reporting to Chicago's minor league complex after the draft, the crafty southpaw pitched in 23 games in 2023 split between Low-A Kannapolis and High-A Winston-Salem, with a combined 3.94 ERA and 121 strikeouts in 107.1 innings.

SCOUTING REPORT: Schweitzer takes the mound with a solid four-pitch mix that grades as average across the board. He commands his low-90s fastball and will occasionally get it into the mid 90s, with good life up in the zone and plenty of spin. His breaking pitches—a slider in the low 80s and a curveball in the mid-to-upper 70s—previously blended too much, but he did a better job of differentiating the two pitches in 2023. He rounds out his arsenal with an average changeup at 82 mph, and he's been working on getting more separation between his curveball and changeup. Scheweitzer has above-average pitchability and feel for throwing strikes and is described as having moxie when he's on the mound.

THE FUTURE: Projected as a potential back-of-the-rotation starter, Schweitzer will get to Double-A at some point in 2024. His stuff isn't flashy, but he gets the job done with his mostly average stuff.

Year	Age	Club (League)	Level	W	L	ERA	G	GS	IP	H	HR	BB	SO	BB%	SO%	WHIP	AVG
2023	22	Kannapolis (CAR)	A	7	2	3.86	13	13	68	62	5	21	76	7.3	26.5	1.23	.234
2023	22	Winston-Salem (SAL)	A+	0	2	4.08	10	9	40	32	5	24	45	13.6	25.6	1.41	.215
Minor League Totals				7	4	3.95	23	22	107	94	10	45	121	9.7	26.1	1.30	.227

Elly De La Cruz electrified with his power and speed.

DYLAN BUELL/GETTY IMAGES

Cincinnati Reds

BY J.J. COOPER

What a difference 18 months makes.

Even as Elly De La Cruz, Hunter Greene, Nick Lodolo and others climbed through the minor leagues for the Reds in 2021 and 2022, there was a realistic fear that it couldn't and wouldn't be enough.

As Jose Barrero's struggles have shown, prospects sometimes fall short of expectations. Sometimes they get hurt. And it's hard to completely turn over a lineup and rotation to rookies and youngsters.

But general manager Nick Krall and the Reds have managed to pull off that tightrope act over the past two years. If any one aspect of the rebuild had failed, Cincinnati could still be a 75-win team. Instead, they head into 2024 with one of the more promising young rosters in baseball on the heels of an 82-win season.

To pull off a complete rebuild requires talent, an organization that has a unified vision and a little bit of luck. When the Reds traded veterans Luis Castillo, Eugenio Suarez, Jesse Winker and Tyler Mahle, they managed to hit on most of the prospect returns. Spencer Steer, Jake Fraley, Christian Encarnacion-Strand and Noelvi Marte were all part of the Reds' lineup down the stretch, while lefthander Brandon Williamson has developed into a solid member of the rotation.

They successfully found value in more modest deals as well. Outfielder Will Benson looked lost for much of his time in the Guardians' farm system. The Reds quickly turned him into a productive big league outfielder.

The development of international signings like De La Cruz and draftees like Matt McLain transformed the Reds into one of the most athletic lineups in the National League, but the team also saw three nondrafted free agents play in Cincinnati in 2023 with outfielder T.J. Friedl leading the way.

Cincinnati revamped its pitching development a few years ago as well. The payoff has included Greene, Graham Ashcraft, Andrew Abbott and

PROJECTED 2027 LINEUP

Catcher	Tyler Stephenson	30
First Base	Christian Encarnacion-Strand	27
Second Base	Matt McLain	27
Third Base	Jonathan India	30
Shortstop	Elly De La Cruz	25
Left Field	Spencer Steer	29
Center Field	Carlos Jorge	23
Right Field	Noelvi Marte	25
Designated Hitter	Sal Stewart	23
No. 1 Starter	Hunter Greene	27
No. 2 Starter	Nick Lodolo	29
No. 3 Starter	Rhett Lowder	25
No. 4 Starter	Andrew Abbott	28
No. 5 Starter	Chase Petty	24
Closer	Connor Phillips	

Lodolo joining the rotation, while Alexis Diaz anchored the bullpen.

Getting from 82 wins to winning a playoff game—something the Reds haven't done since 2012—or a playoff series, which they last accomplished in 1995, will require the Reds to continue to have many more hits than misses.

The 2023 draft gave the Reds a chance to stock up further, thanks to five picks in the top 105 selections. And a lucky set of ping pong balls provided an unexpected bounty for 2024. Despite having tiny odds of landing a lottery pick, Cincinnati wound up with the No. 2 overall pick.

The resulting bonus pool will give the Reds another chance to add depth to a system that remains deep, even if its top-end talent is thinned by the recent graduations of the core of the current big league club.

It will also provide the talent to swing trades. The Reds are currently overstocked with infielders and could use help at the back of the rotation, in the bullpen and in the outfield. Knowing that the 2024 draft can provide reinforcements should help the Reds' front office feel comfortable being more aggressive acquiring big league talent on the trade market.

Cincinnati managed to pick the right prospects when trading away big league talent. Now, they need to see if they can reverse the script. ∎

DEPTH CHART

CINCINNATI REDS

TOP 2024 CONTRIBUTORS   **RANK**
1. Noelvi Marte, 3B   1
2. Connor Phillips, RHP   3

BREAKOUT PROSPECTS   **RANK**
1. Blake Dunn, OF   13
2. Hunter Hollan, LHP   28

SOURCE OF TOP 30 TALENT

Homegrown	24	Acquired	6
College	7	Trade	6
Junior college	2	Rule 5 draft	0
High school	7	Independent league	0
Nondrafted free agent	2	Free agent/waivers	0
International	6		

LF
Blake Dunn (13)
Hector Rodriguez (19)
Jay Allen

CF
Jacob Hurtubise (22)
Sheng-En Lin (27)
TJ Hopkins
Justice Thompson

RF
Rece Hinds (20)
Ariel Almonte (25)
Esmith Pineda

3B
Noelvi Marte (1)
Cam Collier (10)
Ricardo Cabrera (12)
Carlos Sanchez

SS
Edwin Arroyo (4)
Leo Balcazar (8)
Sammy Stafura (15)
Victor Acosta (18)

2B
Carlos Jorge (6)
Tyler Callihan (29)

1B
Sal Stewart (7)
Jack Moss
Ruben Ibarra

C
Alfredo Duno (9)
Connor Burns (30)
Logan Tanner
Daniel Vellojin
Cade Hunter

LHP

LHSP	LHRP
Hunter Hollan (28)	Adam Serwinowski (24)
	Jacob Heatherly
	Bryce Hubbart
	T.J. Sikkema

RHP

RHSP	RHRP
Rhett Lowder (2)	Lyon Richardson (16)
Connor Phillips (3)	Carson Spiers (17)
Chase Petty (5)	Christian Roa (23)
Ty Floyd (11)	Zach Maxwell (26)
Julian Aguiar (14)	Kenya Huggins
Cole Schoenwetter (21)	Levi Stoudt
Jose Acuna	Bryce Bonnin
	Luis Mey
	Braxton Roxby
	Anyer Laureano
	Donovan Benoit
	Hunter Parks

1 NOELVI MARTE, 3B

Born: October 16, 2001. **B-T:** R-R. **HT:** 6-0. **WT:** 216.
Signed: Dominican Republic, 2018.
Signed by: Eddy Toledo/Tim Kissner (Mariners).

TRACK RECORD: A year after the Mariners signed Julio Rodriguez as the star of their 2017 international amateur class, Marte was an equally highly regarded $1.55 million cornerstone of the club's 2018 international crop. Marte immediately became one of the Seattle's top prospects, a title he held until July 2022, when he was traded with Edwin Arroyo to the Reds in a four-prospect swap for righthander Luis Castillo. Marte continues to be a streaky hitter who mixes stretches of dominance with periods where he looks lost at the plate. When he's on, he can carry a lineup. Marte hit seven of his 14 home runs in 2023 in a 16-day stretch in June. Called up to Cincinnati to make his MLB debut on Aug. 19, Marte finished the season with a 13-game hitting streak. A shortstop for most of his pro career, Marte focused exclusively on third base when he reached Triple-A Louisville. He largely stuck to the hot corner in the majors. He started three games at shortstop for Cincinnati in addition to his first pro appearance at second base.

SCOUTING REPORT: Since the day he signed, Marte has faced questions about how his body would age, and whether he would be able to retain most of his impressive athleticism as he filled out. While he has gotten stockier, he has managed so far to retain his speed. Marte is a plus runner, especially once he gets moving. He's also made steady improvements at the plate, and he's now more capable of handling pitchers who stay away. Marte has plus-plus raw power, but so far he's shown only average productive power. There should be more as he develops. He's blessed with exceptional bat speed. Among the Reds on the MLB roster, his average bat speed was second only to Elly De La Cruz. Marte has steadily developed as a hitter. When he runs cold, it's usually because he gets out of sync with his timing. He has a significant timing step and sometimes can get caught on his front foot, but he's in sync more regularly, and he's improved at chasing pitches off the outer third of the plate. He's at his best when he gets his arms extended and has shown the ability to be a solid .260-.270 hitter. At third base, Marte's range, footwork and first step are fringe-average and a hard-hit ball can get on him before he can react, but his

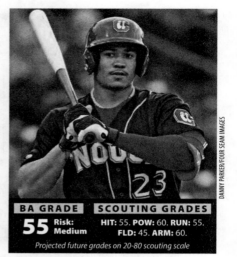

DANNY PARKER/FOUR SEAM IMAGES

BA GRADE	SCOUTING GRADES
55 Risk: Medium	HIT: 55. POW: 60. RUN: 55. FLD: 45. ARM: 60.

Projected future grades on 20-80 scouting scale

BEST TOOLS

BATTING

Best Hitter for Average	Carlos Jorge
Best Power Hitter	Noelvi Marte
Best Strike-Zone Discipline	Sal Stewart
Fastest Baserunner	Jacob Hurtubise
Best Athlete	Blake Dunn

PITCHING

Best Fastball	Zach Maxwell
Best Curveball	Adam Serwinowski
Best Slider	Connor Phillips
Best Changeup	Rhett Lowder
Best Control	Rhett Lowder

FIELDING

Best Defensive Catcher	Logan Tanner
Best Defensive Infielder	Trey Faltine
Best Infield Arm	Noelvi Marte
Best Defensive Outfielder	Justice Thompson
Best Outfield Arm	Yerlin Confidan

plus, accurate arm allows him to make highlight plays, because he doesn't need to set his feet to put something on his throws. He is especially comfortable charging bunts and slow grounders.

THE FUTURE: The Reds have more MLB-ready players than spots to play them, especially in the infield, but Marte showed hints that he can be a long-term fixture thanks to his power-speed combo. He will play the 2024 season as a 22-year-old, so his best years are still ahead of him. His speed and arm would make a move to right field viable if the Reds need to improvise to get his bat in the lineup. ∎

Year	Age	Club	Level	AVG	G	AB	R	H	2B	3B	HR	RBI	BB	SO	SB	OBP	SLG
2023	21	ACL Reds	Rk	.222	3	9	1	2	0	0	0	0	1	1	0	.300	.222
2023	21	Chattanooga (SL)	AA	.281	50	196	37	55	10	1	8	25	22	38	10	.356	.464
2023	21	Louisville (IL)	AAA	.280	39	143	31	40	10	3	3	20	20	31	8	.365	.455
2023	21	Cincinnati (NL)	MLB	.316	35	114	15	36	7	0	3	15	8	25	6	.366	.456
Minor League Totals				.282	379	1502	290	424	89	10	56	238	191	349	82	.367	.467
Major League Totals				.316	35	114	15	36	7	0	3	15	8	25	6	.366	.456

2 RHETT LOWDER, RHP

FB: 55. **SL:** 55. **CHG:** 60. **CTL:** 60. **BA Grade:** 55. **Risk:** High.

Born: March 8, 2002. **B-T:** R-R. **HT:** 6-2. **WT:** 200.
Drafted: Wake Forest, 2023 (1st round). **Signed by:** Charlie Aliano.
TRACK RECORD: Lowder's standout 2023 season with Wake Forest ended with a College World Series duel against LSU's Paul Skenes. Lowder matched Skenes zero for zero in a pitching duel for the ages as both exited with the game still scoreless. That was the only Lowder start all season that Wake Forest didn't win. His 15-0 record and 143 strikeouts both set school records as he won Atlantic Coast Conference player of the year honors for a second straight season. The Reds drafted Lowder seventh overall and signed him for $5.7 million, about 9% under slot. They decided not to ramp Lowder back up after he signed after he had thrown 120 innings for Wake and starred for USA Baseball's Collegiate National Team the previous summer. He'll make his pro debut in 2024.
SCOUTING REPORT: Lowder worked at least five innings in 18 of his 19 starts in 2023 and seven innings in 10 starts, but he did so while never topping 105 pitches in any outing. Lowder has three above-average or plus pitches, and he demonstrates complete confidence in all three. His 93-95 mph above-average four-seam fastball will touch 97 and has plenty of running life. His 93-95 mph two-seam fastball is even more effective because it pairs so well with his changeup, but it's his above-average slider and plus changeup that give hitters the biggest fits. His 85-88 mph slider is a power pitch with more depth than tilt. His 84-88 mph changeup has excellent deception. Lowder's front foot is pointed toward the first-base on-deck circle when he lands. It's unconventional, but it adds deception and hasn't hindered his plus control.
THE FUTURE: Lowder is as close to MLB-ready as any pitcher in the 2023 draft class, and he should move quickly. Scouts generally view him as a relatively safe No. 3 or 4 starter rather than a future ace.

Year	Age	Club	Level	W	L	ERA	G	GS	IP	H	HR	BB	SO	BB%	SO%	WHIP	AVG
2023	21	Did not play															

3 CONNOR PHILLIPS, RHP

FB: 60. **CB:** 55. **SL:** 60. **CHG:** 30. **CTL:** 45 **BA Grade:** 55. **Risk:** High.

Born: May 4, 2001. **B-T:** R-R. **HT:** 6-2. **WT:** 190.
Drafted: McLennan (TX) JC, 2020 (2nd round supp). **Signed by:** Derek Miller (Mariners).
TRACK RECORD: The highest-drafted junior college player in 2020, Phillips was shipped from the Mariners to the Reds with Brandon Williamson for Eugenio Suarez and Jesse Winker in March 2022. Phillips made his MLB debut on Sept. 5. After pitching effectively in back-to-back starts, Phillips' final Reds start saw him throw 12 balls in 12 pitches before he was lifted.
SCOUTING REPORT: Phillips' pure stuff is among the best in the Reds' system, but his control and command run hot and cold. There are outings when Phillips can dominate, but he also had six starts when he failed to make it through the second inning. In every one of those poor outings, he had a strike percentage under 50%, where 63% is average. Phillips presents no glaring delivery flaws. His 95-97 mph four-seam fastball grades as plus and has life and the flat plane to bedevil hitters when he spots it at the top of the strike zone, but he's homer-prone when he loses command and doesn't elevate it. His plus 84-88 mph power slider is his best pitch. He can get swings-and-misses in the zone with it, or run it down and away off the plate for chases. Phillips relies heavily on his above-average, 12-to-6 curveball in the low 80s as a change-of-pace versus lefthanded hitters. His curve has a bigger break, but he has more feel for it than his well below-average 87-88 mph changeup, which he is prone to spiking.
THE FUTURE: Phillips should compete for a spot in a rapidly crowding Reds' big league rotation. Consistency stands between him and MLB success. He has outings when he'll show above-average control and others when it's bottom of the scale. His chance to remain in the rotation depends on more regularly throwing strikes.

Year	Age	Club	Level	W	L	ERA	G	GS	IP	H	HR	BB	SO	BB%	SO%	WHIP	AVG
2023	22	Chattanooga (SL)	AA	2	2	3.34	14	14	65	58	9	27	111	9.5	39.1	1.31	.232
2023	22	Louisville (IL)	AAA	2	3	4.69	11	10	40	33	1	30	43	16.9	24.2	1.56	.224
2023	22	Cincinnati (NL)	MLB	1	1	6.97	5	5	21	18	5	13	26	13.5	27.1	1.50	.220
Minor League Totals				16	17	4.03	66	65	291	242	20	169	415	13.3	32.5	1.42	.224
Major League Totals				1	1	7.20	5	5	21	18	5	13	26	13.5	27.1	1.55	.220

4 EDWIN ARROYO, SS

HIT: 50. **POW:** 45. **RUN:** 55. **FLD:** 55. **ARM:** 60. **BA Grade:** 50. **Risk:** Medium.

Born: August 25, 2003. **B-T:** B-R. **HT:** 6-0. **WT:** 175.
Drafted: HS—Arecibo, PR, 2021 (2nd round). **Signed by:** Rob Mummau (Mariners).
TRACK RECORD: In the 2021 draft, scouts loved Arroyo's glove and worried about his bat. One of the youngest players in his class, Arroyo was 17 for his entire pro debut after the Mariners drafted him 48th overall. He was one of the best hitters in the Low-A California League in 2022, impressing the Reds, who landed him in the Luis Castillo deadline deal. As a Red, Arroyo initially struggled at the plate. He was hitting .197/.249/.329 two months into 2023, but from June onward Arroyo became one of High-A Dayton's best hitters and earned a late-season bump to Double-A Chattanooga.
SCOUTING REPORT: In a system loaded with shortstops, Arroyo is the best and most consistent defender. While every other Reds minor league shortstop also plays additional positions, Arroyo plays only short-stop. He has soft hands, a quick exchange, smooth actions and an accurate, plus arm. His range is aver-age. While his arm allows him to make plays from the hole, balls to his right often end up just out of reach. A switch-hitter who is relatively equally adept from both sides of the plate, Arroyo didn't make any major changes to turn around his season. He kept the same simple, slightly open setup and timing step from both sides of the plate and didn't rework either of his two swings. He chased a little less often, but mainly he just made more contact and found more holes. His below-average present power should steadily improve as he matures. Arroyo is a plus runner with a solid feel for swiping a base.
THE FUTURE: Arroyo is ticketed to be Double-A Chattanooga's shortstop in 2024. There's no rush to push him to Cincinnati. His combination of steady defense and a well-rounded offensive approach gives him a shot to be a future MLB regular at a key defensive position.

Year	Age	Club	Level	AVG	G	AB	R	H	2B	3B	HR	RBI	BB	SO	SB	OBP	SLG
2023	19	Dayton (MWL)	A+	.248	119	475	72	118	26	10	13	55	48	112	28	.321	.427
2023	19	Chattanooga (SL)	AA	.353	4	17	2	6	2	1	0	5	1	6	1	.400	.588
Minor League Totals				.268	260	1030	183	276	55	21	29	154	105	267	60	.344	.447

5 CHASE PETTY, RHP

FB: 50. **SL:** 60. **CHG:** 55. **CTL:** 60. **BA Grade:** 55. **Risk:** High.

Born: April 4, 2003. **B-T:** R-R. **HT:** 6-1. **WT:** 190.
Drafted: HS—Linwood, NJ, 2021 (1st round). **Signed by:** John Wilson (Twins).
TRACK RECORD: Petty's transformation from thrower to pitcher happened remarkably quickly. In high school, he was known for a 100 mph fastball, a high-effort delivery and shaky control. Acquired from the Twins in the March 2022 Sonny Gray trade, Petty now is a clever, consistent strike-thrower who rarely tops 95 mph. His 1.72 ERA, compiled mostly at High-A Dayton, was second-best among minor league pitchers with 60 or more innings.
SCOUTING REPORT: Petty missed the first month of the 2023 season with a minor elbow injury but had no issues taking his turn for 18 starts—though the Reds never let him work past four innings or 65 pitches. Petty's savvy and consistency is notable. A slider/fastball pitcher in high school, he has refined his changeup and added a four-seam fastball as a pro. He commands his average 92-95 mph two-seamer, working low in the zone to his glove side to righties and armside to lefties. He manipulates his plus slider. It's usually a hard, cutter-ish 87-89 mph pitch that can dominate in the zone. He throws it for strikes as consistently as his fastball, which means he can flip a count or get soft contact against hitters looking for his fastball. He can add more depth on his slider for two-strike chases. Petty has complete belief in his above-average, hard 87-89 mph changeup. Against lefty-heavy lineups, he'll rely on it until hitters prove they can handle it.
THE FUTURE: Petty's combination of plus control and command and ability to use three pitches is what scouts look for in a midrotation starter. He has yet to show he can handle the workload of a starter, but caution is understandable, because he won't turn 21 until the 2024 season starts. He's lined up for a return to Chattanooga.

Year	Age	Club	Level	W	L	ERA	G	GS	IP	H	HR	BB	SO	BB%	SO%	WHIP	AVG
2023	20	Dayton (MWL)	A+	0	2	1.95	16	16	60	58	0	14	61	5.8	25.1	1.20	.257
2023	20	Chattanooga (SL)	AA	0	0	0.00	2	2	8	5	0	1	5	3.2	16.1	0.75	.167
Minor League Totals				1	8	2.84	45	39	171	153	7	47	168	6.7	24.0	1.17	.240

6 CARLOS JORGE, 2B/OF

HIT: 60. **POW:** 40. **FLD:** 50. **RUN:** 60. **ARM:** 50. **BA Grade:** 55. **Risk:** High.

Born: Sept. 22, 2003. **B-T:** L-R. **HT:** 5-10. **WT:** 160. **Signed:** Dominican Republic, 2021.
Signed by: Edgard Melo/Enmanuel Cartagena/Richard Jimenez.

TRACK RECORD: Wherever Jorge goes, he hits. He has ranked in the top 10 in on-base percentage, slugging percentage and OPS the last three years while playing in the Dominican Summer, Arizona Complex and Florida State leagues. Jorge's pro odyssey began at shortstop, moved to second base in 2022 and included the addition of center field in 2023 after he moved to High-A Dayton in mid August.

SCOUTING REPORT: In an era of baseball when pitchers love to feed four-seam fastballs at and above the top of the strike zone, Jorge is a high-heat antidote. As a 5-foot-10 lefthanded hitter with quick hands, a short stroke and a flat bat path, he's well-equipped to stay on top of high fastballs. He is also comfortable stinging balls on the outer third to the left center gap. He could flirt with .300 in his best years, and while he's not a 20-home run threat, his sneaky gap power and plus speed should lead to plenty of doubles and triples. Jorge swiped 27 bases in 31 attempts in the first three months of 2023 before he started to tire. Defensively, Jorge is an average second baseman. His hands are fringy, but his average arm, body control, fearlessness to leave his feet and quick release work at the keystone. He's getting acclimated to center field but should be at least average there eventually.

THE FUTURE: Jorge has a lot of ways to help a big league club thanks to his versatility, hitting ability, on-base percentage (career .395 mark as a pro) and basestealing prowess. Jorge wore down in 2023 in his first foray in full-season ball—he had totaled just 89 pro games in his first two seasons—so training to handle the demands of a five-month season is a point of emphasis as he readies to return to High-A Dayton to start 2024.

Year	Age	Club	Level	AVG	G	AB	R	H	2B	3B	HR	RBI	BB	SO	SB	OBP	SLG
2023	19	Daytona (FSL)	A	.295	86	298	70	88	11	9	9	36	47	70	31	.400	.483
2023	19	Dayton (MWL)	A+	.239	23	88	8	21	3	1	3	14	5	30	1	.277	.398
Minor League Totals				.294	198	664	148	195	29	22	22	104	101	173	86	.395	.503

7 SAL STEWART, 3B

HIT: 60. **POW:** 50. **FLD:** 45. **RUN:** 40. **ARM:** 50. **BA Grade:** 55. **Risk:** High.

Born: December 7, 2003. **B-T:** R-R. **HT:** 6-3. **WT:** 215.
Drafted: HS—Miami, 2022 (1st round). **Signed by:** Andrew Fabian.

TRACK RECORD: Stewart is an alum of the same Westminster Christian School program that produced 1993 No. 1 overall pick Alex Rodriguez as well as long-time big leaguers J.P. Arencibia and Doug Mientkiewicz. Stewart stood out in high school for his ability to make hard contact without swinging and missing. As a senior, he hit .514 with more home runs (nine) than strikeouts (six). After sharing time with Cam Collier at third base at Low-A Daytona, Stewart earned a promotion to High-A Dayton in early August. In his final 50 Florida State League games before his promotion, Stewart hit .307/.421/.542 with nine home runs and more walks (35) than strikeouts (34).

SCOUTING REPORT: Stewart is a baseball rat with a savvy understanding of the game. He is a pure hitter but one who is big enough and strong enough to get to average power, especially in the friendly environs of Great American Ball Park. He has an up-the-middle hitting approach, and 10 of his 12 home runs were hit to center field or the power alleys. He's more adept than most teenagers at recognizing and hitting breaking pitches. The pleasant surprise for the Reds was Stewart's athleticism. In high school, the general belief was Stewart's body was headed in the wrong direction and that first base would be his ultimate position. He's worked on his conditioning, and he showed average body control, feet and hands at third base, though he has a tendency to lay back on grounders he should attack. His arm is average.

THE FUTURE: Stewart's bat has largely been as advertised. He's a polished hitter who strings together professional at-bats. His fielding has proven better than expected, which gives him at least a shot to stick at third base. Both Stewart and Collier picked up the pace offensively once they didn't have to share third base, but that job-share could return at High-A Dayton in 2024.

Year	Age	Club	Level	AVG	G	AB	R	H	2B	3B	HR	RBI	BB	SO	SB	OBP	SLG
2023	19	Daytona (FSL)	A	.269	88	316	55	85	19	0	10	60	66	59	10	.395	.424
2023	19	Dayton (MWL)	A+	.291	29	110	16	32	5	0	2	11	18	18	5	.397	.391
Minor League Totals				.276	125	450	76	124	28	0	12	76	88	82	15	.396	.418

8 LEO BALCAZAR, SS

HIT: 60. **POW:** 30. **FLD:** 55. **RUN:** 50. **ARM:** 55. **BA Grade:** 50. **Risk:** High.

Born: June 17, 2004. **B-T:** R-R. **HT:** 5-10. **WT:** 167. **Signed:** Venezuela, 2021.
Signed by: Aguido Gonzalez/Ricardo Quintero/Richard Castro.

TRACK RECORD: On a talented Low-A Daytona team that included first-rounders Cam Collier and Sal Stewart plus emerging talents Carlos Jorge and Hector Rodriguez, it was Balcazar who looked in the early going to be the Tortugas' star. He was the club's everyday shortstop and ranked in the top 10 in the Florida State League in most offensive categories. But Balcazar's season ended prematurely after 18 games. He tore the anterior cruciate ligament in his right knee while scoring the deciding run in Daytona's walk-off win in the second game of a doubleheader on April 30. He had surgery to repair the ligament and missed the remainder of the season.
SCOUTING REPORT: Assuming Balcazar makes a full recovery from his knee surgery, he has the makings of an everyday shortstop who can serve as a top-of-the-order hitter. The Reds have made a recent emphasis on signing and developing polished hitters, and Balcazar, a career .300 hitter in the minor leagues, fits the bill. He has a very simple balanced setup with a modest load and good timing. The righthanded hitter's swing is geared for singles and doubles into the gaps, though he can yank a ball over the left field fence if pitchers make a mistake. Balcazar is a smooth, gliding shortstop with above-average range and an above-average arm. Before the knee injury, he was an average runner and occasional basestealing threat.
THE FUTURE: The Reds have been encouraged by how Balcazar turned a setback into an opportunity. He's added 10 pounds of good weight while rehabbing his knee injury and was taking swings again in October. The recovery time for ACL surgery is about nine months, meaning that Balcazar should be at full speed for Opening Day 2024.

Year	Age	Club	Level	AVG	G	AB	R	H	2B	3B	HR	RBI	BB	SO	SB	OBP	SLG
2023	19	Daytona (FSL)	A	.324	18	68	11	22	5	1	1	11	13	22	2	.427	.471
Minor League Totals				.300	89	323	62	97	16	7	11	52	44	93	23	.392	.495

9 ALFREDO DUNO, C

HIT: 50. **POW:** 60. **FLD:** 55. **RUN:** 40. **ARM:** 60. **BA Grade:** 55. **Risk:** Extreme.

Born: January 7, 2006. **B-T:** R-R. **HT:** 6-2. **WT:** 210.
Signed: Venezuela, 2023. **Signed by:** Reds International Scouting Department.

TRACK RECORD: Venezuela's Ethan Salas was viewed as the top catcher in the 2023 international class, a status he quickly reinforced with an exceptional pro debut for the Padres that saw him reach Double-A as a 17-year-old. Duno, also a Venezuelan, was the second-best catching prospect in the class. Duno is on a more traditional timetable, but he also has a shot to be a long-term major league regular. Duno told the Reds his arm felt sore in the work up to the start of the Dominican Summer League season. Exams found no structural damage, but when the soreness remained, the Reds decided to have him DH exclusively while participating in all catcher's drills except for throwing.
SCOUTING REPORT: Duno is an excellent athlete for an already filled-out teenage catcher with a 6-foot-2, 210-pound frame. He's a fringe-average runner for now and swiped six bags in six attempts in the DSL, though catching will likely sap that speed eventually. Offensively, Duno's combination of excellent bat speed, plus raw power and solid swing decisions gives him a chance to develop into a 20-plus home run hitter with an average hit tool. His bat should play at multiple positions, but he has the mindset and tools to stick behind the plate. Defensively, Duno has the tools to be at least an above-average receiver and blocker with soft hands. While his arm soreness kept the Reds from seeing it in 2023, he's shown a plus to plus-plus arm in the past.
THE FUTURE: Duno should get to go back behind the plate in 2024, when he'll head to the U.S. to play in the Arizona Complex League. He's the Reds' best young catching prospect since the organization drafted Tyler Stephenson in 2015.

Year	Age	Club	Level	AVG	G	AB	R	H	2B	3B	HR	RBI	BB	SO	SB	OBP	SLG
2023	17	DSL Reds	Rk	.303	45	152	36	46	9	1	6	41	38	41	6	.451	.493
Minor League Totals				.303	45	152	36	46	9	1	6	41	38	41	6	.451	.493

10 CAM COLLIER, 3B

HIT: 55. **POW:** 55. **FLD:** 40. **RUN:** 40. **ARM:** 60. **BA Grade:** 50. **Risk:** High.

Born: November 20, 2004. **B-T:** L-R. **HT:** 6-2. **WT:** 210.
Drafted: Chipola (FL) JC, 2022 (1st round). **Signed by:** Sean Buckley

TRACK RECORD: The son of eight-year MLB veteran Lou Collier, Cam followed the same path as Bryce Harper by graduating from high school after his sophomore year, then enrolling at a junior college. That made Collier draft eligible after what would have been his high school junior season. The Reds drafted him 18th overall in 2022 out of Florida juco power Chipola and signed him for $5 million, or 37% over slot. Collier played the entire 2023 season as an 18-year-old, making him one of the younger players in full-season ball.

SCOUTING REPORT: Collier is a relatively mature hitter, despite his youth. He's a potential above-average hitter who has excellent barrel control and makes solid swing decisions. Pitchers rarely fool Collier, and he makes plenty of contact. When he connects, he hits the ball hard. But he hit just .246 with six home runs in 111 games in the Florida State League. The issue for Collier is that he doesn't have a swing that allows him to consistently do damage. Collier hits a lot of pulled ground balls, but he'll need to learn to lift the ball more consistently to get to his above-average power potential. His long-term potential depends a lot on him maintaining his already declining athleticism. He's already slow-footed. Collier lacks lateral range and has poor footwork, which leaves scouts skeptical that he'll be able to stay at third base. He has a strong and accurate arm that grades as plus. He's a below-average runner who is slowing.

THE FUTURE: Collier's upside remains as lofty as it was when he was drafted, but there are reasons to worry. If he maintains or improves his athleticism and develops his power, he's a potential everyday third baseman. But if he can't, his bat will be stretched as a first basemen with no other defensive options. He should head to High-A Dayton for most of 2024.

Year	Age	Club	Level	AVG	G	AB	R	H	2B	3B	HR	RBI	BB	SO	SB	OBP	SLG
2023	18	Daytona (FSL)	A	.246	111	390	40	96	21	2	6	68	57	106	5	.349	.356
Minor League Totals				.254	120	417	47	106	22	2	8	72	64	112	5	.361	.374

11 TY FLOYD, RHP

FB: 65. **SL:** 45. **CB:** 45. **CHG:** 50. **CTL:** 50. **BA Grade:** 50. **Risk:** High.

Born: August 28, 2001. **B-T:** R-R. **HT:** 6-2. **WT:** 200. **Drafted:** Louisiana State, 2023 (1st round supplemental).
Signed by: Mike Partida.

TRACK RECORD: Floyd was a draft-eligible sophomore in 2022, but he returned to Louisiana State both to try to win a national title and to show he could be a dominat starter after spending much of his first two years in the bullpen. Mission accomplished. Floyd showed continual improvement throughout the course of the season, culminating with a standout performance in the College World Series. After tying a career high with 10 strikeouts in his first start in Omaha, Floyd fanned 17 Florida batters in eight innings to help LSU win Game One of the CWS championship series in his final college outing.

SCOUTING REPORT: Floyd still offers some reminders that he was a reliever until relatively recently. Floyd's best pitch is his nearly double-plus four-seam fastball, and he relies on it heavily. When he's on, it's a nearly unhittable pitch at the top of the zone thanks to the combination of 93-98 mph velocity, a flat plane and well above-average carry. He did a solid job of developing his fringe-average slider and curve in 2023, and he's shown some feel for an average changeup that is largely a pitch he uses to neutralize lefthanded hitters.

THE FUTURE: Like fellow College World Series attendee Rhett Lowder, the Reds did not have Floyd throw in games after signing. He'll be making his pro debut in 2024. Floyd's excellent fastball gives him a clear path to at least a relief role, but the Reds will work hard to develop him into a potential mid-rotation starter. Floyd should dominate the Class A levels with his fastball, but he'll need to refine his breaking balls to succeed at the upper levels.

Year	Age	Club	Level	W	L	ERA	G	GS	IP	H	HR	BB	SO	BB%	SO%	WHIP	AVG
2023	21	Did not play															

12 RICARDO CABRERA, 3B/SS

HIT: 50. **POW:** 55. **FLD:** 50. **RUN:** 45. **ARM:** 60. **BA Grade:** 50. **Risk:** High.

Born: October 31, 2004. **B-T:** R-R. **HT:** 5-11. **WT:** 178. **Signed:** Venezuela, 2022.
Signed by: Reds international scouting department.

TRACK RECORD: Cabrera was viewed as one of the most well-rounded hitters in the 2022 international class. So far, he's lived up to that billing. After a modest debut in the Dominican Summer League in 2022, Cabrera was one of the best hitters in the Arizona Complex League in 2023, impressing scouts with his ability to string together quality at-bats. He finished in the top five in the league in batting average, on-base percentage, slugging percentage and stolen bases.

SCOUTING REPORT: Cabrera is an infielder whose success will be dependent on his bat because his body is already thickening. While he played shortstop more than third base in 2023, he's seen as a third baseman in the long-term. If he stays on top of his conditioning, he should be average defensively at the hot corner. His hands work well and he has a plus arm, but he doesn't have much range. Cabrera has a relatively level swing thanks in part to short arms that help him control the barrel. Eventually he should get to more of his above-average power, though it might mostly manifest as doubles from gap to gap.

THE FUTURE: Cabrera isn't going to wow anyone defensively, but he should hit enough that it won't matter. If his bat is as good as advertised, he could be a solid regular. After a brief taste of Low-A Daytona to end 2023, he should return there as one of the Tortugas' stars in 2024.

Year	Age	Club	Level	AVG	G	AB	R	H	2B	3B	HR	RBI	BB	SO	SB	OBP	SLG
2023	18	ACL Reds	Rk	.350	39	143	41	50	7	4	5	21	21	35	21	.469	.559
2023	18	Daytona (FSL)	A	.316	5	19	7	6	0	0	0	2	5	5	3	.519	.316
Minor League Totals				.301	89	312	78	94	13	9	6	42	39	80	29	.423	.458

13 BLAKE DUNN, OF

HIT: 50. **POW:** 50. **FLD:** 50. **RUN:** 60. **ARM:** 40. **BA Grade:** 50. **Risk:** High.

Born: September 5, 1998. **B-T:** R-R. **HT:** 5-9. **WT:** 201. **Drafted:** Western Michigan, 2021 (15th round).
Signed by: Tyler Gibbons.

TRACK RECORD: Dunn is one of the better all-around athletes in Michigan high school state history. He set state records in the 110- and 330-meter hurdles, scored the second-most points (824) in state history in football and set the school record with 51 points in a basketball game. But Dunn's all-out approach leads to injuries. He missed his senior season in high school, then missed a month of his final season at Western Michigan and has played less than 50 games in his first two pro seasons. Finally healthy, he was the Reds' most productive minor leaguer in 2023. He produced an extremely rare 20-50 season, and came just two home runs away from 30-50.

SCOUTING REPORT: Dunn's all-out approach is somewhat reminiscent of how Ryan Freel played his way into an eight-year MLB career. Dunn has speed, power and a knack for getting on base that is both a strength and a concern. Dunn is a well-rounded player who has no glaring flaws. His swing means he's a dartboard for pitchers who like to pitch up and in, as his approach means he ends up close-to-the-plate. His 32 hit-by-pitches were second most in the minors, and he had a knack for immediately stealing second after he's been plunked. Dunn's breakthrough was a surprise, but he has an easy, powerful swing.

THE FUTURE: Unlike most sleeper late-round finds, Dunn is a premium athlete. At this point, he's already played his way from being an org player to someone who could one day help a big league club. If he can show in 2024 that his offensive improvement is sustainable, he could be a regular who can play all three outfield spots and fit in nicely with the Reds' collection of athletic, grinding outfielders.

Year	Age	Club	Level	AVG	G	AB	R	H	2B	3B	HR	RBI	BB	SO	SB	OBP	SLG
2023	24	Dayton (MWL)	A+	.276	47	163	32	45	4	1	8	27	21	46	19	.411	.460
2023	24	Chattanooga (SL)	AA	.332	77	295	75	98	13	4	15	52	41	84	35	.433	.556
Minor League Totals				.302	172	592	132	179	23	6	28	101	89	170	79	.423	.503

14 JULIAN AGUIAR, RHP

FB: 55. **CB:** 45. **SL:** 50. **CHG:** 60. **CTL:** 55. **BA Grade:** 50. **Risk:** High.

Born: June 4, 2001. **B-T:** L-R. **HT:** 6-3. **WT:** 180. **Drafted:** Cypress (CA) JC, 2021 (12th round). **Signed by:** Mike Misuraca.
TRACK RECORD: Aguiar started pitching relatively late in his high school career, but a year at Cypress (Calif.) JC exclusively on the mound helped make him a solid draft prospect. Aguiar was one of the youngest junior college players in the 2021. At 19, he was younger than some of the high school draftees. After a solid 2022 season, Aguiar dominated at times in 2023. His 1.92 ERA in the Midwest League was easily the best among pitchers with 70 or more innings.

SCOUTING REPORT: Aguiar made a big step forward in 2023. He showed that he not only has a big league-caliber array of pitches, but he's also figuring out how to use them. He works up and in on lefties with his four-seamer, then drops in his curveball for strikes. His plus changeup is a weapon he wields against righties and lefties, but it is very much a chase pitch. He has a plus two-seamer in the mid 90s that is hard for righthanded hitters to handle, and there are days when his slider will flash above-average as well. On those days, he's lights out. On others, the slider disappears and he's much more hittable, especially for righthanded hitters.

THE FUTURE: Aguiar's fastball, changeup and developing slider would work well in the bullpen, but he's still got a shot to develop into a No. 4 starter.

Year	Age	Club	Level	W	L	ERA	G	GS	IP	H	HR	BB	SO	BB%	SO%	WHIP	AVG
2023	22	Dayton (MWL)	A+	4	1	1.92	14	14	70	44	2	24	77	8.5	27.2	0.97	.174
2023	22	Chattanooga (SL)	AA	4	4	4.28	11	11	55	57	6	13	61	5.6	26.3	1.28	.266
Minor League Totals				18	13	3.17	55	42	230	200	22	64	265	6.6	27.5	1.15	.229

15 SAMMY STAFURA, SS

HIT: 50. **POW:** 50. **RUN:** 60. **FLD:** 55. **ARM:** 50. **BA Grade:** 55. **Risk:** Extreme.

Born: November 15, 2004. **B-T:** R-R. **HT:** 6-0. **WT:** 188. **Drafted:** HS—Cortlandt Manor, NY, 2023 (2nd round).
Signed by: John Ceprini.

TRACK RECORD: The Reds went very heavy on pitching in the 2023 draft but decided to shut them down after signing, which meant Stafura was the only one of the Reds' top five picks to play in games after the draft. Stafura doubled in his second pro at-bat and doubled in his second to last at-bat of the season. In between, he was 1-for-38 and hit .071/.212/.191 with 23 strikeouts in 53 plate appearances.

SCOUTING REPORT: Stafura's pro debut was concerning and he swung and missed way too much, but there's no need to overreact to 53 plate appearances, especially when you consider that the adjustment Stafura had to make to playing games in the "Fire League." It was 112 degrees for the New York prep product's first game. It's not a total surprise that Stafura may need a bit of time to adjust to pro ball, but he has the potential to be an athletic, well-rounded shortstop with plus speed. Defensively, he shows smooth footwork, good hands and a quick release that helps his average arm play up. Offensively, he's made plenty of contact against top-notch pitching in summer showcases and has steadily gotten stronger, giving hope that he eventually could be an average hitter with average power.

THE FUTURE: Stafura can make any concerns stemming from his rough debut disappear with a strong start in the Florida State League. To make that happen, he's going to need to make better swing decisions and better recognize breaking balls.

Year	Age	Club	Level	AVG	G	AB	R	H	2B	3B	HR	RBI	BB	SO	SB	OBP	SLG
2023	18	ACL Reds	Rk	.071	12	42	7	3	2	0	1	6	8	23	0	.212	.190
Minor League Totals				.071	12	42	7	3	2	0	1	6	8	23	0	.212	.190

16 LYON RICHARDSON, RHP

FB: 60. **CB:** 40. **SL:** 40. **CHG:** 60. **CTL:** 45. **BA Grade:** 50. **Risk:** High.

Born: January 18, 2000. **B-T:** B-R. **HT:** 6-1. **WT:** 200. **Drafted:** HS—Jensen Beach, FL, 2018 (2nd round).
Signed by: Stephen Hunt.

TRACK RECORD: Richardson's return from Tommy John surgery was ... complicated. On one hand, he came into the year with no experience above Class A and he finished it in the majors. His fastball returned from 91-95 mph he'd shown in 2021 to the high 90s he showed in high school. On the other, he also gave up 31 runs and 30 walks in his final 31 innings between Triple-A Louisville and Cincinnati.

SCOUTING REPORT: Richardson is obviously much better than what he showed in his four MLB starts. He's never been homer-prone before, but the way his average control disappeared in August was truly baffling. Even early in the season, Richardson's command and control weren't as sharp as pre-injury, but he went from missing by a few inches to missing by half a foot or more. Feel and command can often improve in the second year back from Tommy John surgery, so there's hope that he can make significant improvements in 2024. There's no complaints about how Richardson's stuff returned. His four-seam plus fastball now sits at 96-98 mph as a starter, which made his already-effective high-80s changeup into a plus pitch. He sells it well with his arm speed, it has above-average depth and he throws it to lefties and righties. His below-average mid-80s slider has to get better. It's too slow, and it's a chase pitch that he can't throw in the strike zone. He also throws a two-seamer and high-70s, below-average curve.

THE FUTURE: Richardson has the strength, build and deep pitch mix to be a starter, but it's easy to find scouts who think his fastball/changeup combination and a refined slider would work even better with a move to the bullpen. As a reliever, he has the stuff to be a potential future closer.

Year	Age	Club	Level	W	L	ERA	G	GS	IP	H	HR	BB	SO	BB%	SO%	WHIP	AVG
2023	23	Daytona (FSL)	A	0	0	1.00	3	3	9	5	0	1	18	3.0	54.5	0.67	.167
2023	23	Chattanooga (SL)	AA	0	2	2.15	15	15	46	35	2	22	58	11.7	30.9	1.24	.213
2023	23	Louisville (IL)	AAA	0	1	9.42	6	6	14	11	0	15	24	21.7	34.8	1.81	.212
2023	23	Cincinnati (NL)	MLB	0	2	8.64	4	4	17	17	6	15	12	18.5	14.8	1.92	.258
Minor League Totals				5	22	4.55	80	79	287	288	24	125	321	9.8	25.2	1.44	.255
Major League Totals				0	2	9.00	4	4	17	17	6	15	12	18.5	14.8	2.00	.258

17 CARSON SPIERS, RHP

FB: 50. **SL:** 45. **CUT:** 45. **CHG:** 45. **CTL:** 55. **BA Grade:** 45. **Risk:** Medium.

Born: November 11, 1997. **B-T:** R-R. **HT:** 6-0. **WT:** 205. **Signed:** Clemson, 2020 (NDFA). **Signed by:** Charlie Aliano.

TRACK RECORD: The nephew of MLB infielder Bill Spiers, Carson was a savvy nondrafted free agent signing of the Reds after the five-round 2020 draft. The one-time Clemson closer saw his velocity improve in pro ball, even as he moved from the bullpen to the starting rotation. Spiers began 2023 as a reliever, but the Reds moved him back into a starting role in July when more than half of the club's MLB rotation was on the injured list. Two months later, Spiers made his MLB debut as a starter before moving back to the bullpen.

SCOUTING REPORT: Spiers has a bucket of usable pitches but no single pitch that gives hitters something to fear. His average 92-95 mph four-seam fastball works if he keeps it at the top or bottom of the zone. Against righthanded hitters he relies more heavily on his two-seamer to get inside, which sets up his average mid-80s slider to break in the opposite direction. His fringe-average changeup was once an above-average pitch but has backed up a little in pro ball. It's effective to generate soft contact when he dots the bottom of the zone.

THE FUTURE: Spiers' future role will depend on the Reds' needs. He has experience in the bullpen and in the rotation, and he's capable of handling either role. More importantly his flexible mindset means he's willing to help in any way possible.

Year	Age	Club	Level	W	L	ERA	G	GS	IP	H	HR	BB	SO	BB%	SO%	WHIP	AVG
2023	25	Chattanooga (SL)	AA	8	3	3.69	28	9	83	71	6	41	106	11.3	29.2	1.35	.226
2023	25	Louisville (IL)	AAA	1	0	0.00	1	0	2	0	0	0	0	0.0	0.0	0.00	.000
2023	25	Cincinnati (NL)	MLB	0	1	6.92	4	2	13	18	1	7	12	10.9	18.8	1.92	.321
Minor League Totals				21	13	4.24	81	52	318	298	42	120	341	8.8	25.1	1.31	.246
Major League Totals				0	1	6.92	4	2	13	18	1	7	12	10.9	18.8	1.92	.321

18 VICTOR ACOSTA, SS

HIT: 50. **POW:** 40. **FLD:** 55. **RUN:** 50. **ARM:** 55. **BA Grade:** 45. **Risk:** High.

Born: June 10, 2004. **B-T:** B-R. **HT:** 5-11. **WT:** 170. **Signed:** Dominican Republic, 2021.
Signed by: Alvin Duran/Trevor Schumm/Chris Kemp (Padres).

TRACK RECORD: A significant part of the Reds' rebuilding effort has come through smart trade acquisitions. Acosta could be another success story, but the payoff might take a bit longer. A $1.8 million Padres' signing in 2021, Acosta was traded to the Reds for Brandon Drury.

SCOUTING REPORT: Acosta is a switch-hitter who can play above-average defense at multiple infield spots, making him a hard guy to take out of the lineup. His lefthanded swing is better than his righthanded swing, but both should be effective and he has plenty of bat speed. He won't be a slugger, but he should hit plenty of doubles. Acosta boosts his on-base percentage by consistently getting hit by pitches. He was once a plus runner, but he's slowed down to average and he's not much of a threat to steal bases. Acosta is an above-average defender at shortstop and is even better at second base. He hasn't been asked to play third, but his hands, feet and arm would be solid there as well.

THE FUTURE: Acosta's most likely profile is as a utility infielder, but he does enough things well to potentially carve out a role as a regular. His defense will give him plenty of opportunities to develop.

Year	Age	Club	Level	AVG	G	AB	R	H	2B	3B	HR	RBI	BB	SO	SB	OBP	SLG
2023	19	Daytona (FSL)	A	.251	100	347	41	87	20	5	2	31	41	85	12	.364	.354
Minor League Totals				.257	198	672	108	173	39	12	9	74	100	167	43	.381	.391

19 HECTOR RODRIGUEZ, OF

HIT: 55. **POW:** 40. **FLD:** 45. **RUN:** 60. **ARM:** 50. **BA Grade:** 45. **Risk:** High.

Born: March 11, 2004. **B-T:** R-R. **HT:** 5-8. **WT:** 186. **Signed:** Dominican Republic, 2021.
Signed by: Moises De La Mota/Oliver Dominguez (Mets).
TRACK RECORD: The Reds acquired Rodriguez and righthander Jose Acuña from the Mets in the July 2022 Tyler Naquin trade. A second baseman and third baseman in the Dominican Summer League, he moved to the outfield after coming stateside and has hit no matter where he's played. He's a .306 career hitter whose 10 triples in 2023 were tied for third-most in the minors.
SCOUTING REPORT: A one-time switch-hitter, Rodriguez's decision to focus on hitting from the left side has paid off. His 2023 season was nearly impeccable. He led the Florida State League in slugging percentage, triples and extra-base hits. As dominating as his season was, there are concerns as to how sustainable his success will be at higher levels. Rodriguez swings at everything. MiLB hitters generally swing at 46-47% of the pitches. Anyone who swings more than 50% of the time is extremely aggressive. Rodriguez swings 63% of the time, and he chases pitches as much as almost anyone in the minors. His exceptional hand-eye and barrel control allowed that approach to work in Class A, but he's going to need to significantly improve his zone awareness against more experienced pitchers. Rodriguez once had blazing speed but he's slowed down to be above-average to plus. The converted infielder is still learning how to play the outfield, where his routes are rarely direct.
THE FUTURE: Rodriguez has the tools to play in the majors. To get there, he's going to need to get significantly better in the outfield and learn to keep the bat on his shoulder from time to time. He should be one of the key players on High-A Dayton's team.

Year	Age	Club	Level	AVG	G	AB	R	H	2B	3B	HR	RBI	BB	SO	SB	OBP	SLG
2023	19	Daytona (FSL)	A	.293	101	410	85	120	23	9	16	56	27	84	18	.347	.510
2023	19	Dayton (MWL)	A+	.294	14	51	6	15	2	1	0	5	1	10	0	.309	.373
Minor League Totals				.304	206	767	142	233	45	20	22	102	53	131	40	.355	.501

20 RECE HINDS, OF

HIT: 30. **POW:** 60. **FLD:** 50. **RUN:** 50. **ARM:** 70. **BA Grade:** 50. **Risk:** Extreme.

Born: September 5, 2000. **B-T:** R-R. **HT:** 6-3. **WT:** 230. **Drafted:** HS—Bradenton, FL, 2019 (2nd round).
Signed by: Sean Buckley
TRACK RECORD: For a slugger who can hit the ball 450-plus feet, Hinds came into 2023 looking for his first real power binge. Injuries hadn't helped, but he entered the year with a career high of 12 home runs, a stunning number for a hitter with 80-grade raw power. In the first two months of 2023, he seemed even more lost. He struck out a remarkable 88 times in his first 210 plate appearances (42%) while hitting just five home runs. He went deep seven more times in a six-game span in mid June and hit a home run every 14 plate appearances from then until the end of the season.
SCOUTING REPORT: When he was struggling, Hinds tweaked his setup. He got closer to the plate to get better plate coverage and simplified his load. Shortly thereafter, he started clearing fences. Hinds will always strike out, but his second-half improvement, which saw his strikeout rate dip to 26%, raises hopes he can get his contact rate to a playable level. Hinds has taken the move to right field well. He's still a little raw, but he should be average eventually and his plus-plus arm is a weapon.
THE FUTURE: The Reds saw enough improvement from Hinds to add him to the 40-man roster heading into 2024. He still has a lot of work to do to carve out a part-time role in the majors, but he is trending in the right direction.

Year	Age	Club	Level	AVG	G	AB	R	H	2B	3B	HR	RBI	BB	SO	SB	OBP	SLG
2023	22	Chattanooga (SL)	AA	.269	109	412	63	111	29	6	23	98	34	151	20	.330	.536
Minor League Totals				.253	245	913	141	231	53	15	47	161	78	344	42	.321	.498

21 COLE SCHOENWETTER, RHP

FB: 60. **CB:** 60. **CHG:** 50. **CTL:** 40. **BA Grade:** 50. **Risk:** Extreme.

Born: October 1, 2004. **B-T:** R-R. **HT:** 6-3. **WT:** 190. **Drafted:** HS—San Marcos, CA, 2023 (4th round).
Signed by: Rick Allen.
TRACK RECORD: At his best, Schoenwetter looked like one of the best prep pitchers in the 2023 draft class. He showed flashes of dominance in summer showcases and had an excellent senior season. He fell to the fourth round in part because of his bonus demands, but that made him the type of high-risk, high-reward pick the Reds could go after because of their large bonus pool. His $1.897 million bonus was the fourth-highest in the Reds' class.

SCOUTING REPORT: Schoenwetter has a 93-95 mph plus fastball that can touch 98, as well as a plus curveball in the high 70s and low 80s that he shows an advanced ability to command and make bigger or smaller depending on the count. Like many high school pitchers, his changeup has further to go, but it will flash average. Schoenwetter needs to get stronger and more consistent with his delivery, and in high school his stuff would back up later in outings.

THE FUTURE: Schoenwetter was yet another Reds pitcher who didn't get officially on the mound in his draft year. The Reds' 2023 draft class will be judged by the development of Rhett Lowder and Ty Floyd, but adding Schoenwetter to the mix gives the club another high-ceiling arm to dream on.

Year	Age	Club	Level	W	L	ERA	G	GS	IP	H	HR	BB	SO	BB%	SO%	WHIP	AVG
2023	18	Did not play															

22 JACOB HURTUBISE, OF

HIT: 55. **POW:** 30. **FLD:** 50. **RUN:** 70. **ARM:** 45. **BA Grade:** 40. **Risk:** Medium.

Born: December 11, 1997. **B-T:** L-R. **HT:** 5-9. **WT:** 186. **Drafted:** Army, 2019 (39th round). **Signed by:** Lee Seras.

TRACK RECORD: The Reds were one of the most aggressive and one of the best teams at aggressively pursuing players as nondrafted free agents when MLB cut the coronavirus-affected 2020 MLB draft to five rounds. Carson Spiers has already made it to the majors as a 2020 Reds' NDFA, and Hurtubise should soon follow. The Army product led all Reds' MiLB hitters with a .330 average and reached Triple-A.

SCOUTING REPORT: Hurtubise has long impressed with his all-out, high-effort approach, but that intensity might also have made it hard to notice what a solid player he's become. He has modest power, but he finished third in the minors with 10 triples. He can yank a ball over the outfielders' heads every now and then, but he's best as a pest. His short swing makes it hard to strike him out, and he knows that a walk can be as good as a double given his plus-plus speed. Hurtubise's speed isn't as useful in the outfield, where he's a choppy runner and an average defender with a fringe-average arm.

THE FUTURE: Hurtubise's speed, contact ability and versatility give him a very solid shot at a lengthy MLB career. He was added to the 40-man roster in November 2023. He's slated to head back to Triple-A Louisville to start 2024, but could make his MLB debut soon.

Year	Age	Club	Level	AVG	G	AB	R	H	2B	3B	HR	RBI	BB	SO	SB	OBP	SLG
2023	25	Chattanooga (SL)	AA	.306	83	242	74	74	7	10	6	36	48	49	33	.453	.492
2023	25	Louisville (IL)	AAA	.390	36	100	28	39	4	0	1	10	29	14	12	.537	.460
Minor League Totals				.296	284	830	206	246	25	15	8	88	158	177	100	.436	.392

23 CHRISTIAN ROA, RHP

FB: 50. **SL:** 55. **CB:** 45. **CHG:** 50. **CTL:** 30. **BA Grade:** 45. **Risk:** High.

Born: April 2, 1999. **B-T:** R-R. **HT:** 6-4. **WT:** 220. **Drafted:** Texas A&M, 2020 (2nd round). **Signed by:** Mike Partida.

TRACK RECORD: The good news for Roa is he was finally able to show he could stay healthy and carry a reasonably heavy workload. His 120 innings in 2023 was nearly 30 more than he'd ever thrown in a season. He has battled a sports hernia and an elbow flexor strain in the past, but he took his turn every time in 2023. He seemed to struggle with the Southern League's sticky baseball at the start of the season, but his control didn't improve after moving to Triple-A..

SCOUTING REPORT: Roa seemed to struggle to repeat his delivery regularly in 2023, which is concerning because his stuff isn't good enough to have success when he's falling behind in counts. There's more effort than ideal, and Roa struggles to keep his arm on time with his lower half, leading to below-average control. His 56% strike rate in 2023 is far below an acceptable level. If Roa can throw more strikes, he has the varied assortment of pitches to survive as a starter. His relatively straight mid-90s fastball could be an average pitch, and his mid-80s slider is above-average but sometimes morphs into more of a cutter. He also has a fringe-average curveball. All of his pitches are usable, but his command and control will need to improve to get the most out of his mix.

THE FUTURE: The Reds had 17 different pitchers make starts in 2023. That's a worst-case scenario, but it shows the value Roa could provide as a useful, reliable Triple-A starter who is ready and waiting when one of the team's regular starters is on the injured list. The Reds added Roa to the 40-man roster for that reason, but he needs to add polish in a return to Triple-A Louisville.

Year	Age	Club	Level	W	L	ERA	G	GS	IP	H	HR	BB	SO	BB%	SO%	WHIP	AVG
2023	24	Chattanooga (SL)	AA	4	5	4.88	13	13	59	41	7	44	87	17.1	33.7	1.44	.199
2023	24	Louisville (IL)	AAA	1	6	5.43	15	12	61	61	12	47	83	16.2	28.6	1.76	.257
Minor League Totals				15	15	4.27	63	58	270	217	31	172	339	14.5	28.5	1.44	.217

24 ADAM SERWINOWSKI, LHP

FB: 60. **CB:** 60. **CHG:** 30. **CTL:** 40. **BA Grade:** 45. **Risk:** High.

Born: January 26, 2001. **B-T:** R-R. **HT:** 6-6. **WT:** 293. **Drafted:** Georgia Tech, 2022 (6th round). **Signed by:** Jerel Johnson.

TRACK RECORD: Serwinowski was viewed as a projectable lefty coming out of high school, but that's a profile that doesn't get drafted as often in a minor league system without short-season leagues. The Reds were willing to take that risk, and it began to pay off when his velocity jumped and transformed him into a very promising power-armed lefty.

SCOUTING REPORT: The Reds have focused on filling the minors with pitchers who make hitters sweat. Sometimes the sweat comes from 97-plus mph at the top of the zone. Sometimes it's because some of these fireballers don't always know where those pitches are going. Serwinowski fits that mold perfectly. He has plus stuff, including a 94-97 mph fastball that's hard to pick up thanks to his funky delivery and the angle he creates more than the movement of the pitch. He has a sweepy breaking ball that has plus potential. He has toyed with a changeup, but it's far from where it needs to be. His control is currently well below-average, but that should improve as he gets stronger and gains experience.

THE FUTURE: Serwinowski is both exceptionally promising and extremely unpolished. He fits the Reds' love of raw pitchers with nasty stuff and lots of polish remaining. He will get a taste of the automated ball-strike system in Low-A Daytona in 2023.

Year	Age	Club	Level	W	L	ERA	G	GS	IP	H	HR	BB	SO	BB%	SO%	WHIP	AVG
2023	19	ACL Reds	Rk	0	0	3.62	11	6	27	13	1	16	43	15.0	40.2	1.06	.149
Minor League Totals				0	0	3.54	12	6	28	14	1	17	44	15.3	39.6	1.11	.156

25 ARIEL ALMONTE, OF

HIT: 40. **POW:** 55. **FLD:** 45. **RUN:** 40. **ARM:** 60. **BA Grade:** 50. **Risk:** Extreme.

Born: December 1, 2003. **B-T:** L-R. **HT:** 6-3. **WT:** 219. **Signed:** Dominican Republic, 2021. **Signed by:** Reds International Scouting Department.

TRACK RECORD: Almonte was seen as a relatively well-polished right field prospect with power and bat-to-ball skills when the Reds signed him as their top target in the 2021 international class. He was exactly as advertised in his 2021 Dominican Summer League debut and his 2022 Arizona Complex League season, but 2023 was a season to forget. Even in the pitcher-friendly Florida State League, a .597 OPS is well below-average.

SCOUTING REPORT: Scouts aren't ready to write off Almonte even if there are worrisome trends. Almonte was never a speedster, but he's going to really have to hit for power as a fringy right fielder who struggles at times to read the ball off the bat. He has above-average bat speed and can create leverage in his swing when he puts it all together, but he never seemed to get comfortable at the plate in the FSL. His struggles against lefties are particularly troublesome. He bails out against breaking balls and had just two extra-base hits against southpaws all season. Almonte has plenty of work to do against righthanders as well, as too often he fell behind in counts, then chased pitchers' pitches. But his swing remains fluid and there's real power potential, offering hope that he still has a shot to develop into a right fielder who gets on base and hits 20-plus home runs.

THE FUTURE: Almonte can't say he's mastered Low-A, so he's most likely ticketed for a return trip to Daytona. His 2024 season can't look like his 2023 season did, but there's still potential to develop into a regular, even if there are a lot more doubts he can get to that point.

Year	Age	Club	Level	AVG	G	AB	R	H	2B	3B	HR	RBI	BB	SO	SB	OBP	SLG
2023	19	Daytona (FSL)	A	.203	97	335	35	68	15	1	5	33	42	133	4	.298	.299
Minor League Totals				.240	187	637	98	153	35	2	16	90	89	234	20	.345	.377

26 ZACH MAXWELL, RHP

FB: 70. **SL:** 70. **CTL:** 20. **BA Grade:** 50. **Risk:** Extreme.

Born: January 26, 2001. **B-T:** R-R. **HT:** 6-6. **WT:** 293. **Drafted:** Georgia Tech, 2022 (6th round). **Signed by:** Jerel Johnson.

TRACK RECORD: Maxwell's career at Georgia Tech was rocky at best. He averaged a walk an inning for his career. An attempt at starting as a junior ended after he walked 18 in 17 innings, but Maxwell's special arm led the Reds to select him in the sixth round in 2022. He evokes some comparisons to former Cincinnati prospect Joe Boyle, a similarly massive righthander with huge pure stuff but big-time command and control concerns who was dealt to the A's in the summer of 2023.

SCOUTING REPORT: Maxwell's frame is a dead ringer for Jonathan Broxton's. There are few pitchers in the world that have Maxwell's combination of extreme velocity and exceptional movement. He sits between

97-99 mph, and has touched 100-101 regularly. He does so while generating more than 20 inches of induced vertical break, which is near the top of the range of fastball carry. It's a plus-plus fastball that is made to climb the ladder at the top of the zone. He's paired it with a plus-plus cutter/slider that has modest movement but big power at 87-89 mph. Maxwell's two-pitch combo could close out big league games if he had average control, which is three grades away. He will repeat his delivery consistently in some outings, but seem lost in others. He struck out half of the batters he faced in the Arizona Fall League, but also walked nine in 12.1 innings.

THE FUTURE: There's a high likelihood that Maxwell becomes yet another flamethrowing reliever whose control problems keep him from ever moving into a high-leverage role, but teams don't quickly give up on pitchers with arms this special.

Year	Age	Club	Level	W	L	ERA	G	GS	IP	H	HR	BB	SO	BB%	SO%	WHIP	AVG
2023	22	Daytona (FSL)	A	3	2	3.79	21	0	36	30	1	23	55	14.6	35.0	1.49	.227
2023	22	Dayton (MWL)	A+	3	2	4.56	13	0	26	17	2	15	41	13.4	36.6	1.25	.185
Minor League Totals				6	4	4.19	39	0	69	52	3	46	106	15.1	34.8	1.43	.205

27 SHENG-EN LIN, SS/OF

HIT: 40. **POW:** 50. **FLD:** 60. **RUN:** 70. **ARM:** 60. **BA Grade:** 50. **Risk:** Extreme.

Born: September 1, 2005. **B-T:** L-R. **HT:** 5-11. **WT:** 185. **Signed:** Taiwan, 2023.
Signed by: Jamey Storvick/Trey Hendricks.

TRACK RECORD: Lin has been a star for Taiwan's junior teams, which also gave U.S. scouts a chance to see him in action against the best of the 2023 draft class. He dominated in two outings on the mound in the 2022 18U World Cup and was named the tournament's top pitcher while also hitting .375 as an outfielder. The Reds signed him for $1.2 million in June 2023. He made his U.S. debut in August in the Arizona Complex League, where he played nine games.

SCOUTING REPORT: The Reds are just getting to fully know Lin, who is just beginning to settle into playing baseball stateside. Lin was a true two-way prospect coming out of Taiwan. Many teams wanted to see him pitch, and he's shown a mid-90s fastball that touches 99. The Reds want to see how well his athleticism and hitting ability plays, but pitching will remain a viable fallback option. Lin played both center field and shortstop in his brief pro debut. Either seems like a plausible option, but his plus-plus speed fits especially well in center.

THE FUTURE: Lin is trying to become the first Taiwanese position player to make a significant impact in the U.S. Yu Chang currently is the most successful of the three Taiwanese position players to play in the major leagues. Lin's athleticism and plus tools give him a shot, but he's years from Cincinnati.

Year	Age	Club	Level	AVG	G	AB	R	H	2B	3B	HR	RBI	BB	SO	SB	OBP	SLG
2023	17	ACL Reds	Rk	.214	9	28	6	6	0	1	0	3	6	16	2	.371	.286
Minor League Totals				.214	9	28	6	6	0	1	0	3	6	16	2	.371	.286

28 HUNTER HOLLAN, LHP

FB: 55. **SL:** 50. **CB:** 50. **CHG:** 50. **CTL:** 50. **BA Grade:** 45. **Risk:** Extreme.

Born: March 5, 2002. **B-T:** L-L. **HT:** 6-5. **WT:** 200. **Drafted:** Arkansas, 2023 (3rd round). **Signed by:** Paul Scott.

TRACK RECORD: As a third-round pick selected out of Southeastern Conference power Arkansas, Hollan may look like a pick that's playing it safe. In reality, he's one of the upside plays of the Reds' 2023 draft class. He spent two years at San Jacinto (Texas) JC before moving to the Razorbacks' weekend rotation for his draft year. He has shown flashes of dominance but moments of inconsistency as well.

SCOUTING REPORT: Hollan generally sat in the low 90s at Arkansas, but there's plenty of hope that he could end up sitting more in the mid 90s as he continues his strength training. He's skinny for now, and he's touched 95-97 mph at times, including pretty regularly in fall ball at Arkansas, so there should be more velocity to come. Hollan has a slider and curveball that can sometimes get too similar and a mid-80s average changeup. None of his secondaries are an above-average pitch, but they should tick up with added velocity.

THE FUTURE: Having five picks in the top 105 gave the Reds the chance to add a pair of safe college pitchers at the top of their class and a pair of more projectable pitchers soon thereafter in Hollan and Cole Schoenwetter. If Hollan keeps adding strength, he could soar up this list over the next two years.

Year	Age	Club	Level	W	L	ERA	G	GS	IP	H	HR	BB	SO	BB%	SO%	WHIP	AVG
2023	21	Did not play															

29 TYLER CALLIHAN, 2B/3B

HIT: 50. **POW:** 30. **FLD:** 55. **RUN:** 55. **ARM:** 55. **BA Grade:** 40. **Risk:** Medium.

Born: June 22, 2000. **B-T:** L-R. **HT:** 6-0. **WT:** 205. **Drafted:** HS—Jacksonville, FL, 2019 (3rd round).
Signed by: Sean Buckley.

TRACK RECORD: Scouting reports are time capsules in a way, because they try as best as they can to project the future while reflecting a player's current skill set. Callihan is an example of how player development and training can dramatically change those projections. Coming out of high school, Callihan was a bad-bodied infielder who didn't seem to have a defensive home. He's now skinnier and more agile than he was in high school, but now he faces many more questions about his bat.
SCOUTING REPORT: Callihan's development path has been rocky. After the coronavirus pandemic wiped out the 2020 season, he missed most of 2021 because of Tommy John surgery. He struggled to string together quality at-bats at High-A Dayton, but he finished with a strong final month and a half as he was promoted to Double-A Chattanooga. The biggest question with Callihan is whether he can do enough damage offensively to find an MLB role. He's shown the type of power that typically produces 5-10 homers in the big leagues, meaning he's more of a solid up-and-down infielder rather than a true utiltyman or platoon player. Callihan has slimmed down as a pro and is now an above-average defender at second who could handle third base. Adding good weight could restore some of his power.
THE FUTURE: Callihan's glove has developed better than expected while his bat hasn't reached anticipated levels. His path to the big leagues depends on him making strides at the plate.

Year	Age	Club	Level	AVG	G	AB	R	H	2B	3B	HR	RBI	BB	SO	SB	OBP	SLG
2023	23	Dayton (MWL)	A+	.236	109	399	44	94	21	5	8	47	37	104	25	.312	.373
2023	23	Chattanooga (SL)	AA	.310	22	87	11	27	10	0	1	11	13	20	4	.396	.460
Minor League Totals				.256	299	1125	144	288	66	15	24	134	95	267	60	.319	.405

30 CONNOR BURNS, C

HIT: 20. **POW:** 45. **FLD:** 60. **RUN:** 40. **ARM:** 70. **BA Grade:** 45. **Risk:** Extreme.

Born: December 25, 2001. **B-T:** R-R. **HT:** 6-1. **WT:** 185. **Drafted:** Long Beach State, 2023 (5th round).
Signed by: Mike Misuraca.

TRACK RECORD: In his first two years at Long Beach State, Burns hit .161/.221/.249, but the Dirtbags never considered benching him because he was so valuable defensively. As a junior, he hit .300/.368/.596 with almost as many extra-base hits (30) as he'd had hits (31) in his first two seasons. That glimpse of offensive potential combined with his impeccable defense made him a fifth-round pick.
SCOUTING REPORT: Defensively, there's little Burns can't do behind the plate. He frames pitches well, blocks pitches well off the plate because of excellent agility and he has a plus-plus arm with a quick release and excellent accuracy. Pro ball carries with it an increased mental load for catchers, but amateur scouts who watched him would be shocked if he is anything less than a plus defender behind the plate. Burns has some power potential but is always going to be a light bat. There's length and little fluidity in his swing. He struck out 47% of the time in his pro debut. If he can be even a .230-.240 hitter that would be a win.
THE FUTURE: The hope is that Burns can develop into a Austin Hedges/Martin Maldonado-type catcher whose glove is so good that teams will overlook his flaws at the plate. That will require his bat getting a good bit better than it is now, but he has shown the willingness to put in the work.

Year	Age	Club	Level	AVG	G	AB	R	H	2B	3B	HR	RBI	BB	SO	SB	OBP	SLG
2023	21	ACL Reds	Rk	.333	4	9	4	3	3	0	0	2	3	4	0	.500	.667
2023	21	Daytona (FSL)	A	.152	19	66	9	10	1	1	3	10	11	39	0	.269	.333
Minor League Totals				.173	23	75	13	13	4	1	3	12	14	43	0	.304	.373

Cleveland Guardians

BY TEDDY CAHILL

The 2023 season was a disappointment for the Guardians. After winning the American League Central in 2022 with the youngest team in MLB, the expectation was that Cleveland would build on that for another strong campaign.

Instead, 2023 was a roller coaster. The team flirted with .500 much of the year and, with it, playoff contention. The Guardians traded Josh Bell, Aaron Civale and Amed Rosario in a series of deadline deals for prospects, only to go on a run in August, cut deeply into the Twins' division lead and then claim Lucas Giolito, Reynaldo Lopez and Matt Moore on waivers to bolster a stretch run. Ultimately, the

Guardians came up short, and then stumbled further upon falling out of contention. Their .469 winning percentage was their worst since a .420 mark in 2012. The season also was the last for manager Terry Francona, who retired following his 11th season with Cleveland.

Despite the ending, the Guardians can look toward 2024 with excitement. The team again had one of the youngest rosters in MLB in 2023, including 24-year-old righthander Tanner Bibee, who finished second in AL Rookie of the Year voting.

He was one of several prospects who graduated to the big leagues. That list includes catcher Bo Naylor, lefthander Logan Allen and righthander Gavin Williams, all of whom had quick success and look like players with long-term futures in Cleveland.

Jose Ramirez remains at the core of the Guardians roster after he made his third straight All-Star Game and finished in the top 10 of MVP voting for the sixth time in seven seasons. Andres Gimenez on the eve of the season signed a seven-year, $106.5 million contract extension, the second-largest deal in franchise history. With Ramirez and Gimenez in the fold for the rest of the decade, as well as the emergence of Steven Kwan in left field and a typically strong, young pitching staff, the core of the Guardians' roster is clear.

To manage it, the Guardians turned to Stephen Vogt, 39, who is only one year removed from his 16-year big-league career as a catcher. He spent his lone season of coaching as the Mariners' bullpen coach and now will take over for the winningest manager in Cleveland history. What Vogt lacks in experience, the Guardians hope he will make up for with his ability to bring along the young players who are breaking through to the major leagues.

The Guardians struck gold in December when they won the second-ever draft lottery to secure the first overall pick in 2024. Cleveland finished

Rookies Gavin Williams (pictured), Tanner Bibee and Logan Allen pitched in the 2023 rotation.

PROJECTED 2027 LINEUP

Catcher	Bo Naylor	27
First Base	Kyle Manzardo	26
Second Base	Andres Gimenez	28
Third Base	Jose Ramirez	34
Shortstop	Brayan Rocchio	26
Left Field	George Valera	26
Center Field	Steven Kwan	29
Right Field	Chase DeLauter	25
Designated Hitter	Josh Naylor	30
No. 1 Starter	Shane Bieber	32
No. 2 Starter	Gavin Williams	28
No. 3 Starter	Tanner Bibee	27
No. 4 Starter	Triston McKenzie	29
No. 5 Starter	Daniel Espino	26
Closer	Emmanuel Clase	29

10th in the reverse standings and had just a 2% chance of winning the lottery, but the ping pong ball bounced its way and now the franchise holds the draft's top pick for the first time.

The Guardians' system remains deep but has fewer impact talents in the upper minors after graduating so many players in 2023. Cleveland continues to find success on the international market, and outfielder Chase DeLauter, the team's first-round pick in 2022, is on the rise.

The No. 1 pick represents an opportunity to inject new, high-level talent into a solid system. With that in mind, 2024 represents a substantial year for the franchise's direction, from the big leagues through to the farm system. ■

CLEVELAND GUARDIANS

TOP 2024 CONTRIBUTORS	RANK
1. Kyle Manzardo, 1B	4
2. George Valera, OF	7
3. Joey Cantillo, LHP	11

BREAKOUT PROSPECTS	RANK
1. Rafael Ramirez Jr., SS	17
2. Dayan Frias, 3B	19

SOURCE OF TOP 30 TALENT

Homegrown	25	Acquired	5
College	6	Trade	4
Junior college	0	Rule 5 draft	1
High school	7	Independent league	0
Nondrafted free agent	1	Free agent/waivers	0
International	11		

LF
Jhonkensy Noel (28)
Guy Lipscomb
Joe Lampe

CF
Chase DeLauter (1)
Jaison Chourio (8)
Petey Halpin (14)
Jake Fox (23)
Jose Pirela

RF
George Valera (7)
Johnathan Rodriguez (24)
Wuilfredo Antuñez

3B
Angel Genao (15)
Dayan Frias (19)
Gabriel Rodriguez

SS
Brayan Rocchio (2)
Angel Martinez (6)
Welbyn Francisca (12)
Rafael Ramirez Jr. (17)
Jose Devers (20)
Kahlil Watson (21)
Alex Mooney
Milan Tolentino

2B
Juan Brito (5)
Jose Tena (22)
Christian Knapczyk
Nate Furman
Fran Alduey

1B
Kyle Manzardo (4)
Deyvison De Los Santos (13)
CJ Kayfus
Joe Naranjo

C
Ralphy Velazquez (9)
Kody Huff
Bryan Lavastida
Cooper Ingle

LHP

LHSP	LHRP
Alex Clemmey (10)	Tim Herrin (30)
Joey Cantillo (11)	Ryan Webb
Jackson Humphries (16)	
Parker Messick (26)	
Will Dion	
Doug Nikhazy	
Steve Hajjar	

RHP

RHSP	RHRP
Daniel Espino (3)	Andrew Walters (18)
Justin Campbell (27)	Cade Smith (25)
Jacob Zibin	Cody Morris (29)
Tommy Mace	Tanner Burns
Yorman Gomez	Hunter Gaddis

1 CHASE DeLAUTER, OF

Born: October 8, 2001. **B-T:** L-L. **HT:** 6-4. **WT:** 235.
Drafted: James Madison, 2022 (1st round).
Signed by: Kyle Bamberger.

TRACK RECORD: DeLauter was unheralded as a prep player at Hedgesville High in West Virginia and went to James Madison as a two-way player. While he played well at JMU in 20202 and 2021, the pandemic severely limited his game time. DeLauter remained under the radar going into summer 2021, when he broke out in the Cape Cod League, tying for the league lead with nine home runs in 34 games. He was off to a strong start in the spring of 2022, but a broken left foot in April brought an end to his junior season after just 24 games. The Guardians drafted DeLauter 16th overall in 2022 and signed him for $3.75 million, which was roughly slot value for the pick. He did not play after the draft and his pro debut was further delayed in 2023 when he required another surgery on his foot, sidelining him until June. DeLauter spent most of 2023 at High-A Lake County, reaching Double-A Akron for six games and then extending his season in the Arizona Fall League. He hit .299/.385/.529 in 23 AFL games, leading the league with 27 RBIs and ranking among the leaders with five home runs.

SCOUTING REPORT: DeLauter first stands out for his size—he is listed at 6-foot-4, 235 pounds—and his powerful lefthanded swing. He's a disciplined hitter with good strike-zone awareness. DeLauter rarely expands the zone and shows good barrel control, making contact on pitches in the zone 88% of the time in 2023 and chasing just 20% of the time. He swings the bat judiciously, making pitchers come into the strike zone and not digging himself into early pitchers' counts. DeLauter has plus raw power and gets to it well, consistently making hard contact. He averaged an 89 mph exit velocity on his batted balls in 2023 and topped out near 111. He gets the ball in the air consistently, with one of the lowest groundball rates in the Guardians' minor league system. DeLauter looks like a prototype corner outfielder, but he has above-average speed, covers ground well and has good instincts in the outfield. He split time in 2023 evenly between center field and right field and could settle in either spot. He has a plus arm.

THE FUTURE: Once DeLauter got underway in 2023, his season couldn't have gone much better. He peaked at Double-A Akron and should return

MIKE JANES/FOUR SEAM IMAGES

BA GRADE	SCOUTING GRADES
60 Risk: High	Hit: 50. Power: 60. Run: 55. Field: 50. Arm: 60.

Projected future grades on 20-80 scouting scale

BEST TOOLS

BATTING

Best Hitter for Average	Chase DeLauter
Best Power Hitter	Jhonkensy Noel
Best Strike-Zone Discipline	Brayan Rocchio
Fastest Baserunner	Guy Lipscomb
Best Athlete	Chase DeLauter

PITCHING

Best Fastball	Daniel Espino
Best Curveball	Alex Clemmey
Best Slider	Daniel Espino
Best Changeup	Joey Cantillo
Best Control	Will Dion

FIELDING

Best Defensive Catcher	Robert Lopez
Best Defensive Infielder	Brayan Rocchio
Best Infield Arm	Kahlil Watson
Best Defensive Outfielder	Petey Halpin
Best Outfield Arm	Johnathan Rodriguez

there to open 2024. The early returns have been great, and more than anything else, DeLauter needs more at-bats to further his development. The Guardians' lineup has a desperate need for power after finishing last in MLB in home runs and 29th in slugging in 2023. DeLauter could add a needed impact bat to Cleveland's lineup, potentially by the end of 2024. ∎

Year	Age	Club (League)	Level	AVG	G	AB	R	H	2B	3B	HR	RBI	BB	SO	SB	OBP	SLG
2023	21	ACL Guardians	Rk	.286	9	28	8	8	3	0	1	4	8	5	3	.447	.500
2023	21	Lake County (MWL)	A+	.366	42	164	24	60	18	0	4	31	10	22	3	.403	.549
2023	21	Akron (EL)	AA	.364	6	22	3	8	1	0	0	4	5	3	0	.464	.409
Minor League Totals				.355	57	214	35	76	22	0	5	39	23	30	6	.417	.528

2 BRAYAN ROCCHIO, SS

HIT: 50. **POW:** 50. **RUN:** 55. **FLD:** 60. **ARM:** 50. **BA Grade:** 55. **Risk:** High.

Born: January 13, 2001. **B-T:** B-R. **HT:** 5-10. **WT:** 170.
Signed: Venezuela, 2017. **Signed by:** Jhonathan Leyba.
TRACK RECORD: Rocchio was nicknamed "The Professor" soon after signing in 2017 because of his preternatural baseball IQ and feel for the game. Those traits helped him hit the ground running in pro ball, and he's been on an accelerated track from the beginning. He reached Double-A Akron in 2021 as a 20-year-old, despite travel issues in 2020 that left him stuck in Venezuela during the pandemic. Rocchio was added to the 40-man roster after that season and the following year reached Triple-A Columbus. He made his major league debut May 16, 2023, and went up and down a couple times during the season, appearing in 23 games for the Guardians.
SCOUTING REPORT: Rocchio doesn't stand out physically, but he has solid all-around tools that play up even further thanks to his game awareness. A switch-hitter, he has a smooth, consistent swing from both sides of the plate and excellent pitch recognition. He's an aggressive hitter and consistently barrels the ball. Rocchio has grown into more power as he's physically matured and worked more on strength training, and now has average power potential. It plays mostly as doubles pop. Rocchio has long since answered any questions about his ability to stick at shortstop. He's an above-average runner, and his hands and arm are good enough for the position. He's also seen time at second and third base to give him more versatility. Even in the big leagues, the vast majority of his time has been spent at shortstop.
THE FUTURE: There are no shortage of options to become Cleveland's shortstop of the future, but Rocchio is the most likely answer and could win the job as soon as Opening Day.

Year	Age	Club (League)	Level	AVG	G	AB	R	H	2B	3B	HR	RBI	BB	SO	SB	OBP	SLG
2023	22	Columbus (IL)	AAA	.280	116	468	81	131	33	6	7	65	60	66	25	.367	.421
2023	22	Cleveland (AL)	MLB	.247	23	81	9	20	6	0	0	8	4	27	0	.279	.321
Minor League Totals				.276	485	1929	316	532	110	19	47	248	182	345	96	.349	.426
Major League Totals				.247	23	81	9	20	6	0	0	8	4	27	0	.279	.321

3 DANIEL ESPINO, RHP

FB: 80. **CB:** 55. **SL:** 70. **CHG:** 50. **CTL:** 55. **BA Grade:** 60. **Risk:** Extreme.

Born: January 5, 2001. **B-T:** R-R. **HT:** 6-2. **WT:** 225.
Drafted: HS—Statesboro, GA, 2019 (1st round). **Signed by:** Ethan Purser.
TRACK RECORD: Espino was born in Panama before his family moved to the U.S. when he was 15. He soon took off on the mound and hit the ground running in pro ball. He opened 2022 with Double-A Akron as one of the younger pitchers in the Eastern League, but he made just four starts before a knee injury sidelined him for the season. Espino was shut down in February 2023 and missed the season after a shoulder strain ultimately resulted in May surgery to repair the anterior capsule.
SCOUTING REPORT: Espino is on the shorter end of what teams look for in a righthanded starter, but his excellent athleticism and a rare combination of explosiveness and flexibility help him access his lower half in a way most pitchers his size cannot. That quality helps him produce elite velocity, and his fastball can reach triple digits and sit 96 mph. Since entering pro ball, Espino has raised his arm slot and now generates significant vertical break on his fastball, adding to its effectiveness. He throws both a curveball and slider. His velocity helps his slider play up, and it's not uncommon for him to throw the pitch in the low 90s. It's a double-plus offering and creates swing-and-miss at an exceptional rate. His curveball is a big, 12-to-6 breaker that works mostly as a chase pitch but also creates groundball outs. Espino's firm changeup is an effective fourth offering and has real promise but needs further refinement because he hasn't needed to use it often. He has a long arm action but typically pitches with average control.
THE FUTURE: Recovery from Espino's surgery is estimated at 12 to 14 months, putting him on target for a midsummer return. Until he gets back on the mound, it's hard to pin down what to expect from him. The Guardians added Espino to the 40-man roster in November to protect him from the Rule 5 draft. He could quickly get in the mix in Cleveland if he returns healthy and effective.

Year	Age	Club (League)	Level	W	L	ERA	G	GS	IP	H	HR	BB	SO	BB%	SO%	WHIP	AVG
2023	22	Did not play—Injured															
Minor League Totals				4	11	3.57	33	33	134	89	15	53	221	9.8	40.9	1.06	.184

4 KYLE MANZARDO, 1B

HIT: 50. POW: 55. RUN: 20. FLD: 50. ARM: 50. BA Grade: 55. Risk: High.

Born: July 18, 2000. **B-T:** L-R. **HT:** 6-0. **WT:** 205.
Drafted: Washington State, 2021 (2nd round). **Signed by:** James Bonnici (Rays).

TRACK RECORD: Manzardo was a three-year starter at Washington State and truly broke out in 2021 as a junior, when he hit .366/.437/.640 with 11 home runs in 47 games. That led him to be drafted in the second round by the Rays and, at pick No. 63 overall, he became the highest drafted Cougar in 30 years. Manzardo has moved quickly in the minor leagues, opening the 2023 season as a 22-year-old at Triple-A Durham. He was sidelined for about six weeks with a dislocated shoulder, costing him an appearance in the Futures Game. The Rays dealt Manzardo to the Guardians at the trade deadline for veteran righthander Aaron Civale and he played well down the stretch after returning from the injury. He shined in the Arizona Fall League, finishing just off the league lead with six home runs and 14 extra-base hits in 22 games.

SCOUTING REPORT: Manzardo has a first base-only profile, which can be limiting, but his bat has lived up to the pressure. The lefthanded hitter has an advanced approach and does an excellent job controlling the strike zone—he struck out in 19.2% of his Triple-A plate appearances. He's not a passive hitter, however. Instead, Manzardo's pitch recognition and batting eye allow him to make excellent swing decisions. He has above-average power and gets to it well in games, particularly in cases when he can pull the ball. Manzardo is a bottom-of-the-scale runner. He's a capable first baseman with good hands.

THE FUTURE: Manzardo is the kind of power hitter the Guardians have long been looking to add to their lineup. Josh Naylor played the bulk of the 2023 season at first base, but there is room at DH. Manzardo will likely figure into the 2024 lineup at those positions, possibly as soon as Opening Day.

Year	Age	Club (League)	Level	AVG	G	AB	R	H	2B	3B	HR	RBI	BB	SO	SB	OBP	SLG
2023	22	ACL Guardians	Rk	.000	3	8	1	0	0	0	0	1	1	1	0	.100	.000
2023	22	Durham (IL)	AAA	.238	73	265	33	63	19	1	11	38	42	65	1	.342	.442
2023	22	Columbus (IL)	AAA	.256	21	78	16	20	8	0	6	16	12	14	0	.348	.590
Minor League Totals				.284	203	718	131	204	58	2	41	144	118	151	2	.384	.542

5 JUAN BRITO, 2B/3B

HIT: 55. POW: 45. RUN: 50. FLD: 55. ARM: 50. BA Grade: 50. Risk: High.

Born: September 24, 2001. **B-T:** B-R. **HT:** 5-11. **WT:** 162.
Signed: Dominican Republic, 2018. **Signed by:** Rolando Fernandez/Frank Roa (Rockies).

TRACK RECORD: Brito was an unheralded signing out of the Dominican Republic by the Rockies in 2018. He's come on strong since, and the Guardians in November 2022 acquired him for Nolan Jones and immediately added him to the 40-man roster. Brito rewarded his new organization in 2023, as he shot through three levels of the minor leagues to reach Triple-A Columbus in September, just a few days before turning 22.

SCOUTING REPORT: Brito fits in well with Cleveland's cadre of young middle infielders. He is a disciplined, patient hitter with good bat-to-ball skills. He has walked about as much as he's struck out over his professional career and has a low chase rate. While he has a contact-oriented approach, the switch-hitter has average power potential. Brito's swing has natural lift, and as he gets stronger he could grow into even more pop. He's already showing it in games. His 31 doubles and 46 extra-base hits in 2023 ranked second and third among Cleveland's minor leaguers, and his .817 OPS ranked third among qualified Eastern League hitters. Brito is an average runner and is aggressive on the bases. He has primarily played second base as a professional and his average athleticism makes him a solid defender at the position. He saw time at both shortstop and third base in 2023 as well, and the Guardians believe his arm strength and range play on the left side of the infield.

THE FUTURE: Brito will return to Columbus to open 2024 and could make his MLB debut later in the season. From there, things are less clear. The Cleveland infield is crowded. Third baseman Jose Ramirez and second baseman Andres Gimenez have long-term deals. Brito is among the best of the Guardians' infielders pushing through the upper minors and gives the organization another high-upside player.

Year	Age	Club (League)	Level	AVG	G	AB	R	H	2B	3B	HR	RBI	BB	SO	SB	OBP	SLG
2023	21	Lake County (MWL)	A+	.265	35	132	29	35	9	0	4	14	24	21	3	.379	.424
2023	21	Akron (EL)	AA	.276	87	315	46	87	21	1	10	60	48	63	3	.373	.444
2023	21	Columbus (IL)	AAA	.214	5	14	1	3	1	0	0	1	6	4	1	.450	.286
Minor League Totals				.285	296	1067	208	304	67	10	31	184	187	195	41	.394	.454

6 ANGEL MARTINEZ, 2B/3B

HIT: 50. **POW:** 50. **RUN:** 50. **FLD:** 55. **ARM:** 60. **BA Grade:** 50. **Risk:** High.

Born: January 27, 2002. **B-T:** B-R. **HT:** 6-0. **WT:** 186.
Signed: Dominican Republic, 2018. **Signed by:** Jhonathan Leyba.
TRACK RECORD: Martinez reached Triple-A Columbus as a 21-year-old in 2023, making him one of the youngest everyday players in the International League. His rise since the pandemic has been meteoric. Martinez's professional experience coming into 2021 was limited to the Dominican Summer League and instructional league, but his experience around baseball—his father is former big league catcher Sandy Martinez, now the Nationals' DSL manager, and his older brother Sandy Martinez Jr. also played professionally—likely eased his transition.
SCOUTING REPORT: Martinez isn't the most tooled-up of Cleveland's middle infielders, but his baseball IQ and maturity make all his tools play up. The switch-hitter has a simple swing from both sides and can drive the ball to all fields with solid power potential, though it plays as doubles pop now. Martinez is a disciplined hitter and makes a lot of contact, priding himself in his ability to make quick adjustments at the plate. After initially struggling in pro ball versus lefthanders, he has improved dramatically as a right-handed hitter as he has matured. Martinez is an average runner but still covers a lot of ground thanks to his instincts and makes sound decisions defensively. He also has worked hard to improve his arm strength, which now grades as plus. Martinez can play anywhere on the infield and in 2023 mostly played second base at Double-A Akron and then mostly third base in Columbus, with a solid amount of time at shortstop at both spots. That versatility should help him find a spot in Cleveland.
THE FUTURE: Martinez has consistently been one of the youngest players at his level, and the way Cleveland has challenged him is indicative of how advanced he is. He'll return to Columbus to start 2024 and could find himself in the mix to be called up later in the season.

Year	Age	Club (League)	Level	AVG	G	AB	R	H	2B	3B	HR	RBI	BB	SO	SB	OBP	SLG
2023	21	Akron (EL)	AA	.245	99	383	55	94	15	4	11	60	37	83	10	.321	.392
2023	21	Columbus (IL)	AAA	.268	37	142	17	38	8	1	3	19	10	36	1	.320	.401
Minor League Totals				.264	390	1487	227	392	76	22	35	196	171	312	47	.347	.415

7 GEORGE VALERA, OF

HIT: 50. **POW:** 55. **RUN:** 50. **FLD:** 50. **ARM:** 50. **BA Grade:** 50. **Risk:** High.

Born: November 13, 2000. **B-T:** L-L. **HT:** 6-0. **WT:** 195.
Signed: Dominican Republic, 2017. **Signed by:** Jhonathan Leyba/Domingo Toribio.
TRACK RECORD: Valera was born in New York and lived there until his family moved to the Dominican Republic when he was 13. In 2017, he was the centerpiece of Cleveland's big play in the international market, signing a $1.3 million deal. He was added to the 40-man roster after the 2021 season and has spent the last two years in the upper minors, primarily at Triple-A. While his progress as a professional has mostly had a consistent upward trend line, Valera's 2023 season was tough. During spring training he had surgery to repair a broken hamate in his right hand and also suffered a hamstring injury. The pair of injuries mostly kept him out of action until mid June, and he never really got on track.
SCOUTING REPORT: Valera has long stood out for his advanced setup at the plate as well as quick hands and an ability to keep the bat in the zone for a long time, traits that enable him to make a lot of hard contact. Despite that loose, easy swing, however, there is some swing-and-miss in his game. Valera has struck out in about one-quarter of his plate appearances in full-season ball. His patience and feel for the zone mean that he also consistently works walks. Valera has above-average raw power and gets to it in games well. He profiles as a corner outfielder with average speed and arm strength. He played more center field in 2023, however.
THE FUTURE: If Valera is able to bounce back after a season to forget, there's still plenty of opportunity for him in Cleveland. He looks like a traditional power-hitting corner outfielder, long a position of need for the Guardians. He'll return to Columbus to begin 2024 and could break through to the big leagues later in the season.

Year	Age	Club (League)	Level	AVG	G	AB	R	H	2B	3B	HR	RBI	BB	SO	SB	OBP	SLG
2023	22	ACL Guardians	Rk	.333	6	21	5	7	4	0	1	3	4	5	2	.423	.667
2023	22	Columbus (IL)	AAA	.211	73	256	40	54	10	1	10	35	50	85	1	.343	.375
Minor League Totals				.242	355	1244	212	301	52	10	63	223	228	387	23	.363	.452

8 JAISON CHOURIO, OF

HIT: 55. **POW:** 45. **RUN:** 60. **FLD:** 55. **ARM:** 50. **BA Grade:** 50. **Risk:** High.

Born: May 19, 2005. **B-T:** B-R. **HT:** 6-1. **WT:** 162.
Signed: Venezuela, 2022. **Signed by:** Jose Stela.
TRACK RECORD: A year after the Brewers made Jackson Chourio the headliner of their 2021 international class, the Guardians made his younger brother Jaison their top signing of the 2022 class at $1.2 million out of Venezuela. Jaison Chourio made his professional debut that June in the Dominican Summer League, where he showed off his advanced skill set. He again impressed in 2023, as he moved up to the Arizona Complex League, where he finished eighth with 19 stolen bases, seventh in he batting race at .349, fifth with 38 walks and third with a .476 on-base percentage. Chourio earned a late-season promotion to Low-A Lynchburg as an 18-year-old.
SCOUTING REPORT: Chourio stands out for his blend of athleticism, tools and projection. The switch-hitter combines excellent pitch recognition and plate discipline, giving him a mature, advanced approach at the plate. He has good bat-to-ball skills and shows a good feel for the barrel. Chourio is hit-over-power now, but there is some hope that he will develop more power in time as he physically matures. There's some leverage to his swing that would help him get to his power, particularly when hitting lefthanded. Chourio is a plus runner with good instincts on the bases and stole 20 bases in 22 attempts in 2023. His speed plays in center field, where he can become an above-average defender or better. He has easy defensive actions, good instincts and an average arm. Chourio works out with his brother Jackson in the offseason.
THE FUTURE: Chourio is already on an aggressive developmental track. He'll return to Lynchburg as a 19-year-old to open the 2024 season, when he'll still be among the youngest everyday players. In a best-case scenario, he could begin to enter the big league picture by 2026, when he will be 21.

Year	Age	Club (League)	Level	AVG	G	AB	R	H	2B	3B	HR	RBI	BB	SO	SB	OBP	SLG
2023	18	ACL Guardians	Rk	.349	39	149	40	52	12	1	1	25	38	37	19	.476	.463
2023	18	Lynchburg (CAR)	A	.200	9	35	7	7	1	0	0	3	6	15	1	.310	.229
Minor League Totals				.298	99	322	81	96	20	4	2	56	87	75	35	.443	.404

9 RALPHY VELAZQUEZ, C

HIT: 55. **POW:** 60. **RUN:** 30. **FLD:** 45. **ARM:** 60. **BA Grade:** 55. **Risk:** Extreme.

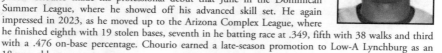

Born: May 28, 2005. **B-T:** L-R. **HT:** 6-2. **WT:** 215.
Drafted: HS—Huntington Beach, CA, 2023 (1st round). **Signed by:** Chirag Nanavati.
TRACK RECORD: Velazquez starred at Southern California prep powerhouse Huntington Beach HS, where he hit 23 home runs in his career and helped the Oilers win the 2023 National High School Invitational. He was the top prep player in the state in 2023 and became the third first-round pick in the program's history, joining Hank Conger (2006) and Nick Pratto (2016). Velazquez made a brief pro debut in the Arizona Complex League after signing and raked. He went 8-for-23 with two home runs and three doubles in six games.
SCOUTING REPORT: Velazquez stands out most for his bat. He has a quick, fluid lefthanded swing and generates easy above-average power. In a tiny ACL sample, Velazquez showed high-end exit velocity with an average reading of 89 mph and max near 109. He has a disciplined approach at the plate and makes good swing decisions, rarely expanding the strike zone. He made contact on pitches in the zone nearly 90% of the time in his brief pro debut, while chasing about 22% of the time. Unlike many young power hitters, Velazquez doesn't sell out for power, instead relying on his bat speed and strength to drive the ball. Velazquez has intriguing tools behind the plate but his glove lags behind his bat. He receives well, has plus arm strength and earns praise for his makeup. To stick at catcher, Velazquez will have to improve his blocking and athleticism behind the plate. He's a below-average runner, meaning first base would be his destination if he ever needed to change positions. As a lefthanded hitter with a chance to develop above-average hitting ability and plus power, Velazquez's bat could one day profile at first base.
THE FUTURE: Velazquez will look to work on his defense as he starts his first full professional season at Low-A Lynchburg.

Year	Age	Club (League)	Level	AVG	G	AB	R	H	2B	3B	HR	RBI	BB	SO	SB	OBP	SLG
2023	18	ACL Guardians	Rk	.348	6	23	7	8	3	0	2	8	3	5	1	.393	.739
Minor League Totals				.348	6	23	7	8	3	0	2	8	3	5	1	.393	.739

10 ALEX CLEMMEY, LHP

FB: 70. **CB:** 60. **CHG:** 40. **CTL:** 40. **BA Grade:** 55. **Risk:** Extreme.

Born: July 18, 2005. **B-T:** L-L. **HT:** 6-6. **WT:** 205.
Drafted: HS—Warwick, RI, 2023 (2nd round). **Signed by:** Kyle Bamberger.
TRACK RECORD: Clemmey had a sensational high school career at Bishop Hendricken—the alma mater of Rocco Baldelli—and in 2023 was named Gatorade Rhode Island Player of the Year. The Guardians drafted him in the second round—58th overall—and Clemmey became the highest selected player from the Rhode Island prep ranks since 2004, when the Twins drafted righthander Jay Rainville at No. 39 overall. It was also the earliest the Guardians have drafted a high school pitcher since taking Daniel Espino 24th overall in 2019. Cleveland went well above slot to sign Clemmey for $2.3 million to buy him out of a Vanderbilt commitment. He did not pitch after signing.
SCOUTING REPORT: Listed at 6-foot-6, 205 pounds, Clemmey has a big, projectable build and high-octane stuff from the left side. His fastball gets up to 98 mph with riding life and typically sits in the mid 90s. Clemmey throws a sharp curveball that at its best is a plus offering and generates swings and misses. He mostly attacks hitters with his fastball and curveball, but he also can mix in a changeup with sinking action. Like most tall, hard-throwing teenagers, Clemmey is still working on his control. His delivery is aggressive and effortful, and he'll need to learn how to more consistently repeat it to allow him to throw more strikes, because he has a history of higher walk rates. That gives him a high-risk, high-reward profile, but it's easy to dream on his upside.
THE FUTURE: Clemmey will make his professional debut in 2024 with Low-A Lynchburg. He was one of the younger players in the draft class and won't turn 19 until July, so the Guardians are likely to take a conservative approach with Clemmey, at least initially.

Year	Age	Club (League)	Level	W	L	ERA	G	GS	IP	H	HR	BB	SO	BB%	SO%	WHIP	AVG
2023	17	Did not play															

11 JOEY CANTILLO, LHP

FB: 55. **CB:** 40. **SL:** 45. **CHG:** 60. **CTL:** 40. **BA Grade:** 50. **Risk:** High.

Born: December 18, 1999. **B-T:** L-L. **HT:** 6-4. **WT:** 220. **Drafted:** Kailua, HI, 2017 (16th round).
Signed by: Justin Baughman (Padres).
TRACK RECORD: Cantillo drew limited draft interest after his fastball sat in the mid 80s in high school, but the Padres were intrigued when he touched 91 mph in a pre-draft workout. They selected him in the 16th round and were able to sign him away from his Kentucky commitment. Cantillo rewarded that belief with a breakout 2019 season, when he led the organization with 144 strikeouts. He was traded to Cleveland at the 2020 trade deadline as a part of the return for Mike Clevinger. He was limited by injuries in his first two seasons with his new organization—an oblique in 2021 and a shoulder in 2022—but he came on strong in 2023 and impressed with Triple-A Columbus.
SCOUTING REPORT: Cantillo long had a projectable look and his velocity had ticked up a bit while still with the Padres. He's since made bigger gains, however, and touched 98 mph in a short stint at the Futures Game. His fastball typically averaged about 93 mph, and with the added velocity—as well as the angle he throws from and the carry he gets on the pitch—it has become an above-average offering that gets swings and misses. His changeup remains a plus pitch and generates swings and misses as well. His slider is his third pitch and is a fringy offering, while he also occasionally shows a below-average curveball. The increased velocity hasn't helped his control, which now rates below-average.
THE FUTURE: Cantillo's strong 2023 put him on the cusp of the big leagues, a year after he was first added to the 40-man roster. Breaking into the Guardians' rotation is no easy task, but he has the tools to be a big league starter. Still, he'll likely return to Columbus to open the 2024 season, with an eye on refining his control.

Year	Age	Club (League)	Level	W	L	ERA	G	GS	IP	H	HR	BB	SO	BB%	SO%	WHIP	AVG
2023	23	Akron (EL)	AA	1	0	1.85	6	6	24	14	2	14	35	14.4	36.1	1.15	.175
2023	23	Columbus (IL)	AAA	6	4	4.64	20	18	95	89	16	55	111	12.9	26.1	1.52	.245
Minor League Totals				24	16	2.94	88	71	362	263	25	163	473	10.9	31.6	1.18	.202

12 WELBYN FRANCISCA, SS

HIT: 55. **POW:** 40. **RUN:** 55. **FLD:** 55. **ARM:** 50. **BA Grade:** 55. **Risk:** Extreme.

Born: May 17, 2006. **B-T:** B-R. **HT:** 5-8. **WT:** 148. **Signed:** Dominican Republic, 2023. **Signed by:** Gustavo Benzan.

TRACK RECORD: Francisca was Cleveland's top signing in the 2023 international market. He made his professional debut later in the year, just a few weeks after his 17th birthday, and started his career in the Dominican Summer League. He is nicknamed "Phosphorus" for his dynamic game and personality.

SCOUTING REPORT: A switch-hitter, Francisca has long stood out for his natural feel for hitting and his offensive profile is a familiar one for the Guardians. He has a rhythmic swing with above-average hand-eye coordination and his feel for the barrel leads to a lot of contact. His profile is hit over power, but he produces above-average bat speed and he could add more power as he physically matures and learns to drive the ball more often. Francisca has the defensive tools to stay up the middle with some viewing a move to second base as likely, while others believe he can stay at shortstop. His above-average speed and average arm give him a chance to develop at shortstop.

THE FUTURE: Francisca has an exciting overall skill set, and his debut summer was encouraging. He'll look to keep progressing in 2024 as he makes his U.S. debut in the Arizona Complex League.

Year	Age	Club (League)	Level	AVG	G	AB	R	H	2B	3B	HR	RBI	BB	SO	SB	OBP	SLG
2023	17	DSL Guardians Blue	Rk	.316	40	152	34	48	7	6	3	24	24	35	11	.419	.500
Minor League Totals				.316	40	152	34	48	7	6	3	24	24	35	11	.419	.500

13 DEYVISON DE LOS SANTOS, 3B/1B

HIT: 40. **POW:** 60. **RUN:** 45. **FLD:** 40. **ARM:** 50. **BA Grade:** 50. **Risk:** Very High.

Born: June 21, 2003. **B-T:** R-R. **HT:** 5-11. **WT:** 185. **Signed:** Dominican Republic, 2019. **Signed by:** Cesar Geronimo Jr./Wil Tejada (D-backs).

TRACK RECORD: De Los Santos' feel for hitting, penchant for loud contact and natural strength got the D-backs' attention as an amateur. After back-to-back strong years in his first two seasons in the minors, he hit his first speed bump in 2023. His struggles at Double-A Amarillo reached a point that the organization paused his season and brought him back to Arizona to clean up his swing. The difference upon his return was night and day, and De Los Santos finished the year as perhaps the hottest hitter in the organization over the final two and a half months of the season. Still, Arizona did not add him to the 40-man roster to protect him from the Rule 5 draft and he was selected by the Guardians.

SCOUTING REPORT: De Los Santos possesses a naturally powerful swing and the ability to drive the ball to all fields with authority, but that power got him into trouble in 2023. He developed bad habits trying to swing as hard as possible, and became too rotational and needed to make swing decisions too early. Once he toned down his approach while on the development list, De Los Santos went on a tear, and went from hitting .207 with a .576 OPS in his first 63 games to .322 with .936 OPS over his final 56. His approach is hyper-aggressive, but he maintained a manageable strikeout rate of 26%. De Los Santos is an average runner who could slow down as he matures. He has enough arm for third base, but his below-average footwork and hands limit his upside and make a shift across the diamond likely.

THE FUTURE: As a Rule 5 pick, De Los Santos must remain on Cleveland's roster for the entire 2024 season or else he will be waived and offered back to Arizona if unclaimed. With Jose Ramirez entrenched at third base, that means the Guardians will mostly use De Los Santos at first base and DH. His righthanded power gives him an impact tool, but he'll also be 20 years old on Opening Day and hasn't appeared in a game above Double-A. For the Guardians, De Los Santos represents a low-risk, high-reward play.

Year	Age	Club (League)	Level	AVG	G	AB	R	H	2B	3B	HR	RBI	BB	SO	SB	OBP	SLG
2023	20	Amarillo (TL)	AA	.254	113	452	73	115	16	2	20	61	25	125	4	.297	.431
Minor League Totals				.284	301	1192	190	339	61	6	50	204	85	339	12	.334	.471

14 PETEY HALPIN, OF

HIT: 55. **POW:** 40. **RUN:** 55. **FLD:** 50. **ARM:** 50. **BA Grade:** 45. **Risk:** High.

Born: May 26, 2002. **B-T:** L-R. **HT:** 6-0. **WT:** 180. **Drafted:** HS—Manhattan Beach, CA, 2020 (3rd round). **Signed by:** Carlos Muniz.

TRACK RECORD: The Guardians have pushed Halpin aggressively since drafting him 95th overall in 2020. He was 20 years old on Opening Day 2023 and spent the season with Double-A Akron, where he was one of the youngest players in the Eastern League.

SCOUTING REPORT: Halpin has a top-of-the-order profile and a well-rounded skill set. He controls the strike zone well and makes adjustments quickly, which helps him make a lot of contact. His swing is geared toward hitting line drives and he's not a slugger, but he drives the ball into gaps often. The combination of that hard contact and his above-average speed makes for a lot of extra-base hits. He's still learning to make the most of his speed on the bases, but he is a threat to run. Halpin has average outfield actions and an average arm. If he can stay in center field—where he's primarily played as a professional—he'll profile well, but if he ends up in a corner it would put more pressure on his bat.

THE FUTURE: Halpin has shown impressive consistency and has not been fazed as he's climbed through the minor leagues. He'll start 2024 with Triple-A Columbus and could give the Guardians an option for their big league outfield sooner than later.

Year	Age	Club (League)	Level	AVG	G	AB	R	H	2B	3B	HR	RBI	BB	SO	SB	OBP	SLG
2023	21	Akron (EL)	AA	.243	113	452	55	110	23	4	9	38	47	126	12	.312	.372
Minor League Totals				.261	272	1055	157	275	58	14	16	92	113	268	39	.335	.388

15 ANGEL GENAO, SS/3B

HIT: 55. **POW:** 40. **RUN:** 50. **FLD:** 55. **ARM:** 60. **BA Grade:** 45. **Risk:** High.

Born: May 19, 2003. **B-T:** B-R. **HT:** 6-0. **WT:** 165. **Signed:** Dominican Republic, 2021. **Signed by:** Anthony Roa.

TRACK RECORD: Genao was Cleveland's top signing in the 2021 international market. He made his professional debut the following year in the Dominican Summer League and his U.S. debut in 2022. He suffered a torn meniscus in his right knee during spring training which delayed his start to the 2023 season until late May. He recovered to turn in a solid season at Low-A Lynchburg as a 19-year-old.

SCOUTING REPORT: Genao is a switch-hitter with an advanced, disciplined approach at the plate. He controls the strike zone well thanks to a feel for the barrel and swing decisions that belie his age. His profile has always been hit-over-power and his 6-foot, 165-pound frame doesn't suggest much power. He has more power in his righthanded swing but he'll need to more consistently elevate the ball if he's to make the most of it, though he did rank in the top 10 in the Carolina League with 20 doubles. Genao evenly split his time between shortstop and third base. His infield actions, hands, arm strength and baseball IQ play well at shortstop, but he's only an average runner now and his range may end up being better suited for third base.

THE FUTURE: Genao so far has lived up to his pre-signing billing and has put himself on an accelerated track. He's quickly joined the Guardians' burgeoning group of young infielders and has significant promise, though he's still a long way from realizing it. He'll still be 19 on Opening Day in 2024 as he moves up to High-A Lake County.

Year	Age	Club (League)	Level	AVG	G	AB	R	H	2B	3B	HR	RBI	BB	SO	SB	OBP	SLG
2023	19	Lynchburg (CAR)	A	.263	72	278	44	73	20	1	4	32	34	49	6	.345	.385
Minor League Totals				.274	164	606	105	166	31	6	7	67	93	123	28	.376	.380

16 JACKSON HUMPHRIES, LHP

FB: 55. **CB:** 55. **SL:** 50. **CHG:** 40. **CTL:** 50. **BA Grade:** 50. **Risk:** Extreme.

Born: July 20, 2004. **B-T:** R-L. **HT:** 6-1. **WT:** 200. **Drafted:** HS—Fuquay-Varina, NC, 2022 (8th round). **Signed by:** Michael Cuva.

TRACK RECORD: Humphries was No. 150 in the 2022 draft rankings but slid a bit on draft day. The Guardians were happy to pick him in the eighth round and signed him to a $600,000 bonus—equivalent to late third-round pick value—to sign him away from his Campbell commitment. He didn't pitch after signing but hit the ground running in 2023. He impressed in the Arizona Complex League and earned a late-season promotion to Low-A Lynchburg.

SCOUTING REPORT: Humphries has a solid all-around skill set. He attacks hitters with a four-pitch arsenal and can run his fastball into the mid 90s. He has a good feel for spin and throws both a big curveball that has plus potential and a hard, biting slider. He also can mix in a changeup. He's an above-average athlete who should have average control. Some scouts note his lack of extension in his delivery will cause his fastball to play down, but he did a nice job of creating swings and misses in his first season.

THE FUTURE: Humphries has an exciting array of tools and pitched well against older competition after his late-season promotion. He has plenty of starter traits and will look to build on his strong debut in 2024 when he returns to Lynchburg.

Year	Age	Club (League)	Level	W	L	ERA	G	GS	IP	H	HR	BB	SO	BB%	SO%	WHIP	AVG
2023	18	ACL Guardians	Rk	0	6	5.61	9	8	34	30	2	21	48	13.8	31.6	1.51	.244
2023	18	Lynchburg (CAR)	A	0	1	5.32	6	6	24	20	3	8	24	7.8	23.3	1.18	.225
Minor League Totals				0	7	5.53	15	14	57	50	5	29	72	11.4	28.2	1.39	.236

17 RAFAEL RAMIREZ JR., SS

HIT: 50. **POW:** 45. **RUN:** 50. **FLD:** 50. **ARM:** 55. **BA Grade:** 50. **Risk:** Extreme.

Born: July 22, 2005. **B-T:** L-R. **HT:** 6-0. **WT:** 159. **Signed:** Dominican Republic, 2022. **Signed by:** Jean Figueroa.

TRACK RECORD: Ramirez is the son of former all-star shortstop Rafael Ramirez and was born in New Jersey and grew up in the Dominican Republic. The Guardians signed him in 2022 and he made his professional debut later that year in the Dominican Summer League. After a solid first year, he made his U.S. debut in 2023 in the Arizona Complex League as a 17-year-old.

SCOUTING REPORT: Ramirez stands out for his advanced feel for hitting. He has a smooth lefthanded swing, controls the barrel well and has above-average bat-to-ball skills. As a result, he makes a lot of contact. He's starting to grow into his frame, and with more physical maturity and his bat speed he looks like he could grow into at least average raw power. Ramirez was signed as a shortstop and that's primarily where he's played. His hands and arm strength play well there, but as he grows it's possible he'll end up at third base.

THE FUTURE: Ramirez was on the younger end of his signing class, and he's been young for his level each of the last two years. He's handled those assignments well and has become another strong signing by the team's international department. He'll look to continue his development in 2024 as he advances to full season ball and Low-A Lynchburg.

Year	Age	Club (League)	Level	AVG	G	AB	R	H	2B	3B	HR	RBI	BB	SO	SB	OBP	SLG
2023	17	ACL Guardians	Rk	.250	41	136	33	34	6	3	4	27	50	54	6	.453	.426
Minor League Totals				.248	88	306	60	76	12	7	6	50	75	88	17	.405	.392

18 ANDREW WALTERS, RHP

FB: 70. **SL:** 50. **CHG:** 40. **CTL:** 55. **BA Grade:** 45. **Risk:** High.

Born: December 8, 2000. **B-T:** R-R. **HT:** 6-4. **WT:** 222. **Drafted:** Miami, 2023 (2nd round supplemental).
Signed by: Gustavo Benzan.

TRACK RECORD: Walters was the best reliever in college baseball in each of the last two seasons, twice earning first-team All-America honors. While he was draft-eligible in 2022—and picked in the 18th round by the Orioles—he opted to return to Miami for a final season. After another impressive season anchoring the Hurricanes' bullpen, the Guardians drafted him 62nd overall.

SCOUTING REPORT: Walters primarily comes right after hitters with his fastball. The pitch can reach triple digits and typically sits in the mid 90s with exceptional ride and carry. The pitch got whiffs 36% of the time, making it one of the best fastballs in the draft class. He mixes in a sweeping slider and a firm changeup with fading life. He pounds the strike zone and pitches with above-average control.

THE FUTURE: While there was some talk of Walters moving to the rotation at Miami after his return to school, that never materialized and he's likely going to continue to develop as a reliever. While that puts a bit of a damper on his prospect value, he has the potential to become a high-leverage reliever. First up will be his professional debut. That will likely come at High-A Lake County, but don't expect him to stay in the Midwest League for long.

Year	Age	Club (League)	Level	W	L	ERA	G	GS	IP	H	HR	BB	SO	BB%	SO%	WHIP	AVG
2023	22	Did not play															

19 DAYAN FRIAS, 3B

HIT: 45. **POW:** 50. **RUN:** 45. **FLD:** 60. **ARM:** 55. **BA Grade:** 45. **Risk:** High.

Born: June 25, 2002. **B-T:** B-R. **HT:** 5-9. **WT:** 180. **Signed:** Colombia, 2018. **Signed by:** Arnold Elles.

TRACK RECORD: Frias was not a high-profile signing in 2018 when the Guardians inked him to an $80,000 bonus out of Colombia. The pandemic slowed his emergence and he didn't make his U.S. debut until 2021 in the Arizona Complex League. Since then, however, Frias has significantly raised his profile. He had a big 2023, first playing for Colombia at the World Baseball Classic and then turning in an impressive season with High-A Lake County.

SCOUTING REPORT: A switch-hitter, Frias has a smooth swing from both sides of the plate and has long shown an impressive feel for the barrel. After getting overly aggressive at the plate in 2022, he worked to reign that in and in 2023 cut his strikeout rate from 24.9% to 20.9% while maintaining his walk rate. He's gained strength since signing and now shows average power potential, especially as a righthanded hitter. Frias has standout defensive tools and was voted best defender in the Midwest League by opposing managers. His infield actions, above-average arm strength and hands give him plus defensive ability at the hot corner.

THE FUTURE: Frias was not added to the 40-man roster in November and went unpicked in the Rule 5 draft. Both of those developments are mostly attributable to the fact he has yet to reach the upper levels. That will change in 2024, when he should progress to Double-A Akron.

Year	Age	Club (League)	Level	AVG	G	AB	R	H	2B	3B	HR	RBI	BB	SO	SB	OBP	SLG
2023	21	Lake County (MWL)	A+	.260	100	338	43	88	19	2	11	49	51	83	8	.356	.426
Minor League Totals				.255	302	1067	164	272	53	10	21	134	180	275	29	.364	.382

20 JOSE DEVERS, SS

HIT: 45. **POW:** 40. **RUN:** 60. **FLD:** 55. **ARM:** 60. **BA Grade:** 45. **Risk:** High.

Born: May 17, 2003. **B-T:** R-R. **HT:** 6-0. **WT:** 140. **Signed:** Dominican Republic, 2019. **Signed by:** Rigo De Los Santos.

TRACK RECORD: Devers, the younger brother of Marlins prospect Jose Devers and the cousin of Red Sox all-star Rafael Devers, signed with the Guardians in 2019 out of the Dominican Republic but the pandemic delayed his professional debut until 2021 in the Arizona Complex League. He moved up to Low-A Lynchburg in 2023, had a breakout season and earned postseason all-star honors in the Carolina League.

SCOUTING REPORT: Devers has the kind of disciplined, hit-over-power approach that so many of Cleveland's hitters employ. He does a nice job of controlling the strike zone and uses his plus speed well on the bases. He came on strong in the second half of the season and did a better job driving the ball as he got more used to facing older competition. Devers is a standout defender at shortstop with all the tools to man the position. His speed and instincts give him above-average range and his plus arm and athleticism play well.

THE FUTURE: The Guardians left him off the 40-man roster and unprotected in the Rule 5 draft, where he went unpicked, though that shouldn't be taken as any slight to a 20-year-old who has yet to play above the Carolina League. Devers has exciting upside and will look to build on his breakout campaign when he advances to High-A Lake County in 2024.

Year	Age	Club (League)	Level	AVG	G	AB	R	H	2B	3B	HR	RBI	BB	SO	SB	OBP	SLG
2023	20	Lynchburg (CAR)	A	.252	111	397	65	100	15	5	11	66	48	92	34	.345	.398
Minor League Totals				.237	174	608	103	144	19	6	15	96	75	156	46	.332	.362

21 KAHLIL WATSON, SS

HIT: 45. **POW:** 50. **RUN:** 55. **FLD:** 50. **ARM:** 60. **BA Grade:** 50. **Risk:** Extreme.

Born: April 16, 2003. **B-T:** L-R. **HT:** 5-10. **WT:** 178. **Drafted:** HS—Wake Forest, NC, 2022 (1st round). **Signed by:** Blake Newsome (Marlins).

TRACK RECORD: Watson went into the 2021 draft regarded as one of the top prep players in the country but slid to No. 16 overall, where the Marlins were happy to draft him. His transition to pro ball hasn't been smooth, however. Watson has struggled offensively in full-season ball and a suspension cost him nearly a month in 2022. The Guardians acquired him at the 2023 trade deadline as a part of the deal that sent Josh Bell to the Marlins.

SCOUTING REPORT: While most of the Guardians' prospects fall into a hit-over-power profile, Watson is different. Though he's not the most physical player, he has electric bat speed and there's no shortage of impact in his swing. He's an aggressive hitter who swings and misses quite often, but he did cut his strikeout rate from 35.1% in 2022 to 26.8% in 2023. Getting back to the more selective approach he showed in high school would help him make the most of his offensive tools. Watson has primarily been a shortstop in pro ball and his plus arm and above-average speed play well there. He'll need to become a more consistent defender to stay at the position, however.

THE FUTURE: Watson is loaded with exciting tools but hasn't been able to put it all together yet in pro ball. There's still time for him to make good on his significant upside after his change of scenery. He'll still be 20 on Opening Day, but 2024 is a big year for him.

Year	Age	Club (League)	Level	AVG	G	AB	R	H	2B	3B	HR	RBI	BB	SO	SB	OBP	SLG
2023	20	FCL Marlins	Rk	.333	2	6	2	2	0	0	2	2	0	1	0	.333	1.333
2023	20	Beloit (MWL)	A+	.206	58	199	26	41	10	0	7	22	35	68	14	.337	.362
2023	20	Lake County (MWL)	A+	.233	23	86	15	20	3	0	5	16	8	24	11	.306	.442
Minor League Totals				.234	180	659	110	154	34	7	24	92	83	232	45	.328	.416

22 JOSE TENA, SS

HIT: 50. **POW:** 45. **RUN:** 55. **FLD:** 50. **ARM:** 55. **BA Grade:** 45. **Risk:** High.

Born: March 20, 2001. **B-T:** L-R. **HT:** 5-10. **WT:** 190. **Signed:** Dominican Republic, 2017.
Signed by: Anthony Roa/Jhonathan Leyba.

TRACK RECORD: Cleveland's 2017 international class has developed into a blockbuster. Outfielder George Valera and shortstop Brayan Rocchio have been the headliners of this group, but Tena, a nephew of Juan Uribe, has made a name for himself. He won the Arizona Fall League batting title after hitting .387 as a 20-year-old in 2021 and made his major league debut in August 2023. He spent most of 2023 at Double-A Akron, where he could play shortstop without competing for time with Rocchio.

SCOUTING REPORT: Tena has a smaller frame that belies his ability. He has a loose, easy swing and above-average feel for the barrel that allows him to consistently square up balls. He's an aggressive hitter who doesn't walk much and struck out in 28.3% of his plate appearances in 2023. His whiff rate is higher than a player of his offensive profile would want and it's something he'll need to manage against high-level pitching. He's an above-average runner and as he's physically matured has grown into more power, though it mostly plays as doubles pop. Tena has an above-average arm, clean hands and solid range thanks to his speed and athleticism. He's mostly played shortstop as a professional, but also has seen time at second and third base.

THE FUTURE: Tena is a part of the growing legion of talented middle infielders in the organization. His defensive versatility is an asset and could help him break through the crowd or emerge as a utility option. He'll start 2024 back in Columbus, where he's played just 20 games so far.

Year	Age	Club (League)	Level	AVG	G	AB	R	H	2B	3B	HR	RBI	BB	SO	SB	OBP	SLG
2023	22	Akron (EL)	AA	.260	81	308	44	80	20	1	4	37	41	104	16	.353	.370
2023	22	Columbus (IL)	AAA	.350	15	60	9	21	5	1	4	11	4	17	0	.394	.667
2023	22	Cleveland (AL)	MLB	.226	18	31	2	7	2	0	0	3	3	13	0	.294	.290
Minor League Totals				.284	430	1702	250	483	92	20	40	215	122	453	50	.336	.432
Major League Totals				.226	18	31	2	7	2	0	0	3	3	13	0	.294	.290

23 JAKE FOX, OF

HIT: 55. **POW:** 40. **RUN:** 60. **FLD:** 50. **ARM:** 45. **BA Grade:** 45. **Risk:** High.

Born: February 12, 2003. **B-T:** L-R. **HT:** 6-0. **WT:** 180. **Drafted:** HS—Lakeland, FL, 2021 (3rd round).
Signed by: Andrew Krause.

TRACK RECORD: Fox went strongly against the grain of the rest of the Guardians' 2021 draft class both as a position player and as a prep player. In both categories, he was one of just two players the club selected with their 21 picks. He's been solid in pro ball and came on strong in the second half of 2023 with High-A Lake County.

SCOUTING REPORT: While Fox was an unusual pick for Cleveland in the context of the rest of its 2021 draft class, he has a familiar offensive profile for the organization. He has an unorthodox setup at the plate but has a loose, easy swing and a patient approach. He has a hit-over-power profile but has gotten stronger since getting into pro ball and he could grow into more. He's a plus runner and is a threat on the bases but is still learning the finer points of basestealing. Fox was drafted as a shortstop but was always unlikely to stay there because of his fringy arm strength. After primarily playing second base in 2022, he moved almost exclusively to the outfield in 2023, primarily playing center field. His speed fits there and he did a nice job learning his new position.

THE FUTURE: Fox is off to a strong start to his professional career and his hitting ability and speed give him a pair of standout tools. He'll face a key challenge in 2024 as he advances to Double-A Akron.

Year	Age	Club (League)	Level	AVG	G	AB	R	H	2B	3B	HR	RBI	BB	SO	SB	OBP	SLG
2023	20	Lake County (MWL)	A+	.256	101	402	61	103	23	5	8	53	45	103	9	.330	.398
Minor League Totals				.260	218	824	145	214	49	9	13	103	125	202	37	.361	.388

24 JOHNATHAN RODRIGUEZ, OF

HIT: 45. **POW:** 55. **RUN:** 40. **FLD:** 45. **ARM:** 60. **BA Grade:** 45. **Risk:** High.

Born: November 4, 1999. **B-T:** R-R. **HT:** 6-0. **WT:** 224. **Drafted:** HS—Florida, PR, 2017 (3rd round).
Signed by: Juan Alvarez.

TRACK RECORD: Rodriguez was one of the youngest players in the 2017 draft class. He was seen as a developmental project at the time and that promise is now getting closer to paying off. He advanced to Triple-A Columbus in 2023 and was added to the 40-man roster in the offseason to prevent him from becoming a minor league free agent.

SCOUTING REPORT: Rodriguez has done a better job of tapping into his power over the last two years, which has helped him emerge as a prospect. His 29 home runs in 2023 led all of the organization's minor leaguers. With improved power has come more swing and miss, though Rodriguez is adept at working walks. Rodriguez is a below-average runner, but his plus arm plays well in right field.

THE FUTURE: Rodriguez will play all of 2024 as a 24-year-old and has put himself in position to make his major league debut sometime during the summer. His powerful righthanded bat gives him intriguing upside, especially for an organization that's short on power hitters.

Year	Age	Club (League)	Level	AVG	G	AB	R	H	2B	3B	HR	RBI	BB	SO	SB	OBP	SLG
2023	23	Akron (EL)	AA	.289	88	322	42	93	14	2	18	55	34	97	3	.364	.512
2023	23	Columbus (IL)	AAA	.280	47	175	32	49	12	2	11	33	25	66	0	.376	.560
Minor League Totals				.276	469	1712	255	472	95	19	69	266	175	508	22	.348	.474

25 CADE SMITH, RHP
FB: 65. **SL:** 45. **CHG:** 40. **CTL:** 50. **BA Grade:** 45. **Risk:** High.

Born: May 9, 1999. **B-T:** R-R. **HT:** 6-5. **WT:** 230. **Signed:** Hawaii, 2020 (NDFA). **Signed by:** Kyle Bamberger.
TRACK RECORD: Smith pitched for the Canadian Junior National Team during high school and was drafted in the 16th round by the Twins in 2018 but opted to attend Hawaii instead of signing. After three years in college, Smith signed with Cleveland as an undrafted free agent after the 2020 draft was shortened to five rounds. He pitched well in three seasons as a professional and in November was added to the 40-man roster.
SCOUTING REPORT: Smith has a big, powerful build and a fastball to match. He relies heavily on the pitch, which averages about 95 mph and gets a lot of swings and misses, both in and out of the zone. The pitch plays up further thanks to the excellent extension he gets in his delivery. His slider is his best secondary offering. It's more of a fringy offering that doesn't miss nearly as many bats, but it's enough to keep batters honest. He also mixes in an occasional below-average changeup and pitches with average control.
THE FUTURE: Smith spent much of 2023 at Triple-A and is now on the 40-man roster, which puts him firmly in contention for a spot in the Guardians' bullpen sooner than later. He'll need to continue refining his slider to become a high-leverage weapon in the big leagues, but he looks to be at least a solid relief option.

Year	Age	Club (League)	Level	W	L	ERA	G	GS	IP	H	HR	BB	SO	BB%	SO%	WHIP	AVG
2023	24	Akron (EL)	AA	1	0	2.86	17	0	22	17	1	9	29	9.8	31.5	1.18	.213
2023	24	Columbus (IL)	AAA	4	3	4.65	30	0	41	37	6	19	66	10.7	37.1	1.38	.236
Minor League Totals				11	8	3.61	124	0	167	117	11	85	262	12.0	37.0	1.21	.193

26 PARKER MESSICK, LHP
FB: 50. **CB:** 50. **SL:** 50. **CHG:** 55. **CTL:** 55. **BA Grade:** 45. **Risk:** High.

Born: October 26, 2000. **B-T:** L-L. **HT:** 6-0. **WT:** 225. **Drafted:** Florida State, 2022 (2nd round). **Signed by:** Matt Linder.
TRACK RECORD: Messick starred at Florida State, where he was the Seminoles' ace for two seasons. He was named Atlantic Coast Conference pitcher of the year in 2021 and an All-American in 2022. He didn't pitch after the Guardians drafted him 54th overall in 2022 and instead made his professional debut in 2023, where he pitched at both Class A levels.
SCOUTING REPORT: Listed at 6-foot, 225 pounds, Messick has a short, stocky build which belies his athleticism—he even showed some two-way ability in college—and he repeats his energetic delivery well, which gives him above-average control. His pure stuff is not overpowering, as his fastball sits in the low 90s and touches 95 mph. He throws from a low release point, which helps him get swings and misses on his fastball at the top of the strike zone. His tumbling changeup is his best pitch and gives him a strong weapon against righthanded hitters. He mixes in a sweeping slider, which he'll need to tighten up to turn it into a more effective pitch. Messick comes right after hitters and his feel for the game helps his entire arsenal play up.
THE FUTURE: Messick's solid but unspectacular stuff makes him a potential back-of-the-rotation starter down the line, but with Cleveland's developmental track record, an eventual tick up for both his stuff and ceiling would be no surprise. While that breakout didn't come in 2023, his solid start gives him a good platform as he advances to Double-A Akron in 2024.

Year	Age	Club (League)	Level	W	L	ERA	G	GS	IP	H	HR	BB	SO	BB%	SO%	WHIP	AVG
2023	22	Lynchburg (CAR)	A	3	2	3.02	13	13	57	48	1	14	61	6.0	26.0	1.09	.221
2023	22	Lake County (MWL)	A+	2	4	4.43	13	11	65	62	10	25	75	8.8	26.3	1.34	.249
Minor League Totals				5	6	3.79	26	24	122	110	11	39	136	7.5	26.2	1.23	.236

27 JUSTIN CAMPBELL, RHP

FB: 55. **CB:** 50. **SL:** 50. **CHG:** 60. **CTL:** 55. **BA Grade:** 45. **Risk:** Very High.

Born: February 14, 2001. **B-T:** L-R. **HT:** 6-7. **WT:** 219. **Drafted:** Oklahoma State, 2022 (1st round supplemental).
Signed by: Ken Jarrett.

TRACK RECORD: Campbell arrived at Oklahoma State as a two-way player and while he made an immediate impact in both roles, he developed into the Cowboys' ace. He was an All-American in 2021 as a two-way player before focusing solely on pitching in 2022. The Guardians drafted him 37th overall, but he has yet to make his professional debut. He was sidelined in 2023 by an elbow injury and in May had surgery to relieve pressure on the ulnar nerve.

SCOUTING REPORT: Listed at 6-foot-7, 219 pounds, Campbell has a long frame and has a loose, easy delivery. When he's healthy, his fastball sits in the low 90s and reaches 95 mph with life up in the zone. He throws both a curveball and a slider. He can throw the curveball for a strike or as a chase pitch, while his slider works to keep righthanded hitters off-balance. His changeup is perhaps his best pitch, earning plus grades thanks to its life and deception. He pitches with solid control and can throw strikes with all his offerings.

THE FUTURE: Coming out of college, Campbell was seen as an advanced player who could move quickly in the minor leagues, but after missing the 2023 season just getting back to full health and on track will be paramount in 2024.

Year	Age	Club (League)	Level	W	L	ERA	G	GS	IP	H	HR	BB	SO	BB%	SO%	WHIP	AVG
2023	22	Did not play—Injured															

28 JHONKENSY NOEL, OF

HIT: 40. **POW:** 70. **RUN:** 45. **FLD:** 45. **ARM:** 50. **BA Grade:** 45. **Risk:** Very High.

Born: July 15, 2001. **B-T:** R-R. **HT:** 6-1. **WT:** 250. **Signed:** Dominican Republic, 2017.
Signed by: Domingo Toribio/Jhonathan Leyba.

TRACK RECORD: Another member of Cleveland's banner 2017 international class, Noel signed on his 16th birthday and debuted the following year in the Dominican Summer League. After a strong 2021 season that ended with High-A Lake County, he was added to the 40-man roster. He's continued his aggressive progress into the upper minors, and his 59 home runs in the last two years led all Guardians minor leaguers.

SCOUTING REPORT: Noel has a big, strong frame and produces tremendous bat speed and raw power. He regularly records elite exit velocities and doesn't have to sell out to get to his premium power. He's an aggressive hitter, though he's maintained manageable strikeout rates in the upper minors including a 24.8% mark in 2024. Noel was a third baseman early in his career but now primarily plays in the outfield. He's not the rangiest player, but he's done a nice job learning the position and has solid-average arm strength.

THE FUTURE: Noel's raw power is tantalizing, and he could be a middle-of-the-order hitter, but as a right-right slugger who will play in a corner, there's a lot riding on his bat and he'll have to continue to develop as an overall hitter. The Guardians are looking to inject more power into their lineup and if Noel continues to perform, he'll likely get an audition in 2024.

Year	Age	Club (League)	Level	AVG	G	AB	R	H	2B	3B	HR	RBI	BB	SO	SB	OBP	SLG
2023	21	Columbus (IL)	AAA	.220	138	519	81	114	23	0	27	85	49	145	1	.303	.420
Minor League Totals				.252	452	1665	277	419	86	3	94	311	158	454	20	.331	.476

29 CODY MORRIS, RHP

FB: 60. **CB:** 45. **CUT:** 50. **CHG:** 55. **CTL:** 50. **BA Grade:** 45. **Risk:** Very High.

Born: November 4, 1996. **B-T:** R-R. **HT:** 6-4. **WT:** 205. **Drafted:** South Carolina, 2018 (7th round).
Signed by: Mike Bradford.

TRACK RECORD: Morris missed his freshman season at South Carolina after having Tommy John surgery before bouncing back to have a solid college career. Morris has continued to deal with injuries in pro ball, including shoulder strains in each of the last two years that have limited him to just 92 innings. When he's been healthy, he's been impressive, however. He made his major league debut in 2022 and was a part of the Guardians' playoff roster that year.

SCOUTING REPORT: Morris has a strong build and a powerful arm. His fastball reaches 98 mph and averages 95.2 mph. He mixes in a changeup, a curveball and a cutter, which he added to his arsenal in 2021. His changeup is above-average and his cutter quickly became a foil to his fastball which he throws about a third of the time. He rarely mixes in his curveball, but it is an effective offering. He pitches with average control, but when he's at his best he shows even better command.

THE FUTURE: Injuries have been Morris' greatest obstacle as a professional and he hasn't had a full season since 2019. Despite that, he's gotten to the big leagues and shown he can have success at the level. He has the stuff to start, but as a 27-year-old who has never thrown more than 90 innings in a season—including college—a role in the bullpen is where Morris fits best. If he's healthy in 2024, he'll have a spot in the Guardians' bullpen.

Year	Age	Club (League)	Level	W	L	ERA	G	GS	IP	H	HR	BB	SO	BB%	SO%	WHIP	AVG
2023	26	Akron (EL)	AA	0	0	0.00	3	3	5	2	0	2	5	10.0	25.0	0.75	.125
2023	26	Columbus (IL)	AAA	2	1	3.74	18	1	34	20	5	25	40	17.4	27.8	1.34	.171
2023	26	Cleveland (AL)	MLB	0	0	6.75	6	0	8	10	3	6	9	15.8	23.7	2.00	.313
Minor League Totals				11	7	3.09	66	44	210	167	17	80	288	9.2	33.0	1.18	.216
Major League Totals				1	2	3.41	13	5	32	31	6	18	32	13.0	23.2	1.55	.261

30 TIM HERRIN, LHP
FB: 60. **SL:** 50. **CB:** 40. **CTL:** 50. **BA Grade:** 40. **Risk:** Medium.

Born: Oct. **8, 1996. B-T:** L-L. **HT:** 6-6. **WT:** 230. **Drafted:** Indiana, 2018 (29th round). **Signed by:** Pete Loizzo.

TRACK RECORD: Herrin rose through the minor leagues after being drafted in the 29th round in 2018. He made the Guardians' Opening Day roster in 2023 for his major league debut and then split the season between Cleveland and Triple-A Columbus.

SCOUTING REPORT: Herrin has a big, powerful build and attacks hitters with a solid fastball-slider combination. In 2023 his fastball averaged 96.6 mph and he threw a lot of strikes with the pitch. His slider flashes above-average and can be a swing-and-miss pitch at its best but isn't as consistent. He also can mix in a curveball, but it's a clear third offering. Herrin pitches with average control.

THE FUTURE: Herrin was much tougher on lefthanded hitters than righthanded hitters in the big leagues thanks to his fastball, which suggests he's perhaps best suited as a lefty specialist. If he can refine his approach in his second big league season, there's still some room for growth, even for a player who will be 27 on Opening Day.

Year	Age	Club (League)	Level	W	L	ERA	G	GS	IP	H	HR	BB	SO	BB%	SO%	WHIP	AVG
2023	26	Columbus (IL)	AAA	7	2	3.38	33	0	37	21	3	20	43	13.4	28.9	1.10	.164
2023	26	Cleveland (AL)	MLB	1	1	5.53	23	0	28	29	3	12	32	9.9	26.4	1.48	.279
Minor League Totals				14	10	3.45	151	2	242	204	17	97	280	9.5	27.5	1.24	.224
Major League Totals				1	1	5.53	23	0	28	29	3	12	32	9.9	26.4	1.48	.279

Ezequiel Tovar was a Gold Glove finalist.

Colorado Rockies

BY GEOFF PONTES

Things finally hit rock bottom in Denver in 2023, when the Rockies finished with their first 100-loss season in franchise history.

The days of offensive juggernaut Rockies teams seem like a distant memory. The team's once-formidable core has moved on to greener pastures.

The Rockies finished in the bottom half of the National League in nearly every offensive category. They fared no better on the pitching side, where a combination of a bad staff and an extremely hitter-friendly run environment yielded poor results.

Things on the farm were mostly positive, and a number of players took big steps forward. Jordan Beck and Sterlin Thompson, a pair of 2022 draft picks, both reached Double-A by the middle of the summer. Thompson hit .293 for the year, while Beck showcased his power and speed by hitting 25 home runs and stealing 20 bases.

Prized international signings Adael Amador and Yanquiel Fernandez reached Double-A by age 20 and were added to the 40-man roster. Amador hit .287/.380/.495 on the season with more walks than strikeouts, and Fernandez hit 17 home runs over his first 58 games and reached Double-A by mid June. The Rockies' international scouting team looks like it struck gold again with outfielder Robert Calaz. The team's top prospect from the 2023 international class impressed offensively in the Dominican Summer League.

The 2023 draft also yielded strong results, and the Rockies landed one of the top college pitchers in the class in Tennessee's Chase Dollander. Colorado also landed two more of its Top 30 Prospects—utility player Cole Carrigg and lefthander Sean Sullivan—in the 2023 draft.

The Rockies will need the reinforcements on the mound because all three of the team's top pitching prospects—Gabriel Hughes, Jackson Cox and

PROJECTED 2027 LINEUP

Catcher	Drew Romo	25
First Base	Elehuris Montero	28
Second Base	Adael Amador	24
Third Base	Ryan McMahon	32
Shortstop	Ezequiel Tovar	25
Left Field	Nolan Jones	29
Center Field	Jordan Beck	26
Right Field	Kris Bryant	35
Designated Hitter	Yanquiel Fernandez	24
No. 1 Starter	Kyle Freeland	34
No. 2 Starter	Chase Dollander	25
No. 3 Starter	Jordy Vargas	23
No. 4 Starter	Carson Palmquist	26
No. 5 Starter	Gabriel Hughes	25
Closer	Justin Lawrence	32

Jordy Vargas—had Tommy John surgery in July. All three will miss all of the 2024 season and eye returns in 2025.

Former top prospect Zac Veen missed most of the season with a left wrist tendon injury that required surgery. Veen was looking to regain his prospect status after a poor showing at Double-A to end 2022.

There were some encouraging bright spots.

Hunter Goodman led the organization in home runs in 2022 and had an even better year in 2023, when he reached the major leagues. Several more rookies showed promise in the major leagues. Chief among that group was Nolan Jones, whom the Rockies acquired via trade from the Guardians after the 2022 season.

Rookie Ezequiel Tovar spent the entire season as the Rockies' starting shortstop, hit 15 home runs and provided jaw-dropping defense. Tovar had an uneven season at the plate, but at just 22 years old he still has the ability to develop into one of the top all-around shortstops in the game within a few years.

Things might be bumpy for the Rockies in the short term, but the organization might get a boost from the wave of prospects in the upper tier of their farm system. ■

COLORADO ROCKIES

TOP 2024 CONTRIBUTORS	RANK
1. Adael Amador, SS	1
2. Sterlin Thompson, 2B	5
3. Drew Romo, C	9

BREAKOUT PROSPECTS	RANK
1. Cole Carrigg, OF	12
2. Sean Sullivan, LHP	16
3. Derek Bernard, 2B	27

SOURCE OF TOP 30 TALENT

Homegrown	28	Acquired	2
College	12	Trade	1
Junior college	0	Rule 5 draft	1
High school	4	Independent league	0
Nondrafted free agent	0	Free agent/waivers	0
International	12		

LF
Jordan Beck (4)
Sean Bouchard (19)
Juan Guerrero

CF
Robert Calaz (10)
Benny Montgomery (11)
Cole Carrigg (12)
Bladimir Restituyo (30)

RF
Yanquiel Fernandez (3)
Zac Veen (6)
Robby Martin Jr.

3B
Warming Bernabel (26)
Andy Perez
Aaron Schunk

SS
Adael Amador (1)
Dyan Jorge (7)
Ryan Ritter (18)
Julio Carreras (21)

2B
Sterlin Thompson (5)
Derek Bernard (28)

1B
Hunter Goodman (13)
Grant Lavigne
Zach Kokoska

C
Drew Romo (9)
Ronaiker Palma
Ben McCabe

LHP

LHSP	LHRP
Carson Palmquist (14)	Evan Justice
Sean Sullivan (16)	Evan Shawver
Michael Prosecky (20)	
Joe Rock (25)	
Mason Albright (29)	

RHP

RHSP	RHRP
Chase Dollander (2)	Angel Chivilli (22)
Jordy Vargas (8)	Juan Mejia (24)
Gabriel Hughes (15)	Victor Vodnik
Jackson Cox (17)	Riley Pint
Anthony Molina (23)	
Victor Juarez (27)	
Case Williams	
Jaden Hill	

1 ADAEL AMADOR, SS/2B

Born: April 11, 2003. **B-T:** B-R. **HT:** 6-0. **WT:** 160.
Drafted: Dominican Republic, 2019.
Signed by: Rolando Fernandez/Martin Cabrera.

TRACK RECORD: A well-known amateur player in his native Dominican Republic, Amador competed for his nation's U15 team before signing with the Rockies for $1.5 million in 2019. Amador debuted in the Arizona Complex League in 2021, hitting .299/.394/.445 while showing some of the most advanced skills in the league that season. He made his full-season debut the following spring with Low-A Fresno, playing in 115 games and hitting .292/.415/.445 with 15 home runs and 26 stolen bases. He was selected a California League all-star after leading the league in runs. He began his 2023 season with an undisclosed injury that delayed his debut with High-A Spokane until April 18. Upon his return, Amador hit .302/.391/.514 in 54 games and showed improved game power. In late June he injured his right hamate bone and required surgery, missing two months. He returned with Double-A Hartford on Aug. 26.

SCOUTING REPORT: One of the most advanced bat-to-ball hitters in the minor leagues, Amador shows uncanny barrel control and a discerning eye. The switch-hitter shows nearly equal skill from each side of the plate, with a slight bump in production as a lefthanded hitter. Amador is adept at staying short to the ball with an efficient swing that he can adjust based on pitch location. Unlike many advanced contact hitters, he is patient, showing the ability to work deep into counts as he waits for mistakes over the plate. While Amador is slight in build with limited projection, he's shown improvements to his game power in each of the last two seasons. Amador added 3 mph onto his average exit velocity in 2023, and hit a ball 110.4 mph to establish a new best. Neither Amador's righthanded or lefthanded swing are optimized for power, and a majority of his hardest-struck drives are to center and the opposite field. Developing the ability to drive the ball consistently to his pull side is an area of potential development. Despite size and swing path concerns, Amador has produced fringe-average power output and projects to hit for average power numbers at peak. He's an above-average straight-line runner with advanced baserunning instincts. Amador shows strong actions and footwork at shortstop but likely lacks the arm for the position. He began to see more time at second base in 2023, including nine of his 10 starts with Double-A. He projects as an above-average second baseman with the ability to fill in at shortstop. Amador's profile is driven by his elite hit tool, but he possesses a variety of skills that make for a well-rounded player.

THE FUTURE: A potential elite leadoff hitter with the ability to play multiple positions in the middle infield, Amador has all-star upside with the ability to win multiple batting titles. He will return to Double-A Hartford to begin 2024. ∎

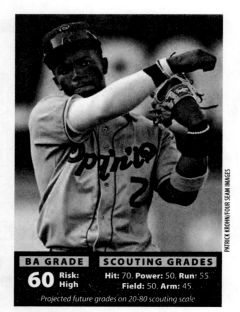

PATRICK KROHN/FOUR SEAM IMAGES

BA GRADE	SCOUTING GRADES
60 Risk: High	Hit: 70. Power: 50. Run: 55. Field: 50. Arm: 45.

Projected future grades on 20-80 scouting scale

BEST TOOLS

BATTING

Best Hitter for Average	Adael Amador
Best Power Hitter	Yanquiel Fernandez
Best Strike-Zone Discipline	Adael Amador
Fastest Baserunner	Braiden Ward
Best Athlete	Jordan Beck

PITCHING

Best Fastball	Victor Vodnik
Best Curveball	Jordy Vargas
Best Slider	Juan Mejia
Best Changeup	Zach Agnos
Best Control	Joe Rock

FIELDING

Best Defensive Catcher	Drew Romo
Best Defensive Infielder	Julio Carreras
Best Infield Arm	Ryan Ritter
Best Defensive Outfielder	Bladimir Restituyo
Best Outfield Arm	Yanquiel Fernandez

Year	Age	Club (League)	Level	AVG	G	AB	R	H	2B	3B	HR	RBI	BB	SO	SB	OBP	SLG
2023	20	ACL Rockies	Rk	.389	5	18	6	7	1	0	2	9	4	3	0	.500	.778
2023	20	Spokane (NWL)	A+	.302	54	222	46	67	14	3	9	35	31	26	12	.391	.514
2023	20	Hartford (EL)	AA	.143	10	35	3	5	0	0	1	2	4	8	3	.244	.229
Minor League Totals				.292	231	888	196	259	49	4	31	127	153	133	51	.401	.461

2 CHASE DOLLANDER, RHP

FB: 60. **CB:** 50. **SL:** 60. **CHG:** 55. **CTL:** 55 **BA Grade:** 55 **Risk:** High.

Born: October 26, 2001. **B-T:** R-R. **HT:** 6-2. **WT:** 200.
Drafted: Tennessee, 2023 (1st round). **Signed by:** Scott Corman.
TRACK RECORD: Dollander slipped under the radar of Power Five conference schools coming out of the 2020 pandemic-shortened season. He pitched one year at Georgia Southern before transferring to Tennessee for 2022, when he was Southeastern Conference pitcher of the year. He headed into 2023 as the top college pitcher in the class but struggled at times as junior. The Rockies drafted him ninth overall and signed him for slot value of $5.72 million. Dollander did not pitch in an affiliated game and has yet to make his professional debut.
SCOUTING REPORT: Dollander has a prototype pitcher's build with lean athleticism. His operation is fluid, clean and repeatable as he delivers from a three-quarters slot with above-average extension and a lower release height. He mixes four pitches, led by his 94-96 mph four-seam fastball that touches 98-99. His unique release characteristics allow his fastball to generate high rates of swings-and-misses when elevated in the zone. His primary secondary is an upper-80s slider with cutter shape and spin rates in the 2,600-2,700 rpm range. He uses his slider almost exclusively as his go-to secondary against righthanded batters, but SEC opponents batted .291/.333/.582 against the pitch in 2023. Dollander's third pitch and primary secondary against lefthanded hitters is his changeup, an upper-80s pitch with some tumble and fade. Lefties hit Dollander's changeup to the tune of .294 despite drawing the highest chase rate of any pitch in his arsenal. His curveball is a clear fourth pitch and sees moderate usage against lefthanded hitters. It sits 75-77 mph with two-plane bite. Dollander's command, which flashed plus throughout his sophomore campaign, backed up to average in 2023.
THE FUTURE: Dollander has midrotation potential but is more likely a fit as a No. 4 starter.

Year	Age	Club (League)	Level	W	L	ERA	G	GS	IP	H	HR	BB	SO	BB%	SO%	WHIP	AVG
2023	21	Did not play															

3 YANQUIEL FERNANDEZ, OF

HIT: 45. **POW:** 60. **RUN:** 40. **FLD:** 40. **ARM:** 60. **BA Grade:** 55. **Risk:** High.

Born: January 1, 2003. **B-T:** L-L. **HT:** 6-2. **WT:** 207.
Signed: Cuba, 2019. **Signed by:** Rolando Fernandez/Marc Russo/Raul Gomez.
TRACK RECORD: A native of Cuba, Fernandez signed for $295,000 in 2019 but had to wait to make his pro debut until the 2021 Dominican Summer League. He impressed by hitting .333/.406/.531, flashing advanced bat-to-ball skills and power. Fernandez made his U.S. debut the following spring with Low-A Fresno. He once again impressed, leading the California League with 109 RBIs. Fernandez began his 2023 with High-A Spokane, hitting .319/.354/.605 with 17 home runs in 58 games to earn a promotion to Double-A Hartford on June 21. Fernandez struggled against more advanced pitchers and should return to Hartford to begin 2024.
SCOUTING REPORT: A power-over-everything profile, Fernandez possesses sneaky bat-to-ball skills, driven by his gifted hands. His hand strength and bat speed allow him to make adjustments mid-swing, still finding his power when he is off-balance. He's an aggressive swinger who can often swing himself into outs. An improvement in swing decisions would go a long way toward cutting down on some of Fernandez's swing and miss. His power is easy plus in games, with a chance to fully tap into his double-plus raw as he refines his plate skills. Fernandez shows easy power to all fields with the ability to pulverize mistakes he gets the barrel on. He's a fringe-average runner who will likely slow down to below-average at peak. This limits him to an outfield corner, where he's playable, mostly due to his plus arm with plus-plus arm strength. His throwing ability will likely allow him to carve out a role in either corner outfield spot despite below-average fielding ability.
THE FUTURE: Fernandez is a potential middle-of-the-order power hitter with all-star potential if he can refine his approach at the plate.

Year	Age	Club (League)	Level	AVG	G	AB	R	H	2B	3B	HR	RBI	BB	SO	SB	OBP	SLG
2023	20	Fresno (CAL)	A	.231	3	13	3	3	1	0	0	3	3	6	0	.375	.308
2023	20	Spokane (NWL)	A+	.319	58	248	47	79	14	3	17	64	14	48	1	.354	.605
2023	20	Hartford (EL)	AA	.206	56	218	20	45	10	0	8	25	15	78	0	.262	.362
Minor League Totals				.284	283	1131	175	321	75	8	52	235	93	272	6	.339	.502

4 JORDAN BECK, OF

HIT: 45. **POW:** 60. **RUN:** 55. **FLD:** 55. **ARM:** 55. **BA Grade:** 50. **Risk:** High.

Born: April 19, 2001. **B-T:** R-R. **HT:** 6-3. **WT:** 225.
Drafted: Tennessee, 2022 (1st round supplemental). **Signed by:** Scott Corman.
TRACK RECORD: Beck developed into one of the best power hitters in college baseball as a Tennessee junior in 2022. The Rockies drafted him 38th overall in the supplemental first round that year and signed him for an above-slot $2.2 million. He slid down the board in part because he faded late in 2022 during Southeastern Conference play, hitting just .252 with a 28% strikeout rate. Beck debuted after the draft and reached Low-A Fresno. He began 2023 with High-A Spokane and struggled over his first few weeks before catching fire. He was promoted to Double-A Hartford following the all-star break and spent 50 games with the Yard Goats. Beck finished the season with 25 home runs and 20 stolen bases, one of eight minor leaguers to reach both thresholds.
SCOUTING REPORT: An impressive athlete with a strong, explosive build and quick-twitch mechanisms, Beck's offensive approach is based on power hitting and getting on base. He's a below-average contact hitter who swings and misses in-zone at a high rate. His swing decisions are above-average, limiting some of his hit tool risk. He's a plus power hitter who gets to his power in games. He makes his best contact at good launch angles and shows the ability to backspin balls to his pull side. He's an above-average runner with the ability to handle center field. His long, fluid strides allow him to cover ground in the outfield. He's likely to fit long term in a corner, where he can be above-average with an above-average throwing arm.
THE FUTURE: Beck is a power hitter with an on-base-focused profile with athleticism and tools that translate to the outfield. He looks like an average everyday regular with 30-home run upside. He should spend much of 2024 in the upper minors.

Year	Age	Club (League)	Level	AVG	G	AB	R	H	2B	3B	HR	RBI	BB	SO	SB	OBP	SLG
2023	22	Spokane (NWL)	A+	.292	76	295	62	86	19	1	20	72	43	71	11	.378	.566
2023	22	Hartford (EL)	AA	.240	50	192	22	46	15	1	5	19	30	71	9	.342	.406
Minor League Totals				.275	152	575	104	158	41	2	28	110	94	162	20	.375	.499

5 STERLIN THOMPSON, 2B/OF

HIT: 55. **POW:** 50. **RUN:** 45. **FLD:** 45. **ARM:** 60. **BA Grade:** 50. **Risk:** High.

Born: June 26, 2001. **B-T:** L-R. **HT:** 6-4. **WT:** 200.
Drafted: Florida, 2022 (1st round). **Signed by:** John Cedarburg.
TRACK RECORD: An advanced hitter dating back to his days on the prep circuit, Thompson went unselected in the five-round 2020 draft. He starred at Florida for two seasons before the Rockies drafted him 31st overall in 2022 and signed him for slot value of $2.41 million. Thompson hit .463/.513/.746 through 18 games at High-A Spokane in 2023 but then missed a month with a left elbow injury suffered on May 1. He returned on June 2 and played another 42 games for Spokane before he was promoted to Double-A Hartford on Aug. 7. Thompson finished the season in the Arizona Fall League.
SCOUTING REPORT: Thompson is a tall, physical player with average athleticism and a hit-over-power profile at the plate. He's an advanced contact hitter who rarely misses in-zone. Thompson likes to use the whole field, and a majority of his hardest contact is to the opposite field. He does a good job of staying in the zone and limiting chase swings, though he's adept at getting extended on pitches on the outside part of the plate. His power is limited by his contact-first approach and his opposite-field contact. He shows average power in games and has the skills to rack up a lot of doubles with 16-20 home runs per season. He's an average runner now who will likely slow down a little with age. He has shown versatility as a pro by playing third base, second base and both corner outfield spots. His best defensive position in the infield is second, where he can develop into a fringe-average defender. He'll likely split time between second base and left field going forward. He is likely done with third base, his primary position in 2023. Thompson has a plus arm and fringe-average instincts and actions.
THE FUTURE: Thompson is a bat-first player who will likely provide quality at-bats, batting average and versatility over a long major league career.

Year	Age	Club (League)	Level	AVG	G	AB	R	H	2B	3B	HR	RBI	BB	SO	SB	OBP	SLG
2023	22	Spokane (NWL)	A+	.323	60	229	42	74	22	1	7	39	23	42	14	.399	.520
2023	22	Hartford (EL)	AA	.238	34	126	14	30	3	0	7	17	15	32	3	.333	.429
Minor League Totals				.296	120	456	74	135	32	1	16	66	43	102	20	.371	.476

6 ZAC VEEN, OF

HIT: 55. **POW:** 50. **RUN:** 55. **FLD:** 50. **ARM:** 50. **BA Grade:** 50. **Risk:** High.

Born: December 12, 2001. **B-T:** L-R. **HT:** 6-4. **WT:** 190.
Drafted: HS—Port Orange, FL, 2020 (1st round). **Signed by:** John Cedarburg.
TRACK RECORD: The Rockies drafted Veen ninth overall in 2020 and signed him for an above-slot $5 million. He had an impressive pro debut in 2021, hitting .301/.399/.501 in 106 games with Low-A Fresno. He was assigned to High-A to begin 2022, once again impressing over 92 games. He struggled in a late-season promotion to Double-A Hartford and returned there to begin 2023. Veen's season never got off the ground. He struggled for the first two months before a left wrist tendon injury required surgery, ending Veen's season in mid June.
SCOUTING REPORT: Veen is a talented hitter with advanced plate approach and remaining power projection. It's difficult to take his 2023 at face value when he likely played through injury for a portion of the season. Veen is an average contact hitter with some swing-and-miss due to his long levers and tendency to dump his barrel in an effort to elevate. At his best, he works deep into counts, rarely expanding the zone and looking for mistakes. In 2023, Veen's swing path looked notably steeper. He also chased at the highest rate of his career. Veen's underlying exit velocity showed early signs of progress in 2023, and he should continue to hit for more power as he ages. Historically, Veen has struggled to drive the ball to his pull side, which caps his power ceiling. He should produce average home run totals in the high teens at peak. Veen is an average runner who will show above-average run times. He is a very instinctual baserunner who should steal 20 or more bases annually. Veen can play center field but is best in a corner, where he profiles as an average defender with an average arm.
THE FUTURE: The 2023 season was one to forget for Veen, but he still projects as an average everyday regular capable of some above-average offensive seasons.

Year	Age	Club (League)	Level	AVG	G	AB	R	H	2B	3B	HR	RBI	BB	SO	SB	OBP	SLG
2023	21	Hartford (EL)	AA	.209	46	172	15	36	7	2	2	24	23	43	22	.303	.308
Minor League Totals				.260	278	1037	182	270	57	9	29	166	151	301	113	.357	.417

7 DYAN JORGE, SS/2B

HIT: 55. **POW:** 45. **RUN:** 60. **FLD:** 55. **ARM:** 55. **BA Grade:** 50 **Risk:** High.

Born: March 18, 2003. **B-T:** R-R. **HT:** 6-3. **WT:** 170.
Signed: Cuba, 2022. **Signed by:** Rolando Fernandez/Raul Gomez/Marc Russo.
TRACK RECORD: Jorge was available to teams late in the 2020-21 international signing period after defecting from Cuba. He waited until the following year, when teams' bonus pools reset, to sign with the Rockies for $2.8 million. Jorge debuted in the Dominican Summer League in 2022, hitting .320/.402/.451 in 53 games. After impressing in minor league camp, Jorge was destined for Low-A Fresno before he broke his right hamate and missed two months. He made his 2023 debut in the Arizona Complex League on June 5, reaching Low-A Fresno a month later.
SCOUTING REPORT: Jorge has a tall, lean frame with wiry strength and looks likely to add good weight in the coming years without sacrificing his athleticism. He's an above-average contact hitter with a patient approach at the plate. His swing is more designed for line-drive contact, with a flatter plane and an approach more focused on making consistent contact and spreading the ball around. His game power is well below-average, and he didn't homer in 49 games in Low-A. Jorge's flatter swing plane and lack of physicality translates to below-average exit velocity and a lack of well-struck fly balls. Jorge is likely to add strength in the coming years, and with adjustments to his swing could find mid-teens power at peak. He's a twitchy, quick runner with speed that translates to both sides of the ball. In the field, Jorge shows range and a quick first step, but he will play too fast at times and lose some plays his hands and feet should make. His throwing arm is above-average with plus arm strength and average accuracy. As Jorge matures, he could grow into a more well-rounded hitter and add polish to his defense.
THE FUTURE: An advanced bat-to-ball hitter with tools and projection, Jorge looks like an average everyday infielder with average hitting ability.

Year	Age	Club (League)	Level	AVG	G	AB	R	H	2B	3B	HR	RBI	BB	SO	SB	OBP	SLG
2023	20	ACL Rockies	Rk	.370	21	73	31	27	5	3	3	18	19	12	9	.495	.644
2023	20	Fresno (CAL)	A	.283	49	198	29	56	11	0	0	22	13	35	10	.322	.338
Minor League Totals				.312	123	477	97	149	29	4	7	65	56	82	32	.386	.434

8 JORDY VARGAS, RHP

FB: 50. **CB:** 60. **CHG:** 45. **CTL:** 50. **BA Grade:** 50. **Risk:** High.

Born: November 6, 2003. **B-T:** R-R. **HT:** 6-3. **WT:** 155.
Signed: Dominican Republic, 2021. **Signed by:** Rolando Fernandez/Manuel Cabrera.
TRACK RECORD: The son of nine-year major league lefthander Yorkis Perez, Vargas signed with the Rockies for $500,000 in 2021. He debuted later that year in the Dominican Summer League, pitching to a 1.30 ERA over 34.2 innings. He made his U.S. debut in the Arizona Complex League the following summer and earned a late-season promotion to Low-A Fresno. He returned to Fresno to begin 2023, making 13 starts and performing well as a 19-year-old in the California League. He suffered a torn ulnar collateral ligament in his right elbow in early July and had Tommy John surgery. Vargas will likely miss all of the 2024 season.
SCOUTING REPORT: Vargas is a tall, projectable righthander with a smooth, athletic delivery and a loose, fast arm. He has a whippy arm action and delivers the ball from a three-quarters arm slot. He mixes a trio of pitches, led by his four-seam fastball that sits 93-95 mph and touches 96-97 at peak with above-average ride and late armside run. Vargas pairs his four-seam primarily with a big-breaking curveball at 75-77 mph with two-plane movement and depth. His curveball is his best bat-missing pitch. In 2023, batters had a 54% whiff rate against the pitch and a 39% in-zone whiff rate, both exceptional marks. Vargas' changeup is a clear third pitch, a low-to-mid-80s offering with tumble and heavy fade. He'll mix in a sinker variation of his fastball on occasion as well. Overall, Vargas shows a good feel for his arsenal, particularly for his fastball/curveball combination. He's still learning his changeup, which will be a point of focus upon returning from Tommy John surgery.
THE FUTURE: A projectable righthander with starter traits, Vargas will likely be an average back-end starter at peak.

Year	Age	Club (League)	Level	W	L	ERA	G	GS	IP	H	HR	BB	SO	BB%	SO%	WHIP	AVG
2023	19	Fresno (CAL)	A	6	3	4.22	13	13	64	55	4	24	69	9.1	26.1	1.23	.239
Minor League Totals				12	4	3.12	37	33	150	106	9	57	179	9.4	29.4	1.09	.198

9 DREW ROMO, C

HIT: 50. **POW:** 40. **RUN:** 50. **FLD:** 70. **ARM:** 60. **BA Grade:** 50. **Risk:** High.

Born: August 29, 2001. **B-T:** B-R. **HT:** 5-11. **WT:** 205.
Drafted: HS—Fountain Valley, CA, 2020 (1st round supp). **Signed by:** Jeff Edwards.
TRACK RECORD: A highly touted prep, Romo was drafted by the Rockies with the 35th overall pick in 2020. He signed for a slot value bonus of $2.1 million and debuted the following spring with Low-A Fresno. The Rockies have moved Romo a level a season. He spent all of 2022 with High-A Spokane before spending a majority of 2023 with Double-A Hartford. After hitting just .208/.254/.312 in the first two months of 2023, Romo caught fire and hit .288/.351/.521 from June 1 onward. The performance earned Romo a late-season promotion to Triple-A Albuquerque. Notably, Romo had two separate three-home run games, occurring on July 28 and Sept. 7. The catcher finished his season in the Arizona Fall League.
SCOUTING REPORT: Romo is a switch-hitter with above-average bat-to-ball skills and a hyper-aggressive approach. The majority of his damage comes as a lefthanded batter, and he hit just .162/.225/.243 from the right side. His lefthanded swing produces better contact quality. Romo doesn't hit the ball particularly hard but is adept at making his best contact at good angles. He flashed more power in 2023 but still projects as a below-average power hitter. He's an average runner who has shown solid basestealing instincts. Long touted for his defensive prowess, Romo is a plus-plus defender with a plus throwing arm. He's comfortable in the crouch and athletic behind the plate. There's little question about his receiving and blocking. Romo has long been viewed as having a defense-driven profile, but in the second half of 2023 he Romo showed a far more impactful offensive performance.
THE FUTURE: Romo is a potential everyday catcher with average production at the plate, driven by his contact hitting.

Year	Age	Club (League)	Level	AVG	G	AB	R	H	2B	3B	HR	RBI	BB	SO	SB	OBP	SLG
2023	21	Hartford (EL)	AA	.254	91	327	45	83	18	2	13	48	29	67	6	.313	.440
2023	21	Albuquerque (PCL)	AAA	.353	4	17	2	6	1	1	0	3	0	4	0	.389	.529
Minor League Totals				.274	275	1030	147	282	55	10	24	156	83	202	47	.327	.417

10 ROBERT CALAZ, OF

HIT: 50. **POW:** 60. **RUN:** 45. **FLD:** 50. **ARM:** 50. **BA GRADE:** 55. **RISK:** EXTREME.

Born: November 11, 2005. **B-T:** R-R. **HT:** 6-2. **WT:** 202.
Signed: Dominican Republic, 2023. **Signed by:** Roberto Fernandez.
TRACK RECORD: Calaz signed with the Rockies for $1.7 million as a 17-year-old in January 2023. He was considered one of the top hitters available in the Dominican Republic in his international signing class. Calaz was noted for his physicality and combination of impact and plate skills. He debuted in the Dominican Summer League and hit .325/.423/.561 with seven home runs, ranking ninth in the league in slugging percentage. Calaz stood as one of the DSL's finest prospects in 2023 and is likely to make his stateside debut in June 2024 in the Arizona Complex League.
SCOUTING REPORT: Calaz is a physical player with size and strength, but plenty of present athleticism for his size. He is still learning his body, but the Rockies are encouraged by his progress in the weight room. Calaz showed above-average bat-to-ball skills and average swing decisions during his pro debut. He rarely missed in-zone and ran an 83% zone contact rate. He has no split issues and destroyed lefthanders with a 1.262 OPS in a small sample. Calaz shows a knack for finding the barrel with the ability to backspin balls over the field. He shows plus-plus raw power with room for more, with plus game power. Calaz had some of the best top-end exit velocity data among teenagers in the minor leagues, with a 90th percentile exit velocity of a 107.2 mph and a max of 113.8. Calaz is an fringe-average runner who can get moving underway. He saw a majority of his time in center field but is expected to move to a corner, where his average arm should play.
THE FUTURE: Calaz is a classic corner outfield masher who showed big exit velocity with solid skills to match.

Year	Age	Club (League)	Level	AVG	G	AB	R	H	2B	3B	HR	RBI	BB	SO	SB	OBP	SLG
2023	17	DSL Colorado	Rk	.325	43	157	38	51	12	2	7	29	22	43	6	.423	.561
Minor League Totals				.325	43	157	38	51	12	2	7	29	22	43	6	.423	.561

11 BENNY MONTGOMERY, OF

HIT: 40. **POW:** 55. **RUN:** 70. **FLD:** 60. **ARM:** 60. **BA Grade:** 55. **Risk:** Extreme.

Born: September 9, 2002. **B-T:** R-R. **HT:** 6-4. **WT:** 200. **Drafted:** HS—Lewisberry, PA, 2021 (1st round).
Signed by: Ed Santa.
TRACK RECORD: Montgomery was a tooled-up high school player with an unusual swing and major questions about his hitting ability. Despite these concerns, the Rockies selected Montgomery with the eighth overall pick and signed him for a $5 million bonus. Montgomery dealt with a quadriceps injury during his full-season debut in 2022, but the Rockies trusted his offseason development enough to assign him to High-A Spokane. He put together a league-average season and participated in the Arizona Fall League following the year.
SCOUTING REPORT: Montgomery has always had loud tools but a lack of baseball skills to make them play to their fullest. He's tinkered with his swing over the years, but still rushes through his mechanics. Montgomery had the highest drop in chase rate of any hitter in minor league baseball in 2023, which led to a climb in walk rate and more consistent plate appearances. Despite the drastic improvement in approach, Montgomery's bat-to-ball skills are still below-average. He has plus raw power, but his lack of barrel control means he rarely gets to it. Montgomery has plus-plus bat speed and could unleash more of his power if he fixes his timing issues. Montgomery is a plus-plus runner who plays a plus center field with a plus arm. He has a high ceiling but won't get to it unless he shows more hitting ability.
THE FUTURE: Montgomery is a tooled-up center fielder who will struggle to consistently hit.

Year	Age	Club (League)	Level	AVG	G	AB	R	H	2B	3B	HR	RBI	BB	SO	SB	OBP	SLG
2023	20	Spokane (NWL)	A+	.251	109	438	62	110	18	2	10	51	52	135	18	.336	.370
Minor League Totals				.277	185	740	120	205	39	7	16	101	78	221	32	.357	.414

12 COLE CARRIGG, C/SS/OF

HIT: 45. **POW:** 45. **RUN:** 60. **FLD:** 60. **ARM:** 70. **BA Grade:** 50. **Risk:** High.

Born: May 8, 2002. **B-T:** S-R. **HT:** 6-3. **WT:** 200. **Drafted:** San Diego State, 2023 (2nd round supplemental).
Signed by: Matt Hattabaugh.
TRACK RECORD: Few players in the 2023 draft class have shown Carrigg's versatility. During his three years at San Diego State, he played every position but first base and made three appearances as a pitcher.

Carrigg had a breakout 2022 summer with Yarmouth-Dennis of the Cape Cod League and carried a late first-round buzz entering the season. He dealt with a shoulder injury and a concussion, which impacted his production. Carrigg dropped to the Rockies in the supplemental second round and signed for an above-slot bonus of $1.3 million. He debuted in the Arizona Complex League, put up gaudy numbers over 13 games and earned a promotion to Low-A Fresno for the final month of the season.

SCOUTING REPORT: Carrigg is a switch-hitting tool shed with a wide range of outcomes but a strong foundation of baseball skills. Some parts of his swing work, but he rotates his hips east to west as opposed to north to south, keeping him from landing before he rotates. He has solid bat-to-ball skills but his approach is overzealous and he expands the zone too often. His swings are similar from both sides, which leads to nearly identical timing issues. Carrigg has never hit for power despite possessing bat speed and a frame that portends at least average power. Carrigg's other tools are outstanding. He's an easy plus runner and his speed translates to the field and on the bases. He has a plus-plus arm that plays anywhere on the field. In his professional debut Carrigg saw time in center field, shortstop and catcher. He projects as a plus center fielder who can provide average defense at shortstop and fringe-average defense behind the plate.

THE FUTURE: Carrigg is a true super-utility player who could be an above-average regular if he fixes his timing issues.

Year	Age	Club (League)	Level	AVG	G	AB	R	H	2B	3B	HR	RBI	BB	SO	SB	OBP	SLG
2023	21	ACL Rockies	Rk	.396	13	48	13	19	6	1	2	13	6	13	7	.464	.688
2023	21	Fresno (CAL)	A	.326	23	92	19	30	4	4	3	16	7	20	6	.376	.554
Minor League Totals				.350	36	140	32	49	10	5	5	29	13	33	13	.408	.600

13 HUNTER GOODMAN, 1B/C

HIT: 40. **POW:** 70. **RUN:** 40. **FLD:** 40. **ARM:** 60. **BA Grade:** 45. **Risk:** Medium.

Born: October 8, 1999. **B-T:** R-R. **HT:** 6-1. **WT:** 210. **Drafted:** Memphis, 2021 (4th round). **Signed by:** Zack Zulli.

TRACK RECORD: Goodman was the first Memphis player to earn freshman All-American when he hit .326/.367/.573 with 13 home runs. The Rockies selected Goodman in the four round in the 2021 draft and signed him for an over-slot bonus of $600,000. In his first full season, Goodman reached Double-A and hit 36 home runs, which tied him for third in the minor leagues. Goodman began 2023 back in Double-A, where he showed an improved approach and contact ability. He was promoted to Triple-A on Aug. 8 and went on a hot streak that included nine home runs over 15 games and helped him earn his first callup.

SCOUTING REPORT: Goodman is a positionless masher with double-plus game power and improving plate skills. He entered the year with well below-average contact and an aggressive approach. Goodman made noticeable changes coming into 2023, which helped him cut his chase rate by 25% and improve his contact rate to a functioning level. Goodman's issues with spin and being overly aggressive resurface in his small major league sample. Goodman's carrying tool is his double-plus raw power which he gets to consistently during games. He swings to do damage and has enough power to drive the ball out of the yard even on mis-hits. He is a below-average defender behind the plate and in left field—where he was used at times in 2023—but is likely destined for first base.

THE FUTURE: Goodman is a power-hitting first baseman with improving but still questionable plate skills.

Year	Age	Club (League)	Level	AVG	G	AB	R	H	2B	3B	HR	RBI	BB	SO	SB	OBP	SLG
2023	23	Hartford (EL)	AA	.239	91	348	53	83	24	0	25	78	41	98	0	.325	.523
2023	23	Albuquerque (PCL)	AAA	.371	15	62	15	23	6	0	9	33	4	17	0	.418	.903
2023	23	Colorado (NL)	MLB	.200	23	70	6	14	4	3	1	17	5	24	1	.247	.386
Minor League Totals				.280	262	993	181	278	70	2	72	229	94	280	7	.352	.572
Major League Totals				.200	23	70	6	14	4	3	1	17	5	24	1	.247	.386

14 CARSON PALMQUIST, LHP

FB: 45. **CB:** 55. **SL:** 45. **CHG:** 55. **CUT:** 40. **CTL:** 50. **BA Grade:** 45. **Risk:** High.

Born: October 17, 2001. **B-T:** L-L. **HT:** 6-3. **WT:** 185. **Drafted:** Miami, 2022 (3rd round). **Signed by:** Rafael Reyes.

TRACK RECORD: Palmquist spent two seasons in the Miami bullpen as one of the top relievers in the country. He earned a USA Baseball Collegiate National Team invite heading into his draft spring and impressed during trials. Palmquist returned to Miami and made the successful jump into the starting rotation, earning first team all-ACC honors for his performance. Palmquist was drafted by the Rockies in the third round and made a single appearance in the Rookie-level Arizona Complex League after signing. Palmquist began the 2023 season with High-A Spokane and struck out 35.7% of hitters over his 15 starts. Palmquist was promoted to Double-A on Aug. 24 making and made four starts with Hartford.

SCOUTING REPORT: A low-slot lefty, Palmquist lacks power on his pitches but also doesn't throw anything straight. He expanded his arsenal in 2023 by adding a slider and a cutter to complement his curveball. His fastball sits between 90-92 mph and touches 93 mph with heavy armside run and a flat approach angle. Despite Palmquist's lack of velocity, his fastball is quite deceptive. His most frequently used secondary is a curveball that sits between 75-76 mph with a difficult horizontal angle. Palmquist's best pitch is his changeup, which sits between 81-82 mph with heavy armside run and tumble. Both his curveball and his changeup drive weak contact and generate whiffs in and out of the zone. Palmquist's slider and cutter are similar variations of the same pitch with a difference of 4-5 mph of average velocity. Palmquist is an average strike thrower with a feel for his entire arsenal.
THE FUTURE: Palmquist's lack of velocity as a starter is a limiting factor and he'll likely settle into a bullpen role.

Year	Age	Club (League)	Level	W	L	ERA	G	GS	IP	H	HR	BB	SO	BB%	SO%	WHIP	AVG
2023	22	Spokane (NWL)	A+	7	2	3.73	15	15	70	61	9	28	106	9.4	35.7	1.27	.238
2023	22	Hartford (EL)	AA	0	2	4.43	4	4	22	19	4	9	28	9.6	29.8	1.25	.226
Minor League Totals				7	4	3.87	20	19	93	80	13	39	135	9.8	34.1	1.28	.234

15 GABRIEL HUGHES, RHP

FB: 50. **CB:** 45. **SL:** 55. **CHG:** 40. **CTL:** 50. **BA Grade:** 50. **Risk:** Extreme.

Born: August 22, 2001. **B-T:** R-R. **HT:** 6-4. **WT:** 220. **Drafted:** Gonzaga, 2022 (1st round). **Signed by:** Matt Pignataro.
TRACK RECORD: After two seasons as a two-way player for Gonzaga, Hughes earned a Collegiate National Team invite prior to his draft spring and converted full-time to pitching. Hughes had a dominant showing with Gonzaga in his draft spring, when he struck out 138 batters over 98 innings and earned second-team All-American honors. The Rockies selected Hughes with the 10th overall pick in the draft. He debuted following the draft with two three-inning outings for Low-A Fresno, one in the regular season and another in the playoffs. Hughes opened 2023 at High-A Spokane and made eight starts before moving to Double-A. After six starts with the Yard Goats, the Rockies announced that Hughes had a torn ulnar collateral ligament and had Tommy John surgery.
SCOUTING REPORT: Hughes is a tall, physical righthander with a four-pitch mix that includes a four-seam fastball, slider, curveball and changeup. His fastball sits between 92-94 mph and touches 95 mph with below-average ride and cut. Hughes shows good command for his fastball and lands it in the zone consistently. His most-used secondary is a slider which sits 84-86 mph with cut. He shows strong command for the pitch, which is a bat-misser. Against lefties, Hughes leans on his curveball. The pitch sits between 77-78 mph with heavy two-plane break. Hughes has a seldom-used changeup that sits between 85-87 mph and is commanded poorly. Overall, Hughes is an average strike-thrower.
THE FUTURE: If Hughes returns healthy, he has the ability to develop into a No. 4 starter.

Year	Age	Club (League)	Level	W	L	ERA	G	GS	IP	H	HR	BB	SO	BB%	SO%	WHIP	AVG
2023	21	Spokane (NWL)	A+	4	3	5.50	8	8	38	30	5	15	54	9.3	33.5	1.19	.208
2023	21	Hartford (EL)	AA	2	2	7.14	6	6	29	34	7	11	29	8.3	22.0	1.55	.286
Minor League Totals				6	5	6.00	15	15	70	65	12	27	84	8.9	27.6	1.33	.238

16 SEAN SULLIVAN, LHP

FB: 55. **SL:** 40. **CHG:** 55. **CTL:** 55. **BA Grade:** 45. **Risk:** High.

Born: July 22, 2002. **B-T:** R-L. **HT:** 6-4. **WT:** 190. **Drafted:** Wake Forest, 2023 (2nd round). **Signed by:** Jordan Czarniecki.
TRACK RECORD: Sullivan spent his freshman season at Northwestern, where he pitched well before impressing over the summer in the Cape Cod League. He transferred to Wake Forest before his sophomore season and dominated, earning all-ACC first team honors. The Rockies selected Sullivan in the second round and signed him for $1.7 million. Sullivan debuted in the Rookie-level Arizona Complex League and made two appearances before he was promoted to Low-A Fresno for a single appearance.
SCOUTING REPORT: Sullivan is a low-slot lefthander who lacks power but has a high level of deception on all of his pitches. He mixes a four-seam fastball, a sweeping slider and a changeup. Sullivan's fastball sits between 90-92 mph and touched 95 mph over the college season. His fastball plays up due to his low release height, deceptive arm action and flat fastball plane. Sullivan's primary secondary is a low-80s changeup that generated a high rate of whiffs and is clearly the better of his two secondary offerings. His low-80s sweeper lacks bite, and it likely won't miss bats in pro ball. He has above-average command of his pitch mix.
THE FUTURE: Sullivan has starter's traits and a deceptive operation that might allow him to overcome his lack of velocity.

Year	Age	Club (League)	Level	W	L	ERA	G	GS	IP	H	HR	BB	SO	BB%	SO%	WHIP	AVG
2023	20	ACL Rockies	Rk	0	0	0.00	2	0	2	0	0	1	4	14.3	57.1	0.50	.000
2023	20	Fresno (CAL)	A	1	0	0.00	1	0	2	0	0	0	6	0.0	100.0	0.00	.000
Minor League Totals				1	0	0.00	3	0	4	0	0	1	10	7.7	76.9	0.25	.000

17 JACKSON COX, RHP

FB: 55. **CB:** 60. **SL:** 40. **CHG:** 40. **CUT:** 40. **CTL:** 45. **BA Grade:** 50. **Risk:** Extreme.

Born: September 25, 2003. **B-T:** R-R. **HT:** 6-0. **WT:** 185. **Drafted:** HS—Toutle, WA, 2022 (2nd round).
Signed by: Matt Pignataro.
TRACK RECORD: Heading into the 2022 draft, Cox was viewed as one of the higher upside prep arms in the class thanks to a high-spin breaking ball that dominated prep competition. The Rockies selected Cox in the second round and signed him for $1.85 million. Cox debuted the following May with Low-A Fresno and made nine starts. Cox suffered an elbow injury in July and had Tommy John surgery. He will miss all of the 2024 season.
SCOUTING REPORT: Cox mixes five pitches: a four-seam fastball, curveball, slider, changeup and cutter. He leans primarily on his fastball and curveball and mixes his other secondaries when necessary. Cox's fastball sits between 93-94 mph and touches 96 mph with above-average ride and late life through the zone. Cox shows command of the pitch, but it did not miss bats in his debut. His most-thrown secondary is his signature curveball, a hellacious two-plane breaking ball with spin rates between 2,800-3,000 rpm. Cox's slider is a mid-80s sweeper and is used roughly as often as his upper-80s changeup and low-90s cutter. Cox's strike-throwing is below-average but should improve as he gets healthy and gains professional experience.
THE FUTURE: Cox has a wide range of outcomes but the upside of a No. 4 starter.

Year	Age	Club (League)	Level	W	L	ERA	G	GS	IP	H	HR	BB	SO	BB%	SO%	WHIP	AVG
2023	19	Fresno (CAL)	A	1	0	7.26	10	9	31	39	2	20	32	13.4	21.5	1.90	.307
Minor League Totals				1	0	7.26	10	9	31	39	2	20	32	13.4	21.5	1.90	.307

18 RYAN RITTER, SS

HIT: 30. **POW:** 55. **RUN:** 55. **FLD:** 55. **ARM:** 55. **BA Grade:** 45. **Risk:** High.

Born: November 10, 2000. **B-T:** R-R. **HT:** 6-2. **WT:** 200. **Drafted:** Kentucky, 2022 (4th round). **Signed by:** Scott Corman.
TRACK RECORD: Ritter spent his freshman season with Logan (Ill.) JC before spending two seasons at Kentucky. The Rockies selected him in the fourth round of the 2022 draft and signed him for a bonus of $530,000. Ritter began 2023 in Low-A Fresno, where he hit .305/.405/.606 over 65 games before a promotion to Spokane on July 3. He hit well for 46 games before a late-season bump to Double-A.
SCOUTING REPORT: Over the last few years Ritter has grown into power but has added more swing and miss to his game. His bat-to-ball skills are below-average, and he struggles particularly to hit spin and offspeed. Despite his hit tool concerns, Ritter shows the ability to discern balls and strikes and is aggressive on pitches in the zone. Ritter has shown a knack for backspinning fly balls to his pull side when and projects to have above-average power. He's an above-average runner, and his speed also helps him show excellent range at shortstop. Ritter is an above-average defender at shortstop with an above-average throwing arm that plays at any spot on the diamond.
THE FUTURE: Ritter could become a power-hitting shortstop with the upside of a second-division regular.

Year	Age	Club (League)	Level	AVG	G	AB	R	H	2B	3B	HR	RBI	BB	SO	SB	OBP	SLG
2023	22	Fresno (CAL)	A	.305	65	246	53	75	14	3	18	58	37	72	6	.405	.606
2023	22	Spokane (NWL)	A+	.265	46	170	33	45	10	1	6	26	22	69	12	.367	.441
2023	22	Hartford (EL)	AA	.160	8	25	4	4	1	0	0	1	3	11	2	.276	.200
Minor League Totals				.283	127	466	99	132	29	5	25	89	64	155	22	.385	.528

19 SEAN BOUCHARD, OF

HIT: 45. **POW:** 55. **RUN:** 40. **FLD:** 40. **ARM:** 40. **BA Grade:** 40. **Risk:** Medium.

Born: May 16, 1996. **B-T:** R-R. **HT:** 6-3. **WT:** 215. **Drafted:** UCLA, 2017 (9th round). **Signed by:** Matt Hattabaugh.
TRACK RECORD: Bouchard was a star at San Diego's Cathedral Catholic High alongside former No. 1 overall pick Brady Aiken. Bouchard made it to campus at UCLA, where he enjoyed a solid career and earned all-Pac-12 team honors as a junior. Drafted by the Rockies in the ninth round in 2017, Bouchard produced solid results over parts of five minor league seasons and made his major league debut on June 19, 2022. Bouchard has dealt with injuries over the past two seasons, including a strained left oblique early in his major league stint with the Rockies in 2022 and then a ruptured left biceps muscle in spring training

2023. He returned to the minor leagues on August 23 and then reached the big leagues again on Sept. 1.
SCOUTING REPORT: Bouchard is a low-risk, low upside, bat-first prospect. He'll turn 28 years old in May, and already has played a few stints in the major leagues. Bouchard shows average bat-to-ball skills with a mildly aggressive approach. He has some difficulty against sliders but is a good fastball hitter who can catch up to velocity at the top of the zone. During Bouchard's month in the big leagues he chased at a higher rate than he had previously. His underlying power data is above-average and he flashed over-the-fence power as well. Bouchard is a below-average runner, a below-average corner outfielder and has a below-average arm.
THE FUTURE: Bouchard is a low-risk major league platoon bat.

Year	Age	Club (League)	Level	AVG	G	AB	R	H	2B	3B	HR	RBI	BB	SO	SB	OBP	SLG
2023	27	ACL Rockies	Rk	.000	1	2	0	0	0	0	0	1	0	0	0	.333	.000
2023	27	Spokane (NWL)	A+	.333	5	18	2	6	2	0	1	4	0	5	0	.368	.611
2023	27	Albuquerque (PCL)	AAA	.222	16	54	11	12	2	0	1	6	17	14	5	.408	.315
2023	27	Colorado (NL)	MLB	.316	21	38	11	12	2	0	4	7	4	14	0	.372	.684
Minor League Totals				.276	437	1643	290	453	122	13	69	283	193	461	61	.356	.492
Major League Totals				.304	48	112	20	34	8	0	7	18	25	39	0	.429	.563

20 MICHAEL PROSECKY, LHP
FB: 55. **CB:** 45. **CHG:** 50. **CUT:** 45. **CTL:** 50. **BA Grade:** 45. **Risk:** High.

Born: February 28, 2001. **B-T:** L-L. **HT:** 6-3. **WT:** 200. **Drafted:** Louisville, 2022 (6th round). **Signed by:** Scott Corman.
TRACK RECORD: Prosecky was drafted in the 35th round by the Phillies in 2019 but honored his commitment to Louisville. He lost his first two seasons to the pandemic and injury, which meant he never cracked the Cardinals' rotation. He made 26 appearances out of the Louisville bullpen in 2022 and was an all-ACC selection. The Rockies took Prosecky in the sixth round of the 2022 draft and signed him for an over-slot bonus of $300,000. He was assigned to Low-A Fresno in 2023 and got an opportunity to start.
SCOUTING REPORT: After pitching exclusively as a reliever in college, Prosecky understandably works with a fastball-heavy mix and threw his heater 67% of the time in 2023. The pitch is above-average and sits between 92-93 mph and touches 95 mph with well above-average ride that helped it miss bats and drive weak contact. Prosecky also throws a mid-70s curveball, a mid-80s changeup and a cutter at 87-88 mph. He showed improved feel for his changeup in 2023 and used it to overwhelm Low-A hitters. Prosecky is an average strike-thrower with the ability to command all of his pitches.
THE FUTURE: Prosecky could blossom into a No. 4 starter with more starting experience. His fastball-heavy approach, however, will likely land him in a relief role.

Year	Age	Club (League)	Level	W	L	ERA	G	GS	IP	H	HR	BB	SO	BB%	SO%	WHIP	AVG
2023	22	Fresno (CAL)	A	11	7	2.72	21	21	109	87	4	41	125	9.1	27.6	1.17	.217
Minor League Totals				11	7	2.70	22	21	110	87	4	41	126	9.0	27.6	1.16	.215

21 JULIO CARRERAS, SS
HIT: 45. **POW:** 30. **RUN:** 55. **FLD:** 60. **ARM:** 60. **BA Grade:** 40. **Risk:** Medium.

Born: January 12, 2000. **B-T:** R-R. **HT:** 6-2. **WT:** 190. **Signed:** Dominican Republic, 2018.
Signed by: Rolando Fernandez/Frank Roa.
TRACK RECORD: Carreras has dealt with injuries and struggles at the plate, but he's still one of the best infield defenders in the organization. After a strong 2022 that saw him reach Double-A, Carreras returned to Hartford to begin 2023. He dealt with nagging injuries throughout the season and landed on the injured list three times. Carreras earned a late-season promotion to Triple-A.
SCOUTING REPORT: Carreras has plenty of tools but the lack of impact in his bat limits his overall upside. He has average bat-to-ball skills and can get his bat on velocity. He's not overly aggressive and does a good job discerning balls from strikes. Carreras' swing is simple but grooved and produces a high rate of grounders. Carreras' impact is below-average but he could still run into 8-10 home runs a season. He had shoulder surgery in 2020, but it's unclear if the procedure affected his power. Carreras is an above-average runner with good range at shortstop, and he has clean actions in the field with a good internal clock and a plus throwing arm.
THE FUTURE: Carreras' plus defense provides him with a low-risk role as a utility infielder.

Year	Age	Club (League)	Level	AVG	G	AB	R	H	2B	3B	HR	RBI	BB	SO	SB	OBP	SLG
2023	23	Hartford (EL)	AA	.235	88	311	48	73	14	1	5	31	33	81	13	.316	.334
2023	23	Albuquerque (PCL)	AAA	.255	16	51	8	13	3	0	1	7	10	14	1	.371	.373
Minor League Totals				.269	462	1676	296	451	103	24	35	223	159	433	78	.344	.422

22 ANGEL CHIVILLI, RHP

FB: 50. **SL:** 55. **CHG:** 55. **CTL:** 55. **BA Grade:** 45. **Risk:** High.

Born: July 28, 2002. **B-T:** R-R. **HT:** 6-2. **WT:** 162. **Signed:** Dominican Republic, 2018.
Signed by: Rolando Fernandez/Manuel Cabrera.

TRACK RECORD: Chivilli was a standout performer for Low-A Fresno in the second half of 2022, and there was talk that he might transition into a starting role in 2023. Instead, Chivilli began the season in High-A Spokane's bullpen. He made 50 appearances at the level and struck out 65 over 57 innings. Chivilli earned a promotion to Double-A Hartford for the final few weeks of the season. Chivilli was added to the 40-man roster following the season.

SCOUTING REPORT: Chivilli mixes a four-seam fastball, slider and changeup. His fastball sits between 95-97 mph with below-average ride but heavy armside run. He shows a knack for landing the pitch in the zone. Chivilli's most-thrown secondary is an above-average changeup that sits between 85-87 mph. His slider, which sits between 85-87 mph, plays like a cutter hybrid and gets swings and misses both in and out of the zone. It's his best pitch. Despite being a reliever so early in his career, Chivilli displays above-average command.

THE FUTURE: With sharp command and an outstanding pitch mix, Chivilli has the makings of a high-leverage reliever.

Year	Age	Club (League)	Level	W	L	ERA	G	GS	IP	H	HR	BB	SO	BB%	SO%	WHIP	AVG
2023	20	Spokane (NWL)	A+	4	9	5.84	50	0	57	62	9	20	65	7.8	25.5	1.44	.274
2023	20	Hartford (EL)	AA	0	0	2.25	3	0	4	4	0	1	3	6.3	18.8	1.25	.267
Minor League Totals				7	19	4.04	108	20	185	186	14	49	209	6.2	26.5	1.27	.257

23 ANTHONY MOLINA, RHP

FB: 55. **SL:** 45. **CHG:** 45. **CTL:** 55. **BA Grade:** 40. **Risk:** High.

Born: January 12, 2002. **B-T:** R-R. **HT:** 6-1. **WT:** 170. **Signed:** Venezuela, 2018. **Signed by:** William Bergolla (Rays).

TRACK RECORD: The Rays signed Molina out of Venezuela during the 2018 international signing period. He was primarily a reliever over his first three professional seasons before the Rays moved him into a starting role late in 2022. In 2023, he made 27 starts between Double-A Montgomery and Triple-A Durham. Molina showed strong control and walked just 6.9% of batters over 122 innings. Molina was left unprotected for the Rule 5 draft and was selected by the Rockies.

SCOUTING REPORT: Molina is an aggressive strike-thrower with a powerful three-pitch mix. He throws a four-seam fastball, slider and changeup and consistently lands all three for strikes. Molina's four-seamer sits 94-96 mph with above-average ride and run, but is a below-average whiff-generator. He mixes his slider and changeup equally but neither misses many bats. His slider sits between 85-86 mph with cutter shape, and his changeup is a mid-80s offering with fade. He has above-average control.

THE FUTURE: Molina has a starter's command but his strike-throwing, above-average velocity and Rule 5 status might push him to the bullpen.

Year	Age	Club (League)	Level	W	L	ERA	G	GS	IP	H	HR	BB	SO	BB%	SO%	WHIP	AVG
2023	21	Montgomery (SL)	AA	2	5	4.61	15	15	66	72	8	20	52	6.8	17.7	1.39	.266
2023	21	Durham (IL)	AAA	3	2	4.37	13	12	56	73	5	18	50	7.1	19.7	1.63	.312
Minor League Totals				23	13	3.64	83	45	302	330	26	74	254	5.7	19.6	1.34	.271

24 JUAN MEJIA, RHP

FB: 55. **SL:** 60. **CHG:** 30. **CTL:** 45. **BA Grade:** 40. **Risk:** High.

Born: July 4, 2000. **B-T:** R-R. **HT:** 6-3. **WT:** 200. **Signed:** Dominican Republic, 2017.
Signed by: Rolando Fernandez/Martin Cabrera.

TRACK RECORD: Mejia signed out of the Dominican Republic as part of the same class as current Rockies shortstop Ezequiel Tovar, but has been brought along slowly. He reached Double-A for the first time in 2023. Mejia broke out in the Arizona Fall League, where he struck out 16 batters over 8.1 innings. Mejia was added to Colorado's 40-man roster in the offseason.

SCOUTING REPORT: Mejia is primarily a two-pitch reliever with power stuff and fringy command. His four-seam fastball sits between 95-97 mph and features heavy cut life. The pitch is an above-average bat-misser pitch that generates whiffs in the zone. His most-thrown secondary is a mid-80s sweeper with an average of between 15-16 inches of horizontal break. Mejia's slider consistently stymied hitters in 2023, when it generated a high rate of chases. Mejia also shows a firm changeup but it's rarely used. Mejia shows below-average command of his fastball but has a good feel for his sweeper.

THE FUTURE: Mejia is a two-pitch middle reliever who could contribute for the Rockies in 2024.

Year	Age	Club (League)	Level	W	L	ERA	G	GS	IP	H	HR	BB	SO	BB%	SO%	WHIP	AVG
2023	22	Spokane (NWL)	A+	2	2	4.81	35	0	43	37	3	23	64	11.6	32.2	1.40	.230
2023	22	Hartford (EL)	AA	1	3	5.74	13	0	16	15	1	9	22	12.9	31.4	1.53	.254
Minor League Totals				15	19	4.54	188	15	274	250	20	130	328	10.7	27.0	1.39	.239

25 JOE ROCK, LHP

FB: 45. **SL:** 55. **CHG:** 45. **CTL:** 45. **BA Grade:** 40. **Risk:** High.

Born: July 29, 2000. **B-T:** L-L. **HT:** 6-6. **WT:** 200. **Drafted:** Ohio, 2021 (2nd round supplemental). **Signed by:** Ed Santa.
TRACK RECORD: Rock broke out during his junior season at Ohio, when he tossed four complete games and led the team in ERA and strikeouts. The Rockies liked what they saw and selected Rock with the 68th overall pick in the supplemental second round. Rock spent a majority of 2022 with High-A Spokane and reached Double-A late in the season. Rock returned to Hartford in 2023 and made 19 starts while striking out more than a batter per inning. Rock made one start with Triple-A Albuquerque in late September.
SCOUTING REPORT: Rock is a big-bodied lefthander who stands at an imposing 6-foot-6, with feel for a three-pitch mix. He mixes two-seam fastball, slider and a changeup, and everything shows heavy horizontal movement due to his low-three quarters slot. His two-seamer sits between 92-93 mph and touches 94 with heavy armside run. Rock's most-used secondary is a mid-80s gyro slider he shows above-average feel to throw. It generates whiffs in the zone and gets lots of ugly chase swings. Rock's changeup sits between 86-88 mph with heavy armside run and good vertical separation from his fastball. Rock has shown fringe-average strike-throwing skills with a chance to develop into average command.
THE FUTURE: Rock is a back-end depth starter who should be capable of eating innings.

Year	Age	Club (League)	Level	W	L	ERA	G	GS	IP	H	HR	BB	SO	BB%	SO%	WHIP	AVG
2023	22	Hartford (EL)	AA	1	10	4.50	19	19	90	94	13	32	108	8.1	27.3	1.40	.266
2023	22	Albuquerque (PCL)	AAA	0	0	10.13	1	1	3	3	1	2	4	15.4	30.8	1.88	.300
Minor League Totals				9	18	4.63	46	44	216	198	26	85	243	9.1	26.2	1.31	.241

26 WARMING BERNABEL, 3B

HIT: 45. **POW:** 40. **RUN:** 45. **FLD:** 45. **ARM:** 50. **BA Grade:** 45. **Risk:** Extreme.

Born: August 6, 2002. **B-T:** R-R. **HT:** 6-0. **WT:** 180. **Signed:** Dominican Republic, 2018.
Signed by: Rolando Fernandez/Martin Cabrera.
TRACK RECORD: Bernabel signed for $900,000 out of the Dominican Republic in 2018 and showed promising hitting skills on the complex and at both Class A levels. After hitting .295/.355/.470 across Low-A and High-A in 2022, the Rockies Bernabel moved to Double-A Hartford. Bernabel's hyper-aggressive approach was exposed against more advanced pitching and he hit just .225/.270/.338 with six home runs over 83 games.
SCOUTING REPORT: During the early portion of his professional career, Bernabel got by on a combination of above-average bat-to-ball skills and a knack for finding the barrel. He shows the ability to make contact with the pitches he swings at in the zone, but his overwhelming tendency to chase adds swing-and-miss to his game. Bernabel's raw power is below-average and his exit velocity numbers went backward in 2023. He has a knack for backspinning fly balls on contact but his approach dilutes some of his output. He is a fringe-average runner with enough range for third base. His hands and actions are sound and his throwing arm is average. Both traits give him a chance to stick at third base.
THE FUTURE: If Bernabel refines his approach and adds strength he has enough skills to carve out a role as an infield depth option.

Year	Age	Club (League)	Level	AVG	G	AB	R	H	2B	3B	HR	RBI	BB	SO	SB	OBP	SLG
2023	21	ACL Rockies	Rk	.333	8	33	9	11	4	0	2	8	1	6	0	.389	.636
2023	21	Hartford (EL)	AA	.225	83	302	30	68	14	1	6	28	15	68	2	.270	.338
Minor League Totals				.276	280	1071	173	296	68	3	33	176	75	185	37	.333	.438

27 VICTOR JUAREZ, RHP

FB: 40. **CB:** 45. **SL:** 40. **CHG:** 55. **CTL:** 55. **BA Grade:** 40. **Risk:** High.

Born: June 19, 2003. **B-T:** R-R. **HT:** 6-0. **WT:** 173. **Signed:** Mexico, 2019.
Signed by: Rolando Fernandez/Alving Mejías/Marc Russo.
TRACK RECORD: Juarez made his full-season debut in 2022 with Low-A Fresno and spent the entire season with the Grizzlies. Juarez jumped to High-A Spokane for 2023. He made 20 starts and struggled to avoid hard contact. Juarez's ERA jumped by a full run but his ERA estimators remained consistent.
SCOUTING REPORT: Juarez mixes a fastball, curveball, slider and changeup. Juarez's fastball sits between

90-92 mph at touches 93 mph with above-average ride and armside run. He commands the pitch well, but it's a below-average bat-misser. He splits the use of his curveball and changeup fairly evenly. His curveball sits in the upper 70s and is a 12-to-6 downer. Juarez's changeup sits between 83-85 mph with tumble and fade and has been his best-performing pitch over the last two seasons. Juarez's slider sits in the mid 80s with gyro shape. He shows above-average control and has the ability to land all of his pitches in the strike zone, but his command lags behind and he'll often miss in the heart of the zone.

THE FUTURE: Juarez took a step backward in 2023, and he now projects as a depth starter in the big leagues.

Year	Age	Club (League)	Level	W	L	ERA	G	GS	IP	H	HR	BB	SO	BB%	SO%	WHIP	AVG
2023	20	Spokane (NWL)	A+	6	6	6.38	20	20	92	116	16	35	94	8.4	22.5	1.65	.314
Minor League Totals				14	12	5.10	51	49	231	242	33	75	241	7.6	24.3	1.37	.273

28 DEREK BERNARD, 2B/OF

HIT: 40. **POW:** 60. **RUN:** 40. **FLD:** 40. **ARM:** 50. **BA Grade:** 45. **Risk:** Extreme.

Born: August 9, 2005. **B-T:** L-R. **HT:** 6-0. **WT:** 190. **Signed:** Dominican Republic, 2022. **Signed by:** Rolando Fernandez.

TRACK RECORD: Bernard grew up in New York City and played travel ball for Canes New York 15U. He signed for $185,000, which was the seventh-highest bonus in the Rockies' 2022 international signing class. Bernard debuted in 2022 in the Dominican Summer League, where he hit .308/.377/.439 with four home runs as a 16-year-old. Bernard repeated the DSL in 2023 due to the tax ramifications of his split bonus. He made the most of it, hitting .324/.421/.576 with seven home runs.

SCOUTING REPORT: Bernard is an aggressive power hitter who looks to do damage. His bat-to-ball skills and approach are fringy, which adds risk that the strikeouts skyrocket when he comes back stateside. Bernard's power is his carrying tool, and he makes lots of hard contact. Bernard's 90th percentile exit velocity of 106.3 mph in 2023 was well above the major league average, and he did so while playing a majority of the season as a 17-year-old. Bernard is likely to slow down to a below-average runner and could end up in left field.

THE FUTURE: Bernard is a young power hitter without a position and a lot of hit tool risk, but his raw juice is double-plus.

Year	Age	Club (League)	Level	AVG	G	AB	R	H	2B	3B	HR	RBI	BB	SO	SB	OBP	SLG
2023	17	DSL Colorado	Rk	.167	4	12	2	2	1	1	0	1	3	1	1	.313	.417
2023	17	DSL Rockies	Rk	.324	38	139	30	45	10	2	7	39	23	31	16	.421	.576
Minor League Totals				.310	98	365	81	113	23	5	11	65	47	98	28	.391	.490

29 MASON ALBRIGHT, LHP

FB: 40. **CB:** 40. **SL:** 50. **CHG:** 55. **CTL:** 45. **BA Grade:** 40. **Risk:** High.

Born: November 26, 2002. **B-T:** L-L. **HT:** 6-0. **WT:** 190. **Drafted:** HS—Bradenton, FL, 2021 (12th round). **Signed by:** Brandon McArthur (Angels).

TRACK RECORD: A Maryland native, Albright transferred to IMG Academy before his senior year of high school. The Angels drafted him in the 12th round and signed him away from a Virginia Tech commitment with a $1,247,500 bonus. After reaching High-A during the 2022 season, Albright returned to Low-A to begin 2023. There, the lefthander found success. He made 14 starts and pitched to a 3.62 ERA with 86 strikeouts to 20 walks over 79.2 innings. Albright was traded to the Rockies alongside Jake Madden for C.J. Cron and Randal Grichuk.

SCOUTING REPORT: Albright is an undersized lefthander with a four-pitch mix. He mixes a four-seam fastball, slider, curveball and changeup. His fastball sits between 92-94 mph with above-average ride and heavy bore. Albright's most-used secondary is a gyro slider at 82-84 mph which is expertly commanded. Albright also mixes in a mid-70s curveball with 1-7 shape and an above-average low-80s changeup with tumble and fade. Albright is a fringe-average strike-thrower.

THE FUTURE: Albright projects as a depth starter.

Year	Age	Club (League)	Level	W	L	ERA	G	GS	IP	H	HR	BB	SO	BB%	SO%	WHIP	AVG
2023	20	Fresno (CAL)	A	1	0	0.00	1	1	5	2	0	2	9	10.5	47.4	0.80	.118
2023	20	Inland Empire (CAL)	A	9	4	3.62	15	14	80	78	10	20	86	6.0	25.7	1.23	.248
2023	20	Spokane (NWL)	A+	2	0	2.88	5	5	25	24	4	12	24	11.2	22.4	1.44	.258
Minor League Totals				14	8	4.87	41	34	173	187	26	64	186	8.4	24.4	1.46	.272

30 BLADIMIR RESTITUYO, OF

HIT: 40. POW: 40. RUN: 60. FLD: 55. ARM: 55. BA Grade: 40. Risk: High.

Born: July 2, 2001. **B-T:** R-R. **HT:** 5-10. **WT:** 155. **Signed:** Dominican Republic, 2017.
Signed by: Rolando Fernandez/Frank Roa.

TRACK RECORD: Restituyo signed for $200,000 out of the Dominican Republic in 2017. The Rockies converted him from the infield to the outfield and he's steadily progressed over the past five seasons. In 2023, Restituyo spent the entire season with Double-A Hartford and hit .258/.277/.414 with a career-high 15 home runs.

SCOUTING REPORT: Restituyo is an undersized outfielder with a high motor and a big swing. He shows above-average bat-to-ball skills but rarely sees a pitch he doesn't want to swing at. Despite a 54.5% chase rate in 2023, Restituyo managed an above-average contact rate and a strikeout rate below 20%. Despite his size, Restituyo has an uncanny ability to cover the plate. He has below-average raw power but his max-effort swings allow him to get to all of his power. Restituyo is a plus runner who covers large swaths of ground in the outfield and has an above-average throwing arm.

THE FUTURE: Restituyo has the look of a defensive replacement outfielder who can run into a home run every now and again.

Year	Age	Club (League)	Level	AVG	G	AB	R	H	2B	3B	HR	RBI	BB	SO	SB	OBP	SLG
2023	21	Hartford (EL)	AA	.258	108	430	61	111	20	1	15	55	8	86	17	.277	.414
Minor League Totals				.272	432	1665	237	453	71	18	36	195	44	366	108	.295	.401

Detroit Tigers

BY J.J. COOPER

Perception is a matter of perspective.

The Tigers won 78 games in 2023, their highest win total since 2016.

Looked at from one angle, it was an encouraging step forward for a team that lost 114 games in 2019 and finished more than 50 games out of first place in the American League Central.

Viewed from another angle, it's a reminder of how much work remains to be done. In the AL East, that record would have placed them in a tie for last. For a team that had World Series dreams a decade ago, it's been a long decline.

But the Tigers get to play in the AL Central. And in this division, they are a team on the rise in part because they are filling a void.

Detroit managed to finish second in the AL Central in 2023 despite a lineup filled with out-makers, and a year when much of its young talent was hobbled by injuries.

President of baseball operations Scott Harris has continued a rather sweeping transformation of the organization. He brought in Jeff Greenberg from the NHL's Chicago Blackhawks to be the team's general manager. Greenberg had extensive baseball experience before he went to the NHL, but his ability to blend analytical knowledge as well as scouting and player development experience that stood out.

Farm director Ryan Garko finished his second season with the Tigers. The 2023 draft was the first for vice president Rob Metzler and scouting director Mark Conner. It was also Metzler's first year in charge of the Tigers' international scouting.

Plenty of work remains, but first baseman Spencer Torkelson's improvement, outfielder Kerry Carpenter's solid work and outfielder Riley Greene's return from Tommy John surgery give the team the starting point for a competent offense. The arrival of Parker Meadows to roam center field, as well as the imminent arrivals of Justyn-Henry Malloy, Colt Keith and Jace Jung should provide additional boosts.

The Tigers are clearly emphasizing adding polished hitters. Keith, Malloy and Jung, as well as 2023 draftees Max Clark and Kevin McGonigle, fit that description. How all of them will fit defensively is still to be determined, but for a team that last finished in the top half of the AL in runs scored in 2016, it's a much-needed adjustment. Detroit has given more at-bats to well below-average hitters than almost any team over the past decade. The new regime is clearly trying to change that trend.

The pitching should be in better shape than 2023 as well, even with Eduardo Rodriguez departing in free agency. Lefthander Tarik Skubal showed signs down the stretch that he's the homegrown

MARK CUNNINGHAM/MLB PHOTOS VIA GETTY IMAGES

The Tigers struck gold with 19th-rounder Kerry Carpenter, the club's most productive hitter.

PROJECTED 2027 LINEUP

Catcher	Jake Rogers	32
First Base	Spencer Torkelson	27
Second Base	Colt Keith	25
Third Base	Jace Jung	26
Shortstop	Kevin McGonigle	23
Left Field	Riley Greene	26
Center Field	Max Clark	21
Right Field	Kerry Carpenter	29
Designated Hitter	Justyn-Henry Malloy	27
No. 1 Starter	Jackson Jobe	23
No. 2 Starter	Tarik Skubal	30
No. 3 Starter	Ty Madden	27
No. 4 Starter	Casey Mize	30
No. 5 Starter	Matt Manning	29
Closer	Troy Melton	26

front-of-rotation starter the team needs. Reese Olson and Matt Manning give the team additional young arms who are established big leaguers with further room to improve. And Casey Mize should be back from Tommy John surgery to join them in 2024. After adding Kenta Maeda via free agency, the Tigers have fewer question marks than they have had in quite a while.

But there remains much work to be done. The Tigers need someone, whether it's Keith, Clark, Torkelson or Greene, to develop into a star, because the lineup has lacked a true impact hitter since J.D. Martinez and Justin Upton were hitting in the middle of the lineup. They are the last two Tigers to post a 130 or better OPS+ in a season. ■

DEPTH CHART

DETROIT TIGERS

TOP 2024 CONTRIBUTORS — **RANK**
1. Colt Keith, 2B — 3
2. Justyn-Henry Malloy, OF — 6

BREAKOUT PROSPECTS — **RANK**
1. Josue Briceño, C — 18
2. Dylan Smith, RHP — 21

SOURCE OF TOP 30 TALENT

Homegrown	26	Acquired	4
College	11	Trade	4
Junior college	0	Rule 5 draft	0
High school	8	Independent league	0
Nondrafted free agent	1	Free agent/waivers	0
International	6		

LF
Justice Bigbie (11)
Cristian Perez
Brady Allen
Brett Callahan

CF
Max Clark (1)
Parker Meadows (7)
Wenceel Perez (20)
Anibal Salas
Roberto Campos
Seth Stephenson

RF
Justyn-Henry Malloy (6)
Jose De La Cruz

3B
Carson Rucker (22)
Izaac Pacheco (23)
Eddys Leonard (28)
Luke Gold
Gage Workman
Adinso Reyes

SS
Kevin McGonigle (8)
Peyton Graham (25)
Cristian Santana (29)
Brailyn Perez
Ryan Kreidler
Franyerber Montilla
Juan Hernandez

2B
Colt Keith (3)
Jace Jung (4)
Hao-Yu Lee (12)
Max Anderson (17)
Samuel Gil (27)
Danny Serretti
Jim Jarvis
John Peck

1B
Andre Lipcius (30)
Chris Meyers

C
Dillon Dingler (9)
Josue Briceño (18)
Enrique Jimenez (27)
Bennett Lee
Eliezer Alfonso

LHP

LHSP	LHRP
Brant Hurter (14)	Adam Wolf
Paul Wilson (16)	Sean Guenther
	Lael Lockhart

RHP

RHSP	RHRP
Jackson Jobe (2)	Keider Montero (13)
Ty Madden (5)	Tyler Mattison (24)
Troy Melton (10)	Jatnk Diaz
Wilmer Flores (15)	
Sawyer Gipson-Long (19)	
Dylan Smith (21)	
Jaden Hamm	
Andrew Dunford	

1 MAX CLARK, OF

Born: December 21, 2004. **B-T:** L-L. **HT:** 6-1. **WT:** 205.
Drafted: HS—Franklin, IN, 2023 (1st round).
Signed by: Harold Zonder.

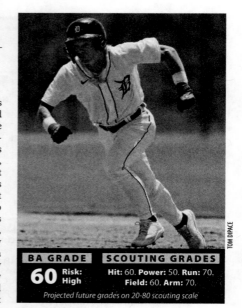

TOM DIPACE

BA GRADE	SCOUTING GRADES
60 Risk: High	Hit: 60. Power: 50. Run: 70. Field: 60. Arm: 70.

Projected future grades on 20-80 scouting scale

TRACK RECORD: In a draft that was viewed as having a five-player top tier, the Tigers picked third with three top outfielders still on the board. Detroit could pick between Florida outfielder Wyatt Langford or high school outfielders Walker Jenkins or Clark. The Tigers chose Clark, valuing his ability to impact the game both at the plate and in the field, where he's viewed as a relatively surefire center fielder. Clark is just the seventh prep position player from Indiana to ever be drafted in the first round. Of the previous six, only Gary Thurman ever reached the majors, though 2021 first-rounder Colson Montgomery will likely change that before long. While Indiana high school baseball isn't as competitive as many of the warm-weather hotbeds, there are few concerns about Clark's ability to handle top-level competition. He consistently performed against the best high school players in the country, even when he was playing against players a year older than him. He was consistently one of the best players on the showcase circuit. After playing wide receiver for Franklin Community High during the fall, Clark hit .646 in 2023 with a state-record 52 walks. He was named BA High School Player of the Year. Clark signed for $7.697 million, the second-highest draft bonus in Tigers history, trailing only Spencer Torkelson, the No. 1 overall pick in 2020.

SCOUTING REPORT: Clark has the potential to be a five-tool player. That's a term that's too often thrown around for players who barely scrape average in one of the five tools, but in Clark's case, it's realistic. He could end up with all five tools grading out as plus. Clark has plus-plus speed, a plus-plus arm, the range to be a plus defender in center field and the bat-to-ball skills to be a plus hitter as well. Projecting his power to be plus is a little more speculative, because he's a hitter whose line-drive swing has generally been more geared to hitting for average. To address this, he lowered his hand setup to get to more power in 2023. With Rob Metzler and Mark Conner leading the scouting department, the Tigers have emphasized adding a slew of advanced hitters, and Clark fits right in with that approach. He stays balanced at the plate and rarely swings and misses. Defensively, he aggressively tracks balls in the gaps, showing why he was also an excellent wide receiver in high school. Unlike most speedy center fielders, Clark's arm is a real weapon as well. He threw in the mid 90s off the mound in high school, and he racked up two assists in just 23 pro games.

THE FUTURE: Clark got a brief taste of the Florida State League in 2023. He's expected to start at Low-A Lakeland in 2024 with a goal of playing his way to High-A West Michigan. His combination of speed, defense and hitting ability gives him a high probability of being a useful big leaguer, and if his power develops, he could become a cornerstone of the Tigers' lineup. ∎

BEST TOOLS

BATTING

Best Hitter for Average	Max Clark
Best Power	Colt Keith
Best Strike-Zone Judgment	Justyn-Henry Malloy
Fastest Baserunner	Parker Meadows
Best Athlete	Max Clark

PITCHING

Best Fastball	Jackson Jobe
Best Curveball	Tyler Mattison
Best Slider	Jackson Jobe
Best Changeup	Jackson Jobe
Best Control	Jackson Jobe

FIELDING

Best Defensive Catcher	Dillon Dinger
Best Defensive Infielder	Reylin Perez
Best Infield Arm	Peyton Graham
Best Defensive Outfielder	Parker Meadows
Best Outfield Arm	Max Clark

Year	Age	Club (League)	Level	AVG	G	AB	R	H	2B	3B	HR	RBI	BB	SO	SB	OBP	SLG
2023	18	FCL Tigers	Rk	.283	12	46	13	13	4	1	2	12	9	10	4	.411	.543
2023	18	Lakeland (FSL)	A	.154	11	39	5	6	1	0	0	7	12	15	1	.353	.179
Minor League Totals				.224	23	85	18	19	5	1	2	19	21	25	5	.383	.376

2 JACKSON JOBE, RHP

FB: 60. **SL:** 70. **CHG:** 60. **CUT:** 50. **CTL:** 60. **BA Grade:** 60. **Risk:** High.

Born: July 30, 2002. **B-T:** R-R. **HT:** 6-2. **WT:** 190.
Drafted: HS—Oklahoma City, 2021 (1st round). **Signed by:** Steve Taylor.
TRACK RECORD: Like organization-mate Max Clark, Jobe was a BA High School Player of the Year winner. Jobe won the award in 2021, the year the Tigers drafted him third overall and signed him for $6.9 million. He reached High-A West Michigan late in 2022 and would have returned there to open 2023 if not for inflammation in his lower back that forced him to miss the first two and a half months of the season. Jobe ended the campaign on a high note with a 22-inning walk-less streak for West Michigan and Double-A Erie, then added four more effective starts in the Arizona Fall League. Jobe's 69.3% strike percentage was among the tops in the minors.
SCOUTING REPORT: Jobe is a hitter's nightmare. He can attack a batter in multiple ways with plus stuff and plus command. Other than missing the first half of the season, Jobe did everything the Tigers could have hoped for in 2023. He dominated hitters, threw strikes and improved his delivery. While he was sidelined, Jobe worked to become more direct to the plate. He also tightened up his plus-plus mid-80s slider, which improved his control of the pitch. His plus 95-97 mph four-seam fastball has above-average life, and he shows plenty of confidence in his plus mid-80s changeup. He also added an average 90-92 mph cutter that can help generate weak contact. Jobe can force hitters to protect the entire plate, because his fastball is effective in the top third of the zone, his slider works glove side and down and his changeup has ride and fade to the armside edge of the zone. His cutter messes with hitters who think they're seeing a fastball.
THE FUTURE: Jobe's slow start meant he only reached Double-A Erie in the final week of the regular season, but if he can stay healthy, it's realistic to think he could advance to Detroit in 2024. He has what scouts look for in a front-of-the-rotation starter.

Year	Age	Club (League)	Level	W	L	ERA	G	GS	IP	H	HR	BB	SO	BB%	SO%	WHIP	AVG
2023	20	FCL Tigers	Rk	0	0	0.00	1	1	2	0	0	0	4	0.0	66.7	0.00	.000
2023	20	Lakeland (FSL)	A	0	1	2.25	6	6	16	14	2	3	20	4.4	29.4	1.06	.222
2023	20	W. Michigan (MWL)	A+	2	3	3.60	8	8	40	39	7	3	54	1.9	33.8	1.05	.252
2023	20	Erie (EL)	AA	0	0	0.00	1	1	6	4	0	0	6	0.0	25.0	0.67	.167
Minor League Totals				6	9	3.38	37	37	141	126	23	36	165	6.1	27.9	1.15	.230

3 COLT KEITH, 2B/3B

HIT: 60. **POW:** 60. **RUN:** 45. **FLD:** 40. **ARM:** 50. **BA Grade:** 55. **Risk:** Medium.

Born: August 14, 2001. **B-T:** L-R. **HT:** 6-3. **WT:** 211.
Drafted: HS—Biloxi, MS, 2020 (5th round). **Signed by:** Mike Smith.
TRACK RECORD: Keith has always hit, regardless of setting. He was the best hitter in Mississippi as a rising high school junior, hitting .527 to win the state's Gatorade player of the year award. While his senior season was wiped away by the coronavirus pandemic, Keith has proven equally adept with the bat in pro ball. The Tigers drafted him in the fifth and final round of the 2020 draft and signed him for $500,000. After a shoulder injury cut short his 2022 season, Keith hit .344 in the Arizona Fall League. In 2023, he forced a midseason promotion to Triple-A Toledo by hitting most everything at Double-A Erie, and he barely slowed down after the promotion.
SCOUTING REPORT: Keith is a pure hitter who gets to plus power without having to sell out for it. He stays in control with a balanced lefthanded swing and above-average bat speed. While his power is primarily to his pull side, he also targets both power alleys. Keith finished third in the minors in 2023 with 68 extra-base hits. He even hits lefthanders well. After working sporadically at second base in 2021, Keith embraced the position after he was promoted to Triple-A Toledo in 2023. Scouts see him as more likely to play second than third base, though he's fringy defensively at either spot thanks to limited range. Keith turns the double play well at second. Though he has arm strength, he doesn't have a quick release, which hinders him, especially at third. Keith runs reasonably well underway, but is a fringe-average runner who should slow further as he matures and is not a stolen base threat.
THE FUTURE: Keith's best position is in the batter's box. The Tigers' goal is to get his defense to a point where he doesn't have to slide to first base or DH. It may not matter, because he has the chance to be one of the best hitters the Tigers have produced in the past few decades.

Year	Age	Club (League)	Level	AVG	G	AB	R	H	2B	3B	HR	RBI	BB	SO	SB	OBP	SLG
2023	21	Erie (EL)	AA	.325	59	246	43	80	18	2	14	50	25	63	2	.391	.585
2023	21	Toledo (IL)	AAA	.287	67	261	45	75	20	1	13	51	35	58	1	.369	.521
Minor League Totals				.300	239	924	167	277	60	11	38	164	123	229	11	.382	.512

4 JACE JUNG, 2B

HIT: 45. **POW:** 60. **RUN:** 40. **FLD:** 45. **ARM:** 50. **BA Grade:** 50. **Risk:** Medium.

Born: October 4, 2000. **B-T:** L-R. **HT:** 6-0. **WT:** 205.
Drafted: Texas Tech, 2022 (1st round). **Signed by:** Steve Taylor.
TRACK RECORD: There have been only three baseball players from Texas Tech who have gone in the first round. The Jung family counts two of them. Just like his older brother Josh, Jace Jung starred for three seasons at Texas Tech and then was a top 15 pick. The Rangers drafted Josh eighth overall in 2019, and he was a key part of the their World Series triumph in 2023. Jace went 12th overall to the Tigers in 2022 and had a breakout 2023 season, reaching Double-A Erie on July 25 and leading all Tigers farmhands with 28 home runs.
SCOUTING REPORT: Much like fellow Tigers infield prospect Colt Keith, Jung has more questions in the field than at the plate. Jung is a reliable defender at second base who will make plays on the balls he can reach. He has soft hands, but he's not particularly rangy. The Tigers let him try third base in the Arizona Fall League. His average arm works, but scouts see him as fringy at either position. At the plate, Jung is a mirror image of his brother. Where Josh was a smooth-swinging righthanded hitter who loves to wear out the opposite field, Jace is a pull-heavy lefthanded hitter with an unconventional setup—he points his bat head to the backstop—and swing. He has a solid understanding of the strike zone and takes his walks, but he's willing to be fooled at times in exchange for doing damage. Praised for his competitive makeup and leadership attributes in college, and those traits have helped him adapt to pro ball and have him poised to reach MLB as quickly as 2024.
THE FUTURE: The Tigers have a slew of bat-first infielders with defensive questions. Much like Keith, Jung will need to keep working on improving defensively, but his power and ability to get on base are valuable, especially for a Tigers team that has lacked impact hitters.

Year	Age	Club (League)	Level	AVG	G	AB	R	H	2B	3B	HR	RBI	BB	SO	SB	OBP	SLG
2023	22	W. Michigan (MWL)	A+	.254	81	303	46	77	18	2	14	43	56	83	5	.377	.465
2023	22	Erie (EL)	AA	.284	47	183	28	52	9	0	14	39	23	56	0	.373	.563
Minor League Totals				.259	158	594	90	154	33	3	29	95	104	167	6	.375	.471

5 TY MADDEN, RHP

FB: 60. **CB:** 40. **SL:** 60. **CHG:** 50. **CUT:** 45. **CTL:** 50. **BA Grade:** 50. **Risk:** Medium.

Born: February 21, 2000. **B-T:** R-R. **HT:** 6-3. **WT:** 215.
Drafted: Texas, 2021 (1st round supplemental). **Signed by:** George Schaefer.
TRACK RECORD: Madden was a reliable college ace for Texas who showed he could maintain his stuff deep into starts. But concerns about how his relatively straight, over-the-top fastball would play in pro ball meant he slid to the 32nd pick in 2021, when the Tigers pounced. Madden lowered his release point in 2022 to help his fastball play better, and it has proven to be effective up in the zone. In 2023, Madden helped lead Double-A Erie to its first Eastern League title. He allowed one run in his final three regular-season starts and won his only postseason start.
SCOUTING REPORT: Madden continues to show that he can carry 97-98 mph through his starts. He tweaked his shoulder tilt later in the 2023 season to improve his direction to the plate, which paid off in better consistency and stuff. His plus fastball is an effective weapon, especially now that he's improved his plus slider as well. Madden's college slider was purely a chase pitch, but he has tightened it, and it's now an 85-87 mph weapon that he can consistently locate in the zone. He mixes in an improved changeup that grades as average and will spot a fringe-average cutter he's developed as a pro. Madden will flip a slow, below-average curveball to lefthanded hitters as well, but the development of his cutter has made that pitch less vital. Madden has generally been a consistent strike-thrower with a clean delivery, but his walk rate climbed in 2023. He should get to average control.
THE FUTURE: Madden's combination of velocity, durability and adaptability has him on the path to a spot in the middle of the Tigers' rotation. Including the postseason, he threw 128 innings in 2023 and won't need much ramping up to handle an MLB workload. He'll head to Triple-A Toledo in 2024, one phone call away from Detroit when a need arises.

Year	Age	Club (League)	Level	W	L	ERA	G	GS	IP	H	HR	BB	SO	BB%	SO%	WHIP	AVG
2023	23	Erie (EL)	AA	3	4	3.43	26	25	118	101	16	50	146	10.2	29.7	1.28	.233
Minor League Totals				11	10	3.23	52	51	241	198	32	88	279	8.9	28.1	1.19	.223

6 JUSTYN-HENRY MALLOY, OF/3B

HIT:: 55. **POW:** 50. **RUN:** 40. **FLD:** 45. **ARM:** 55. **BA Grade:** 50. **Risk:** Medium.

Born: February 19, 2000. **B-T:** R-R. **HT:** 6-3. **WT:** 212.
Drafted: Georgia Tech, 2021 (6th round). **Signed by:** Chris Lionetti (Braves).
TRACK RECORD: After two years of receiving little playing time at Vanderbilt, Malloy transferred to Georgia Tech and quickly became the team's cleanup hitter. The Braves drafted him in the sixth round in 2021, watched him put up a .408 on-base percentage in 2022 and then shipped him to the Tigers that December for reliever Joe Jimenez in what was incoming Tigers president of baseball operations Scott Harris' first transaction. Malloy led Triple-A Toledo in numerous offensive categories in 2023 and led the minor leagues with 110 walks.
SCOUTING REPORT: Malloy manages to get to average or better power—despite modest raw juice—because he's an highly intelligent hitter with a plan at the plate and an excellent idea of the strike zone. He has been an on-base machine in pro ball, with a career .410 OBP. Malloy switched from being Toledo's regular third baseman to playing most days in left or right field in the second half. He slid back to third base in the season's final weeks. Malloy is expected to be a full-time outfielder going forward because he struggled with his throwing accuracy at third base. He made 10 throwing errors in 60 games there compared to one in 44 games in the outfield. Malloy is a below-average runner, but he should be able to play a fringe-average outfield. His above-average arm works in right field better than it did at third.
THE FUTURE: Malloy's move to the outfield clears his path to Detroit. He's not yet on the 40-man roster, and if Riley Greene's recovery from Tommy John surgery goes as planned, the Tigers should have a relatively set outfield for Opening Day. That should only slow Malloy temporarily. On a team that has struggled to score runs, Malloy's ability to get on base and hit for power can't be ignored, and he should reach Detroit in 2024.

Year	Age	Club (League)	Level	AVG	G	AB	R	H	2B	3B	HR	RBI	BB	SO	SB	OBP	SLG
2023	23	Toledo (IL)	AAA	.277	135	487	89	135	25	1	23	83	110	152	5	.417	.474
Minor League Totals				.282	305	1087	203	306	58	1	45	185	231	320	14	.410	.461

7 PARKER MEADOWS, OF

HIT: 40. **POW:** 50. **RUN:** 70. **FLD:** 70. **ARM:** 65. **BA Grade:** 45. **Risk:** Medium.

Born: November 2, 1999. **B-T:** L-R. **HT:** 6-5. **WT:** 205.
Drafted: HS—Loganville, GA, 2018 (2nd round). **Signed by:** Bryson Barber.
TRACK RECORD: Early in the 2022 season, it seemed absurd to suggest that Meadows would be the Tigers' everyday center fielder late in the 2023 season. Meadows was sent back to High-A West Michigan to start 2022 after hitting .221 in the Midwest League in 2019 and .208 in 2021. But Meadows' reworked swing soon began to bear fruit. He more than doubled his career high in home runs in 2022. After a solid stint at Triple-A Toledo in 2023, he earned a callup to Detroit on Aug. 21. Four days later he hit a walk-off home run, the first bomb of his career.
SCOUTING REPORT: Ever since being drafted in 2018, the 6-foot-5 Meadows has worked hard to change his swing. He came into pro ball with a long swing that often left him flailing. Now he's a more controlled hitter with a shorter stroke and, most importantly, better timing. That hasn't turned him into a future batting champ or even an average hitter, but it has helped him become a much tougher out and one who is now a playable big leaguer. He has plus raw power and should get to average productive power if he can make relatively consistent contact. Defensively, Meadows is exceptional. He's a potential plus-plus defender in center field. He's a double-plus runner who is comfortable coming in or going back to the wall. His plus arm is also a weapon. His speed also makes him a stolen base threat any time he reaches.
THE FUTURE: Meadows' glove and speed will make him a valuable regular if he can hit even .240, draw some walks and run into 15 home runs a year. Meadows should start the season as the Tigers' center fielder after claiming the role from Riley Greene in 2023, and his ability to handle Comerica Park's spacious outfield gives Detroit something it has been missing.

Year	Age	Club (League)	Level	AVG	G	AB	R	H	2B	3B	HR	RBI	BB	SO	SB	OBP	SLG
2023	23	Toledo (IL)	AAA	.256	113	449	78	115	27	7	19	65	57	123	19	.337	.474
2023	23	Detroit (AL)	MLB	.232	37	125	19	29	4	2	3	13	17	37	8	.331	.368
Minor League Totals				.244	491	1837	282	448	86	19	58	218	207	477	62	.323	.406
Major League Totals				.232	37	125	19	29	4	2	3	13	17	37	8	.331	.368

8 KEVIN McGONIGLE, SS

HIT: 60. **POW:** 50. **RUN:** 50. **FLD:** 50. **ARM:** 45. **BA Grade:** 50. **Risk:** High.

Born: August 18, 2004. **B-T:** L-R. **HT:** 5-10. **WT:** 187.
Drafted: HS—Drexel Hill, PA, 2023 (1st round supplemental). **Signed by:** Jim Bretz.
TRACK RECORD: Acquiring hitters who can control the strike zone and have a clear plan at the plate is a point of emphasis in drafts under president of baseball operations Scott Harris. So after picking the sweet-swinging Max Clark with the third overall pick in the 2023 draft, the Tigers added McGonigle, another bat-first prep prospect with advanced hitting skills, in the supplemental first round. Drafted 37th overall, McGonigle signed for a bit shy of $2.9 million, and more than $500,000 over slot. He demonstrated his hitting instincts in the Florida Complex and Florida State leagues in his pro debut, reaching base in his first 17 games and 19 of 21 games overall.
SCOUTING REPORT: McGonigle has a long track record of hitting against top opposition in showcases and international competitions, including an impressive stint with USA Baseball's gold medal-winning 18U national team in 2022. He has the barrel control and adjustability in his hands to stay on pitches even when he's fooled initially. McGonigle doesn't show massive power in batting practice, but his bat-to-ball skills makes him a threat to line balls to the gap and clear the fence from time to time. Drafted as a shortstop, McGonigle's likely long-term position is second base. He's average there with a fringe-average but accurate arm that is less stretched on the right side of the infield. He won't embarrass himself at shortstop and has a solid internal clock, but a big league team should have better options.
THE FUTURE: The pairing of McGonigle and Max Clark should make Low-A Lakeland one of the most entertaining and dangerous lineups in the Florida State League to start 2024. Both players have shots to get to High-A West Michigan before long, thanks to their advanced approaches. McGonigle is a bat-first infielder, but he faces fewer defensive questions than some other recent hit-first Tigers' infielders.

Year	Age	Club (League)	Level	AVG	G	AB	R	H	2B	3B	HR	RBI	BB	SO	SB	OBP	SLG
2023	18	FCL Tigers	Rk	.273	9	33	11	9	2	0	0	1	11	5	6	.467	.333
2023	18	Lakeland (FSL)	A	.350	12	40	7	14	2	0	1	5	7	5	2	.438	.475
Minor League Totals				.315	21	73	18	23	4	0	1	6	18	10	8	.452	.411

9 DILLON DINGLER, C

HIT: 30. **POW:** 50. **RUN:** 45. **FLD:** 55. **ARM:** 60. **BA Grade:** 45. **Risk:** Medium.

Born: September 17, 1998. **B-T:** R-R. **HT:** 6-3. **WT:** 210.
Drafted: Ohio State, 2020 (2nd round). **Signed by:** Austin Cousino.
TRACK RECORD: Catching is a brutal occupation. Dingler is a prime example. Drafted in the second round in 2020, he has missed time as a pro with a broken hamate bone, a broken finger and a knee injury. Knee surgery kept Dingler from reaching Double-A Erie until early May in 2023, but he then lit up the Eastern League. He was promoted to Triple-A Toledo in mid August and added to the 40-man roster after the season.
SCOUTING REPORT: Dingler's defense and power give him a clear path to a backup catcher role, but his lack of bat speed could make it tough for him to be a regular. His defense is major league-caliber. Like most young catchers, Dingler can improve at game-calling, but he's an above-average receiver and framer, he blocks well and he has a plus arm with a quick transfer and above-average accuracy. He threw out 50% of basestealers after his promotion to Triple-A and has thrown out 34% for his minor league career. Offensively, there are many more concerns. Dingler has plus raw power, but he has to hunt pitches to get to that power in games, which leaves him vulnerable to being fooled. A lack of bat speed, shaky swing decisions and high strikeout rates make him a well below-average hitter. He runs well for a catcher.
THE FUTURE: Dingler's strengths and weaknesses are quite similar to those of Tigers starting catcher Jake Rogers, and their minor league careers are uncannily similar. Rogers struggled in his first stint with Double-A Erie but dominated in a return to the league before struggling after a promotion to Triple-A. Rogers hit .242/.338/.441 in 1,392 minor league plate appearances. Dingler struggled at Double-A in 2022 but lit up the league in his return. He then struggled after a midseason promotion to Triple-A. He enters 2024 as a .244/.335/.434 career hitter in 1,190 PAs.

Year	Age	Club (League)	Level	AVG	G	AB	R	H	2B	3B	HR	RBI	BB	SO	SB	OBP	SLG
2023	24	Lakeland (FSL)	A	.395	12	43	9	17	4	0	4	8	7	8	3	.509	.767
2023	24	Erie (EL)	AA	.253	51	182	35	46	11	0	9	41	27	63	3	.372	.462
2023	24	Toledo (IL)	AAA	.202	26	99	14	20	7	1	3	9	8	34	0	.266	.384
Minor League Totals				.244	281	1033	164	252	54	8	42	162	109	349	8	.335	.434

10 TROY MELTON, RHP

FB: 60. **SL:** 50. **CHG:** 50. **CTL:** 60. **BA Grade:** 50. **Risk:** High.

Born: December 3, 2000. **B-T:** R-R. **HT:** 6-4. **WT:** 210.
Drafted: San Diego State, 2022 (4th round). **Signed by:** Steve Pack.
TRACK RECORD: Melton seemed headed in the wrong direction when he posted a 6.91 ERA as a starter for San Diego State in 2021. No team would meet his asking price, so he bet on himself and returned to school in 2022. He shortened his arm action and found success. The Tigers astutely drafted him in the fourth round. Melton got even better in 2023 by showing a bit more velocity and plenty of feel for how to work up and down to change hitters' eye levels. He has control to rival nearly any pitcher in the Tigers organization, with a 6.4% walk rate in 2023 that led all starters in the system who pitched at least 70 innings.
SCOUTING REPORT: Melton has a relatively mature, 6-foot-4, 210-pound frame and is somewhat stiff, but he repeats his delivery, throws strikes and his stuff is some of the best in the Tigers' system. His four-seam fastball added another tick in 2023. He now sits 94-96 mph. He can work his fastball to the top of the zone. It doesn't have exceptional life or carry, but he commands it well, and it helps him regularly get ahead in counts. His average low-to-mid-80s slider and above-average mid-80s changeup both have steadily gotten better as well. Melton has plus control, which helps him avoid big innings. He showed as much in 2023 in a season spent primarily at High-A West Michigan. He had 10 different starts in which he walked no one, and only one start all year where he allowed four runs.
THE FUTURE: Melton took his turn every time in 2023, but the Tigers were cautious with his workload, holding him to under 100 innings and never letting him throw 90 pitches in a start. He's ready for a heavier workload as he jumps to Double-A Erie in 2024. He's a potential back-of-the-rotation starter who could also slide to the bullpen if needed.

Year	Age	Club (League)	Level	W	L	ERA	G	GS	IP	H	HR	BB	SO	BB%	SO%	WHIP	AVG
2023	22	Lakeland (FSL)	A	0	0	3.38	7	7	27	26	3	6	33	5.5	30.0	1.20	.252
2023	22	W. Michigan (MWL)	A+	3	1	2.48	16	15	65	55	2	18	61	6.7	22.8	1.12	.225
Minor League Totals				3	1	2.60	25	24	97	84	5	24	99	6.1	25.1	1.11	.231

11 JUSTICE BIGBIE, OF

HIT: 50. **POW:** 50. **FLD:** 40. **RUN:** 50. **ARM:** 40. **BA Grade:** 50. **Risk:** High.

Born: January 24, 1999. **B-T:** R-R. **HT:** 6-3. **WT:** 210. **Drafted:** Western Carolina, 2021 (19th round).
Signed by: Matt Zmuda.
TRACK RECORD: A four-year starter for Western Carolina, Bigbie was a career .352 hitter in college, capping his career with a .395/.500/.621 season for the Catamounts in 2021. The Tigers made him the 555th player picked in the 2021 draft. Bigbie's first two years with the Tigers were nondescript, but he broke out in 2023. After hitting three home runs combined in his first 129 pro games, he hit 19 in 115 games in 2023 while climbing three levels to Triple-A Toledo.
SCOUTING REPORT: While the Tigers had long been impressed with Bigbie's bat-to-ball skills, they worked with him to tweak his swing to more regularly get the ball in the air. Bigbie has always made plenty of hard contact. Now, that impact has gone from outs and singles into doubles and homers thanks to the boost in his flyball rate. He still has work to do because his power is almost entirely to the opposite field. He hit 13 of his 19 home runs to right or right center, and he's yet to show he can pull the ball consistently in the air. Bigbie doesn't have a particularly quick bat, and he will chase, but he has excellent barrel control. Bigbie's offensive breakout also coincided with his move back to the outfield full-time. He was a well below-average defender at first base, but is just below-average in the outfield. He has a below-average arm, but is an average runner.
THE FUTURE: Bigbie put himself on the path to Detroit in 2023. There are still some concerns about whether his breakout is sustainable, but he will return to Toledo to try to prove he can help the Tigers in left field before long.

Year	Age	Club (League)	Level	AVG	G	AB	R	H	2B	3B	HR	RBI	BB	SO	SB	OBP	SLG
2023	24	W. Michigan (MWL)	A+	.333	37	138	25	46	9	1	6	27	15	28	1	.400	.543
2023	24	Erie (EL)	AA	.362	63	243	51	88	13	0	12	43	22	34	5	.421	.564
2023	24	Toledo (IL)	AAA	.275	15	51	5	14	3	0	1	8	5	15	0	.345	.392
Minor League Totals				.303	244	892	138	270	50	7	24	144	89	197	10	.377	.455

12 HAO-YU LEE, 2B

HIT: 60. **POW:** 45. **FLD:** 45. **RUN:** 50. **ARM:** 50. **BA Grade:** 50. **Risk:** High.

Born: February 3, 2003. **B-T:** R-R. **HT:** 5-10. **WT:** 190. **Signed:** Taiwan, 2021. **Signed by:** Youngster Wang (Phillies).

TRACK RECORD: No amateur player from Asia signed by the Phillies has ever reached the big leagues. Lee could become the first, although he won't do so for Philadelphia. The Tigers acquired him in a 1-for-1 deal that sent Michael Lorenzen to the Phillies at the 2023 trade deadline. A native of Taiwan, Lee has been among the youngest players in every league where he's played. That was once again true when he went to the Arizona Fall League in October 2023 and he held his own with a .265/.373/.367 slash line.

SCOUTING REPORT: Lee's above-average bat speed gives him the ability to hit for average with fringe-average power as well. He has a hit-over-power approach, but his sturdy frame gives hope that he'll run into doubles and home runs as he matures. A broken hand slowed Lee in 2022, and he missed time in 2023 with a bruised knee and a quad strain. Lee is stretched at shortstop, but he's worked hard to improve his fringy range and poor footwork. He should develop into average at second base, which is his best position. He turns the double play well and his hands and actions are fine. He's an average runner with a solid understanding of how to steal a base.

THE FUTURE: The Tigers' biggest strength of the farm system is second basemen who can hit. Lee fits that criteria. He should be ready for Double-A, where he'll continue to work on his footwork and range.

Year	Age	Club (League)	Level	AVG	G	AB	R	H	2B	3B	HR	RBI	BB	SO	SB	OBP	SLG
2023	20	FCL Phillies	Rk	.182	3	11	1	2	1	0	0	3	1	3	0	.250	.273
2023	20	Jersey Shore (SAL)	A+	.283	64	247	35	70	12	1	5	26	29	53	14	.372	.401
2023	20	W. Michigan (MWL)	A+	.214	8	28	4	6	1	1	1	3	3	9	2	.313	.429
Minor League Totals				.282	163	607	95	171	31	6	16	90	79	137	30	.376	.432

13 KEIDER MONTERO, RHP

FB: 60. **SL:** 55. **CHG:** 50. **CB:** 50. **CTL:** 55. **BA Grade:** 50. **Risk:** High.

Born: July 6, 2000. **B-T:** R-R. **HT:** 6-1. **WT:** 213. **Signed:** Venezuela, 2016.
Signed by: Alejandro Rodriguez/Delvis Pacheco.

TRACK RECORD: When the 2023 season began, it appeared that Montero's pro career was stuck. A 2016 signee out of Venezuela who had been left available for multiple Rule 5 drafts, he was back at High-A West Michigan for a third straight year. By May, he'd been promoted to Double-A Erie, and he pitched his way to Triple-A Toledo by August. He ended up leading all MiLB pitchers with 15 wins. As a reward for his breakout season, he was added to the 40-man roster in November.

SCOUTING REPORT: Montero has always shown the makings of plus control, and he's never shied away from attacking hitters, but now he has mastered his four-pitch arsenal enough to get hitters out in the strike zone. His plus 94-96 mph fastball has enough life at the top of the zone and a flat enough angle to bedevil hitters when elevated or thrown on hitters' hands. His mid-80s above-average slider is a pitch he can tighten up to get into the strike zone or bury for a chases. He's just as comfortable throwing his mid-80s average changeup and high-70s average curve. Montero weighed 145 pounds when he signed. Now he's 213 pounds and has matured into a solid pitcher's frame with a strong base and a compact delivery.

THE FUTURE: Montero's fastball and breaking balls would play well in the bullpen if the Tigers need immediate help, but he does have a starter's approach and control if Detroit is willing to wait a little longer for him to reach his potential as a No. 4 starter.

Year	Age	Club (League)	Level	W	L	ERA	G	GS	IP	H	HR	BB	SO	BB%	SO%	WHIP	AVG
2023	22	W. Michigan (MWL)	A+	0	0	2.81	4	4	16	10	1	4	22	6.6	36.1	0.88	.175
2023	22	Erie (EL)	AA	10	4	4.93	15	15	69	73	7	31	91	10.1	29.6	1.50	.267
2023	22	Toledo (IL)	AAA	5	2	4.93	8	7	42	42	8	14	47	7.7	25.8	1.33	.258
Minor League Totals				33	29	4.09	106	93	433	444	38	164	450	8.6	23.7	1.40	.263

14 BRANT HURTER, LHP

FB: 50. **SL:** 60. **CHG:** 40. **CUT:** 40. **CTL:** 55. **BA Grade:** 45. **Risk:** Medium.

Born: September 6, 1998. **B-T:** L-L. **HT:** 6-6. **WT:** 250. **Drafted:** Georgia Tech, 2021 (7th round).
Signed by: Bryson Barber.

TRACK RECORD: Hurter bounced back from 2020 Tommy John surgery to pitch effectively for Georgia Tech in 2021 despite not showing the same stuff he'd shown pre-injury. The Tigers trusted there was more to come and were rewarded when his pre-injury velocity returned in 2022. He was one of the organization's standouts that year and quickly climbed three levels. He was just as effective for Erie in 2023, and finished his season by throwing 13 scoreless postseason innings to help Erie win the Eastern League title.

SCOUTING REPORT: Hurter held lefties to a .191/.245/.224 slash line in 2023 and he's yet to give up a home run to one as a pro. His funky delivery, trunk turn, arm slot and deception makes it extremely hard for lefties to pick up the ball. Hurter has worked to find more ways to keep righthanded hitters from getting comfortable swings. He's working on a four-seam fastball and cutter to keep hitters from focusing on the bottom of the zone, but he's still primarily a sinker/slider pitcher. His 90-92 mph average sinker is hard to drive and gets tons of run, while his plus 82-84 mph slider tunnels excellently with it. He's struggled with the consistency of his below-average changeup, and the cutter also needs more work.
THE FUTURE: Hurter should at least be an effective lefty reliever with his sinker/slider combo, but the development of his four-seamer and cutter could keep him a starter. He'll jump to Toledo and could help the big league club late in 2024.

Year	Age	Club (League)	Level	W	L	ERA	G	GS	IP	H	HR	BB	SO	BB%	SO%	WHIP	AVG
2023	24	Erie (EL)	AA	6	7	3.28	26	26	118	108	7	33	133	6.6	26.7	1.19	.242
Minor League Totals				13	13	3.50	51	44	225	207	14	54	269	5.8	28.8	1.17	.242

15 WILMER FLORES, RHP

FB: 50. **SL:** 55. **CB:** 50. **CHG:** 40. **CTL:** 55. **BA Grade:** 50. **Risk:** High.

Born: February 20, 2001. **B-T:** R-R. **HT:** 6-4. **WT:** 225. **Signed:** Arizona Western JC, 2020 (NDFA).
Signed by: Joey Lothrop.
TRACK RECORD: The younger brother of longtime big league infielder Wilmer Flores, the younger Flores is a scouting success story for the Tigers. They signed him as an undrafted free agent out of Arizona Western JC despite the fact that he'd thrown just 11.2 innings in the pandemic-shortened 2020 season. He emerged in 2022 when he reached Double-A, but his 2023 season was a modest step back.
SCOUTING REPORT: Flores missed a month late in the season with a hamstring injury, and he struggled mightily in a rehab stint at High-A West Michigan to end the season. He was better in the Arizona Fall League, but even there batters hit .338 against him. Flores has shown he can touch 97-98 mph in the past, but he sat 92-94 in 2023 and topped out at 95. With a little less velocity, his fastball was fringe-average in many starts, which forced him to rely more on his two breaking balls. His 83-84 mph above-average slider is quite effective largely because of how well he can command it, and his average 77-79 mph curveball is effective at giving lefties something to worry about. His below-average changeup needs improvement, as he hasn't found a grip to let him make it a pitch he can throw with conviction. Flores remains an above-average strike thrower, but with less ability to miss bats, he had to nibble more in 2023.
THE FUTURE: The Tigers added Flores to the 40-man roster to protect him from the 2023 Rule 5 draft. He is one of the team's better pitching prospects, but the Tigers hope he can regain some of his 2022 form.

Year	Age	Club (League)	Level	W	L	ERA	G	GS	IP	H	HR	BB	SO	BB%	SO%	WHIP	AVG
2023	22	W. Michigan (MWL)	A+	0	1	11.88	3	3	8	12	0	1	8	2.6	21.1	1.56	.343
2023	22	Erie (EL)	AA	5	3	3.90	18	18	81	72	5	32	82	9.5	24.3	1.29	.242
Minor League Totals				18	12	3.66	60	58	258	227	16	80	310	7.4	28.8	1.19	.233

16 PAUL WILSON, LHP

FB: 60. **SL:** 60. **CB:** 50. **CHG:** 45. **CTL:** 45. **BA Grade:** 55. **Risk:** Extreme.

Born: December 11, 2004. **B-T:** L-L. **HT:** 6-3. **WT:** 205. **Drafted:** HS—Lake Oswego, OR, 2023 (3rd round).
Signed by: Cal Towey.
TRACK RECORD: The son of Oregon State and Giants lefthander Trevor Wilson, Paul was committed to the Beavers to follow in his father's footsteps, but his velocity took a jump as a senior. Suddenly, his stuff was too alluring to let him get to school. The Tigers paid him nearly $1.7 million to entice him to turn pro. The Tigers were cautious with him, and he won't make his pro debut until 2024.
SCOUTING REPORT: Like his father, Wilson is a relatively polished, athletic lefty with a clear idea of what he's doing on the mound. His plus fastball touched 97 mph this spring, although he generally sat in the low 90s. He mixes a low-80s slider with plus potential and a high-70s curve that is a distinct second breaking ball. It's not as impressive but it should be a useful early-count surprise offering. He will use a fringe-average low-80s changeup as well. Wilson's fringe-average control has steadily improved. His arm slot isn't always consistent and he can lose the strike zone at times. Considering his athleticism, it won't be a stunner if he eventually gets to average or even above-average control as he matures and gets stronger.
THE FUTURE: Wilson has enough starter traits and savvy to develop into a potential mid-rotation starter. He should slot into Lakeland's rotation in 2024.

Year	Age	Club (League)	Level	W	L	ERA	G	GS	IP	H	HR	BB	SO	BB%	SO%	WHIP	AVG
2023	18	Did not play															

17 MAX ANDERSON, 2B

HIT: 50. **POW:** 55. **RUN:** 40. **FLD:** 45. **ARM:** 50. **BA Grade:** 45. **Risk:** High.

Born: February 28, 2002. **B-T:** R-R. **HT:** 6-0. **WT:** 215. **Drafted:** Nebraska, 2023 (2nd round). **Signed by:** Ryan Johnson.
TRACK RECORD: After being named the Big 10 freshman of the year in 2021, Anderson struggled as a sophomore. He answered any questions about his bat with a dominant junior season. Anderson became the first player to hit 15 home runs in Big 10 conference play. He hit 21 home runs overall and finished eighth in Division I with a .414 batting average.
SCOUTING REPORT: Like many recent Tigers' draftees, Anderson's best position is in the batter's box. He has an aggressive approach at the plate, trusts his hands and uses the entire field with a level swing. His power is just as potent going the opposite way as it is when he's yanking a ball down the line. The well-built Anderson has average hitting potential with above-average power, which gives him a path to being an offense-first second baseman. His glove isn't as advanced as his bat. Anderson makes the plays on what he gets to and his average arm is accurate, but his range is below-average thanks to a lack of quickness.
THE FUTURE: After an impressive stint at Low-A Lakeland, Anderson is ready for High-A West Michigan. He joins a conga line of bat-first, defensively limited second basemen that stretches from West Michigan to Erie to Toledo, all of whom will be trying to hit their way to Detroit.

Year	Age	Club (League)	Level	AVG	G	AB	R	H	2B	3B	HR	RBI	BB	SO	SB	OBP	SLG
2023	21	Lakeland (FSL)	A	.289	32	128	18	37	12	1	2	21	12	26	2	.345	.445
Minor League Totals				.289	32	128	18	37	12	1	2	21	12	26	2	.345	.445

18 JOSUE BRICEÑO, C

HIT: 50. **POW:** 55. **FLD:** 40. **RUN:** 30. **ARM:** 40. **BA Grade:** 50. **Risk:** Extreme.

Born: September 23, 2004. **B-T:** L-R. **HT:** 6-4. **WT:** 200. **Signed:** Venezuela, 2022.
Signed by: Jesus Mendoza/Delvis Pacheco/Jose Zambrano.
TRACK RECORD: Briceño was one of the Tigers' top international signees in 2022, and the Tigers were impressed with the long and lanky catcher. He's filled out pretty quickly into a strong, if quite tall at 6-foot-4, catcher. Briceño was one of the stars of the Florida Complex League. He finished top 10 in the league in most offensive categories and earned a late-season promotion to Low-A Lakeland.
SCOUTING REPORT: Briceño, like many tall catchers, needs to continue working on his defense. He has above-average arm strength, but his exchange and long arm stroke keeps him from consistently posting better than fringe-average pop times. His blocking also needs to continue to improve. The Tigers have reason to hope he can become an average defender someday, but opposing scouts see him more likely sliding to first base eventually. He has above-average power for his age, and with his big frame and lever-age, should continue to develop as a power threat. He demonstrated better-than-expected contact skills in 2023 and was consistently a tough out in both the Florida Complex League and Florida State League.
THE FUTURE: Briceño's catching needs lots of work, but his offensive potential is intriguing. He should be one of the best hitters in the Florida State League in 2024.

Year	Age	Club (League)	Level	AVG	G	AB	R	H	2B	3B	HR	RBI	BB	SO	SB	OBP	SLG
2023	18	FCL Tigers	Rk	.325	44	169	40	55	13	2	7	37	23	28	3	.404	.550
2023	18	Lakeland (FSL)	A	.293	11	41	8	12	6	0	0	1	7	8	0	.396	.439
Minor League Totals				.285	99	355	63	101	27	2	11	54	43	73	4	.361	.465

19 SAWYER GIPSON-LONG, RHP

FB: 45. **SL:** 50. **CB:** 45. **CHG:** 45. **CUT:** 45. **CTL:** 60. **BA Grade:** 40. **Risk:** Medium.

Born: December 12, 1997. **B-T:** R-R. **HT:** 6-4. **WT:** 225. **Drafted:** Mercer, 2019 (6th round).
Signed by: Jack Powell (Twins).
TRACK RECORD: Yet another of the Twins' many lower-round pitching finds, Gipson-Long was a sixth-round pick out of Mercer in 2019 despite never posting an ERA below 5.00 in his three-year college career. Traded to the Tigers in the 2022 Michael Fulmer deal, Gipson-Long made his MLB debut in September. He struck out 11 in five innings in just his second big league start, after reaching double-digits in strikeouts just twice in 73 minor league appearances.
SCOUTING REPORT: Gipson-Long succeeds by staying one step ahead of hitters. He doesn't have a single above-average pitch, but at his best he keeps everything out of the middle of the zone. His excellent extension helps his fringe-average 92-94 mph four-seam fastball and sinker survive, but he's mostly dependent on his average, mid-80s downer slider, which is effective against lefties and righties. He's also improved his fringe-average 85-87 mph changeup, and he'll toss in a fringe-average cutter as well. He wants to keep hitters from ever getting comfortable.

THE FUTURE: Gipson-Long's four-start stint with Detroit saw him pitch better than he ever did at Double-A or Triple-A. He's a crafty control specialist in an era of flamethrowers. It's hard to project him as more than a depth up-and-down starter who spends most of his time in Triple-A, but he's already exceeded a lot of expectations.

Year	Age	Club (League)	Level	W	L	ERA	G	GS	IP	H	HR	BB	SO	BB%	SO%	WHIP	AVG
2023	25	Erie (EL)	AA	6	5	3.74	14	13	65	51	12	15	76	5.9	29.8	1.02	.214
2023	25	Toledo (IL)	AAA	2	3	5.45	8	6	35	33	8	14	50	9.2	32.7	1.36	.244
2023	25	Detroit (AL)	MLB	1	0	2.70	4	4	20	14	2	8	26	9.8	31.7	1.10	.189
Minor League Totals				26	25	4.45	73	68	338	327	48	88	405	6.2	28.5	1.23	.248
Major League Totals				1	0	2.70	4	4	20	14	2	8	26	9.8	31.7	1.10	.189

20 WENCEEL PEREZ, OF/2B

HIT: 45. **POW:** 45. **RUN:** 60. **FLD:** 55. **ARM:** 55. **BA Grade:** 45. **Risk:** High.

Born: October 30, 1999. **B-T:** B-R. **HT:** 5-11. **WT:** 203. **Signed:** Dominican Republic, 2016.
Signed by: Ramon Perez/Carlos Santana.
TRACK RECORD: Perez was the standout of the Tigers' 2016 international amateur signing class. After an impressive start to his pro career, he struggled to adapt to the full-season minors at the plate and in the field. He's improved his selectivity to become a tougher out and has regained a little bit of prospect luster.
SCOUTING REPORT: Once an easy out for a pitcher with a plan, Perez has gotten much better at working counts and being a pest in the box. His hand-eye coordination is excellent and he has enough power to punish a pitcher who makes a mistake. Perez started to play center field this year, and that may prove to be the best position to take advantage of his athleticism. He has plus range at second base, but he struggles with throwing issues. He'll sometimes miss his target wildly on routine plays when he has plenty of time, though he has fewer issues when he has to hurry to make the play. He's a plus runner who could develop into an above-average center fielder with more reps.
THE FUTURE: Perez has been a member of the Tigers organization longer than almost anyone on the MLB roster, but he is still just 24 and will head into 2024 with two minor league options remaining. He's likely to be a multi-positional, switch-hitting backup bat with enough offensive pop and speed to find a role.

Year	Age	Club (League)	Level	AVG	G	AB	R	H	2B	3B	HR	RBI	BB	SO	SB	OBP	SLG
2023	23	Lakeland (FSL)	A	.381	5	21	4	8	3	0	0	1	1	5	1	.409	.524
2023	23	Erie (EL)	AA	.271	76	299	56	81	9	2	6	28	35	52	19	.353	.375
2023	23	Toledo (IL)	AAA	.264	35	129	29	34	13	4	3	19	27	29	6	.394	.496
Minor League Totals				.273	565	2143	345	586	102	33	33	240	239	374	116	.347	.398

21 DYLAN SMITH, RHP

FB: 50. **CB:** 40. **SL:** 60. **CHG:** 45. **CTL:** 55. **BA Grade:** 50. **Risk:** Extreme.

Born: May 28, 2000. **B-T:** R-R. **HT:** 6-2. **WT:** 180. **Drafted:** Alabama, 2021 (3rd round). **Signed by:** Mike Smith.
TRACK RECORD: An 18th-round pick of the Padres out of high school, Smith didn't sign and was ineffective and barely pitched at Alabama in his first two years, but he became a star for the Crimson Tide as a junior, even if his 2-8, 3.84 record didn't always make that clear. Alabama scored two or fewer runs in half of his 16 starts. After missing a month in 2022, Smith missed a further three months in 2023 with a right forearm strain. He was sent to the Arizona Fall League to make up for lost innings, but he posted a 7.29 ERA in six starts.
SCOUTING REPORT: As was true in his college career, Smith remains alluring to scouts, even if he's not been healthy long enough to get on a roll in pro ball. When he's feeling good and is stretched out, he can attack hitters with an average 93-95 mph fastball, a plus slider with solid tilt and a fringe-average changeup. He doesn't throw his below-average curve very often anymore. Smith has a high-energy, athletic delivery and he's shown the ability to dot the corners of the zone when he's not knocking off rust from another injured list stint.
THE FUTURE: If Smith can string together a full season when his arm is healthy, he could rocket up these rankings. He spots his fastball, can spin a breaking ball and gets swings and misses.

Year	Age	Club (League)	Level	W	L	ERA	G	GS	IP	H	HR	BB	SO	BB%	SO%	WHIP	AVG
2023	23	FCL Tigers	Rk	0	0	5.79	3	3	5	5	0	3	5	13.6	22.7	1.71	.263
2023	23	W. Michigan (MWL)	A+	1	1	3.67	6	6	27	31	3	5	23	4.3	19.8	1.33	.287
2023	23	Erie (EL)	AA	0	1	12.71	3	2	6	11	0	5	10	15.2	30.3	2.82	.393
Minor League Totals				9	8	4.23	34	32	126	128	9	34	127	6.3	23.6	1.29	.257

22 CARSON RUCKER, 3B/SS

HIT: 45. **POW:** 55. **FLD:** 55. **RUN:** 50. **ARM:** 55. **BA Grade:** 50. **Risk:** Extreme.

Born: August 18, 2004. **B-T:** R-R. **HT:** 6-2. **WT:** 195. **Drafted:** HS—Madison, TN, 2023 (4th round).
Signed by: Harold Zonder.
TRACK RECORD: Tennessee has had a number of pop-up prep prospects who haven't been seen on the showcase circuit, most notably the Rangers' Evan Carter. Rucker isn't on that level, but he established himself as an excellent prospect by hitting everything in sight as a high school senior. He finished the spring hitting .523 with 18 home runs and 31 stolen bases. Area scout Harold Zonder and scouting director Mark Conner saw him a lot and put him firmly on the team's radar for the draft.
SCOUTING REPORT: The Tigers believe they found a day two gem in Rucker. He can flash an above-average run time, he's got an above-average arm and he has the frame to continue to add more good weight and strength. More than anything, Rucker has the ability to develop into above-average power while staying on the left side of the infield. His frame may eventually outgrow shortstop, but he has a chance to play there in the near term, and his long levers and power potential should profile at third base as well.
THE FUTURE: Rucker's power potential and athleticism are worth watching, and his ability to play shortstop and third base are useful for Detroit, as third base is one of the organization's weaker positions. He should be part of a prospect-laden Lakeland team in 2024.

Year	Age	Club (League)	Level	AVG	G	AB	R	H	2B	3B	HR	RBI	BB	SO	SB	OBP	SLG
2023	18	FCL Tigers	Rk	.242	9	33	5	8	1	0	1	9	6	9	4	.390	.364
Minor League Totals				.242	9	33	5	8	1	0	1	9	6	9	4	.390	.364

23 IZAAC PACHECO, 3B

HIT: 30. **POW:** 55. **RUN:** 40. **FLD:** 55. **ARM:** 60. **BA Grade:** 45. **Risk:** High.

Born: November 18, 2002. **B-T:** L-R. **HT:** 6-4. **WT:** 225. **Drafted:** HS—Friendswood, TX, 2021 (2nd round).
Signed by: George Schaefer.
TRACK RECORD: For much of his amateur career, Pacheco's power stood out, but there were just as many concerns he'd struggle to get to that power because he sold out too much to try to hit home runs. So far as a pro, those skeptics' fears have been realized. Pacheco was too often an easy out in 2023. He struck out 31% of the time and needed a late-season surge to get his batting average above .200.
SCOUTING REPORT: Pacheco seemed lost for weeks at a time at the plate. He's got significant power, but his pull-heavy approach is getting picked apart by more advanced pitchers, especially ones who can feed him a steady diet of changeups off the plate. He seemed to be guessing too often. He has plus-plus raw power, but he won't get to it regularly in games until he can string together better at-bats. He is young enough to still figure out a better approach, but the trendlines are concerning. Pacheco's offensive struggles haven't followed him into the field, where he's an above-average defender at third with a plus arm. He's a below-average runner, but isn't a baseclogger.
THE FUTURE: After reaching West Michigan at the end of the 2022 season Pacheco will likely need to return there again in 2024. He has the tools to be a power-hitting third baseman, but he'll need better pitch recognition and plate coverage to get to that potential.

Year	Age	Club (League)	Level	AVG	G	AB	R	H	2B	3B	HR	RBI	BB	SO	SB	OBP	SLG
2023	20	W. Michigan (MWL)	A+	.211	119	455	54	96	22	3	12	50	47	160	6	.283	.352
Minor League Totals				.230	255	951	133	219	49	7	24	109	112	300	19	.309	.372

24 TYLER MATTISON, RHP

FB: 70. **CB:** 55. **SL:** 45. **CTL:** 45. **BA Grade:** 45. **Risk:** High.

Born: September 5, 1999. **B-T:** L-R. **HT:** 6-4. **WT:** 234. **Drafted:** Bryant, 2021 (4th round). **Signed by:** Jim Brentz.
TRACK RECORD: Generally the worst profile in baseball is to be a minor league reliever. Most of the best relievers in the majors were starters who converted to relieving eventually, but the Tigers have had a knack for developing solid bullpen pieces with Corey Knebel and Jason Foley among recent examples. Mattison could be next after he dominated at two levels in 2023.
SCOUTING REPORT: Mattison's plus-plus fastball is exactly what you want to see from a late-inning power arm. He is content to rear back and climb the ladder and gets swings and misses on back-to-back-to-back 96-98 mph fastballs that hitters just can't seem to lay off. He has exceptional carry and solid control and command of the pitch, and he'll cut it as well. There's energy in Mattison's less-than-picturesque delivery, but it works in short relief stints. His low-80s, above-average curveball acts almost as a changeup. It can flummox hitters' timing, as he can drop it in on hitters geared up for 96+ mph. He throws his fringe-average slider for strikes, but he could use a better power secondary offering.

THE FUTURE: Mattison's excellent fastball and effective curve give him the building blocks to be a big league reliever, but the improvement of his slider or a cutter would help as he gets closer to the majors.

Year	Age	Club (League)	Level	W	L	ERA	G	GS	IP'	H	HR	BB	SO	BB%	SO%	WHIP	AVG
2023	23	W. Michigan (MWL)	A+	3	1	3.42	19	2	26	20	5	10	45	9.6	43.3	1.14	.215
2023	23	Erie (EL)	AA	2	0	1.62	22	3	33	20	0	18	46	13.2	33.8	1.14	.171
Minor League Totals				12	2	3.26	68	6	99	69	7	47	145	11.6	35.9	1.17	.194

25 PEYTON GRAHAM, SS

HIT: 50. **POW:** 35. **FLD:** 55. **RUN:** 55. **ARM:** 55. **BA Grade:** 50. **Risk:** Extreme.

Born: January 26, 2001. **B-T:** R-R. **HT:** 6-3. **WT:** 185. **Drafted:** Oklahoma, 2022 (2nd round). **Signed by:** Steve Taylor.

TRACK RECORD: Graham was a star at Oklahoma and helped carry the Sooners to Omaha as a power-hitting, smooth-fielding shortstop. The Tigers' selected him with the 51st overall pick in 2022, but so far his pro career has been a struggle. While most college stars jump to High-A in their first full season, Graham was sent back to Low-A Lakeland. He got off to an awful start but finally started hitting in June, just in time to go on the injured list for almost the entire second half of the season.

SCOUTING REPORT: Graham's future potential depends on him figuring out how to put on some good weight and maintain his strength. He's quite skinny, and wore down in the Florida heat. None of his various soft tissue injuries was particularly severe, but they cost him half a season. Graham has the range, hands and arm to play shortstop when he's at full strength and he should be an above-average defender at second or third, but some scouts wonder if he could be an even better center fielder with his above-average speed and long strides. He's one of the Tigers' better athletes. Graham's power seems limited to the pull side with a wood bat, but that's partly because he's not strong enough yet. He's an excellent baserunner and basestealer.

THE FUTURE: Graham has been working with a nutritionist to try to ensure he's ready for an important 2024 season. He's likely to move up to High-A West Michigan, where he will need to find more of the form that made him a star in college.

Year	Age	Club (League)	Level	AVG	G	AB	R	H	2B	3B	HR	RBI	BB	SO	SB	OBP	SLG
2023	22	FCL Tigers	Rk	.250	3	4	0	1	1	0	0	0	0	1	1	.400	.500
2023	22	Lakeland (FSL)	A	.232	54	203	38	47	11	1	4	29	28	53	15	.339	.355
Minor League Totals				.244	84	307	57	75	17	2	5	42	38	83	23	.342	.362

26 ENRIQUE JIMENEZ, C

HIT: 55. **POW:** 45. **FLD:** 50. **RUN:** 45. **ARM:** 50. **BA Grade:** 50. **Risk:** Extreme.

Born: November 3, 2005. **B-T:** B-R. **HT:** 5-10. **WT:** 170. **Signed:** Venezuela, 2023.
Signed by: Alejandro Rodriguez/Jesus Mendoza/Raul Leiva.

TRACK RECORD: The 2023 international class was viewed as an excellent one for catching prospects. While Ethan Salas and Alfredo Duno grabbed the biggest headlines, Jimenez was the Tigers' top target in the class. He signed for $1.25 million after enticing them with his athleticism, switch-hitting and always-on motor.

SCOUTING REPORT: Jimenez was everything the Tigers expected in his pro debut in the Dominican Summer League. He's got a chance to be a well-rounded catcher with the desire and agility to develop into at least an average defender, with an average, accurate arm that plays up because of a quick release. He's shown the drive and savvy needed in a catcher. He's short and compact, but already has a reasonably strong base. He's got a chance to be an above-average hitter with fringe-average power thanks to short and direct swings from both sides of the plate that produce plenty of line drives. His lefty swing is a little better with more present power. He's an average runner for now, but will likely slow down.

THE FUTURE: Jimenez showed he's ready to make his stateside debut in 2024. He'll likely spend the next few years competing with Josue Briceño to become the Tigers' catcher of the future.

Year	Age	Club (League)	Level	AVG	G	AB	R	H	2B	3B	HR	RBI	BB	SO	SB	OBP	SLG
2023	17	DSL Tigers 1	Rk	.287	36	108	16	31	9	3	0	10	15	24	1	.378	.426
2023	17	DSL Tigers 2	Rk	.242	10	33	7	8	2	0	1	4	9	6	2	.419	.394
Minor League Totals				.277	46	141	23	39	11	3	1	14	24	30	3	.388	.418

27 SAMUEL GIL, 2B/SS

HIT: 55. **POW:** 30. **FLD:** 50. **RUN:** 50. **ARM:** 50. **BA Grade:** 45. **Risk:** High.

Born: November 1, 2004. **B-T:** R-R. **HT:** 5-9. **WT:** 165. **Signed:** Venezuela, 2022. **Signed by:** Jesus Mendoza/Raul Leiva.

TRACK RECORD: Gil has rarely been the most physically impressive or toolsiest player on the field, but he's often been one of the savviest. As a 5-foot-9 middle infielder, he's a little undersized, but he makes that work for him. That's especially true at the plate, where he has a small strike zone and a short stroke. **SCOUTING REPORT:** Gil rarely takes a bad at-bat. He knows the strike zone and is happy to let a wild pitcher walk him. He knows how to use the entire field and was one of the more polished hitters in the Florida Complex League, with a short, line-drive swing that helped him finish in the top 10 in the league in batting average. He has well below-average power. His intelligence is just as apparent in the field. Gil is better at second base than shortstop thanks to his average range and average arm, but he makes the routine play at both spots and always seems to know how much time he has to make the play. With the Tigers' glut of second basemen who can't play shortstop, Gil will likely get plenty of chances to show he can remain playable at short. **THE FUTURE:** Gil's ability to hit for average and get on base are worth watching, even if his lack of loud tools makes it too easy to peg him as a utility infielder. He should pair with Kevin McGonigle and Carson Rucker in the Lakeland infield in 2024.

Year	Age	Club (League)	Level	AVG	G	AB	R	H	2B	3B	HR	RBI	BB	SO	SB	OBP	SLG
2023	18	FCL Tigers	Rk	.298	44	161	34	48	7	2	2	18	29	32	7	.406	.404
Minor League Totals				.278	94	338	67	94	18	5	4	47	54	68	14	.383	.396

28 EDDYS LEONARD, SS/2B/OF

HIT: 40. **POW:** 50. **FLD:** 45. **RUN:** 55. **ARM:** 50. **BA Grade:** 40. **Risk:** Medium.

Born: November 10, 2000. **B-T:** R-R. **HT:** 6-0. **WT:** 195. **Signed:** Dominican Republic, 2017. **Signed by:** Roman Barinas/Luis Marquez/Manelik Pimentel (Dodgers).

TRACK RECORD: A $200,000 signing in the Dodgers' loaded 2017 international class, Leonard's development was slowed by the pandemic. When he finally reached Low-A for good in 2021, he had a breakout season and earned a spot on the 40-man roster. That proved to be a drawback, as the offseason lockout kept him from working with Dodgers coaches. He was slow to get going in 2022, and the Dodgers decided to drop him from their 40-man roster in July 2023. The Tigers acquired him for cash considerations and kept him on their 40-man roster. **SCOUTING REPORT:** Leonard has always had bat speed, and he responded to the trade by having one of the best stretches of his young career after a post-trade promotion to Triple-A Toledo. Leonard makes too much weak contact, but when he squares a ball up he shows off his nearly plus-plus raw power. When it comes to where Leonard will play, it's easier to list the positions where he won't be an option. He doesn't pitch or catch, and a team should always have a better first baseman. Everywhere else is in play. Leonard is below-average at second and shortstop, and fringy most everywhere else, although he should end up as an average defender in the outfield corners. He has an average arm and above-average speed, but he's not a savvy basestealer. **THE FUTURE:** Leonard still has an option remaining, so he'll get a chance to try to carry over his late-season success in a return to Toledo. He profiles as a versatile backup whose power makes him a useful role player.

Year	Age	Club (League)	Level	AVG	G	AB	R	H	2B	3B	HR	RBI	BB	SO	SB	OBP	SLG
2023	22	Tulsa (TL)	AA	.254	92	350	37	89	20	1	11	44	29	85	3	.327	.411
2023	22	Toledo (IL)	AAA	.302	40	149	30	45	10	0	8	31	17	37	2	.374	.530
Minor League Totals				.274	466	1762	302	483	108	13	64	254	198	450	33	.363	.459

29 CRISTIAN SANTANA, SS

HIT: 40. **POW:** 45. **FLD:** 45. **RUN:** 45. **ARM:** 60. **BA Grade:** 50. **Risk:** Extreme.

Born: November 25, 2003. **B-T:** R-R **HT:** 6-0. **WT:** 165. **Signed:** Dominican Republic, 2021. **Signed by:** Aldo Perez/Carlos Santana.

TRACK RECORD: Santana signed for a $2.95 million bonus in 2021 and set a team record for an international amateur signee. After an excellent debut in the Dominican Summer League, the Tigers decided to push him aggressively to Low-A Lakeland. It proved too much, and he still was overmatched in a return to the Florida State League in 2023. **SCOUTING REPORT:** Santana's season was sunk almost before it began. He was the worst hitter in the Florida State League in April and was just as bad in May. His swing was too steep and gave him little chance to make consistent contact. The result was way too many topped grounders and pop-ups. After the Tigers worked to flatten his swing path he hit much better in July, but he was once again lost at the plate in August. Amazingly, Santana cut his chase rate dramatically, but his inability to consistently square up pitches in the zone meant it hasn't paid off yet. Santana draws walks and has above-average raw power but needs to make better contact. Defensively, Santana is slowing down and ended the year playing much more third base than shortstop. He has a plus arm, but his range is limited.

THE FUTURE: Santana will only be 20 for the entirety of the 2024 season, but his career already seems to be at a crossroads. He hasn't earned a spot at High-A West Michigan, but he's already logged 177 games with Low-A Lakeland. He's going to have to fix his swing to have a shot at an eventual big league role.

Year	Age	Club (League)	Level	AVG	G	AB	R	H	2B	3B	HR	RBI	BB	SO	SB	OBP	SLG
2023	19	Lakeland (FSL)	A	.156	97	308	68	48	12	0	12	42	91	116	6	.365	.312
Minor League Totals				.203	233	749	163	152	37	2	31	101	179	253	28	.384	.382

30 ANDRE LIPCIUS, 3B/1B

HIT: 50. **POW:** 35. **FLD:** 40. **RUN:** 30. **ARM:** 45. **BA Grade:** 40. **Risk:** Medium.

Born: May 22, 1998. **B-T:** R-R. **HT:** 6-1. **WT:** 190. **Drafted:** Tennessee, 2019 (3rd round). **Signed by:** Harold Zonder.

TRACK RECORD: A nuclear engineering major at Tennessee, Lipcius was college teammates with his twin brother Luc. The older Lipcius ended up playing six years for Tennessee while getting his masters in aerospace engineering. Meanwhile, Andre was climbing the ladder to Detroit. He made his MLB debut on Sept. 1 and hit his first home run the next day. The TV broadcast found his family celebrating wildly in the stands, with the most energetic celebration coming from Luc.

SCOUTING REPORT: Lipcius is a savvy, smart baseball player with modest tools. He can play multiple positions, and he rarely gives away at-bats. He's an average hitter who works counts, draws walks and gets on base. Whether that will be enough to make him more than an up-and-down player is still to be determined. Despite a corner infielder's build, he's a contact hitter with modest power. His power doesn't fit as a regular at first or third base, and his below-average defense at second meant he never played the position after his big league callup. Lipcius is a well below-average runner with a fringe-average arm.

THE FUTURE: Lipcius will compete for a spot on the Tigers' roster in spring training but his window to establish himself in Detroit may be brief. He's being pushed by the pending arrivals of Colt Keith and Jace Jung, who have more offensive upside and potentially better defense as well. He's most likely to ride the Toledo-Detroit shuttle as a backup.

Year	Age	Club (League)	Level	AVG	G	AB	R	H	2B	3B	HR	RBI	BB	SO	SB	OBP	SLG
2023	25	W. Michigan (MWL)	A+	.286	7	21	3	6	1	0	1	3	4	5	0	.400	.476
2023	25	Toledo (IL)	AAA	.272	97	360	53	98	16	2	11	58	52	74	1	.363	.419
2023	25	Detroit (AL)	MLB	.286	13	35	3	10	1	0	1	4	3	8	0	.342	.400
Minor League Totals				.266	421	1520	223	404	88	8	38	212	220	323	24	.358	.409
Major League Totals				.286	13	35	3	10	1	0	1	4	3	8	0	.342	.400

Houston Astros

BY GEOFF PONTES

Winning cures everything, as the expression goes, but the Astros flipped that on its head.

After winning the 2022 World Series, Houston's second championship in six seasons, there was plenty of turnover in the team's front office. First, general manager James Click's contract expired and he rejected a one-year deal. The Astros brought in veteran scout Dana Brown from the Braves as the team's new GM.

Brown's track record as a talent evaluator is unquestioned, but his lack of front office experience raised eyebrows. In the months that followed Brown's hiring, several tenured members of the Houston front office were replaced.

Despite the turmoil off the field, the Astros remained among the class of the American League, winning their third consecutive AL West title in 2023, and their sixth in the last seven years. The team clinched the division on Oct. 1, securing the second seed in the AL playoffs. The Astros defeated the Twins in four games in the Division Series, securing their seventh consecutive Championship Series appearance.

The in-state rival Rangers waited in the ALCS, in the first all-Texas league finals. The Astros eventually fell to the Rangers in a dramatic seven games, as their in-state rivals would go on to capture their first world championship.

Once again, the Astros saw standout performances from homegrown players. Yordan Alvarez, Kyle Tucker and Framber Valdez were all-stars. Outfielder Chas McCormick had a career year in 2023, hitting .273/.353/.489 with 22 home runs, while righthander J.P. France made 23 starts and impressed as a rookie.

France wasn't the only rookie to make his mark with the Astros. Yainer Diaz established himself as the catcher of the future in Houston by hitting .282/.308/.538 with 23 home runs.

After a strong 2022 draft class brought the farm system back to life, top prospects and 2022 draftees Drew Gilbert and Ryan Clifford were shipped off to the Mets on Aug. 1 for former Astros ace Justin Verlander. With the return of Verlander, the Astros replaced valuable innings they had lost through injuries to Luis Garcia and Lance McCullers Jr..

A year after aggressively targeting college players in the draft, the Astros returned to the well, and selected nine collegians in the first 10 rounds, including first-round Nebraska shortstop Brice Matthews. The Astros once again did well outside the first round, landing four players between

Rookie Yainer Diaz hit 23 home runs in 2023 to rank third among primary catchers.

PROJECTED 2027 LINEUP

Catcher	Yainer Diaz	28
First Base	Zach Dezenzo	27
Second Base	Jose Altuve	37
Third Base	Brice Matthews	25
Shortstop	Jeremy Peña	29
Left Field	Luis Baez	23
Center Field	Jacob Melton	26
Right Field	Kyle Tucker	30
Designated Hitter	Yordan Alvarez	30
No. 1 Starter	Cristian Javier	30
No. 2 Starter	Hunter Brown	28
No. 3 Starter	Spencer Arrighetti	27
No. 4 Starter	Alonzo Tredwell	25
No. 5 Starter	Andrew Taylor	25
Closer	Bryan Abreu	30

rounds two and 11 who rank inside the team's Top 30 Prospects. Despite a lack of draft capital over the last five years, the Astros' farm system has continued to churn out major league contributors, which speaks to the quality of their player development.

With Alex Bregman and Jose Altuve potentially free agents after 2024, the Astros are on the precipice of a potential seismic shift. For 2024, the Astros will look to keep the gang together as they make a final run with their championship core.

Despite potential upcoming departures, the Astros have a strong core of young, controllable players who should be able to supplement some of their departures in coming seasons. ∎

HOUSTON ASTROS

TOP 2024 CONTRIBUTORS — **RANK**
1. Spencer Arrighetti, RHP — 3
2. Joey Loperfido, OF — 6
3. Rhett Kouba, RHP — 17

BREAKOUT PROSPECTS — **RANK**
1. Jake Bloss, RHP — 11
2. Nehomar Ochoa Jr., OF — 24
3. Alberto Hernandez, SS — 29

SOURCE OF TOP 30 TALENT

Homegrown	29	Acquired	1
College	19	Trade	1
Junior college	0	Rule 5 draft	0
High school	3	Independent league	0
Nondrafted free agent	1	Free agent/waivers	0
International	6		

LF
Colin Barber (26)
Kenni Gomez
Ross Adolph
Michael Sandle
Quincy Hamilton

CF
Jacob Melton (1)
Joey Loperfido (6)
Zach Cole (7)
Kenedy Corona (9)
Justin Dirden (29)
Esmil Valencia
Logan Cerny

RF
Luis Baez (2)
Cam Fisher (23)
Nehomar Ochoa Jr. (24)
Pedro Leon
Zach Daniels

3B
Zach Deznezo (5)
David Hensley
Narbe Cruz
Xavier Casserilla
Tyler Whitaker

SS
Brice Matthews (4)
Grae Kessinger (21)
Shay Whitcomb (22)
Camilo Diaz (25)
Alberto Hernandez (30)
Chase Jaworsky
Alejandro Nunez
Tommy Sacco Jr.

2B
Will Wagner (16)
J.C. Correa

1B
Bryan Arias
Scott Schrieber

C
Cesar Salazar
Miguel Palma
Garrett Guillemette
Luke Berryhill
C.J. Stubbs

LHP

LHSP	LHRP
Colton Gordon (18)	Parker Mushinski
Trey Dombroski (20)	Matt Gage
Julio Robaina	Brailyn Marquez
Cristofer Mezquita	Luis Angel Rodriguez
	Jose Nodal

RHP

RHSP	RHRP
Spencer Arrighetti (3)	Forrest Whitley (27)
Alonzo Tredwell (8)	Jimmy Endersby
Andrew Taylor (10)	Ray Gaither
Jake Bloss (11)	
A.J. Blubaugh (12)	
Miguel Ullola (13)	
Michael Knorr (14)	
Jose Fleury (15)	
Rhett Kouba (17)	
Nolan DeVos (19)	
Alimber Santa (28)	

1 JACOB MELTON, OF

Born: September 7, 2000. **B-T:** L-L. **HT:** 6-3. **WT:** 208.
Drafted: Oregon State, 2022 (2nd round).
Signed by: Tim Costic.

TRACK RECORD: After one season at Linn-Benton (Ore.) JC, Melton transferred to Oregon State prior to the 2020 season. He appeared in just seven games before the Covid-19 pandemic canceled the season. Melton worked his way into the starting lineup in 2021, hitting .404/.466/.697 in 32 games. An April shoulder injury ended his season, and Melton went undrafted in 2021 despite being eligible. He returned to Oregon State in 2022 and hit .360/.424/.671 with 17 home runs in 63 games on his way to first-team All-America honors and the Pacific-12 Conference player of the year award. The Astros drafted Melton 64th overall in 2022 and signed him for an under-slot bonus of $1 million. He finished his pro debut with 19 games at Low-A Fayetteville. He began 2023 with High-A Asheville and hit .244/.338/.454 with 18 home runs and 41 stolen bases. He reached Double-A Corpus Christi in late August, hitting five home runs over 13 games. Melton's production varied from month to month. He produced a strong May, July and September and down months in April, June and August. He also had stark home-road splits, surely taking advantage of the friendly confines of Asheville's McCormick Field.

SCOUTING REPORT: Melton is an athletic outfielder with a highly unusual swing and an enticing power-speed combination. At the plate, he sets up open before a big leg kick closes his front side. His swing is rhythmic despite the moving parts, though a slight coil with a late hitch introduces concerns about timing issues versus good major league pitching. He can be beaten with high fastballs and has coverage issues on the outer half of the plate. Melton has fringe-average bat-to-ball skills, but his approach balances aggression and patience well. He rarely misses hittable pitches. Melton's raw power is above-average to plus, and he's gotten to it consistently over the last few seasons. His underlying exit velocity numbers are above the MLB average, with a 106.4 mph 90th percentile exit velocity. Melton hit 23 home runs in 2023 and shows the ability to hit his best-struck drives in the air to his pull side with consistency. He is an above-average to plus straight-line runner who finds another gear when underway. His speed is an asset in the field and a dangerous weapon when on base. He stole 46 bases in 53 attempts in 2023.

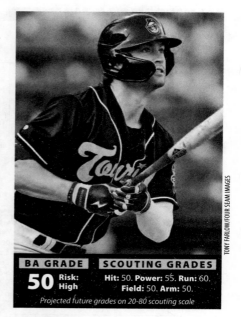

TONY FARLOW/FOUR SEAM IMAGES

BA GRADE	SCOUTING GRADES
50 Risk: High	Hit: 50. **Power:** 55. **Run:** 60. Field: 50. Arm: 50.

Projected future grades on 20-80 scouting scale

BEST TOOLS

BATTING

Best Hitter for Average	Will Wagner
Best Power Hitter	Luis Baez
Best Strike-Zone Discipline	Brice Matthews
Fastest Baserunner	Michael Sandle
Best Athlete	Zachary Cole

PITCHING

Best Fastball	Miguel Ullola
Best Curveball	Shawn Dubin
Best Slider	Forrest Whitley
Best Changeup	Jose Fleury
Best Control	Colton Gordon

FIELDING

Best Defensive Catcher	C.J. Stubbs
Best Defensive Infielder	Tommy Sacco Jr.
Best Infield Arm	Cristian Gonzalez
Best Defensive Outfielder	Kenedy Corona
Best Outfield Arm	Pedro Leon

Melton is an average defender in center field and could develop into an above-average corner outfielder. His arm is average and capable of making the needed throws. Melton is a well-rounded, tooled-up player with an unusual swing.

THE FUTURE: Melton has the tools to develop into an average everyday outfielder capable of above-average offensive seasons. His power-speed combination makes him among the most exciting players in the Astros system.

Year	Age	Club (League)	Level	AVG	G	AB	R	H	2B	3B	HR	RBI	BB	SO	SB	OBP	SLG
2023	22	Asheville (SAL)	A+	.244	86	344	73	84	16	1	18	42	48	83	41	.338	.453
2023	22	Corpus Christi (TL)	AA	.250	13	52	10	13	1	0	5	13	4	16	5	.304	.558
Minor League Totals				.248	122	484	94	120	23	1	27	68	63	125	51	.338	.467

2 LUIS BAEZ, OF

HIT: 45. **POW:** 65. **RUN:** 40. **FLD:** 40. **ARM:** 60. **BA Grade:** 55. **Risk:** Extreme.

Born: January 11, 2004. **B-T:** R-R. **HT:** 6-1. **WT:** 205.
Signed: Dominican Republic, 2022. **Signed by:** Jose Lima.
TRACK RECORD: Baez was eligible to sign during the 2020-21 international signing period but waited until Jan. 15, 2022, to sign with the Astros for $1.3 million. A native of the Dominican Republic, Baez was noted for his physically mature build and present in-game power. Those traits showed up in Baez's pro debut in the Dominican Summer League, when he hit .305/.351/.552 with eye-popping exit velocity to back his production. He made his U.S. debut in 2023 in the Florida Complex League. He hit seven home runs and slugged .661 in 17 games to earn a promotion to Low-A Fayetteville after the MLB all-star break. Baez hit .239/.324/.413 with four homers in 41 games as a 19-year-old in the tough hitting environment of the Carolina League.
SCOUTING REPORT: Baez is a power-over-hit prospect with swing-and-miss present in his game because he has vulnerability to spin. He's a strong fastball hitter with present bat speed and strength. He shows some adjustability in his barrel but can get stiff at times. Baez will need to improve his swing decisions against spin on the outer half after Low-A pitchers exploited his aggression against sliders off the plate. When Baez does make contact, he has the ability to hit the ball out to any part of the park. He hits majestic drives that backspin off his barrel, with the ability to change a game with one swing. Baez has true plus-plus raw power and he's shown the ability to get to it often. He's a below-average runner who will show some closing speed in the outfield but little speed on the bases. He has enough range to handle an outfield corner, with a plus throwing arm that will allow him to run in the grass a little longer.
THE FUTURE: Baez has the ability to grow into a fearsome power-hitting outfielder with the potential for 30-plus home run seasons.

Year	Age	Club (League)	Level	AVG	G	AB	R	H	2B	3B	HR	RBI	BB	SO	SB	OBP	SLG
2023	19	FCL Astros Blue	Rk	.271	17	59	10	16	2	0	7	15	16	14	1	.434	.661
2023	19	Fayetteville (CAR)	A	.239	41	155	20	37	13	1	4	23	17	48	0	.324	.413
Minor League Totals				.276	116	417	70	115	34	3	20	81	47	118	11	.354	.516

3 SPENCER ARRIGHETTI, RHP

FB: 50. **CB:** 45. **SL:** 55. **CHG:** 45. **CTL:** 45. **BA Grade:** 50. **Risk:** High.

Born: January 2, 2001. **B-T:** R-R. **HT:** 6-2. **WT:** 186.
Drafted: Louisiana-Lafayette, 2021 (6th round). **Signed by:** Landon Townsley.
TRACK RECORD: Arrighetti had a well-traveled collegiate career. He attended three schools in three seasons. After stints at Texas Christian in 2019 and Navarro (Texas) JC, Arrighetti spent his 2021 season with Louisiana-Lafayette, earning the Friday night starter role. The Astros drafted Arrighetti in the sixth round in 2021 and signed him for $147,800. He spent the 2022 season primarily at High-A Asheville and saw a late-season promotion to Double-A Corpus Christi. Arrighetti began 2023 at Corpus Christi and made 13 appearances before he was promoted to Triple-A Sugar Land in late June. As the organization's top bat-missing pitching prospect with Triple-A time, Arrighetti was honored with the Astros' minor league pitcher of the year award.
SCOUTING REPORT: Arrighetti has gotten the most out of his high-effort mechanics by relying on his athleticism to make it work. Arrighetti uses a four-seam fastball, slider, curveball and changeup. His fastball sits 92-93 mph and touches 94 mph with a flat vertical approach angle that makes it difficult for hitters to get on plane with the pitch. Arrighetti's primary secondary pitch is a low-80s sweeper slider that is his go-to pitch when ahead in the count. His changeup sits 85-86 mph and is his most-used secondary against lefthanded hitters. His curveball is a clear fourth pitch. It's a mid-to-high-70s two-plane breaking ball that is an effective bat-misser. Arrighetti has fringe-average command across his arsenal but has a tendency to walk too many batters.
THE FUTURE: Arrighetti is positioned to get an opportunity in Houston as a depth starter in the next few seasons. Long term, he projects as a back-end starter with enough command lapses to limit his upside.

Year	Age	Club (League)	Level	W	L	ERA	G	GS	IP	H	HR	BB	SO	BB%	SO%	WHIP	AVG
2023	23	Corpus Christi (TL)	AA	7	2	4.15	13	8	61	48	4	23	79	9.1	31.2	1.17	.218
2023	23	Sugar Land (PCL)	AAA	2	5	4.64	15	13	64	49	7	36	62	13.4	23.1	1.33	.217
Minor League Totals				19	15	4.44	61	40	245	208	21	116	315	11.0	30.0	1.32	.229

4 BRICE MATTHEWS, SS

HIT: 45. **POW:** 55. **RUN:** 55. **FLD:** 55. **ARM:** 45. **BA Grade:** 50. **Risk:** High.

Born: March 16, 2002. **B-T:** R-R. **HT:** 6-0. **WT:** 190.
Drafted: Nebraska, 2023 (1st round). **Signed by:** Drew Pearson.
TRACK RECORD: A breakout junior season at Nebraska in 2023 put Matthews on the prospect map. He drew heavy interest throughout his draft spring, especially as he became the first player in Nebraska history to hit 20 home runs and steal 20 bases in a season. He was drafted by the Astros 28th overall and signed for $2.48 million, roughly 14% below slot value. Matthews debuted in the Florida Complex League after the draft but was quickly promoted to Low-A Fayetteville. He played in 33 games for the Woodpeckers and hit .217/.373/.367.
SCOUTING REPORT: A well-rounded player with a tooled-up skill set, Matthews shows fringe-average bat-to-ball skills, with a good dose of swing-and-miss that surfaced early in his professional debut. Matthews' contact skills are counterbalanced by his selective eye at the plate. He will rarely, if ever, expand the zone. While he can get passive at times, he attacks mostly everything over the plate. Matthews shows above-average game power and has a knack for driving pitches on the inner half of the plate to his pull side. An above-average runner, Matthews is an instinctual baserunner capable of stealing 25 or more bases annually. He stole 18 bases in 22 tries in his 35-game pro debut. His speed translates to good range at shortstop, where he shows good hands and actions. His throwing arm is fringe-average, and he often lacks the strength and accuracy needed for shortstop. Other organizations saw him as a potential center fielder in pro ball.
THE FUTURE: Matthews is an exciting, tooled-up player with a good combination of on-base skills, power and speed. His best-case outlook is a rangy second baseman with above-average offensive contributions.

Year	Age	Club (League)	Level	AVG	G	AB	R	H	2B	3B	HR	RBI	BB	SO	SB	OBP	SLG
2023	21	FCL Astros Blue	Rk	.000	2	5	0	0	0	0	0	0	1	1	2	.167	.000
2023	21	Fayetteville (CAR)	A	.217	33	120	22	26	6	0	4	11	24	40	16	.373	.367
Minor League Totals				.208	35	125	22	26	6	0	4	11	25	41	18	.365	.352

5 ZACH DEZENZO, 3B

HIT: 40. **POW:** 60. **SPD:** 50. **FLD:** 40. **ARM:** 55. **BA Grade:** 50. **Risk:** High.

Born: May 11, 2000. **B-T:** R-R. **HT:** 6-4. **WT:** 220.
Drafted: Ohio State, 2022 (12th round). **Signed by:** Scott Oberhelman.
TRACK RECORD: A four-year starter at Ohio State, Dezenzo went undrafted in 2021 and returned to campus ready to make a statement in 2022. He hit .319/.413/.701 with 19 home runs for the Buckeyes while splitting time between shortstop and first base. The Astros drafted Dezenzo in the 12th round in 2022. He debuted with Low-A Fayetteville following the draft, hitting .255/.342/.402 in 27 games. The Astros assigned Dezenzo to High-A Asheville to begin 2023 and he made quick work of the South Atlantic League, hitting .407/.474/.628 in 31 games. Promoted to Double-A Corpus Christi, Dezenzo hit .257/.339/.486 with 14 home runs and 16 stolen bases.
SCOUTING REPORT: A strong, physical player, Dezenzo looks the part of a power hitter, but he's a better athlete than he appears. His bat-to-ball skills are below-average, but he does a good job of attacking hittable pitches and not expanding the zone. Dezenzo's discerning eye makes up for his lack of natural bat-to-ball ability, minimizing his whiffs and allowing him to get to his plus power. He has double-plus raw power backed by elite exit velocity data, such as a 92.3 mph average EV and a 90th percentile EV of nearly 108. Dezenzo collected 43 extra-base hits in 2023 and should continue to grow as a power hitter as he makes loft adjustments to his swing. He's an average runner and smart baserunner. Dezenzo is a below-average defender at third base but is still learning the position, with an above-average throwing arm that plays on the left side of the infield.
THE FUTURE: Dezenzo is a power-hitting corner infielder who may ultimately end up at first base. His power will be his carrying tool.

Year	Age	Club (League)	Level	AVG	G	AB	R	H	2B	3B	HR	RBI	BB	SO	SB	OBP	SLG
2023	23	Asheville (SAL)	A+	.407	31	113	38	46	11	1	4	20	16	27	6	.474	.628
2023	23	Corpus Christi (TL)	AA	.257	63	245	42	63	12	1	14	41	26	79	16	.339	.486
Minor League Totals				.294	122	460	93	135	26	2	22	76	54	143	26	.374	.503

6 JOEY LOPERFIDO, OF/2B

HIT: 45. **POW:** 55. **RUN:** 55. **FLD:** 45. **ARM:** 40. **BA Grade:** 50. **Risk:** High.

Born: May 11, 1999. **B-T:** L-R. **HT:** 6-4. **WT:** 195.
Drafted: Duke, 2021 (7th round). **Signed by:** Andrew Johnson.
TRACK RECORD: After going unselected in the five-round 2020 draft, Loperfido went back to Duke for his senior year and has since developed into a legitimate position prospect after the Astros drafted him in the seventh round in 2021. After hitting .286/.387/.458 in 2022 across both levels of Class A, Loperfido spent a majority of 2023 with Double-A Corpus Christi. He hit .296/.392/.548 with 19 home runs and 20 stolen bases in 84 games. He was promoted to Triple-A Sugar Land on Aug. 15 but struggled with strikeouts in 32 games.
SCOUTING REPORT: Loperfido is a well-rounded player with no standout tool. At the plate, he sets up with his hands high, equal with the crown of his helmet. A moderate leg lift gives way to an explosive lefthanded swing. Loperfido has shown average bat-to-ball skills and a good balance of aggression and patience as he has climbed the ladder. During his month at Triple-A, he struggled to make contact and expanded at a much higher rate than at any of his previous stops. He shows above-average game power with the ability to get to it by slugging 25 home runs in 2023. Loperfido's groundball rate is on the higher side, capping some of his raw power until an adjustment is made. An above-average runner underway, he is a baserunning threat. He stole 27 bases in 31 attempts in 2023. Loperfido's speed translates to the outfield, where he shows the ability to handle center field. His arm is below-average but has been enough to make him playable at a variety of positions. Loperfido saw playing time at five positions in 2023: first base, second base and all three outfield spots.
THE FUTURE: Loperfido fits the super-utility profile with average or better hitting ability and a nice power and speed combination.

Year	Age	Club (League)	Level	AVG	G	AB	R	H	2B	3B	HR	RBI	BB	SO	SB	OBP	SLG
2023	24	Asheville (SAL)	A+	.265	8	34	4	9	2	2	1	5	2	8	3	.297	.529
2023	24	Corpus Christi (TL)	AA	.296	84	314	60	93	20	1	19	57	47	81	20	.392	.548
2023	24	Sugar Land (PCL)	AAA	.235	32	119	15	28	5	0	5	16	16	45	4	.333	.403
Minor League Totals				.282	251	928	159	262	56	7	39	153	126	266	60	.379	.484

7 ZACHARY COLE, OF

HIT: 30. **POW:** 55. **RUN:** 60. **FLD:** 60. **ARM:** 70. **BA Grade:** 50. **Risk:** Extreme.

Born: August 4, 2000. **B-T:** L-R. **HT:** 6-2. **WT:** 190.
Drafted: Ball State, 2022 (10th round). **Signed by:** Scott Oberhelman.
TRACK RECORD: Cole played in just 22 games during his first two seasons at Ball State before breaking out in his third, hitting .361/.449/.727 with 13 home runs for the Cardinals in 2022. He joined Cotuit of the Cape Cod League after the season and played in 16 games prior to the draft. The Astros selected Cole in the 10th round and signed him for a below-slot $97,500. Cole reached Low-A Fayetteville after the draft and returned to the level to begin 2023. He hit .265/.397/.494 with 11 homers and 25 steals in 70 games. Promoted to High-A Asheville on July 19, he hit .247/.349/.480 with eight homers and 12 steals in 41 games.
SCOUTING REPORT: Cole has an elite athletic capacity, providing the highest ceiling of any Houston prospect. An explosive offensive player, he falls into the category of a three true outcomes hitter. Cole's bat-to-ball skills are well below-average, driving a high strikeout rate. He showed patience against Class A pitching, but many question the quality of his approach and how his swing decisions will translate as he moves up. Cole's plus raw power is his carrying tool and he's shown the ability to get to it in games by hitting 47 extra-base hits in 2023. His underlying exit velocity data is strong with a 91 mph average and a 106.5 mph 90th percentile EV, both numbers well above the major league average. Cole is an easy plus runner with long graceful strides in the outfield and the quick first step to be a basestealing threat. He's a strong defensive outfielder with the range to handle center field and the plus-plus arm to fit in any outfield position. Despite overall hitting questions, Cole is a tooled-up specimen with big upside.
THE FUTURE: A standout defender with an exciting blend of power and speed, Cole looks like an everyday regular with all-star potential if everything breaks right.

Year	Age	Club (League)	Level	AVG	G	AB	R	H	2B	3B	HR	RBI	BB	SO	SB	OBP	SLG
2023	22	Fayetteville (CAR)	A	.265	70	253	48	67	15	5	11	46	45	97	25	.397	.494
2023	22	Asheville (SAL)	A+	.247	41	150	31	37	5	3	8	19	21	58	12	.349	.480
Minor League Totals				.245	144	518	92	127	26	8	21	77	82	192	54	.369	.448

8 ALONZO TREDWELL, RHP

FB: 50. **CB:** 55. **SL:** 50. **CHG:** 40. **CTL:** 55. **BA Grade:** 50. **Risk:** Extreme.

Born: May 8, 2002. **B-T:** L-R. **HT:** 6-8. **WT:** 230.
Drafted: UCLA, 2023 (2nd round). **Signed by:** Tim Costic.
TRACK RECORD: As a rising Junior at Mater Dei High in Southern California, Tredwell had Tommy John surgery and missed all of the summer showcase circuit and his senior year. He arrived at UCLA in 2022 ready to contribute and took over the closer's role as a freshman. Tredwell made the jump to the Bruins' weekend rotation as a draft-eligible sophomore and made nine starts before a back injury cut his season short. Despite his shorter track record and murky injury history, Tredwell intrigued the Astros in the second round in 2023. Tredwell signed for an above-slot bonus of just shy of $1.5 million and did not pitch following the draft.
SCOUTING REPORT: A tall, physical pitcher at 6-foot-8, 230 pounds, Tredwell's size has not equated to durability. he mixes four pitches led by a four-seam fastball with plus ride that sits 92-93 mph and touches 95 at peak. His primary secondary is an upper-70s curveball with heavy two-plane break. Tredwell also throws a slider in the low 80s with tighter gyro shape and a rarely-used changeup. Tredwell's ability to use the north-to-south plan of attack is his bread and butter. He rides his four-seam high and works his curveball off of it. Historically, Tredwell has shown well above-average command. He walked just 18 batters across 92.1 collegiate innings, including a sterling 6% walk rate as a starter in 2023. His ability to land all of his pitches in the zone with great regularity is his standout skill. Tredwell is a refined strikethrower with a starter's frame and pitch mix. It's just a matter of finding consistent health.
THE FUTURE: Tredwell has a future as a No. 4 starter if he can hold up to the rigors of pitching every five days.

Year	Age	Club (League)	Level	W	L	ERA	G	GS	IP	H	HR	BB	SO	BB%	SO%	WHIP	AVG
2023	21	Did not play															

9 KENEDY CORONA, OF

HIT: 40. **POW:** 50. **RUN:** 60. **FLD:** 70. **ARM:** 50. **BA Grade:** 45. **Risk:** High.

Born: March 21, 2000. **B-T:** R-R. **HT:** 5-11. **WT:** 184.
Signed: Venezuela, 2019. **Signed by:** Wilson Peralta (Mets).
TRACK RECORD: The Astros acquired Corona from the Mets for Jake Marisnick following the 2019 season. After an underwhelming 2021, Corona reworked his swing and broke out in 2022, hitting .278/.362/.495 across both levels of Class A. He returned to High-A Asheville to begin 2023 but needed just six games to the earn promotion to Double-A Corpus Christi. In the Texas League, Corona hit .244/.324/.449 with 20 home runs and 31 stolen bases in 111 games and earned rave reviews for his defense, winning a Rawlings minor league Gold Glove award.
SCOUTING REPORT: Corona is a talented defensive outfielder with the tools to be an average offensive contributor. He has fringe-average bat-to-ball skills with moderate swing-and-miss. He struggles against elevated fastballs and soft stuff off the plate. Much of this is due to the steepness of Corona's bat path and the compact nature of his swing, which creates holes at the top of the zone and on the outer half of the plate. Corona has a good balance of patience and aggression, hardly, if ever, taking hittable pitches over the plate. He has average raw power, but he shows an ability to hit his hardest contact at his best launch angles, leading to over-the-fence power. Corona is likely to hit 18-20 home runs per season at peak. He's a plus runner and an instinctual basestealer, capable of swiping 20 or more bases. His speed translates to the field where he is one of the best outfield defenders in the minor leagues. He covers ground in center field, taking strong routes with the ability to make highlight-reel plays. Corona's arm is average but enough for all three outfield positions.
THE FUTURE: Corona has the defensive abilities in center field to earn everyday playing time, but his swing-and-miss will likely limit him to a part-time role.

Year	Age	Club (League)	Level	AVG	G	AB	R	H	2B	3B	HR	RBI	BB	SO	SB	OBP	SLG
2023	23	Asheville (SAL)	A+	.360	6	25	7	9	0	0	2	4	4	9	1	.448	.600
2023	23	Corpus Christi (TL)	AA	.244	111	434	63	106	21	4	20	61	48	127	31	.324	.449
Minor League Totals				.267	344	1289	233	344	71	13	48	183	144	331	98	.349	.454

10 ANDREW TAYLOR, RHP
FB: 55. **CB:** 45. **SL:** 50. **CHG:** 45. **CTL:** 50. **BA Grade:** 45. **Risk:** High.

Born: September 23, 2001. **B-T:** R-R. **HT:** 6-5. **WT:** 190.
Drafted: Central Michigan, 2022 (2nd round supp). **Signed by:** Scott Oberhelman.
TRACK RECORD: A breakout sophomore campaign at Central Michigan put Taylor on the draft radar entering his draft summer. He made seven starts for Cape Cod League runner-up Bourne and returned to campus for his junior season in 2022. His numbers didn't match his sophomore production, but his underlying numbers and fastball shape remained strong. The Astros drafted Taylor with their pick in the supplemental second round in 2022 and signed the righthander for slot value of $807,200. He debuted in 2023 with Low-A Fayetteville and made 24 appearances and threw 84 total innings. While Taylor's 4.61 ERA was disappointing, his 33.8% strikeout rate and 22.3 K-BB% were among the best in the organizations.
SCOUTING REPORT: Taylor's profile centers around the quality of his four-seam fastball. He mixes four pitches, led by a low-90s fastball with elite ride and life at the top of the zone. In his pro debut, Taylor's fastball performed by running high rates for strikes, whiffs and chases. His best secondary is a mid-80s slider with cutter-like shape and is his best swing-and-miss pitch. Taylor throws an upper-70s curveball and a low-to-mid-80s changeup. He shows above-average command of his fastball but consistently struggles to land his breaking pitches. His breaking ball shapes have been altered since Taylor's amateur days, leaving some upside if he can improve their quality. Taylor has good size and fits into the physical characteristics of a typical starting pitching prospect at 6-foot-5, 190 pounds. Refining his secondaries and adding power to his fastball will be points of focus this offseason.
THE FUTURE: Taylor has the traits of a back-of-the-rotation starter with upside for more if his fastball velocity and secondary quality take a step forward in 2024.

Year	Age	Club (League)	Level	W	L	ERA	G	GS	IP	H	HR	BB	SO	BB%	SO%	WHIP	AVG
2023	21	Fayetteville (CAR)	A	4	8	4.61	24	12	84	87	12	43	126	11.5	33.8	1.55	.269
Minor League Totals				4	8	4.61	24	12	84	87	12	43	126	11.5	33.8	1.55	.269

11 JAKE BLOSS, RHP
FB: 60. **CB:** 50. **SL:** 50. **CHG:** 40. **CTL:** 50. **BA Grade:** 45. **Risk:** High.

Born: June 23, 2001. **B-T:** R-R. **HT:** 6-3. **WT:** 205. **Drafted:** Georgetown, 2023 (3rd round). **Signed by:** Bobby St. Pierre.
TRACK RECORD: Bloss spent three seasons with Lafayette College in Pennsylvania, earning an All-Patriot League first-team selection after his third season. He transferred to Georgetown for his fourth season and went 8-4, 2.58 with 96 strikeouts and 24 walks across 76.2 innings. Bloss won Big East pitcher of the year and was a unanimous first-team all conference selection. The Astros took Bloss in the third round of the 2023 draft and signed him for a below-slot bonus of $497,500. Bloss debuted in the Florida Complex League making two appearances before a promotion to Low-A Fayetteville.
SCOUTING REPORT: A strong-framed and athletic pitcher, Bloss has the broad-shouldered build of your typical innings-eater. Bloss mixes primarily a four-seam fastball, a curveball, a slider and a changeup. Bloss' fastball sits 93-95 mph and was clocked as high as 97 while at Georgetown. Due to the spin efficiency and lower release height he's able to create a flat plane of approach on the pitch which makes it difficult for hitters to get on plane. His primary secondary is an upper-70s curveball at 77-78 mph with heavy two-plane break. Bloss's slider is hard at 85-87 mph with heavy cut, and he shows above-average command of the pitch. His changeup is an upper-80s offspeed with two-seam fastball movement. Bloss has fringe-average command but should develop into an average strike-thrower.
THE FUTURE: A late blooming college arm with a four-pitch mix led by a plus fastball, Bloss has a chance to blossom into a back-of-the-rotation starter with the ability to be effective out of the bullpen.

Year	Age	Club (League)	Level	W	L	ERA	G	GS	IP	H	HR	BB	SO	BB%	SO%	WHIP	AVG
2023	22	FCL Astros Blue	Rk	0	0	3.86	2	2	2	2	0	1	3	10.0	30.0	1.29	.222
2023	22	Fayetteville (CAR)	A	1	1	2.76	5	4	16	14	0	11	20	15.9	29.0	1.53	.250
Minor League Totals				1	1	3.00	7	6	19	16	0	12	23	15.2	29.1	1.56	.246

12 A.J. BLUBAUGH, RHP

FB: 50. **CB:** 45. **SL:** 45. **CHG:** 50. **CTL:** 50. **BA Grade:** 45. **Risk:** High.

Born: July 4, 2000. **B-T:** R-R. **HT:** 6-2. **WT:** 190. **Drafted:** Wisconsin-Milwaukee, 2022 (7th round).
Signed by: Drew Pearson.

TRACK RECORD: Blubaugh spent three years at Wisconsin-Milwaukee, winning Horizon League relief pitcher of the year in 2021 and 2022, as well as consecutive first team all-conference selections. Blubaugh was selected by the Astros in the seventh round of the 2022 draft, signing for a below-slot bonus of $172,500. Blubaugh was assigned to High-A Asheville to begin 2023, appearing in 22 games and typically going 3-4 innings in a piggyback fashion with another starter. Blubaugh was promoted to Double-A Corpus Christi on Aug. 26, making four appearances before participating in the Arizona Fall League.
SCOUTING REPORT: Blubaugh has an athletic build with prototypical size for a starter and a clean, athletic operation. He mixes four pitches from a high-three quarters slot. His fastball sits 91-93 mph touching 94 with ride and run. Blubaugh's slider, curveball and changeup are used at a similar rate, with his changeup outperforming the two breaking balls. Blubaugh's changeup sits 81-83 mph with some tumble and fade and is his best swing-and-miss pitch. Blubaugh throws two sweepy breaking balls in a traditional sweeper slider which sits 79-81 mph and a mid-70s curveball with two-plane break. Blubaugh's slider is his primary secondary against righthanded batters, and he uses the changeup and curveball heavily against lefties. He shows above-average command of his fastball but fringe-average command of his secondaries.
THE FUTURE: Blubaugh has a chance to start if he improves command of his secondaries. If not, he could find more velocity and long-term success as a reliever.

Year	Age	Club (League)	Level	W	L	ERA	G	GS	IP	H	HR	BB	SO	BB%	SO%	WHIP	AVG
2023	22	Asheville (SAL)	A+	6	3	4.94	22	9	86	85	10	37	93	10.0	25.1	1.42	.258
2023	22	Corpus Christi (TL)	AA	0	0	1.26	4	3	14	4	1	8	19	15.7	37.3	0.84	.093
Minor League Totals				8	4	4.40	32	15	119	103	11	51	136	10.2	27.3	1.30	.233

13 MIGUEL ULLOLA, RHP

FB: 60. **CB:** 45. **SL:** 50. **CHG:** 40. **CTL:** 40. **BA Grade:** 50. **Risk:** Extreme.

Born: June 19, 2002. **B-T:** R-R. **HT:** 6-1. **WT:** 184. **Signed:** Dominican Republic, 2021.
Signed by: Alfredo Ulloa/Hassan Wessin.

TRACK RECORD: The Astros signed Ullola as an 18-year-old, then moved him quickly. He split his first season between the Dominican Summer League and the Rookie-level Florida Complex League, racking up 38 strikeouts in 24.1 innings. He made his full-season debut in 2022 and has moved a level a year for the past two seasons. Ullola made the jump to High-A in 2023. He made 25 appearances for Asheville but struggled with command and allowed too many home runs. Ullola improved his strike-throwing throughout the season, cutting his walk rate by a third from July 1 forward.
SCOUTING REPORT: Ullola's explosive fastball leads his arsenal and rates as the best in the system. The pitch is a classic four-seamer, sitting 93-94 mph and touching 95 at peak with heavy ride and a tough angle when located at the top of the zone. Ullola shows fringy command of the pitch, but it will generate whiffs in-zone when located. His primary secondary is a mid-80s slider with gyro shape and some late cut. The slider doesn't miss many bats but Ullola has shown average command of the pitch. Ullola also throws an upper-70s curveball with two-plane break but his command of the pitch is fringy. Ullola threw an upper-80s changeup but it was thrown infrequently.
THE FUTURE: Ullola has big stuff and has shown slight command gains but will probably never have the command to start. His future likely lies as a middle reliever where he can air it out.

Year	Age	Club (League)	Level	W	L	ERA	G	GS	IP	H	HR	BB	SO	BB%	SO%	WHIP	AVG
2023	21	Asheville (SAL)	A+	3	9	5.86	25	13	91	87	12	63	116	15.0	27.7	1.65	.251
Minor League Totals				6	12	4.62	57	29	187	138	16	139	274	16.6	32.7	1.48	.201

14 MICHAEL KNORR, RHP

FB: 55. **CB:** 50. **SL:** 50. **CHG:** 40. **CTL:** 45. **BA Grade:** 45. **Risk:** High.

Born: May 12, 2000. **B-T:** R-R. **HT:** 6-5. **WT:** 245. **Drafted:** Coastal Carolina, 2022 (3rd round).
Signed by: Andrew Johnson.

TRACK RECORD: After three subpar seasons at Cal State Fullerton, Knorr transferred to Coastal Carolina. Over that offseason, Knorr made some mechanical changes that unlocked fastball velocity. On the strength of his newfound pitch quality Knorr earned All-Sun Belt conference second-team honors. The Astros selected Knorr in the third round and signed him for a below-slot bonus of $487,500. Knorr was shut down following the draft and debuted with Low-A Fayetteville to start 2023. He made four appearances with Fayetteville before earning a promotion to High-A Asheville, where he pitched 41 innings over 11 outings before suffering a shoulder injury that cost him the final two months of the season.

SCOUTING REPORT: Knorr is a powerful righthander who mixes a four-seam fastball, slider, curveball and changeup. His four-seam fastball sits between 93-95 mph and touches 96 at peak with heavy bore. His primary secondary is a mid-80s slider with gyro shape that works as his main weapon in right-on-right matchups. Knorr's curveball sits between 75-77 mph with two-plane break and is used most frequently against lefthanded hitters. His mid-80s changeup is used in tandem with his curveball to attack lefties. Knorr shows fringe-average command of his stuff and is prone to missing over the heart of the plate.

THE FUTURE: Knorr will likely move to the bullpen, where his above-average fastball and feel for two breaking ball shapes should be a better fit.

Year	Age	Club (League)	Level	W	L	ERA	G	GS	IP	H	HR	BB	SO	BB%	SO%	WHIP	AVG
2023	23	Fayetteville (CAR)	A	2	0	2.60	4	2	17	13	0	7	24	9.9	33.8	1.15	.206
2023	23	Asheville (SAL)	A+	1	5	4.61	11	8	41	39	8	17	54	9.4	30.0	1.37	.242
Minor League Totals				3	5	4.03	15	10	58	52	8	24	78	9.6	31.1	1.31	.232

15 JOSE FLEURY, RHP

FB: 45. **CB:** 50. **SL:** 45. **CHG:** 60. **CTL:** 45. **BA Grade:** 45. **Risk:** High.

Born: March 8, 2002. **B-T:** R-R. **HT:** 6-0. **WT:** 185. **Signed:** Dominican Republic, 2021.
Signed by: Roman Ocumarez/Alfredo Ulloa/Jose Torres.
TRACK RECORD: Fleury signed late in the 2021 international free agency period and slid under the radar of many teams. He debuted in the Dominican Summer League the following June and performed, pitching to a 1.42 ERA, with a 41.1% strikeout rate and a 2.7% walk rate. Fleury made the jump directly to Low-A Fayetteville to begin 2023, where he made 26 appearances totaling 98 innings. It was a successful season for Fleury, who won Carolina League pitcher of the month in August, finished second in the CL in strikeouts with 139 and was selected a league all-star.
SCOUTING REPORT: Fleury mixes four pitches in a four-seam fastball, changeup, curveball and slider. Fleury's four-seam sits 89-91 mph with well above-average ride and gets 20 inches of induced vertical break regularly. His primary secondary is a changeup at 80-82 mph with good vertical and velocity separation from his fastball and is thrown with solid conviction and arm speed. Fleury's slider evolved into a flatter, slightly harder version of his curveball in 2023. Fleury's curveball is his best secondary, though it sometimes blends with his slider. The curveball sits between 77-78 mph with moderate two-plane break. Fleury does a good job commanding his fastball and changeup but lacks consistency with his breaking ball shape and command. Despite a fringy fastball or a true breaking ball, Fleury has shown the ability to navigate an order multiple times. Still, his journey to a spot in a starting rotation has a long way to go.
THE FUTURE: As an undersized, changeup-first righthander, Fleury fits the archetype of starters who move to the pen.

Year	Age	Club (League)	Level	W	L	ERA	G	GS	IP	H	HR	BB	SO	BB%	SO%	WHIP	AVG
2023	21	Fayetteville (CAR)	A	4	3	3.65	26	14	99	63	8	48	139	12.1	34.9	1.13	.182
Minor League Totals				6	3	3.04	36	18	137	90	9	52	199	9.6	36.6	1.04	.185

16 WILL WAGNER, 3B

HIT: 55. **POW:** 45. **RUN:** 40. **FLD:** 40. **ARM:** 40. **BA Grade:** 45. **Risk:** High.

Born: July 29, 1998. **B-T:** L-R. **HT:** 5-11. **WT:** 210. **Drafted:** Liberty, 2021 (18th round). **Signed by:** Andrew Johnson.
TRACK RECORD: The son of seven-time all-star Billy Wagner, Will has gone from an unheralded 18th-round pick to one of the better performers over the last two seasons in the Astros organization. After Wagner hit .261/.374/.394 at two levels in 2022, he returned to Double-A Corpus Christi to begin 2023. After beginning the season on the injured list and struggling over the first month, Wagner was shut down with right wrist discomfort. The injury required surgery to remove the hook of his hamate bone. Wagner returned to Corpus Christi on Aug. 7, hitting .331/.396/.562 over the final 30 games.
SCOUTING REPORT: Wagner is a bat-first infielder whose advanced hit tool drives his profile. He has quick hands, is rarely fooled in the strike zone and hardly ever expands the zone. His strong contact and plate discipline allow him to get the most out of below-average impact. Wagner has shown the ability to make his hardest contact at good launch angles but rarely drives the ball in the air to his pull side. Wagner's advanced barrel control allows him to hit for more power than his raw exit velocity numbers would suggest. He is a below-average runner and lacks range in the field. Wagner has split time between second base and third base but is below-average at each spot.
THE FUTURE: Wagner is a hit-first infielder with an above-average hit tool but no real position in the field, and looks like a bat-first, second-division regular.

Year	Age	Club (League)	Level	AVG	G	AB	R	H	2B	3B	HR	RBI	BB	SO	SB	OBP	SLG
2023	24	FCL Astros Blue	Rk	.313	6	16	5	5	1	0	0	2	7	1	1	.542	.375
2023	24	Corpus Christi (TL)	AA	.309	53	207	36	64	16	2	7	32	26	47	3	.385	.507
2023	24	Sugar Land (PCL)	AAA	.577	6	26	3	15	3	0	0	4	2	2	2	.607	.692
Minor League Totals				.291	213	780	128	227	47	6	19	105	118	181	19	.390	.440

17 RHETT KOUBA, RHP

FB: 40. **CB:** 45. **SL:** 45. **CHG:** 55. **CTL:** 55. **BA Grade:** 40. **Risk:** Medium.

Born: September 3, 1999. **B-T:** R-R. **HT:** 6-0. **WT:** 180. **Drafted:** Dallas Baptist, 2021 (12th round).
Signed by: Jim Stevenson.

TRACK RECORD: Kouba spent two seasons at North Central Texas JC before transferring to Dallas Baptist. After beginning the 2021 season in a relief role, Kouba made a successful jump into the starting rotation. The Astros selected Kouba in the 12th round and signed him for $125,000. Kouba spent 2022 across both Class A levels before beginning 2023 with Double-A Corpus Christi. With Corpus Christi, Kouba posted a 3.27 ERA, struck out 118 against 23 walks and was named the league's pitcher of the year. He was promoted to Triple-A Sugar Land on Aug. 26 and made five appearances over the final month.

SCOUTING REPORT: Kouba is undersized and doesn't have much power behind his pitch mix. His four-seam fastball sits between 91-92 mph and touches 93 but plays up due to his deceptive low three-quarters slot. Kouba commands his fastball extremely well, particularly at the top of the zone where he can generate whiffs. Kouba throws a slider, curveball and changeup and uses them all at a near-equal rate. Kouba's mid-80s changeup with plenty of tumble is his best offspeed. His slider is a low-80s sweeper that is used mostly against righties. Kouba's curveball sits in the high 70s with heavy two-plane break. The curveball is used in tandem with his changeup against lefties. He has strong strike-throwing abilities and shows the ability to command his arsenal. Kouba lacks the power of typical major league starters but he gets the most out of his profile with command and movement.

THE FUTURE: Kouba looks like an up-and down starter with the ability to develop into a No. 5 starter.

Year	Age	Club (League)	Level	W	L	ERA	G	GS	IP	H	HR	BB	SO	BB%	SO%	WHIP	AVG
2023	23	Corpus Christi (TL)	AA	7	5	3.27	23	21	110	95	12	23	118	5.1	26.2	1.07	.231
2023	23	Sugar Land (PCL)	AAA	1	2	4.50	5	3	18	21	2	14	18	16.1	20.7	1.94	.292
Minor League Totals				14	10	3.57	52	37	217	199	25	66	241	7.2	26.3	1.22	.238

18 COLTON GORDON, LHP

FB: 45. **CB:** 45. **SL:** 55. **CHG:** 50. **CTL:** 55. **BA Grade:** 40. **Risk:** Medium.

Born: December 20, 1998. **B-T:** L-L. **HT:** 6-4. **WT:** 225. **Drafted:** Central Florida, 2021 (8th round).
Signed by: Charlie Gonzalez.

TRACK RECORD: After spending a season with Hillsborough (Fla.) JC and a redshirt year at Florida, Gordon transferred to Central Florida in advance of the 2020 season. He joined the Knights' rotation and made nine starts before a torn ulnar collateral ligament required Tommy John surgery. The Astros drafted Gordon in the eighth round in 2021 and signed the lefthander for a below-slot bonus of $125,700. He debuted in 2022 with 15 appearances and reached High-A by season's end. Gordon began the 2023 season with Double-A Corpus Christi and made 20 appearances before earning promotion to Triple-A Sugar Land on Aug. 8. Over his final nine appearances, Gordon struggled with strike-throwing in a way he had not previously.

SCOUTING REPORT: Gordon is a deceptive lefthander who lacks power across his arsenal but features a variety of pitch shapes and the ability to command his repertoire. He mixes four pitches in a fastball in the high 80s to low 90s that he can manipulate to sink or ride, though neither shape is deceptive. He mixes a trio of secondaries, led by his low-80s slider with ride and sweep. Gordon throws a mid-70s curveball with heavy sweep and a mid-80s changeup which he commands at an average rate. Prior to 2023, Gordon's control had been elite. He showed a devolution in strike-throwing throughout the season, which culminated in a messy month-plus at Triple-A, where the unforgiving automated ball-strike system didn't help. Gordon's fastball command is well above-average but he struggles to land his secondaries consistently. All of Gordon's pitches play up due to his long arm action and ability to hide the ball.

THE FUTURE: Gordon profiles as a back-end depth starter with the ability to get the most out of his subpar stuff.

Year	Age	Club (League)	Level	W	L	ERA	G	GS	IP	H	HR	BB	SO	BB%	SO%	WHIP	AVG
2023	24	Corpus Christi (TL)	AA	4	5	3.95	20	18	93	75	9	36	121	9.1	30.7	1.19	.215
2023	24	Sugar Land (PCL)	AAA	3	2	4.63	9	6	35	39	8	22	30	13.5	18.4	1.74	.277
Minor League Totals				9	8	3.61	44	35	182	149	21	66	229	8.7	30.2	1.18	.217

19 NOLAN DEVOS, RHP

FB: 50. **CB:** 45. **SL:** 50. **CHG:** 40. **CTL:** 45. **BA Grade:** 45. **Risk:** High.

Born: August 11, 2000. **B-T:** R-R. **HT:** 6-0. **WT:** 185. **Drafted:** Davidson, 2022 (5th round). **Signed by:** Andrew Johnson.
TRACK RECORD: DeVos spent his first two collegiate seasons pitching out of Davidson's bullpen. He went undrafted as an eligible sophomore and made a successful jump into the Wildcats rotation. DeVos earned first-team all conference honors by going 9-2, 2.40 and leading the Atlantic-10 Conference in strikeouts. He was selected by the Astros in the fifth round of the 2022 draft and signed for a below-slot bonus of $197,500. DeVos began 2023 with Low-A Fayetteville and made 13 appearances before he was promoted to High-A Asheville.
SCOUTING REPORT: DeVos mixes four pitches in a four-seam fastball, slider, curveball and changeup. His fastball and slider see the majority of his usage with his curveball supplementing the slider against lefthanded hitters. DeVos' fastball sits 91-92 mph but what it lacks in power it makes up for in shape, with heavy ride and late life. His primary secondary is a mid-80s slider with ride and around 7-9 inches of sweep. The slider outperformed the rest of DeVos' arsenal this season, driving whiffs in and out of the zone. DeVos' curveball sits 77-78 mph with moderate two-plane break and is his go-to secondary against lefthanders but induces few swings and misses. DeVos' rarely thrown changeup sits 85-86 mph with moderate fade. DeVos shows above-average command of his fastball but fringy to below-average command of his secondaries.
THE FUTURE: DeVos' fastball shape and quality slider give him a chance to make it as back-of-the-rotation starter, but his high-ride fastball and slider might ultimately work best in the bullpen.

Year	Age	Club (League)	Level	W	L	ERA	G	GS	IP	H	HR	BB	SO	BB%	SO%	WHIP	AVG
2023	22	Fayetteville (CAR)	A	2	1	2.24	13	8	52	33	1	27	74	12.8	35.1	1.15	.181
2023	22	Asheville (SAL)	A+	4	3	4.27	12	7	46	48	7	23	43	11.2	20.9	1.53	.262
Minor League Totals				8	4	3.03	31	17	113	90	8	59	139	12.4	29.1	1.32	.217

20 TREY DOMBROSKI, LHP

FB: 40. **CB:** 50. **SL:** 45. **CHG:** 55. **CTL:** 55. **BA Grade:** 45. **Risk:** High.

Born: March 13, 2001. **B-T:** R-L. **HT:** 6-5. **WT:** 235. **Drafted:** Monmouth, 2022 (4th round). **Signed by:** Steve Payney.
TRACK RECORD: Dombroski popped onto the draft radar after a breakout summer with the Harwich Mariners in the Cape Cod League. Dombroski returned to Monmouth where he enjoyed a successful 2022 season, won MAAC pitcher of the year and was a unanimous first team all-conference selection. Dombroski was taken by the Astros in the fourth round of the 2022 draft but did not debut until the following spring with Low-A Fayetteville. He spent the entire 2023 season at Low-A, making 26 appearances spanning 119 innings working to a 7-9, 3.71 mark with 148 strikeouts and 36 walks.
SCOUTING REPORT: Dombroski is a big-bodied lefthander who mixes four pitches in a four-seam fastball, curveball, slider and changeup. Dombroski's fastball lacks power, sitting 89-90 mph on average and peaking at 91-92. His most-used secondary is his upper-70s curveball with two-plane break and late sweep, and he shows excellent feel and command of the pitch. Dombroski's best pitch might be his changeup, which he commands well and uses to generate swings and misses in and out of the zone. His sweeper slider at 79-81 mph can at times blend into his curveball but is his most used secondary in left-on-left matchups. Dombroski has a history of advanced strike-throwing and did not walk more than two batters in any outing from April 28 forward.
THE FUTURE: Dombroski is a potential back-end starter whose ceiling is capped by his fastball's lack of power.

Year	Age	Club (League)	Level	W	L	ERA	G	GS	IP	H	HR	BB	SO	BB%	SO%	WHIP	AVG
2023	22	Fayetteville (CAR)	A	7	9	3.71	26	15	119	97	15	36	148	7.3	30.1	1.12	.216
Minor League Totals				7	9	3.71	26	15	119	97	15	36	148	7.3	30.1	1.12	.216

21 GRAE KESSINGER, SS

HIT: 45. **POW:** 40. **RUN:** 50. **FLD:** 50. **ARM:** 55. **BA Grade:** 40. **Risk:** Medium.

Born: August 25, 1997. **B-T:** R-R. **HT:** 6-2. **WT:** 200. **Drafted:** Mississippi, 2019 (2nd round). **Signed by:** Travis Coleman.
TRACK RECORD: Kessinger spent three seasons at Mississippi, earning first-team all-Southeastern Conference as a junior. He was selected by the Astros in the second round of the 2019 draft and reached Low-A that year. After consecutive subpar seasons in 2021 and 2022 at Double-A Corpus Christi, Kessinger began 2023 with Triple-A Sugar Land. He hit .284/.400/.443 over 52 games with the Space Cowboys, splitting time between shortstop and third base. Kessinger was called up to the major leagues on June 7 and played in 26 games. Kessinger's grandfather is six-time all-star Don Kessinger.

SCOUTING REPORT: A polished infielder with average bat-to-ball skills and some sneaky pull side power, Kessinger shows the ability to make contact consistently and hit spin while rarely swinging and missing. He has solid on-base skills and rarely swings himself into outs. Kessinger's power is fringe-average and he lacks the bat speed to handle premium velocity. Power is not a major part of his game. Kessinger is an average runner who gets the most out of his range in the infield with decisive movements. His arm is above-average, allowing him to handle the demanding throws on the left side of the infield.

THE FUTURE: Kessinger is a utility infielder who can handle multiple positions and provide professional at-bats off the bench.

Year	Age	Club (League)	Level	AVG	G	AB	R	H	2B	3B	HR	RBI	BB	SO	SB	OBP	SLG
2023	25	Corpus Christi (TL)	AA	.286	2	7	0	2	0	0	0	3	1	4	0	.375	.286
2023	25	Sugar Land (PCL)	AAA	.283	54	184	37	52	10	0	6	32	35	45	2	.397	.435
2023	25	Houston (AL)	MLB	.200	26	40	3	8	2	0	1	1	5	12	0	.289	.325
Minor League Totals				.227	325	1120	185	254	42	2	33	139	161	279	46	.331	.356
Major League Totals				.200	26	40	3	8	2	0	1	1	5	12	0	.289	.325

22 SHAY WHITCOMB, SS

HIT: 30. POW: 55. RUN: 45. FLD: 45. ARM: 50. BA Grade: 40. Risk: High.

Born: September 28, 1998. **B-T:** R-R. **HT:** 6-1. **WT:** 202. **Drafted:** UC San Diego, 2020 (5th round). **Signed by:** Ryan Leake.

TRACK RECORD: Whitcomb rode momentum of a loud pre-draft summer in the Cape Cod League into his draft spring before the season was shut down due to the pandemic. The Astros selected Whitcomb in the fifth round and signed him for a below-slot $56,000. He debuted in Low-A Fayetteville in 2021 and hit .293/.363/.530 across Low-A and High-A. He broke camp with Double-A Corpus Christi in 2022 but struggled, hitting .219/.283/.399 over 118 games. Whitcomb returned to Double-A to begin 2023 and showed improved power and defensive skills. He hit .273/.340/.545 over 46 games with Corpus Christi before earning a promotion to Triple-A Sugar Land. Whitcomb finished with 35 home runs, tied for the minor league lead. Whitcomb was left unprotected for the Rule 5 draft and went unselected.

SCOUTING REPORT: After stumbling in 2022, Whitcomb refined several parts of his game heading into 2023. His well below-average contact improved to fringe-average as he showed more consistent control of the barrel. Whitcomb's approach is hyper-aggressive and leads to swing-and-miss driven by poor swing decisions. The contact Whitcomb does make comes with plenty of impact thanks to excellent exit velocity and launch angle numbers. Whitcomb is a fringe-average runner with solid baserunning instincts. After poor defense in the infield in 2022, Whitcomb made the jump to fringe-average at multiple spots in the infield. His once below-average arm has added strength as well.

THE FUTURE: Whitcomb is a difficult profile as a power-first utility infielder. If he can calm his approach, Whitcomb has the impact to push for second-division regular status.

Year	Age	Club (League)	Level	AVG	G	AB	R	H	2B	3B	HR	RBI	BB	SO	SB	OBP	SLG
2023	24	Corpus Christi (TL)	AA	.273	46	176	35	48	12	0	12	36	18	56	8	.340	.545
2023	24	Sugar Land (PCL)	AAA	.224	87	362	44	81	7	0	23	66	24	122	12	.281	.434
Minor League Totals				.248	350	1395	227	346	66	2	77	240	117	477	70	.313	.464

23 CAM FISHER, OF

HIT: 40. POW: 55. RUN: 40. FLD: 45. ARM: 50. BA Grade: 40. Risk: High.

Born: June 12, 2001. **B-T:** L-R. **HT:** 6-2. **WT:** 210. **Drafted:** Charlotte, 2023 (4th round). **Signed by:** Andrew Johnson.

TRACK RECORD: Fisher was well traveled by the time he reached Charlotte in 2022, having spent the 2021 season with Walters State (Tenn.) JC after a redshirt freshman season with Ole Miss in 2020. Fisher impressed across two seasons with the 49ers, earning second team freshman All-American honors in 2022 before making Conference USA first team all-conference in 2023. Fisher was one of three players in Division I with 30 or more home runs in 2023. The Astros selected Fisher in the fourth round, signing him for $497,000. He played one game in the Florida Complex League before making the jump to Low-A Fayetteville.

SCOUTING REPORT: Fisher's profile is driven by his plus raw power and his on-base ability, with legitimate questions around his bat-to-ball skills. His contact quality is impressive, but not always consistent. Fisher is prone to swinging and missing against velocity above 93 mph as well as quality breaking balls. He has mitigated some of his swing and miss with above-average swing decisions and ultimately shows above-average on-base skills. Fisher's power is plus and he has the knack to drive balls to his pull side. He likely will never get to all of his raw power due to his contact concerns. Fisher is a below-average runner and fringe-average fielder in the outfield corners, and his average arm plays in all three outfield spots.

THE FUTURE: As a three-true-outcome slugger with a corner outfielder's defensive profile, Fisher will need to hit to crack a lineup as a second-division regular.

Year	Age	Club (League)	Level	AVG	G	AB	R	H	2B	3B	HR	RBI	BB	SO	SB	OBP	SLG
2023	22	FCL Astros Blue	Rk	.000	1	3	0	0	0	0	0	0	0	1	0	.000	.000
2023	22	Fayetteville (CAR)	A	.273	31	110	16	30	6	2	5	15	22	44	5	.396	.500
Minor League Totals				.265	32	113	16	30	6	2	5	15	22	45	5	.387	.487

24 NEHOMAR OCHOA JR., OF

HIT: 45. POW: 55. RUN: 50. FLD: 50. ARM: 60. BA Grade: 45. Risk: Extreme.

Born: July 31, 2005. **B-T:** R-R. **HT:** 6-4. **WT:** 210. **Drafted:** HS—Galena Park, TX, 2023 (11th round).
Signed by: Brian Sheffler.
TRACK RECORD: Ochoa is the son of a former pitcher by the same name who played parts of three seasons in the Expos system in the early 2000s. A native of Venezuela, Ochoa emigrated to Texas when he was 10 years old. In his senior year, Ochoa hitt .602 with 11 home runs. He was selected by his hometown Astros in the 11th round and signed for a bonus of $300,000. Ochoa debuted in the Florida Complex League hitting three home runs over a dozen games.
SCOUTING REPORT: A physical teenager at 6-foot-4, 210 lbs, Ochoa has flashed the plate skills to consistently tap into his power. Ochoa shows good bat speed and a discerning eye at the plate but also ran into some difficulty against spin on the showcase circuit in 2022. He showed more refined barrel accuracy in the spring and post draft. With a strong approach and improving contact skills, Ochoa now gets to his plus raw power more consistently. At 18 years old, Ochoa's exit velocity data is already near major league average. He is an average runner who will likely move to an outfield corner, and his plus throwing arm that was up to 95 mph on the mound is an asset in the field.
THE FUTURE: A tooled-up power hitter who could climb up the rankings in the coming years, Ochoa has everyday regular upside with some hit tool risk.

Year	Age	Club (League)	Level	AVG	G	AB	R	H	2B	3B	HR	RBI	BB	SO	SB	OBP	SLG
2023	17	FCL Astros Blue	Rk	.222	12	36	10	8	2	0	3	9	3	7	1	.310	.528
Minor League Totals				.222	12	36	10	8	2	0	3	9	3	7	1	.310	.528

25 CAMILO DIAZ, SS

HIT: 30. POW: 55. RUN: 45. FLD: 45. ARM: 60. BA Grade: 45. Risk: Extreme.

Born: September 5, 2005. **B-T:** R-R. **HT:** 6-3. **WT:** 208. **Signed:** Dominican Republic, 2023. **Signed by:** Jose Torres.
TRACK RECORD: One of the Astros' top signings in the 2023 international free agency class, Diaz was lauded for the big impact in his bat and plus throwing arm. He debuted in the summer of 2023 in the Dominican Summer League and hit .209/.374/.353 with four home runs. He struggled to make consistent contact, best exemplified by his 32.8% strikeout rate in the DSL. Diaz has amateur pedigree and loud tools and should make his stateside debut in 2024.
SCOUTING REPORT: Diaz is an explosive young talent with huge bat speed and big swing-and-miss concerns. He was consistently fooled by spin during his professional debut and showed extreme swing and miss with a 40% whiff rate on the season. Diaz's approach—which borders on passive—allows him to mitigate some of his swing and miss. Diaz does have potentially plus raw impact, and his 105.3 mph 90th percentile exit velocity is exemplary. He shows the ability to drive the ball in the air to his pull side on his best contact, but he doesn't make enough contact to consistently tap into that power. Diaz is an average runner likely to slow down as he ages, and he's likely to be a fringe-average defender at third base long term with the plus arm for the position.
THE FUTURE: Diaz is an exciting young infielder with big power and big swing and miss concerns. He could develop into a power-hitting, bat-first infielder.

Year	Age	Club (League)	Level	AVG	G	AB	R	H	2B	3B	HR	RBI	BB	SO	SB	OBP	SLG
2023	17	DSL Astros Blue	Rk	.209	48	153	29	32	6	2	4	15	41	64	7	.374	.353
Minor League Totals				.209	48	153	29	32	6	2	4	15	41	64	7	.374	.353

26 COLIN BARBER, OF

HIT: 50. **POW:** 45. **RUN:** 45. **FLD:** 45. **ARM:** 50. **BA Grade:** 40. **Risk:** High.

Born: December 4, 2000. **B-T:** L-L. **HT:** 6-0. **WT:** 200. **Drafted:** HS—Chico, CA 2019 (4th round).
Signed by: Tim Costic.

TRACK RECORD: After two injury-plagued seasons coming out of the pandemic, Barber managed to stay off the injured list for all of 2023 and played in 79 games for Double-A Corpus Christi. Barber has dealt with shoulder injuries throughout his career and it's uncertain how much that may have affected him over the last few seasons. In 2023, Barber hit .244/.358/.433 while striking out in just 22.7% of at-bats and walking 14% of the time. Barber reached career highs in a variety of statistical categories in 2023 but was left unprotected for the Rule 5 draft.

SCOUTING REPORT: Injuries have likely limited Barber's production over the early part of his career, but he has shown advanced plate skills when healthy. Barber's hands-driven lefthanded swing helps him shoot plenty of line drives to his pull side and helps him have the barrel control to adjust to a variety of pitches. He's more aggressive than his walk rates let on, and also shows a good balance of aggression and patience. Even though Barber has improved his ability to hit the ball in the air to his pull side, his power production and underlying exit velocity data has not taken a corresponding jump. Barber is an average runner with fringe-average defense in a corner outfield spot. His throwing arm is average.

THE FUTURE: Barber is a solid all-around player with refined skills, but he lacks the impact or athleticism to be an everyday player.

Year	Age	Club (League)	Level	AVG	G	AB	R	H	2B	3B	HR	RBI	BB	SO	SB	OBP	SLG
2023	22	Corpus Christi (TL)	AA	.244	79	270	42	66	16	1	11	40	45	73	5	.358	.433
Minor League Totals				.263	189	639	106	168	32	3	23	86	103	182	15	.378	.430

27 FORREST WHITLEY, RHP

FB: 55. **CB:** 50. **SL:** 55. **CHG:** 45. **CTL:** 40. **BA Grade:** 45. **Risk:** Extreme.

Born: September 15, 1997. **B-T:** R-R. **HT:** 6-7. **WT:** 238. **Drafted:** HS—San Antonio, TX, 2016 (1st round).
Signed by: Noel Gonzales-Luna.

TRACK RECORD: At one point, Whitley ranked among the game's best prospects and was the best pitching prospect in the sport heading into the 2019 season. Since then, Whitley has dealt with a rash of injuries and been limited to just 129.2 innings in four years. Whitley dealt with lat and oblique issues in 2018, followed by shoulder fatigue in 2019 and then had Tommy John surgery in 2021. Whitley looked rejuvenated in spring training, showing mid-to-high-90s velocity and a mid-80s curveball, but after eight appearances Whitley was placed on the injured list with a lat strain and did not return for the remainder of the season.

SCOUTING REPORT: Whitley has transformed from physical prep prospect to elite pitching prospect to injury-riddled cautionary tale. When healthy, Whitley's four-pitch mix flashes power and movement. His four-seam fastball sits 95-96 mph and touches 97-98 at peak with four-seam and two-seam shapes. Whitley's upper-80s cutter and mid-80s two-plane curveball offer both power and movement. Of the two, the cutter is thrown the most frequently. Whitley throws a firm upper-80s changeup as well but struggles to command it. Strike-throwing has become a major thorn in Whitley's side over his last few injury-plagued seasons.

THE FUTURE: With premium stuff, a murky track record of health and a 40-man roster spot in jeopardy, Whitley will likely be moved to the bullpen. He could flourish as a reliever if he can throw enough strikes.

Year	Age	Club (League)	Level	W	L	ERA	G	GS	IP	H	HR	BB	SO	BB%	SO%	WHIP	AVG
2023	25	Sugar Land (PCL)	AAA	1	2	5.70	8	6	30	23	6	17	32	12.6	23.7	1.33	.205
Minor League Totals				10	19	5.09	78	64	267	230	26	139	366	11.9	31.3	1.38	.227

28 ALIMBER SANTA, RHP

FB: 55. **CB:** 50. **SL:** 50. **CHG:** 40. **CTL:** 30. **BA Grade:** 45. **Risk:** Extreme.

Born: May 3, 2003. **B-T:** R-R. **HT:** 5-10. **WT:** 163. **Drafted:** Dominican Republic, 2020. **Signed by:** Hassan Wessin.

TRACK RECORD: Santa signed late in the international free agent class of 2019-2020 and quickly transformed into one of the Astros' highest-upside pitching prospects. Santa made a big velocity jump in spring of 2022, peaking at 98 mph on the backfields. He was assigned to Low-A Fayetteville to begin 2022 but an elbow injury in his first appearance forced him to the injured list for the remainder of the season. Santa returned to Fayetteville in 2023, making 26 appearances for the Woodpeckers. He racked up 119 strikeouts but walked 74 over 87.1 innings.

SCOUTING REPORT: Santa's fastball sits 94-95 mph and touches 97-98 at peak with heavy bore. Despite several good characteristics, Santa does not miss many bats with the pitch. His primary secondaries are a slider with heavy cut in the mid-80s and a two-plane curveball in the 78-81 mph range. Each pitch gets whiffs both in and out of the zone. Santa also throws a mid-80s changeup, but it's rarely used. Santa's command is well below-average and strike-throwing is the biggest question mark in the profile.

THE FUTURE: Santa is likely a middle relief candidate if his command improves to fringe-average in the coming years.

Year	Age	Club (League)	Level	W	L	ERA	G	GS	IP	H	HR	BB	SO	BB%	SO%	WHIP	AVG
2023	20	Fayetteville (CAR)	A	3	9	5.98	26	14	87	86	5	74	119	17.9	28.8	1.83	.260
Minor League Totals				3	11	5.65	38	19	110	109	7	84	145	16.3	28.2	1.75	.260

29 JUSTIN DIRDEN, OF

HIT: 30. **POW:** 50. **RUN:** 55. **FLD:** 50. **ARM:** 55. **BA Grade:** 40. **Risk:** High.

Born: July 16, 1997. **B-T:** L-R. **HT:** 6-3. **WT:** 209. **Signed:** Southeast Missouri State, 2020 (NDFA).
Signed by: Jim Stevenson.

TRACK RECORD: Dirden spent five seasons in college before signing as an undrafted free agent following the five-round 2020 draft. Dirden turned heads in his first two professional seasons, hitting .274/.397/.537 in 2022 and .302/.384/.558 in 2023. Dirden returned to Triple-A Sugar Land to start 2023, hitting .276/.345/.489 with 24 extra-base hits over his 58 games until a hamstring injury sent him to the injured list on June 23. Dirden returned on July 16, but hit just .126/.243/.179 over 26 games before returning to the IL on Aug. 30. He was left unprotected for the 2023 Rule 5 draft and went unselected.

SCOUTING REPORT: In 2023, Dirden's contact skills were exposed by Triple-A pitching. It's difficult to know how much of the downturn was because of nagging injuries, but Dirden's contact skills went from fringe-average to well below-average. Dirden chased too often and was consistently fooled by spin. His average power stayed intact, as did his ability to backspin his best contact. When healthy, Dirden is an above-average runner with the ability to play an average outfield corner. His above-average arm plays in all three outfield positions.

THE FUTURE: Major questions around Dirden's ability to hit will likely limit him to a part-time role.

Year	Age	Club (League)	Level	AVG	G	AB	R	H	2B	3B	HR	RBI	BB	SO	SB	OBP	SLG
2023	25	Sugar Land (PCL)	AAA	.231	84	316	39	73	12	5	10	42	37	108	4	.314	.396
Minor League Totals				.274	291	1078	180	295	70	16	49	201	140	342	26	.368	.505

30 ALBERTO HERNANDEZ, SS

HIT: 50. **POW:** 45. **RUN:** 55. **FLD:** 50. **ARM:** 50. **BA Grade:** 45. **Risk:** Extreme.

Born: February 4, 2004. **B-T:** R-R. **HT:** 6-0. **WT:** 169. **Signed:** Cuba, 2022. **Signed by:** Charlie Gonzalez.

TRACK RECORD: Hernandez signed out of Cuba during the 2022 international signing period for $950,000 and was the 21st Cuban-born player in the Astros system, marking the first time one organization rostered more than 20 Cuban players since the 1960s. Hernandez debuted in the 2022 Dominican Summer League and hit .235/.332/.349 over 56 games. He made his stateside debut in 2023 and hit .257/.375/.414 across 40 Florida Complex League games.

SCOUTING REPORT: Despite just league-average production in 2023, Hernandez shows a good balance of plate skills and developing power. Hernandez had previously been a switch-hitter but dropped it, and now hits righthanded full-time. Hernandez shows average bat-to-ball skills and a discerning eye at the plate. With further refinement, he could develop into an above-average hitter. While Hernandez has not shown much over-the-fence power in games, his bat speed and exit velocity data point to untapped potential. Hernandez has above-average speed but has been a subpar baserunner overall. Hernandez is an average defender in the infield with an average arm and saw time at shortstop, second base and third base in 2023.

THE FUTURE: Hernandez is an exciting young infielder with polished plate skills and the ability to stick in the infield.

Year	Age	Club (League)	Level	AVG	G	AB	R	H	2B	3B	HR	RBI	BB	SO	SB	OBP	SLG
2023	19	FCL Astros Blue	Rk	.257	40	140	23	36	14	1	2	20	24	31	9	.375	.414
Minor League Totals				.245	96	306	46	75	20	3	5	42	44	58	18	.352	.379

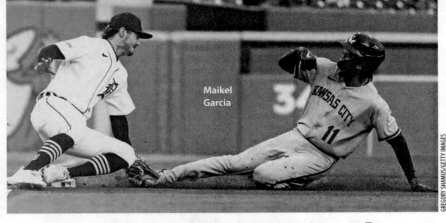

Maikel Garcia

GREGORY SHAMUS/GETTY IMAGES

Kansas City Royals

BY BILL MITCHELL

The Royals' rebuilding process is taking longer than expected, and in 2023 they posted their seventh consecutive losing season.

Kansas City finished 56-106, tied for the worst record in club history, though a 15-12 September provided a glimmer of hope entering the winter.

The 2023 campaign marked the first full year for general manager J.J. Picollo overseeing baseball operations since his promotion and also for manager Matt Quatraro, who came over from the Rays.

Royals domestic minor league affiliates combined for just a 284-318 record and no playoff appearances.

There were a few positive developments, none of which were better than the breakout season by Bobby Witt Jr. The 23-year-old star shortstop hit 30 home runs, stole 49 bases and led the American League with 11 triples.

The Royals' farm system supplemented the big league team with core contributors for the second straight season. Four of the team's top 10 prospects—outfielder Drew Waters, shortstop Maikel Garcia, infielder Nick Loftin and lefthander Angel Zerpa—saw significant playing time in Kansas City.

Improving pitching development at all levels of the organization was a primary goal in 2023. The Royals installed Brian Sweeney as major league pitching coach and turned to Zach Bove as his assistant.

Another success story arrived after the acquisition of 25-year-old lefthander Cole Ragans from the Rangers in the July trade of Aroldis Chapman. Ragans' fastball had already jumped 4 mph from the season before, but the Royals got him back to using his slider. The two-time Tommy John surgery alumnus posted a 2.64 ERA in his 12 starts in Kansas City, striking out 89 in 71.2 innings.

The pitching development in the minor leagues also paid dividends. Lefthander Anthony

PROJECTED 2027 LINEUP

Catcher	Blake Mitchell	22
First Base	Vinnie Pasquantino	29
Second Base	Michael Massey	29
Third Base	Cayden Wallace	25
Shortstop	Bobby Witt Jr.	27
Left Field	Nick Loftin	28
Center Field	Kyle Isbel	30
Right Field	Gavin Cross	26
Designated Hitter	MJ Melendez	28
No. 1 Starter	Cole Ragans	29
No. 2 Starter	Brady Singer	30
No. 3 Starter	Daniel Lynch	30
No. 4 Starter	Frank Mozzicato	24
No. 5 Starter	Anthony Veneziano	29
Closer	Carlos Hernandez	30

Veneziano and righthanders Mason Barnett and Chandler Champlain all moved into the organization's Top 10 prospects with strong seasons. Reliever John McMillon was healthy again in 2023, adding 4-5 mph of velocity as he went through three minor league levels before making his major league debut in August.

The Royals didn't bring any high-end prospect talent to the system at the deadline, but their first postseason deal netted rehabbing Braves righthander Kyle Wright, who is only a year removed from a 21-win season. Kansas City parted with scuffling righthander Jackson Kowar. It's an intriguing buy-low move.

The 2023 draft yielded three highly regarded high school players in the first three rounds. The Royals drafted Texas prep catcher Blake Mitchell No. 8 overall and then landed pitchers Blake Wolters and Hiro Wyatt in the next two rounds. While neither of the pitchers made a pro debut, Wolters impressed observers with a pair of impressive one-inning stints in the last week of instructional league games.

The Royals will add another premium prospect in the 2024 draft, though they're likely lamenting an unlucky drawing in the draft lottery. They entered tied with the best chance to land the No. 1 overall pick and instead fell to sixth. ∎

KANSAS CITY ROYALS

TOP 2024 CONTRIBUTORS	RANK
1. Nick Loftin, 3B/OF	3
2. John McMillon, RHP	16
3. Will Klein, RHP	17

BREAKOUT PROSPECTS	RANK
1. Austin Charles, SS	13
2. David Sandlin, RHP	19
3. Ramon Ramirez, C	21

SOURCE OF TOP 30 TALENT

Homegrown	28	Acquired	2
College	18	Trade	2
Junior college	0	Rule 5 draft	0
High school	7	Independent league	0
Nondrafted free agent	1	Free agent/waivers	0
International	2		

LF
Jared Dickey
Derlin Figueroa
River Town

CF
Gavin Cross (9)
Carson Roccaforte (14)
Spencer Nivens
Diego Hernandez
Milo Rushford
Eric Torres
Henry Ramos

RF
Tyler Gentry (12)
Tony Ruiz

3B
Nick Loftin (3)
Cayden Wallace (4)
Trevor Werner (30)
Devin Mann
Brennon McNair
Stone Russell

SS
Austin Charles (13)
Daniel Vazquez (20)
Tyler Tolbert
Justin Johnson
Dustin Dickerson

2B
Javier Vaz (15)
Peyton Wilson (25)
Samad Taylor
Lisandro Rodriguez

1B
Dillon Shrum

C
Blake Mitchell (1)
Carter Jensen (11)
Ramon Ramirez (21)
Luca Tresh
Hyungchan Um

LHP

LHSP	LHRP
Frank Mozzicato (2)	Asa Lacy
Anthony Veneziano (5)	Christian Chamberlain
Noah Cameron (22)	Cooper McKeehan
Tyson Guerrero (28)	Ben Wereski
Hunter Owen	
Hunter Patteson	
Luis Martinez	
Victor Pena	

RHP

RHSP	RHRP
Mason Barnett (5)	John McMillon (16)
Chandler Champlain (7)	Will Klein (17)
Blake Wolters (8)	Matt Sauer (23)
Ben Kudrna (10)	Eric Cerantola (29)
Jonathan Bowlan (18)	James McArthur
David Sandlin (19)	Anderson Paulino
Hiro Wyatt (24)	Steven Cruz
Steven Zobac (26)	Jacob Wallace
Henry Williams (27)	
Luinder Avila	
Beck Way	
Yunior Marte	
Shane Panzini	
Coleman Picard	
Mauricio Veliz	

1 BLAKE MITCHELL, C

Born: August 3, 2004. **B-T:** L-R. **HT:** 6-1. **WT:** 202.
Drafted: HS—Sinton, TX, 2023 (1st round).
Signed by: Josh Hallgren.

TRACY PROFFITT/FOUR SEAM IMAGES

TRACK RECORD: Mitchell was the top high school catcher in the 2023 draft, and the Royals drafted the Louisiana State commit with the eighth overall pick. They signed him for $4,897,500, which was 18% under slot. High school catchers are often considered to be a riskier profile, and Mitchell went a bit higher than projected, with his under-slot bonus giving the Royals the flexibility to go above slot for second-rounder Blake Wolters. Starring both behind the plate and on the mound, Mitchell had a heralded amateur career at Sinton (Texas) High. He earned Gatorade Texas Player of the Year honors in both his junior and senior years, leading his team to the Texas 4-A title as a junior. He drove in five runs at the 2022 Under Armour All-America Game at Kauffman Stadium, earning MVP honors, and starred for the USA Baseball's 18U National Team, for which he worked both at catcher and pitcher. After starting his pro career with 13 games in the Arizona Complex League, Mitchell participated in the Royals' fall instructional league program, where he showed more of an ease of operation at the plate and began tapping into his raw power. That power comes from a physically mature frame, with well-developed lower and upper halves providing an excellent foundation of strength.

SCOUTING REPORT: With a good eye at the plate and a lefthanded swing geared for bat speed and power to all fields, Mitchell projects to hit for both average and power as he becomes accustomed to pro pitching and consistently higher velocities. His plus bat speed and hand speed allow him to barrel fastballs with plenty of loft. He will swing and miss against all pitch types and needs to improve his bat-to-ball skills to consistently tap into his plus raw power. While Mitchell struggled to make contact in his pro debut, his discerning eye allowed him to draw walks at a high rate. His strong hands help him receive well behind the plate, but his transfer and release need improvement. The plus-plus arm strength that allowed Mitchell to show mid-90s velocity on the mound is his best attribute behind the plate. He recorded elite pop times on throws to second base in the range of 1.8 to 1.9 seconds in high school. He's a well below-average runner.

THE FUTURE: Mitchell showed enough advancement in instructional league that he should be ready for an assignment to Low-A Columbia in 2024 after spring training. His arm strength on the mound gives him another possible path to the big leagues, but that's not in the plans. A lefthanded-hitting catcher with plus raw power is a valuable commodity, and Mitchell will be given every opportunity to develop into an everyday regular. ■

BA GRADE	SCOUTING GRADES
55 Risk: Extreme	**Hit:** 45. **Power:** 55. **Run:** 30. **Field:** 55. **Arm:** 70.

Projected future grades on 20-80 scouting scale

BEST TOOLS

BATTING

Best Hitter for Average	Javier Vaz
Best Power Hitter	Gavin Cross
Best Strike-Zone Discipline	Carter Jensen
Fastest Baserunner	Tyler Tolbert
Best Athlete	Austin Charles

PITCHING

Best Fastball	Mason Barnett
Best Curveball	Eric Cerantola
Best Slider	John McMillon
Best Changeup	Ben Kudrna
Best Control	Steven Zobac

FIELDING

Best Defensive Catcher	Blake Mitchell
Best Defensive Infielder	Daniel Vazquez
Best Infield Arm	Trevor Werner
Best Defensive Outfielder	Carson Roccaforte
Best Outfield Arm	Henry Ramos

Year	Age	Club (League)	Level	AVG	G	AB	R	H	2B	3B	HR	RBI	BB	SO	SB	OBP	SLG
2023	18	ACL Royals	Rk	.147	13	34	8	5	1	0	0	3	17	14	1	.423	.176
Minor League Totals				.147	13	34	8	5	1	0	0	3	17	14	1	.423	.176

2 FRANK MOZZICATO, LHP

FB: 50. **CB:** 60. **CHG:** 45. **CTL:** 40. **BA Grade:** 50. **Risk:** High.

Born: June 10, 2003. **B-T:** L-L. **HT:** 6-3. **WT:** 190.
Drafted: HS—Manchester, CT, 2021 (1st round). **Signed by:** Casey Fahy.
TRACK RECORD: The Royals surprised the industry by drafting Mozzicato seventh overall in 2021, signing the Connecticut high school product for $3,547,500, or 35% under slot value. He raised his stock in his senior season by throwing four straight no-hitters. Mozzicato got off to a fast start at Low-A Columbia in 2023, showing better stuff and pitchability. Through his first nine starts, he posted a 2.14 ERA with 40% strikeouts and an improved walk rate of 13.5%. He then missed time after a collision with a teammate during batting practice and struggled to find his rhythm in July after a promotion to High-A Quad Cities.
SCOUTING REPORT: Mozzicato's fastball sat between 90-94 mph early in 2023 when he was pitching at 200 pounds, but difficulties keeping that weight on caused his heater to dip to 88-92. The pitch plays up due to deception and feel. Mozzicato has room to add strength and velocity, if he can avoid losing 15 pounds during the season as he did in 2023. That would improve the effectiveness of his plus curveball. Mozzicato's 78-81 mph breaking ball is a true power curve with 11-to-5 shape. It's a downer with good gloveside break and vertical movement. His key performance directive in 2023 was to use his changeup more often, and he was up to throwing it 10-12% of the time in 2023. It's a traditional circle-change with armside fade, delivered at 82-84 mph, with a chance to grade near average. Mozzicato's control is inconsistent, in part because of a long arm action, but his athleticism gives him a chance to improve.
THE FUTURE: Mozzicato enters his age-21 season in 2024 with a chance to pitch his way to Double-A if he dominates High-A hitters. Adding velocity and developing his third pitch will help him meet his projection of a No. 4 starter.

Year	Age	Club (League)	Level	W	L	ERA	G	GS	IP	H	HR	BB	SO	BB%	SO%	WHIP	AVG
2023	20	Columbia (CAR)	A	2	5	3.04	12	12	56	36	5	34	85	14.5	36.2	1.24	.180
2023	20	Quad Cities (MWL)	A+	0	4	7.12	9	9	37	34	7	33	45	18.5	25.3	1.83	.239
Minor League Totals				4	15	4.50	40	40	162	125	18	118	219	16.4	30.5	1.50	.211

3 NICK LOFTIN, 3B/2B

HIT: 50. **POW:** 45. **RUN:** 55. **FLD:** 55. **ARM:** 55. **BA Grade:** 45. **Risk:** Medium.

Born: September 25, 1998. **B-T:** R-R. **HT:** 6-1. **WT:** 180.
Drafted: Baylor, 2020 (1st round supplemental). **Signed by:** Josh Hallgren.
TRACK RECORD: One of the top college shortstops in the 2020 draft class, Loftin fell to the Royals at pick No. 32 and signed for $3 million. Since his first pro season in 2021, Loftin has played more third base, second base and center field than his natural position, preparing the Baylor product for being more of a super-utility player in the big leagues. At Triple-A Omaha in 2023, Loftin missed the month of June with a knee injury but returned in time to make his major league debut on Sept. 1. He got into 19 games and batted a respectable .323/.368/.436 while starting at second base, third base and first base.
SCOUTING REPORT: A good contact hitter who makes good decisions at the plate, Loftin improved his numbers by making swing modifications following a 2022 season in which he saw his strikeout rate spike to 24% at Triple-A. Loftin eliminated a toe tap and instead got into an easier operation with a leg kick and leg hang. He's a gap-to-gap hitter with a cerebral approach at the plate. Loftin's average hit tool is not necessarily a separator, but he has the ability to play above his tools. His athleticism and first-step quickness allow him to be at least an average defender at any position. He'll consistently record double-digit stolen base totals because of above-average speed and instincts on the bases. Loftin has a reputation as a winning player who can contribute to his team in a variety of ways, making him suited for the utility role that the Royals are carving out for him.
THE FUTURE: Loftin's versatility and makeup likely guarantee him a spot on the Opening Day roster, and he should spend all of 2024 in Kansas City.

Year	Age	Club (League)	Level	AVG	G	AB	R	H	2B	3B	HR	RBI	BB	SO	SB	OBP	SLG
2023	24	ACL Royals	Rk	.471	6	17	10	8	1	0	1	5	6	4	1	.615	.706
2023	24	Omaha (IL)	AAA	.270	82	315	41	85	13	0	14	56	34	47	6	.344	.444
2023	24	Kansas (AL)	MLB	.323	19	62	10	20	5	1	0	10	4	12	2	.368	.435
Minor League Totals				.272	306	1204	222	327	60	6	42	184	137	209	47	.353	.436
Major League Totals				.323	19	62	10	20	5	1	0	10	4	12	2	.368	.435

4 CAYDEN WALLACE, 3B

HIT: 50. **POW:** 50. **RUN:** 50. **FLD:** 55. **ARM:** 60. **BA Grade:** 50. **Risk:** High.

Born: August 7, 2001. **B-T:** R-R. **HT:** 6-1. **WT:** 205.
Drafted: Arkansas, 2022 (2nd round). **Signed by:** Matt Price.
TRACK RECORD: Wallace reached Double-A before the end of his second pro season after the Royals drafted him in the second round in 2022 following two seasons at Arkansas. He comes from an athletic family, with his father having been a college quarterback and his older brother Paxton a first baseman in the Royals organization in 2023. Wallace opened 2023 as the regular third baseman at High-A Quad Cities, where he hit a solid .261/.341/.431 before returning to his home state for 33 games following a promotion to Double-A Northwest Arkansas.
SCOUTING REPORT: Wallace goes to the plate with a simple, easy operation in terms of swing mechanics. He has a calm demeanor and consistently makes quality contact. Wallace's hands are set just outside his torso, with a quick trigger allowing him to see the ball longer and get the barrel to the ball. While he doesn't make consistent loud contact and is more of a gap hitter, Wallace has strength in his swing and could get to his above-average raw power with more experience. Wallace is a natural third baseman. He's an above-average, reliable defender with a plus arm featuring an unorthodox circular windmill throwing motion. His throws are accurate with good carry and he gets plenty of zip on throws even when he is off-balance. An average runner, Wallace is capable of double-digit stolen base totals thanks to his solid baserunning instincts.
THE FUTURE: Wallace most likely will return to Northwest Arkansas for more seasoning to open 2024, but he should make it to Triple-A during the season. Wallace projects as the regular third baseman the Royals have been seeking for much of the past decade, teaming with shortstop Bobby Witt Jr. to man the left side of the infield for the foreseeable future.

Year	Age	Club (League)	Level	AVG	G	AB	R	H	2B	3B	HR	RBI	BB	SO	SB	OBP	SLG
2023	21	Quad Cities (MWL)	A+	.261	97	376	56	98	22	6	10	64	42	94	15	.341	.431
2023	21	NW Arkansas (TL)	AA	.236	33	127	19	30	5	1	3	20	12	23	3	.300	.362
Minor League Totals				.262	160	619	93	162	35	10	15	101	69	140	26	.340	.423

5 ANTHONY VENEZIANO, LHP

FB: 55. **SL:** 55. **CHG:** 55. **CTL:** 55 **BA Grade:** 45. **Risk:** Medium.

Born: September 1, 1997. **B-T:** L-L. **HT:** 6-5. **WT:** 205.
Drafted: Coastal Carolina, 2019 (10th round). **Signed by:** Joe Barbera.
TRACK RECORD: Veneziano has had an up-and-down pro career since signing with Royals in 2019 as a 10th-round pick from Coastal Carolina. After a down year in 2022 in his first shot at Double-A, he returned to Northwest Arkansas and showed drastically better control. His walk rate dropped from 11.7% to 3%, while his strikeout rate ticked up from 22.8% to 28.4%. The improvement earned him a promotion to Triple-A Omaha before getting to the big leagues late in the season for two short relief appearances.
SCOUTING REPORT: The keys to Veneziano's improvement in 2023 were figuring out his body, gaining confidence and challenging hitters more effectively. His fastball has ticked down a few miles per hour in the last two years, but it's still an effective pitch when sitting 93-94 mph and touching 97. Against right-handers, he likes to use the pitch up and away. Veneziano's heater helps his above-average changeup play up. It's an out pitch for him at 86-88 mph, and he went to it more often in 2023. Veneziano throws his 85-86 mph sweeping slider for strikes, using it as a chase pitch. It's more of a contact pitch than something to use to put hitters away. Veneziano loses the zone at times when he lowers his arm slot, causing him to miss up and away to his arm side, but he usually has a clean delivery from a three-quarters slot.
THE FUTURE: Veneziano can be a solid back-of-the-rotation starter or could thrive as a multi-inning power lefty in the bullpen. Now that he's on the 40-man roster and has gotten a taste of the big leagues, he'll head to spring training with a chance to earn a spot on the Royals' Opening Day pitching staff if he continues throwing consistent strikes.

Year	Age	Club (League)	Level	W	L	ERA	G	GS	IP	H	HR	BB	SO	BB%	SO%	WHIP	AVG
2023	25	NW Arkansas (TL)	AA	5	1	2.13	8	8	42	37	5	5	48	3.0	28.4	0.99	.236
2023	25	Omaha (IL)	AAA	5	4	4.22	18	17	90	83	9	43	79	11.2	20.6	1.41	.249
2023	25	Kansas City (AL)	MLB	0	0	0.00	2	0	2	2	0	2	1	16.7	8.3	1.71	.200
Minor League Totals				25	22	4.51	87	83	395	394	55	164	427	9.5	24.7	1.41	.259
Major League Totals				0	0	0.00	2	0	2	2	0	2	1	16.7	8.3	1.71	.200

6 MASON BARNETT, RHP

FB: 55. **CB:** 55. **SL:** 50. **CHG:** 55. **CTL:** 55. **BA Grade:** 45. **Risk:** High.

Born: November 7, 2000. **B-T:** R-R. **HT:** 6-0. **WT:** 218.
Drafted: Auburn, 2022 (3rd round). **Signed by:** Will Howard.
TRACK RECORD: Barnett took a big step forward in his first full season after the Royals drafted him out of Auburn in the third round in 2022. He turned in a strong season split between High-A Quad Cities and Double-A Northwest Arkansas in 2023, winning the organization's Paul Splittorff pitcher of the year award. Barnett's fastball also was credited as the best in the system. He showed no signs of struggling to adjust to Double-A after an early-August promotion and finished the year with a combined 3.30 ERA and 28.8% strikeout rate and 10.5% walk rate.
SCOUTING REPORT: Barnett has a solid four-pitch mix, highlighted by his fastball and changeup. Both pitches flash as plus offerings, and he's an effective strike-thrower. Barnett's 94-98 mph fastball has good weight to it, and he has good feel for his 86-87 mph changeup that is effective against lefthanded batters. A key performance goal for Barnett is to get more separation between his two breaking pitches, a curveball at 80-83 mph with 12-to-6 break and an above-average slider at 86-87 mph. When they run together, he loses confidence in the pitches. He uses all four of his pitches in good pitcher's counts, and he cut his walk rates during the season when he started attacking hitters more aggressively. Barnett effectively repeats his three-quarters arm slot. His arm stroke gets long and off line on the back end, but he gets out of it in the finish.
THE FUTURE: With improvement to his four-pitch mix and an ability to go deeper in his starts, Barnett projects as a No. 4 or 5 starter. His fastball and changeup combo also would allow him to thrive in a multi-inning relief role.

Year	Age	Club (League)	Level	W	L	ERA	G	GS	IP	H	HR	BB	SO	BB%	SO%	WHIP	AVG
2023	22	Quad Cities (MWL)	A+	4	6	3.18	16	16	82	59	3	38	94	11.2	27.7	1.18	.203
2023	22	NW Arkansas (TL)	AA	2	1	3.58	7	7	33	27	2	12	43	8.8	31.4	1.19	.218
Minor League Totals				7	7	3.10	27	24	123	86	5	51	149	10.2	29.8	1.12	.197

7 CHANDLER CHAMPLAIN, RHP

FB: 55. **CB:** 50. **SL:** 50. **CHG:** 45. **CTL:** 55. **BA Grade:** 45. **Risk:** High.

Born: July 23, 1999. **B-T:** R-R. **HT:** 6-5. **WT:** 240.
Drafted: Southern California, 2021 (9th round). **Signed by:** David Keith (Yankees).
TRACK RECORD: A well-regarded pitching prospect in high school in Rancho Santa Margarita, Calif., Champlain went to nearby Southern California for a disappointing three-year college career. The Yankees drafted the beefy 6-foot-5 righthander in the ninth round in 2021 and began working with him to improve his pitch selection. Champlain got into just 16 Low-A games before being bundled with two other pitchers to the Royals at the 2022 trade deadline for Andrew Benintendi. Champlain ran up a 9.84 ERA in 32 innings at High-A Quad Cities in 2022 but took big steps forward in 2023, with strong performances at both High-A and Double-A Northwest Arkansas.
SCOUTING REPORT: Champlain was given two goals to meet in 2023—improving command of his fastball and using his breaking balls more—and he was successful on both counts. Champlain delivers his fastball at 94-98 mph with good life to both sides of the plate. Both of his breaking pitches project as above-average. His 83-86 mph slider shows more sweep than a true gyro, and his 77-81 mph curveball that he throws for strikes is hard and tight with good shape. Champlain is aggressive on the mound and not afraid to throw his breaking balls when behind in the count. His changeup, which he generally used five or six times per game, is still very much a work in progress. It's a harder pitch at 87-88 mph that resembles a splitter with more vertical drop. It should be an average offering in time. Champlain's energetic delivery lends deception, and his arm works well.
THE FUTURE: Now that he's using his changeup more often, Champlain more safely profiles as a potential back-of-the-rotation starter or possible high-leverage bullpen arm.

Year	Age	Club (League)	Level	W	L	ERA	G	GS	IP	H	HR	BB	SO	BB%	SO%	WHIP	AVG
2023	23	Quad Cities (MWL)	A+	6	3	2.74	11	11	62	48	5	18	61	7.3	24.7	1.06	.214
2023	23	NW Arkansas (TL)	AA	5	5	3.82	14	14	73	64	11	25	64	8.3	21.2	1.22	.234
Minor League Totals				14	16	4.50	49	47	241	242	30	73	241	7.2	23.8	1.31	.262

8 BLAKE WOLTERS, RHP

FB: 60. **SL:** 55. **CHG:** 50. **CTL:** 50. **BA Grade:** 50. **Risk:** Extreme.

Born: October 25, 2004. **B-T:** R-R. **HT:** 6-4. **WT:** 215.
Drafted: HS—Mahomet, IL, 2023 (2nd round). **Signed by:** Scott Melvin.
TRACK RECORD: Wolters didn't participate in many of the big high school showcases, but the Arizona commit certainly popped onto the radar when his fastball velocity jumped significantly just prior to his senior year. The Royals grabbed the Illinois prep product in the second round in 2023 and went over slot to sign him for $2.8 million. The PBR Super 60 Showcase in February, when he broke the event's velocity record with a 97.7 mph fastball, helped put him on the map. With plenty of downtime leading up to the draft, Wolters did not pitch in an official game in 2023 but was very impressive in a pair of one-inning starts late in the fall instructional league.
SCOUTING REPORT: With a strong frame that has been described as the perfect build for a pitcher, Wolters' fastball touches 98 mph with power ride and some bore. It sits in the mid 90s and is delivered with a fast arm from a three-quarters arm slot and a proper finish out in front. He could add velocity with more strength to his frame and better use of his lower half. Wolters pairs his heater with a wipeout 82-84 mph slider that flashes as a plus offering with hard break and 2,700 rpm spin. He lands it to both sides of the plate and can add more sweep when looking for a strikeout. He didn't show a changeup in his brief outings. He used the pitch infrequently in high school, but it projects as an average offering around 80 mph. He repeats his delivery well.
THE FUTURE: Wolters will likely follow the same development path that the Royals have used with previous high school pitchers, staying behind in extended spring training for a month or so in 2024 before heading to Low-A Columbia. Projecting as high as a No. 3 starter, Wolters already has shown enough potential that with more experience he could rocket up the Royals' prospect list.

Year	Age	Club (League)	Level	W	L	ERA	G	GS	IP	H	HR	BB	SO	BB%	SO%	WHIP	AVG
2023	18	Did not play															

9 GAVIN CROSS, OF

HIT: 40. **POW:** 55. **RUN:** 45. **FLD:** 50. **ARM:** 55. **BA Grade:** 45. **Risk:** High.

Born: February 13, 2001. **B-T:** L-L. **HT:** 6-3. **WT:** 210.
Drafted: Virginia Tech, 2022 (1st round). **Signed by:** Tim Bittner.
TRACK RECORD: Looking for a natural hitter who could man the outfield, the Royals drafted Cross ninth overall in 2022 and signed the Virginia Tech product for slot value of $5,200,400. He ranked as the Royals' No. 1 prospect after his first pro season, in which he hit .293/.423/.596 in 26 games at Low-A Columbia before struggling mightily in 94 games at High-A Quad Cities in 2023. Cross hit just .206 as his strikeout rate spiked to near 28%. His season ended after just two games at Double-A Northwest Arkansas due to an illness. Cross reappeared in instructional league, followed by eight games in the Arizona Fall League, where he was slowed by a hamstring issue.
SCOUTING REPORT: Cross is known for his command of the strike zone and above-average power to all fields. The most notable difference from Low-A to High-A was diminished plate discipline as he tried to do too much and was swinging for the fences. Cross' swing and approach looked much better in instructional league, where he worked on keeping his weight more between his hips and not getting too overloaded into his rear hip. That helped his swing work more forward. Cross reads balls well in the outfield and should be able to stay in center field, but he may fit better in right field, where his above-average arm will play. Cross is aggressive on the bases, with his instincts making up for his fringe-average speed. He was successful on 23 of 26 stolen base attempts in 2023. The son of a coach, Cross is a quick learner and makes adjustments well.
THE FUTURE: Cross will return to Double-A in 2024, with a chance to prove that the swing changes he made in instructional league will get him back on track. He projects as an everyday outfielder, and his ability to handle lefthanded pitchers will keep him out of a platoon role.

Year	Age	Club (League)	Level	AVG	G	AB	R	H	2B	3B	HR	RBI	BB	SO	SB	OBP	SLG
2023	22	Quad Cities (MWL)	A+	.206	94	355	49	73	21	3	12	58	42	113	23	.300	.383
2023	22	NW Arkansas (TL)	AA	.000	2	5	0	0	0	0	0	0	1	2	0	.167	.000
Minor League Totals				.228	125	469	73	107	28	5	20	83	67	148	27	.332	.437

10 BEN KUDRNA, RHP

FB: 45. **SL:** 55. **CHG:** 55. **CTL:** 50. **BA Grade:** 45 **Risk:** High.

Born: January 30, 2003. **B-T:** R-R. **HT:** 6-3. **WT:** 215.
Drafted: HS—Overland Park, KS, 2021 (2nd round). **Signed by:** Matt Price.
TRACK RECORD: Kudrna stayed close to home by signing with the Royals after being drafted in the second round in 2021, with the Overland Park native passing on a commitment to Louisiana State. He signed for $3 million, more than $1.25 million above slot, and inked the largest bonus of the second round that year. After making his pro debut in 2022 at Low-A Columbia, Kudrna returned to that team for another 14 outings in 2023 before finishing his season with eight starts for High-A Quad Cities. He improved his strikeout rate from the previous season at Columbia, jumping from 19.6% to 24.1%.
SCOUTING REPORT: Kudrna has added strength to a solid 6-foot-3 frame since joining the Royals organization, but he already has a mature body, raising questions about how much more projection remains. He attacks hitters with a fastball that sits between 92-94 mph and touches 97, but with limited deception. Kudrna can unlock more velocity by using his body better, which he's going to need to do in order to allow his other pitches to play up. He relies heavily on his sharp 82-84 mph gyro slider with late bite and depth that he can throw for strikes. Kudrna's best secondary pitch is a changeup with sink that flashes plus and is delivered at 83-84 mph. His change is effective against both righthanded and lefthanded hitters, but the effort in his delivery from a three-quarters arm slot affects the consistency of the pitch.
THE FUTURE: With the projection of a No. 4 or 5 type starter, Kudrna will return to High-A Quad Cities for more seasoning. His next big test will be a jump to Double-A during the 2024 season, with hopefully a little more zip on his fastball to generate swings and misses across his arsenal.

Year	Age	Club (League)	Level	W	L	ERA	G	GS	IP	H	HR	BB	SO	BB%	SO%	WHIP	AVG
2023	20	Columbia (CAR)	A	4	3	3.56	14	13	68	67	7	30	70	10.3	24.1	1.42	.257
2023	20	Quad Cities (MWL)	A+	1	4	5.36	8	8	40	52	7	15	34	8.5	19.2	1.66	.325
Minor League Totals				7	12	3.93	39	38	181	185	18	77	165	9.9	21.2	1.45	.265

11 CARTER JENSEN, C

Hit: 45. **POW:** 60. **RUN:** 40. **FLD:** 50. **ARM:** 55. **BA Grade:** 45. **Risk:** High.

Born: July 3, 2003. **B-T:** L-R. **HT:** 6-1. **WT:** 215. **Drafted:** HS—Kansas City, MO, 2021 (3rd round). **Signed by:** Matt Price.
TRACK RECORD: Jensen and fellow Kansas City high school product Ben Kudrna were set to attend Louisiana State before both were drafted in 2021 by the hometown Royals, with Jensen signing an over-slot $1,097,500 bonus in the third round. The lefthanded-hitting catcher was still just 19 years old for most of the 2023 season and spent his third pro season at High-A Quad Cities. Jensen hit .211/.356/.363 with a .150 isolated slugging in 116 games, nearly mirroring his production the year prior in Low-A. He hit better as the temperatures warmed and hit his stride in July and August.
SCOUTING REPORT: Jensen has feel for the barrel, quick hands and a compact swing. He gets out in front early on pitches at times, resulting in pull-side foul balls. He will get to his plus raw power when he hits to the middle of the field. Jensen is a contact hitter with a good eye, but he still gets passive at times instead of hunting pitches he can drive. While he's been young for every level so far, Jensen has the tools to develop into a 20-homer hitter with high on-base percentages. He's a stronger hitter against righthanded pitchers but handles southpaws well enough to not require a strict platoon. Jensen is still relatively new to catching. He improved in 2023, showing less stiffness and better mobility behind the plate. Jensen has an above-average arm and threw out 24% of basestealers.
THE FUTURE: Despite his age, Jensen should be ready for the upper levels in 2024 and projects as an everyday catcher.

Year	Age	Club (League)	Level	AVG	G	AB	R	H	2B	3B	HR	RBI	BB	SO	SB	OBP	SLG
2023	19	Quad Cities (MWL)	A+	.211	116	399	61	84	20	4	11	45	92	120	11	.356	.363
Minor League Totals				.223	248	849	136	189	46	7	23	102	185	243	23	.361	.375

12 TYLER GENTRY, OF

Hit: 50. **POW:** 50. **RUN:** 50. **FLD:** 50. **ARM:** 55. **BA Grade:** 45. **Risk:** High.

Born: February 1, 1999. **B-T:** R-R. **HT:** 6-2. **WT:** 210. **Drafted:** Alabama, 2020 (3rd round). **Signed by:** Travis Ezi
TRACK RECORD: The Royals drafted Gentry in the third round in 2020 after a collegiate career split between Tennessee junior college powerhouse Walters State followed by two seasons at Alabama. He hit .253/.370/.421 with 16 homers in 129 games in a full season with Triple-A Omaha in 2023. His strong

performance further validated his 2022 breakout season, which came after an abbreviated debut in 2021 that was slowed by a knee injury. Gentry really broke out in the second half of 2023 after a slow start. He hit .282/.416/.485 in his final 60 games while increasing his walk rate and cutting his strikeouts.

SCOUTING REPORT: Gentry's improvement was sparked by finding more consistency with his toe tap and making better swing decisions at the plate. He has above-average power from the right side with a low-maintenance swing that helps him stay consistent. He continued to show improved plate discipline, increasing his walk rate to 14.2% from 12.4%, though some of that could be entangled with the automated ball-strike system at Triple-A. With an above-average arm, Gentry should be able to stay in right field. He's aggressive chasing after balls hit to the outfield and is at least an average defender. An average runner who will likely slow down as he matures, Gentry stole 14 bases and has sound instincts on the bases.

THE FUTURE: Gentry was added to the 40-man roster after the 2023 season. With a successful run at Triple-A under his belt, he'll head to spring training with a chance to make the big league roster as an extra outfielder or in a platoon role.

Year	Age	Club (League)	Level	AVG	G	AB	R	H	2B	3B	HR	RBI	BB	SO	SB	OBP	SLG
2023	24	Omaha (IL)	AAA	.253	129	475	69	120	28	2	16	71	81	127	14	.370	.421
Minor League Totals				.282	281	1024	177	289	60	3	43	185	170	287	28	.394	.473

13 AUSTIN CHARLES, SS

Hit: 45. **POW:** 60. **RUN:** 50. **FLD:** 55. **ARM:** 60. **BA Grade:** 50. **Risk:** Extreme.

Born: November 13, 2003. **B-T:** R-R. **HT:** 6-6. **WT:** 215. **Drafted:** HS—Bakersfield, CA, 2022 (20th round). **Signed by:** Todd Guggiana.

TRACK RECORD: Charles was one of the top two-way players in the 2022 draft but had to wait until the final round to hear his name called. He was expected to fulfill his commitment to UC Santa Barbara, but the Royals inked him to an over-slot $429,500 bonus right before the signing deadline after bringing him to their Arizona complex for a visit. Charles briefly debuted in the Rookie-level Arizona Complex League in 2022 and spent the bulk of 2023 with Low-A Columbia, where he impressed observers with his size, athleticism and makeup.

SCOUTING REPORT: The report on Charles' hitting ability always starts with his 6-foot-6 height and long levers. He still presents swing-and-miss issues, especially against breaking balls out of the zone, but Charles has plus raw power and has worked hard to develop his game. He gets leverage from his long arms and has gotten stronger since joining the organization, while showing the ability to hit velocity. Evaluators are impressed by his ability to handle shortstop despite his size. His soft hands, limber movements, instincts, internal clock, extreme athleticism and plus arm provide the framework for an above-average defender on the left side of the infield.

THE FUTURE: There's a lot to dream on with Charles, who is one of the most intriguing prospects in the Royals' system. He likely will return to Low-A for more seasoning to open the 2024 season but could push himself to High-A Quad Cities with a strong showing.

Year	Age	Club (League)	Level	AVG	G	AB	R	H	2B	3B	HR	RBI	BB	SO	SB	OBP	SLG
2023	19	ACL Royals	Rk	.455	2	11	5	5	1	1	1	3	0	3	0	.455	1.000
2023	19	Columbia (CAR)	A	.230	69	261	29	60	18	3	3	31	22	73	12	.290	.356
Minor League Totals				.240	74	283	35	68	19	4	4	34	22	80	12	.295	.378

14 CARSON ROCCAFORTE, OF

Hit: 55. **POW:** 45. **RUN:** 55. **FLD:** 55. **ARM:** 50. **BA Grade:** 45. **Risk:** High.

Born: March 9, 2002. **B-T:** L-L. **HT:** 6-1. **WT:** 195. **Drafted:** Louisiana-Lafayette, 2023 (2nd round supplemental). **Signed by:** Cody Clark.

TRACK RECORD: Roccaforte was a productive hitter and outfielder for three college seasons at Louisiana-Lafayette, hitting .325 for his career and setting the school record for doubles in a season with 26 in 2023. That total tied him for fourth in all of Division I. He became the highest Ragin' Cajun drafted since 1995 when the Royals selected him with a supplemental second-round pick in 2023 and signed him to an $897,500 bonus. Roccaforte started his pro career in the Rookie-level Arizona Complex League and went 4-for-4 with four stolen bases in his first game. He finished his season with 27 games at Low-A Columbia, where he hit .257/.377/.356 with 11 stolen bases.

SCOUTING REPORT: A high in-zone contact hitter with good bat-to-ball skills, Roccaforte starts his swing in a traditional position with a small leg kick. While he hit a combined 28 home runs in his college career, he shows more gap-to-gap power now and could add more juice as he gains experience. In his first pro season, he worked on staying through the middle of the field to keep his bat path in line with the pitch as long as possible. Roccaforte is at least an above-average defender with an average arm who is capable of playing all three outfield positions. He was 16-for-19 in stolen base attempts in his pro debut and should have multiple seasons with 20 or more steals in his career.

THE FUTURE: Roccaforte has a chance to break camp with High-A Quad Cities in 2024 after an impressive debut. He projects as a fourth outfielder with a bit more upside because of his makeup.

Year	Age	Club (League)	Level	AVG	G	AB	R	H	2B	3B	HR	RBI	BB	SO	SB	OBP	SLG
2023	21	ACL Royals	Rk	.533	4	15	3	8	1	0	0	3	0	3	5	.500	.600
2023	21	Columbia (CAR)	A	.257	27	101	19	26	6	2	0	12	19	31	11	.377	.356
Minor League Totals				.293	31	116	22	34	7	2	0	15	19	34	16	.391	.388

15 JAVIER VAZ, 2B/OF

Hit: 60. **POW:** 30. **RUN:** 60. **FLD:** 45. **ARM:** 40. **BA Grade:** 45. **Risk:** High.

Born: September 22, 2000. **B-T:** L-R. **HT:** 5-9. **WT:** 151. **Drafted:** Vanderbilt, 2022 (15th round). **Signed by:** Will Howard.
TRACK RECORD: Vaz began his career at Louisiana State-Eunice JC before transferring to Vanderbilt, where he didn't earn regular playing time until his second season with the Commodores. The Royals signed him to a $125,000 bonus in the 15th round of the 2022 draft, and he quickly turned into one of the best pure hitters in their system. The son of Roberto Vaz, a former minor leaguer and current hitting coach in the Cubs system, Javier hit .279 and walked 64 times compared to 50 strikeouts across two levels in 2023 and ended the year with Double-A Northwest Arkansas.
SCOUTING REPORT: Vaz has advanced bat-to-ball skills and defensive versatility. His setup and swing mechanics are efficient, he makes elite swing decisions and consistently finds the barrel. He uses small ball to his advantage, and his 3.3% swinging-strike rate was the third-lowest rate among minor leaguers with at least 400 plate appearances. He has well below-average power but can drive balls to the gaps, and he turned on enough pitches to hit a career-high eight homers in 2023. A plus runner, Vaz is an efficient basestealer who swiped 30 bags on 33 attempts in 2023. A fringe-average defender with a below-average arm, Vaz adds value by playing multiple positions both in the middle infield and outfield.
THE FUTURE: A gamer and fierce competitor, Vaz's advanced contact ability, speed and defensive versatility make him an intriguing prospect in a super utility role. He should reach Triple-A Omaha in 2024, and a late-season callup to Kansas City is not out of the question.

Year	Age	Club (League)	Level	AVG	G	AB	R	H	2B	3B	HR	RBI	BB	SO	SB	OBP	SLG
2023	22	Quad Cities (MWL)	A+	.270	86	333	49	90	14	4	6	39	49	32	26	.367	.390
2023	22	NW Arkansas (TL)	AA	.304	33	112	17	34	4	2	2	12	15	18	4	.391	.429
Minor League Totals				.275	148	553	82	152	25	7	9	63	85	67	35	.376	.394

16 JOHN McMILLON, RHP

FB: 70. **SL:** 60. **CHG:** 40. **CTL:** 45. **BA Grade:** 45. **Risk:** High.

Born: January 27, 1998. **B-T:** R-R. **HT:** 6-3. **WT:** 230. **Signed:** Texas Tech, 2020 (NDFA). **Signed by:** Chad Lee.
TRACK RECORD: McMillon was drafted twice, once out of high school and again after his junior year at Texas Tech. But ultimately he pitched four years in college and signed with the Royals as a nondrafted free agent after the five-round 2020 draft. McMillon started 2023 in Low-A and pitched at two other minor league levels. He struck out 91 batters in 51.1 innings, registering a 45.3% strikeout rate that led all minor league relievers with at least 50 innings. The Royals called him up in August. He made four appearances before a right forearm strain cut his season short.
SCOUTING REPORT: After missing time in his first two pro seasons, McMillon returned with more confidence in his fastball in 2023 and watched his average velocity climb nearly 5 mph compared to 2022. He generally trusted his stuff more, and for good reason. McMillon has an explosive, double-plus 96-100 mph fastball that generates very high whiff rates and is complemented by a plus upper-80s gyro slider that's hard and short. He occasionally dabbles with a mid-to-upper-80s changeup in side sessions, but it's not part of his regular repertoire. McMillon's control is fringe-average at best, but his 12.4% walk rate in 2023 represents progress. He made improvements to his mechanics and repeated his delivery better.
THE FUTURE: McMillon has high-leverage reliever upside on the strength of his ferocious two-pitch arsenal and could even be in the running for the Royals' vacant closer job in 2024.

Year	Age	Club (League)	Level	W	L	ERA	G	GS	IP	H	HR	BB	SO	BB%	SO%	WHIP	AVG
2023	25	Columbia (CAR)	A	1	0	3.38	9	0	11	4	0	6	21	14.0	48.8	0.94	.108
2023	25	Quad Cities (MWL)	A+	3	1	2.70	13	0	20	8	1	8	40	10.4	51.9	0.80	.119
2023	25	NW Arkansas (TL)	AA	3	2	0.87	15	0	21	12	0	11	30	13.6	37.0	1.11	.171
2023	25	Kansas City (AL)	MLB	0	0	2.25	4	0	4	1	1	0	8	0.0	61.5	0.25	.077
Minor League Totals				8	6	4.27	76	1	99	57	7	76	168	17.7	39.2	1.34	.166
Major League Totals				0	0	2.25	4	0	4	1	1	0	8	0.0	61.5	0.25	.077

17 WILL KLEIN, RHP

FB: 70. **CB:** 55. **SL:** 60 **CHG:** 40. **CTL:** 45. **BA Grade:** 45. **Risk:** High.

Born: November 28, 1999. **B-T:** R-R. **HT:** 6-5. **WT:** 235. **Drafted:** Eastern Illinois, 2000 (5th round).
Signed by: Scott Melvin.
TRACK RECORD: Klein was the last of the Royals' six picks in the five-round 2020 draft, and he might have already reached the big leagues if not for a shin injury that ruined his 2022 season. The Eastern Illinois product came back healthy in 2023 and split the season between Double-A Northwest Arkansas and Triple-A Omaha. He shares a similar profile as fellow Royals prospect reliever John McMillon by racking up plenty of strikeouts to go along with a high walk rate.
SCOUTING REPORT: Hitters do not get comfortable at-bats against Klein. He attacks with a double-plus fastball that sits 95-97 mph and touches 100 while playing up in the zone with vertical movement. His above-average 12-to-6 curveball is a hard downer at 82-84 mph that complements his fastball thanks to its hard drop, but he needs to land it more often for strikes down in the zone. Klein resumed throwing a high-80s slider/cutter that is now a plus pitch and a second swing-and-miss offering. Klein varies the usage of the two breaking balls depending on the game, but they are both wipeout offerings. His fourth pitch is a split-grip changeup that he doesn't need much as a reliever. He lacks athleticism, and the stiffness of the body affects his ability to repeat his delivery, thus negatively impacting his control.
THE FUTURE: The Royals added Klein to the 40-man roster, and he has a good chance to earn a bullpen spot out of spring training in 2024. He can work himself into high-leverage situations if he continues to reduce his walk rate.

Year	Age	Club (League)	Level	W	L	ERA	G	GS	IP	H	HR	BB	SO	BB%	SO%	WHIP	AVG
2023	23	NW Arkansas (TL)	AA	0	2	3.38	21	0	29	28	1	14	44	10.7	33.6	1.43	.250
2023	23	Omaha (IL)	AAA	1	3	5.66	28	1	35	40	3	25	49	14.4	28.2	1.86	.276
Minor League Totals				9	7	5.51	115	4	178	166	14	134	269	16.1	32.3	1.69	.244

18 JONATHAN BOWLAN, RHP

FB: 50. **CB:** 40. **SL:** 55. **CHG:** 50. **CTL:** 50. **BA Grade:** 45. **Risk:** High.

Born: December 1, 1996. **B-T:** R-R. **HT:** 6-6. **WT:** 240. **Drafted:** Memphis, 2018 (2nd round). **Signed by:** Travis Ezi.
TRACK RECORD: The Royals drafted Bowlan in the second round in 2018 and he was tracking toward a big league debut in 2021 until an elbow injury required Tommy John surgery that summer. He returned just over a year later, but has been more hittable and also dealt with shoulder and groin issues. Bowlan split his 2023 season between Double-A Northwest Arkansas and Triple-A Omaha before making his big league debut in late September, pitching in a pair of games during the last week of the season.
SCOUTING REPORT: The velocity on Bowlan's mid-90s four-seam fastball returned in 2023. His gyro slider averaged 85-86 mph with good movement and was his best swing-and-miss secondary. Bowlan also throws an upper-80s changeup that has some action but is too firm. He added a low-80s curveball with downward break prior to his surgery, but he needs to rebuild his trust in the pitch. Bowlan was a good strike-thrower early in his career, but his walk rate has nearly doubled upon reaching the upper minors after surgery. There's optimism his control can recover as more time elapses following surgery.
THE FUTURE: The Royals hope Bowlan fully returns to form as he learns to trust his stuff again after the injury. He could factor into the back of the Royals' rotation at some point in 2024.

Year	Age	Club (League)	Level	W	L	ERA	G	GS	IP	H	HR	BB	SO	BB%	SO%	WHIP	AVG
2023	26	NW Arkansas (TL)	AA	1	5	7.20	10	9	35	44	7	13	47	7.9	28.7	1.63	.301
2023	26	Omaha (IL)	AAA	6	6	5.24	14	12	67	72	12	32	58	10.8	19.6	1.55	.275
2023	26	Kansas City (AL)	MLB	0	1	3.00	2	1	3	5	1	0	3	0.0	21.4	1.67	.357
Minor League Totals				22	24	4.70	80	74	362	387	42	102	365	6.6	23.5	1.35	.273
Major League Totals				0	1	3.00	2	1	3	5	1	0	3	0.0	21.4	1.67	.357

19 DAVID SANDLIN, RHP

FB: 55. **CB:** 50. **SL:** 55. **CHG:** 50. **CTL:** 50. **BA Grade:** 45. **Risk:** High.

Born: February 21, 2001. **B-T:** R-R. **HT:** 6-4. **WT:** 215. **Drafted:** Oklahoma, 2022 (11th round). **Signed by:** Bobby Shore.
TRACK RECORD: Sandlin was a successful pitcher at Eastern Oklahoma State JC before transferring to Oklahoma in 2022, where he started for a Sooners team that reached the College World Series. The Royals signed him to an above-slot $397,500 bonus that year in the 11th round. Sandlin was dynamic in his full-season debut in 2023, striking out 79 and walking 13 in 12 starts for Low-A Columbia. He was promoted to High-A Quad Cities on June 23 and made a pair of starts before a lat injury ended his season. Sandlin's 25.5 K-BB% ranked 11th among minor league starters with at least 50 innings.

SCOUTING REPORT: While he has a four-pitch mix, Sandlin relies most heavily on the mid-90s fastball that touches 97 mph and has above-average ride. Sandlin's preferred secondary is a mid-80s slider with horizontal break and high spin rates. He also throws a low-80s curveball with two-plane break and bite, and he mixes in a changeup that breaks like a splitter as well. He's still refining his arsenal—especially his secondaries—so there's a chance they continue to improve. The fastball and slider are above-average offerings right now, and some believe he may profile best in the bullpen, where he can dominate with those pitches alone.

THE FUTURE: Sandlin is a sleeper who could take a jump forward in 2024 if he improves the rest of his arsenal. He should begin the year with High-A Quad Cities.

Year	Age	Club (League)	Level	W	L	ERA	G	GS	IP	H	HR	BB	SO	BB%	SO%	WHIP	AVG
2023	22	Columbia (CAR)	A	4	1	3.38	12	12	59	57	8	13	79	5.5	33.5	1.19	.259
2023	22	Quad Cities (MWL)	A+	0	1	4.50	2	2	8	6	1	5	8	14.3	22.9	1.38	.207
Minor League Totals				4	2	3.44	15	15	69	64	9	18	90	6.5	32.4	1.21	.250

20 DANIEL VAZQUEZ, SS

Hit: 45. **POW:** 40. **RUN:** 55. **FLD:** 55. **ARM:** 60. **BA Grade:** 45. **Risk:** Very High.

Born: December 15, 2003. **B-T:** R-R. **HT:** 6-0. **WT:** 185. **Signed:** Dominican Republic, 2021. **Signed by:** Edis Perez.

TRACK RECORD: Vazquez was Kansas City's top international target in 2021 and signed for $1.5 million. He began his career later that summer in the Dominican Summer League. Instead of the customary second-year assignment to the Arizona Complex League, Vazquez was moved from extended spring training to Low-A Columbia in 2022, where he struggled at the plate and hit just .195/.262/.229. Vazquez returned to Columbia in 2023 with added strength and a couple more inches of height and improved his slash line to .223/.330/.288.

SCOUTING REPORT: Vazquez has a glove-over-hit profile, but he also flashes raw power potential and above-average bat speed after adding more strength. One of his development goals was to get more balls in the air. His groundball rate dropped from 52.2% in 2022 to 41.4% in 2023. Vazquez shows the ability to recognize pitches but gets out of his approach at times. He cut down on strikeouts and drew more walks in his second year at Columbia. Vazquez has good actions at shortstop, projecting as at least an above-average defender. There's a path to plus defense with more consistency, improved footwork and fewer mental mistakes. He flashes a plus arm, with good zip and carry on his throws, which get to their targets on a line.

THE FUTURE: Vazquez has the ability and tools to become an elite defender. Whether that's as a starting shortstop or a utility infielder will depend on how his hit tool develops.

Year	Age	Club (League)	Level	AVG	G	AB	R	H	2B	3B	HR	RBI	BB	SO	SB	OBP	SLG
2023	19	Columbia (CAR)	A	.223	113	400	57	89	15	1	3	43	62	107	32	.330	.288
Minor League Totals				.208	222	795	99	165	28	2	4	84	104	224	46	.299	.263

21 RAMON RAMIREZ, C

Hit: 55. **POW:** 55. **RUN:** 40. **FLD:** 50. **ARM:** 60. **BA Grade:** 50. **Risk:** Extreme.

Born: June 15, 2005. **B-T:** R-R. **HT:** 6-0. **WT:** 180. **Signed:** Venezuela, 2023.
Signed by: Juan Francisco/Daniel Guerrero/Roberto Aquino.

TRACK RECORD: Of the few Dominican Summer League players that the Royals brought to their fall instructional league, Ramirez stood out the most. The native Venezuelan signed for just $57,500 in 2023 but quickly jumped to the head of the Royals' international class after torching the DSL to the tune of a .344/.440/.615 line and eight homers in 41 games. His 1.055 OPS would have ranked among the tops in the DSL had he qualified, and his eight home runs tied for eighth among all hitters.

SCOUTING REPORT: Ramirez has feel to hit with an advanced, powerful swing that shows excellent adjustability and barrel accuracy. He can also handle velocity, projecting the ability to hit for both average and power. His 90th percentile exit velocity of roughly 102 mph in the DSL was well above-average for the level. Like any young catcher, Ramirez has work to do on all facets of his defense. But he has a foundation that indicates he can one day be a plus defender with a plus arm. Both his throwing and receiving improved throughout the season. He's a below-average runner who could slow down as he matures.

THE FUTURE: An exciting prospect at a premium position, Ramirez still has a lot of development ahead. He'll stay in Arizona in 2024 with an assignment to the Rookie-level Arizona Complex League.

Year	Age	Club (League)	Level	AVG	G	AB	R	H	2B	3B	HR	RBI	BB	SO	SB	OBP	SLG
2023	18	DSL Royals Blue	Rk	.344	41	122	26	42	9	0	8	27	21	18	6	.440	.615
Minor League Totals				.344	41	122	26	42	9	0	8	27	21	18	6	.440	.615

22 NOAH CAMERON, LHP

FB: 45. **CB:** 55. **CHG:** 60. **CTL:** 55. **BA Grade:** 45. **Risk:** High.

Born: July 19, 1999. **B-T:** L-L. **HT:** 6-3. **WT:** 225. **Drafted:** Central Arkansas, 2021 (7th round). **Signed by:** Matt Price.

TRACK RECORD: Cameron made just 18 starts at Central Arkansas after losing his junior season to Tommy John surgery. The Royals made him their seventh-round selection in 2021 and signed him to a below-slot $197,500 bonus. Cameron quietly took a step forward in 2022 when he struck out 53 batters in 31 innings with High-A Quad Cities. He returned to the level again in 2023 before earning a promotion to Double-A Northwest Arkansas, where he posted a 6.10 ERA in 72.1 innings with 74 strikeouts.

SCOUTING REPORT: Despite sitting in the low 90s, Cameron generated plenty of whiffs at the lower levels with his fastball because of its deceptive life and carry through the zone. His fastball did not fare as well in his first taste of the upper minors and would benefit from added velocity. The Royals have seen Cameron touch 95 mph and believe there's more in the tank. Cameron struggled with his endurance and holding velocity following surgery and plans to address the issue with an aggressive offseason conditioning plan. His best secondary pitch is a plus low-80s changeup with good vertical separation off his fastball, as well as tumbling action and good command. He also shows feel for an above-average upper-70s curveball with 11-to-5 shape and tight break that he throws for strikes and tunnels well with his fastball. He does a good job repeating his delivery.

THE FUTURE: Cameron will return to Double-A Northwest Arkansas looking for another chance against Texas League hitters.

Year	Age	Club (League)	Level	W	L	ERA	G	GS	IP	H	HR	BB	SO	BB%	SO%	WHIP	AVG
2023	23	Quad Cities (MWL)	A+	2	2	3.60	7	7	35	28	5	9	58	6.3	40.8	1.06	.215
2023	23	NW Arkansas (TL)	AA	3	10	6.10	17	17	72	87	14	26	74	8.0	22.8	1.56	.297
Minor League Totals				7	15	4.63	43	43	173	173	25	51	231	6.9	31.4	1.29	.257

23 MATT SAUER, RHP

FB: 55. **CB:** 40. **SL:** 55. **CHG:** 30. **CTL:** 55. **BA Grade:** 40. **Risk:** Medium.

Born: January 21, 1999. **B-T:** R-R. **HT:** 6-4. **WT:** 230. **Drafted:** HS—Santa Maria, CA, 2017 (2nd round). **Signed by:** Bobby DeJardin (Yankees).

TRACK RECORD: Sauer raised his stock as a high school senior when his velocity ticked up, leading the Yankees to spend $2.5 million on him with their second-round pick in 2017. He had Tommy John surgery early in 2019, then lost the next year when the minor league season was canceled in the midst of the pandemic. Sauer reached Double-A in 2022 but needed another surgery to clean up elbow and forearm issues. He returned to the level in 2023, then was selected by the Royals in the Rule 5 draft.

SCOUTING REPORT: Sauer is a sturdy-bodied righthander who operates with a four-pitch mix dominated by a fastball and slider. His four-seam fastball sat around 94 mph and touched 98, while the slider checked in around 84 mph and peaked at 89. The fastball showed excellent life through the zone and was an effective bat-misser when elevated. Sauer's slider had plenty of sweeping action and a high spin rate of around 2,600 rpm. Both pitches are above-average and can flash a tick higher. Sauer rounds out his mix with a mid-80s changeup and a low-80s curveball. The changeup flashes fade and drop but is inconsistent, and he can give away the pitch by utilizing a more pronounced glove tap than is seen on his other offerings. He has above-average control.

THE FUTURE: If he is to stick in the Royals' bullpen, Sauer will likely do so as a reliever who relies on his fastball and slider and could see a velocity uptick while pitching in shorter bursts.

Year	Age	Club (League)	Level	W	L	ERA	G	GS	IP	H	HR	BB	SO	BB%	SO%	WHIP	AVG
2023	24	FCL Yankees	Rk	0	1	4.91	2	2	4	2	1	2	5	11.8	29.4	1.09	.143
2023	24	Hudson Valley (SAL)	A+	0	0	0.00	1	1	2	0	0	3	5	33.3	55.6	1.50	.000
2023	24	Somerset (EL)	AA	6	4	3.42	14	13	68	49	11	29	83	10.3	29.5	1.14	.196
Minor League Totals				19	25	4.22	83	80	382	320	41	155	419	9.4	25.5	1.24	.222

24 HIRO WYATT, RHP

FB: 55. **SL:** 60. **CHG:** 45. **CTL:** 45. **BA Grade:** 45. **Risk:** Extreme.

Born: August 25, 2004. **B-T:** R-R. **HT:** 6-1. **WT:** 190. **Drafted:** HS—Westport, CT, 2023 (3rd round). **Signed by:** Joe Barbera.

TRACK RECORD: Wyatt attracted attention prior to his senior season when he touched 95 mph at the 2022 World Wood Bat Championship in Jupiter, Fla. The Royals drafted the Connecticut native in the third round and signed him for $1,497,500 to keep him from his Southern California commitment. They took it slowly with the young righthander, who did not pitch during the Arizona Complex League season and then strained his back midway through the Royals' fall instructional league program.

SCOUTING REPORT: Wyatt took a step forward in both stuff and performance as a high school senior. He pitched at 92-95 mph while touching 97 with excellent armside life. His heater pairs well with his low-80s slider, which is a plus pitch with sharp bite and huge sweep away from righthanded hitters to miss bats. He also started throwing a mid-to-upper-80s cutter that doesn't get many whiffs but generates weak contact and tunnels well with his fastball. Wyatt has flashed feel for a changeup in the past, but it's more of a fringe-average pitch that he doesn't throw much. Wyatt is shorter in stature at 6-foot-1, has a longer arm action and historically struggled to command his fastball as an amateur, creating some reliever risk.

THE FUTURE: Like the Royals have done with other prep arms, Wyatt is expected to stay behind in extended spring training to start 2024 before venturing to either the Arizona Complex League or Low-A Columbia.

Year	Age	Club (League)	Level	W	L	ERA	G	GS	IP	H	HR	BB	SO	BB%	SO%	WHIP	AVG
2023	18	Did not play															

25 PEYTON WILSON, 2B/OF

Hit: 45. **POW:** 45. **RUN:** 60. **FLD:** 50. **ARM:** 50. **BA Grade:** 40. **Risk:** High.

Born: November 1, 1999. **B-T:** B-R. **HT:** 5-8. **WT:** 180. **Drafted:** Alabama, 2021 (2nd round supplemental).
Signed by: Cody Clark.

TRACK RECORD: Wilson played two seasons at Alabama before the Royals selected him in 2021 in the supplemental second round as a draft-eligible sophomore. He signed for a bonus just over $1 million. He made it to Double-A Northwest Arkansas in his third pro season, batting .286/.366/.411 while playing all but two games at second base. He finished the year with a strong performance in the Arizona Fall League.

SCOUTING REPORT: Wilson plays with plenty of energy and twitch. He's a plus runner who has the versatility to play multiple positions. His hit tool draws diverse opinions. More optimistic evaluators point toward the hard contact he generates from a compact swing despite his size. Others see the low-impact swing of a slap hitter who is overly aggressive at the plate. There's no questioning Wilson's speed. He averages right around 20 stolen bases a season. He's a fringe-average defender at second base with an average arm, though his arm strength was down a bit from the previous season. His speed and arm should allow him to handle both outfield and third base in a utility role, but he played almost exclusively at second base in 2023.

THE FUTURE: While Wilson played some outfield in the AFL, more time in the grass would be helpful if Wilson's ultimate ceiling is a utility player. He is expected to move to Triple-A Omaha in 2024.

Year	Age	Club (League)	Level	AVG	G	AB	R	H	2B	3B	HR	RBI	BB	SO	SB	OBP	SLG
2023	23	NW Arkansas (TL)	AA	.286	128	489	70	140	33	5	6	65	55	101	19	.366	.411
Minor League Totals				.274	239	903	143	247	55	10	21	117	106	219	49	.361	.426

26 STEVEN ZOBAC, RHP

FB: 55. **SL:** 55. **CHG:** 45. **CTL:** 50. **BA Grade:** 40. **Risk:** High.

Born: October 14, 2000. **B-T:** L-R. **HT:** 6-3. **WT:** 185. **Drafted:** California, 2022 (4th round).
Signed by: Buddy Goldsmith.

TRACK RECORD: Zobac was initially a two-way player at California who didn't focus solely on pitching until his third year. His stuff and draft stock both jumped, and the Royals signed the athletic righthander to a $500,000 bonus in the fourth round in 2022. He posted a 3.47 ERA in 90.2 innings across the Royals' two Class A Affiliates in 2023 despite fading down the stretch with High-A Quad Cities, posting a 6.04 ERA over his last six starts.

SCOUTING REPORT: Zobac pairs well above-average athleticism with a very cerebral mental approach to pitching. His four-seam fastball was a valuable pitch in 2023. His heater sits in the mid 90s and can touch 97 mph with excellent life and above-average ride. He complements the fastball with a potentially plus slider in the mid-to-upper 80s. He rounds out his three-pitch mix with a fringe-average changeup in the low 80s in which he still lacks confidence. He has a simple, repeatable delivery and walked just 6.4% of batters in 2023.

THE FUTURE: Zobac is newer to pitching than a typical 23-year-old college hurler, so he may not move as quickly as his counterparts and could likely head back to High-A to start the 2024 season.

Year	Age	Club (League)	Level	W	L	ERA	G	GS	IP	H	HR	BB	SO	BB%	SO%	WHIP	AVG
2023	22	Columbia (CAR)	A	1	2	2.09	14	10	52	43	2	12	61	5.9	29.9	1.06	.225
2023	22	Quad Cities (MWL)	A+	1	4	5.31	8	8	39	44	3	12	37	7.1	21.8	1.44	.280
Minor League Totals				2	6	3.50	22	18	91	87	5	24	98	6.4	26.2	1.23	.250

27 HENRY WILLIAMS, RHP

FB: 55. **SL:** 60. **CHG:** 50. **CTL:** 50. **BA Grade:** 40. **Risk:** High.

Born: September 18, 2001. **B-T:** R-R. **HT:** 6-5. **WT:** 200. **Drafted:** Duke, 2022 (3rd round).
Signed by: Jake Koenig (Padres).

TRACK RECORD: Williams was regarded as a potential high draft pick entering his junior year at Duke prior to having Tommy John surgery. That didn't scare the Padres, who signed Williams to an over-slot $800,000 as a third-rounder in 2022—the same year they took Dylan Lesko, another righty dealing with elbow surgery, in the first round. Williams returned to the mound late in 2023 spring training and debuted with Low-A Lake Elsinore in May. The Royals acquired him at the trade deadline for closer Scott Barlow.

SCOUTING REPORT: Williams' fastball settled into the 92-94 mph range after the injury, which is a tick below the 94-98 range he displayed as an amateur. He has a clean delivery with good arm action from a three-quarters slot. He also has a short, tight low-80s gyro slider that has plus potential and he shows the ability to command an average mid-80s changeup. Williams can throw every pitch in his arsenal for strikes, and there's hope more velocity returns as he gets some distance from his surgery.

THE FUTURE: After finishing the 2023 season on a high note, Williams will be ready to move up at least another level in 2024. His most likely landing spot is High-A Quad Cities. Williams projects as a durable back-of-the-rotation starter.

Year	Age	Club (League)	Level	W	L	ERA	G	GS	IP	H	HR	BB	SO	BB%	SO%	WHIP	AVG
2023	21	Lake Elsinore (CAL)	A	1	5	5.74	12	12	42	39	6	21	40	11.5	22.0	1.42	.250
2023	21	Columbia (CAR)	A	2	1	3.38	5	5	24	18	3	13	23	12.9	22.8	1.29	.209
Minor League Totals				3	6	4.91	17	17	66	57	9	34	63	12.0	22.3	1.38	.236

28 TYSON GUERRERO, LHP

FB: 55. **CB:** 50. **SL:** 60. **CHG:** 55. **CTL:** 55. **BA Grade:** 40. **Risk:** High.

Born: February 16, 1999. **B-T:** L-L. **HT:** 6-1. **WT:** 188. **Drafted:** Washington, 2021 (12th round). **Signed by:** Joe Ross

TRACK RECORD: The Centralia, Wash., native spent time with three different in-state colleges as an amateur, ultimately surfacing at Washington in 2021 and posting a 2.96 ERA. That performance caught the attention of the Royals, who signed Guerrero to a $127,500 bonus in the 12th round. He pitched sparingly his first two years as a professional because of shoulder injuries. He broke out in 2023 with a solid performance in 18 games with High-A Quad Cities, where he struck out 106 batters and walked just 29 in 84.1 innings.

SCOUTING REPORT: Finally healthy, Guerrero pounded the strike zone with an above-average fastball at 91-95 mph. His best secondary is a potentially plus slider in the mid to upper 80s with 10-to-4 shape. He also throws a low-80s curveball that differs from his slider with more downer action. An inconsistent mid-80s changeup completes his repertoire. Guerrero is a control-over-command pitcher with a clean delivery that he sometimes has issues repeating. His determination and composure are among his best attributes on the mound.

THE FUTURE: Profiling best as a No. 5 starter, Guerrero should return to Double-A Northwest Arkansas to begin the 2024 season.

Year	Age	Club (League)	Level	W	L	ERA	G	GS	IP	H	HR	BB	SO	BB%	SO%	WHIP	AVG
2023	24	Quad Cities (MWL)	A+	2	4	3.63	18	17	84	65	10	29	106	8.5	31.0	1.11	.215
2023	24	NW Arkansas (TL)	AA	1	2	6.55	3	3	11	10	2	5	15	10.2	30.6	1.36	.233
Minor League Totals				4	10	4.47	36	33	136	117	19	52	163	9.1	28.6	1.25	.233

29 ERIC CERANTOLA, RHP

FB: 70. **CB:** 70. **CHG:** 55. **CTL:** 40. **BA Grade:** 40. **Risk:** High.

Born: May 2, 2000. **B-T:** R-R. **HT:** 6-5. **WT:** 225. **Drafted:** Mississippi State, 2021 (5th round). **Signed by:** Cody Clark.

TRACK RECORD: The Montreal native was more highly regarded as a hockey player in high school, but he ultimately honored his baseball commitment to Mississippi State. He pitched limited innings during his three-year career with the Bulldogs due to his inability to throw consistent strikes. The Royals believed they could work with Cerantola's strengths and signed him for $500,000 in the fifth round in 2021. He began to turn the corner in 2023, pitching 76.1 innings between High-A Quad Cities and Double-A Northwest Arkansas. He posted a combined 4.13 ERA with 11.7 strikeouts and 5.4 walks per nine innings.

SCOUTING REPORT: Cerantola's work in the offseason allowed him to gain confidence in his stuff and key his development. His 94-97 mph fastball can touch triple digits and is a double-plus pitch that he is throwing more consistently. His downer curveball also has double-plus potential. It's a 12-to-6 breaker that he throws 83-86 mph and can be a major league strikeout pitch against both righties and lefties. Rounding out Cerantola's electric arsenal is a split-changeup at 85-87 mph that he uses just 10% of the time and has solid-average potential. His control is still below-average and continues to be his weak spot. **THE FUTURE:** Cerantola has late-inning relief potential with even a marginal improvement in control. He should return to Double-A in 2024.

Year	Age	Club (League)	Level	W	L	ERA	G	GS	IP	H	HR	BB	SO	BB%	SO%	WHIP	AVG
2023	23	Quad Cities (MWL)	A+	3	3	4.04	29	2	62	46	3	41	80	14.6	28.6	1.40	.199
2023	23	NW Arkansas (TL)	AA	0	1	1.93	3	2	14	9	0	5	19	9.3	35.2	1.00	.196
Minor League Totals				4	7	4.04	46	16	111	91	8	67	144	13.6	29.3	1.42	.220

30 TREVOR WERNER, 3B

Hit: 40. **POW:** 50. **RUN:** 50. **FLD:** 50. **ARM:** 70. **BA Grade:** 45. **Risk:** Extreme.

Born: September 3, 2000. **B-T:** R-R. **HT:** 6-3. **WT:** 225. **Drafted:** Texas A&M, 2023 (7th round). **Signed by:** Josh Hallgren.
TRACK RECORD: Injuries marred Werner's four-year career at Texas A&M, where he was a two-way contributor, but he rebounded as a senior to lead the Aggies to the College World Series. The Royals signed Werner for $350,000 in the seventh round of the 2023 draft. He produced arguably the best pro debut of any Kansas City draft pick, hitting .354/.459/.699 with eight home runs in 113 at-bats at Low-A Columbia.
SCOUTING REPORT: The rap on Werner in college was that his difficulty barreling premium velocity contributed to his rather high 25% strikeout rate. He immediately went to work combatting that issue with the Royals' hitting development program. He showed above-average plate skills with an improved contact and chase rate in his debut, producing a well above-average 90th percentile exit velocity of 108 mph. Werner is an agile defender at third base with a double-plus arm. Though he was officially drafted as a two-way player, Werner pitched sparingly out of Texas A&M's bullpen in college. The Royals have no plans to develop him as a pitcher. He's an average runner, though stolen bases are not expected to be a major part of his game.
THE FUTURE: Werner's next challenge is seeing if the improvements made in 2023 stick against better pitching at one of the Royals' Class A affiliates.

Year	Age	Club (League)	Level	AVG	G	AB	R	H	2B	3B	HR	RBI	BB	SO	SB	OBP	SLG
2023	22	ACL Royals	Rk	.333	4	15	4	5	1	1	1	4	1	6	2	.375	.733
2023	22	Columbia (CAR)	A	.354	31	113	32	40	11	2	8	36	21	31	8	.459	.699
Minor League Totals				.352	35	128	36	45	12	3	9	40	22	37	10	.450	.703

Los Angeles Angels

BY TAYLOR BLAKE WARD

In their most pivotal season in decades, the Angels once again fell short of their high expectations in 2023.

Despite having two generational talents in Shohei Ohtani and Mike Trout on their roster, the Angels finished with their eighth consecutive losing season and missed the postseason for the ninth straight year. Both are the longest active streaks in the majors.

Now, Ohtani's departure in free agency—and the seismic missed opportunity that represents—hangs over the franchise.

Front office inconsistency has dogged the Angels for the better part of that stretch. They've had three full-time general managers since the middle of 2015. Current GM Perry Minasian has received praise across baseball for his vision, though owner Arte Moreno has hamstrung the organization with limited budgeting for scouting and development staffs.

Moreno is frequently criticized. While he has attempted to field a winning team every year since purchasing the club in 2003, the constant pursuit of high-dollar free agents and lack of spending on procurement and development has hindered the Angels' homegrown talent. That has led to struggles finding and developing internal impact talent or making a splash on the trade market.

Not every problem with the Angels falls at the feet of Moreno. Former GMs Jerry Dipoto and Billy Eppler both struggled on the amateur market, with Eppler's high-risk athletes failing to produce and Dipoto focusing his allocations on one player, Roberto Baldoquin for $8 million, which did not fare well for either party.

The Angels are 15 years removed from the epic 2009 draft that landed Mike Trout, Randal Grichuk, Tyler Skaggs, Garrett Richards and Patrick Corbin. They have struggled bringing amateur talent into the organization since. From 2010 to 2019, just three players drafted or signed internationally have produced at least 5 bWAR for the organization: Ohtani, Kole Calhoun and David Fletcher.

Minasian and his staff implemented a new draft philosophy, placing an emphasis on selecting players at the top of the draft who were near major league ready. They're already seeing the benefits. The Angels have had the first player to reach MLB from each of the last four drafts: Reid Detmers (2020), Chase Silseth (2021), Zach Neto (2022) and Nolan Schanuel (2023).

Minasian hired Brian Parker as international scouting director, and the Angels have seen more results on the international market. The

Logan O'Hoppe missed three months with shoulder surgery but slugged .581 in September.

PROJECTED 2027 LINEUP

Catcher	Logan O'Hoppe	27
First Base	Nolan Schanuel	25
Second Base	Kyren Paris	25
Third Base	Denzer Guzman	23
Shortstop	Zach Neto	26
Left Field	Mike Trout	35
Center Field	Nelson Rada	21
Right Field	Jo Adell	28
Designated Hitter	Mickey Moniak	29
No. 1 Starter	Reid Detmers	27
No. 2 Starter	Chase Silseth	27
No. 3 Starter	Patrick Sandoval	30
No. 4 Starter	Caden Dana	23
No. 5 Starter	Barrett Kent	22
Closer	Sam Bachman	27

international scouting staff has done a great job identifying players of both high-profile value, such as Nelson Rada, while also bringing in low-bonus signees like Joel Hurtado who have become notable prospects.

Most of the Angels' farm system is loaded with high-variance prospects who have yet to develop, particularly the hitters. Some optimism can be found in the Angels using 22 rookie-eligible players in Anaheim in 2023, with 11 making their MLB debuts—though the impact of most of those players is in question.

The future of the organization will rely on finding impact within the farm system. The sooner, the better. ∎

DEPTH CHART

LOS ANGELES ANGELS

TOP 2024 CONTRIBUTORS — **RANK**
1. Nolan Schanuel, 1B — 1
2. Sam Bachman, RHP — 5
3. Ben Joyce, RHP — 6

BREAKOUT PROSPECTS — **RANK**
1. Dario Laverde, C — 12
2. Walbert Urena, RHP — 14
3. Anthony Scull, OF — 25

SOURCE OF TOP 30 TALENT

Homegrown	29	Acquired	1
College	8	Trade	1
Junior college	0	Rule 5 draft	0
High school	7	Independent league	0
Nondrafted free agent	0	Free agent/waivers	0
International	14		

LF
Alberto Rios (11)
Jorge Ruiz (23)
Joe Redfield Jr. (29)
Orlando Martinez

CF
Nelson Rada (2)
Jordyn Adams (22)
Anthony Scull (25)
David Calabrese (28)
Raudi Rodriguez
D'Shawn Knowles

RF
Jadiel Sanchez (19)
Tucker Flint
Randy de Jesus
Alexander Ramirez

3B
Werner Blakely (24)
Cole Fontenelle
Arol Vera
Luis Rodriguez

SS
Kyren Paris (4)
Denzer Guzman (9)
Felix Morrobel (15)
John Wimmer
Livan Soto

2B
Adrian Placencia (13)
Capri Ortiz (27)

1B
Nolan Schanuel (1)
Trey Cabbage
Luis Torres
Sonny Dichiara

C
Dario Laverde (12)
Juan Flores

LHP
LHSP
Francis Texido
Jhonathan Diaz

LHRP
Nick Jones

RHP
RHSP
Caden Dana (3)
Sam Bachman (5)
Barrett Kent (7)
Jack Kochanowicz (8)
Victor Mederos (10)
Walbert Urena (14)
Ryan Costeiu (17)
Joel Hurtado (20)
Jorge Marcheco (30)
Riley Bauman
Keythel Key
Bryce Osmond
Davis Daniel
Chris Clark
Mason Erla
Brett Kerry
Ubaldo Soto

RHRP
Ben Joyce (6)
Kelvin Caceres (18)
Camden Minacci (21)
Adrian Acosta (26)
Luke Murphy
Kenyon Yovan
Hayden Seig
Sadrac Franco
Erik Martinez
Jared Southard

1 NOLAN SCHANUEL, 1B

Born: February 14, 2002. **B-T:** L-R. **HT:** 6-4. **WT:** 220.
Drafted: Florida Atlantic, 2023 (1st round).
Signed by: Brandon McArthur.

TRACK RECORD: Schanuel was a three-year start-er for Florida Atlantic who regularly posted video game numbers. Following his sophomore year, he struggled in the Cape Cod League, which led to an eye doctor appointment where he was diagnosed with an astigmatism. He had a correc-tive lens placed in his right eye in January 2023. Schanuel went on to a huge junior season, slash-ing .447/.615/.868 with 71 walks to 14 strikeouts and a Division I-leading 1.483 OPS. The Angels loved his performance and mental aptitude for hitting and drafted him 11th overall in 2023. They signed him for the slot value of $5.253 million. Schanuel hit well at Double-A in his pro debut, and the Angels called him up after just 22 minor league games. Schanuel's 40 days between draft day and MLB debut is the fifth-shortest timeline in history. He rewarded the Angels by reaching base in each of his 29 games. He drew 20 walks against 19 strikeouts on his way to a .402 on-base percentage. He drew the most MLB plate appearances in his draft year since the Braves' Bob Horner in 1978.

SCOUTING REPORT: Schanuel is a lefthanded-hitting first baseman with substantial offensive upside. His operation starts with an unorthodox setup, with his hands held high over his head while incorporating a high leg kick as he loads. Despite an atypical setup, Schanuel keeps his body and swing in sync and remains balanced. He has an innate feel for hitting and understand-ing of the hitting process, aided by excellent barrel control and zone coverage. Schanuel's power has yet to appear in pro ball—he hit two home runs in 51 games after signing—though he made the unorthodox setup to help tap into power by creating better separation. He shows above-average raw power in batting practice but used more of a downhill swing in pro ball. His swing lacks explosiveness, leaving him reli-ant on his contact skills and swing decisions to get to average power production. He has an inherent aptitude for hitting with an advanced approach which results in high walk rates and minimal swing-and-miss. Schanuel's corrected vision enhanced his feel for the strike zone and he profiles as a high-average, on-base threat. He

MITCHELL LEFF GETTY IMAGES

BA GRADE	SCOUTING GRADES
50 Risk: Medium	Hit: 60. Power: 50. Run: 40. Field: 50. Arm: 40.

Projected future grades on 20-80 scouting scale

BEST TOOLS

BATTING
Best Hitter for Average	Nolan Schanuel
Best Power Hitter	Trey Cabbage
Best Strike-Zone Discipline	Nolan Schanuel
Fastest Baserunner	Jordyn Adams
Best Athlete	Jordyn Adams

PITCHING
Best Fastball	Ben Joyce
Best Curveball	Kelvin Caceres
Best Slider	Sam Bachman
Best Changeup	Ryan Costeiu
Best Control	Jorge Marcheco

FIELDING
Best Defensive Catcher	Juan Flores
Best Defensive Infielder	Denzer Guzman
Best Infield Arm	Denzer Guzman
Best Defensive Outfielder	Nelson Rada
Best Outfield Arm	Jadiel Sanchez

is an aggressive and high-energy runner making him an occasional basestealer, though his speed is just below-average. After playing first base exclusively in college and pro ball, he handles the position with ease and may be athletic enough to test in the corner outfield.

THE FUTURE: Schanuel is viewed as the Angels' everyday first baseman starting in 2024. If he grows into more natural power, he could develop into a first-division starter. But without enhanced power, he faces a future as a hit-over-power first baseman. ■

Year	Age	Club (League)	Level	AVG	G	AB	R	H	2B	3B	HR	RBI	BB	SO	SB	OBP	SLG
2023	21	ACL Angels	Rk	.250	3	8	3	2	1	0	0	1	4	1	1	.500	.375
2023	21	Inland Empire (CAL)	A	.833	2	6	2	5	0	0	0	2	1	0	0	.778	.833
2023	21	Rocket City (SL)	AA	.333	17	60	15	20	3	1	1	12	16	9	1	.474	.467
2023	21	Los Angeles (AL)	MLB	.275	29	109	19	30	3	0	1	6	20	19	0	.402	.330
Minor League Totals				.365	22	74	20	27	4	1	1	15	21	10	2	.505	.486
Major League Totals				.275	29	109	19	30	3	0	1	6	20	19	0	.402	.330

2 NELSON RADA, OF

HIT: 55. **POW:** 45. **RUN:** 60. **FLD:** 60. **ARM:** 55. **BA Grade:** 50. **Risk:** High.

Born: August 24, 2005. **B-T:** L-L. **HT:** 5-10. **WT:** 160.
Signed: Venezuela, 2022. **Signed by:** Marlon Urdaneta/Joel Chicarelli.
TRACK RECORD: One week shy of being ineligible for the 2022 international signing period, Rada signed with the Angels for $1.85 million as a high-profile prospect. He was among the offensive league leaders in his pro debut in the Dominican Summer League later that summer. The Angels aggressively assigned him to Low-A Inland Empire as a 17-year-old in 2023 as the youngest player on any full-season Opening Day roster. Rada performed honorably, slashing .276/.395/.346 while leading the California League with 55 stolen bases.
SCOUTING REPORT: Rada is an advanced lefthanded hitter with everyday upside. His short, line-drive swing allows him to make contact to all fields with innate bat-to-ball skills and feel for the barrel. Though his lean, 5-foot-10 frame doesn't permit much physical projection, any muscle gains could give him fringe-average power with his ability to frequently find the barrel. It may take years for him to become stronger naturally, but his ability to make barrel adjustments and drive the ball in the air more consistently will help. A highly selective hitter who handled the zone against older pitchers, Rada rarely swings and misses. He occasionally gets beat on the inner half, which should improve as he shortens up and gains barrel strength. With above-average speed, Rada's instinctual baserunning aggression gives him a plus run tool and makes him a basestealing threat. He makes good reads and is a smooth defender in center field, where he has plus potential at a premium position. Rada is the same age as players in the 2024 high school class, so most of his everyday projection rests in his physical maturity.
THE FUTURE: Rada is on track to be a table-setting everyday center fielder but will need to get stronger to maximize his upside.

Year	Age	Club (League)	Level	AVG	G	AB	R	H	2B	3B	HR	RBI	BB	SO	SB	OBP	SLG
2023	17	Inland Empire (CAL)	A	.276	115	439	94	121	13	6	2	48	73	98	55	.395	.346
Minor League Totals				.285	165	603	144	172	25	9	3	74	99	124	82	.410	.371

3 CADEN DANA, RHP

FB: 55. **CB:** 50. **SL:** 60. **CHG:** 45. **CTL:** 50. **BA Grade:** 50. **Risk:** High.

Born: December 17, 2003. **B-T:** L-R. **HT:** 6-4. **WT:** 215.
Drafted: HS—Ramsey, NJ, 2022 (11th round). **Signed by:** Drew Dominguez.
TRACK RECORD: Dana was an advanced New Jersey prep with physicality when the Angels drafted him in the 11th round in 2022. They signed him for a post-10th round record $1,497,500 bonus. They also drafted older brother Casey in the 16th round. Caden performed well in his pro debut in the Arizona Complex League with one late-season start in Low-A, where he returned to start 2023. He earned a late-April promotion to High-A Tri-City, where he performed modestly as the youngest pitcher in the Northwest League before the Angels shut him down in mid July because of workload limitations and arm fatigue.
SCOUTING REPORT: Dana is a physical, 6-foot-4 righthander who has taken a step forward toward his midrotation upside. With an uncanny ability to backspin his fastball, he added carry to its natural high spin while sitting 93-95 mph and touching 97. It's a swing-and-miss weapon for Dana, who improved his arm strength to hold velocity through outings. He added a mid-80s slider in pro ball that is now his best offspeed offering with good sweep and depth that hitters from both sides of the plate swung through. He uses his curveball against lefthanders in lieu of his changeup. It is a high-spin breaker that he sometimes struggles to feel. His fading changeup was believed to be his best future offspeed offering, though he barely used it in 2023. Dana has advanced ability to regain feel for his pitches when his command lapses. An easy operator on the mound, he works in and out of the zone well with a build and physicality for long-term rotation projection.
THE FUTURE: Dana has the ingredients to be an innings-eating No. 4 starter. He needs to continue building his workload, adding touch to his repertoire and getting comfortable in different situations.

Year	Age	Club (League)	Level	W	L	ERA	G	GS	IP	H	HR	BB	SO	BB%	SO%	WHIP	AVG
2023	19	Inland Empire (CAL)	A	1	1	1.20	3	3	15	6	1	6	18	10.5	31.6	0.80	.120
2023	19	Tri-City (NWL)	A+	2	4	4.22	11	11	53	45	3	24	71	10.7	31.7	1.29	.228
Minor League Totals				3	5	3.91	18	18	77	63	4	31	97	9.7	30.5	1.24	.223

4 KYREN PARIS, SS/2B

HIT: 40. **POW:** 50. **RUN:** 60. **FLD:** 55. **ARM:** 50. **BA Grade:** 45. **Risk:** Medium.

Born: November 11, 2001. **B-T:** R-R. **HT:** 6-0. **WT:** 180.
Drafted: HS—Oakley, CA, 2019 (2nd round). **Signed by:** Brian Tripp.
TRACK RECORD: The Angels drafted Paris 55th overall in 2019 as one of the youngest players in the class and signed him for an over-slot $1.4 million. After breaking his hamate three games into his pro career, Paris lost game reps to the pandemic and a broken tibia that held him to just 50 games from 2019 to 2021. In his first full healthy season in 2022, he struggled initially at High-A before hitting .299 in July and August to earn a promotion to Double-A Rocket City. In 2023, he struggled with strikeouts during the first half of the Southern League season, when the league experimented with a pre-tacked baseball, before posting an .840 OPS in the 40 games following. That earned Paris a September callup that saw him appear in 15 games.
SCOUTING REPORT: Paris is an athletic, versatile infielder with roughly average tools. He has a strong, compact swing from the right side which helps him make hard contact on pitches in the zone. Swing-and-miss is a big part of his offensive package, though he has started to get into better counts and has always been able to draw walks. His surprising power helped pay off a 29% strikeout rate at Double-A in 2023. If he can continue making better swing decisions, he could have enough power and on-base prowess to be a regular. An aggressive baserunner with plus speed, Paris is a constant stolen base threat. He showed dramatic improvements in his footwork and throwing at shortstop in 2023. Experience at both middle infield positions and brief time in center field gives him defensive versatility.
THE FUTURE: Paris' ability to limit his swing-and-miss will dictate whether he becomes a regular or more of a utility player. He is part of the Angels' MLB middle infield picture for 2024.

Year	Age	Club (League)	Level	AVG	G	AB	R	H	2B	3B	HR	RBI	BB	SO	SB	OBP	SLG
2023	21	Rocket City (SL)	AA	.255	113	415	79	106	23	1	14	45	88	151	44	.393	.417
2023	21	Los Angeles (AL)	MLB	.100	15	40	4	4	0	0	0	1	4	17	3	.200	.100
Minor League Totals				.252	268	971	191	245	51	13	30	114	182	353	99	.381	.424
Major League Totals				.100	15	40	4	4	0	0	0	1	4	17	3	.200	.100

5 SAM BACHMAN, RHP

FB: 60. **SL:** 60. **CHG:** 40. **CTL:** 40. **BA Grade:** 45. **Risk:** Medium.

Born: September 30, 1999. **B-T:** R-R. **HT:** 6-1. **WT:** 235.
Drafted: Miami (Ohio), 2021 (1st round). **Signed by:** John Burden.
TRACK RECORD: A three-year starter for Miami (Ohio), Bachman saw a velocity spike and improved control his junior season that led to first-round chatter. Angels general manager Perry Minasian attended Bachman's final college start and saw enough for the club to draft him ninth overall in 2021 and sign him for $3,847,500, about 22% under slot. Much of Bachman's first full season at Double-A in 2022 was lost to back spasms and bicep inflammation, which led to inconsistent command and velocity. Returned to Rocket City in 2023, he got off to a strong start that earned him a late-May callup to Anaheim before shoulder inflammation ended his season in early July.
SCOUTING REPORT: Bachman is a burly righthander with a two-pitch power arsenal. His fastball sits 96-97 mph and touches 99, with immense armside run and sink from a low three-quarters arm slot. His slider is a plus, swing-and-miss pitch despite its odd shape. It's a low-spin, mid-to-upper-80s breaker that works more as a cutter in the upper register, with late dive to his glove side. His slider-heavy approach works in relief, because the opposing movement of his slider and fastball play well from his arm slot. His changeup shows glimpses of being an effective pitch against lefthanded hitters with sink to his arm side, though he'll need to throw it more frequently with better command. Bachman has poor control, though his high-effort delivery, arm action and injury history would indicate a future relief role.
THE FUTURE: The Angels will continue developing Bachman as a starter, though he'll have to remain healthy and improve his changeup to see a contact-management, rotation future. His two plus-plus pitches and aptitude could lead to a late-inning relief role with closer upside.

Year	Age	Club (League)	Level	W	L	ERA	G	GS	IP	H	HR	BB	SO	BB%	SO%	WHIP	AVG
2023	23	Rocket City (SL)	AA	3	2	5.81	6	6	26	15	3	20	29	16.9	24.6	1.33	.163
2023	23	Los Angeles (AL)	MLB	1	2	3.18	11	0	17	17	0	11	14	14.3	18.2	1.65	.262
Minor League Totals				4	5	4.50	23	23	84	69	8	49	74	13.3	20.1	1.40	.223
Major League Totals				1	2	3.18	11	0	17	17	0	11	14	14.3	18.2	1.65	.262

6 BEN JOYCE, RHP

FB: 80. **SL:** 55. **CHG:** 30. **CTL:** 40. **BA Grade:** 45. **Risk:** High.

Born: September 17, 2000. **B-T:** R-R. **HT:** 6-5. **WT:** 225.
Drafted: Tennessee, 2022 (3rd round). **Signed by:** Joel Murrie.
TRACK RECORD: Joyce spent two seasons at Walters State (Tenn.) JC before transferring to Tennessee. Growth-plate issues, arm injuries and the pandemic limited him to just five appearances from 2019-21. Returning from Tommy John surgery in 2022, Joyce averaged 101 mph, touched 105 and stayed healthy enough to strike out 53 in 32.1 innings and be drafted by the Angels in the third round. He missed bats in his pro debut in Double-A and did much of the same for the first two months of 2023 before earning a May 29 callup. Suffering ulnar neuritis after five appearances with the Angels, he spent three months on the injured list before returning in September.
SCOUTING REPORT: Joyce has unicorn-like velocity with a fastball that averaged 100.8 mph in MLB in 2023 and surpassed 103 multiple times. His fastball can flatten when not properly executed but shows armside run down in the zone and is hard to barrel in the upper quadrants. The pitch plays up from Joyce's low three-quarters arm slot. His fastball usage hovers around 80%, with the remainder going to a hard-sweeping slider that flashes plus in the mid-to-upper 80s with a peak of 90 mph. Joyce's feel for his slider has improved with an ability to front-door righthanded hitters, but his offspeed command is well below-average. He generally works around the zone but will never be much of a strike-thrower. His premier stuff would fit as a closer, but to reach that designation he will have to show durability enough to pitch on back-to-back days, which he has not done as a collegian or a pro.
THE FUTURE: Joyce has top-of-the-scale velocity that would fit in a closing role, but he will have to throw more strikes and remain healthy to be an impact reliever. He is ready for a full season in Anaheim.

Year	Age	Club (League)	Level	W	L	ERA	G	GS	IP	H	HR	BB	SO	BB%	SO%	WHIP	AVG
2023	22	Inland Empire (CAL)	A	0	0	0.00	2	0	2	1	0	1	2	14.3	28.6	1.00	.167
2023	22	Rocket City (SL)	AA	0	1	4.60	14	0	16	7	1	13	24	18.6	34.3	1.28	.135
2023	22	Los Angeles (AL)	MLB	1	1	5.40	12	0	10	9	1	9	10	18.8	20.8	1.80	.243
Minor League Totals				1	1	3.30	29	0	31	19	1	18	46	13.4	34.3	1.23	.176
Major League Totals				1	1	5.40	12	0	10	9	1	9	10	18.8	20.8	1.80	.243

7 BARRETT KENT, RHP

FB: 55. **CB:** 45. **SL:** 55. **CHG:** 50. **CTL:** 50. **BA Grade:** 50. **Risk:** Extreme.

Born: September 29, 2004. **B-T:** R-R. **HT:** 6-4. **WT:** 215.
Drafted: HS—Pottsboro, TX, 2023 (8th round). **Signed by:** K.J. Hendricks.
TRACK RECORD: Kent was a standout on the summer showcase circuit before seeing his velocity and performance waver as a Texas high school senior in 2023. The Angels followed his progress over the spring and were impressed during a private workout, enough to draft him in the eighth round and sign him for $997,500, which is third-round money. Kent performed well after the draft, pitching 8.2 scoreless innings. He spent time in the offseason working on strength and conditioning, with a focus on his lower half.
SCOUTING REPORT: Kent is a tall, projectable righthander with a solid four-pitch mix. He works primarily off his 92-94 mph fastball. The pitch ranges from 94-96 early in outings while touching 98 with good armside run. Kent's primarily developmental focus is to add strength to his lower half, with hopes of holding velocity through his whole workload. His low-80s slider is an above-average offering with two-plane action that drifts away from righthanded hitters. The pitch plays well off his fastball, which has similar plane. He is working on a high-arching, upper-70s curveball that shows glimpses of promise, but he has not used it in games. Kent has decent feel for a low-80s changeup that is thrown with conviction and flashes above-average potential with fade. Most of his repertoire works downhill and plays up to his arm side, but he will need to use the rest of the zone to make his arsenal more well-rounded. An easy operator on the mound, Kent has solid control for a young pitcher, with good command of his fastball and slider. Strength gains should improve his ability to repeat and hold velocity.
THE FUTURE: Kent has a rotation future with four pitches he can land for strikes. Strength gains could allow him to reach his No. 4 starter upside.

Year	Age	Club (League)	Level	W	L	ERA	G	GS	IP	H	HR	BB	SO	BB%	SO%	WHIP	AVG
2023	18	ACL Angels	Rk	1	0	0.00	2	0	5	2	0	3	5	15.0	25.0	1.07	.125
2023	18	Inland Empire (CAL)	A	0	0	0.00	1	1	4	2	0	1	5	6.3	31.3	0.75	.143
Minor League Totals				1	0	0.00	3	1	9	4	0	4	10	11.1	27.8	1.00	.133

8 JACK KOCHANOWICZ, RHP

FB: 55. **CB:** 45. **SL:** 50. **CHG:** 55. **CTL:** 55. **BA Grade:** 45. **Risk:** High.

Born: December 22, 2000. **B-T:** L-R. **HT:** 6-7. **WT:** 228.
Drafted: HS—Bryn Mawr, PA, 2019 (3rd round). **Signed by:** Kennard Jones.
TRACK RECORD: Kochanowicz was a projectable high school pitcher from Pennsylvania when the Angels drafted him in the third round in 2019. They signed him for nearly double slot value at $1,247,500. Part of the Angels' alternate training site in 2020, Kochanowicz's pro debut was slowed by the pandemic and an oblique injury before having two rocky seasons with Low-A Inland Empire. Altering his delivery and arm slot at the end of spring training 2023 helped him find new velocity and early season success at High-A Tri-City, earning a May promotion to Double-A Rocket City where he ran up a 6.53 ERA in 70.1 innings.
SCOUTING REPORT: Kochanowicz is a 6-foot-7, strike-throwing righthander with a groundball-inducing repertoire. Lowering his arm slot to low three-quarters at the end of spring training helped him become more confident in his fastball. Kochanowicz favors a two-seam fastball to a four-seam grip with which he began his pro career. While altering the shape of how his fastball approaches the plate, he added 3-4 ticks to his heater which now sits 95-97 mph and touches 99. That makes him tough for righthanded hitters to square up and yields a high rate of ground balls. Kochanowicz's velo gains added separation to his sinking changeup, making it a swing-and-miss weapon in the upper 80s. He has mostly scrapped a loopy curveball in the early stages of development, instead favoring a sweeping slider in the mid-to-upper 80s that will flash above-average. Kochanowicz throws strikes at a high clip but will need to expand the zone, because he throws too many pitches over the heart of the plate.
THE FUTURE: Kochanowicz has the makings of a groundball-oriented back-end rotation arm or possible reliever. Added to the 40-man roster in November, he could get an opportunity in Anaheim in 2024.

Year	Age	Club (League)	Level	W	L	ERA	G	GS	IP	H	HR	BB	SO	BB%	SO%	WHIP	AVG
2023	22	Tri-City (NWL)	A+	1	0	1.52	5	5	24	22	0	3	14	3.1	14.6	1.06	.247
2023	22	Rocket City (SL)	AA	4	5	6.53	16	16	70	81	15	22	55	7.1	17.7	1.46	.290
Minor League Totals				13	11	5.78	58	48	235	262	33	78	195	7.5	18.8	1.45	.277

9 DENZER GUZMAN, SS

HIT: 40. **POW:** 30. **RUN:** 45. **FLD:** 55. **ARM:** 60. **BA Grade:** 45. **Risk:** High.

Born: February 8, 2004. **B-T:** R-R. **HT:** 6-1. **WT:** 180.
Signed: Dominican Republic, 2021. **Signed by:** Domingo Garcia.
TRACK RECORD: Guzman signed with the Angels for $2 million in January 2021. Following a mediocre pro debut in the Dominican Summer League, he hit well in his U.S. debut in the Arizona Complex League and was the biggest standout at instructional league following the 2022 season. Assigned to Low-A Inland Empire in 2023, Guzman struggled offensively against older competition as one of the youngest players in the California League, posting a .680 OPS.
SCOUTING REPORT: Guzman is a young, glove-first shortstop with some feel for hitting. He is a rhythmic hitter with a simple line-drive swing from the right side who has a natural feel for the barrel. He consistently makes hard contact to his pull side and to the gaps, with most of his power coming from hard doubles as opposed to over-the-fence authority. Guzman handles fastballs well, with his biggest hurdles coming from recognizing and adjusting to offspeed pitches from righthanders. His solid approach and eye for the zone means could help him improve as he gains more experience, and doing so will be the biggest marker in his future offensive impact. Guzman is a fringe-average runner who is better underway than in quick bursts, making him an extra-base threat more than a basestealer. He is an above-average defender at shortstop with the rhythm and cadence for longevity at a premium defensive position. He maintained his agility and athleticism while physically maturing, allowing him to keep his solid range up the middle with improved footwork, backed by a plus arm.
THE FUTURE: Guzman will need reps and success against non-fastballs to prove his bat can handle an everyday starting spot near the back of a lineup. His glove will carry him to utility consideration at minimum.

Year	Age	Club (League)	Level	AVG	G	AB	R	H	2B	3B	HR	RBI	BB	SO	SB	OBP	SLG
2023	19	Inland Empire (CAL)	A	.239	111	426	62	102	21	7	7	52	42	131	8	.309	.371
Minor League Totals				.245	212	776	123	190	42	11	13	114	83	209	23	.320	.378

10 VICTOR MEDEROS, RHP

FB: 55. **CB:** 50. **SL:** 60. **CHG:** 45. **CTL:** 45. **BA Grade:** 45. **Risk:** High.

Born: June 8, 2001. **B-T:** R-R. **HT:** 6-2. **WT:** 227.
Drafted: Oklahoma State, 2022 (6th round). **Signed by:** K.J. Hendricks.
TRACK RECORD: A touted Florida high school arm, Mederos' strong commitment to Miami landed him on campus, where he was immediately thrown into the Hurricanes' rotation. He transferred to Oklahoma State as a draft-eligible sophomore in 2022. Mederos ran up a 5.40 ERA in two college seasons, but the Angels liked his premium arsenal and drafted him in the sixth round in 2022 and signed him for an under-slot $227,750. Assigned to Double-A Rocket City in 2023, Mederos struggled with the pre-tacked baseball in the Southern League. The Angels again took a flier by calling him up twice over the summer. He made three bumpy relief appearances.
SCOUTING REPORT: Mederos is a strong, tall righthander with multiple swing-and-miss weapons. His fastball has ticked up in pro ball and now sits 94-98 mph and peaks at 99. He has improved his command while adding powerful sink and armside run. Mederos' primary out pitch is a mid-to-upper-80s, two-plane slider that flashes plus and is effective against hitters on both sides of the plate. He has added power to his downer curveball, which now ranges from 80-86 mph, though he needs to throw it for more strikes to make it an effective swing-and-miss pitch. He has a firm, upper-80s changeup with fade that he rarely uses. Praised for his makeup and leadership, Mederos is working on harnessing his emotions. He gets into trouble while getting into hitters' counts too often. With a high-effort delivery, his projected control is limited and may never be more than fringe-average.
THE FUTURE: Mederos' power sinker and bat-missing breaking stuff could play in high-leverage relief role, though the Angels see his upside as a groundball-heavy back-end rotation arm.

Year	Age	Club (League)	Level	W	L	ERA	G	GS	IP	H	HR	BB	SO	BB%	SO%	WHIP	AVG
2023	22	Rocket City (SL)	AA	4	9	5.67	20	20	92	93	21	43	99	10.4	23.9	1.48	.258
2023	22	Los Angeles (AL)	MLB	0	0	9.00	3	0	3	5	0	3	3	17.6	17.6	2.67	.417
Minor League Totals				4	10	5.67	26	26	108	108	22	52	114	10.7	23.4	1.48	.255
Major League Totals				0	0	9.00	3	0	3	5	0	3	3	17.6	17.6	2.67	.417

11 ALBERTO RIOS, OF/C

HIT: 55. **POW:** 45. **RUN:** 45. **FLD:** 40. **ARM:** 40. **BA Grade:** 45. **Risk:** High.

Born: March 19, 2002. **B-T:** R-R. **HT:** 6-0. **WT:** 203. **Drafted:** Stanford, 2023 (3rd round). **Signed by:** Scott Richardson.
TRACK RECORD: Rios spent his first two years at Stanford as a bullpen catcher who accumulated just eight plate appearances. He earned a starting role in left field with Stanford his junior year and went on to slash .384/.485/.707, leading to Pacific-12 Conference player of the year honors. Angels scout Scott Richardson followed his progress closely, and the team selected him in the third round of the 2023 draft, signing him under slot for $847,500. After the draft, he struggled offensively with Low-A Inland Empire before hitting well at instructs while catching.
SCOUTING REPORT: Rios has a short and compact stroke from the right side with great balance and feel for the barrel. Not selling out for power, he swings with intent, allowing his natural strength to help make hard contact to the gaps with near-average power projection. He is a disciplined hitter with good pitch recognition and zone awareness, giving more confidence to his ability to hit for average and reach base with limited swing-and-miss. He is a serviceable defender at best in the outfield who played left field exclusively his junior year and early pro career. He continued catching at instructs, with promising raw traits and glimpses of a fine arm, but his throwing mechanics need attention to stick behind the plate and control the running game. His defensive home is in question, and he'll play multiple positions during development with catching and left field being the focus.
THE FUTURE: With a limited track record, Rios needs more offensive reps to reach his above-average offensive upside while also needing to find a true defensive home. If he can catch, his profile will grow significantly with his offensive prowess.

Year	Age	Club (League)	Level	AVG	G	AB	R	H	2B	3B	HR	RBI	BB	SO	SB	OBP	SLG
2023	21	ACL Angels	Rk	.200	3	10	3	2	0	0	0	1	2	0	1	.333	.200
2023	21	Inland Empire (CAL)	A	.181	33	127	19	23	4	2	3	18	14	37	7	.269	.315
Minor League Totals				.182	36	137	22	25	4	2	3	19	16	37	8	.274	.307

12 DARIO LAVERDE, C

HIT: 50. **POW:** 40. **RUN:** 45. **FLD:** 45. **ARM:** 50. **BA Grade:** 45. **Risk:** High.

Born: February 26, 2005. **B-T:** L-R. **HT:** 5-10. **WT:** 160. **Signed:** Venezuela, 2022. **Signed by:** Marlon Urdaneta.

TRACK RECORD: Laverde signed with the Angels out of Venezuela for $350,000 at the start of the 2022 international signing period. He performed well in his pro debut that summer in the Dominican Summer League, posting an .807 OPS while throwing out 41% of basestealers. He carried his performance into a standout showing at instructs. Laverde again impressed in his stateside debut in 2023, slashing .306/.419/.455 in the Arizona Complex League with 28 walks to 31 strikeouts, flashing shades of former Angels catching prospect Edgar Quero.

SCOUTING REPORT: Laverde is a well-rounded, athletic lefthanded-hitting catcher. He has a flat plane, line-drive swing with high in-zone contact and the ability to manipulate the barrel. A patient hitter who focuses on contact, he has shown an advanced ability to make adjustments and rarely chases out of the zone. Laverde is strong and has a mature frame. He can impact the ball to the gaps with hopes of tapping into more over-the-fence power as he grows. A converted outfielder, Laverde is new to catching. His hands and feet worked well while honing his technique in his setup with Angels catching coordinators. He has a good foundation for lateral movement and receives well. Laverde has above-average arm strength, but his throwing mechanics and release need work. He is an near-average runner with aggressive baserunning instincts and is praised for his elite makeup.

THE FUTURE: Laverde has a lot of work to become an everyday catcher, but his hitting ability gives him a chance to be on the strong side of a platoon. He will make his full-season debut as a teenager in 2024.

Year	Age	Club (League)	Level	AVG	G	AB	R	H	2B	3B	HR	RBI	BB	SO	SB	OBP	SLG
2023	18	ACL Angels	Rk	.306	43	134	23	41	9	4	1	32	28	31	7	.419	.455
Minor League Totals				.302	88	285	58	86	13	10	1	60	49	50	16	.411	.428

13 ADRIAN PLACENCIA, 2B

HIT: 50. **POW:** 40. **RUN:** 40. **FLD:** 55. **ARM:** 45. **BA Grade:** 45. **Risk:** High.

Born: June 2, 2003. **B-T:** B-R. **HT:** 5-11. **WT:** 173. **Signed:** Dominican Republic, 2019. **Signed by:** Jochy Cabrera/Rusbell Cabrera.

TRACK RECORD: Placencia was one of the youngest players in the 2019-20 international class when he signed with the Angels for $1.1 million, but his pro debut stalled a year due to the coronavirus pandemic. After struggling in the Arizona Complex League in 2021, he had a standout season with Low-A Inland Empire in 2022, posting an .814 OPS with 13 home runs while also striking out in 30.3% of his plate appearances. He performed around league average with a 96 wRC+ with High-A Tri-City in 2023 before finishing his season with brief stints in Double-A and the Arizona Fall League.

SCOUTING REPORT: Placencia is an undersized switch-hitting middle infielder. He shows a feel for hitting from both sides of the plate with quick hands and fair barrel control. He knows the strike zone and will draw walks but will get anxious leading to poor pitch selection and swing-and-miss on both breaking balls and moderate-velocity fastballs. He needs to develop his approach to limit mistakes that lead to easy outs. He has solid strength and plus bat speed with sneaky pop and hard contact, but his diminutive frame limits his power. Signed as a shortstop, he lacks the actions and arm to stick on the left side of the infield. His range could make him an above-average defender at second base if he maintains his athleticism while physically maturing. He is an instinctual baserunner with below-average speed.

THE FUTURE: Just 20 years old entering 2024, Placencia is trending in a positive direction offensively. He'll start the season at Double-A and projects as a future second-division regular at second base.

Year	Age	Club (League)	Level	AVG	G	AB	R	H	2B	3B	HR	RBI	BB	SO	SB	OBP	SLG
2023	20	Tri-City (NWL)	A+	.218	109	390	59	85	15	2	9	46	82	133	24	.354	.336
2023	20	Rocket City (SL)	AA	.170	14	53	5	9	0	0	1	4	4	24	0	.237	.226
Minor League Totals				.223	270	968	176	216	41	7	28	133	190	348	49	.357	.367

14 WALBERT URENA, RHP

FB: 70. **SL:** 45. **CHG:** 55. **CTL:** 40. **BA Grade:** 45. **Risk:** High.

Born: January 25, 2004. **B-T:** R-R. **HT:** 6-0. **WT:** 170. **Signed:** Dominican Republic, 2021. **Signed by:** Jochy Cabrera.

TRACK RECORD: Urena signed for $140,000 two months into the 2021 international signing period, but arm injuries delayed his debut by a year. He raised his stock by regularly touching 100 mph during extended spring training and in the Arizona Complex League in 2022, although walks dogged his performance. Walks continued to hinder his performance with Low-A Inland Empire in 2023 until Urena incorporated a sinker and began throwing more strikes, leading to a 3.68 ERA over his final 13 starts.

SCOUTING REPORT: Urena is a lean, undersized righty with special arm strength and velocity. His fastball touches 102 mph and sits 98, but the shape needs work. He added a sinker that sits 94-98 mph and improved his shaky fastball command to fringe-average in the process. Urena could ultimately sit in the triple digits in short stints if he adds strength to his lean frame. He tinkered with multiple grips to find semblance of a real breaking ball, eventually landing on a fringe-average mid-80s slider with depth. His mid-to-upper 80s changeup will flash plus with fade, though the feel for his off-speed needs work. Urena has a basic delivery and shows on-mound athleticism. His control has improved with more reps and confidence throwing strikes, though it may never be better than below-average.

THE FUTURE: Urena has to throw more strikes and find a true breaking ball to reach his immense upside, but his premium velocity and small-stature point toward a future as a power reliever.

Year	Age	Club (League)	Level	W	L	ERA	G	GS	IP	H	HR	BB	SO	BB%	SO%	WHIP	AVG
2023	19	Inland Empire (CAL)	A	4	7	5.66	22	21	99	94	5	60	97	13.5	21.7	1.56	.253
Minor League Totals				7	11	5.16	34	31	136	119	7	92	142	14.9	23.1	1.55	.235

15 FELIX MORROBEL, SS

HIT: 50. **POW:** 40. **RUN:** 50. **FLD:** 55. **ARM:** 50. **BA Grade:** 45. **Risk:** High.

Born: September 24, 2005. **B-T:** B-R. **HT:** 6-0. **WT:** 175. **Signed:** Dominican Republic, 2023. **Signed by:** Rusbell Cabrera.
TRACK RECORD: Morrobel was one of the top infield prospects in the Dominican Republic and was the Angels' primary target when he signed for $900,000 in the 2023 international signing period. He performed well in his pro debut in the Dominican Summer League, hitting .286 with 11 stolen bases.
SCOUTING REPORT: Morrobel is an athletic, switch-hitting shortstop with solid tools across the board. He has a line-drive swing from both sides of the plate with excellent barrel control. He makes hard gap-to-gap power but has virtually nonexistent home run power because of a lack of strength. He has a chance for below-average power as he grows. A highly aggressive hitter, he rarely walked or struck out in his pro debut. He has a solid eye, but also a strong desire to swing because of his ability to make frequent contact. He will have to become more selective as he climbs the development ladder. An average runner, he is an instinctual baserunner who will steal the occasional base. He is an above-average defender at shortstop with good actions and a natural feel for the position that allow him to slow the pace of the game, while his quick release and average arm give him long-term defensive projection at a premium position.
THE FUTURE: Morrobel's defense and ability to hit for average give him utility infield projection, and even below-average power could turn him into a table-setting regular if he adds strength.

Year	Age	Club (League)	Level	AVG	G	AB	R	H	2B	3B	HR	RBI	BB	SO	SB	OBP	SLG
2023	17	DSL Angels	Rk	.286	42	161	21	46	4	2	0	20	8	13	11	.322	.335
Minor League Totals				.286	42	161	21	46	4	2	0	20	8	13	11	.322	.335

16 JUAN FLORES, C

HIT: 30. **POW:** 50. **RUN:** 40. **FLD:** 60. **ARM:** 70. **BA Grade:** 40. **Risk:** Medium.

Born: February 13, 2006. **B-T:** R-R. **HT:** 5-10. **WT:** 180. **Signed:** Venezuela, 2023. **Signed by:** Vicente Lupo.
TRACK RECORD: Viewed as one of Venezuela's best defensive amateur catchers in his class, the Angels signed Flores for $280,000 at the start of the 2023 international signing period. He struggled during the first two weeks of his pro debut in the Dominican Summer League before finishing strong, posting a .767 OPS and 112 wRC+ with six homers in his final 40 games. His 53.1% caught-stealing percentage ranked second in the DSL in 2023.
SCOUTING REPORT: Flores is a small but strong defense-first teenage catcher. He has made harder contact than expected early in development, with a rhythmic line-drive swing from the right side. His swing isn't always synced up and can be upper-body heavy, leading to swinging over the top of balls. When he stays on plane, he can create some over-the-fence impact. He has good hitting instincts with a fine approach and will draw his share of walks while keeping his strikeouts limited, but he'll likely always be power-over-hit with a well below-average hit tool. His calling card will always be his big-league caliber defense behind the plate. Flores has quiet receiving skills, lateral mobility and a plus-plus arm, regularly posting pop times under two seconds. He is a below-average runner. He is praised highly for his makeup.
THE FUTURE: Flores has a chance to be a major league backup on the strength of his defensive ability, but further hitting development could increase his upside. The Angels may challenge his advanced defensive skill set at a full-season affiliate in 2024.

Year	Age	Club (League)	Level	AVG	G	AB	R	H	2B	3B	HR	RBI	BB	SO	SB	OBP	SLG
2023	17	DSL Angels	Rk	.236	46	165	32	39	7	0	6	26	15	25	6	.352	.388
Minor League Totals				.236	46	165	32	39	7	0	6	26	15	25	6	.352	.388

17 RYAN COSTEIU, RHP

FB: 55. **CB:** 45. **CHG:** 60. **CTL:** 45. **BA Grade:** 40. **Risk:** Medium.

Born: November 28, 2000. **B-T:** R-R. **HT:** 6-0. **WT:** 200. **Drafted:** Arkansas, 2021 (7th round). **Signed by:** Joel Murrie.

TRACK RECORD: A two-year starter for Sacramento City (Calif.) JC, Costeiu transferred to Arkansas for his junior season where he worked as a high-leverage reliever. The Angels liked his data-driven arsenal in the seventh round of the 2021 draft and signed him to a near-slot $220,500 bonus. Costeiu struck out 41.9% of hitters in his pro debut between Class A affiliates. He returned to High-A in 2022 with solid results until a mid-July elbow injury required Tommy John surgery and ended his season. He missed all of 2023 and did not throw off a mound before instructional league play.

SCOUTING REPORT: The 6-foot Costeiu is a pitchability righty. He works primarily off his high-spin fastball that sits 92-94 and can reach 95. He works the ball north-to-south with top-of-the-scale carry. His low-80s circle changeup regularly grades plus as a swing-and-miss or weak contact weapon in his arsenal. He has confidence in an upper-70s, big-breaking curveball that he uses as a setup pitch, though its shape—which he had started to alter before the injury—makes it a fringe-average offering. He works around the zone with fringe-average control, with fastball command improvements needed to keep his rotation upside.

THE FUTURE: The Angels will keep Costeiu on a starter track, but his size and limited track record of health could ultimately push him to a middle relief role, where his two above-average pitches could be effective against both righties and lefties. He's expected to make a fully healthy return in 2024.

Year	Age	Club (League)	Level	W	L	ERA	G	GS	IP	H	HR	BB	SO	BB%	SO%	WHIP	AVG
2023	22	Did not play—Injured															
Minor League Totals				4	5	3.45	27	10	86	75	10	25	112	7.2	32.1	1.16	.237

18 KELVIN CACERES, RHP

FB: 60. **CB:** 60. **CHG:** 50. **CTL:** 40. **BA Grade:** 40. **Risk:** Medium.

Born: January 26, 2000. **B-T:** R-R. **HT:** 6-1. **WT:** 205. **Signed:** Dominican Republic, 2018. **Signed by:** Jochy Cabrera.

TRACK RECORD: Caceres signed for $10,000 near the end of the 2017-18 signing period and was a pedestrian performer in a swingman role early in his pro career. He moved to the bullpen almost exclusively in 2022 and missed enough bats with Low-A Inland Empire to earn a trip to the Arizona Fall League. Caceres went unselected in the Rule 5 draft and continued to pitch well in relief in 2023 across three levels. He earned a big league callup and a spot on the 40-man roster during the final week of the season, making a pair of relief appearances.

SCOUTING REPORT: Caceres is a smaller righthanded reliever with a full swing-and-miss arsenal. Both versions of his fastball miss bats. His power four-seamer sits 96-98 mph and flirts with triple digits. But Caceres prefers to use his 95-97 mph two-seamer that induces groundballs at a high clip. His two-plane, low-80s curveball is a swing-and-miss offering that flashes plus and generates 3,000-3,200 rpm of spin. He occasionally throws a changeup that flashes above-average and the Angels hope he utilizes it more often in 2024. Caceres still possesses below-average control despite improving his general strike-throwing in 2023. He's a solid athlete, so there's a chance his control could improve, but his herky-jerky delivery may always keep it fringe-average or worse.

THE FUTURE: Caceres will see time in the upper minors and could reach the majors at some point in 2024. His power swing-and-miss arsenal could play in high-leverage situations if he throws more strikes.

Year	Age	Club (League)	Level	W	L	ERA	G	GS	IP	H	HR	BB	SO	BB%	SO%	WHIP	AVG
2023	23	Tri-City (NWL)	A+	0	0	2.45	11	0	11	8	0	5	21	11.1	46.7	1.18	.205
2023	23	Rocket City (SL)	AA	5	1	5.61	34	0	34	30	3	22	53	13.8	33.3	1.54	.229
2023	23	Salt Lake (PCL)	AAA	1	0	0.90	7	0	10	5	0	5	11	12.5	27.5	1.00	.152
2023	23	Los Angeles (AL)	MLB	0	0	6.75	2	0	1	2	0	2	1	25.0	12.5	3.00	.400
Minor League Totals				12	16	4.53	128	29	262	196	16	178	333	15.0	28.1	1.43	.200
Major League Totals				0	0	6.75	2	0	1	2	0	2	1	25.0	12.5	3.00	.400

19 JADIEL SANCHEZ, OF

HIT: 50. **POW:** 45. **RUN:** 50. **FLD:** 50. **ARM:** 60. **BA Grade:** 40. **Risk:** Medium.

Born: May 10, 2001. **B-T:** B-R. **HT:** 6-2. **WT:** 185. **Drafted:** HS—Arroyo, PR, 2019 (12th round). **Signed by:** Luis Raffan (Phillies).

TRACK RECORD: The Puerto Rico native had a quiet pro debut after signing an above-slot $300,000 bonus in 2019. He hit .297 over 21 games in a stint with Low-A Clearwater in 2021, but struggled to replicate those results at the same level in 2022. The Angels acquired Sanchez along with Mickey Moniak at the 2022 trade deadline in exchange for Noah Syndergaard. Lower body soft tissue injuries hindered the start of his Angels tenure, but he sustained more success in 2023, hitting .304 with a .903 OPS between May and September with Low-A Inland Empire.

SCOUTING REPORT: Sanchez is a physically talented switch-hitting outfielder with interesting offensive tools. He has an aesthetically pleasing swing from both sides of the plate with solid bat-to-ball skills despite an immense bat wrap. He'll show above-average raw power in batting practice and has started to tap into that power in games to his pull side as he's physically matured, but his contact-driven mindset deteriorates from his overall power projection. His zone coverage make him a rare strikeout victim, while he is a patient hitter from the right side and much more aggressive from the left. An average runner, he lacks the range and athleticism for center field but is capable in corner outfield spots with a plus arm.

THE FUTURE: A fifth-year pro who is 22 years old with no experience above Low-A, Sanchez will have to continue gaining regular reps and hitting at a high clip to meet his bat-first bench bat projection.

Year	Age	Club (League)	Level	AVG	G	AB	R	H	2B	3B	HR	RBI	BB	SO	SB	OBP	SLG
2023	22	Inland Empire (CAL)	A	.297	105	381	59	113	15	10	11	66	47	64	7	.378	.475
Minor League Totals				.277	197	711	97	197	27	14	20	105	74	130	10	.350	.439

20 JOEL HURTADO, RHP

FB: 70. **CB:** 45. **SL:** 55. **CTL:** 45. **BA Grade:** 40. **Risk:** Medium.

Born: February 6, 2001. **B-T:** R-R. **HT:** 6-2. **WT:** 180. **Signed:** Dominican Republic, 2022.
Signed by: Jonathan Genao/Rusbell Cabrera.

TRACK RECORD: Angels international scouts discovered the 21-year-old Hurtado late in the 2022 signing period and the team signed him for just $10,000. Hurtado was passable in his Dominican Summer League pro debut in 2022, but struggled stateside in 2023 with Low-A Inland Empire.

SCOUTING REPORT: Hurtado is a strong, lean righthanded pitcher with two above-average pitches. He works primarily off his power sinker that sits 95-99 mph with considerable armside run, with the ability to hold peak velocity deep into outings. Still maturing physically, he could add more strength to his lean frame and see his fastball flirt with triple digits more regularly in shorter stints. His mid-to-upper-80s slider flashes plus and is his primary swing-and-miss offering. The pitch dramatically improved under the tutelage of Angels development coach Elmer Dessens, showing more depth than sweep. He'll alter the shape and velocity of his breaking ball, turning it into a fringe-average downer curve that he uses in lieu of a changeup. With a basic three-quarters delivery, Hurtado operates around the zone with fringe-average control, while improvements to his breaking ball command could turn his control into average.

THE FUTURE: Hurtado has back-of-the-rotation upside if he can find a true third pitch, but his two above-average pitchers provide a fallback as a potential quick-moving, multi-inning power reliever.

Year	Age	Club (League)	Level	W	L	ERA	G	GS	IP	H	HR	BB	SO	BB%	SO%	WHIP	AVG
2023	22	Inland Empire (CAL)	A	6	5	5.42	22	10	78	78	2	31	90	9.1	26.3	1.40	.260
Minor League Totals				7	6	5.06	27	14	96	90	5	40	111	9.6	26.7	1.35	.248

21 CAMDEN MINACCI, RHP

FB: 60. **SL:** 60. **CTL:** 45. **BA Grade:** 40. **Risk:** Medium.

Born: January 14, 2002. **B-T:** L-R. **HT:** 6-3. **WT:** 215. **Drafted:** Wake Forest, 2023 (6th round). **Signed by:** Nick Gorneault.

TRACK RECORD: Minacci secured Wake Forest's closer role as a sophomore and spent two years as one of the top closers in college. He saved 13 games and pitched to a 2.78 ERA his junior year. The Angels liked his fire and energy, drafting him in the sixth round and signing him to a $328,500 bonus in 2023. Minacci pitched to a 5.40 ERA and allowed 18 hits in 8.1 innings with Low-A Inland Empire.

SCOUTING REPORT: A strong righty, Minacci is a relief-only pitching prospect with two plus pitches. He sets up and attacks hitters with his fastball that sits 93-96 mph and touches 99 with notable ride. His mid-to-upper-80s slider is a swing-and-miss offering that flashes plus when he stays on top of it, with more vertical depth than sweep that he will work away from righthanders and around the hands of lefthanders. Though his highly active delivery results in fringe-average control, he has steadily improved his fastball command. He keeps his heater around the zone and allows his slider to tunnel well off of it. Minacci has a fearless approach and shows a high intensity on the mound.

THE FUTURE: Minacci has the aptitude and arsenal suited for a role in middle relief. He could move quickly and has a shot to reach the majors at some point in 2024.

Year	Age	Club (League)	Level	W	L	ERA	G	GS	IP	H	HR	BB	SO	BB%	SO%	WHIP	AVG
2023	21	Inland Empire (CAL)	A	0	0	5.40	7	0	8	18	0	1	10	2.3	23.3	2.28	.450
Minor League Totals				0	0	5.63	7	0	8	18	0	1	10	2.3	23.3	2.38	.450

22 JORDYN ADAMS, OF

HIT: 30. **POW:** 40. **RUN:** 80. **FLD:** 60. **ARM:** 45. **BA Grade:** 40. **Risk:** Medium.

Born: October 18, 1999. **B-T:** R-R. **HT:** 6-2. **WT:** 181. **Drafted:** HS—Cary, NC, 2018 (1st round).
Signed by: Chris McAlpin.
TRACK RECORD: The Angels banked on the athleticism of Adams, a three-sport athlete committed to play football and baseball at North Carolina, when they drafted him No. 17 overall in 2018 and signed him to an over-slot $4.1 million bonus. He impressed in his first two seasons in the low minors, but struggled mightily upon returning from the 2020 shutdown. Adams hit enough with Triple-A Salt Lake (.817 OPS) to earn a big league callup in August, where he hit .128 with 16 strikeouts in 17 games.
SCOUTING REPORT: Adams is a premium athlete with game-changing speed. He has tinkered with multiple swing alterations during his development, even showing irregularities from swing to swing. Adams' tinkering led to weak contact and erratic swing-and-miss. He made adjustments that returned his natural athleticism and strength to his swing, allowing him to hit the ball harder and tap into his power more consistently. He doesn't have a bad approach and swings at strikes, but swing-and-miss will likely always be part of his game. Adams is an 80-grade runner both on the basepaths and in center field. He tracks flyballs like a wide receiver and his closing speed makes him a plus defender at a premium defensive position.
THE FUTURE: Adams will have to hit more consistently to be more than a late-inning pinch runner and defensive replacement. He has an opportunity to carve out a big league role in 2024.

Year	Age	Club (League)	Level	AVG	G	AB	R	H	2B	3B	HR	RBI	BB	SO	SB	OBP	SLG
2023	23	Salt Lake (PCL)	AAA	.267	109	415	74	111	25	6	15	67	53	133	44	.351	.465
2023	23	Los Angeles (AL)	MLB	.128	17	39	1	5	0	0	0	1	0	16	1	.125	.128
Minor League Totals				.249	438	1645	251	409	73	19	32	185	193	514	116	.333	.374
Major League Totals				.128	17	39	1	5	0	0	0	1	0	16	1	.125	.128

23 JORGE RUIZ, OF

HIT: 50. **POW:** 30. **RUN:** 55. **FLD:** 50. **ARM:** 45. **BA Grade:** 40. **Risk:** High.

Born: June 30, 2004. **B-T:** L-L. **HT:** 5-10. **WT:** 163. **Signed:** Venezuela, 2021. **Signed by:** Felix Feliz.
TRACK RECORD: Ruiz has hit ever since signing for $10,000 four months into the 2021 international signing period. He fell two points shy of the Arizona Complex League batting title in 2022 and followed that with a standout performance at Angels instructs. Ruiz went on to hit .304 through 73 games with Low-A Inland Empire in 2023 until an ankle injury sustained while sliding for a ball in the outfield required season-ending surgery.
SCOUTING REPORT: Despite being undersized, Ruiz is an offensive-minded outfielder. He has a slap-and-dash swing from the left side with excellent barrel control and zone coverage. A highly aggressive hitter, he believes he can hit any pitch and has done so thus far in his career. He will need to be more selective as he continues developing. Ruiz is also lacking physically and needs strength gains to prove he can turn on the ball to project more than well below-average power. He is an above-average runner who can steal bases and cover ground in the outfield, but played left field strictly in 2023 in deference to fellow prospect Nelson Rada. His fringe arm and inexperience in center field may one day make him a better fit for left field anyway.
THE FUTURE: Ruiz projects as an offense-first bench outfielder with the chance to become more if he adds strengths and shows he can handle center field.

Year	Age	Club (League)	Level	AVG	G	AB	R	H	2B	3B	HR	RBI	BB	SO	SB	OBP	SLG
2023	18	Inland Empire (CAL)	A	.304	73	296	49	90	19	3	3	52	28	54	13	.379	.419
Minor League Totals				.305	179	673	117	205	40	7	4	90	62	99	40	.380	.403

24 WERNER BLAKELY, 3B

HIT: 40. **POW:** 50. **RUN:** 60. **FLD:** 50. **ARM:** 55. **BA Grade:** 40. **Risk:** High.

Born: February 21, 2002. **B-T:** L-R. **HT:** 6-3. **WT:** 185. **Drafted:** HS—Detroit, 2020 (4th round).
Signed by: Drew Dominguez.
TRACK RECORD: Blakely missed his senior season at Detroit-area Edison Academy because of the pandemic. But the Angels were enticed enough by his tools to sign him for $900,000 in the fourth round of the 2020 draft to buy him out of an Auburn commitment. Fluky injuries have limited Blakely to just 211 professional games through three seasons, where he has hit .227/.358/.356 but shown promising signs during stretches of good health.
SCOUTING REPORT: Blakely is a tall and athletic infielder with intriguing power and speed tools. He has a loose and whippy swing from the left side with plus bat speed that allows him to tap into his plus raw

power as he grows into his lean 6-foot-3 frame. He hasn't seen quality pitches regularly, though, because of lost reps due to injury, resulting in poor chase and strikeout rates. Still, he's shown the ability to make adjustments in the box. He has improved his defensive consistency at third base with better footwork and range to his glove side. There's confidence he can stick at third, where his plus arm plays, but he's athletic enough to maneuver center field and the Angels may opt to develop him there. He's a plus runner.

THE FUTURE: Blakely has impact tools and is trending in the right direction but will need to be healthy to make up for lost reps and find consistency to reach his substantial upside.

Year	Age	Club (League)	Level	AVG	G	AB	R	H	2B	3B	HR	RBI	BB	SO	SB	OBP	SLG
2023	21	Tri-City (NWL)	A+	.214	92	323	45	69	17	3	5	28	44	137	22	.316	.331
2023	21	Rocket City (SL)	AA	.000	2	7	0	0	0	0	0	0	2	5	0	.222	.000
Minor League Totals				.227	193	661	103	150	36	5	13	87	124	281	61	.358	.356

25 ANTHONY SCULL, OF

HIT: 50. **POW:** 45. **RUN:** 55. **FLD:** 50. **ARM:** 50. **BA Grade:** 40. **Risk:** High.

Born: January 26, 2004. **B-T:** L-L. **HT:** 6-0. **WT:** 165. **Signed:** Cuba, 2021. **Signed by:** Rusbell Cabrera.

TRACK RECORD: The son of 19-year Cuban major league star Antonio Scull, Anthony signed with the Angels late in the 2021 international signing period for $235,000. He hit .306 in his brief Arizona Complex League debut in 2022, but a shoulder injury limited him to 13 games. He returned to the ACL with a clean bill of health and hit .300 with an .830 OPS, then earned MVP honors at the Angels' instructional league series at Angel Stadium.

SCOUTING REPORT: Scull is an athletic lefthanded-hitting outfielder with a well-rounded toolset. He has a compact swing from the left side with solid bat speed that allows him to make optimal contact and drive the ball to the gaps with authority. He has the ability to do damage, while his flat swing plane doesn't always allow him to tap into his above-average pull side raw power. An aggressive hitter, he is working on finding a more balanced approach while making better swing decisions and keeping his strikeouts in check. He is an above-average runner which helps him steal the occasional base and cover ground across all three outfield positions, while his athleticism and aggression could keep him in center field long term. He has an average arm.

THE FUTURE: Scull's physical maturation will dictate whether he can grow into enough power to fit a corner profile. He will make his full-season affiliate debut in 2024 at 20 years old.

Year	Age	Club (League)	Level	AVG	G	AB	R	H	2B	3B	HR	RBI	BB	SO	SB	OBP	SLG
2023	19	ACL Angels	Rk	.300	48	170	31	51	7	5	3	30	12	41	10	.377	.453
Minor League Totals				.279	72	233	45	65	7	8	3	43	20	64	14	.361	.416

26 ADRIAN ACOSTA, RHP

FB: 55. **SL:** 55. **CHG:** 40. **CTL:** 45. **BA Grade:** 40. **Risk:** Very High.

Born: May 20, 2005. **B-T:** R-R. **HT:** 6-1. **WT:** 170. **Signed:** Dominican Republic, 2022. **Signed by:** Jochy Cabrera.

TRACK RECORD: The Angels signed Acosta for a modest $10,000 late in the 2022 international signing period. He remained unheralded as a swingman in his Dominican Summer League debut. But he showed improved fastball command and an uptick in velocity in 2023, blossoming in a full-time starting role. Acosta led the DSL with a 1.17 ERA and started the league's all-star game, earning the victory.

SCOUTING REPORT: Acosta is a strong and athletic 6-foot-1 righthander with two above-average pitches. He has drastically improved the command of his fastball, which sits 92-95 and touches 96, and could tick up even more in relief. He shows good feel for a low-to-mid-80s sweeping slider that has become his bat-missing out pitch. Acosta's sparsely-used changeup is in the rudimentary stages of development and is a distant third pitch with fringy potential. He has shown below-average command, but has a sound delivery and the athletic markers to suggest his command could improve over time. Acosta's natural strength gives him the ability to hold velocity deep into outings.

THE FUTURE: Acosta will have to develop his changeup and improve his command to keep his backend rotation upside. He will make his U.S. debut in 2024 as a teenager.

Year	Age	Club (League)	Level	W	L	ERA	G	GS	IP	H	HR	BB	SO	BB%	SO%	WHIP	AVG
2023	18	DSL Angels	Rk	2	3	1.17	10	10	46	28	1	22	64	11.7	34.0	1.08	.174
Minor League Totals				4	4	3.23	23	17	78	57	5	45	101	12.9	29.0	1.31	.201

27 CAPRI ORTIZ, SS

HIT: 50. **POW:** 30. **RUN:** 70. **FLD:** 55. **ARM:** 50. **BA Grade:** 40. **Risk:** Very High.

Born: April 1, 2005. **B-T:** B-R. **HT:** 6-0. **WT:** 150. **Signed:** Dominican Republic, 2022. **Signed by:** Rusbell Cabrera.

TRACK RECORD: Ortiz signed for $125,000 during the 2022 international signing period and made his pro debut in the Dominican Summer League later that summer, finishing strong after early struggles. During his stateside debut in 2023, he hit .273 while learning to switch-hit in the Arizona Complex League, while setting a new single-season affiliate record with 30 stolen bases.

SCOUTING REPORT: Ortiz is an athletic, undersized and speedy shortstop. He's a natural righthanded hitter, but began switch-hitting midway through the 2023 complex league season. He's more of a slap-and-dash hitter with solid bat-to-ball skills and well below-average power. Ortiz infrequently shows a line drive swing more geared to drive the ball from both sides. He can be strikeout prone and struggles to make adjustments to his aggressive approach, but he causes havoc when putting the ball in play with game-changing speed. He is a 70-grade runner with the ability and aggression to use that speed on the basepaths. He has quick feet and an average arm at shortstop but will have to improve his actions to stick there in the long run. He has the athleticism to stay up the middle and played center field as an amateur.

THE FUTURE: Ortiz needs serious strength gains and a more consistent swing to see any offensive impact, but his defensive upside and elite speed give him a strong chance at a super utility type bench role. He will make his full-season affiliate debut in 2024 at 19 years old.

Year	Age	Club (League)	Level	AVG	G	AB	R	H	2B	3B	HR	RBI	BB	SO	SB	OBP	SLG
2023	18	ACL Angels	Rk	.273	53	194	39	53	8	3	0	22	29	68	30	.374	.345
Minor League Totals				.257	106	385	67	99	15	8	2	48	43	120	46	.341	.353

28 DAVID CALABRESE, OF

HIT: 40. **POW:** 45. **RUN:** 70. **FLD:** 60. **ARM:** 50. **BA Grade:** 40. **Risk:** Very High.

Born: September 26, 2002. **B-T:** L-R. **HT:** 5-11. **WT:** 160. **Drafted:** HS—Thornhill, ON, 2020 (3rd round). **Signed by:** Chris Cruz.

TRACK RECORD: Calabrese reclassified to become draft eligible in 2020, but was sparsely seen by scouts that spring because of the coronavirus pandemic. The Angels liked his tools and youth, and signed him to a $744,200 bonus in the third round to keep him from an Arkansas commitment. Injuries and the pandemic slowed the start of his career, but he turned a corner in 2022, hitting .301 with an .843 OPS in his final 57 games with Low-A Inland Empire. The Angels assigned him aggressively to Double-A in 2023 at 20 years old and he performed poorly.

SCOUTING REPORT: Calabrese is an athletic lefthanded-hitting outfielder with intriguing tools. He has a loose and rhythmic swing that has been altered throughout development to make him more upright and get his hands in a better hitting position to drive the ball with more authority. Calabrese is a patient hitter, but also deals with significant swing-and-miss. He has sacrificed contact to tap into his fringe-average power as he has physically matured. He is a plus-plus runner who uses his instincts well on the basepaths. He is a plus defender at all three outfield positions with an accurate arm.

THE FUTURE: His speed and defense make him a candidate for a bench role, but Calabrese needs to hit to unlock more. He's only 21 years old, but the clock is ticking as he approaches Rule 5 eligibility following the 2024 season.

Year	Age	Club (League)	Level	AVG	G	AB	R	H	2B	3B	HR	RBI	BB	SO	SB	OBP	SLG
2023	20	Rocket City (SL)	AA	.194	122	458	63	89	18	3	15	48	70	164	14	.309	.345
Minor League Totals				.218	276	1026	156	224	49	12	23	129	140	334	45	.315	.357

29 JOE REDFIELD JR., OF

HIT: 50. **POW:** 40. **RUN:** 55. **FLD:** 50. **ARM:** 50. **BA Grade:** 40. **Risk:** Very High.

Born: October 18, 2001. **B-T:** L-R. **HT:** 6-2. **WT:** 200. **Drafted:** Sam Houston State, 2023 (4th round). **Signed by:** Brian Gordon.

TRACK RECORD: Redfield spent two seasons at Temple (Texas) JC before transferring to Sam Houston State for his junior season. He was among the nation's top performers, slashing .402/.485/.683 while ranking top 10 in Division I in hits (100) and runs (81). He signed an under-slot $472,500 deal in the fourth round of the 2023 draft. Redfield was limited to 12 games with High-A Tri-City because of a concussion, although he was a full participant in instructs. He is the son of former big league third baseman Joe Redfield, who made his MLB debut with the 1988 Angels.

SCOUTING REPORT: Redfield is an athletic outfielder with a well-rounded toolset, albeit without an obvious carrying tool. He has a quick, compact swing from the left side while staying low through his operation with minimal stride and load focused toward the barrel. He has solid bat speed and natural strength, but his swing plane can get downhill which limits his ability to frequently impact the ball and suggests fringe power potential. He controls the zone well, rarely expanding, while his barrel control permits good zone coverage and ability to handle velocity. He is an above-average runner with good baserunning instincts and the ability to cover ground in center field.

THE FUTURE: Redfield fits a fourth outfielder profile, although he could ultimately fit on the strong side of a platoon if he shows he can handle center field at the upper levels.

Year	Age	Club (League)	Level	AVG	G	AB	R	H	2B	3B	HR	RBI	BB	SO	SB	OBP	SLG
2023	21	ACL Angels	Rk	.200	3	10	1	2	1	0	0	1	1	1	1	.333	.300
2023	21	Tri-City (NWL)	A+	.255	12	47	8	12	3	1	1	8	5	10	2	.340	.426
Minor League Totals				.246	15	57	9	14	4	1	1	9	6	11	3	.338	.404

30 JORGE MARCHECO, RHP

FB: 40. **CB:** 30. **SL:** 45. **CHG:** 40. **CTL:** 60. **BA Grade:** 40. **Risk:** Very High.

Born: August 6, 2002. **B-T:** R-R. **HT:** 6-1. **WT:** 185. **Signed:** Cuba, 2021. **Signed by:** Frank Tejeda.

TRACK RECORD: Marcheco signed for $35,000 in September 2021 and was stellar in his pro debut later that month, striking out 20 of the 28 batters he faced. He pitched well in his stateside debut in 2022 and again in 2023, earning a promotion to High-A Tri-City, where he posted a 1.88 ERA in 28.2 innings. The Angels sent Marcheco back to Low-A Inland Empire for its playoff push but his numbers ballooned after allowing 20 runs in 22 innings.

SCOUTING REPORT: Marcheco is an undersized righthanded pitcher who relies on pitchability and deception. He is reliant on a fastball that sits 87-89 mph and touches 91. While it lacks in velocity, his ability to command it makes it successful in getting chases above the zone. He manipulates the shape and speed of his slider, working it 74-81 mph, altering a sweepy breaker and slurve, though both variations are fringe-average. He has some feel for a changeup, but it lags behind his slider. He will occasionally throw an eephus-like curveball in the mid-to-upper-60s as a change-of-pace breaker, though it wouldn't work being thrown multiple times in an outing. He has plus command of his full arsenal and finds success through deception, altering his arm slot and pace of his delivery.

THE FUTURE: Marcheco needs to add velocity and find a better breaking ball to turn over a Major League lineup multiple times and reach his back-of-the-rotation upside.

Year	Age	Club (League)	Level	W	L	ERA	G	GS	IP	H	HR	BB	SO	BB%	SO%	WHIP	AVG
2023	20	Inland Empire (CAL)	A	7	5	4.06	17	17	93	77	11	23	91	6.1	24.1	1.08	.223
2023	20	Tri-City (NWL)	A+	3	1	1.88	5	5	29	22	4	3	33	2.8	30.6	0.87	.210
Minor League Totals				15	9	3.38	39	36	193	149	19	41	234	5.3	30.4	0.99	.210

BaseballAmerica.com   Baseball America 2024 Prospect Handbook · **225**

Los Angeles Dodgers

BY KYLE GLASER

The Dodgers don't rebuild. They reload. That maxim held true once again in 2023. Despite losing Trea Turner, Justin Turner and Cody Bellinger in free agency and losing Walker Buehler, Gavin Lux, Tony Gonsolin and Dustin May to injuries, the Dodgers still went 100-62 and won their 10th National League West title in the last 11 seasons. They used 16 rookies, led by righthander Bobby Miller and center fielder James Outman, and again flexed their unparalleled organizational depth to win the division by 16 games.

But for all their regular-season success, the Dodgers once again disappointed in the postseason. The Dodgers were unceremoniously swept by the D-backs in the National League Division Series, their most underwhelming postseason performance yet. It was the first time the Dodgers had been swept in a playoff series since 2006. Their 11-2 loss in Game 1 was their largest loss in Dodger Stadium playoff history.

Despite 11 straight postseason appearances, the Dodgers have only one World Series title to show for it, and that came in the shortened 2020 season.

After losing so much core talent in recent years, the Dodgers stand to lose more. Franchise icon Clayton Kershaw battled a shoulder injury throughout the season's final months and is nearing retirement. Lefthander Julio Urias, already set to be a free agent after the season, was placed on administrative leave in September after being arrested on domestic violence charges. Key offseason acquisition J.D. Martinez is a free agent after 2023 and longtime slugger Max Muncy will be a free agent after 2024.

Once again, the Dodgers will rely on their stable of homegrown talent to keep them rolling. Rookie righthanders Miller, Emmet Sheehan and Ryan Pepiot helped keep the Dodgers' rotation afloat after injuries to Kershaw, May and Gonsolin and Urias' arrest. Outman was a revelation in center field, while infielder Michael Busch, outfielder Jonny Deluca and righthander Kyle Hurt made their big league debuts and showed flashes of their ability.

Even after graduating substantial talent from their farm system in recent years, the Dodgers have plenty more. Busch won the Pacific Coast League MVP award in 2023 and is ready for a bigger role in the Dodgers lineup. Double-A Tulsa's rotation was the talk of the minors with Sheehan, Hurt, Nick Frasso, River Ryan and the since-traded Nick Nastrini. The organization's rich history of homegrown catchers continued with the development of 2022 first-round pick Dalton Rushing and the emergence of 20-year-old Thayron Liranzo, who

Bobby Miller finished second on the Dodgers' depleted pitching staff with 124 innings.

PROJECTED 2027 LINEUP

Catcher	Will Smith	32
First Base	Dalton Rushing	26
Second Base	Miguel Vargas	27
Third Base	Michael Busch	29
Shortstop	Gavin Lux	29
Left Field	Andy Pages	26
Center Field	James Outman	30
Right Field	Mookie Betts	34
Designated Hitter	Freddie Freeman	37
No. 1 Starter	Bobby Miller	28
No. 2 Starter	Dustin May	29
No. 3 Starter	Tony Gonsolin	33
No. 4 Starter	Ryan Pepiot	29
No. 5 Starter	Emmet Sheehan	27
Closer	Evan Phillips	32

led all minor league catchers with a .962 OPS. He also lead the Cal League with 24 home runs.

It won't just be up to homegrown talents to help the Dodgers continue their NL West success and get over their playoff hump. The Dodgers are expected to be the top suitor in free agency for Shohei Ohtani and have the financial resources to add any player they deem necessary.

With stable ownership willing to spend, a starstudded roster and deep farm system, the Dodgers are in position to contend for World Series titles for years to come.

But merely contending for World Series titles isn't good enough anymore. The task, with increasing urgency, is to start winning them. ∎

LOS ANGELES DODGERS

TOP 2024 CONTRIBUTORS	RANK
1. Michael Busch, 3B	1
2. Gavin Stone, RHP	3
3. Andy Pages, OF	4

BREAKOUT PROSPECTS	RANK
1. Payton Martin, RHP	18
2. Joendry Vargas, SS	19

SOURCE OF TOP 30 TALENT

Homegrown	27	Acquired	3
College	12	Trade	3
Junior college	1	Rule 5 draft	0
High school	4	Independent league	0
Nondrafted free agent	1	Free agent/waivers	0
International	9		

LF
Samuel Muñoz (28)
Kyle Nevin
Ryan Ward

CF
Jonny Deluca (13)
Kendall George (15)
Jose Ramos (24)
Chris Newell (30)
Eduardo Quintero
Drew Avans

RF
Andy Pages (4)
Josue De Paula (6)
Damon Keith

3B
Michael Busch (1)
Jake Gelof (26)
Rayne Doncon
Jeral Perez

SS
Joendry Vargas (19)
Alex Freeland (25)
Alexander Albertus
Jose Izarra

2B
Jorbit Vivas (17)
Austin Gauthier (20)
Kenneth Betancourt
Oswaldo Osorio

1B
Griffin Lockwood-Powell

C
Dalton Rushing (2)
Diego Cartaya (9)
Thayron Liranzo (12)
Yeiner Fernandez (21)
Hunter Feduccia
Jesus Galiz

LHP

LHSP	LHRP
Maddux Bruns (10)	Ronan Kopp (16)
Justin Wrobleski (13)	John Rooney (29)
Wyatt Crowell	Alec Gamboa
	Ben Harris

RHP

RHSP	RHRP
Gavin Stone (3)	Gus Varland (22)
Nick Frasso (5)	Ben Casparius (23)
Kyle Hurt (7)	Ryan Sublette
River Ryan (9)	Jake Pilarski
Landon Knack (11)	Chris Campos
Payton Martin (18)	Patrick Copen
Peter Heubeck (27)	Lucas Wepf
Jerming Rosario	Braydon Fisher
Jared Karros	Livan Reinoso
Hyun-il Choi	
Yon Castro	
Kendall Williams	

1 MICHAEL BUSCH, 3B/2B

Born: November 9, 1997. **B-T:** L-R. **HT:** 6-1. **WT:** 210.
Drafted: North Carolina, 2019 (1st round).
Signed by: Jonah Rosenthal.

TRACK RECORD: One of eight children in his family, Busch starred as one of the best athletes in recent Minnesota prep history at Simley High. He led the Spartans football team to the state final as the quarterback, captained the hockey team and was a two-time all-state baseball player. He chose baseball as his path and started all three years at North Carolina, where he hit 32 career home runs and finished second in school history with 143 career walks. The Dodgers drafted him 31st overall in 2019 and signed him for $2.312 million. Injuries to his right hand hindered Busch his first two seasons, but he broke out with full health in 2022 and led the minor leagues in runs scored. He followed up with an even better season in 2023 at Triple-A Oklahoma City. Busch hit .323/.431/.618, all career highs, and finished second in the minors with a 1.049 OPS. He received three different callups to the majors with the Dodgers, won the Pacific Coast League MVP award and was named the Dodgers' minor league player of the year.

SCOUTING REPORT: Busch is a polished, well-rounded offensive performer. He has a calm, controlled presence in the batter's box and maintains elite strike-zone discipline. He recognizes pitches early and barrels both high-end velocity and quality secondary stuff with a balanced, powerful lefthanded stroke. He drives balls hard in the air from foul pole to foul pole and is a true all-fields hitter who can take what the pitcher gives him. He can be overly passive at times, but he has improved his approach to jump on hittable pitches and get the most from his natural strength, hand-eye coordination and plate discipline. He projects to be an at least above-average hitter who draws lots of walks and gets to his plus power in games. The Dodgers drafted Busch as a first baseman and attempted to turn him into a second baseman, but his lack of range makes him a liability without the help of a shift. He's a below-average runner who lacks quickness and agility and is a below-average defender at the keystone. He began playing third base in 2023 and started most of his games there in Triple-A and the majors. He shows a good feel for body positioning and reading angles at the hot corner but is still a below-average defender learning the nuances of the position. Busch has also seen time

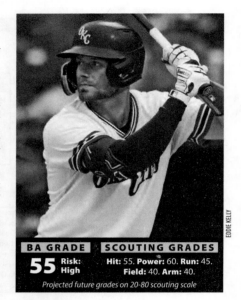

EDDIE KELLY

BA GRADE	SCOUTING GRADES
55 Risk: High	Hit: 55. Power: 60. Run: 45.
	Field: 40. Arm: 40.

Projected future grades on 20-80 scouting scale

BEST TOOLS

BATTING

Best Hitter for Average	Josue De Paula
Best Power Hitter	Dalton Rushing
Best Strike-Zone Discipline	Michael Busch
Fastest Baserunner	Kendall George
Best Athlete	Jonny Deluca

PITCHING

Best Fastball	Nick Frasso
Best Curveball	Maddux Bruns
Best Slider	River Ryan
Best Changeup	Kyle Hurt
Best Control	Landon Knack

FIELDING

Best Defensive Catcher	Diego Cartaya
Best Defensive Infielder	Alex Freeland
Best Infield Arm	Mairoshendrick Martinus
Best Defensive Outfielder	Jonny Deluca
Best Outfield Arm	Jose Ramos

in left field, but his best position remains first base. He has below-average arm strength.

THE FUTURE: Busch projects to be a middle-of-the-order force who gets on base and hits for power, but he is blocked at first base by Freddie Freeman and has to find a position to break into the Dodgers' lineup. The Dodgers received multiple offers for Busch at the trade deadline but held onto him because of his offensive potential. He will try to improve his defense at third base enough to be the eventual successor to Max Muncy. ∎

Year	Age	Club (League)	Level	AVG	G	AB	R	H	2B	3B	HR	RBI	BB	SO	SB	OBP	SLG
2023	25	Okla. City (PCL)	AAA	.323	98	390	85	126	26	4	27	90	65	88	4	.431	.618
2023	25	Los Angeles (NL)	MLB	.167	27	72	9	12	3	0	2	7	8	27	1	.247	.292
Minor League Totals				.283	357	1375	292	389	91	5	79	267	216	389	10	.390	.529
Major League Totals				.167	27	72	9	12	3	0	2	7	8	27	1	.247	.292

2 DALTON RUSHING, C

HIT: 45. **POW:** 65. **RUN:** 45. **FLD:** 45. **ARM:** 55. **BA Grade:** 55. **Risk:** High.

Born: February 21, 2001. **B-T:** L-R. **HT:** 6-1. **WT:** 220.
Drafted: Louisville, 2022 (2nd round). **Signed by:** Marty Lamb.

TRACK RECORD: Rushing spent his first two seasons at Louisville as the back-up catcher behind 2021 first overall pick Henry Davis but flourished once he got the chance to start. He hit a team-high 23 homers for the Cardinals in his lone season as the starter in 2022 and was drafted 40th overall by the Dodgers. He hit .424 in 28 games for Low-A Rancho Cucamonga after signing and continued to shine in his first full season in 2023. Rushing went on the injured list twice with a lingering concussion but still had 15 home runs in 89 games at High-A Great Lakes.

SCOUTING REPORT: A hard-hitting linebacker in high school, Rushing is a muscular, broad-chested specimen who can squat 700 pounds. He's a patient hitter with excellent strike-zone discipline and demolishes pitches over the plate with a violent, compact swing. He frequently posts exit velocities over 110 mph and shows nearly plus-plus power with towering home runs to right field. Rushing's hands aren't particularly fluid and he can be beat by velocity up in the zone, but his discipline and power give him a chance to be a fringe-average hitter who reaches 30 home runs per season. Rushing is a good athlete behind the plate and flashes soft hands, but his receiving remains raw. He is still honing his technique and stances and projects to be a fringe-average defender. He has above-average arm strength that is hamstrung by poor accuracy. Rushing is a fiery competitor, but sometimes he gets too intense and gets off track with his game-calling and management.

THE FUTURE: Rushing will continue to develop as a catcher but may end up at first base, with Will Smith entrenched behind the plate for the Dodgers. He has the bat to be an impact, middle-of-the-order hitter at any position.

Year	Age	Club (League)	Level	AVG	G	AB	R	H	2B	3B	HR	RBI	BB	SO	SB	OBP	SLG
2023	22	Great Lakes (MWL)	A+	.228	89	290	55	66	18	1	15	53	72	93	1	.404	.452
Minor League Totals				.274	119	394	82	108	29	1	23	83	94	115	2	.435	.528

3 GAVIN STONE, RHP

FB: 55. **SL:** 50. **CUT:** 40. **CHG:** 65. **CTL:** 55. **BA Grade:** 50. **Risk:** Medium.

Born: October 15, 1998. **B-T:** R-R. **HT:** 6-1. **WT:** 175.
Drafted: Central Arkansas, 2020 (5th round). **Signed by:** Brian Kraft

TRACK RECORD: While Bobby Miller, Ryan Pepiot and Emmet Sheehan all played big roles as midseason callups on the Dodgers' pitching staff in 2023, Stone fell behind. The 2020 fifth-rounder won the minor league ERA title in 2022 and appeared primed for a role on the Dodgers' staff, but he suffered a blister on his toe in spring training that threw off his delivery, leading to a decline in his stuff and control. He got crushed for a 9.00 ERA and .338 opponent average over his eight appearances with the Dodgers and posted the worst ERA (4.74), walk rate (10.7%) and strikeout rate (27.8%) of his career at Triple-A Oklahoma City. He managed to finish on a high note with 6.1 innings and 10 strikeouts to win the deciding game of the Pacific Coast League championship series.

SCOUTING REPORT: Stone is a slight but athletic righthander with a fierce competitive streak. His fastball sits 94 mph and touches 98 out of a low release point that gives it added carry. His 83-87 mph changeup is nearly a plus-plus pitch with late run and dive, and his mid-80s slider flashes average with depth and late bite. Stone's arsenal is loud, but his pitch selection needs improvement. He falls in love with his changeup and major league hitters took advantage, ignoring his slider and sitting on his change to make him a two-pitch pitcher. He added a 89-91 cutter during the season to give him another option, but it's a below-average offering in its nascent stages. Stone throws strikes with above-average control when his delivery is right, but his fastball command is only average and he'll catch too much of the plate.

THE FUTURE: Stone has to incorporate his slider more to get batters off his fastball and changeup. He projects to be a No. 4 starter if he makes that adjustment.

ear	Age	Club (League)	Level	W	L	ERA	G	GS	IP	H	HR	BB	SO	BB%	SO%	WHIP	AVG
2023	24	Okla. City (PCL)	AAA	7	4	4.74	21	19	101	86	12	46	120	10.7	27.8	1.31	.226
2023	24	Los Angeles (NL)	MLB	1	1	9.00	8	4	31	46	8	13	22	8.6	14.5	1.90	.338
Minor League Totals				18	12	3.19	70	66	313	265	22	115	426	8.8	32.6	1.21	.225
Major League Totals				1	1	9.00	8	4	31	46	8	13	22	8.6	14.5	1.90	.338

4 ANDY PAGES, OF

HIT: 40. **POW:** 60. **RUN:** 45. **FLD:** 50. **ARM:** 70. **BA Grade:** 55. **Risk:** High.

Born: December 8, 2000. **B-T:** R-R. **HT:** 6-1. **WT:** 212.
Signed: Cuba, 2018. **Signed by:** Luis Marquez/Roman Barinas/Manelik Pimentel
TRACK RECORD: Pages signed with the Dodgers for $300,000 out of Cuba and immediately asserted himself as one of the top power hitters in the minor leagues. He blasted 19 home runs in 63 games as an 18-year-old for Rookie-level Ogden in 2019. He won the 2021 Midwest League MVP award after hitting a Great Lakes franchise-record 31 home runs and finished third in the Texas League with 26 home runs for Double-A Tulsa in 2022. Pages earned a quick promotion to Triple-A Oklahoma City in 2023 and was nearing his first big league callup, but he tore his labrum in his left shoulder on a swing May 16 and had season-ending surgery.
SCOUTING REPORT: Previously a heavyset slugger, Pages dropped 25 pounds going into last season and improved his athleticism without losing any power. He generates plus power with a fast, uphill swing and sends towering fly balls out to all fields. He frequently clears scoreboards and can hit balls out of any stadium. Pages pulverizes pitches low in the zone, but his swing path creates a hole above his belt that leaves him vulnerable to swings and misses. He is a cerebral hitter who controls the strike zone and makes enough contact to be a below-average hitter even with that vulnerability. He's particularly strong in clutch situations. Pages ticked up to a fringe-average runner after losing weight and gets good jumps in the outfield. He is an average defender in right field and can play center in a pinch, although he struggles with focus at times. He has plus-plus arm strength but inconsistent accuracy.
THE FUTURE: Pages' power and approach give him a chance to be a low-average, high on-base percentage slugger. He began hitting again in mid October and is on track to be fully ready in time for spring training.

Year	Age	Club (League)	Level	AVG	G	AB	R	H	2B	3B	HR	RBI	BB	SO	SB	OBP	SLG
2023	22	Tulsa (TL)	AA	.284	33	109	23	31	12	1	3	25	25	32	7	.430	.495
2023	22	Okla. City (PCL)	AAA	.000	1	3	0	0	0	0	0	0	1	2	0	.250	.000
Minor League Totals				.257	401	1438	284	370	97	7	89	284	220	420	36	.378	.520

5 NICK FRASSO, RHP

FB: 70. **SL:** 60. **CHG:** 50. **CTL:** 50. **BA Grade:** 55. **Risk:** High.

Born: October 18, 1998. **B-T:** R-R. **HT:** 6-5. **WT:** 200.
Drafted: Loyola Marymount, 2020 (4th round). **Signed by:** Bud Smith (Blue Jays).
TRACK RECORD: Frasso grew up in suburban Los Angeles as a Dodgers fan who idolized Clayton Kershaw. He stayed close to home at Loyola Marymount and blossomed into a potential first-round pick before forearm tightness ended his junior season. The Blue Jays drafted him in the fourth round in 2020 and signed him for $459,000. Frasso had Tommy John surgery after signing, but he impressed enough in his return for the Dodgers to acquire him in the 2022 deadline trade that sent Mitch White to Toronto. Frasso opened 2023 at Double-A Tulsa and dominated early before a stomach bug caused him to lose 15 pounds, sapping his stuff and durability.
SCOUTING REPORT: A high-flying basketball star in high school, Frasso has a long, lean 6-foot-5 frame and explosive athleticism. He hides the ball well behind his big frame and comes across his body in his delivery, generating deception that helps his stuff play up. His fastball sits 93-96 mph and touches 98 with late run and projects to be a plus-plus pitch with his deception. His short, hard slider at 86-89 mph is an above-average pitch that plays particularly well against righthanded batters. Frasso mostly relies on his fastball and slider, but he sells his average 84-86 mph changeup well and can use it to get swings and misses and weak contact below the zone. His exceptional athleticism allows him to repeat his cross-body delivery and throw strikes with average control. Frasso has ingredients to start, but he has never pitched 100 innings in a season and his velocity drops early in outings. He has trouble holding weight and must get stronger to maintain a starter's workload.
THE FUTURE: Frasso has midrotation potential if he can improve his durability. If not, he projects to be a late-inning relief weapon.

Year	Age	Club (League)	Level	W	L	ERA	G	GS	IP	H	HR	BB	SO	BB%	SO%	WHIP	AVG
2023	24	Tulsa (TL)	AA	3	4	3.91	21	21	74	68	4	24	94	7.6	29.8	1.25	.242
2023	24	Okla. City (PCL)	AAA	1	2	3.26	4	4	19	19	0	7	13	8.3	15.5	1.34	.257
Minor League Totals				4	6	2.96	44	43	152	123	6	50	191	7.9	30.2	1.14	.217

6 JOSUE DE PAULA, OF

HIT: 60. **POW:** 55. **RUN:** 45. **FLD:** 30. **ARM:** 55. **BA Grade:** 55. **Risk:** High.

Born: May 24, 2005. **B-T:** L-L. **HT:** 6-3. **WT:** 185.
Signed: Dominican Republic, 2022. **Signed by:** Laiky Uribe

TRACK RECORD: A cousin of former NBA players Stephon Marbury and Sebastian Telfair, De Paula was born and raised in New York but moved to the Dominican Republic when he was 15 to sign as an international free agent. The Dodgers signed him for $397,500 on the first day of the 2022 signing period. De Paula starred in the Dominican Summer League after signing and hit his way out of extended spring training to Low-A Rancho Cucamonga in 2023. He hit .284/.396/.372 as an 18-year-old and posted a .924 OPS in the playoffs to help the Quakes reach the California League championship series.

SCOUTING REPORT: De Paula is a tall, 6-foot-3, projectable teenager with tantalizing offensive potential. He has a calm, patient approach and a picturesque lefthanded swing that leaves few holes for pitchers to attack. He has a unique ability to look over a baseball for his age and drives hittable pitches on a line with a balanced, efficient swing. He projects to be a plus hitter, if not more, and should grow into above-average power as he packs muscle onto his developing frame. De Paula is advanced in the batter's box, but he has a long way to go defensively. He's a fringe-average runner and timid right fielder and who takes poor routes and struggles to track fly balls. He is prone to overrunning grounders and whiffing on catchable balls in the air, especially on the move. He committed six errors in 87 chances in 2023 for a poor .931 fielding percentage. De Paula projects to be a well below-average defender even with improvement and will have to move to DH unless he can catch the ball more consistently.

THE FUTURE: De Paula's offensive potential gives him the chance to be an impact player even as a DH. He requires lots of projection and will need time to mature into his power.

Year	Age	Club (League)	Level	AVG	G	AB	R	H	2B	3B	HR	RBI	BB	SO	SB	OBP	SLG
2023	18	R. Cucamonga (CAL)	A	.284	74	282	55	80	15	2	2	40	46	61	14	.396	.372
Minor League Totals				.310	127	468	97	145	28	4	7	70	78	92	30	.417	.432

7 KYLE HURT, RHP

FB: 60. **SL:** 55. **CB:** 50. **CHG:** 60. **CTL:** 45. **BA Grade:** 50. **Risk:** Medium.

Born: May 30, 1998. **B-T:** R-R. **HT:** 6-3. **WT:** 240.
Drafted: Southern California, 2020 (5th round). **Signed by:** Tim McDonnell (Marlins).

TRACK RECORD: A top draft prospect in high school, Hurt showed premium stuff at Southern California but posted a 5.06 ERA in a frustrating college career. The Marlins drafted him in the fifth round in 2020 and quickly traded him to the Dodgers with Alex Vesia for Dylan Floro in February 2021. Hurt continued to tease and got crushed at Double-A in 2022, but he used his struggles as motivation. He spent the offseason improving his fitness, confidence and execution and responded with his best season in 2023. He posted the highest strikeout rate in the minors (39.2%) among pitchers with at least 90 innings and rose from Double-A to the majors, where he retired Fernando Tatis Jr., Juan Soto and Manny Machado in order in his first big league inning.

SCOUTING REPORT: Hurt is a large-bodied righthander with a fast arm. His plus fastball sits 94-96 mph and touches 98-99 with late, riding life and gets swings-and-misses in the strike zone. His changeup is another plus pitch at 87-88 mph that falls off the table with late dive. He has advanced command of his change and can throw it for strikes or bury it for chase swings. Hurt rounds out his arsenal with an above-average, 86-89 mph vertical slider that keeps improving and an average 79-81 mph curveball he'll mix in. He previously had below-average control and poor fastball command, but after dropping 30 pounds, he now maintains his delivery better and throws strikes at a fringy but effective clip. He has yet to throw more than five innings in a start and must improve his durability.

THE FUTURE: Hurt's improvements give him a chance to remain a starter if he can continue building on them. He projects to be a hard-throwing No. 4 starter or a high-octane reliever.

Year	Age	Club (League)	Level	W	L	ERA	G	GS	IP	H	HR	BB	SO	BB%	SO%	WHIP	AVG
2023	25	Tulsa (TL)	AA	2	3	4.15	19	15	65	50	7	33	110	11.8	39.4	1.28	.207
2023	25	Okla. City (PCL)	AAA	2	1	3.33	7	1	27	19	3	11	42	10.1	38.5	1.11	.198
2023	25	Los Angeles (NL)	MLB	0	0	0.00	1	0	2	0	0	0	3	0.0	50.0	0.00	.000
Minor League Totals				11	13	4.63	63	39	185	143	16	113	297	13.9	36.5	1.39	.208
Major League Totals				0	0	0.00	1	0	2	0	0	0	3	0.0	50.0	0.00	.000

8 RIVER RYAN, RHP

FB: 65. **CB:** 55. **SL:** 60. **CHG:** 55. **CTL:** 45. **BA Grade:** 50. **Risk:** Medium.

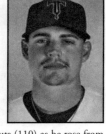

Born: August 17, 1998. **B-T:** R-R. **HT:** 6-2. **WT:** 195.
Drafted: UNC Pembroke, 2021 (11th rd). **Signed by:** Jake Koenig/Nick Brannon (Padres).
TRACK RECORD: Ryan played both ways as a shortstop/second baseman and relief pitcher at Division II North Carolina-Pembroke. He hit exclusively in his pro debut after the Padres drafted him in the 11th round in 2021, but he impressed on the mound in instructional league after the season, leading the Dodgers to acquire him for Matt Beaty. Ryan's stuff ticked up with his focus exclusively on pitching as he conquered the Class A levels in 2022. He took another jump in 2023 and set new career highs in innings (104.1) and strikeouts (110) as he rose from Double-A to Triple-A.
SCOUTING REPORT: Ryan is an elite athlete with a quick arm out of a strong, 6-foot-2 frame. His high-spin fastball sits 94-96 mph and touches 99 with late ride and tail up in the zone. His hard, 88-91 mph slider with depth and late movement is another plus pitch. Ryan also has an 80-84 mph power curveball with downward break and an 86-88 mph changeup with late fade that project to be above-average pitches, though his execution of them is inconsistent. He is a good athlete with a clean delivery and throws strikes with average control. Ryan has a promising blend of stuff, control and athleticism, but he is still new to starting and learning the finer points of pitch sequencing and execution. He mixes dominant outings with clunkers and is still learning how to last deep into games. He has yet to complete more than five innings in a start in his career.
THE FUTURE: Ryan is 25 years old but still young as a pitcher. He has the stuff to be a midrotation starter if he can improve his execution and durability. If not, he projects to be a flame-throwing, high-leverage reliever.

Year	Age	Club (League)	Level	W	L	ERA	G	GS	IP	H	HR	BB	SO	BB%	SO%	WHIP	AVG
2023	24	Tulsa (TL)	AA	1	6	3.33	24	22	97	78	8	44	98	10.7	23.7	1.25	.221
2023	24	Okla. City (PCL)	AAA	0	1	10.29	2	2	7	12	2	2	12	5.7	34.3	2.00	.364
Minor League Totals				3	11	3.38	41	37	152	128	14	67	180	10.3	27.7	1.28	.227

9 DIEGO CARTAYA, C

HIT: 30. **POW:** 55. **RUN:** 40. **FLD:** 50. **ARM:** 60. **BA Grade:** 50. **Risk:** High.

Born: September 7, 2001. **B-T:** R-R. **HT:** 6-3. **WT:** 219. **Signed:** Venezuela, 2018.
Signed by: Luis Marquez/Roman Barinas/Cliff Nuiter/Jean Castro.
TRACK RECORD: A star on Venezuela's junior national teams, Cartaya emerged as arguably the top prospect in the 2018 international class and signed with the Dodgers for $2.5 million. He played just 80 games combined his first three years due to the coronavirus pandemic and a pair of back injuries, but he stayed healthy in 2022 and hit 22 home runs with an .892 OPS to win the Dodgers' minor league player of the year award. Cartaya rose to Double-A Tulsa in 2023 and ably handled a high-octane Drillers pitching staff, but his offense cratered. He hit .189 with a .657 OPS, the lowest batting average and fourth-lowest OPS in the Texas League, and was transferred to the development list for the final month of the season.
SCOUTING REPORT: Cartaya is a physical righthanded hitter with explosive power. He makes thunderous contact when he connects and sends long home runs out from left field to right-center. Cartaya previously had a short, compact swing, but as his body has matured and changed, his swing has gotten overly long. He struggles to catch up to velocity with his swing length and has lost his plate discipline as his struggles have compounded, frequently chasing sliders low and away. The Dodgers have worked with Cartaya on shortening his swing but have yet to see results. While Cartaya's offense has declined, his defense has improved. He has strong hands and has improved his receiving and blocking technique enough to project to be an average defender. He's just a fair athlete but makes up for it with meticulous preparation. He's a smart game-caller who is bilingual and works hard for his pitchers.
THE FUTURE: Cartaya has to shorten his swing to fulfill his potential as an everyday, power-hitting catcher. That will be his primary goal in 2024.

Year	Age	Club (League)	Level	AVG	G	AB	R	H	2B	3B	HR	RBI	BB	SO	SB	OBP	SLG
2023	21	Tulsa (TL)	AA	.189	93	354	51	67	10	0	19	57	37	117	0	.278	.379
Minor League Totals				.241	268	1015	192	245	50	3	55	182	134	315	2	.346	.459

10 MADDUX BRUNS, LHP

FB: 60. **CB:** 60. **SL:** 60. **CHG:** 50. **CTL:** 30. **BA Grade:** 50. **Risk:** High.

Born: June 20, 2002. **B-T:** L-L. **HT:** 6-2. **WT:** 205.
Drafted: HS—Mobile, AL, 2021 (1st round). **Signed by:** Benny Latino.
TRACK RECORD: Bruns touched 97 mph at the Perfect Game National showcase to establish himself as one of the top prep pitchers in the 2021 draft class,
though control problems surfaced throughout his senior year. The Dodgers
drafted him 29th overall and signed him for $2,197,500. Bruns showed loud
stuff but walked more than a batter per inning in his first full season at Low-A
Rancho Cucamonga and repeated the level to start 2023. He improved his
control and composure to earn a quick promotion to High-A Great Lakes and finished the year second
in the Dodgers system with 126 strikeouts.
SCOUTING REPORT: Bruns has a strong, powerful 6-foot-2 frame and buzzworthy stuff. His plus fastball
sits 94-96 mph and touches 98 with heavy armside life from the left side. His plus 74-78 mph curveball
is a hammer with late snap and depth, and his 82-86 mph slider with angle and late bite is a third plus
offering. He also has a fading, mid-80s changeup that flashes average potential, though he rarely throws
it. Bruns shortened his arm stroke and became more consistent with his delivery in 2023 to improve his
control, but he's still a well below-average strike-thrower. He relies on overpowering hitters and must
improve the control of his secondaries to get the most from his arsenal. Bruns has matured after frequently
melting down on the mound in his first full season, but he still occasionally displays his frustration when
his defense makes errors behind him. The Dodgers have worked with him on bouncing back better from
adversity.
THE FUTURE: Bruns is moving in the right direction with his control and composure. He has a chance to
be a hard-throwing, back-end starter or power reliever if he can continue those upward trends.

Year	Age	Club (League)	Level	W	L	ERA	G	GS	IP	H	HR	BB	SO	BB%	SO%	WHIP	AVG
2023	21	R. Cucamonga (CAL)	A	0	0	1.29	6	6	21	11	0	13	33	14.8	37.5	1.14	.149
2023	21	Great Lakes (MWL)	A+	0	7	4.74	20	20	76	56	7	54	93	15.8	27.2	1.45	.205
Minor League Totals				0	12	4.93	51	51	146	111	10	119	198	17.6	29.3	1.58	.210

11 LANDON KNACK, RHP

FB: 55. **CB:** 45. **SL:** 55. **CHG:** 55. **CTL:** 55. **BA Grade:** 45. **Risk:** Medium.

Born: July 15, 1997. **B-T:** R-R. **HT:** 6-2. **WT:** 220. **Drafted:** East Tennessee State, 2020 (2nd round).
Signed by: Marty Lamb.
TRACK RECORD: Knack experienced a velocity bump his senior year at East Tennessee State that sent
him rising up draft boards. The Dodgers selected him in the second round in 2020 and signed him for
a below-slot $712,500. Knack struggled with his weight and conditioning and suffered repeated injuries
early in his pro career, but he overhauled his diet in 2023 and had his best season. Knack set new career-
bests with a 2.51 ERA, 100.1 innings pitched and 99 strikeouts as he rose from Double-A to Triple-A.
Forearm tightness ended his season in late August.
SCOUTING REPORT: Knack is a thick, burly righthander who relies on precision. His fastball ranges from
90-96 mph and is above-average with his ability to command it to both sides of the plate. He gives his
fastball tail and run to his armside and drives it down to his glove side. Knack's short, vertical 82-84 mph
slider is an above-average pitch he locates well. His fading, 79-81 mph changeup is a third above-average
pitch that plays against both lefties and righties. He also has a fringy, 76-79 mph curveball he throws
for strikes early in counts. Nothing Knack throws is exceptional, but his stuff plays up with his surgical
precision and execution. He has above-average control and stays off of barrels to induce ground balls.
Knack has some effort in his delivery and will occasionally spin out of it, but he pitches efficiently to last
deep into games.
THE FUTURE: Knack projects to be a back-end starter if he can stay healthy. His big league debut may
come in 2024.

Year	Age	Club (League)	Level	W	L	ERA	G	GS	IP	H	HR	BB	SO	BB%	SO%	WHIP	AVG
2023	25	Tulsa (TL)	AA	2	0	2.20	12	12	57	42	3	12	61	5.4	27.4	0.94	.202
2023	25	Okla. City (PCL)	AAA	3	1	2.93	10	10	43	44	6	18	38	9.6	20.2	1.44	.262
Minor League Totals				14	12	3.40	55	50	227	200	25	65	261	6.9	27.8	1.17	.231

12 THAYRON LIRANZO, C

HIT: 40. **POW:** 55. **RUN:** 30. **FLD:** 50. **ARM:** 60. **BA Grade:** 50. **Risk:** High.

Born: July 5, 2003. **B-T:** B-R. **HT:** 6-3. **WT:** 195. **Signed:** Dominican Republic, 2021. **Signed by:** Domingo Toribio.

TRACK RECORD: Liranzo fell under the radar in the 2021 international signing class and signed with the Dodgers for $30,000 out of the Dominican Republic. He emerged as a potential steal in the complex leagues and broke out in his full-season debut at Low-A Rancho Cucamonga in 2023. Liranzo hit .272/.400/.562, led the California League with 24 home runs and led all qualified minor league catchers with a .962 OPS. He also guided the Quakes' pitching staff to the most strikeouts and lowest opponent average in the league.

SCOUTING REPORT: Liranzo has a strong, mature body and above-average power from both sides of the plate. He has a smooth, rhythmic lefthanded swing that punishes balls to all fields. His righthanded swing is stiffer, but he has the strength to hit long drives when he connects. Liranzo has solid strike-zone discipline, but he tends to overswing and will swing and miss in the zone. He projects to be a below-average hitter with above-average power and may need to drop his righthanded swing. Liranzo is a solid receiver and blocker who moves well behind the plate. He has plus arm strength and the ability to throw runners out from multiple arm angles, although his accuracy is inconsistent. He projects to be an average defender overall.

THE FUTURE: Liranzo holds promise as a potential power-hitting catcher, but he has to prove he can make enough contact against better pitching. He'll aim to do that at High-A Great Lakes in 2024.

Year	Age	Club (League)	Level	AVG	G	AB	R	H	2B	3B	HR	RBI	BB	SO	SB	OBP	SLG
2023	19	R. Cucamonga (CAL)	A	.272	94	345	81	94	24	2	24	70	70	112	2	.400	.562
Minor League Totals				.260	156	561	115	146	39	3	33	109	105	174	5	.383	.517

13 JONNY DELUCA, OF

HIT: 40. **POW:** 50. **RUN:** 60. **FLD:** 55. **ARM:** 55. **BA Grade:** 45. **Risk:** Medium.

Born: July 10, 1998. **B-T:** R-R. **HT:** 6-0. **WT:** 200. **Drafted:** Oregon, 2019 (25th round). **Signed by:** Jeff Stevens.

TRACK RECORD: A top long jumper and relay runner in high school, Deluca showed immense athleticism as Oregon's center fielder, but hit just .226 in two seasons with the Ducks. The Dodgers drafted him in the 25th round as a draft-eligible sophomore and signed him for $300,000, equivalent to sixth-round money. Deluca dropped switch-hitting as a pro and flourished at the plate while maintaining his athleticism. He rapidly climbed the minors and made his major league debut in 2023, batting .262 with two homers in 24 games.

SCOUTING REPORT: Deluca started hitting righthanded only as a pro and found his offensive stride. He takes big, powerful swings and generates above-average raw power with his muscular forearms. He has above-average plate discipline and crushes fastballs at any velocity. Deluca struggles against secondary stuff and is more masher than pure hitter, but he battles through at-bats and projects to be a below-average hitter who gets to his power. He hits lefties particularly hard. Deluca is a plus runner who steals bases and covers wide swaths of ground in the outfield. He runs down balls in all directions and has the athleticism to make highlight-reel plays at all three spots. He is an above-average defender and keeps runners honest with his above-average arm strength.

THE FUTURE: Deluca projects to be a valuable role player who crushes lefties and plays strong defense at all three outfield positions. He will have a chance to win a bench job in 2024.

Year	Age	Club (League)	Level	AVG	G	AB	R	H	2B	3B	HR	RBI	BB	SO	SB	OBP	SLG
2023	24	Tulsa (TL)	AA	.279	32	122	29	34	8	0	10	18	14	26	9	.380	.590
2023	24	Okla. City (PCL)	AAA	.306	41	157	27	48	13	2	7	35	21	29	3	.397	.548
2023	24	Los Angeles (NL)	MLB	.262	24	42	5	11	1	0	2	6	3	8	1	.311	.429
Minor League Totals				.271	298	1146	223	310	70	14	65	201	134	218	58	.357	.526
Major League Totals				.262	24	42	5	11	1	0	2	6	3	8	1	.311	.429

14 JUSTIN WROBLESKI, LHP

FB: 55. **SL:** 55. **CUT:** 50. **CHG:** 40. **CTL:** 50. **BA Grade:** 45. **Risk:** High.

Born: July 14, 2000. **B-T:** L-L. **HT:** 6-1. **WT:** 194. **Drafted:** Oklahoma State, 2021 (11th round). **Signed by:** Heath Holliday.

TRACK RECORD: An unsigned 36th-round pick out of high school, Wrobleski attended three colleges in three years before settling at Oklahoma State. He had Tommy John surgery after just nine starts for the Cowboys, but the Dodgers saw enough to draft him in the 11th round and sign him for an over-slot $197,500 bonus. Wrobleski returned midway through the 2022 season and flashed exciting stuff in short stints. He built on that in 2023 and finished second in the Midwest League with a 2.90 ERA and 109 strikeouts at High-A Great Lakes.

SCOUTING REPORT: Wrobleski's stuff has ticked up the further he's moved away from surgery. His fastball sits 93-96 mph, touches 98, and gets ugly swings with the angle and deception he creates from a closed-off delivery and short arm stroke. His fastball occasionally flattens out when he spins out of his delivery, but it's an above-average pitch at its best. Wrobleski has a natural feel for spin and can manipulate the shape and power of his above-average, two-plane slider anywhere from 78-86 mph. He also has an average, 87-91 mph cutter he'll mix in. Wrobleski's 86-90 mph changeup has progressed to become a below-average pitch that gives him just enough to handle righthanded hitters. He throws strikes with average control and works quickly.

THE FUTURE: Wrobleski's stuff, deception and improving durability gives him a chance to be an effective No. 5 starter or long reliever. He'll move to Double-A Tulsa in 2024.

Year	Age	Club (League)	Level	W	L	ERA	G	GS	IP	H	HR	BB	SO	BB%	SO%	WHIP	AVG
2023	22	Great Lakes (MWL)	A+	4	4	2.90	25	23	102	93	6	35	109	8.3	26.0	1.25	.244
Minor League Totals				5	7	2.90	38	33	124	113	7	40	135	7.9	26.6	1.23	.246

15 KENDALL GEORGE, OF

HIT: 55. **POW:** 30. **RUN:** 80. **FLD:** 55. **ARM:** 40. **BA Grade:** 50. **Risk:** Extreme.

Born: October 29, 2004. **B-T:** L-L. **HT:** 5-10. **WT:** 170. **Drafted:** HS—Humble, TX, 2023 (1st round supp).
Signed by: Clint Bower.

TRACK RECORD: George hit .364 with five stolen bases as the center fielder on USA Baseball's 18U national team in 2022. He got stronger throughout his senior season at Atasocita (Humble, Texas) High and was targeted by the Dodgers for their second-round pick, but they instead jumped up to take him 36th overall. He signed for $1,847,500 to forgo an Arkansas commitment. George surprised the Dodgers with how advanced he was offensively after signing and earned a quick promotion to Low-A Rancho Cucamonga. He hit .381 in 12 games to help the Quakes reach the California League championship series.

SCOUTING REPORT: George is a small but speedy outfielder with a knack for contact. He's a patient hitter with a good feel for the strike zone and makes consistent contact with a short, slashing lefthanded swing. George primarily hits ground balls and low line drives, but he can beat out almost any ball in play with his 80-grade speed. He turns in sub 4.0–second run times down the line and is an excellent baserunner with advanced basestealing instincts. George flashes surprising power in batting practice, but he doesn't show it in games. He projects to be an above-average hitter with limited power who racks up steals. George is still raw defensively in center field. He has the speed to run down balls but needs to polish his routes and tracking. He has below-average arm strength.

THE FUTURE: George projects to be a contact and speed-driven center fielder similar to Juan Pierre. He'll begin 2024 back at Rancho Cucamonga.

Year	Age	Club (League)	Level	AVG	G	AB	R	H	2B	3B	HR	RBI	BB	SO	SB	OBP	SLG
2023	18	ACL Dodgers	Rk	.362	16	58	11	21	3	0	0	7	11	11	11	.451	.414
2023	18	R. Cucamonga (CAL)	A	.381	12	42	13	16	2	0	0	3	6	9	6	.469	.429
Minor League Totals				.370	28	100	24	37	5	0	0	10	17	20	17	.458	.420

16 RONAN KOPP, LHP

FB: 60. **CB:** 50. **SL:** 55. **CUT:** 50. **CHG:** 40. **CTL:** 30. **BA Grade:** 45. **Risk:** High.

Born: July 29, 2002. **B-T:** L-L. **HT:** 6-7. **WT:** 250. **Drafted:** South Mountain (AZ) JC, 2021 (12th round).
Signed by: Brian Compton.

TRACK RECORD: Kopp frustrated scouts as a talented but enigmatic lefthander in high school. He made his way to South Mountain (Ariz.) JC and improved enough for the Dodgers to draft him in the 12th round and sign him for an above-slot $250,000. Kopp continued his upward trend at Low-A Rancho Cucamonga in his first full season and built on it with High-A Great Lakes in 2023. He led the Midwest League with a .184 opponent average and tied for third with 107 strikeouts, but his 16.7% walk rate was the league's second-highest.

SCOUTING REPORT: Kopp is physically huge at 6-foot-7, 250 pounds. His fastball sits 92-95 mph and touches 98 with hard downhill plane and gets on batters quickly with the extension generated by his long limbs. He complements his fastball with a lateral, mid-80s slider with late break that flashes above-average, although it's inconsistent. Kopp's changeup is below-average, so he added an 86-89 mph cutter that ties up righthanded hitters and projects to be average. He also has a big-breaking, 73-75 mph curveball that flashes average. Kopp is difficult to hit in the strike zone, but he's a poor athlete and lumbering giant who struggles to repeat his release point and delivery. He has well below-average control and caps out at about 3-4 innings.

THE FUTURE: Kopp projects to be a lefthanded relief weapon who can pitch multiple innings. He'll open 2024 at Double-A Tulsa.

Year	Age	Club (League)	Level	W	L	ERA	G	GS	IP	H	HR	BB	SO	BB%	SO%	WHIP	AVG
2023	20	Great Lakes (MWL)	A+	0	4	2.99	30	21	72	45	6	50	107	16.7	35.8	1.31	.184
Minor League Totals				5	7	2.83	60	32	137	86	9	94	220	16.0	37.4	1.32	.178

17 JORBIT VIVAS, 2B

HIT: 50. **POW:** 30. **RUN:** 45. **FLD:** 50. **ARM:** 45. **BA Grade:** 45. **Risk:** High.

Born: March 9, 2001. **B-T:** L-R. **HT:** 5-10. **WT:** 171. **Signed:** Venezuela, 2017.
Signed by: Luis Marquez/Roman Barinas/Andres Simancas.

TRACK RECORD: Vivas compiled a long track record of hitting as an amateur in Venezuela and signed with the Dodgers for $300,000 in 2017. He continued to hit in the low minors and earned a spot on the 40-man roster before playing a game above High-A. Vivas made the jump to the upper minors in 2023 and continued to show advanced offensive ability. He finished second in the Dodgers system with 136 hits and 98 runs scored as he rose from Double-A to Triple-A.

SCOUTING REPORT: Vivas is a small lefthanded hitter with a keen eye for the strike zone. He recognizes pitches and stays in the zone with a disciplined approach, helping him record nearly as many walks (69) as strikeouts (71) last season. Vivas has a natural feel for contact, but his swing has gotten longer and more aggressive as he's tried to add power. He still has good bat speed and extension, and possesses an advanced ability to manipulate bat angles and drive the ball in all parts of the zone. He projects to be an average hitter and could reach double-digit homers as he gets stronger. Vivas has gotten faster and added range at second base to improve to an average defender. He makes the routine plays with solid actions and has fringe-average arm strength.

THE FUTURE: Vivas' contact and on-base skills give him a chance to be a second-division starter. He'll begin 2024 back at Triple-A.

Year	Age	Club (League)	Level	AVG	G	AB	R	H	2B	3B	HR	RBI	BB	SO	SB	OBP	SLG
2023	22	Tulsa (TL)	AA	.280	109	404	82	113	23	2	12	54	54	52	21	.391	.436
2023	22	Okla. City (PCL)	AAA	.225	26	102	16	23	2	1	1	9	15	19	4.	.339	.294
Minor League Totals				.281	474	1773	320	498	98	18	39	259	217	250	61	.383	.422

18 PAYTON MARTIN, RHP

FB: 60. **SL:** 60. **CHG:** 55. **CTL:** 55. **BA Grade:** 50. **Risk:** Extreme.

Born: May 19, 2004. **B-T:** R-R. **HT:** 6-0. **WT:** 170. **Drafted:** HS—Clemmons, NC, 2022 (17th round).
Signed by: Jonah Rosenthal.

TRACK RECORD: Martin primarily played shortstop at East Forsyth High and started only six games as a pitcher in high school. The Dodgers were intrigued by his arm action and athleticism in those limited looks and drafted him in the 17th round in 2022, signing him for $125,000 to forgo an East Carolina commitment. Martin's stuff ticked up with his focus on pitching and led to a breakout pro debut in 2023. He posted a 2.04 ERA in 14 appearances (12 starts) at Low-A Rancho Cucamonga before reaching his innings limit.

SCOUTING REPORT: Martin is a lean, twitchy righthander with exceptional athleticism. His plus fastball sits 93-96 mph and touches 98 out of a clean, compact delivery and fast arm. His 86-89 mph power slider is another potential plus pitch that starts in the strike zone before shooting out late for empty chase swings. He also has a firm, 89-92 mph changeup that has been a point of emphasis and flashes above-average. Martin has rapidly assimilated to pitching and pounds the strike zone with above-average control. He is a confident, aggressive competitor who throws strikes with no fear.

THE FUTURE: Martin is still physically slight and threw only 39.2 innings in his pro debut. He has the foundation to be a mid-rotation starter, but has years of strength gains ahead.

Year	Age	Club (League)	Level	W	L	ERA	G	GS	IP	H	HR	BB	SO	BB%	SO%	WHIP	AVG
2023	19	R. Cucamonga (CAL)	A	2	1	2.04	14	12	40	30	1	15	48	9.4	30.2	1.13	.213
Minor League Totals				2	1	2.08	14	12	40	30	1	15	48	9.4	30.2	1.15	.213

19 JOENDRY VARGAS, SS

HIT: 55. **POW:** 55. **RUN:** 45. **FLD:** 55. **ARM:** 60. **BA Grade:** 50. **Risk:** Extreme.

Born: Nov. **8,** 2005. **B-T:** R-R. **HT:** 6-4. **WT:** 175. **Signed:** Dominican Republic, 2023. **Signed by:** Alant Moncon.

TRACK RECORD: Vargas grew up as a switch-hitter before deciding to bat righthanded only as a teenager. The change helped him emerge as one of the top offensive players in the 2023 international signing class. The Dodgers signed him for $2,077,500, half of their bonus pool, the day the signing period opened. Vargas lived up to his pedigree with a sensational pro debut in the Dominican Summer League. He hit .328/.423/.529 with seven home runs, 31 RBIs, 19 stolen bases and nearly as many walks (30) as strike-outs (31) to lead DSL Dodgers Bautista to a 42-11 record and the DSL championship.

SCOUTING REPORT: Vargas has a long, projectable 6-foot-4 frame and an advanced aptitude for making adjustments in the batter's box. He had a long, rotational swing when he signed, but he quickly adopted a shorter, more dynamic swing and became a force. Vargas is a high-contact hitter who controls the strike zone and drills balls into the gaps with his bat speed and natural feel for the barrel. He has natural strength and leverage in his swing and projects to be an above-average hitter with above-average power as he adds muscle to his frame. Vargas is an average runner with good range at shortstop, but he projects to slow down and outgrow the position as he matures. He has plus arm strength and will profile well at third base.

THE FUTURE: Vargas projects to be an everyday third baseman, but he's many years and developmental steps away. He'll make his stateside debut in 2024.

Year	Age	Club (League)	Level	AVG	G	AB	R	H	2B	3B	HR	RBI	BB	SO	SB	OBP	SLG
2023	17	DSL Dodgers Bautista	Rk	.328	48	174	47	57	12	1	7	31	30	31	19	.423	.529
Minor League Totals				.328	48	174	47	57	12	1	7	31	30	31	19	.423	.529

20 AUSTIN GAUTHIER, 3B/SS

HIT: 50. **POW:** 40. **RUN:** 50. **FLD:** 45. **ARM:** 50. **BA Grade:** 45. **Risk:** High.

Born: May 7, 1999. **B-T:** R-R. **HT:** 6-0. **WT:** 188. **Signed:** Hofstra, 2021 (NDFA). **Signed by:** Will Rhymes.

TRACK RECORD: Gauthier started all four years at shortstop for Hofstra and was one of the Colonial Athletic Association's top hitters as an upperclassman. He went undrafted as a senior, but Dodgers farm director Will Rhymes, a former CAA shortstop at William & Mary, found Gauthier and led the team to sign him as an undrafted free agent. Gauthier led the Dodgers system with a .441 on-base percentage in his first full season and followed with an even better year in 2023. He hit .312/.435/.476 and led the organization in hits (148), walks (100) and runs (111) while advancing to Double-A.

SCOUTING REPORT: Gauthier is a disciplined hitter with elite strike-zone recognition. He has more walks (226) than strikeouts (221) in his career and consistently conducts high-level at-bats. Gauthier has a good feel for picking out pitches to drive and makes consistent contact with a compact, level righthanded swing. He uses the whole field and turns around both fastballs and secondary offerings. Gauthier doesn't hit the ball overly hard, but he reworked his body to get stronger and has started to drive balls. He projects to be an average hitter, who posts high on-base percentages and reaches double-digit home runs. Gauthier doesn't have a true home defensively, but he is an average defender at second base and is playable at third base, shortstop and left field. He makes the routine plays and has average arm strength.

THE FUTURE: Gauthier's ability to reach base and play multiple positions give him a path to be a bat-driven utilityman. He should see Triple-A in 2024.

Year	Age	Club (League)	Level	AVG	G	AB	R	H	2B	3B	HR	RBI	BB	SO	SB	OBP	SLG
2023	24	Great Lakes (MWL)	A+	.365	40	148	39	54	10	1	6	25	36	30	4	.487	.568
2023	24	Tulsa (TL)	AA	.293	84	321	72	94	19	4	6	34	64	54	15	.411	.433
Minor League Totals				.291	259	929	223	270	53	11	19	130	226	221	36	.433	.433

21 YEINER FERNANDEZ, C/2B

HIT: 50. **POW:** 30. **RUN:** 50. **FLD:** 40. **ARM:** 55. **BA Grade:** 45. **Risk:** High.

Born: September 19, 2002. **B-T:** R-R. **HT:** 5-9. **WT:** 170. **Signed:** Venezuela, 2019.
Signed by: Roman Barinas/Jean Castro/Cristian Guzman.

TRACK RECORD: Fernandez played for Venezuela in the 2015 Little League World Series and hit two home runs in four games at Williamsport. He remained a top hitter through his teenage years and signed with the Dodgers for $717,500. Fernandez has continued to hit as a pro, but he has yet to find a position. He hit .274/.360/.375 with nearly as many walks (47) as strikeouts (56) at High-A Great Lakes in 2023, but was primarily a DH by season's end.

SCOUTING REPORT: Previously a short, pudgy righthanded hitter, Fernandez grew taller and thinned out to improve his athleticism and explosiveness. He's an aggressive hitter with elite hand-eye coordination and barrel control that allows him to consistently put the ball in play. Fernandez doesn't always swing at the best pitches to hit and overwhelmingly hits the ball on the ground, but his pure contact skills give him a chance to be an average hitter if he refines his approach. He mostly makes soft contact and doesn't have much room to add strength to his frame. Fernandez has decent hands at catcher, but he lacks subtlety in his framing and blocking, and is a below-average defender. He is adequate at second base with above-average arm strength and has begun seeing time at third base, first base and shortstop.

THE FUTURE: Fernandez's contact skills give him a chance to be a utilityman if he improves his defense. He'll head to Double-A in 2024.

Year	Age	Club (League)	Level	AVG	G	AB	R	H	2B	3B	HR	RBI	BB	SO	SB	OBP	SLG
2023	20	Great Lakes (MWL)	A+	.273	99	373	47	102	14	3	6	50	47	56	4	.360	.375
Minor League Totals				.296	230	908	151	269	42	6	19	143	105	141	8	.379	.419

22 GUS VARLAND, RHP

FB: 70. **SL:** 50. **CHG:** 40. **CTL:** 45. **BA Grade:** 40. **Risk:** Medium.

Born: November 6, 1996. **B-T:** L-R. **HT:** 6-1. **WT:** 213. **Drafted:** Concordia-St. Paul (MN), 2018 (14th round). **Signed by:** Derek Lee (Athletics).

TRACK RECORD: Varland posted a 1.04 ERA as a junior at Division II Concordia-St. Paul and was drafted by the Athletics in the 14th round after the 2018 season. The Dodgers acquired him in the trade that sent Adam Kolarek to Oakland, but lost him when the Brewers selected him in the Rule 5 draft. Varland made his major league debut with the Brewers in 2023 and logged an 11.42 ERA in eight appearances, but he flourished after being returned to the Dodgers in May. Varland emerged as a dominant setup man at Triple-A Oklahoma City and posted a 3.09 ERA in eight Dodgers appearances before right knee inflammation ended his season.

SCOUTING REPORT: Varland is an aggressive, hard-throwing reliever who relies on arm strength. His plus-plus, riding fastball sits 96-97 mph, touches 99, and overwhelms hitters at the top of the strike zone. He throws his fastball liberally and is not afraid to challenge hitters with it. Varland's short, 89-91 mph slider flashes average to give him a viable secondary, but it's extremely inconsistent and needs refinement. He also has a below-average changeup he rarely throws. Varland has an effortful delivery and fringe-average control, but he throws his fastball for strikes enough to be effective in short bursts.

THE FUTURE: Varland's arm strength gives him a chance to be a middle-to-late inning reliever if he can refine his secondaries. He'll be in the Dodgers' bullpen mix in 2024.

Year	Age	Club (League)	Level	W	L	ERA	G	GS	IP	H	HR	BB	SO	BB%	SO%	WHIP	AVG
2023	26	Wisconsin (MWL)	A+	0	1	13.50	2	0	2	4	0	1	0	9.1	0.0	2.50	.400
2023	26	Nashville (IL)	AAA	0	1	9.82	3	0	4	3	2	4	3	23.5	17.6	1.91	.250
2023	26	Okla. City (PCL)	AAA	2	1	2.16	30	1	33	29	2	8	39	6.0	29.3	1.11	.236
2023	26	Los Angeles (NL)	MLB	1	1	3.09	8	0	12	12	0	8	14	15.4	26.9	1.71	.279
2023	26	Milwaukee (NL)	MLB	0	0	11.42	8	0	9	15	3	8	6	15.7	11.8	2.65	.357
Minor League Totals				9	13	4.15	110	37	209	194	26	84	226	9.4	25.4	1.34	.249
Major League Totals				1	1	6.64	16	0	20	27	3	16	20	15.5	19.4	2.12	.318

23 BEN CASPARIUS, RHP

FB: 45. **SL:** 60. **CHG:** 55. **CTL:** 45. **BA Grade:** 45. **Risk:** High.

Born: February 11, 1999. **B-T:** R-R. **HT:** 6-2. **WT:** 215. **Drafted:** Connecticut, 2021 (5th round). **Signed by:** John Pyle.

TRACK RECORD: Casparius played both ways for two seasons at North Carolina before transferring to Connecticut and becoming a pitcher exclusively. He led the Big East Conference with 127 strikeouts as a junior and was drafted by the Dodgers in the fifth round. Casparius has an unsightly 5.18 ERA as a pro, but he's shown promising underlying stuff. He struck out 120 batters, tied for third-most in the Dodgers system, and rose to Double-A Tulsa in 2023.

SCOUTING REPORT: Casparius is an athletic, physical righthander with a deep pitch mix. His fastball sits 93-94 mph and touches 96 with downhill plane. His primary pitch is a plus, 84-87 mph slider with hard, downward break he can both land in the strike zone or use to get chase swings. He commands his slider better than his fastball and can manipulate it to give it added sweep. Casparius' 83-86 mph changeup with late fade is an above-average pitch he is comfortable throwing to both lefties and righties. He also mixes in an occasional curveball and cutter. Casparius' fastball gets hit hard, so he leans heavily on his secondaries. He tends to spin off in his delivery and has fringe-average control.

THE FUTURE: Casparius' delivery and secondary-heavy mix portend an eventual move to the bullpen. He projects to be an effective middle reliever.

Year	Age	Club (League)	Level	W	L	ERA	G	GS	IP	H	HR	BB	SO	BB%	SO%	WHIP	AVG
2023	24	Great Lakes (MWL)	A+	4	0	2.68	8	8	37	23	5	18	44	11.9	29.1	1.11	.173
2023	24	Tulsa (TL)	AA	2	7	6.62	18	13	71	73	15	37	76	11.5	23.5	1.56	.264
Minor League Totals				8	13	5.18	58	38	203	190	34	104	240	11.5	26.4	1.45	.240

24 JOSE RAMOS, OF

HIT: 30. **POW:** 50. **RUN:** 50. **FLD:** 55. **ARM:** 70. **BA Grade:** 45. **Risk:** High.

Born: January 1, 2001. **B-T:** R-R. **HT:** 6-1. **WT:** 200. **Signed:** Panama, 2018. **Signed by:** Luis Marquez/Cliff Nuitter.

TRACK RECORD: Ramos signed with the Dodgers for $30,000 out of Panama and looked like a steal early in his career, but his aggressive approach was eventually exploited by higher-level pitching. He went unprotected and unpicked in the 2022 Rule 5 draft and used it as motivation. Ramos hit .313/.353/.500 as Panama's center fielder in the World Baseball Classic and followed with a solid showing at Double-A Tulsa in 2023. He cut his strikeout rate, improved his walk rate and finished tied for second on the team with 19 home runs.

SCOUTING REPORT: Ramos flashes tantalizing tools that can impact a game. He has extraordinary bat speed and annihilates fastballs at any velocity with plus raw power. He regularly crushes balls 400-plus feet and can use the whole field. Ramos has long struggled to recognize or hit breaking pitches, but he is slowly improving. He has a chance to be a well below-average hitter with average power production if he can cut down his chase swings on secondary stuff. Ramos is an average runner who plays above-average defense in center field and plus defense in right. He goes back to the wall and into the gaps with remarkable ease and plays comfortably at both positions. He has plus-plus arm strength and makes jaw-dropping throws.

THE FUTURE: Ramos' power and defense give him a path to playing time in the majors. He'll see Triple-A in 2024.

Year	Age	Club (League)	Level	AVG	G	AB	R	H	2B	3B	HR	RBI	BB	SO	SB	OBP	SLG
2023	22	Tulsa (TL)	AA	.240	113	416	55	100	13	0	19	68	54	140	7	.333	.409
Minor League Totals				.266	355	1352	215	359	74	9	57	251	154	426	22	.352	.460

25 ALEX FREELAND, SS

HIT: 45. **POW:** 40. **RUN:** 40. **FLD:** 50. **ARM:** 60. **BA Grade:** 45. **Risk:** High.

Born: August 24, 2001. **B-T:** R-R. **HT:** 6-2. **WT:** 200. **Drafted:** Central Florida, 2022 (3rd round). **Signed by:** Wes Sargent.

TRACK RECORD: Freeland was born with a clubfoot and had multiple surgeries as an infant to correct it. His right foot is smaller than his left and he has limited ankle mobility, but he never let it derail his baseball aspirations. Freeland hit 18 home runs in two seasons as Central Florida's starting shortstop and was drafted by the Dodgers in the third round as a draft-eligible sophomore. He played his first full season at High-A Great Lakes in 2023 and showed standout defensive ability as well as promising underlying offensive metrics.

SCOUTING REPORT: Freeland is a physical, athletic switch-hitter who competes at a high effort level. He's an aggressive swinger, but he controls the strike zone and shows the potential to hit for average and power from the left side. He has an explosive lefthanded swing and hit .262 with a .740 OPS from the left side last year compared to .149 with a .579 OPS batting righthanded. He has to improve his plate coverage and potentially drop his righthanded swing, but he has the potential to be a fringe-average hitter who reaches double-digit home runs. Freeland is a loose mover at shortstop despite his big, 6-foot-2 frame and below-average speed. He positions himself well with excellent instincts and covers enough ground to stay at the position. He projects to be a steady, average defender with a plus, accurate arm.

THE FUTURE: Freeland's abilities to play shortstop and hit lefthanded give him a path to the majors. He'll move to Double-A in 2024.

Year	Age	Club (League)	Level	AVG	G	AB	R	H	2B	3B	HR	RBI	BB	SO	SB	OBP	SLG
2023	21	Great Lakes (MWL)	A+	.240	106	392	58	94	17	2	9	57	60	131	31	.345	.362
Minor League Totals				.245	114	424	65	104	18	2	12	63	62	142	33	.348	.382

26 JAKE GELOF, 3B

HIT: 40. **POW:** 60. **RUN:** 40. **FLD:** 45. **ARM:** 50. **BA Grade:** 45. **Risk:** High.

Born: February 25, 2002. **B-T:** R-R. **HT:** 6-1. **WT:** 195. **Drafted:** Virginia, 2023 (2nd round). **Signed by:** Paul Murphy.

TRACK RECORD: The younger brother of A's second baseman Zack Gelof, Jake set Virginia's single-season (23) and career (48) home runs records in a decorated three-year career. The Dodgers drafted him in the second round, No. 60 overall, and signed him for $1,334,400. Gelof did little for six weeks after the college season ended and fell out of shape, leading to a disappointing .226/.325/.429 slash line in his pro debut. He hit seven home runs in his final 12 games, including the postseason, at Low-A.

SCOUTING REPORT: Gelof is a strong, thick-bodied righthanded hitter with plus raw power. He posts loud exit velocities and hits balls out to all fields, even when he's off-balance. Gelof's power is undeniable, but his swing is long and he expands the strike zone against better stuff. He struggled against top competition in the Cape Cod League and during USA Baseball's College National team trials. He has to shorten his swing to be a below-average hitter who gets to his power. Gelof is a sneaky athlete despite his frame and has advanced instincts and feel for the game. He's a below-average runner and workmanlike defender at third base with an average arm.

THE FUTURE: Gelof has a chance to be a power-hitting third baseman if he shortens his swing and monitors his conditioning. He'll open at High-A Great Lakes in 2024.

Year	Age	Club (League)	Level	AVG	G	AB	R	H	2B	3B	HR	RBI	BB	SO	SB	OBP	SLG
2023	21	ACL Dodgers	Rk	.231	4	13	6	3	1	1	1	4	4	5	2	.412	.692
2023	21	R. Cucamonga (CAL)	A	.225	30	120	23	27	8	1	5	23	16	41	2	.314	.433
Minor League Totals				.226	34	133	29	30	9	2	6	27	20	46	4	.325	.459

27 PETER HEUBECK, RHP
FB: 60. **CB:** 60. **SL:** 55. **CHG:** 50. **CTL:** 30. **BA Grade:** 50. **Risk:** Extreme.

Born: July 22, 2002. **B-T:** R-R. **HT:** 6-3. **WT:** 170. **Drafted:** HS—Baltimore, 2021 (3rd round). **Signed by:** Paul Murphy.

TRACK RECORD: Heubeck pitched Baltimore's Gilman High to the 2021 Maryland state championship as a senior and was drafted by the Dodgers in the third round. He signed for an above-slot $1.272 million to forgo a Wake Forest commitment. Heubeck flashed loud stuff but horrendous control in his first full season at Low-A Rancho Cucamonga, and repeated the level to start 2023. He cut his walk rate by nearly one-third while maintaining his premium stuff and earned a late promotion to High-A Great Lakes.

SCOUTING REPORT: Heubeck is a lean, projectable righthander, who keeps getting stronger. His lively, riding fastball sits 92-93 mph, touches 96 and has room to keep adding velocity as he fills out. His big-breaking, 78-80 mph curveball is a potentially plus pitch with depth and power, and he added a tight-spinning, mid-80s slider that already shows above-average potential. He rarely throws his 84-87 mph changeup, but it flashes average with fade and sink. Heubeck has the pitch mix and clean, easy delivery of a starter, but his control is well below-average. He struggles to repeat his delivery and misses his spots by large margins, leading to excessive wild pitches.

THE FUTURE: Heubeck's stuff is potent, but he needs to add strength and coordination and improve his control. Those will be his main goals in 2024.

Year	Age	Club (League)	Level	W	L	ERA	G	GS	IP	H	HR	BB	SO	BB%	SO%	WHIP	AVG
2023	20	R. Cucamonga (CAL)	A	3	5	5.11	19	19	69	55	7	34	91	11.5	30.7	1.30	.219
2023	20	Great Lakes (MWL)	A+	2	2	8.47	6	5	17	21	4	9	16	11.4	20.3	1.76	.304
Minor League Totals				5	8	6.02	42	38	121	99	18	70	158	13.1	29.6	1.40	.222

28 SAMUEL MUÑOZ, OF
HIT: 55. **POW:** 50. **RUN:** 40. **FLD:** 50. **ARM:** 45. **BA Grade:** 50. **Risk:** Extreme.

Born: September 22, 2004. **B-T:** L-R. **HT:** 6-3. **WT:** 190. **Signed:** Dominican Republic, 2022. **Signed by:** Paul Brazon.

TRACK RECORD: Muñoz showed some of the best offensive tools in the 2022 international class and signed with the Dodgers for $757,000 out of the Dominican Republic. He lived up to his pedigree by batting .347 in the Dominican Summer League in his pro debut and continued to burnish his reputation in 2023. He finished fourth in the Arizona Complex League with 59 hits, led the league with seven triples and finished seventh with 89 total bases.

SCOUTING REPORT: Muñoz has a big, projectable 6-foot-3 frame that is easy to dream on. He has a smooth, rhythmic swing from the left side and drives the ball to all fields. He manages at-bats well and has a good feel for the strike zone. Muñoz struggles against lefties, but his swing and plate discipline give him the foundation to grow into an above-average hitter. Muñoz primarily focuses on contact, but he has the frame to get stronger and grow into average power as he matures. He drives balls hard for extra-base hits that should eventually turn into home runs. Muñoz is a below-average runner, but he's coordinated and plays center field well. He will likely end up in left field as an average defender with a fringy arm.

THE FUTURE: Muñoz's raw foundation to hit for average and power is promising. He'll move to Low-A Rancho Cucamonga in 2023.

Year	Age	Club (League)	Level	AVG	G	AB	R	H	2B	3B	HR	RBI	BB	SO	SB	OBP	SLG
2023	18	ACL Dodgers	Rk	.273	52	216	35	59	10	7	2	32	21	41	9	.338	.412
Minor League Totals				.306	99	389	74	119	22	12	3	74	47	75	13	.380	.447

29 JOHN ROONEY, LHP

FB: 45. **SL:** 50. **CHG:** 45. **CTL:** 50. **BA Grade:** 40. **Risk:** Medium.

Born: January 28, 1997. **B-T:** R-L. **HT:** 6-5. **WT:** 215. **Drafted:** Hofstra, 2018 (3rd round). **Signed by:** Paul Murphy.

TRACK RECORD: Rooney finished second in the nation with a 1.23 ERA as a junior at Hofstra and set school records with 108 strikeouts and 95 innings pitched in a season. The Dodgers drafted him in the third round and signed him for $563,240. Rooney struggled as a starter against upper-level hitters, but his stuff ticked up with a move to the bullpen in 2023. He gained more than 4 mph on his fastball and posted a 2.86 ERA in 53 appearances across Double-A and Triple-A.

SCOUTING REPORT: Rooney is a long, lanky lefthander who generates deception with an extreme crossfire delivery and low arm slot. His fastball sits 92-93, touches 95 and plays up with his deception and tough angle. His primary pitch is a horizontal, 83-85 mph slider that sweeps across the zone and is effective against both lefties and righties. Rooney also has a fringy, mid-80s changeup, but it's not a significant part of his arsenal in the bullpen. He throws strikes with average and control, and keeps traffic off the bases with an elite pickoff move. Rooney is especially dominant against lefties and held them to a .202/.297/.247 slash line in 2023.

THE FUTURE: Rooney projects to be a deceptive middle reliever, who matches up against lefties. His big league debut should come in 2024.

Year	Age	Club (League)	Level	W	L	ERA	G	GS	IP	H	HR	BB	SO	BB%	SO%	WHIP	AVG
2023	26	Tulsa (TL)	AA	3	2	2.38	29	0	34	33	3	9	37	6.4	26.2	1.24	.262
2023	26	Okla. City (PCL)	AAA	3	1	3.31	24	1	35	27	4	13	32	9.2	22.7	1.13	.214
Minor League Totals				20	16	3.91	113	51	321	299	36	138	320	10.2	23.6	1.37	.254

30 CHRIS NEWELL, OF

HIT: 30. **POW:** 50. **RUN:** 45. **FLD:** 50. **ARM:** 55. **BA Grade:** 40. **Risk:** High

Born: April 23, 2001. **B-T:** L-L. **HT:** 6-3. **WT:** 200. **Drafted:** Virginia, 2022 (13th round). **Signed by:** Paul Murphy.

TRACK RECORD: An unsigned 37th-round pick of the Cardinals in high school, Newell flashed huge tools but struggled to translate them into consistent production at Virginia. He posted a .952 OPS for Harwich in the Cape Cod League after his junior season, leading the Dodgers to draft him in the 13th round and sign him for an above-slot $147,500. Newell underwent a swing change with the Dodgers and got off to a loud start at Low-A Rancho Cucamonga in 2023, but his production fell off after a promotion to High-A Great Lakes. He battled elbow problems late in the year and had season-ending surgery to remove a bone chip.

SCOUTING REPORT: Newell is a strong, athletic lefthanded hitter, who knows the strike zone and crushes balls when he connects. He has plus-plus raw power and sends towering home runs out to all fields. He routinely posts exit velocities over 100 mph. Newell takes big, aggressive cuts and swings and misses in the strike zone alarmingly often, especially against elevated fastballs. He projects to be a well below-average hitter reliant on getting to his power. Newell is a fringy runner, but he runs clean routes and is playable in center field. He's a technically sound defender with an above-average arm and can play all three outfield spots.

THE FUTURE: Newell has a chance to be a backup outfielder who provides power from the left side. He'll try to prove he can hit higher-level pitching in 2024.

Year	Age	Club (League)	Level	AVG	G	AB	R	H	2B	3B	HR	RBI	BB	SO	SB	OBP	SLG
2023	22	R. Cucamonga (CAL)	A	.312	41	154	41	48	8	2	14	38	32	52	7	.426	.662
2023	22	Great Lakes (MWL)	A+	.222	42	158	24	35	9	1	7	22	24	58	8	.321	.424
Minor League Totals				.261	94	353	70	92	20	3	22	62	57	121	18	.361	.521

Miami Marlins

BY PETER FLAHERTY

In 2023, the Marlins made their first playoff appearance in a 162-game season since 2003. They had a blend of young, exciting talent and a core of veterans that helped snap their decades-long playoff drought and put the franchise in a strong position for the foreseeable future. While the major league club gave the fan base plenty to cheer about, the Marlins have a number of prospects who are poised to one day make an impact in the big leagues.

The Marlins are a pitching-heavy organization from top to bottom. Their major league rotation is chalk-full of young talent and profiles to be one of the better staffs in the National League going forward. Not only is it set up well in the short term, but poten-

tially for years to come with the talent waiting in the wings. Top prospect Noble Meyer has frontline starter potential, and fellow top 10 prospects Thomas White, Max Meyer and Dax Fulton all have what it takes to be in a future big league rotation.

Anywhere you look in the Marlins system, there are prospects that fit nearly any pitcher archetype: there are rotation pieces with thunderous pure stuff, pitchability specialists, and effective relievers. This might be both a blessing and a curse, however. The Marlins almost have an embarrassment of riches on the pitching side, and it will be interesting to see how the front office manages their many key pieces. It is clear that under general manager Kim Ng the Marlins placed a heavy emphasis on pitching, an ideology that has already paid dividends at all levels of the organization—but following the season Ng declined a mutual option in the final year of her contract as owner Bruce Sherman planned to hire a president of baseball operations above her.

Things get murkier for the Marlins on the hitting side, though much of its offensive core from the 2023 season figures to anchor the lineup for years to come. Luis Arraez (.354/.393/.469), Jazz Chisholm Jr. (.250/.304/.457), Jesus Sanchez (.253/.327/.450) and others enjoyed productive 2023 campaigns and will look to keep the momentum they built rolling. One hole for Miami defensively was up the middle at shortstop, but No. 10 prospect Jacob Amaya has already gotten a taste of the big leagues and packs an advanced defensive skill set. While not as far along as Amaya, there is also excitement surrounding fellow shortstop and No. 6 prospect Yiddi Cappe.

Looking at the future of another premium position, catcher Will Banfield had a strong season in Double-A Pensacola in which he slashed .258/.302/.472 while setting new career highs in

The Marlins' enviable pitching pipeline produced 20-year-old Eury Perez in 2023.

PROJECTED 2027 LINEUP

Position	Player	Age
Catcher	Will Banfield	27
First Base	Jacob Berry	26
Second Base	Luis Arraez	29
Third Base	Xavier Edwards	27
Shortstop	Jacob Amaya	28
Left Field	Victor Mesa Jr.	25
Center Field	Jazz Chisholm Jr.	29
Right Field	Jesus Sanchez	29
Designated Hitter	Bryan De La Cruz	30
No. 1 Starter	Sandy Alcantara	31
No. 2 Starter	Jesus Luzardo	29
No. 3 Starter	Eury Perez	23
No. 4 Starter	Noble Meyer	22
No. 5 Starter	Trevor Rogers	29
Closer	Edward Cabrera	28

home runs (23), doubles (25), and RBIs (76). In addition to his raw power, Banfield brings strong defense behind the plate with a plus throwing arm. Outfielder Victor Mesa Jr. provides an enticing power-speed combination, but he will need to cut down on his swing-and-miss tendencies to reach his ceiling.

The calling card of future Marlins clubs should be the depth and ability of its pitching staff, but there is also some impact talent on the hitting front. The window for the Marlins to be a postseason regular and perhaps go on a run in October is open, and the next handful of seasons could be the best potential stretch for the franchise in quite some time. ■

DEPTH CHART

MIAMI MARLINS

TOP 2024 CONTRIBUTORS	RANK
1. Xavier Edwards, 2B	4
2. Jacob Amaya, SS	10

BREAKOUT PROSPECTS	RANK
1. Andres Valor, OF	12
2. Anthony Maldonado, RHP	21
3. Mark Coley, OF	26

SOURCE OF TOP 30 TALENT

Homegrown	27	Acquired	3
College	13	Trade	2
Junior College	0	Rule 5 Draft	1
High School	7	Independent League	0
Nondrafted free agent	0	Free agent/waivers	0
International	7		

LF
Antony Peguero
Jake DeLeo

CF
Andres Valor (12)
Dane Myers (14)
Osiris Johnson

RF
Victor Mesa Jr. (5)
Jose Gerardo (20)
Kemp Alderman (19)
Mark Coley (26)
Peyton Burdick
Griffin Conine
Brett Roberts

3B
Jordan Groshans
Cobie Vance

SS
Jacob Amaya (10)
Fabian Lopez (13)

2B
Xavier Edwards (4)
Yiddi Cappe (6)
Javier Sanoja (16)
Jose Devers
Ian Lewis
Cody Morissette

1B
Jacob Berry (9)
Troy Johnston (17)
Brock Vradenburg (18)
Torin Montgomery (30)

C
Will Banfield (15)
Joe Mack (22)
Paul McIntosh

LHP

LHSP	LHRP
Thomas White (3)	Josh Simpson
Dax Fulton (8)	Caleb Wurster
Patrick Monteverde (23)	Justin Storm
Emmett Olson (29)	Dale Stanavich
Janero Miller	Evan Taylor
	Jhon Cabral

RHP

RHSP	RHRP
Noble Meyer (1)	Anthony Maldonado (21)
Max Meyer (2)	Nigel Belgrave (27)
Karson Milbrandt (7)	Xavier Meachem (28)
Jacob Miller (11)	Matt Pushard
Juan De La Cruz (24)	Zach McCambley
Ike Buxton (25)	Nick Maldonado
Sixto Sanchez	Eliazar Dishmey
Alex Williams	
Gabe Bierman	
Evan Fitterer	

1 NOBLE MEYER, RHP

Born: January 10, 2005. **B-T:** R-R. **HT:** 6-5. **WT:** 185.
Drafted: HS—Beaverton, OR, 2023 (1st round).
Signed by: Scott Fairbanks

TOM DIPACE

TRACK RECORD: A high school All-American and the Gatorade Player of the Year for Oregon, Meyer excelled at Jesuit High in 2023 and pitched his way to a minuscule 0.33 ERA with a strikeout-to-walk ratio of 128-to-19 in 63 innings. Meyer was the first high school pitcher off the board in 2023, selected 10th overall by the Marlins and signed him for $4.5 million. That was 18% under the slot value of $5,480,000 for the pick. Meyer threw 11 innings between the Florida Complex League and Low-A Jupiter in his pro debut. He notched 15 strikeouts against seven walks.

SCOUTING REPORT: The 6-foot-5 Meyer features a lively 93-95 mph fastball that tops out at 96 and 97. It has plenty of natural armside run given Meyer's three-quarters arm slot as well as heavy sink at times. It bears in on the hands of right-handed hitters, making for a rather uncomfortable at-bat. Meyer's command of the pitch was a bit scattered in his pro debut, but the sample was extremely small and his overall control is above-average. Meyer supplements his heater with a double-plus slider that has plenty of sharp, horizontal movement. It generates tons of swings and is a true out pitch. The spin rate of the pitch has eclipsed the 3,000 rpm mark, which is well above the major league average. To round out his arsenal, Meyer features a mid-80s changeup that he occasionally throws. It is an inconsistent offering, but it has flashed armside fade. Given Meyer's arm slot, it is easy to dream on what the changeup might become, but for now it is an average pitch. The continued development of the offering will be key when it comes to maximizing Meyer's upside as a starter. In high school, Meyer displayed above-average control and command of his arsenal, but it wavered in his pro debut. He moves well on the mound and has a loose, whippy arm stroke with exceptional arm speed. Meyer falls off toward the first-base side, which was certainly a contributing factor in his spotty control. Cleaning up his direction should not be too tall a task, and will likely lead to improved strike-throwing. As Meyer continues to mature physically and fill out his frame, he could add a few ticks of velocity.

THE FUTURE: Meyer projects to start the 2024 season at Low-A Jupiter, but will likely be promoted to High-A Beloit at some point. There is

BA GRADE	SCOUTING GRADES
60 Risk: Extreme	FB: 60. SL: 70. CHG: 50. Control: 55.

Projected future grades on 20-80 scouting scale

BEST TOOLS

BATTING

Best Hitter for Average	Xavier Edwards
Best Power Hitter	Kemp Alderman
Best Strike-Zone Discipline	Xavier Edwards
Fastest Baserunner	Xavier Edwards
Best Athlete	Mark Coley

PITCHING

Best Fastball	Noble Meyer
Best Curveball	Thomas White
Best Slider	Max Meyer
Best Changeup	Patrick Monteverde
Best Control	Patrick Monteverde

FIELDING

Best Defensive Catcher	Will Banfield
Best Defensive Infielder	Fabian Lopez
Best Infield Arm	Jacob Amaya
Best Defensive Outfielder	Victor Mesa Jr.
Best Outfield Arm	Jose Gerardo

no reason to rush Meyer, but there is an outside chance he makes it to Double-A Pensacola by season's end. His potential MLB debut is still years away, but he could make his debut by 2026 or 2027. Meyer is a top-of-the-line pitching prospect and has the potential to be a future No. 1 or No. 2 starter. ∎

Year	Age	Club (League)	Level	W	L	ERA	G	GS	IP	H	HR	BB	SO	BB%	SO%	WHIP	AVG
2023	18	FCL Marlins	Rk	0	1	4.50	2	2	4	2	0	3	6	17.6	35.3	1.25	.143
2023	18	Jupiter (FSL)	A	0	0	3.86	3	3	7	9	0	4	9	11.8	26.5	1.86	.310
Minor League Totals				0	1	4.09	5	5	11	11	0	7	15	13.7	29.4	1.64	.256

2 MAX MEYER, RHP

FB: 55. **SL:** 70. **CHG:** 55. **CTL:** 55. **BA Grade:** 55 **Risk:** High.

Born: March 12, 1999. **B-T:** L-R. **HT:** 6-0. **WT:** 196.
Drafted: Minnesota, 2020 (1st round). **Signed by:** Shaeffer Hall.
TRACK RECORD: After starring as a two-way player at Minnesota for three years with a career 2.13 ERA and 187 strikeouts in 148 innings, Meyer was drafted third overall in the 2020 draft and signed to an under-slot deal worth $6.7 million. He started his professional career at Double-A Pensacola in 2021 and he carved his way to a 2.41 ERA with 113 strikeouts in 101 innings. Meyer ended the season at Triple-A Jacksonville, where he had similar success. After making a dozen starts in Jacksonville to start the 2022 season in which he struck out 65 in 58 innings, Meyer was called up to Miami. He was off to a promising start before a July elbow injury led to Tommy John surgery and he missed the entire 2023 season.
SCOUTING REPORT: Meyer has an explosive fastball that sits in the 93-95 mph range and tops out at 97. It jumps out of his hand and takes on a unique shape with an average of 12 inches of induced vertical break and 5 inches of horizontal break. Most of batters' swings and misses against the pitch come at the top of the zone. The main attraction with Meyer is his soul-snatching, high-80s power slider. It has tight spin with serious late teeth and is effective against hitters on either side of the plate. Meyer's advanced feel for the pitch makes it all the more lethal. He also has a high-80s changeup that boasts ample armside fade and is an above-average pitch. Meyer is an athletic mover on the mound and has some effort to his delivery. He attacks from a high-three quarters slot and is consistently around the strike zone.
THE FUTURE: Meyer is poised to head into spring training healthy and will have the opportunity to make the big league Opening Day roster. He projects either as a midrotation arm or perhaps even a high-leverage reliever down the road.

Year	Age	Club (League)	Level	W	L	ERA	G	GS	IP	H	HR	BB	SO	BB%	SO%	WHIP	AVG
2023	24	Did not play—Injured															
Minor League Totals				9	8	2.77	35	35	172	130	13	61	199	8.8	28.7	1.11	.207
Major League Totals				0	1	7.50	2	2	6	7	2	2	6	7.7	23.1	1.50	.292

3 THOMAS WHITE, LHP

FB: 60. **CB:** 60. **CHG:** 55. **CTL:** 45. **BA Grade:** 55. **Risk:** Extreme.

Born: September 29, 2004. **B-T:** L-L. **HT:** 6-5. **WT:** 210.
Drafted: HS—Andover, MA, 2023 (1st round supplemental). **Signed by:** Alex Smith
TRACK RECORD: White ranked as the top lefthander in the 2023 draft class after an illustrious prep career. He took home back-to-back Massachusetts Gatorade Player of the Year awards in 2022 and 2023 and was also named a 2023 High School All-American. In his senior season at Phillips Academy, White had a 1.66 ERA with 95 strikeouts in 42 innings. He was selected 35th overall by the Marlins and signed for $4.1 million, an amount nearly $2 million more than slot value. White's pro career got off to a rocky start. Across three appearances spanning 4.1 innings between the Florida Complex League and Low-A Jupiter, he had a 6.23 ERA with seven strikeouts, six walks and three hits allowed.
SCOUTING REPORT: White features a plus fastball that will sit in the 94-96 mph range and routinely top out at 97. It has plenty of carry through the strike zone and consistently gets above the barrel of opposing hitters. He also has a high-70s curveball with big shape and sharp, two-plane break. White has inconsistent feel for the pitch, but when it's on it is a plus offering. Rounding out his repertoire is a mid-80s changeup that is an above-average pitch with tumble and fade. The 6-foot-5 White has an effortless delivery with a long, loose arm action. Strike-throwing has been a bugaboo at times, and tightening up his command will be key.
THE FUTURE: White is slated to begin 2024 at Low-A Jupiter with an opportunity to be promoted to High-A Beloit at some point. Adding polish will go a long way toward maximizing his potential, and he has No. 3 starter upside. White profiles to be in the big leagues no sooner than 2027, when he will be 22 years old.

Year	Age	Club (League)	Level	W	L	ERA	G	GS	IP	H	HR	BB	SO	BB%	SO%	WHIP	AVG
2023	18	FCL Marlins	Rk	0	0	0.00	1	0	1	0	0	2	2	33.3	33.3	3.00	.000
2023	18	Jupiter (FSL)	A	0	1	7.36	2	2	4	3	0	4	5	22.2	27.8	1.91	.214
Minor League Totals				0	1	6.75	3	2	4	3	0	6	7	25.0	29.2	2.25	.167

4 XAVIER EDWARDS, 2B/OF

HIT: 55. **POW:** 30. **RUN:** 70. **FLD:** 50. **ARM:** 50. **BA Grade:** 45. **Risk:** Medium.

Born: August 9, 1999. **B-T:** S-R. **HT:** 5-10. **WT:** 175.
Drafted: HS—Coconut Creek, FL, 2018 (1st round supp). **Signed by:** Brian Cruz (Padres).
TRACK RECORD: Edwards was selected 38th overall in 2018 by the Padres after a standout high school career at North Broward Prep. He had a productive first two pro seasons, hitting a combined .328 with nearly as many walks (75) as strikeouts (79). He was traded to the Rays in 2019, where he continued to show off his advanced bat-to-ball skills. After reaching Triple-A Durham in 2022, Edwards was traded to Miami that fall. Edwards made his MLB debut in 2023 during a productive season with Triple-A Jacksonville in which he hit .351 with 32 stolen bases and 52 walks to 30 strikeouts. He played to his strengths in Miami, hitting .295 and stealing five bases in 30 games.
SCOUTING REPORT: Edwards has a direct, compact swing from both sides of the plate with quickness in his hands. His operation is geared toward putting the ball in play and spraying line drives to all fields. Edwards has an undoubted hit-over-power profile, but he sometimes laces the ball down the line or into a gap. He has excellent bat-to-ball skills. Across Triple-A and MLB in 2023, he had an overall contact rate of 87% and an in-zone contact rate of 91%. Edwards will sometimes struggle to pick up spin, which will lead to him expanding the strike zone at times. He is a double-plus runner who has turned in 80-grade home-to-first times and has the ability to wreak havoc on the basepaths. Edwards focused his MLB time at second base and center field and is capable at both. He also played third base and shortstop in Triple-A.
THE FUTURE: Having already gotten an MLB taste, Edwards projects to crack the Opening Day roster in 2024. His contact and speed-oriented profile bodes well with the new rules aiding basestealers. He can affect the game in a number of ways, and his versatility will help keep him in the lineup.

Year	Age	Club (League)	Level	AVG	G	AB	R	H	2B	3B	HR	RBI	BB	SO	SB	OBP	SLG
2023	23	Jacksonville (IL)	AAA	.351	93	370	80	130	14	2	7	47	52	30	32	.429	.457
2023	23	Miami (NL)	MLB	.295	30	78	12	23	3	0	0	3	3	14	5	.329	.333
Minor League Totals				.312	433	1672	284	521	72	15	13	166	206	226	114	.386	.396
Major League Totals				.295	30	78	12	23	3	0	0	3	3	14	5	.329	.333

5 VICTOR MESA JR., OF

HIT: 45. **POW:** 55. **RUN:** 50. **FLD:** 55. **ARM:** 60. **BA Grade:** 50. **Risk:** High.

Born: September 8, 2001. **B-T:** L-L. **HT:** 6-0. **WT:** 195.
Signed: Cuba, 2018. **Signed by:** Fernando Seguignol.
TRACK RECORD: The younger brother of former blue-chip Cuban prospect Victor Victor Mesa, Victor Jr. signed for $1 million alongside his older brother in fall 2018. The pair defected from Cuba in May 2018 in order to sign with an MLB team. While Victor Victor was the more highly touted of the two, Victor Jr. has surpassed him as a prospect. He had a fantastic pro debut in the Gulf Coast League in 2019, slashing .284/.366/.398 as a 17-year-old. He has steadily ascended the Marlins' system, most recently completing a full season in Double-A Pensacola, where he flashed power and speed with 18 home runs, 24 doubles and 16 stolen bases.
SCOUTING REPORT: Mesa operates out of a slightly open, upright stance in the box with a medium-high handset. His swing is rather along with a noticeable barrel tip, but he does a nice job of extending through the ball and creating leverage in his swing. While Mesa hit for the most power in his pro career in 2023, it also came with a strikeout rate near 23%. He had an overall contact rate of just 71% with a chase rate of 33%. Cutting down on the movement in his operation should lead to less swing-and-miss and susceptibility to offspeed offerings. Mesa has above-average raw power and most of his damage is done between center and to his pull side. He is a strong defender in center field with range to either gap and an above-average throwing arm.
THE FUTURE: Mesa will likely begin the 2024 season at either Pensacola or Triple-A Jacksonville, but with a strong performance he could be on the big league club before the end of the season. While he might slide to an outfield corner, he has the potential to be a big league regular with overall offensive production near average.

Year	Age	Club (League)	Level	AVG	G	AB	R	H	2B	3B	HR	RBI	BB	SO	SB	OBP	SLG
2023	21	Pensacola (SL)	AA	.242	123	483	73	117	24	2	18	76	41	122	16	.308	.412
Minor League Totals				.254	402	1547	231	393	80	20	29	221	151	353	45	.322	.388

6 YIDDI CAPPE, 2B/SS

HIT: 45. **POW:** 50. **RUN:** 40. **FLD:** 45. **ARM:** 50. **BA Grade:** 50. **Risk:** High.

Born: September 17, 2002. **B-T:** R-R. **HT:** 6-3. **WT:** 175.
Signed: Cuba, 2021. **Signed by:** Adrian Lorenzo

TRACK RECORD: Cappe was one of the more highly touted prospects in the 2021 international signing period and signed with Miami for $3 million when he was 18 years old. Cappe's first pro experience came in the Dominican Summer League that year. The lanky shortstop showed well, hitting .270 with 20 extra-base hits. After a productive 2022 campaign that was split between the Florida Complex League and Low-A Jupiter, Cappe spent the entire 2023 season at High-A Beloit. He hit just .220 but laced 26 doubles and swiped 19 bases while making three quarters of his starts at second base.

SCOUTING REPORT: Cappe has a tall, upright stance with a low handset and a loose operation. He has a slight load with his hands, a high leg kick and some present bat speed. Much of his damage and power is to the pull side, but given his physical projection and the likelihood of his frame to fill out, there is more impact on the way. Cappe struck out nearly 20% in 2023 and his approach will need refining as his overall chase rate was 38%. He particularly struggles against spin, which is the root of most of his swing-and-miss. However, he was just 20 years old in the notoriously pitcher-friendly Midwest League and has a track record of showing an advanced hit tool. Cappe has a chance to grow into at least average power, a tool he can supplement with a potentially above-average hit tool. He is an average runner and a bit clunky defensively, and his future home could be in the outfield.

THE FUTURE: Cappe will have a chance to progress to Double-A Pensacola by the end of the 2024 season. Once his positional future is solidified, he has the potential to be an impact bat as an everyday member of a big league lineup.

Year	Age	Club (League)	Level	AVG	G	AB	R	H	2B	3B	HR	RBI	BB	SO	SB	OBP	SLG
2023	20	Beloit (MWL)	A+	.220	123	509	53	112	26	2	5	53	18	102	18	.250	.308
Minor League Totals				.249	244	974	125	243	55	4	16	120	52	178	40	.288	.363

7 KARSON MILBRANDT, RHP

FB: 55. **CB:** 55. **CHG:** 50. **CTL:** 45. **BA Grade:** 50. **Risk:** Extreme.

Born: April 21, 2004. **B-T:** R-R. **HT:** 6-2. **WT:** 190.
Drafted: HS—Liberty, MO, 2022 (3rd round). **Signed by:** Ryan Cisterna.

TRACK RECORD: Milbrandt was a two-sport star at Liberty High, starring in basketball as well as baseball. He was named the 2022 Missouri Baseball Gatorade Player of the Year. Milbrandt would go on to be selected in the third round—85th overall—of the 2022 draft and signed for an over-slot deal worth $1.5 million. Milbrandt in 2023 enjoyed a productive first full professional season, working a 5.09 ERA with 94 strikeouts and 51 walks in 97.1 innings across Low-A Jupiter and High-A Beloit.

SCOUTING REPORT: At 6-foot-2 and 190 pounds, Milbrandt has an athletic build and moves well on the mound. He has an easy, low-effort delivery as well as blistering arm speed. Milbrandt works primarily on the third base side of the rubber and attacks hitters from a mid-three-quarters slot. His fastball will sit in the 94-97 mph range and explodes out of the hand. Most of the swing-and-miss Milbrandt gets on the pitch is when it is located in the top half of the strike zone, where it displays run and ride through the zone. His go-to out pitch is a tight-spinning, low-80s curveball. It flashes big shape at times and has sharp, two-plane break. Milbrandt maintains his trademark arm speed well and it is effective against batters on both sides of the plate. It is an above-average offering and has out pitch potential down the road. Though he threw the pitch sparingly, Milbrandt also has a high-80s changeup in his arsenal that shows promise, showing run and fade to the arm side at times. A key for Milbrandt going forward will be continuing to refine his command, which in 2023 was inconsistent at times.

THE FUTURE: Milbrandt is on track to start the 2024 season at High-A Beloit and could reach Double-A Pensacola. He has the potential to be an effective No. 3 or 4 starter.

Year	Age	Club (League)	Level	W	L	ERA	G	GS	IP	H	HR	BB	SO	BB%	SO%	WHIP	AVG
2023	19	Jupiter (FSL)	A	3	3	5.33	12	12	52	50	4	26	52	11.4	22.7	1.45	.251
2023	19	Beloit (MWL)	A+	0	3	4.60	11	11	43	46	1	24	41	12.3	21.0	1.63	.274
Minor League Totals				3	6	5.10	24	24	97	98	5	51	94	11.8	21.7	1.54	.261

8 DAX FULTON, LHP

FB: 55. **SL:** 60. **CHG:** 50. **CTL:** 55. **BA Grade:** 50. **Risk:** Extreme.

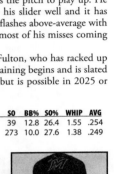

Born: October 16, 2001. **B-T:** L-L. **HT:** 6-7. **WT:** 235.
Drafted: HS—Mustang, OK, 2020 (2nd round). **Signed by:** James Vilade
TRACK RECORD: Fulton had a standout high school career at Mustang High and was one of the most coveted prep arms in the 2020 draft class. Fulton had Tommy John surgery as a senior and saw his draft stock slip. The Marlins called his name 40th overall in the shortened five-round draft and signed him for an over-slot $2.4 million. When healthy, Fulton has proved to be a quality starter option. After a successful first stint at Double-A Pensacola in 2022, Fulton ran up a 5.18 ERA with 19 walks in 33 innings before he had a repair procedure on his UCL in June, ending his season.
SCOUTING REPORT: At 6-foot-7 and 235 pounds, Fulton is an imposing figure on the mound. He has the prototypical build of a starter and has a thick lower half. His fastball sits in the 92-94 mph range and tops out at 95. It has life through the zone and generates a fair share of swing-and-miss. Fulton attacks from a high-three quarters slot and has some funk in his delivery, which allows the pitch to play up. He also features a mid-80s slider that serves as his go-to out pitch. Fulton spins his slider well and it has plenty of depth with two-plane break. Lastly, he has a high-80s changeup that flashes above-average with late fade. Fulton has above-average command and control of his arsenal, with most of his misses coming to his arm side.
THE FUTURE: Getting healthy and staying healthy will be the biggest key for Fulton, who has racked up 273 strikeouts in 230 pro innings. He will likely be ready by the time spring training begins and is slated to start the season at Double-A Pensacola. The potential of a major league debut is possible in 2025 or late 2024.

Year	Age	Club (League)	Level	W	L	ERA	G	GS	IP	H	HR	BB	SO	BB%	SO%	WHIP	AVG
2023	21	Pensacola (SL)	AA	2	4	5.18	7	6	33	32	4	19	39	12.8	26.4	1.55	.254
Minor League Totals				10	16	4.28	51	48	230	216	18	99	273	10.0	27.6	1.38	.249

9 JACOB BERRY, 3B

HIT: 45. **POW:** 50. **RUN:** 40. **FLD:** 35. **ARM:** 40. **BA Grade:** 45. **Risk:** High.

Born: May 5, 2001. **B-T:** S-R. **HT:** 6-0. **WT:** 212.
Drafted: Louisiana State, 2022 (1st round). **Signed by:** Chris Joblin.
TRACK RECORD: Berry was one of the top college hitters in two seasons split between Arizona and Louisiana State. He hit .352 with 17 home runs as a freshman and earned an invitation to USA Baseball's Collegiate National Team. Berry followed head coach Jay Johnson to LSU in 2022 and had similar success in the Southeastern Conference, hitting .370 with 15 home runs. The Marlins drafted him sixth overall in the 2022 and signed him for $6 million. Through two professional seasons, Berry has not had the same success as he did collegiately. In 144 games, he has hit just 12 home runs and has seen his approach and bat-to-ball skills take a step back.
SCOUTING REPORT: Berry has a simple setup in the box with a slight load and small stride. He has some physicality in his lower half, and there is minimal unnecessary movement in his swing. The switch-hitting Berry does a nice job, particularly from the right side, in creating leverage in his swing and getting the ball in the air. He hit .275/.300/.517 with four of his nine home runs in 103 plate appearances batting righthanded in 2023. He has present power to his pull side, but his hit tool will need refining in order to maximize his offensive upside. In 2023 he struck out at a 22% clip and struggled mightily to pick up offspeed offerings. Berry was susceptible to expanding the strike zone and his swing decisions lacked polish. He is both a below-average runner and below-average defender at third base. He faces a likely future at first base.
THE FUTURE: Berry figures to start the 2024 season at Double-A Pensacola, where he will have an opportunity to earn a promotion to Triple-A by the end of the year. His major league debut is unlikely to occur before the 2025 season. As things stand, he will likely be a bench option.

Year	Age	Club (League)	Level	AVG	G	AB	R	H	2B	3B	HR	RBI	BB	SO	SB	OBP	SLG
2023	22	Beloit (MWL)	A+	.227	79	317	28	72	19	7	4	37	16	70	5	.278	.369
2023	22	Pensacola (SL)	AA	.248	28	113	22	28	5	1	5	22	9	26	5	.301	.442
Minor League Totals				.236	144	571	70	135	31	8	12	85	39	125	11	.300	.382

10 JACOB AMAYA, SS

HIT: 45. **POW:** 50. **RUN:** 45. **FLD:** 55. **ARM:** 60. **BA Grade:** 40. **Risk:** Medium.

Born: September 3, 1998. **B-T:** R-R. **HT:** 6-0. **WT:** 180.
Drafted: HS—West Covina, CA, 2017 (11th round). **Signed by:** Bobby Darwin (Dodgers).
TRACK RECORD: Amaya has a lengthy track record in the minors, having spent five seasons in the Dodgers system before being traded to the Marlins in 2023 for infielder Miguel Rojas. In 2022 he had the most productive season of his professional career and posted a combined slash line of .261/.369/.427 with 20 doubles, 17 home runs and 71 RBIs. At Triple-A Jacksonville, Amaya slashed .252/.345/.407 with 26 doubles and 15 home runs before being called up to the big league club for a brief four-game stint.
SCOUTING REPORT: Amaya has a quiet setup in the box with a slight bend in his lower half and normal handset. He has a minimal load with a small stride and average bat speed. Amaya extends well through the baseball and does a nice job creating leverage in his swing. He has shown the ability to drive the baseball to all fields, but has borderline above-average power the pull side. Amaya has a decent approach and above average bat-to-ball skills, as evident by his 87% in-zone contact rate. His best tool is his defense, where he shows quick feet and smooth actions with a plus arm.
THE FUTURE: Amaya will have a strong chance to crack the big league roster out of camp, especially with Joey Wendle becoming a free agent. Should the club bring in no further reinforcements from outside the organization, Amaya seems destined to be the Opening Day shortstop. If the club does elect to sign a free agent to fill the void left by Wendle, Amaya could be on the move.

Year	Age	Club (League)	Level	AVG	G	AB	R	H	2B	3B	HR	RBI	BB	SO	SB	OBP	SLG
2023	24	Jacksonville (IL)	AAA	.252	128	484	85	122	26	2	15	65	70	106	6	.345	.407
2023	24	Miami (NL)	MLB	.222	4	9	1	2	0	0	0	2	0	1	1	.222	.222
Minor League Totals				.255	591	2186	383	557	103	17	57	297	350	491	40	.358	.396
Major League Totals				.222	4	9	1	2	0	0	0	2	0	1	1	.222	.222

11 JACOB MILLER, RHP

FB: 50. **SL:** 55. **CB:** 50. **CHG:** 45. **CTL:** 50. **BA Grade:** 50. **Risk:** Extreme.

Born: August 10, 2003. **B-T:** R-R. **HT:** 6-2. **WT:** 180. **Drafted:** HS—Baltimore, OH, 2022 (2nd round). **Signed by:** JT Zink.
TRACK RECORD: Miller was named the Ohio Baseball Gatorade Player of the Year in 2022 after a sparkling senior season when he posted a 0.35 ERA with an incredible strikeout-to-walk ratio of 94-to-6 across 40 innings. The Marlins then drafted him with the 46th overall pick and signed him to a slightly over-slot deal of $1,700,400. In his first full pro season with Low-A Jupiter, Miller posted a 4.70 ERA in 14 starts and 59.1 innings and struck out 50 batters.
SCOUTING REPORT: Miller stands at 6-foot-2, 180 pounds with some physicality in his lower half. There is a bit of effort in his delivery and he has an abbreviated arm stroke while attacking from a high three-quarters slot. His fastball sits 91-94 with some carrying life through the zone, though opposing batters hit .344 against it in 2023. Miller features two distinct breaking balls with a high-70s curveball and mid-80s slider. His curveball takes on a big shape and has some downward teeth, but his slider is the more effective pitch. In 2023 it generated a 42% miss rate and flashed tight, two-plane break. Miller throws a high-80s changeup sparingly, but it does show some promise with late tumbling life.
THE FUTURE: Miller should spend most of the 2024 season with High-A Beloit. He has No. 3 or 4 starter upside with continued progression.

Year	Age	Club (League)	Level	W	L	ERA	G	GS	IP	H	HR	BB	SO	BB%	SO%	WHIP	AVG
2023	19	FCL Marlins	Rk	0	0	0.00	2	1	5	2	0	2	5	12.5	31.3	0.86	.143
2023	19	Jupiter (FSL)	A	2	4	4.70	14	14	59	46	3	25	50	10.1	20.2	1.20	.213
Minor League Totals				2	6	4.43	20	19	70	53	4	29	61	10.0	21.1	1.19	.209

12 ANDRES VALOR, OF

HIT: 50. **POW:** 55. **RUN:** 55. **FLD:** 60. **ARM:** 55. **BA Grade:** 50. **Risk:** Extreme.

Born: November 8, 2005. **B-T:** R-R. **HT:** 6-3. **WT:** 180. **Signed:** Venezuela, 2023. **Signed by:** Nestor Moreno.
TRACK RECORD: Valor was a part of the Marlins' 2023 international free agent class and signed for $520,000. He had a strong first professional season in the Dominican Summer League in which he hit .294/.360/.466 with 16 doubles, five home runs, 25 RBIs and 21 stolen bases in 51 games.
SCOUTING REPORT: Valor has a great body at 6-foot-3, 180 pounds. He has an incredibly athletic build with plenty of present strength, but he still has room to add more mass and impact potential. Valor stands

almost completely upright in the box with a medium-high handset. He has a twitchy, compact operation with a small load, hardly any stride and scissor action in his back leg with lightning-fast hands. At just 17 years old, Valor has already posted a max exit velocity of 108 mph. His bat-to-ball skills at this point are solid, with an in-zone contact rate of 80%. Valor's approach should only get better as he continues to get acclimated to professional baseball. He is a great athlete in the outfield with a quick first step and strong throwing arm. Valor covers plenty of ground to either gap and he has the defensive chops to stick in center long term. He oozes upside and is one of the most exciting prospects in the organization.

THE FUTURE: Valor this year figures to get his first taste of stateside baseball and is likely to start the year in the Florida Complex League. There is no reason to rush him, but there's a chance he's able to earn a promotion to Jupiter by season's end. Valor's big league debut is still a ways away, but he has all the tools to be an impact player.

Year	Age	Club (League)	Level	AVG	G	AB	R	H	2B	3B	HR	RBI	BB	SO	SB	OBP	SLG
2023	17	DSL Miami	Rk	.294	51	204	39	60	16	2	5	25	21	55	21	.360	.466
Minor League Totals				.294	51	204	39	60	16	2	5	25	21	55	21	.360	.466

13 FABIAN LOPEZ, SS

HIT: 50. **POW:** 50. **RUN:** 55. **FLD:** 60. **ARM:** 60. **BA Grade:** 50. **Risk:** Extreme.

Born: September 18, 2005. **B-T:** B-R. **HT:** 6-0. **WT:** 165. **Signed:** Dominican Republic, 2023.
Signed by: Miguel Beltre/Roman Ocumarez.

TRACK RECORD: Lopez was a part of Miami's 2023 international free agent class, alongside outfielder Andres Valor, and signed for $650,000. The switch-hitting shortstop made a strong first impression in the Dominican Summer League and hit .265/.327/.405 with 12 doubles, four home runs, 22 RBIs and 15 stolen bases in 49 games.

SCOUTING REPORT: Lopez has two distinct looks in the box. From the left side, he has an open front side with a somewhat high handset and his bat completely horizontal above his back shoulder. He takes a small stride and rotates well in his swing with solid leverage to the pull side. From the right side, Lopez's front side is a bit more closed off with his bat more vertical in his stance. He has shown the ability to impact the baseball, especially from the left side, and has strong bat-to-ball skills given his 83% in-zone contact rate. As he continues to age and mature physically, Lopez projects to add impact from both sides. Lopez is a plus defender at shortstop, where he has quick feet, athletic actions and an above-average internal clock. He is comfortable going up the middle and to the backhand side and has a plus arm. Lopez is a safe bet to stick at the position and has the makings of an everyday shortstop. He is also an above-average runner and effective basestealer—another reason why his fingerprints are regularly all over the box score.

THE FUTURE: Lopez is likely to start the 2024 season in the Florida Complex League before earning a promotion to Low-A Jupiter. He is unlikely to make his big league debut before the 2027 or 2028 season, but he could be the club's shortstop of the future.

Year	Age	Club (League)	Level	AVG	G	AB	R	H	2B	3B	HR	RBI	BB	SO	SB	OBP	SLG
2023	17	DSL Miami	Rk	.265	49	200	28	53	12	2	4	22	16	53	15	.327	.405
Minor League Totals				.265	49	200	28	53	12	2	4	22	16	53	15	.327	.405

14 DANE MYERS, OF

HIT: 45. **POW:** 50. **RUN:** 55. **ARM:** 55. **FLD:** 55. **BA Grade:** 40. **Risk:** Medium.

Born: March 8, 1996. **B-T:** R-R. **HT:** 6-0. **WT:** 205. **Drafted:** Rice, 2017 (6th round). **Signed by:** Matt Lea (Tigers).

TRACK RECORD: A seventh-round pick after a monster junior season at Rice, Myers had a lengthy five-year stint in the Tigers system that was headlined by a productive 2022 season. After not being added to Detroit's 40-man roster, Myers was picked up by Miami in the minor league phase of the 2022 Rule 5 Draft. He had an excellent 100-game stretch between Double-A Pensacola and Triple-A Jacksonville where he hit .316/.406/.489 with 14 doubles, 15 home runs, 62 RBIs and 20 stolen bases. Myers also spent 22 games in the majors and hit .269 with four extra-base hits and nine RBIs.

SCOUTING REPORT: Myers has an interesting setup in the box and stands completely upright with a slightly open front side and low handset. He has a small stride with plus bat speed and has shown the ability to catch pitches deep in the zone and drive them with authority the opposite way. Myers does most of his damage against fastballs. Between Double-A and Triple-A he hit .328 with five doubles and 11 home runs while working an above-average in-zone contact rate of 89%. He does have a tendency to expand the strike zone and struggles to pick up spin at times. Myers is a sound defender In center field where his athleticism and above-average speed play well. He takes efficient routes to the baseball and has an above-average arm.

THE FUTURE: Myers is close to a finished product with a bench player or fourth outfielder role in the majors. He'll play in his age-28 season in 2024 and should start the season with Triple-A Jacksonville, though he's likely to get big league time.

Year	Age	Club (League)	Level	AVG	G	AB	R	H	2B	3B	HR	RBI	BB	SO	SB	OBP	SLG
2023	27	Pensacola (SL)	AA	.291	49	182	34	53	6	2	7	25	27	37	14	.395	.462
2023	27	Jacksonville (IL)	AAA	.339	51	192	43	65	8	1	8	37	23	43	6	.417	.516
2023	27	Miami (NL)	MLB	.269	22	67	9	18	3	0	1	9	2	19	1	.286	.358
Minor League Totals				.291	269	983	168	286	45	6	44	165	94	262	46	.364	.483
Major League Totals				.269	22	67	9	18	3	0	1	9	2	19	1	.286	.358

15 WILL BANFIELD, C

HIT: 30. **POW:** 50. **RUN:** 35. **FLD:** 60. **ARM:** 70. **BA Grade:** 45. **Risk:** High.

Born: November 18, 1999. **B-T:** R-R. **HT:** 6-0. **WT:** 215. **Drafted:** HS—Snellville, GA, 2018 (2nd round).
Signed by: Christian Castorri

TRACK RECORD: Entering the 2023 season, Banfield had established a less-than-stellar track record at the plate. However, he had what was by far the most productive season offensively and produced a career-best .258 average. He also laced a career-high 25 doubles, 23 home runs, and 76 RBIs. Banfield's production at the plate brought optimism for the future, especially given his defensive prowess.
SCOUTING REPORT: Banfield has an interesting setup in the box with a fairly open front side and low handset. He stands nearly upright with a normal load and stride and shows plenty of bat speed. Banfield has above-average raw power that he tapped into more frequently in 2023, although his pure hit tool lacks polish. He has below-average bat-to-ball skills with an overall contact rate of just 71% and has an aggressive approach and a 38% chase rate. The root of his struggles are below-average pitch recognition and lackluster swing decisions and led to a 26.6% strikeout rate. Banfield has long been known for his defense. He moves well behind the plate, receives well, and has a railgun of a throwing arm. Banfield consistently has quick transfers and his throws have excellent carry through the bag.
THE FUTURE: Banfield appears to be on track to make his Major League debut at some point in 2024, though he will likely begin the year at Triple-A Jacksonville. Banfield's defense is already big league caliber, but a questionable hit tool could limit his overall upside.

Year	Age	Club (League)	Level	AVG	G	AB	R	H	2B	3B	HR	RBI	BB	SO	SB	OBP	SLG
2023	23	Pensacola (SL)	AA	.258	115	458	70	118	25	2	23	76	25	122	3	.302	.472
Minor League Totals				.221	424	1636	199	362	78	8	52	242	102	474	5	.273	.374

16 JAVIER SANOJA, OF/2B

HIT: 50. **POW:** 30. **RUN:** 60. **FLD:** 55. **ARM:** 50. **BA Grade:** 45. **Risk:** High.

Born: September 3, 2022. **B-T:** R-R. **HT:** 5-7. **WT:** 150. **Signed:** Venezuela, 2019. **Signed by:** Fernando Seguignol.

TRACK RECORD: Sanoja signed for $500,000 as an international free agent in 2019, but was unable to make his professional debut until 2021 due to the pandemic. He has seen year-over-year improvement in each of his three professional seasons with 2023 being his most productive. Between Low-A Jupiter and High-A Beloit, Sanoja slashed .298/.348/.388 with 20 doubles, eight triples, four home runs, 67 RBIs and 37 stolen bases. Most of his production came in Jupiter, but Sanoja held his own in the notoriously pitcher-friendly Midwest League.
SCOUTING REPORT: Sanoja has an unorthodox setup in the box with his front side way open and a somewhat low handset, with his hands far away from his chest. As odd as his pre-swing look might be, it is an aesthetically pleasing and rhythmic operation. Sanoja consistently gets into a good hitter's position and has some quickness in his hands. Given his astronomically high contact rates, there is no reason to make a ton of tweaks. Between Low-A and High-A, Sanoja had a 90% overall contact rate and a 94% in-zone contact rate. He has minimal impact, but he sprays base hits to all fields. Sanoja is a Swiss Army Knife defensively and has earned meaningful reps in center field, at shortstop, and at second base. He has advanced baseball sense with silky smooth hands and an average arm. Sanoja is also a plus runner who regularly makes his presence felt on the basepaths. Sanoja profiles best as a second baseman.
THE FUTURE: Sanoja should start the 2024 season in Beloit, but is likely to earn a promotion to Double-A Pensacola. Sanoja will be a nice utility option in the majors given his defensive versatility, but he is unlikely to debut before 2026.

Year	Age	Club (League)	Level	AVG	G	AB	R	H	2B	3B	HR	RBI	BB	SO	SB	OBP	SLG
2023	20	Jupiter (FSL)	A	.308	102	400	51	123	18	8	1	57	31	32	31	.356	.400
2023	20	Beloit (MWL)	A+	.267	30	131	10	35	2	0	3	10	10	10	6	.324	.351
Minor League Totals				.273	288	1125	168	307	47	14	13	137	85	100	66	.326	.374

17 TROY JOHNSTON, 1B

HIT: 55. **POW:** 60. **RUN:** 30. **FLD:** 50. **ARM:** 45. **BA Grade:** 45. **Risk:** High.

Born: June 22, 1997. **B-T:** L-L. **HT:** 5-11. **WT:** 205. **Drafted:** Gonzaga, 2019 (17th round). **Signed by:** Scott Fairbanks

TRACK RECORD: Johnston had a productive three-year career at Gonzaga where he hit .312/.387/.515 with 46 extra-base hits and 69 RBIs in 109 games. He was taken in the 17th round of the 2019 draft and signed for $125,000. Though Johnston is older than the prototypical prospect, he has carved out a nice professional career. He had a productive 2021 campaign in which he hit .300 with 27 doubles, 15 home runs and 85 RBIs between Low-A Jupiter and High-A Beloit. In 2023, Johnston had a breakout year and slashed .307/.399/.549 between Double-A Pensacola and Triple-A Jacksonville. He set a new career high with 36 doubles, 26 home runs and 116 RBIs and was perhaps the best hitter in the Marlins system.

SCOUTING REPORT: Johnston stands straight up in the box with a slightly open front side, his right heel in the air, and wiggles his bat horizontally over his back shoulder. He has plenty of natural strength and physicality in his 5-foot-11, 205-pound frame. Johnston has above-average bat speed and a beautiful lefthanded stroke in which he extends extremely well through the baseball and does a nice job generating torque. He does big-time damage to all fields and consistently gets the ball in the air. Johnston does chase at times, although his 2023 strikeout-to-walk ratio was respectable. Johnston has an above-average pure hit tool with plus raw power. He is limited to first base defensively, but his productivity at the plate will offset any defensive concerns.

THE FUTURE: Johnston is expected to compete in spring training to be the Marlins 2024 opening day first baseman. If he doesn't break camp, he will start the season in Triple-A Jacksonville with a big league callup on the horizon.

Year	Age	Club (League)	Level	AVG	G	AB	R	H	2B	3B	HR	RBI	BB	SO	SB	OBP	SLG
2023	26	Pensacola (SL)	AA	.296	83	314	71	93	23	4	18	83	42	64	16	.396	.567
2023	26	Jacksonville (IL)	AAA	.323	51	198	31	64	13	1	8	33	20	44	8	.403	.520
Minor League Totals				.288	427	1591	253	459	103	8	58	293	209	357	35	.381	.473

18 BROCK VRADENBURG, 1B

HIT: 50. **POW:** 45. **RUN:** 45. **FLD:** 45. **ARM:** 40. **BA Grade:** 45. **Risk:** High.

Born: March 20, 2002. **B-T:** L-R. **HT:** 6-7. **WT:** 230. **Drafted:** Michigan State, 2023 (3rd round). **Signed by:** JT Zink.

TRACK RECORD: Vradenburg was one of the best pure hitters in college in 2023 and produced a gaudy .400/.492/.721 slash line with 22 doubles, 13 home runs and 69 RBIs across 55 games played. He was a third team All-American and first team All-Big 10 selection for his performance. Vradenburg was selected 78th overall and signed for the full slot value of $916,000. He had a quiet introduction to professional baseball and hit .236/.368/.291 with just four extra-base hits in 34 games with Low-A Jupiter.

SCOUTING REPORT: Vradenburg stands at a towering 6-foot-7, 230 pounds with physicality throughout his massive frame. He stands almost completely upright in the box and holds the bat practically straight up and down with his hands a bit far from his chest. Vradenburg has average bat speed as well as average raw power that he has yet to flash in-game as a pro. He has a sound approach with an overall chase rate of 16.7%, but his bat-to-ball skills are slightly below average given his 71% overall contact rate. Vradenburg isn't a great athlete, but holds his own over at first base which is where he will stick.

THE FUTURE: Given his overall profile, Vradenburg will need to mash in order to produce at a respectable clip. He has less than a full pro season under his belt and will have plenty of time to get adjusted, but his initial showing was underwhelming. Vradenburg figures to start the 2024 season in Low-A before a promotion to High-A Beloit.

Year	Age	Club (League)	Level	AVG	G	AB	R	H	2B	3B	HR	RBI	BB	SO	SB	OBP	SLG
2023	21	Jupiter (FSL)	A	.236	34	110	15	26	3	0	1	10	22	37	3	.368	.291
Minor League Totals				.236	34	110	15	26	3	0	1	10	22	37	3	.368	.291

19 KEMP ALDERMAN, OF

HIT: 40. **POW:** 65. **RUN:** 40. **FLD:** 45. **ARM:** 55. **BA Grade:** 40. **Risk:** High.

Born: August 20, 2002. **B-T:** R-R. **HT:** 6-3. **WT:** 250. **Drafted:** Mississippi, 2023 (2nd round). **Signed by:** Davis Knapp

TRACK RECORD: Alderman was one of the premier collegiate hitters in 2023, when he slashed .376/.440/.709 with 14 doubles, 19 home runs and 61 RBIs. He was a second team All-SEC selection and was subsequently selected 47th overall. Alderman signed for $1.4 million, which was roughly $425,000 less than slot value. Alderman experienced growing pains in his first professional season and hit just .205/.286/.316 with 10 extra-base hits and 15 RBIs in 34 games with Low-A Jupiter. Perhaps most concerning was Alderman's 33.3% strikeout rate.

SCOUTING REPORT: At 6-foot-3, 250 pounds, Alderman is as physical as they come. He stands in the box with a slightly open front side and low handset. Alderman has a normal stride, but his swing is lengthy. When Alderman makes contact he generates extremely high-quality impact—the struggle has just been making contact. In his first pro season, Alderman made contact at just a 63% clip, including a well below-average in-zone contact rate of 69%. Similar to his time at Mississippi, Alderman displayed below-average pitch-recognition skills and poor swing decisions. He does have borderline double-plus raw power, but there's a risk he doesn't get to it consistently in games. Alderman moves surprisingly well in the outfield and has an above-average arm, though there is some first base risk.

THE FUTURE: Alderman will begin 2024 with Low-A Jupiter and should get a taste of High-A Beloit before the end of the season. His offensive potential is exciting, though his approach will need to improve. In the majors Alderman might fit best at first base.

Year	Age	Club (League)	Level	AVG	G	AB	R	H	2B	3B	HR	RBI	BB	SO	SB	OBP	SLG
2023	20	Jupiter (FSL)	A	.205	34	117	13	24	8	1	1	15	7	39	4	.286	.316
Minor League Totals				.205	34	117	13	24	8	1	1	15	7	39	4	.286	.316

20 JOSE GERARDO, OF

HIT: 35. **POW:** 50. **RUN:** 55. **FLD:** 55. **ARM:** 70. **BA Grade:** 45. **Risk:** Extreme.

Born: June 12, 2005. **B-T:** R-R. **HT:** 6-0. **WT:** 179. **Signed:** Dominican Republic, 2022. **Signed by:** Sahir Fersobe.

TRACK RECORD: Gerardo was part of Miami's 2022 international free agent class and signed for $180,000. In 2022, he showed flashes of his immense upside in the Dominican Summer League and hit .284/.417/.551 with 12 doubles, 11 home runs, 31 RBIs and 18 stolen bases. However, Gerardo struggled in the Florida Complex League in his stateside debut, producing a .192/.345/.319 slash line and a sky-high strikeout rate of 42.5%.

SCOUTING REPORT: Gerardo has a lean, athletic build at 6-foot, 179 pounds. He has a relaxed setup in the box, standing tall with a slightly open front side. Gerardo has hardly any stride, though his swing can get long at times, but he has plus bat speed and has already generated high-quality impact at a young age. His max exit velocity last year was 108 mph, and his overall offensive upside is exciting given his remaining physical projection. Gerardo struggled to make contact in 2023 with an incredibly low overall contact rate of just 54% and an in-zone contact rate of 66%. His pitch-recognition skills will need to drastically improve in order to unlock his full offensive potential. Gerardo has a double-plus arm in the outfield, where he is a solid defender. He split time between center and right field last year, but would be a slam dunk fit in right field given his arm strength.

THE FUTURE: Gerardo is on track to begin 2024 in the Florida Complex League and will likely spend a fair amount of time there given his 2023 struggles. He figures to make his Low-A debut at some point next year, but his potential big league debut will not be until at least 2027. Gerardo has as much upside as any prospect in the system, but will need to refine his plate skills.

Year	Age	Club (League)	Level	AVG	G	AB	R	H	2B	3B	HR	RBI	BB	SO	SB	OBP	SLG
2023	18	FCL Marlins	Rk	.192	49	182	40	35	6	1	5	29	37	96	17	.345	.319
Minor League Totals				.237	99	358	84	85	18	2	16	60	70	162	35	.381	.433

21 ANTHONY MALDONADO, RHP

FB: 45. **CUT:** 60. **SL:** 60. **CTL:** 55. **BA Grade:** 40. **Risk:** High.

Born: February 6, 1998. **B-T:** R-R. **HT:** 6-4. **WT:** 220. **Drafted:** Bethune-Cookman, 2019 (11th round). **Signed by:** Hank LaRue

TRACK RECORD: An 11th round draft choice out of Bethune-Cookman, Maldonado has established himself as one of the best relief pitchers in the Marlins organization. After spending time at both Double-A Pensacola and Triple-A Jacksonville in 2022, Maldonado had an outstanding full season in Triple-A in 2023. He worked to a 1.76 ERA with 71 strikeouts to 21 walks across 46 innings and looked the part of an effective big league reliever.

SCOUTING REPORT: Maldonado is high-waisted at 6-foot-4 and features a lethal three-pitch mix that includes a mid-80s cutter, low-80s slider and low-90s two-seam fastball. He throws each offering the same amount, but his cutter-slider combination is especially deadly. Maldonado hides the ball well and attacks from a mid three-quarters slot. He has some arm speed and throws each offering with conviction. His cutter generated an absurd 63% miss rate and held opposing hitters to a minuscule .048 average. Maldonado manipulates its shape well and it consistently flashes late, two-plane break. His slider was just as effective with a 50% miss rate and .102 opponent's batting average. It takes on a similar look to his cutter, but has a bit more horizontal break. Maldonado's two-seam fastball isn't necessarily a bat-misser, but it generates plenty of soft contact with its sinking action.

THE FUTURE: Maldonado will have an opportunity to make the big league roster out of camp and could fit in a late-inning role. With two plus pitches, he has the stuff to be an above-average major league reliever.

Year	Age	Club (League)	Level	W	L	ERA	G	GS	IP	H	HR	BB	SO	BB%	SO%	WHIP	AVG
2023	25	Jupiter (FSL)	A	0	0	0.00	3	0	4	1	0	0	7	0.0	53.8	0.25	.077
2023	25	Jacksonville (IL)	AAA	7	3	1.76	34	0	46	23	5	21	71	11.7	39.4	0.96	.148
Minor League Totals				14	13	2.71	110	2	153	107	16	49	213	8.0	34.7	1.02	.192

22 JOE MACK, C
HIT: 30. **POW:** 40. **RUN:** 35. **FLD:** 55. **ARM:** 60. **BA Grade:** 40. **Risk:** High.

Born: December 27, 2002. **B-T:** L-R. **HT:** 6-1. **WT:** 210. **Drafted:** HS—East Amherst, NY, 2021 (1st round supplemental).
Signed by: Alex Smith
TRACK RECORD: Mack was drafted 31st overall in 2021 after a senior season when he hit .500 with eight home runs. He signed for an over-slot deal worth $2.5 million but has failed to live up to expectations thus far. Through three professional seasons, Mack has had minimal production at the plate. He showed some signs of life in 2023 at High-A Beloit, where he finished with a .218/.295/.287 slash line with 13 doubles, six home runs, and 36 RBIs but a 26.2% strikeout rate hindered his production.
SCOUTING REPORT: A defense-first catcher, Mack finally showed at least some prowess with the bat in 2023. He has an ultra-high handset in the box and uses a toe tap as a timing mechanism. Mack has some impact to the pull side, but that's about it when it comes to the overall offensive profile. He has both below-average bat-to-ball skills and a below-average approach, and struggles mightily to pick up spin. In 2023, Mack had miss rates of 52%, 45%, and 44% against sliders, changeups, and curveballs respectively. One positive is he does fare relatively well against heaters, as evidenced by his 88% in-zone contact rate and 13 extra-base hits against the offering. The best part of Mack's game is his defense. He receives well and has a plus arm, and in 2023 he threw out an impressive 26% of potential basestealers.
THE FUTURE: While Mack could conceivably begin the 2024 campaign with Double-A Pensacola, it makes sense for him to start back in Beloit for his bat to continue to make strides. He has the defensive chops to profile as a backup if he can improve his offensive approach or contact skills.

Year	Age	Club (League)	Level	AVG	G	AB	R	H	2B	3B	HR	RBI	BB	SO	SB	OBP	SLG
2023	20	Beloit (MWL)	A+	.218	120	449	46	98	13	0	6	36	42	118	0	.295	.287
Minor League Totals				.217	183	650	75	141	18	1	12	53	95	187	0	.324	.303

23 PATRICK MONTEVERDE, LHP
FB: 50. **SL:** 50. **CB:** 45. **CHG:** 55. **CTL:** 60. **BA Grade:** 40. **Risk:** High.

Born: September 24, 1997. **B-T:** R-L. **HT:** 6-2. **WT:** 200. **Drafted:** Texas Tech, 2021 (8th round).
Signed by: Ryan Wardinsky
TRACK RECORD: After putting together a quality four-year collegiate career between Division II Seton Hill and Texas Tech, Monteverde was selected in the eighth round of the 2021 draft. Monteverde was excellent during his 2023 stint with Double-A Pensacola and pitched his way to a 10-5 record with a 3.32 ERA and 114 strikeouts in 114 innings pitched. Monteverde eventually was promoted to Triple-A Jacksonville, but he got hit around in his two starts. For his performance in Pensacola, Monteverde represented the National League in the 2023 Futures Game.
SCOUTING REPORT: Monteverde has a true four-pitch mix and features a high-80s fastball, high-70s curveball, mid-80s slider and low-80s changeup. He has a lean frame and attacks hitters from a high three-quarters slot with above-average arm speed. Monteverde relies on his heater and in 2023 he threw it 52% of the time. While it lacks premium velocity, it plays up due to its ample riding life through the zone. It generated a 25% miss rate and is at its best when located in the top half of the strike zone. His slider has short, late horizontal break and is especially effective given his advanced feel for the pitch. Monteverde's curveball takes on a bigger shape with plenty of depth and has also proven to be a viable secondary pitch. His changeup might be the most effective of his secondary offerings. Like his slider, it also had a 42% miss rate and flashes tumbling and fading life to his arm side.
THE FUTURE: Monteverde will most likely begin 2024 with Triple-A Jacksonville where he will look to potentially earn a big league callup. He profiles as a swingman or back end starter.

Year	Age	Club (League)	Level	W	L	ERA	G	GS	IP	H	HR	BB	SO	BB%	SO%	WHIP	AVG
2023	25	Pensacola (SL)	AA	10	5	3.32	21	21	114	91	13	46	114	9.9	24.5	1.20	.220
2023	25	Jacksonville (IL)	AAA	1	1	15.58	2	2	9	15	4	6	7	12.5	14.6	2.42	.375
Minor League Totals				15	10	3.68	51	45	247	219	31	88	259	8.6	25.2	1.24	.237

24 JUAN DE LA CRUZ, RHP

FB: 55. **CB:** 60. **CHG:** 45. **CTL:** 40. **BA Grade:** 45. **Risk:** Extreme.

Born: March 4, 2005. **B-T:** R-R. **HT:** 6-3. **WT:** 180. **Signed:** Dominican Republic, 2022. **Signed by:** Angel Izquierdo

TRACK RECORD: De La Cruz signed at 16 years old in 2022 for $150,000 as an international free agent. He progressed quickly and made his affiliated debut in 2023. After appearing twice in the Florida Complex League, De La Cruz was promoted to Low-A Jupiter, where he showed flashes of an exciting arsenal. In 12 starts that spanned 43.1 innings, De La Cruz posted a 4.57 ERA with 42 strikeouts and 32 walks.

SCOUTING REPORT: De La Cruz has a projectable, high-waisted frame and is a high-upside ball of clay for player development to mold. He has a low-effort delivery with a short arm action and plenty of arm speed. De La Cruz's fastball sits in the 92-94 range with carry through the zone. At just 18 years old, it is easy to envision De La Cruz eventually pitching in the mid-to-upper 90s with the offering. His breaking ball blends shape at times, but it is a plus offering with plenty of horizontal break and in 2023 generated a miss rate north of 40%. De La Cruz also features a high-80s changeup, but he threw it sparingly in 2023 and will need to continue to refine it to help complete his repertoire. In addition to the development of a third pitch, De La Cruz's command will also need to improve.

THE FUTURE: De La Cruz will begin the 2024 season in Low-A Jupiter, but should earn a promotion to High-A Beloit before long. He has an electric two-pitch mix and No. 3 starter upside, but he will need to prove he can stick in the rotation. There is plenty of reliever risk with De La Cruz and his future could be in the bullpen.

Year	Age	Club (League)	Level	W	L	ERA	G	GS	IP	H	HR	BB	SO	BB%	SO%	WHIP	AVG
2023	18	FCL Marlins	Rk	1	1	2.00	2	1	9	4	0	6	8	16.2	21.6	1.11	.129
2023	18	Jupiter (FSL)	A	1	4	4.57	12	12	43	48	3	32	42	15.0	19.7	1.85	.282
Minor League Totals				5	7	4.16	25	23	93	90	6	56	78	13.1	18.2	1.57	.254

25 IKE BUXTON, RHP

FB: 50. **SL:** 55. **CHG:** 60. **CTL:** 45. **BA Grade:** 40. **Risk:** High.

Born: July 18, 2000. **B-T:** R-R. **HT:** 6-3. **WT:** 208. **Drafted:** Lipscomb, 2022 (15th round). **Signed by:** Hank LaRue.

TRACK RECORD: After being selected in the 15th round of the 2022 draft, Buxton had an impressive first full professional season in 2023 in which he spent time with Low-A Jupiter and High-A Beloit before finishing the season with Double-A Pensacola. Across three levels, he compiled a 2.45 ERA with 73 strikeouts to 43 walks in 77 innings.

SCOUTING REPORT: Buxton has a durable build with plenty of physicality in his lower half. He has an abbreviated arm action and attacks hitters from a low three-quarters slot and low release height. Buxton has a true four-pitch mix and features a four-seam fastball, two-seam fastball, slider, and changeup. He relies heavily on his fastball, a pitch he threw 57% of the time in 2023. Both his four and two-seam heaters sit in the 92-95 MPH range and feature life through the zone. His two-seamer has plenty of armside run and bears in on the hands of righthanded hitters, while his four-seam fastball has more carry and is most effective when located at the top of the zone. Buxton's low-80s slider has tons of tight, late sweeping action. Its miss rate in 2023 was an impressive 45% and held opposing hitters to a .219 average. He also throws a potentially plus mid-80s changeup that flashes both late tumbling life and fade to his armside. It plays well against lefthanded hitters and in 2023 opposing hitters hit just .087 against it.

THE FUTURE: While it does make the most sense for Buxton to begin the 2024 season with High-A Beloit, he will likely only make a handful of starts before being promoted back to Double-A Pensacola. With how quickly he has been ascending through the system, Buxton could be on track to make his Triple-A debut before the season ends.

Year	Age	Club (League)	Level	W	L	ERA	G	GS	IP	H	HR	BB	SO	BB%	SO%	WHIP	AVG
2023	22	Jupiter (FSL)	A	4	0	1.62	12	5	39	20	1	25	46	15.6	28.8	1.15	.152
2023	22	Beloit (MWL)	A+	2	2	3.71	7	7	34	31	3	15	23	10.1	15.5	1.35	.235
2023	22	Pensacola (SL)	AA	0	0	0.00	1	1	4	1	0	3	4	17.6	23.5	1.00	.077
Minor League Totals				6	2	2.87	23	13	82	55	4	51	78	14.6	22.3	1.30	.188

26 MARK COLEY, OF

HIT: 35. **POW:** 60. **RUN:** 60. **FLD:** 50. **ARM:** 60. **BA Grade:** 40. **Risk:** High.

Born: November 22, 2000. **B-T:** R-R. **HT:** 6-2. **WT:** 194. **Drafted:** Rhode Island, 2023 (17th round).
Signed by: Alex Smith

TRACK RECORD: Coley was a four-year player for Rhode Island who enjoyed a strong 2023 season that propelled him into a late day three draft selection. He had a strong pro debut and in Low-A Jupiter he hit .265/.395/.480 with eight doubles, three home runs and 17 RBIs in 33 games.

SCOUTING REPORT: Coley has plenty of present strength in his lean and athletic frame. He has a quiet yet explosive operation in the box with a minimal load and stride. Coley's barrel explodes through the hitting zone and he has thunderous bat speed that enables him to generate big-time impact from the right side. He has plus power that he has gotten to in games, although his pure hit tool lacks refinement. Coley has below-average pitch-recognition skills and has the tendency to expand the strike zone given his overall contact rate of 57% and a 29% chase rate. Coley is a plus runner whose speed and athleticism translate well to center field, where he has a chance to stick long term, though his plus arm strength could also fit in right field.

THE FUTURE: Coley will likely begin 2024 back with Low-A Jupiter, although a promotion to High-A Beloit seems imminent. While he is already 23 years old, Coley's potential big league debut could come as soon as 2026. He has an exciting toolset and could be a solid fourth outfielder.

Year	Age	Club (League)	Level	AVG	G	AB	R	H	2B	3B	HR	RBI	BB	SO	SB	OBP	SLG
2023	22	Jupiter (FSL)	A	.265	33	98	20	26	8	2	3	17	16	36	9	.395	.480
Minor League Totals				.265	33	98	20	26	8	2	3	17	16	36	9	.395	.480

27 NIGEL BELGRAVE, RHP
FB: 40. **SL:** 60. **CTL:** 45. **BA Grade:** 45. **Risk:** Extreme.

Born: May 12, 2002. **B-T:** R-R. **HT:** 6-4. **WT:** 195. **Drafted:** Maryland, 2023 (15th round). **Signed by:** Alex Smith.

TRACK RECORD: While no back of the baseball card stats jump out when looking at Belgrave, he was a decent reliever during his time at Maryland and struck out nearly 12 hitters per nine innings pitched. He went on to be selected in the 15th round of the 2023 draft and enjoyed a strong start to his professional career. While he threw just 8.1 innings, Belgrave at Low-A Jupiter posted a 2.16 ERA with 14 strikeouts.

SCOUTING REPORT: Belgrave has a lean build at 6-foot-4, 195 pounds and features an effective fastball-slider combination. He has a short arm stroke and attacks from a low three-quarters slot. Belgrave's fastball sits in the 94-97 range and features some running and sinking life at times, although it has a bit of a dead zone profile. Improving the shape of the pitch will be a key going forward. Belgrave's mid-80s slider is a legit sweeper and is by far his best pitch. He has above-average feel for the pitch and during the 2023 college season, it generated an impressive miss rate of 54%. Belgrave has below-average command, but it plays in his favor at times given his effectively wild track record.

THE FUTURE: Belgrave is a reliever through and through, but he profiles as a quality one who could potentially ascend quickly through the system. Adding more life to his fastball and improving his strike-throwing ability would go a long way for Belgrave. He figures to begin 2024 at Low-A Jupiter, but has a chance to pitch his way to Double-A Pensacola by season's end.

Year	Age	Club (League)	Level	W	L	ERA	G	GS	IP	H	HR	BB	SO	BB%	SO%	WHIP	AVG
2023	21	FCL Marlins	Rk	0	1	6.00	2	0	3	1	0	3	3	23.1	23.1	1.33	.100
2023	21	Jupiter (FSL)	A	2	0	2.16	4	0	8	5	0	7	14	18.9	37.8	1.44	.167
Minor League Totals				2	1	3.27	6	0	11	6	0	10	17	20.0	34.0	1.45	.150

28 XAVIER MEACHEM, RHP
FB: 50. **SL:** 55. **CTL:** 45. **BA Grade:** 45. **Risk:** Extreme.

Born: September 6, 2002. **B-T:** R-R. **HT:** 5-11. **WT:** 200. **Drafted:** North Carolina A&T, 2023 (10th round). **Signed by:** Blake Newsome.

TRACK RECORD: Meachem had an up-and-down three-year career at North Carolina A&T, where he split time between the starting rotation and the bullpen. Seven of his 16 appearances last year were starts, but he was at his best when pitching in relief. Before the draft, Meachem had a strong stint with Team USA's Collegiate National Team. He was selected in the 10th round and signed for $169,500. Meachem had a quality introduction to professional baseball, and at Low-A Jupiter he posted a 1.64 ERA with 16 strikeouts in 11 innings.

SCOUTING REPORT: Meachem has a compact frame at 5-foot-11, 200 pounds, with some thickness in his lower half. He pitches from a three-quarters arm slot and features a mid-90s fastball and low-80s slider. Meachem will pitch in the 92-95 range with his fastball, but it tops out at 97. It has run and ride through the zone and is at its best when elevated. Meachem's high-spin slider flashes sharp two-plane break with some depth. He spins it well and it has a chance to eventually be a true out pitch.

THE FUTURE: Meachem is likely to begin 2024 back with Low-A Jupiter, but should earn a promotion to High-A Beloit quickly. While he projects to pitch out of the bullpen, Meachem has the makings of a fast-moving reliever who could close out the 2024 season in Double-A.

Year	Age	Club (League)	Level	W	L	ERA	G	GS	IP	H	HR	BB	SO	BB%	SO%	WHIP	AVG
2023	20	FCL Marlins	Rk	0	0	3.86	4	0	9	5	2	6	12	15.8	31.6	1.18	.156
2023	20	Jupiter (FSL)	A	1	0	1.64	6	0	11	8	1	6	16	13.3	35.6	1.27	.205
Minor League Totals				1	0	2.70	10	0	20	13	3	12	28	14.5	33.7	1.25	.183

29 EMMETT OLSON, LHP

FB: 45. **SL:** 40. **CB:** 55. **CHG:** 45. **CTL:** 55. **BA Grade:** 40. **Risk:** High.

Born: May 15, 2002. **B-T:** L-L. **HT:** 6-4. **WT:** 230. **Drafted:** Nebraska, 2023 (4th round). **Signed by:** Eric Wordekemper.

TRACK RECORD: Olson had a standout collegiate career at Nebraska, where he compiled a 3.83 ERA with 161 strikeouts in 160 innings across three seasons. 2023 was the first time Olson spent a full season as a starter, and he pitched his way to a 4.50 ERA with 80 strikeouts in 82 innings. Olson was selected in the fourth round of the 2023 draft and signed an under-slot deal worth $460,000. He made just one professional appearance after signing and threw 1.2 innings in the Florida Complex League.

SCOUTING REPORT: Olson has a thick, durable frame and is an imposing presence on the mound. He works almost exclusively on the third base side of the rubber and has a slightly up-tempo delivery and a high leg lift. Olson has a short arm action and throws from a high three-quarters slot. His fastball sits in the 91-93 range, but has been up to 95 with riding life through the zone. His mid-80s slider has some sweeping life, but opposing hitters posted a .340 average against it. Lefthanded hitters hit .429 against Olson's slider while righthanded hitters hit just .240. His mid-70s curveball is by far his best pitch and has huge depth with a bit of sharp, 12-to-6 bite. It worked an impressive 56% miss rate and held opposing hitters to a minuscule .077 average. Finally, Olson has inconsistent feel for a mid-80s changeup. It's not much of a speed difference from his fastball, but will flash some tumble.

THE FUTURE: Olson is on track to start 2024 at Low-A Jupiter and could earn a promotion to High-A Beloit at some point. He is consistently around the strike zone, but his command will need to further improve in order for him to reach his ceiling of a potential fifth starter.

Year	Age	Club (League)	Level	W	L	ERA	G	GS	IP	H	HR	BB	SO	BB%	SO%	WHIP	AVG
2023	21	FCL Marlins	Rk	0	0	5.40	1	0	2	1	0	1	2	14.3	28.6	1.20	.167
Minor League Totals				0	0	9.00	1	0	2	1	0	1	2	14.3	28.6	2.00	.167

30 TORIN MONTGOMERY, 1B

HIT: 50. **POW:** 45. **RUN:** 30. **FLD:** 55. **ARM:** 45. **BA Grade:** 40. **Risk:** High.

Born: May 2, 2001. **B-T:** R-R. **HT:** 6-3. **WT:** 230. **Drafted:** Missouri, 2022 (14th round). **Signed by:** Ryan Cisterna

TRACK RECORD: Following the disbanding of the Boise State baseball program, Montgomery transferred to Missouri, where he had a productive two-year stint. In 2022, he hit .365/.462/.547 with 12 doubles, seven home runs, and 49 RBIs in as many games. Montgomery was selected in the first half of day three in the 2022 draft, and had a breakout 2023 season with Low-A Jupiter. During his time with the Hammerheads, Montgomery posted a .341/.481/.487 slash line with 14 doubles, three home runs, and 32 RBIs. He earned a promotion to High-A Beloit, but he struggled in the pitcher-friendly Midwest League and produced a .214 average with seven extra-base hits across 35 games.

SCOUTING REPORT: At 6-foot-3 and 230-pounds, Montgomery has an ultra-physical build. He packs loads of natural strength, though he is currently a hit-over-power guy. Montgomery has a simple setup in the box with his knees slightly bent and his bat rested on his back shoulder. He has a short, quick swing and takes a direct path to contact with above average bat speed. Montgomery's swing is geared towards spraying line drives all over the field, but he can also generate big-time impact as evident by his 2023 max exit velocity of 119.6 mph. He has a sound approach and above-average bat-to-ball skills. Going forward, Montgomery will need to tweak his swing to create more leverage and loft which will allow him to get the ball in the air on a more consistent basis. Doing so will enable him to tap into his power in-game and also maximize his offensive upside. Montgomery is a sure-handed defender at first base and there is no reason for him to move off the position.

THE FUTURE: Montgomery figures to begin the 2024 season with High-A Beloit. With an increase in production, he could earn a promotion to Double-A Pensacola. An advanced hitter, Montgomery has the chance to progress reasonably quickly through the system and could make his major league debut as early as 2026.

Year	Age	Club (League)	Level	AVG	G	AB	R	H	2B	3B	HR	RBI	BB	SO	SB	OBP	SLG
2023	22	Jupiter (FSL)	A	.341	63	185	36	63	14	2	3	32	42	47	4	.481	.486
2023	22	Beloit (MWL)	A+	.214	35	131	11	28	6	0	1	12	16	35	1	.304	.282
Minor League Totals				.282	133	440	68	124	28	2	8	63	69	118	5	.395	.409

Milwaukee Brewers

BY BEN BADLER

Twenty years ago, the Brewers had the best farm system in baseball.

Ranked No. 1 heading into the 2004 season, the Brewers had Rickie Weeks, Prince Fielder, J.J. Hardy, Corey Hart and Chris Capuano as prospects, though they were never able to parlay that core of young talent into a perennial playoff contender.

Today, the Brewers farm system is the best it has been in 20 years. Even more impressive is that the Brewers have done it while simultaneously building a team that has reached the playoffs five of the last six seasons. Despite typically picking toward the back of the first round, the Brewers have created a strong, balanced system through the draft, international free agency and trades.

The crown jewel, of course, is center fielder Jackson Chourio, who went from signing out of Venezuela on Jan. 15, 2021, for $1.8 million when he was 16 to in December 2023 signing an eight-year, $82 million contract with club options for two more years. Chourio has yet to play a big league game, but he has the chance to be Milwaukee's version of Ronald Acuña Jr., a potential franchise cornerstone with an electric mix of power and speed.

Milwaukee's international scouting department has blanketed Venezuela as well as any organization, with catcher Jeferson Quero and outfielder Luis Lara both Top 10 Prospects in the system. Quero is one of the elite defensive catchers in the minor leagues and hit well as a 20-year-old in Double-A in 2023. Lara jumped straight from the Dominican Summer League in 2022 to Low-A Carolina in 2023 as an 18-year-old, finishing the year in High-A.

Even with the graduation of second baseman Brice Turang and outfielders Sal Frelick and Joey Wiemer in 2023, the Brewers have more homegrown draft prospects on the way. Righthander Jacob Misiorowski is in the conversation for the best stuff in the minor leagues, armed with an electric fastball that reaches triple digits and nightmare breaking stuff. His control remains a huge risk, but his upside is gigantic.

Tyler Black, who played primarily third base in 2023 but has moved around the diamond in pro ball as they try to find his best defensive fit, has been an on-base machine who reached Triple-A and should be in the big leagues early in 2024.

Lefthander Robert Gasser, whom the Brewers picked up in the 2022 trade for Josh Hader, pitched well in the second half with Triple-A Nashville and should join Chourio and Black as rookies in Milwaukee in 2024.

PATRICK MCDERMOTT/GETTY IMAGES

The Brewers graduated four key prospects, including 2021 first-round outfielder Sal Frelick.

PROJECTED 2027 LINEUP

Catcher	Jeferson Quero	24
First Base	Brock Wilken	25
Second Base	Brice Turang	27
Third Base	Tyler Black	26
Shortstop	Willy Adames	31
Left Field	Sal Frelick	27
Center Field	Jackson Chourio	23
Right Field	Garrett Mitchell	28
Designated Hitter	Christian Yelich	35
No. 1 Starter	Jacob Misiorowski	25
No. 2 Starter	Freddy Peralta	31
No. 3 Starter	Aaron Ashby	28
No. 4 Starter	Robert Gasser	28
No. 5 Starter	Carlos Rodriguez	25
Closer	Abner Uribe	27

Still, the team enters 2024 with significant questions. Former president of baseball operations David Stearns officially left after the 2023 season to lead the Mets. Manager Craig Counsell left to take the same job with the Cubs, with Pat Murphy promoted from bench coach to replace him. And the Brewers non-tendered righthander Brandon Woodruff, whose shoulder surgery was expected to keep him out for the 2024 season.

Now the challenge is for general manager Matt Arnold to take the Brewers from their most successful stretch in franchise history and leverage their collection of young talent into a new wave of postseason appearances for the remainder of the decade. ■

MILWAUKEE BREWERS

TOP 2024 CONTRIBUTORS	RANK
1. Jackson Chourio, OF	1
2. Tyler Black, 3B	4
3. Robert Gasser, LHP	5

BREAKOUT PROSPECTS	RANK
1. Yophery Rodriguez, OF	11
2. Luke Adams, 3B	13
3. Cooper Pratt, SS	14

SOURCE OF TOP 30 TALENT

Homegrown	27	Acquired	3
College	7	Trade	3
Junior college	4	Rule 5 draft	0
High school	6	Independent league	0
Nondrafted free agent	0	Free agent/waivers	0
International	10		

LF
Hedbert Perez
Carlos D. Rodriguez

CF
Jackson Chourio (1)
Garrett Mitchell (6)
Luis Lara (7)

RF
Yophery Rodriguez (11)
Luis Castillo

3B
Tyler Black (4)
Brock Wilken (8)
Eric Bitonti (12)
Luke Adams (13)
Mike Boeve (15)
Juan Baez (23)

SS
Cooper Pratt (14)
Daniel Guilarte (22)
Eric Brown Jr. (24)
Filippo Di Turi (29)
Gregory Barrios (30)
Freddy Zamora
Ethan Murray
Kevin Ereu
Eduardo Garcia

2B
Oliver Dunn (19)
Dylan O'Rae (20)
Jadher Areinamo (21)
Pedro Ibarguen (25)
Felix Valerio
Jheremy Vargas

1B
Wes Clarke (16)
Zavier Warren
Jesus Chirinos

C
Jeferson Quero (3)
Matt Wood (28)
Darrien Miller

LHP

LHSP	LHRP
Robert Gasser (5)	Ethan Small
	Russell Smith

RHP

RHSP	RHRP
Jacob Misiorowski (2)	Patricio Aquino
Carlos Rodriguez (9)	Quinton Low
Josh Knoth (10)	Craig Yoho
Bradley Blalock (17)	
Logan Henderson (18)	
Ryan Birchard (26)	
Bishop Letson (27)	
Janson Junk	
Will Rudy	
Jason Woodward	

1 JACKSON CHOURIO, OF

Born: March 11, 2004. **B-T:** R-R. **HT:** 5-11. **WT:** 165.
Signed: Venezuela, 2021. **Signed**
by: Fernando Veracierto/Luis Perez.

TRACK RECORD: Chourio excited scouts with his quick-twitch athleticism during the tryout process in Venezuela. A shortstop and center fielder at the time, Chourio had a wiry build and the potential for an enticing power/speed combination as a 16-year-old that prompted the Brewers to make him the centerpiece of their international class when the signing period opened on Jan. 15, 2021, giving him a $1.8 million bonus. Less than two years later, Chourio catapulted himself into the discussion as the best prospect in baseball. He jumped to Low-A Carolina in 2022 as an 18-year-old and continued to hit well in High-A Wisconsin before a late-season bump to Double-A Biloxi. After an uneven first half back in Biloxi to open 2023, his performance skyrocketed in the second half. After the season, Chourio signed an eight-year, $82 million contract with club options for two more seasons.

SCOUTING REPORT: Hitters in the Double-A Southern League were at a disadvantage in the first half, when MLB experimented with a pretacked ball that led to more extreme pitch movements and higher whiff rates. Through July 6, Chourio hit .239/.304/.410 with 11 home runs in 71 games with a 7% walk rate and 21% strikeout rate. After that—when the Southern League reverted to the traditional baseball—Chourio hit .323/.380/.544 in 51 games with 11 home runs, an 8% walk rate and a 14% strikeout rate before a mid-September promotion to Triple-A Nashville. How much of those splits were because of the baseball itself or a 19-year-old making adjustments and getting more comfortable during the season was a wide topic of discussion inside and outside the organization. What's clear is that Chourio is an electric talent with standout tools and skills at a premium position. His explosiveness is evident in his bat speed, which helps him drive the ball out to any part of the park. He has plus-plus raw power and is content letting the ball travel deep and hammering the ball to right-center field, with more than half of his home runs going to center or right field. Chourio is a good hitter who doesn't swing and miss much at pitches in the strike zone, though he will need to tighten up his plate discipline. He's not a free-swinger, and he did chase less as the season progressed, but continued improvement with his swing decisions will be critical for him to achieve his potential. A

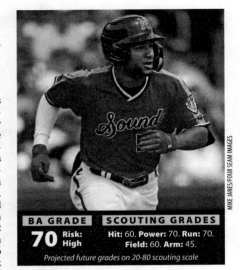

MIKE JANES/FOUR SEAM IMAGES

BA GRADE	SCOUTING GRADES
70 Risk: High	Hit: 60. Power: 70. Run: 70. Field: 60. Arm: 45.

Projected future grades on 20-80 scouting scale

BEST TOOLS

BATTING

Best Hitter for Average	Tyler Black
Best Power Hitter	Jackson Chourio
Best Strike-Zone Discipline	Tyler Black
Fastest Baserunner	Garrett Mitchell
Best Athlete	Garrett Mitchell

PITCHING

Best Fastball	Jacob Misiorowski
Best Curveball	Josh Knoth
Best Slider	Jacob Misiorowski
Best Changeup	Logan Henderson
Best Control	Logan Henderson

FIELDING

Best Defensive Catcher	Jeferson Quero
Best Defensive Infielder	Gregory Barrios
Best Infield Arm	Brock Wilken
Best Defensive Outfielder	Jackson Chourio
Best Outfield Arm	Garrett Mitchell

plus-plus runner, Chourio has the speed, acceleration and lateral range to be an above-average defender in center field. He's still learning to finish plays at the wall consistently, but his reads and routes have all improved since getting more full-time reps in center field. Chourio had an issue with his right elbow as an amateur and has a fringe-average arm that is his lightest tool.

THE FUTURE: Chourio has a chance to be a franchise cornerstone, a potential perennial all-star with 30-30 potential who could hit in the middle of the Brewers' lineup. Given Milwaukee's outfield situation, the organization can be patient with Chourio, but he's now squarely in position to make the team's Opening Day roster. ■

Year	Age	Club (League)	Level	AVG	G	AB	R	H	2B	3B	HR	RBI	BB	SO	SB	OBP	SLG
2023	19	Biloxi (SL)	AA	.280	122	510	84	143	23	3	22	89	41	103	43	.336	.467
2023	19	Nashville (IL)	AAA	.333	6	21	4	7	3	0	0	2	2	1	1	.375	.476
Minor League Totals				.286	272	1090	194	312	63	9	47	191	98	250	68	.347	.490

2 JACOB MISIOROWSKI, RHP

FB: 80. **CB:** 60. **SL:** 70. **CHG:** 40. **CTL:** 40. **BA Grade:** 60. **Risk:** High.

Born: April 3, 2002. **B-T:** R-R. **HT:** 6-7. **WT:** 190.
Drafted: Crowder (MO) JC, 2022 (2nd round). **Signed by:** Riley Bandelow.
TRACK RECORD: The Brewers drafted shortstop Eric Brown Jr. with their first-round pick in 2022, but their highest bonus ($2.35 million) of that draft class went to Misiorowski, their second-rounder. In Misiorowski's first full season in 2023, the Brewers tightly controlled his workload early—he threw more than four innings only once in the first two months—but he rose through three levels, finishing at Double-A Biloxi.
SCOUTING REPORT: Misiorowski's raw stuff stacks up among the best of any pitching prospect in the game. He's a gangly 6-foot-7 righthander with an explosive fastball, sitting at 95-99 mph and topping at 102. Misiorowski generates a ton of extension from a low release height out of his low three-quarters arm slot, allowing his already outstanding velocity to play up because of the unusual look. His slider flashes as a plus-plus pitch, producing a high whiff rate against both righties and lefties. He throws a power slider in the mid-to-upper 80s at 2,400-2,600 rpm. The pitch snaps off with late bite to dive underneath barrels. His curveball, which he shelved in college but reintroduced in pro ball, is a plus pitch that gets whiffs as well. Misiorowski's changeup is a firm, below-average offering in the low 90s that he rarely throws. While his control took a step forward in 2023, it still remains a concern. He walked 13% of batters, while his 18 hit batsmen tied for fourth in the minors. It's a challenge for Misiorowski to sync up his long limbs in his high-effort delivery, which might always make it difficult for him to corral his stuff in the zone.
THE FUTURE: Misiorowski has the stuff to be a frontline starter or a wipeout reliever. His mechanics and control lead some scouts to think his future is in the bullpen, but if he can throw enough strikes and handle a bigger workload, he could develop into one of the game's best starters.

Year	Age	Club (League)	Level	W	L	ERA	G	GS	IP	H	HR	BB	SO	BB%	SO%	WHIP	AVG
2023	21	Carolina (CAR)	A	1	1	3.04	9	9	27	10	0	12	46	11.9	45.5	0.83	.118
2023	21	Wisconsin (MWL)	A+	1	0	1.90	6	6	24	15	0	14	28	13.2	26.4	1.23	.176
2023	21	Biloxi (SL)	AA	2	1	5.57	5	5	21	17	2	16	36	15.0	33.6	1.57	.215
Minor League Totals				4	2	3.45	22	22	73	43	2	49	113	14.9	34.5	1.26	.169

3 JEFERSON QUERO, C

HIT: 50. **POW:** 50. **RUN:** 40. **FLD:** 70. **ARM:** 70. **BA Grade:** 55. **Risk:** High.

Born: October 8, 2002. **B-T:** R-R. **HT:** 5-11. **WT:** 215.
Signed: Venezuela, 2019. **Signed by:** Reinaldo Hidalgo.
TRACK RECORD: When the Brewers signed Quero out of Venezuela for $200,000 in 2019, they quickly realized he was one of the best international catching prospects in the class. As a 20-year-old in 2023, he was one of the youngest players in the Double-A Southern League. He threw out 35% of basestealers and allowed 1.05 attempts per game, both rates among the best by minor league catchers with at least 50 games caught.
SCOUTING REPORT: Quero is one of the best defensive catchers in the minors. Pitchers love throwing to Quero, who is an energetic leader with a high baseball IQ with polished catch-and-throw skills. He's a good receiver and an agile defender with a knack for blocking breaking balls in the dirt. With his plus arm and quick release, Quero controls the running game well with pop times often under 1.9 seconds on throws to second base. Quero shines with the glove, but his offensive game took a leap forward in 2023 as well to solidify his status as one of the game's best catching prospects. With a slightly simpler load, he has a simple lower half load with a small toe tap, quiet hands and is a good fastball hitter who doesn't swing and miss often at pitches in the strike zone. He is an aggressive hitter who will need to develop more selectivity, particularly against offspeed stuff, but he has good bat control and added more power to his game in 2023, with exit velocities up to 111 mph and a chance to be a 20-25 home run hitter.
THE FUTURE: Ticketed to open 2024 in Triple-A Nashville, Quero will likely spend most of the year there, though he could make his major league debut by the end of the season, when he will still be just 21 years old. If he can continue to refine his swing decisions, he has the upside to develop into a plus regular behind the plate.

Year	Age	Club (League)	Level	AVG	G	AB	R	H	2B	3B	HR	RBI	BB	SO	SB	OBP	SLG
2023	20	Biloxi (SL)	AA	.262	90	336	47	88	12	0	16	49	38	68	5	.339	.440
Minor League Totals				.278	208	771	116	214	39	3	28	114	80	154	19	.349	.445

4 TYLER BLACK, 3B

HIT: 60. **POW:** 45. **RUN:** 60. **FLD:** 40. **ARM:** 45. **BA Grade:** 50. **Risk:** Medium.

Born: July 26, 2000. **B-T:** L-R. **HT:** 5-10. **WT:** 204.
Drafted: Wright State, 2021 (1st round supplemental). **Signed by:** Pete Vukovich Jr.
TRACK RECORD: Black was an on-base machine at Wright State, where he hit .383/.496/.683 in 2021, when the Brewers drafted him 33rd overall. His first full season in 2022 ended after 64 games when he fractured his scapula while making a diving catch in center field. He returned in 2023, spending most of his time at third base and posting the highest OPS of any prospect in the organization with at least 200 plate appearances.
SCOUTING REPORT: Black has elite plate discipline and consistently works himself into favorable counts and piles up walks. His lefthanded swing starts with a high, hanging leg kick and he's typically on time, leading to a high contact rate. Black keeps his hands inside the ball well with a tight barrel turn, allowing him to cover the inner third of the plate while maintaining an all-fields approach. He's a good low-ball hitter, though he had trouble making contact with fastballs up in the zone. Black showed more power in 2023, though it's still fringe-average raw power that mostly comes to his pull side. Black is a good athlete, a plus runner and a smart, aggressive baserunner who gets good jumps, leading the organization with 55 stolen bases. Black has long been an offensive-oriented player trying to find a position. Primarily a second baseman in college, he played mostly second base and center field in 2022, then became a primary third baseman in 2023. While he made progress during the season, he's a below-average defender there with a fringe-average arm, limited range and footwork that needs improvement. He got time at first base as well.
THE FUTURE: Black's hitting polish should allow him to make his major league debut early in 2024, potentially as Milwaukee's starting third baseman. He's a potential league-average regular, with more upside if he can tap into more power or improve his defense.

Year	Age	Club (League)	Level	AVG	G	AB	R	H	2B	3B	HR	RBI	BB	SO	SB	OBP	SLG
2023	22	Biloxi (SL)	AA	.273	84	308	70	84	16	8	14	48	61	77	47	.411	.513
2023	22	Nashville (IL)	AAA	.310	39	142	35	44	9	4	4	25	27	23	8	.428	.514
Minor League Totals				.279	213	768	165	214	42	16	23	116	159	175	73	.415	.465

5 ROBERT GASSER, LHP

FB: 50. **SL:** 55. **CUT:** 50. **CHG:** 45. **CTL:** 50. **BA Grade:** 50. **Risk:** Medium.

Born: May 31, 1999. **B-T:** L-L. **HT:** 6-0. **WT:** 192.
Drafted: Houston, 2021 (2nd round). **Signed by:** Kevin Ham (Padres).
TRACK RECORD: Gasser's strong 2021 season at Houston, when he showed improved stuff and performance, bolstered his draft stock and led the Padres to take him that year in the second round. During Gasser's first full season in 2022, the Brewers acquired him in the trade deadline deal that sent reliever Josh Hader to San Diego. In the first two months of 2023, Gasser had trouble with strikes, posting a 4.59 ERA in 49 innings with an 11.7% walk rate and 60% strike rate, but he turned things around after that, posting a 3.34 ERA in 86.1 innings, slicing his walk rate nearly in half to 6.5%, with 67% strikes the rest of the season. He led all Triple-A pitchers with 166 strikeouts.
SCOUTING REPORT: With a fastball that sits at 89-93 mph and will occasionally tickle 95, Gasser doesn't overpower hitters. Instead he relies on his pitchability and willingness to liberally mix in all of his pitches to keep hitters guessing. He throws both a four-seamer and a two-seam fastball, with his two-seamer producing lively armside run with 16 inches of horizontal break from a low release height. He added an average cutter to his mix as well in the upper-80s that he uses more against righties. Gasser uses those fastballs and his cutter in about a 50-50 mix with his slider and changeup. His low-80s slider is his best pitch, with deep lateral movement at 16-18 inches of horizontal break to run away from lefties or to throw to the back foot of a righty. Gasser's changeup has a lot of fade away from lefties, but it's an upper-80s pitch that doesn't have much separation from his fastball.
THE FUTURE: After spending all of 2023 in Triple-A, Gasser is ready for a rotation spot in Milwaukee. He's likely a back-end starter, though some scouts see enough upside for more.

Year	Age	Club (League)	Level	W	L	ERA	G	GS	IP	H	HR	BB	SO	BB%	SO%	WHIP	AVG
2023	24	Nashville (IL)	AAA	9	1	3.79	26	25	135	123	12	50	166	8.4	28.0	1.28	.236
Minor League Totals				16	13	3.73	59	58	287	260	24	104	352	8.5	28.7	1.27	.239

6 GARRETT MITCHELL, OF

HIT: 40. **POW:** 50. **RUN:** 80. **FLD:** 60. **ARM:** 60. **BA Grade:** 50. **Risk:** High.

Born: September 4, 1998. **B-T:** L-R. **HT:** 6-3. **WT:** 225.
Drafted: UCLA, 2020 (1st round). **Signed by:** Daniel Cho/Corey Rodriguez.
TRACK RECORD: Mitchell hit .349/.418/.566 for UCLA in 2019, but the coronavirus pandemic ended his junior season early in 2020. While Mitchell had some of the best tools and athleticism in that draft, the Brewers were able to get him with the 20th overall pick. In three seasons of pro ball, Mitchell has played 64, 96 and 27 games due to different injuries. While he made his MLB debut in August 2022, he remains prospect eligible with fewer than 131 major league at-bats, as a torn labrum in his left shoulder that required surgery limited him to just 19 games in 2023.
SCOUTING REPORT: The injuries add more uncertainty to a player who was already challenging to project. Mitchell's combination of size, athleticism and tools is rare to find, though it comes with offensive question marks. At 6-foot-3, 225 pounds, his physicality sticks out, as does his 80 speed on the 20-80 scouting scale. He combines that speed with plus raw power, with exit velocities up to 112 mph. That power is evident in batting practice, but to be able to get to that power in games will require adjustments. His attack angle and swing path aren't geared to drive the ball in the air, and while he has shown solid patience, his elevated swing-and-miss rate against pitches in the strike zone led to a 38% strikeout rate in the majors. Mitchell's speed makes him a rangy defender in center field, where he has a plus arm and should be a plus defender.
THE FUTURE: Few players in the organization can match Mitchell's upside if he can make enough contact and elevate the ball consistently, but he carries more risk than most players entering their age-25 season. The Milwaukee outfield is getting crowded, so Mitchell will have to show health and productivity.

Year	Age	Club (League)	Level	AVG	G	AB	R	H	2B	3B	HR	RBI	BB	SO	SB	OBP	SLG
2023	24	Nashville (IL)	AAA	.188	8	32	3	6	0	1	0	0	2	6	3	.257	.250
2023	24	Milwaukee (NL)	MLB	.246	19	65	10	16	2	1	3	7	7	26	1	.315	.446
Minor League Totals				.268	140	504	101	135	22	5	13	64	78	151	37	.375	.409
Major League Totals				.278	47	126	19	35	5	1	5	16	13	54	9	.343	.452

7 LUIS LARA, OF

HIT: 60. **POW:** 30. **RUN:** 60. **FLD:** 55. **ARM:** 55. **BA Grade:** 50. **Risk:** High.

Born: November 17, 2004. **B-T:** B-R. **HT:** 5-7. **WT:** 155.
Signed: Venezuela, 2022. **Signed by:** Jose Rodriguez.
TRACK RECORD: As a skinny 5-foot-6 outfielder, Lara didn't get a ton of attention early in the scouting process in Venezuela. The Brewers were drawn to his mix of quick-twitch athleticism, hitting ability and defense at a premium position, signing him for $1.1 million when the international signing period opened on Jan. 15, 2022. Lara made his pro debut in the Dominican Summer League that year and was so advanced that the Brewers pushed him in 2023 to Low-A Carolina as an 18-year-old before another an August promotion to High-A Wisconsin.
SCOUTING REPORT: Lara is a small, athletic switch-hitter with an accurate barrel and solid grasp of the strike zone who struck out in just 15% of his plate appearances in 2023. He starts his swing with his barrel tipped toward the pitcher but is able to keep his hands direct to the ball with good balance and the bat control to make consistent contact against fastballs and breaking stuff. He's comfortable letting the ball travel deep into the hitting zone, using the whole field and shooting line drives the opposite way. Lara's future power is a question mark. He's small and has just two home runs in 145 career games, so he might never have more than below-average power. More bullish evaluators can point to his youth, high upper-end exit velocities—up to 110 mph—and potential to develop more impact once he learns which pitches to turn on with pull power as reasons to believe there's more impact coming. He draws strong reviews for his defense in center field, where he's a potential above-average defender with plus speed, a quick first step, athletic movements and an above-average arm.
THE FUTURE: Lara's hitting ability is polished for his age, but the key will be to prove he can hit for more power. He will again be one of the youngest players in the league when he opens 2024 in Wisconsin.

Year	Age	Club (League)	Level	AVG	G	AB	R	H	2B	3B	HR	RBI	BB	SO	SB	OBP	SLG
2023	18	Carolina (CAR)	A	.285	70	274	55	78	11	1	2	21	39	46	22	.379	.354
2023	18	Wisconsin (MWL)	A+	.290	17	69	13	20	2	2	0	8	5	15	8	.351	.377
Minor League Totals				.276	145	543	107	150	24	7	4	50	65	89	37	.361	.368

8 BROCK WILKEN, 3B

HIT: 45. **POW:** 70. **RUN:** 30. **FLD:** 45. **ARM:** 70. **BA Grade:** 50. **Risk:** High.

Born: June 17, 2002. **B-T:** R-R. **HT:** 6-4. **WT:** 225.
Drafted: Wake Forest, 2023 (1st round). **Signed by:** Taylor Frederick.

TRACK RECORD: Wilken was one of the most dangerous sluggers in college baseball. He mashed 31 home runs in 66 games for Wake Forest in 2023, when he hit .345/.506/.807 while setting the school's single-season record for home runs and walks (69). Wilken's 71 career home runs are also the most in school history and tied for the Atlantic Coast Conference career record. The Brewers drafted him with their first-round pick at 18th overall and signed him for $3.15 million. He moved quickly upon signing, finishing 2023 at Double-A Biloxi.

SCOUTING REPORT: Power is Wilken's calling card. He has quiet hands, a simple lower-half load and the strength in his 6-foot-4 frame to drive the ball with plus-plus raw power. He's generally a pull-oriented hitter, but he has the juice to go deep to any part of the park. From 2022 to 2023 at Wake Forest, Wilken cut his strikeout rate from 24% to 18% while increasing his walk rate from 12% to 21%. That helped answer questions scouts had about his pure hitting ability, though he will likely always have a power-over-hit offensive profile with some swing-and-miss to his game. A well below-average runner, Wilken showed better lateral agility than expected at third base after signing. He has a plus-plus arm, though his hands and footwork might restrict him from being better than a fringe-average defender at third base, with a chance he outgrows the position and moves to first base.

THE FUTURE: If everything clicks, Wilken has the chance to be a 30-plus home run hitter who draws a lot of walks in the middle of a lineup, though he will have to prove he can keep his contact rate high enough against better pitchers and continue developing defensively to stick at third base. He's likely ticketed for Double-A to open 2024.

Year	Age	Club (League)	Level	AVG	G	AB	R	H	2B	3B	HR	RBI	BB	SO	SB	OBP	SLG
2023	21	ACL Brewers Gold	Rk	.333	7	21	3	7	0	1	1	6	4	6	1	.464	.571
2023	21	Wisconsin (MWL)	A+	.289	34	121	21	35	6	3	2	15	27	32	3	.427	.438
2023	21	Biloxi (SL)	AA	.217	6	23	3	5	2	0	2	8	2	9	0	.280	.565
Minor League Totals				.285	47	165	27	47	8	4	5	29	33	47	4	.414	.473

9 CARLOS RODRIGUEZ, RHP

FB: 45. **CB:** 45. **SL:** 50. **CHG:** 55. **CUT:** 45. **CTL:** 50. **BA Grade:** 45. **Risk:** Medium.

Born: November 27, 2001. **B-T:** R-R. **HT:** 6-0. **WT:** 206.
Drafted: Florida Southwestern State JC, 2021 (6th round). **Signed by:** Mike Burns.

TRACK RECORD: Rodriguez could be another junior college pitching success story for the Brewers, who signed him for $250,000 as a sixth-round pick from Florida Southwestern State JC in 2021. Rodriguez was the organization's minor league pitcher of the year in 2022 and shared the honor with lefthander Robert Gasser again in 2023, when he led the Double-A Southern League with a 2.77 ERA.

SCOUTING REPORT: Rodriguez continues to surprise and has now proven successful at the upper levels. He lacks a big fastball or a wipeout secondary pitch but continually finds a way to mix and match his arsenal. Rodriguez has good control of a fastball that sits at 90-94 mph and can scrape 95 and mixes four- and two-seamers. His 83-85 changeup is his best pitch, an above-average offering with 17 inches of horizontal run to fade away from lefties. It's the pitch that gets the highest rate of swing-and-miss and a key reason why his OPS allowed was near equal against lefties (.566) and righties (.563) in 2023. His 78-82 mph slider is a fringe-average pitch that flashes better at times, with a low-to-mid-70s curveball that he will sprinkle in occasionally when he's ahead in the count and a mid-80s cutter that gives him six pitches to attack hitters. With a stocky, strong build, Rodriguez has been a solid strike-thrower, though his success comes more from his ability to mix his stuff and location rather than precise command.

THE FUTURE: There are still scouts who think Rodriguez could end up in a relief role, but he now looks more likely to be able to stick as a starter, most likely toward the back of the rotation, though he could continue to surprise. Rodriguez most likely opens 2024 in Triple-A, but if his success there continues, he should be in the mix for starts in Milwaukee when a need arises.

Year	Age	Club (League)	Level	W	L	ERA	G	GS	IP	H	HR	BB	SO	BB%	SO%	WHIP	AVG
2023	21	Biloxi (SL)	AA	9	6	2.77	25	25	124	82	10	53	152	10.3	29.5	1.09	.183
2023	21	Nashville (IL)	AAA	0	0	5.79	1	1	5	5	0	4	6	17.4	26.1	1.93	.313
Minor League Totals				15	11	2.94	52	46	236	161	17	97	287	10.0	29.7	1.09	.192

10 JOSH KNOTH, RHP

FB: 55. **CB:** 60. **SL:** 65. **CHG:** 45. **CTL:** 55. **BA Grade:** 55. **Risk:** Extreme.

Born: August 10, 2005. **B-T:** R-R. **HT:** 6-1. **WT:** 190.
Drafted: HS—Medford, NY, 2023 (1st round supplemental). **Signed by:** Steve DiTrolio.
TRACK RECORD: Entering his senior season in 2023, Knoth had encouraging projection indicators, with the buzz around him increasing during the spring as his stuff took another leap forward at his Long Island high school. A 19-strikeout perfect game only enhanced his profile for scouts. One of the youngest pitchers in the 2023 class, Knoth was 17 on draft day when the Brewers selected him in the supplemental first round at No. 33 overall and signed him for $2 million.
SCOUTING REPORT: Knoth is an athletic pitcher with sound arm action and an efficient delivery that he repeats well, helping him throw consistent strikes with his fastball. His velocity increased during the 2023 season and now sits at 92-96 mph and peaks at 98. It's a strong fastball, but the separator for Knoth is his ability to spin a pair of tight breaking pitches that both eclipse 3,000 rpm. His low-to-mid-80s slider is a potential plus-plus pitch. He snaps it off with sharp break and two-plane depth to miss bats. He throws his curveball with power at 79-82 mph, and while it can blend together with his slider at times, it's another pitch that flashes plus with good depth. Some scouts prefer his curve to his slider. Knoth's changeup has solid fade, though it comes in firm and he doesn't use it much yet, as is the case with most high school power pitchers.
THE FUTURE: Knoth is still several years away from being a major league contributor, but he has the potential to develop into a high-end starter who can rack up whiffs with his breaking stuff. He will make his pro debut in 2024, likely with Low-A Carolina. Knoth will be just 18 all season, and his development will take time.

Year	Age	Club (League)	Level	W	L	ERA	G	GS	IP	H	HR	BB	SO	BB%	SO%	WHIP	AVG
2023	17	Did not play															

11 YOPHERY RODRIGUEZ, OF

HIT: 55. **POW:** 55. **Run:** 55. **Field:** 50. **ARM:** 50. **BA Grade:** 55. **Risk:** Extreme.

Born: December 5, 2005 **B-T:** L-L. **HT:** 6-1. **WT:** 185. **Signed:** Dominican Republic, 2023. **Signed by:** Jose Morales.
TRACK RECORD: Rodriguez was one of the most advanced hitters in the Dominican Republic for 2023, when the Brewers made him their highest-paid prospect of the class with a $1.5 million bonus. Rodriguez backed up the Brewers' belief in him as a 17-year-old in the Dominican Summer League, where he showed a promising mix of bat control, plate discipline and power.
SCOUTING REPORT: Rodriguez stands out for his maturity at the plate. He's a selective hitter who recognizes spin and has the hand-eye coordination that leads to a low swing-and-miss rate. He has fast bat speed from the left side and showed flashes of what should be above-average raw power. His flatter bat path means he doesn't fully tap into that power yet, but he can hit deep home runs and should have more power coming as he gets stronger and learns how to turn on pitches for loft with more frequency. Rodriguez has the athleticism and tick above-average speed to handle center field in the lower levels, though most likely will shift to a corner as he moves up. He has an average arm that could fit in either outfield corner.
THE FUTURE: While the Brewers have built a strong group of homegrown Venezuelan prospects, Rodriguez is one of the best Dominican prospects to come through the system in recent years. He's talented enough that he could follow the path of Milwaukee's top signings from their last two classes— outfielders Jackson Chourio and Luis Lara—by skipping the Rookie-level Arizona Complex League and instead playing in Low-A Carolina in 2024.

Year	Age	Club (League)	Level	AVG	G	AB	R	H	2B	3B	HR	RBI	BB	SO	SB	OBP	SLG
2023	17	DSL Brewers 1	Rk	.253	52	178	34	45	13	2	6	36	41	40	12	.393	.449
Minor League Totals				.253	52	178	34	45	13	2	6	36	41	40	12	.393	.449

12 ERIC BITONTI, 3B/SS

HIT: 40. **POW:** 60. **RUN:** 40. **FLD:** 55. **ARM:** 60. **BA Grade:** 55. **Risk:** Extreme.

Born: November 17, 2005. **B-T:** L-R. **HT:** 6-4. **WT:** 218. **Drafted:** HS—San Bernardino, CA, 2023 (3rd round).
Signed by: Daniel Cho.
TRACK RECORD: Bitonti didn't turn 18 until four months after the 2023 draft, making him extremely young for that year's high school class. A third-round pick in 2023, Bitonti signed for an above-slot bonus

of $1.75 million, then made his pro debut in the Rookie-level Arizona Complex League.
SCOUTING REPORT: Bitonti immediately grabs attention for his size. He's a physical 6-foot-4 infielder with big lefthanded power. He has the strength, leverage and bat speed to generate plus raw power now with a chance to grow into 70 raw power on the 20-80 scale. There is some length to Bitonti's swing that leaves holes and creates a higher swing-and-miss rate. He has been able to keep the strikeouts manageable, but it will likely always be something he has to monitor in what projects as a power-over-hit offensive profile. While Bitonti's size is more typical of a first baseman, he has surprisingly good body control on the left side of the infield. He played shortstop in high school and spent some time there in the ACL, though he spent more time at third base after signing. While his speed is limited, his defensive actions are sound and his arm is plus, so he could stick at third base. He has experience at first base as well and could be a plus defender if he had to move to the position.
THE FUTURE: As a teenager who has yet to get to a full-season league, Bitonti carries plenty of risk, but he has some of the biggest upside in the organization. He should spend 2024 in Low-A Carolina.

Year	Age	Club (League)	Level	AVG	G	AB	R	H	2B	3B	HR	RBI	BB	SO	SB	OBP	SLG
2023	17	ACL Brewers Gold	Rk	.179	12	39	8	7	1	1	2	9	9	15	0	.333	.410
Minor League Totals				.179	12	39	8	7	1	1	2	9	9	15	0	.333	.410

13 LUKE ADAMS, 3B
HIT: 45. **POW:** 55. **RUN:** 50. **FLD:** 40. **ARM:** 50. **BA Grade:** 45. **Risk:** High.

Born: April 4, 2004. **B-T:** R-R. **HT:** 6-4. **WT:** 210. **Drafted:** HS—Hinsdale, IL, 2022 (12th round).
Signed by: Ginger Poulson.
TRACK RECORD: In high school, Adams was a Michigan State commit who was not a prominent prospect at national events. After his senior season, he hit .404/.478/.737 in 68 plate appearances in the summer collegiate Prospect League, which enhanced his draft stock. The Brewers signed him for $282,500 as a 12th-round pick in 2022, and after a strong pro debut that summer in the Rookie-level Arizona Complex League, Adams followed with a solid campaign with Low-A Carolina in 2023.
SCOUTING REPORT: Adams is a split camp player with an unorthodox look. He's a strong, physical player who can drive the ball with impact. He has above-average raw power with exit velocities up to 112 mph, he's a patient hitter who has piled up walks and doesn't have much swing-and-miss on pitches in the strike zone. He does it with an extremely funky swing that starts with a big, hanging leg kick and a significant hitch, starting his hands up by his ear, dropping them to his waist, then raising them back up to his shoulder. Adams is a good fastball hitter who can punish mistakes, but there's length to his swing and a lack of adjustability that will get tested against better pitching. An average runner, Adams typically makes the routine plays at third base with an average arm from a lower slot, but his heavy feet and limited range mean he's probably ticketed for an outfield corner or first base.
THE FUTURE: The upper levels of the minors will be the big jump for Adams to prove that his offensive skill set will translate against more advanced competition. He could get there in 2024 after likely opening in High-A Wisconsin.

Year	Age	Club (League)	Level	AVG	G	AB	R	H	2B	3B	HR	RBI	BB	SO	SB	OBP	SLG
2023	19	Carolina (CAR)	A	.233	99	339	74	79	18	3	11	54	76	99	30	.400	.401
Minor League Totals				.245	110	371	83	91	21	3	12	61	83	107	39	.410	.415

14 COOPER PRATT, SS
HIT: 50. **POW:** 45. **RUN:** 50. **FLD:** 50. **ARM:** 60. **BA Grade:** 50. **Risk:** Extreme.

Born: August 18, 2004. **B-T:** R-R. **HT:** 6-4. **WT:** 195. **Drafted:** HS—Senatobia, Miss, 2023 (6th round).
Signed by: Scott Nichols.
TRACK RECORD: Pratt's barrel accuracy and high baseball IQ stood out in high school, making him the No. 63 prospect for the 2023 draft. The Brewers drafted him in the sixth round, signed him for well above-slot at $1.35 million and Pratt went on to hit well in the Rookie-level Arizona Complex League in the summer. After the season, Pratt was the buzziest player at the organization's instructional league, standing out in a system that's relatively light on shortstops.
SCOUTING REPORT: A lanky 6-foot-4 righthanded hitter, Pratt showed a knack for putting the ball in play as an amateur that continued into his pro debut. He has a calm, relaxed swing, trusting his hands with a fluid path to the ball. Pratt has an accurate barrel with the ability to consistently square up both fastballs and offspeed stuff, showing solid strike-zone judgment for his age. Pratt has mainly been a singles hitter with gap power, and while the strength projection remaining in his frame suggests more over-the-fence juice should come, it's likely going to be a hit-over-power profile. An average runner, Pratt doesn't have the first-step explosion that some scouts prefer at shortstop, but he plays under control at shortstop

with a good internal clock and a plus arm. He impressed defensively at shortstop in his pro debut, though as he fills out there's a chance he could slide over to third base.

THE FUTURE: The early returns have arrows pointing up on Pratt, who could take a significant leap forward if he's able to unlock more power. He's likely ticketed for Low-A Carolina to open 2024.

Year	Age	Club (League)	Level	AVG	G	AB	R	H	2B	3B	HR	RBI	BB	SO	SB	OBP	SLG
2023	18	ACL Brewers Gold	Rk	.356	12	45	9	16	2	1	0	8	5	11	4	.426	.444
Minor League Totals				.356	12	45	9	16	2	1	0	8	5	11	4	.426	.444

15 MIKE BOEVE, 3B/2B

HIT: 55. **POW:** 40. **RUN:** 40. **FLD:** 45. **ARM:** 50. **BA Grade:** 45. **Risk:** High.

Born: May 5, 2002 **B-T:** L-R. **HT:** 6-2. **WT:** 210. **Drafted:** Nebraska-Omaha, 2023 (2nd round).
Signed by: Riley Bandelow.

TRACK RECORD: As a junior at Nebraska-Omaha in 2023, Boeve struck out just nine times in 211 plate appearances as he hit .401/.512/.563, an OBP that ranked 14th in the nation. The Brewers drafted him in the second round that year and signed him for $1.25 million.

SCOUTING REPORT: Boeve has a strong frame with a thick lower half, though it's his contact skills that stand out more than his power. He loads with a small toe tap, has little movement in his swing with a short path to the ball. Boeve has a good sense of the strike zone and doesn't miss much, with the hand-eye coordination and approach to spread the ball around the field. Boeve makes hard contact, though his bat path results in more ground balls and low line drives than loft, so he doesn't project to hit for big power without a swing adjustment. An offensive-minded player, Boeve is primarily a third baseman, though he played more second base after signing while 2023 first-round pick Brock Wilken got most of the reps at third. He's a below-average runner whose lack of first-step quickness limits him. Some scouts think he could end up in an outfield corner or at first base, while others think his defensive actions and average arm will be enough to be a fringe-average defender at third.

THE FUTURE: If Boeve can continue to progress defensively and tap into more game power, he has the upside to develop into an everyday third baseman. High-A Wisconsin is likely his next stop.

Year	Age	Club (League)	Level	AVG	G	AB	R	H	2B	3B	HR	RBI	BB	SO	SB	OBP	SLG
2023	21	ACL Brewers Gold	Rk	.500	9	30	8	15	3	0	4	12	4	6	0	.556	1.000
2023	21	Wisconsin (MWL)	A+	.250	19	72	11	18	3	0	1	18	10	19	1	.333	.333
Minor League Totals				.324	28	102	19	33	6	0	5	30	14	25	1	.400	.529

16 WES CLARKE, 1B/C

HIT: 30. **POW:** 70. **RUN:** 30. **FLD:** 40. **ARM:** 45. **BA Grade:** 45. **Risk:** High.

Born: October 13, 1999. **B-T:** R-R. **HT:** 6-0. **WT:** 228. **Drafted:** South Carolina, 2021 (10th round).
Signed by: Taylor Frederick.

TRACK RECORD: Clarke was a third-team All-American in 2021 at South Carolina, where his 23 home runs tied for the most in the country. The Brewers—who drafted Clarkee out of high school in the 40th round in 2018—picked him again in 2021 in the 10th round, signing him for $75,000. He elevated his status with a big 2023 campaign in Double-A, leading the system in both walks and home runs before continuing to perform well in the Arizona Fall League.

SCOUTING REPORT: Clarke has as much raw power as any player in the organization. It's 70 raw power on the 20-80 scale with exit velocities up to 115 mph and the ability to go deep to any part of the park. Clarke is strong with a simple lower half move to the ball, punishing fastballs and changeups left over the plate. Clarke does have patience to take his walks, but his steep swing leaves him vulnerable to swing and miss, especially against breaking stuff, leading to a 29% strikeout rate. Clarke still played 34 games at catcher last year, but he spent most of his time at first base and most likely will become a full time first baseman. He's a well below-average runner whose value will be tied to what he does in the batter's box.

THE FUTURE: To prove he can be more than a 4-A slugger, Clarke will have to continue to trim his swing-and-miss tendencies, but he has the patience and power to profile at first base. He will open 2024 in Triple-A Nashville.

Year	Age	Club (League)	Level	AVG	G	AB	R	H	2B	3B	HR	RBI	BB	SO	SB	OBP	SLG
2023	23	Biloxi (SL)	AA	.241	118	398	68	96	24	0	26	80	89	147	6	.392	.497
Minor League Totals				.233	241	806	118	188	48	0	45	162	174	272	6	.378	.460

17 BRADLEY BLALOCK, RHP

FB: 55. **CB:** 50. **SL:** 45. **SPLT:** 50. **CTL:** 50. **BA Grade:** 45. **Risk:** High.

Born: December 25, 2000. **B-T:** R-R. **HT:** 6-2. **WT:** 200. **Drafted:** HS—Loganville, GA, 2019 (32nd round).
Signed by: Brian Moehler (Red Sox).
TRACK RECORD: Blalock signed with the Red Sox for $250,000 as a 32nd-round pick in the 2019 draft. After the pandemic wiped out the 2020 season, Blalock spent 2021 with Low-A Salem, but Tommy John surgery erased his 2022 season. He was back pitching in 2023 when the Red Sox dealt him to the Brewers in the trade deadline deal that brought infielder Luis Urias to Boston. The Brewers added Blalock to the 40-man roster after the season.
SCOUTING REPORT: Blalock's best pitch is his fastball, which he throws for strikes, sitting at 91-95 mph and touching 96. He throws from a near over-the-top arm slot, getting excellent carry on his fastball with 21 inches of induced vertical break, enabling him to get swing-and-miss up in the zone. There's no wipeout secondary pitch for Blalock, whose main offspeed offering has been a low-to-mid 80s slider that flashes as an average pitch with spin in the 2,500-2,600 rpm range. The 2023 addition of an 84-88 mph split-changeup has been an asset. It's an average pitch that plays well off his high-slot fastball to induce chase and give him a weapon against lefties. Blalock's mid-70s curveball has good depth and is a solid-average pitch, one that could make him more effective if he increases its usage.
THE FUTURE: Blalock's repertoire and ability to throw strikes give him a chance to be a back-end starter. If not, his stuff could play up in relief. He should open 2024 in Double-A.

Year	Age	Club (League)	Level	W	L	ERA	G	GS	IP	H	HR	BB	SO	BB%	SO%	WHIP	AVG
2023	22	Salem (CAR)	A	1	0	1.50	4	4	18	10	1	4	22	6.2	33.8	0.78	.167
2023	22	Greenville (SAL)	A+	5	1	2.55	7	7	35	31	3	9	36	6.2	24.8	1.13	.233
2023	22	Wisconsin (MWL)	A+	0	0	5.27	4	4	14	13	3	7	17	11.5	27.9	1.46	.245
Minor League Totals				9	9	3.77	42	41	160	155	12	60	164	8.7	23.8	1.34	.251

18 LOGAN HENDERSON, RHP

FB: 45. **SL:** 40. **CHG:** 60. **CTL:** 55. **BA Grade:** 45. **Risk:** High.

Born: March 2, 2002. **B-T:** R-R. **HT:** 5-11. **WT:** 194. **Drafted:** McLennan (TX) JC. **Signed by:** K.J. Hendrick.
TRACK RECORD: The NJCAA Division I pitcher of the year as a freshman for national champion McLennan (Texas), Henderson led the nation in strikeouts and signed for $495,000 that year as a fourth-round pick. In spring training in 2022, an avulsion fracture in his throwing elbow required surgery and sidelined him until August. He pitched all of 2023 at Low-A, where he struck out 35% of batters.
SCOUTING REPORT: Henderson throws strikes at a high clip with his four-seam fastball, which sits at 89-92 mph and touches 94. He lacks big velocity, but his fastball rides up in the zone to help him miss bats when he elevates. Henderson's best pitch is his 78-81 mph changeup, which he leans on heavily against both lefties and righties. It's a plus changeup that typically has 11-12 mph of separation off his fastball and excellent fade, enabling him to pile up whiffs. Henderson throws his fastball/changeup mix more than 90% of the time. He sprinkles in an occasional slider, but it's a distant third pitch.
THE FUTURE: Henderson carved Low-A hitters with his fastball/changeup attack, but he will likely need a better breaking ball to continue his success in the upper levels. If he's able to do that, there's a chance for him to develop into a back-end starter.

Year	Age	Club (League)	Level	W	L	ERA	G	GS	IP	H	HR	BB	SO	BB%	SO%	WHIP	AVG
2023	21	Carolina (CAR)	A	4	3	2.75	18	18	79	50	8	26	106	8.6	35.2	0.97	.185
Minor League Totals				4	4	2.93	25	25	92	65	8	32	129	8.7	35.2	1.05	.199

19 OLIVER DUNN, 2B

HIT: 40. **POW:** 55. **RUN:** 55. **FLD:** 40. **ARM:** 40. **BA Grade:** 40. **Risk:** Medium.

Born: September 2, 1997. **B-T:** L-R. **HT:** 5-10. **WT:** 185. **Drafted:** Utah, 2019 (11th round).
Signed by: Mike Thurman (Yankees).
TRACK RECORD: A Yankees 11th-round pick out of Utah in 2019, Dunn reached Triple-A in 2022, then after the season the Phillies selected him with the final pick in the minor league phase of the Rule 5 draft. Dunn never hit more than seven home runs in a season in either college or pro ball, but he slugged 21 homers in 2023 for Double-A Reading, then continued his success in the Arizona Fall League. In November, the Brewers acquired him in a prospect swap for second baseman Robert Moore and outfielder Hendry Mendez, then added Dunn to the 40-man roster.
SCOUTING REPORT: Entering his age-26 season, Dunn is old for a prospect, and while Reading is a hitter's park, there are reasons to believe his steps forward in 2023 will carry over. He has a compact,

physically mature frame at 5-foot-10, 185 pounds and a patient approach, walking at a 16% clip with his 82 walks the most in the Phillies farm system in 2023. Reading is a band box, but Dunn has at least plus raw power with an average exit velocity of 92 mph that would put him only behind Wes Clarkee among Brewers' minor leaguers last year. Dunn has a short, simple lefthanded swing, but he did post a 28% strikeout rate. He's a good fastball-hitter who squares up high-end velocity, but he struggled with swing-and-miss against changeups. A solid-average runner, Dunn is a below-average defender with a below-average arm, primarily playing second base but with time at third and left field as well.

THE FUTURE: At 26, Dunn doesn't have much projection left, but his ability to draw walks and hit for power could allow him to carve out a major league role. He should start 2024 in Triple-A Nashville but could make his MLB debut later in the year.

Year	Age	Club (League)	Level	AVG	G	AB	R	H	2B	3B	HR	RBI	BB	SO	SB	OBP	SLG
2023	25	Reading (EL)	AA	.271	119	417	65	113	27	4	21	78	82	139	16	.396	.506
Minor League Totals				.246	278	874	140	215	49	9	34	143	165	296	35	.370	.439

20 DYLAN O'RAE, 2B/OF/SS

HIT: 50. **POW:** 20. **RUN:** 70. **FLD:** 55. **ARM:** 45. **BA Grade:** 45. **Risk:** High.

Born: February 14, 2004. **B-T:** L-R. **HT:** 5-7. **WT:** 160. **Drafted:** HS—Sarnia, ON, 2022 (3rd round). **Signed by:** Pete Orr.
TRACK RECORD: O'Rae was one of the surprise picks of the top three rounds in 2022 when the Brewers drafted him in the third round. Since signing, O'Rae has shown outstanding bat-to-ball skills, albeit without much power, leading the Brewers' farm system in OBP in 2023 as he reached Low-A Carolina.
SCOUTING REPORT: O'Rae's skill set is one of extremes. He's just 5-foot-7, but he is the best contact hitter in the system. He has superb bat control and a small strike zone that he doesn't often expand. He's a plus-plus runner, giving him the components for a high-contact, high on-base threat. O'Rae is strong for his size, but he has well below-average raw power and a short, downhill swing geared to slap the ball on the ground. He rarely pulls a ball in the air, so he has yet to homer in 68 career games and has just nine extra-base hits. O'Rae's fringe-average arm is light for shortstop, but he's a good defender at second base and got exposure to center field, a position he could see more time at going forward because of his speed..
THE FUTURE: O'Rae's ability to get on base and play a premium position make for an intriguing foundation, but he will have to find a way to unlock more power to maintain those high OBPs at higher levels.

Year	Age	Club (League)	Level	AVG	G	AB	R	H	2B	3B	HR	RBI	BB	SO	SB	OBP	SLG
2023	19	ACL Brewers Gold	Rk	.362	37	130	44	47	4	1	0	15	40	23	28	.522	.408
2023	19	Carolina (CAR)	A	.330	23	88	14	29	4	0	0	8	17	14	16	.439	.375
Minor League Totals				.344	68	244	64	84	8	1	0	26	63	44	48	.484	.385

21 JADHER AREINAMO, 2B/3B/SS

HIT: 50. **POW:** 30. **RUN:** 40. **FLD:** 55. **ARM:** 50. **BA Grade:** 45. **Risk:** High.

Born: November 28, 2003. **B-T:** R-R. **HT:** 5-8. **WT:** 160. **Signed:** Venezuela, 2021.
Signed by: Jose Rodriguez/Javier Castillo.
TRACK RECORD: Areinamo's lack of size and tools worked against him during the tryout process in Venezuela, but the Brewers were drawn to his ability to hit and high baseball IQ. Areinamo signed for $150,000 in 2021 and reached Low-A Carolina as an 18-year-old at the end of the 2022 season. He returned there for 2023 and finished runner-up for the Carolina League batting title.
SCOUTING REPORT: Areinamo has an unorthodox bat waggle. He sets his hands at his back shoulder, drops them as he begins his leg kick, then snaps his wrists down so his barrel gets near parallel to the ground before snapping them back up just before the pitcher's release. There's a lot of noise involved, but Areinamo has good bat-to-ball skills and regularly squares up all types of pitches with little swing-and-miss in the zone. He covers the inner third of the plate well, smacking line drives everywhere with an all-fields approach. Areinamo will need to develop a more selective approach, as he is prone to chasing outside the zone. His power is well below-average, but after just 14 extra-base hits the first four months of the season, he hit 14 doubles in August alone. A below-average runner with an average arm, Areinamo is an instinctive fielder and a potential a potential above-average defender at second base, where he gets most of his work, with time at third base and some at shortstop as well.
THE FUTURE: If Areinamo can get stronger and develop more extra-base impact, he could be a significant riser in the system, though he could ultimately fit best in a utility role. He's ready for High-A Wisconsin.

Year	Age	Club (League)	Level	AVG	G	AB	R	H	2B	3B	HR	RBI	BB	SO	SB	OBP	SLG
2023	19	Carolina (CAR)	A	.306	103	396	52	121	26	1	4	52	17	52	16	.333	.407
Minor League Totals				.294	216	798	131	235	46	6	5	95	62	115	27	.351	.386

22 DANIEL GUILARTE, SS

HIT: 45. **POW:** 20. **RUN:** 60. **FLD:** 50. **ARM:** 60. **BA Grade:** 45. **Risk:** High.

Born: October 29, 2003. **B-T:** R-R. **HT:** 6-0. **WT:** 170. **Signed:** Venezuela, 2021. **Signed by:** Trino Aguilar.

TRACK RECORD: Jackson Chourio was the prize signing of Milwaukee's international class in 2021, but they also signed Guilarte that year for $1 million. After a shoulder injury kept him off the field in 2021, Guilarte debuted in the Rookie-level Arizona Complex League in 2022 before jumping in 2023 to Low-A Carolina, where he made a lot of contact, albeit with little power.

SCOUTING REPORT: Guilarte split time between shortstop and second base last year because the Brewers also had Gregory Barrios in Carolina, but he has the tools to stick at shortstop. He's a good athlete and a plus runner with a quick first step and a plus arm. Unlike a lot of young shortstops who can play out of control and get error-prone, Guilarte doesn't make many mistakes in the field. At the plate, Guilarte has a handsy swing and doesn't swing and miss much in the zone, though he has minimal power with no home runs in 99 career games. Guilarte will need to get stronger and will likely need to adjust a downhill swing path, as he rarely pulls a ball in the air, often shooting line drives the other way or hitting a lot of groundballs.

THE FUTURE: There's still room for Guilarte to layer more strength on to his lean frame, giving him a chance to potentially unlock more power that will be key for his development. He should head to High-A Wisconsin for 2024.

Year	Age	Club (League)	Level	AVG	G	AB	R	H	2B	3B	HR	RBI	BB	SO	SB	OBP	SLG
2023	19	ACL Brewers Gold	Rk	.450	5	20	9	9	0	0	0	2	1	2	5	.500	.450
2023	19	Carolina (CAR)	A	.269	58	223	35	60	6	2	0	31	35	66	26	.377	.314
Minor League Totals				.292	99	367	61	107	14	2	0	53	55	99	39	.392	.341

23 JUAN BAEZ, SS/3B

HIT: 50. **POW:** 45. **RUN:** 40. **FLD:** 45. **ARM:** 50. **BA Grade:** 50. **Risk:** Extreme.

Born: June 27, 2005. **B-T:** R-R. **HT:** 5-9. **WT:** 175. **Signed:** Dominican Republic, 2022.
Signed by: Julio De La Cruz/Gary Peralta.

TRACK RECORD: Baez had a low profile as an amateur player in the Dominican Republic when he signed with the Brewers at 16 for $10,000 on Jan. 15, 2022. After a decent pro debut that year in the Dominican Summer League, Baez in 2023 hit .370/.395/.557 to finish runner-up for the batting title in the Rookie-level Arizona Complex League, then drew a promotion to Low-A Carolina at the end of August.

SCOUTING REPORT: At 5-foot-9, 175 pounds, Baez has a strong, stocky build with a thick lower half. He's an aggressive hitter who loads with a big leg kick and his swing has some length, yet he consistently puts the ball in play at a high clip, striking out in just 11% of his plate appearances in 2023. Baez also walked just 4% of the time, as he's a free-swinger who will need to develop a more selective approach. Baez does make frequent contact though and shows flashes of average raw power that he should be able to tap into more if he's able to add more loft to his stroke and make better swing decisions. Baez spent time at shortstop and third base but he's a below-average runner with limited range who projects best at third or second base.

THE FUTURE: Baez started to break through in 2023 and could make a bigger name for himself in 2024 if his offensive success continues in Low-A Carolina.

Year	Age	Club (League)	Level	AVG	G	AB	R	H	2B	3B	HR	RBI	BB	SO	SB	OBP	SLG
2023	18	ACL Brewers Gold	Rk	.370	48	192	39	71	16	4	4	42	8	23	17	.395	.557
2023	18	Carolina (CAR)	A	.233	9	30	7	7	3	0	0	6	2	4	2	.265	.333
Minor League Totals				.312	111	420	79	131	28	4	7	70	27	58	36	.352	.448

24 ERIC BROWN JR., SS

HIT: 45. **POW:** 40. **RUN:** 55. **FLD:** 50. **ARM:** 50. **BA Grade:** 45. **Risk:** High.

Born: December 19, 2000. **B-T:** R-R. **HT:** 5-10. **WT:** 190. **Drafted:** Coastal Carolina, 2022 (1st round).
Signed by: Taylor Frederick.

TRACK RECORD: Brown was a standout in the 2021 Cape Cod League, then hit .330/.460/.544 at Coastal Carolina in 2022, when the Brewers drafted him in the first round (27th overall) and signed him for $2.05 million. Brown's bat was supposed to be his calling card, but he didn't do much to distinguish himself offensively in 2023, with a non-displaced hairline fracture of his left shoulder blade that kept him out for six weeks in July and August.

SCOUTING REPORT: Brown doesn't have big-time tools or explosiveness, but he made a ton of contact in college and his low swing-and-miss rate carried over into pro ball. In college, Brown had an unconventional swing, with his hands above his head and away from his body and a big leg kick, but he has condensed some of those bigger movements, lowering his hands and shortening his leg kick. Brown has good strike-zone judgment and is a high-contact hitter, but it's typically lighter contact. He can occasionally sneak a ball over the fence to his pull side, but he will need to develop more extra-base impact. An above-average runner with an average arm, Brown has the actions to stick in the dirt, with several scouts thinking he would fit better at second base than shortstop.

THE FUTURE: Brown will need to rebound in 2024, with more damage on contact the key for his development. He should start 2024 in Double-A Biloxi.

Year	Age	Club (League)	Level	AVG	G	AB	R	H	2B	3B	HR	RBI	BB	SO	SB	OBP	SLG
2023	22	ACL Brewers Gold	Rk	.182	4	11	5	2	0	0	2	2	3	3	1	.400	.727
2023	22	Wisconsin (MWL)	A+	.265	63	245	48	65	8	0	4	25	32	48	37	.362	.347
2023	22	Biloxi (SL)	AA	.000	5	7	1	0	0	0	0	0	1	3	1	.125	.000
Minor League Totals				.258	99	360	77	93	15	1	9	35	51	75	58	.365	.381

25 PEDRO IBARGUEN, 2B/3B/OF

HIT: 50. **POW:** 40. **RUN:** 50. **FLD:** 50. **ARM:** 55. **BA Grade:** 45. **Risk:** Extreme.

Born: July 2, 2006. **B-T:** R-R. **HT:** 5-10. **WT:** 185. **Signed:** Venezuela, 2023. **Signed by:** Javier Meza.

TRACK RECORD: Ibarguen signed with the Brewers for just $60,000 out of Venezuela when the international signing period opened on Jan. 15, 2023, but his hitting ability and athleticism made him an intriguing sleeper. He showed why in his first pro season in the Dominican Summer League, turning 17 in July and hitting well overall before finishing on fire with a .341/.436/.659 tear in August.

SCOUTING REPORT: At 5-foot-10, 185 pounds, Ibarguen isn't that tall, but he has a strong, compact frame. He's a disciplined hitter for his age who didn't chase much and has the bat control to make contact at a high clip, with a barrel tip to the pitcher in his swing but the ability to keep his hands inside the ball well. Ibarguen mostly has doubles power now but he makes hard contact for his age, with a chance for more of those doubles to turn into home runs. Ibarguen is a good athlete who signed as a shortstop but didn't play there in the DSL, instead bouncing around between all three outfield spots and second and third base. He's an average runner whose above-average arm could fit at third base, though he probably will continue to move around the field to develop at multiple positions.

THE FUTURE: Ibarguen has become one of the Brewers' more promising sleepers in the lower levels of the system. If he continues to hit like he did in the DSL when he comes to the Rookie-level Arizona Complex League in 2024, he could take a big leap up the rankings.

Year	Age	Club (League)	Level	AVG	G	AB	R	H	2B	3B	HR	RBI	BB	SO	SB	OBP	SLG
2023	16	DSL Brewers 2	Rk	.311	43	132	27	41	7	1	3	26	25	32	7	.437	.447
Minor League Totals				.311	43	132	27	41	7	1	3	26	25	32	7	.437	.447

26 RYAN BIRCHARD, RHP

FB: 55. **CB:** 55. **SL:** 55. **CHG:** 40. **CTL:** 40. **BA Grade:** 40. **Risk:** High.

Born: July 12, 2003. **B-T:** L-R. **HT:** 6-0. **WT:** 207. **Drafted:** Niagara County (NY) JC, 2023 (5th round). **Signed by:** Steve DiTrolio.

TRACK RECORD: The Brewers were among the handful of teams that made the trip out to remote Niagara County (N.Y.) JC to see Birchard, who struck out 95 in 50 innings in 2023. After the season, Birchard pitched in the MLB Draft League, where he dominated and showed high-octane stuff, making him more well known leading into the draft. The Brewers drafted him in the fifth round and signed him for $322,500, and while he didn't pitch in games after signing, he threw well during instructional league.

SCOUTING REPORT: Birchard has a strong, compact 6-foot frame with a high-effort delivery and a power arm. His fastball sits in the mid-90s, reaching 98 mph with riding life up in the zone. Birchard has a pair of breaking balls that can miss bats and flash above-average, including a mid-80s slider with good lateral break and an upper-70s curveball with tight rotation and big depth. Birchard walked 15% of the batters he faced his final year at Niagara, though his control was better in the MLB Draft League. He should develop in the minor leagues as a starter but some scouts see him fitting best as a reliever in the majors.

THE FUTURE: The Brewers have shown a knack for identifying and developing quality junior college arms. Birchard could be next in line from that path.

Year	Age	Club (League)	Level	W	L	ERA	G	GS	IP	H	HR	BB	SO	BB%	SO%	WHIP	AVG
2023	19	Did not play															

27 BISHOP LETSON, RHP

FB: 50. **SL:** 55. **CHG:** 45. **CTL:** 50. **BA Grade:** 45. **Risk:** Extreme.

Born: September 15, 2004. **B-T:** R-R. **HT:** 6-4. **WT:** 170. **Drafted:** HS—Floyd Knobs, IN, 2023 (11th round).
Signed by: Ginger Poulson.
TRACK RECORD: As a high school underclassman, Letson generated little attention and wasn't heavily recruited before he committed to Purdue. After pitching in the upper 80s and touching 90 mph in 2022, Letson during his senior year in 2023 was pitching more regularly into the low 90s and touching 93 mph. The brewers drafted him in the 11th round that year and signed him for an above-slot bonus of $482,600.
SCOUTING REPORT: Letson doesn't have the power or polish of some of the other high school pitchers drafted in 2023, but he has an array of promising projection indicators. He has good arm speed and a classic projectable build, a skinny 6-foot-4 frame with tons of space to fill out, which should help him add velocity to a fastball with good armside run. His 78-82 mph slider slider has above-average potential, getting slurvy at times but with late break and two-plane depth when it's at its best. Letson's changeup is less refined, but it has a ton of fade that could make it a bigger weapon for him with more reps. Letson is a good athlete, though he's still growing into his coordination to throw consistent strikes.
THE FUTURE: Letson is a deeper projection arm with a lot of risk, but he has some of the best upside among the organization's lower-level pitchers. He should pitch in Low-A Carolina in 2024.

Year	Age	Club (League)	Level	W	L	ERA	G	GS	IP	H	HR	BB	SO	BB%	SO%	WHIP	AVG
2023	18	Did not play															

28 MATT WOOD, C

HIT: 40. **POW:** 40. **RUN:** 40. **FLD:** 50. **ARM:** 50. **BA Grade:** 40. **Risk:** High.

Born: March 2, 2001. **B-T:** L-R. **HT:** 5-10. **WT:** 190. **Drafted:** Penn State, 2022 (4th round). **Signed by:** James Fisher.
TRACK RECORD: Wood ranked second in the Big Ten Conference in OPS while at Penn State in 2022, finishing top five in batting average, on-base percentage and slugging when the Brewers drafted him in the fourth round. In 2023, Wood raked for a month at Low-A Carolina, but cooled off considerably after his promotion to High-A Wisconsin.
SCOUTING REPORT: Like a lot of hitters the Brewers have targeted in recent drafts, Wood has little swing and miss in the strike zone and makes good swing decisions. He recognizes pitches well, doesn't chase much and can manipulate the barrel to use the whole field, drawing more walks than strikeouts. What Wood lacks is power, with only one home run and 10 extra-base hits in 83 games with Wisconsin. and he seemed fatigued toward the end of the year. Wood projects to stick at catcher, where he moves well and has an average arm, though he threw out just 23% of basestealers.
THE FUTURE: Wood's ability to control the strike zone and put balls in play give him a chance at a big league role—likely as a backup catcher—if he can find a way to tap into more power.

Year	Age	Club (League)	Level	AVG	G	AB	R	H	2B	3B	HR	RBI	BB	SO	SB	OBP	SLG
2023	22	Carolina (CAR)	A	.293	25	82	13	24	7	0	3	20	26	15	1	.468	.488
2023	22	Wisconsin (MWL)	A+	.242	83	306	28	74	8	1	1	43	47	53	2	.349	.284
Minor League Totals				.252	110	393	41	99	15	1	4	64	73	68	3	.375	.326

29 FILIPPO DI TURI, SS

HIT: 40. **POW:** 20. **RUN:** 45. **FLD:** 45. **ARM:** 60. **BA Grade:** 45. **Risk:** Extreme.

Born: November 9, 2005. **B-T:** B-R. **HT:** 5-11. **WT:** 165. **Signed:** Venezuela, 2023. **Signed by:** Jose Rodriguez.

TRACK RECORD: When the international signing period opened on Jan. 15, 2023, the Brewers signed there players to bonuses of at least $1 million, with Di Turi landing a $1.3 million deal. He showed a mature offensive approach in his pro debut en route to becoming a Dominican Summer League all-star.

SCOUTING REPORT: Di Turi has a discerning eye at the plate. He tracks pitches well, recognizes spin early and doesn't swing at many pitches outside the strike zone, drawing more walks than strikeouts in his pro debut. His bat-to-ball skills are good from both sides of the plate, but it's usually light, shallow contact with minimal power. Di Turi's defensive skills have progressed over the last couple years, with the hands, actions and body control to stick in the infield, though his lack of first-step quickness and range might push him off shortstop. A fringe-average runner with a plus arm, Di Turi split time between shortstop and second base last year and could move all around the infield, with some scouts curious if he could convert to catcher, though the Brewers don't plan to make that move.

THE FUTURE: While he will probably never be a slugger, getting stronger to develop more power will be critical for Di Turi's development. He will jump to the Rookie-level Arizona Complex League in 2024.

Year	Age	Club (League)	Level	AVG	G	AB	R	H	2B	3B	HR	RBI	BB	SO	SB	OBP	SLG
2023	17	DSL Brewers 2	Rk	.282	52	181	35	51	9	2	0	27	38	32	12	.414	.354
Minor League Totals				.282	52	181	35	51	9	2	0	27	38	32	12	.414	.354

30 GREGORY BARRIOS, SS

HIT: 30. **POW:** 30. **RUN:** 55. **FLD:** 60. **ARM:** 55. **BA Grade:** 40. **Risk:** High.

Born: April 8, 2004. **B-T:** R-R. **HT:** 6-0. **WT:** 180. **Signed:** Venezuela, 2021.
Signed by: Jose Rodriguez/Fernando Veracierto.

TRACK RECORD: Barrios stood out for his glove when the Brewers signed him out of Venezuela for $1 million when he was 16 in Jan. 2021. A switch-hitter at the time, Barrios hit exclusively from the right side in 2022 and made his full-season debut in 2023 with Low-A Carolina, where he continued to shine in the field, though with muted results at the plate.

SCOUTING REPORT: Barrios is the best defensive shortstop in the Brewers' farm system and one of the better defensive shortstops in the minors. He's a smart, instinctive defender with good body control and easy actions. He's an above-average runner who can make the acrobatic, highlight-reel plays with his quick reactions, soft hands and swift exchange to a tick above-average arm, with the internal clock to slow the game down. The key for Barrios will be what he does offensively. He has a short, balanced swing and one of the lowest swing-and-miss rates in the system against pitches in the strike zone. However, he's an aggressive hitter who walked just 5% of the time in 2023 and doesn't have much bat speed or power, with only one home run in 184 career games.

THE FUTURE: Barrios has value as a potential plus defender at a premium position with a high-contact bat, but getting stronger to be able to do more damage on contact will be essential for Barrios.

Year	Age	Club (League)	Level	AVG	G	AB	R	H	2B	3B	HR	RBI	BB	SO	SB	OBP	SLG
2023	19	Carolina (CAR)	A	.232	106	410	52	95	20	3	1	37	24	60	32	.283	.302
Minor League Totals				.243	184	686	104	167	29	5	1	69	55	104	54	.306	.305

Minnesota Twins

BY J.J. COOPER

While it ended in frustration, the Twins' 2023 season was a clear success.

The Twins not only ended an 18-game postseason losing streak, but they swept the Blue Jays in the Wild Card Series to win their first playoff series since 2002.

Minnesota was the best team in a very weak American League Central, but more importantly, thanks to the recent additions of Sonny Gray and Pablo Lopez, the team had the starting pitching to go head-to-head against other playoff teams—something that had clearly been lacking in many of the Twins' quick playoff exits.

Minnesota will no longer need to hear about 0-18, but producing a solid follow-up in 2024 will be a challenge. Gray and Kenta Maeda, two-fifths of the rotation, quickly left in free agency. While many MLB teams face revenue concerns because of the steady decline of regional sports networks, it's a present challenge for the Twins, who did not have a local TV contract for 2024 as of mid December.

With so much revenue uncertainty, Twins president Derek Falvey has indicated that the team's payroll will decrease in 2024. That means the depth that helped the Twins survive multiple injuries in 2023 will most likely have to be filled with homegrown youngsters and low-cost additions.

The Twins sacrificed prospect depth in the failed attempt at a playoff run in 2022, as well as the successful run in 2023. Spencer Steer had an excellent rookie season with the Reds, and Christian Encarnacion-Strand joined him in Cincinnati's lineup in the second half. Yennier Cano was one of the best rookie relievers in baseball for the Orioles.

The cupboard was clearly not bare even after those moves. Third baseman Royce Lewis emerged as one of the Twins' stars as a rookie, while second baseman Edouard Julien showed he can get on base in the majors, just like he did in the minors. Matt Wallner's power is a nice addition to the outfield, and Louie Varland became the latest late-round pitcher to find his way to Minnesota as well.

Thanks in part to winning a surprise lottery pick in 2023, the Twins' farm system is still in solid shape. First-round picks Walker Jenkins and Brooks Lee form an excellent top two, and while the team's pitching depth is less than it was a few years ago, there are a number of potential role players at the upper levels of the system.

But the best news for the Twins is that they still play in the AL Central.

The AL Central hasn't had two teams finish with winning records in a full 162-game season since 2019.

Third baseman Royce Lewis showed the impact that made him the 2017 No. 1 overall pick.

CARMEN MANDATO/GETTY IMAGES

PROJECTED 2027 LINEUP

Catcher	Ryan Jeffers	30
First Base	Edouard Julien	28
Second Base	Brooks Lee	26
Third Base	Royce Lewis	28
Shortstop	Carlos Correa	32
Left Field	Emmanuel Rodriguez	24
Center Field	Walker Jenkins	22
Right Field	Matt Wallner	29
Designated Hitter	Byron Buxton	33
No. 1 Starter	Pablo Lopez	31
No. 2 Starter	Louie Varland	29
No. 3 Starter	David Festa	27
No. 4 Starter	Marco Raya	24
No. 5 Starter	C.J. Culpepper	26
Closer	Jhoan Duran	29

The Tigers are on the rise, but they still have many lineup holes. The Guardians have remained semi-competitive, but their payroll constraints make the Twins seem like a big-market club. The White Sox and Royals are both dealing with the after effects of rebuilds that failed to take.

Thanks to Lopez, the Twins have a front-of-the-rotation starter. The return of Chris Paddack last September offered hints that he will be able to fill Maeda's role in the rotation in 2024. It will be tougher to replace Gray, but Joe Ryan, Bailey Ober and Varland give the team decent rotation depth.

It will be hard for the Twins to repeat the success of 2023. But if they can be as good, that might be enough to get them back to the postseason. ∎

MINNESOTA TWINS

TOP 2024 CONTRIBUTORS	RANK
1. Brooks Lee, SS/2B	2
2. Austin Martin, 2B/OF	9

BREAKOUT PROSPECTS	RANK
1. Luke Keaschall, 2B	11
2. Dameury Pena, 2B	27

SOURCE OF TOP 30 TALENT			
Homegrown	26	Acquired	4
College	14	Trade	3
Junior college	0	Rule 5 draft	0
High school	7	Independent league	0
Nondrafted free agent	0	Free agent/waivers	1
International	5		

LF
Yoyner Fajardo
Jayson Bass

CF
Austin Martin (9)
Yasser Mercedes (18)
DaShawn Keirsey Jr. (21)
Michael Helman (30)
Ariel Castro

RF
Walker Jenkins (1)
Emmanuel Rodriguez (3)
Kala'i Rosario (13)
Brandon Winokur (15)

3B
Rafael Cruz
Moises Lopez

SS
Danny De Andrade (12)
Noah Miller (22)
Jose Salas
Hendry Chivilli

2B
Brooks Lee (2)
Tanner Schobel (7)
Luke Keaschall (11)
Dameury Pena (27)
Ben Ross
Bryan Acuna
Will Holland

1B
Yunior Severino (19)
Jose Rodriguez (20)
Chris Williams
Aaron Sabato

C
Jair Camargo (25)
Andrew Cossetti (26)
Noah Cardenas
Daniel Pena
Patrick Winkel
Carlos Silva

LHP

LHSP	LHRP
Connor Prielipp (16)	Kody Funderburk (23)
	Brent Headrick (29)

RHP

RHSP	RHRP
David Festa (4)	Matt Canterino (6)
Marco Raya (5)	Cory Lewis (17)
C.J. Culpepper (8)	Jordan Balazovic (24)
Charlee Soto (10)	Simeon Woods Richardson (28)
Zebby Matthews (14)	Pierson Ohl
	Ronny Henriquez
	Andrew Morris
	Tanner Hall
	Sean Mooney

1 WALKER JENKINS, OF

Born: February 19, 2005. **B-T:** L-R. **Ht.:** 6-3. **Wt.:** 210.
Drafted: HS—Southport, NC, 2023 (1st round).
Signed by: Ty Dawson.

TOM DIPACE

TRACK RECORD: As rising juniors, Jenkins and Max Clark battled for the title of best high school prospect in the 2023 draft class. A year later when the draft arrived, the debate seemed no closer to a resolution. A hamate injury slowed Jenkins during the summer, but he went out and performed week after week during the spring at South Brunswick High to stamp himself as an elite prospect. Jenkins is the bigger and stronger of the two, with a typical right fielder's profile thanks to his bat speed, strength and power. Deciding which player is better will be a tough call for years to come, but the Twins' decision on draft day was rather easy. They picked fifth in a draft that was viewed as having a five-player top tier. The fact that the Twins could pick Jenkins was because of a few lucky bounces of ping-pong balls in the draft lottery. Minnesota landed the No. 5 pick despite having less than 2% odds to win a top-six pick. Under the previous draft format, the Twins would have picked 13th. Negotiations with Jenkins came down to the July 25 signing deadline, but he agreed to a Twins-record $7.144 million bonus. Despite the late start, he had an impressive pro debut in which he finished with 14 multi-hit games out of 26.

SCOUTING REPORT: Jenkins is one of the toolsiest players the Twins have drafted in the 21st century. His exceptional bat speed gives him the potential to develop into a nearly plus-plus power hitter. He's a relatively polished hitter as well. Coming into this senior year, there were some concerns that he sold out too much for power, but those concerns have been somewhat allayed by Jenkins' ability to string together consistent at-bats, something that was apparent in his brief pro debut. He has above-average hand-eye coordination and excellent timing. Jenkins also showed that he runs well enough to make center field an option. A team may eventually have a better center fielder who pushes Jenkins to right, but his reads and range are above-average in right and average for center, giving him a chance to stay up the middle early in his pro career. He has a plus arm.

THE FUTURE: Jenkins got a brief taste of the Florida State League at Low-A Fort Myers to end 2023. While he may begin 2024 there, he's likely to also get a lot of time in High-A Cedar Rapids if he progresses as expected. Jenkins has drawn comparisons to Austin Meadows, but some veteran scouts compare him to Josh Hamilton, another North Carolina prep outfielder. Jenkins has the tools and skills to become a foundational player for the Twins. The early reviews from his pro debut are glowing, and if anything his star is even brighter than it was pre-draft. ■

BA GRADE | SCOUTING GRADES

60 Risk: High

Hit: 60. Power: 65. Run: 55.
Field: 55. Arm: 60.

Projected future grades on 20-80 scouting scale

BEST TOOLS

BATTING

Best Hitter for Average	Brooks Lee
Best Power	Emmanuel Rodriguez
Best Strike-Zone Judgment	Austin Martin
Fastest Baserunner	DaShawn Keirsey
Best Athlete	Walker Jenkins

PITCHING

Best Fastball	Zebby Matthews
Best Curveball	Jordan Balazovic
Best Slider	Marco Raya
Best Changeup	Samuel Perez
Best Control	Zebby Matthews

FIELDING

Best Defensive Catcher	Noah Cardenas
Best Defensive Infielder	Noah Miller
Best Infield Arm	Noah Miller
Best Defensive Outfielder	DaShawn Keirsey
Best Outfield Arm	Dylan Neuse

Year	Age	Club (League)	Level	AVG	G	AB	R	H	2B	3B	HR	RBI	BB	SO	SB	OBP	SLG
2023	18	FCL Twins	Rk	.333	14	54	6	18	3	1	2	12	5	8	4	.390	.537
2023	18	Fort Myers (FSL)	A	.392	12	51	10	20	2	3	1	10	4	6	2	.446	.608
Minor League Totals				.362	26	105	16	38	5	4	3	22	9	14	6	.417	.571

2 BROOKS LEE, SS

HIT: 60. **POW:** 50. **RUN:** 50. **FLD:** 50. **ARM:** 50. **BA Grade:** 55. **Risk:** Medium.

Born: February 14, 2001. **B-T:** B-R. **HT:** 6-2. **WT:** 205.
Drafted: Cal Poly, 2022 (1st round). **Signed by:** Brian Tripp.
BACKGROUND: Lee was born to be a baseball player. His grandfather Tom Lee was a Cal Poly baseball coach. His uncle Terry was the Giants' 1974 first-round pick, and Brooks himself is the son of long-time Cal Poly coach Larry Lee. In fact, Brooks is named in honor of Orioles Hall of Fame third baseman Brooks Robinson. Lee played for his father for three years at Cal Poly. He fell to eighth overall in the 2022 draft, where the Twins scooped him up and signed him for $5,675,000. He spent most of 2023 at Double-A Wichita before a late bump to Triple-A St. Paul.
SCOUTING REPORT: Lee is a prospect who stands out more because he's a well-rounded player with few weaknesses rather than any one outlier tool. He's not particularly twitchy, but the game seems to move a little slower for him than most. He's a polished hitter from both sides of the plate, though his lefthanded swing is a little shorter and more fluid than his righthanded one. Lee will never be a slugger, but his ability to make consistent contact and produce bushels of doubles leads scouts to expect that he'll develop average power. Lee isn't particularly rangy, but his internal clock is excellent, and he is reliable, which makes him playable as an average shortstop. He has a knack for getting just enough on the throw to beat the runner. He's average at third base as well. He's yet to play second base as a pro, but some scouts think that will be his best position eventually, and that he could be above-average there, because his arm fits better with a shorter throw. He is an average runner.
THE FUTURE: Lee missed time with back and hamstring injuries as an amateur, but he's been healthy so far as a pro. He should begin 2024 at Triple-A, but his versatility and polish should get him to Minnesota at some point. With Carlos Correa and Royce Lewis established, second base seems like his clearest path.

Year	Age	Club (League)	Level	AVG	G	AB	R	H	2B	3B	HR	RBI	BB	SO	SB	OBP	SLG
2023	22	Wichita (TL)	AA	.292	87	349	63	102	31	0	11	61	41	63	6	.365	.476
2023	22	St. Paul (IL)	AAA	.237	38	152	20	36	8	3	5	23	15	28	1	.304	.428
Minor League Totals				.281	156	623	100	175	45	3	20	99	72	111	7	.355	.459

3 EMMANUEL RODRIGUEZ, OF

HIT: 50. **POW:** 65. **RUN:** 55. **FLD:** 50. **ARM:** 60. **BA Grade:** 55 **Risk:** High.

Born: February 28, 2003. **B-T:** L-L. **HT:** 5-10. **WT:** 210.
Signed: Dominican Republic, 2019. **Signed by:** Manuel Luciano.
TRACK RECORD: The Twins made Rodriguez the cornerstone of their 2019 international signing class, signing him for $2.5 million in a class that also included righthander Yennier Cano. Because of the pandemic, he didn't make his pro debut until 2021. In 2022, he got off to a fast start for Low-A Fort Myers before a left knee sprain ended his season early. An abdominal strain slowed him early in 2023 as well. Rodriguez was hitting just .155/.318/.214 at the end of May, but he was one of the best hitters in the Midwest League for the rest of the season. In the playoffs, he hit three home runs in six games to lead the Kernels to the league title.
SCOUTING REPORT: Rodriguez offers a tantalizing combination of risk and reward. He's an on-base machine, but part of the reason he draws so many walks is his extreme passivity. Keeping his bat on his shoulder has been effective against wild Class A pitchers, but as he advances it will more often leave him behind in the count. Rodriguez is exceptional at not swinging at pitches out of the strike zone, but he doesn't have elite bat-to-ball skills. He can be beaten in the zone by a pitcher who can locate, especially if the pitcher mixes his pitches. Rodriguez has plus-plus raw power and has consistently posted some of the best exit velocities in the organization. His body is thickening up, but he remains an above-average runner for now and is an average center fielder. His plus arm would fit in right field.
THE FUTURE: The Twins added Rodriguez to the 40-man roster in November to protect him from the Rule 5 draft. If he can more often ambush pitchers early in counts, he could be one of the better hitters in the Double-A Texas League in 2024. His combination of on-base skills and power gives him middle-of-the-lineup potential.

Year	Age	Club (League)	Level	AVG	G	AB	R	H	2B	3B	HR	RBI	BB	SO	SB	OBP	SLG
2023	20	Cedar Rapids (MWL)	A+	.240	99	354	87	85	13	9	16	55	92	134	20	.400	.463
Minor League Totals				.242	183	616	153	149	23	14	35	103	172	242	40	.413	.495

4 DAVID FESTA, RHP

FB: 55. **SL:** 55. **CHG:** 55. **CTL:** 50. **BA Grade:** 50. **Risk:** High.

Born: March 8, 2000. **B-T:** R-R. **HT:** 6-6. **WT:** 185.
Drafted: Seton Hall, 2021 (13th round). **Signed by:** John Wilson.

TRACK RECORD: The Twins' 2021 draft is shaping up to be excellent, but a lot of the best picks are performing elsewhere now. Four of the Twins' top five picks that year—Chase Petty, Steve Hajjar, Cade Povich and Christian Encarnacion-Strand—have been traded, but Festa, a 13th-round pick out of Seton Hall, has blossomed to become a Twins later-round pitching find. That group includes Bailey Ober, Louie Varland and Josh Winder, none drafted earlier than the seventh round. Festa cruised through both Class A levels in 2022, posting a 2.43 ERA in 103.2 innings, paving the way for a 2023 season spent primarily at Double-A Wichita and also including 12.1 innings at Triple-A St. Paul. He represented the Twins at the Futures Game and threw a scoreless inning with one strikeout.

SCOUTING REPORT: Festa has steadily added velocity in pro ball and now is among the hardest throwers in the Twins' system. He is a skinny-legged skyscraper of a pitcher at 6-foot-6 who attacks hitters by working up in the zone with his above-average 94-95 mph fastball. Against righthanded batters, he follows up with an above-average 86-88 mph slider down and away. For lefthanded batters, Festa favors his above-average changeup down and to his arm side. When he's on, Festa has three swing-and-miss pitches to go with average control.

THE FUTURE: After the Twins lost Sonny Gray and Kenta Maeda to free agency, Festa should be an important part of the team's rotation depth in 2024. He should begin the season in Triple-A St. Paul, but he's just down the road for when the team needs a fill-in starter. That should be preparation for him stepping into a rotation role later in 2024 or 2025.

Year	Age	Club (League)	Level	W	L	ERA	G	GS	IP	H	HR	BB	SO	BB%	SO%	WHIP	AVG
2023	23	Wichita (TL)	AA	3	3	4.39	21	19	80	76	8	33	104	9.6	30.4	1.36	.249
2023	23	St. Paul (IL)	AAA	1	1	2.92	3	3	12	10	1	9	15	16.7	27.8	1.54	.222
Minor League Totals				14	8	3.31	49	40	204	168	15	80	239	9.5	28.4	1.22	.225

5 MARCO RAYA, RHP

FB: 55. **CB:** 55. **SL:** 65. **CHG:** 40. **CTL:** 50. **BA Grade:** 55. **Risk:** Extreme.

Born: August 7, 2002. **B-T:** R-R. **HT:** 6-1. **WT:** 170.
Drafted: HS—Laredo, Texas, 2020 (4th round). **Signed by:** Trevor Brown.

TRACK RECORD: The Twins had just four picks in the shortened five-round 2020 draft. To this point, the top two picks—college hitters Aaron Sabato and Alerick Soularie—have struggled to live up to expectations. But the Twins' two high school picks—Raya, a fourth-rounder; and outfielder Kala'i Rosario, a fifth-rounder—have given that draft hope. Raya's stuff has continually impressed, but his slight, 6-foot-1, 170-pound frame and extremely limited workload has also raised concern. He made 22 starts in 2023, totaling 62.2 innings and carved up High-A competition before meeting more resistance with Double-A Wichita, where he racked up a 5.28 ERA in 29 innings.

SCOUTING REPORT: Raya has some of the best stuff of any Twins' starting pitching prospect. His 94-96 mph fastball has above-average carry at the top of the zone, but his nearly double-plus slider and above-average curveball are even more impressive than his fastball. Raya's slider has above-average horizontal movement, and he has the ability to get swings-and-misses in the zone with it. He actually has better command of his slider than his fastball. Raya is very athletic, helping him field his position like a middle infielder and repeat his delivery. He throws a slower low-80s curveball with plenty of depth. He throws strikes with his curve, which shows above-average potential. He has average control.

THE FUTURE: The biggest question surrounding Raya continues to be his durability. Raya averaged just 45 pitches per start in 2023 and never threw 80 pitches in any pro game. He has yet to throw 60 pitches in any pro game. Until he shows he can turn over a lineup multiple times and maintain his stuff for five-plus innings, it's difficult to know how well he can fare as a starter. His stuff would also excel in the bullpen. While Raya should start 2024 in Wichita, Triple-A St. Paul is beckoning before too long.

Year	Age	Club (League)	Level	W	L	ERA	G	GS	IP	H	HR	BB	SO	BB%	SO%	WHIP	AVG
2023	20	Cedar Rapids (MWL)	A+	0	1	2.94	11	11	34	23	4	8	39	6.1	29.5	0.92	.192
2023	20	Wichita (TL)	AA	0	3	5.28	11	11	29	22	2	14	26	11.2	20.8	1.24	.204
Minor League Totals				3	6	3.54	41	39	128	92	14	45	141	8.7	27.1	1.08	.198

6 MATT CANTERINO, RHP

FB: 60. **SL:** 60. **CHG:** 70. **CTL:** 45. **BA Grade:** 50. **Risk:** High.

Born: December 14, 1997. **B-T:** R-R. **HT:** 6-2. **WT:** 222.
Drafted: Rice, 2019 (2nd round). **Signed by:** Greg Runser.

TRACK RECORD: When he has been healthy, Canterino has shown some of the best stuff in the Twins' organization, but staying healthy has been a struggle. Drafted in the second round in 2019 out of Rice, Canterino tried to rehab an elbow injury multiple times, but the elbow pain kept returning, limiting him to 23 innings in 2021. He finally decided to have Tommy John surgery to reconstruct his elbow ligament in August 2022, which caused him to miss the entire 2023 season.

SCOUTING REPORT: Canterino's delivery has always been effortful and funky, but that's part of what makes him effective. He's not easy to time, especially when he's ripping off plus 94-97 mph fastballs with above-average hop. He has long had a plus slider as well. Before surgery, it was a high-80s pitch that was effective because of its top-tier velocity. As a pro, Canterino found a changeup grip that works for him, and it's now a plus-plus weapon. Until 2022, Canterino showed above-average control, but with a balky elbow, he struggled more to throw strikes. Often, command and feel are slow to return after Tommy John surgery. Despite his funky delivery, Canterino should have at least fringe-average control.

THE FUTURE: It's easy to forget about Canterino because he's been injured, but he's among the organization's best pitching prospects. The Twins will face a decision on how to develop him. If they are willing to move Canterino to the bullpen, he could make a quicker impact, but he has a starter's assortment. He should be ready to go for spring training. After dominating Double-A Wichita in his short stint in 2022, he's ready to head to Triple-A St. Paul.

Year	Age	Club (League)	Level	W	L	ERA	G	GS	IP	H	HR	BB	SO	BB%	SO%	WHIP	AVG
2023	25	Did not play—Injured															
Minor League Totals				2	2	1.48	26	25	85	38	3	35	130	10.5	39.2	0.86	.130

7 TANNER SCHOBEL, 2B/3B

HIT: 55. **POW:** 40. **RUN:** 50. **FLD:** 55. **ARM:** 50. **BA Grade:** 50. **Risk:** High.

Born: June 4, 2001. **B-T:** R-R. **HT:** 5-10. **WT:** 170.
Drafted: Virginia Tech, 2022 (2nd round supplemental). **Signed by:** John Wilson.

TRACK RECORD: After a solid but unremarkable freshman season at Virginia Tech, Schobel impressed in the Cape Cod League, hitting .302 with an .843 OPS in 29 games in 2021. He then rose further up draft boards with a standout sophomore season in 2022 in which he hit .362/.445/.689 with 19 home runs while playing shortstop. The Twins drafted Schobel in the supplemental second round in 2022, signing him for $1 million as the 68th pick as a draft-eligible sophomore.

SCOUTING REPORT: Schobel is the type of well-rounded baseball rat who often figures out a path to a big league role. He's undersized at 5-foot-10, 170 pounds, but he has pull-side power and could run into 10-15 home runs in the big leagues. Schobel's short, simple swing generates plenty of contact. Pitchers don't enjoy facing him, because he strings together focused, consistent at-bats with above-average contact abilities. There's no plus tool on Schobel's scouting report, but he does everything relatively well. Drafted as a shortstop, he is fringy defensively there but playable in a pinch because he is consistent and reliable at handling balls hit his way. Schobel has a quick release that helps his average arm play. He's more comfortable at second base, where he's above-average, and he can play an average third base. He runs well enough that he should be able to add the corner outfield spots as well if the need arises.

BACKGROUND: Schobel shares some similarities with Spencer Steer, the former Twins prospect who was traded to the Reds in 2022 and had an excellent rookie season in 2023. Like Steer, Schobel is a versatile, undersized college infielder who will have to keep proving himself. Schobel's versatility and reliability give him a chance to be an everyday second baseman or a utilityman who can make an offensive impact.

Year	Age	Club (League)	Level	AVG	G	AB	R	H	2B	3B	HR	RBI	BB	SO	SB	OBP	SLG
2023	22	Cedar Rapids (MWL)	A+	.288	77	302	53	87	10	5	14	61	36	64	9	.366	.493
2023	22	Wichita (TL)	AA	.226	49	177	19	40	6	1	2	18	25	40	3	.329	.305
Minor League Totals				.260	158	593	86	154	20	6	17	90	80	130	19	.352	.400

8 C.J. CULPEPPER, RHP

FB: 55. **CB:** 40. **SL:** 55. **CHG:** 45. **CUT:** 50. **CTL:** 50. **BA Grade:** 50. **Risk:** High.

Born: November 2, 2001. **B-T:** R-R. **HT:** 6-3. **WT:** 195.
Drafted: California Baptist, 2022 (13th round). **Signed by:** John Leavitt.
TRACK RECORD: Cal Baptist has become somewhat of a pitching factory. The one-time Division II school has produced big leaguers Trevor Oaks and Tyson Miller as well as an array of additional draftees. Culpepper has quickly emerged as a later-round pick after the Twins drafted him in the 13th round in 2022. In college, Culpepper's stuff dipped when he moved from the bullpen to the rotation, but he showed in his first full season that he is a potential starter. He wore down late in the 2023 season, with 25 of the 40 runs he allowed all year coming in his final 23.2 innings for High-A Cedar Rapids after spending the first half at Low-A Fort Myers.
SCOUTING REPORT: Culpepper quickly demonstrated he's one of the Twins' best starting pitching prospects thanks to his solid stuff and highly varied repertoire. Culpepper throws both a four-seam and two-seam fastball, a changeup, a cutter, a slider and a curveball. He works inside and out to both lefties and righties with a largely east-west approach. His 93-95 mph four-seamer is an above-average pitch, and his 92-93 two-seamer is nearly as effective because of the way it pairs with his above-average mid-80s slider. His slider runs away from righthanders, while his two-seamer runs in on their hands. His average low-90s cutter doesn't move a lot, but he throws it for strikes and it just helps further scramble a hitter's brain. He breaks out his below-average 1-to-7 curveball occasionally, but it often ends below the zone. But because hitters aren't looking for it, it can surprise a hitter.
THE FUTURE: Culpepper has a starter's array of pitches, and the confidence to keep hitters uncomfortable. There's nothing in his arsenal to blow big leaguers away, but his ability to mix such a large number of pitches gives him a shot at being a potential No. 4 starter.

Year	Age	Club (League)	Level	W	L	ERA	G	GS	IP	H	HR	BB	SO	BB%	SO%	WHIP	AVG
2023	21	Fort Myers (FSL)	A	4	3	2.33	11	11	46	32	2	15	53	8.3	29.4	1.01	.196
2023	21	Cedar Rapids (MWL)	A+	2	2	4.99	10	10	40	40	2	16	36	9.0	20.2	1.41	.260
Minor League Totals				6	5	3.52	22	21	87	72	4	32	90	8.8	24.8	1.20	.225

9 AUSTIN MARTIN, 2B/OF

HIT: 55. **POW:** 30. **RUN:** 55. **FLD:** 55. **ARM:** 45. **BA Grade:** 45. **Risk:** Medium.

Born: March 23, 1999. **B-T:** R-R. **HT:** 6-0. **WT:** 185.
Drafted: Vanderbilt, 2020 (1st round). **Signed by:** Nate Murrie (Blue Jays).
TRACK RECORD: Martin was a consistent performer in his three years at Vanderbilt, though the coronavirus pandemic meant his draft season was cut short after just 16 games. The Blue Jays selected him fifth overall in 2020, but dealt him just a year later along with Simeon Woods Richardson to acquire righthander Jose Berrios. Martin's time with the Twins has been marred by injuries. He missed the first three months of the 2023 season with a right elbow sprain. He also missed a month in 2022 because of a sprain of his left, non-throwing elbow.
SCOUTING REPORT: Because he was a top five overall pick and a key part of a big trade, Martin has carried lofty expectations that now appear unrealistic. He's unlikely to develop significant power—he has never hit 20 doubles or 10 home runs in a season—and now projects to have well below-average juice. His throwing issues have made shortstop unrealistic as well. If you focus on what he can do—and if he can stay healthy—he could still be a useful player. Martin has an excellent understanding of the strike zone, which gives him a shot to be an above-average hitter who consistently gets on base. He draws plenty of walks and has some of the best contact skills in the organization, but his approach and swing trade impact for contact. Defensively, Martin is an athletic, rangy second baseman who is also a competent center and left fielder. He's played more in the dirt than in the outfield, but his range and arm appear more comfortable in the grass.
THE FUTURE: The dreams of Martin being an impact shortstop are long gone, but he could be a useful multi-positional player for the Twins in 2024. The hope is that he can be a Willi Castro type who gets on base, steals bases and provides defensive versatility.

Year	Age	Club (League)	Level	AVG	G	AB	R	H	2B	3B	HR	RBI	BB	SO	SB	OBP	SLG
2023	24	FCL Twins	Rk	.429	3	7	2	3	0	0	1	1	2	1	2	.600	.857
2023	24	Fort Myers (FSL)	A	.158	5	19	0	3	0	0	0	1	1	2	1	.200	.158
2023	24	St. Paul (IL)	AAA	.263	59	205	33	54	11	0	6	28	36	43	16	.386	.405
Minor League Totals				.256	252	905	162	232	43	5	14	100	148	184	68	.388	.361

10 CHARLEE SOTO, RHP

FB: 60. **SL:** 55. **CHG:** 60. **CTL:** 45. **BA Grade:** 55. **Risk:** Extreme.

Born: August 31, 2005. **B-T:** B-R. **HT:** 6-3. **WT:** 210.
Drafted: HS—Kissimmee, Fla., 2023 (1st round supplemental). **Signed by:** Brett Dowdy.
TRACK RECORD: A shortstop for much of his amateur career, Soto made a quick transition once he began to focus on pitching at Reborn Christian Academy outside Orlando. He leapt up teams' pref lists when his velocity jumped from the low 90s as a rising junior to the high 90s over the 2022 summer showcase circuit as a rising senior. That velocity spike made Soto's already impressive changeup even more effective. The Twins drafted Soto 34th overall in the supplemental first round of the 2023 draft. He signed for a slot bonus of $2.48 million, which was one of the larger bonuses the Twins have handed out for a high school pitcher.
SCOUTING REPORT: Unlike many young fireballers, Soto showed true conviction in his changeup, often doubling up on it. At his best, he shows feel for pitching to go with his stuff. Soto was a little inconsistent in the spring, but at his best he showed exceptional velocity and advanced savvy as one of the younger pitchers in the 2023 draft class. Soto may eventually touch 100 mph, but his fastball is unlikely to be his best pitch. While it has premium velocity, it's not expected to miss a ton of bats in pro ball because it has relatively average movement. His plus 84-88 mph changeup is a present weapon. It has sink, fade and deception. Soto also throws a high-80s slider that's also an above-average pitch. Soto's delivery is clean, but like many young pitchers, he needs to improve his fringe-average control.
THE FUTURE: The Twins didn't have Soto pitch in any official games after he signed, so he'll make his pro debut in 2024, likely for Low-A Fort Myers. Soto will pitch almost all of the 2024 season as an 18-year-old. He has present physicality and polish, so he offers a pretty well-rounded package.

Year	Age	Club (League)	Level	W	L	ERA	G	GS	IP	H	HR	BB	SO	BB%	SO%	WHIP	AVG
2023	17	Did not play															

11 LUKE KEASCHALL, 2B

HIT: 55. **POW:** 40. **RUN:** 55. **FLD:** 50. **ARM:** 50. **BA Grade:** 50. **Risk:** High.

Born: August 5, 2002. **B-T:** R-R. **HT:** 6-1. **WT:** 190. **Drafted:** Arizona State, 2023, (2nd round).
Signed by: Chandler Wagoner.
TRACK RECORD: After winning West Coast Conference freshman of the year in the first of two excellent seasons at San Francisco, Keaschall transferred to Arizona State for his junior season. It paid off as he more than doubled his home run total while hitting .353. He made an immediate impact as a pro, got on base and stole 11 bags in 11 tries.
SCOUTING REPORT: Keaschall is a well-rounded player. He can play numerous positions and is an above-average runner, but it's his bat that most interests evaluators. He has a long track record of hitting with a short and quick swing that produces plenty of contact and low strikeout rates. He should be able to produce .270-.280 batting averages, low strikeout rates and plenty of doubles. His below-average power relies on him getting pitches to pull, but he showed more pop than expected with a wood bat in his pro debut. Keaschall played shortstop at San Francisco and second base at Arizona State, and second, third and center as a Twin. His funky arm action and fringe-average arm limit him in the infield, but his hands are soft and he makes the routine play.
THE FUTURE: Most who watch Keaschall seem to fall in love with his ability to make whatever team he plays for better. He seems to be a favorite of most scouts who see him. No one is sure exactly where he'll end up defensively, but there's plenty of belief he'll hit and figure out a way to make an impact.

Year	Age	Club (League)	Level	AVG	G	AB	R	H	2B	3B	HR	RBI	BB	SO	SB	OBP	SLG
2023	20	FCL Twins	Rk	.143	3	7	4	1	0	0	0	0	2	2	2	.500	.143
2023	20	Fort Myers (FSL)	A	.292	20	72	20	21	8	1	1	9	15	20	8	.426	.472
2023	20	Cedar Rapids (MWL)	A+	.313	8	32	5	10	2	0	2	6	2	3	1	.353	.563
Minor League Totals				.288	31	111	29	32	10	1	3	15	19	25	11	.414	.477

12 DANNY DE ANDRADE, SS

HIT: 50. **POW:** 40. **RUN:** 50. **FLD:** 50. **ARM:** 60. **BA Grade:** 50. **Risk:** High.

Born: April 10, 2004. **B-T:** R-R. **HT:** 5-11. **WT:** 173. **Signed:** Venezuela, 2021. **Signed by:** Fred Guerrero/Luis Lajara.
TRACK RECORD: The Twins made De Andrade their top target in 2021 and signed him for $2.2 million. Even then, he was more of a skilled baseball player than a player with massive tools, and that's become

even more true as he's developed as a pro. De Andrade was one of the better hitters in the Florida State League in 2023, where he finished in the top 10 in extra base hits, runs and total bases. De Andrade's younger brother Sebastian is now a catching prospect in the Mariners' organization after signing in 2023.
SCOUTING REPORT: De Andrade isn't particularly twitchy, but he has proven to be a solid-average short-stop thanks to his plus arm and solid footwork. He can play a little deeper than most. He's a leader on the field, and plays with a steady intensity. He has skinny legs now, but there's room to fill out which may eventually push him to second or third base. Offensively, he's vulnerable to a good slider, and his swing decisions need to improve, but he rarely misses a hittable pitch in the strike zone. He has a pull-heavy approach—almost all of his home runs went to left or left center field.
THE FUTURE: De Andrade has been a slow-and-steady developing middle infielder, but he's showing the baseball acumen to develop into at least a useful multi-position infielder, and he could be a future regular if his bat continues to develop.

Year	Age	Club (League)	Level	AVG	G	AB	R	H	2B	3B	HR	RBI	BB	SO	SB	OBP	SLG
2023	19	Fort Myers (FSL)	A	.244	105	394	72	96	21	3	11	67	58	103	20	.354	.396
Minor League Totals				.248	203	750	115	186	43	5	15	106	92	164	30	.346	.379

13 KALA'I ROSARIO, OF

HIT: 40. **POW:** 60. **RUN:** 45. **FLD:** 50. **ARM:** 60. **BA Grade:** 50. **Risk:** High.

Born: July 2, 2002. **B-T:** R-R. **HT:** 6-0. **WT:** 205. **Drafted:** HS—Hilo, Hawaii, 2020 (5th round). **Signed by:** John Leavitt.
TRACK RECORD: If you draft a high school position player from Hawaii, you'll need to have some patience. Even if they played in summer showcases, most prep hitters from the islands usually have to catch up to the level of competition in pro ball. Shane Sasaki, a 2019 Rays pick, blossomed in 2022 in his third pro season. A similar timetable played out for Rosario, as the 2020 draftee became the Midwest League MVP in 2023.
SCOUTING REPORT: Rosario has always had two exceptional tools: he has plus-plus raw power and a plus arm that makes him a prototypical right fielder. After hitting 21 home runs for Cedar Rapids, he tied for the Arizona Fall League lead with seven home runs, but he also struck out 33% of the time. Rosario got to his power much more consistently in 2023, thanks in part to a shortened stride that helped his timing, as well as better pitch recognition. He remains a hitter with clear holes in his swing with little adjustability. If a pitcher tries to challenge Rosario on the inner third or at the top of the zone, Rosario will feast—he's adept at hitting elevated fastballs. But a pitcher who can work down and away to Rosario doesn't have much to worry about. He's an average defender and fringe-average runner with that cannon of an arm.
THE FUTURE: Rosario has made big strides already, but he needs to continue to make big improvements to get to a future MLB regular role. His power is legitimate, but as he heads to Double-A Wichita, he'll need to make more contact.

Year	Age	Club (League)	Level	AVG	G	AB	R	H	2B	3B	HR	RBI	BB	SO	SB	OBP	SLG
2023	20	Cedar Rapids (MWL)	A+	.252	118	445	71	112	27	3	21	94	75	157	2	.364	.467
Minor League Totals				.251	278	1006	156	253	58	10	38	180	128	359	13	.344	.442

14 ZEBBY MATTHEWS, RHP

FB: 55. **SL:** 50. **CB:** 45. **CHG:** 45. **CUT:** 55. **CTL:** 60. **BA Grade:** 50. **Risk:** High.

Born: May 22, 2000. **B-T:** R-R. **HT:** 6-5. **WT:** 225. **Drafted:** Western Carolina, 2022 (8th round). **Signed by:** Ty Dawson.
TRACK RECORD: There has never been a big leaguer named Zebby. But Daniel Zebulon Matthews could become the first Zebby to the bigs, which is an impressive development of yet another later-round Twins pitching find. Matthews had a solid frame and fastball at Western Carolina, but he moved to the bullpen late in his draft year to help the team's chances. As a pro, he's figured out how to separate his cutter and slider, which has turned him from a fringe prospect to one worth keeping an eye on.
SCOUTING REPORT: A massive righthander who seems to be larger than his listed 6-foot-5, 225 pounds, Matthews doesn't have a plus pitch, but he has five different ones he's comfortable throwing regularly with plus control. Because of that, it's easy to like his chances to develop into a back-of-the-rotation starter or multi-inning reliever. His development of that 90 mph cutter helped unlock another level for Matthews as a starter. The cutter gives him a weapon to keep lefties off balance, while the horizontal movement on his sweepy slider runs away from righthanded hitters. His above-average four-seam fastball touches 96 mph and sits at 93-94, and he mixes in a fringe-average curveball and changeup as well.
THE FUTURE: Matthews' dominance at Low-A Fort Myers turned into effectiveness at High-A Cedar Rapids. He'll be 24 for most of 2024, so there's reason to start to speed his development.

Year	Age	Club (League)	Level	W	L	ERA	G	GS	IP	H	HR	BB	SO	BB%	SO%	WHIP	AVG
2023	23	Fort Myers (FSL)	A	3	1	2.56	8	7	39	31	1	5	53	3.3	35.3	0.93	.217
2023	23	Cedar Rapids (MWL)	A+	4	2	4.59	14	13	67	65	13	10	59	3.6	21.5	1.13	.248
Minor League Totals				7	3	3.75	24	20	108	97	14	15	118	3.5	27.2	1.04	.234

15 BRANDON WINOKUR, OF/SS

HIT: 40. **POW:** 55. **RUN:** 55. **FLD:** 55. **ARM:** 60. **BA Grade:** 50. **Risk:** Extreme.

Born: December 16, 2004. **B-T:** R-R. **HT:** 6-5. **WT:** 210. **Drafted:** HS—Huntington Beach, Calif., 2023 (3rd round).
Signed by: John Leavitt.
TRACK RECORD: Winokur was one of the more interesting draft prospects on the West Coast. If you liked him, his athletic lanky build and present power made him an alluring future right fielder or third baseman. If you didn't, you worried that inconsistencies in his swing and his struggles to catch up to top-notch fastballs could lead to too many strikeouts. The Twins were willing to gamble on Winokur's potential and spent $1.5 million to buy him out of his UCLA commitment.
SCOUTING REPORT: The Twins' selections of Walker Jenkins and Luke Keaschall were viewed as some of the safest picks in the draft at their respective positions. In righthander Charlee Soto and Winokur, the Twins also took some big swings at the top of the draft. Winokur had some of the best raw power in the draft class, but there are plenty of scouts who think he'll have to simplify his swing and tone down a lot of early movement and a big leg kick to get to his 25+ home run potential. The Twins played Winokur nearly equally between center field and shortstop in his debut. Very few believe he'll stay at shortstop for long, and as he fills out he's most likely a right fielder or third baseman. His plus arm works at either spot, and his athleticism and quickness could help him stick in the dirt.
THE FUTURE: Winokur showed the power and strikeouts that were expected in his brief pro debut with nine extra-base hits and a 32% strikeout rate. He's got a chance to develop into one of the best prospects in the Twins' system, but it will take a lot of work in the batting cage to get there.

Year	Age	Club (League)	Level	AVG	G	AB	R	H	2B	3B	HR	RBI	BB	SO	SB	OBP	SLG
2023	18	FCL Twins	Rk	.288	17	66	14	19	5	0	4	17	4	23	0	.338	.545
Minor League Totals				.288	17	66	14	19	5	0	4	17	4	23	0	.338	.545

16 CONNOR PRIELIPP, LHP

FB: 55. **SL:** 60. **CHG:** 50. **CTL:** 50. **BA Grade:** 50. **Risk:** Extreme.

Born: January 10, 2001. **B-T:** L-L. **HT:** 6-2. **WT:** 210. **Drafted:** Alabama, 2022 (2nd round). **Signed by:** Matt Williams.
TRACK RECORD: If you saw Prielipp on the right day, he has been one of those pitchers whose dominance sticks in your brain. Prielipp has flashed the ability to be a front-of-the-rotation starter in his best healthy moments. He began his college career by throwing 26 scoreless innings and appeared to be in the mix to be the No. 1 pick in the 2022 draft. Unfortunately for Prielipp, those moments have been exceedingly fleeting. Since that scoreless streak, he's thrown just 8.2 innings in the past two seasons. He was shut down because of elbow soreness and had Tommy John surgery in 2021. He pitched in instructional league in 2022 and spring training in 2023, but had further elbow soreness. When a rehab stint ended because of more elbow soreness, he eventually needed internal brace surgery to reinforce his elbow ligament.
SCOUTING REPORT: Until Prielipp gets back on the mound and shows he can handle a starting pitcher's workload, it's hard to have a comfortable projection on his long-term potential. Prielipp has thrown less than 40 innings in the past four seasons, so he's got a lot of catching up to do. Pre-injury, he had a plus fastball and a plus-plus slider with above-average control, but it's difficult to feel confident that he'll shrug off four seasons of rust and injuries with no ill effects.
THE FUTURE: Internal brace surgery usually has a six-month timetable to return to action, so Pirelipp should get to show what he can do in 2024. If he makes a full recovery from his multiple elbow surgeries, he has the highest ceiling of any other pitcher in the Twins system.

Year	Age	Club (League)	Level	W	L	ERA	G	GS	IP	H	HR	BB	SO	BB%	SO%	WHIP	AVG
2023	22	FCL Twins	Rk	0	0	6.75	1	1	3	3	0	2	4	15.4	30.8	1.88	.300
2023	22	Cedar Rapids (MWL)	A+	0	0	6.75	1	1	4	5	0	2	3	10.5	15.8	1.75	.294
Minor League Totals				0	0	7.50	2	2	7	8	0	4	7	12.5	21.9	2.00	.296

17 CORY LEWIS, RHP

FB: 50. **CB:** 45. **SL:** 45. **CHG:** 45. **KNUCKLE:** 55. **CTL:** 50. **BA Grade:** 45. **Risk:** High.

Born: November 9, 2000. **B-T:** R-R. **HT:** 6-5. **WT:** 220. **Drafted:** UC Santa Barbara, 2022 (9th round). **Signed by:** Brian Tripp.

TRACK RECORD: Lewis was UC Santa Barbara's Friday starter, and fellow Big West alum and now Twins teammate Brooks Lee described him as one of the toughest pitchers he's faced. The Twins picked him in the ninth round, in part because of his excellent fastball movement and feel for pitching, but also because he had an intriguing knuckleball. His .198 opponent average was one of the best in the minors among starters with 100+ innings.

SCOUTING REPORT: While most knuckleballers throw that pitch as their main weapon, Lewis has a four-pitch repertoire that would give him a chance even if he didn't throw his knuckler. Adding in the knuckleball is what turns a tough at-bat into a brain-scrambler. Lewis' average fastball has below-average velocity at 90-92 mph but exceptional carry. He has three fringe-average secondary offerings including a low-80s top-down curveball, a low-80s bullet slider that doesn't move much but works because of everything else he has and a 79-80 mph changeup. None of those are true weapons, but he throws all of them enough to keep them in a hitter's head. And then there's the knuckleball. It's the hardest knuckleball anyone has really seen. It dances like a knuckler, but at 80-84 mph, it comes in at slider speed. He only throws it a few times a game, but it's a weapon because hitters usually have never seen anything like it.

THE FUTURE: Lewis is a hard pitcher to peg. Some scouts see a crafty but vanilla starting pitching prospect who will be challenged by more advanced hitters. Others see a pitcher who already has multiple ways to get hitters out as well as a knuckleball that makes him a truly unique pitcher.

Year	Age	Club (League)	Level	W	L	ERA	G	GS	IP	H	HR	BB	SO	BB%	SO%	WHIP	AVG
2023	22	Fort Myers (FSL)	A	4	3	2.75	9	9	39	26	3	15	55	9.2	33.7	1.04	.179
2023	22	Cedar Rapids (MWL)	A+	5	1	2.32	13	13	62	48	3	18	63	7.2	25.3	1.06	.211
Minor League Totals				9	4	2.50	22	22	101	74	6	33	118	8.0	28.6	1.06	.198

18 YASSER MERCEDES, OF

HIT: 45. **POW:** 55. **RUN:** 60. **FLD:** 60. **ARM:** 45. **BA Grade:** 50. **Risk:** Extreme.

Born: November 16, 2004. **B-T:** R-R. **HT:** 6-2. **WT:** 175. **Signed:** Dominican Republic, 2021. **Signed by:** Fred Guerrero.

TRACK RECORD: The Twins' top target in the 2021 international class, Mercedes had an excellent debut in the Dominican Summer League in 2022 but a promotion to the Florida Complex League exposed some rawness to his approach. He has some of the best tools in the organization, but he's going to have to develop a better understanding of the strike zone for it to matter. He didn't have a day in the Florida Complex League season where he had a batting average above .225.

SCOUTING REPORT: Mercedes is going to require some patience, but he's one of the few players in the system who could have three plus tools. He shows flashes of becoming a plus defender in center and he has plus speed. He once had an above-average arm as well, but that's a tool that has backed up in pro ball. With his above-average bat speed, he has plus raw power that could help him develop into a competent power hitter as well. But Mercedes' below-average bat-to-ball skills are a detriment for now. He expands out of the zone and makes poor contact on pitches he probably shouldn't be swinging at.

THE FUTURE: The Twins face a tough call. Mercedes may need to return to the Florida Complex League, as it's hard to say he mastered the level in any way, but there's always a worry that players grow stale if they have to repeat the complex leagues where games are played in front of almost no fans on a never-ending routine of Groundhog Days. It has often been described as the level almost designed to sap the love of baseball.

Year	Age	Club (League)	Level	AVG	G	AB	R	H	2B	3B	HR	RBI	BB	SO	SB	OBP	SLG
2023	18	FCL Twins	Rk	.196	25	97	14	19	4	1	4	17	6	23	6	.248	.381
Minor League Totals				.294	66	252	48	74	17	4	8	37	24	58	36	.356	.488

19 YUNIOR SEVERINO, 1B/3B

HIT: 30. **POW:** 60. **RUN:** 30. **FLD:** 40. **ARM:** 50. **BA Grade:** 40. **Risk:** Medium.

Born: November 3, 1999. **B-T:** B-R. **HT:** 6-0. **WT:** 189. **Signed:** Dominican Republic, 2016. **Signed by:** Jonathan Cruz (Braves).

TRACK RECORD: Severino was supposed to help the Braves win a World Series by this point. He was one of the numerous players, topped by Kevin Maitan, who were the vaunted Braves' international class that was declared free agents because of the Braves' rules violations. After missing out on signing Shohei Ohtani, the Twins' consolation prize was they had enough bonus pool remaining to sign Severino for

$2.5 million. After hitting 20 home runs in his first four seasons combined, he hit 19 in 2022. In 2023, he led the minors with 35 homers.

SCOUTING REPORT: When he signed with the Twins, Severino was a relatively live-bodied middle infielder with modest power. But there was an expectation that he would eventually get much bigger and stronger. Officially, he's listed at 189 pounds, but that undersells his weight by at least 30 pounds. That transformation happened in 2022 and 2023. He now has some of the best raw power in the Twins organization. When he stays back and gets his full body into a pitch, he hits some truly majestic home runs that clear batter's eyes and concourses. But he's also become a slow-twitch first baseman who is stretched to be a below-average third baseman. His hands offer reminders that he once could play shortstop, but his range is now quite limited.

THE FUTURE: Severino was added to the 40-man roster in November 2023. There's a chance that his power will help him carve out a useful career as a regular, but a number of scouts see him as a bad-ball hitter whose swing is too grooved to get to that power consistently in the majors. He should start 2024 at Triple-A St. Paul, but could get big league at-bats in 2024 if injuries thin the Twins' corner infield depth.

Year	Age	Club (League)	Level	AVG	G	AB	R	H	2B	3B	HR	RBI	BB	SO	SB	OBP	SLG
2023	23	Wichita (TL)	AA	.287	84	334	56	96	15	2	24	62	36	117	3	.365	.560
2023	23	St. Paul (IL)	AAA	.233	36	133	24	31	2	1	11	22	15	56	0	.320	.511
Minor League Totals				.270	436	1656	252	447	98	11	74	286	190	541	6	.352	.476

20 JOSE RODRIGUEZ, OF

HIT: 45. **POW:** 60. **RUN:** 30. **FLD:** 40. **ARM:** 50. **BA Grade:** 50. **Risk:** Extreme.

Born: June 10, 2005. **B-T:** R-R. **HT:** 6-2. **WT:** 196. **Signed:** Dominican Republic, 2022. **Signed by:** Fred Guerrero.

TRACK RECORD: It's hard to make a name for yourself in baseball as Jose Rodriguez, because there have been more than 80 Jose Rodriguez's who have played professionally, including seven currently. But the Twins' Jose Rodriguez has a shot to be known as a slugger with enough hitting ability to get to his power.

SCOUTING REPORT: Rodriguez has plus-plus raw power and has shown already that he can get to that juice in games. He led the Dominican Summer League in home runs in 2022 and in 2023 his six home runs were good for 10th in the Florida Complex League. Rodriguez will take some big hacks, but he has acceptable bat-to-ball skills and doesn't just grip-and-rip. What's more concerning for Rodriguez's long-term potential is how quickly he's filling out. When he signed, he looked like he could be a solid right fielder. He's gained a lot of weight since and is now a well below-average runner. He started playing some first base and may end up with that and DH as his only options.

THE FUTURE: Rodriguez has plenty of power potential and a decent idea of how to get to it, but he's going to need to work on his conditioning and maintain his already declining speed and agility.

Year	Age	Club (League)	Level	AVG	G	AB	R	H	2B	3B	HR	RBI	BB	SO	SB	OBP	SLG
2023	18	FCL Twins	Rk	.262	49	187	28	49	10	0	6	23	18	41	0	.325	.412
Minor League Totals				.276	104	377	67	104	25	3	19	72	39	93	5	.343	.509

21 DASHAWN KEIRSEY JR., OF

HIT: 40. **POW:** 30. **RUN:** 70. **FLD:** 70. **ARM:** 45. **BA Grade:** 40. **Risk:** Medium.

Born: May 13, 1997. **B-T:** L-L. **HT:** 6-0. **WT:** 195. **Drafted:** Utah, 2018 (4th round). **Signed by:** Andrew Ayers.

TRACK RECORD: A promising wide receiver in high school, Keirsey Jr. quickly realized that his size/speed combination may fit better in baseball. He had an excellent career at Utah, and his speed and defense has been apparent from his first day as a pro, but he's had to work hard to get to a point where he can hit enough to be a potential big leaguer.

SCOUTING REPORT: Keirsey seems to believe that any ball hit in the air in the stadium is catchable. He often proves that true, but it also means that sometimes he's found outfield walls getting in the way. He missed time in college when he fractured and dislocated a hip in a particularly ferocious wall collision that saw him wheeled off the field on a stretcher. Keirsey is a plus-plus defender in center field with a fringe-average arm who could fit as a backup thanks to the expanded 26-man rosters. He also has plus-plus speed and is a threat to steal anytime he's standing on first base. As a hitter, Keirsey has made significant improvements, but there's not a lot of fluidity to his swing and scouts are skeptical as to whether he can consistently hit premium velocity. His 15 home runs in 2023 more than doubled his career totals dating back to 2018, but he's projected as a below-average hitter with well below-average power.

THE FUTURE: Keirsey will turn 27 early in the 2024 season, and he went unpicked in the Rule 5 draft, so this late-bloomer still has skeptics to win over. But with Michael A. Taylor gone and Andrew Stevenson headed to Japan, Keirsey's exceptional defense and speed could help the Twins in a backup or up-and-down role.

Year	Age	Club (League)	Level	AVG	G	AB	R	H	2B	3B	HR	RBI	BB	SO	SB	OBP	SLG
2023	26	Wichita (TL)	AA	.305	91	361	59	110	17	5	13	48	31	93	31	.363	.488
2023	26	St. Paul (IL)	AAA	.264	39	129	20	34	1	3	2	13	19	31	8	.375	.364
Minor League Totals				.261	368	1317	194	344	56	19	29	160	136	351	99	.336	.399

22 NOAH MILLER, SS

HIT: 40. **POW:** 30. **RUN:** 50. **FLD:** 65. **ARM:** 60. **BA Grade:** 45. **Risk:** High.

Born: November 12, 2002. **B-T:** B-R. **HT:** 6-0. **WT:** 185. **Drafted:** HS—Fredonia, Wisc., 2021 (1st round supplemental).
Signed by: Joe Bisenius.

TRACK RECORD: The younger brother of Brewers infielder Owen Miller, Noah has been one of the smoothest, slickest-fielding shortstops in pretty much every league he's played in. That was the case again in 2023 as Miller helped lead Cedar Rapids to the Midwest League title with his range and reliability at shortstop. His bat has yet to catch up to his glove.

SCOUTING REPORT: Miller is a joy to watch play defense. He has above-average range, smooth and flowing actions, soft hands and an innate understanding of where everyone is and where they are going when the ball is put in play. His plus arm allows him to make the play deep in the hole that many shortstops know better than to even attempt. His body control also allows him to quickly get rid of the ball if he leaves his feet. If the Twins needed a shortstop to step in and play solid defense in an emergency role, Miller could handle the job capably. He's also an excellent baserunner despite having only average speed. At the plate, Miller doesn't make pitchers sweat. He can hit a fastball, but even then, he's likely to just line a single. He has a lot of work to do at recognizing and making better contact against breaking balls and changeups and he has very limited power.

THE FUTURE: Miller's defense is hard to criticize, but if he doesn't learn to make a little more offensive impact, it's going to be hard to get to the big leagues. Even defensive wizards like Nick Ahmed and Jose Iglesias showed some offensive acumen in the minors.

Year	Age	Club (League)	Level	AVG	G	AB	R	H	2B	3B	HR	RBI	BB	SO	SB	OBP	SLG
2023	20	Cedar Rapids (MWL)	A+	.223	120	462	71	103	20	5	8	60	58	108	12	.309	.340
Minor League Totals				.220	250	929	144	204	35	10	12	98	143	244	36	.326	.318

23 KODY FUNDERBURK, LHP

FB: 50. **SL:** 55. **CHG:** 40. **CTL:** 50. **BA Grade:** 40. **Risk:** Medium.

Born: November 27, 1996. **B-T:** L-L. **HT:** 6-4. **WT:** 230. **Drafted:** Dallas Baptist, 2018 (15th round).
Signed by: Trevor Brown.

TRACK RECORD: In two years at Mesa (Ariz.) JC, Funderburk was a junior college All-American as a hitter who sometimes pitched. In his only year at Dallas Baptist, he posted a 6.84 ERA and hit .300 with 13 home runs. Even though he looked more like a first baseman, the Twins drafted him as a late-round pitcher. He had a rocky start to full-time pitching, but began to dominate midway through 2022. In his late-season MLB debut, Funderburk posted a 0.75 ERA with nine consecutive scoreless appearances to end his first MLB season. It was an impressive highlight for a former two-way player who embraced the chance to reshape his body to be a pitcher.

SCOUTING REPORT: Funderburk added a sinker as a pro, and it's helped him become a solid reliever. While none of his pitches is dominating, he's a lefty who is equally effective against righties and lefties thanks to a four-seam and fringy mid-80s changeup for righties and a sinker-slider at the bottom of the zone against lefties. His 90-92 mph four-seamer keeps hitters from getting too comfortable in protecting the bottom of the zone and he throws his above-average sinker a tick harder in the 91-93 mph range.

THE FUTURE: Funderburk's career found a new gear as soon as the Twins moved him to the bullpen. He has a solid shot to be a regular in the Twins' 2024 bullpen, and add yet another pitcher to the list of recent Twins' late-round pitching scouting and development success stories.

Year	Age	Club (League)	Level	W	L	ERA	G	GS	IP	H	HR	BB	SO	BB%	SO%	WHIP	AVG
2023	26	Wichita (TL)	AA	1	0	1.00	5	0	9	8	0	6	14	15.0	35.0	1.56	.235
2023	26	St. Paul (IL)	AAA	4	1	2.60	37	2	52	34	1	21	75	10.0	35.7	1.06	.183
2023	26	Minnesota (AL)	MLB	2	0	0.75	11	0	12	6	1	5	19	10.6	40.4	0.92	.146
Minor League Totals				22	13	3.20	115	48	323	279	14	140	363	10.1	26.3	1.30	.229
Major League Totals				2	0	0.75	11	0	12	6	1	5	19	10.6	40.4	0.92	.146

24 JORDAN BALAZOVIC, RHP

FB: 50. **SL:** 55. **CB:** 40. **CHG:** 40. **CTL:** 40. **BA Grade:** 40. **Risk:** Medium.

Born: September 17, 1998. **B-T:** R-R. **HT:** 6-5. **WT:** 215. **Drafted:** HS—Mississauga, Ont., 2016 (5th round).
Signed by: Walt Burrows.

TRACK RECORD: Balazovic's career has had more peaks and valleys than the Rockies. He once was one of the Twins' best young starting pitching prospects but in 2022 he showed up too heavy, saw his stuff take a step back and struggled all year to regain his 2021 form. In 2023, things got worse when he broke his jaw in a fight during spring training. With time running out in his development, the Twins moved him to the pen and he made his MLB debut in June.

SCOUTING REPORT: Balazovic has always had plenty of arm strength. As a reliever, his average fastball settled into the mid 90s and his above-average slider sits in the 85-87 mph range. He'll mix in a high-80s changeup and low-80s curveball as well. If Balazovic's command improves, his stuff is good enough to be an effective reliever, but he misses his spots too often, and there's just nothing here that's good enough to beat hitters when he makes a mistake.

THE FUTURE: Balazovic has already used three options, so it's time for him to stake a consistent claim to a spot in the Twins' bullpen. He's most likely to end up in a lower-leverage role, but with the transient nature of bullpens, he could have stretches where his arm strength helps him get key outs.

Year	Age	Club (League)	Level	W	L	ERA	G	GS	IP	H	HR	BB	SO	BB%	SO%	WHIP	AVG
2023	24	St. Paul (IL)	AAA	1	1	5.32	22	3	46	47	5	32	54	15.2	25.7	1.73	.269
2023	24	Minnesota (AL)	MLB	1	0	4.44	18	0	24	26	5	12	17	11.1	15.7	1.56	.274
Minor League Totals				24	24	4.31	114	82	443	445	49	175	485	9.0	24.9	1.40	.257
Major League Totals				1	0	4.44	18	0	24	26	5	12	17	11.1	15.7	1.56	.274

25 JAIR CAMARGO, C

HIT: 30. **POW:** 55. **RUN:** 40. **FLD:** 40. **ARM:** 55. **BA Grade:** 40. **Risk:** Medium.

Born: July 1, 1999. **B-T:** R-R. **HT:** 5-10. **WT:** 230. **Signed:** Colombia, 2015. **Signed by:** Francisco Cartaya (Dodgers).

TRACK RECORD: Camargo signed with the Dodgers in 2015 and commenced a very slow and steady climb through the minors. He needed three years in rookie ball before he reached full-season ball and the Twins acquired him in the 2020 Kenta Maeda trade. Camargo didn't reach Double-A until his eighth year in pro ball. He had his best year as a pro in 2023 where he hit 21 home runs for St. Paul. He was added to the 40-man roster in November 2023.

SCOUTING REPORT: Camargo's power is his calling card. He hits the ball as hard as nearly anyone in the Twins farm system, and should pile up home runs even if he's struggling to hit for average. He swings at most everything, and his over-aggressiveness leads to plenty of strikeouts. All that would be fine if Camargo's defense was a little better. He's playable, but he's fringe-average as a pitch framer, receiver and blocker. It's not bad enough to make him unplayable, but it means a big league team will usually have a better defender on the roster. His above-average arm is his best defensive asset.

THE FUTURE: Camargo's 2024 depends in large part on external factors. With Ryan Jeffers and Christian Vazquez under contract, Camargo is slated to return to Triple-A St. Paul unless there's a trade or an injury. His defense makes it tough to see him fitting as a typical backup profile, but he's an excellent third catcher option to have sitting in Triple-A.

Year	Age	Club (League)	Level	AVG	G	AB	R	H	2B	3B	HR	RBI	BB	SO	SB	OBP	SLG
2023	23	St. Paul (IL)	AAA	.259	90	332	56	86	16	1	21	63	29	119	2	.323	.503
Minor League Totals				.252	427	1562	213	393	72	8	63	244	96	524	24	.303	.429

26 ANDREW COSSETTI, C

HIT: 40. **POW:** 50. **RUN:** 30. **FLD:** 40. **ARM:** 50. **BA Grade:** 45. **Risk:** High.

Born: January 31, 2000. **B-T:** R-R. **HT:** 6-0. **WT:** 215. **Drafted:** St. Joseph's, 2022 (11th round). **Signed by:** Nick Venuto.

TRACK RECORD: If you want a catcher who seems as invested in a pitcher's success from pitch to pitch as the pitcher himself, Cossetti's your guy. He's an 11th-round grinder who showed his polish at the plate in an impressive 2023 season. Cossetti was a four-year starter at St. Joseph's who slugged over .700 in his final two seasons.

SCOUTING REPORT: Cossetti's bat gives him a chance to hit more than most catchers. Now the question is going to be whether or not his glove is enough to make him a usable backup or even a second-division regular. He understands how to work with pitchers but he's not very athletic which is why he's a below-average defender for now. His willingness to work gives hope that he'll develop into a fringe-average or even average receiver and blocker, but for now, he still has plenty of work to do. He'll flash average pop times, but will also show some below-average ones. As a hitter, Cossetti can be beaten by quality stuff, but he rarely beats himself. He has the ability to yank 15-20 home runs a year if he gets steady playing time, and he'll also draw his walks.

THE FUTURE: Cossetti is the kind of grinder that scouts, coaches and pitchers love. His defense is going to have to keep improving for him to find a way to the big leagues, but he's passed the first test by handling both Class A levels.

Year	Age	Club (League)	Level	AVG	G	AB	R	H	2B	3B	HR	RBI	BB	SO	SB	OBP	SLG
2023	23	Fort Myers (FSL)	A	.330	35	112	20	37	11	1	6	33	22	25	1	.462	.607
2023	23	Cedar Rapids (MWL)	A+	.262	60	195	45	51	12	3	9	30	42	54	0	.406	.492
Minor League Totals				.285	96	309	66	88	23	4	15	63	65	79	1	.427	.531

27 DAMEURY PENA, 2B

HIT: 60. POW: 40. RUN: 45. FLD: 40. ARM: 45. BA Grade: 50. Risk: Extreme.

Born: September 1, 2005. **B-T:** R-R. **HT:** 5-10. **WT:** 150. **Signed:** Dominican Republic, 2023. **Signed by:** Manuel Luciano.

TRACK RECORD: Pena's thumbnail scouting report may sound familiar to Twins fans: he's a second baseman who will have to work to stay there and doesn't really have a chance to play shortstop. His power is modest at best. He doesn't run particularly well. Pretty much everything other than his hitting ability is fringy at best, but he's such a polished, competent hitter that it may not matter, as he's got a chance to hit .300 regularly if he develops as hoped.

SCOUTING REPORT: Pena can really hit. He just missed qualifying, but with a few more plate appearances he would have finished second in the Dominican Summer League in batting average. He has plenty of barrel control and adaptability to his swing, which allows him to make tons of contact. Pitchers quickly learn that getting a swing and miss from Pena is worthy of a celebration—his 10% swing-and-miss rate was best among all Twins minor leaguers with 20 or more plate appearances. It's generally hard to put a plus hit tool on a 18-year-old who has yet to play in the U.S., but Pena inspires a lot of confidence. He should eventually get to below-average power but it's a swing geared for average more than pop. Defensively, he's going to need to take thousands of ground balls. His hands are hard, his range is limited and his arm is fringe-average.

THE FUTURE: Pena is going to need to be an elite hitter to have MLB value, but as Luis Arraez has shown before him, if you can challenge for batting titles, teams can live with a lot of fringe tools otherwise. Pena is more than ready to come to make his stateside debut.

Year	Age	Club (League)	Level	AVG	G	AB	R	H	2B	3B	HR	RBI	BB	SO	SB	OBP	SLG
2023	17	DSL Twins	Rk	.382	39	123	25	47	8	3	0	16	14	9	13	.453	.496
Minor League Totals				.382	39	123	25	47	8	3	0	16	14	9	13	.453	.496

28 SIMEON WOODS RICHARDSON, RHP

FB: 45. SL: 45. CHG: 55. CTL: 40. BA Grade: 40. Risk: Medium.

Born: September 27, 2000. **B-T:** R-R. **HT:** 6-3. **WT:** 210. **Drafted:** HS—Sugar Land, Texas, 2018 (2nd round). **Signed by:** Ray Corbett (Mets).

TRACK RECORD: A second-round pick of the Mets back in 2018, Woods Richardson was one of the youngest players in his draft class and an arm with rapidly improving velocity. He touched 95-97 mph early in his pro career, which enticed the Blue Jays to acquire him in the Marcus Stroman trade in 2019. He was then dealt again, this time with Austin Martin, in the 2021 Jose Berrios trade. He made his MLB debut on April 22, 2023, but after giving up five runs in four innings in a relief appearance, he spent the remainder of the season at Triple-A St. Paul.

SCOUTING REPORT: Woods Richardson's arm speed isn't what it once was, so he now has to survive with fringy stuff. In most starts, he sits at 89-91 mph and rarely tops 92. That's brought down the quality of his fringe-average slider as well, as it lacks the power it once had. He has grown to rely more and more on his above-average low-80s changeup. It has some fade and he's comfortable mixing it in as a right-on-right weapon. Woods Richardson is able to cut his fastball exceptionally well, which does help him avoid the sweet spot and he is an example of a pitcher who has better command than control. He locates his pitches well, but because he has to nibble, he'll pile up walks rather than give in to throw a strike in hitters' counts.

THE FUTURE: If Woods Richardson was sitting at 93-94 instead of 89-91, he would be a viable back-end rotation option. But unless he gets back some of his lost arm speed, he has a very small margin of error, as was apparent in his MLB debut. He should head back to St. Paul, but could get starts or multi-inning relief appearances with the Twins on a fill-in basis.

Year	Age	Club (League)	Level	W	L	ERA	G	GS	IP	H	HR	BB	SO	BB%	SO%	WHIP	AVG
2023	22	St. Paul (IL)	AAA	7	6	4.91	24	22	114	109	13	61	96	12.3	19.3	1.50	.253
2023	22	Minnesota (AL)	MLB	0	0	9.64	1	0	5	7	1	3	5	12.5	20.8	2.14	.350
Minor League Totals				22	24	4.02	95	88	398	345	31	159	440	9.5	26.4	1.27	.230
Major League Totals				0	1	6.52	2	1	10	10	2	5	8	11.4	18.2	1.55	.263

29 BRENT HEADRICK, LHP

FB: 45. **SL:** 45. **SPLT:** 45. **CTL:** 60. **BA Grade:** 40. **Risk:** Medium.

Born: December 17, 1997. **B-T:** L-L. **HT:** 6-6. **WT:** 227. **Drafted:** Illinois State, 2019 (9th round). **Signed by:** Jeff Pohl.

TRACK RECORD: In college Headrick showed he could dominate with guile and modest stuff. He was the Missouri Valley Conference pitcher of the year in 2019 with a fastball that often sat in the high 80s. As a Twin, he's added velocity to now touch 93-94 mph. He was a surprise callup in April 2023 and his first MLB appearance resulted in his first save since he pitched in the Appalachian League in 2019. A starter throughout his minor league career, Headrick pitched exclusively out of the bullpen in the majors.

SCOUTING REPORT: Headrick's profile is the baseball version of vanilla frozen yogurt. He's a Nissan Versa. Teams need dependable low-leverage multi-inning relievers, but it's easy to overlook them to focus on higher-ceiling prospects. Headrick has largely been a starter in the minors, but he only relieved in the majors, and his future MLB role is more likely out of the pen. He doesn't have a plus pitch, and he may not have an average one. He has excellent command of his 91-94 mph fringe-average four-seam fastball and a 79-81 mph fringe-average slider. He's added a low-80s splitter that serves as his changeup, but it's something he uses almost exclusively against righthanded hitters. Headrick throws strikes but without a swing-and-miss pitch he's also quite homer prone.

THE FUTURE: Headrick has long shown he has the durability to carry a starter's workload, but it's hard to see him being one of the Twins' best six or seven starting pitcher options. His more likely role is as a crafty multi-inning reliever who can eat innings. He has multiple options left to bounce back and forth between St. Paul and Minnesota.

Year	Age	Club (League)	Level	W	L	ERA	G	GS	IP	H	HR	BB	SO	BB%	SO%	WHIP	AVG
2023	25	St. Paul (IL)	AAA	4	2	4.68	19	12	75	72	11	26	83	8.1	25.9	1.31	.251
2023	25	Minnesota (AL)	MLB	3	0	6.31	14	0	26	27	7	10	30	8.5	25.6	1.44	.267
Minor League Totals				17	12	3.78	63	52	250	231	34	91	309	8.6	29.1	1.29	.240
Major League Totals				3	0	6.31	14	0	26	27	7	10	30	8.5	25.6	1.44	.267

30 MICHAEL HELMAN, OF/2B

HIT: 50. **POW:** 40. **RUN:** 55. **FLD:** 50. **ARM:** 45. **BA Grade:** 40. **Risk:** Medium.

Born: May 23, 1996. **B-T:** R-R. **HT:** 5-11. **WT:** 195. **Drafted:** Texas A&M, 2018 (11th round). **Signed by:** Greg Runser.

TRACK RECORD: A dislocated shoulder may have kept Helman from making it to the majors in 2023. After a solid 2022 season, he seemed poised to be a useful callup as a backup who could plausibly play four positions. But he dislocated his shoulder sliding headfirst to score on an infield grounder on May 11. That injury kept him sidelined until the end of August. After the season he went to play for Licey in the Dominican Winter League to try to make up for lost at-bats.

SCOUTING REPORT: Helman is the type of well-rounded player who can help a club without having any real standout tool. He's an average hitter with below-average power, and he's proven to be an exceptional basestealer despite only above-average speed. Helman is 48-for-54 on stolen bases in 173 games since the rules were liberalized to encourage more steals. He's an average defender in all three outfield spots, a fringe-average defender at second and a below-average but playable defender in an emergency at shortstop or third base.

THE FUTURE: Helman was unprotected and unpicked in the Rule 5 draft, but he could find his way to Minnesota at some point in 2024. Until then, he'll be one of St. Paul's most valuable players as a solid hitter and baserunner who can play almost anywhere.

Year	Age	Club (League)	Level	AVG	G	AB	R	H	2B	3B	HR	RBI	BB	SO	SB	OBP	SLG
2023	27	Fort Myers (FSL)	A	.421	5	19	7	8	3	1	0	4	3	3	3	.542	.684
2023	27	Wichita (TL)	AA	.227	6	22	2	5	1	0	1	5	1	5	0	.250	.409
2023	27	St. Paul (IL)	AAA	.296	27	108	22	32	7	1	6	31	7	16	5	.356	.546
Minor League Totals				.258	405	1490	257	384	74	12	53	204	149	281	82	.330	.430

New York Mets

BY MATT EDDY

The Mets are embarking on a new direction. Again.

The 2024 season will be the fourth since Steve Cohen assumed ownership of the club. The organization enters the season with its fourth head of baseball operations and third field manager during Cohen's tenure.

This time should be different.

The day after the 2023 season ended, the Mets announced a five-year pact with David Stearns as president of baseball operations. He replaced general manager Billy Eppler, who built a 101-win team in 2022 that dropped to 75 wins in 2023 when injuries and decline visited the oldest roster in the National League—and the highest payroll ever.

The 38-year-old Stearns grew up in New York a Mets fan, as did Cohen, and the union between executive, club and owner was long rumored.

Stearns is most famous as the former Brewers general manager. Between 2017 and 2023, Milwaukee made five postseason appearances in seven years. The 2018 Brewers were Organization of the Year after winning 96 games and coming within one win of the World Series.

The hallmarks of Stearns' Brewers teams were disciplined decision-making, pitching development and a refusal to tank. Stearns inherited a 94-loss Brewers team but never tore things all the way down to improve draft position and exploit bonus pool allowances.

One other key to Stearns' success with the Brewers was his close relationship with manager Craig Counsell. The two prided themselves on "stacking good decisions" to achieve results, often ahead of schedule.

Stearns will look to mimic that symbiotic relationship with Carlos Mendoza, his handpicked manager who replaces Buck Showalter.

A longtime Yankees minor league coach and manager, Mendoza joined the big league staff in 2018 and became bench coach in 2020.

Stearns also hired Eduardo Brizuela, formerly a trusted lieutenant with the Brewers, as a special assistant. He hired former Astros scouting director Kris Gross to head Mets amateur scouting. He hired former Cubs bench coach Andy Green as vice president of player development.

The challenges facing Stearns are myriad. To build a sustainable winner, the Mets need to build organizational depth—especially on the pitching side—and become younger and more athletic to fit the new MLB milieu introduced by rules changes.

Mets minor league pitching development is largely unproven, though it took strides under

TODD KIRKLAND/MLB PHOTOS VIA GETTY IMAGES

Rookie Francisco Alvarez blasted 25 home runs, one of the highest totals ever for a 21-year-old.

PROJECTED 2027 LINEUP

Catcher	Francisco Alvarez	25
First Base	Brett Baty	27
Second Base	Luisangel Acuña	25
Third Base	Ronny Mauricio	26
Shortstop	Francisco Lindor	33
Left Field	Brandon Nimmo	34
Center Field	Jett Williams	23
Right Field	Drew Gilbert	26
Designated Hitter	Pete Alonso	32
No. 1 Starter	Kodai Senga	34
No. 2 Starter	David Peterson	31
No. 3 Starter	Christian Scott	28
No. 4 Starter	Blade Tidwell	26
No. 5 Starter	Mike Vasil	27
Closer	Edwin Diaz	33

first-year director Eric Jagers in 2023. Test cases Christian Scott, Mike Vasil and Blade Tidwell are poised for potential MLB debuts in 2024.

The Mets have a middle-of-the-pack farm system topped by dynamic shortstop Jett Williams, who was a focal point on a Double-A Binghamton team that advanced to the Eastern League finals.

Binghamton featured many of the system's top prospects, including Williams, Scott and Tidwell as well as Drew Gilbert and Luisangel Acuña. Those last two plus Ryan Clifford are products of 2023 deadline deals that saw the Mets exchange Max Scherzer, Justin Verlander and at least $70 million to the Rangers and Astros for top prospects. ∎

DEPTH CHART

NEW YORK METS

TOP 2024 CONTRIBUTORS	RANK
1. Christian Scott, RHP	7
2. Mike Vasil, RHP	9
3. Jose Butto, RHP	19

BREAKOUT PROSPECTS	RANK
1. Nolan McLean, RHP	14
2. Jesus Baez, SS	16
3. Jeremy Rodriguez, SS	17

SOURCE OF TOP 30 TALENT

Homegrown	24	Acquired	6
College	11	Trade	6
Junior college	0	Rule 5 draft	0
High school	5	Independent league	0
Nondrafted free agent	0	Free agent/waivers	0
International	8		

LF
Matt Rudick (25)

CF
Drew Gilbert (3)
Alex Ramirez (13)
Rowdey Jordan (28)
Nick Morabito
Rhylan Thomas

RF
Ryan Clifford (5)
Stanley Consuegra
Jeffry Rosa

3B
Jacob Reimer (15)
Jesus Baez (16)
William Lugo
Jeremiah Jackson
Jose Peroza
Mateo Gil

SS
Jett Williams (1)
Colin Houck (8)
Jeremy Rodriguez (17)
Boston Baro (22)
Branny De Oleo (23)
Cristopher Larez

2B
Ronny Mauricio (2)
Luisangel Acuña (4)
Marco Vargas (18)
A.J. Ewing

1B
JT Schwartz

C
Kevin Parada (10)
Ronald Hernandez (24)
Daiverson Gutierrez
Hayden Senger
Vincent Perozo

LHP

LHSP	LHRP
Luis Rodriguez	Felipe De La Cruz

RHP

RHRP	RHRP
Christian Scott (7)	Tyler Stuart (21)
Blade Tidwell (8)	Raimon Gomez (26)
Mike Vasil (9)	Saul Garcia (30)
Brandon Sproat (11)	Layonel Ovalles
Dominic Hamel (12)	Grant Hartwig
Nolan McLean (14)	Eric Orze
Jose Butto (19)	Junior Santos
Kade Morris (20)	Paul Gervase
Calvin Ziegler (27)	Joander Suarez
Joel Diaz (29)	Landon Marceaux
Justin Jarvis	Candido Cuevas
Coleman Crow	
Jordany Ventura	
Luis Moreno	
Matt Allan	

1 JETT WILLIAMS, SS/OF

Born: November 3, 2003. **B-T:** R-R. **HT:** 5-6. **WT:** 175.
Drafted: HS—Heath, Texas, 2022 (1st round).
Signed by: Gary Brown.

TRACK RECORD: The Mets were linked to Williams throughout the 2022 draft cycle and got their man with the 14th overall pick. Little more than a year later, he was in Double-A helping Binghamton reach the Eastern League finals as a 19-year-old. Williams was a favorite of scouts on the high school showcase circuit because of his swing decisions, speed and aggressive style of play. Those traits were on display in an outstanding first full season in pro ball. Williams hit .263/.425/.451 with 13 home runs and 45 stolen bases in 121 games, spending most of the season at Low-A St. Lucie and High-A Brooklyn. He was especially productive from June 1 onward, putting up a .943 OPS that ranked him top 50 in the full-season minors among a sample of hitters who averaged 24 years of age. Williams drew 104 walks to rank second in the minors. Williams was one of four teenagers who drew at least 100 walks—fellow 2022 first-rounders Jackson Holliday and Termarr Johnson were two others—which had not been done by a teen in the full-season minor leagues since 1996.

SCOUTING REPORT: Williams plays with a confidence born out of always being doubted because of his 5-foot-6 stature. The Dallas-Fort Worth metroplex product has at least average tools across the board, with a chance to develop standout hitting and on-base ability to go with plus speed. Using a simple hitting setup and minimal leg kick, Williams hits the ball with authority to all fields. He gets outstanding carry to right field because he has the rare ability to drive the ball on a line the other way, with no slicing action. While his power may be no better than average, he gets to all of it. Swing decisions are Williams' strong suit. He had one of the lower chase rates in the minor leagues in 2023 and rarely swings and misses in the zone. He works a lot of deep counts because he makes pitchers work. He is a plus runner and constant stolen base threat. Williams entered pro ball as an unrefined shortstop defender, but he made many strides at the position in 2023 and could get to average with continued work. Williams also made 21 starts in center field, and many prefer him there to maximize his speed, athleticism and above-average arm. He hasn't played second base as a pro, but the Mets expect he could pick it up quickly if needed.

MIKE JANES/FOUR SEAM IMAGES

BA GRADE	SCOUTING GRADES
55 Risk: High	Hit: 60. Power: 50. Run: 60. Field: 50. Arm: 55.

Projected future grades on 20-80 scouting scale

BEST TOOLS

BATTING

Best Hitter for Average	Jett Williams
Best Power Hitter	Ronny Mauricio
Best Strike-Zone Discipline	Jett Williams
Fastest Baserunner	Luisangel Acuña
Best Athlete	Nolan McLean

PITCHING

Best Fastball	Blade Tidwell
Best Curveball	Calvin Ziegler
Best Slider	Blade Tidwell
Best Changeup	Eric Orze
Best Control	Christian Scott

FIELDING

Best Defensive Catcher	Hayden Senger
Best Defensive Infielder	Luisangel Acuña
Best Infield Arm	Mateo Gil
Best Defensive Outfielder	Rhylan Thomas
Best Outfield Arm	Stanley Consuegra

THE FUTURE: Williams plays with a chip on his shoulder reminiscent of former Red Sox all-star Dustin Pedroia. As a potential on-base machine with average power and plus basestealing ability, Williams could develop into a first-division leadoff man who plays up the middle. After reaching Double-A as a teenager, he is primed to advance to Triple-A at age 20 and enter the major league picture in late 2024 or early 2025. ■

Year	Age	Club (League)	Level	AVG	G	AB	R	H	2B	3B	HR	RBI	BB	SO	SB	OBP	SLG
2023	19	St. Lucie (FSL)	A	.249	79	261	51	65	12	6	6	35	69	76	32	.422	.410
2023	19	Brooklyn (SAL)	A+	.299	36	127	25	38	9	2	7	18	33	32	12	.451	.567
2023	19	Binghamton (EL)	AA	.227	6	22	5	5	1	0	0	2	2	10	1	.308	.273
Minor League Totals				.262	131	442	88	116	23	9	14	61	108	124	51	.421	.450

2 RONNY MAURICIO, 2B/SS

HIT: 40. **POW:** 55. **RUN:** 55. **FLD:** 50. **ARM:** 60. **BA Grade:** 50. **Risk:** Medium.

Born: April 4, 2001. **B-T:** B-R. **HT:** 6-3. **WT:** 166.
Signed: Dominican Republic, 2017. **Signed by:** Marciano Alvarez/Gerardo Cabrera.
TRACK RECORD: Power potential has been Mauricio's selling point since the day he signed as a 16-year-old in 2017. Over time, that potential has turned into production. Mauricio hit 20 or more home runs in each of the past three seasons, and just 14 minor leaguers have hit more than his total of 69 in that time. Mauricio spent nearly a full season with Triple-A Syracuse in 2023 before making his major league debut on Sept. 1.
SCOUTING REPORT: Mauricio has a carrying tool in his plus power, but his below-average on-base ability has generally weighed down his overall offensive production. Mauricio has the electric bat speed and twitch to produce majestic drives to his pull side, and his first MLB hit was a 117.3 mph double that was the hardest hit ball by any Mets hitter in 2023. He also led the Mets with one of the highest chase rates in MLB, undone by poor swing decisions against sliders and changeups. The switch-hitting Mauricio is much stronger from the left side, hitting .284/.334/.497 with a 21% strikeout rate against righthanders in the upper minors and majors. He is an above-average runner and efficient basestealer who went 7-for-7 in his MLB debut. Mauricio is a steady defensive shortstop with a plus arm who fanned out to second base, third base and left field at Triple-A to create avenues for a MLB role. Playing outfield was abandoned in August, but he looked at home at second and third base in New York.
THE FUTURE: Mauricio is an exceptional athlete who has added muscle mass and mental maturity. The Mets hope that his athleticism enables him to improve his hitting ability. Mauricio stood poised to assume a large MLB role in 2024, but that was before he tore the anterior cruciate ligament in his knee in the Dominican League in December. Surgery to repair it will probably cost him the season.

Year	Age	Club (League)	Level	AVG	G	AB	R	H	2B	3B	HR	RBI	BB	SO	SB	OBP	SLG
2023	22	Syracuse (IL)	AAA	.292	116	490	76	143	30	3	23	71	35	97	24	.346	.506
2023	22	New York (NL)	MLB	.248	26	101	11	25	4	0	2	9	7	31	7	.296	.347
Minor League Totals				.268	520	2119	299	568	107	18	76	296	121	473	63	.311	.443
Major League Totals				.248	26	101	11	25	4	0	2	9	7	31	7	.296	.347

3 DREW GILBERT, OF

HIT: 55. **POW:** 50. **RUN:** 50. **FLD:** 55. **ARM:** 60. **BA Grade:** 50. **Risk:** Medium.

Born: September 27, 2000. **B-T:** L-L. **HT:** 5-9. **WT:** 195.
Drafted: Tennessee, 2022 (1st round). **Signed by:** Freddy Perez (Astros).
TRACK RECORD: Gilbert starred for a Tennessee team that led the nation in home runs and ranked No. 1 for much of the 2022 season. The Astros drafted him 35th overall that summer, and a year later he climbed quickly to Double-A in his first full pro season. The Mets acquired Gilbert and 19-year-old outfielder Ryan Clifford at the 2023 trade deadline, sending Justin Verlander and at least $35.5 million to Houston. New York will owe the Astros another $17.5 million if Verlander reaches 140 innings in 2024. Gilbert hit well for the Mets after the trade, helping Double-A Binghamton reach the Eastern League finals.
SCOUTING REPORT: The 5-foot-9 Gilbert is short for an MLB hitter but not exactly undersized. He is strong and powerfully built with plus athletic ability, a high energy level and excellent bat speed. Gilbert plays to his strengths by hunting fastballs early in counts and looking to inflict pull-side damage, but otherwise works deep counts and stays within his zone. While with the Astros, he made an effort to contact the ball out in front of the plate to unlock more power. His flyball and pull rates spiked as a result. Ultimately, he probably settles in with average power. Gilbert is an above-average center fielder with a plus arm—he also pitched as a Tennessee underclassman—that will play in right field. He is a solid-average runner with strong baserunning instincts.
THE FUTURE: At the end of the day, Gilbert may grade out average to above in every category, without a true carrying tool. On-base ability may end up being his best asset. Gilbert's outfield versatility gives him a chance to be a regular wherever he is needed, depending on the makeup of the club.

Year	Age	Club (League)	Level	AVG	G	AB	R	H	2B	3B	HR	RBI	BB	SO	SB	OBP	SLG
2023	22	Asheville (SAL)	A+	.360	21	86	21	31	8	1	6	18	6	21	4	.421	.686
2023	22	Binghamton (EL)	AA	.325	35	123	22	40	7	2	6	21	19	30	2	.423	.561
2023	22	Corpus Christi (TL)	AA	.241	60	224	36	54	11	0	6	20	33	46	6	.342	.371
Minor League Totals				.290	126	465	88	135	27	3	20	65	62	99	18	.383	.490

4 LUISANGEL ACUÑA, SS/2B

HIT: 50. **POW:** 40. **RUN:** 60. **FLD:** 60. **ARM:** 60. **BA Grade:** 50. **Risk:** Medium.

Born: March 12, 2002. **B-T:** R-R. **HT:** 5-8. **WT:** 181.
Signed: Venezuela, 2018. **Signed by:** Rafic Saab (Rangers).
TRACK RECORD: Acuña signed with the Rangers in 2018, the same summer that older brother Ronald Jr. was building his National League Rookie of the Year credentials with the Braves. The Acuña brothers are a study in contrasts. Ronald is a powerful outfielder, while Luisangel is a small-in-stature middle infielder. Both are now NL East rivals. Luisangel was in the midst of a Double-A breakout in 2023 when Texas dealt him to the Mets for Max Scherzer plus $35 million at the trade deadline. Acuña helped Double-A Binghamton advance to the Eastern League finals.
SCOUTING REPORT: Acuña is a plus runner and standout defender who has strong bat-to-ball skills and hand-eye coordination. He likes to swing the bat and will expand his zone early, but he fights off pitches with two strikes and takes his share of walks. Acuña is strong and twitchy, with more raw power than his 5-foot-8 frame suggests. He hits the ball hard but on the ground and the other way frequently, capping his projected home run totals as below-average. He is at least a plus runner who was successful on 57 of 67 stolen base attempts in 2023 and has swiped at least 40 bags in each full season. Acuña has strong range, solid feet, clean actions and a plus arm at both middle infield positions, but his internal clock may be a tick slow for shortstop. Most scouts prefer him at second base, and he also played center field in the Rangers system.
THE FUTURE: Acuña could develop into a standout defensive second baseman whose on-base ability and speed could lengthen a lineup. On a first-division club, he might fit best as a second tablesetter at the bottom of the order. After a full Double-A season, he's ready for Triple-A and his MLB debut at some point in 2024.

Year	Age	Club (League)	Level	AVG	G	AB	R	H	2B	3B	HR	RBI	BB	SO	SB	OBP	SLG
2023	21	Binghamton (EL)	AA	.243	37	148	25	36	3	0	2	12	15	30	15	.317	.304
2023	21	Frisco (TL)	AA	.315	84	362	68	114	25	2	7	51	37	76	42	.377	.453
Minor League Totals				.289	374	1482	297	428	70	10	34	213	186	338	158	.369	.418

5 RYAN CLIFFORD, OF/1B

HIT: 55. **POW:** 55. **RUN:** 30. **FLD:** 50. **ARM:** 70. **BA Grade:** 55. **Risk:** High.

Born: July 20, 2003. **B-T:** L-L. **HT:** 6-3. **WT:** 200.
Drafted: HS—Cary, NC, 2022 (11th round). **Signed by:** Andrew Johnson (Astros).
TRACK RECORD: The Mets liked Clifford's bat as a potential early-round pick out of high school in the 2022 draft, but they couldn't make the money work. He fell to the Astros in the 11th round, and since Houston had gone college-heavy with its draft class, it was able to go over slot to sign Clifford for a tick more than $1.25 million. That equates to second-round money. Making his full-season debut in 2023, Clifford hit his way to High-A in May. He was raking at hitter-happy Asheville when the Astros traded him and Drew Gilbert to the Mets for Justin Verlander—plus $35.5 million—at the trade deadline. Clifford struggled at High-A Brooklyn after the trade, hitting .188 with a 36% strikeout rate.
SCOUTING REPORT: Clifford combines plus raw power and strong swing decisions for his age. He hit the ball as hard as nearly any fellow 20-year-old in 2023, with a 90th percentile exit velocity of 107.1 mph and one of the highest home run totals (24) among his age peers. Clifford's approach can tend toward passivity and resulted in many deep counts, walks and strikeouts. He really struggled hitting at Brooklyn, a park notorious for suppressing lefthanded power and one where he struggled to pick the ball up because of outfield signage. Despite his large 6-foot-3 frame, Clifford is agile enough to play corner outfield, though he saw nearly as many reps at first base. His double-plus arm and throwing accuracy would be wasted if he settles at first base. He is a well below-average runner who is no threat to steal bases.
THE FUTURE: Clifford's future value is tied to his bat. If he develops plus power and on-base ability, he could hit in the middle of a big league lineup. If not, he becomes more of a 4-A hitter. Seeing him outside Brooklyn and against more advanced Double-A arms will be a fitting test in 2024.

Year	Age	Club (League)	Level	AVG	G	AB	R	H	2B	3B	HR	RBI	BB	SO	SB	OBP	SLG
2023	19	Fayetteville (CAR)	A	.337	25	92	22	31	5	0	2	15	25	27	3	.488	.457
2023	19	Asheville (SAL)	A+	.271	58	214	35	58	11	0	16	46	21	62	1	.356	.547
2023	19	Brooklyn (SAL)	A+	.188	32	117	13	22	4	0	6	20	18	51	1	.307	.376
Minor League Totals				.260	140	500	83	130	25	0	26	91	86	171	7	.382	.466

6 CHRISTIAN SCOTT, RHP

FB: 60. **CB:** 40. **SL:** 55. **CHG:** 50. **CTL:** 60. **BA Grade:** 55. **Risk:** High

Born: June 15, 1999. **B-T:** R-R. **HT:** 6-4. **WT:** 215.
Drafted: Florida, 2021 (5th round). **Signed by:** Jon Updike.
TRACK RECORD: Scott had worked primarily as a reliever in three years at Florida when the Mets drafted him in the fifth round in 2021. He shifted to a starter and bulk pitcher role at Class A in 2022, his first full season, before taking on a traditional starter role and upping his workload to a career high 87.2 innings in 2023. Scott spent the final three months of the season at Double-A Binghamton and his overall numbers reflect a dominant season. Scott walked just 3.6% of batters, the fourth-best rate among minor league pitchers with at least 80 innings. His 28.4 K-BB% ranked first at that threshold.
SCOUTING REPORT: Scott has the best mix of stuff and starter traits in the system. That is a credit to both him and Mets pitching development. A sinker/slider pitcher in college, Scott has remade his repertoire in pro ball to feature a four-seam fastball, slider, split-changeup and occasional curveball. He also added greater core strength and stability to help key his breakout. Scott pitches at 94 mph and touches 98 with plus ride and horizontal life. He throws a ton of strikes with his fastball and can get whiffs with it both in and out of the zone. Scott also throws strikes with a solid-average mid-80s slider that he favors when working ahead in the count. His mid-80s split-changeup has rapidly become a key pitch for whiffs and chases. He throws an occasional curve to steal a strike. Scott has plus control and holds runners well, with just 11 stolen base attempts against him in 19 starts in 2023.
THE FUTURE: Scott's feel for strikes, sequencing and competitive makeup give him a pitchability edge that he has worked hard to refine in pro ball. He has No. 3 starter upside and might not be far off from making his MLB debut.

Year	Age	Club (League)	Level	W	L	ERA	G	GS	IP	H	HR	BB	SO	BB%	SO%	WHIP	AVG
2023	24	St. Lucie (FSL)	A	0	1	9.00	1	1	2	4	0	0	3	0.0	30.0	2.00	.400
2023	24	Brooklyn (SAL)	A+	1	0	2.28	6	6	24	15	0	4	27	4.4	30.0	0.80	.176
2023	24	Binghamton (EL)	AA	4	3	2.47	12	12	62	44	5	8	77	3.4	32.8	0.84	.198
Minor League Totals				8	7	3.31	40	28	149	127	7	35	185	5.8	30.5	1.08	.226

7 BLADE TIDWELL, RHP

FB: 60. **SL:** 60. **CHG:** 50. **CTL:** 45. **BA Grade:** 50. **Risk:** High.

Born: June 8, 2001. **B-T:** R-R. **HT:** 6-4. **WT:** 207.
Drafted: Tennessee, 2022 (2nd round). **Signed by:** Nathan Beuster.
TRACK RECORD: Tidwell entered the 2022 season as one of the top college pitching prospects, but a sore shoulder cost him two months. He pitched just 39 innings for Tennessee and fell to the second round, where the Mets went 25% over slot to sign him for $1.85 million. Tidwell struggled to throw strikes during 2023 spring training, and that wildness initially carried over to High-A Brooklyn, where he walked 29 through his first 34.2 innings.
SCOUTING REPORT: Tidwell looked like a different pitcher after his early control misadventures, both in terms of results and repertoire. In his final 16 starts, the last eight at Double-A Binghamton, he recorded a 2.99 ERA with 103 strikeouts and 34 walks in 81.1 innings. Tidwell pitches at 94 mph and tops near 98 with good ride up in the zone. He gets whiffs on the pitch at a plus rate but has more present fastball control than command. Tidwell's low-80s slider has bat-missing sweeper action with plus horizontal break. He throws it both ahead and behind in the count. Tidwell took giant strides with his low-80s changeup in 2023 and ended up throwing it more than 10% of the time to help him combat lefthanded hitters. He learned to catch a seam with his ring finger when releasing the ball, which imparted extreme depth and sinking action. He disguises his arm path well to help his pitches play up. After Tidwell walked nearly 13% of batters in 2023, throwing more quality strikes and gaining greater mechanical consistency will be keys to helping him stay in the rotation.
THE FUTURE: Gaining confidence in his changeup gave Tidwell a third quality pitch to go with his plus fastball and slider. With improved command, he has the upside of a No. 2 or 3 starter. The fallback option for Tidwell is high-leverage power reliever. He should see plenty of Double-A time in 2024.

Year	Age	Club (League)	Level	W	L	ERA	G	GS	IP	H	HR	BB	SO	BB%	SO%	WHIP	AVG
2023	22	Brooklyn (SAL)	A+	8	3	3.09	17	17	82	55	8	46	112	13.6	33.0	1.24	.190
2023	22	Binghamton (EL)	AA	3	3	4.72	8	8	34	32	6	17	41	11.5	27.7	1.43	.254
Minor League Totals				11	7	3.46	30	30	125	91	14	70	164	13.3	31.1	1.29	.204

8 COLIN HOUCK, SS

HIT: 55. **POW:** 55. **RUN:** 55. **FLD:** 55. **ARM:** 55. **BA Grade:** 55. **Risk:** Extreme

Born: September 30, 2004. **B-T:** R-R. **HT:** 6-2. **WT:** 190.
Drafted: HS—Lilburn, GA, 2023 (1st round). **Signed by:** Marlin McPhail.

TRACK RECORD: Houck starred for Atlanta-area prep power Parkview High and shined on the showcase circuit heading into his senior year of 2023. The Mets were pleased to scoop him up at pick No. 32 and sign him for $2,750,000, about 5% over slot value. Houck was a two-sport athlete in high school who also was a three-star quarterback, and many believe he can take a leap in pro ball after he tailors his body for baseball. He made a brief pro debut in the Florida Complex League after signing and then impressed the Mets by volunteering to spend his offseason in Port St. Lucie to train at the organization's complex.

SCOUTING REPORT: Houck has a well-rounded tool set and is lauded for his competitive makeup. His simple righthanded swing and small leg kick produce a clean bat path through the zone. Houck showed off his bat speed by hammering mid-90s velocity in high school and exercised swing decisions in pro ball with a patient approach, high contact rate and discerning eye to not chase breaking pitches. His power is mostly gap-to-gap but should improve as he matures his 6-foot-2 body and approach. Houck is a sound fundamental shortstop who ultimately may be a touch short in terms of range and arm to stick there. A move to third base or second base could be in his future. He has flashed plus run times but probably settles as above-average.

THE FUTURE: Houck can hit and has the potential to hit for power. He has a lot of polish for a high school product and has no glaring weakness. If he can take one of his average to above-average tools to plus, he could become a first-division regular. His journey begins as the shortstop for Low-A St. Lucie in 2024.

Year	Age	Club (League)	Level	AVG	G	AB	R	H	2B	3B	HR	RBI	BB	SO	SB	OBP	SLG
2023	18	FCL Mets	Rk	.241	9	29	6	7	0	1	0	4	7	8	0	.389	.310
Minor League Totals				.241	9	29	6	7	0	1	0	4	7	8	0	.389	.310

9 MIKE VASIL, RHP

FB: 55. **CB:** 45. **SL:** 60. **CHG:** 50. **CTL:** 55. **BA Grade:** 50. **Risk:** High

Born: March 19, 2000. **B-T:** L-R. **HT:** 6-5. **WT:** 225.
Drafted: Virginia, 2021 (8th round). **Signed by:** Daniel Coles.

TRACK RECORD: Vasil scuffled through three years at Virginia but has emerged as one of the Mets' top starting pitcher prospects since they drafted him in the eighth round in 2021. Bone spurs in his elbow truncated his 2022 full-season debut, but he made 26 starts in 2023 and logged a career-high 124 innings, most of them at Triple-A Syracuse. Vasil walked just 4% of batters with Double-A Binghamton, but that rate shot up near 12% at Triple-A, where the automated ball-strike system wreaked havoc with pitchers' walk rates.

SCOUTING REPORT: Vasil has worked hard to turn himself from a pitcher who had a 4.74 ERA in 161 college innings to a four-pitch starter on the cusp of making his MLB debut. He came into the 2023 season in better shape and focused his attention on loading the back side of his delivery to throw harder and with more precision. Vasil pitches at 93-94 mph and tops near 95 with a four-seam fastball he uses to set up the rest of his repertoire. Like many pitchers contending with the ABS system at Triple-A, he had trouble registering called high strikes with the tight zone. Vasil's mid-to-high-80s slider is his standout offering and grades as plus based on his ability to throw it for strikes or induce chases. He throws his slider both ahead and behind in the count. Vasil's mid-80s changeup has developed into a trusty chase pitch he uses to try to put away batters. He will drop in an occasional low-80s curveball when ahead in the count.

THE FUTURE: Vasil's ability to command all four pitch types to both sides of the plate helps him keep hitters guessing. He is a high-probability starter who might fit at No. 4 or 5 in a rotation. Vasil is poised to make his MLB debut in 2024.

Year	Age	Club (League)	Level	W	L	ERA	G	GS	IP	H	HR	BB	SO	BB%	SO%	WHIP	AVG
2023	23	Binghamton (EL)	AA	1	2	3.71	10	10	51	35	8	8	57	4.1	28.9	0.84	.187
2023	23	Syracuse (IL)	AAA	4	4	5.30	16	16	73	70	10	38	81	11.7	24.9	1.48	.250
Minor League Totals				9	8	4.14	47	46	202	159	22	72	233	8.6	27.8	1.14	.209

10 KEVIN PARADA, C

HIT: 50. **POW:** 50. **RUN:** 40. **FLD:** 40. **ARM:** 40. **BA Grade:** 50. **Risk:** High.

Born: August 3, 2001. **B-T:** R-R. **HT:** 6-1. **WT:** 197.
Drafted: Georgia Tech, 2022 (1st round). **Signed by:** Marlin McPhail.
TRACK RECORD: Parada made huge strides both offensively and defensively as a Georgia Tech sophomore in 2022 following offseason strength gains. The Mets drafted him 11th overall that year and signed him for $5,019,735, or 5% over slot value. Parada helped Low-A St. Lucie win the Florida State League title in his pro debut, then spent most of the 2023 season at High-A Brooklyn. He was promoted to Double-A at the end of August.
SCOUTING REPORT: Parada's first full pro season was a trying one. He hit well for Brooklyn until an August ankle injury and rough adjustment to Double-A muddied his final line. But any discussion of Parada's future value begins with his defense. He allowed 129 stolen bases—fourth most in the minors—on 157 attempts, showing an erratic arm that was short for catcher. Parada has average raw arm strength but has struggled to get into position to properly turn and load his throws, costing him velocity and accuracy. He also struggled to frame pitches at the top of the zone because he was late loading his glove for the high pitch. At the plate, Parada uses a unique reverse barrel tip as a timing mechanism but is generally good at getting out early and on time, especially for pull-side power. His hitting ability was compromised by higher-than-expected miss rates on pitches both in and out of the zone. If he can iron out his approach, he could be an average hitter with average power.
THE FUTURE: The Mets praise Parada for his aptitude and work ethic, and he focused his Arizona Fall League time working on catching drills. If he has to move off catcher, he should be able to pick up first base. Some rival scouts would like to see him try second base. The 2024 season will be pivotal for Parada's development.

Year	Age	Club (League)	Level	AVG	G	AB	R	H	2B	3B	HR	RBI	BB	SO	SB	OBP	SLG
2023	21	St. Lucie (FSL)	A	.077	4	13	2	1	0	0	0	1	2	7	0	.200	.077
2023	21	Brooklyn (SAL)	A+	.265	87	340	44	90	21	4	11	42	30	96	1	.340	.447
2023	21	Binghamton (EL)	AA	.185	14	54	4	10	2	0	3	11	4	23	0	.250	.389
Minor League Totals				.251	118	447	56	112	26	4	15	62	48	139	1	.338	.427

11 BRANDON SPROAT, RHP

FB: 55. **SL:** 55. **CB:** 45. **CHG:** 60. **CTL:** 45. **BA Grade:** 50. **Risk:** High.

Born: September 17, 2000. **B-T:** R-R. **HT:** 6-3. **WT:** 215. **Drafted:** Florida, 2023 (2nd round). **Signed by:** Brett Campbell.
TRACK RECORD: A Rangers seventh-round pick out of Pace (Fla.) High in 2019, Sproat made it to campus at Florida, where he worked primarily as a reliever for two seasons before joining the rotation in 2022. He held high-90s velocity and reduced his walk rate as a starter, prompting the Mets to draft him in the third round in 2022. Sproat didn't sign and returned to the Gators for his senior year. He finished seventh in the nation with 134 strikeouts in 2023 for the College World Series runners-up. He was again drafted by the Mets, this time in the second round, and signed for slot value of $1,474,500. He did not pitch after the draft.
SCOUTING REPORT: Sproat is a 6-foot-3 righthander with requisite velocity, repertoire and athleticism to start. The question will be control after he walked nearly 10% of collegiate batters as a junior and senior. Sproat was one of the hardest-throwing starters in Division I in 2023. He sits in the mid 90s and has touched as high as 101 mph with a two-seam fastball with armside run. As they did with fellow Florida product Christian Scott, the Mets will probably emphasize a four-seam grip in pro pitching development. Sproat has solid feel for a plus, high-80s changeup with fading life to his arm side. His breaking stuff is less refined, but he has flashed a plus, mid-80s slider with two-plane break and a fringy curveball that won't be a big part of his repertoire. Sproat's long arm stroke may inhibit his strike-throwing and lead to fringe control.
THE FUTURE: If the Mets can improve Sproat's fastball shape and slider consistency, he has major league rotation value. If not, he has a high-leverage relief profile. He should ease into pro ball at High-A Brooklyn and finish in Double-A in 2024.

Year	Age	Club (League)	Level	W	L	ERA	G	GS	IP	H	HR	BB	SO	BB%	SO%	WHIP	AVG
2023	22	Did not play															

12 DOMINIC HAMEL, RHP

FB: 60. **CB:** 40. **SL:** 55. **CHG:** 45. **CUT** 45. **CTL:** 50. **BA Grade:** 45. **Risk:** Medium.

Born: March 2, 1999. **B-T:** R-R. **HT:** 6-2. **WT:** 206. **Drafted:** Dallas Baptist, 2021 (3rd round). **Signed by:** Gary Brown.

TRACK RECORD: Hamel ranked ninth in Division I with 136 strikeouts in 2021 as a fourth-year player for Dallas Baptist, prompting the Mets to draft him in the third round. He won organization pitcher of the year honors in 2022 as he climbed to High-A Brooklyn, then spent the entire 2023 season with Double-A Binghamton. Hamel topped the Mets system with 160 strikeouts, 124 innings and a 21.1 K-BB%.

SCOUTING REPORT: Hamel threw his fastball 57% of the time in 2023 and got results despite ordinary 93-mph velocity. He delivers the ball from a low attack angle and imparts plus vertical ride on the pitch to miss bats up in the zone. He throws a ton of strikes and tops near 95 mph. Hamel throws four other average or near-average pitches. He modified his slider to more of a low-80s sweeper, while also adding a cutter to work glove side to lefthanded hitters. His mid-80s changeup has become a trusted weapon that helps him limit platoon damage. His high-70s curveball has enough depth to generate chases and steal strikes. Hamel needs to throw his secondaries for strikes more consistently, but he holds his velocity, misses bats and holds baserunners well.

THE FUTURE: Hamel's pitching style would have been a poor fit for the tight automated ball-strike system at Triple-A, which might have factored in him spending all of 2023 at Double-A. He will advance to Syracuse in 2024 and hope the ABS system has been refined. If he pitches well, he could see big league innings as a swingman or spot starter. Ultimately he fits toward the back of a rotation.

Year	Age	Club (League)	Level	W	L	ERA	G	GS	IP	H	HR	BB	SO	BB%	SO%	WHIP	AVG
2023	24	Binghamton (EL)	AA	8	6	3.85	26	25	124	108	12	49	160	9.3	30.4	1.27	.230
Minor League Totals				18	9	3.51	53	51	246	191	17	103	312	10.0	30.4	1.20	.212

13 ALEX RAMIREZ, OF

HIT: 40. **POW:** 50. **RUN:** 60. **FLD:** 65. **ARM:** 55. **BA Grade:** 50. **Risk:** High.

Born: January 13, 2003. **B-T:** R-R. **HT:** 6-3. **WT:** 170. **Signed:** Dominican Republic, 2019. **Signed by:** Gerardo Cabrera/Fernando Encarnacion.

TRACK RECORD: The Mets centered their 2019 international class on Ramirez, signing the athletic Dominican outfielder for $2.05 million. Following the lost 2020 season, he raced to Low-A as an 18-year-old in 2021 and reached High-A Brooklyn while still a teenager in 2022. Returning to the South Atlantic League in 2023, Ramirez scuffled through a disappointing season in which he hit .221 and put up a .627 OPS that was eighth-worst among 56 qualifiers. The Mets made Ramirez their lone addition to the 40-man roster at the November reserve deadline.

SCOUTING REPORT: Ramirez is a loose, athletic 6-foot-3 center fielder with raw power but questionable feel for hitting. Despite showing more swing restraint, making more contact and chasing less, Ramirez's surface production nosedived in 2023. He continued to hit the ball as hard as ever at peak but without enough frequency. The Mets have worked with Ramirez to smooth out his handsy load while still allowing him to get his hands where he feels they need to be. His bat speed and projectable frame would allow him to access at least average power if he makes enough quality contact. Ramirez's separating ability is his glove in center field. When he's locked in, he's a plus defender with a chance at double-plus with consistent effort. The same applies to baserunning, where Ramirez has plus speed but inconsistent focus. His throws are above-average and accurate, and the Mets point to him as a success story in their new arm care regimen for position players.

THE FUTURE: Ramirez's downbeat season reinforces the need for him to grind, and to that end he spent a lot of time at the Mets' Dominican academy in the offseason. His youth and athleticism stand out, and thanks to his secondary tools he has a path to a major league role even if he doesn't hit.

Year	Age	Club (League)	Level	AVG	G	AB	R	H	2B	3B	HR	RBI	BB	SO	SB	OBP	SLG
2023	20	Brooklyn (SAL)	A+	.221	120	457	66	101	21	1	7	53	56	114	21	.310	.317
Minor League Totals				.254	317	1257	169	319	66	12	23	159	123	340	58	.328	.380

14 NOLAN McLEAN, RHP/DH

FB: 55. **CB:** 55. **SL:** 60. **CHG:** 45. **CTL:** 40. **BA Grade:** 55. **Risk:** Extreme.

Born: July 24, 2001. **B-T:** R-R. **HT:** 6-4. **WT:** 214. **Drafted:** Oklahoma State, 2023 (3rd round). **Signed by:** Scott Thomas.

TRACK RECORD: McLean starred in baseball and football in high school outside Raleigh, N.C., and briefly played both sports at Oklahoma State before dropping football. He continued as a two-way player for the Cowboys, playing third base and then right field while notching 11 career saves as a reliever. The Orioles drafted McLean in the third round in 2022 as an eligible sophomore but did not sign him. One year later, the Mets drafted him in the third round and signed him for slot value of $747,600. McLean made six lineup appearances at DH and two on the mound in a brief pro debut.

SCOUTING REPORT: The Mets will let McLean serve as DH on occasion in 2024—he slugged .561 in three collegiate seasons with a 35% strikeout rate—but his developmental focus will be pitching. The organization is excited by the raw stuff he showed in an offseason pitching camp and believes he can move quickly in pro ball. McLean averages 95 mph on his two-seamer with an easy motion and has topped at 98. His velocity could climb as he adapts to a pro starter's routine. McLean's high-spin slider has plus potential with mid-80s velocity—up to 88 mph—and two-plane break. He also throws a quality high-70s curveball on occasion. McLean didn't throw a changeup as a college reliever, but the Mets like what they have seen in side sessions. His athleticism and strong frame stand out. McLean walked nearly 13% of collegiate batters as a reliever, so control is a giant question mark.

THE FUTURE: The Mets have turned college relievers Tylor Megill and Christian Scott into notable pro starters and will look to do the same with McLean. He should break camp with High-A Brooklyn in 2024 and deepen the organization's growing store of athletic pitchers drafted out of college.

Year	Age	Club (League)	Level	W	L	ERA	G	GS	IP	H	HR	BB	SO	BB%	SO%	WHIP	AVG
2023	21	St. Lucie (FSL)	A	0	0	2.70	2	1	3	1	0	2	2	16.7	16.7	0.90	.100
Minor League Totals				0	0	3.00	2	1	3	1	0	2	2	16.7	16.7	1.00	.100

15 JACOB REIMER, 3B

HIT: 50. **POW:** 50. **RUN:** 40. **FLD:** 45. **ARM:** 50. **BA Grade:** 50. **Risk:** High.

Born: February 2, 2004. **B-T:** R-R. **HT:** 6-2. **WT:** 205. **Drafted:** HS—Yucaipa, CA, 2022 (4th round).
Signed by: Glenn Walker.

TRACK RECORD: Most teams wanted to see Reimer continue his development in college, but the Mets were convinced in his ability and went over slot to sign him for $775,000 in the fourth round in 2022. He stumbled through the early stages of the season at Low-A St. Lucie in 2023 before he put up a .995 OPS in his final 40 games at the level and moved to High-A Brooklyn as a 19-year-old on Aug. 1. Reimer's .399 on-base percentage trailed only Jett Williams in the system and ranked top 10 among minor league teenagers with at least 400 plate appearances.

SCOUTING REPORT: Reimer is a disciplined hitter who can handle third base but needs to get to more game power to round out his profile. To that end, he worked to improve his bat speed at Driveline in the offseason. Reimer has a large 6-foot-2 frame with large hands and above-average raw power, so if he can sculpt his body and add more oomph to his batted balls, he could deliver average-or-better hitting ability and power. A high school shortstop, Reimer is a capable third baseman in pro ball with near-average potential and an average arm. He has occasionally played first base, and the Mets have considered adding corner outfielder versatility to his profile. He is a below-average runner who won't factor for stolen bases.

THE FUTURE: Reimer adapted to pro ball because of his excellent swing decisions, even if his surface production was muted by tough hitting environments in St. Lucie and Brooklyn. His age-20 season in 2024 will give the Mets a better idea of his hitting upside and whether he might develop a carrying tool.

Year	Age	Club (League)	Level	AVG	G	AB	R	H	2B	3B	HR	RBI	BB	SO	SB	OBP	SLG
2023	19	FCL Mets	Rk	.429	2	7	2	3	0	0	1	4	1	1	0	.444	.857
2023	19	St. Lucie (FSL)	A	.280	75	250	48	70	10	0	6	37	44	61	3	.412	.392
2023	19	Brooklyn (SAL)	A+	.203	25	79	13	16	3	0	1	8	17	22	0	.354	.278
Minor League Totals				.265	109	359	68	95	13	1	9	56	68	87	3	.400	.382

16 JESUS BAEZ, SS

HIT: 40. **POW:** 55. **RUN** 30. **FLD:** 50. **ARM:** 60. **BA Grade:** 50. **Risk:** High.

Born: February 26, 2005. **B-T:** R-R. **HT:** 5-10. **WT:** 180. **Signed:** Dominican Republic, 2022.
Signed by: Oliver Dominguez/Moises De La Mota.

TRACK RECORD: Exemplary bat speed and raw power drew the Mets to sign Baez for $275,000 out of the Dominican Republic in 2022. He blasted seven homers and won the organization's Dominican Summer League player of the year award in his 2022 pro debut. Baez found the going tougher in the Rookie-level Florida Complex League in 2023, where he hit .210 but supplied enough extra-base thump that his .123 isolated slugging ranked 14th among qualified 18-and-younger hitters in the power-suppressing league.

SCOUTING REPORT: Baez hits the ball harder than most 18-year-olds, and the ball sounds different coming off his bat when he barrels it. He identifies pitches well by staying within his zone and making contact at a high rate for a hitter with power. Baez started slowly in the FCL and began to press, which led to an elevated groundball rate, less-than-ideal angles and a .245 batting average on balls in play that was among the lowest in the league. Being more selectively aggressive could enable him to grow into a

.240-type hitter with above-average power and on-base ability. Baez has cleaned up his shortstop actions and has soft hands, but his thickening 5-foot-10 frame, plus arm and lack of twitchiness mark him as a future third baseman. He is a well below-average runner.

THE FUTURE: With a likely corner profile, Baez must figure things out offensively. He has plenty of time to do so and will be a part of the Low-A St. Lucie infield picture in 2024. With Colin Houck and Marco Vargas also projected to the Florida State League, Baez may begin playing more third base.

Year	Age	Club (League)	Level	AVG	G	AB	R	H	2B	3B	HR	RBI	BB	SO	SB	OBP	SLG
2023	18	FCL Mets	Rk	.210	40	138	18	29	9	1	2	17	19	28	5	.306	.333
Minor League Totals				.228	94	324	54	74	18	1	9	51	45	74	13	.326	.373

17 JEREMY RODRIGUEZ, SS

HIT: 55. **POW:** 50. **RUN:** 45. **FLD:** 50. **ARM:** 50. **BA Grade:** 55. **Risk:** Extreme.

Born: July 4, 2006. **B-T:** L-R. **HT:** 6-0. **WT:** 170. **Signed:** Dominican Republic, 2023.
Signed by: Cesar Geronimo Jr./Peter Wardell/Jose Ortiz (D-backs).
TRACK RECORD: The Diamondbacks signed Rodriguez out of the Dominican Republic for $1.25 million as the headliner of their 2023 international class. As one of the younger players eligible to sign, Rodriguez debuted as a 16-year-old in the Dominican Summer League. Arizona dealt him to the Mets just minutes before the 2023 trade deadline, and acquired veteran outfielder Tommy Pham and $820,000 to pay down half of his expiring contract. Rodriguez's .878 OPS ranked inside the top 10 among qualified 17-and-under DSL shortstops.
SCOUTING REPORT: Rodriguez has a wiry 6-foot frame and the type of bat speed and approach that portends significant offensive growth. His focal point early in his career will be adding strength to hit the ball harder. He averaged an 81 mph exit velocity in his pro debut, a figure that was low even among his age peers. Where the lefthanded-hitting Rodriguez shines is swing decisions. His miniscule in-zone miss rate stands out, while his low swing rate translated to few strikeouts and a high walk rate. Assuming strength gains as he matures, Rodriguez projects as an above-average hitter with solid-average power. Rodriguez's range and instincts are short for shortstop, though his fringe-average speed and average arm would fit at second base.
THE FUTURE: Rodriguez will make his U.S. debut in 2024, likely in the Florida Complex League. He will be 17 years old for the first month of the FCL season and could receive a late cameo with Low-A St. Lucie. In time, Rodriguez has the attributes to develop into a regular major league second baseman.

Year	Age	Club (League)	Level	AVG	G	AB	R	H	2B	3B	HR	RBI	BB	SO	SB	OBP	SLG
2023	16	DSL D-backs Black	Rk	.246	38	122	24	30	6	2	2	18	22	27	12	.363	.377
2023	16	DSL Mets Orange	Rk	.422	13	45	13	19	4	3	1	15	11	4	7	.536	.711
Minor League Totals				.293	51	167	37	49	10	5	3	33	33	31	19	.411	.467

18 MARCO VARGAS, SS/2B

HIT: 60. **POW:** 30. **RUN:** 40. **FLD:** 50. **ARM:** 50. **BA Grade:** 50. **Risk:** High.

Born: May 14, 2005. **B-T:** L-R. **HT:** 6-0. **WT:** 170. **Signed:** Mexico, 2022.
Signed by: Andres Guzman/Adrian Puig (Marlins).
TRACK RECORD: The Marlins signed Vargas out of Mexico for just $17,500 in late May 2022 after they came up short on infielders to stock their two Dominican Summer League affiliates. He hit .319 with more walks than strikeouts in his pro debut and continued to shine in the Florida Complex League in 2023. Miami dealt Vargas plus 19-year-old FCL catcher Ronald Hernandez to the Mets ahead of the 2023 trade deadline for closer David Robertson. Vargas completed a strong U.S. debut and led the FCL with 48 walks, ranked second with 14 doubles and third with a .434 on-base percentage.
SCOUTING REPORT: Vargas is a lefthanded-hitting middle infielder with outstanding bat-to-ball skill, strong strike-zone judgment and an all-fields hitting approach. He doesn't often attack the ball for impact or hit the ball hard consistently but has flashed glimpses of power in batting practice. The attractions for Vargas are his swing decisions and feel for the barrel, with some scouts projecting a plus hit tool. He is a sound defender at shortstop with soft hands, but his near-average arm and ordinary range mark him as a likely future second baseman or, if his arm improves, third baseman. Vargas is not a stolen base threat as a below-average runner who might slow down as ages. He has strong baseball instincts that help him play above his tools.
THE FUTURE: Like fellow 2023 trade deadline pickup Jeremy Rodriguez, Vargas must add strength and batted-ball authority as he develops. His bat is his ticket to a major league role, potentially as a multi-position infielder who hits for average and gets on base. He will get middle-infield reps at Low-A St. Lucie at the outset of 2024.

Year	Age	Club (League)	Level	AVG	G	AB	R	H	2B	3B	HR	RBI	BB	SO	SB	OBP	SLG
2023	18	FCL Marlins	Rk	.283	33	120	32	34	11	1	2	19	38	22	8	.457	.442
2023	18	FCL Mets	Rk	.234	15	47	9	11	3	0	0	5	10	9	2	.368	.298
2023	18	St. Lucie (FSL)	A	.308	6	26	5	8	0	0	0	4	5	7	3	.419	.308
Minor League Totals				.296	107	375	76	111	27	4	4	66	88	70	27	.427	.421

19 JOSE BUTTO, RHP

FB: 50. **CB:** 40. **SL:** 50. **CHG:** 60. **CTL:** 45. **BA Grade:** 45. **Risk:** Medium.

Born: March 19, 1998. **B-T:** R-R. **HT:** 6-1. **WT:** 205. **Signed:** Venezuela, 2017. **Signed by:** Hector Rincones.

TRACK RECORD: Butto gained steam as a prospect by shining at the alternate training site in 2020. He finished 2021 at Double-A and then reached Triple-A in 2022, when he made his major league debut with an Aug. 21 start against the Phillies. Butto began the 2023 season with Triple-A Syracuse and received three separate callups to New York, including a run of five September starts in which he logged a 3.29 ERA in 27.1 innings that included 28 strikeouts and nine walks.

SCOUTING REPORT: Butto's separating pitch has always been his changeup. The plus mid-80s pitch drops and fades to his arm side, and induces batters to swing over it, especially if they're looking for something else. Butto's 93-95 mph four-seam fastball rides to the top of the zone, which hurt him with the automated ball-strike system in use at Triple-A. High strikes were in short supply, and Butto's walk rate spiked to a career-high 12%. He added a two-seam grip to compensate, and the addition helped him get back into counts and, he said, gain greater feel for his four-seam. Butto's slider made strides in 2023. He amped up the pitch to the high 80s and used it with greater frequency to give him a second putaway weapon. He mixes in an occasional 80 mph curveball as a disruptor. Butto is an extreme flyball pitcher who walks a tightrope without excellent stuff or control.

THE FUTURE: Butto reached the majors in 2022 and 2023 and has one minor league option remaining. He will be 26 years old in what will be a crucial 2024. He has a chance to pitch his way into the rotation or serve in a long reliever/swingman role similar to the one Trevor Williams filled in 2022.

Year	Age	Club (League)	Level	W	L	ERA	G	GS	IP	H	HR	BB	SO	BB%	S0%	WHIP	AVG
2023	25	Syracuse (IL)	AAA	3	7	5.93	19	19	91	99	17	49	82	11.8	19.8	1.63	.278
2023	25	New York (NL)	MLB	1	4	3.64	9	7	42	33	3	23	38	12.8	21.2	1.33	.212
Minor League Totals				23	32	3.86	121	108	541	501	68	179	535	7.8	23.4	1.26	.242
Major League Totals				1	4	4.70	10	8	46	42	5	25	43	12.4	21.3	1.46	.237

20 KADE MORRIS, RHP

FB: 50. **CB:** 45. **SL:** 50. **CHG:** 50. **CTL:** 55. **BA Grade:** 45. **Risk:** High.

Born: June 21, 2002. **B-T:** R-R. **HT:** 6-3. **WT:** 190. **Drafted:** Nevada, 2023 (3rd round). **Signed by:** Rich Morales.

TRACK RECORD: Morris pitched primarily relief during his first two seasons at Nevada but made a memorable start late in his sophomore season. He pitched 8.2 strong innings against rival Nevada-Las Vegas in the elimination game of the Mountain West Conference finals. Morris moved to the rotation in 2023 and struck out 85 in 81.1 innings and posted a 5.42 ERA that looks better in light of the extreme hitting environments of the MWC, where the overall ERA was 6.08. The Mets drafted Morris with the final pick of the third round and signed him for slot value of $666,500. He made two abbreviated starts in his pro debut.

SCOUTING REPORT: Morris has a deep and well-rounded repertoire, a history of throwing strikes and an athletic 6-foot-3 frame that will fit in a pro rotation. He favored his two-seam fastball and slider in college but has a true four-pitch mix. Morris sits at 93 mph and has touched as high as 97 in the past, focusing more on generating weak groundball contact than blowing the ball past hitters up in the zone. His mid-80s slider is his go-to pitch for whiffs and has above-average potential. Morris upsets hitters' timing with a mid-70s curveball and mid-80s changeup, which both have flashed solid-average potential. He will need to throw those pitches more often—and maybe a four-seam fastball as well—to reach his upside. He ties together his repertoire of average pitches with above-average control.

THE FUTURE: Morris' athleticism, arm strength and clean delivery should take him far in pro ball, potentially to the back of a big league rotation if he continues improving. Getting him out of Reno and into a more neutral run environment in the Mets' system could help him see better results across his repertoire.

Year	Age	Club (League)	Level	W	L	ERA	G	GS	IP	H	HR	BB	SO	BB%	S0%	WHIP	AVG
2023	21	FCL Mets	Rk	0	0	0.00	1	1	1	1	0	0	0	0.0	0.0	1.00	.200
2023	21	St. Lucie (FSL)	A	0	0	3.86	1	1	2	1	0	2	3	18.2	27.3	1.29	.111
Minor League Totals				0	0	3.00	2	2	3	2	0	2	3	12.5	18.8	1.33	.143

21 TYLER STUART, RHP

FB: 50. **SL:** 50. **CHG:** 40. **CUT:** 45. **CTL:** 45. **BA Grade:** 45. **Risk:** High.

Born: October 8, 1999. **B-T:** R-R. **HT:** 6-9. **WT:** 250. **Drafted:** Southern Mississippi, 2022 (6th round).
Signed by: Jet Butler.
TRACK RECORD: Stuart spent four years at Southern Mississippi but pitched only in the final two because he redshirted his first year and lost his second to the pandemic. The Mets drafted him in the sixth round in 2022. Stuart served as a workhorse reliever in college, but the Mets installed him in the High-A Brooklyn rotation in 2023, to positive results. He advanced to Double-A Binghamton on July 15 and overall led qualified minor league pitchers with a 2.20 ERA and ranked 11th with a 1.10 WHIP.
SCOUTING REPORT: Stuart moves well for his 6-foot-9, 250-pound frame and throws strikes with a 93-95 mph tailing fastball and sweepy low-80s slider. The pitches are solid-average but leave him somewhat vulnerable to lefthanded hitters. Stuart has worked to add a changeup and a cutter to become more platoon neutral, and developing a third trusted pitch will be key to him staying in the rotation. Some scouts see him settling in as a multi-inning reliever based on repertoire and command. Stuart's control is solid for a long-levered pitcher, but his command is more scattered. He worked to tighten his delivery in 2023 to limit the running game after allowing 23 stolen base attempts.
THE FUTURE: Stuart threw more sliders than any pitch type in 2023. Emphasizing new pitch types, such as cutter, four-seam fastball and changeup, will be developmental keys in the upper minors in 2024. He has back-end rotation or bullpen upside.

Year	Age	Club (League)	Level	W	L	ERA	G	GS	IP	H	HR	BB	SO	BB%	SO%	WHIP	AVG
2023	23	Brooklyn (SAL)	A+	4	0	1.55	14	14	76	56	3	23	84	7.6	27.8	1.04	.204
2023	23	Binghamton (EL)	AA	3	2	3.60	7	7	35	34	4	9	28	6.2	19.3	1.23	.258
Minor League Totals				7	2	2.45	24	23	114	94	7	35	119	7.5	25.5	1.13	.224

22 BOSTON BARO, SS/2B

HIT: 50. **POW:** 30. **RUN:** 50. **FLD:** 50. **ARM:** 55. **BA Grade:** 50. **Risk:** Extreme.

Born: August 23, 2004. **B-T:** L-R. **HT:** 6-2. **WT:** 170. **Drafted:** HS—Mission Viejo, CA, 2023 (8th round).
Signed by: Glenn Walker.
TRACK RECORD: Baro shined on the 2022 high school showcase circuit and emerged as a rising prospect for the 2023 draft after he added strength and transferred to Capistrano Valley High in Southern California to face better competition. The Mets liked his athleticism and chance to add good weight in college and viewed him as a potential top-three-rounds pick in 2026 after three years at UCLA. New York drafted Baro in the eighth round in 2023 and went more than $500,000 over slot to sign him for $700,000. He made a brief pro debut in the Florida Complex League.
SCOUTING REPORT: Baro is a lefthanded-hitting shortstop with a lean 6-foot-1 frame, command of the strike zone and a future in the middle infield. He emphasizes contact at the plate and struck out only once in seven games in his debut. Baro's line-drive swing is geared to find the gaps, with only occasional loft to his pull side. He projects for well below-average power without significant strength gains. Baro has strong defensive instincts that might keep him at shortstop, where he shows clean footwork, natural actions and an above-average arm. A rangier shortstop on the same team could push Baro to second base. His run times are merely average, but he earns high marks for his effort level and defensive consistency.
THE FUTURE: Baro is in the growth stage of his career. In three years he could look more like a scrappy big league second baseman that some scouts expect him to become. He faces a likely summer in the FCL in 2024 as he gains experience.

Year	Age	Club (League)	Level	AVG	G	AB	R	H	2B	3B	HR	RBI	BB	SO	SB	OBP	SLG
2023	18	FCL Mets	Rk	.316	7	19	4	6	2	0	0	2	5	1	0	.458	.421
Minor League Totals				.316	7	19	4	6	2	0	0	2	5	1	0	.458	.421

23 BRANNY DE OLEO, SS

HIT: 50. **POW:** 45. **RUN:** 50. **FLD:** 55. **ARM:** 55. **BA Grade:** 50. **Risk:** Extreme.

Born: May 15, 2005. **B-T:** R-R. **HT:** 6-1. **WT:** 156. **Signed:** Dominican Republic, 2023. **Signed by:** Felix Romero.
TRACK RECORD: De Oleo signed for just $10,000 out of the Dominican Republic as a "passed over" player in January 2023. He was already 18 years old when he debuted in the Dominican Summer League that June, but he quickly proved he belonged. De Oleo hit .313 with an .879 OPS in 46 games, drawing 14 walks against just 18 strikeouts. The Mets would have considered transferring him to the Florida Complex League if it weren't so challenging to adhere to player limits for domestic minor league rosters.
SCOUTING REPORT: De Oleo stands out as an up-the-middle athlete with encouraging bat-to-ball skill.

He has a tapered 6-foot-1 physique capable of adding good weight as he matures. De Oleo likes to swing the bat and put the first pitch he can handle in play. He contacts most pitches in the zone but will get himself out with weak contact by chasing. His power is well below-average currently, but his projectable frame and wiry athleticism encourage future growth. De Oleo is a reliable shortstop with the requisite actions, range and arm to continue developing at the position. He also played second base in the DSL and will probably move around the infield as he progresses.

THE FUTURE: De Oleo was one of the Mets' most pleasant development surprises in 2023. They will see if he can keep momentum going in the Florida Complex League in 2024.

Year	Age	Club (League)	Level	AVG	G	AB	R	H	2B	3B	HR	RBI	BB	SO	SB	OBP	SLG
2023	18	DSL Mets Blue	Rk	.313	46	166	36	52	12	3	3	25	14	18	6	.403	.476
Minor League Totals				.313	46	166	36	52	12	3	3	25	14	18	6	.403	.476

24 RONALD HERNANDEZ, C

HIT: 50. POW: 30. RUN: 40. FLD: 50. ARM: 50. BA Grade: 45. Risk: High.

Born: October 23, 2003. **B-T:** B-R. **HT:** 5-11. **WT:** 155. **Signed:** Venezuela, 2021.
Signed by: Fernando Seguignol (Marlins).

TRACK RECORD: The Marlins signed Hernandez out of Venezuela in 2021 and assigned him to Rookie complex leagues for his first three pro seasons. He repeated the Florida Complex League in 2023 and experienced a mini-breakthrough that caught the Mets' attention. They acquired Hernandez plus 18-year-old shortstop Marco Vargas from the Marlins for closer David Robertson at the 2023 trade deadline. Hernandez led the FCL with a .476 on-base percentage, finished second with 47 walks and 10th with a .295 average.

SCOUTING REPORT: Hernandez is a switch-hitting catcher with strong command of the strike zone and a contact-oriented, up-the-middle approach. He has some natural power but deemphasizes it in games, and makes himself more of an on-base threat than a threat to go yard. Hernandez has the potential to get to average defense behind the plate. He receives well and shows leadership and character traits the Mets value. His arm strength, transfers and throwing accuracy need to improve and should get better with work and experience. He is a below-average runner who will slow down as catching takes its toll on his knees.

THE FUTURE: With the notable exception of Francisco Alvarez, the Mets have not truly developed a catcher of note since Todd Hundley, which speaks to the lack of catching depth they typically have in the organization. Hernandez helps address that, though he is years away from a big league role, most likely as backup catcher candidate. He will get everyday reps at Low-A St. Lucie in 2024.

Year	Age	Club (League)	Level	AVG	G	AB	R	H	2B	3B	HR	RBI	BB	SO	SB	OBP	SLG
2023	19	FCL Marlins	Rk	.298	31	104	27	31	5	1	3	25	32	27	3	.464	.452
2023	19	FCL Mets	Rk	.286	14	35	6	10	4	0	1	11	15	10	1	.509	.486
2023	19	St. Lucie (FSL)	A	.172	8	29	3	5	2	0	0	7	6	13	0	.333	.241
Minor League Totals				.242	137	442	80	107	20	5	9	91	98	114	9	.390	.371

25 MATT RUDICK, OF

HIT: 50. POW: 30. RUN: 55. FLD: 55. ARM: 55. BA Grade: 45. Risk: High.

Born: July 2, 1998. **B-T:** L-L. **HT:** 5-7. **WT:** 172. **Drafted:** San Diego State, 2021 (13th round). **Signed by:** Glenn Walker.

TRACK RECORD: Rudick hit .341 in four years at San Diego State—including .410 to rank 10th in the nation as a senior—and struck out just 8% of the time. But the 5-foot-6 lefthanded hitter totaled just five home runs in 176 games, which pushed him down the board to the Mets in the 13th round in 2021. After a nondescript 2022 season at High-A Brooklyn, Rudick experienced a first-half breakthrough at Double-A Binghamton in 2023. He hit .289/.435/.478 with a career-high nine home runs in 58 games before a shoulder injury sidelined him and ultimately led to offseason surgery.

SCOUTING REPORT: Rudick is an undersized lefthanded-hitting outfielder with outsized plate discipline, a quality glove and improving power production. While he is unlikely to reach double-digit home runs in MLB, he did a better job picking his spots to pull the ball in 2023, a fact reflected in a career-high pull rate of 44%. Rudick's bat-to-ball skills and swing decisions are among the strongest in the system. He rarely goes outside his zone and was the only upper-level Mets prospect to compile more walks than strikeouts. Rudick is an above-average runner and strong defensive outfielder who plays all three positions. He also pitched in high school and has an above-average arm.

THE FUTURE: Former Mets farm director Kevin Howard evoked Jon Jay as a comparison point for Rudick, whose baseball instincts elevate his profile as a future fourth outfielder. He will be 25 in 2024, so if he hits at Triple-A he could get an MLB look.

Year	Age	Club (League)	Level	AVG	G	AB	R	H	2B	3B	HR	RBI	BB	SO	SB	OBP	SLG
2023	24	FCL Mets	Rk	.235	6	17	2	4	2	0	0	2	2	2	0	.316	.353
2023	24	Binghamton (EL)	AA	.271	61	214	45	58	11	0	9	31	46	42	12	.414	.449
Minor League Totals				.256	178	625	117	160	34	7	13	73	108	118	35	.383	.395

26 RAIMON GOMEZ, RHP

FB: 60. SL: 60. CUT: 30. CTL: 40. BA Grade: 50. Risk: Extreme.

Born: September 6, 2001. **B-T:** R-R. **HT:** 6-2. **WT:** 224. **Signed:** Venezuela, 2021. **Signed by:** Carlos Perez.

TRACK RECORD: Gomez signed as a 19-year-old out of Venezuela in 2021 and pitched mostly in relief during his first two pro seasons, including at Low-A St. Lucie in 2022. He came out firing in spring 2023 to catch the attention of scouts on the minor league backfields with high-90s heat and a sharp high-80s slider. Assigned to High-A Brooklyn to work as a starter, Gomez struck out 12 in seven innings before succumbing to Tommy John surgery after three starts.

SCOUTING REPORT: Gomez is a solidly-built 6-foot-2 righthander who showed double-plus 97 mph velocity and above-average riding life prior to having TJS. His sharp, power slider tops near 89 mph and is a true swing-and-miss pitch with plus potential. Gomez toyed with a low-90s cutter briefly before going under the knife. He should get back on the mound around midseason 2024, when he will continue working to refine his strike-throwing and develop a changeup. Gomez was primarily a two-pitch pitcher in 2023, and given his relief background and below-average control—he walked nine of 33 batters faced in 2023—a move to the bullpen could be in his future.

THE FUTURE: Gomez will be just 22 years old when he returns and has obvious big league arm talent if he makes a full recovery. He could get on the MLB radar as soon as 2025 if moved to the bullpen.

Year	Age	Club (League)	Level	W	L	ERA	G	GS	IP	H	HR	BB	SO	BB%	SO%	WHIP	AVG
2023	21	Brooklyn (SAL)	A+	0	0	6.43	3	3	7	4	1	9	12	27.3	36.4	1.86	.174
Minor League Totals				5	6	3.76	36	7	67	57	3	35	80	11.9	27.3	1.37	.231

27 CALVIN ZIEGLER, RHP

FB: 60. CB: 55. SL: 40. SPLT: 40. CTL: 40. BA Grade: 50. Risk: Extreme.

Born: October 3, 2002. **B-T:** R-R. **HT:** 6-0. **WT:** 205. **Drafted:** HS—Ocoee, FL, 2021 (2nd round). **Signed by:** Jon Updike/John Kosciak.

TRACK RECORD: Because of travel restrictions, Canadian prep Ziegler had to enroll at a Florida charter school to be scouted for the 2021 draft. The Mets drafted Ziegler in the second round and signed him for $910,000, more than $700,000 under slot. They expected to apply the bonus pool savings to first-rounder Kumar Rocker, but he didn't sign. In his 2022 pro debut, Ziegler struck out 35% of batters for Low-A St. Lucie, though he walked nearly 18% and pitched just 46.2 innings. At 2023 spring training, his range of motion was restricted and led to surgery to remove bone spurs from his elbow.

SCOUTING REPORT: During his rehab from elbow surgery, Ziegler tore his right quad, which delayed his return. He made it back for one Sept. 9 start for St. Lucie in which he struck out the side in one clean inning of work. Known for his power fastball and curveball as an amateur, Ziegler gets excellent ride on his 95 mph fastball and both power and depth on his low-80s curveball. He experimented with a splitter in 2022 but could not control it. He tried a spread-finger changeup grip in 2023 but didn't throw it in his lone appearance. Ziegler worked to incorporate a power slider at the fall pitching camp, and developing it was his offseason project. If he can rein it in, that would give him a pitch to use to get back into counts. When healthy in 2022, his control was well below-average, hinting at a possible future in the bullpen.

THE FUTURE: Elbow injuries are tricky, and Ziegler has had incomplete seasons in each of the past four. A healthy 2024 would help clarify his upside and timetable.

Year	Age	Club (League)	Level	W	L	ERA	G	GS	IP	H	HR	BB	SO	BB%	SO%	WHIP	AVG
2023	20	St. Lucie (FSL)	A	0	0	0.00	1	1	1	0	0	0	3	0.0	100.0	0.00	.000
Minor League Totals				0	6	4.40	17	17	48	26	3	35	73	17.3	36.1	1.30	.163

28 JOEL DIAZ, RHP

FB: 60. CB: 50. CHG: 45. CTL: 50. BA Grade: 50. Risk: Extreme.

Born: February 26, 2004. **B-T:** R-R. **HT:** 6-2. **WT:** 200. **Signed:** Dominican Republic, 2021. **Signed by:** Moises de Mota/Oliver Dominguez.

TRACK RECORD: Diaz experienced a velocity spike right before he signed with the Mets in January 2021 and then laid waste to Dominican Summer League competition as a 17-year-old that summer. He allowed three earned runs in 50.1 innings and struck out 63 in his pro debut. Assigned to Low-A St. Lucie in

May 2022, Diaz grappled with shaky command of his secondary stuff and the Florida Stage League's automated ball-strike system on his way to a 5.86 ERA in 55.1 innings. He looked good at minor league spring training in 2023 but ultimately had Tommy John surgery in late March that will keep him out until at least May 2024.

SCOUTING REPORT: When healthy in 2021 and 2022, Diaz showed a swing-and-miss fastball, improving velocity and an athletic 6-foot-2 frame that could support augmented strength. He throws strikes with a 93-mph fastball that has peaked at 97 and comes from a low release height with riding life. Diaz has worked hard to improve the shape, execution and consistency of his secondary pitches, primarily a mid-70s curveball and developing changeup. He has solid feel for his curve as a potential putaway pitch, especially if he can add more power to it.

THE FUTURE: Diaz has the raw ingredients to remain in the rotation and will be just 20 years old in 2024. Getting back on the mound at Low-A and finishing the season healthy are key objectives for Diaz.

Year	Age	Club (League)	Level	W	L	ERA	G	GS	IP	H	HR	BB	SO	BB%	SO%	WHIP	AVG
2023	19	Did not play—Injured															
Minor League Totals				3	4	3.32	31	25	106	91	7	34	114	7.7	25.8	1.18	.230

29 ROWDEY JORDAN, OF

HIT: 45. **POW:** 30. **RUN:** 55. **FLD:** 50. **ARM:** 50. **BA Grade:** 40. **Risk:** High.

Born: January 27, 1999. **B-T:** B-R. **HT:** 5-10. **WT:** 190. **Drafted:** Mississippi State, 2021 (11th round). **Signed by:** Jet Butler.

TRACK RECORD: The leadoff man and center fielder for Mississippi State's 2021 national championship team, Jordan was drafted by the Mets in the 11th round that year after four college seasons. He spent a full season at Double-A Binghamton in 2023 and ranked top 10 in the Eastern League with 30 stolen bases, 65 walks and 67 runs as the club's primary No. 2 hitter in the first half before the likes of Jett Williams, Drew Gilbert, Luisangel Acuña and Kevin Parada arrived.

SCOUTING REPORT: Jordan is a 5-foot-10 switch-hitter with an on-base-oriented game, the capability to play outfield plus second base and limited power. For Jordan, it's all about contact, swing decisions and grinding out at-bats. His swing is more natural from the left side, but he takes competitive at-bats from the right side. Jordan is a quality defender at all three outfield positions and made a career-high 41 starts at second base in 2023. He is an average defensive outfielder and playable on the dirt with an average arm. Jordan is an above-average runner with sharp baserunning instincts.

THE FUTURE: A switch-hitter with infield-outfield flexibility, Jordan could become a utility player or up-down option for a winning club. He played in the Arizona Fall League after the 2023 season and will head to Triple-A Syracuse as a 25-year-old in 2024.

Year	Age	Club (League)	Level	AVG	G	AB	R	H	2B	3B	HR	RBI	BB	SO	SB	OBP	SLG
2023	24	Binghamton (EL)	AA	.230	119	427	67	98	23	3	13	63	65	116	30	.344	.389
Minor League Totals				.236	245	886	126	209	48	7	18	109	135	236	46	.344	.367

30 SAUL GARCIA, RHP

FB: 60. **CB:** 30. **SL:** 50. **CHG:** 30. **CTL:** 40. **BA Grade:** 40. **Risk:** High.

Born: June 11, 2003. **B-T:** R-R. **HT:** 6-0. **WT:** 180. **Signed:** Venezuela, 2021. **Signed by:** Andres Nuñez.

TRACK RECORD: The Mets signed Garcia out of Venezuela when he was 18 in 2021. He spent two seasons in Rookie complex leagues before joining Low-A St. Lucie in 2023. He made three late appearances for High-A Brooklyn, and despite running up a cumulative 5.04 ERA and near 15% walk rate, Garica has pitch traits that grade well in stuff models.

SCOUTING REPORT: Garcia is a 6-foot righthander with a low release height and a riding 91-93 mph fastball that generates an above-average rate of in-zone whiffs for a two-seamer. The pitch has armside run in addition to ride and is especially difficult for righthanded hitters to handle. They hit .196 with five extra-base hits and a 32% strikeout rate against Garcia in 2023. He also throws a low-80s slider that flashes above-average but requires more consistent shape and location. Garcia mixes in the occasional four-seamer, curveball and changeup but is primarily a two-pitch pitcher and likely reliever.

THE FUTURE: Garcia is one of the hardest pitchers to hit in the Mets system, but without improved velocity or control he looks like a prime relief candidate. He is ready for a longer look at High-A Brooklyn.

Year	Age	Club (League)	Level	W	L	ERA	G	GS	IP	H	HR	BB	SO	BB%	SO%	WHIP	AVG
2023	20	St. Lucie (FSL)	A	5	9	5.35	22	8	67	49	3	48	96	15.9	31.9	1.44	.203
2023	20	Brooklyn (SAL)	A+	1	0	3.46	3	2	13	12	0	4	10	7.4	18.5	1.23	.240
Minor League Totals				9	12	5.15	44	12	117	95	4	79	163	14.9	30.8	1.49	.220

New York Yankees

BY JOSH NORRIS

The 2023 Yankees represented a tipping point. They finished in fourth place in the American League East and wound up with the franchise's worst record since 1993.

The club's biggest acquisitions over the past season and a half were either injured or ineffective, including lefthander Carlos Rodon and righthanders Frankie Montas, Scott Effross and Tommy Kahnle. In addition, all-stars Anthony Rizzo, Aaron Judge and Giancarlo Stanton each missed significant chunks of the season.

In the midst of a year when its offense was inconsistent at best, the team fired hitting coach Dillon Lawson mid-year and replaced him with Sean Casey, a former teammate of manager Aaron Boone who was working as an analyst with MLB Network.

Amid all of this, they were surpassed by the Orioles, whose youthful core vaulted them to 101 wins and the division crown.

There were a few bright spots. Gerrit Cole was the unanimous choice for the American League Cy Young Award. Rookie shortstop Anthony Volpe made the club out of spring training and won a Gold Glove while also producing a 20-20 season.

Late in the season, the team also got debuts from several of its best prospects, including outfielders Jasson Dominguez and Everson Pereira and catcher Austin Wells. Dominguez, the team's top prospect, made an instant impact when he homered off Justin Verlander in his first big league at-bat.

Unfortunately, Dominguez tore his ulnar collateral ligament a few days later and had Tommy John surgery.

After the season, the team set about making a series of trades to reverse its fortunes and return to the playoffs. The first of those moves was to swing a trade with the Red Sox to acquire outfielder Alex Verdugo.

The second step, which came a day later, landed them Juan Soto, a 25-year-old lefthanded superstar who could pair with Judge in the middle of the lineup.

The cost for both players included righthander Drew Thorpe—who at the time of the deal ranked as the system's top pitching prospect—and five other pitchers with big league experience.

Even after the trade, the Yankees' farm system was in a strong position. The moves for Soto and Verdugo did not cost New York any of its top position prospects, and at the lower levels another wave of young talent began to bubble.

In particular, their affiliate in the Florida Complex League featured a cluster of players that

Rookie Anthony Volpe hit 21 homers, stole 24 bases and won a Gold Glove as a 22-year-old.

SARAH STIER/GETTY IMAGES

PROJECTED 2027 LINEUP

Position	Player	Age
Catcher	Jose Trevino	34
First Base	Austin Wells	27
Second Base	Oswald Peraza	27
Third Base	Roderick Arias	22
Shortstop	Anthony Volpe	26
Left Field	Jasson Dominguez	24
Center Field	Everson Pereira	26
Right Field	Spencer Jones	26
Designated Hitter	Aaron Judge	35
No. 1 Starter	Gerrit Cole	36
No. 2 Starter	Carlos Rodon	34
No. 3 Starter	Nestor Cortes Jr.	32
No. 4 Starter	Chase Hampton	25
No. 5 Starter	Henry Lalane	23
Closer	Clarke Schmidt	31

led scouts to say it was the best club they'd seen at the Rookie level in decades.

The group was led by shortstop Roderick Arias, a top signing in the 2022 international class who showed a tool set replete with enough pluses to give him a potential future as a franchise player. Arias was complemented by lefthander Henry Lalane, a tall southpaw whose athleticism, poise and stuff gives him a sky-high ceiling that could make him the team's best homegrown lefthander since at least Jordan Montgomery.

Soto is signed for one more season, and Judge and Cole are in the primes of their careers, giving the Yankees a sense of urgency to use the trio to return to meaningful October baseball. ∎

DEPTH CHART

NEW YORK YANKEES

TOP 2024 CONTRIBUTORS — **RANK**

1. Jasson Dominguez, OF — 1
2. Everson Pereira, OF — 3
3. Will Warren, RHP — 10

BREAKOUT PROSPECTS — **RANK**

1. Carlos LaGrange, RHP — 13
2. Jerson Alejandro, RHP — 25

SOURCE OF TOP 30 TALENT

Homegrown	27	Acquired	3
College	8	Trade	3
Junior college	1	Rule 5 draft	0
High school	2	Independent league	0
Nondrafted free agent	1	Free agent/waivers	0
International	15		

LF
Jasson Dominguez (1)
Elijah Dunham
Christopher Familia
Jared Wegner

CF
Spencer Jones (2)
Everson Pereira (3)
Brando Mayea (11)
Estevan Florial
Brandon Lockridge
Willy Montero
Wilson Rodriguez

RF
John Cruz (24)

3B
Trey Sweeney (15)
Tyler Hardman

SS
Roderick Arias (4)
George Lombard Jr. (8)
Hans Montero

2B
Jared Serna (20)
Keiner Delgado (21)
Enmanuel Tejeda (26)
Roc Riggio (27)
Caleb Durbin

1B
TJ Rumfield (28)

C
Austin Wells (5)
Ben Rice (12)
Agustin Ramirez (19)
Engelth Ureña (22)
Rafael Flores (30)
Edinson Duran
Antonio Gomez

LHP

LHSP	LHRP
Henry Lalane (7)	Edgar Barclay
Kyle Carr (10)	
Brock Selvidge (14)	

RHP

RHSP	RHRP
Chase Hampton (6)	Clayton Beeter (16)
Will Warren (9)	Yoendrys Gomez (17)
Carlos LaGrange (13)	Luis Gil (18)
Angel Benitez (24)	Jordarlin Mendoza (23)
Jerson Alejandro (25)	Jack Neely (29)
Luis Serna	Kervin Castro
Zach Messinger	Jackson Fristoe
Omar Gonzalez	Tyrone Yulie
Chalniel Arias	Brian Hendry
Christian Zazueta	Danny Watson
	Justin Lange

1 JASSON DOMINGUEZ, OF

Born: February 7, 2003. **B-T:** B-R. **HT:** 5-9. **WT:** 190.
Signed: Dominican Republic, 2019.
Signed by: Juan Rosario/Lorenzo Piron/Edgar Mateo.

TRACK RECORD: When he signed in 2019, Dominguez instantly became one of the most celebrated Yankees prospects in recent memory. His pro debut got pushed back a year when the pandemic canceled the 2020 minor league season. The spotlight got even brighter in summer 2021, when Dominguez was named to his first Futures Game before he had played a game outside the Florida Complex League. He returned to the Futures Game in 2022 and hit a booming home run to center field at Dodger Stadium. He finished the season in Double-A with a flourish, homering from both sides of the plate in the game that clinched the Eastern League championship for Somerset. In 2023, Dominguez returned to Somerset, where he started slowly before turning it on in the summer months, and especially after a promotion to Triple-A. He opened his big league career with a bang on Sept. 1, when he homered off Justin Verlander in his first major league at-bat. He homered three more times over the next seven games before tearing the ulnar collateral ligament in his right elbow and having Tommy John surgery.

SCOUTING REPORT: Dominguez's 2023 season started slowly and strangely. From Opening Day until June 30, he hit .197/.345/.357 and had the look of a three-true-outcomes hitter. At that time, nearly half of his plate appearances ended in either a walk (56), a strikeout (85) or a home run (10). He hit the ball plenty hard all year long, with an average exit velocity of 91.4 mph and a 90th percentile EV of 105.7 mph, both above-average marks compared to his peers. His plate discipline was also excellent, with above-average in-zone and overall miss rates of 17.5% and 26.8%. Once the calendar hit July, Dominguez's numbers started to look more in line with his tools. In 42 games until he was promoted to Triple-A, he hit .331/.399/.492. His combination of plate discipline, contact and power could make him at least an above-average hitter with potentially plus power. Dominguez split his time in the minors nearly evenly between left field and center field and got all of his defensive reps in the big leagues in center. The presence of Everson Pereira, who is a stronger defender up the middle, could push Dominguez into a corner.

RICH SCHULTZ/GETTY IMAGES

BA GRADE	SCOUTING GRADES
60 Risk: High	Hit: 55. Power: 60. Run: 60. Field: 50. Arm: 60.

Projected future grades on 20-80 scouting scale

BEST TOOLS

BATTING

Best Hitter for Average	Ben Rice
Best Power Hitter	Jasson Dominguez
Best Strike-Zone Discipline	Jasson Dominguez
Fastest Baserunner	Jasson Dominguez
Best Athlete	Jasson Dominguez

PITCHING

Best Fastball	Chase Hampton
Best Curveball	Chase Hampton
Best Slider	Henry Lalane
Best Changeup	Luis Serna
Best Control	Will Warren

FIELDING

Best Defensive Catcher	Carlos Narvaez
Best Defensive Infielder	Roderick Arias
Best Infield Arm	Roderick Arias
Best Defensive Outfielder	Brandon Lockridge
Best Outfield Arm	Jasson Dominguez

If that happens, his bat should easily fit the necessary profile. Scouts saw above-average run times Dominguez, and his sprint speed in his major league cameo fit the bill for a potentially plus runner once he gets underway. Tommy John surgery clouds his long-term arm strength, which scouts pegged as at least plus before the surgery. They also noted he did a good job getting himself into a strong position to throw.

THE FUTURE: Recovery from Tommy John surgery is quicker for position players, and Dominguez should be back in MLB at some point in 2024. If he reaches his ceiling, he's a potential all-star who hits in the middle of a lineup. ∎

Year	Age	Club (League)	Level	AVG	G	AB	R	H	2B	3B	HR	RBI	BB	SO	SB	OBP	SLG
2023	20	Somerset (EL)	AA	.254	109	425	83	108	19	2	15	66	77	130	37	.367	.414
2023	20	Scranton/W-B (IL)	AAA	.419	9	31	6	13	3	1	0	10	6	3	3	.514	.581
2023	20	New York (AL)	MLB	.258	8	31	6	8	1	0	4	7	2	8	1	.303	.677
Minor League Totals				.266	294	1113	212	296	54	11	36	154	182	334	86	.372	.431
Major League Totals				.258	8	31	6	8	1	0	4	7	2	8	1	.303	.677

2 SPENCER JONES, OF

HIT: 40. **POW:** 60. **RUN:** 55. **FLD:** 50. **ARM:** 50. **BA Grade:** 60. **Risk:** Very High.

Born: May 14, 2001. **B-T:** L-L. **HT:** 6-7. **WT:** 225.
Drafted: Vanderbilt, 2022 (1st round). **Signed By:** Chuck Bartlett.

TRACK RECORD: Jones was a two-way talent as a high schooler, but a broken elbow helped him make it to campus at Vanderbilt. The Yankees drafted him 25th overall in 2022 and signed him for $2,880,800. Jones reached Low-A in his pro debut, then split his first full season between High-A and Double-A. His 155 strikeouts were the most in the system, and his 109 mph 90th-percentile exit velocity tied for the highest in the organization.

SCOUTING REPORT: See Jones on the right day and he looks like one of the best prospects in baseball. See him on the wrong day and his strikeout issues appear to put a sizable roadblock in his path. Jones improved as the 2023 season went on, going from a 34.6% strikeout rate in April and May to a 26% rate from June onward. To achieve that success, he had to improve his approach and swing decisions. He was selling out to crush fastballs, which made him vulnerable to breaking balls. Sliders overall were particularly vexing, and he had trouble with breaking balls below the zone in general. Once he started adjusting his approach to the way pitchers were attacking him, he got better. Jones' power is one of his calling cards, and his 93.8 mph average exit velocity was among the 10 best in the minor leagues among players with 100 or more plate appearances. Jones' long strides allow him to cover a lot of ground in center field, but scouts are split about whether he'll remain there. If he moves off the position, his average arm would fit in either corner.

THE FUTURE: The 2024 season will be big for Jones. He'll spend an entire season facing upper-level pitchers with the quality stuff and command to demonstrate how much further Jones will need to improve to reach his ceiling as an athletic middle-order thumper.

Year	Age	Club (League)	Level	AVG	G	AB	R	H	2B	3B	HR	RBI	BB	SO	SB	OBP	SLG
2023	22	Hudson Valley (SAL)	A+	.268	100	411	62	110	28	4	13	56	42	133	35	.337	.450
2023	22	Somerset (EL)	AA	.261	17	69	9	18	1	0	3	10	7	22	8	.333	.406
Minor League Totals				.279	142	573	92	160	35	4	20	78	60	175	55	.351	.459

3 EVERSON PEREIRA, OF

HIT: 45. **POW:** 55. **RUN:** 60. **FLD:** 55. **ARM:** 55. **BA Grade:** 55. **Risk:** High.

Born: April 10, 2001. **B-T:** R-R. **HT:** 5-11. **WT:** 191.
Signed: Venezuela, 2017. **Signed by:** Roney Calderon.

TRACK RECORD: In 2017, the Yankees used some of the money they had allocated for Shohei Ohtani to sign Pereira. His career has been waylaid time and again by injuries, and 2022 is his only season with more than 100 games. Pereira was excellent at the upper levels in 2023 and made his big league debut on Aug. 22. He struggled mightily in the majors, striking out nearly 39% of the time.

SCOUTING REPORT: Pereira has plenty of tools. Now, he needs to make more contact to help them turn into skills. His raw power is among the best in the system, with some scouts putting it at nearly double-plus, and his 90th percentile exit velocity of 109 mph was tied with Spencer Jones for tops in the organization. In the minors, his miss rate was 36%. In a small big league sample, that figure jumped to 43%, which coincided with a 4% increase in swing rate. If he becomes more selective, Pereira could be a fringe-average hitter with above-average power. The Yankees also worked with him to simplify the movement with his hands from a season ago, and also helped him learn which swings to deploy in which situations and against which pitches. Of the Yankees' upper-level options, Pereira is the best bet to stick in center field, where his plus speed helps him track down balls from gap to gap. He has an above-average arm as well, which would allow him to play in a corner if needed.

THE FUTURE: After a taste of the big leagues, Pereira will be given every opportunity in spring training to earn a spot on the Opening Day roster, especially with Jasson Dominguez recovering from Tommy John surgery. If he can cut down on his swing-and-miss issues, he has a chance to be a well-rounded center fielder.

Year	Age	Club (League)	Level	AVG	G	AB	R	H	2B	3B	HR	RBI	BB	SO	SB	OBP	SLG
2023	22	Somerset (EL)	AA	.291	46	165	24	48	10	1	10	31	19	54	7	.362	.545
2023	22	Scranton/W-B (IL)	AAA	.312	35	138	29	43	7	1	8	33	13	44	4	.386	.551
2023	22	New York (AL)	MLB	.151	27	93	6	14	4	0	0	10	8	40	4	.233	.194
Minor League Totals				.279	291	1129	206	315	55	14	56	205	122	369	47	.353	.501
Major League Totals				.151	27	93	6	14	4	0	0	10	8	40	4	.233	.194

4 RODERICK ARIAS, SS

HIT: 55. **POW:** 60. **RUN:** 55. **FLD:** 60. **ARM:** 70. **BA Grade:** 60. **Risk:** Extreme.

Born: September 9, 2004. **B-T:** B-R. **HT:** 6-0. **WT:** 178.
Signed: Dominican Republic, 2022. **Signed by:** Esdras Abreu.
TRACK RECORD: Arias was the Yankees' top signing in the 2022 international period, garnering a $4 million bonus that was the second-highest in the class. The shortstop spent his first pro season in the Dominican Summer League, but his year was limited by injury to just 31 games. He moved stateside to the Florida Complex League in 2023 and showed flashes of potential all-star upside before a broken thumb brought his season to a close after just 27 games.
SCOUTING REPORT: In an FCL loaded with talent, Arias stood above nearly all the rest as one of the clear-cut top prospects in the league. He came by his accolades thanks to a set of eye-popping tools that could make him a fixture in the middle of the Yankees' lineup in a few years. He has the potential to be at least an above-average hitter thanks to an outstanding feel for the strike zone and an unwillingness to chase, albeit with a slightly elevated rate of in-zone miss relative to age and level. When Arias connects, he does damage. His exit velocities and barrel rate were better than average, including a 90th percentile EV of 103.5 mph. He hit six home runs before the injury, including one off the batter's eye against big leaguer Alek Manoah. Arias has a strong shot to stick at shortstop and got better as the year went along. He handles most anything hit his way and has the elite arm strength to erase runners on balls hit deep in the hole. Arias is an extremely athletic player who is a plus runner who glides around the basepaths, especially when he gets underway.
THE FUTURE: Arias will get his first test of full-season ball in 2024, when he will continue down a development path that could lead him to a starring role in New York. He's got a long way to go until then, and he must stay healthy as well.

Year	Age	Club (League)	Level	AVG	G	AB	R	H	2B	3B	HR	RBI	BB	SO	SB	OBP	SLG
2023	18	FCL Yankees	Rk	.267	27	101	32	27	2	2	6	26	27	29	17	.423	.505
Minor League Totals				.230	58	209	57	48	8	4	9	37	55	75	27	.400	.435

5 AUSTIN WELLS, C

HIT: 45. **POW:** 55. **RUN:** 30. **FLD:** 40. **ARM:** 40. **BA Grade:** 55. **Risk:** High.

Born: July 12, 1999. **B-T:** L-R. **HT:** 6-2. **WT:** 220.
Drafted: Arizona, 2020 (1st round). **Signed by:** Troy Afenir.
TRACK RECORD: Wells was drafted twice by the Yankees—once in high school and then again in 2020, when was an eligible sophomore at Arizona after the pandemic-shortened 2020 season. He missed time in 2022 with a ruptured testicle and then missed more time in 2023 with a fractured rib during spring training. He made his season debut on April 25, then put forth an .897 OPS in a season split mostly at Double-A and Triple-A. He made his big league debut on Sept. 1 and hit three home runs in 19 games.
SCOUTING REPORT: One of Wells' main objectives in 2023 was to improve his bat path. When he was slumping, he'd hang too long on his backside and then let his swing get too steep and uphill, which created a hole at the top of the zone. When he flattened his path, he became more of a complete hitter, especially when combined with his stellar knack for contact, impact and strong swing decisions. He has the skills to hit roughly .250 with a high on-base percentage and 20-25 home runs a season. Defensively, Wells draws raves for his work ethic and dedication to improvement. Scouts noticed better receiving skills and a quicker transfer on his throws, which helps counteract arm strength that is improved but is still below-average and led to him throwing out just 13% of basestealers. Scouts also noticed Wells' strong leadership skills and ability to command a pitching staff. He is a well below-average runner.
THE FUTURE: The Yankees' current catching situation features Jose Trevino in front and five more backstops on the 40-man roster vying for the backup job. Wells should have a chance in spring training to grab that spot, with a chance to earn more and more time as the season progresses.

Year	Age	Club (League)	Level	AVG	G	AB	R	H	2B	3B	HR	RBI	BB	SO	SB	OBP	SLG
2023	23	Tampa (FSL)	A	.176	5	17	2	3	0	0	1	2	3	3	0	.300	.353
2023	23	Somerset (EL)	AA	.237	58	228	28	54	14	0	11	50	29	60	5	.327	.443
2023	23	Scranton/W-B (IL)	AAA	.254	33	126	16	32	10	0	5	20	16	34	2	.349	.452
2023	23	New York (AL)	MLB	.229	19	70	8	16	6	0	4	13	3	14	0	.257	.486
Minor League Totals				.260	291	1089	188	283	64	6	53	213	175	304	39	.370	.476
Major League Totals				.229	19	70	8	16	6	0	4	13	3	14	0	.257	.486

6 CHASE HAMPTON, RHP

FB: 60. **CB:** 55. **SL:** 55. **CHG:** 45. **CUT:** 50. **CTL:** 60 **BA Grade:** 55. **Risk:** High.

Born: August 7, 2001. **B-T:** R-R. **HT:** 6-2. **WT:** 220.
Drafted: Texas Tech, 2022 (6th round). **Signed by:** Brian Rhees.
TRACK RECORD: The Yankees drafted Hampton out of Texas Tech in 2022, then shut him down in favor of work behind the scenes in their pitching program. That work included adding a slider and cutter to his repertoire. Hampton made his pro debut in 2023 and almost immediately ascended into the upper echelon of the system's pitching prospects. He split his season between High-A and Double-A and finished with 12.2 strikeouts per nine innings.
SCOUTING REPORT: Hampton's bread-and-butter pitches are his fastball and slider, which he threw the most frequently. The former is around 94 mph and has touched a few ticks higher while showing outstanding vertical break. The latter is a mid-80s pitch that scouts see as a potentially above-average breaking pitch. His curveball is on equal footing with his slider, though it is thrown more in the high 70s with top-down break that garnered whiffs both in and out of the zone. Hampton's cutter—one of the weapons the Yankees introduced when he turned pro—is an excellent weapon that he can land to both his glove and arm side with short, sharp break. Hampton has a fringy, seldom-used changeup in the high 80s. He ties the package together with control that is at least above-average and could get to plus with further refinement. When he was at High-A, he found he could simply dominate hitters with his stuff. Upon moving to Double-A, he spent time learning how to become more of a complete pitcher. He learned which pitches to throw in certain situations, and the Yankees still would like to see him throw his fastball more often.
THE FUTURE: Hampton should begin 2024 in Triple-A with a chance to make his big league debut in the second half. He has the upside of a No. 3 starter if everything comes together in his development.

Year	Age	Club (League)	Level	W	L	ERA	G	GS	IP	H	HR	BB	SO	BB%	SO%	WHIP	AVG
2023	21	Hudson Valley (SAL)	A+	2	1	2.68	9	9	47	31	5	16	77	8.4	40.5	1.00	.179
2023	21	Somerset (EL)	AA	2	2	4.37	11	11	60	54	8	21	68	8.5	27.4	1.26	.240
Minor League Totals				4	3	3.65	20	20	107	85	13	37	145	8.4	33.1	1.15	.214

7 HENRY LALANE, LHP

FB: 60. **SL:** 65. **CHG:** 60. **CTL:** 60. **BA Grade:** 55. **Risk:** Extreme.

Born: May 18, 2004. **B-T:** L-L. **HT:** 6-7. **WT:** 211.
Signed: Dominican Republic, 2021. **Signed by:** Jose Ravelo.
TRACK RECORD: Lalane was part of the Yankees' 2021 international signing class. The lefthander comes from athletic bloodlines, with a father who played basketball collegiately in New York, then for the Dominican national team and professionally in Europe, and a mother who played volleyball. Both parents passed their athleticism to their son, who spent two seasons in the Dominican Summer League before moving to the Florida Complex League in 2023. He was the clear-cut best pitching prospect on the circuit, with a 34-to-4 strikeout-to-walk ratio in 21.2 innings.
SCOUTING REPORT: Lalane's hallmark is not a single pitch but the combination of size, athleticism and stuff that gives him an extremely high upside. The 6-foot-7 lefty works with a four-pitch mix, starting with a mid-90s fastball that peaked at 97 mph. The pitch has strong movement properties and gains deception because of its low release height. He backs up his fastball primarily with a mid-80s changeup and a high-70s slider. Each projects to at least a plus pitch. Lalane's changeup was deceptive enough to get whiffs at a nearly 53% clip, and his slider was nasty enough that he could throw it at the back foot of righthanders and get plenty of awkward swings and misses. Lalane tied his mix together with impressive coordination of his massive frame and long levers, to the point where he could throw strikes in both quality and volume. The next steps will be to work to keep his slider shape more consistent and to get stronger in order to add more velocity to all his pitches.
THE FUTURE: Lalane will graduate to full-season ball in 2024 and could see time at both Class A levels. If he continues to show the same combination of stuff, athleticism and coordination, he could be the best lefthander New York has developed since Jordan Montgomery.

Year	Age	Club (League)	Level	W	L	ERA	G	GS	IP	H	HR	BB	SO	BB%	SO%	WHIP	AVG
2023	19	FCL Yankees	Rk	1	0	4.57	8	5	22	17	3	4	34	4.5	38.6	0.97	.207
Minor League Totals				5	6	3.57	31	28	111	94	5	43	125	9.1	26.4	1.23	.227

8 GEORGE LOMBARD JR., SS

HIT: 55. **POW:** 55. **RUN:** 55. **FLD:** 55. **ARM:** 60. **BA Grade:** 55. **Risk:** Extreme.

Born: June 2, 2005. **B-T:** R-R. **HT:** 6-3. **WT:** 190.
Drafted: HS—Miami, 2023 (1st round). **Signed by:** Ronnie Merrill.
TRACK RECORD: Lombard is the son of former big leaguer George Lombard, who played for four teams over parts of six seasons and is now on the Tigers' coaching staff. Lombard Jr. was one of the youngest players in the 2023 draft class and upped his prospect stock over the summer by showing up with increased strength that showed up in his power and speed. The Yankees drafted Lombard 26th overall and signed him away from a Vanderbilt commitment for $3.3 million. He split his first pro test between the Florida Complex League and Low-A.
SCOUTING REPORT: Lombard is a well-rounded player who has five tools that all grade as at least average, with power and speed that could get to above-average. His swing, which starts with a slow leg kick, is both controlled and powerful. It allowed him to produce a .989 OPS on the showcase circuit and then rack up more walks (13) than strikeouts (12) in 13 pro games. He handles both velocity and spin well, doesn't show any obvious flaws and posted solid exit velocity numbers in his small pro sample. His first step out of the box is a little bit slower, but he can produce above-average run times and kick it up a shade higher underway. Lombard has solid actions up the middle and plus arm strength, which should give him a strong chance to stick at shortstop. If he fills out his frame further, it might push him toward third base, which would put more pressure on his bat. If more power comes with the strength, he could profile at the position.
THE FUTURE: Lombard will open his first full year as a pro with Low-A Tampa, where he could share shortstop with fellow top prospect Roderick Arias. He has the upside of a middle infielder who provides value on both sides of the ball.

Year	Age	Club (League)	Level	AVG	G	AB	R	H	2B	3B	HR	RBI	BB	SO	SB	OBP	SLG
2023	18	FCL Yankees	Rk	.417	4	12	3	5	1	0	0	2	5	2	3	.588	.500
2023	18	Tampa (FSL)	A	.273	9	33	6	9	1	0	0	4	8	10	1	.415	.303
Minor League Totals				.311	13	45	9	14	2	0	0	6	13	12	4	.466	.356

9 WILL WARREN, RHP

FB: 60. **CB:** 40. **SL:** 60. **CHG:** 45. **CUT:** 45. **CTL:** 55. **BA Grade:** 50. **Risk:** High.

Born: June 16, 1999. **B-T:** R-R. **HT:** 6-2. **WT:** 175.
Drafted: Southeastern Louisiana, 2021 (8th round). **Signed by:** Mike Leuzinger.
TRACK RECORD: An eighth-round pick in 2021, Warren was shut down after signing in favor of more controlled instruction at the team's minor league complex in Tampa. When he emerged, he put forth a breakout 2022 season between High-A and Double-A that included 125 strikeouts in 129 innings and earned him the organization's minor league pitcher of the year honors. He split 2023 between Double-A and Triple-A, where he struck out 149 in 129 innings.
SCOUTING REPORT: Warren works with a varied arsenal that includes four- and two-seam fastballs, as well as a cutter, slider, changeup and curveball. Both fastballs are thrown around 94 mph and occasionally bump a tick higher. He changed the grip on his four-seamer this season in an attempt to give it more life. Warren's sweeping slider is also a potential plus pitch, and it pairs well with his two-seamer to form an excellent east-west attack. He rounds out his repertoire with a fringy changeup in the high 80s. Warren added a cutter in 2023 to help him attack lefthanded hitters more effectively. His cutter and curveball were thrown a combined 5% of the time. The Yankees want Warren to continue to learn the best ways to deploy his mix, and part of the reason behind his promotion to Triple-A was to show him that more advanced hitters are less prone to chasing pitches than those at the lower levels. Those hitters, plus a stricter strike zone enforced by the automated ball-strike system, led to a slightly elevated walk rate and about a 2% lower strike rate. Warren has plenty of weapons. Now, he needs to learn the best ways to use them.
THE FUTURE: Warren's likely role is as a starter toward the back end of a rotation with a fallback option as a powerful multi-inning reliever. He should make his MLB debut in 2024.

Year	Age	Club (League)	Level	W	L	ERA	G	GS	IP	H	HR	BB	SO	BB%	SO%	WHIP	AVG
2023	24	Somerset (EL)	AA	3	0	2.45	6	6	29	26	0	12	39	9.9	32.2	1.30	.239
2023	24	Scranton/W-B (IL)	AAA	7	4	3.61	21	19	100	83	15	47	110	10.9	25.6	1.30	.223
Minor League Totals				19	13	3.63	53	51	258	228	25	101	274	9.2	25.1	1.28	.236

10 KYLE CARR, LHP

FB: 60. **SL:** 50. **CH:** 40. **CTL:** 55. **BA Grade:** 55. **Risk:** Extreme

Born: May 6, 2002. **B-T:** L-L. **HT:** 6-1. **WT:** 175.
Drafted: Palomar (CA) JC, 2023 (3rd round). **Signed by:** Troy Afenir/Scott Lovekamp.
TRACK RECORD: Carr's arrow started pointing up in high school during the summer of 2020, but the shortened five-round draft led him to honor his commitment to San Diego. He made nine appearances with the Toreros and pitched with Orleans of the Cape Cod League. He transferred to Palomar JC for the 2023 season, then struck out 111 hitters in 78 innings. The Yankees took him with their third-round pick, signed him for $692,000 and then shut him down in favor of targeted instruction after the regular season.
SCOUTING REPORT: In high school, Carr's fastball sat between 92-95 mph and touched 97. He still has projection remaining, which could lead to longer bouts of that velocity band. Carr pairs the fastball with a nasty sweeping slider in the mid 80s with huge break away from lefties. He's got a developing changeup in the mid 80s, but it's a clear third pitch at this point and was a focal point during the team's instructional league camp. Carr ties it together with outstanding athleticism—he ran 6.6-second 60-yard dashes—that helps him repeat his delivery and get to his best stuff with ease. He was a two-way player at Palomar and hit .500 in the spring.
THE FUTURE: Carr will make his pro debut in 2024, when he should at least reach Low-A Tampa at some point during the season, if not on Opening Day. In a system typically low and lefthanders, he the upside to fit in the middle of a rotation.

Year	Age	Club (League)	Level	W	L	ERA	G	GS	IP	H	HR	BB	SO	BB%	SO%	WHIP	AVG
2023	21	Did not play															

11 BRANDO MAYEA, OF

HIT: 55. **POW:** 50. **SPD:** 70. **FLD:** 50. **ARM:** 60. **BA Grade:** 55. **Risk:** Extreme.

Born: September 12, 2005. **B-T:** R-R. **HT:** 5-11. **WT:** 205. **Signed:** Cuba, 2023. **Signed by:** Juan Piron.
TRACK RECORD: Mayea defected from Cuba at an early age and established residency in the Dominican Republic. He signed with the Yankees on Jan. 15, 2023 for $4.35 million, the third-highest bonus of any player signed in the class. He spent his first pro season in the Dominican Summer League, where produced a .782 OPS with three homers and 18 RBIs. He missed about 10 days of action after a minor ankle injury sustained on Opening Day while trying to stretch a double into a triple.
SCOUTING REPORT: Mayea was one of the most coveted player on the international market thanks to a well-rounded set of tools that should help him provide value on both sides of the ball. He turned in a solid pro debut that included excellent bat-to-ball skills compared to his peers and max exit velocities up to 108 mph. To turn those traits into more production, he'll need to get more balls in the air. In the DSL, 58% of his contact was on the ground. His speed and athleticism should help him stick in center field, where he can be an average defender with an arm that could get to plus if he gains strength. He's a double-plus runner who can cover plenty of ground. .
THE FUTURE: Mayea should move to the Florida Complex League in 2024, when he'll get his first test stateside and should continue the wave of high-impact talent that the Yankees have sent through the low minors in recent years.

Year	Age	Club (League)	Level	AVG	G	AB	R	H	2B	3B	HR	RBI	BB	SO	SB	OBP	SLG
2023	17	DSL Yankees	Rk	.276	38	145	27	40	7	1	3	18	22	27	22	.382	.400
Minor League Totals				.276	38	145	27	40	7	1	3	18	22	27	22	.382	.400

12 BEN RICE, C

HIT: 50. **POW:** 55. **SPD:** 30. **FLD:** 40. **ARM:** 40. **BA Grade:** 50. **Risk:** High.

Born: February 22, 1999. **B-T:** L-R. **HT:** 6-1. **WT:** 215. **Drafted:** Dartmouth, 2021 (12th round). **Signed by:** Matt Hyde.
TRACK RECORD: After a season and change at Dartmouth, Rice's college career ended when the pandemic canceled the remainder of the 2020 season and the Ivy League chose to cancel the 2021 season as well. By the time he was drafted, he had nearly three times as many plate appearances in summer college leagues as he did with Dartmouth. Yankees area scout Matt Hyde stayed on him the whole time, and New York pounced in the 12th round. After two seasons spent mostly at Low-A, Rice broke out in 2023 and was one of the system's biggest risers despite a left oblique injury that limited his season to just 73 games.
SCOUTING REPORT: Throughout his career, Rice's hallmark has been his strong plate discipline and bat-

to-ball skills. The results have been strikeout and walk rates of roughly 19% and 13%. He was also one of just three minor leaguers with 20 or more homers and fewer than 70 strikeouts. The lefty hitter hits the ball quite hard, with average (91) and 90th percentile (104) exit velocities that ranked among the best in the system. His barrel accuracy was also excellent. When he's going bad, Rice has a tendency to hook balls. To fix the problem, the Yankees worked with him to keep his body in the proper position to stay behind pitches and drive them across the field. Rice catches in a one-knee down stance and did a good job keeping pitches in front of him—he allowed just one passed ball all year—but he's going to have to really improve his arm to control the running game. He caught just 5 of 68 potential basestealers between High-A and Double-A. Rice also got into 18 games at first base, which could be his long-term home.

THE FUTURE: Rice will play all of the 2024 season as a 25-year-old, when he'll likely make his Triple-A debut. He could be an offensive-minded player who bounces between first base and catcher but plays regularly.

Year	Age	Club (League)	Level	AVG	G	AB	R	H	2B	3B	HR	RBI	BB	SO	SB	OBP	SLG
2023	24	Tampa (FSL)	A	.286	10	35	7	10	3	0	2	10	5	10	1	.405	.543
2023	24	Hudson Valley (SAL)	A+	.341	15	44	15	15	2	0	2	10	18	10	3	.559	.523
2023	24	Somerset (EL)	AA	.327	48	196	40	64	13	1	16	48	21	42	7	.401	.648
Minor League Totals				.287	163	547	102	157	29	1	32	117	85	124	16	.398	.519

13 CARLOS LAGRANGE, RHP

FB: 70. **CB:** 40. **SL:** 70. **CHG:** 30. **CTL:** 40. **BA Grade:** 55. **Risk:** Extreme.

Born: May 25, 2003. **B-T:** R-R. **HT:** 6-7. **WT:** 195. **Signed:** Dominican Republic, 2022.
Signed by: Luis Brito/Ethan Sander.

TRACK RECORD: The Yankees signed Lagrange in 2022 out of the Dominican Republic. He spent his first pro season in the Dominican Summer League, where he allowed just 10 hits over 33 innings while striking out 43. He advanced stateside in 2023 and was part of an extraordinarily talented Florida Complex League that advanced to the championship round. His 63 strikeouts were the most in the league since 2018.

SCOUTING REPORT: Lagrange is a big, powerful righthander who cuts an intimidating presence on the mound and has the stuff to match. He primarily uses four- and two-seam fastballs that each sit between 95-97 mph and can reach triple-digits. The four-seamer is a monster, with high spin and horizontal break and a 44% miss rate. The two-seamer comes in a tick slower. His slider sits around 83 mph and induced a whiff rate of 48%. Lagrange has both a curveball and a changeup in his mix, but neither is thrown often and both have a long way to go before they're truly viable parts of his arsenal. His control and command are below-average but showed improvement throughout the course of the season and he made his movement toward the plate more direct and consistent.

THE FUTURE: Lagrange is part of a pack of high-upside arms lurking at the back of the Yankees' system. He has the ceiling of a No. 3 starter but could also be a bullpen hammer in the mold of Dellin Betances if he doesn't improve his control or bring forward a third pitch.

Year	Age	Club (League)	Level	W	L	ERA	G	GS	IP	H	HR	BB	SO	BB%	SO%	WHIP	AVG
2023	20	FCL Yankees	Rk	0	0	4.97	12	11	42	34	4	24	63	12.4	32.5	1.39	.214
Minor League Totals				0	1	4.14	23	21	75	44	5	43	106	13.3	32.7	1.18	.166

14 BROCK SELVIDGE, LHP

FB: 55. **SL:** 60. **CHG:** 40. **CUT:** 40. **CTL:** 50. **BA Grade:** 50. **Risk:** High.

Born: August 28, 2002. **B-T:** R-L. **HT:** 6-3. **WT:** 205. **Drafted:** HS—Chandler, AZ, 2021 (3rd round).
Signed by: Troy Afenir.

TRACK RECORD: The Yankees took Selvidge out of an Arizona high school in the third round of the 2021 draft and signed him to a $1.5 million bonus, the second-highest in their class. He spent both of his first two seasons in the Florida Complex League before advancing to full-season ball in 2023. He split the year between both Class A levels and racked up 137 strikeouts, the seventh-most in the system.

SCOUTING REPORT: The vast majority of Selvidge's mix is made up of two pitches: a low-90s four-seam fastball with late ride and a mid-80s bullet slider. The former pitch posted elite spin rates around 2,700 rpm, while the latter spun at roughly the same rate that was good for both called strikes and chases. Mechanical adjustments to get him a bit more north-south in his delivery helped Selvidge's velocity tick up a touch. The next step is to use his mid-80s changeup and high-80s cutter more often to give himself a more complete arsenal. Scouts notice that Selvidge slows his arm on his offspeeds and cutter, which will allow upper-level hitters to capitalize. He also needs to get stronger in his lower half in order to avoid spinning off and spraying the ball all over the zone.

THE FUTURE: Selvidge has a chance to fit around a No. 4 starter if he brings his changeup or cutter forward and irons out the kinks in his delivery. If not, his fastball and slider should fit in the bullpen.

Year	Age	Club (League)	Level	W	L	ERA	G	GS	IP	H	HR	BB	SO	BB%	SO%	WHIP	AVG
2023	20	Tampa (FSL)	A	4	4	3.38	15	14	77	72	3	21	91	6.5	28.0	1.20	.240
2023	20	Hudson Valley (SAL)	A+	4	1	3.58	9	9	50	44	2	14	46	6.6	21.7	1.15	.226
Minor League Totals				11	6	3.31	38	34	174	155	7	53	194	7.2	26.5	1.20	.232

15 TREY SWEENEY, SS

HIT: 45. **POW:** 50. **RUN:** 45. **FLD:** 45. **ARM:** 50. **BA Grade:** 45. **Risk:** High.

Born: April 24, 2000. **B-T:** L-R. **HT:** 6-4. **WT:** 2000. **Drafted:** Eastern Illinois, 2021 (1st round). **Signed by:** Steve Lemke.
TRACK RECORD: After an excellent career at Eastern Illinois, Sweeney was selected by the Yankees in the first round of the 2021 draft. He's moved steadily through the system since then, reaching Double-A in 2022 for the team's run to the Eastern League championship and spending 100 games at the level in 2023. He spent a month on the injured list late in the season with an unspecified injury.
SCOUTING REPORT: The Yankees spent the season simplifying Sweeney's mechanics, including eliminating a bat tip and reducing the movement in his load. Sweeney also opened his stance a little bit and set his hands higher in order to let his barrel travel through the zone on a higher plane. Sweeney saw a jump in his exit velocity data, moving from an 86.2 mph average in 2022 to 87.1 mph in 2023, and also lowered his miss rate year over year. The results, scouts noticed, was more authoritative contact and a much-improved bat path that was more direct to the ball. He had a noticeable issue against breaking balls, with miss rates of worse than 30% against both sliders and curveballs. He's a fringy defender with fringy speed and an average arm which should allow him to play shortstop without standing out at the position.
THE FUTURE: Sweeney will advance to Triple-A in 2024. He has the ceiling of a second-division shortstop.

Year	Age	Club (League)	Level	AVG	G	AB	R	H	2B	3B	HR	RBI	BB	SO	SB	OBP	SLG
2023	23	Somerset (EL)	AA	.252	100	397	67	100	20	2	13	49	65	90	20	.367	.411
Minor League Totals				.248	243	945	173	234	43	10	36	119	153	239	55	.361	.429

16 CLAYTON BEETER, RHP

FB: 55. **CB:** 30. **SL:** 60. **CHG:** 45. **CTL:** 40. **BA Grade:** 45. **Risk:** High.

Born: October 9, 1998. **B-T:** R-R. **HT:** 6-2. **WT:** 220. **Drafted:** Texas Tech, 2020 (2nd round supplemental). **Signed by:** Clint Bowers (Dodgers).
TRACK RECORD: Beeter was the Dodgers' second-round pick in 2020 out of Texas Tech, where he was teammates with current system-mate TJ Rumfield. He was dealt from Los Angeles to New York in the 2022 deal that sent Joey Gallo west. He split his 2023 season between Double-A and Triple-A, was the Yankees' representative in the Futures Game and finished with 165 strikeouts, the eighth-most in the minors.
SCOUTING REPORT: Beeter works primarily with a combination of a low-90s fastball and a low-80s slider. Together, the pair accounted for roughly 90% of his pitches in 2023. Scouts believe the deception in Beeter's delivery helps his fastball play better than its velocity. His sweepy slider has the makings of a plus pitch and will be his primary offspeed weapon no matter his future role. He ties his repertoire together with a curveball at around 81 mph and a changeup around 85 mph. Both pitches were sparingly used, but scouts thought the changeup had potential to be at least fringy. The curveball is mostly a strike-stealer. The Yankees believe Beeter's struggles at Triple-A, where his strikeout rate stayed static but his walk rate ballooned to 5.6 per nine innings, showed him that he needs to pitch with more finesse rather than throwing his mix with max effort.
THE FUTURE: Beeter was added to the 40-man roster this offseason, suggesting that he could make his big league debut in 2024. While he has an outside shot to start, his likely future is as a reliever who can pitch in short bursts or bulk innings.

Year	Age	Club (League)	Level	W	L	ERA	G	GS	IP	H	HR	BB	SO	BB%	SO%	WHIP	AVG
2023	24	Somerset (EL)	AA	6	2	2.08	12	12	61	44	3	31	76	12.1	29.7	1.24	.204
2023	24	Scranton/W-B (IL)	AAA	3	5	4.94	15	14	71	61	15	44	89	13.9	28.1	1.48	.227
Minor League Totals				9	16	3.86	80	76	261	207	34	143	372	12.6	32.8	1.34	.215

17 YOENDRYS GOMEZ, RHP

FB: 55. **CB:** 40. **SL:** 50. **CHG:** 40. **CTL:** 45. **BA Grade:** 40. **Risk:** Medium.

Born: October 15, 1999. **B-T:** R-R. **HT:** 6-3. **WT:** 212. **Signed:** Venezuela, 2016. **Signed by:** Alan Atacho.

TRACK RECORD: Gomez signed with the Yankees in 2016 and was one the system's most intriguing arms in the years before the pandemic. Tommy John surgery ended his 2021 season early and limited his 2022 season to just 47 innings. He dealt with right shoulder tendinitis in 2023 but recovered enough to make his big league debut on Sept. 28.

SCOUTING REPORT: After showing depressed stuff in 2022, Gomez looked closer in 2023 to his pre-surgery form. The righthander works with a four-pitch mix dominated by a combination of his four-seam fastball and slider. The former pitch averages roughly 94 mph with excellent shape and decent miss rates. The latter is thrown around 84 mph and features more sweep than vertical break. His curveball sits in the high 70s while the cutter averages around 88 mph. The Yankees have worked with Gomez to become more consistent with the length of his stride, which they believe will improve control and command that were slipshod in 2023.

THE FUTURE: Now that he's made his debut, 2024 will be a big year for Gomez. He's likely out of options and would need to make the big club out of spring training. He's likely a middle reliever at this point..

Year	Age	Club (League)	Level	W	L	ERA	G	GS	IP	H	HR	BB	SO	BB%	SO%	WHIP	AVG
2023	23	Somerset (EL)	AA	0	3	3.58	19	19	65	47	6	37	78	13.5	28.5	1.29	.200
2023	23	New York (AL)	MLB	0	0	0.00	1	0	2	1	0	0	4	0.0	50.0	0.50	.143
Minor League Totals				9	12	3.44	78	75	275	222	16	123	292	10.6	25.2	1.25	.219
Major League Totals				0	0	0.00	1	0	2	1	0	0	4	0.0	50.0	0.50	.143

18 LUIS GIL, RHP

FB: 60. **SL:** 60. **CHG:** 45. **CTL:** 45. **BA Grade:** 40. **Risk:** Medium.

Born: June 3, 1998. **B-T:** R-R. **HT:** 6-2. **WT:** 185. **Signed:** Dominican Republic, 2014. **Signed by:** Luis Lajara (Twins).

TRACK RECORD: Gil was traded to the Yankees from the Twins in 2018 in a deal that sent outfielder Jake Cave to Minnesota. He made six big league starts in 2021 and one more in 2022 before suffering a torn ulnar collateral ligament that required Tommy John surgery. He did not pitch in the big leagues in 2023 but made two rehab starts at Low-A Tampa.

SCOUTING REPORT: At his best, Gil works with a three-pitch mix. Before the surgery his fastball showed the markings of a true plus pitch, with mid-90s velocity and high spin and hop through the zone. In his brief 2023 showing, the pitch averaged 96 mph. He backed it with a slider that also had a chance to rank as a 60 on the 20-to-80 scouting scale. At Tampa, the pitch sat around 86 mph and got whiffs on the half the swings it induced. Gil completes his mix with a low-90s changeup that before the surgery showed fringe-average potential His command and control were fringe-average during his major league stint.

THE FUTURE: Gil will be ready to start fresh come spring training, when he will battle for a spot on the big league staff. His time away will make a starter's workload tricky, and he still needs to prove that his changeup and control need to come forward a bit to reach his former ceiling. His fastball and slider could make him a useful weapon out of the bullpen, especially if he gets a few more ticks of velocity when deployed in shorter bursts.

Year	Age	Club (League)	Level	W	L	ERA	G	GS	IP	H	HR	BB	SO	BB%	SO%	WHIP	AVG
2023	25	Tampa (FSL)	A	0	0	11.25	2	2	4	6	0	3	6	14.3	28.6	2.25	.333
Minor League Totals				13	16	3.52	90	71	312	235	22	187	418	13.7	30.7	1.35	.203
Major League Totals				1	1	3.78	7	7	33	25	4	21	43	14.2	29.1	1.38	.198

19 AGUSTIN RAMIREZ, C

HIT: 45. **POW:** 60. **RUN:** 30. **FLD:** 40. **ARM:** 60. **BA Grade:** 45. **Risk:** High.

Born: September 10, 2001. **B-T:** R-R. **HT:** 6-0. **WT:** 210. **Signed:** Dominican Republic, 2018. **Signed by:** Juan Piron.

TRACK RECORD: Ramirez was signed out of the Dominican Republic in 2018 and has moved slowly through the system. He repeated the Florida Complex League in 2022 and didn't reach full-season ball until 2023, when he got on a rocket ship through the system. Ramirez zoomed from Low-A to Double-A, slugging 18 home runs along the way. The total bested his previous career mark by four longballs.

SCOUTING REPORT: Ramirez's calling card is going to be the damage he can do with his bat. He marries bat speed with a stroke that keeps the barrel in the zone a long time. The combination helped him produce big-time average (91 mph) and 90th percentile (106.6 mph) exit velocities that will give him a ceiling as a thumper. Ramirez also makes a lot of contact in the strike zone but needs to rein in his chase rates a touch. He also could stand to make his path to the zone a little less steep. He has plus arm strength

but needs plenty of polish when it comes to receiving and blocking. He's a well below-average runner.
THE FUTURE: The Yankees protected Ramirez on the 40-man roster, and he'll return to Double-A in 2024. If he can rein in chase rate, he'll make the most of his strength and bat speed and could be an offensive-minded backstop. He also got a few games at first base upon moving to Double-A, and his bat would profile at the position.

Year	Age	Club (League)	Level	AVG	G	AB	R	H	2B	3B	HR	RBI	BB	SO	SB	OBP	SLG
2023	21	Tampa (FSL)	A	.245	56	184	35	45	7	0	7	35	43	41	7	.384	.397
2023	21	Hudson Valley (SAL)	A+	.384	27	112	21	43	10	0	9	23	8	17	2	.430	.714
2023	21	Somerset (EL)	AA	.211	31	128	17	27	7	0	2	11	10	27	3	.273	.313
Minor League Totals				.266	231	846	147	225	58	1	32	161	111	183	26	.352	.450

20 JARED SERNA, 2B

HIT: 50. **POW:** 40. **RUN:** 40. **FLD:** 45. **ARM:** 40. **BA Grade:** 45. **Risk:** High.

Born: June 1, 2002. **B-T:** R-R. **HT:** 5-6. **WT:** 168. **Signed:** Mexico, 2019. **Signed by:** Lee Sigman.
TRACK RECORD: Serna was inked out of Mexico in 2019 but the pandemic canceled the minor league season and pushed his debut until 2021. The righthanded hitter walked more often than he struck out at both stops in the complex leagues. He had a rough introduction to full-season ball in 2022 but rebounded in 2023 with an excellent year across both Class A affiliates.
SCOUTING REPORT: Serna is an intriguing hitter who makes sound swing decisions with decent thump but needs to improve the trajectory of his contact. He has quick hands and a quick bat and rarely misses pitches inside the zone. Serna's chase rate was a bit high, which leads to weak contact on pitches he cannot impact. He did a better job elevating the ball when he was at Low-A but regressed into beating the ball into the ground when he moved to High-A. He projects as an average hitter with below-average power and doesn't have a frame that looks like it can add much more strength. Serna is a steady defender who could be fringe-average at second base, where his below-average arm is less of an issue because of the new shift restrictions that limit positioning infielders in the outfield.
THE FUTURE: The 2024 season will be a big test for Serna, who will reach the upper levels for the first time. His limited defensive profile will mean he needs to hit to his complete potential to reach his ceiling of a bat-first everyday second baseman.

Year	Age	Club (League)	Level	AVG	G	AB	R	H	2B	3B	HR	RBI	BB	SO	SB	OBP	SLG
2023	21	Tampa (FSL)	A	.283	95	400	72	113	21	1	19	71	40	75	19	.350	.483
2023	21	Hudson Valley (SAL)	A+	.287	27	108	18	31	7	2	0	8	9	15	10	.350	.389
Minor League Totals				.273	221	827	170	226	48	6	28	125	111	156	70	.371	.447

21 KEINER DELGADO, SS

HIT: 55. **POW:** 30. **RUN:** 60. **FLD:** 55. **ARM:** 50. **BA Grade:** 50. **Risk:** Extreme.

Born: January 5, 2004. **B-T:** B-R. **HT:** 5-7. **WT:** 145. **Signed:** Venezuela, 2021.
Signed by: Luis Delgado/Jose Gavidia/Ricardo Finol.
TRACK RECORD: Delgado was signed out of Venezuela in 2021 and opened his career with a standout season in the Dominican Summer League. He finished the year with more walks (58) than strikeouts (28). His walks and OBP (.504) were the second-best on the circuit. He moved stateside in 2023 and fit right in on a spectacularly talented Florida Complex League team. His hits (58) and total bases (96) were second in the league.
SCOUTING REPORT: Scouts universally tabbed Delgado with two words: Baseball player. The infielder rarely misses or chases and has a knack for manipulating the barrel, but there wasn't a whole lot of impact paired with his contact. The Yankees worked hard to add some strength to his frame through plenty of time in the weight room, but his average and 90th percentile exit velocities were still well below-average. He bounced between both middle-infield spots and scouts believe he fits best at second base because of an average arm and just fair range. He has soft hands and strong instincts that pair well with speed that can get to plus underway. Scouts ooze about Delgado's instinct and makeup.
THE FUTURE: Delgado gets the most out of his tools and will have no problem reaching his ceiling as a quality backup who earns ample playing time.

Year	Age	Club (League)	Level	AVG	G	AB	R	H	2B	3B	HR	RBI	BB	SO	SB	OBP	SLG
2023	19	FCL Yankees	Rk	.293	49	198	54	58	12	1	8	31	36	31	36	.414	.485
Minor League Totals				.301	101	366	104	110	28	5	11	59	94	59	70	.459	.495

22 ENGELTH UREÑA, C

HIT: 55. **POW:** 55. **RUN:** 40. **FLD:** 40. **ARM:** 55. **BA Grade:** 50. **Risk:** Extreme.

Born: August 17, 2004. **B-T:** R-R. **HT:** 6-0. **WT:** 196. **Signed:** Dominican Republic, 2022.
Signed by: Jose Ravelo/Edgar Mateo.
TRACK RECORD: Ureña inked for $275,000 as part of the Yankees' 2022 signing class—the jewel of which was shortstop Roderick Arias—and then made a quick impression in the Dominican Summer League, but a broken hand meant Ureña played just 11 games. The damage was worse in 2023, when surgery on his left knee kept him off the field all season long.
SCOUTING REPORT: When healthy, Ureña has shown the skills necessary to be the latest in the Yankees' line of offense-first catchers. He showed a taste of those skills in 2022 when he homered in his first professional at-bat. The blast became even more impressive when the team found out afterward that he'd done so with a broken hand suffered earlier in the game. The lack of reps has also cost Ureña much-needed development time on defense, where he was already raw thanks to an amateur career spent mostly as an outfielder. He showed an above-average arm but needs to continue to polish the rest of his defensive skills in order to stick at the position.
THE FUTURE: If Ureña returns healthy in 2024, he should make his stateside debut in the Florida Complex League, where he'd be part of another wave of talented prospects working their way through the Yankees' lower levels.

Year	Age	Club (League)	Level	AVG	G	AB	R	H	2B	3B	HR	RBI	BB	SO	SB	OBP	SLG
2023	18	Did not play															

23 JORDARLIN MENDOZA, RHP

FB: 60. **SL:** 60. **CTL:** 40. **BA Grade:** 50. **Risk:** Extreme.

Born: November 14, 2003. **B-T:** R-R. **HT:** 6-0. **WT:** 175. **Signed:** Dominican Republic, 2021. **Signed by:** Esdras Abreu.
TRACK RECORD: Mendoza signed on June 30, 2021 and got into one game in the DSL. He's a former center fielder who caught the Yankees eye thanks to the athleticism that comes from his background as a center fielder and a clean arm stroke. He returned to the DSL in 2022 for a full workload and led the league with 77 strikeouts. He moved stateside in 2023 and spent the year in the Florida Complex League, where he pitched in a piggyback role and showed dominant stuff over the course of 10 outings. Despite never making a start, his six wins led the FCL.
SCOUTING REPORT: Mendoza works with two pitches—a mid-90s four-seam fastball and a nasty slider in the mid 80s. His fastball can show hard sinking and boring action in on the hands of righthanded hitters, while the slider sweeps away from their barrels. The Yankees have worked with Mendoza to improve his delivery and get him moving in a better direction toward the plate, which they believe will help improve his control and command. He's shown feel for a changeup but did not throw any in 2023.
THE FUTURE: Scouts see Mendoza as a pure relief prospect with the upside and arsenal to be a late-inning force. He'll move to full-season for the first time in 2024.

Year	Age	Club (League)	Level	W	L	ERA	G	GS	IP	H	HR	BB	SO	BB%	SO%	WHIP	AVG
2023	19	FCL Yankees	Rk	6	0	4.40	10	0	29	16	2	24	39	18.6	30.2	1.40	.162
Minor League Totals				7	1	3.39	24	12	86	62	5	44	119	12.1	32.8	1.25	.205

24 JOHN CRUZ, OF

HIT: 50. **POW:** 60. **RUN:** 55. **FLD:** 55. **ARM:** 55. **BA Grade:** 50. **Risk:** Extreme.

Born: August 29, 2005. **B-T:** L-L. **HT:** 6-3. **WT:** 171. **Signed:** Dominican Republic, 2022.
Signed by: Dennis Woody/Juan Piron.
TRACK RECORD: The Yankees' club in the Florida Complex League had evaluators buzzing all summer long, with headliners like Roderick Arias and Henry Lalane getting the bulk of the ink. Cruz's combination of youth and production opened eyes, and he finished the year as one of three players in the league with double-digit home runs.
SCOUTING REPORT: The Yankees signed Cruz on the strength of a loose, powerful swing from the left side with a body that could add plenty more strength. Those traits showed up in spades in the FCL, where scouts saw a player with less rawness than one would expect for a player his age. There's some mechanical issues in his swing that causes a bit of a hole at the top of the zone, and he needs to make better swing decisions in order to make high-quality contact more often. His whiff rates are better than average for his age, but he often hits pitcher's pitches and makes weak contact. Scouts are split about whether Cruz will stick in center field. If he moves to a corner, his above-average arm strength and speed would fit well

in right field.

THE FUTURE: Cruz will get his first taste of full-season ball in 2024, when he will move to Low-A Tampa. He likely fits as a corner outfielder with power and hittability who can man center field in a pinch.

Year	Age	Club (League)	Level	AVG	G	AB	R	H	2B	3B	HR	RBI	BB	SO	SB	OBP	SLG
2023	17	FCL Yankees	Rk	.294	48	177	28	52	6	3	10	47	22	44	9	.376	.531
Minor League Totals				.260	102	346	66	90	14	6	15	71	70	106	19	.394	.465

25 JERSON ALEJANDRO, RHP
FB: 70. **SL:** 50. **CHG:** 65. **CTL:** 50. **BA Grade:** 50. **Risk:** Extreme.

Born: February 23, 2006. **B-T:** R-R. **HT:** 6-6. **WT:** 255. **Signed:** Dominican Republic, 2023.
Signed by: Juan Brito/Edgar Mateo.
TRACK RECORD: Alejandro was the top pitching prospect the Yankees added in their most recent international signing class. He was lauded for his combination of size, athleticism and present stuff. He spent his first season in the Dominican Summer League, where he showed flashes of high-end stuff and struck out 36 hitters in as many innings.
SCOUTING REPORT: Alejandro cuts an intimidating presence on the mound at 6-foot-6 and 255 pounds and shows the stuff to match. His fastball in 2023 sat in the low 90s and peaked around 94, though it was up to 98 in his amateur days. He backs the fastball with a nasty changeup in the low 80s that has flashed plus and might get even better with more use. As an amateur he threw a curveball that flashed average and would be a third pitch to round out his arsenal, but now the pitch has become a low-80s slider with short, sharp shape. He should have average control as he develops into his frame and learns to sync his massive frame.
THE FUTURE: Alejandro will move stateside in 2024, when he will be part of what should be part of another high-upside group in the Florida Complex League.

Year	Age	Club (League)	Level	W	L	ERA	G	GS	IP	H	HR	BB	SO	BB%	SO%	WHIP	AVG
2023	17	DSL Yankees	Rk	1	4	4.50	10	9	36	30	3	17	36	10.8	22.9	1.31	.224
Minor League Totals				1	4	4.50	10	9	36	30	3	17	36	10.8	22.9	1.31	.224

26 ENMANUEL TEJEDA, 2B/3B
HIT: 50. **POW:** 30. **RUN:** 60. **FLD:** 50. **ARM:** 45. **BA Grade:** 45. **Risk:** Extreme.

Born: December 25, 2004. **B-T:** R-R. **HT:** 5-11. **WT:** 158. **Signed:** Dominican Republic, 2022.
Signed by: Luis Brito/Victor Mata/Edgar Mateo.
TRACK RECORD: Tejeda signed out of the Dominican Republic in 2022, then put forth a strong debut that summer that saw him rack up more walks (41) than strikeouts (22). He repeated the performance after moving stateside, where his .465 on-base percentage ranked second in the Florida Complex League and his 24 stolen bases were second only to teammate Keiner Delgado.
SCOUTING REPORT: Tejeda is a smaller player who makes plenty of contact but lacks impact at this point. His average and 90th percentile exit velocities were well below-average, but his offensive skills were buoyed by outstanding rates of miss and chase and excellent swing decisions. Tejeda was a shortstop as an amateur but split his 2023 season between second and third base in deference to a host of other middle infielders, like Roderick Arias and Keiner Delgado and George Lombard Jr. Second base is his best position, and he'll likely be average there thanks to strong instincts and speed that grades as at least plus. He has average arm strength but needs to improve his accuracy.
THE FUTURE: Tejeda will move to Low-A Tampa in 2024, where he'll again be clustered with Lombard, Arias and Delgado on the infield. He could be a utility infielder with skills on both sides of the ball.

Year	Age	Club (League)	Level	AVG	G	AB	R	H	2B	3B	HR	RBI	BB	SO	SB	OBP	SLG
2023	18	FCL Yankees	Rk	.307	50	166	37	51	4	3	5	30	44	44	24	.465	.458
Minor League Totals				.299	96	308	72	92	10	10	8	52	85	69	35	.464	.474

27 ROC RIGGIO, 2B
HIT: 50. **POW:** 50. **RUN:** 40. **FLD:** 45. **ARM:** 45. **BA Grade:** 40. **Risk:** High.

Born: June 11, 2002. **B-T:** L-R. **HT:** 5-9. **WT:** 180. **Drafted:** Oklahoma State, 2023 (4th round). **Signed by:** Matt Ranson.
TRACK RECORD: As a high schooler, Riggio was part of the same California club that also produced A's prospect Max Muncy. Riggio landed at Oklahoma State and was a key part of the Cowboys' lineup for two seasons before becoming a draft-eligible sophomore. The Yankees took him in the fourth-round in 2023 and signed him for $693,000, which was above slot by roughly 37%.

SCOUTING REPORT: Riggio doesn't have a standout tool on the card, but he's solid across the board. The lefthanded hitter cut his strikeouts and raised his walk rate in 2023 and reached max exit velocities of 110 mph. He has a filled-out body without much room for more strength, but he's got enough thump behind the ball right now. Riggio made it to Low-A and spent his time as a pro working to improve his swing decisions against non-fastballs. He's a fringy defender who hangs in on double plays. He has strong makeup that will help him work to improve his trouble spots.

THE FUTURE: Riggio's college pedigree should allow him to advance to High-A out the gate in 2023. He has the ceiling of a solid middle infielder who does a little bit of everything but won't overwhelm in any one area.

Year	Age	Club (League)	Level	AVG	G	AB	R	H	2B	3B	HR	RBI	BB	SO	SB	OBP	SLG
2023	21	FCL Yankees	Rk	.188	5	16	2	3	0	0	0	0	4	6	0	.381	.188
2023	21	Tampa (FSL)	A	.193	17	57	11	11	2	0	0	9	18	18	3	.395	.228
Minor League Totals				.192	22	73	13	14	2	0	0	9	22	24	3	.392	.219

28 TJ RUMFIELD, 1B

HIT: 45. POW: 50. RUN: 40. FLD: 50. ARM: 55. BA Grade: 40. Risk: High.

Born: May 17, 2000. **B-T:** L-R. **HT:** 6-4. **WT:** 225. **Drafted:** Virginia Tech, 2021 (12th round). **Signed by:** Kellan McKeon (Phillies).

TRACK RECORD: The Phillies drafted Rumfield out of Virginia Tech in 2021, and he made his pro debut with Low-A Clearwater. The Yankees acquired him the following offseason in a trade that sent Nick Nelson and Donny Sands to Philadelphia. His 2022 season was limited by injuries to just 57 games, though he made up for lost time in the Arizona Fall League. He dealt with injuries again in 2023 but still homered 17 times in 86 games.

SCOUTING REPORT: In 2023, Rumfield worked to simplify his mechanics and load in order to create a more direct path to the ball so he could get to his power more frequently. The result was strong contact ability despite slightly elevated chase rates. He hit just .219 on the season, part of which could be attributed to swing decisions that lead to a bit of poor contact. Another part of the equation was a BABIP of just .227. Rumfield's an average defender at first base with an above-average arm. His speed is below-average.

THE FUTURE: Rumfield should move to Triple-A in 2024, when he'll look to stay healthy for a full season and let his offensive skills show for an extended period of time. His plate discipline will be tested by the automatic ball-strike system

Year	Age	Club (League)	Level	AVG	G	AB	R	H	2B	3B	HR	RBI	BB	SO	SB	OBP	SLG
2023	23	Hudson Valley (SAL)	A+	.286	4	14	2	4	2	0	0	3	1	2	0	.313	.429
2023	23	Somerset (EL)	AA	.219	82	297	43	65	14	0	17	55	39	75	8	.320	.438
Minor League Totals				.243	170	596	85	145	30	0	21	100	90	135	12	.351	.399

29 JACK NEELY, RHP

FB: 60. SL: 65. CTL: 55. BA Grade: 40. Risk: High.

Born: June 5, 2000. **B-T:** R-R. **HT:** 6-8. **WT:** 245. **Drafted:** Ohio State, 2021 (11th round). **Signed by:** Mike Gibbons.

TRACK RECORD: Neely began his career at Texas, then transferred to Ohio State in 2021, after the sport resumed post-pandemic. He worked to a 6.10 ERA in his lone season with the Buckeyes but also struck out 62 hitters in 41.1 innings. The Yankees popped him in the 11th round in 2021, then let him get his feet wet in Low-A. He was one of the system's most dominant relievers and was the only pitcher in the minors to strike out 100 hitters without making a start.

SCOUTING REPORT: Neely cuts an imposing figure on the mound at 6-foot-8 and 245 pounds, and he gets outs with a pair of pitches that each grade as plus or better. His fastball averaged 95 mph and touched a tick higher with plenty of life through the zone. Neely's biggest weapon, however, is his slider. The pitch sits in the mid 80s with short, sharp life and more sweep than depth. He threw the pitch nearly half the time and got whiffs at a 58% clip. His arsenal plays up thanks to the deception in his delivery, and he ties everything together with above-average control and command that's maybe a tick below.

THE FUTURE: After finishing 2024 in Double-A, he should return to the level in 2024 and could make his big league debut late in the season. He has the stuff to be a late-game weapon.

Year	Age	Club (League)	Level	W	L	ERA	G	GS	IP	H	HR	BB	SO	BB%	SO%	WHIP	AVG
2023	23	Hudson Valley (SAL)	A+	5	3	2.03	31	0	49	27	4	17	74	9.0	39.2	0.90	.160
2023	23	Somerset (EL)	AA	1	2	2.55	11	0	18	12	4	3	26	4.3	37.1	0.85	.182
Minor League Totals				10	6	2.75	82	0	119	77	11	46	192	9.5	39.8	1.04	.180

30 RAFAEL FLORES, C/1B

HIT: 40. **POW:** 50. **RUN:** 20. **FLD:** 40. **ARM:** 45. **BA Grade:** 40. **Risk:** High.

Born: October 5, 1999. **B-T:** R-R. **HT:** 6-4. **WT:** 220. **Signed:** Rio Hondo (CA) JC, 2022 (NDFA). **Signed by:** Dave Keith.

TRACK RECORD: Flores played his college ball with Rio Hondo (Calif.) JC and also played with the Alaska Goldpanners—a barnstorming summer college team—after the 2022 season. He went undrafted in 2022 but the Yankees signed him as a free agent. He got into four games in the Florida Complex League after signing, then spent all of 2023 at High-A Hudson Valley, where he split time between catcher and first base.

SCOUTING REPORT: At first blush, Flores' season doesn't jump off the page. Look a little deeper, and you can see a player who performed a bit better than his stats. His OPS was just .712, but he hit the ball hard. His average (89.6 mph) and 90th percentile (104.3) exit velocities were both above-average compared to his peers. Flores mostly did a good job staying within the zone, but he did show a weakness against offspeed pitches. His barrel accuracy is solid, but he needs to tighten his approach against non-fastballs. Flores is a passable defender who frames well but needs to continue to add polish to his blocking. He has average arm strength that plays down because he is a bigger-bodied player who takes a while to get rid of the ball out of his one-knee setup.

THE FUTURE: Flores will move up to Double-A in 2024, where he is likely to once again split backstop duties with Ramirez. He's a sneaky prospect who could jump further onto the radar if his hard-hit rates begin translating into more production.

Year	Age	Club (League)	Level	AVG	G	AB	R	H	2B	3B	HR	RBI	BB	SO	SB	OBP	SLG
2023	22	Hudson Valley (SAL)	A+	.259	105	382	49	99	15	1	8	41	49	108	3	.346	.366
Minor League Totals				.265	109	396	53	105	16	1	10	47	49	111	3	.348	.386

Oakland Athletics

BY MARK CHIARELLI

The 2023 season represented a painful nadir for the Athletics' time in Oakland.

The A's entered the season with the lowest payroll in baseball and lost a franchise-record 112 games. They finished at least 40 games out of first place in the American League West for the second consecutive season.

Yet things were even worse off the field.

Oakland's entire season was set against the backdrop of relocation rumors amid ownership's inability to reach an agreement with the city on a new ballpark. A painful split seemed inevitable, even more so after team president Dave Kaval announced an agreement to purchase land in late April for a new ballpark in Las Vegas.

Fans protested the move, staging a reverse boycott of John Fisher and ownership in mid June at the Oakland Coliseum, but to little avail. MLB owners voted in mid November to approve Oakland's relocation to Las Vegas. The A's are likely to become just the second MLB team to relocate in the past 50 years, following the Expos' move to Washington in 2005.

The overall uncertainty created an unfortunate and difficult situation across all levels of the organization. It's unclear where the A's will play after their ballpark lease with the city of Oakland ends in 2024, and it has not announced interim plans until a stadium in Vegas is ready in 2028. And it's also not particularly clear which players will make up their core, either.

The A's had a few bright spots in 2023. Rookie second baseman Zack Gelof emerged as a foundational piece. Outfielder Brent Rooker, who was claimed on waivers last November, became an all-star. Players the team hopes are part of its future, such as Mason Miller, Tyler Soderstrom and Lawrence Butler, all made their debuts.

But there's a prevailing concern the A's haven't infused their system with enough high-end talent, especially after stripping down their big league roster and dealing the likes of Matt Olson, Matt Chapman and Sean Murphy. The Chapman haul from the Blue Jays looks especially haunting. Of the four players acquired, only righthander Gunnar Hoglund remains in the organization, but injuries have kept him mostly on the shelf.

Some high-profile first-round misses in the back half of the 2010s hurt. An unlucky draw in MLB's first draft lottery didn't help, either. The A's entered tied for the best odds to land the No. 1 overall pick in 2023 but instead fell to No. 6, where they selected Grand Canyon shortstop Jacob Wilson, a standout defender who may lack the offensive upside of those who went before him.

All Zack Gelof has done is hit since the Athletics drafted him in the second round in 2021.

GREG FIUME/GETTY IMAGES

PROJECTED 2027 LINEUP

Catcher	Shea Langeliers	27
First Base	Tyler Soderstrom	25
Second Base	Zack Gelof	27
Third Base	Darell Hernaiz	25
Shortstop	Jacob Wilson	25
Left Field	Esteury Ruiz	28
Center Field	Denzel Clarke	26
Right Field	Lawrence Butler	26
Designated Hitter	Max Muncy	26
No. 1 Starter	Mason Miller	28
No. 2 Starter	Luis Morales	24
No. 3 Starter	JP Sears	31
No. 4 Starter	Royber Salinas	25
No. 5 Starter	Jack Perkins	27
Closer	Joe Boyle	27

The A's hope under-the-radar trade acquisitions like shortstop Darell Hernaiz and righthander Joe Boyle help to slowly turn the tide. The team remains excited about Soderstrom's hitting potential, even despite a shaky pro debut.

While Oakland has struggled to develop high-priced international signees, Cuban righthander Luis Morales could quickly change that trend. And the team's player development apparatus is savvy at turning unheralded players into MLB contributors.

The 2024 season could get a little better, especially with several prominent prospects expected to settle into big league roles. But Oakland's road to contention figures to be a long and winding one, and it's unclear when—and where—it ends. ∎

DEPTH CHART

OAKLAND ATHLETICS

TOP 2024 CONTRIBUTORS	RANK
1. Mason Miller, RHP	1
2. Tyler Soderstrom, 1B/C	2
3. Lawrence Butler, OF	6

BREAKOUT PROSPECTS	RANK
1. Henry Bolte, OF	13
2. Jack Perkins, RHP	15
3. Colby Thomas, OF	20

SOURCE OF TOP 30 TALENT

Homegrown	23	Acquired	7
College	13	Trade	7
Junior college	0	Rule 5 draft	0
High school	7	Independent league	0
Nondrafted free agent	0	Free agent/waivers	0
International	0		

LF
Lazaro Armenteros
Clark Elliott
Junior Perez

CF
Denzel Clarke (5)
Ryan Lasko (18)
Jonah Cox (28)
Brayan Buelvas
Max Schuemann
Caeden Trenkle
Pedro Pineda

RF
Lawrence Butler (6)
Henry Bolte (13)
Colby Thomas (20)
Nate Nankil
Joseph Rodriguez

3B
Myles Naylor (12)
Brett Harris (17)
Yeniel Laboy

SS
Jacob Wilson (3)
Darell Hernaiz (7)
Max Muncy (9)
Drew Swift
Bjay Cooke
Angel Arevalo

2B
Cooper Bowman (21)
Euribiel Angeles
Colby Halter

1B
Tyler Soderstrom (2)
Will Simpson (29)
Brennan Milone
Logan Davidson
Drew Lugbauer
Mario Gomez

C
Daniel Susac (11)
Cesar Gonzalez (26)
Kyle McCann

LHP

LHSP	LHRP
Brady Basso (22)	Garrett Irvin
Eduardo Rivera	
James Gonzalez	

RHP

RHSP	RHRP
Mason Miller (1)	Freddy Tarnok (24)
Luis Morales (4)	Ryan Cusick (25)
Joe Boyle (8)	Jacob Watters (30)
Steven Echavarria (10)	Tyler Baum
Royber Salinas (14)	Grant Holman
Jack Perkins (15)	Drew Conover
Joey Estes (16)	Stevie Emanuels
Cole Miller (19)	Pedro Santos
Nathan Dettmer (23)	Blake Beers
Mitch Spence (27)	Billy Sullivan
Gunnar Hoglund	Jack Weisenburger
J.T. Ginn	Yunior Tur
Joelvis Del Rosario	
Jose Dicochea	
Jefferson Jean	
Tzu-Chen Sha	

1 MASON MILLER, RHP

Born: August 24, 1994. **B-T:** R-R. **HT:** 6-5. **WT:** 220.
Drafted: Gardner-Webb, 2021 (3rd round).
Signed by: Neil Avent.

TRACK RECORD: Miller posted an ERA above 7.00 each of his first two seasons at Division III Waynesburg (Pa.) and walked more batters than he struck out as a sophomore while pitching with a nondescript mid-80s fastball. Of more concern, he struggled to keep on weight, losing 20 pounds during that time. It wasn't until Miller underwent a routine blood test—required by a potential summer internship—that doctors flagged an issue, ultimately identified as Type 1 diabetes. The discovery changed his career. Miller retooled his diet and steadily added physicality, leading to more effectiveness on the mound. He transferred to Gardner-Webb as a fifth-year senior in 2021 and struck out 121 batters in 92.2 innings. Oakland signed him for $599,100 as a third-round selection that year and was immediately impressed. Injuries, though, have led to an unusual development arc. Miller has thrown just 39.1 minor league innings. He missed nearly all of 2022 with a right rotator cuff strain, returning in August and subsequently shining in the Arizona Fall League. He made such an impression on the Athletics' big league staff at 2023 spring training that Oakland fast-tracked him to the majors, where he debuted in late April and posted a 3.78 ERA in 33.1 innings. He also missed three months between May and September with a right UCL sprain.

SCOUTING REPORT: When healthy, Miller flashes a dazzling arsenal that misses plenty of barrels. The righthander has a prototypical starter's build and a four-seam fastball that averaged 98.3 mph and touched 102 in the majors. The pitch possesses above-average carry and elicits whiffs at the top of the strike zone. Big league hitters batted just .186 against Miller's heater, and minor leaguers whiffed on the pitch 46% of the time within the strike zone. They had an even tougher time dealing with his plus slider. The mid-80s offering has sweep and depth, racking up a 47% whiff rate in his truncated big league showing. Mason reintroduced his mid-90s cutter in 2023 after shelving the pitch during his rehab a year prior, using it primarily against lefties. He also sparingly flashes a low-90s changeup. Miller has solid command and throws more than enough strikes to remain in a starting role—that is, if his body holds up. Miller explodes down the mound with force and has a short, quick arm path. His mechanics are fairly sound, but the A's believe there are some slight biomechanical improvements, such as staying better stacked and on line as he gets down the mound, that he can make to his delivery and finish to marginally aid his durability.

THE FUTURE: While Miller's stuff belongs near the front of a rotation, the A's are debating internally whether he's better suited for shorter stints given the arm issues. General manager David Forst indicated at the Winter Meetings—at least for 2024—that Miller will likely serve as a reliever. ∎

BA GRADE / SCOUTING GRADES

55 Risk: High

FB: 70. **SL:** 60. **CHG:** 50.
CUT: 60. **CTL:** 50.

Projected future grades on 20-80 scouting scale

BEST TOOLS

BATTING

Best Hitter for Average	Darell Hernaiz
Best Power Hitter	Tyler Soderstrom
Best Strike-Zone Discipline	Max Schuemann
Fastest Baserunner	Cooper Bowman
Best Athlete	Henry Bolte

PITCHING

Best Fastball	Joe Boyle
Best Curveball	Jacob Watters
Best Slider	Royber Salinas
Best Changeup	Tyler Baum
Best Control	Jack Cushing

FIELDING

Best Defensive Catcher	Kyle McCann
Best Defensive Infielder	Drew Swift
Best Infield Arm	Jacob Wilson
Best Defensive Outfielder	Denzel Clarke
Best Outfield Arm	Henry Bolte

Year	Age	Club (League)	Level	W	L	ERA	G	GS	IP	H	HR	BB	SO	BB%	SO%	WHIP	AVG
2023	24	Stockton (CAL)	A	0	0	4.91	2	2	4	3	1	2	4	13.3	26.7	1.36	.231
2023	24	Midland (TL)	AA	0	0	4.91	1	1	4	2	2	0	8	0.0	61.5	0.55	.154
2023	24	Las Vegas (PCL)	AAA	1	0	0.00	4	4	12	3	0	3	23	7.1	54.8	0.50	.077
2023	24	Oakland (AL)	MLB	0	3	3.78	10	6	33	24	2	16	38	11.5	27.3	1.20	.203
Minor League Totals				1	3	2.52	16	15	39	20	6	11	69	7.6	47.9	0.79	.150
Major League Totals				0	3	3.78	10	6	33	24	2	16	38	11.5	27.3	1.20	.203

2 TYLER SODERSTROM, C/1B

HIT: 50. **POW:** 60. **RUN:** 40. **FLD:** 45. **ARM:** 55. **BA Grade:** 55. **Risk:** High.

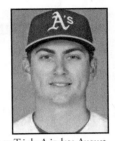

Born: November 24, 2001. **B-T:** L-R. **HT:** 6-2. **WT:** 200.
Drafted: HS—Turlock, CA, 2020 (1st round). **Signed by:** Kevin Mello.

TRACK RECORD: Oakland has moved Soderstrom assertively since he signed for an above-slot $3.3 million in 2020 on the strength of his amateur hitting prowess. He mostly enjoyed success as he ascended the minors, hitting 29 home runs at three levels in 2022 while reaching Triple-A. He hit a stumbling block in 2023, when he returned to Triple-A Las Vegas and posted an 88 wRC+ in 77 games. Oakland called up Soderstrom, along with Zack Gelof, on July 14. He hit .160 with a 31% strikeout rate in 45 games sandwiched around a return trip to Triple-A in late August.

SCOUTING REPORT: Evaluators have long coveted Soderstrom's swing, which is geared for damage to all fields and has become more powerful as he gets older. He led all A's minor leaguers in 90th percentile exit velocity in 2023 and showed an ability to find the barrel. Soderstrom's approach did not mature in the same manner. Triple-A pitchers exposed his willingness to expand the strike zone, especially on velocity up in the strike zone. Big leaguers only further exacerbated the issue. The A's don't believe Soderstrom has poor pitch recognition, but he hasn't shown much patience and the struggles compounded as the season progressed, sometimes following him to the field. Soderstrom caught roughly 40% of the time in Oakland. Evaluators were pleasantly surprised with his defense. Some give him a shot at becoming an average receiver with a solid-average arm, but there's work remaining to get there. He may ultimately settle into a hybrid role, mixing in at catcher, first base and DH.

THE FUTURE: The ingredients remain for Soderstrom to become an impact middle-of-the-order of the bat if he can develop the requisite patience after an eye-opening big league debut.

Year	Age	Club (League)	Level	AVG	G	AB	R	H	2B	3B	HR	RBI	BB	SO	SB	OBP	SLG
2023	21	Las Vegas (PCL)	AAA	.252	77	306	49	77	17	2	21	62	25	88	2	.307	.526
2023	21	Oakland (AL)	MLB	.160	45	125	9	20	1	0	3	7	11	43	0	.232	.240
Minor League Totals				.271	268	1033	154	280	58	8	62	216	92	294	4	.334	.523
Major League Totals				.160	45	125	9	20	1	0	3	7	11	43	0	.232	.240

3 JACOB WILSON, SS

HIT: 60. **POW:** 40. **RUN:** 50. **FLD:** 55. **ARM:** 55. **BA Grade:** 55 **Risk:** High.

Born: March 30, 2002. **B-T:** R-R. **HT:** 6-3. **WT:** 190.
Drafted: Grand Canyon, 2023 (1st round). **Signed by:** Jeff Urlaub.

TRACK RECORD: The son of all-star shortstop Jack Wilson, Jacob was coached by his father at Thousand Oaks (Calif.) High before enjoying a decorated collegiate career at Grand Canyon. He hit .412 as a junior while striking out just five times in 49 games. Wilson was Baseball America's No. 9 prospect in the 2023 draft class and landed with Oakland sixth overall, signing a $5.5 million bonus that was 17% under slot. In his pro debut he hit .318/.378/.455 in 23 games with High-A Lansing.

SCOUTING REPORT: Wilson's hallmark ability has long been his freakish bat-to-ball skills which carried into his professional debut. He's a twitchy athlete and greets pitchers in a unique manner. He employs an open stance and a bouncy pre-pitch routine before settling into a crouch as the pitch is delivered and lashing at the ball. He rarely misses, especially on pitches within the strike zone. The operation results in plenty of contact—but not all of the contact was particularly hard or on the barrel. Wilson posted below-average exit velocities in his debut and has faced concerns about his power output dating back to his college career. Wilson is aware of the criticisms and has shown some predilection for pull-side launch, and the A's are optimistic more power could come once he adds muscle to his frame after rarely lifting weights as an amateur. He'll also have to find the right balance between trusting his contact ability and chasing suboptimal offerings on the edges of the zone as he faces better pitchers. Defensively, Wilson shows off good hands, arm strength and instincts, albeit with average range.

THE FUTURE: Wilson has the potential to move quickly. His hitting skills and sound defense provide a high floor as an everyday shortstop, but his ceiling for offensive impact is somewhat capped without a material change in power.

Year	Age	Club (League)	Level	AVG	G	AB	R	H	2B	3B	HR	RBI	BB	SO	SB	OBP	SLG
2023	21	ACL Athletics	Rk	.455	3	11	4	5	2	0	0	5	0	1	0	.500	.636
2023	21	Lansing (MWL)	A+	.318	23	88	13	28	9	0	1	8	6	10	4	.378	.455
Minor League Totals				.333	26	99	17	33	11	0	1	13	6	11	4	.391	.475

4 LUIS MORALES, RHP

FB: 70. **CB:** 55. **SL:** 60. **CHG:** 45. **CTL:** 50. **BA Grade:** 60. **Risk:** Extreme.

Born: September 24, 2002. **B-T:** R-R. **HT:** 6-3. **WT:** 190.
Signed: Cuba, 2023. **Signed by:** Javier Agelvis.
TRACK RECORD: Morales struck out 135 batters over 82.2 innings in Cuba's 18U national league in 2020. He defected in 2021 and trained on his own outside of Mexico City until the Athletics signed him for $3 million in January 2023. That marked the largest deal for an international pitcher in the hard-capped era and Oakland's biggest bonus to an international arm since signing Michael Ynoa in 2008. The A's initially planned to move Morales slowly, but he forced their hand with a strong Dominican Summer League. He ultimately posted a 2.86 ERA in 44 innings across four different levels and ended the year with High-A Lansing at 20 years old.
SCOUTING REPORT: Morales is a highly projectable righthander who already sits 97 mph with a sinewy, high-waisted frame and loose, athletic delivery. He has one of the better fastballs in Oakland's system and showed average command for the pitch considering age and level. He also showed the feel to spin two separate breaking balls at nearly 3,000 rpm. His sweeping slider has plus potential as a swing-and-miss offering, and he also throws a curveball with more depth. The pitches sometimes blend together, and he struggled at times to land them in the zone. The A's want him to prioritize developing his slider. Morales' changeup is more of a developmental pitch, but it flashed solid-average potential. Some international scouts were concerned Morales' inconsistent command would ultimately push him to the bullpen. The A's were optimistic with Morales' strike-throwing in his pro debut and hope his athleticism will allow for continued improvement.
THE FUTURE: While Morales' profile is risky, it's easy to dream on his stuff and his relatively low-mileage arm. He has midrotation upside with more refinement of his strike-throwing.

Year	Age	Club (League)	Level	W	L	ERA	G	GS	IP	H	HR	BB	SO	BB%	SO%	WHIP	AVG
2023	20	DSL Athletics	Rk	0	0	0.82	4	3	11	4	0	2	16	5.1	41.0	0.55	.108
2023	20	ACL Athletics	Rk	0	2	6.00	3	3	9	10	0	2	11	5.0	27.5	1.33	.270
2023	20	Stockton (CAL)	A	0	3	2.20	5	5	16	13	0	8	18	11.6	26.1	1.29	.217
2023	20	Lansing (MWL)	A+	0	0	3.52	2	2	8	6	2	3	8	9.4	25.0	1.17	.207
Minor League Totals				0	5	2.86	14	13	44	33	2	15	53	8.3	29.4	1.09	.202

5 DENZEL CLARKE, OF

HIT: 45. **POW:** 60. **RUN:** 70. **FLD:** 70. **ARM:** 50. **BA Grade:** 55. **Risk:** Very High.

Born: May 1, 2000. **B-T:** R-R. **HT:** 6-5. **WT:** 225.
Drafted: Cal State Northridge, 2021 (4th round). **Signed by:** Dillon Tung.
TRACK RECORD: Clarke was a decorated amateur for Canada's junior national team, but he was more raw than the average college outfielder when the A's drafted him in the fourth round in 2021. He accrued just 326 at-bats over three college seasons at Cal State Northridge, so it was a mild surprise when he opened 2023 with Double-A Midland in late April after missing time with a left shoulder strain. Clarke blitzed the competition, hitting four homers over his first three games. He cooled off a bit in May and June, but still hit .261 with 12 homers through 64 games until a left shoulder injury ended his season in late July.
SCOUTING REPORT: Clarke has long faced questions about whether his hitting instincts and contact ability can improve to the point where his dynamic power and speed flourish regularly. He made meaningful progress toward addressing those concerns in 2023, albeit in a shortened season. Clarke showed more consistent timing and cut both his whiff and chase rates, allowing his plus raw power and solid on-base skills play more consistently. He still has some rather unique moves—Clarke holds his hands high and heel off the ground prior to the pitch—but tinkered with his stance and setup less in 2023. Clarke still battled bouts of swing-and-miss and was susceptible at times to good four-seam fastballs, especially up in the zone. Laying off breaking stuff down and away has also been a point of emphasis. Clarke is a plus defender who covers ample ground and is capable of making highlight-type plays in center field, with a strong arm. He's also a plus runner who has stolen 42 bases in 48 tries in pro ball.
THE FUTURE: Clarke will turn 24 in May and still has yet to reach Triple-A, but he has a relatively high ceiling if he can sustain his contact gains against more skilled pitching.

Year	Age	Club (League)	Level	AVG	G	AB	R	H	2B	3B	HR	RBI	BB	SO	SB	OBP	SLG
2023	23	Midland (TL)	AA	.261	64	234	54	61	11	4	12	43	37	85	11	.381	.496
Minor League Totals				.255	164	596	123	152	36	8	28	91	96	226	42	.373	.483

6 LAWRENCE BUTLER, OF

HIT: 45. **POW:** 60. **RUN:** 55. **FLD:** 50. **ARM:** 50. **BA Grade:** 50. **Risk:** High.

Born: July 10, 2000. **B-T:** L-R. **HT:** 6-1. **WT:** 223.
Drafted: HS—Atlanta, 2018 (6th round). **Signed by:** Jemel Spearman.
TRACK RECORD: Butler was a toolsy developmental pick in the sixth round in 2018 with swing-and-miss issues early in his pro career. He returned from the 2020 shutdown as a revelation since and has steadily ascended. Butler hit .284/.350/.475 across 89 games in 2023 between Double-A Midland and Triple-A Las Vegas before making his big league debut on Aug. 11, where he struggled to a .211/.240/.341 line and a 60 wRC+.
SCOUTING REPORT: Butler is a dynamic athlete. Originally drafted as a first baseman, he played almost exclusively in center field upon reaching Oakland in 2023. He's a powerful hitter with a strong, loose swing that produces good launch angles. Butler again posted some of the best 90th percentile exit velocities of any Oakland minor leaguer. A historically selective hitter, Butler also made meaningful adjustments to his approach in the minors in an attempt to reach that power more consistently. He cut his miss rate by roughly 8% and also reduced his chase rate despite increasing his swing rate for the second consecutive year. There will likely always be swing-and-miss elements to his game—he especially struggled with quality breaking balls in 2023—but there's a chance for fringe-average contact ability. Butler is a good runner who stole 21 bases in the minors. He covers enough ground to adequately play center field, but he needs to refine his routes to the ball. Most evaluators believe he's ultimately better suited for a corner. Butler draws positive reviews for his clubhouse presence and magnetic personality.
THE FUTURE: It may take some time to fully click, but Butler has the upside of an everyday power-speed corner threat who could become a foundational piece as Oakland tries to emerge from its rebuild.

Year	Age	Club (League)	Level	AVG	G	AB	R	H	2B	3B	HR	RBI	BB	SO	SB	OBP	SLG
2023	22	Midland (TL)	AA	.285	67	284	53	81	17	2	10	47	30	60	13	.352	.465
2023	22	Las Vegas (PCL)	AAA	.280	22	82	14	23	2	1	5	23	8	18	8	.340	.512
2023	22	Oakland (AL)	MLB	.211	42	123	10	26	4	0	4	10	4	35	0	.240	.341
Minor League Totals				.257	376	1351	235	347	71	14	50	223	181	466	67	.343	.441
Major League Totals				.211	42	123	10	26	4	0	4	10	4	35	0	.240	.341

7 DARELL HERNAIZ, SS/2B

HIT: 55. **POW:** 45. **RUN:** 50. **FLD:** 55. **ARM:** 45. **BA Grade:** 50. **Risk:** High.

Born: August 3, 2001. **B-T:** R-R. **HT:** 6-1. **WT:** 190.
Drafted: HS—El Paso, 2019 (5th round). **Signed by:** John Gillette (Orioles).
TRACK RECORD: Drafted by the Orioles in 2019, Hernaiz kickstarted his ascent through the minors by hitting .273 with 12 homers across three levels in 2022 and finishing at Double-A. The Athletics took notice and acquired him that winter in the deal that sent Cole Irvin to Baltimore. Hernaiz hit .321 in 131 games between Double-A and Triple-A in 2023.
SCOUTING REPORT: Hernaiz makes ample contact via a direct path to the ball and strong feel for the barrel. He also has a solid understanding of the strike zone and posted a nearly even strikeout-to-walk ratio at Triple-A in his age-21 season. He's an aggressive hitter, especially early in the count, employing an all-fields approach. While he produces above-average exit velocities for his age, he has a bit of a BABIP-dependent profile. His downhill swing plane isn't geared toward launch, tempering his power potential. Hernaiz posted a 51.6% groundball rate in his first taste of Triple-A. He also had significant reverse splits in 2023, particularly struggling against offspeed pitches from lefthanders. Defensively, Hernaiz benefited from working with A's Double-A manager Bobby Crosby, who will join Oakland's big league staff in 2024. Hernaiz has the hands and range to stay at shortstop, but his fringe-average arm is tested on more difficult throws. Some within the organization believe he ultimately moves to either second or third base. Hernaiz is a solid runner with good baserunning instincts, but there are concerns he may slow down as his body continues to fill out.
THE FUTURE: While he may have an opportunity to win Oakland's starting shortstop job out of spring training, Hernaiz could ultimately settle into a super-utility type role once other shortstops arrive.

Year	Age	Club (League)	Level	AVG	G	AB	R	H	2B	3B	HR	RBI	BB	SO	SB	OBP	SLG
2023	21	Midland (TL)	AA	.338	71	278	43	94	20	3	5	43	26	48	7	.393	.486
2023	21	Las Vegas (PCL)	AAA	.300	60	220	44	66	12	1	4	28	24	27	6	.376	.418
Minor League Totals				.291	359	1375	240	400	67	10	29	193	130	252	72	.357	.417

8 JOE BOYLE, RHP

FB: 70. **CB:** 50. **SL:** 70. **CUT:** 45. **CTL:** 30. **BA Grade:** 55. **Risk:** Extreme.

Born: August 14, 1999. **B-T:** R-R. **HT:** 6-7. **WT:** 240.
Drafted: Notre Dame, 2020 (5th round). **Signed by:** Tyler Gibbons (Reds).

TRACK RECORD: Boyle burnished a reputation for premium stuff and extreme erraticism as an amateur that continued as a pro. So much so that Boyle's 19.4% walk rate with Double-A Chattanooga in 2023 actually represented a subtle improvement. The ability to miss bats continued, though. The A's took notice and acquired Boyle from the Reds for reliever Sam Moll in a no-fanfare deadline deal. Boyle's strike-throwing drastically improved afterward. He made his MLB debut on Sept. 17 and posted a 1.69 ERA with 16 strikeouts over 15 innings in three starts.

SCOUTING REPORT: The 6-foot-7 Boyle cuts a formidable mound presence and backs it up with two premium pitches. He attacks hitters with an elite fastball that touches triple-digits and sat at 97-98 mph in 2023. It's a classic high-spin four-seamer thrown from an over-the-top release. His upper-80s slider may be even better and is his best putaway offering. He also showed the feel to spin a downer low-80s curveball that flashes plus, which he used more often in the minors. Boyle infrequently mixes in a low-90s cutter, and the A's would like him to explore adding a changeup. He has historically shown bottom-of-the-scale command despite a relatively fluid delivery and clean arm action. He made no major mechanical adjustments after the trade, though the A's noted he sometimes fights the timing of his delivery and his front side swings open early. They are optimistic he's learning to trust his fastball in the zone.

THE FUTURE: There's a healthy amount of sample-size skepticism with Boyle's drastic strike-throwing improvement, but the rebuilding A's can let him continue to start. He has the floor of a high-leverage reliever and a chance for much more if everything coalesces.

Year	Age	Club (League)	Level	W	L	ERA	G	GS	IP	H	HR	BB	SO	BB%	SO%	WHIP	AVG
2023	23	Chattanooga (SL)	AA	6	5	4.50	19	19	84	63	6	75	122	19.4	31.5	1.64	.211
2023	23	Midland (TL)	AA	2	1	2.08	3	3	17	12	0	7	28	10.1	40.6	1.10	.197
2023	23	Las Vegas (PCL)	AAA	0	2	2.25	3	3	16	8	1	11	18	16.7	27.3	1.19	.151
2023	23	Oakland (AL)	MLB	2	0	1.69	3	3	16	8	1	5	15	8.3	25.0	0.81	.148
Minor League Totals				11	14	3.30	56	55	238	138	14	191	362	18.7	35.4	1.39	.172
Major League Totals				2	0	1.69	3	3	16	8	1	5	15	8.3	25.0	0.81	.148

9 MAX MUNCY, SS

HIT: 45. **POW:** 55. **RUN:** 55. **FLD:** 50. **ARM:** 50. **BA Grade:** 50. **Risk:** High.

Born: August 25, 2002. **B-T:** R-R. **HT:** 6-1. **WT:** 180.
Drafted: HS—Thousand Oaks, CA, 2021 (1st round). **Signed by:** Dillon Tung.

TRACK RECORD: Muncy starred under the tutelage of former big leaguer Jack Wilson at Thousand Oaks High, the alma mater of Oakland 2023 first-rounder Jacob Wilson before Wilson attended Grand Canyon. The A's drafted Muncy 25th overall in 2021 and signed him for $2.85 million on the strength of his hitting ability and athleticism. He has been an inconsistent performer as a pro, but took a step forward after a July 2023 promotion to Double-A Midland.

SCOUTING REPORT: While his physicality, athleticism and impact power potential remain intact, Muncy has battled more swing-and-miss concerns than expected given his amateur track record. He can do damage when he connects and shows a propensity to lift and pull pitches, but his pitch selection is a work in progress. He's an aggressive hitter who hunts fastballs but also gets himself into trouble expanding the strike zone against breaking balls early in the count. His career strikeout rate hovered around 30% prior to arriving in Midland, where it dropped to 23% in 233 plate appearances. Muncy made changes to simplify his approach, toned down his leg kick throughout the season, and also modified his pregame routine at High-A Lansing to encouraging results. His athleticism also translates to shortstop, where he has good lateral quickness. Muncy made fewer mistakes in 2023, cutting his errors nearly in half, but he needs to continue to clean up his footwork. External evaluators note Muncy needs to improve his adjustability to make different types of throws at shortstop, especially with his average arm strength.

THE FUTURE: Muncy has the upside of an offensive-minded second-division regular at shortstop, but he needs to prove he can sustain his newfound approach against upper-level pitching to realize his offensive potential. The pressure on the bat will only intensify if he is pushed to a different infield position.

Year	Age	Club (League)	Level	AVG	G	AB	R	H	2B	3B	HR	RBI	BB	SO	SB	OBP	SLG
2023	20	Lansing (MWL)	A+	.255	72	275	36	70	18	0	6	31	31	92	9	.327	.385
2023	20	Midland (TL)	AA	.302	51	202	40	61	17	0	4	31	21	54	4	.387	.446
Minor League Totals				.248	257	980	148	243	63	3	29	136	124	327	33	.340	.407

10 STEVEN ECHAVARRIA, RHP

FB: 55. **SL:** 55. **CHG:** 50. **CTL:** 50. **BA Grade:** 50. **Risk:** Extreme.

Born: August 6, 2005. **B-T:** R-R. **HT:** 6-1. **WT:** 180.
Drafted: HS—Millburn, NJ, 2023 (3rd round). **Signed by:** Ron Vaughn.
TRACK RECORD: Echavarria's velocity jumped during the spring of his senior year at Millburn (N.J.) High and he was just 17 years old on draft day, which helped propel him up draft boards. Still, even Echavarria expected to make it to college and honor his commitment to Florida. The Athletics pounced in the third round and signed him for $3 million—equivalent to late first-round money—to pry him away from the college ranks. The bonus is the largest the A's have given to a prep pitcher and their biggest draft deal for a pitcher since signing A.J. Puk—himself a former Florida Gator—for $4,069,200 as the No. 6 overall pick in 2016. Echavarria needed time to build back up and did not make his professional debut in 2023, but he did pitch in Oakland's fall instructional camp.
SCOUTING REPORT: Echavarria's ease of operation and chance for three above-average pitches is intriguing. The well-rested righthander sat 94-96 mph and touched 97 in instructs. There's room for more physical projection on his 6-foot-1 frame, too. Echavarria has shown feel to spin a slider—which showed sharp break and 2,500-2,600 rpm spin at its best in high school—and has shown feel for a changeup. Neither was a particularly dominant swing-and-miss offering as an amateur, but the A's believe both have above-average potential with a chance for more because he has shown a feel for throwing strikes. Echavarria is athletic and generates solid velocity with a loose, easy delivery that he repeats well. He employs a rather large leg swing in his delivery and gets down the mound well.
THE FUTURE: Some in the Oakland organization believe they've landed a gem in Echavarria. He has midrotation upside and will make his pro debut in 2024.

Year	Age	Club (League)	Level	W	L	ERA	G	GS	IP	H	HR	BB	SO	BB%	SO%	WHIP	AVG
2023	17	Did not play															

11 DANIEL SUSAC, C

HIT: 55. **POW:** 50. **RUN:** 40. **FLD:** 45. **ARM:** 55. **BA Grade:** 45. **Risk:** High.

Born: May 14, 2001. **B-T:** R-R. **HT:** 6-4. **WT:** 218. **Drafted:** Arizona, 2022 (1st round). **Signed by:** Jeff Urlaub.
TRACK RECORD: Susac was the Pacific-12 Conference freshman of the year at Arizona in 2021 and ranked as the No. 11 prospect in the draft a year later when the A's selected him No. 19 overall and signed him to a bonus just north of $3.53 million. He has continued to hit for a high average since turning pro, albeit with just nine career homers. Susac posted a .301/.365/.428 line across 112 games between High-A Lansing and Double-A Midland in 2023.
SCOUTING REPORT: The 6-foot-4 Susac is an offensive-oriented catcher with a strong frame and long levers. He keeps his swing in the zone for quite some time and showed feel for contact in 2023. A lot of Susac's hits were either up the middle or to the opposite field, though, and there's some trepidation regarding his approach and underlying power metrics. His power output hasn't quite matched his raw potential given his strength. The A's worked with Susac in the second half of the season to both eliminate a hole in his swing on the inside of the plate and to get in better position to pull the ball. Susac also needs to tighten his plate discipline, especially against offspeed pitches, after chasing more than a third of the time in 2023. Susac has the defensive tools to stick behind the plate with proper maintenance. He has a strong throwing arm defensively, but his sheer size can stress his agility and footwork when getting out of his crouch behind the plate. His receiving must continue to improve as well.
THE FUTURE: Susac has the ceiling of a second-division regular if he can tighten his approach and grow into more power.

Year	Age	Club (League)	Level	AVG	G	AB	R	H	2B	3B	HR	RBI	BB	SO	SB	OBP	SLG
2023	22	Lansing (MWL)	A+	.303	99	366	47	111	18	5	7	54	39	88	8	.373	.437
2023	22	Midland (TL)	AA	.280	13	50	2	14	1	0	1	8	2	14	1	.304	.360
Minor League Totals				.300	139	520	64	156	27	5	9	77	48	127	9	.363	.423

12 MYLES NAYLOR, SS/3B

HIT: 45. **POW:** 55. **RUN:** 40. **FLD:** 45. **ARM:** 50. **BA Grade:** 50. **Risk:** Extreme.

Born: April 15, 2005. **B-T:** R-R. **HT:** 6-2. **WT:** 195. **Drafted:** HS—Mississauga, ON, 2023 (2nd round).
Signed by: Matt Higginson.

TRACK RECORD: The youngest of three Naylor brothers, Myles has considerable baseball bloodlines. His brothers Josh and Bo are entrenched in the Guardians' lineup, and he's also cousins with A's farmhand Denzel Clarke. The A's signed the youngest Naylor to a $2,202,500 bonus after drafting him No. 39 overall in 2023. He debuted in late July and hit .208 with six homers and a 39.4% strikeout rate over 32 games with Low-A Stockton.

SCOUTING REPORT: Naylor impressed amateur evaluators with his toolsy mixture of bat-to-ball skills and raw power potential. He's advanced for his age in terms of his ability to launch and pull the ball. He also has a good understanding of the strike zone. But Naylor's overeagerness to do damage led to trouble in his limited pro debut and much more swing-and-miss than expected. Naylor whiffed a concerning 43% of the time in Stockton and particularly struggled with spin. Still, the skills are there if he can calm down the approach. Some in the A's organization were pleasantly surprised at Naylor's defensive ability at shortstop, but there's still a prevailing sentiment that he moves to third base as he climbs the ladder and grows into his body. He's also a below-average runner.

THE FUTURE: Naylor turns 19 in April. He has the potential of an everyday third baseman with impact potential at the plate, but needs to dial in his approach and swing-and-miss.

Year	Age	Club (League)	Level	AVG	G	AB	R	H	2B	3B	HR	RBI	BB	SO	SB	OBP	SLG
2023	18	ACL Athletics	Rk	.333	2	6	2	2	1	0	0	0	1	3	0	.429	.500
2023	18	Stockton (CAL)	A	.208	32	120	16	25	2	0	6	17	11	52	2	.280	.375
Minor League Totals				.214	34	126	18	27	3	0	6	17	12	55	2	.288	.381

13 HENRY BOLTE, OF

HIT: 40. **POW:** 60. **RUN:** 60. **FLD:** 55. **ARM:** 55. **BA Grade:** 50. **Risk:** Extreme.

Born: August 4, 2003. **B-T:** R-R. **HT:** 6-3. **WT:** 195. **Drafted:** HS—Palo Alto, CA, 2022 (2nd round).
Signed by: Troy Stewart.

TRACK RECORD: Oakland drafted the Palo Alto native No. 56 overall in 2022 and signed him to a $2 million bonus. Bolte briefly debuted in the Arizona Complex League that year and expected to open 2023 in full-season ball. Instead, the A's held him back in extended spring training to work extensively with a high-velocity pitching machine to further develop his hit tool and selectivity. Bolte ultimately debuted with Low-A Stockton in late April and remained in the lineup nearly every day from that point on, hitting .257 with a 113 wRC+ while also leading all A's minor leaguers in strikeouts (164).

SCOUTING REPORT: The A's raved about Bolte's progress throughout 2023. The toolsy outfielder has methodically rebuilt his swing since turning pro in an effort to make enough contact to allow his immense power to play more consistently. Bolte has closed his stance, worked to sync up his lower half and shortened his path to the ball. There's still considerable swing-and-miss—he owned a 33.4% strikeout rate in Low-A—but he improved his contact as the season progressed. His approach and pitch recognition still need more maturation. The majority of his power is to the opposite field, and there's still a hole on the inside of the plate. The rest of Bolte's skill set remains dynamic. He's a plus runner and an above-average defender and thrower who can play both center and right field.

THE FUTURE: Bolte still has a long road to travel, but he has dynamic power-speed potential if he can continue to refine his hitting ability.

Year	Age	Club (League)	Level	AVG	G	AB	R	H	2B	3B	HR	RBI	BB	SO	SB	OBP	SLG
2023	19	Stockton (CAL)	A	.257	112	420	77	108	17	5	14	68	62	164	32	.356	.421
Minor League Totals				.254	123	453	82	115	17	5	14	70	67	183	32	.355	.406

14 ROYBER SALINAS, RHP

FB: 55. **CB:** 55. **SL:** 65. **CUT:** 50. **CTL:** 45. **BA Grade:** 50. **Risk:** Extreme.

Born: April 10, 2001. **B-T:** R-R. **HT:** 6-3. **WT:** 205. **Signed:** Venezuela, 2018. **Signed by:** Carlos Sequera (Braves).

TRACK RECORD: The Venezuela native was an under-the-radar signing by the Braves in 2018. He enjoyed a breakout 2022 season, striking out 175 batters over 109 innings in the lower levels. The A's acquired Salinas along with three others in a December 2022 deal that sent catcher Sean Murphy to Atlanta. He spent all of 2023 with Double-A Midland, striking out 89 batters in 67.1 innings despite a somewhat unlucky 5.48 ERA. He also missed nearly two months with a forearm injury.

SCOUTING REPORT: Salinas' inconsistency provides a tough evaluation for opposing scouts. He has electric days when he touches 97 mph with his fastball and pairs it with a plus slider, but also struggles with command, sequencing and stranding runners. That evened out to a 30.9% to 10.8% strikeout-to-walk ratio in 2023. His fastball averaged nearly 95 mph and has riding life, although slightly less induced vertical break compared to his time in the Braves system. He also introduced a cutter in 2023. Salinas' tight mid-80s slider is his best pitch and a plus offering. He can land it in the zone and it elicited whiffs nearly 60% of the time. He can also bury his low-80s curve in the dirt as a chase pitch. He needs to throw more strikes to remain in a starting role. There are also concerns about Salinas' conditioning—he weighs far closer to 250 pounds than his listed 205 pounds.

THE FUTURE: Salinas has dynamite stuff, but plenty to clean up. He has the floor of a high-leverage reliever if the strike-throwing doesn't improve.

Year	Age	Club (League)	Level	W	L	ERA	G	GS	IP	H	HR	BB	SO	BB%	SO%	WHIP	AVG
2023	22	ACL Athletics	Rk	0	0	4.15	2	2	4	6	0	0	4	0.0	20.0	1.38	.316
2023	22	Midland (TL)	AA	1	5	5.48	18	16	67	59	9	31	89	10.8	30.9	1.34	.232
Minor League Totals				11	19	3.91	75	52	253	193	20	140	372	12.8	34.1	1.32	.207

15 JACK PERKINS, RHP

FB: 55. **CUT:** 55. **SL:** 50. **CHG:** 50. **CTL:** 45. **BA Grade:** 45. **Risk:** High.

Born: December 26, 1999. **B-T:** R-R. **HT:** 6-1. **WT:** 220. **Drafted:** Indiana, 2022 (5th round). **Signed by:** Rich Sparks.

TRACK RECORD: Perkins showed explosive stuff as an amateur and piqued the A's interest after throwing more strikes upon transferring from Indiana to Louisville in 2022. They signed him for $270,750 in the fifth round and he trended up in his first full season of pro ball in 2023, posting a 4.10 ERA in 107.2 innings between High-A Lansing and Double-A Midland. Perkins continued on to the Arizona Fall League and did not allow an earned run in 12.1 innings.

SCOUTING REPORT: A full offseason committed to a plyo-ball routine helped Perkins' velocity tick up in 2023. His four-seamer averaged nearly 95 mph and has decent shape, playing well at the top of the zone because of his lower release angle. He also throws a low-90s cutter that has above-average potential. Perkins missed fewer bats upon reaching Double-A. Settling on a more precise slider could help improve his swing-and-miss potential at the upper levels. His mid-80s offering flashes above-average potential, but has inconsistent shape and sometimes blends into a slurve-like offering. There's some debate internally whether the pitch is better suited by adding more sweep or more depth. Perkins also throws a firm upper-80s changeup that elicited the most whiffs of any offering in the zone. He has been an average strike-thrower so far, and utilizes a quick, compact delivery and shorter arm stroke.

THE FUTURE: Perkins needs to unlock more consistent secondaries to stay on a starter track, although his stuff might play up in a high-leverage relief role.

Year	Age	Club (League)	Level	W	L	ERA	G	GS	IP	H	HR	BB	SO	BB%	SO%	WHIP	AVG
2023	23	Lansing (MWL)	A+	3	3	2.52	10	9	54	34	3	18	49	8.5	23.2	0.97	.182
2023	23	Midland (TL)	AA	1	0	5.67	12	11	54	70	2	29	44	11.5	17.5	1.83	.329
Minor League Totals				4	4	3.98	28	22	118	111	5	49	107	9.8	21.4	1.36	.249

16 JOEY ESTES, RHP

FB: 55. **CUT:** 50. **SL:** 50. **CB:** 50. **CHG:** 50. **CTL:** 50. **BA Grade:** 45. **Risk:** High.

Born: October 8, 2001. **B-T:** R-R. **HT:** 6-2. **WT:** 195. **Drafted:** HS—Lancaster, CA, 2019 (16th round). **Signed by:** Kevin Martin (Braves).

TRACK RECORD: The A's acquired Estes from the Braves in the March 2022 Matt Olson trade, less than a year after the righty broke out for Low-A Augusta. He has proven a steady and durable option since arriving in Oakland's system. Estes climbed the minors and made his big league debut at 21 years old.

SCOUTING REPORT: Estes made modifications to both his delivery and arsenal in 2023. He attacks hitters in an athletic, aggressive manner with a funky release. The A's worked with Estes to better leverage the ball and move down the mound more efficiently. The changes reduced the amount of horizontal break on his 93 mph fastball, which previously had nearly equal ride and run, but the pitch is still an above-average offering that he trusts in every quadrant of the zone. He also introduced two variants of his slider—a low-80s sweeper and a separate, slightly slower breaker with more depth that is sometimes classified as a curveball. He also added a mid-80s cutter to go along with his solid-average changeup. Estes' delivery has historically raised reliever risk, but he continues to throw enough strikes to remain on a starter track. Now, he needs those strikes to start missing more bats. He yielded below-average in-zone whiff rates on all his secondaries, furthering concerns he lacks a true swing-and-miss offering.

THE FUTURE: Estes shows a deep arsenal, competitiveness, and pitchability, but the lack of whiffs limits his ceiling to a back-of-the-rotation starter.

OAKLAND ATHLETICS

Year	Age	Club (League)	Level	W	L	ERA	G	GS	IP	H	HR	BB	SO	BB%	SO%	WHIP	AVG
2023	21	Midland (TL)	AA	6	6	3.28	20	17	104	84	14	31	100	7.2	23.3	1.10	.215
2023	21	Las Vegas (PCL)	AAA	3	0	5.23	7	6	33	32	10	12	31	8.3	21.5	1.35	.246
2023	21	Oakland (AL)	MLB	0	1	7.20	2	2	10	12	4	2	7	4.3	14.9	1.40	.286
Minor League Totals				15	20	3.85	72	68	337	278	48	109	358	7.8	25.5	1.15	.220
Major League Totals				0	1	7.20	2	2	10	12	4	2	7	4.3	14.9	1.40	.286

17 BRETT HARRIS, 3B

HIT: 55. POW: 45. RUN: 45. FLD: 55. ARM: 50. BA Grade: 45. Risk: High.

Born: June 24, 1998. **B-T:** R-R. **HT:** 6-3. **WT:** 210. **Drafted:** Gonzaga, 2021 (7th round). **Signed by:** James Coffman.

TRACK RECORD: Harris has flown under the radar despite being a favorite of scouts and coaches alike, dating back to his time at Gonzaga. The A's drafted him in the seventh round of the 2021 draft and signed him for just $120,000. He has been productive since turning pro and hit .279/.383/.424 with nine homers in 105 games across Double-A Midland and Triple-A Las Vegas in 2023 before heading off to the Arizona Fall League.

SCOUTING REPORT: Harris is a smart, polished player with strong bat-to-ball skills to all fields, but just average power potential. He has some of the best contact ability in the A's system, whiffing on pitches in the strike zone just 11% of the time in 2023. He has a good understanding of the strike zone, but his approach was strained for the first time against Triple-A pitching. In particular, Harris was challenged with velocity at the top of the strike zone. He adjusted by moving to a more upright posture near the end of the season. Harris is fairly athletic and posted slightly above-average exit velocities, so there's some optimism he can develop more power, but he also hit the ball on the ground more in 2023. As a professional, Harris has predominantly played third base, where he's a sound defender with savvy instincts, and has also dabbled at second base.

THE FUTURE: A quintessential example of an all-around player without a true carrying tool, Harris has a better chance of reaching his ceiling as a low-end regular at third base if his power takes another step.

Year	Age	Club (League)	Level	AVG	G	AB	R	H	2B	3B	HR	RBI	BB	SO	SB	OBP	SLG
2023	25	Midland (TL)	AA	.283	69	258	44	73	16	3	5	48	40	42	6	.399	.426
2023	25	Las Vegas (PCL)	AAA	.271	36	129	19	35	7	0	4	14	10	27	4	.347	.419
Minor League Totals				.280	245	888	152	249	48	5	29	139	110	172	24	.376	.444

18 RYAN LASKO, OF

HIT: 45. POW: 45. RUN: 55. FLD: 60. ARM: 70. BA Grade: 45. Risk: High.

Born: June 24, 2002. **B-T:** R-R. **HT:** 6-0. **WT:** 190. **Drafted:** Rutgers, 2023 (2nd round). **Signed by:** Ron Vaughn.

TRACK RECORD: The Jackson, New Jersey native stayed home to attend Rutgers and enjoyed a very productive career, leading the Big Ten in hits as a sophomore. He wasn't as prolific the ensuing summer with a wood bat, posting a .600 OPS in 34 Cape Cod League games, but he bounced back to hit .330 as a junior. The A's signed him to a $1.7 million bonus after drafting him No. 41 overall in 2023. Lasko hit .154 over 10 games in the Arizona Complex League and was slowed by injury.

SCOUTING REPORT: Lasko plays with an unapologetic intensity, especially defensively. He takes good routes to the ball in center field and is a plus defender despite just above-average speed. He's capable of making dazzling plays and willing to sacrifice his body—even if it means hurtling into the outfield wall. He also has a plus-plus throwing arm. There's less conviction among evaluators regarding his hitting ability. Lasko showed a decent eye in college and has physical strength, but the raw power potential didn't always translate to games. There's some rigidity and stiffness to his swing at times, and amateur evaluators were concerned he may need to alter his swing to better combat velocity, especially at the top of the strike zone.

THE FUTURE: Lasko doesn't turn 22 until June. He has the physical tools to stick in center and the ceiling of a second-division regular if he improves at the plate.

Year	Age	Club (League)	Level	AVG	G	AB	R	H	2B	3B	HR	RBI	BB	SO	SB	OBP	SLG
2023	21	ACL Athletics	Rk	.154	10	26	3	4	2	0	0	3	3	5	1	.233	.231
Minor League Totals				.154	10	26	3	4	2	0	0	3	3	5	1	.233	.231

19 COLE MILLER, RHP

FB: 55. **SL:** 50. **CHG:** 45. **CTL:** 45. **BA Grade:** 50. **Risk:** Extreme.

Born: May 2, 2005. **B-T:** R-R. **HT:** 6-6. **WT:** 225. **Drafted:** HS—Thousand Oaks, CA, 2023 (4th round).
Signed by: Dillon Tung.
TRACK RECORD: One of several Thousand Oaks natives in Oakland's system, Miller was a standout at Newbury Park High, like his older brother Jake, who is now a pitcher in the Guardians system. Cole was committed to UCLA, but a velocity spike moved him up draft boards during his senior spring. The A's signed him for $1 million at No. 103 overall in the 2023 draft.
SCOUTING REPORT: The 6-foot-6 righty has a powerful frame with a low-90s fastball that touched 94-95 mph in spurts this spring. The A's think he can ultimately sit in that range, with potential for even a tick or two more, as he continues to add functional strength. Miller's fastball bores in on righthanded hitters and he throws it assertively to any quadrant of the zone. It pairs well with his low-80s breaking ball, which flashes average potential and slurve-like shape. He also shows feel for a mid-80s changeup. Miller repeats his delivery fairly well, but struggled to hold velocity deeper into outings as an amateur. There's ample time for the 18-year-old to alleviate those concerns as he gets stronger and fills out his frame.
THE FUTURE: There's a lot of projection left for Miller, who has back-of-the-rotation upside if his three-pitch mix comes together. He will make his professional debut in 2024.

Year	Age	Club (League)	Level	W	L	ERA	G	GS	IP	H	HR	BB	SO	BB%	SO%	WHIP	AVG
2023	18	Did not play															

20 COLBY THOMAS, OF

HIT: 40. **POW:** 55. **RUN:** 55. **FLD:** 45. **ARM:** 55. **BA Grade:** 50. **Risk:** Extreme.

Born: January 26, 2001. **B-T:** R-R. **HT:** 6-0. **WT:** 190. **Drafted:** Mercer, 2022 (3rd round). **Signed by:** Jemel Spearman.
TRACK RECORD: Thomas was a power-speed threat at Mercer, albeit with hit tool questions after batting .228 in the Cape Cod League in 2021. He was in the midst of a productive junior spring in 2022 until a right shoulder labrum injury in May required season-ending surgery. The A's signed him for $750,000 in the third round that year, and he made his pro debut in 2023, hitting .286/.351/.493 across Low-A Stockton and High-A Lansing.
SCOUTING REPORT: Based on tools and athleticism, Thomas stacks up with almost any player in Oakland's system. He has plus raw power, mostly geared toward right-center field, and averaged 104 mph 90th percentile exit velocity in 2023. Thomas' plus running ability translates to both his defense and bas-erunning, where he stole 25 bases in 31 attempts. But there are concerns his hitting approach won't hold up against better pitching. Thomas struck out 29.5% of the time compared to a 4.6% walk rate against High-A pitching. He chases too frequently, especially early in the count against breaking balls. Thomas plays with a high motor and covers plenty of ground defensively. He has a strong throwing arm, but his route-running needs refining. He's likely best suited to right field.
THE FUTURE: Thomas has some of the higher upside among position players in Oakland's system. There's risk involved, though, and his pitch recognition and plate coverage require considerable refinement to help reach that ceiling.

Year	Age	Club (League)	Level	AVG	G	AB	R	H	2B	3B	HR	RBI	BB	SO	SB	OBP	SLG
2023	22	Stockton (CAL)	A	.283	72	290	49	82	24	4	8	49	26	76	14	.364	.476
2023	22	Lansing (MWL)	A+	.290	54	217	38	63	15	2	10	33	11	70	11	.333	.516
Minor League Totals				.286	126	507	87	145	39	6	18	82	37	146	25	.351	.493

21 COOPER BOWMAN, 2B

HIT: 50. **POW:** 45. **RUN:** 70. **FLD:** 50. **ARM:** 50. **BA Grade:** 45. **Risk:** High.

Born: January 25, 2000. **B-T:** R-R. **HT:** 6-0. **WT:** 205. **Drafted:** Louisville, 2021 (4th round).
Signed by: Mike Gibbons (Yankees).
TRACK RECORD: Bowman hit .293 during his lone season with Louisville in 2021 after transferring from Iowa Western JC. The Yankees signed him to a $353,000 bonus that year and traded him to the A's in 2022 along with three others in a deal for Frankie Montas. Bowman was more productive in 2023 despite dealing with multiple injuries, hitting .262/.360/.431 with 38 steals in 72 games.
SCOUTING REPORT: A quick-twitch athlete, Bowman is the fastest baserunner in Oakland's system with the instincts to match. He consistently leveraged that speed on the bases as an amateur by using his solid contact ability and discipline at the plate. Upon turning pro, the Yankees tried to tap more into Bowman's raw strength to unlock more power, but it led to significantly more swing-and-miss. Bowman restored

a more line-drive-oriented approach in Oakland's system and was impactful over the second half of the season, posting an .853 OPS over his final 38 games with Double-A Midland. Durability has been a concern for Bowman. He's a solid defender at second base, but he worked on his outfield play after the season, and his average arm may be better suited for the grass.

THE FUTURE: If Bowman can stay healthy and continue to enhance his versatility, he could reach Oakland by the end of 2024 in a utility role.

Year	Age	Club (League)	Level	AVG	G	AB	R	H	2B	3B	HR	RBI	BB	SO	SB	OBP	SLG
2023	23	ACL Athletics	Rk	.250	4	12	4	3	1	0	0	2	1	4	3	.400	.333
2023	23	Midland (TL)	AA	.262	68	271	49	71	17	3	8	38	36	68	35	.358	.435
Minor League Totals				.237	215	799	139	189	44	5	23	110	112	237	98	.343	.390

22 BRADY BASSO, LHP

FB: 45. **CUT:** 55. **CB:** 50. **CHG:** 40. **CTL:** 55. **BA Grade:** 45. **Risk:** High.

Born: October 8, 1997. **B-T:** R-L. **HT:** 6-2. **WT:** 210. **Drafted:** Oklahoma State, 2019 (16th round). **Signed by:** William Avent.

TRACK RECORD: Basso has a relatively limited professional track record since signing for $75,000 in 2019. The son of former minor league manager and scout Mike Basso, the lefty pitched primarily out of the bullpen at Oklahoma State, but the A's have stretched him out as a starter. Basso missed all of 2022 due to Tommy John surgery and was built up slowly in 2023. The A's added him to their 40-man roster after the season.

SCOUTING REPORT: While his velocity didn't quite reach pre-injury levels, Basso returned with a deeper arsenal that lacks an obvious plus offering. His four-seam fastball sat between 92-93 mph. His upper-80s cutter showed more encouraging shape and performance and has a chance to be his best pitch. Basso's 12-6 curveball descends on hitters from his over-the-top slot, but the mid-70s offering could be more easily detected by better hitters. He uses the curve almost exclusively as a putaway pitch and it's his best swing-and-miss offering. Basso deployed a mid-80s changeup sparingly. His command has been much sharper as a professional compared to his amateur career. Basso owned the second-best strikeout-to-walk ratio (20.2) of any pitcher with 50 or more innings in Oakland's system. He fills up the strike zone with his two fastballs, although he'd benefit from sharper command of his secondaries.

THE FUTURE: The 26-year-old has yet to reach Triple-A, but there's an opportunity to push into a back-end role in Oakland at some point in 2024—especially if his stuff ticks up following a normal offseason.

Year	Age	Club (League)	Level	W	L	ERA	G	GS	IP	H	HR	BB	SO	BB%	SO%	WHIP	AVG
2023	25	Lansing (MWL)	A+	2	4	2.64	15	12	44	34	4	11	45	6.4	26.0	1.02	.211
2023	25	Midland (TL)	AA	2	0	1.89	5	5	19	13	1	4	19	5.7	27.1	0.89	.203
Minor League Totals				6	6	2.70	42	22	110	88	7	30	128	6.8	29.0	1.07	.217

23 NATHAN DETTMER, RHP

FB: 50. **SL:** 55. **CHG:** 45. **CTL:** 40. **BA Grade:** 45. **Risk:** High.

Born: April 26, 2002. **B-T:** R-R. **HT:** 6-4. **WT:** 230. **Drafted:** Texas A&M, 2023 (5th round). **Signed by:** Kelcey Mucker.

TRACK RECORD: Dettmer dependably slotted into Texas A&M's rotation for the better part of three seasons. His command waned in his junior spring, though, leading to a 6.32 ERA. Still, Dettmer ranked as the No. 81 prospect in the draft and the A's landed him in the fifth round at No. 139 overall for a $425,000 bonus. Dettmer threw three innings over two outings in a brief Arizona Complex League cameo later that summer.

SCOUTING REPORT: The A's were encouraged by Dettmer's fall instructional league and believe some tweaks to his sinker can help him regain his form from earlier in his college career. The 6-foot-4, 230-pound righty has a powerful frame and arsenal. When he's on, it's easy to see how his three-pitch mix works together. Dettmer's low-spin fastball sat 93-94 mph and topped out at 96. He throws it from a three-quarters slot with armside run, racking up grounders. He added more power to his above-average mid-80s slider and the pitch has a comparable amount of horizontal break to his fastball, working in the opposite direction of righties. He needs to show more feel for a mid-80s changeup that tunnels off his fastball.

THE FUTURE: Dettmer profiles as a grounder-oriented back-of-the-rotation starter if he can throw more consistent strikes. He's ready for the lower levels in 2024.

Year	Age	Club (League)	Level	W	L	ERA	G	GS	IP	H	HR	BB	SO	BB%	SO%	WHIP	AVG
2023	21	ACL Athletics	Rk	0	0	0.00	2	2	3	2	0	1	3	9.1	27.3	1.00	.200
Minor League Totals				0	0	0.00	2	2	3	2	0	1	3	9.1	27.3	1.00	.200

24 FREDDY TARNOK, RHP

FB: 55. **CB:** 50. **SL:** 45. **CHG:** 55. **CTL:** 40. **BA Grade:** 40. **Risk:** Medium.

Born: November 24, 1998. **B-T:** R-R. **HT:** 6-4. **WT:** 210. **Drafted:** HS—Riverview, FL, 2017 (3rd round).
Signed by: Justin Clark (Braves).
TRACK RECORD: Tarnok was a two-way player committed to Division II Tampa until the Braves signed him for $1,445,000 in 2017, setting off a steady climb through their system that culminated with his big league debut in 2022. The A's acquired him that winter as part of the deal that sent Sean Murphy to Atlanta. Injuries have thwarted Tarnok with his new club. He pitched just 21.2 innings in 2023, missing time with shoulder, blister and calf ailments before a hip injury required season-ending surgery.
SCOUTING REPORT: When healthy, Tarnok's mid-90s fastball plays well at the top of the strike zone with good spin and carry. He pitched off his fastball/curveball combination as he ascended the minors. His upper-70s downer curve was once one of the best in Atlanta's system, but has backed up. Tarnok has relied more frequently on a tighter upper-80s slider over the last year, especially in a limited big league look in 2023. His changeup has plus shape, albeit with inconsistent results. Tarnok battled his delivery at times as a minor leaguer and his command was below-average in 2023, although injuries may have factored into the shaky strike-throwing.
THE FUTURE: There is ample opportunity for Tarnok in Oakland in 2024, although his command and durability woes may ultimately push him toward a relief role.

Year	Age	Club (League)	Level	W	L	ERA	G	GS	IP	H	HR	BB	SO	BB%	SO%	WHIP	AVG
2023	24	ACL Athletics	Rk	0	0	0.00	1	1	2	1	0	1	2	14.3	28.6	1.00	.167
2023	24	Las Vegas (PCL)	AAA	1	1	1.83	5	5	20	12	2	11	11	13.9	13.9	1.17	.176
2023	24	Oakland (AL)	MLB	1	1	4.91	5	1	15	11	4	11	14	16.9	21.5	1.50	.204
Minor League Totals				19	24	3.92	104	84	399	350	37	165	430	9.6	25.1	1.29	.233
Major League Totals				1	1	4.91	6	1	15	12	4	11	15	16.2	22.1	1.50	.211

25 RYAN CUSICK, RHP

FB: 60. **SL:** 50. **CB:** 55 **CHG:** 40. **CTL:** 40. **BA Grade:** 45. **Risk:** Very High.

Born: November 12, 1999. **B-T:** R-R. **HT:** 6-6. **WT:** 235. **Drafted:** Wake Forest, 2021 (1st round).
Signed by: Billy Best (Braves).
TRACK RECORD: Cusick was a fireballer at Wake Forest whom the Braves drafted No. 24 overall in 2021. They dealt him to the Athletics a year later in 2022 in the Matt Olson trade. Cusick's tenure in Oakland's system has not gone well. He dealt with a rib injury in 2022 and walked 66 batters in 100 innings in 2023. Oakland sent Cusick to its Arizona complex to rework his delivery in mid July and he returned to action a month later.
SCOUTING REPORT: Cusick once touched triple digits as an amateur, so his diminished velocity early in 2023 was alarming. He made changes to his delivery prior to the season in an attempt to work more downhill and improve his strike-throwing. His heater dipped to 92-94 mph as a result. He worked on restoring the ride-cut characteristics of his fastball in Arizona and his velocity bounced back to the 95-97 mph range by the end of the season with Triple-A Las Vegas. At its best, Cusick's heater should play well at the top of the zone, although he struggles to spot it there. He has the potential to throw two distinct breaking balls with solid-average or above-average potential and occasionally throws a below-average low-90s changeup.
THE FUTURE: The A's may continue to give Cusick a chance to start, but a future as a two-pitch power reliever in the middle innings seems increasingly likely.

Year	Age	Club (League)	Level	W	L	ERA	G	GS	IP	H	HR	BB	SO	BB%	SO%	WHIP	AVG
2023	23	ACL Athletics	Rk	0	0	0.00	1	1	3	1	0	2	5	16.7	41.7	1.00	.100
2023	23	Midland (TL)	AA	5	7	4.77	22	22	94	83	17	57	84	14.1	20.7	1.48	.239
2023	23	Las Vegas (PCL)	AAA	0	1	16.88	1	1	3	3	0	7	2	38.9	11.1	3.75	.300
Minor League Totals				6	15	5.31	43	40	159	158	22	100	171	14.0	24.0	1.62	.260

26 CESAR GONZALEZ, C

HIT: 55. **POW:** 50. **RUN:** 40. **FLD:** 45. **ARM:** 50. **BA Grade:** 45. **Risk:** Extreme.

Born: January 13, 2005. **B-T:** R-R. **HT:** 6-2. **WT:** 165. **Signed:** Venezuela, 2022. **Signed by:** Andri Garcia.
TRACK RECORD: The A's made Gonzalez one of their top international signings in 2022 on the strength of his offensive-oriented profile and makeup. He debuted that year and returned to the Dominican Summer League in 2023, hitting .218/.361/.320 in 44 games while walking nearly as many times as he struck out despite dealing with nagging injuries.

SCOUTING REPORT: Gonzalez's profile derives considerable value from his bat. He has a chance for above-average hitting and average power. Gonzalez is at his best utilizing the whole field with a quick swing and a line drive-oriented approach. He has shown feel for the barrel and a mature understanding of the strike zone, posting solid chase and whiff rates for an 18-year-old. Gonzalez has above-average raw power, but gets himself into trouble when he sells out to reach it. Gonzalez's receiving and throwing accuracy is far more raw. He has solid arm strength and aptitude, but questions about whether he'll stick behind the plate continue to linger. He's a fringe-average runner now and will likely slow down as his 6-foot-2 frame continues to fill out. Some think he's athletic enough to handle a move to left field, though, if he ultimately moves out from behind the plate.

THE FUTURE: Gonzalez has the upside of an offensive-minded backstop. He should begin 2024 in the Arizona Complex League, where he must show better durability and consistency.

Year	Age	Club (League)	Level	AVG	G	AB	R	H	2B	3B	HR	RBI	BB	SO	SB	OBP	SLG
2023	18	DSL Athletics	Rk	.218	44	147	25	32	6	0	3	23	27	29	1	.361	.320
Minor League Totals				.234	66	197	33	46	7	0	3	31	41	37	2	.394	.315

27 MITCH SPENCE, RHP

FB: 45. **CUT:** 55. **SL:** 55. **CHG:** 45. **CTL:** 50. **BA Grade:** 40. **Risk:** High.

Born: May 6, 1998. **B-T:** R-R. **HT:** 6-1. **WT:** 185. **Drafted:** South Carolina-Aiken, 2019 (10th round). **Signed by:** Billy Godwin (Yankees).

TRACK RECORD: A velocity spike during his junior spring at South Carolina-Aiken sent Spence up draft boards in 2019 and the Yankees pounced in the 10th round, signing him to a $122,500 bonus. Spence spent all of 2022 and 2023 in the upper levels of the Yankees system, posting a 4.47 ERA with 153 strikeouts in 163 innings for Triple-A Scranton/Wilkes-Barre in 2023. New York left him off its 40-man roster and the A's took him No. 1 overall in the 2023 Rule 5 draft.

SCOUTING REPORT: Spence shows the ability to manipulate his fastball to both sides of the plate, although his arsenal would benefit from adding a bit more power. He primarily attacks hitters with a low-90s four-seamer that has cutting action and also mixes in a two-seamer with armside run that is a tick or two harder. He pairs it with a low-to-mid-80s breaking ball that elicits whiffs both inside and outside the strike zone. He'll occasionally work in a low-spin mid-80s changeup.

THE FUTURE: Spence will have ample opportunity to carve out a role in 2024 as a Rule 5 selection. He can provide the A's length in the back of their rotation, although his arsenal may take a step forward in shorter spurts and allow for a role as a low-leverage reliever.

Year	Age	Club (League)	Level	W	L	ERA	G	GS	IP	H	HR	BB	SO	BB%	SO%	WHIP	AVG
2023	25	Scranton/W-B (IL)	AAA	8	8	4.47	29	29	163	162	30	53	153	7.5	21.8	1.32	.254
Minor League Totals				23	24	4.35	95	74	426	415	58	136	427	7.5	23.5	1.29	.250

28 JONAH COX, OF

HIT: 55. **POW:** 40. **RUN:** 70. **FLD:** 55. **ARM:** 45. **BA Grade:** 40. **Risk:** High.

Born: August 4, 2001. **B-T:** R-R. **HT:** 6-3. **WT:** 190. **Drafted:** Oral Roberts, 2023 (6th round). **Signed by:** Fletcher Byrd.

TRACK RECORD: Cox transferred to Oral Roberts prior to the 2023 season and won Summit League Player of the Year, hitting .412 with 11 homers and 28 steals. The A's signed him to a $300,000 bonus in the sixth round of the draft, and he hit .264 with 14 steals in 28 games with Low-A Stockton. Cox's father, Darron, was a fifth-round pick in 1989 and briefly reached the majors with the Expos in 1999.

SCOUTING REPORT: A's staffers frequently compare both Cox and fellow 2023 draft pick Ryan Lasko to former Oakland outfielder Eric Byrnes because of their frenetic play styles. Cox is a twitchy athlete and plus-plus runner with speed that excels on both the basepaths and in center field. He takes a slasher's mentality to the plate with an unconventional swing and downward bat path. He makes plenty of contact to all fields—Cox had a 47-game hit streak at Oral Roberts—but generates just fringe-average exit velocities. His aggressive mentality also leads to bouts of chase out of the strike zone. A former shortstop, Cox doesn't have the strongest throwing arm, but he covers plenty of ground and should remain in center field.

THE FUTURE: Cox faces questions about his ultimate impact with the bat, but his contact ability, speed and aptitude provide a nice foundation for a potential fourth outfielder with room for more.

Year	Age	Club (League)	Level	AVG	G	AB	R	H	2B	3B	HR	RBI	BB	SO	SB	OBP	SLG
2023	21	ACL Athletics	Rk	.421	7	19	6	8	1	1	0	5	4	1	6	.560	.579
2023	21	Stockton (CAL)	A	.264	28	110	16	29	2	2	2	10	5	40	14	.325	.373
Minor League Totals				.287	35	129	22	37	3	3	2	15	9	41	20	.366	.403

29 WILL SIMPSON, 1B

HIT: 45. **POW:** 55. **RUN:** 40. **FLD:** 40. **ARM:** 45. **BA Grade:** 40. **Risk:** High.

Born: August 28, 2001. **B-T:** R-R. **HT:** 6-4. **WT:** 225. **Drafted:** Washington, 2023 (15th round). **Signed by:** Jim Coffman.

TRACK RECORD: The Pirates drafted the Sammamish, Wash. native in the 18th round of the 2019 draft, but Simpson opted to stay home and attend Washington. He hit .299 and 36 homers over four college seasons. He proved to be a productive senior sign for the A's after they signed him for $150,000 in the 15th round of the 2023 draft. Simpson hit .322/.373/.522 with four homers in 29 games with Low-A Stockton.

SCOUTING REPORT: The A's were intrigued by Simpson's above-average power potential and feel for launch in his pro debut. They were also impressed with his analytical aptitude upon arriving in Stockton. Simpson's power plays to all fields, but comes with a tradeoff for contact ability. He faced swing-and-miss questions as an amateur, and there's some concern his bat speed may be tested against better velocity. Simpson's defensive profile also puts more strain on his bat. He was a below-average defender at first base as an amateur. Some within the A's system believe he could be passable in a corner outfield spot, where he played sparingly in college, but there's far more opportunity at first base in Oakland's system.

THE FUTURE: Simpson has a high bar to clear as a power-over-hit righthanded first baseman, but he has the opportunity to move quickly in Oakland's system after his pro debut put him on some internal radars.

Year	Age	Club (League)	Level	AVG	G	AB	R	H	2B	3B	HR	RBI	BB	SO	SB	OBP	SLG
2023	21	ACL Athletics	Rk	.304	7	23	9	7	2	0	2	7	1	5	0	.333	.652
2023	21	Stockton (CAL)	A	.322	29	115	18	37	11	0	4	16	10	29	3	.373	.522
Minor League Totals				.319	36	138	27	44	13	0	6	23	11	34	3	.367	.543

30 JACOB WATTERS, RHP

FB: 55. **CB:** 70. **CHG:** 55. **CTL:** 30. **BA Grade:** 45. **Risk:** Extreme.

Born: March 3, 2001. **B-T:** R-R. **HT:** 6-4. **WT:** 230. **Drafted:** West Virginia, 2022 (4th round). **Signed by:** Tripp Faulk.

TRACK RECORD: Watters spent three seasons at West Virginia and pitched briefly over two summers in the Cape Cod League before the A's signed him to a $491,750 bonus in the fourth round of the 2022 draft. His high-octane stuff and erratic control have carried over to his professional career. Watters spent all of 2023 with High-A Lansing, striking out 94 batters in 84.1 innings while issuing 59 free passes.

SCOUTING REPORT: The righthander cuts an imposing figure at 6-foot-4, 230 pounds and has the stuff to back it up. Watters' fastball averaged 95 mph and touched 98, and his hammer of a mid-80s curveball is the best in Oakland's system. Despite the velocity, Watters generated below-average in-zone whiff rates with his fastball. He could benefit from more distinction between his four-seamer and two-seamer, which has considerable armside run. He also throws a solid-average mid-80s changeup with good tumble and fade. Watters' strike-throwing has always been his bugaboo. He's a fair athlete despite his size, but there's some rigidity in his delivery, and he showed below-average control in 2023, especially with his secondaries.

THE FUTURE: Watters' stuff allows for a long runway to keep starting in the hopes he throws more strikes, although a potential mid-leverage relief role seems more likely.

Year	Age	Club (League)	Level	W	L	ERA	G	GS	IP	H	HR	BB	SO	BB%	SO%	WHIP	AVG
2023	22	Lansing (MWL)	A+	2	9	6.62	22	21	84	83	8	59	94	14.9	23.7	1.68	.254
Minor League Totals				2	9	6.34	25	23	88	84	8	63	97	15.2	23.4	1.67	.246

Philadelphia Phillies

BY JOSH NORRIS

After falling to the Astros in the 2022 World Series, the Phillies once again had high hopes entering 2023. The core of their pennant-winning club was still intact, even if they had to wait a little longer for Bryce Harper to return from Tommy John surgery.

They'd also supplemented the club with superstar shortstop Trea Turner, who signed an 11-year, $300 million deal in the offseason. Zack Wheeler and Aaron Nola were still at the front of the rotation, with JT Realmuto behind the dish to complete a star-studded battery.

They finished the year with 90 wins, good enough to place second in the NL East behind the Braves, who used one of the most potent offenses in history to power their way to the division crown.

In October, of course, everything flipped. After dispatching the Marlins in the Wild Card series, the Phillies shut down Atlanta's big bats—with a dose of extra motivation provided by Braves shortstop Orlando Arcia—en route to the NLCS.

There, they ran into the upstart Diamondbacks, who'd buzzsawed their way through their side of the bracket. Arizona edged Philadelphia in seven games en route to their first World Series appearance since 2001, and the Phillies were sent to another offseason after falling just short of the ultimate prize.

One of the biggest blows to the season came early, when top prospect Andrew Painter felt something barking in his elbow during spring training. The righthander, who if healthy would certainly have been a factor for the major league club, tried rehab until the summer, when he eventually had Tommy John surgery. The procedure will likely keep him from his big league debut until 2025.

When he makes his first appearance in Citizens Bank Park, he'll still be part of a rotation with ace Aaron Nola, who re-upped with Philadelphia on a seven-year, $172 million contract.

The farm system did produce one of sport's fastest rising prospects in dynamic reliever Orion Kerkering. The righthander bullied his way through four levels of the minor leagues with a fastball-slider combination that proved poison to anyone in its path. The South Florida alum made his big league debut in April and earned a spot on the postseason roster.

The team's biggest offensive success on the farm came from outfielder Justin Crawford, who was the Phillies' first-round pick in 2022. The son of former all-star Carl Crawford, Justin ran roughshod through the lower levels of the minor leagues with the slash-and-dash skill set that runs

Swift center fielder Johan Rojas started for the Phillies throughout the postseason.

PROJECTED 2027 LINEUP

Catcher	JT Realmuto	36
First Base	Bryce Harper	34
Second Base	Bryson Stott	29
Third Base	Aidan Miller	23
Shortstop	Trea Turner	34
Left Field	Justin Crawford	23
Center Field	Johan Rojas	26
Right Field	Gabriel Rincones Jr.	26
Designated Hitter	Darick Hall	31
No. 1 Starter	Aaron Nola	34
No. 2 Starter	Andrew Painter	24
No. 3 Starter	Mick Abel	25
No. 4 Starter	Ranger Suarez	31
No. 5 Starter	Cristopher Sanchez	30
Closer	Orion Kerkering	26

in the family. He earned a spot in the Futures Game in Seattle.

Elsewhere in the minor leagues, international prospects Starlyn Caba and Eduardo Tait made big impressions at the lowest levels. Caba in particular had evaluators buzzing, and Tait showed a particularly advanced bat for one of the youngest players in the sport.

They added another offensive-minded infielder in the draft when they selected high school infielder Aidan Miller with their first-round selection.

The pieces are in place in Philadelphia for further runs deep into October. Now, they just need one more boost to get over the final hump and bring the city its first title since 2008. ∎

PHILADELPHIA PHILLIES

TOP 2024 CONTRIBUTORS | **RANK**
1. Orion Kerkering, RHP | 6

BREAKOUT PROSPECTS | **RANK**
1. Devin Saltiban, SS | 12
2. TJayy Walton, OF | 13
3. Kehden Hettiger, C | 21

SOURCE OF TOP 30 TALENT

Homegrown	29	Acquired	1
College	7	Trade	1
Junior college	2	Rule 5 draft	0
High school	10	Independent league	0
Nondrafted free agent	2	Free agent/waivers	0
International	8		

LF
Carlos De La Cruz (15)
Hendry Mendez (24)

CF
Justin Crawford (2)
Simon Muzziotti (22)
Emaarion Boyd (23)
Yhoswar Garcia

RF
Gabriel Rincones Jr (10)
TJayy Walton (13)
Raylin Heredia (21)
Cade Fergus
Ethan Wilson

3B
Aidan Miller (4)
Kendall Simmons

SS
Starlyn Caba (5)
Bryan Rincon (7)
William Bergolla Jr. (8)
Devin Saltiban (12)

2B
Nikau Pouaka-Grego
Trevor Schwecke

1B
Bryce Ball

C
Eduardo Tait (9)
Caleb Ricketts (19)
Kehden Hettiger (21)
Rafael Marchan
Jordin Dissin
Rickardo Perez
William Simoneit
Carson Taylor

LHP

LHSP	LHRP
Samuel Aldegheri (14)	Jordi Martinez

RHP

RHSP	RHRP
Andrew Painter (1)	Orion Kerkering (6)
Mick Abel (3)	Griff McGarry (11)
Christian McGowan (16)	Alex McFarlane (18)
Wen Hui Pan (17)	Andrew Baker (25)
	George Klassen (26)
	Tommy McCollum (27)
	Jake Eddington (28)
	Cam Brown (29)
	Enrique Segura (30)
	McKinley Moore
	Michael Mercado
	Mitch Neunborn
	Dominic Pipkin

1 ANDREW PAINTER, RHP

Born: April 10, 2003. **B-T:** R-R. **HT:** 6-7. **WT:** 215.
Drafted: HS—Fort Lauderdale, FL, 2021 (1st round).
Signed by: Victor Gomez.

BRACE HEMMELGARN/MINNESOTA

TRACK RECORD: In 2021, Painter was a unanimous member of Baseball America's Preseason High School All-America team, as voted on by amateur scouting directors. Later that summer, the Phillies drafted him 13th overall out of Calvary Christian Academy in Fort Lauderdale, Fla. They signed him for an under-slot bonus of $3.9 million. He pitched six shutout innings in his pro debut, then used his first full season to establish himself as one of the best pitching prospects in the sport. He moved from Low-A to Double-A—a rare feat for a prep pitcher in his first full year. Other pitchers to do the same include Zack Greinke, Clayton Kershaw, Dylan Bundy, Chad Billingsley and Forrest Whitley. He struck out 155 hitters in 103.2 innings and won BA's inaugural Minor League Pitcher of the Year award. His strikeout total was good enough to lead the organization by 22. Painter also earned the Paul Owens award, given annually to the top hitter and pitcher in the Phillies' minor league system. In 2023, he was invited to big league spring training and made one appearance before elbow pain cropped up. He made several attempts to rehab the injury before having Tommy John surgery in late July. He will likely miss all of 2024.

SCOUTING REPORT: When healthy, Painter showed an elite combination of stuff, command and poise. His fastball, which parked in the mid 90s and topped out at 101 mph, showed excellent induced vertical break and spin rates in the 2,400 rpm range. All of those factors make the pitch a potential double-plus offering. He backs the fastball with an array of offspeed weapons, the best of which is a potentially plus slider. In 2022, the pitch, which is thrown in the low 80s, produced spin rates in the range of 2,500 rpm and averaged roughly 12 inches of horizontal break. As the season wore on, he showed more conviction in the rest of his repertoire, a high-80s changeup and a high-70s curveball. The former produced respective whiff and chase rates of 55% and 38%, while the latter could blend with his slider but showed average potential at its best. He tied his pitch mix together with uncommon poise for a pitcher of his age and experience and a smooth, repeatable delivery with excellent extension. He has the potential for double-plus control, which showed up when he walked just two hitters in 28.1 innings at Double-A Reading, which is one

BA GRADE | SCOUTING GRADES

70

Risk: Extreme

FB: 70. CB: 50. SL: 60.
CHG: 55. CTL: 70.

Projected future grades on 20-80 scouting scale

BEST TOOLS

BATTING

Best Hitter for Average	Justin Crawford
Best Power Hitter	Carlos De La Cruz
Best Strike-Zone Discipline	William Bergolla Jr.
Fastest Baserunner	Emaarion Boyd
Best Athlete	Justin Crawford

PITCHING

Best Fastball	Andrew Painter
Best Curveball	Mick Abel
Best Slider	Orion Kerkering
Best Changeup	Wen Hui Pan (splitter)
Best Control	Sam Aldegheri

FIELDING

Best Defensive Catcher	Jordan Dissin
Best Defensive Infielder	Bryan Rincon
Best Infield Arm	Bryan Rincon
Best Defensive Outfielder	Justin Crawford
Best Outfield Arm	Cade Fergus

of the most hitter-friendly atmospheres in the minor leagues.

THE FUTURE: If he had been healthy, Painter was a candidate to reach the big leagues in 2023. Now, his first start at Citizens Bank Park will not likely come until sometime in the 2025 season. If he arrives showing the same combination of stuff, control and poise he displayed in 2022, he has a chance to pitch at the front of Philadelphia's rotation for years to come. ■

Year	Age	Club (League)	Level	W	L	ERA	G	GS	IP	H	HR	BB	SO	BB%	SO%	WHIP	AVG
2023	20	Did not play—Injured															
Minor League Total				6	2	1.48	26	26	110	71	5	25	167	5.8	39.6	0.88	.181

2 JUSTIN CRAWFORD, OF

HIT: 50. **POW:** 40. **RUN:** 70. **FLD:** 55. **ARM:** 50. **BA Grade:** 55. **Risk:** High.

Born: January 13, 2004. **B-T:** L-R. **HT:** 6-3. **WT:** 175.
Drafted: HS—Las Vegas, 2022 (1st round). **Signed by:** Zach Friedman.
TRACK RECORD: Crawford is the son of 15-year big leaguer and four-time all-star Carl Crawford. The younger Crawford was selected out of high school in Las Vegas in the first round of the 2022 draft. In his first full season, split between Low-A Clearwater and High-A Jersey Shore, Crawford produced a .332 average that was seventh overall in the minors and the best for any player without upper-level experience. He represented Philadelphia in the Futures Game.
SCOUTING REPORT: Crawford's goals entering the year revolved around improving the quality of his at-bats and adding more strength to his lower half. Now, the next step is improving his bat path and catching pitches in front of the strike zone in order to get them in the air more often. He was one of the most extremely groundball-oriented hitters in the minors in 2023, with an average launch angle of -9 degrees and a groundball rate of roughly 70% between both stops. He hits the ball plenty hard—his 90th percentile exit velocity was 103.1 mph—now he needs to get it off the ground. Crawford's chase rate was a bit high, but his in-zone miss rate of 13.4% was excellent. Defensively, Crawford's double-plus speed helps him make up plenty of ground in center field, but there's work to be done to make the most of his capabilities. Presently, his speed helps mask reads, routes and jumps that scouts believe could stand to be sharpened. If he makes those improvements, he could develop into an above-average defender. If he does have to move to a corner, his average arm strength would fit in left field, but his offensive game fits much better in center.
THE FUTURE: Crawford's skill set evokes the classic turn-and-burn hitter at the top of a lineup. He'll return to High-A in 2024 with a chance at reaching the upper levels by the summertime.

Year	Age	Club (League)	Level	AVG	G	AB	R	H	2B	3B	HR	RBI	BB	SO	SB	OBP	SLG
2023	19	Clearwater (FSL)	A	.344	69	276	51	95	16	6	3	60	25	53	40	.399	.478
2023	19	Jersey Shore (SAL)	A+	.288	18	73	20	21	6	2	0	4	7	16	7	.366	.425
Minor League Totals				.319	103	407	79	130	22	9	3	69	39	84	57	.383	.440

3 MICK ABEL, RHP

FB: 70. **CB:** 60. **SL:** 55. **CHG:** 60. **CTL:** 40. **BA Grade:** 55. **Risk:** High.

Born: August 18, 2001. **B-T:** R-R. **HT:** 6-5. **WT:** 190.
Drafted: HS—Portland, OR, 2020 (1st round). **Signed By:** Zach Friedman.
TRACK RECORD: Abel was the Phillies' first-round pick in the 2020 draft, which was shortened to five rounds due to the pandemic. When he was selected, he became the highest prep pick from the state of Oregon since 1994. Since turning pro, he has showcased an exciting array of pure stuff but has been hampered at times by slipshod command. In 2023, he finished second in both the system and the Double-A Eastern League in strikeouts.
SCOUTING REPORT: Abel's raw stuff is excellent, but the Phillies made a few tweaks to his arsenal in 2023. His repertoire is led by an outstanding mid-90s fastball that garnered a 29% whiff rate and showed excellent life through the zone. Now, he complements the four-seamer with a two-seamer to help him attack the inside part of the plate against righthanded hitters before shifting his focus toward the outer half. Abel's best offspeed pitch is his low-80s curveball, which projects as plus. His slider went through several changes in 2023. First, he changed the pitch from a gyro shape to a sweeper, then split the difference and settled on a gyro slider/cutter hybrid when the sweeper blended too closely with his plus, low-80s curveball. The current version also gives him a harder breaking ball, and is most effective when it is thrown in the mid 80s or harder. His changeup has also earned plus grades from scouts outside the organization. The biggest remaining focus is improving his control and command, which led to walk rates of worse than 5 per nine innings in a season spent mostly at Double-A Reading. To address this, the Phillies want Abel to strengthen his lower half and shorten his arm stroke.
THE FUTURE: Abel finished 2023 at Triple-A, where he'll return in 2024. If he can sharpen his strike-throwing, he could fit in the middle of a rotation.

Year	Age	Club (League)	Level	W	L	ERA	G	GS	IP	H	HR	BB	SO	BB%	SO%	WHIP	AVG
2023	21	Reading (EL)	AA	5	5	4.14	22	22	109	73	15	62	126	13.5	27.5	1.24	.188
2023	21	Lehigh Valley (IL)	AAA	0	1	3.86	1	1	5	5	0	3	6	12.5	25.0	1.71	.278
Minor League Totals				14	20	4.09	60	60	266	199	31	142	328	12.4	28.7	1.28	.205

4 AIDAN MILLER, 3B

HIT: 55. **POW:** 60. **RUN:** 50. **FLD:** 50. **ARM:** 60. **BA Grade:** 55. **Risk:** Extreme.

Born: June 9, 2004. **B-T:** R-R. **HT:** 6-2. **WT:** 205.
Drafted: HS—Dunedin, FL, 2023 (1st round). **Signed by:** Bo Way.

TRACK RECORD: Miller's pedigree with Team USA is about as prolific as you'll find. He was a part of the organization's 12U, 15U and 18U national teams, and his .478 average was the best on an 18U team that included four other 2023 first-round picks. The Phillies used a $3.1 million bonus to break Miller from his commitment to Arkansas. He debuted with 10 games apiece in the Florida Complex and Florida State leagues in the regular season. His first pro home run was the deciding blow in the win that pushed Clearwater into the FSL finals.

SCOUTING REPORT: Miller earned a rep as one of the best hitters available in the prep class thanks to tremendous bat speed, plus raw power and an excellent understanding of the strike zone. He did an superb job controlling the zone in his pro debut, producing respective miss and chase rates of 15.4% and 14.4%. He loads the bat with a downward movement and has a bit of a barrel tip and a big leg kick, but the Phillies ultimately believed Miller offered the best prep combination of hitting ability and power in the draft. Miller will begin his career at shortstop, but the prevailing thinking both inside and outside the organization is that he will likely wind up at third base as he matures and adds strength to his already-physical frame. If that happens, his plus arm strength will be an asset at the position. He also had experience as an amateur both corner-outfield positions, where his bat would easily profile. He's an average runner now but could slow down as he ages.

THE FUTURE: Miller should begin 2024 back at Low-A Clearwater with a chance to reach High-A Jersey Shore in the second half of the season. He has the offensive skills to profile an middle-order hitter who mans third base.

Year	Age	Club (League)	Level	AVG	G	AB	R	H	2B	3B	HR	RBI	BB	SO	SB	OBP	SLG
2023	19	FCL Phillies	Rk	.414	10	29	6	12	2	0	0	2	6	5	0	.528	.483
2023	19	Clearwater (FSL)	A	.216	10	37	4	8	1	1	0	0	6	10	4	.341	.297
Minor League Totals				.303	20	66	10	20	3	1	0	2	12	15	4	.425	.379

5 STARLYN CABA, SS

HIT: 60. **POW:** 40. **RUN:** 60. **FLD:** 60. **ARM:** 55. **BA Grade:** 55. **Risk:** Extreme.

Born: December 6, 2005. **B-T:** B-R. **HT:** 5-10. **WT:** 160.
Signed: Dominican Republic, 2023. **Signed by:** Luis Garcia.

TRACK RECORD: The biggest bonus the Phillies handed out in the international class that opened on Jan. 15, 2023 went to Caba, a Dominican shortstop who inked his deal as a 17-year-old. Caba got $3 million from Philadelphia, then began his career a few months later in the Dominican Summer League. He was outstanding for 38 games before an injury to his left elbow suffered on a slide required a season-ending surgical cleanup.

SCOUTING REPORT: As an amateur, Caba earned a reputation as an excellent defensive shortstop with outstanding bat-to-ball skills. Both of those traits showed up in his pro debut. At the plate, he hit the ball with slightly below-average exit velocities when compared to his peers, but his contact skills were the real story. Caba's overall and zone-miss rates over the course of 164 plate appearances were 9.5% and 4.2%—exemplary for any level, but especially so for someone his age. Caba is not a particularly physical player and doesn't project to add much more muscle to his frame, so his power will likely come from doubles and line drives from gap to gap. His plus speed could help him leg out a few triples, too. Defensively, Caba shows elite instincts and actions at shortstop as one of the quickest infield defenders in the Phillies' system. He has strong footwork to go with plus arm strength, which should help keep him at shortstop for the long run. Caba is also praised for his outstanding makeup, which internal evaluators say helps him act like another coach on the field.

THE FUTURE: After recovering from elbow surgery, Caba should be ready in plenty of time for spring training. He'll make his U.S. debut in 2024 and has the ceiling of a standout defensive shortstop who hits toward the top of an order.

Year	Age	Club (League)	Level	AVG	G	AB	R	H	2B	3B	HR	RBI	BB	SO	SB	OBP	SLG
2023	17	DSL Phillies White	Rk	.301	38	133	29	40	2	2	0	17	28	16	16	.423	.346
Minor League Totals				.301	38	133	29	40	2	2	0	17	28	16	16	.423	.346

6 ORION KERKERING, RHP

FB: 60. **SL:** 70. **CTL:** 45. **BA Grade:** 45. **Risk:** Medium.

Born: April 4, 2001. **B-T:** R-R. **HT:** 6-2. **WT:** 204.
Drafted: South Florida, 2022 (5th round). **Signed by:** Bryce Harman.

TRACK RECORD: In his first two seasons at South Florida, Kerkering was almost exclusively a reliever. In his draft season, he shuttled between the rotation and the bullpen and achieved mixed results. Confident in what they'd seen in previous seasons, the Phillies drafted Kerkering in the fifth round in 2022. He moved through all four levels of the minor leagues in 2023, made his big league debut on Sept. 24 and was a part of the Phillies' playoff roster.
SCOUTING REPORT: Kerkering works largely with two pitches—a high-90s two-seam fastball and a monster of a mid-80s slider that won Best Breaking Pitch in the Florida State, South Atlantic and Eastern leagues in BA's Best Tools voting. The combination helped him rack up 79 strikeouts in 53.2 innings before his callup. He then added six more punchouts in three big league innings. The slider is so good, in fact, that he uses it to set up his fastball. He threw it 53% of the time in the minor leagues, then went even further by throwing it on 51 of his 60 big league pitches in the regular season. The slider's effectiveness can be explained by two factors: The velocity and fierce, two-plane movement that includes roughly 17 inches of sweep. The results were a 51% miss rate in the minors and a 40% rate in the big leagues. Kerkering also has thrown a changeup and a curveball but used neither in the majors or minors. The biggest holes scouts could find in Kerkering's game were a lack of elite life on his fastball and a need to better learn how to deploy his arsenal in the types of situations he'd face in pressure situations in the big leagues.
THE FUTURE: Kerkering is a near-lock to make Philadelphia's bullpen on Opening Day. He should be an elite reliever for a long time.

Year	Age	Club (League)	Level	W	L	ERA	G	GS	IP	H	HR	BB	SO	BB%	SO%	WHIP	AVG
2023	22	Clearwater (FSL)	A	1	0	0.00	9	0	10	2	0	1	18	2.9	51.4	0.29	.061
2023	22	Jersey Shore (SAL)	A+	2	0	1.77	18	0	20	13	2	6	27	7.5	33.8	0.93	.178
2023	22	Reading (EL)	AA	0	1	2.05	21	0	22	19	2	5	33	5.7	37.5	1.09	.229
2023	22	Lehigh Valley (IL)	AAA	1	0	0.00	1	0	1	2	0	0	1	0.0	20.0	2.00	.400
2023	22	Philadelphia (NL)	MLB	1	0	3.00	3	0	3	3	0	2	6	14.3	42.9	1.67	.250
Minor League Totals				5	1	1.80	55	0	61	43	4	13	86	5.5	36.4	0.93	.195
Major League Totals				1	0	3.00	3	0	3	3	0	2	6	14.3	42.9	1.67	.250

7 BRYAN RINCON, SS

HIT: 40. **POW:** 40. **RUN:** 55. **FLD:** 60. **ARM:** 60. **BA Grade:** 50 **Risk:** High

Born: February 8, 2004. **B-T:** S-R. **HT:** 5-10. **WT:** 185.
Drafted: HS—Pittsburgh, 2022 (14th round). **Signed by:** Jeff Zona Jr.

TRACK RECORD: Rincon was the Phillies' 14th-round selection in 2022, drafted out of Shaler Area High in Pittsburgh. He began his career with a dozen games—including two home runs—in the Florida Complex League before getting a bit more experience at instructional league that fall. He showed excellent plate discipline at a pair of Class A stops in 2023, finishing with nearly as many walks (68) as strikeouts (76).
SCOUTING REPORT: When the Phillies drafted Rincon, they expected an excellent defensive shortstop but were surprised with the offensive aptitude and output he showed in 2023. Rincon did an excellent job controlling the zone and making contact, with in-zone miss and chase rates of 11.7% and 16.6% between both levels. There's still a bit of work to be done, and scouts say he needs to adopt an approach that lets him better use the whole field. Scouts observed near-identical setups from both sides of the plate but a more controlled swing from the left side compared to more powerful, violent cuts when hitting righthanded. Despite a smaller stature that is mostly filled out, Rincon's advanced idea of the strike zone and strong wrists give him a chance to add some power if he can add more of a load to his swing mechanics. Defensively, he's likely to stick at shortstop but could move off the position if his lower half gets too thick. He shows strong defensive instincts, the footwork to move to his left and just enough arm strength to make the throws from the 5.5 hole. If he does move from shortstop, he has the chops to earn regular playing time at any infield spot.
THE FUTURE: Rincon has the top-end ceiling of an everyday shortstop who hits toward the bottom of the order but is more likely to settle in as a super-utility player who provides plenty of defensive value.

Year	Age	Club (League)	Level	AVG	G	AB	R	H	2B	3B	HR	RBI	BB	SO	SB	OBP	SLG
2023	19	Clearwater (FSL)	A	.228	81	276	49	63	13	1	8	45	59	63	23	.369	.370
2023	19	Jersey Shore (SAL)	A+	.258	18	62	13	16	4	0	0	7	9	13	4	.364	.323
Minor League Totals				.228	111	372	69	85	19	1	10	61	74	83	31	.363	.366

8 WILLIAM BERGOLLA JR., SS

HIT: 50. **POW:** 30. **RUN:** 60. **FLD:** 50. **ARM:** 55. **BA Grade:** 50. **Risk:** High.

Born: October 20, 2004. **B-T:** L-R. **HT:** 5-10. **WT:** 155.
Signed: Venezuela, 2022. **Signed by:** Rafael Alvarez/William Mota.

TRACK RECORD: Bergolla was the gem of the Phillies' signing class in the international period that opened on Jan. 15, 2022. The Venezuelan native got a signing bonus of $2.05 million and put together an excellent pro debut in the Dominican Summer League, where he hit .380/.470/.423 with just three strikeouts in 83 plate appearances. The Phillies showed their faith in him in 2023 by skipping him over the Florida Complex League and straight to the Florida State League, where he racked up more walks (30) than strikeouts (17) in 55 games. His father, William Sr., was a middle infielder who appeared in 17 games for the 2005 Reds.

SCOUTING REPORT: Bergolla's game is centered on putting the bat on the ball and playing steady, reliable defense at shortstop. The 18-year-old made a remarkable amount of contact at Low-A, producing an overall miss rate of just 5.4%, a minuscule in-zone whiff rate of 3.3% and a chase rate of 18.1%. But that contact came with minimal impact. His exit velocities were well below-average and he found the barrel less often than he whiffed. The Phillies acknowledge the Bergolla needs to get much stronger to access any sort of power and to hold up over the rigors of a long season against more advanced pitchers. Bergolla has the skills to be an average defender who makes all the plays at shortstop and the above-average arm strength to stick at the position. He's a plus runner but needs to sharpen his basestealing instincts to make that aspect of his game more successful.

THE FUTURE: Bergolla could return to Low-A to begin the 2024 season with a shot at High-A Jersey Shore by sometime in the summer. If he adds strength, he has the ceiling of an everyday big league shortstop who can hit toward the bottom of an order.

Year	Age	Club (League)	Level	AVG	G	AB	R	H	2B	3B	HR	RBI	BB	SO	SB	OBP	SLG
2023	18	Clearwater (FSL)	A	.255	55	192	26	49	2	2	0	20	30	17	2	.351	.286
Minor League Totals				.289	79	263	44	76	5	2	0	34	41	20	4	.383	.323

9 EDUARDO TAIT, C

HIT: 50. **POW:** 60. **RUN:** 40. **FLD:** 50. **ARM:** 55. **BA Grade:** 55. **Risk:** Extreme.

Born: August 27, 2006. **B-T:** L-R. **HT:** 6-0. **WT:** 175.
Signed: Panama, 2006. **Signed by:** Abdiel Ramos.

TRACK RECORD: Were he born five days later, Tait would have been a prospect for the international class that opens on Jan. 15, 2024. Instead, he was one of the youngest players in his class and a sleeper prospect whom the Phillies scooped up and signed for $90,000 in 2023. Tait played the majority of his season at 16 years old—he didn't turn 17 until the first game of the Dominican Summer League's championship series—and spent the summer reinforcing the knack for barreling balls he showed as an amateur. He was selected for the DSL's all-star game and put together a standout postseason performance that included five doubles in six games.

SCOUTING REPORT: Tait projects to be a bat-first backstop, and his offensive game showed up in spades in his pro debut. The foundation of his tool set starts with a strong body, a clean swing and excellent raw power from the left side, and he used those traits to hit balls harder than his peers. Tait's average and 90th percentile exit velocities were 88.8 and 92.9 mph, both of which were considerably better than most players his age or in the DSL. The power in his game showed up early, too, with home runs to dead center and the opposite way during spring training in the Dominican Republic. His swing also features smooth enough rhythm to help him get the barrel to the ball on time more often than not. Tait's game will likely always be focused on his offense, but the Phillies believe his defense could get to average as he develops and learns the finer points of the position. His arm has the potential to get to above-average and he will likely settle in as a below-average runner.

THE FUTURE: After a boffo season in the DSL, Tait will move stateside in 2024 to the Florida Complex League. He's got the upside be a bat-first everyday catcher in the big leagues.

Year	Age	Club (League)	Level	AVG	G	AB	R	H	2B	3B	HR	RBI	BB	SO	SB	OBP	SLG
2023	16	DSL Phillies Red	Rk	.331	35	121	25	40	12	3	3	27	9	24	3	.396	.554
2023	16	DSL Phillies White	Rk	.346	9	26	3	9	0	0	0	9	3	7	1	.419	.346
Minor League Totals				.333	44	147	28	49	12	3	3	36	12	31	4	.400	.517

10 GABRIEL RINCONES JR., OF

HIT: 40. **POW:** 55. **RUN:** 30. **FLD:** 40. **ARM:** 60. **BA Grade:** 45. **Risk:** High.

Born: March 3, 2001. **B-T:** L-R. **HT:** 6-4. **WT:** 225.
Drafted: Florida Atlantic, 2022 (3rd round). **Signed by:** Victor Gomez.
TRACK RECORD: Rincones started his collegiate career with two years at St. Petersburg (Fla.) JC before transferring to Florida Atlantic for his junior season. In his lone season with the Owls, Rincones produced 19 home runs in 58 games. He returned to FAU for his senior year, but a tear in his right shoulder kept him off the field the entire season. Nonetheless, the Phillies selected him in the third round in 2022. He made his pro debut in 2023 and hit 15 home runs in a season spent primarily at High-A Jersey Shore.
SCOUTING REPORT: Rincones—the son of a former Mariners minor leaguer by the same name—has a game based around big-time power. His combination of size and strength produced high-end exit velocities, including a 90th-percentile mark of 106.3 mph that was well above-average compared to his peers in Class A. To become a more complete hitter, he'll have to do better against same-side pitching. In his first pro test, Rincones hit .209 with a .665 OPS against southpaws. Unless he closes that hole, he projects as no more than a below-average hitter. Rincones moved between both corner outfield spots and DH, with the majority of his defensive time coming in right field. He's likely never going to be better than a below-average outfield defender, and scouts speculate he could get some exposure to first base. His plus arm plays well in right field, but his well below-average speed could lead to moves elsewhere. If he continues to show power at the upper levels, his bat will play on a corner.
THE FUTURE: In 2024, Rincones will move to Double-A Reading, an extremely hitter-friendly environment that should allow for an strong season at the plate. At peak, he could be a classic corner outfield masher whose booming bat makes up for defensive shortcomings.

Year	Age	Club (League)	Level	AVG	G	AB	R	H	2B	3B	HR	RBI	BB	SO	SB	OBP	SLG
2023	22	Clearwater (FSL)	A	.264	48	178	31	47	13	2	5	21	28	55	24	.388	.444
2023	22	Jersey Shore (SAL)	A+	.238	72	281	50	67	18	1	10	39	33	79	8	.326	.416
Minor League Totals				.248	120	459	81	114	31	3	15	60	61	134	32	.351	.427

11 GRIFF McGARRY, RHP

FB: 60. **CB:** 40. **SL:** 60. **CHG:** 45. **CTL:** 40. **BA Grade:** 50. **Risk:** Extreme.

Born: June 8, 1999. **B-T:** R-R. **HT:** 6-2. **WT:** 190. **Drafted:** Virginia, 2021 (5th round). **Signed by:** Kellan McKeon.
TRACK RECORD: Ever since his days at Virginia, McGarry has been a pitcher with tremendous stuff which has its effectiveness muted by poor control and command. The Phillies saw enough upside to take a chance on McGarry in the fifth round of the 2021 draft and sign him for $322,500. McGarry opened the season on the injured list but showed his signature mix of whiffs and walks at Double-A Reading before running into enough control problems at Triple-A to necessitate a stint on the Development List.
SCOUTING REPORT: There's zero doubt about the filthiness of McGarry's stuff. At his best, his mix features a four-seam fastball that averages around 94 mph and has excellent life through the zone. Its quality is amplified by the low vertical approach angle in McGarry's delivery. The righthander backs the heat with a filthy mid-80s slider with sweepy break. The Phillies are working with McGarry to shorten the pitch to help it land in the zone more often. McGarry also has a low-80s curveball he can flip in for a strike, as well as a cutter and changeup which are thrown in the high 80s and used sparingly. Now the Phillies need to figure out how to get him to throw just enough strikes to make his repertoire effective. To that end, they used the time away from competition to begin re-tooling McGarry's delivery. They believe a shorter arm path and fewer big movements in his delivery will help him find the zone at somewhere near an average rate.
THE FUTURE: If McGarry can get his delivery and control in a good place, he still has a slight chance to fit somewhere in a rotation. His more likely role, however, is as a fire-breathing monster in the late innings, though even that outcome will require him to throw strikes with more frequency and quality.

Year	Age	Club (League)	Level	W	L	ERA	G	GS	IP	H	HR	BB	SO	BB%	SO%	WHIP	AVG
2023	24	Clearwater (FSL)	A	0	0	9.00	1	1	1	1	1	0	2	0.0	50.0	1.00	.250
2023	24	Reading (EL)	AA	1	1	3.13	13	13	55	31	4	36	74	15.6	32.0	1.23	.163
2023	24	Lehigh Valley (IL)	AAA	0	2	41.54	3	3	4	8	0	14	5	40.0	14.3	5.08	.400
Minor League Totals				6	11	4.42	52	40	172	106	14	117	254	15.9	34.6	1.30	.177

12 DEVIN SALTIBAN, SS

HIT: 50. **POW:** 55. **RUN:** 55. **FLD:** 50. **ARM:** 55. **BA Grade:** 50. **Risk:** Extreme.

Born: February 14, 2005. **B-T:** R-R. **HT:** 5-10. **WT:** 180. **Drafted:** HS—Hilo, HI, 2023 (3rd round).
Signed by: Demerius Pittman.

TRACK RECORD: Saltiban was the highest-rated Hawaiian prospect in the class and began opening the eyes of evaluators during his draft spring after showing an impressive set of tools. The Phillies drafted him in the third round and signed him away from a commitment to Hawaii with a bonus of $602,500. The selection came with a twist. As an amateur, Saltiban was an outfielder, but Phillies crosschecker Shane Bowers saw him taking grounders before a game and believed he had the chops to handle the position as a pro. He got into 10 games in the Florida Complex League.

SCOUTING REPORT: Saltiban has a smooth, simple swing that the Phillies believe should produce a combination of average and power, and noted that his amateur exit velocities were better than average for the typical 18-year-old. The biggest caveat is that he hasn't had much experience against the type of high-velocity fastballs he'll see in pro ball. He has plenty of bat speed, however, which should help him get to 55-grade power. Saltiban's last experience at shortstop came when he was in Little League, so his development at the position might take a bit of patience. In a system with Trea Turner in the big leagues and a host of prospects already at the position, he'll have plenty of leash to develop. Saltiban earns above-average marks for his speed and throwing arm.

THE FUTURE: Saltiban should reach Low-A in 2024, depending on how the team deploys the rest of its young middle infielders. He's a risky prospect who could provide plenty of value one day.

Year	Age	Club (League)	Level	AVG	G	AB	R	H	2B	3B	HR	RBI	BB	SO	SB	OBP	SLG
2023	18	FCL Phillies	Rk	.333	10	42	10	14	2	0	1	7	3	7	5	.391	.452
Minor League Totals				.333	10	42	10	14	2	0	1	7	3	7	5	.391	.452

13 TJAYY WALTON, OF

HIT: 50. **POW:** 60. **RUN:** 50. **FLD:** 50. **ARM:** 55. **BA Grade:** 50. **Risk:** Extreme.

Born: January 29, 2005. **B-T:** R-R. **HT:** 6-3. **WT:** 225. **Drafted:** HS—Bradenton, FL, 2023 (4th round). **Signed by:** Bo Way.

TRACK RECORD: Walton missed much of the 2022 showcase circuit with an arm injury but rebounded enough the following spring to become the Phillies' fourth-round pick in 2023. He was taken out of Florida's powerhouse IMG Academy, then was signed for $499,100 to lure him away from a commitment to Miami. Before transferring to IMG, Walton was a two-sport athlete at Greensville County High in Virginia, where he also played basketball. He got a quick look in the Florida Complex League after signing and went 5-for-13 in five games with three extra-base hits.

SCOUTING REPORT: Walton was IMG's leading hitter in 2023, and slashed 473/.526/.770 with six home runs and more walks than strikeouts. He has a flat swing geared for line drives, but the Phillies believe he'll ultimately have a power-over-hit profile when he adds more loft to his cut and taps into a body that already looks like a slugger's frame and has produced exit velocities in excess of 110 mph. He's an above-average runner, though he could slow down as he fills out, and has above-average arm strength. Those traits, combined with the power the team believes will blossom, should lead him to a future as an average defender in an outfield corner, likely right field.

THE FUTURE: Walton should see Low-A Clearwater at some point during 2024, if not on Opening Day. If the expected power begins to show up, he'll begin on a path toward a classic corner-outfield masher.

Year	Age	Club (League)	Level	AVG	G	AB	R	H	2B	3B	HR	RBI	BB	SO	SB	OBP	SLG
2023	18	FCL Phillies	Rk	.385	5	13	4	5	2	1	0	4	3	6	0	.529	.692
Minor League Totals				.385	5	13	4	5	2	1	0	4	3	6	0	.529	.692

14 CARLOS DE LA CRUZ, OF

HIT: 40. **POW:** 60. **RUN:** 40. **FLD:** 40. **ARM:** 40. **BA Grade:** 45. **Risk:** High.

Born: October 6, 1999. **B-T:** R-R. **HT:** 6-8. **WT:** 210. **Signed:** HS—New York, 2017 (NDFA). **Signed by:** Alex Agostino.

TRACK RECORD: De La Cruz went unselected out of high school in 2017, when the draft was still 40 rounds. He signed as a free agent on the strength of breathtaking raw power. De La Cruz began to put things together in 2022, when he split the year between High-A Jersey Shore and Double-A Reading and crushed 17 home runs. He upped that total to 24 in 2023, when he spent the entire season at Double-A.

SCOUTING REPORT: De La Cruz has a huge frame at 6-foot-8 and the power that would be expected from someone that size. His 90.6-mph average and 106.6-mph 90th percentile exit velocities are among the best in the system, but he also has the miss rates that usually come from someone who stands at 6-foot-8. He's an aggressive swinger who rarely walks, leading scouts to believe his hit tool will be below-average at best. De La Cruz bounced through all three outfield positions in 2023 and got a good chunk of time at first base as well. Scouts like him better in the outfield because he's a long strider who can cover plenty of ground. His below-average arm would fit best in left field. He's a big target at first base but his footwork is suspect and his hands are too stiff to scoop balls with regularity.

THE FUTURE: De La Cruz was left unprotected and unselected in each of the last two Rule 5 drafts. His raw power will give him plenty of chances but his likely role in the big leagues is as a bench bat who can provide a jolt every now and then. He'll move to Triple-A in 2024.

Year	Age	Club (League)	Level	AVG	G	AB	R	H	2B	3B	HR	RBI	BB	SO	SB	OBP	SLG
2023	23	Reading (EL)	AA	.259	129	509	80	132	25	1	24	67	54	160	3	.344	.454
Minor League Totals				.244	454	1654	211	404	81	7	59	211	145	582	23	.317	.409

15 SAMUEL ALDEGHERI, LHP

FB: 50. **CB:** 45. **SL:** 50. **CHG:** 45. **CTL:** 50. **BA Grade:** 45. **Risk:** High.

Born: September 19, 2001. **B-T:** L-L. **HT:** 6-1. **WT:** 180. **Signed:** Italy, 2019. **Signed by:** Claudio Scerrato.

TRACK RECORD: The Phillies signed Aldegheri out of Italy in 2019 as part of an international class that also included Curtis Mead, who was used in a trade to bring Cristopher Sanchez into the system. Aldegheri is light on experience thanks to the pandemic and injuries to his elbow, back and shoulder that have limited him to just 117 innings.

SCOUTING REPORT: Aldegheri doesn't have the high-octane stuff of some of the other arms in the system, but he knows how to mix, match and locate. The lefty works with four- and two-seam fastballs in front of a five-pitch mix that is complemented by the standard offspeed array. The lefty's fastball sits in the low 90s and has peaked at 95 with cutting and riding action through the zone. Aldegheri's slider is his only average secondary, but both his curveball and changeup grade out as fringe-average. He sells the changeup well. Aldegheri does a nice job pounding the strike zone and lowered his walk rate in a small sample at High-A toward season's end. Scouts like his overall command and feel to pitch despite not having a knockout weapon in his mix. They also note a much better body than in season's past.

THE FUTURE: Aldegheri will likely reach Double-A for the first time in 2024. If healthy, he might fit as a No. 5 starter or a swingman. He was left unprotected but didn't get picked in the Rule 5 draft.

Year	Age	Club (League)	Level	W	L	ERA	G	GS	IP	H	HR	BB	SO	BB%	SO%	WHIP	AVG
2023	21	Clearwater (FSL)	A	3	1	3.86	16	15	68	59	8	30	79	10.3	27.1	1.32	.234
2023	21	Jersey Shore (SAL)	A+	1	0	5.63	4	4	16	19	1	5	20	6.9	27.8	1.50	.288
Minor League Totals				5	2	3.62	36	26	117	104	9	52	148	10.2	29.1	1.33	.234

16 CHRISTIAN McGOWAN, RHP

FB: 60. **SL:** 55. **CHG:** 40. **CTL:** 40. **BA Grade:** 45. **Risk:** High.

Born: March 7, 2000. **B-T:** R-R. **HT:** 6-3. **WT:** 205. **Drafted:** Eastern Oklahoma State JC, 2021 (7th round). **Signed by:** Tommy Field.

TRACK RECORD: McGowan was the Phillies seventh-round selection in 2021 out of Eastern Oklahoma State JC. He spent three seasons at the school and blossomed in his draft year after switching from a four-seamer to a sinker and upping his velocity considerably. The righthander was committed to Texas Tech but signed for $577,000. He had Tommy John surgery in 2022 and didn't make his 2023 debut until July. He made up for lost time in the Arizona Fall League.

SCOUTING REPORT: McGowan operates primarily with his sinker-slider combo but will mix in a change-up every so often as well. The fastball sits in the mid 90s and can touch 98 with wicked running life that helped him get grounders by the bushel. The pitch is thrown from a higher than average release height for a sinking fastball. McGowan actually has two types of sliders: a sweeper for whiffs and a tighter-breaking gyro to drop in for called strikes. He throws a high-80s changeup, though some scouts think he might be a candidate for a splitter that would give him a weapon to attack north-south. He has below-average control and the Phillies would like him to learn that it's OK to pitch to contact.

THE FUTURE: McGowan will pitch at an upper-level stop in 2024 and could be a candidate for a late-season big league debut if things fall into place. He has an outside chance for a back-end role but more likely fits as a late-inning power arm.

Year	Age	Club (League)	Level	W	L	ERA	G	GS	IP	H	HR	BB	SO	BB%	SO%	WHIP	AVG
2023	23	FCL Phillies	Rk	0	0	3.60	2	2	5	2	0	6	6	33.3	0.40	.118	
2023	23	Clearwater (FSL)	A	0	1	18.00	1	1	2	5	1	2	2	15.4	15.4	3.50	.455
2023	23	Jersey Shore (SAL)	A+	0	0	2.81	5	5	16	15	0	5	17	7.7	26.2	1.25	.259
2023	23	Lehigh Valley (IL)	AAA	0	0	0.00	1	1	3	2	0	3	3	25.0	25.0	1.88	.222
Minor League Totals				0	2	3.55	15	12	38	34	2	13	43	8.4	27.7	1.24	.243

17 ALEX McFARLANE, RHP

FB: 60. SL: 60. CHG: 40. CTL: 30. BA Grade: 50. Risk: Extreme.

Born: June 9, 2001. **B-T:** R-R. **HT:** 6-4. **WT:** 205. **Drafted:** Miami, 2022 (4th round). **Signed by:** Victor Gomez.

TRACK RECORD: McFarlane was a coveted prospect out of high school, and the Cardinals drafted him in the 25th round, but didn't sign him. The Phillies popped McFarlane out of Miami in the fourth round of the 2022 draft. He was mostly a reliever in college but spent his first full season as a pro in the rotation at Low-A Clearwater, where he struggled with control and command. He had Tommy John surgery after the season and will likely miss all of 2024 while recovering.

SCOUTING REPORT: The most important part of McFarlane's career involved his move from a four-seam to a two-seam fastball. The former did not work well with McFarlane's arm slot, while the latter proved adept at getting grounders while maintaining its velocity in the mid-to-high 90s. He's still learning how to control his sinker and where to start it before letting its movement do the rest. The slider has high spin rates and plenty of sweep in the mid 80s and could get to plus with plenty of refinement. Like the rest of his arsenal, he needs to greatly improve the command of the pitch. He rounds out his mix with a split-change in the high 80s with hard running life away from lefthanders that could get to below-average with further refinement. He has well below-average control.

THE FUTURE: McFarlane's development is on hold until 2025 while he recovers from the surgery. He'll likely fit as a reliever when he reaches the big leagues, though scouts believe he has the potential and pitch mix to work high-leverage situations.

Year	Age	Club (League)	Level	W	L	ERA	G	GS	IP	H	HR	BB	SO	BB%	SO%	WHIP	AVG
2023	22	Clearwater (FSL)	A	0	4	5.72	16	16	50	46	4	38	69	16.3	29.6	1.67	.246
Minor League Totals				0	7	6.21	19	19	58	58	5	41	81	15.2	30.1	1.71	.264

18 WEN HUI PAN, RHP

FB: 70. SL: 55. CHG: 60. CTL: 45. BA Grade: 45. Risk: High.

Born: September 19, 2002. **B-T:** R-R. **HT:** 6-3. **WT:** 220. **Signed:** Taiwan, 2023. **Signed by:** Youngster Wang.

TRACK RECORD: Pan was signed out of Taiwan as part of the international period that opened on Jan. 15, 2023. At 20 years old, he was quickly put on a more advanced track and caught the attention of scouts during his first spring training. Pan split his first year between both Class A levels, though the bulk of his time came at Low-A Clearwater. He pitched almost exclusively out of the bullpen, save for a four-inning start in early May.

SCOUTING REPORT: Pan works with a three-pitch mix fronted by a four-seam fastball that averaged 96 mph and touched triple digits. He backed the fastball with a nasty splitter that the Phillies believe stands as the best change of pace in the system. When combined, the two pitches make for an effective north-south attack. He rounds out his mix with a low-80s slider that flashed above-average. The Phillies worked with Pan all season to help the slider gain more velocity to complete a mix based on power and a variety of shapes. He showed solid control but inconsistent command of his repertoire. He's shown a slow curveball and a two-seamer in the past, but going forward he's likely to phase out those two pitches.

THE FUTURE: Pan's role out of the bullpen saw him go multiple innings on all but nine occasions. The organization plans to stretch him out in 2024 in advance of a move into a starter's workload. If he succeeds, he could fit as a back-end starter, but his likeliest still fit still is as a late-inning reliever.

Year	Age	Club (League)	Level	W	L	ERA	G	GS	IP	H	HR	BB	SO	BB%	SO%	WHIP	AVG
2023	20	Clearwater (FSL)	A	4	1	2.81	27	1	58	31	2	19	81	8.5	36.2	0.87	.154
2023	20	Jersey Shore (SAL)	A+	0	0	15.00	6	0	6	13	1	5	7	13.9	19.4	3.00	.419
Minor League Totals				4	1	4.00	33	1	64	44	3	24	88	9.2	33.8	1.08	.190

19 CALEB RICKETTS, C

HIT: 50. POW: 55. RUN: 30. FLD: 45. ARM: 45. BA Grade: 45. Risk: High.

Born: May 10, 2000. **B-T:** L-R. **HT:** 6-3. **WT:** 225. **Drafted:** San Diego, 2022 (7th round). **Signed by:** Zach Friedman.

TRACK RECORD: Ricketts' amateur career started at California prep powerhouse Orange Lutheran High, where he caught future first-rounder Cole Winn and led his club to its first two of three consecutive wins at the prestigious National High School Invitational. He spent four years at San Diego before the Phillies selected him in the seventh round in the 2022 draft. He debuted at Low-A in 2022 then split his 2023 season between the Class A levels. An injury limited him to 70 regular season games. He made up lost reps in the Arizona Fall League.

SCOUTING REPORT: Early in the season, Ricketts caught scouts' attention because of a combination of strong bat-to-ball skills and burgeoning power. He did an excellent job making contact on pitches in the zone but could stand to chase a little less often, though scouts praised his willingness to use the whole field. He's not a standout defender and he has below-average arm strength that plays up a bit because of a quick transfer. He's a fair receiver and blocker and gets high marks for the way he manages a game. Ricketts is a well below-average runner.

THE FUTURE: Ricketts entered the year as one of the biggest up-arrow prospects in the system but looked a bit diminished after returning from injury. An offseason to heal could get him back in the swing of things and help him bounce back to the form he showed in early 2023. He could fit as an offensive-minded backup.

Year	Age	Club (League)	Level	AVG	G	AB	R	H	2B	3B	HR	RBI	BB	SO	SB	OBP	SLG
2023	23	FCL Phillies	Rk	.222	3	9	0	2	1	0	0	2	2	1	0	.364	.333
2023	23	Clearwater (FSL)	A	.368	23	95	16	35	10	2	1	23	3	13	2	.390	.547
2023	23	Jersey Shore (SAL)	A+	.218	44	170	21	37	1	2	3	25	15	35	4	.287	.300
Minor League Totals				.268	92	355	50	95	12	4	7	60	31	79	6	.333	.383

20 RAYLIN HEREDIA, OF
HIT: 40. **POW:** 60. **RUN:** 55. **FLD:** 50. **ARM:** 60. **BA Grade:** 50. **Risk:** Extreme.

Born: November 10, 2003. **B-T:** R-R. **HT:** 6-0. **WT:** 174. **Signed:** Dominican Republic, 2021.
Signed by: Carlos Salas/Juan Feliciano.
TRACK RECORD: Heredia is a pop-up prospect from the Phillies' 2021 international signing class. He put together a solid 2022 season in the Dominican Summer League, including a white-hot postseason run. He was one of the best prospects in the Florida Complex League in 2023, then finished the year with Low-A Clearwater. His .947 OPS was the third-best in the FCL.
SCOUTING REPORT: Heredia is one of the more tooled-up players in Philadelphia's low minors. He grades as average to plus in every area except hitting, where he's not likely to be better than below-average. Scouts both inside and outside the organization believe Heredia will need to improve his bat-to-ball skills, and his rates of miss and chase were below-average across the board. In particular, he needs to firm up his approach with two strikes. When he did connect, Heredia showed excellent bat speed and did a good job of finding the barrel. His 102.5 mph 90th percentile exit velocity was above-average when compared to his peers in the FCL. Heredia's above-average speed and plus arm should allow him to profile in right field, where he should be an average defender.
THE FUTURE: Heredia has a blend of tools that could lead to a future as a power-hitting corner outfielder who hits toward the bottom of a lineup. He'll face a big test in 2024 when he spends his first year solely at full-season levels.

Year	Age	Club (League)	Level	AVG	G	AB	R	H	2B	3B	HR	RBI	BB	SO	SB	OBP	SLG
2023	19	FCL Phillies	Rk	.326	35	141	30	46	9	4	4	25	17	42	7	.415	.532
2023	19	Clearwater (FSL)	A	.288	18	66	9	19	3	1	1	9	6	23	4	.342	.409
Minor League Totals				.298	106	383	66	114	28	10	7	68	36	115	18	.367	.478

21 KEHDEN HETTIGER, C
HIT: 50. **POW:** 55. **RUN:** 40. **FLD:** 55. **ARM:** 50. **BA Grade:** 50. **Risk:** Extreme.

Born: May 25, 2004. **B-T:** B-R. **HT:** 6-2. **WT:** 205. **Drafted:** HS—Chatsworth, CA, 2023 (11th round).
Signed by: Zach Friedman.
TRACK RECORD: Hettiger was the Phillies' 11th-round pick in 2023 but earned the fourth-highest bonus in the class at $397,500. The California prep product opened evaluators' eyes during a brief look in the Florida Complex League. He added strength between his junior and senior seasons in high school and showed big-time power gains, which elevated his draft stock.
SCOUTING REPORT: Hettiger sticks out because of a well-rounded set of tools both offensively and defensively. He has a flexible body with plenty of athleticism and average arm strength that should allow him to stick behind the plate. In the box he shows a wider stance with plenty of separation that helps create a whippy, powerful swing. He projects as an average hitter who has above-average power now and a chance for more thanks to remaining projection in his frame. There's a couple of mechanical issues in his swing that could be smoothed out as he moves up the ladder.
THE FUTURE: Hettiger impressed evaluators both internally and externally with his defense and now has a better chance than expected to stick at catcher. He'll open 2023 at Low-A Clearwater.

Year	Age	Club (League)	Level	AVG	G	AB	R	H	2B	3B	HR	RBI	BB	SO	SB	OBP	SLG
2023	19	FCL Phillies	Rk	.190	10	21	5	4	1	0	0	3	6	7	0	.370	.238
Minor League Totals				.190	10	21	5	4	1	0	0	3	6	7	0	.370	.238

22 SIMON MUZZIOTTI, OF

HIT: 40. **POW:** 45. **RUN:** 55. **FLD:** 50. **ARM:** 50. **BA Grade:** 40. **Risk:** Medium.

Born: December 27, 1998. **B-T:** L-L. **HT:** 6-1. **WT:** 198. **Signed:** Venezuela, 2016. **Signed by:** Claudio Scerrato.

TRACK RECORD: Muzziotti initially signed with the Red Sox in 2015 but was declared a free agent again after Boston was deemed to have violated international signing rules. He inked with the Phillies a year later. His development has been stunted by the pandemic and a visa issue that kept him in Venezuela in 2021. He made his big league debut in 2022 but has amassed just seven big league at-bats in his career. He spent all of 2023 with Triple-A Lehigh Valley.

SCOUTING REPORT: Muzziotti is a solid player without a standout tool, but he's in the wrong organization. The Phillies are well-stocked with lefthanded-hitting outfielders and could not find a spot for him all season. He's got decent enough impact but has to do a much better job staying within the strike zone and improving his barrel accuracy. Muzziotti is a decent defender who can handle center field in a pinch but is best suited for a corner, where his fringy power would put pressure on his bat. He's an above-average runner.

THE FUTURE: Muzziotti retained his spot on the Phillies' 40-man roster and will likely report to Triple-A again in 2024. He's a backup outfielder on a championship club with a chance at more playing time on a non-contender.

Year	Age	Club (League)	Level	AVG	G	AB	R	H	2B	3B	HR	RBI	BB	SO	SB	OBP	SLG
2023	24	Lehigh Valley (IL)	AAA	.296	124	473	67	140	22	4	7	61	45	81	26	.358	.404
Minor League Totals				.275	463	1782	231	490	74	22	16	179	146	257	93	.330	.368
Major League Totals				.143	9	7	0	1	0	0	0	0	0	2	0	.250	.143

23 EMAARION BOYD, OF

HIT: 40. **POW:** 30. **RUN:** 70. **FLD:** 55. **ARM:** 50. **BA Grade:** 45. **Risk:** Extreme.

Born: August 22, 2003. **B-T:** R-R. **HT:** 6-1. **WT:** 177. **Drafted:** HS—Batesville, MS, 2022 (11th round).
Signed by: Mike Stauffer.

TRACK RECORD: Boyd was one of the toolsiest players in the 2022 draft class. The Phillies took him in the 11th round and signed him to a $647,500 bonus that was the second-highest bonus the team handed out that year. Boyd hit well in his pro debut, then showed hints of promise in the Low-A Florida State League in his first full season. His 56 stolen bases placed second in the FSL.

SCOUTING REPORT: When everything is going right, it's easy to see why the Phillies took a chance on Boyd. He has game-breaking speed that plays both in the outfield and on the bases. He already has a knack for contact which allows his quickness to accentuate his offensive game and make up for a lack of thump. There's still plenty of refinement to go and he needs to add strength and polish, and doing so could get him to his ceiling as a below-average hitter with 30-grade power. His speed makes up for some of his suspect route-running in the outfield, and without improvement he might be relegated to a corner. If that happens, he would face more pressure to add power to his offensive game. He has an average arm that would fit in either corner, where he would likely be a 55-grade defender.

THE FUTURE: Boyd should move to High-A Jersey Shore in 2024, when he'll be tested against more advanced pitching. He has the ceiling of a fourth outfielder who provides value mainly with his glove and legs.

Year	Age	Club (League)	Level	AVG	G	AB	R	H	2B	3B	HR	RBI	BB	SO	SB	OBP	SLG
2023	19	Clearwater (FSL)	A	.262	91	343	68	90	8	5	1	36	35	60	56	.366	.324
Minor League Totals				.272	102	379	75	103	9	5	1	38	40	65	64	.377	.330

24 HENDRY MENDEZ, OF

HIT: 50. **POW:** 40. **RUN:** 50. **FLD:** 45. **ARM:** 50. **BA Grade:** 45. **Risk:** Extreme.

Born: November 7, 2003. **B-T:** L-L. **HT:** 6-2. **WT:** 175. **Signed:** Dominican Republic, 2021.
Signed by: Gary Peralta (Brewers).

TRACK RECORD: Mendez's contact skills steadily improved as an amateur, leading the Brewers to sign him in 2021 for $800,000. He made it to Low-A in his first full year as a pro and was one of the youngest players in the Carolina League. He missed significant time in 2023 with injuries to his ankle and hamstring, then made up for lost time in the Arizona Fall League. He was traded to the Phillies as part of a two-player package that brought Oliver Dunn to Milwaukee.

SCOUTING REPORT: After being limited to just 66 regular-season games, Mendez still makes plenty of contact but with very little impact. Just 16 of his 64 hits went for extra-bases. He rarely misses when he swings, but he didn't find the barrel particularly often either. His bat path is more of a chopping stroke that naturally produces far too many grounders. He has speed enough to be serviceable in a corner but still needs to improve his routes and jumps. His average arm strength would fit in both left or right field. Because he's limited to a corner, there's more pressure to add strength to his frame and produce more thump.

THE FUTURE: Mendez will play all of the 2024 season at 20 years old and could begin at High-A Jersey Shore.

Year	Age	Club (League)	Level	AVG	G	AB	R	H	2B	3B	HR	RBI	BB	SO	SB	OBP	SLG
2023	19	ACL Brewers Gold	Rk	.600	4	15	5	9	3	0	0	5	0	0	0	.600	.800
2023	19	Wisconsin (MWL)	A+	.236	62	233	29	55	8	2	3	25	23	40	0	.307	.326
Minor League Totals				.260	211	742	97	193	31	6	9	88	102	122	10	.354	.354

25 ANDREW BAKER, RHP

FB: 60. **CB:** 40. **SL:** 55. **CTL:** 30. **BA Grade:** 40. **Risk:** High.

Born: March 24, 2000. **B-T:** R-R. **HT:** 6-3. **WT:** 190. **Drafted:** Chipola (FL) JC, 2021 (11th round).
Signed by: Mike Stauffer.

TRACK RECORD: Baker was a catcher in high school but converted to pitching in college. He spent the 2019 and 2021 seasons at Chipola (Fla.) JC sandwiched around six games at Auburn in the pandemic-shortened 2020 season. The Phillies gambled on his arm strength in 2021 and have spent his career trying to mold him into a pitcher.

SCOUTING REPORT: Baker's signature is his fastball, which sits between 97-100 mph and can touch a few ticks higher. The pitch is straight, however, and he doesn't command it well. That equation leads to more contact than would be expected against that velocity. He complements the fastball with two breaking balls: a sweeper slider in the mid 80s and a power curveball a couple of ticks slower. Baker doesn't throw with much finesse at this point and the slider will sometimes morph into more of a cutter. He doesn't throw nearly enough strikes to get the most out of his stuff, and will likely never have better than 30-grade control.

THE FUTURE: Baker is the kind of pitcher who will get plenty of chances because of the flashes of brilliance he'll show every now and again. If he can become more of a pitcher and less of a thrower, his stock will jump.

Year	Age	Club (League)	Level	W	L	ERA	G	GS	IP	H	HR	BB	SO	BB%	SO%	WHIP	AVG
2023	23	Reading (EL)	AA	0	6	8.12	41	0	41	35	6	48	64	22.9	30.5	2.02	.226
Minor League Totals				5	9	6.20	96	1	107	84	12	94	156	18.6	30.9	1.66	.208

26 GEORGE KLASSEN, RHP

FB: 70. **CB:** 60. **SL:** 40. **CHG:** 30. **CUT:** 45. **CTL:** 40. **BA Grade:** 40. **Risk:** High.

Born: January 26, 2002. **B-T:** R-R. **HT:** 6-2. **WT:** 170. **Drafted:** Minnesota, 2023 (6th round). **Signed by:** Derrick Ross.

TRACK RECORD: Klassen was taken by the Phillies in the sixth round of the 2023 draft, then signed for $297,500. He missed his freshman season with Minnesota after having Tommy John surgery, pitched out of the Golden Gophers' rotation in his draft year, then was shut down after signing. He dealt with back spasms after turning pro and will make his debut in 2024.

SCOUTING REPORT: The Phillies chose Klassen knowing he was going to be a bit of a project, but his pure stuff was too loud to overlook. He was one of the hardest throwers in the college class, with a fastball that sat in the upper 90s and touched triple-digits. He pairs the fastball with a potentially plus slider with depth and sweep in the mid 80s that should be his best offspeed weapon as a pro. In college, his primary breaking ball was a low-80s curveball with a similar shape to his slider. He pitched at the MLB Draft Combine and showed a hard, high-80s cutter as well. Klassen rounds out his mix with a seldom-thrown changeup in the high 80s. The Phillies made some small tweaks to his delivery and arm action in the hopes of more consistent strike throwing.

THE FUTURE: Klassen will be developed as a starter initially but could make for a solid fallback option in the bullpen if he doesn't take to the role.

Year	Age	Club (League)	Level	W	L	ERA	G	GS	IP	H	HR	BB	SO	BB%	SO%	WHIP	AVG
2023	21	Did not play															

27 TOMMY McCOLLUM, RHP

FB: 60. **SL:** 55. **CHG:** 55. **CTL:** 30. **BA Grade:** 40. **Risk:** High.

Born: June 8, 1999. **B-T:** R-R. **HT:** 6-5. **WT:** 260. **Signed:** Wingate (NC), 2021 (NDFA). **Signed by:** Kellan McKeon.

TRACK RECORD: McCollum was a reliever at Division II Wingate in North Carolina for three seasons but a poor draft year led him to go unselected in 2021. He signed with the Phillies as a free agent then made a solid 2022 season but struggled with control between High-A and Double-A in 2023 and had a stint on the development list as a way to manage his workload. He also dealt with a blister issue.

SCOUTING REPORT: McCollum is a big, strong righthander who comes at hitters from a near-overhand slot with a lower release height and extension that creates an element of deception. He works mostly with a mid-90s fastball that got heavy dose of whiffs and a split-changeup in the low 80s that at its best shows hard drop out of the zone. The quality of the pitch is inconsistent but flashes above-average. He rounds out his mix with a short slider in the high 80s that opened up the outer part of the plate and got plenty of swings and misses. His control is still well below-average.

THE FUTURE: McCollum has excellent stuff but needs to greatly improve his control and command for it to be useful. If he throws more strikes, he could fit as a reliever. If not, he'll be relegated to the minor leagues.

Year	Age	Club (League)	Level	W	L	ERA	G	GS	IP	H	HR	BB	SO	BB%	SO%	WHIP	AVG
2023	24	Jersey Shore (SAL)	A+	0	0	2.31	34	0	35	17	0	23	56	16.1	39.2	1.14	.143
2023	24	Reading (EL)	AA	1	0	3.86	10	0	9	3	0	9	11	21.4	26.2	1.29	.100
Minor League Totals				2	0	2.76	76	0	88	40	4	64	134	17.4	36.4	1.18	.136

28 JAKE EDDINGTON, RHP

FB: 60. **SL:** 60. **CHG:** 40. **CTL:** 30 **BA Grade:** 40. **Risk:** High.

Born: April 26, 2001. **B-T:** R-R. **HT:** 6-2. **WT:** 185. **Drafted:** Missouri State, 2023 (7th round). **Signed by:** Justin Munson.

TRACK RECORD: Eddington pitched his freshman season at Alabama then transferred to Missouri State. He missed his sophomore season with an injury, then broke out in his draft year as part of the Bears' rotation. He showed big stuff but scattershot control and command. The Phillies bet on the stuff in the seventh round, then signed him for $225,000. He did not pitch after signing.

SCOUTING REPORT: Eddington is a loose, athletic righthander with a frame that leaves plenty of room for projection. He delivers from a three-quarters slot and has a crossfire landing that adds deception. His high-spin fastball sits between 92-94 mph and has been up to 97. He backs the pitch with a low-80s slider with similarly high spin rates that projects as a plus weapon. His changeup is a clear third pitch but it has potential considering its sharp drop at its best. His control is well below-average thanks in part to a violent, winding arm action.

THE FUTURE: Like many of the pitchers in the Phillies' 2023 class, Eddington pairs big stuff with scattered control and command. If he throws more strikes, he could be a powerful reliever who works in the late innings.

Year	Age	Club (League)	Level	W	L	ERA	G	GS	IP	H	HR	BB	SO	BB%	SO%	WHIP	AVG
2023	22	Did not play															

29 CAM BROWN, RHP

FB: 60. **SL:** 60. **CHG:** 40. **CTL:** 40. **BA Grade:** 40. **Risk:** High.

Born: October 15, 2001. **B-T:** R-R. **HT:** 6-3. **WT:** 225. **Drafted:** Texas Christian, 2023 (10th round).
Signed by: Tommy Field.

TRACK RECORD: Brown's three-pitch mix made him highly regarded in high school, but the five-round draft in 2020 meant he made it to campus at Texas Christian. He also pitched for Chatham of the Cape Cod League in 2022. With TCU, Brown showed big stuff but subpar control and command. The Phillies selected him in the 10th round of the 2023 draft and let him get his feet wet with a few innings in the Florida Complex League and at Low-A.

SCOUTING REPORT: Brown is a physical righthander with a powerful arsenal. His fastball sits in the mid 90s and can get up to 98 mph. Post-draft, he worked with the Phillies' player development staff to determine whether a four-seam or two-seam heater would make the most sense as he moved up the ladder. Brown backs the fastball with a potentially plus slider in the mid 80s that showed two-plane break and generated a 45% whiff rate in college. He has a firm changeup in the upper 80s as well. Brown has well below-average control that the Phillies hope will improve with tweaks to his delivery.

THE FUTURE: Brown has high-octane stuff that will be more effective if he can throw more strikes. Considering his age and college pedigree, he could jump to High-A Jersey Shore in 2024.

Year	Age	Club (League)	Level	W	L	ERA	G	GS	IP	H	HR	BB	SO	BB%	SO%	WHIP	AVG
2023	21	FCL Phillies	Rk	0	0	54.00	1	0	0	1	0	3	0	60.0	0.0	12.00	.500
2023	21	Clearwater (FSL)	A	0	1	20.25	2	0	1	3	0	5	1	45.5	9.1	6.00	.500
Minor League Totals				0	1	45.00	3	0	2	4	0	8	1	50.0	6.3	12.00	.500

30 ENRIQUE SEGURA, RHP

FB: 60. **SL:** 55. **CHG:** 50. **CTL:** 40. **BA Grade:** 45. **Risk:** Extreme.

Born: December 19, 2004. **B-T:** R-R. **HT:** 6-3. **WT:** 175. **Signed:** Dominican Republic, 2022.
Signed by: Carlos Salas/Bernardo Perez.

TRACK RECORD: Segura signed with the Phillies in 2022 and showed his potential in his first pro test, which came in the Dominican Summer League, where he struck out 39 hitters in 43 innings. He moved to the Rookie-level Florida Complex League in 2023 and continued piquing the interest of pro scouts despite underwhelming stats.

SCOUTING REPORT: Segura's delivery features a quick arm and a unique arm slot, which adds layers of deception to his pitch mix. He works with four- and two-seam fastballs in the low 90s that play up thanks to excellent extension. He complements his heaters with a sweeping, slurvy slider in the high 70s and a mid-80s changeup that ranks as a clear third pitch and was thrown roughly 10% of the time. His well below-average control could tick up a grade if he adds strength to his frame, which has plenty of room for remaining projection. Scouts also were heartened by Segura's makeup on the mound. He showed plenty of competitiveness and an even-keeled attitude despite his struggles.

THE FUTURE: Segura is likely a reliever at the highest level, but he has enough upside for a bit more if he adds strength and throws more strikes. He'll move to Low-A Clearwater in 2024 where he'll pitch all year as a 19-year-old.

Year	Age	Club (League)	Level	W	L	ERA	G	GS	IP	H	HR	BB	SO	BB%	SO%	WHIP	AVG
2023	18	FCL Phillies	Rk	1	3	6.87	11	10	37	32	4	29	33	17.1	19.4	1.66	.254
Minor League Totals				6	4	4.44	24	18	79	68	5	51	72	14.6	20.6	1.51	.243

Pittsburgh Pirates

BY JOSH NORRIS

There was never any real expectation that the Pirates would compete in 2023, but at least there was some hope that the season could serve as a coming-out party for powerful, toolsy shortstop Oneil Cruz and some of the team's top prospects.

That dream didn't last long.

Cruz broke his leg in the early days of the season and spent the rest of the year rehabbing. The injury deprived Pittsburgh and the sport at large of one of its most dynamic young talents, a Statcast-melting monster with outlier tools on both sides of the ball.

As the season wore on, Pirates fans did get early previews at some of the young talents lurking in the upper levels of their minor leagues.

Henry Davis, the No. 1 overall pick in 2021, and young catcher Endy Rodriguez debuted in June and July, and each showed flashes of their potential in largely uneven seasons. The team also got a boost from third baseman Jared Triolo, who produced 2.1 bWAR in 54 games.

Righthander Quinn Priester spent a good amount of time in the big leagues as well, coming one out short of graduating from prospect qualification. He showed the potential to sit in the back of the rotation with a bit more refinement.

On the farm, the Pirates' pitching pipeline is poised to produce a few more options in the coming years. Righthanders Jared Jones and Bubba Chandler each reached the upper levels and showed flashes of dominance. So, too, did lefthander Anthony Solometo.

Their top position prospect is second baseman Termarr Johnson, who showed flashes of hitting ability and power but rarely showed both skills at the same time.

And then there's Paul Skenes. The Pirates made the righthanded Louisiana State product their choice with the No. 1 overall pick in the 2023 draft. Skenes turned in the most dominant season from a collegiate pitcher, and in doing so helped lead LSU to College World Series championship.

Skenes also was part of history when his college teammate Dylan Crews was selected by the Nationals with the No. 2 overall pick. In doing so, Skenes and Crews became the first pair of players from the same college to go with the first and second picks in the draft.

Skenes made it to Double-A in his pro debut, but was shut down just before a series in Harrisburg, where he would have gotten to face Crews for the first time as professionals.

There is no behemoth in the National League

The Pirates graduated several key prospects in 2023, but Jared Triolo outperformed them all.

PROJECTED 2027 LINEUP

Catcher	Endy Rodriguez	26
First Base	Jared Triolo	29
Second Base	Liover Peguero	26
Third Base	Ke'Bryan Hayes	30
Shortstop	Oneil Cruz	28
Left Field	Jack Suwinski	28
Center Field	Bryan Reynolds	32
Right Field	Henry Davis	27
Designated Hitter	Termarr Johnson	23
No. 1 Starter	Paul Skenes	25
No. 2 Starter	Bubba Chandler	24
No. 3 Starter	Mitch Keller	31
No. 4 Starter	Jared Jones	25
No. 5 Starter	Anthony Solometo	24
Closer	David Bednar	32

Central, and MLB's expanded playoffs give more teams than ever before a chance to at least reach the postseason.

For the Pirates to work their way back to October, they'll need strong sophomore seasons from Davis, Rodriguez, Priester, Triolo and the rest of their young big leaguers, with the hope that they can supplement that group with the next wave of upper-level pitching waiting for their turn.

They'll also need a bit more offensive firepower—some of which should come when Cruz returns in 2024.

If everything comes together, they might have a chance to return to the playoffs for the first time since 2015. ∎

DEPTH CHART

PITTSBURGH PIRATES

TOP 2024 CONTRIBUTORS / **RANK**
1. Paul Skenes, RHP — 1
2. Jared Jones, RHP — 3
3. Anthony Solometo, LHP — 4

BREAKOUT PROSPECTS / **RANK**
1. Lonnie White Jr., OF — 17
2. Jun-Seok Shim, RHP — 19
3. Estuar Suero, OF — 29

SOURCE OF TOP 30 TALENT

Homegrown	27	Acquired	3
College	12	Trade	3
Junior college	0	Rule 5 draft	0
High school	11	Independent league	0
Nondrafted free agent	0	Free agent/waivers	0
International	4		

LF
Tres Gonzalez (27)
Charles McAdoo

CF
Matt Gorski (15)
Lonnie White Jr. (17)
Jase Bowen (26)
P.J. Hilson
Shalin Polanco

RF
Estuar Suero (23)
Canaan Smith-Njigba

3B
Jack Brannigan (12)
Marcos Cabrera
Jesus Castillo

SS
Tsung-Che Cheng (7)
Mitch Jebb (11)
Alika Williams (22)
Yordany De Los Santos

2B
Termarr Johnson (4)
Nick Gonzales (9)

1B
Garrett Forrester (24)
Tony Blanco Jr. (30)
Seth Beer

C
Carter Bins
Axiel Plaz

LHP

LHSP	LHRP
Anthony Solometo (5)	Nick Dombkowski
Hunter Barco (18)	J.C. Flowers
Michael Kennedy (20)	Tyler Samaniego
Jackson Wolf (21)	Luis Peralta

RHP

RHSP	RHRP
Paul Skenes (1)	Kyle Nicolas (13)
Bubba Chandler (2)	Michael Burrows (14)
Jared Jones (3)	Carlson Reed (25)
Quinn Priester (8)	Brandan Bidois (28)
Thomas Harrington (6)	Colin Selby (29)
Braxton Ashcraft (10)	Cody Bolton
Zander Mueth (16)	Ryan Harbin
Jun-Seok Shim (19)	Fineas Del Bonta-Smith
Po-Yu Chen	David Matoma

1 PAUL SKENES, RHP

Born: May 29, 2002. **B-T:** R-R. **HT:** 6-6. **WT:** 235.
Drafted: Louisiana State, 2023 (1st round).
Signed by: Wayne Mathis.

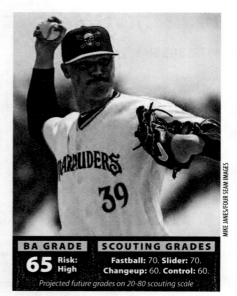

MIKE JANES/FOUR SEAM IMAGES

TRACK RECORD: For two seasons at Air Force, Skenes was a talented two-way prospect with upside on the mound and in the batter's box. He also spent summers in the Cape Cod League and with USA Baseball's Collegiate National Team. He transferred to Louisiana State before the 2023 season, ditched the lumber and entered his draft year as one of the best pitchers in his class. Five months later, he had helped lead LSU to a College World Series championship while cementing himself as the best arm on the board and one of a handful of serious candidates—along with LSU teammate Dylan Crews—to go No. 1 overall. The Pirates called Skenes' name first on draft day, then signed him for a draft-record $9.2 million. A pick later, the Nationals chose Crews, marking the first time two teammates had gone off the board with the first two selections. Skenes moved quickly in pro ball, reaching Double-A on Aug. 26. He was shut down just before a scheduled start with Altoona against Harrisburg, which could have led to his first showdown with Crews as a professional.

SCOUTING REPORT: One of the biggest keys to Skenes' success in pro ball will revolve around the quality of his fastball. Questions arose about the pitch's shape and whether—even if he can maintain its upper-90s velocity on a professional schedule—it would play against better hitters. If it becomes an issue, there are multiple avenues to explore, including changing the grip or the emphasis of a two-seamer as a way to continue the east-west profile created by his sweeping slider. In pro ball, Skenes threw his two-seamer at a 44% clip, far more often than his four-seamer. His sweeper was an adjustment that came about through work at LSU, where pitching coach Wes Johnson helped him alter the pitch's shape from its former, shorter-breaking iteration. As an amateur, scouts projected Skenes' changeup as a potentially plus pitch. To reach that upside, he'll need to throw the pitch more often. At LSU, Skenes threw the changeup just 7% of the time. In his brief pro experience, that jumped to 17%. At its best, the pitch is thrown in the upper 80s and features sharp fade and drop, but there's work to do in order to get it consistently to that ceiling. The Pirates have already worked with Skenes to find a grip that works best. Skenes also

BA GRADE	SCOUTING GRADES
65 Risk: High	Fastball: 70. Slider: 70. Changeup: 60. Control: 60.

Projected future grades on 20-80 scouting scale

BEST TOOLS

BATTING

Best Hitter for Average	Termarr Johnson
Best Power Hitter	Tony Blanco Jr.
Best Strike-Zone Discipline	Mitch Jebb
Fastest Baserunner	Jesus Castillo
Best Athlete	Lonnie White Jr.

PITCHING

Best Fastball	Paul Skenes
Best Curveball	Quinn Priester
Best Slider	Jared Jones
Best Changeup	Po-Yu Chen
Best Control	Thomas Harrington

FIELDING

Best Defensive Catcher	Carter Bins
Best Defensive Infielder	Jack Brannigan
Best Infield Arm	Jack Brannigan
Best Defensive Outfielder	Hudson Head
Best Outfield Arm	Canaan Smith-Njigba

has size, athleticism and an outstanding work ethic that should allow him to get the most out of his ability, while also keeping himself open to attacking new challenges as he develops.

THE FUTURE: Between college and pro ball, Skenes threw 129.1 innings in 2023, well beyond the 89.1 he threw in 2022 between Air Force and summer ball. After an offseason of rest, he will return poised to begin climbing toward his ceiling as a top-end starter who could make his MLB debut in 2024. ■

Year	Age	Club (League)	Level	W	L	ERA	G	GS	IP	H	HR	BB	SO	BB%	SO%	WHIP	AVG
2023	21	FCL Pirates	Rk	0	0	0.00	1	1	1	0	0	0	1	0.0	33.3	0.00	.000
2023	21	Bradenton (FSL)	A	0	0	0.00	2	2	3	1	0	0	4	0.0	36.4	0.33	.091
2023	21	Altoona (EL)	AA	0	0	13.50	2	2	3	4	0	2	5	14.3	35.7	2.25	.333
Minor League Totals				0	0	6.00	5	5	7	5	0	2	10	7.1	35.7	1.17	.192

2 BUBBA CHANDLER, RHP

FB: 60. **SL:** 55. **CHG:** 55. **CTL:** 45. **BA Grade:** 55. **Risk:** High.

Born: September 14, 2022. **B-T:** B-R. **HT:** 6-3. **WT:** 200.
Drafted: HS—Bogart, GA, 2021 (3rd round). **Signed by:** Cam Murphy.

TRACK RECORD: In 2021, the Pirates had the No. 1 overall pick in the draft. With no consensus player available, they chose Henry Davis, signed him to an under-slot deal, and used the savings to gamble on several high-upside prep prospects. One such prospect was Chandler, a two-way talent from Georgia with considerable athleticism and a high ceiling as a pitcher. He continued hitting for the first two seasons of his pro career before focusing solely on pitching in 2023, when he began polishing his rough edges and hinting at what could be a very bright future. He spun five no-hit innings with eight strikeouts in his lone start for Double-A Altoona.
SCOUTING REPORT: Though Chandler struggled early in the season, there was no point when his pure stuff was questioned. His four-seam fastball, which sat in the mid 90s and peaked a few ticks higher, showed above-average life and got plenty of misses and chases. Chandler's primary offspeed weapon is a mid-80s slider with snappy action that scouts project as at least a future above-average pitch. His third pitch is a changeup that averaged around 88 mph and was thrown roughly 10% of the time. The pitch showed above-average life and projects to be a 55 on the 20-80 scouting scale. The key to Chandler's improvements in 2023 was an improved ability to throw his offspeed pitches for strikes. Once that happened, hitters could no longer eliminate them immediately as pitches designed solely to be chased. That improvement was stark after the first two months of the season. In April and May, Chandler walked 27 hitters and struck out 39. From June on, he walked 24 hitters and struck out 89.
THE FUTURE: Chandler will return to Double-A in 2024 and will get a full year of experience against savvier hitters. There's still plenty of development remaining, but he has the upside of a No. 3 starter.

Year	Age	Club (League)	Level	W	L	ERA	G	GS	IP	H	HR	BB	SO	BB%	SO%	WHIP	AVG
2023	20	Greensboro (SAL)	A+	9	4	4.75	24	24	106	108	15	51	120	10.9	25.6	1.50	.265
2023	20	Altoona (EL)	AA	1	0	0.00	1	1	5	1	0	0	8	0.0	50.0	0.20	.063
Minor League Totals				11	5	4.03	39	36	152	132	18	79	188	12.0	28.6	1.39	.233

3 JARED JONES, RHP

FB: 70. **CB:** 50. **SL:** 60. **CHG:** 45. **CTL:** 45. **BA Grade:** 55. **Risk:** High.

Born: August 6, 2001. **B-T:** L-R. **HT:** 6-1. **WT:** 190.
Drafted: HS—La Mirada, CA, 2020 (2nd round). **Signed by:** Brian Tracy.
TRACK RECORD: Jones was the Pirates' third pick in the shortened 2020 draft, but his $2.2 million bonus was the second-highest in their class. He was a two-way talent as an amateur and was a regular on USA Baseball's national teams. Jones spent all of 2022 at High-A Greensboro, where he racked up a system-high 122.2 innings. His track accelerated in 2023, when he split his season between Double-A Altoona and Triple-A Indianapolis. His 146 strikeouts were tied at the top of the system with 2022 supplemental first-rounder Thomas Harrington.
SCOUTING REPORT: In 2022, one of Jones' biggest focuses was becoming a more mature pitcher and finding a way to respond more constructively to failure. That season, he would let mistakes spiral and begin to overthrow, leading to poor command and big innings for his opponent. A more even keel in 2023 helped Jones blossom, but it wasn't the only factor. The righthander also altered the way he threw his changeup. Instead of pronating his wrist, he snapped down and through the ball in a way that mimicked his hand action on his four-seam fastball. He also changed the grip on his slider to help him hold its higher-end velocity deeper into games. All together, Jones' arsenal—fronted by a potentially double-plus mid-90s fastball and a plus high-80s slider and backed by an above-average downer curveball and a fringy changeup—includes weapons for both righties and lefties. After a stellar turn in Double-A, Jones ran into a bit more trouble at Triple-A, where his walk rate dropped but his home run rate rose. He'll also need to maintain consistency in his delivery, which led to some of his more uneven outings in 2023.
THE FUTURE: In 2024, Jones will return to Triple-A, where he'll work to sharpen his command. He should see the big leagues at some point and has the ceiling of a midrotation starter.

Year	Age	Club (League)	Level	W	L	ERA	G	GS	IP	H	HR	BB	SO	BB%	SO%	WHIP	AVG
2023	21	Altoona (EL)	AA	1	4	2.23	10	10	44	32	3	16	47	8.9	26.3	1.08	.201
2023	21	Indianapolis (IL)	AAA	4	5	4.72	16	15	82	74	9	34	99	9.7	28.3	1.32	.240
Minor League Totals				13	22	4.31	70	66	315	284	37	135	391	9.9	28.7	1.33	.238

4 TERMARR JOHNSON, 2B

HIT: 55. **POW:** 50. **RUN:** 50. **FLD:** 50. **ARM:** 50. **BA Grade:** 55. **Risk:** High.

Born: June 11, 2004. **B-T:** L-R. **HT:** 5-8. **WT:** 175.
Drafted: HS—Atlanta, 2022 (1st round). **Signed by:** Cam Murphy.
TRACK RECORD: In 2022, Johnson was one of a handful of candidates to be drafted first overall. The Orioles chose Jackson Holliday at 1-1 rather than Druw Jones or Johnson, who fell to Pittsburgh at fourth overall. The Pirates signed him for $7,219,000, the third-highest bonus in franchise history behind only Gerrit Cole and Paul Skenes. Lauded as one of the purest prep hitters in years, Johnson reached Low-A Bradenton in his draft year, then split 2023 between Low-A and High-A Greensboro. He played a bit of catchup in the early going after a hamstring injury sidelined him for much in the spring and delayed his season debut until April 21.
SCOUTING REPORT: After roughly a season's worth of games, Johnson appears to have two distinct paths as a hitter. If he continues his trend from 2023, he will be a player who hits for a low average, draws a ton of walks and uses electric bat speed to hit long home runs to his pull side. If he varies his approach a bit and makes better swing decisions, he can trade some of those walks for hits and live up to his amateur billing as a player who can use a supremely gifted set of hands and a whip-quick bat to hit for both average and power. Though he was drafted as a shortstop, Johnson has played second base nearly exclusively as a pro and did not get a game on the left side after moving to High-A. He has an average arm and has a chance to be average at second base, though scouts noted his thicker lower half, which will have to be maintained as he matures in order to keep the necessary range. He's an average runner, though evaluators have seen him kick it up a notch when he smells extra bases.
THE FUTURE: Johnson is likely to return to High-A to begin 2024. His future hinges on the offensive approach he decides to employ as he moves through the minor leagues.

Year	Age	Club (League)	Level	AVG	G	AB	R	H	2B	3B	HR	RBI	BB	SO	SB	OBP	SLG
2023	19	Bradenton (FSL)	A	.244	75	250	57	61	10	1	13	44	72	88	7	.419	.448
2023	19	Greensboro (SAL)	A+	.242	30	99	26	24	2	0	5	15	29	32	3	.427	.414
Minor League Totals				.240	128	412	90	99	18	1	19	65	117	141	16	.413	.427

5 ANTHONY SOLOMETO, LHP

FB: 60. **SL:** 60. **CHG:** 55. **CTL:** 50. **BA Grade:** 55. **Risk:** High.

Born: December 2, 2002. **B-T:** L-L. **HT:** 6-2. **WT:** 208.
Drafted: HS—Pennsauken Township, NJ, 2021 (2nd round). **Signed by:** Dan Radcliff.
TRACK RECORD: When the Pirates cut an under-slot deal with catcher Henry Davis—whom they selected No. 1 overall in 2021—they used the savings to add high-end high school talent to their system. One such pitcher was Solometo, who got $2.8 million to break his commitment to North Carolina. Solometo did not pitch in his draft year, then made his pro debut with 13 outings at Low-A Bradenton. He split the 2023 season between High-A Greensboro and Double-A Altoona. His overall 3.26 ERA ranked inside the top 20 for pitchers with at least 100 innings.
SCOUTING REPORT: Solometo's long, winding arm action from the left side evokes the obvious comparisons and spurs the expected questions. His delivery calls to mind Madison Bumgarner, and scouts wonder if he'll throw a high volume of quality strikes. Early in 2023, his command was not good. Over his first seven starts, Solometo issued 21 walks in 29.2 innings. The Pirates challenged Solometo to pound the zone and let his stuff do its job, and the results were stark. He walked just four hitters over his next five starts—a span of 29 innings—and earned a bump to Double-A. Solometo's mix includes four- and two-seam fastballs in the low 90s, a slider in the mid 80s and a low-80s changeup. His two-seamer and slider each have a chance to be plus pitches. Scouts believe his changeup, though it is a bit further behind, could get to above-average with further development. Solometo will always have work to maintain the consistency of his slinging arm action to achieve average control and command. If 2023 is any indication, he's up to the challenge.
THE FUTURE: Solometo should reach Triple-A at some point in 2024—if not on Opening Day—and his major league debut sometime in the second half is a possibility. He could fit in the middle of a rotation.

Year	Age	Club (League)	Level	W	L	ERA	G	GS	IP	H	HR	BB	SO	BB%	SO%	WHIP	AVG
2023	20	Greensboro (SAL)	A+	2	3	2.30	12	12	59	43	2	25	68	10.7	29.1	1.16	.207
2023	20	Altoona (EL)	AA	2	4	4.35	12	12	52	49	6	14	50	6.5	23.0	1.22	.247
Minor League Totals				9	8	3.08	37	32	158	123	8	58	169	9.1	26.4	1.15	.215

6 THOMAS HARRINGTON, RHP

FB: 60. **SL:** 55. **CHG:** 50. **CUT:** 45. **CTL:** 60. **BA Grade:** 50. **Risk:** High.

Born: July 12, 2001. **B-T:** R-R. **HT:** 6-2. **WT:** 185.
Drafted: Campbell, 2022 (1st round supplemental). **Signed by:** Mike Bradford.
TRACK RECORD: Harrington's profile involves more than a bit of projection and development. He didn't start pitching full-time until his junior year of high school in Sanford, N.C., and the pandemic limited his senior year to one start. He walked on at Campbell and became the team's Friday starter by the time he was drafted in 2022, when he was a sophomore. Pittsburgh chose him with their supplemental first-round pick and signed him for $2.047 million. He pitched at two Class A levels in his 2023 pro debut, primarily High-A Greensboro.
SCOUTING REPORT: Harrington's mix starts with a four-seam fastball that sits around 93 mph but plays up because of high spin rates and excellent life through the zone. The pitch is further amplified by a lower release height and angle created in his delivery. Harrington threw his fastball effectively in and out of the zone, earning high rates of both miss and chase. The righthander backs up his fastball primarily with two pitches. The first is a short, sweeping slider in the low 80s that he can land in the zone for a called strike or spin out of the zone for chases. He rounds out his mix with a mid-80s changeup that he shows solid feel to throw but still could use further development and consistency. Harrington also throws a two-seam fastball in the same velocity range as his four-seamer and will flip in an occasional cutter as well. The latter pitch could become a bigger part of his arsenal in coming seasons. He threw all of his pitches for strikes in volume and quality. All together, Harrington's mix gives him a variety of shapes and velocities to disperse throughout the strike zone to hitters of both hands.
THE FUTURE: The 2024 season, which will likely begin in Double-A, should provide a clearer picture of Harrington's direction and future. For now, he could fit in the back of a rotation.

Year	Age	Club (League)	Level	W	L	ERA	G	GS	IP	H	HR	BB	SO	BB%	SO%	WHIP	AVG
2023	21	Bradenton (FSL)	A	4	1	2.77	8	8	39	31	3	12	40	8.0	26.7	1.10	.230
2023	21	Greensboro (SAL)	A+	3	5	3.87	18	18	88	86	11	29	106	7.7	28.2	1.30	.255
Minor League Totals				7	6	3.54	26	26	127	117	14	41	146	7.8	27.8	1.24	.248

7 TSUNG-CHE CHENG, SS/2B

HIT: 55. **POW:** 45. **RUN:** 60. **FLD:** 55. **ARM:** 55. **BA Grade:** 50. **Risk:** High.

Born: July 26, 2001. **B-T:** L-R. **HT:** 5-7. **WT:** 174.
Signed: Taiwan, 2019. **Signed by:** Fu-Chan Chiang.
TRACK RECORD: Cheng was signed out of Taiwan in 2019 but didn't make his official pro debut until 2021, when the minor leagues resumed following the canceled 2020 season. He moved a level a year in 2021 and 2022—first in the Florida Complex League and then at Low-A—before kicking it into overdrive in 2023, when he split the season between High-A Greensboro and Double-A Altoona. At both stops, Cheng showed his signature mix of contact, speed and a smattering of power. His overall numbers were boosted by the hitter-friendly atmosphere at Greensboro, but two strong months at Double-A lent credence to his level of skill.
SCOUTING REPORT: Cheng's game is built around contact, which shows up in person and in batted-ball data. Scouts report a player with excellent bat control, and he finished the year with respective overall and zone miss rates of 21.6% and 15.8%. He doesn't hit the ball particularly hard, but he has just enough thump to shoot balls from gap to gap and let his plus speed play on the basepaths. Internal evaluators would like him to narrow his approach to center more around pitches he can damage rather than simply putting the bat on the ball. Cheng must also improve against lefthanders, who carved him during his time at Double-A. He's a slick, twitchy defender at shortstop with more than enough arm for the position, but he also moved over to second base for 40 games to help increase his versatility. That could come in handy considering the glut of potential middle infielders in the Pirates organization.
THE FUTURE: Cheng will likely return to Double-A to begin 2024 and should finish the year on the precipice of the big leagues. He's one of the system's sneakier hitting prospects and could be a player who finds everyday time and provides value on both sides of the ball.

Year	Age	Club (League)	Level	AVG	G	AB	R	H	2B	3B	HR	RBI	BB	SO	SB	OBP	SLG
2023	21	Greensboro (SAL)	A+	.308	57	214	45	66	12	9	9	31	35	47	13	.406	.575
2023	21	Altoona (EL)	AA	.251	66	247	35	62	11	1	4	25	17	53	13	.304	.352
Minor League Totals				.279	265	968	191	270	56	18	23	139	145	209	75	.375	.445

8 QUINN PRIESTER, RHP

FB: 50. **CB:** 60. **SL:** 55. **CHG:** 50. **CTL:** 45. **BA Grade:** 45. **Risk:** Medium.

Born: September 15, 2000. **B-T:** R-R. **HT:** 6-3. **WT:** 210.
Drafted: HS—Cary, IL, 2019 (1st round). **Signed by:** Anthony Wycklendt.

TRACK RECORD: Priester was the Pirates' first-round pick in 2019, when the Illinois prep product earned a $3.4 million bonus. The righthander was impressive in his first taste of pro ball, split between the Florida Complex League and Low-A. He spent 2020 at the team's alternate training site, then moved quickly once the minor leagues resumed. After missing time early in 2023 with an oblique injury, Priester reached Triple-A before his 22nd birthday, then made his MLB debut on July 17. He will graduate from prospect status with his next out in the major leagues.

SCOUTING REPORT: Priester dealt with fluctuations to his fastball velocity early in 2023 and was hit hard as a result. He and the Pirates worked to steady his lower half, which helped him regain the ticks he'd lost on his heater, and he averaged 93 mph in the big leagues. Priester's best offspeed pitch is his curveball, a high-70s downer that has been one of his signatures throughout his career. The righthander also had to learn to show more trust in his slider, which the team believed he had been babying to achieve better shape rather than throwing it with conviction. Priester's changeup lost effectiveness at points during the season because its velocity did not drop along with his fastball's, which led to much less separation between the pitches. Now, Priester will have to throw more strikes after walking nearly 12% of big league batters faced. If he can improve that figure a few ticks, he could fit in the back of the Pirates' rotation.

THE FUTURE: Priester will enter 2024 with a clear chance to seize a roster spot in Pittsburgh on Opening Day. To do so, he'll need to maintain consistency throughout his repertoire and improve his control. If he does that, he has the upside of a No. 4 starter.

Year	Age	Club (League)	Level	W	L	ERA	G	GS	IP	H	HR	BB	SO	BB%	SO%	WHIP	AVG
2023	22	Indianapolis (IL)	AAA	9	4	4.00	22	20	108	97	6	47	116	10.2	25.3	1.33	.240
2023	22	Pittsburgh (NL)	MLB	3	3	7.74	10	8	50	58	12	27	36	11.5	15.4	1.70	.290
Minor League Totals				22	14	3.44	70	67	333	290	21	130	344	9.3	24.5	1.26	.232
Major League Totals				3	3	7.74	10	8	50	58	12	27	36	11.5	15.4	1.70	.290

9 NICK GONZALES, 2B

HIT: 45. **POW:** 50. **RUN:** 55. **FLD:** 45. **ARM:** 50. **BA Grade:** 45. **Risk:** Medium.

Born: May 27, 1999. **B-T:** R-R. **HT:** 5-9. **WT:** 190.
Drafted: New Mexico State, 2020 (1st round). **Signed by:** Derrick Van Dusen.

TRACK RECORD: Gonzales was celebrated as one of the best pure hitters in the nation as a New Mexico State junior in 2020, when he was drafted No. 7 overall and signed for $5,432,400. His early career was marred by injuries—including a broken finger in 2021 and a torn plantar fascia in his heel in 2022—but he stayed healthy enough in 2023 to play a career-high 134 games. That mark included 36 games in the big leagues, where he struggled with strikeouts before being optioned back to Triple-A for August and most of September.

SCOUTING REPORT: Gonzales hit .399 in three college seasons in the thin New Mexico air, but despite those gaudy numbers he faced questions. Specifically, evaluators wondered how much of his success was a product of the quality of Western Athletic Conference pitching and high elevation. The root of Gonzales' MLB struggles is his swing, which is short, quick and powerful, but also takes the barrel in and out of the zone too quickly. The result is a swing that gives pitchers many holes to exploit, especially with offspeed pitches. The Pirates believe Gonzales' struggles in that area were made clear in the big leagues and are pleased with the progress he made upon returning to the minor leagues. Gonzales' batted-ball data points to a potentially average slugger, and his speed is above-average. He's a fringy defender at second base with an average arm.

THE FUTURE: Gonzales' ceiling is as an offensive-minded second baseman, but he'll have to continue to improve his swing to reach those heights. He will have to outplay Oneil Cruz, Termarr Johnson and Liover Peguero for regular play in the Pirates' middle infield of the future.

Year	Age	Club (League)	Level	AVG	G	AB	R	H	2B	3B	HR	RBI	BB	SO	SB	OBP	SLG
2023	24	Indianapolis (IL)	AAA	.281	99	377	75	106	27	8	14	49	53	118	4	.379	.507
2023	24	Pittsburgh (NL)	MLB	.209	35	115	12	24	8	1	2	13	6	36	0	.268	.348
Minor League Totals				.284	253	970	176	275	71	14	39	140	137	312	17	.382	.506
Major League Totals				.209	35	115	12	24	8	1	2	13	6	36	0	.268	.348

10 BRAXTON ASHCRAFT, RHP

FB: 60. **CB:** 55. **SL:** 60. **CHG:** 45. **CTL:** 60. **BA Grade:** 50. **Risk:** High.

Born: October 5, 1999. **B-T:** L-R. **HT:** 6-5. **WT:** 195.
Drafted: HS—Waco, TX, 2018 (2nd round). **Signed by:** Phil Huttmann.
TRACK RECORD: In high school, Ashcraft's big frame and athleticism made him an outstanding enough wide receiver to catch 37 touchdowns in his junior season. He focused on the diamond exclusively in his senior year and showed well both on the mound and in the batter's box. The Pirates drafted him in the second round in 2018 and signed him for $1.825 million. Since then, his career has been waylaid a bit, first by the pandemic and then by Tommy John surgery which limited his 2021 season to 38.2 innings and erased his 2022 season entirely. He got back on the hill in 2023 and impressed at High-A and Double-A while dealing with a carefully managed workload.
SCOUTING REPORT: In his return to the mound, Ashcraft impressed by mixing power stuff with superb control. He starts his repertoire with a four-seam fastball that sat at 95 mph and showed impressive life through the zone. The fastball was backed with a slider, a curveball and an occasional cutter. Part of Ashcraft's development will involve making sure he varies the shapes on the cutter and slider to make them distinct offerings. Scouts peg his slider, which sat around 87 mph, as a potentially plus pitch, and rated his low-80s curveball as a future above-average offering. His cutter sat around the same velocity as his slider but was thrown just 5% of the time. Ashcraft has thrown a changeup but mostly shelved it in 2023 in order to focus on other areas of development. He ties his mix together with outstanding control that allowed him to throw strikes at a rate of 70% across all three of his stops.
THE FUTURE: The Pirates will have to continue to carefully manage Ashcraft's workload in 2024, but what they saw in 2023 adds yet another interesting pitching prospect to their system. He should reach Triple-A and has an outside chance of making his MLB debut at some point in the second half.

Year	Age	Club (League)	Level	W	L	ERA	G	GS	IP	H	HR	BB	SO	BB%	SO%	WHIP	AVG
2023	23	Bradenton (FSL)	A	0	0	0.00	2	2	6	3	0	1	11	4.2	45.8	0.63	.130
2023	23	Greensboro (SAL)	A+	0	2	3.76	9	9	26	29	4	5	29	4.5	26.4	1.29	.279
2023	23	Altoona (EL)	AA	0	1	1.35	8	8	20	14	0	5	23	6.3	29.1	0.95	.194
Minor League Totals				2	14	4.44	45	45	162	146	18	50	155	7.4	22.8	1.21	.235

11 MITCH JEBB, SS

HIT: 55. **POW:** 40. **RUN:** 60. **FLD:** 50. **ARM:** 45. **BA Grade:** 45. **Risk:** High.

Born: May 13, 2002. **B-T:** L-R. **HT:** 6-1. **WT:** 185. **Drafted:** Michigan State, 2023 (2nd round).
Signed by: Anthony Wycklendt.
TRACK RECORD: After a decorated career at Michigan State, Jebb was the Pirates' choice with their second-round selection and signed for a bonus of $1,647,500. He made the Big Ten's All-Freshman team in 2021. He was even better in his sophomore season, then put together a standout stint in the Cape Cod League. He began his pro career in Low-A Bradenton and put together a solid opening act, including a .780 OPS and 11 stolen bases. He finished his college career with more walks (82) than strikeouts (68) and continued that trend in the first stages of his professional career.
SCOUTING REPORT: Jebb's game is based around contact and speed. His swing is unorthodox but he can be short and quick to the ball and manipulate the barrel to different sectors of the strike zone. Though he's never hit for much impact, the Pirates believe there's more to come after seeing him reach the upper deck at PNC Park in a pre-draft workout. He's also shown the chops to filet balls to the opposite field. Jebb has plus speed, but his fringy throwing arm might force him off of shortstop as he moves up the ladder. He's an average defender at the position now, and his speed might make center field an option as well.
THE FUTURE: Jebb will move to High-A Greensboro in 2024. The hitter-friendly environment there will give him a power boost. If he reaches his ceiling, he could be a middle-diamond defender who hits toward the bottom of the lineup.

Year	Age	Club (League)	Level	AVG	G	AB	R	H	2B	3B	HR	RBI	BB	SO	SB	OBP	SLG
2023	21	Bradenton (FSL)	A	.297	34	128	26	38	6	2	1	13	17	11	11	.382	.398
Minor League Totals				.297	34	128	26	38	6	2	1	13	17	11	11	.382	.398

12 JACK BRANNIGAN, SS/3B

HIT: 40. **POW:** 55. **RUN:** 60. **FLD:** 60. **ARM:** 70. **BA Grade:** 45. **Risk:** High.

Born: March 11, 2001. **B-T:** R-R. **HT:** 6-0. **WT:** 190. **Drafted:** Notre Dame, 2022 (3rd round).
Signed by: Anthony Wycklendt.

TRACK RECORD: Brannigan was a two-way talent at Notre Dame, where he was a fireballing reliever out of the bullpen who brought his fastball into the upper 90s. That same arm strength served him well as the team's everyday third baseman. The Pirates took Brannigan in the third round of the 2022 draft and signed him for $770,700. He reached Low-A in his first pro season, then returned to the level in 2023. Brannigan made it to High-A but missed enough time with quad injuries that he made up for lost time in the Arizona Fall League.

SCOUTING REPORT: Brannigan's best assets are on display when he's in the field. He's the best infield defender in the organization and has the strongest throwing arm as well. Scouts have him as a plus short-stop with double-plus arm strength. Brannigan has plenty of power too, but he has too much swing-and-miss in his game and the Pirates would like him to create a more varied bat path and add more stability in his lower half. He struck out at a clip of nearly 30% in the minors, then saw that figure escalate during his time in the AFL. His chase rates are roughly average, but he whiffs too often at pitches both in and out of the zone.

THE FUTURE: Brannigan should reach Double-A Altoona in 2024. If he cuts down his swing and miss, he could greatly raise his stock. At worst, his defense could make him an asset in the big leagues who hits at the bottom of the order and provides the occasional longball.

Year	Age	Club (League)	Level	AVG	G	AB	R	H	2B	3B	HR	RBI	BB	SO	SB	OBP	SLG
2023	22	Bradenton (FSL)	A	.253	49	162	38	41	7	2	7	17	32	54	17	.398	.451
2023	22	Greensboro (SAL)	A+	.299	38	147	26	44	7	1	12	37	21	58	7	.382	.605
Minor League Totals				.259	115	409	78	106	17	3	22	68	69	142	30	.377	.477

13 KYLE NICOLAS, RHP

FB: 70. **CB:** 40. **SL:** 60. **CTL:** 40. **BA Grade:** 40. **Risk:** Medium

Born: February 22, 1999. **B-T:** R-R. **HT:** 6-4. **WT:** 223. **Drafted:** Ball State, 2020 (2nd round supplemental).
Signed by: Joe Dunigan (Marlins).

TRACK RECORD: Nicolas showcased plenty of high-octane stuff as an amateur, but really began shooting up draft boards when he started throwing more strikes during his junior year at Ball State. The Marlins popped him with their second-round pick, then traded him to the Pirates with outfielder Connor Scott in exchange for catcher Jacob Stallings. He made his big league debut on Sept. 19 and got into four games.

SCOUTING REPORT: Nicolas is a big, strong righthander with stuff as powerful as his build would suggest. As a starter, he worked with a full four-pitch complement that included four- and two-seam fastballs, a pair of breaking balls and a changeup. After shifting to a relief role, that mix winnowed to a combination predicated upon his four-seamer and slider with an occasional curveball. His fastball averaged 97 mph, while his slider came in around 90 mph. His pitch mix plays up because of extension close to 7 feet. Now, he needs to throw more strikes. The Pirates believe the move to the bullpen will increase his margin for error and will allow him to have a more aggressive mindset. Doing so, they believe, will also help him get more swings and misses. Nicolas is a hard worker who loves to challenge hitters so the move into a relief role could be for the best.

THE FUTURE: Nicolas is likely a reliever only from now on. If he can improve his strike-throwing, he could be a weapon at the end of games.

Year	Age	Club (League)	Level	W	L	ERA	G	GS	IP	H	HR	BB	SO	BB%	SO%	WHIP	AVG
2023	24	Altoona (EL)	AA	3	5	4.36	12	12	54	56	8	23	63	9.6	26.4	1.47	.267
2023	24	Indianapolis (IL)	AAA	1	2	6.20	23	6	45	42	8	29	64	13.9	30.8	1.58	.243
2023	24	Pittsburgh (NL)	MLB	0	0	11.81	4	0	5	7	1	4	7	15.4	26.9	2.06	.333
Minor League Totals				12	15	4.47	80	60	288	249	41	148	364	11.7	28.8	1.38	.230
Major League Totals				0	0	11.81	4	0	5	7	1	4	7	15.4	26.9	2.06	.333

14 MICHAEL BURROWS, RHP

FB: 60. **CB:** 60. **CHG:** 40. **CTL:** 50. **BA Grade:** 40. **Risk:** Medium

Born: November 8, 1999. **B-T:** R-R. **HT:** 6-1. **WT:** 190. **Drafted:** HS—Waterford, CT, 2018 (11th round).
Signed by: Eddie Charles.

TRACK RECORD: After spending his high school days in Connecticut, Burrows was slated to join the home-state Huskies for his collegiate career. Instead, the Pirates came calling in the 11th round and signed him for $500,000. He got to the upper levels in 2022 and also made an appearance in Dodger Stadium for the Futures Game. He's missed significant time with injuries, including ones to his oblique in 2021, shoulder in 2022 and Tommy John surgery in April of 2023.

SCOUTING REPORT: At his best, Burrows works primarily with two pitches: a mid-90s four-seam fastball with plenty of carry through the zone and a 77-81 mph downer curveball with spin rates that average around 2,900 rpm. In tandem, the two pitches create a powerful north-south attack. He also mixes in a changeup in the mid 80s. The Pirates believe he can get the pitch to average, and he threw it more often in 2022, but the injury and missed development time have curtailed that progress. The Pirates were also planning to add a second breaking ball to his mix that could have helped him navigate lineups second and third times in his quest to remain a starter. He has a repeatable delivery and an overhand slot with potentially average control.

THE FUTURE: Before the injury, Burrows had a path to becoming a No. 4 starter with the fallback of landing as a powerful reliever toward the end of a game. After a return from the surgery, the latter path is more likely. He could make his big league debut in 2024.

Year	Age	Club (League)	Level	W	L	ERA	G	GS	IP	H	HR	BB	SO	BB%	SO%	WHIP	AVG
2023	23	Indianapolis (IL)	AAA	0	0	2.70	2	2	7	4	2	2	3	8.0	12.0	0.90	.174
Minor League Totals				9	11	3.34	54	51	208	161	15	77	232	9.0	27.1	1.15	.210

15 MATT GORSKI, OF

HIT: 40. **POW:** 50. **RUN:** 60. **FLD:** 60. **ARM:** 70. **BA Grade:** 40. **Risk:** Medium.

Born: December 22, 1997. **B-T:** R-R. **HT:** 6-2. **WT:** 215. **Drafted:** Indiana, 2019 (2nd round).
Signed by: Anthony Wycklendt.

TRACK RECORD: After being selected in the second round of the 2019 draft, Gorski immediately earned a rep as a tooled-up player who could be polished into a high-upside player if he could bring his hitting ability forward. He showed major progress in that regard during the 2022 season after rebuilding his swing in the offseason and produced a .956 OPS before a quad injury ended his season. Gorski's issues with swinging and missing popped up again in 2023, which was spent mostly at Double-A.

SCOUTING REPORT: As ever, Gorski's biggest questions revolve around his hit tool. He struck out at a 25% clip in 2023. His rates of chase and miss—both in zone and out—were subpar, and he was particularly vexed upon a promotion to Triple-A. When he did connect, he produced a 90th percentile exit velocity of 105.9 mph, well above-average when compared to his peers. Even if he doesn't hit, Gorski's defense and speed could get him to the big leagues. He's a plus runner who can deftly man center field and both corners. If he moves to a corner, his double-plus arm would fit easily in right field or make him even more of an asset if he sticks in center field.

THE FUTURE: For the second straight season, Gorski was unprotected and unpicked in the Rule 5 draft. To reach his ceiling, he'll need to control the strike zone better. If he does, his strength and power will play up. If not, he fits as a fourth outfielder who provides speed and outstanding defense.

Year	Age	Club (League)	Level	AVG	G	AB	R	H	2B	3B	HR	RBI	BB	SO	SB	OBP	SLG
2023	25	Altoona (EL)	AA	.238	93	357	56	85	16	2	17	54	27	101	19	.296	.437
2023	25	Indianapolis (IL)	AAA	.190	15	58	9	11	4	0	3	7	6	15	4	.262	.414
Minor League Totals				.239	333	1238	221	296	58	8	64	205	119	382	73	.309	.454

16 ZANDER MUETH, RHP

FB: 60. **SL:** 55. **CHG:** 55. **CTL:** 45. **BA Grade:** 50. **Risk:** Extreme.

Born: June 22, 2005. **B-T:** R-R. **HT:** 6-6. **WT:** 205. **Drafted:** HS—Belleville, IL, 2023 (2nd round supplemental).
Signed by: Anthony Wycklendt.

TRACK RECORD: As an amateur, Mueth was lauded for his combination of present stuff and remaining projection. The Pirates took him in the supplemental second round and signed him away from a commitment to Mississippi with a bonus of $1,797,500. He didn't pitch after signing and instead focused on developing a routine and getting on a throwing program that would help him better acclimate to pro ball.

SCOUTING REPORT: Mueth has a quick arm and throws from a tough angle that varies from low three-quarters to fully sidearm. His fastball can sit between 92-95 and touch up to 97 mph with armside run and sink that should induce plenty of grounders. He pairs the fastball with an above-average slider with sweeping break that should get plenty of swings and misses at the end of at-bats. He rounds out the mix with a changeup in the low 80s that also gets plenty of drop. Like his slider, the changeup flashes the potential to be above-average. When his delivery is together, he's extremely difficult to hit. Now, he needs to do that more often. Streamlining his delivery and making it repeatable will be job one as soon as he makes his professional debut.

THE FUTURE: If it all comes together he could be a dominant part of a starting rotation. That's especially if he continues packing good weight and strength onto his frame. If not, his fastball-slider combination would be an excellent addition to the back of a bullpen. He'll likely debut in the Florida Complex League with a chance to reach Low-A by the end of the 2024 season.

Year	Age	Club (League)	Level	W	L	ERA	G	GS	IP	H	HR	BB	SO	BB%	SO%	WHIP	AVG
2023	18	Did not play															

17 LONNIE WHITE JR., OF

HIT: 40. **POW:** 55. **RUN:** 60. **FLD:** 55. **ARM:** 50. **BA Grade:** 50. **Risk:** Extreme.

Born: December 31, 2002. **B-T:** R-R. **HT:** 6-3. **WT:** 212. **Drafted:** HS—Malvern, PA, 2021 (2nd round supplemental). **Signed by:** Dan Radcliff.

TRACK RECORD: White was a highly valued prospect in the 2021 draft based on an athletic skill set that earned him a scholarship offer to play baseball and football at Penn State. Instead, the Pirates chose him with the No. 64 pick and gave him a $1.5 million bonus. Three seasons later, injuries have kept him off the field and his talent under wraps. Sixty-one of his 71 career games came in 2023.

SCOUTING REPORT: Though the early portion of his career has been extremely limited, White's tools still are intact and intriguing. Scouts see a player with three above-average or plus tools, including speed that grades out as a 60. His hit tool lags behind, but the Pirates are working with White to get it closer to average. Specifically, they're working to get his body a bit more loose and improve his bat angle to create a better path through the zone that adds a little more loft. White was rusty as expected, and he whiffed in-zone at rates that don't indicate a pure hitter. He didn't chase much, however, and his exit velocities were solid. White is a pure center fielder with above-average defense and an average arm.

THE FUTURE: Simply staying on the field for an extended period was a boon for White's career. He should spend his 2024 season at the Class A levels, and he is one of the system's prime breakout candidates if he can stay healthy. He has a ceiling as a well-rounded center fielder.

Year	Age	Club (League)	Level	AVG	G	AB	R	H	2B	3B	HR	RBI	BB	SO	SB	OBP	SLG
2023	20	FCL Pirates	Rk	.317	17	63	13	20	5	0	1	10	11	19	6	.434	.444
2023	20	Bradenton (FSL)	A	.259	44	162	36	42	11	1	8	30	32	56	12	.395	.488
Minor League Totals				.274	72	263	56	72	19	1	12	48	45	92	18	.392	.490

18 HUNTER BARCO, LHP

FB: 50. **SL:** 55. **CHG:** 50. **CTL:** 55. **BA Grade:** 50. **Risk:** Extreme.

Born: December 15, 2000. **B-T:** L-L. **HT:** 6-4. **WT:** 210. **Drafted:** Florida, 2022 (2nd round). **Signed by:** Cam Murphy.

TRACK RECORD: Barco was a first-round talent out of high school but instead landed on campus in Gainesville, where he was part of Florida's rotation for three seasons. The Pirates popped him in the second round of the 2022 draft and signed him for $1.52 million. He had Tommy John surgery in May of his junior season and didn't make his pro debut until July 20. He split the 2023 season between the Florida Complex League and Low-A Bradenton.

SCOUTING REPORT: The Pirates selected Barco after he'd had his surgery because they believed his upside was worth the wait. In limited action, they began to see some of his potential. His two-seam fastball sat between 92-94 mph with solid sinking life, and his four-seamer sat in the same range with excellent horizontal break. Barco pairs his fastballs with a short slider in the low 80s. The Pirates had Barco tweak the grip on the pitch during instructional league to give it more of a gyro shape. He also throws a split-changeup in the mid 80s. In combination, Barco has weapons to attack both vertically and horizontally. He's a strong worker who is motivated to get back to the version of himself he showed before the surgery.

THE FUTURE: The 2024 season will be big for Barco as he gets further away from surgery. Scouts believed the lefthander had a high floor when he came out of college. Now, it's about getting him healthy enough to begin to show it again.

Year	Age	Club (League)	Level	W	L	ERA	G	GS	IP	H	HR	BB	SO	BB%	SO%	WHIP	AVG
2023	22	FCL Pirates	Rk	0	0	1.17	3	2	8	4	0	2	9	6.9	31.0	0.78	.148
2023	22	Bradenton (FSL)	A	0	2	5.06	6	6	11	13	0	4	19	8.2	38.8	1.59	.289
Minor League Totals				0	2	3.50	9	8	18	17	0	6	28	7.7	35.9	1.28	.236

19 JUN-SEOK SHIM, RHP

FB: 60. **CB:** 60. **SL:** 55. **CTL:** 50. **BA Grade:** 50. **Risk:** Extreme.

Born: April 9, 2004. **B-T:** R-R. **HT:** 6-4. **WT:** 215. **Signed:** South Korea, 2023. **Signed by:** Jong Hoon Na.

TRACK RECORD: Shim was the top signing in Pittsburgh's 2023 international class, which opened on Jan. 15. He was coveted because of his combination of physicality, polish and present stuff. He dealt with an elbow injury that cut short his 2021 season and then missed significant time again in 2023 with an injury to his pectoral muscles. He struck out 13 hitters in the eight innings he pitched before landing on the IL.

SCOUTING REPORT: In the brief time he was on the mound, Shim showed some of the best pure stuff in the Florida Complex League. His fastball sat between 95-98 mph with carry through the zone, and his curveball showed spin rates better than 3,000 rpm. He throws a slider as well, though sometimes the two breaking balls blend together. He and the Pirates worked to add a changeup to his mix as well. There were concerns about whether Shim had enough mobility in his hips to eventually handle a starter's workload. They believe there was progress in that regard, but also acknowledge it might have led to the chest injury. Even in the brief time Shim pitched in games, scouts were impressed with his stuff, poise and calm demeanor on the hill.

THE FUTURE: Shim will turn 20 in the first week of the minor league season, and he might be advanced enough to jump to Low-A instead of returning to the FCL. He has some of the most eye-opening upside of any of the youngest arms in the Pirates' system.

Year	Age	Club (League)	Level	W	L	ERA	G	GS	IP	H	HR	BB	SO	BB%	SO%	WHIP	AVG
2023	19	FCL Pirates	Rk	0	0	3.38	4	4	8	3	1	3	13	10.0	43.3	0.75	.111
Minor League Totals				0	0	3.38	4	4	8	3	1	3	13	10.0	43.3	0.75	.111

20 MICHAEL KENNEDY, LHP

FB: 45. **SL:** 50. **CHG:** 45. **CTL:** 55. **BA Grade:** 45. **Risk:** High.

Born: November 30, 2004. **B-T:** L-L. **HT:** 6-1. **WT:** 204. **Drafted:** HS—Troy, NY, 2022 (4th round).
Signed by: Eddie Charles.

TRACK RECORD: In 2021, Kennedy was part of USA Baseball's 18U national team, where he was teammates with fellow Pirates prospect Termarr Johnson. He was the most talented player from New York available in the 2022 draft, and Pittsburgh chose him in the fourth round. He signed for a double-slot bonus of $1 million instead of heading to Louisiana State. He didn't pitch after signing and made his pro debut in 2023. Kennedy split the year between the Florida Complex League and Low-A Bradenton and surrendered just 27 hits in 46.1 innings. His 55 strikeouts were the fourth-most in the FCL.

SCOUTING REPORT: Despite his eye-popping stats, Kennedy's stuff doesn't jump off the page. His fastball sits between 87-89 mph and plays up a little bit because of a lower release height. He pairs the pitch with a low-80s slider with spin rates around 2,500 rpm that gets whiffs at an above-average rate. Kennedy rounds out his mix with a mid-80s changeup he throws about 10% of the time. The lefty's shorter arm path gives him a bit of deception, but there are concerns he doesn't have enough remaining projection to add the necessary power to his arsenal.

THE FUTURE: Kennedy will return to Low-A in 2024. He needs to add strength to his frame to bring his stuff forward enough to survive as he moves through the system. Otherwise, he's going to have trouble being more than a smoke-and-mirrors lefty who gets by on deception instead of stuff.

Year	Age	Club (League)	Level	W	L	ERA	G	GS	IP	H	HR	BB	SO	BB%	SO%	WHIP	AVG
2023	18	FCL Pirates	Rk	2	1	2.13	11	7	42	25	1	19	55	11.1	32.2	1.04	.171
2023	18	Bradenton (FSL)	A	0	0	2.08	2	0	4	2	0	6	8	30.0	40.0	1.85	.154
Minor League Totals				2	1	2.15	13	7	47	27	1	25	63	13.1	33.0	1.13	.170

21 JACKSON WOLF, LHP

FB: 40. **SL:** 45. **CHG:** 50. **CTL:** 55. **BA Grade:** 40. **Risk:** Medium.

Born: April 22, 1999. **B-T:** L-L. **HT:** 6-7. **WT:** 205. **Drafted:** West Virginia, 2021 (4th round).
Signed by: Danny Sader (Padres).

TRACK RECORD: Wolf was drafted out of West Virginia in the fourth round of the 2021 draft and signed for $300,000. He lost most of his draft year when the pandemic cut short the 2020 college season, then returned for his senior campaign after going unselected. He was traded in 2023 as part of a three-player package that brought Rich Hill and Ji-Man Choi to San Diego. Wolf made his big league debut on July 22, when he was still with the Padres. He went five innings against the Tigers that day and earned his first big league win.

SCOUTING REPORT: Wolf's raw stuff isn't overpowering, but he gets his outs on the strength of his long levers and excellent extension. His fastball averages around 91 mph, and he backs the pitch with a slurvy slider in the mid 70s and a low-80s split-changeup. The changeup is his best secondary for swings and misses, while the breaking ball is a pitch he can land for strikes early in counts. He throws plenty of strikes and can deftly move his pitches around the zone to induce weak contact.

THE FUTURE: Aside from the spot start, Wolf spent his season at Double-A with both of his clubs. He'll move to Triple-A in 2024 and fits best as a bulk reliever or a No. 5 starter on a second-division club.

Year	Age	Club (League)	Level	W	L	ERA	G	GS	IP	H	HR	BB	SO	BB%	SO%	WHIP	AVG
2023	24	Altoona (EL)	AA	0	4	4.25	8	8	36	32	5	10	30	6.6	19.9	1.17	.232
2023	24	San Antonio (TL)	AA	8	9	4.08	18	18	88	74	12	22	105	6.3	29.8	1.09	.228
2023	24	San Diego (NL)	MLB	1	0	5.40	1	1	5	6	0	1	1	4.5	4.5	1.40	.286
Minor League Totals				15	23	4.18	58	57	269	222	35	89	301	8.1	27.3	1.16	.223
Major League Totals				1	0	5.40	1	1	5	6	0	1	1	4.5	4.5	1.40	.286

22 ALIKA WILLIAMS, SS
HIT: 30. **POW:** 30. **RUN:** 60. **FLD:** 60. **ARM:** 45. **BA Grade:** 40. **Risk:** Medium.

Born: March 12, 1999. **B-T:** R-R. **HT:** 6-1. **WT:** 180. **Drafted:** Arizona State, 2020 (1st round supplemental). **Signed by:** David Hamlett (Rays).

TRACK RECORD: Williams was part of a star-studded Arizona State infield that in 2020 produced five draft picks, including four within the first 102 selections and No. 1 overall pick Spencer Torkelson. Williams went to Tampa Bay in the supplemental first round on the strength of standout defense that has been the hallmark of his career. He was dealt in 2023 in the deal that brought Robert Stephenson to the Rays.

SCOUTING REPORT: Six weeks after being traded, Williams made his big league debut. With Pittsburgh, he played to script and provided solid defense at shortstop with almost no offensive impact. He's got excellent range and can make all the plays at shortstop, although his arm strength in the big leagues was below-average. He's a plus runner, which helps him provide range to his right and left. He's a passive hitter who makes solid contact on pitches in the zone but chased a bit too much during his time in the minor leagues. Despite decent exit velocities, his power is well below-average and he's unlikely to produce double-digit home runs even if given regular playing time.

THE FUTURE: Williams stanched a wound left by the season-ending injury to Oneil Cruz. Once he returns, Williams' playing time is likely to diminish and he'll settle in as a defensive replacement in the late innings with a start every now and again.

Year	Age	Club (League)	Level	AVG	G	AB	R	H	2B	3B	HR	RBI	BB	SO	SB	OBP	SLG
2023	24	Montgomery (SL)	AA	.237	42	156	21	37	11	1	5	23	15	34	3	.314	.417
2023	24	Indianapolis (IL)	AAA	.305	36	128	25	39	8	0	7	20	15	22	3	.384	.531
2023	24	Pittsburgh (NL)	MLB	.198	46	101	7	20	5	0	0	6	9	35	0	.270	.248
Minor League Totals				.261	247	952	157	248	47	4	27	151	103	195	19	.338	.403
Major League Totals				.198	46	101	7	20	5	0	0	6	9	35	0	.270	.248

23 ESTUAR SUERO, OF
HIT: 50. **POW:** 55. **RUN:** 55. **FLD:** 50. **ARM:** 60. **BA Grade:** 50. **Risk:** Extreme.

Born: August 29, 2005. **B-T:** S-R. **HT:** 6-5. **WT:** 180. **Signed:** Dominican Republic, 2022. **Signed by:** Jose Salado/Alvin Duran (Padres).

TRACK RECORD: Suero was part of the Padres' 2022 international signing class that has already produced players who figured into two trades. Massive righthander Jarlin Susana was shipped to the Nationals in the Juan Soto deal, and Suero was dealt to the Pirates in the deal that brought Rich Hill and Ji-Man Choi to the Padres. Suero opened eyes during spring training and is one of the more intriguing prospects in the lower levels of Pittsburgh's system.

SCOUTING REPORT: Suero is a classic tool shed who has a ceiling that needs plenty of time to develop. He's a twitchy athlete with smooth swings from both sides of the plate and the potential for above-average power. His frame is loose and lanky, but there's plenty of room to add more bulk. If that happens, his impact should be amplified. As it is, he produced below-average exit velocities and swung and missed a touch too often. He gets good reads in the outfield and can play center field for now but might move to a corner as his body fills out. Scouts who saw him this spring believe enough in his body's future to project plus raw power one day.

THE FUTURE: When they dealt for him, the Pirates were betting on Suero's upside. It will take years to reach that ceiling, but it might be worth the wait. He'll head to Low-A Bradenton in 2024.

Year	Age	Club (League)	Level	AVG	G	AB	R	H	2B	3B	HR	RBI	BB	SO	SB	OBP	SLG
2023	17	ACL Padres	Rk	.216	35	139	22	30	4	1	4	23	16	49	7	.306	.345
2023	17	FCL Pirates	Rk	.217	13	46	7	10	0	1	1	6	12	12	2	.379	.326
Minor League Totals				.231	95	337	62	78	11	5	8	50	49	113	23	.335	.365

24 GARRET FORRESTER, 3B

HIT: 55. **POW:** 50. **RUN:** 40. **FLD:** 50. **ARM:** 50. **BA Grade:** 40. **Risk:** High.

Born: November 11, 2001. **B-T:** R-R. **HT:** 6-1. **WT:** 208. **Drafted:** Oregon State, 2023 (3rd round). **Signed by:** Brett Evert.
TRACK RECORD: In three seasons at Oregon State, Forrester proved himself as one of the Pac-12's best hitters. He was part of the conference's all-freshman team in 2021 and finished his career with 26 home runs in 177 games. The Pirates selected him in the third round, signed him for $772,500 and assigned him to Low-A Bradenton to begin his career. Forrester's father played three seasons as a Dodgers minor leaguer.
SCOUTING REPORT: Forrester doesn't have the skills for a prototype first baseman, but he can hit. He's got solid bat-to-ball abilities and a keen eye for the strike zone. He walked more than he struck out during his college career, then did the same thing in his first test as a pro. Forrester shows an all-fields approach and should get to average power in time, and he posted an average exit velocity of 88 mph during his junior season with the Beavers. The righthanded hitter is an average defender with an average arm, though teams tried him at catcher in a few workouts before the draft.
THE FUTURE: Forrester will move to High-A in 2024 and will need to boost his power to profile as a first baseman. Greensboro's cozy confines should help him in that regard.

Year	Age	Club (League)	Level	AVG	G	AB	R	H	2B	3B	HR	RBI	BB	SO	SB	OBP	SLG
2023	21	Bradenton (FSL)	A	.278	6	18	4	5	0	0	0	3	10	7	0	.552	.278
Minor League Totals				.278	6	18	4	5	0	0	0	3	10	7	0	.552	.278

25 CARLSON REED, RHP

FB: 60. **SL:** 55. **CHG:** 50. **CTL:** 35. **BA Grade:** 40. **Risk:** High

Born: November 27, 2002. **B-T:** L-R. **HT:** 6-4. **WT:** 200. **Drafted:** West Virginia, 2023 (4th round).
Signed by: Dan Radcliff.
TRACK RECORD: Reed has an ideal pitcher's build and remaining projection, which intrigued Pittsburgh enough to call his name in the fourth round of the 2023 draft. Reed worked exclusively as a reliever in his draft year, then signed for $597,500. He pitched in the Cape Cod League before his junior year and then in the MLB Draft League afterward. Reed made his pro debut with four outings in the Florida Complex League.
SCOUTING REPORT: Reed is almost certainly a relief-only prospect as a professional, but he has the big-time arsenal to be solid in that role. His fastball sits in the mid 90s and touches 98 with heavy sinking action. The velocity is amplified by the extension he gets from his lanky frame. Reed backs the fastball with a potentially plus slider in the low 80s and a changeup in the mid 80s that flashed average in his early pro outings. He has plenty of room on his frame to add more strength and velocity and might get to 100 mph on his fastball one day. His long arm action suggests that command and control will never be big parts of his game and will keep him in a reliever's role long-term.
THE FUTURE: Reed will move to High-A in 2024 and could move quickly as a bullpen arm.

Year	Age	Club (League)	Level	W	L	ERA	G	GS	IP	H	HR	BB	SO	BB%	SO%	WHIP	AVG
2023	20	FCL Pirates	Rk	1	2	2.57	4	2	7	7	0	3	6	8.8	17.6	1.43	.233
Minor League Totals				1	2	2.57	4	2	7	7	0	3	6	8.8	17.6	1.43	.233

26 JASE BOWEN, OF

HIT: 30. **POW:** 55. **RUN:** 60. **FLD:** 60. **ARM:** 50. **BA Grade:** 40. **Risk:** High

Born: September 2, 2000. **B-T:** R-R. **HT:** 6-0. **WT:** 190. **Drafted:** HS—Toledo, OH, 2019 (11th round).
Signed by: Adam Bourassa.
TRACK RECORD: Bowen was taken by the Pirates in the 11th round of the 2019 draft. He played baseball and football in high school and was a three-star prospect as a wide receiver. He chose baseball and earned a $392,500 bonus to break his commitment to Michigan State. He got his feet wet in the Florida Complex League before the pandemic pushed back his first full season until 2021. He made it to Double-A for the first time in 2023 and then spent six weeks in the Arizona Fall League.
SCOUTING REPORT: Bowen has plenty of tools but will need to make much more contact to put everything together. The righthander hits the ball plenty hard—his 90th percentile exit velocity was 102.7 mph, maxed out at 112 mph and he led the system with 23 home runs—but he needs to make more

contact. He missed at pitches both in and out of the zone and chased at a worse-than-average rate as well. He's a plus runner and is one of the system's best outfield defenders.

THE FUTURE: Bowen has plenty of tools and remaining upside to fit into a power-speed profile. If he can make more contact, he has a chance to move up this list in 2024, when he'll spend most of the season in Double-A against much craftier pitchers than he faced in Class A.

Year	Age	Club (League)	Level	AVG	G	AB	R	H	2B	3B	HR	RBI	BB	SO	SB	OBP	SLG
2023	22	Greensboro (SAL)	A+	.257	110	435	80	112	15	4	23	88	35	121	24	.333	.469
2023	22	Altoona (EL)	AA	.219	8	32	6	7	3	2	0	7	1	7	2	.242	.438
Minor League Totals				.244	382	1420	223	346	55	15	54	236	125	419	72	.319	.418

27 TRES GONZALEZ, OF

HIT: 55. **POW:** 40. **RUN:** 50. **FLD:** 45. **ARM:** 45. **BA Grade:** 40. **Risk:** High.

Born: October 4, 2000. **B-T:** L-L. **HT:** 5-11. **WT:** 185. **Drafted:** Georgia Tech, 2022 (5th round). **Signed by:** Cam Murphy.

TRACK RECORD: In three seasons at Georgia Tech and a stint in the Cape Cod League, Gonzalez earned a rep as a professional hitter with an outstanding feel for the strike zone. He had more walks (91) than strikeouts (74) in college, though those numbers came without much power. The Pirates took him in the fifth round of the 2022 draft and signed him for $347,500. He spent most of the 2023 season at High-A Greensboro, where continued to show solid plate skills but without the impact needed for a corner outfield spot.

SCOUTING REPORT: Gonzalez's offensive game is predicated on his strong idea of the strike zone. His exit velocities are below-average, but he does a nice job connecting with pitches in the zone. His barrel accuracy could stand to improve, and his bat path doesn't keep the barrel in the zone long enough. Gonzalez is a fringy defender with a fringy arm who fits in a corner, which adds more pressure to develop the power necessary to profile at the position. Gonzalez is an average runner.

THE FUTURE: Gonzalez will head to Double-A in 2024. At Altoona, his developmental goals will involve cleanup of his bat path in order to tap into more impact. He's likely a backup outfielder whose value is in the batter's box.

Year	Age	Club (League)	Level	AVG	G	AB	R	H	2B	3B	HR	RBI	BB	SO	SB	OBP	SLG
2023	22	Bradenton (FSL)	A	.299	19	67	15	20	4	0	1	12	15	11	6	.427	.403
2023	22	Greensboro (SAL)	A+	.287	94	366	73	105	18	0	8	46	65	84	22	.400	.402
Minor League Totals				.293	138	515	101	151	26	1	9	70	89	107	35	.405	.400

28 BRANDAN BIDOIS, RHP

FB: 60. **CB:** 50. **CUT:** 55. **CTL:** 40. **BA Grade:** 45. **Risk:** Extreme.

Born: June 21, 2001. **B-T:** R-R. **HT:** 6-2. **WT:** 158. **Signed:** Australia, 2019. **Signed by:** Tony Harris.

TRACK RECORD: Bidois signed with the Pirates out of Australia in 2019 but has had his career severely stymied in the proceeding years. He lost the 2020 season to the pandemic, then missed the 2022 season after having Tommy John surgery. Bidois re-emerged in 2023 with a full season out of the Low-A Bradenton bullpen. He dominated with the Marauders, going 3-0, 1.99 with 42 strikeouts in 22.2 innings.

SCOUTING REPORT: After working as a starter in the Florida Complex League in 2021, Bidois shifted to the pen in full-season ball after recovering from his surgery. He showed a powerful arsenal dominated by a four-seam fastball that averaged 95 mph and touched 99. The pitch has excellent life through the zone and got whiffs at a 30% clip. He backs the fastball with a curveball in the mid 70s that averaged nearly 3,000 rpm of spin that projects to be average. At its best, the pitch shows 1-to-7 shape with hard finish. He rounds out his mix with a nasty cutter with plenty of life that appears like a sweeping slider. The pitch has lots of spin and gets whiffs at a high rate and should be at least above-average. Bidois' control was spotty in his first year post-surgery, and he'll need to show improvement in that regard to reach his ceiling as a late-inning reliever.

THE FUTURE: Bidois will move to High-A Greensboro in 2024, when he'll look to improve his command to help his excellent arsenal become even nastier. If he succeeds early, he could see Double-A.

Year	Age	Club (League)	Level	W	L	ERA	G	GS	IP	H	HR	BB	SO	BB%	SO%	WHIP	AVG
2023	22	Bradenton (FSL)	A	3	0	1.99	22	0	23	14	1	15	42	14.9	41.6	1.28	.173
Minor League Totals				3	0	2.51	25	3	29	22	1	19	48	14.6	36.9	1.43	.206

29 COLIN SELBY, RHP

FB: 60. **SL:** 60. **CB:** 30. **CTL:** 30. **BA Grade:** 40. **Risk:** High.

Born: October 24, 1997. **B-T:** R-R. **HT:** 6-2. **WT:** 220. **Drafted:** Randolph-Macon (VA), 2018 (16th round).
Signed by: Dan Radcliff.
TRACK RECORD: After three seasons at Division III Randolph-Macon (Va.), Selby was selected by the Pirates in the 16th round of the 2018 draft. The team had plans for him to develop as a starter, but Tommy John surgery during the 2020 shutdown led to his conversion into a reliever. He's been outstanding over the last two seasons at the upper levels, made his big league debut on Aug. 9 and pitched in 21 games. He struck out 30 in that time, but also walked 15 hitters in 24 innings.
SCOUTING REPORT: Selby works with a mix of velocity and spin, and his three-pitch mix is fronted by a two-seamer that averaged 97 mph. He backed the pitch with a slider in the high 80s and a curveball in the low 80s. Both breaking balls feature spin rates in the 2,600 rpm range. In the big leagues, Selby favored the slider over the curveball. His curveball is well below-average, however, and he issued far too many walks at both Triple-A and in the big leagues.
THE FUTURE: Simply put, Selby needs to throw more strikes. His stuff is excellent, but it will make no difference if he cannot find the zone with much greater frequency. If he does, he fits as a late-inning reliever. If he doesn't, he will ride the shuttle back and forth to Indianapolis.

Year	Age	Club (League)	Level	W	L	ERA	G	GS	IP	H	HR	BB	SO	BB%	SO%	WHIP	AVG
2023	25	Indianapolis (IL)	AAA	0	0	3.86	28	0	30	19	0	22	41	16.5	30.8	1.35	.176
2023	25	Pittsburgh (NL)	MLB	2	2	9.00	21	5	24	29	4	15	30	13.2	26.3	1.83	.296
Minor League Totals				12	10	3.51	116	29	261	201	21	114	278	10.3	25.2	1.21	.208
Major League Totals				2	2	9.00	21	5	24	29	4	15	30	13.2	26.3	1.83	.296

30 TONY BLANCO JR., OF

HIT: 30. **POW:** 70. **RUN:** 30. **FLD:** 40. **ARM:** 50. **BA Grade:** 45. **Risk:** Extreme.

Born: May 14, 2005. **B-T:** R-R. **HT:** 6-6. **WT:** 243. **Signed:** Dominican Republic, 2023. **Signed by:** Omelis Corporan.
TRACK RECORD: Blanco is the son of the former big leaguer of the same name. He was born in Boston but was raised in the Dominican Republic, where he signed out of 2022. He played eight games in the Dominican Summer League in 2022, then added 40 more at the same level in 2023, where he homered five times.
SCOUTING REPORT: Blanco is attractive as a prospect because of true outlier power. He homered five times in the DSL, but that output doesn't tell the whole story. His average exit velocity was 92.9 mph, a figure that sat between those produced by Julio Rodriguez and Rafael Devers in the big leagues. His 113.2 mph 90th percentile EV was the best of any player in the minor leagues with more than 30 plate appearances. That power, however, came with significant swing and miss, including a 37% strikeout rate in the DSL. He's a below-average runner who is already a massive human being and is likely to move to first base in the coming years.
THE FUTURE: Blanco faces a long road to the big leagues that will require serious improvements with his contact. He has the type of power that will give him plenty of chances, and could wind up as a Franchy Cordero-type of player if everything clicks.

Year	Age	Club (League)	Level	AVG	G	AB	R	H	2B	3B	HR	RBI	BB	SO	SB	OBP	SLG
2023	18	DSL Pirates Gold	Rk	.235	40	136	21	32	7	0	5	25	17	59	0	.325	.397
Minor League Totals				.232	48	155	22	36	7	0	6	29	17	69	0	.313	.394

St. Louis Cardinals

BY GEOFF PONTES

The 91-loss Cardinals had a massively disappointing season and finished with a losing record for the first time since 2007.

It was only the second time this century St. Louis failed to finish above .500. The Cardinals struggled with their rotation and ranked in the bottom five in the league with a 5.08 starters' ERA and just a 17.4% strikeout rate. Only the Rockies at 15.7% were worse.

The St. Louis offense under-performed its lofty expectations as both Paul Goldschmidt and Nolan Arenado had down years. Their big free agent signing of Willson Contreras fell flat, and he was removed from catching duties for a stretch early in

the season. They also struggled to find health for Brendan Donovan or Tyler O'Neill, which cut into the positional depth that was viewed as a strength entering the season.

While the 2023 season was one of dashed hopes and missed expectations, there were bright spots down on the farm. The Cardinals have used continuity to their strength and have executed well in scouting and player development to continually put together solid systems ripe with homegrown talent.

The current core of the team is heavily homegrown. Seven of the team's top 10 hitters by plate appearances were drafted and developed by the Cardinals. This homegrown core and depth of close-to-the-majors position talent is a strength of the organization heading into the 2024 season, and it could be used as an avenue for trades to infuse more talent in other areas of need.

The Cardinals debuted Jordan Walker on Opening Day and he proved to be a solid contributor who hit .276/.342/.445 in 117 games. Outfielder Alec Burleson saw significant time as a rookie and logged the ninth-most at-bats on the team, and lefthander Matthew Liberatore made 22 appearances and showed flashes of the pitcher the Cardinals hope he can grow into. On top of that, the Cardinals debuted No. 1 prospect Masyn Winn as well as slugger Luken Baker in 2023.

St. Louis showed a willingness to move MLB pieces to retool the farm system at the trade deadline. They dealt lefthander Jordan Montgomery to the Rangers, reliever Jordan Hicks to the Blue Jays and righthander Jack Flaherty to the Orioles. This netted seven players who now rank in the Top 30 Prospects, including two in the Top 10.

Second baseman Thomas Saggese, one of the acquisitions, took home Double-A Texas League MVP honors, while Springfield teammate Tekoah Roby, a righthander, looked dominant post-trade.

It was a change in direction for a religiously competitive club but perhaps just what was needed

At age 21, Jordan Walker was the youngest position player to bat at least 400 times.

PROJECTED 2027 LINEUP

Position	Player	Age
Catcher	Willson Contreras	35
First Base	Brendan Donovan	30
Second Base	Thomas Saggese	25
Third Base	Nolan Arenado	36
Shortstop	Masyn Winn	25
Left Field	Jordan Walker	25
Center Field	Victor Scott II	26
Right Field	Lars Nootbaar	29
Designated Hitter	Nolan Gorman	27
No. 1 Starter	Matthew Liberatore	27
No. 2 Starter	Tekoah Roby	25
No. 3 Starter	Tink Hence	24
No. 4 Starter	Gordon Graceffo	27
No. 5 Starter	Sem Robberse	25
Closer	Ryan Helsley	32

for the long-term health of the organization. A byproduct of the down season is the Cardinals will now have a top 10 draft selection for the first time since they picked No. 5 overall in 1998.

The Cardinals were aggressive early in free agency and targeted veteran starters as reinforcements for a pitching staff that struggled mightily. They reached agreements with free agent righthanders Sonny Gray, Lance Lynn and Kyle Gibson. The Cardinals now have one of the oldest rotations in baseball, but Gray is a top-of-the-rotation arm and both Lynn and Gibson should be durable.

It was an unusual season in St. Louis, but it may prove to be the reset button the organization needed. ∎

DEPTH CHART

ST. LOUIS CARDINALS

TOP 2024 CONTRIBUTORS — **RANK**
1. Masyn Winn, SS — 1
2. Tekoah Roby, RHP — 3
3. Ivan Herrera, C — 6

BREAKOUT PROSPECTS — **RANK**
1. Travis Honeyman, OF — 16
2. Zach Levenson, OF — 18
3. Zack Showalter, RHP — 22

SOURCE OF TOP 30 TALENT			
Homegrown	**21**	**Acquired**	**9**
College	14	Trade	8
Junior college	4	Rule 5 draft	1
High school	3	Independent league	0
Nondrafted free agent	0	Free agent/waivers	0
International	0		

LF
Zach Levenson (18)
Matt Koperniak
Alex Iadisernia
Nathan Church

CF
Victor Scott II (3)
Chase Davis (7)
Mike Antico

RF
Won-Bin Cho (13)
Joshua Baez (30)
Moises Gomez

3B
Michael Curialle
Jacob Buchberger

SS
Masyn Winn (1)
Jeremy Rivas
Jonathan Mejia

2B
Thomas Saggese (5)
Cesar Prieto (17)
Buddy Kennedy
Nick Dunn

1B
Luken Baker (26)
Chandler Redmond

C
Ivan Herrera (6)
Leonardo Bernal (10)
Jimmy Crooks (15)
Pedro Pages (19)

LHP

LHSP	LHRP
Cooper Hjerpe (8)	Nathanael Heredia
Brycen Mautz (20)	Jack Ralston
Quinn Mathews (23)	
Drew Rom (25)	
Pete Hansen (27)	

RHP

RHSP	RHRP
Tekoah Roby (2)	Edwin Nuñez (21)
Tink Hence (4)	Nick Robertson (24)
Gordon Graceffo (9)	Ryan Fernandez (29)
Sem Robberse (11)	Ryan Loutos
Max Rajcic (12)	Andre Granillo
Michael McGreevy (14)	
Zack Showalter (22)	
Adam Kloffenstein (28)	

1 MASYN WINN, SS

Born: March, 21, 2002. **B-T:** R-R. **HT:** 5-11. **WT:** 180.
Drafted: HS—Kingswood, TX, 2020 (2nd round).
Signed by: Jabari Bennett.

TRACK RECORD: A two-way star on the high school summer showcase circuit, Winn was a tooled-up shortstop who could touch the upper 90s from the mound. Drafted in the second round in 2020, Winn joined Jordan Walker and Tink Hence as three high school players drafted by the Cardinals inside the first two rounds that year. Winn signed for an above-slot $2.1 million and debuted the following season at Class A Palm Beach. He saw time at both Class A levels, hitting .242/.324/.356 with five home runs. Coming into the 2022 season, Winn made adjustments to his swing, ironing out synchronization issues between his upper and lower halves. He hit the ground running and hit .349/.404/.566 in 33 games at High-A Peoria, showing a more refined hit tool. Winn was promoted to Double-A Springfield, where he produced a league-average batting line over 86 games. His star began to shine bright at the 2022 Futures Game when he unleashed a Statcast-record 100.5 mph throw from shortstop. Winn began his 2023 with Triple-A Memphis and hit .288/.359/.474 with 18 home runs in 105 games, earning a callup to St. Louis on Aug. 18. Winn retains his rookie eligibility for 2024.

SCOUTING REPORT: The advancements in Winn's swing and subsequent contact ability has driven his profile. He now possesses plus bat-to-ball skills and limits swing-and-miss in the zone at an elite rate. Winn's swing decisions often get him into trouble, and he bites on pitches out of the zone he should take. He struggled against velocity this year, producing poor numbers against pitches 95 mph or faster as he struggled to find his timing. Winn excels against lefthanders, and produced a .926 OPS against them in 2023. His numbers in same-side matchups are not as rosy. Winn's lack of impact wasn't evident by his home run totals this year, but his underlying exit velocity data is below-average. His high-end power is particularly concerning. His 90th percentile exit velocity of 101.9 mph is fringe-average for his age and level. Winn's ability to hit his best-struck drives at optimal launch angles allows him to max out his impact. He's an easy plus runner and threat to steal whenever he's on base. Winn's running is a true weapon under MLB's new rules.

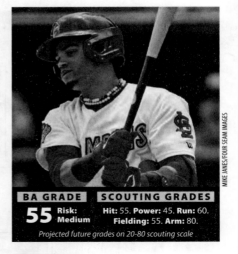

MIKE JANES/FOUR SEAM IMAGES

BA GRADE	SCOUTING GRADES
55 Risk: Medium	Hit: 55. Power: 45. Run: 60. Fielding: 55. Arm: 80.

Projected future grades on 20-80 scouting scale

BEST TOOLS

BATTING

Best Hitter for Average	Cesar Prieto
Best Power Hitter	Luken Baker
Best Strike-Zone Discipline	Noah Mendlinger
Fastest Baserunner	Victor Scott II
Best Athlete	Victor Scott II

PITCHING

Best Fastball	Tink Hence
Best Curveball	Tekoah Roby
Best Slider	Andre Granillo
Best Changeup	Joseph King
Best Control	Max Rajcic

FIELDING

Best Defensive Catcher	Pedro Pages
Best Defensive Infielder	Masyn Winn
Best Infield Arm	Masyn Winn
Best Defensive Outfielder	Victor Scott II
Best Outfield Arm	Joshua Baez

In the field, Winn possesses one of the few 80 tools in his throwing arm. His arm allows him to make plays his hands can't, though he has become adept at keeping the ball in front of him. When Winn can do that, he can make a majority of plays. His hands, actions and transfers are just average, but the package plays up due to his range and arm strength.

THE FUTURE: Winn is a skills-driven hitter with the ability to make consistent contact. Added bat speed and strength will allow him to take his offensive game to the next level. In the field, Winn has the ability to play shortstop every day because of his range and elite throwing arm. He is a future regular shortstop with above-average offensive potential. ∎

Year	Age	Club	Level	AVG	G	AB	R	H	2B	3B	HR	RBI	BB	SO	SB	OBP	SLG
2023	21	Memphis (IL)	AAA	.288	105	445	99	128	15	7	18	61	44	83	17	.359	.474
2023	21	St. Louis (NL)	MLB	.172	37	122	8	21	2	0	2	12	10	26	2	.230	.238
Minor League Totals				.272	322	1304	266	355	70	20	35	168	153	298	92	.351	.437
Major League Totals				.172	37	122	8	21	2	0	2	12	10	26	2	.230	.238

2 TEKOAH ROBY, RHP

FB: 55. **CB:** 60. **SL:** 50. **CHG:** 50. **CTL:** 60. **BA Grade:** 60. **Risk:** Extreme.

Born: September 18, 2001. **B-T:** R-R. **HT:** 6-1. **WT:** 185.
Drafted: HS—Pensacola, FL, 2020 (3rd round). **Signed by:** Brian Morrison (Rangers).
TRACK RECORD: Roby was a summer pop-up and spring riser heading into the 2020 draft, showing high-spin stuff and projectable power. The Rangers drafted him in the third round and signed him for an above-slot $775,000. His 2021 debut was cut short by an elbow strain, but he returned in 2022 to make 21 starts with High-A Hickory. Roby was assigned to Double-A Frisco in 2023 but went down in early June with a shoulder injury. He was traded

to the Cardinals with Thomas Saggese for Jordan Montgomery and Chris Stratton. Roby debuted with Double-A Springfield on Aug. 26 and headed to the Arizona Fall League following the season.
SCOUTING REPORT: Roby has a prototype pitcher's build with broad shoulders, a lean and muscular body and strong lower half. He mixes four pitches, led by a fastball sitting 94-95 mph touching 97 at peak. His fastball has average ride and armside run but moves toward the plate on an efficient plane, allowing the pitch to play when elevated. His primary secondary is a hammer curveball in the 79-81 mph range with big depth and enough tilt to generate glove-side break. Roby's curveball generates above-average whiff rates in and out of the zone. His slider is his third pitch and is used primarily to righthanded hitters. It's a mid-80s pitch with tight gyro shape and is most effective when thrown out of the zone. His changeup is a low-80s offering with tumble and fade, but he struggled to command it consistently throughout the season. Roby throws a high rate of strikes with a high pitching IQ. He's still learning to command his changeup and slider, but each pitch projects to reach average.
THE FUTURE: Health permitting, Roby has the ability to develop into a midrotation starter with above-average stuff, pitchability and a competitive fire.

Year	Age	Club	Level	W	L	ERA	G	GS	IP	H	HR	BB	SO	BB%	SO%	WHIP	AVG
2023	21	Frisco (TL)	AA	2	3	5.05	10	10	46	49	5	12	50	25.6	1.32	.274
2023	21	Springfield (TL)	AA	0	0	3.00	4	4	12	6	1	3	19	6.8	43.2	0.75	.146
Minor League Totals				7	16	4.38	42	41	185	164	26	57	230	7.4	29.8	1.19	.233

3 VICTOR SCOTT II, OF

HIT: 55. **POW:** 40. **RUN:** 80. **FLD:** 70. **ARM:** 50. **BA Grade:** 55. **Risk:** High.

Born: February 12, 2001. **B-T:** L-L. **HT:** 5-10. **WT:** 190.
Drafted: West Virginia, 2022 (5th round). **Signed by:** TC Calhoun.
TRACK RECORD: The Cardinals drafted Scott in the fifth round in 2022 after three seasons at West Virginia. He debuted with Low-A Palm Beach and produced a .358 on-base percentage with 13 steals in 31 games. Scott saw time with the big league team in 2023 spring training, filling in for players who had left for the World Baseball Classic. Assigned to High-A Peoria out of camp, Scott hit .282 and stole 50 bases in 66 games to earn a promotion to Double-A Springfield on June 28. He hit .323 and stole 45 bases in the second half. Scott tied for the minor league lead with 94 stolen bases then participated in the Arizona Fall League following the season.
SCOUTING REPORT: One of the best athletes in the Cardinals system, Scott is an explosive but undersized outfielder with quick-twitch mechanisms. He has advanced as a hitter during his time as a professional and now shows an advanced approach and plus bat-to-ball skills. Scott employs two separate approaches depending upon the opposing pitcher's handedness. Against righthanders, he uses a more traditional approach by looking to make consistent hard contact. Against lefthanders, he looks to put the ball in play. He doesn't get overly aggressive but often shortens his swing and uses his double-plus speed as an advantage. Scott bunted 28 times in 2023, 24 times against lefties. It's a viable strategy for Scott, who hit .708 on bunts this season. He flies out of the lefthanded batter's box and consistently puts pressure on defenders. He's an elite basestealer whose speed allows him to cover large swaths of ground in center field. Scott is a difference-maker on defense.
THE FUTURE: Scott is a standout defensive center fielder and basestealer with an approach at the plate that fits his tools. He should see ample Triple-A time in 2024, with a chance to make his MLB debut.

Year	Age	Club	Level	AVG	G	AB	R	H	2B	3B	HR	RBI	BB	SO	SB	OBP	SLG
2023	22	Peoria (MWL)	A+	.282	66	266	44	75	9	8	2	29	28	52	50	.365	.398
2023	22	Springfield (TL)	AA	.323	66	282	51	91	11	2	7	34	18	45	44	.373	.450
Minor League Totals				.290	163	656	115	190	24	14	11	75	70	123	107	.367	.419

4 TINK HENCE, RHP

FB: 55. **CB:** 45. **SL:** 50. **CHG:** 55. **CTL:** 45. **BA Grade:** 55. **Risk:** High.

Born: August, 6, 2002. **B-T:** R-R. **HT:** 6-1. **WT:** 175.
Drafted: HS—Pine Bluff, AR, 2020 (2nd round supplemental). **Signed by:** Dirk Kinney.
TRACK RECORD: Drafted by the Cardinals in the supplemental second round in 2020, Hence saw limited action in his 2021 pro debut and started his 2022 season late with strict innings and pitch limits. The training wheels were removed in 2023 as Hence made 23 starts split between High-A Peoria and Double-A Springfield. After an impressive 11-start stretch with Peoria, Hence was promoted to Double-A where he struggled across a dozen starts.
SCOUTING REPORT: While Hence is of average height for a major league starter, he has a slight build. His lack of physicality leads to questions about his long-term viability in a rotation. He took a big step forward from a workload standpoint in 2023, making 23 starts and jumping from 52.1 innings in 2022 to 96. After taking the Florida State League by storm in 2022 with his plus fastball and three quality secondaries, Hence took a step backward in 2023. He struggled to command his fastball, particularly at Double-A. Sitting 95-96 mph, Hence's fastball has outlier plane to the plate that is difficult for hitters to square. When elevated, the pitch is a bat-missing weapon, but Hence struggled to consistently elevate it in 2023. His slider sits in the mid 80s with cut and has become his primary secondary against righthanded hitters. It was an ineffective pitch in the zone in 2023 and is best used for chases. Hence pocketed his curveball usage in 2023, leaning into his 82-84 mph changeup with great results. It has heavy fade and has developed into his best bat-missing pitch. Hence throws strikes with all of his pitches but struggled to hit his target with his fastball. His slider and changeup are best when thrown for chases.
THE FUTURE: Hence proved he could stay healthy while handling a larger workload, but his breaking ball quality backed up and he now profiles as a changeup-first righthander with fastball command issues.

Year	Age	Club	Level	W	L	ERA	G	GS	IP	H	HR	BB	SO	BB%	SO%	WHIP	AVG
2023	20	Peoria (MWL)	A+	2	1	2.81	11	11	42	34	4	12	46	7.3	27.9	1.10	.224
2023	20	Springfield (TL)	AA	2	5	5.47	12	12	54	60	8	22	53	9.2	22.2	1.51	.283
Minor League Totals				4	8	3.57	47	40	156	136	14	52	194	8.1	30.3	1.20	.234

5 THOMAS SAGGESE, 2B

HIT: 55. **POW:** 50. **RUN:** 45. **FLD:** 45. **ARM:** 45. **BA Grade:** 50 **Risk:** Medium.

Born: April, 10, 2002. **B-T:** R-R. **HT:** 5-11. **WT:** 175.
Drafted: HS—Carlsbad, CA, 2020 (5th round). **Signed by:** Steve Flores (Rangers).
TRACK RECORD: The Rangers selected Saggese with their final pick in the five-round 2020 draft. He signed for an above-slot $800,000 and debuted the following spring. Over his first two pro seasons Saggese hit .291/.365/.490 across 176 games. He took another step forward in 2023, hitting .313/.379/.512 in 93 games with Double-A Frisco. He was traded alongside Tekoah Roby to the Cardinals for Jordan Montgomery at the 2023 trade deadline. Saggese was voted Texas League MVP after the season.
SCOUTING REPORT: Saggese is a bat-first middle infielder with above-average bat-to-ball skills and an aggressive approach at the plate. He looks to do damage early in counts, and 23 of his 26 home runs came on the first three pitches of the at-bat. This aggressive approach has its drawbacks. Saggese struggles to control the at-bat when behind in the count. He has just fringe-average raw power but gets the most out of his game power due to his innate feel for the barrel. Saggese shows a knack for making his best contact at optimal launch angles with consistency, allowing him to over-perform many of his underlying metrics. How his aggressive approach will translate against major league pitchers is a lingering question. Saggese is a fringe-average runner with solid baserunning instincts. He spent time at second base, third base and shortstop over the last few seasons but profiles best as a second baseman. His actions and arm are fringy, but he makes a majority of the plays.
THE FUTURE: Saggese has a bat-driven profile and shows an ability to get the most out of his contact and an aggressive approach that can often get him into trouble. He profiles as an average everyday second baseman capable of above-average hitting seasons at peak.

Year	Age	Club	Level	AVG	G	AB	R	H	2B	3B	HR	RBI	BB	SO	SB	OBP	SLG
2023	21	Frisco (TL)	AA	.313	93	367	67	115	22	3	15	78	34	96	8	.379	.512
2023	21	Springfield (TL)	AA	.331	33	130	25	43	7	3	10	29	15	34	3	.403	.662
2023	21	Memphis (IL)	AAA	.207	13	58	9	12	5	0	1	4	3	14	1	.270	.345
Minor League Totals				.298	315	1198	206	357	73	13	51	218	124	326	35	.369	.508

6 IVAN HERRERA, C

HIT: 55. **POW:** 50. **RUN:** 30. **FLD:** 50. **ARM:** 45. **BA Grade:** 45. **Risk:** Medium.

Born: June 1, 2000. **B-T:** R-R. **HT:** 5-11. **WT:** 220.
Drafted: Panama, 2016. **Signed by:** Damaso Espino.
TRACK RECORD: Signed out of Panama for $200,000 in July 2016, Herrera has hit his way up the Cardinals' minor league ladder, seeing major league time in each of the past two seasons. He hit .297 with a .409 on-base percentage over his limited MLB action in 2023. After producing a .951 OPS, which led all Triple-A catchers with at least 300 plate appearances, Herrera was selected as an International League all-star.
SCOUTING REPORT: A stocky backstop with no physical projection remaining, Herrera's profile is driven by his above-average contact skills and patient approach. His approach borders on overly passive, but he has a history of producing elite walk rates. He rarely expands the zone and consistently makes contact when he does swing. He shows above-average raw power but has yet to fully tap into it in games. Herrera makes a high rate of opposite-field contact and a majority of his best-hit balls come in the form of line drives or hard hit ground balls. Herrera hits lefthanders well and has no platoon split issues. He's an average receiver and blocker with a fringe-average arm. His throwing improved slightly in 2023, as did his blocking and receiving following an injury-plagued 2022. Herrera has a balance of skills that allow him to do a little of everything well. If he can find more over-the-fence power without sacrificing his contact skills, he could unlock another gear at the plate.
THE FUTURE: Herrera is a low-risk catcher with above-average hitting and on-base ability. He should be in the mix for a share of catching duties with the Cardinals in 2024. He will vie for time with Willson Contreras and Andrew Knizner to be the long-term answer at catcher.

Year	Age	Club	Level	AVG	G	AB	R	H	2B	3B	HR	RBI	BB	SO	SB	OBP	SLG
2023	23	Memphis (IL)	AAA	.297	83	290	66	86	27	1	10	60	75	77	11	.451	.500
2023	23	St. Louis (NL)	MLB	.297	13	37	6	11	2	0	0	4	5	11	0	.409	.351
Minor League Totals				.280	413	1484	249	416	81	6	44	256	242	355	22	.391	.432
Major League Totals				.236	24	55	6	13	2	0	0	5	7	19	0	.338	.273

7 CHASE DAVIS, OF

HIT: 50. **POW:** 55. **RUN:** 50. **FLD:** 50. **ARM:** 60. **BA Grade:** 55 **Risk:** Extreme.

Born: December, 5, 2001. **B-T:** L-L. **HT:** 6-1. **WT:** 216.
Drafted: Arizona, 2023 (1st round). **Signed by:** Scott Cousins.
TRACK RECORD: Davis was a touted amateur dating back to his days as a Sacramento area prep. He lost his senior high school season to the pandemic and made it to campus at Arizona, where he hit .362/.489/.742 as a junior to earn All-Pacific-12 Conference honors and inclusion on the Golden Spikes Award watch list. The Cardinals drafted Davis with the 21st overall pick in 2023 and signed him for $3.62 million. He debuted with Low-A Palm Beach.
SCOUTING REPORT: Davis has a big league body, which includes an athletic build with strength throughout his frame. His bat-to-ball skills have come a long way in the last few years and now project as average. Davis' approach has always been advanced and he shows a discerning eye at the plate with the ability to draw walks at a high rate. He struggled to hit lefthanders in his pro debut, but it's uncertain how much of that was simply the product of a small sample. While his college splits favored righthanders, Davis had solid production in left-on-left matchups while at Arizona. His power didn't show with Palm Beach, leading to some concerns of it translating with a wood bat. In college, Davis showed plus power backed by strong exit velocity numbers. His overall EV data and power production was down in his pro debut. He's an average runner who will show above-average run times. He's an average fielder in an outfield corner capable of making a highlight reel play from time to time. His throwing arm is plus and plays in either outfield corner and should keep baserunners honest.
THE FUTURE: Davis is a strong all-around player who will look to prove he can hit professional pitching in his first full season. He projects as an everyday corner outfielder with a chance to grow into an above-average hitter if his recent contact gains prove to be legitimate.

Year	Age	Club	Level	AVG	G	AB	R	H	2B	3B	HR	RBI	BB	SO	SB	OBP	SLG
2023	21	Palm Beach (FSL)	A	.212	34	104	15	22	6	0	0	23	25	34	3	.366	.269
Minor League Totals				.212	34	104	15	22	6	0	0	23	25	34	3	.366	.269

8 COOPER HJERPE, LHP

FB: 55. **CB:** 40. **SL:** 50. **CHG:** 55. **CUT:** 40. **CTL:** 50 **BA Grade:** 50. **Risk:** High.

Born: March, 16, 2001. **B-T:** L-L. **HT:** 6-3. **WT:** 200.
Drafted: Oregon State, 2022 (1st round). **Signed by:** Chris Rodriguez/Donnie Marbut.
TRACK RECORD: Hjerpe led the nation in strikeouts as an Oregon State junior and intrigued analytically slanted front offices heading into the 2022 draft. He was drafted 22nd overall by the Cardinals and signed for $3.18 million. He was held out of play following the draft and debuted the following spring with High-A Peoria. After eight starts with Peoria, Hjerpe went down with an elbow injury on May 23. He had a procedure to remove loose bodies from his pitching elbow and did not return until early September, making two appearances with Peoria. Following the season, Hjerpe participated in the Arizona Fall League.
SCOUTING REPORT: Hjerpe's sidearm slot is the defining characteristic of the lefthander's profile and the driving force behind his outlier analytic traits. He mixes five pitches, but his primary mix consists of his fastball, slider and changeup. His fastball sits 88-90 mph and touches 91 at peak. While his velocity is well below-average, Hjerpe's combination of unique release traits and fastball shape allows it to miss bats and generate whiffs in zone. His slider is his primary secondary pitch in left-on-left matchups, but is also effective when he backdoors it to righthanders. It's a slower sweeper-style pitch that sits 77-79 mph. He can manipulate it for more depth and produce a slower curveball-like version of his breaking ball. He mixed in a cutter in the mid 80s in spurts, but it is a fairly new pitch. His command of his entire mix is strong and he showed a knack for not only strike-throwing but landing all of his pitches in the zone.
THE FUTURE: After an injury-plagued debut, Hjerpe will look to prove he can complete a season healthy in 2024. The traits that made him a viable first-round pick are still evident, and he projects as a No. 5 starter with unique deceptive traits that would work in relief.

Year	Age	Club	Level	W	L	ERA	G	GS	IP	H	HR	BB	SO	BB%	SO%	WHIP	AVG
2023	22	Peoria (MWL)	A+	2	3	3.51	10	8	41	26	8	25	51	14.6	29.8	1.24	.183
Minor League Totals				2	3	3.51	10	8	41	26	8	25	51	14.6	29.8	1.24	.183

9 GORDON GRACEFFO, RHP

FB: 50. **CB:** 45. **SL:** 55. **CHG:** 45. **CTL:** 50. **BA Grade:** 50 **Risk:** High

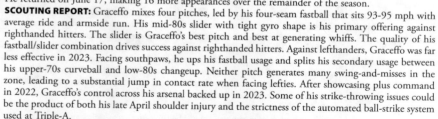

Born: March, 17, 2000. **B-T:** R-R. **HT:** 6-4. **WT:** 210.
Drafted: Villanova, 2021 (5th round). **Signed by:** Jim Negrych.
TRACK RECORD: Graceffo sat 90-93 mph in spring 2021, but his fastball steadily gained steam, peaking at 100 mph on the backfields at 2022 spring training. He dominated High-A competition out of camp, earning a promotion to Double-A. He broke camp with Triple-A Memphis in 2023 but hit the injured list following his April 28 start at Durham. Graceffo missed nearly two months with right shoulder inflammation, his first injury since high school. He returned on June 17, making 16 more appearances over the remainder of the season.
SCOUTING REPORT: Graceffo mixes four pitches, led by his four-seam fastball that sits 93-95 mph with average ride and armside run. His mid-80s slider with tight gyro shape is his primary offering against righthanded hitters. The slider is Graceffo's best pitch and best at generating whiffs. The quality of his fastball/slider combination drives success against righthanded hitters. Against lefthanders, Graceffo was far less effective in 2023. Facing southpaws, he ups his fastball usage and splits his secondary usage between his upper-70s curveball and low-80s changeup. Neither pitch generates many swing-and-misses in the zone, leading to a substantial jump in contact rate when facing lefties. After showcasing plus command in 2022, Graceffo's control across his arsenal backed up in 2023. Some of his strike-throwing issues could be the product of both his late April shoulder injury and the strictness of the automated ball-strike system used at Triple-A.
THE FUTURE: Graceffo fits the mold of a back-end starter capable of providing average performance with the ability to handle a starter's workload. His profile could take a substantial jump if he establishes a true go-to secondary against lefthanded hitters.

Year	Age	Club	Level	W	L	ERA	G	GS	IP	H	HR	BB	SO	BB%	SO%	WHIP	AVG
2023	23	Memphis (IL)	AAA	4	3	4.92	21	18	86	87	9	45	81	11.6	20.9	1.53	.261
Minor League Totals				15	9	3.51	58	45	251	218	27	82	257	7.8	24.5	1.20	.230

10 LEONARDO BERNAL, C

HIT: 50. **POW:** 50. **RUN:** 30. **FLD:** 45. **ARM:** 50. **BA Grade:** 50. **Risk:** Extreme.

Born: February, 13, 2004. **B-T:** B-R. **HT:** 6-0. **WT:** 200.
Drafted: Panama, 2021. **Signed by:** Damaso Espino.
TRACK RECORD: Signed out of Panama in January 2021 for $680,000, Bernal has established himself as one of the top young players in the Cardinals' system over his first three seasons. After debuting in the Dominican Summer League in 2021, Bernal skipped the Florida Complex League and made his U.S. debut with Low-A Palm Beach in 2022. He returned to Palm Beach in 2023, playing 78 games before hitting the injured list on Aug. 10.
SCOUTING REPORT: A switch-hitting catcher with a mature physical frame, Bernal showed a noticeable improvement in plate skills this season. After whiffing and chasing at high rates in 2022, he made adjustments to his setup to make more contact and chase less this season. The changes worked and Bernal improved his contact rate, in-zone miss rate and cut down on his chase swings. Bernal has always possessed plus raw power dating back to his days as an amateur but has yet to fully actualize his game power due to flatter angles on contact. His power hitting took a step back in 2023 and his isolated slugging dropped more than a hundred points year over year. This was in large part due to a drop in launch angles on his balls in play over 95 mph and a drop in pull-side launch. Behind the plate, Bernal struggled at times with his blocking and didn't show the same plus arm he showed in 2022. Much of this looks to be a product of Bernal's body backing up and a subsequent drop in athleticism. He is a young switch-hitting catcher with improving contact and approach, but he faces questions around his in-game power and catching ability.
THE FUTURE: Bernal's overall skills project him as a backup big league catcher with the upside to blossom into an average everyday catcher.

Year	Age	Club	Level	AVG	G	AB	R	H	2B	3B	HR	RBI	BB	SO	SB	OBP	SLG
2023	19	Palm Beach (FSL)	A	.265	78	268	45	71	15	1	3	44	49	55	4	.381	.362
Minor League Totals				.247	167	582	90	144	32	3	15	102	78	115	8	.342	.390

11 SEM ROBBERSE, RHP

FB: 40. **CB:** 55. **SL:** 55. **CHG:** 45. **CUT:** 45. **CTL:** 45. **BA Grade:** 45. **Risk:** High.

Born: October 12, 2001. **B-T:** R-R. **HT:** 6-1. **WT:** 180. **Signed:** Netherlands, 2019. **Signed by:** Andrew Tinnish (Blue Jays).
TRACK RECORD: A Netherlands native, Robberse is the rare prospect born and raised in Europe. He signed with the Blue Jays in 2019 and steadily climbed the minor league ladder, reaching Double-A by the end of his second full season. He returned to Double-A in 2023 and made 18 starts before he was traded to the Cardinals as part of the exchange for Jordan Hicks. Robberse made seven starts with Triple-A Memphis after the trade.
SCOUTING REPORT: A projectable righthander with an athletic operation, Robberse mixes five pitches in his fastball, slider, curveball, changeup and cutter. Robberse's fastball sits 91-93 mph and touches 94, with pedestrian movement. He threw it less than 40% of the time because it lacks vertical movement and velocity. Robberse's feel for spinning a pair of breaking ball shapes is his carrying tool. His slider sits 84-86 mph with sweeper shape, but less horizontal movement than a typical sweeper. Robberse's curveball might be his best performing pitch and sits 82-84 mph with more sweep and depth than his slider. Robberse's changeup is a fringe-average and firm offspeed pitch that sits 87-89 mph with tumble and moderate fade. He'll also throw a cutter as bridge pitch between his fastball and two breaking balls. Robberse is still learning to command his vast arsenal and projects as a fringe-average strike thrower.
THE FUTURE: Robberse could make the jump to a potential back-end starter with command improvements. If not, he could make it as a low-leverage reliever who heavily relies on his breaking ball.

Year	Age	Club	Level	W	L	ERA	G	GS	IP	H	HR	BB	SO	BB%	SO%	WHIP	AVG
2023	21	New Hampshire (EL)	AA	3	5	4.06	18	18	89	71	14	33	86	8.9	23.1	1.17	.213
2023	21	Memphis (IL)	AAA	2	1	4.84	8	7	35	39	6	24	44	14.3	26.2	1.78	.279
Minor League Totals				16	20	3.85	74	69	334	301	38	129	326	9.0	22.8	1.29	.236

12 MAX RAJCIC, RHP

FB: 45. **CB:** 50. **SL:** 45. **CHG:** 55. **CTL:** 50. **BA Grade:** 45. **Risk:** High.

Born: August 3, 2001. **B-T:** R-R. **HT:** 6-1. **WT:** 205. **Drafted:** UCLA, 2022 (6th round). **Signed by:** Michael Garciaparra.
TRACK RECORD: Rajcic had a noteworthy high school career as the ace for Southern California powerhouse Orange Lutheran. He made it to campus as the Bruins' top recruit in the 2020 class. As a freshman, Rajcic served as UCLA's closer and transitioned to a starter's role as a draft-eligible sophomore. The

Cardinals selected Rajcic in the sixth round of the 2022 draft and signed him for an above-slot $600,000. He debuted with Low-A Palm Beach in 2023 and split his season across both Class A levels and was named the Cardinals' minor league pitcher of the year.

SCOUTING REPORT: Rajcic pitches with a tried and true approach: he gets ahead with his fastball and then attacks with secondaries. Rajcic mixes four pitches in a four-seam fastball, curveball, slider and changeup. His fastball sits 92-94 mph and features a good combination of ride and armside run and he does an excellent job commanding the pitch. This sets up Rajcic's trio of secondaries, led by his signature low-80s curveball with two-plane break and above-average depth. The curveball is a solid bat-misser, but succeeds due to poor quality of contact against it. Rajcic also shows solid feel for a mid-80s changeup, which is his best bat-misser and drives whiffs in and out of the zone. His 82-84 mph slider has sweeper shape, but less sweep than is typical. Rajcic is an average strike thrower who could push to above-average at peak.

THE FUTURE: Rajcic looked like a fringe starting pitching candidate entering affiliated ball, but is trending toward No. 5 starter.

Year	Age	Club	Level	W	L	ERA	G	GS	IP	H	HR	BB	SO	BB%	SO%	WHIP	AVG
2023	21	Palm Beach (FSL)	A	6	3	1.89	12	12	62	41	4	9	68	3.8	28.6	0.81	.183
2023	21	Peoria (MWL)	A+	3	3	3.08	11	11	61	57	2	18	55	7.2	21.9	1.22	.251
Minor League Totals				9	6	2.49	23	23	123	98	6	27	123	5.5	25.2	1.02	.217

13 WON-BIN CHO, OF

HIT: 50. **POW:** 45. **RUN:** 50. **FLD:** 50. **ARM:** 55. **BA Grade:** 50. **Risk:** Extreme.

Born: August 2, 2003. **B-T:** L-L. **HT:** 6-1. **WT:** 200. **Signed:** South Korea, 2022. **Signed by:** Matt Slater.

TRACK RECORD: After Cho turned heads in the annual High School Power Showcase, the South Korean slugger was very much on the radar of MLB teams. The rare international amateur from Asia, Cho signed with the Cardinals for a $500,000 bonus in January of 2022. He debuted in the Florida Complex League the following summer and played in 26 games. Cho was assigned to Low-A Palm Beach to begin 2023 and hit .270 in 105 games with a 14.2% walk rate.

SCOUTING REPORT: Cho is bat-first corner outfielder with enough supporting skills to project everyday upside. He shows a good balance of skills at the plate, with average bat-to-ball ability and a discerning eye. He shows a lack of adjustability in his swing and struggles to adjust to soft stuff, but is adept at hitting high fastballs thanks to his more linear bat plane at contact. Cho shows above-average raw power, but struggles to get to it due to his struggles with certain pitches inside and the lack of loft in his bat path. Cho will likely slow down as his body matures, but at present he's an above-average runner with a quick first step and an effective basestealer. Cho spent time in all three outfield positions but should settle in an outfield corner where his above-average arm will play.

THE FUTURE: Cho has solid all-around skills and could develop into a regular with swing adjustments.

Year	Age	Club	Level	AVG	G	AB	R	H	2B	3B	HR	RBI	BB	SO	SB	OBP	SLG
2023	19	Palm Beach (FSL)	A	.270	105	378	64	102	14	5	7	52	64	98	32	.376	.389
Minor League Totals				.260	131	454	74	118	17	6	8	55	84	125	38	.380	.377

14 MICHAEL McGREEVY, RHP

FB: 45. **CB:** 45. **SL:** 55. **CHG:** 45. **CTL:** 60. **BA Grade:** 40. **Risk:** Medium.

Born: July 8, 2000. **B-T:** R-R. **HT:** 6-4. **WT:** 215. **Drafted:** UC Santa Barbara, 2021 (1st round). **Signed by:** Michael Garciaparra.

TRACK RECORD: A freshman All-American reliever in 2019, McGreevy made the jump to the rotation with UC Santa Barbara as a sophomore. McGreevy broke out in 2021 and struck out 115 batters with just 11 walks in 101.2 innings during his draft spring. The Cardinals selected McGreevy in the first round of the 2021 draft and he debuted in 2022. McGreevy reached Double-A in 2022 and returned to the level to begin 2023. He dominated over three starts and earned the promotion to Triple-A.

SCOUTING REPORT: McGreevy mixes two fastball variants, a slider, curveball and changeup, but his primary mix is sinker and slider. McGreevy's sinker sits 90-92 mph and touches 93 mph with moderate sink and armside run. While his raw stuff is poor on the pitch, he shows plus command and avoids trouble spots in the zone. His slider is his primary secondary and McGreevy's best pitch. It sits 84-85 mph with cut and he tunnels it off of the fastball well. His changeup is a firm upper-80s pitch that can blend into his sinker at times, but he showed improved feel for the pitch in 2023. McGreevy's curveball was once his go-to secondary and is now used in tandem with his changeup against lefthanded hitters. McGreevy shows plus command and has a strong track record of strike-throwing.

THE FUTURE: McGreevy is a low-upside back-end starter who can eat innings.

Year	Age	Club	Level	W	L	ERA	G	GS	IP	H	HR	BB	SO	BB%	SO%	WHIP	AVG
2023	22	Springfield (TL)	AA	2	0	1.45	3	3	19	17	0	1	16	1.4	22.5	0.96	.246
2023	22	Memphis (IL)	AAA	11	6	4.49	24	24	134	160	17	37	107	6.2	18.0	1.47	.291
Minor League Totals				22	13	4.19	62	62	305	341	33	70	247	5.4	19.1	1.35	.281

15 JIMMY CROOKS, C

HIT: 45. **POW:** 45. **RUN:** 30. **FLD:** 55. **ARM:** 55. **BA Grade:** 45. **Risk:** High.

Born: July 19, 2001. **B-T:** L-R. **HT:** 6-1. **WT:** 210. **Drafted:** Oklahoma, 2022 (4th round). **Signed by:** Pete Parise.

TRACK RECORD: Crooks began his college career with one season with McLennan (Texas) JC before transferring to Oklahoma. With the Sooners, Crooks handled a bulk of the catching duties for two seasons and hit .297/.409/.504. The Cardinals selected Crooks in the fourth round and he debuted following the draft with Low-A Palm Beach. Crooks was assigned to High-A Peoria to begin 2023 and played 114 games for the Chiefs before a late-season cameo at Triple-A.

SCOUTING REPORT: Crooks has a well-rounded profile with potential average skills on both sides of the ball. Crooks is a fringe-average hitter with fringe-average bat-to-ball skills and tendency to get passive at the plate. He shows average raw power, but has not gotten to it consistently, though he does have enough raw power to project for mid-teens home run totals over a full season. Crooks is a well below-average runner who moves from station-to-station when on base. His defensive skills have taken a sizable jump over the last few seasons thanks to improved blocking and receiving that now look like above-average tools. Crooks also cleaned up his mechanics and is now an above-average thrower with a career caught stealing rate near 30%.

THE FUTURE: While he lacks loud offensive skills, Crooks provides value as a sum-of-its-parts profile who could carve out a role as a platoon catcher thanks to his above-average defense.

Year	Age	Club	Level	AVG	G	AB	R	H	2B	3B	HR	RBI	BB	SO	SB	OBP	SLG
2023	21	Peoria (MWL)	A+	.271	114	413	71	112	29	1	12	73	52	101	2	.358	.433
Minor League Totals				.270	138	492	83	133	32	3	15	80	64	123	2	.364	.439

16 TRAVIS HONEYMAN, OF

HIT: 50. **POW:** 45. **RUN:** 55. **FLD:** 45. **ARM:** 50. **BA Grade:** 50. **Risk:** Extreme.

Born: October 2, 2001. **B-T:** R-R. **HT:** 6-2. **WT:** 190. **Drafted:** Boston College, 2023 (3rd round). **Signed by:** Jim Negrych.

TRACK RECORD: Honeyman played sparingly at Boston College as a freshman but broke out after earning a starting role as a sophomore and .329/.402/.506 in 41 games. He followed that up with a standout showing in the Cape Cod League in 2022 where he hit .289/.400/.530 in 24 games. He returned to Boston College for his draft spring but was limited to 39 games due to a shoulder injury. The Cardinals selected Honeyman in the third round and signed him for a below-slot bonus of $700,000.

SCOUTING REPORT: Honeyman's bat-to-ball skills are above-average and that's been the case throughout his college career. He shows strong plate coverage skills with a short swing and loose hands, though his swing does have some moving parts with a leg kick and a hand pump. After showing plate discipline as a sophomore Honeyman's chase rate jumped as a junior. Some of this is explained by an adjustment to a more aggressive approach, but his struggles versus spin were evident. Honeyman shows above-average raw power and will turn on a pitch to his pull side, but his more linear bat path is more conducive to line drives than back-spinning fly balls. Honeyman is an above-average runner and has some success as a basestealer. That speed translates to the outfield where he's seen time in all three positions as an amateur, though his route running is currently subpar and will need to improve. He has an average throwing arm.

THE FUTURE: Honeyman has everyday regular potential if he can stay on the field and everything comes together.

Year	Age	Club	Level	AVG	G	AB	R	H	2B	3B	HR	RBI	BB	SO	SB	OBP	SLG
2023	21	Did not play															

17 CESAR PRIETO, 2B

HIT: 55. **POW:** 30. **RUN:** 40. **FLD:** 50. **ARM:** 50. **BA Grade:** 45. **Risk:** High.

Born: May 10, 1999. **B-T:** L-R. **HT:** 5-9. **WT:** 175. **Signed:** Cuba, 2022. **Signed by:** Koby Perez (Orioles).

TRACK RECORD: Prieto signed with the Orioles as one of the top players out of Cuba in January 2022, after defecting the previous May from Cuba's national team during an Olympic qualifying trip in Miami. Prieto debuted that spring with High-A Aberdeen and reached Double-A by late May. He returned to Double-A to begin 2023 and earned a promotion to Triple-A Norfolk on June 20 before he was traded to the Cardinals as a part of the trade for Jack Flaherty.

SCOUTING REPORT: Prieto is an advanced contact hitter with a .299 career minor league average in more than 1,000 plate appearances. He utilizes a line drive-focused swing with an aggressive approach focused on putting the ball in play. Prieto makes this approach work with an uncanny ability to get his bat on pitches all over the strike zone, on the fringes and out of the zone. This hyper-aggressive approach limits Prieto's walks. Prieto has fringe-average raw power, but his swing and approach are not optimized for power. He's likely to produce 8-11 home runs per season with full time at-bats. Prieto is a below-average runner who's unlikely to steal more than a few bases, though his average fielding at second base and average arm give him supporting skills beyond his hitting ability. He saw extensive time at third base in 2022, but played primarily second in 2023.

THE FUTURE: Prieto is a hit-first utility player with second-division regular upside.

Year	Age	Club	Level	AVG	G	AB	R	H	2B	3B	HR	RBI	BB	SO	SB	OBP	SLG
2023	24	Bowie (EL)	AA	.364	58	231	33	84	12	1	4	29	15	17	5	.406	.476
2023	24	Memphis (IL)	AAA	.270	38	163	24	44	5	1	4	20	7	25	2	.314	.387
2023	24	Norfolk (IL)	AAA	.317	27	104	16	33	8	1	2	20	8	10	2	.365	.471
Minor League Totals				.299	238	963	130	288	53	3	21	126	50	126	14	.342	.426

18 ZACH LEVENSON, OF

HIT: 50. **POW:** 50. **RUN:** 45. **FLD:** 45. **ARM:** 45. **BA Grade:** 45. **Risk:** High.

Born: March 6, 2002. **B-T:** R-R. **HT:** 6-2. **WT:** 211. **Drafted:** Miami, 2023 (5th round). **Signed by:** Josh Lopez.

TRACK RECORD: After one season with Seminole State (Fla.) JC, Levenson transferred to Miami, where he spent two seasons with the Hurricanes and hit .295/.406/.546. He was selected to the all-Atlantic Coast Conference third team in 2023 after hitting .292/.397/.554 with 14 home runs. The Cardinals drafted Levenson in the fifth round in 2023 and signed him for $381,300. He debuted with Low-A Palm Beach after signing and hit .268/.331/.480 in 34 games.

SCOUTING REPORT: Levenson showed a combination of plate skills and average or better power both as an amateur and in his short pro sample. Levenson has a simple righthanded swing with strong wrists and loose hands which allow him to adjust to a variety of pitch types. He has a good balance of aggression and patience and rarely swings himself into outs. Levenson's raw power is average at present and he shows the ability to get to it by hitting the ball consistently at good angles. Levenson is an average runner who could slow down to fringe-average. He has enough speed for the corner outfield where he's a fringe-average defender with a fringe-average arm.

THE FUTURE: Levenson is an offensive-driven corner outfielder with second-division regular upside.

Year	Age	Club	Level	AVG	G	AB	R	H	2B	3B	HR	RBI	BB	SO	SB	OBP	SLG
2023	21	Palm Beach (FSL)	A	.268	34	123	24	33	6	1	6	22	12	32	2	.331	.480
Minor League Totals				.268	34	123	24	33	6	1	6	22	12	32	2	.331	.480

19 PEDRO PAGES, C

HIT: 50. **POW:** 45. **RUN:** 30. **FLD:** 55. **ARM:** 55. **BA Grade:** 45. **Risk:** High.

Born: September 17, 1998. **B-T:** R-R. **HT:** 6-1. **WT:** 234. **Drafted:** Florida Atlantic, 2019 (6th round). **Signed by:** Mike Dibiase.

TRACK RECORD: Pages made his bones early in his career as a defensive catcher, but took a big step forward in 2023. He technically played down a level in 2023 after spending 44 games with Triple-A Memphis in 2022. Pages hit .267/.362/.443 in 117 games with Springfield and his 16 home runs nearly equaled his total from the previous two seasons combined. Pages was added to the Cardinals 40-man roster after the season.

SCOUTING REPORT: Pages improved his contact and chase rates in 2023 which led to the best season of his career. He now shows above-average contact rates and low chase rates which point towards sustainable offensive production. Pages' power is average currently, with average exit velocity data and consistent contact at positive launch angles. With the improvements to his approach Pages projects for fringe-average game power. After using a more traditional stance behind the plate, Pages adopted a one-knee-down catching style on the suggestion of Yankees catcher Jose Trevino. This led to more consistent framing and blocking, and paired with an above-average throwing arm and natural catching instincts, give Pages a strong defensive foundation.

THE FUTURE: Pages is a potential platoon catcher with above-average defensive ability and a chance for a league average bat.

Year	Age	Club	Level	AVG	G	AB	R	H	2B	3B	HR	RBI	BB	SO	SB	OBP	SLG
2023	24	Springfield (TL)	AA	.267	117	424	63	113	23	2	16	72	59	96	3	.362	.443
Minor League Totals				.256	333	1195	158	306	67	4	37	176	159	319	6	.348	.412

20 BRYCEN MAUTZ, LHP

FB: 45. **CB:** 40. **SL:** 55. **CHG:** 50. **CTL:** 40. **BA Grade:** 45. **Risk:** High.

Born: July 17, 2001. **B-T:** L-L. **HT:** 6-3. **WT:** 190. **Drafted:** San Diego, 2022 (2nd round). **Signed by:** Chris Rodriguez.

TRACK RECORD: After two seasons in and out of the San Diego bullpen, Mautz made the jump to the starting rotation in 2022. He produced a standout season, went 10-2 with 122 strikeouts and 22 walks in 90.2 innings and earned all-West Coast Conference first team honors. Mautz was selected by the Cardinals in the second round of the 2022 draft and signed for a below-slot bonus of $1.1 million. Mautz debuted in 2023 with Low-A Palm Beach where he made 23 starts.

SCOUTING REPORT: Mautz is more than a sinker and slider lefty and also has feel for a changeup and the ability to generate heavy rates of chase swings outside the zone. Mautz technically mixes four pitches, but the vast majority of his pitch usage is his sinker, slider and changeup. Mautz's fastball sits 91-93 mph with moderate sink and armside run, and while he doesn't miss many barrels with it, he does consistently generate weak ground ball contact. Mautz's slider is his best whiff inducing pitch and he gets swings and misses in and out of the zone. The chase rate against the pitch in 2023 was unusually high and likely the product of overwhelming Low-A hitters. His changeup is thrown more than any other pitch against righthanded batters and he typically goes straight to the pitch after getting strike one. He also throws a rarely-used curveball. Mautz's control is below-average and will likely be exposed as he progresses through the minors.

THE FUTURE: Mautz is a back-end starter candidate with the ability to transition to the pen on the strength of his groundball-generating skills.

Year	Age	Club	Level	W	L	ERA	G	GS	IP	H	HR	BB	SO	BB%	SO%	WHIP	AVG
2023	21	Palm Beach (FSL)	A	4	9	3.98	23	23	104	94	4	45	115	9.9	25.2	1.34	.237
Minor League Totals				4	9	3.98	23	23	104	94	4	45	115	9.9	25.2	1.34	.237

21 EDWIN NUÑEZ, RHP

FB: 60. **CB:** 45. **CHG:** 50. **CTL:** 40. **BA Grade:** 45. **Risk:** High.

Born: November 5, 2001. **B-T:** R-R. **HT:** 6-3. **WT:** 185. **Signed:** Dominican Republic, 2020. **Signed by:** Alix Martinez.

TRACK RECORD: Nuñez was suspended a year by MLB for an age discrepancy which pushed his official signing date back to June of 2020. Nuñez signed for $525,000 and debuted in 2021 with Low-A Palm Beach. He struggled with his command mightily over his first two professional seasons and returned to Low-A Palm Beach for his third consecutive season in 2023. He took a step forward in 2023, cut his walk rate, earned a promotion to High-A Peoria and then pitched in the Arizona Fall League after the season.

SCOUTING REPORT: Nuñez mixes four pitches with a fastball, curveball, slider and changeup. Nuñez sits 95-97 mph and touches 98, with four-seam and two-seam shapes on his fastball. His two-seam has a steeper plane and heavier armside run. Neither pitch has tremendous ride or sink, but they each feature above-average run and premium velocity. Nuñez commands his fastball shapes with above-average feel, but his command for his secondaries is shaky. Nuñez's primary secondary is an upper-80s changeup with tumble and fade that generates high rates of swings and misses and lots of chase swings out of the zone. His go-to breaking ball is a slurvy upper-70s curveball with two-plane break. It drives whiffs but is rarely swung at or in the zone. Nuñez has improved his control to below-average after having bottom of the scale control early in his career.

THE FUTURE: Nuñez is a high-powered one-inning reliever who lacks the breaking ball feel for high-leverage work.

Year	Age	Club	Level	W	L	ERA	G	GS	IP	H	HR	BB	SO	BB%	SO%	WHIP	AVG
2023	21	Palm Beach (FSL)	A	3	3	3.62	19	0	27	23	1	14	35	11.7	29.2	1.35	.219
2023	21	Peoria (MWL)	A+	3	1	3.22	22	0	36	33	4	16	30	10.1	19.0	1.35	.236
Minor League Totals				10	9	6.57	100	2	151	148	14	112	154	15.5	21.3	1.73	.253

22 ZACK SHOWALTER, RHP

FB: 55. **CB:** 40. **SL:** 50. **CHG:** 40. **CTL:** 45. **BA Grade:** 50. **Risk:** Extreme.

Born: January 23, 2004. **B-T:** R-R. **HT:** 6-2. **WT:** 195. **Drafted:** HS—Wesley Chapel, FL, 2022 (11th round).
Signed by: Brandon Verley (Orioles).

TRACK RECORD: Showalter was committed to South Florida but blew up on the showcase circuit in his pre-draft summer. The Orioles selected him in the 11th round and signed him for fifth-round money with a $440,000 bonus. Showalter debuted the following summer in the Florida Complex League and impressed over three appearances before he was promoted to Low-A Delmarva. At the trade deadline he was dealt to the Cardinals as a part of the Jack Flaherty deal, then after one appearance with Palm Beach was placed on the injured list and missed the remainder of the season.

SCOUTING REPORT: Showalter is a projectable righthander with unique release characteristics that play up his fastball. He mixes four pitches with a fastball, curveball, slider and changeup. His fastball sits 92-93 mph and touches 95 from a sub-five foot release height that creates deception. Showalter's four-seam fastball is an above-average pitch that could grade plus with added velocity. His three secondaries are all below-average at the moment with his slider showing the best projection of the trio. Showalter's strike-throwing is below-average but should develop to fringe-average as he tones down his violent operation.

THE FUTURE: Showalter is an intriguing projection righthander with a quality fastball but a wide range of outcomes.

Year	Age	Club	Level	W	L	ERA	G	GS	IP	H	HR	BB	SO	BB%	SO%	WHIP	AVG
2023	19	FCL Orioles	Rk	0	0	0.90	3	3	10	7	0	4	16	10.0	40.0	1.10	.194
2023	19	Delmarva (CAR)	A	0	2	3.10	6	5	20	19	1	10	25	11.2	28.1	1.43	.253
2023	19	Palm Beach (FSL)	A	0	0	0.00	1	0	1	0	0	1	1	25.0	25.0	1.00	.000
Minor League Totals				0	2	2.32	10	8	31	26	1	15	42	11.3	31.6	1.32	.228

23 QUINN MATHEWS, LHP

FB: 45. **CB:** 40. **SL:** 50. **CHG:** 55. **CTL:** 55. **BA Grade:** 45. **Risk:** High.

Born: October 4, 2000. **B-T:** L-L. **HT:** 6-4. **WT:** 192. **Drafted:** Stanford, 2023 (4th round). **Signed by:** Stacey Pettis.

TRACK RECORD: Mathews was a 19th-round draft pick by the Rays in 2022, but didn't sign and returned to Stanford for his senior year. That was a smart move. He had his best college season, won Pac-12 pitcher of the year and led Stanford to the College World Series. Mathews had a viral moment when he threw a 156-pitch complete game against Texas in super regionals. The Cardinals selected Mathews in the fourth round and signed him to a $600,000 bonus.

SCOUTING REPORT: Mathews is a polished strike thrower with a four-pitch mix and average stuff. His fastball sits 90-92 mph and touches 94 mph with above-average ride. His best pitch is an above-average changeup that generates swings and misses. Mathews has a low-80s slider with moderate sweep and a mid-70s curveball that's hardly used. His command took a jump to above-average in 2023 after often nibbling around the zone too much as an underclassman. Mathews has a high level of pitchability and touch for execution and throws lots of strikes while consistently working deep into games.

THE FUTURE: Mathews is a low-risk, back-end starter and innings-eater who could take a jump with a few added ticks of velocity.

Year	Age	Club	Level	W	L	ERA	G	GS	IP	H	HR	BB	SO	BB%	SO%	WHIP	AVG
2023	22	Did not play															

24 NICK ROBERTSON, RHP

FB: 60. **SL:** 50. **CHG:** 55. **CTL:** 50. **BA Grade:** 40. **Risk:** Medium.

Born: July 16, 1998. **B-T:** R-R. **HT:** 6-6. **WT:** 265. **Drafted:** James Madison, 2019 (7th round).
Signed by: Paul Murphy (Dodgers).

TRACK RECORD: Robertson had a whirlwind few months to end 2023. After being left off the Dodgers' 40-man roster and exposed to the 2022 Rule 5 draft, Robertson pitched his way onto the 40-man in 2023. He was then shipped to the Red Sox for Enrique Hernandez a week before the 2023 trade deadline. Robertson spent the remainder of the season moving back and forth between Triple-A Worcester and Boston and had three stints with the Red Sox. On Dec. 8, Robertson was one of the players traded to the Cardinals for outfielder Tyler O'Neill.

SCOUTING REPORT: An imposing righthanded reliever, Robertson mixes a fastball, slider and changeup. Robertson's four-seam fastball sits 95-96 mph and touches 97, and misses bats when located at the top of the zone. His best secondary is an upper-80s changeup with heavy tumble and fade. He shows remarkable feel for the pitch despite its dynamic movement and generates whiffs in and out of the zone with it. Robertson's breaking ball is a mid-80s sweeper slider that generates few whiffs but lots of bad contact. Robertson shows strong command for his entire arsenal and is a candidate for the opening day bullpen.

THE FUTURE: Robertson is a middle reliever with a powerful three pitch mix and solid command.

Year	Age	Club	Level	W	L	ERA	G	GS	IP	H	HR	BB	SO	BB%	SO%	WHIP	AVG
2023	24	Okla. City (PCL)	AAA	2	0	2.54	27	0	28	19	2	9	42	8.0	37.5	0.99	.184
2023	24	Worcester (IL)	AAA	2	1	4.40	15	0	14	14	3	4	16	6.3	25.4	1.26	.241
2023	24	Boston (AL)	MLB	0	0	6.00	9	1	12	13	2	5	13	8.9	23.2	1.50	.265
2023	24	Los Angeles (NL)	MLB	0	1	6.10	9	0	10	17	1	4	13	8.0	26.0	2.03	.370
Minor League Totals				7	8	3.62	150	3	185	159	17	61	231	7.8	29.7	1.20	.227
Major League Totals				0	1	6.04	18	1	22	30	3	9	26	8.5	24.5	1.75	.316

25 DREW ROM, LHP

FB: 45. **SL:** 50. **CHG:** 40. **CTL:** 40. **BA Grade:** 40. **Risk:** Medium.

Born: December 15, 1999. **B-T:** L-L. **HT:** 6-2. **WT:** 170. **Drafted:** HS—Fort Thomas, KY, 2018 (4th round).
Signed by: Adrian Dorsey (Orioles).

TRACK RECORD: After reaching Triple-A over the final few months of 2022, Rom returned to the level to begin 2023. He made 18 starts with Norfolk before he was traded to the Cardinals as a part of the return for Jack Flaherty. Rom was called up to the majors in Augusta and made seven starts for the Cardinals to close the season.

SCOUTING REPORT: Rom mixes three pitches with two fastball variations as well as a sweeper slider and a splitter. His fastball sits 90-91 mph and touches 92 with average ride and cut but plays up due to his above-average feel. Rom shows a two-seam as well in the 89-90 mph range with sink. His primary secondary is a low-80s sweeper that he throws to both righties and lefties and had the highest swinging strike rate in his arsenal. Rom's splitter is his least-thrown pitch and he needs to do a better job landing it in the zone. Rom is a below-average strike-thrower, but he does a decent job avoiding the middle of the zone.

THE FUTURE: Rom is a ready-made up-and-down starter with the ability to handle mop-up duty out of the bullpen.

Year	Age	Club	Level	W	L	ERA	G	GS	IP	H	HR	BB	SO	BB%	SO%	WHIP	AVG
2023	23	Memphis (IL)	AAA	2	0	0.82	2	2	11	2	1	4	18	9.8	43.9	0.55	.056
2023	23	Norfolk (IL)	AAA	7	6	5.34	19	18	86	100	7	46	100	11.5	25.1	1.70	.291
2023	23	St. Louis (NL)	MLB	1	4	8.02	8	8	34	51	7	19	32	11.2	18.8	2.08	.340
Minor League Totals				34	15	3.72	101	89	451	430	36	162	532	8.4	27.5	1.32	.249
Major League Totals				1	4	8.02	8	8	34	51	7	19	32	11.2	18.8	2.08	.340

26 LUKEN BAKER, 1B

HIT: 40. **POW:** 60. **RUN:** 20. **FLD:** 40. **ARM:** 55. **BA Grade:** 40. **Risk:** Medium.

Born: March 10, 1997. **B-T:** R-R. **HT:** 6-4. **WT:** 280. **Drafted:** Texas Christian, 2018 (2nd round supplemental).
Signed by: Tom Lipari.

TRACK RECORD: Baker had a legendary freshman season at Texas Christian when he helped lead the Horned Frogs to the 2016 College World Series. Baker spent close to five full seasons in the minors before a standout performance in 2023 skyrocketed him to the majors. Baker hit 18 home runs over his first 54 games and earned his first callup to the majors on June 4th.

SCOUTING REPORT: Significant improvements to Baker's approach yielded eye-popping results in 2023. Baker had a substantial decrease in chase rate year-over-year and it materialized in both higher contact quantity and quality. While Baker hit Triple-A pitching, he showed elevated swing-and-miss in the major leagues against better quality stuff. Baker's power is his carrying tool and he showed an ability to consistently get to it this season. He can send balls into orbit when he makes his best contact with a leveraged, power swing. Baker is a bottom-of-the-scale runner who's limited to first base defensively where he is a below-average defender.

THE FUTURE: Baker is a near-ready reserve player who can provide power off the bench.

Year	Age	Club	Level	AVG	G	AB	R	H	2B	3B	HR	RBI	BB	SO	SB	OBP	SLG
2023	26	Memphis (IL)	AAA	.334	84	314	71	105	22	0	33	98	59	76	0	.439	.720
2023	26	St. Louis (NL)	MLB	.209	33	86	9	18	3	0	2	10	13	31	0	.313	.314
Minor League Totals				.264	468	1733	248	458	100	1	94	309	205	457	1	.343	.486
Major League Totals				.209	33	86	9	18	3	0	2	10	13	31	0	.313	.314

27 PETE HANSEN, LHP

FB: 40. CB: 40. SL: 55. CHG: 50. CTL: 55. BA Grade: 40. Risk: High.

Born: July 28, 2000. **B-T:** R-L. **HT:** 6-2. **WT:** 205. **Drafted:** Texas, 2022 (3rd round). **Signed by:** Joseph Quezada.

TRACK RECORD: Hansen was a rock in the Texas rotation for three years and earned all-Big 12 first team honors as a redshirt sophomore. The Cardinals selected Hansen in the third round of the 2022 draft and signed him for $629,800. Hansen debuted in the spring of 2023 with Low-A Palm Beach and made 23 starts. He received a late-season promotion to Triple-A where he made one appearance.

SCOUTING REPORT: A soft-tossing lefty with a feel for a trio of secondaries and above-average command, Hansen mixes four pitches and can land all of them for strikes. His fastball sits 89-91 mph with some cut and is a below-average swing-and-miss pitch. His primary secondary is a sweeper slider in the low 80s that generates an above-average whiff rate. His mid-80s changeup is an average pitch that generates whiffs and is effective against righthanded hitters. Hansen will show a mid-70s curveball with two-plane break a few times a start. He has above-average command of his entire arsenal that allows him to maximize his fairly pedestrian pure stuff.

THE FUTURE: Hansen is an up-and-down starter with the upside of a back-of-the-rotation innings eater.

Year	Age	Club	Level	W	L	ERA	G	GS	IP	H	HR	BB	SO	BB%	SO%	WHIP	AVG
2023	22	Palm Beach (FSL)	A	11	3	3.12	23	23	113	92	10	39	126	8.4	27.1	1.16	.220
2023	22	Memphis (IL)	AAA	0	0	0.00	1	0	1	0	0	0	0	0.0	0.0	0.00	.000
Minor League Totals				11	3	3.11	24	23	114	92	10	39	126	8.3	26.9	1.16	.218

28 ADAM KLOFFENSTEIN, RHP

FB: 45. CB: 40. SL: 55. CHG: 40. CUT: 45. CTL: 45. BA Grade: 40. Risk: High.

Born: August 25, 2000. **B-T:** R-R. **HT:** 6-5. **WT:** 243. **Drafted:** HS—Magnolia, TX, 2018 (3rd round). **Signed by:** Brian Johnston (Blue Jays).

TRACK RECORD: Kloffenstein toiled in the minors for three seasons before he took a noticeable step forward in 2023. He made 17 starts for New Hampshire to begin the season and pitched to a 3.24 ERA while driving ground balls at a better than 50% rate and posting a 27.1% strikeout rate. The Cardinals acquired Kloffenstein as a part of the Jordan Hicks trade with Toronto, and assigned him to Triple-A Memphis where he made eight starts to finish the season.

SCOUTING REPORT: Kloffenstein has a deep repertoire and mixes six different pitches, including a sinker, slider, changeup, cutter, four-seam fastball and curveball. Kloffenstein's bread and butter is his slider and sinker combination. His sinker is a low-90s offering with heavy sink from a steeper approach angle that added two ticks of velocity in 2023. His slider is a sweeper in the low-to-mid 80s he shows advanced feel for. His cutter, changeup, curveball and four-seam fastball are all fringe to below-average offerings. Kloffenstein's strike-throwing is fringe-average but he's typically around the zone.

THE FUTURE: Kloffenstein is a potential depth starter who could fit in long relief duty thanks to a sinker/slider combination that allows him to drive high groundball rates and miss bats.

Year	Age	Club	Level	W	L	ERA	G	GS	IP	H	HR	BB	SO	BB%	SO%	WHIP	AVG
2023	22	New Hampshire (EL)	AA	5	5	3.24	17	17	89	79	8	34	105	8.9	27.6	1.27	.236
2023	22	Memphis (IL)	AAA	2	1	3.00	9	8	39	29	6	21	35	12.7	21.2	1.28	.209
Minor League Totals				20	24	4.42	89	87	408	378	44	196	433	10.9	24.2	1.41	.244

29 RYAN FERNANDEZ, RHP

FB: 50. SL: 50. CUT: 55. CTL: 50. BA Grade: 40. Risk: High.

Born: June 11, 1998. **B-T:** R-R. **HT:** 6-0. **WT:** 170. **Drafted:** Hillsborough (FL) JC, 2018 (23rd round). **Signed by:** Tom Kotchman (Red Sox).

TRACK RECORD: Fernandez had no college offers out of high school and ended up at Hillsborough (Fla.) JC on a recommendation from his high school coach. Once there, Fernandez transformed his body and jumped from 88 to 96 mph on his fastball. The Red Sox drafted him in the 23rd round with the 700th pick in 2018. Fernandez dealt with injuries toward the end of 2022 and was shut down in late July with right elbow inflammation. Fernandez returned and pitched his way to Triple-A Worcester by mid June. He was left unprotected for the 2023 Rule 5 draft and was selected by the Cardinals.

SCOUTING REPORT: While Fernandez's upper-90s fastball lights up radar guns, it's his unusual feel for spin that makes him successful. He mixes three pitches in a fastball, slider and cutter after scrapping a curveball in 2022. His fastball sits 95-96 mph and touches 97-98 with generic movement and release traits and doesn't miss many bats. Fernandez's low-90s cutter is his bread and butter, and he shows tremendous feel for the pitch by locating in the zone consistently and getting chases with it when he needs them.

His tight gyro slider is thrown at 87-88 mph with high spin rates. Fernandez shows average feel for the entirety of his arsenal.

THE FUTURE: Fernandez is a middle relief candidate for the Cardinals in 2024. As a Rule 5 pick, he will have to stick on the active MLB roster to remain with the organization.

Year	Age	Club	Level	W	L	ERA	G	GS	IP	H	HR	BB	SO	BB%	SO%	WHIP	AVG
2023	25	Salem (CAR)	A	1	0	0.00	2	0	3	1	0	0	6	0.0	60.0	0.30	.100
2023	25	Portland (EL)	AA	2	1	1.77	14	0	20	14	1	8	26	9.9	32.1	1.08	.192
2023	25	Worcester (IL)	AAA	3	3	6.16	26	0	31	38	7	10	35	7.2	25.2	1.57	.302
Minor League Totals				17	10	3.33	128	8	216	197	22	60	252	6.7	28.2	1.19	.238

30 JOSHUA BAEZ, OF

HIT: 30. **POW:** 55. **RUN:** 45. **FLD:** 45. **ARM:** 60. **BA Grade:** 45. **Risk:** Extreme.

Born: June 28, 2003. **B-T:** R-R. **HT:** 6-3. **WT:** 220. **Drafted:** HS—Brookline, MA, 2021 (2nd round).
Signed by: Jim Negrych.

TRACK RECORD: Baez got national recognition as a two-way talent with loud tools including huge raw power and a fastball up to 97 mph. After concerns around his hit tool dropped him out of the first round, the Cardinals swooped in and selected Baez in the second round of the 2021 draft and signed him for $2.25 million. Since that time Baez has struggled to make contact and repeated Low-A in consecutive seasons.

SCOUTING REPORT: Baez's struggles to make consistent contact have plagued him, but he showed signs of improvement in 2023. His swing-and-miss issues are rooted in his difficulty tracking pitches and adjusting his swing to make contact. When Baez does make contact he has the ability to put the ball out to all parts of the field with bat speed and a leveraged swing that has an upward path. Baez's raw power is easily plus—it's just a matter of making enough contact to get to it. Baez's body has backed up as a professional and he's thickened up and slowed down to a fringe-average runner. Baez is also fringe-average in a corner outfield spot though he does boast a plus throwing arm.

THE FUTURE: Baez is a low-average, power-hitting outfielder who needs to improve his plate skills to tap into his impressive natural tools.

Year	Age	Club	Level	AVG	G	AB	R	H	2B	3B	HR	RBI	BB	SO	SB	OBP	SLG
2023	20	Palm Beach (FSL)	A	.218	91	298	54	65	20	4	7	36	45	122	30	.341	.383
Minor League Totals				.219	146	475	87	104	31	6	13	65	75	194	45	.344	.392

San Diego Padres

BY JEFF SANDERS

The Padres entered the 2023 season with World Series aspirations and the third-highest payroll. Instead, it all came crashing down.

The Padres went 82-80 in a nightmare season that was yet another underachieving campaign under president of baseball operations A.J. Preller. Now, the Padres are in for a world of change.

Manager Bob Melvin was allowed to leave for the division-rival Giants after the season despite having a year left on his contract. Preller's marching orders were to trim payroll some $50 million for 2024, leading to outfielder Juan Soto being traded to the Yankees and pitchers Blake Snell, Michael Wacha, Seth Lugo and Nick Martinez all being allowed to hit free agency.

The biggest change of all came when owner and chairman Peter Seidler died in November. Seidler had been in declining health toward the end of the season and passed away shortly after issuing a public statement of support for Preller and Melvin. Seidler was a San Diego icon who changed perceptions of the team and the market with his willingness to spend on par with baseball's marquee franchises.

Shortly after Seidler's death, Preller hired former Cardinals manager Mike Shildt as Melvin's replacement. The hire came as the Padres headed into a critical 2024 season having made the playoffs just twice in nine years under Preller.

"He is familiar with our players, our staff, the minor leagues," Preller said at Shildt's introductory press conference. "We feel really confident this is a team that can win games and play in the playoffs (in 2024). So I think not having to get Mike up to speed on kind of where we're at and what this group is capable of—he knows it, he has seen it firsthand the last couple of years—that was definitely a factor for us."

Shildt, Preller's fourth full-time managerial hire, appears to be on the same page as the front office after spending the last two years working throughout the organization as an adviser. The long-term direction of the franchise, however, is unknown as new chairman Eric Kutsenda, Seidler's friend and business partner, takes control of the team.

Whatever the payroll looks like, the farm system Shildt spent the last two years familiarizing himself with figures to play a larger role in constructing more cost-efficient big league rosters.

Top catching prospect Ethan Salas made his pro debut in full-season ball before his 17th birthday and finished the year at Double-A San Antonio alongside several prospects who zoomed to the Texas League in their first full year of pro ball. That includes BA Minor League Pitcher of the

Luis Campusano missed May and June with a thumb injury but raked when he returned.

THEARON W. HENDERSON/GETTY IMAGES

PROJECTED 2027 LINEUP

Catcher	Ethan Salas	21
First Base	Jake Cronenworth	34
Second Base	Xander Bogaerts	34
Third Base	Manny Machado	35
Shortstop	Jackson Merrill	24
Left Field	Samuel Zavala	23
Center Field	Dillon Head	22
Right Field	Fernando Tatis Jr.	28
Designated Hitter	Luis Campusano	28
No. 1 Starter	Joe Musgrove	34
No. 2 Starter	Robby Snelling	23
No. 3 Starter	Dylan Lesko	24
No. 4 Starter	Drew Thorpe	26
No. 5 Starter	Yu Darvish	41
Closer	Jairo Iriarte	25

Year Robby Snelling, Arizona Fall League MVP Jakob Marsee and breakout prospect Graham Pauley, who led the system with 23 home runs across three levels.

Beyond that group, 2021 first-rounder Jackson Merrill is inching closer to his major league debut, 2022 first-rounder Dylan Lesko reached High-A Fort Wayne in his first year back from Tommy John surgery, and the Padres' international scouting department remains among the game's best.

The Padres have long been heralded for the strength of their farm systems, but that hasn't consistently translated to results in the majors. After nearly a decade, the pressure is on Preller to finally deliver the results long promised. ■

SAN DIEGO PADRES

TOP 2024 CONTRIBUTORS	RANK
1. Drew Thorpe, RHP	5
2. Adam Mazur, RHP	8
3. Jakob Marsee, OF	11

BREAKOUT PROSPECTS	RANK
1. Homer Bush Jr., OF	15
2. Braden Nett, RHP	19
3. Jagger Haynes, LHP	27

SOURCE OF TOP 30 TALENT

Homegrown	27	Acquired	3
College	11	Trade	3
Junior college	0	Rule 5 draft	0
High school	0	Independent league	0
Nondrafted free agent	1	Free agent/waivers	0
International	6		

LF
Samuel Zavala (6)
Jorge Oña
Tyler Robertson

CF
Dillon Head (7)
Jakob Marsee (11)
Homer Bush Jr. (15)
Korry Howell

RF
Tirso Ornelas
Albert Fabian
Joshua Mears

3B
Graham Pauley (10)
Eguy Rosario (16)
Marcos Castañon (26)
Jose Sanabria

SS
Jackson Merrill (2)
Ismael Javier
Jarryd Dale
Kervin Pichardo
Yendry Rojas

2B
Rosman Verdugo
Nerwilian Cedeño
Ripken Reyes

1B
Nathan Martorella (17)
Cole Cummings
Griffin Doersching

C
Ethan Salas (1)
J.D. Gonzalez (14)
Brandon Valenzuela (28)
Lamar King Jr.

LHP

LHSP	LHRP
Robby Snelling (3)	Ray Kerr (23)
Blake Dickerson (21)	Gabriel Morales
Jagger Haynes (27)	
Austin Krob (30)	
Jay Groome	

RHP

RHSP	RHRP
Dylan Lesko (4)	Alek Jacob (25)
Drew Thorpe (5)	Stephen Kolek
Jairo Iriarte (7)	Carter Loewen
Adam Mazur (8)	Kevin Kopps
Randy Vasquez (12)	Moises Lugo
Ryan Bergert (13)	Drew Carlton
Victor Lizarraga (18)	Sean Reynolds
Braden Nett (19)	
Isaiah Lowe (20)	
Kannon Kemp (22)	
Matt Waldron (24)	
Garrett Hawkins (29)	
Jared Kollar	
Gabe Mosser	
Henry Baez	

1 ETHAN SALAS, C

Born: June 1, 2006. **B-T:** L-R. **HT:** 6-2. **WT:** 185.
Signed: Venezuela, 2023.
Signed by: Luis Prieto/Trevor Schumm/Jake Koenig.

TRACK RECORD: The Padres had $5.8 million to spend in the 2023 international signing class and they gave almost all of it—$5.6 million, tops among all international bonuses last year—to Salas. He is a rare five-tool catcher and a third-generation talent from one of his country's best-known baseball families. Salas landed on the Padres' radar while they courted his older brother Jose, who signed with the Marlins for $2.8 million in 2019, and they expected him to move quickly given his bloodlines, familiarity with professional baseball and pure talent. A sore throwing shoulder delayed the start of Salas' pro debut season in 2023, but the Padres still assigned him to Low-A Lake Elsinore in late May while he was still a few days shy of his 17th birthday. A 16-year-old playing in full-season ball is exceedingly rare. The only others in recent history are Adrian Beltre in 1996 and Edgar Renteria in 1993, two players who, it was later learned, were illegally signed at age 15. Salas hit the ground running in the California League, winning the league's player of the month award for July, which played into the Padres' decision to aggressively promote him to High-A Fort Wayne in early August. Salas put up just a .472 OPS in nine games, but the Padres believed in his makeup and skill enough to promote him to Double-A San Antonio well before the Midwest League season ended. The move kept Salas developing alongside the organization's next wave of talent. A knee sprain ended Salas' season after nine games in the Texas League, but he should be ready by spring training.

SCOUTING REPORT: Salas boasts a quick, compact swing and keeps his barrel in the hitting zone for a long time. He doesn't yet have the raw power that Francisco Alvarez or Gary Sanchez showed as prospects, but he was already taking 97 mph fastballs over the wall as a teenager during his pro debut and is easy to project for more over-the-fence pop as he matures. Salas also already shows the ability to make adjustments on the fly. For example, he got back in the zone for a standout July after chasing early in his stay in Lake Elsinore. That's an excellent profile for a corner outfielder, but what makes Salas' potential even greater is that he's an excellent defensive catcher for his age, showcasing soft

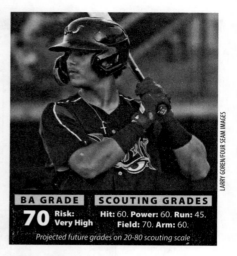

Photo credit: LARRY GOREN/FOUR SEAM IMAGES

BA GRADE	SCOUTING GRADES
70 Risk: Very High	Hit: 60. Power: 60. Run: 45. Field: 70. Arm: 60.

Projected future grades on 20-80 scouting scale

BEST TOOLS

BATTING

Best Hitter for Average	Jackson Merrill
Best Power Hitter	Ethan Salas
Best Strike-Zone Discipline	Jakob Marsee
Fastest Baserunner	Homer Bush Jr.
Best Athlete	Dillon Head

PITCHING

Best Fastball	Jairo Iriarte
Best Curveball	Robby Snelling
Best Slider	Adam Mazur
Best Changeup	Dylan Lesko
Best Control	Drew Thorpe

FIELDING

Best Defensive Catcher	Ethan Salas
Best Defensive Infielder	Jackson Merrill
Best Infield Arm	Eguy Rosario
Best Defensive Outfielder	Dillon Head
Best Outfield Arm	Samuel Zavala

hands, athletic blocking ability and outstanding receiving and exchanges. He also has a slightly above-average arm that should tick up to at least plus with natural strength progression. His arm already plays up because of his efficient transfer and release, leading to pop times under 1.9 seconds on throws to second base. Salas' maturity showed as he emerged as a proactive partner in game-planning with older pitchers after getting his legs under him in pro ball.

THE FUTURE: The Padres' unquestioned catcher of the future—and perhaps sooner than many realize—Salas is a superstar in the making who could one day earn MVP votes, a la Buster Posey, for his ability to impact the game with his bat, defense and leadership skills with a pitching staff. ∎

Year	Age	Club (League)	Level	AVG	G	AB	R	H	2B	3B	HR	RBI	BB	SO	SB	OBP	SLG
2023	17	Lake Elsinore (CAL)	A	.267	48	191	35	51	11	2	9	35	24	57	5	.350	.487
2023	17	Fort Wayne (MWL)	A+	.200	9	35	3	7	1	0	0	3	2	10	0	.243	.229
2023	17	San Antonio (TL)	AA	.179	9	28	2	5	1	0	0	3	4	8	0	.303	.214
Minor League Totals				.246	67	256	40	63	13	2	9	41	32	75	5	.333	.418

2 JACKSON MERRILL, SS

HIT: 60. **POW:** 55. **RUN:** 50. **FLD:** 55. **ARM:** 55. **BA Grade:** 60. **Risk:** High.

Born: April 19, 2003. **B-T:** L-R. **HT:** 6-3. **WT:** 195.
Drafted: HS—Severna Park, MD, 2021 (1st round). **Signed by:** Danny Sader.
TRACK RECORD: The flu and a subsequent stomach bug slowed Merrill to start the 2023 season at High-A Fort Wayne, then a hamstring strain hobbled him late in his time at Double-A San Antonio. The latter injury kept him from the field in the Texas League playoffs. In between, Merrill continued to return surplus value as a below-slot signee as the 27th overall pick in the 2021 draft. He finished the first half strong at Fort Wayne heading into his Futures Game appearance, helping him earn a move to Double-A afterward. The front office even kicked around the idea of bringing Merrill to San Diego as a multi-positional piece for their late-season postseason push before opting to leave him in San Antonio to develop alongside the next talent wave.
SCOUTING REPORT: A growth spurt added nearly 30 pounds to Merrill's frame in the months leading up to the 2021 draft, boosting the raw power that was one of his calling cards. He's since developed advanced offspeed coverage for his age and an impressive left-on-left approach, reasons that many in the organization believe a smooth swing will eventually produce 30 homers annually in the majors. Merrill has also improved his range, agility and arm strength at shortstop since turning pro. Though he's an average runner, his first-step efficiency contributes to his overall profile as a smooth defender. More than that, internal evaluators rave about culture-changing makeup that will be an asset in a big league clubhouse.
THE FUTURE: Merrill continues to show he can stick at shortstop, though his ultimate landing spot likely depends on the big league roster. That decision may come as soon as 2024, because he is poised to make his MLB debut as a 21-year-old. Merrill's athleticism will be an asset wherever he plays, and his bat will ultimately help him profile as a middle-of-the-order threat.

Year	Age	Club (League)	Level	AVG	G	AB	R	H	2B	3B	HR	RBI	BB	SO	SB	OBP	SLG
2023	20	Fort Wayne (MWL)	A+	.280	68	279	50	78	12	2	10	33	17	37	10	.318	.444
2023	20	San Antonio (TL)	AA	.273	46	187	26	51	13	2	5	31	18	25	5	.338	.444
Minor League Totals				.295	200	800	133	236	45	10	21	114	65	133	31	.347	.455

3 ROBBY SNELLING, LHP

FB: 55. **CB:** 60. **SL:** 55. **CHG:** 50. **CTL:** 60. **BA Grade:** 60. **Risk:** High.

Born: December 19, 2003. **B-T:** R-L. **HT:** 6-3. **WT:** 210.
Drafted: HS—Reno, NV 2022 (1st round supplemental). **Signed by:** Tim Reynolds.
TRACK RECORD: The Padres lured Snelling away from a commitment to Louisiana State in 2022 with a $3 million bonus, which was $1 million over slot for the 39th pick. In high school he starred in baseball and was a four-star recruit as a linebacker in football. Snelling was worth every penny. He breezed through 11 starts in his pro debut at Low-A Lake Elsinore with a 1.57 ERA, then made seven starts at High-A Fort Wayne and four more at Double-A San Antonio, including five no-hit innings in his second Texas League start. Snelling's 1.82 ERA was the lowest of any minor league pitcher with at least 100 innings. He finished his first season in pro ball as the BA Minor League Pitcher of the Year.
SCOUTING REPORT: Broad shouldered with a thick, muscular lower half, Snelling shed roughly 10 pounds in the offseason following his draft year to become more whippy with his delivery. A spike-grip, 11-to-5 curveball was one of the better breakers in his prep class, but it has played up because of the way he locates and tunnels it off of a 95-96 mph fastball with ride. His curve velocity ranges from the mid 70s to the mid 80s. Snelling began developing a changeup after the draft and it has some bottom, even if it is a bit firm at 4-5 mph slower than his heater. He also began throwing a tight, above-average slider in 2023, another weapon against lefthanded hitters. Still very much a linebacker on the mound, Snelling is an intense competitor who is unfazed by umpires' questionable calls and the plays that do not go his way, which contributes to his profile as a sum-of-his-parts pitcher.
THE FUTURE: A dominant first season cemented Snelling's floor as at least a No. 3 starter. He should receive an invite to big league spring training and could be on the MLB radar as soon as 2024.

Year	Age	Club (League)	Level	W	L	ERA	G	GS	IP	H	HR	BB	SO	BB%	SO%	WHIP	AVG
2023	19	Lake Elsinore (CAL)	A	5	1	1.57	11	11	52	39	2	13	59	6.5	29.6	1.01	.211
2023	19	Fort Wayne (MWL)	A+	4	2	2.34	7	7	35	31	1	11	40	7.6	27.8	1.21	.237
2023	19	San Antonio (TL)	AA	2	0	1.56	4	4	17	12	1	10	19	13.7	26.0	1.27	.190
Minor League Totals				11	3	1.83	22	22	104	82	4	34	118	8.2	28.4	1.13	.216

4 DYLAN LESKO, RHP

FB: 70. **CB:** 55. **CHG:** 70. **CTL:** 60. **BA Grade:** 60. **Risk:** Extreme.

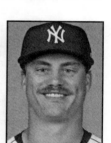

Born: September 7, 2003. **B-T:** R-R. **HT:** 6-2. **WT:** 195.
Drafted: HS—Buford, GA, 2022 (1st round). **Signed by:** Tyler Stubblefield.
TRACK RECORD: Lesko was the 2021 Gatorade National Player of the Year after striking out 112 in 60 innings with a 0.35 ERA as a high school junior. He appeared ticketed for a top-five selection in the 2022 draft before Tommy John surgery ended his senior season months ahead of the draft. The Padres drafted him 15th overall and signed him for $3.9 million and unveiled him in the Arizona Complex League in June 2023. Lesko made four starts in the ACL, five at Low-A Lake Elsinore and three at High-A Fort Wayne, flashing upside at each level of his progression. The highlight was striking out nine over five shutout innings of one-hit ball in his second-to-last start of the season in the Midwest League.
SCOUTING REPORT: As with most Tommy John rehabbers, Lesko's command fluctuated throughout his first year back on the mound. When he was right, he still boasts a four-seamer that touches 98 mph with carry at the top of the zone. Lesko's dastardly low-80s, fading changeup also still grades as a plus-plus pitch and perhaps the best offering of any pitcher in the system. There's power to his 12-to-6 curveball that can push 3,000 rpm, though it's a pitch he will need to refine with the repetition it didn't get as an afterthought in his prep career. Given Lesko's work ethic and aptitude for spinning a baseball, the Padres are optimistic that his curve will continue to improve as he moves further away from Tommy John surgery.
THE FUTURE: Lesko could become a No. 3 starter—and perhaps more—based on his repertoire and assuming his command sharpens as he moves further past surgery. Look for him to start 2024 back at Fort Wayne and catch up with Robby Snelling as the two race toward San Diego.

Year	Age	Club (League)	Level	W	L	ERA	G	GS	IP	H	HR	BB	SO	BB%	SO%	WHIP	AVG
2023	19	ACL Padres	Rk	0	1	10.80	4	4	5	8	1	3	9	12.5	37.5	2.20	.381
2023	19	Lake Elsinore (CAL)	A	0	3	4.50	5	5	16	13	1	8	23	11.8	33.8	1.31	.228
2023	19	Fort Wayne (MWL)	A+	1	1	4.50	3	3	12	8	1	11	20	20.8	37.7	1.58	.190
Minor League Totals				1	5	5.45	12	12	33	29	3	22	52	15.2	35.9	1.55	.242

5 DREW THORPE, RHP

FB: 50. **CB:** 40. **SL:** 50. **CHG:** 70. **CUT:** 40. **CTL:** 60. **BA Grade:** 55. **Risk:** High.

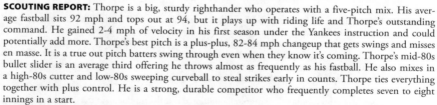

Born: October 1, 2000. **B-T:** L-R. **HT:** 6-4. **WT:** 212.
Drafted: Cal Poly, 2022 (2nd round). **Signed by:** Tyler Robertson (Yankees).
TRACK RECORD: A college standout who starred in both the Cape Cod League and for USA Baseball's Collegiate National team, Thorpe finished second in the nation with 149 strikeouts his junior year at Cal Poly and was drafted by the Yankees in the second round. He worked to gain velocity in their system and continued to rack up whiffs with a dominant pro debut in 2023. Thorpe went 14-2, 2.52 and led the minors with 182 strikeouts as he climbed to Double-A. The Padres acquired him as one of five players in the trade for Juan Soto after the season.
SCOUTING REPORT: Thorpe is a big, sturdy righthander who operates with a five-pitch mix. His average fastball sits 92 mph and tops out at 94, but it plays up with riding life and Thorpe's outstanding command. He gained 2-4 mph of velocity in his first season under the Yankees instruction and could potentially add more. Thorpe's best pitch is a plus-plus, 82-84 mph changeup that gets swings and misses en masse. It is a true out pitch batters swing through even when they know it's coming. Thorpe's mid-80s bullet slider is an average third offering he throws almost as frequently as his fastball. He also mixes in a high-80s cutter and low-80s sweeping curveball to steal strikes early in counts. Thorpe ties everything together with plus control. He is a strong, durable competitor who frequently completes seven to eight innings in a start.
THE FUTURE: Thorpe doesn't light up a radar gun, but he's an accomplished pitcher who knows how to get the most from his stuff. He projects to be a No. 3 or 4 starter and could be more if he continues to add velocity.

Year	Age	Club (League)	Level	W	L	ERA	G	GS	IP	H	HR	BB	SO	BB%	SO%	WHIP	AVG
2023	22	Hudson Valley (SAL)	A+	10	2	2.81	18	18	109	84	10	33	138	7.7	32.4	1.07	.215
2023	22	Somerset (EL)	AA	4	0	1.48	5	5	30	15	3	5	44	4.5	40.0	0.66	.144
Minor League Totals				14	2	2.53	23	23	139	99	13	38	182	7.1	34.0	0.99	.200

6 SAMUEL ZAVALA, OF

HIT: 50. **POW:** 50. **RUN:** 55. **FLD:** 55. **ARM:** 55. **BA Grade:** 55. **Risk:** Very High.

Born: July 15, 2004. **B-T:** L-L. **HT:** 6-1. **WT:** 175.
Signed: Venezuela, 2021. **Signed by:** Luis Prieto/Trevor Schumm/Chris Kemp.
TRACK RECORD: Regarded as one of the best pure hitters in the 2020-21 international class, Zavala signed for $1.2 million and has been pushed aggressively each year in the system. With injuries dogging Zavala early in his career, the Padres challenged him to stay on the field in 2023 and he did just that as a Low-A California League all-star. He finished one home run shy of joining a rare list of teenagers to log 20 doubles, 15 homers and 20 steals in a season. Zavala spiraled after a late promotion to High-A Fort Wayne, though he was playing through an oblique injury at the end of the season.
SCOUTING REPORT: Zavala has been young for the level at every stop, so it's taken time for strength to catch up to natural gifts that include a smooth, whip-like swing. He has a knack for putting the barrel on the ball, though the Padres would like Zavala to continue to add muscle in the hope that he regularly unlocks average power. He does not chase much, but there's a bit of swing-and-miss in the zone, the result of a leg kick that can get big. An above-average runner, Zavala makes up for a lack of closing speed in center field with good reads, a good first step and fluid movement. Above-average arm strength would likely push him to left field if he outgrows center. Bilingual and a heady player, Zavala has also taken well to coaching and the examples of older teammates when it came to finding a routine that allowed him to get his legs under him after a slow start in Lake Elsinore.
THE FUTURE: Still the best true outfield prospect in the system, Zavala should begin his age-19 season back at Fort Wayne, where he'll be one of the younger players in the Midwest League. He could develop into a starting-caliber corner outfielder with across-the-board skills.

Year	Age	Club (League)	Level	AVG	G	AB	R	H	2B	3B	HR	RBI	BB	SO	SB	OBP	SLG
2023	18	Lake Elsinore (CAL)	A	.267	101	348	83	93	22	0	14	71	89	121	20	.420	.451
2023	18	Fort Wayne (MWL)	A+	.078	14	51	4	4	1	0	0	6	5	19	1	.161	.098
Minor League Totals				.263	213	745	161	196	48	9	25	149	149	224	37	.389	.452

7 DILLON HEAD, OF

HIT: 55. **POW:** 40. **RUN:** 70. **FLD:** 60. **ARM:** 55. **BA Grade:** 55. **Risk:** Extreme.

Born: October 11, 2004. **B-T:** L-L. **HT:** 6-0. **WT:** 185.
Drafted: HS—Flossmoor, IL, 2023 (1st round). **Signed by:** Troy Hoerner.
TRACK RECORD: The Padres certainly have an amateur type under general manager A.J. Preller—young, toolsy and plays up the middle. See: Jackson Merrill and James Wood in the 2021 draft, Robert Hassell III in 2020 and CJ Abrams in 2019. Head, the Padres' first-rounder in 2023, fits the bill. He was the best position prospect in Homewood-Flossmoor High history as he hit .485/.568/.814 as a senior while striking out just five times in 118 plate appearances and going 31-for-31 in stolen bases. The Padres signed Head for a slightly-under slot $2.8 million as the 25th overall pick, and he finished his first pro summer at Low-A Lake Elsinore after dominating the Arizona Complex League in 14 games.
SCOUTING REPORT: Blessed with a ton of natural athletic ability, Head has plus-plus speed. The Padres clocked him at 6.3 seconds in the 60-yard dash ahead of the draft. That will serve Head well on the bases as he gets more comfortable reading pitchers, as well as in the outfield, where he has good instincts and solid arm strength. Presently, Head is a gap-to-gap hitter with a hit-it-where-it's-pitched approach that allows him to put the ball in play and showcase his wheels. The lefthanded hitter cut down a high leg kick heading into the draft, improving his timing and balance. His hit tool is well ahead of the power, but the Padres believe Head could develop 15-20 homer power as he fills out a wiry strong frame. He showed strong swing decisions with 15 walks, 19 strikeouts and an elite in-zone chase rate of 7.6%.
THE FUTURE: Head is a good bet to develop into an everyday center fielder and could impact games with menacing speed and surprising pop for a leadoff hitter. He finished his first summer in pro ball in Lake Elsinore and will likely return to the California League to start 2024.

Year	Age	Club (League)	Level	AVG	G	AB	R	H	2B	3B	HR	RBI	BB	SO	SB	OBP	SLG
2023	18	ACL Padres	Rk	.294	14	51	15	15	4	1	1	8	11	9	3	.413	.471
2023	18	Lake Elsinore (CAL)	A	.241	13	54	3	13	1	2	0	3	4	10	1	.311	.333
Minor League Totals				.267	27	105	18	28	5	3	1	11	15	19	4	.363	.400

8 JAIRO IRIARTE, RHP

FB: 60. **SL:** 50. **CHG:** 55. **CTL:** 45. **BA Grade:** 50. **Risk:** High.

Born: December 15, 2001. **B-T:** R-R. **HT:** 6-2. **WT:** 210.
Signed: Venezuela, 2018. **Signed by:** Trevor Schumm/Luis Prieto.

TRACK RECORD: Standing at 6-foot-2 and 160 pounds when he signed for $75,000 in 2018, Iriarte has matured into an imposing figure. The bullpen has long been a fallback option, but shaving nearly two runs off his ERA in his second full year in full-season ball will keep him in the rotation for at least another year. He shined at High-A Fort Wayne and flashed well in spurts in his first taste of Double-A, which included a stint in relief to both manage his workload and see what it looked like as the big league team sorted through bullpen issues over the summer.

SCOUTING REPORT: Iriarte's growth spurt pushed his fastball to 95-97 mph, and there's little doubt that it would touch triple-digits regularly in short bursts. It plays up with carry through the top of the zone and teams with a mid-80s slider to produce silly swings and misses. Iriarte's changeup has late fading action and could be a future plus offering, but it's a bit firm and is clearly the third pitch in a bullpen-ready mix. Averaging more than four walks per nine innings as a pro, Iriarte might have already moved to relief if it weren't for the gains he made in 2023. He's added strength and strengthened his shoulders to better withstand a starter's workload and made tremendous strides in repeating a loose delivery with huge extension. He was in the zone more in Fort Wayne than he was at San Antonio but also pushed his strikeout rate to 40.5% in the Texas League.

THE FUTURE: Iriarte continues to intrigue in the rotation, but the Padres could need him sooner as a reliever as they look to replace high-priced arms over the next couple of seasons. He'll head back to Double-A San Antonio to start the year and could be the first man up when a need arises in the rotation or the bullpen.

Year	Age	Club (League)	Level	W	L	ERA	G	GS	IP	H	HR	BB	SO	BB%	SO%	WHIP	AVG
2023	21	Fort Wayne (MWL)	A+	3	3	3.10	14	14	61	50	2	28	77	10.8	29.7	1.28	.224
2023	21	San Antonio (TL)	AA	0	1	4.30	13	7	29	21	2	17	51	13.5	40.5	1.30	.198
Minor League Totals				8	18	5.03	72	50	247	232	27	114	292	10.4	26.6	1.40	.246

9 ADAM MAZUR, RHP

FB: 55. **CB:** 50. **SL:** 60. **CHG:** 50. **CTL:** 70. **BA Grade:** 50. **Risk:** High.

Born: April 20, 2001. **B-T:** R-R. **HT:** 6-2. **WT:** 180.
Drafted: Iowa, 2022 (2nd round). **Signed by:** Troy Hoerner.

TRACK RECORD: Mazur began moving up draft boards with an impressive stay as an all-star in the Cape Cod League, where he posted a 1.55 ERA and 0.83 WHIP with 34 strikeouts in 29 innings in 2021. He followed up as the Big Ten Conference pitcher of the year in 2022, when the Padres went slightly under slot to sign him for $1.25 million as the 53rd overall pick. Mazur made his professional debut in 2023 in the High-A Midwest League and finished a standout first full year in pro ball in Double-A San Antonio's postseason rotation.

SCOUTING REPORT: Mazur added 10 pounds after signing and could probably still stand to add mass if he's going to withstand a starter's workload. His fastball sits 92-96 mph, and his tight slider has been up to 90 mph in becoming a plus power pitch. Mazur also has a mid-80s changeup with two-seam action and armside life as well as a 12-to-6 curveball that keep hitters off-balance. Both breaking pitches fetch swings and misses in and out of the zone. It all comes together out of a loose, easy delivery with a three-quarters arm slot that adds deception to the total package. Mazur also boasts a double-plus ability to fill up the zone. It's everything you want in a starter. Mazur's stuff figures to play up even more if he falls into a bullpen role, and the Padres experimented with that look a bit after his promotion to San Antonio while managing his workload in his first full year as a pro. Mazur has projection left in his wiry build.

THE FUTURE: The Padres need homegrown options in the upper levels, and Mazur has done nothing but thrive so far in the system. He looks to return to Double-A to build upon last year's innings base and see if he can indeed develop into a midrotation starter.

Year	Age	Club (League)	Level	W	L	ERA	G	GS	IP	H	HR	BB	SO	BB%	SO%	WHIP	AVG
2023	22	Fort Wayne (MWL)	A+	4	1	2.02	12	11	58	50	2	10	47	4.3	20.4	1.03	.227
2023	22	San Antonio (TL)	AA	2	3	4.03	12	7	38	47	3	7	43	4.3	26.2	1.42	.301
Minor League Totals				6	4	2.81	24	18	96	97	5	17	90	4.3	22.8	1.19	.258

10 GRAHAM PAULEY, 3B

HIT: 55. **POW:** 50. **RUN:** 45. **FLD:** 50. **ARM:** 50. **BA Grade:** 50. **Risk:** High.

Born: September 24, 2000. **B-T:** L-R. **HT:** 6-1. **WT:** 200.
Drafted: Duke, 2022 (13th round). **Signed by:** Jake Koenig.
TRACK RECORD: Covid barred Pauley from the field entirely at Duke in 2020, and the backlog of players going to college when the majors shortened the draft limited his playing time his sophomore season. Rather than transferring, Pauley used that as fuel in seizing a starting job as a junior, and the limited exposure may have landed the Padres a steal in the 13th round in 2022. His first summer in pro ball was halted just before the California League playoffs as Pauley returned to Duke to finish his economics degree, but he breezed through three levels in 2023 as the organization's hitter of the year, finishing the regular season in Double-A San Antonio.
SCOUTING REPORT: A slightly open stance allows Pauley to get a longer look at pitches, and his strike-zone discipline is a strength. He also tapped into more power than even the Padres expected. He led the system with 23 home runs, including 16 in 45 games after a promotion to High-A Fort Wayne. He uses a short lefthanded swing with some loft. He made a point of keeping his front shoulder closed in 2023, and the change allowed him to hit lefthanders better than he had at any point in his career. His aptitude for picking out pitches to damage has also improved as a professional. He's an average defender with the ability to move around the diamond. He saw time at third base, second base and both corner outfield spots in 2023. He's athletic and smart enough to steal some bases, but first-step quickness and agility are points of emphasis moving forward in the field. He is a natural leader with an exemplary work ethic, one the Padres highlighted for Pauley's younger teammates to mirror at each of his stops.
THE FUTURE: At first glance, Pauley profiles as a utilityman in the majors, but off-the-charts makeup will allow him to squeeze every ounce out of his ability—and then some.

Year	Age	Club (League)	Level	AVG	G	AB	R	H	2B	3B	HR	RBI	BB	SO	SB	OBP	SLG
2023	22	Lake Elsinore (CAL)	A	.309	62	230	50	71	14	5	4	36	40	40	12	.422	.465
2023	22	Fort Wayne (MWL)	A+	.300	45	170	33	51	8	0	16	46	13	41	8	.358	.629
2023	22	San Antonio (TL)	AA	.321	20	81	15	26	10	0	3	12	7	12	2	.375	.556
Minor League Totals				.302	159	586	121	177	39	6	27	119	81	110	28	.395	.527

11 JAKOB MARSEE, OF

HIT: 55. **POW:** 50. **RUN:** 50. **FLD:** 60. **ARM:** 50. **BA Grade:** 45. **Risk:** Medium.

Born: June 28, 2001. **B-T:** L-L. **HT:** 6-0. **WT:** 180.
Drafted: Central Michigan, 2022 (6th round). **Signed by:** Matt Maloney.
TRACK RECORD: Marsee lettered in baseball, football and basketball at Allen Park (Mich.) High but was not drafted out of high school. He largely went under the radar at Central Michigan while hitting .345/.467/.550 with seven homers and 18 steals in 2022. The Padres went slightly under slot to sign him for $250,000 in the sixth round. Marsee finished his first summer in pro ball as the leadoff hitter for Low-A Lake Elsinore's championship team and remained in that role while moving from High-A Fort Wayne to Double-A San Antonio in 2023. Along the way, Marsee led the system with 46 steals, added power to his profile and continued to flash both tools in the Arizona Fall League.
SCOUTING REPORT: A blue-collar baseball rat, Marsee wears out pitchers with a discerning eye at the plate, plus bat-to-ball skills and the ability to handle velocity. While he entered the system with below-average power, he took a step forward in that department in 2023. The organization asked for an uptick in aggression—picking out pitches to damage—and Marsee hit four homers over his final 12 games at High-A Fort Wayne and three more in 16 games to close the season at Double-A San Antonio. Even better, Marsee accomplished this while walking more than he struck out for a second year in a row. He has average speed but a good baseball IQ has made him the best baserunner in the system. He has an average arm, and a knack for reads and correct first steps makes him a quality defender. Plus makeup also gives Marsee a good chance to outperform his tools.
THE FUTURE: Presently viewed as an extra outfielder, Marsee will have to continue to show that his power uptick is real. He finished 2023 strong at Double-A and will likely return there to start 2024.

Year	Age	Club (League)	Level	AVG	G	AB	R	H	2B	3B	HR	RBI	BB	SO	SB	OBP	SLG
2023	22	Fort Wayne (MWL)	A+	.273	113	400	91	109	16	3	13	41	87	82	41	.413	.425
2023	22	San Antonio (TL)	AA	.286	16	56	12	16	0	0	3	5	11	15	5	.412	.446
Minor League Totals				.268	160	556	134	149	23	5	18	57	128	122	61	.416	.425

12 RANDY VASQUEZ, RHP

FB: 55 **CB:** 60 **CHG:** 50. **CUT:** 50. **CTL:** 45. **BA Grade:** 45. **Risk:** Medium.

Born: November 3, 1998. **B-T:** R-R. **HT:** 6-0. **WT:** 185. **Signed:** Dominican Republic, 2018.
Signed by: Arturo Peña (Yankees).

TRACK RECORD: Vasquez signed with the Yankees in 2018 out of the Dominican Republic and was nearly traded to the Rangers as part of the deal for Joey Gallo. He instead remained in the system as part of a rearranged deal and finished the 2022 season on a high note by throwing the first eight innings of a combined no-hitter that sealed Double-A Somerset's Eastern League championship. Vasquez made his big league debut in 2023 and posted a 2.87 ERA in 37.2 innings while working as a spot starter and long reliever for the Yankees. The Padres acquired him as one of five players for Juan Soto after the season.

SCOUTING REPORT: Vasquez is an athletic righthander who works with a deep arsenal. He throws four-seam, two-seam and cut fastballs that are above-average, has an average changeup and rounds out his arsenal with a plus, sweeping breaking ball that he calls a curveball but moves like a slider. None of his pitches got a large amount of swings and misses, but he generally does a good job of keeping them off the barrel. Vasquez's main goal is to add polish. He needs to be more aggressive in setting hitters up with his fastball so he can use his breaking pitches in advantage counts. He could also stand to move the ball around more. Vasquez walked more than four hitters per nine innings in his big league debut and needs to tighten his control.

THE FUTURE: Vasquez projects to be a No. 5 starter if he reaches his ceiling. At worst, he'll fit on a staff as a bulk reliever or spot starter.

Year	Age	Club (League)	Level	W	L	ERA	G	GS	IP	H	HR	BB	SO	BB%	SO%	WHIP	AVG
2023	24	Scranton/W-B (IL)	AAA	3	8	4.59	17	17	80	78	10	40	96	11.2	26.9	1.47	.257
2023	24	New York (AL)	MLB	2	2	2.87	11	5	38	30	5	18	33	10.8	19.9	1.27	.211
Minor League Totals				18	21	3.41	85	81	388	327	32	159	427	9.6	25.9	1.25	.223
Major League Totals				2	2	2.87	11	5	38	30	5	18	33	10.8	19.9	1.27	.211

13 RYAN BERGERT, RHP

FB: 55. **CB:** 40. **SL:** 55. **CHG:** 45. **CTL:** 50. **BA Grade:** 50. **Risk:** High.

Born: March 8, 2000. **B-T:** R-R. **HT:** 6-1. **WT:** 210. **Drafted:** West Virginia, 2021 (6th round). **Signed by:** Danny Sader.

TRACK RECORD: Bergert mostly pitched in the bullpen as a freshman at West Virginia in 2020 and made just four starts as a sophomore before the coronavirus pandemic canceled the season. He continued to trend upward in the collegiate summer Northwoods League but had Tommy John surgery and missed his junior season. The Padres considered him a second-round talent in 2021 and snagged him in the sixth round, signing him for an above-slot $500,000. Bergert struggled in his first season back from surgery, but he flourished in 2023. He posted a 2.73 ERA over 105.2 innings and finished the year in Double-A San Antonio's playoff rotation.

SCOUTING REPORT: Bergert features a classic four-pitch mix and continues to improve the further he moves away from surgery. His above-average fastball sits between 93-94 mph and touches 97-98 with extreme horizontal break after he lowered his arm slot to take advantage of its natural east-west movement. His sweeping 82-85 mph slider flashes above-average and is his primary secondary pitch. Bergert's 84-87 mph changeup flashes average with late dive but is inconsistent. His 80-83 mph curveball is a below-average pitch he'll occasionally flip in for an early strike. Bergert commands his fastball and moves it around to keep hitters guessing and has average control overall. He rarely allows hard contact in the air and has gotten more consistent in his delivery as he's gained mound time.

THE FUTURE: Bergert keeps trending up and improving every year. He has mid-to-back-of-the-rotation potential as long as he continues in his current direction.

Year	Age	Club (League)	Level	W	L	ERA	G	GS	IP	H	HR	BB	SO	BB%	SO%	WHIP	AVG
2023	23	Fort Wayne (MWL)	A+	5	2	2.63	14	12	62	45	3	28	75	11.0	29.5	1.18	.202
2023	23	San Antonio (TL)	AA	1	2	2.86	9	8	44	32	1	18	51	10.2	28.8	1.14	.206
Minor League Totals				11	14	4.05	54	47	220	204	22	88	269	9.4	28.6	1.33	.242

14 J.D. GONZALEZ, C

HIT: 50. **POW:** 55. **RUN:** 40. **FLD:** 55. **ARM:** 70. **BA Grade:** 50. **Risk:** Extreme.

Born: October 3, 2005. **B-T:** L-R. **HT:** 6-0. **WT:** 182. **Drafted:** HS—Humacao, PR, 2023 (3rd round).
Signed by: Willie Ronda/Cliff Terracuso.

TRACK RECORD: Gonzalez impressed during Perfect Game's WWBA World Championship in the fall of his senior year, but a knee injury limited his exposure in the spring. He regained his draft helium with a strong showing at the draft combine and was selected by the Padres in the third round in 2023. He signed for a below-slot $550,000 to forgo an Indiana State commitment. Gonzalez did not play in an official game after signing, but he stood out in instructional league and briefly played winter ball in Puerto Rico as an 18 year old.

SCOUTING REPORT: Gonzalez is a raw, projectable catcher with a chance to make an impact on both sides of the ball. He makes solid contact with a quick, whippy swing and flashes above-average power. He can get a little pull-happy at times, but he has the foundation to be an average hitter. Though Gonzalez is a below-average runner, he moves well behind the plate and has a chance to be an above-average defender as he improves his footwork. He has tremendous arm speed and plus-plus arm strength that has the potential to shut down running games as he fine-tunes his accuracy.

THE FUTURE: Gonzalez will make his pro debut in the Arizona Complex League in 2024. He projects to be a starting catcher but will require time and patience to fulfill his potential.

Year	Age	Club (League)	Level	AVG	G	AB	R	H	2B	3B	HR	RBI	BB	SO	SB	OBP	SLG
2023	17	Did not play															

15 HOMER BUSH JR., OF

HIT: 50. **POW:** 40. **RUN:** 80. **FLD:** 55. **ARM:** 45. **BA Grade:** 45. **Risk:** High.

Born: October 13, 2001. **B-T:** R-R. **HT:** 6-3. **WT:** 200. **Drafted:** Grand Canyon, 2023 (4th round). **Signed by:** Will Scott.

TRACK RECORD: The son of former Padres prospect and longtime major leaguer Homer Bush, the younger Bush was limited by a hamstring injury in high school and the coronavirus pandemic in college at Grand Canyon. With scouts flocking to see GCU shortstop and eventual first-round pick Jacob Wilson, Bush hit .370/.478/.500 while showing the elite athleticism to become a top draft prospect himself. The Padres drafted him in the fourth round and signed him for $511,600. Bush moved quickly in his pro debut and finished the year on Double-A San Antonio's postseason roster.

SCOUTING REPORT: Bush is an 80-grade runner whose game revolves around his legs. He puts balls in play with a quick, level swing and uses his legs to beat out grounders and stretch singles into doubles. The Padres have asked him to improve his bunting to give him another weapon. Bush has a good sense of the strike zone and walked nearly as often as he struck out after being drafted. He hit just four home runs in three years in college, but the Padres believe he could reach double-digit home runs as he learns to backspin balls. Bush's defense in center field is raw, but his speed allows him to outrun his mistakes and gives him a chance to be an above-average center fielder. He has exceptional makeup that provides optimism he'll get the most from his abilities.

THE FUTURE: Bush has the potential to challenge for an everyday job as the Padres center fielder. He'll open 2024 back at Double-A.

Year	Age	Club (League)	Level	AVG	G	AB	R	H	2B	3B	HR	RBI	BB	SO	SB	OBP	SLG
2023	21	ACL Padres	Rk	.409	12	44	16	18	3	0	2	4	7	7	10	.509	.614
2023	21	Lake Elsinore (CAL)	A	.247	24	85	16	21	5	0	1	10	12	15	11	.369	.341
2023	21	San Antonio (TL)	AA	.429	8	28	2	12	1	0	0	3	1	2	1	.448	.464
Minor League Totals				.325	44	157	34	51	9	0	3	17	20	24	22	.422	.439

16 EGUY ROSARIO, 2B/3B

HIT: 45. **POW:** 45. **RUN:** 55. **FLD:** 50. **ARM:** 60. **BA Grade:** 40. **Risk:** Medium.

Born: August 25, 1999. **B-T:** R-R. **HT:** 5-9. **WT:** 204. **Signed:** Dominican Republic, 2015. **Signed by:** Felix Felix/Trevor Schumm/Chris Kemp.

TRACK RECORD: Rosario signed with the Padres for $300,000 on his 16th birthday and was among the youngest players in his league every year. He was overmatched early but broke out in Double-A and was added to the Padres' 40-man roster after the 2021 season. Rosario made his major league debut in 2022 and was primed to contend for a 2023 Opening Day roster spot before he fractured his ankle training in the Dominican Republic. He returned to the majors in September and became the Padres' primary third baseman while Manny Machado battled tennis elbow down the stretch.

SCOUTING REPORT: Rosario is built like a fire hydrant at 5-foot-9, 204 pounds but is surprisingly twitchy and athletic despite his stocky build. He has a short, quick righthanded swing that shoots balls from gap to gap when his approach is locked into the middle of the field. Rosario gets too big in his swing at times, but he makes enough contact to be a fringy hitter with double-digit home run production. He is an above-average runner who has improved his ability to put that speed to use on the bases. Rosario is playable at shortstop, but his range and actions fit better at second base and third base. His plus arm is the best among infielders in the Padres' system.

THE FUTURE: Rosario projects to be a reserve utilityman who can play around the infield. He'll contend for an Opening Day roster spot in 2024.

Year	Age	Club (League)	Level	AVG	G	AB	R	H	2B	3B	HR	RBI	BB	SO	SB	OBP	SLG
2023	23	ACL Padres	Rk	.714	2	7	3	5	2	0	1	4	1	1	0	.750	1.429
2023	23	El Paso (PCL)	AAA	.265	43	166	24	44	9	1	5	28	20	39	4	.348	.422
2023	23	San Diego (NL)	MLB	.250	11	36	6	9	1	1	2	6	1	12	0	.270	.500
Minor League Totals				.274	689	2615	408	717	172	27	58	364	275	617	141	.349	.427
Major League Totals				.244	18	41	6	10	1	1	2	6	2	14	0	.279	.463

17 NATHAN MARTORELLA, 1B

HIT: 45. **POW:** 50. **RUN:** 20. **FLD:** 40. **ARM:** 50. **BA Grade:** 45. **Risk:** High.

Born: February 18, 2001. **B-T:** L-L. **HT:** 6-1. **WT:** 224. **Drafted:** California, 2022 (5th round). **Signed by:** Tim Reynolds.
TRACK RECORD: An unsigned 30th-round pick of the Red Sox out of high school, Martorella became a three-year starter at California and posted a .430 on-base percentage with Cotuit in the Cape Cod League. He hit a career-best .333 with 11 home runs and a .977 OPS as a junior, leading the Padres to draft him in the fifth round and sign him for $325,000. After an impressive pro debut, Martorella climbed to Double-A in his first full season in 2023. He finished tied for second in the Padres' system with 19 home runs and went to the Arizona Fall League after the season.
SCOUTING REPORT: A physical lefthanded hitter who gets into a low crouch similar to former Padres slugger Phil Plantier, Martorella will go as far as his bat takes him. He is an all-fields masher who overpowers balls with his brute strength and has average power. Martorella's bat speed is merely average and his swing path can be flat, but he manages the strike zone well enough to hold his own against advanced pitching. Martorella is a 20-grade runner who has to improve defensively. He is a below-average defender at first base and left field with slow reaction times. He has an exceptional makeup and work ethic that should allow him to improve.
THE FUTURE: Martorella's lack of athleticism limits his ceiling, but his bat gives him a path to the majors as a power-hitting reserve. He'll open 2024 back at Double-A.

Year	Age	Club (League)	Level	AVG	G	AB	R	H	2B	3B	HR	RBI	BB	SO	SB	OBP	SLG
2023	22	Fort Wayne (MWL)	A+	.259	112	398	71	103	26	1	16	73	73	87	5	.371	.450
2023	22	San Antonio (TL)	AA	.236	23	89	12	21	4	0	3	15	9	14	0	.313	.382
Minor League Totals				.265	163	577	97	153	38	1	22	109	98	122	5	.370	.449

18 VICTOR LIZARRAGA, RHP

FB: 55. **CB:** 55. **CHG:** 50. **CTL:** 50. **BA Grade:** 45. **Risk:** High.

Born: November 30, 2003. **B-T:** R-R. **HT:** 6-3. **WT:** 180. **Signed:** Mexico, 2021.
Signed by: Bill McLaughlin/Emmanuel Rangel/Trevor Schumm/Chris Kemp.
TRACK RECORD: Lizarraga ranked as Mexico's best pitching prospect in the 2021 international class and signed with the Padres for $1 million. Highly advanced for his age, he jumped straight to the Arizona Complex League at 17 years old and started a California League playoff game at 18. Lizarraga hit his first speed bump at High-A Fort Wayne in 2023 as the Midwest League's youngest player on Opening Day. He had a 5.02 ERA through early August but adjusted to hold opponents scoreless in three of his final four starts.
SCOUTING REPORT: Lizarraga boasts a long, lean, athletic 6-foot-3 frame and is a good bet to add strength and velocity as he gets older. His fastball presently sits between 90-94 mph and projects to be an above-average pitch when he is fully mature. His best secondary offering is an upper-70s curveball that projects to be an out pitch. He rounds out his arsenal with a hard, fading changeup that flashes average but doesn't have enough separation from his fastball at times. None of Lizarraga's pitches projects to be a plus offering, but he reads swings well and is a good competitor who outlasts opposing hitters. He has average control and should gain body control as he gets stronger.
THE FUTURE: Lizarraga's stuff has to tick up for him to be more than a long reliever, but he's young and has plenty of time to get stronger. He is bound for Double-A as a 20 year old.

Year	Age	Club (League)	Level	W	L	ERA	G	GS	IP	H	HR	BB	SO	BB%	SO%	WHIP	AVG
2023	19	Fort Wayne (MWL)	A+	4	7	4.09	21	21	95	85	5	34	78	8.4	19.2	1.26	.237
Minor League Totals				12	14	3.95	52	51	219	197	15	83	208	8.8	22.0	1.28	.238

19 BRADEN NETT, RHP

FB: 65. **SL:** 55. **CHG:** 40. **CTL:** 40. **BA Grade:** 50. **Risk:** Extreme.

Born: June 18, 2002. **B-T:** R-R. **HT:** 6-3. **WT:** 185. **Signed:** St. Charles (MO) JC, 2022 (NDFA).
Signed by: Kurt Kemp/Chris Kemlo.

TRACK RECORD: Post-pandemic, the Padres have prized themselves on adding to smaller draft classes with undrafted free agents. Nett is quickly becoming the best of the bunch. Nett did not pitch in college, recorded just two outs in the Appalachian League and posted a 6.48 ERA in the MLB Draft League, but the Padres saw enough raw stuff to sign him for $10,000 after the 2022 draft. Shoulder weakness limited Nett's first pro summer and he was inconsistent in the complex league and Low-A Lake Elsinore in 2023, but his command took a leap forward in the Arizona Fall League. He emerged as one of the AFL's breakout prospects, was selected for the Fall Stars Game and started the league's championship game.
SCOUTING REPORT: Nett is a wiry, 6-foot-3 righthander with a fresh, emerging arm. His fastball sits between 94-96 mph and touches 98 with late explosion and carry at the top of the strike zone. It's a border-line plus-plus pitch he can blow by hitters. Nett's best secondary offering is sweepy breaking ball with tight spin and good shape that projects to be an above-average pitch, although it's inconsistent. He also flashes a below-average, rarely used changeup that is a bit firm in the low 90s. Nett's effectiveness comes down to control. He jumps forward in an effortful delivery and is prone to losing his hat. His stuff plays with even below-average control, but it is often worse than that.
THE FUTURE: Nett projects to be a hard-throwing reliever if he can throw enough strikes. He'll see High-A Fort Wayne in 2024.

Year	Age	Club (League)	Level	W	L	ERA	G	GS	IP	H	HR	BB	SO	BB%	SO%	WHIP	AVG
2023	21	ACL Padres	Rk	1	2	4.28	11	9	27	17	0	25	32	20.7	26.4	1.54	.187
2023	21	Lake Elsinore (CAL)	A	1	0	4.85	3	2	13	11	0	12	13	19.0	20.6	1.77	.220
Minor League Totals				2	2	4.36	17	11	43	30	0	39	50	19.6	25.1	1.59	.192

20 ISAIAH LOWE, RHP

FB: 65. **SL:** 55. **CHG:** 50. **CTL:** 50. **BA Grade:** 50. **Risk:** Extreme.

Born: May 7, 2003. **B-T:** R-R. **HT:** 6-1. **WT:** 220. **Drafted:** HS—Lincolnton, NC, 2022 (11th round).
Signed by: Jake Koenig.

TRACK RECORD: The Padres considered taking Lowe as early as the fourth or fifth round in 2022 and believe they netted a steal when they grabbed him in the 11th round and signed him for an over-slot bonus of $400,000. Lowe made his pro debut at Low-A Lake Elsinore in 2023 and impressed in three starts before shoulder fatigue forced him to the injured list. He tried to come back in August and during instructional league after the season, but both times had to shelve his comeback due to shoulder setbacks.
SCOUTING REPORT: Lowe is a strong, physical 6-foot-1 righthander with a sturdy lower half. His fastball sits between 93-95 mph and reaches 97 with carry at the top of the zone out of a three-quarters arm slot. He generates excellent extension in his delivery to help his fastball jump on batters faster than they expect. Lowe's best secondary offering is a sweepy slider that he lands for strikes and projects to be an above-average pitch. He also has a firm but deceptive changeup that flashes average. Lowe has demonstrated a good feel for pitching despite his lack of mound time and throws strikes with average control.
THE FUTURE: Lowe profiles as a back-end starter or a middle reliever if he can stay healthy. He's avoided surgery so far and is expected to be ready for 2024 Opening Day.

Year	Age	Club (League)	Level	W	L	ERA	G	GS	IP	H	HR	BB	SO	BB%	SO%	WHIP	AVG
2023	20	ACL Padres	Rk	0	0	9.00	1	1	1	1	0	1	1	20.0	20.0	2.00	.250
2023	20	Lake Elsinore (CAL)	A	0	1	1.59	3	3	11	9	1	4	17	8.2	34.7	1.15	.205
Minor League Totals				0	1	2.25	4	4	12	10	1	5	18	9.3	33.3	1.25	.208

21 BLAKE DICKERSON, LHP

FB: 55. **SL:** 55. **CHG:** 40. **CTL:** 50. **BA Grade:** 50. **Risk:** Extreme.

Born: January 7, 2005 **B-T:** L-L. **HT:** 6-6. **WT:** 210. **Drafted:** HS—Virginia Beach, 2023 (12th round).
Signed by: Danny Sader.

TRACK RECORD: Dickerson struggled with his control while pitching for USA Baseball's 18U National team but took a star turn at the WWBA World Championships in the fall. He fell in the draft due to a strong commitment to Virginia Tech, but the Padres were confident they could sign him and selected him in the 12th round. They signed him for a $500,000 bonus—equivalent to fourth-round money—and sent him out for his first game action in instructional league.

SCOUTING REPORT: Dickerson is a lean, projectable 6-foot-6 lefthander His fastball sits between 89-91 mph and is too straight, but he projects to add a lot of velocity as he adds strength. His best secondary pitch is a 79-83 mph slider with late bite that projects to be above-average as he fills out and adds power. He also has a below-average, mid-80s changeup that he rarely throws and needs to refine. Despite his size and long levers, Dickerson moves well through an easy delivery and shows fast arm speed out of a three-quarters slot. He has a good feel for pitching and throws strikes with average control, although he deals with bouts of inconsistency.
THE FUTURE: Dickerson has a chance to jump straight to Low-A Lake Elsinore for his pro debut in 2023. He projects to be a No. 4 or 5 starter who has a fallback as a middle reliever if his changeup doesn't develop.

Year	Age	Club (League)	Level	W	L	ERA	G	GS	IP	H	HR	BB	SO	BB%	SO%	WHIP	AVG
2023	18	Did not play															

22 KANNON KEMP, RHP

FB: 65. **SL:** 45. **CHG:** 40. **CTL:** 55. **BA Grade:** 50. **Risk:** Extreme.

Born: September 3, 2004. **B-T:** R-R. **HT:** 6-6. **WT:** 225. **Drafted:** HS—Weatherford, TX, 2023 (8th round).
Signed by: Matt Schaffner.
TRACK RECORD: A late-bloomer on the mound, Kemp didn't start pitching until eighth grade and was a reliever his sophomore year at Weatherford (Texas) High. He blossomed into a top pitching prospect as an upperclassman and was committed to Oklahoma before the Padres drafted him in the eighth round and signed him for $625,000, nearly triple the recommended slot amount. Kemp didn't pitch in an official game after signing but began throwing at the Padres' complex during instructional league.
SCOUTING REPORT: Large and physical at 6-foot-6, 225 pounds, Kemp sat 88-92 mph in high school but had already began pushing his 94-96 mph after getting on a throwing program with the Padres. It projects to be a borderline plus-plus pitch as he continues to mature. Kemp's secondaries are still raw. He has the makings of a high-spin slider that sits 78-82 mph and he flashes a good feel for a mid-80s changeup with two-seam action, but both are fringy to below-average pitches that need improvement. Despite his size, Kemp has a compact delivery and fast arm speed out a three-quarters slot. He fills up the strike zone with above-average control and shows the ability to manipulate and cut his fastball.
THE FUTURE: Kemp is on track to make his pro debut at Low-A Lake Elsinore in 2024. He projects to be a No. 4 starter with continued velocity gains and secondary development.

Year	Age	Club (League)	Level	W	L	ERA	G	GS	IP	H	HR	BB	SO	BB%	SO%	WHIP	AVG
2023	18	Did not play															

23 RAY KERR, LHP

FB: 65. **CB:** 55. **CHG:** 45. **CTL:** 45. **BA Grade:** 40. **Risk:** Medium.

Born: September 10, 1994. **B-T:** L-L. **HT:** 6-3. **WT:** 185. **Signed:** Lassen (CA) JC, 2017 (NDFA).
Signed by: Jordan Bley (Mariners).
TRACK RECORD: Kerr pitched Lassen (Calif.) JC to the verge of a conference title in 2017 and followed with a star turn in the Alaska Baseball League. The Mariners signed him for $5,000 as an undrafted free agent and dabbled with him as a starter before making him a full-time reliever. The Padres acquired Kerr in the deal that sent Adam Frazier to the Mariners and have called up him several times over the last two years. He had his best season in 2023, when his strikeout rate jumped from 14.3% to 30.7% and his walk rate shriveled from 19.1% to 7.9%.
SCOUTING REPORT: Moving to relief made Kerr one of the hardest-throwing lefthanders in the minors. His fastball averages 97 mph and can touch triple-digits out a low arm slot. His fastball gets on batters quicker than they expect out of his low-effort delivery, resulting in late swings and misses. Kerr backs up his fastball with an above-average, bendy curveball in the low-80s that has emerged as his best swing-and-miss pitch. He also has a fringy, firm, seldom-used changeup in the low-90s. Kerr has fringy control and struggles to throw strikes at times, but his stuff is good enough to get outs even when he misses his spots.
THE FUTURE: Kerr will get every opportunity to seize a middle relief job in 2024. He has the stuff to pitch in high-leverage situations.

Year	Age	Club (League)	Level	W	L	ERA	G	GS	IP	H	HR	BB	SO	BB%	SO%	WHIP	AVG
2023	28	El Paso (PCL)	AAA	6	0	2.25	36	0	36	24	2	17	42	11.7	29.0	1.14	.189
2023	28	San Diego (NL)	MLB	1	1	4.33	22	0	27	25	5	9	35	7.9	30.7	1.26	.243
Minor League Totals				22	19	3.88	180	36	324	297	23	163	367	11.6	26.0	1.42	.242
Major League Totals				1	1	4.33	22	0	27	25	5	9	35	7.9	30.7	1.26	.243

24 MATT WALDRON, RHP

FB: 45. **SL:** 45. **CUT:** 40. **KNUCKLE:** 55. **CTL:** 45. **BA Grade:** 40. **Risk:** Medium.

Born: September 26, 1997. **B-T:** R-R. **HT:** 6-2. **WT:** 185. **Drafted:** Nebraska, 2019 (18th round).
Signed by: Kyle Bamberger (Guardians).
TRACK RECORD: Waldron spent four years in Nebraska's rotation and signed with the Guardians for just $5,000 after they made him an 18th-round pick in 2019. The Padres acquired him the following year in the deal that brought Mike Clevinger to San Diego. Waldron began to set himself apart by toying with a knuckleball the following spring and became a full-fledged knuckleballer during the season. His confidence in the pitch wavered in the hitter-friendly Pacific Coast League, but he overcame it to make his big league debut in 2023 and finished the year in the Padres rotation.
SCOUTING REPORT: Waldron's repertoire is rather nondescript aside from his knuckleball. His fringy fastball sits 91-93 mph with sink, his soft slider is a fringy offering at 79-81 mph and his mid-80s cutter doesn't fool big leaguers. Waldron's knuckleball, however, gives him a chance to stand out. He throws it harder than most traditional knuckleballs at 75-78 mph and it consistently fools hitters. He had his most success in the majors when he increased his usage of the pitch and is particularly effective against younger hitters, many of whom have never seen a knuckleball. He is still working to control his knuckler but throws enough strikes with fringe-average control.
THE FUTURE: Waldron projects to be a long reliever or spot starter used to mess with hitters' timing. He'll head into 2024 in contention for an Opening Day roster spot.

Year	Age	Club (League)	Level	W	L	ERA	G	GS	IP	H	HR	BB	SO	BB%	SO%	WHIP	AVG
2023	26	El Paso (PCL)	AAA	2	10	7.31	20	18	92	118	18	30	99	7.2	23.8	1.60	.313
2023	26	San Diego (NL)	MLB	1	3	4.35	8	6	41	39	9	12	31	6.9	17.9	1.23	.244
Minor League Totals				14	28	5.52	79	64	355	388	43	108	355	7.0	23.0	1.40	.274
Major League Totals				1	3	4.35	8	6	41	39	9	12	31	6.9	17.9	1.23	.244

25 ALEK JACOB, RHP

FB: 30. **SL:** 50. **CHG:** 70. **CTL:** 70. **BA Grade:** 40. **Risk:** Medium.

Born: June 16, 1998. **B-T:** L-R. **HT:** 6-3. **WT:** 190. **Drafted:** Gonzaga, 2021 (16th round). **Signed by:** Justin Baughman.
TRACK RECORD: Jacob threw just 84-88 mph at Gonzaga but was watched closely by the Padres because their analytics staff identified his changeup as a potential outlier. He threw a no-hitter against Pepperdine and a shutout against Louisiana State in the NCAA Tournament as a senior to convince skeptical evaluators. The Padres drafted him in the 16th round and signed him for $75,000. Jacob continued to confound hitters at every level of the minors and received his first big league callup in July, He made three scoreless appearances before he suffered a season-ending flexor and ulnar collateral ligament strain.
SCOUTING REPORT: Jacob is a throwback reliever who succeeds on deception. His fastball sits 85-87 mph with late sink out of a whippy, sidearm slot. His fastball plays up because it pairs well with his plus-plus, 70-74 mph changeup with heavy fade and sink. He hides the ball well and sells his changeup to make it difficult for hitters to recognize pitches out of his hand. Jacob also has an average, sweeping slider in the low 70s that he commands well. He varies his delivery and attacks the zone with the confidence of someone who throws much harder.
THE FUTURE: Jacob will get every opportunity to win a middle-relief job in spring training if he's healthy. He earns frequent comparisons to former Padres reliever Adam Cimber.

Year	Age	Club (League)	Level	W	L	ERA	G	GS	IP	H	HR	BB	SO	BB%	SO%	WHIP	AVG
2023	25	San Antonio (TL)	AA	1	0	1.32	18	0	27	19	1	8	32	7.3	29.4	0.99	.192
2023	25	San Diego (NL)	MLB	0	0	0.00	3	0	3	0	0	1	5	10.0	50.0	0.33	.000
Minor League Totals				8	1	1.82	74	1	104	82	6	25	138	6.0	32.9	1.03	.212
Major League Totals				0	0	0.00	3	0	3	0	0	1	5	10.0	50.0	0.33	.000

26 MARCOS CASTAÑON, 3B/2B

HIT: 50. **POW:** 45. **RUN:** 30. **FLD:** 30. **ARM:** 40. **BA Grade:** 40. **Risk:** High.

Born: March 23, 1999. **B-T:** R-R. **HT:** 6-0. **WT:** 195. **Drafted:** UC Santa Barbara, 2021 (12th round).
Signed by: Josh Emmerick.
TRACK RECORD: Castañon has been an overachiever since his time in high school, where he frequently outperformed higher profile players in Southern California. He left Carter High in Rialto as the career hits leader and hit .404/.492/.716 his final year at UC Santa Barbara despite missing nearly two months with a broken hand. He signed for $125,000 as a 12th-round pick, was a California League all-star in 2022 and finished second in the system in hits (142) and total bases (234) as he rose to Double-A in 2023.

SCOUTING REPORT: Strong at a sturdy 6 feet, 195 pounds, Castañon has solid bat speed and natural timing, controls the strike zone and has a keen ability to put the barrel on the ball. He uses the big part of the field well and has begun tapping into more power with a swing adjustment that keeps him from pulling off of pitches. Castañon is a smart baserunner, but he has a thick lower half and well below-average speed. He's a well below-average defender who lacks the range for second base or the arm strength for third base and will have to find a position. Castañon's athleticism is lacking, but he's scrappy and has always hit.
THE FUTURE: Castañon has a chance to develop into at least a platoon hitter who crushes lefties. He should see Triple-A El Paso in 2024.

Year	Age	Club (League)	Level	AVG	G	AB	R	H	2B	3B	HR	RBI	BB	SO	SB	OBP	SLG
2023	24	Fort Wayne (MWL)	A+	.287	77	289	47	83	20	0	13	58	29	70	1	.352	.491
2023	24	San Antonio (TL)	AA	.280	54	211	24	59	19	1	4	26	18	49	0	.335	.436
Minor League Totals				.266	266	972	157	259	68	1	42	181	129	257	1	.361	.468

27 JAGGER HAYNES, LHP
FB: 55. **CB:** 50. **CHG:** 50. **CTL:** 45. **BA Grade:** 45. **Risk:** Extreme.

Born: September 20, 2002. **B-T:** L-L. **HT:** 6-3. **WT:** 170. **Drafted:** HS—Cerro Gordo, NC, 2020 (5th round).
Signed by: Jake Koenig.
TRACK RECORD: Haynes played just one game his senior year due to the coronavirus pandemic, but then-Padres minor leaguer Seth Frankoff worked out with Haynes during the shutdown and recommended him to the club. The Padres drafted Haynes in the fifth round in 2020 and signed him for an above-slot $300,000. Haynes has struggled to stay healthy since signing. He had Tommy John surgery that delayed his pro debut until 2023 and pitched only 25.1 innings at Low-A Lake Elsinore while being hampered by blisters. He was scheduled to pitch in the Arizona Fall League after the season but was shut down with a balky shoulder.
SCOUTING REPORT: A tall, lanky lefthander, Haynes got stronger during his Tommy John rehab and saw his fastball velocity jump. His fastball sits 92-95, up from 87-91 mph in high school, and projects to be an above-average pitch as he gets stronger. His slurvy, 83-86 mph curveball flashes average, and he effectively sells his average, mid-80s changeup with fade. Haynes is a good athlete with a repeatable delivery and projects to have fringe-average control.
THE FUTURE: Haynes is talented but has to stay healthy to fulfill his back-of-the-rotation potential. He'll move to High-A Fort Wayne in 2024.

Year	Age	Club (League)	Level	W	L	ERA	G	GS	IP	H	HR	BB	SO	BB%	SO%	WHIP	AVG
2023	20	Lake Elsinore (CAL)	A	0	3	3.91	11	11	25	22	2	12	29	11.0	26.6	1.34	.234
Minor League Totals				0	3	3.96	11	11	25	22	2	12	29	11.0	26.6	1.36	.234

28 BRANDON VALENZUELA, C
HIT: 45. **POW:** 30. **RUN:** 30. **FLD:** 60. **ARM:** 55. **BA Grade:** 40. **Risk:** High.

Born: October 2, 2000. **B-T:** B-R. **HT:** 6-0. **WT:** 225. **Signed:** Mexico, 2017.
Signed by: Bill McLaughlin/Trevor Schumm/Chris Kemp.
TRACK RECORD: Valenzuela enjoyed a growth spurt after the Padres purchased his rights from the Mexican League's Mexico City franchise for $100,000. He rose quickly up the minors but regressed across the board in 2022, leading him to buy into the organization's wishes for him to improve his conditioning. Valenzuela arrived at 2023 spring training with 12 pounds and 4-5% of body fat shaved off his frame and had a bounceback season. He hit his way to Double-A San Antonio before having season-ending surgery on his MCL in his left knee in August.
SCOUTING REPORT: Valenzuela is a thick, physical catcher who looks the part of a big league backstop. A switch-hitter, Valenzuela doesn't possess great bat speed but knows the strike zone and which pitches to attack. He sprays line drives all over the field with a short, sound swing from both sides and has developed a newfound aggressiveness that allows him to do damage. Valenzuela is a highly advanced catcher who stands head and shoulders above his peer group in his ability to call a game, learn hitters' tendencies and manage a pitching staff. He has an above-average arm and is a plus receiver and blocker, especially with a better body helping to improve his agility.
THE FUTURE: Valenzuela is set to return in 2024. He projects to be a dependable backup catcher.

Year	Age	Club (League)	Level	AVG	G	AB	R	H	2B	3B	HR	RBI	BB	SO	SB	OBP	SLG
2023	22	Fort Wayne (MWL)	A+	.279	39	136	22	38	10	1	4	15	17	37	0	.372	.456
2023	22	San Antonio (TL)	AA	.181	27	94	10	17	4	0	1	6	13	29	2	.287	.255
Minor League Totals				.252	358	1296	180	326	61	9	23	184	225	352	8	.366	.366

29 GARRETT HAWKINS, RHP

FB: 60. **SL:** 45. **CHG:** 50. **CTL:** 55. **BA Grade:** 45. **Risk:** Extreme.

Born: February 10, 2000. **B-T:** R-R. **HT:** 6-5. **WT:** 230. **Drafted:** British Columbia, 2021 (9th round).
Signed by: Chris Kemlo.

TRACK RECORD: A 6-foot-5, 230-pound Saskatchewan native, Hawkins saw his junior season at British Columbia wiped out by Canada's Covid-19 protocols. He impressed with a 2.63 ERA in six starts in the MLB Draft League and was drafted by the Padres in the ninth round, signing for a below-slot $75,000. Hawkins showed loud stuff in his first full seasons and was viewed as a potential breakout candidate in 2023. He made only four starts before suffering a season-ending elbow injury that required Tommy John surgery in August.

SCOUTING REPORT: Hawkins is a tall righthander with incredibly long arms and gets significant extension down the mound. His high-spin fastball sits 93-96 mph and gets on hitters faster than they expect thanks to his extension. He generates impressive carry with his ability to backspin the ball and gets swings and misses with his heater in all quadrants of the strike zone. Hawkins' secondaries are much more raw. His best secondary pitch is an 82-84 split-changeup that flashes average but is inconsistent. His downward-breaking, 81-84 mph slider is a fringy offering that gets slurvy. Hawkins throws his fastball for strikes with above-average control and has slowly improved his walk rate. He has a durable frame and showed the ability to log innings before getting hurt.

THE FUTURE: Hawkins will miss all of 2024 recovering. He projects to be a middle reliever who dominates with his fastball.

Year	Age	Club (League)	Level	W	L	ERA	G	GS	IP	H	HR	BB	SO	BB%	SO%	WHIP	AVG
2023	23	Fort Wayne (MWL)	A+	0	2	3.60	4	4	15	17	2	6	15	8.8	22.1	1.53	.283
Minor League Totals				8	11	4.32	32	25	123	127	18	38	162	7.2	30.6	1.34	.262

30 AUSTIN KROB, LHP

FB: 50. **SL:** 45. **CHG:** 45. **CTL:** 50. **BA Grade:** 40. **Risk:** High.

Born: September 20, 1999. **B-T:** L-L. **HT:** 6-3. **WT:** 205. **Drafted:** Texas Christian, 2022 (12th round).
Signed by: Matt Schaffner.

TRACK RECORD: Lightly recruited out of high school, Krob pitched mostly out of the bullpen in his one season at Kirkwood (Iowa) JC and his first year at Texas Christian. He moved into the Horned Frogs' rotation as a junior and impressed before falling back as a senior. The Padres saw enough to draft him in the 12th round and sign him for $125,000. Krob got back on track in his first full professional season and cruised to a 2.72 ERA in 22 appearances (21 starts) across the Class A levels. He joined Double-A San Antonio's bullpen for the Texas League playoffs.

SCOUTING REPORT: Krob is a crafty lefthander who keeps hitters off-balance with his ability to mix and match. His two-seam fastball sits 91-92 mph and touches 95 with natural sink to induce a heavy dose of grounders. His low-80s slider is fringy but effective against lefties and his straight, 84-88 mph is fringy but plays against righthanders. Krob has an easy, simple delivery and effectively moves the ball around the strike zone. Almost everything to lefties is either in or on their hands. Krob has a solid feel for pitching and thrives under pressure. His control is average and improving.

THE FUTURE: Krob is already 24 years old and doesn't have much room for growth. He projects to be a swingman or mop-up reliever who is particularly effective against lefties.

Year	Age	Club (League)	Level	W	L	ERA	G	GS	IP	H	HR	BB	SO	BB%	SO%	WHIP	AVG
2023	23	Lake Elsinore (CAL)	A	0	1	2.34	11	10	50	46	1	22	59	10.2	27.3	1.36	.243
2023	23	Fort Wayne (MWL)	A+	5	3	3.03	11	11	59	57	4	21	65	8.3	25.6	1.31	.251
Minor League Totals				5	4	3.03	25	23	114	109	6	45	128	9.1	26.0	1.36	.250

Rookie catcher Patrick Bailey

EZRA SHAW/GETTY IMAGES

San Francisco Giants

BY JOSH NORRIS

Two years after leading the majors with 107 wins, the Giants finished fourth in the National League West. It was their second straight season missing the playoffs and their first full season under .500 since 2019.

To make matters worse, the rival Diamondbacks finished just five games better but clawed their way to the pennant thanks to MLB's newly expanded playoffs and a core of young talent. Those two factors could have San Francisco staring up at both Arizona and the rival Dodgers in the coming seasons.

San Francisco dismissed manager Gabe Kapler after the season and replaced him with Bob Melvin, whom they pried from the Padres. Kapler was hired by Miami as an assistant general manager.

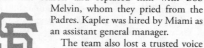

The team also lost a trusted voice in the amateur scouting department when the Royals hired national cross-checker Brian Bridges to be their scouting director.

With a new skipper in tow, the team's next task involves overhauling the roster he'll oversee. In 2023, the team got a taste of some of the players who may take on central roles.

That list includes lefthander Kyle Harrison and shortstop Marco Luciano, who each made their big league debut in 2023. Harrison in particular had flashes of brilliance, including five no-hit innings in a duel with Dodgers righthander Bobby Miller on the season's final day.

Luciano will have plenty of opportunities to seize the starting shortstop job in 2024 after stalwart Brandon Crawford hung up his cleats after a 13-year big league career that featured three all-star nods.

San Francisco also got contributions from outfielder Luis Matos, third baseman Casey Schmitt, catcher Patrick Bailey and outfielder Blake Sabol. Bailey was particularly outstanding on defense and finished as one of three finalists for the NL Gold Glove.

PROJECTED 2027 LINEUP

Catcher	Patrick Bailey	26
First Base	Bryce Eldridge	21
Second Base	Marco Luciano	24
Third Base	Casey Schmitt	27
Shortstop	Walker Martin	22
Left Field	Wade Meckler	25
Center Field	Grant McCray	26
Right Field	Luis Matos	25
Designated Hitter	Mike Yastrzemski	36
No. 1 Starter	Logan Webb	30
No. 2 Starter	Kyle Harrison	26
No. 3 Starter	Carson Whisenhunt	26
No. 4 Starter	Hayden Birdsong	24
No. 5 Starter	Reggie Crawford	25
Closer	Camilo Doval	29

The Giants have the makings of a young core. Now, they need a nucleus around which it can be built. The team came close to landing one before the 2023 season, when it nearly added Aaron Judge or Carlos Correa to the fold. Judge re-signed with the Yankees and Correa's deal was scuttled by medical issues, leaving the roster without an obvious centerpiece.

The rotation has a clear ace in righthander Logan Webb, who finished second to Padres lefty Blake Snell for the NL Cy Young Award, but there is no similar player on offense. Luciano might one day fill that role, but such a star turn could be a couple of years away.

San Francisco fortified its farm system with high-upside two-way talent Bryce Eldridge, who has the size and strength to be a classic middle-order thumper in a couple of seasons.

Several prospects took steps forward, too, including lefthander Carson Whisenhunt—who appeared in the 2023 Futures Game—and righty Hayden Birdsong, who each claimed spots in the organization's Top 10 Prospects.

San Francisco has plenty of pieces to supplement a potential rise back to the playoffs, but now it needs something to tie everything together. If it can't find a player or players who fit that bill, it might be hard to overtake the Dodgers and D-backs for the next few years. ∎

SAN FRANCISCO GIANTS

TOP 2024 CONTRIBUTORS	RANK
1. Kyle Harrison, LHP	1
2. Marco Luciano, SS	2
3. Wade Meckler, OF	15

BREAKOUT PROSPECTS	RANK
1. Joe Whitman, LHP	14
2. Onil Perez, C	17
3. Trevor McDonald, RHP	19

SOURCE OF TOP 30 TALENT

Homegrown	29	Acquired	1
College	13	Trade	1
Junior college	1	Rule 5 draft	0
High school	7	Independent league	0
Nondrafted free agent	0	Free agent/waivers	0
International	8		

LF
Vaun Brown (11)
Heliot Ramos (25)

CF
Grant McCray (10)
Wade Meckler (15)

RF
Bryce Eldridge (3)
Rayner Arias (7)
Carter Howell

3B
Carter Aldrete
Dariel Lopez
Will Wilson

SS
Marco Luciano (2)
Walker Martin (5)
Aeverson Arteaga (16)
Maui Ahuna (18)

2B
Cole Foster (22)
Diego Velasquez (23)
Quinn McDaniel
Jose Ramos

1B
Luis Toribio
Victor Bericoto

C
Onil Perez (17)
Adrian Sugastey (24)
Luke Shliger

LHP

LHSP	LHRP
Kyle Harrison (1)	Erik Miller
Carson Whisenhunt (4)	Nick Swiney
Reggie Crawford (9)	John Michael Bertrand
Joe Whitman (13)	Jack Choate
Timmy Manning	Hayden Wynja

RHP

RHSP	RHRP
Hayden Birdsong (6)	Landen Roupp (14)
Mason Black (8)	William Kempner (27)
Keaton Winn (12)	Jose Cruz (28)
Trevor McDonald (19)	Gerelmi Maldonado (29)
Carson Seymour (20)	Liam Simon (30)
Eric Silva (21)	Josh Bostick
Ryan Murphy (26)	RJ Dabovich
	Randy Rodriguez
	Will Bednar
	Carson Ragsdale
	Nick Garcia

1 KYLE HARRISON, LHP

Born: August 12, 2001. **B-T:** L-L. **HT:** 6-2. **WT:** 200.
Drafted: HS—Concord, CA, 2020 (3rd round).
Signed by: Keith Snider.

THEARON W. HENDERSON/GETTY

BA GRADE	SCOUTING GRADES
60 Risk: High	**FB:** 60. **SL:** 60. **CHG:** 40. **CUT:** 50. **CTL:** 45.

Projected future grades on 20-80 scouting scale

TRACK RECORD: Harrison was the Giants' third-rounder—but their fifth pick—in the five-round 2020 draft, but he earned the second-highest bonus in San Francisco's class at $2,497,500. The class has been wildly successful, producing three big leaguers already: catcher Patrick Bailey, third baseman Casey Schmitt and Harrison, who made his first start with the Giants on Aug. 22. Before then, Harrison had spent his time in the minor leagues carving hitters with a mix of stuff and deception that led to 295 strikeouts over the last two seasons. That figure includes 186 strikeouts in 2022, which ranked second in the minors. Harrison's 2023 season began with his first test at Triple-A, which meant a trip to the hitter-friendly Pacific Coast League. Beyond that, the league introduced an automated ball-strike system that led to tighter, less-forgiving strike zones. Harrison struggled to adjust to the ABS-enforced zone, and it led to 21 walks in 15.2 April innings. Though his command and control were never sparkling, he calmed down for the remainder of his tenure with Sacramento. Harrison closed his season on a high note, tossing five hitless innings against the Dodgers.

SCOUTING REPORT: After a month in the PCL, Harrison and the Giants realized his arsenal would need some tweaking in order to cross the final hurdles. First, they tried adding a gyro slider to his mix but scrapped it because he didn't throw it with enough velocity. Eventually, they settled on a cutter in addition to his sweeper breaking ball in order to give him a pair of breaking pitches with a wider range of velocity separation. Harrison's slider is thrown in the low 80s, while his cutter is thrown a few ticks higher in the upper 80s. The two pitches complement an excellent, mid-90s fastball with exceptional horizontal movement and a whiff rate of nearly 25% in MLB. The next piece of the puzzle is the continued development of the changeup. Harrison's version of the pitch is thrown with a two-seam grip and comes in around 86 mph. In the minors, Harrison threw the changeup roughly 6% of the time, a figure that nearly doubled once he reached MLB. He still needs to show more consistency with the pitch overall, and he needs to prove he can throw it for a called strike

BEST TOOLS

BATTING

Best Hitter for Average	Wade Meckler
Best Power Hitter	Marco Luciano
Best Strike-Zone Discipline	Wade Meckler
Fastest Baserunner	Tyler Fitzgerald
Best Athlete	Walker Martin

PITCHING

Best Fastball	Reggie Crawford
Best Curveball	Landen Roupp
Best Slider	Reggie Crawford
Best Changeup	Carson Whisenhunt
Best Control	John Michael Bertrand

FIELDING

Best Defensive Catcher	Adrian Sugastey
Best Defensive Infielder	Aeverson Arteaga
Best Infield Arm	Aeverson Arteaga
Best Defensive Outfielder	Grant McCray
Best Outfield Arm	Grant McCray

instead of merely as a chase pitch. Harrison's fastball and slider give him two potentially plus weapons. Now, it's about cementing one or both of the changeup and cutter as reliable third and fourth options. He'll also have to keep working to maintain his delivery, which gives him plenty of deception but also can negatively affect his control and command, which is unlikely to ever be better than fringy.

THE FUTURE: If Harrison can solidify either his cutter or changeup as a reliable third option and improve his control and command, he has the ceiling of a No. 2 starter. If not, he still should fit in the rotation, but perhaps more toward the middle or back. After an extended run in the big leagues in 2023, he'll have the inside track at earning a rotation spot in 2024 and beyond. ◾

Year	Age	Club (League)	Level	W	L	ERA	G	GS	IP	H	HR	BB	SO	BB%	SO%	WHIP	AVG
2023	21	ACL Giants Black	Rk	0	0	0.00	1	1	2	0	0	0	4	0.0	66.7	0.00	.000
2023	21	Sacramento (PCL)	AAA	1	3	4.66	20	20	66	52	10	48	105	16.3	35.6	1.52	.215
2023	21	San Francisco (NL)	MLB	1	1	4.15	7	7	35	29	8	11	35	7.5	23.8	1.15	.221
Minor League Totals				9	9	3.32	69	69	279	217	26	149	452	12.3	37.4	1.31	.212
Major League Totals				1	1	4.15	7	7	35	29	8	11	35	7.5	23.8	1.15	.221

2 MARCO LUCIANO, SS

HIT: 50. **POW:** 60. **RUN:** 40. **FLD:** 50. **ARM:** 60. **BA Grade:** 55 **Risk:** High.

Born: September 10, 2001. **B-T:** R-R. **HT:** 6-2. **WT:** 178.
Signed: Dominican Republic, 2018. **Signed by:** Jonathan Bautista.
TRACK RECORD: When the Giants signed him in 2018, Luciano immediately vaulted into the upper tier of their system. Since then, most of the bumps in his path have revolved around health. An offseason stress fracture in his back kept him out all of spring training and delayed his regular season debut at Double-A until early May. After a slow start, Luciano hit his stride at mid-summer, then earned a promotion to Triple-A on July 18. Eight days later, he received his first big league callup.
SCOUTING REPORT: No matter where he winds up on the diamond, Luciano's bat will lead the way. He's a well-built player with plenty of raw and usable power that could play up further if he becomes a little bit more disciplined in the batter's box. Injuries have limited his experience severely, and he has not played more than 100 games in a season since 2021. The time on the IL has somewhat stunted his development and kept him from getting the requisite at-bats against high-quality pitching he'll need in order to reach his ceiling. He'll also need to refine his approach to be a little less aggressive early in counts. To stick at shortstop—where he played primarily during his look in the big leagues—he'll have to work hard to maintain his range and focus on taking better angles to the ball. He has more than enough arm for the left side, but his speed is no better than below-average. If he has to move off the position, his plus throwing arm will play just fine at third base and his bat would likely profile at either outfield corner.
THE FUTURE: After getting his feet wet this season, Luciano will likely get a long look in San Francisco in 2024. If he reaches his ceiling, he'll be a force in the middle of the lineup and the diamond.

Year	Age	Club (League)	Level	AVG	G	AB	R	H	2B	3B	HR	RBI	BB	SO	SB	OBP	SLG
2023	21	Richmond (EL)	AA	.228	56	202	32	46	12	0	11	32	36	72	6	.339	.450
2023	21	Sacramento (PCL)	AAA	.209	18	67	10	14	2	0	4	8	10	28	0	.321	.418
2023	21	San Francisco (NL)	MLB	.231	14	39	4	9	3	0	0	0	6	17	1	.333	.308
Minor League Totals				.259	292	1070	195	277	56	7	55	189	152	325	21	.356	.479
Major League Totals				.231	14	39	4	9	3	0	0	0	6	17	1	.333	.308

3 BRYCE ELDRIDGE, OF/RHP

HIT: 50. **POW:** 60. **RUN:** 30. **FLD:** 50. **ARM:** 55. **BA Grade:** 60. **Risk:** Extreme.

Born: October 20, 2004. **B-T:** L-R. **HT:** 6-7. **WT:** 223.
Drafted: HS—Vienna, VA, 2023 (1st round). **Signed by:** John DiCarlo.
TRACK RECORD: For the second year in a row, the Giants took a two-way player with their first-round pick. In 2022, it was Connecticut's Reggie Crawford. This time around, it was Eldridge, who entering his junior season at Madison High looked more like a pitcher than a hitter. After his senior season, the opposite appeared true. The massive, lefthanded-hitting slugger clubbed a team-best eight home runs for USA Baseball's 18U National Team in 2022, and the Giants selected him with their first choice. Eldridge made a strong first impression as a pro, belting five homers and slugging .647 in 16 games in the Arizona Complex League, and reached Low-A by season's end.
SCOUTING REPORT: Eldridge is a massive human being at 6-foot-7 and 223 pounds, and he packs the corresponding punch in his bat. Despite that frame, the Giants were attracted to Eldridge's solid ability to control the strike zone, manageable whiff rates for a player with long levers and a knack for finding the barrel. Scouts who saw Eldridge as a pro were similarly encouraged by his controlled approach in the box and easy double-plus power. Evaluators both inside and outside of the organization agree that will have to work on recognition of secondary pitches, though he did get positive marks for swing decisions in his initial pro tests. As a pro, Eldridge played exclusively in right field on the days he wasn't used as a DH, though it's likely he winds up at first base as he moves forward in his career. He's a well below-average runner. As a pitcher in high school, Eldridge sat in the low 90s and topped out at 96 mph with great plane thanks to his height. Body control helped him throw strikes with his slider and nascent changeup.
THE FUTURE: Eldridge has a chance to be a true middle-of-the-order bat who lands either in right field or first base. He'll get his first full test in 2024.

Year	Age	Club (League)	Level	AVG	G	AB	R	H	2B	3B	HR	RBI	BB	SO	SB	OBP	SLG
2023	18	ACL Giants Orange	Rk	.294	16	51	8	15	3	0	5	13	9	16	0	.393	.647
2023	18	San Jose (CAL)	A	.293	15	58	7	17	2	0	1	5	11	18	1	.406	.379
Minor League Totals				.294	31	109	15	32	5	0	6	18	20	34	1	.400	.505

4 CARSON WHISENHUNT, LHP

FB: 60. **CB:** 40. **CHG:** 70. **CTL:** 55. **BA Grade:** 50 **Risk:** High

Born: October 10, 2000. **B-T:** L-L. **HT:** 6-3. **WT:** 209.
Drafted: East Carolina, 2022 (2nd round). **Signed by:** DJ Jauss.

TRACK RECORD: Whisenhunt's junior year at East Carolina ended before it began. The lefthander tested positive for a performance-enhancing substance and was suspended for the entirety of the season. The Giants were convicted enough by their previous looks and a cameo in the Cape Cod League to draft him with their second-round pick in 2022. In his first full season in 2023, Whisenhunt raced from Low-A to Double-A—with a stop at the Futures Game as well—before his season ended with tightness in his left forearm.

SCOUTING REPORT: The crown jewel of Whisenhunt's arsenal is his changeup—or, more accurately, his changeups. He has three variations of the pitch—differentiated by the placement of his fingers—that he can use to vary the depth of its break and land it in the zone for a called strike, add a touch of fade or let the bottom completely fall out. He complements the changeup with a four-seam fastball and curveball. The former averaged 94 mph and topped at 97 while showing excellent life through the zone. Now, the key is the development of Whisenhunt's curveball, which is a 1-to-7 bender with decent power at an average of 79 mph. He threw the pitch just 12% of the time, a figure that will need to be increased to help Whisenhunt gain more trust in the pitch and make it more of a viable weapon. Evaluators inside and outside the organization believe adding a cutter could be helpful. Whisenhunt has potentially above-average control.

THE FUTURE: Whisenhunt didn't pitch after July 22 but had recovered well enough to begin a throwing program in the offseason. His future hinges on the development of the breaking ball. If he can find one that becomes a true third option, he could fit as a No. 4 starter with a chance at a bit more.

Year	Age	Club (League)	Level	W	L	ERA	G	GS	IP	H	HR	BB	SO	BB%	SO%	WHIP	AVG
2023	22	San Jose (CAL)	A	0	0	3.29	4	4	14	12	1	4	20	7.0	35.1	1.17	.231
2023	22	Eugene (NWL)	A+	1	0	1.42	6	6	25	9	1	8	36	8.5	38.3	0.67	.107
2023	22	Richmond (EL)	AA	0	1	3.20	6	6	20	16	1	11	27	13.1	32.1	1.37	.219
Minor League Totals				1	1	2.17	20	19	66	43	3	24	97	9.1	36.6	1.01	.181

5 WALKER MARTIN, SS

HIT: 55. **POW:** 50. **RUN:** 55. **FLD:** 50. **ARM:** 50. **BA Grade:** 55. **Risk:** Extreme.

Born: February 20, 2004. **B-T:** L-R. **HT:** 6-2. **WT:** 188.
Drafted: HS—Greeley, CO, 2023 (2nd round). **Signed by:** Chuck Hensley Jr.

TRACK RECORD: Martin was not only one of the best prospects in the country's Four Corners region, he was one of more productive prep players in the nation in 2023. His 20 home runs at Eaton (Colo.) High were the most in the country, and he backed them up with a .636 batting average. The Giants were intrigued enough to make him their second-round pick and sign him for a $2,997,500 bonus that was nearly double the recommended slot. Some teams might have been scared away by Martin's age. He was 19 for his entire senior season.

SCOUTING REPORT: Martin's greatest allure is his potential as a hitter with a pure lefthanded swing. His swing is short, quick and balanced and allows for an excellent feel for the barrel. Because he didn't face the same level of competition as would be provided in the more talent-rich parts of the country, Martin might have a steeper learning curve. The Giants would also like to see him add strength and learn how best to deploy his swing depending on the situation he is facing. Martin pairs that hitting ability with outstanding athleticism that helped him star in three sports in high school. He played basketball briefly and was starting quarterback for two Class 2A state champions in football. Martin excelled among his prep peers in Loden testing, an evaluation that assesses athletes' power, quickness, speed, symmetry and brain speed. He has soft hands and strong footwork, which will help him stick at shortstop for the time being. If he has to move over to third base his average arm strength should play just fine. He is an average runner and has excellent makeup.

THE FUTURE: Martin didn't play after signing, so 2024 will give him his first test as a pro. His ceiling is as an offensive-minded infielder on the left side of the diamond.

Year	Age	Club (League)	Level	AVG	G	AB	R	H	2B	3B	HR	RBI	BB	SO	SB	OBP	SLG
2023	19	Did not play															

6 HAYDEN BIRDSONG, RHP

FB: 60. **CB:** 60. **SL:** 55. **CHG:** 40. **CTL:** 50. **BA Grade:** 50. **Risk:** High.

Born: August 30, 2001. **B-T:** R-R. **HT:** 6-4. **WT:** 215.
Drafted: Eastern Illinois, 2022 (6th round). **Signed by:** Tom Shafer.

TRACK RECORD: After a year at Lake Land (Ill.) JC in 2020, Birdsong transferred to Eastern Illinois for his final two collegiate seasons. The Giants popped him in the sixth round, then watched him carve the competition at the lower levels in his pro debut. He put up a 2.67 ERA with 36% strikeouts at two Class A stops. Birdsong continued bullying hitters in his first full season as a pro, moving from Low-A to Double-A and striking out 149 hitters in 100.2 innings along the way. Only one minor league pitcher had a higher strikeout rate than Birdsong's 34.9% at the 100 inning threshold.

SCOUTING REPORT: Birdsong is already a physically imposing presence at 6-foot-4 and 215 pounds, but the Giants believe there's even more room to grow and add even more power to his arsenal. He works with a full four-pitch complement, led by a mid-90s fastball with carry through the zone and a potentially plus curveball in the low 80s that hitters simply did not touch in 2023. Birdsong rounds out the arsenal with a slider that averaged around 83 mph and could be an above-average pitch and a fringy, infrequently thrown changeup in the high 80s that is a clear fourth pitch. He will have to refine his control and command, which took a significant hit in terms of both strike percentage and walk rate once he reached Double-A.

THE FUTURE: The 2024 season will be key for Birdsong, who will likely spend the entirety of the year at the upper levels. If he can return his control and command to the standards he maintained at Low-A and High-A, he has the ceiling of a rotation piece. If not, he might fit more as an overpowering option in the late innings.

Year	Age	Club (League)	Level	W	L	ERA	G	GS	IP	H	HR	BB	SO	BB%	SO%	WHIP	AVG
2023	21	San Jose (CAL)	A	0	0	2.16	12	10	42	34	0	22	70	12.0	38.0	1.34	.218
2023	21	Eugene (NWL)	A+	2	2	3.25	8	7	36	24	4	9	46	6.5	33.1	0.92	.190
2023	21	Richmond (EL)	AA	0	3	5.48	8	8	23	21	2	13	33	12.5	31.7	1.48	.236
Minor League Totals				3	5	3.29	35	25	112	89	6	47	172	9.9	36.2	1.21	.215

7 RAYNER ARIAS, OF

HIT: 55. **POW:** 60. **RUN:** 50. **FLD:** 50. **ARM:** 55. **BA Grade:** 50. **Risk:** Extreme.

Born: April 29, 2006. **B-T:** R-R. **HT:** 6-2. **WT:** 185.
Signed: Dominican Republic, 2023. **Signed by:** Jonathan Bautista.

TRACK RECORD: Arias signed with San Francisco at the opening of the 2023 international signing period. The lithe Dominican outfielder earned the Giants' top bonus of $2,697,500 and began his career in the Dominican Summer League. Arias is the son of longtime scout Pablo Arias, which meant Rayner grew up around the game. His season was limited to just 16 games by a broken left wrist suffered on a diving catch on June 30. He made a big impression in a small sample, hitting .414 with 12 extra-base hits, including four homers.

SCOUTING REPORT: Despite the limited sample, Arias made a big impression in his short time on the field. He was one of the youngest players in the class and will not turn 18 until late April 2024. He already shows an enticing combination of both strength and projectability that makes him one of the highest-upside prospects in the system. In the short sample, Arias produced average and 90th percentile exit velocities of 86.1 and 100.9 mph, both of which were elite figures for his age level and would be around the average EVs produced by Low-A hitters in 2023. Arias controls the zone as well, with more walks (15) than strikeouts (11) before the injury. He also swung less frequently and made contact more often than most DSL players. Arias will have plenty of leash when it comes to staying in center field, where his speed and lithe body should fit well. If he gets too big, however, his bat, average speed and above-average arm strength would profile in right field.

THE FUTURE: After an offseason to recover, Arias should begin 2024 in the Arizona Complex League. He has a chance to be a well-rounded player who fits near the top of an order and provides value on both sides of the ball.

Year	Age	Club (League)	Level	AVG	G	AB	R	H	2B	3B	HR	RBI	BB	SO	SB	OBP	SLG
2023	17	DSL Giants Black	Rk	.414	16	58	19	24	6	2	4	21	15	11	4	.539	.793
Minor League Totals				.414	16	58	19	24	6	2	4	21	15	11	4	.539	.793

8 MASON BLACK, RHP

FB: 60. **SL:** 60. **CTL:** 50. **BA Grade:** 50. **Risk:** High.

Born: December 10, 1999. **B-T:** R-R. **HT:** 6-3. **WT:** 230.
Drafted: Lehigh, 2021 (3rd round). **Signed by:** John DiCarlo.
TRACK RECORD: Black was San Francisco's third-round pick in 2021, out of Lehigh University, where his struggles down the stretch in his draft year affected his stock to the point where he fell into the Giants' lap. He followed an excellent pro debut in 2022 with another outstanding season in 2023, when he split time between Double-A and Triple-A. His 155 strikeouts were the second-most in the organization, behind only Kai-Wei Teng, and ranked 16th overall in the minor leagues.
SCOUTING REPORT: By and large, Black is a classic sinker/slider pitcher. His primary two weapons are a mid-90s sinker and a sweepy slider in the low 80s. He will mix in the occasional four-seam fastball as well, and he added a gyro slider later in the year as an early-count offspeed pitch that helps him steal strikes and can be landed in the zone more easily than a sweeper. He went through a renaissance in the middle of the season. From June 8 through July 1—a span of five starts and 22.1 innings—he surrendered just eight hits, gave up no runs and struck out 29 while walking just five. Black has the potential for average control, though his walk rate spiked sharply at Triple-A, where the automated ball-strike system has created a less-welcoming environment for pitchers who live on the edges of the zone. He's an extremely hard worker who is constantly looking for ways to up his game and shows a particularly intense demeanor on days when he starts.
THE FUTURE: Black will return to Triple-A in 2024 and has the ceiling of a back-end starter who can eat innings. Because his arsenal is so limited, however, his more likely home is in the bullpen. He should make his MLB debut in 2024.

Year	Age	Club (League)	Level	W	L	ERA	G	GS	IP	H	HR	BB	SO	BB%	SO%	WHIP	AVG
2023	23	Richmond (EL)	AA	1	5	3.57	16	16	63	45	7	21	83	8.3	32.7	1.05	.197
2023	23	Sacramento (PCL)	AAA	3	4	3.86	13	13	61	53	9	31	72	12.0	27.9	1.38	.242
Minor League Totals				10	13	3.49	53	53	236	193	28	88	291	9.0	29.8	1.20	.223

9 REGGIE CRAWFORD, LHP/1B

FB: 70. **CB:** 60. **CHG:** 40. **CTL:** 45. **BA Grade:** 55. **Risk:** Extreme.

Born: December 4, 2000. **B-T:** L-L. **HT:** 6-4. **WT:** 235.
Drafted: Connecticut, 2022 (1st round). **Signed by:** Ray Callari.
TRACK RECORD: At Connecticut, Crawford's career was stunted on both the mound and in the batter's box. The pandemic and Tommy John surgery limited him to just eight innings and 290 plate appearances. Undaunted, the Giants drafted Crawford 30th overall in 2022 and have let him continue his career as a two-way prospect. Unfortunately, his problems staying on the field have carried to his pro career. His 2023 season was delayed by a bout of mononucleosis in the spring and ended in August with a strained oblique. He made up time in the Arizona Fall League, where he was a hitter only.
SCOUTING REPORT: In his limited time, Crawford showed the same kind of stuff that made him such an intriguing prospect in the first place. His arsenal starts with a fastball that averaged 97 mph and featured excellent horizontal break and vertical approach angle. The fastball was backed by a powerful, short-breaking curveball in the low 80s that worked to get both called strikes and whiffs. Those two pitches alone could help Crawford profile as an excellent reliever. Now, he needs to continue to develop his changeup. Currently, the pitch sits around 87 mph and shows effective shape, but Crawford needs to learn how to throw it in the strike zone more often. In 2023, his changeup was thrown for a strike just 42% of the time.
THE FUTURE: The Giants knew Crawford's development would take time. The time away from the field in 2023 further complicates things, especially considering none of his 13 starts lasted longer than two innings. His time in the AFL will help the Giants determine how much Crawford should continue hitting, but internally the organization believes his future is on the mound.

Year	Age	Club (League)	Level	W	L	ERA	G	GS	IP	H	HR	BB	SO	BB%	SO%	WHIP	AVG
2023	22	San Jose (CAL)	A	0	0	4.09	7	7	11	9	3	4	18	8.7	39.1	1.18	.220
2023	22	Eugene (NWL)	A+	0	0	1.13	6	6	8	6	0	6	14	16.7	38.9	1.50	.207
Minor League Totals				0	0	2.84	13	13	19	15	3	10	32	12.2	39.0	1.32	.214

10 GRANT McCRAY, OF

HIT: 45. **POW:** 55. **RUN:** 70. **FLD:** 60. **ARM:** 55. **BA Grade:** 50. **Risk:** High.

Born: December 7, 2000. **B-T:** L-R. **HT:** 6-2. **WT:** 190.
Drafted: HS—Bradenton, FL, 2019 (3rd round). **Signed by:** Jim Gabella.
TRACK RECORD: McCray was part of an excellent one-two punch of low-profile prospects identified by Florida area scout Jim Gabella, who found McCray in 2019 and then Vaun Brown in 2021. In his first two years as a pro, McCray showed tools but little in the way of production. The next year, 2022, was a different story. Mechanical changes helped him turn his tools into production, and he put himself on the map as one of the better prospects in San Francisco's system by hitting .289/.383/.514 with 23 home runs and 43 stolen bases, mostly at Low-A San Jose.
SCOUTING REPORT: After a breakout 2022 season, McCray struggled with consistency but showed flashes of his big-time potential. His 2023 began on a low note with a .554 OPS at High-A Eugene in April. A month later, that figure was .909. At his best, McCray should fit into a hit-over-power mold. When he tries to reverse that profile, things tend to go awry. McCray hits the ball plenty hard—his 103 mph 90th percentile exit velocity was above-average for his level—but his miss rates on pitches both in and out of the zone were concerning. His 171 strikeouts were the most in the Northwest League and the second-most in all of High-A. McCray's defense alleviates a bit of the pressure on his bat. He's got a plus glove in center field, a plus throwing arm and double-plus speed. NWL managers voted McCray the best outfield defender on the circuit.
THE FUTURE: McCray has plenty of tools. Now, he needs to settle on a consistent approach in order to put them together more often. The 2024 season—which will likely be spent at Double-A—will represent the biggest test of McCray's career. If he puts it together, he could be a classic table-setter at the top of San Francisco's lineup.

Year	Age	Club (League)	Level	AVG	G	AB	R	H	2B	3B	HR	RBI	BB	SO	SB	OBP	SLG
2023	22	Eugene (NWL)	A+	.255	127	494	101	126	26	6	14	66	72	171	52	.360	.417
Minor League Totals				.272	340	1302	272	354	59	20	41	174	184	445	119	.370	.442

11 VAUN BROWN, OF

HIT: 40. **POW:** 55. **RUN:** 70. **FLD:** 55. **ARM:** 50. **BA Grade:** 50. **Risk:** High.

Born: June 23, 1998. **B-T:** R-R. **HT:** 6-1. **WT:** 215. **Drafted:** Florida Southern, 2021 (10th round). **Signed by:** Jim Gabella.
TRACK RECORD: In 2022, Brown was one of the biggest pop-up prospects in San Francisco's system. Area scout Jim Gabella navigated strict pandemic restrictions at Florida Southern to get as good a look as possible at Brown, whom the Giants took in the 10th round and signed him for $75,000. In his first full season as a pro, the selection looked like a heist while he bullied the lower levels of the minor leagues. Brown's 2023 was limited to just 59 games with an early knee injury and then a broken leg suffered later in the year on a hit by pitch.
SCOUTING REPORT: At his best, Brown shows the makings of the kind of power-speed combination coveted by teams. To help those skills reach their peak, he'll need to do a much better job controlling the zone and make better swing decisions. He missed both in and out of the zone at rates that were below-average compared to his peers. Even during his banner 2022 season, scouts believed he'd have trouble with high fastballs and soft stuff away. Those traits could make him a below-average hitter with 55-grade power. He's a double-plus runner, which should help him stick in center field. He has the potential to be an above-average defender and has average arm strength.
THE FUTURE: Brown is already 25 years old, so time is not on his side. He should move to Triple-A in 2024 and with a return to health could make his big league debut during the summer.

Year	Age	Club (League)	Level	AVG	G	AB	R	H	2B	3B	HR	RBI	BB	SO	SB	OBP	SLG
2023	25	San Jose (CAL)	A	.412	4	17	4	7	2	0	0	1	2	5	3	.500	.529
2023	25	Eugene (NWL)	A+	.300	5	20	2	6	2	0	1	3	2	5	2	.391	.550
2023	25	Richmond (EL)	AA	.221	50	190	27	42	10	2	8	34	13	78	15	.284	.421
Minor League Totals				.313	187	693	157	217	45	13	34	127	71	236	72	.403	.563

12 KEATON WINN, RHP

FB: 60. **SL:** 40. **SPLT:** 60. **CTL:** 55. **BA Grade:** 45. **Risk:** Medium.

Born: February 20, 1998. **B-T:** R-R. **HT:** 6-4. **WT:** 238. **Drafted:** Iowa Western JC, 2018 (5th round).
Signed by: Todd Coryell.

TRACK RECORD: After two seasons at Iowa Western JC, Winn had planned to move to Texas Christian. Instead, the Giants selected him in the fifth round of the 2018 draft and signed him for $500,000. He missed the 2021 season after having Tommy John surgery, then re-emerged in 2022 with one of the better seasons in the Giants' system. Winn made his big league debut on June 13 and made nine appearances—including five starts—in the big leagues.

SCOUTING REPORT: Winn's bread and butter is his combination of a mid-90s fastball and a nasty splitter in the high 80s that helps him execute a quality north-south approach that will play well at least in a bulk reliever's role. If he can improve his slider, which is a clear third pitch at this point, he'll have a chance to raise his ceiling. Right now, both his fastball and splitter grade as plus pitches, while his slider checks in as a below-average offering. He uses the slider roughly 10% of the time and will need to up that rate if he is to fit in the rotation. He also uses a two-seamer that adds another east-west option to his mix. Winn has had plus control throughout his minor league career except for a blip in Triple-A, where the automatic ball-strike system does not pair well with pitchers who live at the top of the zone.

THE FUTURE: Winn will likely spend most of 2024 in the big leagues, where he can eat innings either in the back of the rotation or as a bulk reliever.

Year	Age	Club (League)	Level	W	L	ERA	G	GS	IP	H	HR	BB	SO	BB%	SO%	WHIP	AVG
2023	25	Sacramento (PCL)	AAA	0	6	4.81	17	14	58	66	7	26	66	9.9	25.1	1.59	.284
2023	25	San Francisco (NL)	MLB	1	3	4.68	9	5	42	36	6	8	35	4.7	20.3	1.04	.231
Minor League Totals				16	20	4.02	85	64	336	349	29	97	326	6.7	22.7	1.33	.268
Major League Totals				1	3	4.68	9	5	42	36	6	8	35	4.7	20.3	1.04	.231

13 JOE WHITMAN, LHP

FB: 55. **SL:** 60. **CHG:** 50. **CTL:** 55. **BA Grade:** 50. **Risk:** High.

Born: September 17, 2001. **B-T:** L-L. **HT:** 6-5. **WT:** 200. **Drafted:** Kent State, 2023 (2nd round supp).
Signed by: Todd Coryell.

TRACK RECORD: In a draft class notable for its lack of quality lefthanders, Whitman stood out as the best southpaw available from the college ranks. In three years at Kent State, he established himself as a quality prospect who got plenty of whiffs and pounded the strike zone. San Francisco selected him with its second-round supplemental pick and signed him for $805,575. He reached Low-A in his first pro test and made six appearances between the Arizona Complex League and the California League.

SCOUTING REPORT: Whitman has excellent arm speed and works from a low slot with a three-pitch mix. His repertoire is fronted by a low-90s fastball with tailing action. The pitch peaked at 96 mph. His best offspeed is a sharp slider in the low 80s. The pitch has two-plane break and spin rates around 3,000 rpm. Those qualities make it effective against both lefthanders and righthanders. He finishes his mix with a changeup that sits in the mid 80s and flashed average potential, especially during his time in the Cape Cod League. Bringing the changeup to its ceiling will be a fulcrum in his career. If he can get it there, he'll have a chance to fit in the back of a rotation. He should have above-average control and did a good job pounding the strike zone in his professional outings.

THE FUTURE: Whitman should reach High-A Eugene in his first full season. If his changeup improves, he has a ceiling as a No. 4 starter. If not, he could be an effective left-on-left reliever.

Year	Age	Club (League)	Level	W	L	ERA	G	GS	IP	H	HR	BB	SO	BB%	SO%	WHIP	AVG
2023	21	ACL Giants Black	Rk	0	0	0.00	3	3	4	1	0	1	4	6.3	25.0	0.50	.071
2023	21	San Jose (CAL)	A	1	0	3.18	3	2	6	3	0	2	9	9.1	40.9	0.88	.158
Minor League Totals				1	0	2.00	6	5	10	4	0	3	13	7.9	34.2	0.78	.121

14 LANDEN ROUPP, RHP

FB: 55. **CB:** 65. **SL:** 40. **CHG:** 40. **CTL:** 55. **BA Grade:** 45. **Risk:** High.

Born: September 10, 1998. **B-T:** R-R. **HT:** 6-2. **WT:** 205. **Drafted:** UNC Wilmington, 2021 (12th round).
Signed by: Mark O'Sullivan.

TRACK RECORD: Roupp spent four years at UNC Wilmington and mixed in a stint in the Cape Cod League as well. San Francisco took a flier on him in the 12th round in 2021, then watched as he racked up 152 strikeouts in his first full season as a pro. Roupp missed roughly half the season with a lower back injury but was healthy enough to pitch during instructional league.

SCOUTING REPORT: Roupp works primarily with two pitches: a sinker at around 93 mph and a high-70s curveball with two-plane break. The curveball is particularly nasty and grades as the best of its kind in the system. It got whiffs at a 48% clip and was thrown for a strike nearly 70% of the time. The sinker and curveball are the bulk of Roupp's mix, but he will also mix in a below-average slider and changeup. Neither pitch was thrown more than 4% of the time. To become a strong rotation candidate, he'll need to develop at least one of those pitches into a usable third option. He has above-average control as well, and threw strikes for both quality and volume at Double-A.

THE FUTURE: More than anything, Roupp needs to stay healthy. He has a forearm strain and a back injury on his record already. After that, he'll need to find a quality third pitch. If he checks those boxes, he might wind up in the back of a rotation.

Year	Age	Club (League)	Level	W	L	ERA	G	GS	IP	H	HR	BB	SO	BB%	SO%	WHIP	AVG
2023	24	Richmond (EL)	AA	0	0	1.74	10	10	31	22	1	9	42	7.5	35.0	1.00	.206
Minor League Totals				10	3	2.40	41	24	146	99	7	47	208	8.1	35.7	1.00	.189

15 WADE MECKLER, OF

HIT: 45. **POW:** 20. **RUN:** 70. **FLD:** 45. **ARM:** 40. **BA Grade:** 45. **Risk:** Medium.

Born: April 21, 2000. **B-T:** L-R. **HT:** 5-10. **WT:** 178. **Drafted:** Oregon State, 2022 (8th round). **Signed by:** Larry Casian.

TRACK RECORD: Meckler's story is one of perseverance. As a freshman in high school, he was just 4-foot-10 and 75 pounds and initially made Oregon State's roster as a walk-on. He got just 10 at-bats in his freshman season and was cut before the 2020 season, which was ultimately canceled by the pandemic. He thrived over the next two seasons, however, and the Giants took a flier on him in the eighth round. In his first full year, he hit his way to the big leagues, debuting on Aug. 14 and getting 56 at-bats.

SCOUTING REPORT: Meckler's calling card is his extreme ability to put the bat on the ball. He struck out just 58 times in 363 minor league plate appearances, good for a rate just shy of 16%. All that contact, however, comes with almost no power. His exit velocity in the big leagues was 81.6 mph, which would have been the lowest among all qualified hitters. He also struggled mightily against breaking balls. At all levels, he hit just .145/.224/.232 against those pitch types. Given that profile, it is paramount Meckler stays in center field, and while he will be aided by double-plus speed, it isn't a slam dunk at this point.

THE FUTURE: Evaluators inside and outside the organization believe he is still refining his defensive chops.

Year	Age	Club (League)	Level	AVG	G	AB	R	H	2B	3B	HR	RBI	BB	SO	SB	OBP	SLG
2023	23	Eugene (NWL)	A+	.456	20	79	14	36	6	1	2	17	6	9	2	.494	.633
2023	23	Richmond (EL)	AA	.336	39	149	36	50	7	2	2	23	25	29	4	.431	.450
2023	23	Sacramento (PCL)	AAA	.354	24	82	12	29	4	1	2	10	18	20	7	.465	.500
2023	23	San Francisco (NL)	MLB	.232	20	56	6	13	1	0	0	4	6	25	0	.328	.250
Minor League Totals				.370	106	389	83	144	28	4	7	64	69	74	15	.465	.517
Major League Totals				.232	20	56	6	13	1	0	0	4	6	25	0	.328	.250

16 AEVERSON ARTEAGA, SS

HIT: 40. **POW:** 50. **RUN:** 50. **FLD:** 55. **ARM:** 60. **BA Grade:** 45. **Risk:** High.

Born: March 16, 2003. **B-T:** R-R. **HT:** 6-1. **WT:** 170. **Signed:** Venezuela, 2019. **Signed by:** Edgar Fernandez.

TRACK RECORD: Arteaga's $1 million bonus was the highest in San Francisco's 2019 international signing class, but his debut was delayed a year by the pandemic. He was part of Low-A San Jose's championship club in 2021, then went a level a year in 2022 and 2023, first at San Jose and then at High-A Eugene. His 17 home runs were the most for his Emeralds club and ranked fifth in the Northwest League.

SCOUTING REPORT: All season, Arteaga looked like a player caught in between two approaches. He'd added strength in the offseason and was regularly swinging with an all-or-nothing mentality. The result was the highest home run total of his career, but also a dip in the rest of his offensive game. He chased too many pitches and walked just 7.3% of the time, a dip of roughly 1.3% from the 2022 season. The combination of whiffs and chases masked solid contact skills on pitches within the strike zone and led to career lows in batting average (.235) and on-base percentage (.299). Arteaga is an above-average defender with a plus arm who should easily stick at shortstop, though his body appeared thicker than it did in 2022 in San Jose. He's an average runner who shows plenty of hustle on the bases.

THE FUTURE: Arteaga opened 2023 as the third-youngest player in the NWL and still has time on his side. If he improves his approach, he could be an everyday shortstop on a second-division club.

Year	Age	Club (League)	Level	AVG	G	AB	R	H	2B	3B	HR	RBI	BB	SO	SB	OBP	SLG
2023	20	Eugene (NWL)	A+	.235	126	493	66	116	29	3	17	73	40	132	8	.299	.410
Minor League Totals				.259	305	1196	195	310	76	6	40	200	112	357	27	.329	.433

17 ONIL PEREZ, C

HIT: 40. **POW:** 30. **RUN:** 40. **FLD:** 60. **ARM:** 70. **BA Grade:** 45. **Risk:** High.

Born: September 10, 2002. **B-T:** R-R. **HT:** 6-1. **WT:** 182. **Signed:** Dominican Republic, 2019. **Signed by:** Gabriel Elias.

TRACK RECORD: Perez was signed for $200,000 out of the Dominican Republic in 2019 as part of the same class that also brought shortstop Aeverson Arteaga into the fold. He, too, had to wait until 2021 to make his official professional debut. He spent his first two seasons in the complex leagues before splitting his 2023 season between Low-A San Jose and High-A Eugene.

SCOUTING REPORT: Perez's calling card is his excellent defense. He's a quick mover behind the dish who mostly does an excellent job blocking and receiving but could stand to be a shade more consistent in both departments. His arm is a double-plus showpiece that regularly produces pop times in the 1.9-second range, and his arm strength would play up even further with a shortened throwing stroke. Perez makes plenty of contact—he struck out just 38 times in 331 plate appearances—but has yet to show much impact at all. His 90th percentile exit velocity (97.2 mph) was well below-average for his level, and he has just four home runs in 636 career plate appearances. Part of this can be attributed to the fact that while he does an excellent job hitting pitches in the zone, he tends to chase a bit too much and makes weak contact. His open stride also creates holes on the outer half of the plate. Perez is a solid athlete who runs well for a catcher. He also earns high marks for his leadership and the way he works with pitchers.

THE FUTURE: Even with further improvement, Perez is not likely to be a factor offensively. Instead, he has a ceiling as a defense-first regular on a second-division club or a strong backup on a contender.

Year	Age	Club (League)	Level	AVG	G	AB	R	H	2B	3B	HR	RBI	BB	SO	SB	OBP	SLG
2023	20	San Jose (CAL)	A	.300	62	253	46	76	12	4	2	36	23	31	21	.364	.403
2023	20	Eugene (NWL)	A+	.289	13	45	4	13	0	1	0	1	3	7	2	.333	.333
Minor League Totals				.291	158	550	92	160	27	8	4	72	72	83	32	.374	.391

18 MAUI AHUNA, SS

HIT: 40. **POW:** 45. **RUN:** 55. **FLD:** 60. **ARM:** 60. **BA Grade:** 50. **Risk:** Extreme.

Born: March 11, 2002. **B-T:** L-R. **HT:** 6-1. **WT:** 170. **Drafted:** Tennessee, 2023 (4th round). **Signed by:** Nick Long.

TRACK RECORD: After two excellent seasons at Kansas, Ahuna entered the transfer portal and became one of its most highly coveted players. He chose Tennessee but did not quite perform to the degree he did with the Jayhawks. Ahuna also had two stints in the Cape Cod League and also played for the 2022 Collegiate National Team. He played hurt for most of the season and finished with nearly as many strikeouts as he had in his previous two seasons combined. Nonetheless, the Giants banked on what they'd seen in the past and chose him in the fourth round of the 2023 draft and signed him for $497,500. He did not play after signing.

SCOUTING REPORT: After struggling in the Southeastern Conference, Ahuna's biggest question is contact. The Giants believe some of those issues stemmed from the injury and will improve when he returns to full health but they do acknowledge that the strikeouts will need to be addressed and could be improved with simplified swing mechanics. Ideally, Ahuna will adopt a hit-first mindset and let the power, which projects as fringe-average, come naturally. He should easily stick at shortstop, where he is a plus defender with plus arm strength. Ahuna is an above-average runner.

THE FUTURE: Ahuna has the pedigree to begin the year at High-A Eugene but the Giants have a tendency to slow-cook their prospects, so he might open at Low-A San Jose. If he reaches his ceiling, he should be a standout defensive shortstop who hits toward the bottom of an order.

Year	Age	Club (League)	Level	AVG	G	AB	R	H	2B	3B	HR	RBI	BB	SO	SB	OBP	SLG
2023	21	Did not play															

19 TREVOR McDONALD, RHP

FB: 65. **SL:** 40. **CB:** 60. **CTL:** 60. **BA Grade:** 40. **Risk:** High.

Born: February 26, 2001. **B-T:** R-R. **HT:** 6-2. **WT:** 200. **Drafted:** HS—Mobile, AL, 2019 (11th round). **Signed by:** Jeff Wood.

TRACK RECORD: McDonald was the Giants' 11th-round pick in 2019. They drafted him from a high school in Alabama and signed him for $800,000, the highest bonus in the round and the third-highest figure in San Francisco's class. McDonald pitched well in 2022 but really broke out in 2023, when he dominated at High-A Eugene and earned a spot on the 40-man roster.

SCOUTING REPORT: McDonald works with a pair of fastballs and a pair of breaking balls. He added strength to his frame and saw his four- and two-seam fastball each average around 94 mph and peak at

98. He used the two-seamer most frequently, which helped him post a groundout-to-flyout ratio of more than 4.5-to-1. He backs the fastballs with a slider and a curveball. He deployed both at a near-equal rate. The low-80s curveball is the superior offering. It's a potentially plus pitch with high spin, deep break and rates of miss and chase that grade out as nearly double-plus. McDonald's slider is a mid-80s offering that gives hitters an extra option to consider. He has potentially plus control as well.

THE FUTURE: McDonald's biggest test will come in 2024, when he'll move to Double-A Richmond. He has a chance to start but could be a dynamic weapon out of the bullpen thanks to his nasty sinker.

Year	Age	Club (League)	Level	W	L	ERA	G	GS	IP	H	HR	BB	SO	BB%	SO%	WHIP	AVG
2023	22	ACL Giants Black	Rk	0	1	1.04	4	4	9	8	0	2	11	5.7	31.4	1.15	.250
2023	22	ACL Giants Orange	Rk	0	0	18.00	1	1	1	1	0	1	1	16.7	16.7	2.00	.333
2023	22	Eugene (NWL)	A+	3	1	0.96	9	8	38	24	1	8	39	5.7	27.7	0.85	.185
Minor League Totals				11	9	2.66	62	40	223	191	9	89	250	9.4	26.5	1.26	.233

20 CARSON SEYMOUR, RHP

FB: 60. **SL:** 60. **CHG:** 30. **CTL:** 55. **BA Grade:** 40. **Risk:** High.

Born: December 16, 1998. **B-T:** R-R. **HT:** 6-6. **WT:** 260. **Drafted:** Kansas State, 2021 (6th round).
Signed by: Scott Thomas (Mets).

TRACK RECORD: Seymour was originally selected by the Mets in the sixth round of the 2021 draft. He was traded in 2022 with lefty Nick Zwack as part of a four-player package that brought outfielder Darin Ruf to the Mets. Seymour split his 2022 season between the Class A levels, then spent all of 2023 at Double-A Richmond. His 114 strikeouts were the third-most in the system.

SCOUTING REPORT: Early in the year, Seymour made too many mistakes in the middle of the plate. To correct the issue, he and the Giants worked on refining the way he mixed his four- and two-seam fastballs, which each sit around 94 mph and have peaked at 97. As a result, scouts say, Seymour's slider became more effective. The pitch is thrown between 88-92 mph and shows tight gyro shape with short, sharp break. He threw a curveball during the season but now exclusively uses the slider. Seymour's changeup is a clear fourth pitch in his mix and was thrown just 2% of the time in 2023. It's a well below-average offering that will need to take serious steps forward if Seymour is to remain a rotation option. He works from the stretch only and has a short arm action in the back.

THE FUTURE: Seymour will move to Triple-A in 2023, where he will be tested by the confines of the automatic ball-strike system. He looks like a reliever who leans heavily on his fastball-slider combination.

Year	Age	Club (League)	Level	W	L	ERA	G	GS	IP	H	HR	BB	SO	BB%	SO%	WHIP	AVG
2023	24	Richmond (EL)	AA	5	3	3.99	28	23	113	96	8	43	114	9.2	24.5	1.23	.231
Minor League Totals				12	11	3.51	56	42	228	192	17	80	253	8.5	26.7	1.19	.227

21 ERIC SILVA, RHP

FB: 55. **CB:** 50. **SL:** 55. **CHG:** 50. **CTL:** 40. **BA Grade:** 45. **Risk:** Extreme.

Born: October 3, 2002. **B-T:** R-R. **HT:** 6-1. **WT:** 185. **Drafted:** HS—San Juan Capistrano, CA, 2021 (4th round).
Signed by: Brad Cameron.

TRACK RECORD: Silva was taken out of high school in California in the fourth round of the 2021 draft. The Giants coaxed him out of his commitment to UCLA with a bonus of $1,497,500. Silva spent his first full year as a pro at Low-A San Jose, where he pitched to mixed results. He advanced to High-A Eugene in 2023 and struggled enough that he required time in the Arizona Complex League for a bit of a reset.

SCOUTING REPORT: The Giants still believe in Silva's ceiling, but the results have to begin showing up, and his offseason work will be crucial in determining his long-term role. His final 10 appearances were out of the bullpen. As a starter, Silva works with a five-pitch mix fronted by 92-94 mph four- and two-seam fastballs and backed with a slider that could be above-average and a potentially average curveball and changeup. He spins the ball well, gets high miss rates on both of his breaking pitches and throws from a lower release height. Scouts haven't given up on Silva's ceiling, but he needs to learn the best ways to deploy his mix. He doesn't sequence well, leading to predictable patterns that play into hitters' hands. Silva has a smaller frame but is also quite athletic, which should help him repeat his delivery.

THE FUTURE: Silva is likely to return to Eugene for more seasoning. This might be his last chance to prove he can start before moving to the bullpen on a full-time basis.

Year	Age	Club (League)	Level	W	L	ERA	G	GS	IP	H	HR	BB	SO	BB%	SO%	WHIP	AVG
2023	20	ACL Giants Black	Rk	0	0	5.06	2	2	5	7	0	0	13	0.0	52.0	1.31	.292
2023	20	Eugene (NWL)	A+	2	7	5.92	28	18	76	78	7	39	73	11.4	21.3	1.54	.269
Minor League Totals				5	15	6.05	54	42	168	166	18	81	187	10.9	25.2	1.47	.261

22 COLE FOSTER, SS

HIT: 45. **POW:** 50. **RUN:** 50. **FLD:** 50. **ARM:** 50. **BA Grade:** 40. **Risk:** High.

Born: October 8, 2001. **B-T:** B-R. **HT:** 6-1. **WT:** 193. **Drafted:** Auburn, 2023 (3rd round). **Signed by:** Jeff Wood.

TRACK RECORD: Foster spent three seasons at Auburn, including a 2023 campaign that saw him club a career-best 13 home runs. The Giants took Foster in the third round and signed him for a bonus of $747,500. He split his pro debut between Rookie ball and Low-A and hit seven home runs.

SCOUTING REPORT: The Giants were drawn to Foster for his combination of athleticism, power and middle-diamond skills. He's a more powerful hitter from the left side but a more complete hitter when batting righthanded and could stand to improve his swing decisions overall. He needs to tighten his approach to cut down on his swing-and-miss and better learn to use the whole field. Foster is a solid shortstop but has trouble getting to balls hit to his right. He has short-area quickness and is an average runner but will have to learn to take better angles to reach grounders hit his way.

THE FUTURE: After finishing the year at Low-A, Foster may return to the level in 2024 or could head to High-A Eugene. No matter the assignment, he'll need to improve his zone control and polish his defense.

Year	Age	Club (League)	Level	AVG	G	AB	R	H	2B	3B	HR	RBI	BB	SO	SB	OBP	SLG
2023	21	ACL Giants Black	Rk	.333	7	30	8	10	2	0	3	8	1	10	0	.355	.700
2023	21	San Jose (CAL)	A	.230	25	100	14	23	4	0	4	15	8	35	2	.306	.390
Minor League Totals				.254	32	130	22	33	6	0	7	23	9	45	2	.317	.462

23 DIEGO VELASQUEZ, SS/2B

HIT: 50. **POW:** 40. **RUN:** 55. **FLD:** 60. **ARM:** 50. **BA Grade:** 40. **Risk:** High.

Born: October 1, 2003. **B-T:** B-R. **HT:** 6-1. **WT:** 150. **Signed:** Venezuela, 2021. **Signed by:** Robert Moron.

TRACK RECORD: Velasquez was the Giants' top international signee in the period that opened on Jan. 15, 2021. He was lauded for his defensive skills and contact-oriented approach, and spent the bulk of his first two seasons in the complex leagues. He reached Low-A toward the end of 2022 and then spent all of 2023 at the level, where he led the league with 127 hits and 32 doubles.

SCOUTING REPORT: None of Velasquez's tools jumps off the page, but the whole package could give him a ceiling of a versatile big leaguer who plays every day. His offensive game is geared for contact over impact, although his righthanded swing tends to go in and out of the zone fairly quickly. Scouts believe he has a chance to get to average raw power as he matures. He's a solid defender who will likely wind up at second base, where he has the chance to be plus, but could survive at either shortstop or third base in a pinch thanks to quickness and impressive instincts, above-average speed and an average throwing arm. His range isn't quite enough to stick at shortstop full time, however.

THE FUTURE: After an excellent year at Low-A, Velasquez will move to High-A Eugene in 2024.

Year	Age	Club (League)	Level	AVG	G	AB	R	H	2B	3B	HR	RBI	BB	SO	SB	OBP	SLG
2023	19	San Jose (CAL)	A	.298	111	426	76	127	32	1	8	69	56	82	23	.387	.434
Minor League Totals				.269	219	789	119	212	41	3	9	99	93	147	32	.354	.362

24 ADRIAN SUGASTEY, C

HIT: 40. **POW:** 40. **RUN:** 30. **FLD:** 55. **ARM:** 60. **BA Grade:** 40. **Risk:** High.

Born: October 23, 2002. **B-T:** R-R. **HT:** 6-1. **WT:** 210. **Signed:** Panama, 2019. **Signed by:** Rogelio Castillo.

TRACK RECORD: Sugastey was part of Panama's junior national team and signed with San Francisco in 2019 for a bonus of $525,000. He skipped the Dominican Summer League, reached Low-A quickly in 2022 and then spent all of 2023 at High-A Eugene. He was limited to just 63 games by injuries. It was the second straight year when Sugastey was limited to fewer than 100 games.

SCOUTING REPORT: Sugastey has a blend of skills on both sides of the ball but little that necessarily stands out as a carrying tool. He does a decent job of making contact in the zone but chases far too frequently. Scouts also note that he struggles against fastballs with premium velocity. He doesn't hit the ball particularly hard, either, with average (83.5 mph) and 90th percentile (99.2 mph) exit velocities that grade as below-average. Sugastey has slowed down a bit as he's matured but still has the mobility to project as an above-average defender behind the dish with a plus throwing arm. He is a well below-average runner.

THE FUTURE: After missing half the season, Sugastey will likely head back to High-A and split time at catcher with Onil Perez in 2024. He could become a second-division backup.

Year	Age	Club (League)	Level	AVG	G	AB	R	H	2B	3B	HR	RBI	BB	SO	SB	OBP	SLG
2023	20	Eugene (NWL)	A+	.298	63	248	23	74	15	2	4	40	13	37	1	.333	.423
Minor League Totals				.284	190	722	91	205	33	4	11	99	59	121	3	.346	.386

25 HELIOT RAMOS, OF

HIT: 40. **POW:** 45. **RUN:** 45. **FLD:** 45. **ARM:** 40. **BA Grade:** 40. **Risk:** High.

Born: September 7, 1999. **B-T:** R-R. **HT:** 5-9. **WT:** 233. **Drafted:** HS—Guaynabo, PR, 2017 (1st round).
Signed by: Junior Roman.
TRACK RECORD: Ramos was the team's first-round pick in 2017, when he was one of the youngest players in the class. He's appeared in three Futures Games and has been a part of the Giants' 40-man roster since 2021. He made his big league debut in 2022 and got back to San Francisco for 56 games in 2023.
SCOUTING REPORT: Ramos dealt with a pair of strains to his right oblique in 2023 but otherwise performed well at Triple-A Sacramento. The same can not be said for his big league time. He still hits the ball fairly hard but shows elevated rates of miss and chase that will likely limit him to a fringy offensive skill set. Ramos is not much of a defender either and his chances of being serviceable in center field have been all but extinguished. He's a passable left fielder thanks to fringe-average speed and a below-average arm, but his bat does not appear to be anywhere near the caliber required to profile in a corner as a regular.
THE FUTURE: Without serious improvements, Ramos will likely be limited to an up-down player who only gets extended playing time in emergencies. At just 24 years old, he still has time somewhat on his side.

Year	Age	Club (League)	Level	AVG	G	AB	R	H	2B	3B	HR	RBI	BB	SO	SB	OBP	SLG
2023	23	San Jose (CAL)	A	.353	5	17	2	6	3	0	2	6	2	4	0	.421	.882
2023	23	Sacramento (PCL)	AAA	.300	62	227	44	68	14	3	12	45	27	66	9	.382	.546
2023	23	San Francisco (NL)	MLB	.179	25	56	5	10	4	0	1	2	4	20	0	.233	.304
Minor League Totals				.265	552	2132	331	565	118	22	72	286	199	622	56	.338	.442
Major League Totals				.158	34	76	9	12	4	0	1	2	6	26	0	.220	.250

26 RYAN MURPHY, RHP

FB: 50. **CB:** 50. **SL:** 50. **CHG:** 45. **CTL:** 50. **BA Grade:** 40. **Risk:** High.

Born: October 8, 1999. **B-T:** R-R. **HT:** 6-1. **WT:** 190. **Drafted:** Le Moyne (NY), 2020 (5th round). **Signed by:** Ray Callari.
TRACK RECORD: Murphy was selected in the fifth round of the pandemic-shortened 2020 draft out of Division II Le Moyne (N.Y), which also produced Nationals righthander Josiah Gray. Murphy was a revelation in his first pro season, when he struck out 164 hitters in 107.1 innings split between both of the Giants' Class A levels. His encore performance was cut short by back and elbow injuries, though he did reach Double-A. He returned to the level in 2023 and tied the career high innings total he'd set in 2021.
SCOUTING REPORT: Murphy does not have a knockout arsenal but at his best shows the ability to mix and match four pitches in and out of the strike zone. The righthander leaned heavily on his four-seamer and two breaking pitches in 2023, with the trio making up a full 90% of his arsenal. The fastball averages around 92 mph with solid spin and life through the zone, while the curveball and slider respectively sit at 81 and 85 mph. None of his pitches garnered a high whiff rate, but he still struck out a solid 23% of batters. His control took a step backwards and now he looks to be more average than plus in that department.
THE FUTURE: Murphy may return to Double-A in 2024 for further seasoning. He projects as a bulk reliever or swingman unless one of his offspeed pitches takes a step forward.

Year	Age	Club (League)	Level	W	L	ERA	G	GS	IP	H	HR	BB	SO	BB%	SO%	WHIP	AVG
2023	23	Richmond (EL)	AA	2	9	4.36	29	27	107	102	15	51	107	11.0	23.0	1.43	.252
Minor League Totals				10	14	3.64	61	57	257	208	32	100	328	9.4	30.8	1.20	.221

27 WILLIAM KEMPNER, RHP

FB: 60. **SL:** 60. **CHG:** 40. **CTL:** 40. **BA Grade:** 40. **Risk:** High.

Born: June 18, 2001. **B-T:** R-R. **HT:** 6-0. **WT:** 222. **Drafted:** Gonzaga, 2022 (3rd round). **Signed by:** Larry Casian.
TRACK RECORD: Kempner was a standout at Gonzaga for three seasons before the Giants popped him in the third round of the 2022 draft. He signed for $525,000 and has spent the majority of his career pitching in a relief role. He moved from Low-A to Double-A in his first full season and finished the year with 78 strikeouts and 30 walks in 62.2 innings.
SCOUTING REPORT: Kempner's aggression and arm action will relegate him to a bullpen role, where his pitch mix could be overpowering. The primary pieces of his arsenal are a mid-90s two-seam fastball and a sweeper slider in the low 80s that projects as plus. He also throws high-80s changeup, but it accounted for just 1% of his mix in 2023. He's got a thick body with surprising twitch and can make hitters look silly when everything clicks. Kempner's control is below-average, which might make the difference between which role he fills in the big leagues.
THE FUTURE: Kempner will likely return to Double-A in 2024, when he'll look to tighten his control and

improve his changeup enough to make it a viable third option. He's a straight reliever who could fill an impact role with further development.

Year	Age	Club (League)	Level	W	L	ERA	G	GS	IP	H	HR	BB	SO	BB%	SO%	WHIP	AVG
2023	22	San Jose (CAL)	A	1	3	4.67	14	5	27	21	0	15	29	12.1	23.4	1.33	.208
2023	22	Eugene (NWL)	A+	3	2	2.91	23	0	34	28	5	13	47	9.0	32.6	1.21	.224
2023	22	Richmond (EL)	AA	0	0	5.40	1	0	2	3	0	2	2	20.0	20.0	3.00	.375
Minor League Totals				5	5	3.93	43	7	72	62	6	36	89	11.2	27.7	1.38	.231

28 JOSE CRUZ, RHP

FB: 60. **SL:** 30. **CHG:** 55. **CTL:** 40. **BA Grade:** 40. **Risk:** High.

Born: May 18, 2000. **B-T:** R-R. **HT:** 6-1. **WT:** 178. **Signed:** Dominican Republic, 2017. **Signed by:** Gabriel Elias.

TRACK RECORD: After signing out of the Dominican Republic in 2017, Cruz moved through the minors fairly anonymously until breaking out in 2022. He lowered his arm slot and switched from a four-seam to a two-seam fastball, which led to an outstanding season and culminated with a spot on the 40-man roster. He split the 2023 season between High-A Eugene and Double-A Richmond, where he ran into serious control issues.

SCOUTING REPORT: Cruz works primarily with his two-seamer and changeup, and each projects to be above-average or better. He sprinkles in a slider as well, but it is well below-average and stands as a clear third pitch in his arsenal. He delivers all three pitches from a low slot with a crossfire finish that creates plenty of deception. Now Cruz needs to figure out how to improve his control and command while maintaining the same level of deception. He ran into big-time issues at Double-A, where his strike rate dropped from 65% to just 55% and he issued 31 walks in 25.2 innings.

THE FUTURE: There's little question about Cruz's stuff, but it won't mean much if he can't find the strike zone consistently. Further development of his slider would give hitters another wrinkle to consider.

Year	Age	Club (League)	Level	W	L	ERA	G	GS	IP	H	HR	BB	SO	BB%	SO%	WHIP	AVG
2023	23	Eugene (NWL)	A+	0	0	1.45	13	0	19	7	0	7	28	9.6	38.4	0.75	.113
2023	23	Richmond (EL)	AA	0	2	6.66	23	0	26	16	5	31	39	23.8	30.0	1.83	.170
Minor League Totals				9	9	3.91	127	3	198	136	13	114	271	13.3	31.5	1.26	.190

29 GERELMI MALDONADO, RHP

FB: 65. **SL:** 60. **CHG:** 45. **CTL:** 40. **BA Grade:** 40. **Risk:** High.

Born: December 21, 2003. **B-T:** R-R. **HT:** 6-2. **WT:** 170. **Signed:** Dominican Republic, 2021. **Signed by:** Robert Moron.

TRACK RECORD: Maldonado was signed out of the Dominican Republic in 2021 as a sleeper in a class that was led by shortstop Diego Velasquez. He's advanced a level year since signing and made his full-season debut in 2023 at Low-A San Jose. He was limited to 65 innings because of a forearm strain that landed him on the 60-day injured list in August.

SCOUTING REPORT: Maldonado worked in a starter's role at San Jose but has the explosive pitch mix to become a powerful late-inning reliever. He works mostly with two pitches: a mid-90s fastball and a mid-80s slider that flashes plus but needs more consistency to reach its ceiling. He has a changeup that might settle in around fringe-average and could function as a solid third option. His control is spotty now but could get to below-average with further refinement or if he moves to the bullpen and airs it out for an inning or two at a time. He's gained significant weight since signing and will need to keep his conditioning in check to reach his ceiling.

THE FUTURE: Maldonado will move to High-A Eugene in 2024 and has a likely future as a power reliever who can pitch the late innings.

Year	Age	Club (League)	Level	W	L	ERA	G	GS	IP	H	HR	BB	SO	BB%	SO%	WHIP	AVG
2023	19	San Jose (CAL)	A	1	1	4.71	19	16	65	52	5	40	81	13.9	28.2	1.42	.221
Minor League Totals				3	4	4.10	46	30	134	109	8	76	170	12.9	29.0	1.38	.222

30 LIAM SIMON, RHP

FB: 60. **SL:** 55. **CTL:** 40. **BA Grade:** 40. **Risk:** High.

Born: October 16, 2000. **B-T:** R-R. **HT:** 6-4. **WT:** 220. **Drafted:** Notre Dame, 2022 (5th round). **Signed by:** Todd Coryell.

TRACK RECORD: After splitting his junior year between the rotation and the bullpen at Notre Dame, Simon was selected by the Giants in the fifth round of the 2022 draft. He signed for $317,500 and split his first full year between the Arizona Complex League and Low-A. He returned to Low-A in 2023 but had Tommy John surgery in early May.

SCOUTING REPORT: Before the injury, Simon showed an overwhelming two-pitch mix of a mid-90s sinker and a low-80s slider. As a collegian, Simon struggled to throw strikes but had improved in that regard during his time as a pro, though his control numbers were by no means standout. Before the injury, scouts noted a need for Simon to find consistency with the shape of his slider. Sometimes it had cutting action while other times it showed more tilt. He's got a solid, repeatable delivery, though there should be some expected rust when he gets back on the mound.

THE FUTURE: Simon should be back sometime in the first half of the season. If his stuff comes back in full, he has a chance to pitch in late-inning situations. He'll have to improve his control and find a consistent slider shape to reach that role.

Year	Age	Club (League)	Level	W	L	ERA	G	GS	IP	H	HR	BB	SO	BB%	SO%	WHIP	AVG
2023	22	San Jose (CAL)	A	1	1	3.86	6	2	21	18	1	9	32	10.1	36.0	1.29	.234
Minor League Totals				1	1	3.38	12	4	32	24	1	15	44	11.0	32.4	1.22	.205

Bryce Miller

HAYDEN CARROLL/TEXAS RANGERS/GETTY IMAGES

Seattle Mariners

BY KYLE GLASER

The Mariners have emerged from their rebuild and become the perennial playoff contender hoped for. Now the goal is to erase the stain of being the only team to never reach a World Series.

The Mariners went 88-74 in 2023 and remained in the American League playoff picture until the season's final weekend. Logan Gilbert and George Kirby cemented their status as two of the AL's best young pitchers and fellow homegrown righthanders Bryce Miller and Bryan Woo had two of the best seasons among rookie pitchers. Franchise center fielder Julio Rodriguez posted a 30-30 campaign and finished fourth in AL MVP voting, while 20-something franchise staples J.P. Crawford and Cal Raleigh had their best offensive seasons.

But despite those positives, issues surfaced that must be resolved for the Mariners to finally reach the Fall Classic.

For the second time in three years, general manager Jerry Dipoto traded away the Mariners' closer at the deadline despite the fact the team was in playoff contention. Just as the trade of Kendall Graveman led to a player revolt in 2021, the trade of closer Paul Sewald to the Diamondbacks went over poorly in a clubhouse that felt the team needed to add, not subtract.

"Losing Paul at the trade deadline definitely hurt and I think was a big spot in our season," Raleigh said after the Mariners were eliminated from playoff contention.

"I think we've done a great job of growing some players here and within the farm system, but sometimes you got to go out and you have to buy and that's just the name of the game."

Said Crawford: "I think Cal had some great comments . . . I know there's a big controversy about that and I'm with him on that. I think we need to go out there and really make a move to help this team win."

PROJECTED 2027 LINEUP

Catcher	Cal Raleigh	30
First Base	Tyler Locklear	26
Second Base	Cole Young	23
Third Base	Colt Emerson	21
Shortstop	J.P. Crawford	32
Left Field	Harry Ford	24
Center Field	Julio Rodriguez	26
Right Field	Gabriel Gonzalez	23
Designated Hitter	Lazaro Montes	22
No. 1 Starter	Luis Castillo	34
No. 2 Starter	George Kirby	29
No. 3 Starter	Logan Gilbert	30
No. 4 Starter	Bryce Miller	28
No. 5 Starter	Bryan Woo	27
Closer	Andres Muñoz	28

Dipoto doubled down in his end-of-season press conference, stating the franchise's goal was to win 54% of its games—an 87-win pace—over a 10-year period and that it would reach a World Series merely by doing that.

"If what you're doing is focusing year to year on, 'What do we have to do to win the World Series this year?', you might be one of the teams that's laying in the mud and can't get up for another decade," Dipoto said. "So we're actually doing that fanbase a favor in asking for their patience to win the World Series while we continue to build a sustainably good roster."

Dipoto apologized a day later, but the damage was done. The perception the front office isn't willing to make the bold additions needed to get the Mariners to the World Series has calcified.

The Mariners have homegrown talent on the way. Through the draft and international signings, they've developed a promising wave of position players in the lower levels that is on the rise to complement their homegrown arms in the major leagues.

But without a change in philosophy, that won't matter. Unless the Mariners start aggressively making the additions needed to reach a World Series and make doing so their focus, all the talent they've amassed will be for naught. ■

SEATTLE MARINERS

TOP 2024 CONTRIBUTORS	RANK
1. Emerson Hancock, RHP	10
2. Prelander Berroa, RHP	12
3. Zach DeLoach, OF	14

BREAKOUT PROSPECTS	RANK
1. Aidan Smith, OF	19
2. Darren Bowen, RHP	24
3. Jeter Martinez, RHP	30

SOURCE OF TOP 30 TALENT

Homegrown	27	Acquired	3
College	13	Trade	3
Junior college	0	Rule 5 draft	0
High school	8	Independent league	0
Nondrafted free agent	0	Free agent/waivers	0
International	6		

LF
Zach DeLoach (14)
Spencer Packard (22)
Isiah Gilliam

CF
Jonny Farmelo (8)
Jonatan Clase (11)
Aidan Smith (19)
Bill Knight
Victor Labrada

RF
Lazaro Montes (4)
Gabriel Gonzalez (5)
Alberto Rodriguez (20)

3B
Ben Williamson (16)
Ben Ramirez
Starlin Aguilar
Milkar Perez

SS
Cole Young (1)
Colt Emerson (3)
Felnin Celesten (7)
Tai Peete (13)
Axel Sanchez

2B
Michael Arroyo (9)
Ryan Bliss (17)
Brock Rodden (25)
Kaden Polcovich
Josh Hood

1B
Tyler Locklear (6)
Hogan Windish (27)
Luis Suisbel
Gabe Moncada

C
Harry Ford (2)
Freuddy Batista
Tatem Levins
Sebastian De Andrade
Jake Anchia

LHP

LHSP	LHRP
Reid VanScoter (29)	Raul Alcantara
Juan Pinto	
Brandon Schaeffer	

RHP

RHSP	RHRP
Emerson Hancock (10)	Prelander Berroa (12)
Taylor Dollard (15)	Darren Bowen (24)
Teddy McGraw (18)	Jimmy Joyce (26)
Walter Ford (21)	Troy Taylor (28)
Michael Morales (23)	Carlos Vargas
Jeter Martinez (30)	Marcelo Perez
Cole Phillips	Travis Kuhn
Logan Evans	Luis Curvelo
Ashton Izzi	Ty Cummings
Brody Hopkins	Natanel Garabitos
Shaddon Peavyhouse	
Tyler Cleveland	
Nick Davila	

1 COLE YOUNG, SS

Born: July 29, 2003. **B-T:** L-R. **HT:** 6-0. **WT:** 180.
Drafted: HS—Wexford, PA, 2022 (1st round).
Signed by: Jackson Laumann.

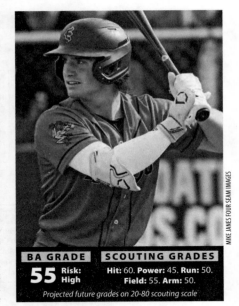

MIKE JANES FOUR SEAM IMAGES

TRACK RECORD: Young first emerged on the baseball scene as a 10-year-old when he won MLB's Pitch, Hit and Run competition for his age bracket at Minnesota's Target Field during 2014 All-Star Weekend. He parlayed that into continued success as a teenager and blossomed into one of the top hitters in the 2022 draft at North Allegheny High just outside Pittsburgh. He hit .428 in a decorated three-year career and showed he could compete with warm-weather players with repeated standout performances on the summer showcase circuit. The Mariners drafted him 21st overall in 2022 and signed him for $3.3 million to forgo a Duke commitment. Young hit .367 in his pro debut and continued to assert himself as a premium hitter in his first full season in 2023. He hit .277/.399/.449 with 34 doubles, a system-high nine triples, 11 home runs and 22 stolen bases across the Class A levels and recorded nearly as many walks (88) as strikeouts (90).

SCOUTING REPORT: Young is a natural hitter with a sweet lefthanded swing. He has a fast, direct stroke with natural loft and consistently finds the barrel. He has exceptional hand-eye coordination and natural timing and is rarely fooled or caught off-balance. He uses the whole field and is particularly adept at driving the ball the other way. Young doesn't have overwhelming bat speed or strength, but he finds the barrel so frequently he's able to make consistent quality contact. He pulls balls in the air for home runs to right field or laces them on a line for doubles into the left-center gap. He expertly manages the strike zone, rarely swings and misses and projects to be a plus hitter who averages around 15 home runs per season. He should post high on-base percentages and rack up doubles. Young is an average runner with a quick first step and good instincts on the basepaths. He is faster underway than out of the box and has a good feel for knowing when to take an extra base. Young is more steady than flashy defensively in the middle infield. He positions himself well with good instincts, plays low to the ground and has soft, reliable hands at shortstop. His lateral range is a tick short and he loses accuracy on longer throws, so he is likely to move to second base in the long term. He has average arm strength and projects to be an above-average defender at the

BA GRADE	SCOUTING GRADES
55 Risk: High	Hit: 60. Power: 45. Run: 50. Field: 55. Arm: 50.

Projected future grades on 20-80 scouting scale

BEST TOOLS

BATTING

Best Hitter for Average	Cole Young
Best Power Hitter	Lazaro Montes
Best Strike-Zone Discipline	Harry Ford
Fastest Baserunner	Jonatan Clase
Best Athlete	Harry Ford

PITCHING

Best Fastball	Natanel Garabitos
Best Curveball	Jimmy Joyce
Best Slider	Prelander Berroa
Best Changeup	Emerson Hancock
Best Control	Taylor Dollard

FIELDING

Best Defensive Catcher	Jake Anchia
Best Defensive Infielder	Axel Sanchez
Best Infield Arm	Felnin Celesten
Best Defensive Outfielder	Johnny Farmelo
Best Outfield Arm	Gabriel Gonzalez

keystone. Young lacks explosive tools and rarely stands out on a first look, but he is the type of player whom observers gain increased appreciation for over time. He is a calm, composed individual with a slow heartbeat and is rarely rattled in pressure situations.

THE FUTURE: Young projects to be a productive No. 2 hitter who hits for a high average, draws walks and does occasional damage while playing steady defense in the middle infield. He will open 2024 at Double-A Arkansas and is the Mariners' second baseman of the future. ■

Year	Age	Club (League)	Level	AVG	G	AB	R	H	2B	3B	HR	RBI	BB	SO	SB	OBP	SLG
2023	19	Modesto (CAL)	A	.267	78	303	60	81	20	7	5	39	54	52	17	.396	.429
2023	19	Everett (NWL)	A+	.292	48	192	32	56	14	2	6	23	34	38	5	.404	.479
Minor League Totals				.286	143	555	109	159	35	10	13	76	96	98	26	.402	.456

2 HARRY FORD, C

HIT: 50. **POW:** 50. **RUN:** 60. **FLD:** 45. **ARM:** 55. **BA Grade:** 55. **Risk:** High.

Born: February 21, 2003. **B-T:** R-R. **HT:** 5-10. **WT:** 200.
Drafted: HS—Kennesaw, GA, 2021 (1st round). **Signed by:** John Wiedenbauer
TRACK RECORD: The son of two British nationals, Ford was born and raised in Georgia and emerged as the top high school catcher in the 2021 draft class. The Mariners drafted him 12th overall and signed him for $4,366,400 after he dazzled general manager Jerry Dipoto in a pre-draft workout. Ford finished fourth in the California League with a .425 on-base percentage in his first full season and blossomed on an international stage in 2023. He hit .308 with two home runs as Great Britain's cleanup hitter and starting catcher in the World Baseball Classic and led the Brits to their first WBC win. He finished second in the Northwest League with an .840 OPS in 2023 and started the Futures Game in Seattle.
SCOUTING REPORT: Ford is an exceptional athlete by any measure, but especially for a catcher. He is a plus runner with twitchy, explosive actions and a strong frame. He has a short, impactful righthanded swing and drives the ball in the air from gap to gap. He is an exceedingly patient hitter and almost never chases out of the strike zone. Ford draws walks and hits the ball hard on contact but is prone to swinging and missing in the zone. He can be passive early in counts and gets beat by good velocity. He has the athleticism to adjust and be an average hitter with average power in time. Ford's athleticism translates behind the plate. He gets out of the crouch quickly to corral popups and dribblers and controls running games with his above-average arm strength and quick release. His blocking and receiving are fringy but improving with experience. He is an advanced game-caller and natural leader.
THE FUTURE: Ford projects to be an everyday catcher who gets on base and provides versatility with his athleticism. He'll open at Double-A Arkansas in 2024.

Year	Age	Club (League)	Level	AVG	G	AB	R	H	2B	3B	HR	RBI	BB	SO	SB	OBP	SLG
2023	20	Everett (NWL)	A+	.257	118	444	89	114	24	4	15	67	103	109	24	.410	.430
Minor League Totals				.267	241	889	190	237	54	8	29	142	200	238	50	.416	.443

3 COLT EMERSON, SS

HIT: 60. **POW:** 50. **RUN:** 45. **FLD:** 50. **ARM:** 55. **BA Grade:** 55 **Risk:** High.

Born: July 20, 2005. **B-T:** L-R. **HT:** 6-1. **WT:** 195.
Drafted: HS—New Concord, OH, 2023 (1st round). **Signed by:** Jackson Laumann.
TRACK RECORD: Emerson hails from the small Ohio town of Cambridge—population: 10,014—but his talent has long made him known to evaluators. He played on USA Baseball's 12U and 18U national teams and hit .360 to lead Team USA to the gold medal at the 2022 WBSC U-18 Baseball World Cup. He emerged as one of the top hitters in the 2023 draft class throughout his senior spring and was drafted 22nd overall by the Mariners. He signed for an over-slot $3.8 million to forgo an Auburn commitment. Emerson immediately made good on his pedigree with a sterling pro debut. He hit .374/.496/.550 in 24 games between the Arizona Complex League and Low-A Modesto, capped by going 4-for-6 with four RBIs in the clinching game of the California League championship series.
SCOUTING REPORT: Emerson is a polished offensive player with a sweet, lefthanded swing. He's a disciplined hitter who knows the strike zone and makes hard contact off the barrel with a fast, simple stroke. He's exceptionally consistent with his swing and approach and has few holes for pitchers to attack. He uses the whole field and projects to be a plus hitter. Emerson primarily hits ground balls and low line drives, but he hits the ball hard. He's strong in his frame and has a chance to reach 15-20 home runs as he learns to elevate. Emerson has fringe-average speed and isn't the rangiest shortstop, but he positions himself well with good instincts and makes the routine plays. He plays low to the ground, has reliable hands and makes every throw with above-average arm strength. He may move to third base as he gets bigger and slows down.
THE FUTURE: Emerson projects to be a solid everyday infielder who produces on both sides of the ball. He'll begin 2024 back at Modesto.

Year	Age	Club (League)	Level	AVG	G	AB	R	H	2B	3B	HR	RBI	BB	SO	SB	OBP	SLG
2023	17	ACL Mariners	Rk	.536	8	28	10	15	4	0	1	5	6	6	4	.629	.786
2023	17	Modesto (CAL)	A	.302	16	63	17	19	6	0	1	8	11	14	4	.436	.444
Minor League Totals				.374	24	91	27	34	10	0	2	13	17	20	8	.496	.549

4 LAZARO MONTES, OF

HIT: 40. **POW:** 70. **RUN:** 20. **FLD:** 30. **ARM:** 50. **BA Grade:** 55. **Risk:** Very High.

Born: October 22, 2004. **B-T:** L-R. **HT:** 6-4. **WT:** 256.
Signed: Cuba, 2022. **Signed by:** Ismael Rosado.

TRACK RECORD: Born and raised in Cuba, Montes moved to the Dominican Republic as a teenager to train with famed hitting instructor Aldo Marrero, who is best known for training Astros slugger Yordan Alvarez. Montes blossomed into one of the premier power hitters in the 2022 international class under Marrero and signed with the Mariners for $2.5 million. He experienced some ups and downs in his pro debut in the Dominican Summer League but he flourished in his U.S. debut in 2023. He hit .303/.440/.560 with 13 home runs in 70 games between the Arizona Complex League and Low-A Modesto and led the Nuts to a California League championship.

SCOUTING REPORT: Montes is a massive lefthanded slugger at 6-foot-4, 256 pounds. He possesses plus-plus power and demolishes pitches for scorching line drives and mesmerizing home runs. He posts some of the highest exit velocities in the Mariners' system and is strong enough to hit balls out even when he mis-hits them. Montes knows the strike zone and limits his chases, but he swings and misses an alarming amount in the zone. He is still learning to recognize spin and struggles to hit anything above the belt with his uphill swing plane. He projects to be a below-average hitter who makes an impact with 30-plus home run power. Montes plays hard and hustles in right field, but he's a bottom-of-the scale runner with a heavy lower half. He doesn't move well enough to stick in the outfield and projects to move to first base or DH. Montes is a big personality with a charismatic, energetic presence and celebrates demonstratively. He keeps his teammates loose in the dugout as the life of the party.

THE FUTURE: Montes projects to be a power-hitting DH similar to a lefthanded Franmil Reyes in both production and personality. He'll see High-A Everett in 2024.

Year	Age	Club (League)	Level	AVG	G	AB	R	H	2B	3B	HR	RBI	BB	SO	SB	OBP	SLG
2023	18	ACL Mariners	Rk	.282	37	110	31	31	10	1	6	31	33	37	1	.452	.555
2023	18	Modesto (CAL)	A	.321	33	131	27	42	9	1	7	30	21	39	1	.429	.565
Minor League Totals				.295	125	417	92	123	32	7	23	102	89	150	5	.432	.571

5 GABRIEL GONZALEZ, OF

HIT: 45. **POW:** 60. **RUN:** 30. **FLD:** 40. **ARM:** 70. **BA Grade:** 55. **Risk:** Very High.

Born: January 4, 2004. **B-T:** B-R. **HT:** 5-10. **WT:** 220.
Signed: Venezuela, 2021. **Signed by:** Luis Martinez.

TRACK RECORD: Gonzalez signed with the Mariners for $1.3 million out of Venezuela and moved quickly after signing. He reached Low-A Modesto as an 18-year-old in his first season in the U.S. and opened back in Modesto in 2023. Gonzalez overcame an early arm injury to demolish California League pitching and earned a promotion to High-A Everett in the second half. He hit .298/.361/.476 with 18 homers between the two levels and finished second in the Mariners organization with 142 hits.

SCOUTING REPORT: Gonzalez is a thick, stocky righthanded hitter with a bowling ball frame. He has strong hands, excellent hand-eye coordination and a fast, powerful swing that generates loud contact from line to line. He is particularly adept driving the ball the opposite way to right-center field and has a knack for delivering in clutch moments. Gonzalez impacts the ball when he finds the barrel, but he's an extremely aggressive free-swinger who swings at too many pitches he can't drive. His aggressiveness was exploited by more advanced pitchers in High-A, and he must reel in his approach to hit enough as he moves up. His strength gives him plus power potential if he improves his approach. Gonzalez continues to get larger every year and has slowed to a well below-average runner. He has regressed to a below-average defender in right field with limited range and is prone to misjudging fly balls. He has plus-plus arm strength and recorded 12 outfield assists in 88 games on defense last year.

THE FUTURE: Gonzalez's natural hitting gifts are exciting, but his size and aggressiveness create concern both inside and outside the Mariners organization. He needs to improve his conditioning and approach to fulfill his potential as an everyday, power-hitting right fielder.

Year	Age	Club (League)	Level	AVG	G	AB	R	H	2B	3B	HR	RBI	BB	SO	SB	OBP	SLG
2023	19	Modesto (CAL)	A	.348	73	296	51	103	19	4	9	54	23	46	8	.403	.530
2023	19	Everett (NWL)	A+	.215	43	181	27	39	4	0	9	30	13	43	2	.290	.387
Minor League Totals				.302	237	917	168	277	52	9	32	154	78	167	28	.377	.483

6 TYLER LOCKLEAR, 1B

HIT: 45. **POW:** 65. **RUN:** 40. **FLD:** 45. **ARM:** 50. **BA Grade:** 50. **Risk:** High.

Born: November 24, 2000. **B-T:** R-R. **HT:** 6-1. **WT:** 210.
Drafted: Virginia Commonwealth, 2022 (2nd round). **Signed by:** Jackson Laumann.
TRACK RECORD: A star tight end in high school, Locklear blossomed into one of college baseball's top power hitters at Virginia Commonwealth and set a school record with 20 home runs his junior season. The Mariners drafted him in the second round in 2022 and signed him for $1,276,500. Locklear played his first full season in 2023 and missed two months after he was hit by a pitch that broke a bone in his right hand, but he starred when he was on the field. He hit .288/.405/.502 with 13 home runs and 52 RBIs in 85 games and advanced from High-A Everett to Double-A Arkansas even with his injury. His .907 OPS led all Mariners prospects with at least 325 plate appearances.
SCOUTING REPORT: Locklear is a chiseled, physical righthanded hitter with borderline plus-plus power. He is one of the strongest players in the Mariners organization, with muscular legs and huge forearms, and punishes balls on contact. Locklear has an unconventional setup with a bat waggle over the plate, but he's a patient hitter who works long at-bats and turns around fastballs at any velocity. He hits towering home runs to all fields and gets to his power with little effort. Locklear can be a bit stiff and struggles to hit righthanded breaking balls, but he knows the strike zone and makes enough contact to be a fringy hitter who accesses his power in games. A third baseman when he was drafted, Locklear moved to first base full time in 2023. He's a below-average runner but moves well for his size and has the potential to be an average defender at first base. He has average arm strength.
THE FUTURE: Locklear projects to be an everyday first baseman and middle-of-the-order slugger. He'll begin 2024 back at Double-A.

Year	Age	Club (League)	Level	AVG	G	AB	R	H	2B	3B	HR	RBI	BB	SO	SB	OBP	SLG
2023	22	ACL Mariners	Rk	.000	2	6	0	0	0	0	0	0	0	2	0	.000	.000
2023	22	Everett (NWL)	A+	.305	61	226	40	69	19	0	12	44	36	60	10	.422	.549
2023	22	Arkansas (TL)	AA	.260	22	77	11	20	6	1	1	8	11	14	2	.383	.403
Minor League Totals				.287	116	432	70	124	31	1	20	83	55	106	12	.395	.502

7 FELNIN CELESTEN, SS

HIT: 50. **POW:** 60. **RUN:** 60. **FLD:** 55. **ARM:** 60. **BA Grade:** 55. **Risk:** Extreme

Born: September 15, 2005. **B-T:** B-T. **HT:** 6-1. **WT:** 175.
Signed: Dominican Republic, 2023. **Signed by:** Rafael Mateo.
TRACK RECORD: Celesten emerged early as a top prospect in the Dominican Republic and trained in the same program as Athletics shortstop prospect Robert Puason. Celesten attracted clubs as a switch-hitter with a mechanically-sound swing from both sides of the plate and vaulted into the upper echelon of the 2023 international class. The Mariners signed him for $4.7 million, the second-largest bonus in the class, the day the signing period opened. Celesten impressed in the spring, but he suffered a Grade 2 hamstring strain during an intrasquad game in June and missed the Dominican Summer League season. He returned in the fall for instructional league in Arizona and stood out as one of the Mariners' top players in camp.
SCOUTING REPORT: Celesten has some of the best tools and biggest upside in the Mariners system. He's a lean but strong 6-foot-2, 175 pounds and has physical projection still remaining. He has a direct, powerful righthanded swing that produces plus power and could grow into more thump as he gets stronger. His lefthanded swing is longer but flashes plus power when it connects. Celesten has an aggressive approach and will need to be more selective against higher-level pitching, but he has a track record of hitting in games. He projects to be an average hitter who accesses power in games. Celesten is a plus runner with loose, long strides and smooth actions at shortstop. He has a plus, accurate arm that will allow him to remain on the left side of the infield. Celesten may slow down as he fills out, but he projects to remain at shortstop with his athleticism and actions.
THE FUTURE: Celesten has the tools to be a power-hitting, everyday shortstop, but he has yet to play a professional game and has a long road ahead. He'll make his pro debut in the Arizona Complex League.

Year	Age	Club (League)	Level	AVG	G	AB	R	H	2B	3B	HR	RBI	BB	SO	SB	OBP	SLG
2023	17	Did not play—Injured															

8 JONNY FARMELO, OF

HIT: 45. **POW:** 55. **RUN:** 70. **FLD:** 60. **ARM:** 50. **BA Grade:** 55. **Risk:** Extreme.

Born: September 9, 2004. **B-T:** L-R. **HT:** 6-2. **WT:** 205.
Drafted: HS—Chantilly, VA, 2023 (1st round supplemental). **Signed by:** Ty Holub.
TRACK RECORD: Farmelo emerged as one of the 2023 draft's toolsiest players with a standout showing at East Coast Pro. He solidified himself as a potential first-round pick in the spring, headlined by a strong showing against prep righthander Bryce Eldridge in a marquee in-state showdown. The Mariners drafted Farmelo 29th overall, using the Prospect Promotion Incentive pick earned from Julio Rodriguez's Rookie of the Year season in 2022, and signed him for an above-slot $3.2 million. Farmelo's pro debut was delayed by a concussion, but he joined Low-A Modesto for the California League playoffs and helped lead the Nuts to a title. He hit a tie-breaking, three-run homer in Game 1 of the championship series.
SCOUTING REPORT: Farmelo is built like a linebacker with a physical, 6-foot-2, 205-pound frame and has the strength and athleticism to match. He flashes plus raw power from the left side and flies around the field with plus-plus speed and a powerful gait. Farmelo's power-speed combination is tantalizing, but he's raw as a hitter. He has a funky, unconventional setup and gets happy feet in the box, negatively affecting his timing. He has plenty of bat speed and is short to the ball, but his swing is rigid with limited adjustability. Farmelo shows a pure swing when he's on time and is geared to drive balls the opposite way to left-center field. He projects to be a fringe-average hitter with 20-plus homer potential if he can iron out his swing and setup. Farmelo is a plus defender in center field with solid instincts and outstanding jumps on top of his speed. He has average arm strength and has flashed higher.
THE FUTURE: Farmelo has the tools to be an everyday center fielder who goes 20-20, but he needs time to develop as a hitter. He'll open 2024 back at Modesto.

Year	Age	Club (League)	Level	AVG	G	AB	R	H	2B	3B	HR	RBI	BB	SO	SB	OBP	SLG
2023	18	Did not play															

9 MICHAEL ARROYO, 2B

HIT: 55. **POW:** 45. **RUN:** 40. **FLD:** 45. **ARM:** 55. **BA Grade:** 55. **Risk:** Extreme.

Born: November 3, 2004. **B-T:** R-R. **HT:** 5-10. **WT:** 180.
Signed: Colombia, 2022. **Signed by:** David Brito.
TRACK RECORD: Arroyo starred for Colombia's junior national teams at tournaments across the globe as a teenager to emerge as one of the top prospects in the 2022 international signing class. The Mariners signed him on Jan. 15, 2022, for $1.375 million, the largest bonus ever given to a Colombian amateur. Arroyo hit a team-best .314 in his pro debut in the Dominican Summer League and hit his way out of the Arizona Complex League after four games in his U.S. debut in 2023. He joined Low-A Modesto and helped lead the Nuts to the California League championship, highlighted by going 5-for-5 in the clinching game of the semifinals.
SCOUTING REPORT: Arroyo is a mature, confident hitter who is highly advanced for his age. He is unfazed by high velocity or quality breaking stuff and makes consistent contact with a fast, compact righthanded swing. He stays balanced through his swing and has the preternatural ability to manipulate his hands and get the barrel to all parts of the zone. He can be too aggressive at times, but he stays in the strike zone and projects to be an above-average hitter. Arroyo isn't the biggest player, but he's strong in his 5-foot-10 frame and hits the ball hard to all fields. He projects to rack up doubles and could grow into 15-home run power as he learns to elevate more. Signed as a shortstop, Arroyo's defense at second base is less polished. He's a fringy runner with a stocky build and lacks fluidity in his actions. His hands are just OK and he struggles to make backhanded plays. He projects to be a fringy second baseman and finished the year as a DH for Modesto.
THE FUTURE: Arroyo projects to be a bat-first, everyday second baseman. His youth and hitting ability have made him a popular trade target for opposing teams.

Year	Age	Club (League)	Level	AVG	G	AB	R	H	2B	3B	HR	RBI	BB	SO	SB	OBP	SLG
2023	18	ACL Mariners	Rk	.636	4	11	3	7	0	0	1	5	1	1	3	.692	.909
2023	18	Modesto (CAL)	A	.234	57	209	45	49	17	3	2	23	36	53	5	.389	.373
Minor League Totals				.279	110	373	94	104	27	5	7	50	64	87	12	.426	.434

10 EMERSON HANCOCK, RHP

FB: 55. **SL:** 40. **CHG:** 60. **CTL:** 50 **BA Grade:** 45. **Risk:** Medium.

Born: May 31, 1999. **B-T:** R-R. **HT:** 6-4. **WT:** 213.
Drafted: Georgia, 2020 (1st round). **Signed by:** John Wiedenbauer.
TRACK RECORD: A top draft prospect in high school, Hancock made it to campus at Georgia and spent three seasons in the Bulldogs' rotation. The Mariners drafted him sixth overall in the shortened 2020 draft and signed him for $5.7 million. Hancock's pedigree was lofty, but repeated injuries have hampered him as a pro. He battled recurring shoulder soreness his first season, missed the first six weeks of the 2022 season with a lat strain and was again felled by a shoulder injury in 2023. When healthy, he went 11-5, 4.20 at Double-A Arkansas and made his big league debut in August but suffered a shoulder strain in his third start and finished the year on the 60-day injured list.
SCOUTING REPORT: Hancock is a big, physical righthander whose stuff has been up and down with his health. He has a riding four-seam fastball and sinking two-seam fastball that both sit 92-93 mph and touch 95, with his sinker the better of the two pitches. His tumbling, mid-80s changeup plays well off his sinker and is a plus pitch that gets swings and misses from both lefthanded and righthanded hitters. His mid-80s slider is a soft, loose offering he lacks touch or feel for and is a below-average pitch. Hancock's control is just average and he lacks overpowering stuff, but he reads swings and sequences well to get ground balls. He rarely allows hard contact in the air and does a good job of limiting home runs. Hancock's primary issue is his delivery. He opens up early and puts lots of strain on his shoulder with his short arm action and low arm slot, leading to his injuries.
THE FUTURE: Hancock projects to be a steady back-of-the-rotation starter or long reliever but has to stay healthy. That will be his main goal in 2024.

Year	Age	Club (League)	Level	W	L	ERA	G	GS	IP	H	HR	BB	SO	BB%	SO%	WHIP	AVG
2023	24	Arkansas (TL)	AA	11	5	4.32	20	20	98	83	9	38	107	9.2	26.0	1.23	.230
2023	24	Seattle (AL)	MLB	0	0	4.50	3	3	12	13	1	3	6	6.1	12.2	1.33	.283
Minor League Totals				21	10	3.77	53	53	241	192	26	93	242	9.3	24.1	1.18	.217
Major League Totals				0	0	4.50	3	3	12	13	1	3	6	6.1	12.2	1.33	.283

11 JONATAN CLASE, OF

HIT: 30. **POW:** 45. **RUN:** 70. **FLD:** 55. **ARM:** 50. **BA Grade:** 50. **Risk:** High.

Born: May 23, 2002. **B-T:** B-R. **HT:** 5-9. **WT:** 180. **Signed:** Dominican Republic, 2018. **Signed by:** Audo Vicente.
TRACK RECORD: The Mariners signed Clase for $35,000 out of the Dominican Republic in 2018 and quickly realized they had a potential steal. Injuries and the coronavirus pandemic limited him to 70 games combined in his first three seasons, but he broke out at Low-A Modesto in 2022 and continued his ascent in 2023. Clase hit a career-high 20 home runs, finished third in the minors with 79 steals and earned a selection to the Futures Game as he climbed to Double-A Arkansas. He also struck out 165 times, second-most in the Mariners system, and hit .222/.331/.396 in 108 games at Double-A.
SCOUTING REPORT: Clase has prolific tools but is learning to translate them into skills. He has plus-plus speed, plus raw power from both sides of the plate and the athleticism to be an above-average defender in center field. Clase's tools are evident, but he is a wild swinger with poor instincts in every facet of the game. He has poor barrel accuracy and chases pitches he can't hit. He tries to do too much at the plate and needs to tone down his aggressiveness to be even a well below-average hitter. Despite his raw power, Clase doesn't project to make enough contact to hit more than 10-15 home runs per season. Clase's speed allows him to outrun bad jumps and indirect routes on the basepaths and in the outfield. He is an aggressive and energetic player, who alternately excites and frustrates.
THE FUTURE: Clase has to mature as a player to fulfill his potential as a bottom-of-the-order, speed-driven center fielder. That will be his main goal in 2024.

Year	Age	Club (League)	Level	AVG	G	AB	R	H	2B	3B	HR	RBI	BB	SO	SB	OBP	SLG
2023	21	Everett (NWL)	A+	.333	21	87	23	29	9	1	7	17	18	28	17	.453	.701
2023	21	Arkansas (TL)	AA	.222	108	414	79	92	19	7	13	51	64	137	62	.331	.396
Minor League Totals				.262	313	1196	269	313	63	26	37	149	204	369	181	.375	.451

12 PRELANDER BERROA, RHP

FB: 70. **SL:** 70. **CTL:** 30. **BA Grade:** 50. **Risk:** High.

Born: April 18, 2000. **B-T:** R-R. **HT:** 5-11. **WT:** 170. **Signed:** Dominican Republic, 2016.
Signed by: Fred Guerrero (Twins).

TRACK RECORD: Berroa bounced around before finding a home with the Mariners. He originally signed with the Twins for $200,000, was traded to the Giants at the 2019 deadline for reliever Sam Dyson and was traded again to the Mariners in 2022 for utilityman Donnie Walton. Berroa flourished under the Mariners' instruction and dominated as a starter in 2022 before moving to the bullpen in 2023. He posted a 2.89 ERA in 43 appearances at Double-A Arkansas and made his major league debut with two scoreless appearances in Seattle.

SCOUTING REPORT: Berroa is short in stature at 5-foot-11, but he's strong in his frame and has a big right arm. His potentially plus-plus fastball sits 96-97 mph, reaches 100 and explodes through the strike zone with late life and finish. His 86-89 mph slider has improved rapidly with the Mariners and is another potential plus-plus offering with hard, late downward break. He can both land his slider for called strikes or drop it below the zone for swings and misses over the top. Berroa previously had a firm, well-below average changeup, but he scrapped it with his move to relief. Berroa's shortcoming is his control. He has a maximum-effort delivery that he struggles to repeat and is prone to spinning off the mound. He only throws strikes consistently in short bursts and has well below-average control.

THE FUTURE: Berroa has the stuff to be a setup man if he can improve his control even slightly. He'll see the majors again in 2024.

Year	Age	Club (League)	Level	W	L	ERA	G	GS	IP	H	HR	BB	SO	BB%	SO%	WHIP	AVG
2023	23	Arkansas (TL)	AA	5	1	2.89	43	5	65	45	2	39	101	14.1	36.6	1.29	.193
2023	23	Seattle (AL)	MLB	0	0	0.00	2	0	2	0	0	3	3	37.5	37.5	1.80	.000
Minor League Totals				21	12	3.58	124	77	375	284	26	210	498	13.2	31.3	1.32	.208
Major League Totals				0	0	0.00	2	0	2	0	0	3	3	37.5	37.5	1.80	.000

13 TAI PEETE, SS/OF

HIT: 40. **POW:** 55. **RUN:** 60. **FLD:** 45. **ARM:** 60. **BA Grade:** 55. **Risk:** Extreme.

Born: August 11, 2005. **B-T:** L-R. **HT:** 6-2. **WT:** 193. **Drafted:** HS—Sharpsburg, GA, 2023 (1st round supplemental).
Signed by: Terry McClure.

TRACK RECORD: A two-way player in high school, Peete touched 95 mph as a pitcher, but suffered an elbow injury that kept him off the mound his senior year. He blossomed as a position player with his focus exclusively on hitting, leading the Mariners to draft him 30th overall and sign him for $2.5 million to forgo a Georgia Tech commitment. Peete hit his way out of the Arizona Complex League and authored a signature performance when he hit grand slams in consecutive innings for Low-A Modesto on Aug. 27. He became a staple of the Nuts lineup and helped them win the California League championship.

SCOUTING REPORT: Peete is a loose, springy athlete, who is still growing as a baseball player. He has fast hands and flashes a short, quick lefthanded swing, but other times his swing gets too big. He constantly tinkers and is an aggressive swinger who has to tighten his strike zone discipline to be even a below-average hitter. His natural strength and leverage give him above-average raw power when he connects. Peete is a plus runner with the athleticism to play multiple positions, but he needs polish. He sits back on his heels in the infield and his footwork is poor on routine ground balls. He is better at making plays on the move and will likely end up in the outfield, where he can roam with his athleticism and long strides.

THE FUTURE: Peete will take time to develop. He has the potential to be a dynamic power-speed outfielder if everything clicks.

Year	Age	Club (League)	Level	AVG	G	AB	R	H	2B	3B	HR	RBI	BB	SO	SB	OBP	SLG
2023	17	ACL Mariners	Rk	.351	10	37	4	13	1	1	0	6	5	11	3	.429	.432
2023	17	Modesto (CAL)	A	.242	14	62	7	15	3	0	2	14	5	19	3	.299	.387
Minor League Totals				.283	24	99	11	28	4	1	2	20	10	30	6	.349	.404

14 ZACH DeLOACH, OF

HIT: 45. **POW:** 45. **RUN:** 50. **FLD:** 50. **ARM:** 40. **BA Grade:** 45. **Risk:** Medium.

Born: August 8, 1998. **B-T:** L-R. **HT:** 6-1. **WT:** 205. **Drafted:** Texas A&M, 2020 (2nd round). **Signed by:** Derek Miller.

TRACK RECORD: DeLoach struggled to hit his first two seasons at Texas A&M before breaking out with Falmouth in the Cape Cod League. He started his junior year hot before the coronavirus pandemic ended the season, leading the Mariners to draft him 43rd overall. DeLoach steadily produced at each level before delivering his best season in 2023. He batted .286 and set career highs with 23 home runs, 88 RBIs and

an .868 OPS at Triple-A Tacoma. The Mariners added him to the 40-man roster in November.
SCOUTING REPORT: DeLoach is a steady player who does everything well if nothing spectacularly. He's a patient hitter who identifies pitches well and rarely chases outside the strike zone. DeLoach added loft to his swing to hit for more power and saw his strikeouts spike as a result, but he has enough plate discipline and barrel feel to be an adequate, albeit fringy, hitter. He improved against lefties (.306, .905 OPS) to quiet concerns about being limited to a platoon. DeLoach's power is fringy, but he knows which pitches to attack and has improved at getting the ball in the air. He crushes fastballs in particular. DeLoach is an average runner and has improved to be an average defender in the outfield. His below-average arm fits best in left field, but he can fill in at all three spots.
THE FUTURE: DeLoach's lefthanded bat and ability to do a little bit of everything give him a chance to stick as a reserve outfielder. His major league debut should come in 2024.

Year	Age	Club (League)	Level	AVG	G	AB	R	H	2B	3B	HR	RBI	BB	SO	SB	OBP	SLG
2023	24	Tacoma (PCL)	AAA	.286	138	528	90	151	30	2	23	88	83	173	8	.387	.481
Minor League Totals				.275	359	1380	253	379	78	9	51	220	214	413	19	.377	.455

15 TAYLOR DOLLARD, RHP

FB: 50. CB: 45. SL: 60. CHG: 50. CTL: 60. BA Grade: 45. Risk: Medium.

Born: August 17, 1999. **B-T:** R-R. **HT:** 6-3. **WT:** 195. **Drafted:** Cal Poly, 2020 (5th round). **Signed by:** Ryan Holmes.
TRACK RECORD: Dollard began his career at Cal Poly as a shutdown reliever before transitioning to the rotation as a junior. He made only four starts before the coronavirus pandemic canceled the season but showed enough for the Mariners to draft him in the fifth round. Dollard flourished at Double-A Arkansas in 2022 and won the Texas League pitcher of the year award. He entered the 2023 season in the Mariners' big-league plans, but he made just three starts at Triple-A Tacoma before suffering a labrum injury in his right shoulder that required season-ending surgery.
SCOUTING REPORT: Dollard is a good athlete with a smooth, easy delivery and exquisite command. He locates his entire four-pitch arsenal and effectively reads swings to exploit batters' holes. Dollard's command needs to be sharp because his stuff is pedestrian. His average fastball sits 91-93 mph with just enough extension and ride to play in the strike zone. His two-plane, 78-82 mph slider lacks exceptional power or spin, but plays as a plus pitch with his ability to locate it. His 81-83 mph split-changeup is an average pitch that induces ground balls and he mixes in a big-breaking, 68-72 mph curveball to disrupt hitters' timing. Dollard has a good feel for mixing his pitches and is a tough, aggressive competitor. He's strong in his frame and showed he was durable before his injury.
THE FUTURE: Dollard is set to return in 2024. He projects to be a valuable swingman.

Year	Age	Club (League)	Level	W	L	ERA	G	GS	IP	H	HR	BB	SO	BB%	SO%	WHIP	AVG
2023	24	Tacoma (PCL)	AAA	0	2	7.56	3	3	8	9	4	3	8	8.3	22.2	1.44	.273
Minor League Totals				25	8	3.61	49	48	257	233	27	58	272	5.4	25.5	1.13	.237

16 BEN WILLIAMSON, 3B

HIT: 50. POW: 40. RUN: 45. FLD: 60. ARM: 55. BA Grade: 50. Risk: High.

Born: November 5, 2000. **B-T:** R-R. **HT:** 6-0. **WT:** 190. **Drafted:** William & Mary, 2023 (2nd round). **Signed by:** Ty Holub.
TRACK RECORD: Williamson flashed solid ability his first three seasons at William & Mary, but went undrafted as a junior due to a lack of strength. He put on 15 pounds of muscle as a senior and set new career highs with a .391 batting average, 12 home runs and a 1.175 OPS to win Colonial Athletic Association player of the year. He followed with a strong showing for Hyannis in the Cape Cod League and was drafted by the Mariners in the second round, No. 57 overall. He signed for a below-slot $600,000.
SCOUTING REPORT: Williamson is a disciplined hitter, who expertly manages the strike zone. He has a flat righthanded swing that makes consistent contact and generates hard line drives to all fields. He doesn't elevate the ball yet, but he hits the ball hard enough to project to be an average hitter with 12-15 home run power. He makes excellent swing decisions and rarely strikes out. Williamson shines brightest on defense. He is a plus defender at third base and can play shortstop if needed. Though he's just a fringy runner, he has easy, athletic actions in the infield and is gifted at reading hops. He syncs up his hands and feet to be a consistent, reliable defender, who makes all the routine plays. He has above-average arm strength.
THE FUTURE: Williamson profiles as a solid everyday third baseman. He'll open at High-A in 2024.

Year	Age	Club (League)	Level	AVG	G	AB	R	H	2B	3B	HR	RBI	BB	SO	SB	OBP	SLG
2023	22	ACL Mariners	Rk	.500	2	6	1	3	0	1	0	0	0	2	0	.500	.833
2023	22	Modesto (CAL)	A	.229	10	35	3	8	2	1	0	6	2	10	1	.289	.343
Minor League Totals				.268	12	41	4	11	2	2	0	6	2	12	1	.318	.415

17 RYAN BLISS, 2B/SS

HIT: 50. **POW:** 40. **RUN:** 60. **FLD:** 50. **ARM:** 45. **BA Grade:** 45. **Risk:** Medium.

Born: December 13, 1999. **B-T:** B-T. **HT:** 5-6. **WT:** 165. **Drafted:** Auburn, 2021 (2nd round).
Signed by: Kerry Jenkins (D-backs).
TRACK RECORD: A three-year starter at Auburn, Bliss hit .365 with a career-high 15 home runs as a junior and was drafted by the Diamondbacks in the second round. He struggled in his first full pro season as he started chasing power, but he returned to a contact-oriented approach in 2023 and had a standout year. He finished third in the minors in runs (110) and total bases (284) and tied for fourth in hits (164) as he climbed from Double-A to Triple-A. The Mariners acquired him as one of three players for closer Paul Sewald at the trade deadline.
SCOUTING REPORT: Bliss is one of the smallest players in professional baseball at 5-foot-6, 165 pounds. He uses his size to his advantage with a quick, compact righthanded swing and drives the ball to all fields. He catches up to fastballs at any velocity, crushes breaking stuff and has the strength to run into double-digit home runs despite his size. Bliss is aggressive at the plate and gets pull-happy, but he shows the ability to be an average hitter when he's locked into the right-center gap. He's a plus runner with excellent basestealing instincts. Bliss has split time at shortstop and second base and is a good athlete with natural actions and reliable hands at both positions. His fringe-average arm strength plays better at second base.
THE FUTURE: Bliss projects to be a second-division starter or utilityman similar to Tony Kemp, albeit righthanded. His major league debut should come in 2024.

Year	Age	Club (League)	Level	AVG	G	AB	R	H	2B	3B	HR	RBI	BB	SO	SB	OBP	SLG
2023	23	Amarillo (TL)	AA	.358	68	293	67	105	25	4	12	47	24	55	30	.414	.594
2023	23	Reno (PCL)	AAA	.196	13	56	6	11	2	2	1	4	5	12	5	.274	.357
2023	23	Tacoma (PCL)	AAA	.251	47	191	37	48	7	2	10	35	29	52	20	.356	.466
Minor League Totals				.264	277	1131	201	299	63	12	39	147	114	279	99	.340	.445

18 TEDDY McGRAW, RHP

FB: 60. **SL:** 60. **CHG:** 50. **CTL:** 40. **BA Grade:** 50. **Risk:** Extreme.

Born: October 30, 2001. **B-T:** R-R. **HT:** 6-3. **WT:** 210. **Drafted:** Wake Forest, 2023 (3rd round). **Signed by:** Ty Holub.
TRACK RECORD: McGraw had Tommy John surgery in high school but recovered to become a top draft prospect after two seasons at Wake Forest. He became a favorite of Mariners general manager Jerry Dipoto and entered his junior year considered a potential first-round pick, but he blew out his elbow in January and had a second Tommy John surgery. The Mariners saw an opportunity to get a premium talent at a discount and drafted him in the third round, No. 92 overall. He signed him for a below-slot $600,000.
SCOUTING REPORT: McGraw is a physical righthander with power stuff. His fastball sits 93-95 mph and touches 98 with sinking action at the bottom of the strike zone. His best pitch is a high-spin, vertical slider in the mid-80s that misses bats and projects to be a plus pitch. McGraw primarily throws those two pitches, but he also has an average, mid-80s changeup with sinking action that keeps balls on the ground. He's a heavy groundball pitcher who avoids serving up home runs. McGraw relies on overpowering hitters rather than hitting his spots and has below-average command and control. He has the look and physicality of a starter but has to prove he can stay healthy.
THE FUTURE: McGraw is slated to make his pro debut in 2024. He has mid-rotation upside if his stuff returns intact and he proves he can hold up.

Year	Age	Club (League)	Level	W	L	ERA	G	GS	IP	H	HR	BB	SO	BB%	SO%	WHIP	AVG
2023	21	Did not play—Injured															

19 AIDAN SMITH, OF

HIT: 45. **POW:** 50. **RUN:** 60. **FLD:** 65. **ARM:** 55. **BA Grade:** 50. **Risk:** Extreme.

Born: July 23, 2004. **B-T:** R-R. **HT:** 6-3. **WT:** 190. **Drafted:** HS—Lucas, TX, 2023 (4th round). **Signed by:** Patrick O'Grady.
TRACK RECORD: Smith largely stayed off the summer showcase circuit and wasn't well known, but Mariners area scout Patrick O'Grady identified him early and kept highlighting Smith to his superiors. Smith made that look prescient by batting .491 in a huge senior season at Lovejoy (Lucas, Texas) High and followed with an impressive showing at the draft combine. The Mariners drafted him in the fourth round and signed him for an above-slot $1.2 million bonus to forgo a Mississippi State commitment.
SCOUTING REPORT: Smith is a physical athlete whose baseball skills are rapidly progressing. He has a projectable 6-foot-3, 190-pound frame and drives balls 400-plus feet in batting practice with plus raw power. He hits balls hard when he connects and has room to keep getting stronger and add more power. Smith

is still a raw hitter with a top-heavy, rotational swing and poor breaking ball recognition. He has good hand-eye coordination but needs time to improve his swing and pitch recognition. He has the potential to be a fringe-average hitter with 20-home run power if everything clicks. Smith is much more polished on defense. He's a plus runner underway who runs pristine routes and is a borderline plus-plus defender in center field. He has above-average arm strength that flashes higher.

THE FUTURE: Smith's defense in center field will give him time to develop as a hitter. He has a chance to be an everyday center fielder if everything clicks.

Year	Age	Club (League)	Level	AVG	G	AB	R	H	2B	3B	HR	RBI	BB	SO	SB	OBP	SLG
2023	18	ACL Mariners	Rk	.261	8	23	7	6	0	2	0	3	6	8	6	.433	.435
2023	18	Modesto (CAL)	A	.184	14	49	11	9	2	1	1	5	4	16	0	.259	.327
Minor League Totals				.208	22	72	18	15	2	3	1	8	10	24	6	.321	.361

20 ALBERTO RODRIGUEZ, OF

HIT: 50 **POW:** 45. **RUN:** 40. **FLD:** 40. **ARM:** 55. **BA Grade:** 45. **Risk:** High.

Born: Oct. 6, 2000. **B-T:** L-L. **HT:** 5-11. **WT:** 180. **Signed:** Dominican Republic, 2017.
Signed by: Sandy Rosario/Lorenzo Perez/Luciano del Rosario (Blue Jays).

TRACK RECORD: Rodriguez originally signed with the Blue Jays for $500,000 out of the Dominican Republic and was traded to the Mariners in 2020 as the player to be named later for Taijuan Walker. He earned a spot on the Mariners 40-man roster after a productive first season in the organization, but he ballooned out of shape in 2022 and was outrighted after a miserable year. Rodriguez slimmed down and had a bounceback year in 2023. He led the Mariners system with a .300 batting average and 38 doubles, and rose from High-A to Double-A.

SCOUTING REPORT: Rodriguez has long struggled with his weight and is two different players depending on his fitness. When he's in shape, he has solid bat-to-ball skills from the left side and good direction at the plate that allows him to stay on balls and drive them on a line from gap to gap. He makes loud contact and has improved at elevating the ball to project for 15-20 home run power. Rodriguez is an average runner and average defensive right fielder when he's in shape, but he's well below average at both when he's not. He has above-average arm strength with inconsistent accuracy. Rodriguez gets bored at times and performs best when the stakes are highest. He lacks natural drive and needs coaches to stay on him.

THE FUTURE: Rodriguez's outlook depends solely on if he stays in shape. He has a chance to be a second-division regular in right field if he does.

Year	Age	Club (League)	Level	AVG	G	AB	R	H	2B	3B	HR	RBI	BB	SO	SB	OBP	SLG
2023	22	Everett (NWL)	A+	.306	72	281	61	86	30	7	11	58	31	69	3	.393	.580
2023	22	Arkansas (TL)	AA	.291	46	179	17	52	8	0	3	27	20	51	5	.361	.385
Minor League Totals				.281	445	1727	280	485	119	17	41	259	205	447	63	.362	.441

21 WALTER FORD, RHP

FB: 55. **CB:** 55. **SL:** 50. **CHG:** 40. **CTL:** 50. **BA Grade:** 50. **Risk:** Extreme.

Born: December 28, 2004. **B-T:** R-R. **HT:** 6-3. **WT:** 198. **Drafted:** HS—Pace, FL, 2022 (2nd round supplemental).
Signed by: Rob Mummau.

TRACK RECORD: Nicknamed the "Vanilla Missile", Ford was one of the top pitchers in the 2023 draft class before reclassifying to be eligible a year earlier. The Mariners drafted him in the supplemental second round and signed him for an above-slot $1.25 million to forgo an Alabama commitment. Ford made his pro debut in the Arizona Complex League in 2023, but pitched only 22.2 innings due to a series of minor injuries. He was never quite at full strength and saw his velocity drop 4-5 mph from high school.

SCOUTING REPORT: Ford is a long, lean 6-foot-3 righthander, who requires lots of projection. His fastball sat 88-92 mph in his pro debut, down from 92-97 when he was drafted, and he needs to get stronger to better hold his stuff. He has an explosive, athletic delivery and projects to add velocity as he fills out. Ford complements his fastball with a potentially above-average, 78-82 mph curveball with 11-to-5 shape and an average short slider in the 85-89 mph range. He also has a below-average, mid-80s changeup he rarely throws. Ford struggled with walks in his pro debut, but he projects to have average control as he gains strength and improves his body control.

THE FUTURE: Ford needs to get stronger to stay healthy and fulfill his mid-to-back of the rotation potential. He'll move to Low-A Modesto in 2024.

Year	Age	Club (League)	Level	W	L	ERA	G	GS	IP	H	HR	BB	SO	BB%	SO%	WHIP	AVG
2023	18	ACL Mariners	Rk	0	0	3.57	9	8	23	25	1	10	23	9.7	22.3	1.54	.284
Minor League Totals				0	0	3.68	9	8	23	25	1	10	23	9.7	22.3	1.59	.284

22 SPENCER PACKARD, OF

HIT: 50. **POW:** 45. **RUN:** 30. **FLD:** 40. **ARM:** 40. **BA Grade:** 40. **Risk:** Medium.

Born: October 12, 1997. **B-T:** L-L. **HT:** 6-1. **WT:** 205. **Drafted:** Campbell, 2021 (9th round). **Signed by:** Ty Holub.

TRACK RECORD: A three-year starter at Campbell, Packard led the Big South Conference in hits and RBIs as a senior and was drafted by the Mariners in the ninth round. He signed for a below-slot $25,000. Packard emerged as a potential steal with a stellar offensive campaign in his pro debut and delivered another in 2023. He hit .291 with 14 home runs, 82 RBIs and an .839 OPS at Double-A Arkansas, a notorious pitchers park, and finished fifth in the Texas League with 136 hits.

SCOUTING REPORT: Packard lacks big tools but can flat-out hit. He has excellent strike zone discipline, consistently works high-quality at-bats and drives hittable pitches with a quick, direct lefthanded swing. He previously flared balls the other way with an inside-out stroke, but he has learned to lift and pull the ball more and now uses the whole field. He hits all pitch types, handles both righties and lefties and projects to be an average hitter with double-digit home runs. Packard is a well-below average runner with limited athleticism and has to move between left field, right field and first base to avoid being overexposed. He's a below-average defender with a below-average arm everywhere.

THE FUTURE: Packard's hitting ability gives him a chance to carve out a role as a reserve outfielder. He'll move to Triple-A Tacoma in 2024.

Year	Age	Club (League)	Level	AVG	G	AB	R	H	2B	3B	HR	RBI	BB	SO	SB	OBP	SLG
2023	25	Arkansas (TL)	AA	.292	121	466	66	136	27	2	14	82	68	86	1	.391	.448
Minor League Totals				.286	225	857	133	245	47	4	29	142	126	155	8	.390	.452

23 MICHAEL MORALES, RHP

FB: 50. **CB:** 55. **SL:** 45. **CHG:** 45. **CTL:** 50. **BA Grade:** 45. **Risk:** High.

Born: August 13, 2002. **B-T:** R-R. **HT:** 6-2. **WT:** 205. **Drafted:** HS—Enola, PA, 2021 (3rd round). **Signed by:** Dave Pepe.

TRACK RECORD: Morales intrigued as a talented, but raw pitcher from cold-weather Pennsylvania as a prep. The Mariners drafted him in the third round in 2021 and signed him for an above-slot $1.5 million to forgo a Vanderbilt commitment. Morales posted a league-worst 5.91 ERA in his pro debut at Low-A Modesto in 2022 and repeated the level in 2023. He lowered his ERA to 4.53 in his second turn through the league while showing a slight uptick in stuff.

SCOUTING REPORT: Morales is an athletic 6-foot-2, 205-pound righthander with a polished delivery and growing stuff. His fastball sits 90-94 mph with late life up in the zone and gets swings and misses when he elevates it. His best pitch is an above-average, 75-78 mph downer curveball with depth that he has a consistent feel for. Morales also has an 81-83 mph depth slider that flashes average but is inconsistent. He rounds out his arsenal with a fringy, 78-81 mph changeup with armside fade. Morales repeats his delivery and has average control, but he shies away from contact at times. His confidence is slowly growing and projects to improve as he gets stronger and throws harder.

THE FUTURE: Morales needs to make gains both physically and mentally to fulfill his back-of-the-rotation potential. He'll open at High-A Everett in 2024.

Year	Age	Club (League)	Level	W	L	ERA	G	GS	IP	H	HR	BB	SO	BB%	SO%	WHIP	AVG
2023	20	Modesto (CAL)	A	5	4	4.53	22	22	101	92	7	40	106	9.2	24.4	1.30	.238
Minor League Totals				10	11	5.35	49	49	223	237	21	91	232	9.1	23.2	1.48	.270

24 DARREN BOWEN, RHP

FB: 55. **SL:** 55. **CUT:** 50. **CHG:** 45. **CTL:** 40. **BA Grade:** 45. **Risk:** Very High.

Born: February 3, 2001. **B-T:** R-R. **HT:** 6-3. **WT:** 180. **Drafted:** UNC Pembroke, 2022 (13th round). **Signed by:** Ty Holub.

TRACK RECORD: Bowen struggled to a 5.43 ERA over three seasons as a starter and reliever at Division II UNC Pembroke, but the Mariners liked his athleticism and arm strength and drafted him in the 12th round. Bowen rewarded their faith with a strong pro debut at Low-A Modesto in 2023. He joined the Nuts at midseason and worked his way from the bullpen to the rotation, posting a 3.88 ERA over 19 appearances (15 starts) to help them win the California League championship.

SCOUTING REPORT: Bowen is a lean, athletic righthander with lots of room for growth. His fastball sits 92-94 mph with late run and ride and projects to add velocity as he gets stronger. His main secondary is a sweepy, 81-85 mph slider with tight spin that flashes above average, but is inconsistent. Bowen also has a fringy, 84-87 mph changeup with sink he is still learning to command and an 86-89 mph cutter that flashes average, but blends with his slider. Bowen is a good athlete, but he doesn't repeat his delivery and has below-average control. He has never thrown more than 90 pitches in a start and still has to build durability.

THE FUTURE: Bowen's athleticism and projection excite, but he still needs a lot of development to fulfill his starter potential. He'll open at High-A Everett in 2024.

Year	Age	Club (League)	Level	W	L	ERA	G	GS	IP	H	HR	BB	SO	BB%	SO%	WHIP	AVG
2023	22	Modesto (CAL)	A	4	2	3.88	19	15	56	36	2	25	59	10.9	25.7	1.10	.182
Minor League Totals				4	2	3.93	19	15	56	36	2	25	59	10.9	25.7	1.11	.182

25 BROCK RODDEN, 2B/3B

HIT: 50. **POW:** 30. **RUN:** 55. **FLD:** 50. **ARM:** 50. **BA Grade:** 40. **Risk:** High.

Born: May 25, 2000. **B-T:** B-R. **HT:** 5-9. **WT:** 170. **Drafted:** Wichita State, 2023 (5th round). **Signed by:** Joe Saunders.

TRACK RECORD: The son of a high school baseball coach, Rodden started his college career at Seminole State (Okla.) JC before transferring to Wichita State. The A's drafted him in the 10th round after his junior year, but he returned to school and won American Athletic Conference player of the year as a senior. The Mariners drafted him in the fifth round and signed him for a below-slot $200,000. Rodden moved quickly to Low-A Modesto after signing and batted .319 as the Nuts' leadoff hitter to help them win the California League championship.

SCOUTING REPORT: Rodden is a scrappy, undersized player, who plays with a chip on his shoulder. He's a switch-hitter who gets into a low crouch, chokes up on the handle and makes frequent contact with a quick, level swing from both sides of the plate. He's an aggressive swinger and doesn't walk much, but he has the hand-eye coordination to make contact and avoid striking out. He has more power righthanded than lefthanded and projects to be an average hitter whose power manifests in doubles. Rodden is an above-average runner with good instincts and a quick first step at second base. He projects to be an average defender with average arm strength at the keystone and can fill in at shortstop, third base or left field.

THE FUTURE: Rodden's well-rounded toolset and high effort level give him a chance to be a utilityman. He'll open at High-A Everett in 2024.

Year	Age	Club (League)	Level	AVG	G	AB	R	H	2B	3B	HR	RBI	BB	SO	SB	OBP	SLG
2023	23	ACL Mariners	Rk	.143	2	7	0	1	0	0	0	0	0	2	1	.143	.143
2023	23	Modesto (CAL)	A	.319	32	144	33	46	11	2	2	20	11	24	1	.376	.465
Minor League Totals				.311	34	151	33	47	11	2	2	20	11	26	2	.366	.450

26 JIMMY JOYCE, RHP

FB: 55. **CB:** 55. **CHG:** 50. **CTL:** 45. **BA Grade:** 40. **Risk:** High.

Born: January 13, 1999. **B-T:** R-R. **HT:** 6-2. **WT:** 210. **Drafted:** Hofstra, 2021 (16th round). **Signed by:** Dave Pepe.

TRACK RECORD: Joyce led Wantagh (N.Y.) High to back-to-back state championship games as a prep and arrived at Hofstra as a top recruit. Initially a two-way player, he focused on pitching as an upperclassman and led the Pride in strikeouts, wins and ERA as a senior. The Mariners drafted him in the 16th round and signed him for $25,000. Joyce's pitch analytics jumped out when he was drafted, and that translated into results in 2023. He logged a 2.57 ERA in 16 starts across High-A and Double-A, and led the Mariners system with a 59.3% groundball rate.

SCOUTING REPORT: Joyce is a strong, athletic righthander with lively stuff. He hides the ball with a deep turn in his delivery and unleashes 92-94 mph two-seam fastballs with exceptional sink and run. He generates lots of called strikes and check swings from batters who have trouble tracking his heater. Joyce complements his two-seamer with an above-average, 82-84 mph power curveball with hard break and depth. He rounds out his arsenal with an average, 83-85 mph changeup that effectively mirrors his fastball. Joyce's pitches have so much movement he struggles to command them at times, but he throws strikes at a fringe-average clip. His starts typically cap out at 3-5 innings.

THE FUTURE: Joyce projects to be a groundball–inducing middle reliever in the major leagues. His debut may come in 2024.

Year	Age	Club (League)	Level	W	L	ERA	G	GS	IP	H	HR	BB	SO	BB%	SO%	WHIP	AVG
2023	24	Everett (NWL)	A+	2	0	1.60	9	9	39	28	4	10	54	6.3	34.0	0.97	.200
2023	24	Arkansas (TL)	AA	0	3	3.82	7	7	31	29	1	10	29	7.8	22.7	1.27	.250
Minor League Totals				9	15	4.35	47	47	213	190	21	81	254	8.7	27.4	1.27	.236

27 HOGAN WINDISH, 1B

HIT: 30. **POW:** 50. **RUN:** 30. **FLD:** 40. **ARM:** 40. **BA Grade:** 40. **Risk:** High.

Born: May 10, 1999. **B-T:** R-R. **HT:** 5-11. **WT:** 224. **Drafted:** UNC Greensboro, 2022 (7th round). **Signed by:** Ty Holub.

TRACK RECORD: A four-year starter at UNC Greensboro, Windish led the Southern Conference in batting average (.380) and on-base percentage (.496) as a senior and followed with a solid performance for Wareham in the Cape Cod League. The Mariners drafted him in the seventh round and signed him for a below-slot $20,000. Windish spent his first full season at High-A Everett in 2023 and led the Northwest League with 22 home runs, 84 RBIs and an .878 OPS, but he also had the league's fourth-highest strikeout rate at 30.8%.

SCOUTING REPORT: Windish is a chiseled righthanded hitter with bulging biceps, massive forearms and strong, powerful legs. He does enormous damage with his brute strength, hitting both towering home runs and scorched liners that carry out to all fields. Windish has plus raw power, but his swing is stiff and lacks adjustability, leading to lots of swings and misses and mis-hit balls. He projects to be a well below-average hitter with average power production. Windish is a stiff athlete with well below-average speed and poor agility. He is a below-average defender at first base with an average arm.

THE FUTURE: Windish's power gives him a carrying tool. He'll need to make more contact to find a reserve role in the majors.

Year	Age	Club (League)	Level	AVG	G	AB	R	H	2B	3B	HR	RBI	BB	SO	SB	OBP	SLG
2023	24	Everett (NWL)	A+	.270	105	385	64	104	17	4	22	84	55	139	10	.372	.506
Minor League Totals				.286	138	514	95	147	30	5	24	119	73	174	14	.388	.504

28 TROY TAYLOR, RHP

FB: 60. **SL:** 55. **CTL:** 45. **BA Grade:** 40. **Risk:** High.

Born: September 9, 2001. **B-T:** R-R. **HT:** 6-0. **WT:** 195. **Drafted:** UC Irvine, 2022 (12th round). **Signed by:** Ryan Holmes.

TRACK RECORD: Taylor primarily played shortstop in high school before converting to pitching in college. He started at Long Beach State, transferred to Cypress (Calif.) JC and finished his career as a dominant closer at UC Irvine. The Mariners drafted him in the 20th round out of Cypress in 2021 and failed to sign him, but they selected him again in the 12th round out of Irvine in 2022 and inked him for $125,000. Taylor showed why the Mariners drafted him twice with an eye-opening pro debut in 2023. He struck out 62 batters in 45.1 innings of relief across the Class A levels and posted a 1.74 ERA in the Arizona Fall League.

SCOUTING REPORT: Taylor is a 6-foot righthander with a powerful two-pitch mix. His two-seam fastball sits 94-96 mph and touches 98 with hard, late armside run. He locates his two-seamer to both sides of the plate and has the unique ability to elevate it to make it a plus pitch. Taylor complements his fastball with an 85-87 mph power slider with sharp vertical break and late sweep. It's an above-average offering he primarily uses as a chase pitch. Taylor's pitches have so much movement they get away from him at times and yield fringy control, but he throws enough strikes to be effective in short bursts.

THE FUTURE: Taylor has the stuff to be a mid-leverage reliever with further development. He'll move to Double-A in 2024.

Year	Age	Club (League)	Level	W	L	ERA	G	GS	IP	H	HR	BB	SO	BB%	SO%	WHIP	AVG
2023	21	Modesto (CAL)	A	1	1	4.11	32	0	35	26	1	19	51	11.8	31.7	1.29	.197
2023	21	Everett (NWL)	A+	0	0	0.87	8	0	10	5	0	2	11	5.1	28.2	0.68	.147
Minor League Totals				1	1	3.38	40	0	45	31	1	21	62	10.5	31.0	1.15	.186

29 REID VanSCOTER, LHP

FB: 40. **CB:** 50. **SL:** 50. **CHG:** 45. **CTL:** 55. **BA Grade:** 40. **Risk:** High.

Born: November 25, 1998 **B-T:** L-L. **HT:** 6-0. **WT:** 190. **Drafted:** Coastal Carolina, 2022 (5th round). **Signed by:** Ty Holub.

TRACK RECORD: VanScoter spent his first two college seasons at Binghamton before transferring to Coastal Carolina. He won Sun Belt Conference pitcher of the year as a redshirt senior and was drafted by the Mariners in the fifth round, signing for $20,000. VanScoter made his pro debut at High-A Everett in 2023 and dominated the level. He led the Northwest League in ERA (3.27) and strikeouts (157) despite pitching his home games in one of the minors' most hitter-friendly stadiums.

SCOUTING REPORT: VanScoter is a crafty lefthander with a low, three-quarters arm slot that presents an uncomfortable look for hitters. His below-average two-seam fastball sits just 89-91 mph, but it's not a significant part of his arsenal. He primarily throws his sweepy, 82-86 mph slider that is an average pitch he can land in the strike zone or get chase swings with. He backs up his slider with an 11-to-5 curveball in the 75-78 mph range that has more depth than his slider. He also has a fringy, 82-85 mph changeup that is usable against righthanders. VanScoter throws all four of his pitches for strikes with above-average control and keeps the ball on the ground.

THE FUTURE: VanScoter's low slot and quality breaking pitches give him a chance to be a low-leverage reliever who handles lefties in the majors. He'll move to Double-A Arkansas in 2024.

Year	Age	Club (League)	Level	W	L	ERA	G	GS	IP	H	HR	BB	SO	BB%	SO%	WHIP	AVG
2023	24	Everett (NWL)	A+	10	6	3.27	25	25	143	141	6	35	157	5.8	26.0	1.23	.255
Minor League Totals				10	6	3.27	25	25	143	141	6	35	157	5.8	26.0	1.23	.255

30 JETER MARTINEZ, RHP

FB: 60. **SL:** 40. **CHG:** 40. **CTL:** 50. **BA Grade:** 45. **Risk:** Extreme.

Born: February 16, 2006. **B-T:** R-R. **HT:** 6-4. **WT:** 180. **Signed:** Mexico, 2023. **Signed by:** David Velazquez.

TRACK RECORD: Martinez originally developed as a position player in Mexico before converting to pitching when he was 15. He took to pitching rapidly and emerged as one of the most intriguing righthanders in the 2023 international class, leading the Mariners to sign him for $600,000 when the signing period opened. Martinez made his pro debut in the Dominican Summer League after signing, and starred as one of the league's top pitchers. He led the DSL with a 0.79 WHIP and .109 opponent batting average among qualified pitchers, and finished fifth with a 1.72 ERA.

SCOUTING REPORT: Martinez is a broad-shouldered righthander with a projectable 6-foot-4, 180-pound frame. His heavy fastball sits 92-93 mph and reaches the mid 90s out of a quick arm and easy, athletic delivery. His velocity has already increased rapidly in a short time and should continue ticking up as he fills out. Martinez shows aptitude for throwing a curveball and changeup, but both are raw due to his lack of pitching experience. His athleticism and easy delivery should yield at least average control as he gains strength.

THE FUTURE: Martinez is as projectable as any pitcher in the Mariners system, but he has years of development left. He'll make his stateside debut in the Arizona Complex League in 2024.

Year	Age	Club (League)	Level	W	L	ERA	G	GS	IP	H	HR	BB	SO	BB%	SO%	WHIP	AVG
2023	17	DSL Mariners	Rk	2	2	1.72	10	8	47	17	1	20	55	11.2	30.7	0.79	.109
Minor League Totals				2	2	1.72	10	8	47	17	1	20	55	11.2	30.7	0.79	.109

Taj
Bradley

Tampa Bay Rays

BY J.J. COOPER

The Rays' 99 wins in 2023 were the second-most in franchise history. The team scored a franchise-record 860 runs and set a franchise record by starting the season 13-0.

So it may seem odd to say that the season ended in disappointment. For the first two months of the season, the Rays were clearly the best team in baseball. But by October, they weren't very frightening.

The Rays scored only one run in a two-game sweep at the hands of eventual World Series-champion Rangers. It was a second consecutive feeble exit for Tampa Bay. They also scored one one run in a two-game sweep to Cleveland in 2022.

Since making it to the World Series in 2020, the Rays have won once in eight playoff games.

In 2022, the team's offensive struggles in the postseason seemed like a logical continuation of the team's regular season struggles to hit for power.

In 2023, it was much less expected. The 2022 Rays hit 139 home runs. The 2023 Rays hit 230. Power had been the Rays' strength all season. It just disappeared at the wrong time.

Injuries played a factor. Second baseman Brandon Lowe was sidelined with a fractured kneecap, but it was the rotation that truly suffered. Shane McClanahan, Jeffrey Springs, Shane Baz and Drew Rasmussen were all on the 60-day injured list for the playoffs.

Those injuries leave the Rays somewhat hobbled heading into 2024 as well. Baz should be ready to go early in the season, but Springs, Rasmussen and McClanahan all had Tommy John surgery during the 2023 season.

Springs (April surgery) should be the first to return, but Rasmussen (July) and McClanahan (August) will be likely to miss most or all of the 2024 season.

There's an even more serious issue that hangs over the team. Shortstop Wander Franco, the team's franchise player, spent the final two months of the 2023 season on the restricted list. He was being investigated in the Dominican Republic on allegations

PROJECTED 2027 LINEUP

Catcher	Rene Pinto	30
First Base	Xavier Isaac	23
Second Base	Curtis Mead	26
Third Base	Brayden Taylor	25
Shortstop	Carson Williams	24
Left Field	Josh Lowe	29
Center Field	Jose Siri	31
Right Field	Junior Caminero	23
Designated Hitter	Jonathan Aranda	29
No. 1 Starter	Shane McClanahan	30
No. 2 Starter	Shane Baz	28
No. 3 Starter	Jeffrey Springs	34
No. 4 Starter	Drew Rasmussen	31
No. 5 Starter	Taj Bradley	26
Closer	Yoniel Curet	24

of inappropriate relationships with underage girls.

No charges had been filed as of mid December, but the investigations continue. The off-the-field realities far outdistance the baseball aspects of the Franco investigation, but on the field, it means the Rays have no idea if or when the team's best player will play for them.

The Rays' farm system has continued to produce. Third baseman Junior Caminero had a breakout season. He began the season playing in High-A with less than two months of Low-A experience on his résumé. He finished it in the Rays' lineup for the playoffs, as he showed the kind of power that could make him a star.

Curtis Mead also made the postseason roster, and shortstop Carson Williams and first baseman Xavier Isaac are also quite promising.

The team's pitching prospect depth is not what it once was, however, which is more troubling because of Tampa Bay's injuries in the MLB rotation.

The Rays face more uncertainty going into 2024 than they have in quite a while. Tampa Bay is a poker player who never goes all-in. The Rays' trades often will provide a short-term hit in the goal of ensuring the team remains successful for the long term.

The 2024 season seems to be one where the team's short-term success is more in peril.

But with a team that has made the playoffs for five straight seasons and has won 59% of its games over that span, it's hard to count them out. ∎

DEPTH CHART

TAMPA BAY RAYS

TOP 2024 CONTRIBUTORS — **RANK**
1. Junior Caminero, 3B — 1
2. Curtis Mead, 2B — 3
3. Shane Baz, RHP — 4

BREAKOUT PROSPECTS — **RANK**
1. Jose Urbina, RHP — 14
2. Erick Lara, 3B — 30

SOURCE OF TOP 30 TALENT

Homegrown	19	Acquired	11
College	8	Trade	11
Junior college	1	Rule 5 draft	0
High school	6	Independent league	0
Nondrafted free agent	0	Free agent/waivers	0
International	4		

LF
Colton Ledbetter (11)
Dru Baker (28)
Heriberto Hernandez

CF
Chandler Simpson (18)
Shane Sasaki (20)
Mason Auer (24)
Kameron Misner (25)
Greg Jones
Brock Jones

RF
Brailer Guerrero (21)
Ryan Cermak

3B
Junior Caminero (1)
Brayden Taylor (6)
Willy Vasquez (23)
Erick Lara (30)

SS
Carson Williams (2)
Osleivis Basabe (7)
Adrian Santana (8)
Hunter Haas
Carlos Colmenarez
Ryan Spikes

2B
Curtis Mead (3)
Cooper Kinney (29)
Ronny Simon
Wilian Trinidad

1B
Xavier Isaac (5)
Austin Shenton (17)
Tre' Morgan (22)
Bobby Seymour

C
Dominic Keegan (9)
Logan Driscoll
Kenny Piper
Cam James

LHP

LHSP	LHRP
Jacob Lopez (26)	Mason Montgomery (15)
	Ian Seymour (16)
	Keyshawn Askew
	Dalton Fowler
	Patrick Wicklander

RHP

RHSP	RHRP
Shane Baz (4)	Colby White
Yoniel Curet (10)	Andrew Lindsey
Santiago Suarez (12)	Austin Vernon
Marcus Johnson (13)	Adam Boucher
Jose Urbina (14)	Garrett Edwards
Cole Wilcox (19)	T.J. Nichols
Ben Peoples (27)	
Trevor Martin	
Trevor Harrison	
Drew Dowd	
JJ Goss	

1 JUNIOR CAMINERO, 3B/SS

Born: July 5, 2003. **B-T:** R-R. **HT:** 5-11. **WT:** 210.
Signed: Dominican Republic, 2019.
Signed by: Amiro Santana (Guardians).

MIKE JANES/FOUR SEAM IMAGES

BA GRADE	SCOUTING GRADES
70 Risk: High	**Hit:** 55. **Power:** 80. **Run:** 55. **Field:** 50. **Arm:** 60.

Projected future grades on 20-80 scouting scale

TRACK RECORD: The Rays have consistently poured resources into scouting the Dominican Summer League to try to find prospects who could be useful trade pickups. It's a high-risk, high-reward strategy. Often the Rays acquire modest talents, but sometimes the effort yields trades like the one that landed Caminero for Tobias Myers, a righthander who needed to be added to the 40-man roster when the Rays sent him to Cleveland after the 2021 season. Myers was soon designated for assignment, while Caminero turned into one of the top prospects in baseball. After a stint in the Florida Complex League in 2022, he earned a late-season promotion to Low-A Charleston in 2022. He hit .471 in four playoff games to help the RiverDogs win the Carolina League title. Caminero was slated to spend most of 2023 at High-A Bowling Green, but he tore up those plans by blitzing the league, and he got even better after a promotion to Double-A Montgomery. When he made his MLB debut on Sept. 23, he became the second-youngest big leaguer in Rays history, trailing only B.J. Upton.

SCOUTING REPORT: Caminero hits the ball harder than almost anyone in baseball. His bat speed is top-of-the-scale, trailing only Giancarlo Stanton, Franchy Cordero and Jo Adell in average bat speed among big leaguers with 25 or more plate appearances, and he had the best 90th percentile exit velocity of any qualifying minor leaguer in 2023. As that bat speed list attests, a fast bat by itself is just a building block for offensive success, but Caminero pairs it with rapidly improving bat-to-ball skills and pitch recognition. He will expand his zone at times, but when he gets a hittable pitch, he rarely misses it. He doesn't have to sell out to get to his power, and he rarely gets pull-happy. He can wait a little longer on pitches and still drive the ball, and if a pitcher tries to work him away, he can flick his wrists to drive balls to the opposite field. Sixteen of his 32 home runs in 2023 went to right or right-center field. Caminero is an average at defender at third base with a chance to eventually be above-average. He moves well side-to-side but is still learning when to stay back and when to charge balls. His plus arm helps a lot and allows him

BEST TOOLS

BATTING

Best Hitter for Average	Xavier Isaac
Best Power Hitter	Junior Caminero
Best Strike-Zone Discipline	Chandler Simpson
Fastest Baserunner	Chandler Simpson
Best Athlete	Brock Jones

PITCHING

Best Fastball	Yoniel Curet
Best Curveball	Santiago Suarez
Best Slider	Shane Baz
Best Changeup	JJ Goss
Best Control	Marcus Johnson

FIELDING

Best Defensive Catcher	Logan Driscoll
Best Defensive Infielder	Carson Williams
Best Infield Arm	Carson Williams
Best Defensive Outfielder	Mason Auer
Best Outfield Arm	Mason Auer

to be fringy but playable at shortstop. Caminero moves really well for his size. He'll flash above-average to plus run times and could probably handle right field if the Rays desired.

THE FUTURE: The Rays haven't produced many consistent sluggers, which helps explain why Caminero has the potential to quickly become one of the most prolific home run hitters in team history. His defensive versatility helps with the Rays' mix-and-match lineup approach. Tampa Bay doesn't usually call up players straight from Double-A, but having already done so in Caminero's case, it will be hard to keep him in Triple-A for long in 2024. While he has more power than hitting ability, as a 20-year-old who makes plenty of contact, he could be the rare player who hits for average while challenging for home run crowns. ∎

Year	Age	Club (League)	Level	AVG	G	AB	R	H	2B	3B	HR	RBI	BB	SO	SB	OBP	SLG
2023	19	Bowling Green (SAL)	A+	.356	36	146	30	52	9	3	11	32	10	40	2	.409	.685
2023	19	Montgomery (SL)	AA	.309	81	314	55	97	9	3	20	62	32	60	3	.373	.548
2023	19	Tampa Bay (AL)	MLB	.235	7	34	4	8	1	0	1	7	2	8	0	.278	.353
Minor League Totals				.316	222	845	148	267	33	8	51	178	85	171	19	.383	.555
Major League Totals				.235	7	34	4	8	1	0	1	7	2	8	0	.278	.353

2 CARSON WILLIAMS, SS

HIT: 40. **POW:** 60. **RUN:** 55. **FLD:** 65. **ARM:** 70. **BA Grade:** 60. **Risk:** High.

Born: June 24, 2003. **B-T:** R-R. **HT:** 6-2. **WT:** 180.
Drafted: HS—San Diego, 2021 (1st round). **Signed by:** Jaime Jones.

TRACK RECORD: It seems hard to believe now, but at San Diego's Torrey Pines High Williams was viewed as a pitcher who also played shortstop for most of his career. He added muscle as a senior and began to show newfound power, which convinced the Rays to draft him 28th overall and spend $2.35 million to buy him out of his California commitment. He led Low-A Charleston to a Carolina League title in 2022 and followed it up by leading the High-A South Atlantic League with 48 extra-base hits while finishing second with 23 home runs.

SCOUTING REPORT: Williams is one of the better defensive shortstops in the minor leagues thanks largely to his plus-plus arm. He's a smooth, gliding fielder with fluid actions, above-average lateral range and a quick transfer, but his ability to make strong and accurate throws without having to set his feet or build momentum allows him to make plays other shortstops don't even attempt. He's an above-average runner. At the plate, Williams can carry a team when he's locked in, but he struggles to maintain his timing. He uses a significant leg lift at the start of his swing that sometimes gets him out of sync. He will have stretches where he is an easy out, and others where his power plays. He can clear batter's eyes in center field and is comfortable driving the ball to right field as well.

THE FUTURE: Depending on how Wander Franco's legal issues are resolved, Williams has the glove and power to give him a chance to be the Rays' shortstop of the not-too-distant future. His offensive game somewhat resembles that of Dansby Swanson as a shortstop who doesn't always hit for average but gets on base at a solid clip and hits for enough power to make an impact. He's ready for Double-A Montgomery.

Year	Age	Club (League)	Level	AVG	G	AB	R	H	2B	3B	HR	RBI	BB	SO	SB	OBP	SLG
2023	20	Bowling Green (SAL)	A+	.254	105	401	69	102	18	7	23	77	53	147	17	.351	.506
2023	20	Montgomery (SL)	AA	.429	6	21	4	9	2	0	0	4	4	5	3	.538	.524
2023	20	Durham (IL)	AAA	.077	4	13	3	1	1	0	0	0	2	6	0	.200	.154
Minor League Totals				.256	239	926	165	237	47	18	42	159	122	339	50	.354	.482

3 CURTIS MEAD, 2B/3B

HIT: 60. **POW:** 55. **RUN:** 40. **FLD:** 50. **ARM:** 30. **BA Grade:** 50. **Risk:** Medium.

Born: October 26, 2000. **B-T:** R-R. **HT:** 6-2. **WT:** 171.
Signed: Australia, 2018. **Signed by:** Howard Norsetter/Roberto Aquino/Derrick Chung (Phillies).

TRACK RECORD: The Rays acquired Mead from the Phillies in the November 2019 trade that sent Class A lefthander Cristopher Sanchez to Philadelphia. Sanchez blossomed into a solid starter for the Phillies in 2023, while Mead is ready to break into the Rays' lineup in 2024, so the trade may prove to be a win for both teams. After missing time in 2022 with an elbow injury, Mead missed almost two months with a wrist injury in 2023 after being hit by a pitch. He dominated the Triple-A International League upon his return, made his MLB debut in August and started both playoff games for the Rays, driving in Tampa Bay's lone postseason run.

SCOUTING REPORT: Mead is one the Rays' best pure hitters. He has the rare combination of above-average plate discipline and exceptional bat-to-ball skills. Mead looks to pull or go up the middle to do damage, but with two strikes the Australia native shortens up and pokes the ball to right field. He has plus power potential, though so far it has led to more doubles than home runs because he hits balls to the power alleys. Mead feasts on fastballs. He's not a very adept breaking ball hitter, but he recognizes them and doesn't chase. Mead's well below-average arm is an issue for him at either second base or third. He has solid short-area quickness and a solid first step. His hands are average as well, but if he has to leave his feet, go to his knees or move away from his target, he struggles to get anything on his throws. The shift restrictions help him at second by eliminating long throws from short right field.

THE FUTURE: Mead's bat fits in Tampa Bay's 2024 lineup, ideally as someone who bounces between second and third base, depending on where fewer balls are expected to be hit.

Year	Age	Club (League)	Level	AVG	G	AB	R	H	2B	3B	HR	RBI	BB	SO	SB	OBP	SLG
2023	22	FCL Rays	Rk	.167	4	12	0	2	1	0	0	4	1	1	0	.214	.250
2023	22	Durham (IL)	AAA	.294	61	235	41	69	21	2	9	45	35	48	4	.385	.515
2023	22	Tampa Bay (AL)	MLB	.253	24	83	12	21	3	1	1	5	7	21	0	.326	.349
Minor League Totals				.302	291	1104	188	333	99	6	41	187	119	205	26	.376	.514
Major League Totals				.253	24	83	12	21	3	1	1	5	7	21	0	.326	.349

4 SHANE BAZ, RHP

FB: 70. **CB:** 45. **SL:** 60. **CHG:** 50. **CTL:** 55. **BA Grade:** 60. **Risk:** Extreme.

Born: June 17, 1999. **B-T:** R-R. **HT:** 6-2. **WT:** 190.
Drafted: HS—Tomball, TX, 2017 (1st round). **Signed by:** Wayne Mathis (Pirates).

TRACK RECORD: The Pirates drafted Baz 12th overall in 2017 then made him the player to be named in the 2018 trade with the Rays trade that sent Chris Archer to Pittsburgh for Baz, Austin Meadows and Tyler Glasnow. Baz reached the majors in 2021, and even made a start for Tampa Bay in the 2021 post-season, but he needed surgery to remove loose bodies in his elbow at the start of the 2022 season. He suffered further elbow pain upon his return and ended up having Tommy John surgery in September 2022 that sidelined him for all of 2023. Baz's development has taken long enough that Archer has both returned to the Rays post-trade and now been out of baseball. He didn't pitch anywhere in 2023.

SCOUTING REPORT: No one will know for sure what Baz looks like now until he returns to the mound. The Rays say his rehabilitation has gone as expected and that he should be full speed for the opening of spring training. Before the injury, Baz had a Gerrit Cole-like high-90s plus-plus fastball that can over-whelm hitters with its combination of exceptional velocity and above-average carry. He complements his heater with a high-80s bullet slider that relies more on velocity than movement to handcuff hitters. Baz will flip over a low-80s fringe-average curveball to get ahead in counts, and he has used an average high-80s changeup to combat lefthanded hitters.

THE FUTURE: The Rays may start Baz slowly in 2024 as he re-acclimates to the mound, but he's a big part of Tampa Bay's big league rotation plans, with the stuff to serve as a front-of-the-rotation playoff starter. The Rays ran out of starters in 2023 as elbow injuries claimed Shane McClanahan, Jeffrey Springs and Drew Rasmussen, so having a healthy Baz pitch in October 2024 would be a big improvement.

Year	Age	Club (League)	Level	W	L	ERA	G	GS	IP	H	HR	BB	SO	BB%	SO%	WHIP	AVG
2023	24	Did not play—Injured															
Minor League Totals				12	14	3.00	60	60	249	203	20	97	298	9.3	28.6	1.20	.219
Major League Total				3	2	4.02	9	9	40	33	8	12	48	7.2	28.9	1.12	.216

5 XAVIER ISAAC, 1B

HIT: 55. **POW:** 65. **RUN:** 40. **FLD:** 50. **ARM:** 50. **BA Grade:** 55. **Risk:** High.

Born: December 17, 2003. **B-T:** L-L. **HT:** 6-0. **WT:** 240.
Drafted: HS—Kernersville, NC, 2022 (1st round). **Signed by:** Landon Lassiter.

TRACK RECORD: Isaac was hard to scout as an amateur because a foot injury kept him from playing for most of the summer as a rising high school senior outside Winston-Salem, N.C. The Rays were one of the teams who stayed on him, drafting him 29th overall in 2022 and signing him for slot value of $2,548,900. Isaac has rewarded Tampa Bay by steadily exceeding expectations. Isaac cut 20 pounds in offseason workouts heading into 2023, which paid off both at the plate and in the field in a season he spent primarily with Low-A Charleston.

SCOUTING REPORT: Isaac's massive frame and raw power understandably led to him being pegged as a slugger coming out of high school, but he's shown himself to be more of a pure hitter than a grip-it-and-rip-it slugger. His natural approach is to work counts, wait until he gets a pitch he likes and then line the ball around the field. Isaac has top-of-the-scale raw power, and the Rays will work to get him to try to let loose more often in hitter's counts to get to his 30-plus home run potential. He proved in 2023 that he should be more than a DH. His improved agility paid off in better range to go with soft hands at first base. He's now an average defender with an accurate, average arm, a promising sign for an organization that emphasizes first base defense. Isaac is a below-average runner, but he's not a clogger, and he swiped 12 bases in 12 tries in 2023.

THE FUTURE: It's hard to impress scouts with a first-base only profile, because the hitting demands are so severe, but Isaac is a rarity as an above-average hitter with massive power. He'll need to stay on top of his conditioning, but he's already demonstrated his willingness to put in the work. He'll head back to High-A Bowling Green to start 2024 and could eventually be Yandy Diaz's replacement at first base.

Year	Age	Club (League)	Level	AVG	G	AB	R	H	2B	3B	HR	RBI	BB	SO	SB	OBP	SLG
2023	19	Charleston (CAR)	A	.266	90	312	58	83	16	3	13	56	56	80	10	.380	.462
2023	19	Bowling Green (SAL)	A+	.408	12	49	13	20	4	1	6	16	8	12	2	.491	.898
Minor League Totals				.282	107	380	75	107	23	4	19	77	66	95	12	.390	.513

6 BRAYDEN TAYLOR, 3B

HIT: 60. **POW:** 50. **RUN:** 50. **FLD:** 50. **ARM:** 50. **BA Grade:** 55. **Risk:** High.

Born: May 22, 2002. **B-T:** L-R. **HT:** 6-1. **WT:** 180.
Drafted: Texas Christian, 2023 (1st round). **Signed by:** Chris Hom.

TRACK RECORD: Heading into the 2023 season, Taylor was viewed as one of the better hitters in his draft class. As a Texas Christian junior, he answered some of the questions about his power by hitting 23 home runs in 67 games after hitting 25 bombs in his previous two seasons combined. The Rays drafted Taylor 19th overall and signed him for a slot value bonus of $3.877 million, the seventh highest for a drafted player in franchise history.

SCOUTING REPORT: Taylor fits the Rays' desire for developing players who are hitters with power potential rather than sluggers who may develop as hitters. He walked more than he struck out over his college career and impressed evaluators with his ability to hit for average and make plenty of contact. Taylor's swing could use a little cleanup. He tends to pull off the ball at times and his swing path could get more direct, but he has excellent pitch recognition and bat-to-ball skills. He has the potential to sell out for more power, but he's likely better off focusing on being a plus hitter with average power. Taylor's eventual defensive home is not fully set. While he played third base exclusively in his pro debut, he has the tools to be a solid second baseman, and it wouldn't be a shock to see him try his hand at shortstop in the minor leagues 2024. Taylor doesn't have a standout tool aside from his bat, but he does a lot of things well. For example, he has average speed and has stolen 48 bases successfully since his last caught stealing, which occurred early in his freshman year at TCU.

THE FUTURE: Taylor is the kind of offensive infielder with bat-to-ball skills that the Rays love. He's set to head to High-A Bowling Green in 2024. If he develops as expected, Taylor could become an everyday second or third baseman for Tampa Bay in a couple of years.

Year	Age	Club (League)	Level	AVG	G	AB	R	H	2B	3B	HR	RBI	BB	SO	SB	OBP	SLG
2023	21	FCL Rays	Rk	.222	3	9	4	2	1	1	0	0	3	3	2	.417	.556
2023	21	Charleston (CAR)	A	.244	22	82	15	20	3	2	5	15	14	31	9	.354	.512
Minor League Totals				.242	25	91	19	22	4	3	5	15	17	34	11	.361	.516

7 OSLEIVIS BASABE, SS/2B

HIT: 55. **POW:** 30. **RUN:** 60. **FLD:** 50. **ARM:** 50. **BA Grade:** 45. **Risk:** Medium.

Born: September 13, 2000. **B-T:** R-R. **HT:** 6-1. **WT:** 165.
Signed: Venezuela, 2000. **Signed by:** Carlos Plaza (Rangers).

TRACK RECORD: The Rays don't win every trade in which they flip a major leaguer for a package of minor leaguers, and the December 2020 trade that sent Nathaniel Lowe to the Rangers for Basabe, Heriberto Hernandez and Alexander Ovalles is one Tampa Bay might want back. But Basabe has given the Rays some usefulness. He made his MLB debut in August 2023, becoming the Rays' everyday shortstop when Taylor Walls was on the injured list and Wander Franco was placed on the restricted list.

SCOUTING REPORT: In an organization that has been filled with middle infield prospects, Basabe has climbed the ladder and pushed other prospects to the side because of his steady, reliable production. The Rays have traded away Xavier Edwards, Vidal Brujan and Tristan Gray, clearing a path for Basabe. While he struggled in his first MLB action, Basabe has shown he can be an above-average hitter but with limited power. He's an aggressive hitter who feasts on pitches up in the zone and has above-average contact skills, but he's a line-drive hitter who doesn't hit many home runs. The Rays have bounced Basabe all around the infield. He's a reliable, average defender at shortstop and third base with an average, accurate arm. He's above-average at second base, but his ability to make the routine play at any infield position led to his callup. He's a plus runner, but he's not a particularly aggressive basestealer.

THE FUTURE: Ideally, Basabe is a part-time player or utility infielder who can provide reliable defense at three positions. With Walls recovering from hip surgery and Franco facing legal issues, Basabe could end up as Tampa Bay's Opening Day shortstop in 2024.

Year	Age	Club (League)	Level	AVG	G	AB	R	H	2B	3B	HR	RBI	BB	SO	SB	OBP	SLG
2023	22	Durham (IL)	AAA	.296	94	385	45	114	24	7	4	58	31	66	16	.351	.426
2023	22	Tampa Bay (AL)	MLB	.218	31	87	15	19	5	0	1	12	6	25	0	.277	.310
Minor League Totals				.311	365	1476	244	459	91	26	12	207	130	216	74	.369	.432
Major League Totals				.218	31	87	15	19	5	0	1	12	6	25	0	.277	.310

8 ADRIAN SANTANA, SS

HIT: 50. **POW:** 40. **RUN:** 70. **FLD:** 60. **ARM:** 55. **BA Grade:** 55. **Risk:** Extreme.

Born: July 18, 2005. **B-T:** B-R. **HT:** 5-11. **WT:** 155.
Drafted: HS—Doral, FL, 2023 (1st round supplemental). **Signed by:** Victor Rodriguez.
TRACK RECORD: The son of former Cleveland minor league outfielder Osmany Santana, who peaked at Double-A in 2001, Adrian headed into his senior year at Doral (Fla.) Academy in 2023 with a solid shot of making it to campus at Miami. He answered many of the questions about his bat by leading Doral County preps with 11 home runs while showing one of the best gloves in the draft class. The Rays drafted Santana 31st overall, making him the fourth shortstop they've picked in their past five competitive balance picks and paying him $2 million to forgo his college commitment to Miami.
SCOUTING REPORT: Santana is one of the smoother shortstops to come out of high school in the past few years. He's not yet Carson Williams' equal defensively, but he has a chance to get there thanks to his exceptional twitchiness, body control and smooth hands. His arm is above-average, and there's reason to believe it will get better as he gets stronger. The switch-hitting Santana faces many more questions offensively. His lefthanded swing will need a whole lot of work in the cage. It has more length to it than the righthanded swing he uses much less often, and he struggles with his timing from the left side. Santana weighs just 155 pounds but has shown surprising pop for such a slight frame. Still, his lack of strength will be a challenge early in his pro career. He is a plus-plus runner who should steal bushels of bases.
THE FUTURE: Santana would have been better served by the old minor league structure where he could spend his first full pro season in the Appalachian or New York-Penn leagues. Now, the Rays will have to decide whether to push him to Low-A Charleston or send him back to the Florida Complex League. He's more than ready defensively, but his bat may not be up to the Carolina League challenge.

Year	Age	Club (League)	Level	AVG	G	AB	R	H	2B	3B	HR	RBI	BB	SO	SB	OBP	SLG
2023	17	FCL Rays	Rk	.205	10	39	6	8	2	0	0	3	7	9	3	.340	.256
Minor League Totals				.205	10	39	6	8	2	0	0	3	7	9	3	.340	.256

9 DOMINIC KEEGAN, C

HIT: 55. **POW:** 40. **RUN:** 40. **FLD:** 45. **ARM:** 40. **BA Grade:** 50. **Risk:** High.

Born: August 1, 2000. **B-T:** R-R. **Ht.:** 6-0. **Wt.:** 205.
Drafted: Vanderbilt, 2022 (4th round). **Signed by:** Steve Ames.
TRACK RECORD: For four years at Vanderbilt, all Keegan did was hit. He toyed with catching in college but generally found himself playing first base whenever the Commodores' best pitchers were on the mound. The Rays were willing to give Keegan a chance to catch every day after drafting him in the fourth round in 2022, and while he has moved slowly, he has rewarded that faith by steadily improving defensively while showing a polished bat.
SCOUTING REPORT: Keegan has worked hard to improve his catching, and it's paid off. He's an above-average receiver and has become a fringe-average blocker on balls in the dirt. He works well with pitchers. His big hurdle behind the plate is his throwing. His arm is average, but he takes a long time to make the exchange and get rid of the ball, leading to plenty of below-average pop times on throws to second base. He threw out 30% of basestealers during the regular season at Low-A Charleston and High-A Bowling Green, but he gave up 35 stolen bases in 40 attempts in 13 games in the Arizona Fall League. Offensively, Keegan has been a consistent performer, but considering his four years of experience at Vanderbilt, he's been playing at a level or two below his hitting ability while his glove tries to catch up. He's rarely fooled and draws walks with a contact-heavy approach, though there is plus raw power that could lead to more power down the road.
THE FUTURE: Catcher remains a question mark for the Rays both in the short and long terms, though that's been true for much of the 21st century. Keegan is the next Rays' minor leaguer who could get a shot. He has shown the desire to put in the work to improve defensively, and his bat is above-average for a catcher, but he still has plenty of work to do to get to St. Petersburg.

Year	Age	Club (League)	Level	AVG	G	AB	R	H	2B	3B	HR	RBI	BB	SO	SB	OBP	SLG
2023	22	Charleston (CAR)	A	.315	58	200	34	63	9	4	5	35	31	48	2	.402	.475
2023	22	Bowling Green (SAL)	A+	.254	48	173	26	44	11	0	8	30	28	42	0	.367	.457
Minor League Totals				.291	118	413	66	120	24	4	15	76	64	100	3	.389	.477

10 YONIEL CURET, RHP

FB: 70. **SL:** 60. **CTL:** 40. **BA Grade:** 55. **Risk:** Extreme.

Born: November 3, 2002. **B-T:** R-R. **Ht.:** 6-2. **Wt.:** 190.
Signed: Dominican Republic, 2019. **Signed by:** Daniel Santana.
TRACK RECORD: The Rays signed numerous position players in their 2019 international class who landed bigger bonuses than Curet's $150,000, but after he dominated Class A hitters, he was the only player from that signing class to be added to the 40-man roster in November to protect him from selection in the Rule 5 draft.
SCOUTING REPORT: Curet already touched 95 mph when the Rays signed him, but he has now blossomed into the best arm in the system—with the exception of the rehabbing Shane Baz. There are plenty of pitchers in the system with less risk, but Curet's ability to throw a fastball and hard slider that have proven nearly impossible to square up gives him the highest upside. His plus-plus fastball checks all the boxes. He sits at 96-98 mph as a starter, and his combination of above-average carry and a flat plane bedevils hitters. His plus high-80s slider never gets very big, and at its hardest it's more of a cutter. Curet has largely shelved the slower curveball that once was his best breaking pitch. As basic as Curet's assortment is, it's extremely effective. Class A hitters hit .142 with a .193 slugging percentage against him in 2023. He allowed 11 extra-base hits among 432 batters faced. He's around the zone, but his control is below-average and needs to improve after his walk rate approached 17% in 2023. Hs delivery is relatively clean with no glaring flaws, suggesting he could one day throw more strikes.
THE FUTURE: Curet is emerging as the Rays' best pitching prospect, but he's several notches below the recent standard for that trait. He carries plenty of reliever risk, because everything he throws is hard, and he needs plenty of development and refinement before he'll be big league ready. But his fastball is special, and hitters rarely square him up, which is the perfect start for a pitching prospect.

Year	Age	Club (League)	Level	W	L	ERA	G	GS	IP	H	HR	BB	SO	BB%	SO%	WHIP	AVG
2023	20	Charleston (CAR)	A	6	1	2.46	20	17	80	34	1	54	111	16.7	34.4	1.10	.132
2023	20	Bowling Green (SAL)	A+	2	0	4.56	6	5	24	17	1	19	33	17.4	30.3	1.52	.200
Minor League Totals				12	6	2.97	55	40	197	113	5	128	265	15.3	31.7	1.22	.170

11 COLTON LEDBETTER, OF

HIT: 55. **POW:** 50. **RUN:** 50. **FLD:** 50. **ARM:** 50. **BA Grade:** 50. **Risk:** High.

Born: November 15, 2001. **B-T:** L-R. **Ht.:** 6-2. **Wt.:** 205. **Drafted:** Mississippi State, 2023 (2nd round).
Signed by: Rickey Drexler.
TRACK RECORD: Ledbetter has always hit. In two years at Samford, he was one of the best hitters in the Southern Conference. He then was one of the best players in the New England Collegiate League during summer 2022. And to prove that he could handle a jump in level of competition, Ledbetter transferred to Mississippi State for his junior year, where he showed that he was just as capable of hitting Southeastern Conference pitching. He hit .320/.452/.574 while stealing 17 bases in 2023, making himself the Rays' second-round pick. Ledbetter finished his pro debut with Low-A Charleston as starting center fielder during the postseason. He homered in Game 1 of the championship series to help the RiverDogs win their third straight title.
SCOUTING REPORT: Ledbetter is a well-rounded outfielder who has a chance to have five average tools. He doesn't do anything exceptionally, but he also has no glaring weakness. He doesn't chase too frequently. He doesn't get himself out and shouldn't strike out too much. Ledbetter has average power, and he's an above-average defender in the corners who can plausibly play center field, though probably not for the Rays who always seem to have plus defenders in center.
THE FUTURE: As a capable SEC hitter who has already gotten a taste of the Carolina League, a push to High-A Bowling Green to start 2024 is likely. There are plenty of Rays outfield prospects who do something better than Ledbetter. But the Rays don't have an outfield prospect who can do as many things well as Ledbetter.

Year	Age	Club (League)	Level	AVG	G	AB	R	H	2B	3B	HR	RBI	BB	SO	SB	OBP	SLG
2023	21	FCL Rays	Rk	.400	3	10	4	4	0	0	1	4	2	1	1	.500	.700
2023	21	Charleston (CAR)	A	.254	18	63	11	16	6	0	1	8	10	16	2	.356	.397
Minor League Totals				.274	21	73	15	20	6	0	2	12	12	17	3	.376	.438

12 SANTIAGO SUAREZ, RHP

FB: 55. **CB:** 60. **CHG:** 40. **CTL:** 60. **BA Grade:** 50. **Risk:** High.

Born: January 11, 2005. **B-T:** R-R. **Ht.:** 6-2. **Wt.:** 175. **Signed:** Venezuela, 2022.
Signed by: Manuel Padron/Clifford Nuitter/Tibaldo Hernandez (Marlins).

TRACK RECORD: Much like his Florida Complex League teammate Jose Urbina in 2023, Suarez is a relatively polished Venezuelan righthander who has made massive gains in the past couple of years. Suarez was originally a scouting success story for the Marlins. Miami signed him just before the 2022 Dominican Summer League season. After a solid stint in the DSL, he was traded to the Rays with Marcus Johnson for Xavier Edwards and J.T. Chargois.

SCOUTING REPORT: Suarez was one of the best pitchers in the Florida Complex League in his Rays debut and made a start in the playoffs for Low-A Charleston. He simply overwhelmed hitters by rarely falling behind. He threw his above-average 93-94 mph fastball for strikes an absurd 75% of the time. Suarez's fastball has a tick above-average carry and he elevates it well. His 77-79 mph downer curveball is a plus pitch. Suarez didn't seem as confident in his nascent changeup this year as he was in 2022. It needs to develop significantly if he's going to be a starter.

THE FUTURE: Suarez is one of the most promising and most polished young pitchers in the Rays' system. He'll need to add a third pitch eventually, but his plus control and ability to spin a breaking ball gives him a great foundation.

Year	Age	Club (League)	Level	W	L	ERA	G	GS	IP	H	HR	BB	SO	BB%	SO%	WHIP	AVG
2023	18	FCL Rays	Rk	4	0	1.13	10	3	40	28	0	8	38	5.3	25.3	0.91	.199
2023	18	Charleston (CAR)	A	1	2	2.29	5	5	20	21	1	3	14	3.7	17.1	1.22	.269
Minor League Totals				6	3	1.84	26	19	98	85	2	17	90	4.4	23.4	1.04	.234

13 MARCUS JOHNSON, RHP

FB: 50. **SL:** 45. **CB:** 45. **CHG:** 45. **CTL:** 65. **BA Grade:** 50. **Risk:** High.

Born: December 11, 2000. **B-T:** R-R. **Ht.:** 6-0. **Wt.:** 200. **Drafted:** Duke, 2022 (4th round).
Signed by: Blake Newsome (Marlins).

TRACK RECORD: For much of his career at Duke, Johnson was a successful reliever. A move to the rotation as a junior didn't go as well, and he posted a near 6.00 ERA in his 2022 pro debut as a starter in the Marlins system as well. The Rays liked his control and delivery anyway and acquired him with Santiago Suarez in the deal that sent Xavier Edwards and J.T. Chargois to Miami. Johnson responded by being one of the better starters in the Low-A Carolina League in 2023. In late July and early August, Johnson hit a minor speed bump, as he struggled with his control in back-to-back starts. Those eight walks in 8.2 innings were more than one-third of all the walks he issued in 2023.

SCOUTING REPORT: Even if Johnson's stuff can be described as average at best, it's hard to ignore what plus control does for a pitcher. Johnson locates both arm side and glove side. His 92-94 mph fastball is an average pitch, and his low-80s sweepy slider and bigger breaking high-70s curveball with 1-to-7 shape are both fringe average, as is his mid-80s changeup. For skeptical scouts, he's just a dime-a-dozen, back-end starter. But because he throws strikes and locates all four pitches, hitters are often caught on their back foot.

THE FUTURE: Johnson's upside is likely as a back-of-the-rotation starter, but No. 5 starters don't dot the corners like this. He has a chance to exceed expectations because of his excellent control and command.

Year	Age	Club (League)	Level	W	L	ERA	G	GS	IP	H	HR	BB	SO	BB%	SO%	WHIP	AVG
2023	22	Charleston (CAR)	A	5	6	3.74	26	24	130	130	12	21	114	3.9	21.3	1.16	.258
Minor League Totals				6	9	4.01	31	28	147	142	14	32	143	5.3	23.5	1.19	.251

14 JOSE URBINA, RHP

FB: 55. **CB:** 60. **CHG:** 40. **CTL:** 45. **BA Grade:** 50. **Risk:** Extreme.

Born: November 2, 2005. **B-T:** R-R. **Ht.:** 6-3. **Wt.:** 180. **Signed:** Venezuela, 2023.
Signed by: Angel Contreras/Juan Castillo.

TRACK RECORD: In the 1990s and 2000s, teams often spent big to sign the best arms in Latin America. But after high-priced arm after high-priced arm failed to make it to the major leagues, the approach changed. Now, even the best international pitchers don't come close to matching the bonuses handed out to the top hitters. But even considering that, Urbina is an unusual case. He signed with the Rays for $210,000 out of Venezuela in January 2023, but he's already one of the team's most promising pitching prospects.

SCOUTING REPORT: When teams were scouting Urbina, he was an athletic, well-built righthander with a clean delivery and a fast arm, but he maxed out at 90 mph. There was a hope that he'd add more velocity, but it would have been hard to expect it would happen this quickly. The Rays skipped the polished Urbina over the Dominican Summer League, and he debuted as a 17-year-old in the Florida Complex League. While his statistics weren't particularly impressive, he showed some of the best stuff and feel in the league. Urbina sits in the mid 90s and touches 97 mph with a potentially plus fastball with above-average life. He also spins a future plus curveball and will flash feel for his still-developing changeup.

THE FUTURE: For years, the Rays seemed to produce front-line starters at will, but at present there are few pitchers in the system who the organization projects as even midrotation starters. Urbina has arguably the highest upside of any of them. His athleticism, clean delivery and feel for spinning a breaking ball to go with rapidly improving velocity makes him an arm to watch.

Year	Age	Club (League)	Level	W	L	ERA	G	GS	IP	H	HR	BB	SO	BB%	SO%	WHIP	AVG
2023	17	FCL Rays	Rk	0	3	5.32	11	8	24	23	4	12	21	11.4	20.0	1.48	.258
Minor League Totals				0	3	5.48	11	8	24	23	4	12	21	11.4	20.0	1.52	.258

15 MASON MONTGOMERY, LHP

FB: 60. **SL:** 40. **CHG:** 40. **CTL:** 45. **BA Grade:** 45. **Risk:** High.

Born: June 17, 2000. **B-T:** L-L. **Ht.:** 6-2. **Wt.:** 200. **Drafted:** Texas Tech, 2021 (6th round). **Signed by:** Pat Murphy.

TRACK RECORD: The Rays' minor league pitcher of the year in 2022, Montgomery seemed to struggle with the experimental pre-tacked ball being used in the Double-A Southern League in the first half of 2023. After a rocky start, he found his form in the final six weeks, allowing two runs in a five-start stretch while earning a promotion to Triple-A Durham.

SCOUTING REPORT: When Montgomery was dominating in stretches in 2022, there was reason to hope that he would take a further step forward in 2023 by developing his slider. Instead, his fastball lost some of its carry and his slider seemed stuck where it was in 2022. Montgomery didn't take a step forward in 2023, but in reaching Triple-A he also didn't take a step back. Montgomery's fastball can be a plus pitch when he's throwing it in the 92-93 mph range with plus life. But when it backs up, it becomes a pitch that can get squared up. In one game against Biloxi, he gave up four home runs in a 10-batter stretch. His short-arm delivery imparts deception on everything he throws. Montgomery's body stays between the ball and the batter until late in his delivery. His short-breaking, low-80s slider has cutterish action and is below-average. It has the movement of a power slider, but not the velocity. And he doesn't seem to have much feel or conviction in his below-average mid-80s changeup.

THE FUTURE: Montgomery has had plenty of success in the minors, and there's still time for him to develop his secondary offerings to give him a shot to remain a starter. But with each passing year, it gets harder to believe that transformation will occur. More likely he'll be a quality lefthanded reliever whose hard-to-hit fastball plays effectively in short stints, even if his slider doesn't frighten hitters.

Year	Age	Club (League)	Level	W	L	ERA	G	GS	IP	H	HR	BB	SO	BB%	SO%	WHIP	AVG
2023	23	Montgomery (SL)	AA	5	4	4.18	25	25	108	98	18	49	131	10.5	28.0	1.37	.238
2023	23	Durham (IL)	AAA	2	0	2.70	4	4	17	7	2	11	13	15.9	18.8	1.08	.127
Minor League Totals				14	7	2.95	61	60	259	198	31	104	335	9.7	31.2	1.17	.207

16 IAN SEYMOUR, LHP

FB: 50. **CHG:** 60. **SL:** 40. **CTL:** 45. **BA Grade:** 45. **Risk:** High.

Born: December 13, 1998. **B-T:** L-L. **Ht.:** 6-0. **Wt.:** 210. **Drafted:** Virginia Tech, 2020 (2nd round). **Signed by:** Landon Lassiter.

TRACK RECORD: At Virginia Tech and then with the Rays, Seymour has proven to be a funky lefty who always seemed to leave hitters wondering why and how he got them out. Something seemed off to start 2022, which proved to be a torn elbow ligament that needed Tommy John surgery. He made it back to the mound late in 2023 and once again looked like his old funky self. In 2021 and 2023 combined, he recorded a 1.76 ERA.

SCOUTING REPORT: Seymour has an exaggerated and high-tempo hip turn to begin his delivery. Not only does it seem odd to watch, but it also hides the ball well and seems to aid in the deception of his plus low-80s changeup. Seymour's changeup has solid separation and exceptional deception. Even hitters who are looking for it see fastball out of his hand. Seymour's low-90s fastball is a solid pitch in its own right thanks to plus life when he gets it above hitters' hands. He has a below-average slider and slow curve, but both seem almost superfluous because he has yet to develop feel for either of them. He is an average strike-thrower.

THE FUTURE: While Seymour has long been a starter, the expectation of most evaluators is that he will eventually move to the bullpen, where his fastball/changeup approach will bedevil hitters an inning or two at a time. He should get a chance to return to Double-A Montgomery for a third and hopefully final time to start 2024, but he should get to Triple-A Durham soon if everything goes as hoped.

Year	Age	Club (League)	Level	W	L	ERA	G	GS	IP	H	HR	BB	SO	BB%	SO%	WHIP	AVG
2023	24	FCL Rays	Rk	0	0	1.35	4	4	7	4	0	4	11	14.3	39.3	1.20	.167
2023	24	Charleston (CAR)	A	1	0	1.64	6	6	22	12	1	5	22	6.5	28.6	0.77	.171
2023	24	Bowling Green (SAL)	A+	0	0	2.08	2	2	9	4	1	5	9	14.7	26.5	1.04	.143
2023	24	Montgomery (SL)	AA	0	0	0.00	1	1	5	1	0	2	4	12.5	25.0	0.64	.071
Minor League Totals				5	2	2.68	32	31	114	69	8	47	156	10.4	34.7	1.02	.176

17 AUSTIN SHENTON, 1B/3B

HIT: 50. **POW:** 60. **FLD:** 40. **RUN:** 30. **ARM:** 30. **BA Grade:** 40. **Risk:** Medium.

Born: January 28, 1998. **B-T:** R-R. **Ht.:** 6-0. **Wt.:** 205. **Drafted:** Florida International, 2019 (5th round). **Signed by:** Dan Rovetto (Mariners).

TRACK RECORD: Shenton was in the middle of a breakout season for the Mariners' Double-A Arkansas club when he was traded to the Rays in a July 2021 deal for reliever Diego Castillo. Shenton's 2022 season was wrecked by a hip injury. He began 2023 with a third-straight assignment to the Double-A Southern League. He hit his way to Triple-A on July 14 and had the second-best OPS in the International League from that day until the end of the season.

SCOUTING REPORT: Shenton has plus productive power. He works counts until he gets a pitch to drive. He hit .304 in 2023. Still, evaluators generally see him as a .240-.250 hitter in the majors with solid on-base percentages. Strikeouts are going to be part of the tradeoff for his power. Despite his offensive upside, defensive limitations will make it harder for him to become a regular. Shenton is a slower-twitch athlete, a well below-average runner and somewhat stiff fielder with below-average range at third and first base. He sometimes struggles with accuracy issues at third base, especially on throws to second, and his arm strength simply isn't adequate for the position. His 74.1 mph average velocity on throws at third in Triple-A was worse than any MLB regular third baseman in 2023. At first base he's below-average.

THE FUTURE: Shenton's power is real and gives him a shot to carve out a big league role. Even after his addition to the 40-man roster, he's more likely to find a backup or fill-in role.

Year	Age	Club (League)	Level	AVG	G	AB	R	H	2B	3B	HR	RBI	BB	SO	SB	OBP	SLG
2023	25	Montgomery (SL)	AA	.307	73	254	45	78	21	0	15	49	46	79	0	.415	.567
2023	25	Durham (IL)	AAA	.301	61	219	57	66	24	0	14	50	48	75	0	.432	.603
Minor League Totals				.290	319	1181	225	342	103	6	58	234	188	355	1	.395	.534

18 CHANDLER SIMPSON, OF

HIT: 50. **POW:** 20. **FLD:** 60. **RUN:** 80. **ARM:** 30. **BA Grade:** 45. **Risk:** High.

Born: November 18, 2000. **B-T:** L-R. **Ht.:** 6-0. **Wt.:** 170. **Drafted:** Georgia Tech, 2022 (2nd round supplemental). **Signed by:** Milt Hill.

TRACK RECORD: In his first year at Georgia Tech in 2022, Simpson led Division I in batting when he hit .433/.506/.517. In his first full season in pro ball, Simpson led the minors with 94 steals. He actually tied his good friend and Cardinals prospect Victor Scott II for the title, continuing a friendly basestealing rivalry they've had stretching back to their days in the summer wood bat Northwoods League. Back then Simpson edged Scott for the stolen base crown by stealing a league-record 55 bags.

SCOUTING REPORT: Simpson's exceptional speed makes it easy to overlook the fact that he's actually a smart and effective hitter. He rarely swings at pitches outside of the strike zone, and his bat-to-ball skills are well above-average. Simpson posted one of the best contact rates in the minors and walked more than he struck out in 2023. He fully understands that any time he's swinging for the fences, he's helping the pitcher—he has one home run in the past four years between college and pro ball. Most of his hits land in front of outfielders. But he doesn't get the bat knocked out of his hand. Simpson's well below-average arm was unplayable in the infield, so the Rays immediately moved him to center field as a pro. He projects as a plus defender thanks largely to his top-of-the-scale speed.

THE FUTURE: Simpson's speed evokes comparisons to Terrance Gore and Billy Hamilton, but his hitting ability gives him a better shot at a regular or semi-regular role. While former Vanderbilt star and 2023 first-rounder Enrique Bradfield Jr. is more famous than Simpson, the pair shares a lot of similarities.

Year	Age	Club (League)	Level	AVG	G	AB	R	H	2B	3B	HR	RBI	BB	SO	SB	OBP	SLG
2023	22	Charleston (CAR)	A	.285	91	354	66	101	9	4	0	24	38	35	81	.358	.333
2023	22	Bowling Green (SAL)	A+	.326	24	89	22	29	4	1	0	7	16	9	13	.429	.393
Minor League Totals				.298	123	470	93	140	16	5	0	34	60	48	102	.379	.353

19 COLE WILCOX, RHP

FB: 45. **SL:** 55. **CHG:** 45. **CTL:** 45. **BA Grade:** 45. **Risk:** High.

Born: July 14, 1999. **B-T:** R-R. **Ht.:** 6-5. **Wt.:** 232. **Drafted:** Georgia, 2020 (3rd round).
Signed by: Tyler Stubblefield (Padres).

TRACK RECORD: Wilcox was a third-round pick of the Padres who got first-round money. The Rays acquired Wilcox as one of three players the team received when Blake Snell was traded to San Diego. Wilcox looked like a potential front-of-the-rotation starter early in his Rays career, but he tore his elbow ligament early in 2021 and had Tommy John surgery. He returned to action late in 2022. In 2023, he was durable but rarely dominated.

SCOUTING REPORT: While Tommy John surgery has a high recovery rate, Wilcox is a cautionary tale. Wilcox sat at 93-95 mph both in college and early in his pro career. He had touched 100 mph and regularly got to the high 90s. Post surgery, Wilcox's fastballs—he throws a two- and four-seamer—have dipped into the 91-93 mph range and he rarely tops 94. His slider is still above-average, but it doesn't have the same power and effectiveness in the 85-87 mph range that it did when he was 88-89. The same can be said for his fringe-average, hard 87-89 mph changeup. Wilcox is now a sinker/slider pitcher who is looking to generate ground balls and weak contact. He has to nibble more, which has also spiked his once impressive walk rate.

THE FUTURE: The Rays left Wilcox off their 40-man roster, gambling correctly that no team would be willing to pick him in the Rule 5 draft. His ranking here and his prospect status in general is buoyed by what everyone saw before his elbow injury. The hope remains that he will regain some of that arm speed, but right now he's more of a savvy righthander with modest stuff.

Year	Age	Club (League)	Level	W	L	ERA	G	GS	IP	H	HR	BB	SO	BB%	SO%	WHIP	AVG
2023	23	Montgomery (SL)	AA	6	8	5.23	25	25	107	95	14	44	99	9.7	21.8	1.30	.239
Minor League Totals				7	10	4.26	42	42	167	143	16	53	175	7.6	25.1	1.17	.228

20 SHANE SASAKI, OF

HIT: 50. **POW:** 40. **RUN:** 65. **FLD:** 55. **ARM:** 45. **BA Grade:** 45. **Risk:** High.

Born: July 1, 2000. **B-T:** R-R. **Ht.:** 6-0. **Wt.:** 175. **Drafted:** HS—Honolulu, HI, 2019 (3rd round). **Signed by:** Casey Onaga.

TRACK RECORD: After a solid but modest debut in the Florida Complex League in 2021, Sasaki was one of the better players in the Low-A Carolina League in 2022 as he helped the RiverDogs to their second of three straight titles. Sasaki was once again one of the more polished hitters in 2023, this time in the High-A South Atlantic League. He then had a solid stint in the Arizona Fall League, where he stole 13 bases in 13 tries in 22 games.

SCOUTING REPORT: Sasaki has simplified his setup as a pro, raising his hands but toning down a coil and timing step he once used. It has helped him get on time more consistently, and he's developed into a line-drive hitter who tries to hit the ball up the middle or to right field, the opposite field for the righthanded hitter. Sasaki is a top- or bottom-of-the-order tablesetter with below-average power. A nearly double-plus runner, Sasaki is also an above-average defender in center field and left. He can play right, but his arm is fringe-average.

THE FUTURE: Sasaki was Rule 5 eligible and unpicked, which isn't all that surprising because he's yet to play above Class A. He most likely profiles as a fourth outfielder who can play left and center field, run and hit for average. There is still some concern about how well he can hold up over a full season. He'll jump to Double-A Montgomery in 2024.

Year	Age	Club (League)	Level	AVG	G	AB	R	H	2B	3B	HR	RBI	BB	SO	SB	OBP	SLG
2023	22	FCL Rays	Rk	.250	4	12	2	3	0	1	0	0	4	4	4	.438	.417
2023	22	Bowling Green (SAL)	A+	.301	64	256	53	77	15	3	7	39	30	65	12	.375	.465
Minor League Totals				.302	203	782	165	236	48	9	18	113	104	216	86	.386	.455

21 BRAILER GUERRERO, OF

HIT: 45. **POW:** 60. **FLD:** 45. **RUN:** 45. **ARM:** 60. **BA Grade:** 50. **Risk:** Extreme.

Born: June 25, 2006. **B-T:** L-R. **Ht.:** 6-1. **Wt.:** 215. **Signed:** Dominican Republic, 2023.
Signed by: Daniel Santana/Remmy Hernandez.

TRACK RECORD: The Rays placed a big bet on Guerrero's big power, signing him in January 2023 for a $3.7 million bonus that ranked as the fifth-highest in a relatively loaded international amateur class. There's no need to really project Guerrero's power. He's already 6-foot-1, 215 pounds and hits the ball as hard as many big leaguers.

SCOUTING REPORT: Guerrero's 2023 debut in the Dominican Summer League was cut short by a shoulder injury that required surgery, but not before he showed exactly what the Rays were expecting. He hits the ball exceptionally hard for a teenager, with 110 mph or faster exit velocities at his best already. What makes Guerrero an especially interesting prospect is he shows signs that he's already able to combine quality swing decisions with that power to punish any pitcher who makes a mistake. Guerrero's an average runner now with a plus arm that would fit in right field, but he could keep getting bigger and stronger, which likely means he would get slower as well. If so, his power and patience would fit at first base.

THE FUTURE: Guerrero should be fully healthy and ready to go for spring training. He's more polished than many young international signees, but after playing just seven games in the DSL, an assignment to the Florida Complex League would be a possible but aggressive assignment.

Year	Age	Club (League)	Level	AVG	G	AB	R	H	2B	3B	HR	RBI	BB	SO	SB	OBP	SLG
2023	17	DSL Rays	Rk	.261	7	23	3	6	3	0	0	5	4	6	0	.379	.391
Minor League Totals				.261	7	23	3	6	3	0	0	5	4	6	0	.379	.391

22 TRE' MORGAN, 1B

HIT: 55. **POW:** 40. **RUN:** 55. **FLD:** 70. **ARM:** 40. **BA Grade:** 45. **Risk:** High.

Born: July 16, 2002. **B-T:** L-L. **Ht.:** 6-1. **Wt.:** 215. **Drafted:** Louisiana State, 2023 (3rd round). **Signed by:** Rickey Drexler.

TRACK RECORD: Morgan will be a hero in Baton Rouge for the rest of his life. His play against Wake Forest was the signature highlight of Louisiana State's 2023 national championship run. In an eighth-inning scoreless tie with a runner on third base, Morgan charged a bunt, fielded it cleanly and short-arm flipped it home to keep the game scoreless, setting up Tommy White's extra-inning heroics. Morgan was named to the College World Series all-tournament team. The Rays picked him in the third round a couple of weeks later. His 2023 pro debut ended because of a minor arm injury, but he should be fine for 2024.

SCOUTING REPORT: It's odd to start a scouting report on a first baseman by talking about his defense, but Morgan isn't a typical first baseman. He plays the position like a shortstop, with excellent range, quick reactions and soft hands. There have been sporadic attempts to try to see what he can do in the outfield, but he's a below-average defender out there despite his plus-plus defense at first. Offensively, Morgan is a line-drive hitter who aims to hit for average and hit doubles. James Loney's offensive approach and impact is an optimistic ceiling, but Morgan has shown hints of more power in batting practice.

THE FUTURE: The Rays emphasize defense more than most organizations, which is good news for Morgan, who has a light bat for a first baseman, but the Rays' love for gloves could help a plus-plus defender find a way to a useful MLB role.

Year	Age	Club (League)	Level	AVG	G	AB	R	H	2B	3B	HR	RBI	BB	SO	SB	OBP	SLG
2023	20	FCL Rays	Rk	.417	3	12	1	5	1	0	1	4	0	1	0	.417	.750
2023	20	Charleston (CAR)	A	.389	11	36	7	14	1	1	0	2	8	2	4	.500	.472
Minor League Totals				.396	14	48	8	19	2	1	1	6	8	3	4	.482	.542

23 WILLY VASQUEZ, 3B

HIT: 40. **POW:** 55. **FLD:** 50. **RUN:** 50. **ARM:** 60. **BA Grade:** 50. **Risk:** Extreme.

Born: September 6, 2001. **B-T:** R-R. **HT:** 6-0. **WT:** 191. **Signed:** Dominican Republic, 2019.
Signed by: Remmy Hernandez/Daniel Santana.

TRACK RECORD: In 2022, the Rays had a pair of high-ceiling shortstop/third base prospects at their Port Charlotte, Fla., complex. It wasn't hard to find evaluators who thought Vasquez was the better prospect than teammate Junior Caminero. Caminero found another gear in 2023, rocketing from High-A Bowling Green to the major leagues, while Vasquez struggled at High-A Bowling Green. But while he no longer compares to Caminero, Vasquez is still young enough to forge his own path to Tampa Bay.

SCOUTING REPORT: Vasquez still has the tools and potential to be an everyday regular, but he'll need to take a significant step forward. He has excellent bat speed, plus raw power and the potential to be an above-average third baseman. Otherwise, he remains a step behind. Vasquez's swing can get too long at times, and he has a hitch, which disrupts his timing. He has exceptional raw power but struggles to hit the ball in the air enough for it to play in games. Vasquez has moved to third base, but could still end up at second, where his long limbs and plus arm might be a better fit.

THE FUTURE: Vasquez spent his winter in the Dominican League to get more seasoning. He faces a crucial year as he heads to Double-A Montgomery. A bounce-back season would make a case for a spot on the 40-man roster, but he needs to make more consistent quality contact and lift the ball more frequently.

Year	Age	Club (League)	Level	AVG	G	AB	R	H	2B	3B	HR	RBI	BB	SO	SB	OBP	SLG
2023	21	Bowling Green (SAL)	A+	.233	114	420	53	98	11	4	16	62	46	109	17	.310	.393
Minor League Totals				.256	278	1059	163	271	40	17	28	171	103	266	58	.324	.405

24 MASON AUER, OF

HIT: 30. **POW:** 50. **FLD:** 65. **RUN:** 70 **ARM:** 70. **BA Grade:** 50. **Risk:** Extreme.

Born: March 1, 2001. **B-T:** R-R. **Ht.:** 6-0. **Wt.:** 210. **Drafted:** San Jacinto (TX) JC, 2021 (5th round).
Signed by: Pat Murphy.

TRACK RECORD: A two-way player at San Jacinto (Texas) JC, Auer was the Ray's breakout prospect in 2022. His 2023 season was the opposite. Auer seemed lost at the plate from the first day of the season until almost the last. He hit .074 in May for Double-A Montgomery with a 43% strikeout rate, and only by hitting .295 in September did he drag his batting average back above .200.

SCOUTING REPORT: Auer may not be as good as he looked in 2022, but he's also not as bad as he appeared to be in 2023. The Rays were encouraged with how he just kept grinding and refused to get too discouraged, which explains why he was never demoted. But he also never found a swing he was comfortable with. Auer started the year in a closed setup and ended up open. He kept trying different places to start his hands. Nothing seemed to work. His lower half seemed disconnected from his hands, he was pull-happy, too rotational in his swing and chased way too many sliders off the plate. Auer will get to reset for 2024, but he'll need to show that he's more than a bottom-of-the-order hitter who can ambush a mistake. Defensively, Auer is a big league-ready, plus-plus center fielder with a plus-plus arm. His defensive acumen is why he remains an intriguing prospect, and his plus-plus speed makes him one of the organization's best basestealers as well.

THE FUTURE: Auer faces a pivotal year. Another year like 2023 in a return to Montgomery would leave him as a fringy prospect despite three plus or plus-plus tools on his scouting report. But if he can just make modest improvements offensively, his speed and glove will give him a shot at a big league role.

Year	Age	Club (League)	Level	AVG	G	AB	R	H	2B	3B	HR	RBI	BB	SO	SB	OBP	SLG
2023	22	Montgomery (SL)	AA	.205	124	454	59	93	18	7	11	51	49	184	47	.292	.348
Minor League Totals				.248	250	946	150	235	41	19	26	116	110	301	105	.335	.414

25 KAMERON MISNER, OF

HIT: 30. **POW:** 50. **FLD:** 60. **RUN:** 60. **ARM:** 60 **BA Grade:** 45. **Risk:** High.

Born: January 8, 1998. **B-T:** L-L. **HT:** 6-4. **WT:** 219. **Drafted:** Missouri, 2019 (1st round supplemental).
Signed by: Joe Dunigan (Marlins).

TRACK RECORD: When Misner was at Missouri, he was a toolsy outfield prospect who showed the potential to be a power-speed center fielder, but there were concerns about whether he would hit enough to let his tools play. Five seasons later—and following a November 2021 trade to Tampa Bay—he remains toolsy, but his 186 strikeouts in 2023 were third-most in the minors.

SCOUTING REPORT: Misner is a plus defender at all three outfield spots with a plus arm. He's also a plus runner who should be good for 20 steals a year. And he set a career high with 21 home runs for Triple-A Durham in 2023, showing power and the ability to draw walks, though sometimes his passivity leads to three and four-pitch strikeouts. The Rays have tried to help Misner string together better at-bats against lefties, but he remains largely helpless against them. He hit .140 against same-siders in 2023 while striking out 46% of the time. He's actually competent against righthanders, hitting .252/.387/.520 with 42 extra-base hits. He's a bottom-of-the-scale hitter if asked to play every day but could produce better numbers in a more limited role.

THE FUTURE: Misner's chances of hitting lefties well enough to be a regular are fading, and the fact that no team picked him in the 2023 Rule 5 draft is a clear indication that no other team is willing to make him a big leaguer just yet. But his defense, speed and power could make him a platoon outfielder, as long as he's yanked anytime a lefty steps onto the mound.

Year	Age	Club (League)	Level	AVG	G	AB	R	H	2B	3B	HR	RBI	BB	SO	SB	OBP	SLG
2023	25	Durham (IL)	AAA	.226	130	421	85	95	25	5	21	58	91	186	21	.363	.458
Minor League Totals				.246	391	1394	262	343	88	9	51	203	264	519	90	.370	.432

26 JACOB LOPEZ, LHP

FB: 40. **SL:** 50. **CHG:** 50. **CTL:** 50. **BA Grade:** 40. **Risk:** Medium.

Born: March 11, 1998. **B-T:** L-L. **Ht.:** 6-4. **Wt.:** 220. **Drafted:** JC of the Canyons (CA), 2018 (26th round).
Signed by: Charles Fick (Giants).

TRACK RECORD: The Rays constantly churn their big league and minor league rosters, looking to figure out how to add talent in blockbuster trades, but just as much on less-noticed moves. Lopez was acquired by the Rays from the Giants for Joe McCarthy in 2019. He missed all of 2022 because of Tommy John surgery, but he sped from Double-A to the majors in 2023.

SCOUTING REPORT: An ideal outcome for Lopez is for him to become the Rays' next Ryan Yarbrough. He's a bulk-innings pitcher who may do better when a team can pick the spot for which 12-15 outs he's set to get by following an opener. Lopez is not a fun at-bat for hitters because he has a deceptive delivery, excellent extension and he makes it hard for lefties to pick him up thanks to a low three-quarters arm slot. Nothing Lopez throws is sexy. He's a sinker/slider lefty with below-average 89-91 mph velocity who lives at the very edges of the strike zone. He wants to get in just off the plate with his below-average fastball to lefties, and then get them to chase the slider out of the zone. Similarly, he nibbles on the outer edge against righthanded hitters with his fastball and slider, but will sneak a changeup down in the zone as well. If Lopez is in the top half of the strike zone, he's missed his spot.

THE FUTURE: Lopez's success relies on guile and command and he has a low margin of error. But he's making it work, and should ride the Durham-Tampa Bay shuttle in 2024 as a multi-inning reliever/spot starter.

Year	Age	Club (League)	Level	W	L	ERA	G	GS	IP	H	HR	BB	SO	BB%	SO%	WHIP	AVG
2023	25	Montgomery (SL)	AA	0	0	2.57	8	6	28	14	2	9	45	8.3	41.7	0.82	.144
2023	25	Durham (IL)	AAA	4	5	2.72	18	18	79	58	7	47	87	14.0	26.0	1.32	.207
2023	25	Tampa Bay (AL)	MLB	1	0	4.38	4	1	12	14	0	2	8	3.7	14.8	1.30	.280
Minor League Totals				12	10	2.53	62	51	249	182	21	91	319	9.0	31.6	1.10	.202
Major League Totals				1	0	4.38	4	1	12	14	0	2	8	3.7	14.8	1.30	.280

27 BEN PEOPLES, RHP
FB: 60. SL: 45. CHG: 50. CTL: 45. BA Grade: 45. Risk: High.

Born: May 1, 2001. **B-T:** L-R. **Ht.:** 6-1. **Wt.:** 175. **Drafted:** HS—Pulaski, TN, 2019 (22nd round). **Signed by:** Steve Ames.

TRACK RECORD: It's fair to wonder whether a player like Peoples would ever be drafted in the current minor league structure. It's not only because he was drafted in a round that no longer exists—the 22nd—but because he was drafted at a time when the Rays had Appalachian and New York-Penn league affiliates. Prior to 2021, the Rays would expect raw prospects like Peoples to spend two or three years climbing the ladder before reaching full-season ball. Instead, he spent two years in Rookie complex ball and spent all of this his fifth pro season at High-A Bowling Green.

SCOUTING REPORT: The Rays loved to move high school pitchers at a slow pace under the old minor league system, and Peoples may be one of the Rays' last pitchers to follow the old development plan. Five years into his pro career, he's only just starting to display the glimmers of what the Rays saw back in 2019. He has a plus 93-95 mph fastball and an average 85-87 mph changeup that could some day get to above-average. He has now improved his long fringy slider into a more powerful 87-89 mph pitch with modest downward bite. He has fringe-average control and should get to average in time.

THE FUTURE: Peoples is a starter for now, but most likely he develops into a reliever who can work up and down in the zone with his fastball and changeup. The Rays didn't need to protect him from the Rule 5 draft because they rightfully believed no one would consider taking a pitcher so far away. In 2024, he and the Rays hope that will be a more difficult decision.

Year	Age	Club (League)	Level	W	L	ERA	G	GS	IP	H	HR	BB	SO	BB%	SO%	WHIP	AVG
2023	22	Bowling Green (SAL)	A+	4	6	4.06	22	22	84	76	7	45	96	12.3	26.3	1.43	.240
Minor League Totals				11	15	3.59	60	51	208	171	17	111	262	12.5	29.5	1.36	.223

28 DRU BAKER, OF
HIT: 45. POW: 40. FLD: 55. RUN: 60. ARM: 50. BA Grade: 45. Risk: High.

Born: March 22, 2000. **B-T:** R-R. **Ht.:** 5-11. **Wt.:** 195. **Drafted:** Texas Tech, 2021 (4th round). **Signed by:** Pat Murphy.

TRACK RECORD: Baker was Texas Tech's shortstop for part of his freshman year, but while the Red Raiders loved his bat, they quickly realized he was better in the outfield. Baker spent most of two seasons in Class A before reaching Double-A Montgomery at the end of the 2023 season.

SCOUTING REPORT: If Colton Ledbetter can be described as a well-rounded outfielder with potentially five average tools, Baker's profile is similar, but with a little less pop and a lot more strikeouts. Baker's 14 home runs in 2023 were a surprise—he had hit 15 in the previous four years combined. His power is almost entirely pull-side shots that just clear the left field fence, and he's more of a line-drive and ground-ball hitter. Baker is a capable, fringe-average hitter, but there are worries that more advanced pitchers will make his solid 22% strikeout rate climb. He's average in center field and above-average in the corners with an average arm. As a basestealer, Baker is exceptional. He has swiped 76 of 85 in his pro career.

THE FUTURE: If Baker can keep this up, he could end up as a well-rounded fourth outfielder. He can play all three outfield spots, he steals bases in bunches and hits well enough to pinch-hit. It would just be an easier path for him if he hit lefthanded rather than righthanded.

Year	Age	Club (League)	Level	AVG	G	AB	R	H	2B	3B	HR	RBI	BB	SO	SB	OBP	SLG
2023	23	Bowling Green (SAL)	A+	.307	90	326	58	100	11	5	13	39	40	86	38	.396	.491
2023	23	Montgomery (SL)	AA	.287	30	115	24	33	6	3	1	15	7	28	11	.346	.417
Minor League Totals				.299	179	668	128	200	28	12	20	96	79	171	76	.386	.467

29 COOPER KINNEY, 2B

HIT: 55. **POW:** 45. **FLD:** 40. **RUN:** 40. **ARM:** 50. **BA Grade:** 50. **Risk:** Extreme.

Born: January 27, 2003. **B-T:** L-R. **Ht.:** 6-3. **Wt.:** 200. **Drafted:** HS—Chattanooga, TN, 2021 (1st round supplemental).
Signed by: Steve Ames.

TRACK RECORD: Kinney is trying to make up for a lot of lost time. A shoulder injury sidelined him for all of 2022 and meant that when he returned in 2023, he spent the whole year at Low-A Charleston, a level below many of his 2021 draft contemporaries. While his season wasn't a particularly loud one, Kinney impressed with his consistent approach at the plate.
SCOUTING REPORT: Kinney's bat will likely always be a couple of steps ahead of his glove. He's a second baseman, but the most realistic hope is that he'll be a below-average defender who is playable in certain situations. Third base may be a better option, but even there his lack of first-step quickness and slow feet will make it a struggle, and he's going to have to really hit for first base to be an option. Offensively, he uses the whole field and can drive the ball to the gaps. He's a little too aggressive at times and will strike out, but he has solid bat-to-ball skills and should be an above-average hitter.
THE FUTURE: Kinney's swing leaves a lot of evaluators convinced he's going to hit. There's a lot of other aspects of his game that will need a lot of diligent work, but the most important tool for any position player is the ability to hit, which is Kinney's best tool.

Year	Age	Club (League)	Level	AVG	G	AB	R	H	2B	3B	HR	RBI	BB	SO	SB	OBP	SLG
2023	20	Charleston (CAR)	A	.274	121	456	61	125	24	0	10	61	42	107	3	.341	.393
Minor League Totals				.275	132	491	70	135	25	1	10	66	52	116	5	.351	.391

30 ERICK LARA, SS/3B

HIT: 45. **POW:** 55. **FLD:** 50. **RUN:** 50. **ARM:** 55. **BA Grade:** 50. **Risk:** Extreme.

Born: June 10, 2006. **B-T:** L-R. **Ht.:** 6-2. **Wt.:** 165. **Signed:** Dominican Republic, 2023.
Signed by: Sahir Fersobe (Marlins).

TRACK RECORD: At $85,000, Lara was a relatively low-cost signing by the Marlins at the start of the 2023 international signing period. But he quickly established himself as a promising hitter with a solid Dominican Summer League debut. Right after the Marlins announced long-time Rays executive Peter Bendix as the team's new general manager, Bendix acquired Vidal Brujan and Calvin Faucher from his old team for Lara and righthander Andrew Lindsey.
SCOUTING REPORT: Lara is relatively strong for his size and a lefthanded hitter who already shows he knows how to drive the ball, even if he doesn't yet have much strength to actually drive it. He has some adaptability in his swing, but he's so young and relatively inexperienced that it's hard to project whether he develops more as a hitter or a slugger. Defensively, Lara seems athletic enough to stay on the left side of the infield, but his 6-foot-2, 165-pound has plenty of room to fill out and force him to third base or a corner outfield spot.
THE FUTURE: Lara is an interesting flier of a prospect. The Rays like his bat and his athleticism, but there's a massive amount of risk and variability remaining in his projection, because he's a 17-year-old who is just getting settled in as a pro.

Year	Age	Club (League)	Level	AVG	G	AB	R	H	2B	3B	HR	RBI	BB	SO	SB	OBP	SLG
2023	17	DSL Marlins	Rk	.305	34	128	21	39	8	2	2	32	23	37	5	.416	.445
Minor League Totals				.305	34	128	21	39	8	2	2	32	23	37	5	.416	.445

Texas Rangers

BY JOSH NORRIS

In 2023, the Rangers won their first World Series.

The championship was the culmination of two years of smart acquisitions through free agency, trades and the draft. Moreover, the team—led by ownership's willingness to spend, general manager Chris Young and a cadre of veteran scouts in both the amateur and professional ranks—was aggressive enough to find replacements when players succumbed to injuries.

Even then, the Rangers barely made the playoffs. Texas squeaked into the tournament in the final days of the regular season, then proceeded to sweep through the Rays and Orioles in the first two rounds.

Their Texas showdown with the Astros in the Championship Series lasted seven games, and they capped their championship run with a five-game World Series victory against the Diamondbacks.

The Rangers' commitment to winning up and down the organization also earned them Baseball America's Organization of the Year award.

Now comes the tricky part: Sustaining it.

In that regard, the Rangers are also well positioned, thanks to a roster replete with established all-stars and players who one day could be described the same way.

No player better fits that bill than Evan Carter, a highway robbery of a draft pick as part of a stunningly excellent 2020 draft class that should produce four major leaguers out of its five selections. After two seasons displaying a precocious skill set in the minors, Carter was called up in September and made a big enough impression to land a spot on the postseason roster.

He finished October with a .917 OPS, 10 extra-base hits and, most importantly, a World Series ring.

Two of the players from that draft class—infielder Thomas Saggese and righty Tekoah Roby—were used to pry lefthander Jordan Montgomery from the Cardinals. Montgomery was a standout in the postseason, especially in the ALCS, where he started two of the team's wins against Houston. The Rangers also spun shortstop Luisangel Acuña, one of the team's top prospects, to the Mets to add righthander Max Scherzer.

After the trades, the Rangers system has thinned, but the top still houses one of the most enviable trios in the minors. Carter ranks as the system's best prospect, but behind him are two outstanding talents added in 2023.

The first was Sebastian Walcott, a firecracker of a Bahamian shortstop signed in January. The 17-year-old moved stateside quickly and showed

Josh Jung hit .266/.315/.467 with 23 homers and placed fourth for AL Rookie of the Year.

PROJECTED 2027 LINEUP

Catcher	Jonah Heim	32
First Base	Nathaniel Lowe	31
Second Base	Marcus Semien	36
Third Base	Josh Jung	29
Shortstop	Corey Seager	33
Left Field	Wyatt Langford	25
Center Field	Evan Carter	24
Right Field	Sebastian Walcott	21
Designated Hitter	Justin Foscue	28
No. 1 Starter	Jacob deGrom	39
No. 2 Starter	Owen White	27
No. 3 Starter	Brock Porter	24
No. 4 Starter	Dane Dunning	32
No. 5 Starter	Cody Bradford	29
Closer	Kumar Rocker	27

an explosive set of tools, including power that helped him swat seven home runs in the ACL.

The second premium prospect the Rangers added was Wyatt Langford, a dynamic outfielder from Florida who was drafted with the No. 4 overall pick. Like Carter, Langford is one of the best prospects in the sport. He reinforced that reputation by cruising to Triple-A in his first pro season.

The Rangers have an all-star middle infield, young talents like Carter, Langford and Walcott waiting in the wings, and a group of executives and evaluators who are willing to do whatever it takes to improve the roster's weak spots.

In other words, the future deep in the heart of Texas looks big and bright. ∎

TEXAS RANGERS

<table>
<tr><td colspan="2">TOP 2024 CONTRIBUTORS</td><td>RANK</td></tr>
<tr><td colspan="2">1. Evan Carter, OF</td><td>1</td></tr>
<tr><td colspan="2">2. Wyatt Langford, OF</td><td>2</td></tr>
<tr><td colspan="2">3. Owen White, RHP</td><td>5</td></tr>
</table>

BREAKOUT PROSPECTS

	RANK
1. Aidan Curry, RHP	13
2. Emiliano Teodo, RHP	14
3. Izack Tiger, RHP	20

SOURCE OF TOP 30 TALENT

Homegrown	27	Acquired	3
College	8	Trade	2
Junior college	1	Rule 5 draft	0
High school	5	Independent league	1
Nondrafted free agent	2	Free agent/waivers	0
International	7		

LF
Wyatt Langford (2)
Aaron Zavala (11)
Pablo Guerrero
Yeremi Cabrera

CF
Evan Carter (1)
Anthony Gutierrez (10)
Yeison Morrobel (21)
Daniel Mateo
Jose De Jesus
Jojo Blackmon

RF
Braylin Morel (18)
Marcos Torres
Tommy Specht
Quincy Scott
Geisel Cepeda
Maxton Martin

3B
Gleider Figuereo (19)

SS
Sebastian Walcott (3)
Cam Cauley (8)
Jonathan Ornelas (30)

2B
Echedry Vargas (16)
Danyer Cueva
Jayce Easley

1B
Justin Foscue (4)
Dustin Harris (6)
Abimelec Ortiz (15)
Blaine Crim
Josh Hatcher

C
Liam Hicks (23)
Jesus Lopez
Cody Freeman
Matt Whatley
Cooper Johnson
Daniel Bruzal

LHP

LHSP	LHRP
Mitch Bratt (28)	Antoine Kelly
Thomas Ireland	Grant Wolfram
Dylan MacLean	
Brayan Mendoza	
Larson Kindreich	

RHP

RHSP	RHRP
Owen White (5)	Emiliano Teodo (14)
Brock Porter (7)	Alejandro Rosario (22)
Kumar Rocker (9)	Skylar Hales (26)
Jack Leiter (12)	Zak Kent (27)
Aidan Curry (13)	Grant Anderson
Jose Corniell (17)	Alex Speas
Izack Tiger (20)	Anthony Hoopii-Tuionetoa
Josh Stephan (24)	Marc Church
Caden Scarborough (26)	Dane Acker
Joseph Montalvo (29)	Carson Coleman
Winston Santos	
Cole Winn	

1 EVAN CARTER, OF

Born: August 29, 2002. **B-T:** L-R. **HT:** 6-2. **WT:** 190.
Drafted: HS—Elizabethton, TN, 2020 (2nd round).
Signed by: Derrick Tucker/Ryan Coe.

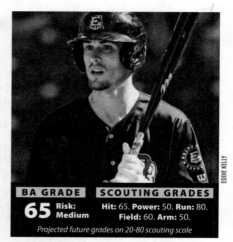

EDDIE KELLY

BA GRADE	SCOUTING GRADES
65 Risk: Medium	**Hit:** 65. **Power:** 50. **Run:** 80. **Field:** 60. **Arm:** 50.

Projected future grades on 20-80 scouting scale

TRACK RECORD: If the Rangers hadn't made the playoffs, Carter would have been assigned to the Arizona Fall League, where he would have been part of the champion Surprise Saguaros. Instead, he made Texas' postseason roster and was a key piece of their run to the franchise's first World Series title. Carter's rise to top prospect and post-season hero was unforeseeable in 2020, when the Rangers shocked the industry by popping him with their second-round pick. Nearly imme-diately after entering pro ball, Carter looked like that draft's biggest steal. He was assigned to Low-A Down East as an 18-year-old in 2021 and immediately showed a strong combination of plate discipline and bat-to-ball skills before a back injury cut short his season. The lefthanded hitter broke out in 2022, when he spent nearly all of the regular season in High-A before a cameo with Double-A Frisco that culminated in a Texas League championship. Before making his big league debut on Sept. 8, 2023, Carter was excel-lent in a year split between Frisco and Triple-A Round Rock, hitting .288/.413/.450 with 13 home runs and 26 stolen bases in 108 games.

SCOUTING REPORT: Carter is among the most well-rounded prospects in baseball, with an array of average to plus tools across the board. The Tennessee native is an advanced hitter with an excellent knowledge of the strike zone that led to miss and chase rates of 26.1% and 18.7%, as well as an in-zone whiff rate of just 17.3%. Now, the question is whether he'll add the thump to complete the package. His average exit velocity in the minors was a pedestrian 85.5 mph, but that figure jumped significantly in his small sample size in the big leagues. Carter's output also ticked up. After hitting 13 home runs in the minors, he slammed five in 23 big league games and one more in the postseason. To sustain the jump, part of Carter's offseason plan involves dedicating himself to a serious strength program for the first time. In the past, both as a pro and in high school, weightlifting was more of a comple-mentary piece of his workout regimen. He also could stand to add a bit more loft to his swing. Carter's other target area includes improving against lefthanders, against whom he showed on-base skills but racked up only one extra-base hit in 2023. Though the presence of Leody Taveras pushed Carter to left field in the big leagues, he has the instincts and long, gliding strides to allow him to play center field at a potentially Gold Glove level. He will be excellent in left—where his average arm fits best—as long as he stays there, but there will be more pressure to develop the power that comes with a corner-outfield job.

THE FUTURE: Carter will play nearly all of the 2024 season as a 21-year-old, and his body still has opportunity to fill out. If he adds strength and closes his hole against southpaws, he could be yet another piece of a tantalizing Rangers line-up blessed with a mix of pedigree and promise. ∎

BEST TOOLS

BATTING

Best Hitter for Average	Justin Foscue
Best Power Hitter	Abimelec Ortiz
Best Strike-Zone Discipline	Evan Carter
Fastest Baserunner	Evan Carter
Best Athlete	Sebastian Walcott

PITCHING

Best Fastball	Jack Leiter
Best Curveball	Owen White
Best Slider	Jose Corniell
Best Changeup	Brock Porter
Best Control	Jose Corniell

FIELDING

Best Defensive Catcher	Matt Whatley
Best Defensive Infielder	Cam Cauley
Best Infield Arm	Cam Cauley
Best Defensive Outfielder	Evan Carter
Best Outfield Arm	Daniel Mateo

Year	Age	Club (League)	Level	AVG	G	AB	R	H	2B	3B	HR	RBI	BB	SO	SB	OBP	SLG
2023	20	ACL Rangers	Rk	.222	3	9	3	2	1	0	1	2	3	2	1	.417	.667
2023	20	Frisco (TL)	AA	.284	97	377	68	107	15	6	12	62	74	103	22	.411	.451
2023	20	Round Rock (PCL)	AAA	.353	8	34	8	12	1	0	0	3	4	6	3	.436	.382
2023	20	Texas (AL)	MLB	.306	23	62	15	19	4	1	5	12	12	24	3	.413	.645
Minor League Totals				.285	246	923	187	263	46	17	27	152	179	220	66	.410	.459
Major League Totals				.306	23	62	15	19	4	1	5	12	12	24	3	.413	.645

2 WYATT LANGFORD, OF

HIT: 60. **POW:** 70. **RUN:** 60. **FLD:** 45. **ARM:** 45. **BA Grade:** 70. **Risk:** High.

Born: November 15, 2001. **B-T:** R-R. **HT:** 6-1. **WT:** 225.
Drafted: Florida, 2023 (1st round). **Signed by:** John Wiedenbauer.
TRACK RECORD: Langford went undrafted out of Trenton (Fla.) High, then spent his sophomore and junior seasons at Florida building himself into one of the best players in the country. He spent the summer after his sophomore season with USA Baseball's College National Team. In 2023 he helped propel the Gators to College World Series finals. The Rangers drafted Langford fourth overall and signed him to an over-slot deal of $8 million, then watched as he had the loudest pro debut of any 2023 draftee, hitting .360/.480/.677 in 44 games and reaching Triple-A.
SCOUTING REPORT: Pound for pound, Langford is one of the best prospects in the sport. He was unchallenged at any of his minor league stops and was the only player on the Rangers' postseason taxi squad who was not part of the 40-man roster. The righthanded hitter has a simple, powerful swing that keeps the barrel in the zone long enough to hit for a high average and with enough strength and loft to eventually achieve double-plus power. Langford also makes stellar swing decisions. He doesn't chase often, and he rarely misses pitches in the zone. He should be an offensive force in Texas in short order. Defensively, Langford has a bit more work to do. He needs to improve his reads, routes and jumps in order to grade near average on an outfield corner. His fringe-average arm makes him fit best in left field, where his bat would certainly profile. He is a plus runner.
THE FUTURE: Langford finished the season on the precipice of the big leagues. In 2024, he should make the final leap. He has the skills and the pedigree to be a cornerstone in the Rangers' lineup.

Year	Age	Club (League)	Level	AVG	G	AB	R	H	2B	3B	HR	RBI	BB	SO	SB	OBP	SLG
2023	21	ACL Rangers	Rk	.385	3	13	3	5	3	0	1	4	1	3	1	.429	.846
2023	21	Hickory (SAL)	A+	.333	24	87	22	29	8	2	5	15	18	18	7	.453	.644
2023	21	Frisco (TL)	AA	.405	12	42	7	17	3	0	4	10	11	7	1	.519	.762
2023	21	Round Rock (PCL)	AAA	.368	5	19	4	7	3	0	0	1	6	6	3	.538	.526
Minor League Totals				.360	44	161	36	58	17	2	10	30	36	34	12	.480	.677

3 SEBASTIAN WALCOTT, SS

HIT: 50. **POW:** 60. **RUN:** 55. **FLD:** 45. **ARM:** 60. **BA Grade:** 60. **Risk:** Extreme.

Born: March 14, 2006. **B-T:** R-R. **HT:** 6-4. **WT:** 190.
Signed: Bahamas, 2023. **Signed by:** Jonny Clum.
TRACK RECORD: Walcott signed two months before he turned 17, earned a bonus north of $3 million and immediately showed a wealth of high-end tools. Walcott speaks more English than Spanish, which was part of the reason the Rangers promoted him out of the Dominican Summer League after just six games. It's also why he skipped Low-A after playing 35 games in the Arizona Complex League. At High-A Hickory, Walcott could be around English speakers like Cam Cauley instead of the group of mostly Spanish-speaking prospects clustered at Low-A Down East.
SCOUTING REPORT: After moving stateside to the ACL, Walcott immediately put on a show. The 17-year-old swatted a home run in his first game and finished with seven, tied for fifth in the Rookie-level league. Walcott is twitchy with huge bat speed that helps him generate nearly elite raw power that translates into games. To get to that ceiling, he'll need to greatly reduce his whiffs. He struggled overall to handle offspeed pitches, right-on-right sliders in particular. The end result was a strikeout rate of 29.7% across all three of his stops and a rate of 32.4% in the ACL. Walcott also showed a tendency to let the his frustration compound and occasionally threw helmets and bats after strikeouts, leading to removal from games. He has a chance to remain at shortstop, but if he gets too big he might have to move to third base or the outfield. Walcott has the plus arm to handle third base, and his bat would certainly profile at the position. His athleticism and above-average speed would play well in an outfield corner.
THE FUTURE: Whether Walcott starts at Low-A or High-A, he has a chance to blossom into a perennial all-star. Better plate discipline is the first step toward reaching that ceiling.

Year	Age	Club (League)	Level	AVG	G	AB	R	H	2B	3B	HR	RBI	BB	SO	SB	OBP	SLG
2023	17	DSL Rangers Blue	Rk	.161	9	31	4	5	3	1	0	3	10	8	3	.381	.323
2023	17	ACL Rangers	Rk	.273	35	143	26	39	9	3	7	19	10	51	9	.325	.524
2023	17	Hickory (SAL)	A+	.154	4	13	2	2	1	0	0	2	3	5	0	.313	.231
Minor League Totals				.246	48	187	32	46	13	4	7	24	23	64	12	.335	.471

4 JUSTIN FOSCUE, 2B/1B

HIT: 60. **POW:** 50. **RUN:** 30. **FLD:** 40. **ARM:** 40. **BA Grade:** 50. **Risk:** Medium.

Born: March 2, 1999. **B-T:** R-R. **HT:** 5-11. **WT:** 205.
Drafted: Mississippi State, 2020 (1st round). **Signed by:** Brian Morrison.

TRACK RECORD: Foscue was the Rangers' first-round pick in the five-round 2020 draft, part of a treasure trove of talent that also included postseason star Evan Carter as well as righthander Tekoah Roby and shortstop Thomas Saggese, who were used in tandem to acquire lefthander Jordan Montgomery from the Cardinals for the playoffs. All season long at Triple-A, Foscue showed a combination of selectivity and bat-to-ball skills that led to more walks (85) than strikeouts (70). After beginning his career as a second baseman, Foscue has begun to transition to the corners. In 2023, he made 35 starts at third base and nine more at first base.

SCOUTING REPORT: Wherever he lands on the diamond, Foscue's value will come from what he does at the plate. When he swings, he usually makes contact. His rate of miss (17.8%) and in-zone miss (8.9%) were both excellent, but his impact was just average. To improve, Foscue will need to add some more loft to his bat path, which was an area of focus at Texas' postseason instructional camp. If he can make that change successfully, some of the 62 doubles he's amassed over the past two seasons might leave the park. Defensively, Foscue does not have the range, mobility or arm strength to stick up the middle or at third base. He's also blocked by Josh Jung, Corey Seager and Marcus Semien. That leaves first base, where he might serve as an effective platoon partner for Nathaniel Lowe. Foscue is a well below-average runner as well.

THE FUTURE: After two seasons at the upper levels, Foscue will get a chance in spring training to win a spot on Texas' crowded roster. If he hits enough in spring training, he could earn a job spelling Lowe against lefthanders while also serving as the DH on other days.

Year	Age	Club (League)	Level	AVG	G	AB	R	H	2B	3B	HR	RBI	BB	SO	SB	OBP	SLG
2023	24	Round Rock (PCL)	AAA	.266	122	462	94	123	31	4	18	84	85	70	14	.394	.468
Minor League Totals				.276	285	1091	206	301	81	6	50	216	155	208	19	.380	.499

5 OWEN WHITE, RHP

FB: 50. **CB:** 55. **SL:** 55. **CHG:** 50. **CUT:** 45. **CTL:** 50. **BA Grade:** 45. **Risk:** Low.

Born: August 9, 1999. **B-T:** R-R. **HT:** 6-3. **WT:** 199.
Drafted: HS—China Grove, NC, 2018 (2nd round). **Signed by:** Jay Heafner.

TRACK RECORD: Like many Rangers pitching prospects of a certain vintage, White has had a checkered injury history. He did not pitch post-draft in 2018, then missed the 2019 season with Tommy John surgery before the pandemic wiped out the 2020 season. A broken hand limited White to 35.1 innings in 2021, and he lost two months to arm fatigue in 2022. In 2023, he pitched a career-high 112.2 innings, including four over two big league starts.

SCOUTING REPORT: Despite reaching the big leagues, White's stuff took a severe dip in quality. That was particularly true of his four-seam fastball, which dropped nearly 2 mph in velocity as well as a corresponding loss of vertical break. Those two factors led to his whiff rate on four-seamers nearly being cut in half, from 33% in 2022 to 17% in 2023. White's downgraded fastball can be explained in part by even more health issues. He dealt with nagging injuries to his hip and shoulder throughout the season and struggled to get down the mound with any sort of authority. The Rangers would also like to see White improve his nutrition. The biggest change to White's arsenal involved his slider, which was switched to a sweeper shape during the season in an effort to induce more swings and misses against righthanders. His above-average curveball is the best in a system that trends heavily toward sliders, and he rounds out his mix with an average changeup and a fringy cutter. White's control was solid at Double-A but suffered at Triple-A, where the automated ball-strike system punishes pitchers who attack north to south.

THE FUTURE: White will look for a reset in 2024, when he'll have a chance to make the Opening Day roster but will likely head back to Triple-A. The Rangers system overall is thin on pitching, so he should have plenty of chances to return to Texas.

Year	Age	Club (League)	Level	W	L	ERA	G	GS	IP	H	HR	BB	SO	BB%	SO%	WHIP	AVG
2023	23	Frisco (TL)	AA	2	3	3.51	12	12	56	40	5	23	48	10.1	21.1	1.12	.205
2023	23	Round Rock (PCL)	AAA	2	2	4.99	13	12	52	52	10	32	32	13.5	13.5	1.61	.264
2023	23	Texas (AL)	MLB	0	1	11.25	2	0	4	5	2	2	4	10.5	21.1	1.75	.313
Minor League Totals				17	8	3.81	49	46	224	188	25	90	240	9.6	25.7	1.24	.227
Major League Totals				0	1	11.25	2	0	4	5	2	2	4	10.5	21.1	1.75	.313

6 DUSTIN HARRIS, 1B/OF

HIT: 50. **POW:** 50. **RUN:** 50. **FLD:** 45. **ARM:** 45. **BA Grade:** 50. **Risk:** High.

Born: July 8, 1999. **B-T:** L-R. **HT:** 6-3. **WT:** 185.

Drafted: St. Petersburg (FL) JC, 2019 (11th round). **Signed by:** Trevor Schaeffer (Athletics).

TRACK RECORD: Harris was drafted by the Athletics out of junior college in 2019, then dealt to the Rangers in 2020 as part of a two-player package that sent Mike Minor to Oakland. In 2021, Harris made that deal look like a heist by hitting .327/.401/.542 with 20 home runs and winning the organization's minor league player of the year award. He earned a berth in the 2022 Futures Game and collected two hits and a stolen base. A sprained left wrist in August ended his season. Harris split 2023 between Double-A Frisco and Triple-A Round Rock, finishing as one of eight minor leaguers with 20 or more doubles, 80 or more walks and 40 or more stolen bases.

SCOUTING REPORT: Harris' season flipped when he was promoted to Triple-A. Part of that was because the automated ball-strike system plays into hitters' hands at the top of the zone, which is an area of weakness for Harris. Opposing hitters noticed that Harris was having trouble keeping his upper and lower halves connected during his swing. To remedy this, he began starting his stride earlier, which helped. He also cleaned up some of the excess movement in his swing to help get a cleaner, more efficient path to the ball. Harris' exit velocities were subpar in 2023, and the Rangers would like him to work on putting on more weight to get more oomph behind the ball. Harris has gotten experience in left field but he's likely going to wind up at first base, where he'll compete with Justin Foscue for a potential roster spot. Despite 41 stolen bases, Harris is more of a skilled baserunner than he is a true burner. His speed is roughly average.

THE FUTURE: Harris will return to Triple-A in 2024 to try to continue his strong finish from 2023. If he can show more power, he'll have a shot to make his big league debut.

Year	Age	Club (League)	Level	AVG	G	AB	R	H	2B	3B	HR	RBI	BB	SO	SB	OBP	SLG
2023	23	Frisco (TL)	AA	.245	60	229	42	56	14	4	5	29	44	65	24	.374	.406
2023	23	Round Rock (PCL)	AAA	.273	67	242	47	66	11	3	9	31	40	63	17	.382	.455
Minor League Totals				.288	380	1415	266	407	74	13	52	237	198	314	94	.381	.469

7 BROCK PORTER, RHP

FB: 60. **SL:** 55. **CHG:** 60. **CTL:** 40. **BA Grade:** 55. **Risk:** Extreme.

Born: June 3, 2003. **B-T:** R-R. **HT:** 6-4. **WT:** 208.

Drafted: HS—Orchard Lake, MI, 2022 (4th round). **Signed by:** Chris Collias.

TRACK RECORD: In 2022, the Rangers forfeited their second- and third-round picks as a penalty for signing World Series cornerstones Corey Seager and Marcus Semien. They took Kumar Rocker with their first-round choice, signed him for an under-slot deal and used the savings to sign Porter, one of the highest-upside high school arms in the class. Porter's bonus was $3.7 million, the fourth-round record by a wide margin. The righthander spent all of his first full season in 2023 at Low-A Down East, which advanced to the Carolina League finals.

SCOUTING REPORT: Porter's bread and butter is his changeup, a filthy pitch that is a true plus offering. His changeup sits in the low 80s and features late, hard drop and is thrown with enough velocity separation and conviction to get swings and misses from both lefthanded and righthanded batters. His changeup complements a four-seam fastball that also grades out as a future plus. It sits around 94 mph and earns high marks for its nearly 2,500 rpm spin rate and a nearly 30% whiff rate. The question all year long was whether Porter could find a suitable breaking ball, and late in the year he found one. After scrapping a curveball, he opted for a sweeping slider in the low 80s that featured more than 15 inches of horizontal break. The next step is improving his control, which was poor all season long and resulted in a 14% walk rate and an overall strike rate of just 57%. Scouts suggested that part of the reason for the control issues was because his delivery, while repeatable, was too uptempo and would leave him fatigued after a few innings. He pitched five innings just twice all season.

THE FUTURE: Porter will advance to High-A in 2024, when he'll work on continuing to sharpen his breaking ball and throwing more strikes. If he can check those boxes, he has midrotation upside.

Year	Age	Club (League)	Level	W	L	ERA	G	GS	IP	H	HR	BB	SO	BB%	SO%	WHIP	AVG
2023	20	Down East (CAR)	A	0	3	2.47	21	21	69	39	1	42	95	14.3	32.4	1.17	.160
Minor League Totals				0	3	2.48	21	21	69	39	1	42	95	14.3	32.4	1.17	.160

8 CAMERON CAULEY, SS/2B

HIT: 40. **POW:** 45. **RUN:** 65. **FLD:** 60. **ARM:** 60. **BA Grade:** 50 **Risk:** High.

Born: February 6, 2003. **B-T:** R-R. **HT:** 5-10. **WT:** 170.
Drafted: HS—Mount Belvieu, TX, 2021 (3rd round). **Signed by:** Josh Simpson.

TRACK RECORD: Cauley has baseball bloodlines thanks to a father who played in the minor leagues with the White Sox. He was the Rangers' first prep choice in 2021, after the team had already drafted Jack Leiter (Vanderbilt) and Aaron Zavala (Oregon) with its first two picks. Cauley's $1 million bonus was the second-highest the Rangers handed out that season. He has moved deliberately through the system, including significant time at Low-A in each of the past two seasons. He reached High-A in 2023, then closed with six weeks in the Arizona Fall League.

SCOUTING REPORT: Cauley is one of the twitchier athletes in the system, but he also has plenty of refinement to go before he can make the most of those gifts. The biggest action item on Cauley's list involves cutting down his swing-and-miss and making better swing decisions. He hits the ball plenty hard, with average and 90th percentile exit velocities of 89 and 102 mph—but his whiff rates were concerning. His in-zone miss rate of 25.8% was a particularly red flag. The Rangers hope adding strength will lead to a more consistent bat path, something outside scouts noticed was an issue as well. When Cauley does connect, there's plenty of thump behind the ball. His 34 extra-base hits—including 12 home runs—exceeded his career total by 10. Cauley ranks as the system's best infield defender. He's a graceful shortstop with a strong arm that should get to plus once he gets stronger and can get the most on his throws without having to put everything he's got behind them. He's a blazing runner whose speed borders on double-plus.

THE FUTURE: Cauley will make his upper-level debut in 2024, when his efforts to improve his bat-to-ball skills and swing decisions will meet their toughest test. If he passes, he can get to an everyday shortstop with bottom-of-the-order offensive skills.

Year	Age	Club (League)	Level	AVG	G	AB	R	H	2B	3B	HR	RBI	BB	SO	SB	OBP	SLG
2023	20	Down East (CAR)	A	.244	66	242	43	59	12	3	7	35	30	89	22	.331	.405
2023	20	Hickory (SAL)	A+	.248	34	125	25	31	7	0	5	24	17	44	14	.336	.424
Minor League Totals				.233	200	748	124	174	34	10	14	97	93	255	84	.320	.361

9 KUMAR ROCKER, RHP

FB: 60. **SL:** 60. **CHG:** 45. **CTL:** 50. **BA Grade:** 55. **Risk:** Extreme.

Born: November 22, 1999. **B-T:** R-R. **HT:** 6-5. **WT:** 245.
Drafted: Frontier League, 2022 (1st round). **Signed by:** Tyler Carroll.

TRACK RECORD: Rocker's winding journey to pro ball is well documented. A standout Georgia prep, he raised his profile in three years at Vanderbilt, winning Freshman of the Year in 2019 and tying Commodores co-ace Jack Leiter for the national lead with 179 strikeouts in 2021. Rocker was drafted by the Mets 10th overall in 2021 but went unsigned after medical issues popped up. He pitched in the independent Frontier League in 2022, then was taken by Texas with the No. 3 overall pick and signed to an under-slot deal of $5.2 million. His first pro work came in the Arizona Fall League, where he struck out 18 but walked 12 over 14 innings over six short starts. He looked sharp at High-A Hickory to open 2023 but had Tommy John surgery on May 16.

SCOUTING REPORT: Before the injury, Rocker was outstanding. His fastball sat in the mid 90s and his slider was at times a wipeout pitch that got swings and misses both in and out of the zone. He continued to throw his fringy, high-80s changeup, but it was a clear fourth piece of his arsenal. Rocker's biggest change in pro ball was the addition of a two-seam fastball, added to give him more of a weapon against righthanders. The pitch sat around 95 mph and got swings and misses at a 27% clip, much higher than the 16% induced by his four-seamer. Rocker's control was much better in the South Atlantic League than in the AFL, but scouts who saw him early would like to see better command. His delivery also showed more repeatability than in the AFL, especially when it came to finding a consistent arm slot.

THE FUTURE: There have been no setbacks in Rocker's rehab, and he should be ready to go at some point during the 2024 season. If he can show the same kind of stuff he did at Hickory, he could fit in the middle of the rotation with the fallback of a nasty late-inning reliever.

Year	Age	Club (League)	Level	W	L	ERA	G	GS	IP	H	HR	BB	SO	BB%	SO%	WHIP	AVG
2023	23	Hickory (SAL)	A+	2	2	3.86	6	6	28	21	2	7	42	6.3	37.8	1.00	.202
Minor League Totals				2	2	3.86	6	6	28	21	2	7	42	6.3	37.8	1.00	.202

10 ANTHONY GUTIERREZ, OF

HIT: 45. **POW:** 55. **RUN:** 50. **FLD:** 60. **ARM:** 55. **BA Grade:** 55. **Risk:** Extreme.

Born: November 25, 2004. **B-T:** R-R. **HT:** 6-3. **WT:** 180.
Signed: Venezuela, 2022. **Signed by:** Rafic Saab/Willy Espinal.

TRACK RECORD: Gutierrez was the jewel of Texas' 2022 international signing class, signing for $1.97 million on Jan. 15. He's been pushed aggressively over his two pro seasons, moving stateside in his first year and opening 2023 as the youngest position player in the Low-A Carolina League. Unsurprisingly, Gutierrez struggled against older competition. He also dealt with a pair of injuries, including a sprained wrist and a fractured finger toward the end of the year.

SCOUTING REPORT: Gutierrez is still extremely young—he'll play all of 2024 as a 19-year-old—so he has plenty of leash remaining, but there's little question his stock is down. In his first year outside a complex league setting, Gutierrez was a free-swinger who did a good job making contact on pitches in the zone but strayed outside it too often. His chase rate of 41% was well below-average, even considering his level. He also needs to get the ball in the air much more often. To do so, the Rangers would like him to adjust his bat path to turn some of his grounders into line drives. Gutierrez's raw power shows up in batting practice but produced just 16 extra-base hits in 76 Low-A games. Gutierrez is an excellent center fielder, with long, gliding strides that help him track down balls with ease no matter whether they were hit behind him or from side to side. He's still young enough that his body could take him into a corner, where there would be even more pressure on his bat to take big strides forward. Gutierrez's instincts in center field mask the fact that he is an average runner, which shows up in times to first base.

THE FUTURE: Scouts inside and outside the organization still believe in Gutierrez, though they acknowledge that the road to his ceiling has not gotten shorter. If everything clicks, he can be a center fielder with a well-rounded skill set. He'll return to Low-A in 2024.

Year	Age	Club (League)	Level	AVG	G	AB	R	H	2B	3B	HR	RBI	BB	SO	SB	OBP	SLG
2023	18	ACL Rangers	Rk	.350	6	20	4	7	0	2	0	2	1	6	2	.381	.550
2023	18	Down East (CAR)	A	.259	78	293	39	76	11	3	2	34	25	72	30	.326	.338
Minor League Totals				.280	129	485	78	136	24	7	6	60	37	112	43	.340	.396

11 AARON ZAVALA, OF

HIT: 50. **POW:** 40. **RUN:** 50. **FLD:** 50. **ARM:** 50. **BA Grade:** 50. **Risk:** High.

Born: June 24, 2000. **B-T:** L-R. **HT:** 6-0. **WT:** 193. **Drafted:** Oregon, 2021 (2nd round). **Signed by:** Gary McGraw.

TRACK RECORD: After a breakout season at Oregon that saw him produce a 1.124 OPS and establish himself as one of the best lefthanded bats on the board, Zavala was selected in the second round of the 2021 draft. A medical issue complicated things, but he eventually signed for a bonus of $830,000. Just five games into his stint in the 2022 Arizona Fall League, he suffered an injury that required the implantation of a surgical brace. He didn't make his 2023 debut until May 27, and then struggled to get off the ground all year long.

SCOUTING REPORT: At his best, Zavala's bat is his calling card. He was not at his best in 2023. Scouts outside the organization noted a player who didn't have the same burst as in past years despite solid bat speed and bat-to-ball skills. The Rangers believe the surgery affected Zavala's bat angle, which was lower than before and led to him consistently being under fastballs and lower exit velocities and hard-hit rates than when he was at his best. He is an extremely selective hitter who swung just 37.5% of the time in 2023 but did a good job finding the barrel when he cut it loose. Now he needs to regain the thump he lost before the surgery. The results from the team's fall instructional camp seemed to point in the right direction. As a corner outfielder with secondary tools that are only average across the board, the pressure is on Zavala's bat to return to its prior levels.

THE FUTURE: Zavala might return to Double-A in 2024 to get a clean slate at a level where he struggled mightily in 2023. If he can rebound, he has the ceiling of an average left fielder on a second division club.

Year	Age	Club (League)	Level	AVG	G	AB	R	H	2B	3B	HR	RBI	BB	SO	SB	OBP	SLG
2023	23	Frisco (TL)	AA	.194	95	341	47	66	16	0	5	40	72	159	7	.343	.284
Minor League Totals				.244	228	827	154	202	39	3	22	111	174	287	30	.388	.378

12 JACK LEITER, RHP

FB: 60. **CB:** 45. **SL:** 50. **CHG:** 45. **CTL:** 40. **BA Grade:** 50. **Risk:** Extreme.

Born: April 21, 2000. **B-T:** R-R. **HT:** 6-1. **WT:** 205. **Drafted:** Vanderbilt, 2021 (1st round). **Signed by:** Derrick Tucker.

TRACK RECORD: Leiter's collegiate career was limited to just a season and change thanks to the pandemic and sophomore eligibility. Nonetheless, the Rangers selected Leiter—the son and nephew of big leaguers Al and Mark Leiter—second overall. After resting him post-draft, the Rangers assigned Leiter to Double-A to begin his pro career. He's spent two rocky seasons at the level, where he's struggled with command and control and made several alterations to his delivery and pitch mix.

SCOUTING REPORT: Leiter made two stints on the development list in 2023. Part of the reason for those assignments was to change the way he used his lower half in his delivery. Specifically, the Rangers wanted him to keep his heel in connection with the rubber longer. They also simplified other aspects of his mechanics in an effort to help him throw more strikes and improve a walk rate that has been 10% or higher for the entirety of his career. Further improvements to the delivery were a target of his offseason work. Leiter works with a four-pitch mix, starting with a mid-90s fastball with high spin and promising life through the zone. If he can throw more strikes, it could be a plus offering. None of his offspeed pitches grade as better than average, and even his best pitch, his slider, went through a major overhaul. The pitch, which comes in around 86 mph, needs to show sharper break because the current version acts more like a cutter. If he can add some break, it has the power to get to average. Leiter's changeup and curveball are fringe-average, and his control will have to take a big step forward to get to below-average.

THE FUTURE: After two seasons spent tinkering, Leiter needs to show something in 2024. If he does, he might have a chance to fit in the back of a rotation. If not, he might have a future as a setup man.

Year	Age	Club (League)	Level	W	L	ERA	G	GS	IP	H	HR	BB	SO	BB%	SO%	WHIP	AVG
2023	23	Frisco (TL)	AA	2	6	5.07	19	19	82	67	14	47	110	13.4	31.3	1.40	.226
2023	23	Round Rock (PCL)	AAA	0	0	8.10	1	1	3	8	2	2	4	10.0	20.0	3.00	.444
Minor League Totals				5	16	5.39	43	42	178	163	27	105	223	13.2	28.0	1.51	.243

13 AIDAN CURRY, RHP

FB: 60. **SL:** 60. **CHG:** 50. **CUT:** 50. **CTL:** 50. **BA Grade:** 50. **Risk:** High.

Born: July 25, 2002. **B-T:** R-R. **HT:** 6-5. **WT:** 205. **Signed:** HS—Bronx, NY, 2020 (NDFA). **Signed by:** Takeshi Sakurayama.

TRACK RECORD: As if their haul in the 2020 draft weren't enough, the Rangers also cleaned up on undrafted free agents. One of their biggest coups was Curry, a tall righthander from a New York high school. Curry got a cameo at Low-A in 2022, then returned to the level in 2023 for most of the season. He was one of six Rangers prospects to strike out more than 100 hitters last season.

SCOUTING REPORT: Curry's size and age made him an upside play, and in 2023 he began to scratch the surface of that potential by becoming more in sync with his upper and lower halves. His stuff is plenty good, too. Curry works primarily with two pitches: A low-90s fastball and a low-80s slider. The former has excellent shape, with roughly 18 inches of induced vertical break and a spin rate around 2,400 rpm. The slider is a slicing, downer breaking ball that got Low-A hitters to swing and miss at a rate of 46%. He mixes in a cutter around 89 mph and a changeup in the mid 80s that scouts believe could have average potential once he begins throwing it more often. Curry could get to average control as he gains further coordination and strength, and evaluators noted that his fastball command winnowed at the upper end of its velocity.

THE FUTURE: Curry ended the season at High-A Hickory and will return there in 2024. His upside lies in his projection, and the top of his ceiling could see him slot in toward the back of a rotation.

Year	Age	Club (League)	Level	W	L	ERA	G	GS	IP	H	HR	BB	SO	BB%	SO%	WHIP	AVG
2023	20	Down East (CAR)	A	6	3	2.30	19	15	82	47	4	29	99	9.0	30.8	0.93	.163
2023	20	Hickory (SAL)	A+	0	0	8.53	2	2	6	9	3	10	5	27.8	13.9	3.00	.346
Minor League Totals				7	5	4.37	44	28	142	117	12	75	183	12.2	29.8	1.35	.221

14 EMILIANO TEODO, RHP

FB: 70. **CB:** 60. **CTL:** 40. **BA Grade:** 50. **Risk:** High.

Born: February 14, 2001. **B-T:** R-R. **HT:** 6-0. **WT:** 175. **Signed:** Dominican Republic, 2020.
Signed by: JC Alvarez/Jack Marino.

TRACK RECORD: Teodo is a strong-armed righthander who signed for a five-figure bonus and spent his first pro season as a reliever in the Arizona Complex League. He moved into a starter's role in 2022, and has been part of the rotation at both Class A levels over the past two seasons. Teodo missed time in 2023 with a forearm injury, then made up the innings with a dominant stint in the Arizona Fall League.

SCOUTING REPORT: The story of Teodo's season can be told in two parts. In the beginning, his four-seam fastball played way down from its upper-90s velocity and was ineffective at missing bats. Once Teodo switched to a two-seamer, his season swung. Teodo made the switch on July 16, and from that point on he struck out 57 and walked just 18 over the season's final 37.2 innings. He was even more overpowering in the AFL, where he allowed three hits and struck out 18 hitters over 11 frames. Teodo backs the fastball with a nasty curveball in the mid 80s whose break and velocity makes it appear like a slider. The pitch's shape is inconsistent, and the Rangers have worked with him to improve in that area. When he threw the four-seamer, he would often alter his tempo in an effort to coax the ball into the strike zone. By changing to the two-seamer, Teodo could aim down the middle and allow the combination of movement and velocity to bedevil hitters. He is not likely to have better than below-average control and command.
THE FUTURE: Teodo might get a few more cracks at starting, but he's a near-certain reliever. If it all clicks, he could be a force at the back of the bullpen.

Year	Age	Club (League)	Level	W	L	ERA	G	GS	IP	H	HR	BB	SO	BB%	SO%	WHIP	AVG
2023	22	Hickory (SAL)	A+	5	3	4.52	18	14	62	53	10	33	84	12.3	31.3	1.39	.231
Minor League Totals				12	11	3.64	59	31	175	128	17	95	247	12.7	32.9	1.27	.199

15 ABIMELEC ORTIZ, 1B

HIT: 40. **POW:** 55. **RUN:** 30. **FLD:** 40. **ARM:** 40. **BA Grade:** 45. **Risk:** High.

Born: February 22, 2002. **B-T:** L-L. **HT:** 6-0. **WT:** 230. **Signed:** Florida SouthWestern State JC, 2021 (NDFA).
Signed by: Rafael Santiago.

TRACK RECORD: Ortiz went to high school at the Carlos Beltran Baseball Academy in Puerto Rico and then played one season at Florida Southwestern State JC, where he hit .349 with nine home runs. He signed as an undrafted free agent after the 2021 draft and in 2023 hit 33 home runs, which was tied for fourth in the minors.
SCOUTING REPORT: Ortiz's first two seasons as a pro were fairly nondescript. His career turned when he was diagnosed with astigmatism and got corrective lenses. Once he was able to see the ball, he began hitting it hard and often. He made loud contact all year long, and his average (90 mph) and 90th percentile (106.1) exit velocities were some of the best in the system. He also simplified his mechanics to turn a leg lift into a toe-tap. Now, Ortiz must do better against premium velocity. He whiffed more than 35% against fastballs thrown 95 mph or harder, and was particularly susceptible when they were thrown up in the zone. Ortiz has seen some time in the outfield, but first base and DH are his likely homes. He's a below-average defender and a well below-average runner, so all of his value is going to have to come when he's in the batter's box.
THE FUTURE: Ortiz will move to Double-A in 2024, when he'll try to improve against hard fastballs in order to let his strength and power play to their fullest. He could be an everyday first baseman on a second-division club.

Year	Age	Club (League)	Level	AVG	G	AB	R	H	2B	3B	HR	RBI	BB	SO	SB	OBP	SLG
2023	21	Down East (CAR)	A	.307	29	101	19	31	7	1	7	20	16	36	0	.392	.604
2023	21	Hickory (SAL)	A+	.290	80	290	59	84	13	3	26	81	33	90	1	.363	.624
Minor League Totals				.260	242	812	148	211	38	7	55	173	114	250	12	.358	.527

16 ECHEDRY VARGAS, SS/2B

HIT: 45. **POW:** 50. **RUN:** 55. **FLD:** 50. **ARM:** 55. **BA Grade:** 50. **Risk:** Extreme.

Born: February 27, 2005. **B-T:** R-R. **HT:** 5-11. **WT:** 170. **Signed:** Dominican Republic, 2022.
Signed by: JC Alvarez/Jack Marino.

TRACK RECORD: Vargas was signed out of the Dominican Republic in 2022 for a small bonus. His career is in its early stages, but he's already proved a shrewd signing. The versatile infielder stood out in the Rookie-level Arizona Complex League, where his 11 home runs tied for the league lead, and his 27 extra-base hits and 112 total bases stood alone atop the circuit.
SCOUTING REPORT: Vargas has a well-rounded skill set without a standout tool on defense or in the batter's box. He's a tightly packed athlete who can put plenty of thump behind the ball but will need to improve his approach in order to do so more often. His chase and miss rates were not good, but his 103.9 mph 90th percentile exit velocity stood out among his peers. If he can better recognize and lay off spin, his knack for barreling balls will show up more frequently. Vargas improved his walk rate year over year but the Rangers would like to see that figure improve. He mostly split his defensive reps between shortstop and second base but got seven starts at third base as well. He could be an average defender at second but has enough arm strength to fill in on the left side from time to time. He's an above-average runner who can get to plus underway.

THE FUTURE: Vargas made a one-game cameo with Low-A Down East, and he'll return to the level in 2024. He has the ceiling of a utilityman who gets regular playing time around the diamond.

Year	Age	Club (League)	Level	AVG	G	AB	R	H	2B	3B	HR	RBI	BB	SO	SB	OBP	SLG
2023	18	ACL Rangers	Rk	.315	52	197	46	62	15	1	11	39	21	54	17	.387	.569
2023	18	Down East (CAR)	A	.500	1	2	1	1	0	0	0	0	0	1	0	.500	.500
Minor League Totals				.309	107	395	87	122	34	6	15	66	34	82	30	.378	.539

17 JOSE CORNIELL, RHP

FB: 55. **SL:** 60. **CHG:** 50. **CUT:** 45. **CTL:** 55. **BA Grade:** 45. **Risk:** High.

Born: June 22, 2003. **B-T:** R-R. **HT:** 6-3. **WT:** 165. **Signed:** Dominican Republic, 2019.
Signed by: Francisco Rosario (Mariners).
TRACK RECORD: Corniell was signed by Seattle in 2019 for $330,000, the highest bonus awarded by the Mariners in that year's signing class. He never threw a pitch in a Seattle uniform. Instead, the Rangers acquired him—along with infielder Andres Mesa—following the 2020 season as the return for reliever Rafael Montero. He's moved slowly through the system but broke through in 2023, when he reached High-A for the first time and struck out 119 hitters, second-most in the system.
SCOUTING REPORT: As Corniell has matriculated through the minors, his repertoire has undergone a metamorphosis. His four-seam fastball, which sits around 94 mph, worked in concert with a sweepy, potentially plus slider around 84 mph to give righthanded hitters fits. Lefthanders, however, fared much better. To remedy that issue, Corniell introduced a cutter to steal strikes early in counts and give hitters another option to consider. He was also encouraged to throw his mid-80s changeup more often to give himself a putaway pitch against lefties. The strike, chase and miss rates on the changeup were all plus in 2023. Corniell also throws a two-seam fastball, which comes in a few ticks slower than his four-seamer. Scouts reported a bit of inconsistency in Corniell's slider shape, which may stem from not getting on top of the pitch regularly. The Rangers were also impressed by Corniell's improved maturity, and rewarded him with the organization's pitcher of the year award.
THE FUTURE: Corniell was added to the 40-man roster and will reach Double-A for the first time in 2024. He has the upside of a back-end starter.

Year	Age	Club (League)	Level	W	L	ERA	G	GS	IP	H	HR	BB	SO	BB%	SO%	WHIP	AVG
2023	20	Down East (CAR)	A	4	1	2.70	10	6	43	26	4	14	56	8.4	33.7	0.92	.174
2023	20	Hickory (SAL)	A+	4	2	3.09	13	11	58	44	7	17	63	7.3	26.9	1.05	.208
Minor League Totals				12	11	4.50	58	30	206	172	27	79	234	9.1	27.0	1.22	.226

18 BRAYLIN MOREL, OF

HIT: 50. **POW:** 60. **RUN:** 45. **FLD:** 45. **ARM:** 55. **BA Grade:** 50. **Risk:** Extreme.

Born: January 19, 2006. **B-T:** R-R. **HT:** 6-2. **WT:** 180. **Signed:** Dominican Republic, 2023.
Signed by: Nelson Muniz/Willy Espinal.
TRACK RECORD: Morel signed with Texas in 2023 for a bonus of $97,500 on the strength of an intriguing but raw tool set. He spent his first pro season in the Dominican Summer League, where he led the league with 17 doubles, eight triples, 32 extra-base hits and 116 total bases. The XBH total was the most in the league since 2019, when Luis Matos had 33.
SCOUTING REPORT: Morel's game is centered around his offense, which has the potential to profile at right field if he makes some improvements. Chiefly, he must make better swing decisions. He didn't strike out at an extreme rate—just 24.5%—but his miss rates both in and out of the zone were a touch high for the level. If he improves in those areas, he'll be able to access his plus power as he moves up the ladder. There's work to be done on defense, where Morel must clean up his routes and jumps to remain in right field. He's a fringy runner right now, and if he slows down he might have to move to first base.
THE FUTURE: Morel will advance stateside in 2024 and has the ceiling of a classic everyday right fielder.

Year	Age	Club (League)	Level	AVG	G	AB	R	H	2B	3B	HR	RBI	BB	SO	SB	OBP	SLG
2023	17	DSL Rangers Red	Rk	.344	47	180	40	62	17	8	7	43	21	50	2	.417	.644
Minor League Totals				.344	47	180	40	62	17	8	7	43	21	50	2	.417	.644

19 GLEIDER FIGUEREO, 3B

HIT: 40. **POW:** 60. **RUN:** 30. **FLD:** 40. **ARM:** 65. **BA Grade:** 50. **Risk:** Extreme.

Born: June 27, 2004. **B-T:** L-R. **HT:** 6-0. **WT:** 165. **Signed:** Dominican Republic, 2021. **Signed by:** Willy Espinal.
TRACK RECORD: Figuereo signed out of the Dominican Republic in 2021 and put himself on the map a

year later with a scorching performance in the Rookie-level Arizona Complex League that included nine home runs. He was part of a very young group that moved to Low-A and took their lumps all season.
SCOUTING REPORT: Catch him on the right day, and you can clearly see Figuereo's ceiling. He's a muscularly gifted player with more than enough raw power to profile at third base. He needs to do a better job recognizing and laying off spin so he can actually get pitches he can drive. His chase and whiff numbers are high, and he needs to tone down his aggression so he can take a few more walks. He's also vexed by lefthanders, who held him to just a .493 OPS in 2023. Figuereo will make highlight-reel plays that allow him to show off a nearly double-plus arm, but he has to get more consistent on routine plays. He needs to improve the finer points, including footwork and transfers. He's a well below-average runner.
THE FUTURE: Figuereo will likely return to Low-A in 2024 and will have to show significant improvement to reach his ceiling.

Year	Age	Club (League)	Level	AVG	G	AB	R	H	2B	3B	HR	RBI	BB	SO	SB	OBP	SLG
2023	19	Down East (CAR)	A	.220	107	396	51	87	14	0	9	51	42	132	8	.300	.323
Minor League Totals				.233	196	701	103	163	25	9	20	111	87	204	18	.323	.379

20 IZACK TIGER, RHP
FB: 60. **SL:** 60. **CUT** 45. **SPLIT:** 55. **CTL:** 45. **BA Grade:** 50. **Risk:** Extreme.

Born: February 8, 2001. **B-T:** R-R. **HT:** 6-2. **WT:** 175. **Drafted:** Butler (KS) JC, 2023 (7th round). **Signed by:** Dustin Smith.
TRACK RECORD: The Rangers have not been shy about hunting for upside in the draft, and Tiger is one of their latest projects. The righthander spent three seasons at Butler (KS) JC, where he caught the eye of area scout Dustin Smith, whose intrigue was piqued further by Tiger's short stint in the Cape Cod League in 2022. In his draft season, Tiger whiffed 121 hitters against just 29 walks in 84.2 innings. Texas took Tiger in the seventh round in 2023 and sent him for a quick stint in the Arizona Complex League before he moved to Low-A for the playoffs, where he struck out six hitters over three hitless frames.
SCOUTING REPORT: Tiger works mostly with three pitches: a mid-90s fastball, a hard-diving slider in the high-80s and a splitter that serves as his changeup. The righthander used to throw a circle changeup but the Rangers believed his delivery—with its overhand stroke—was better suited for a splitter. The fastball played up in relief and touched 100 mph in the playoffs. He's also utilized a low-90s cutter that grades out as fringe-average. Tiger is an above-average mover on the mound and has the arm action and delivery to give him the upside of a starter if he can add the requisite polish. He has fringe-average control.
THE FUTURE: Tiger is likely to spend 2024 at the Class A levels, where he will work toward a ceiling in the rotation with the fallback option of a weapon out of the bullpen.

Year	Age	Club (League)	Level	W	L	ERA	G	GS	IP	H	HR	BB	SO	BB%	SO%	WHIP	AVG
2023	22	ACL Rangers	Rk	0	0	2.25	3	1	4	7	0	2	4	11.1	22.2	2.25	.438
Minor League Totals				0	0	2.25	3	1	4	7	0	2	4	11.1	22.2	2.25	.438

21 YEISON MORROBEL, OF
HIT: 55. **POW:** 45. **RUN:** 50. **FLD:** 50. **ARM:** 55. **BA Grade:** 45. **Risk:** Extreme.

Born: December 8, 2003. **B-T:** L-L. **HT:** 6-1. **WT:** 190. **Signed:** Dominican Republic, 2021.
Signed by: Willy Espinal/JC Alvarez.
TRACK RECORD: Morrobel earned the highest bonus in Texas' 2021 international class and showed signs of promise early in his pro career, which was spent at the lowest levels of the minor leagues. The outfielder was part of an extremely young pack of prospects assigned to Low-A Down East. He took his lumps during the season but missed roughly half the year with injuries to his hamstring and shoulder, the latter of which required season-ending surgery.
SCOUTING REPORT: Morrobel showed the best control of the strike zone among the young prospects at Low-A, but he did not show nearly enough impact and homered just once in 128 at-bats. The Rangers are heartened by his solid swing mechanics and excellent decisions, but he doesn't have high-end bat speed and absolutely has to start putting bigger charges into balls. That's especially true if he moves to a corner-outfield spot, which some scouts believe will be a necessity as he matures and adds strength. Evaluators see an average defender in right field because of above-average arm strength. He's an average runner.
THE FUTURE: Morrobel was healthy enough to see action at Texas' fall instructional league camp and should return to Low-A Down East in 2024. It is imperative that he adds strength and power to help him profile in an outfield corner. Otherwise, he fits more as a backup.

Year	Age	Club (League)	Level	AVG	G	AB	R	H	2B	3B	HR	RBI	BB	SO	SB	OBP	SLG
2023	19	Down East (CAR)	A	.273	37	128	16	35	2	0	1	13	22	34	12	.384	.313
Minor League Totals				.287	137	491	83	141	27	7	5	67	72	99	27	.391	.401

22 LIAM HICKS, C

HIT: 50. **POW:** 40. **RUN:** 40. **FLD:** 40. **ARM:** 40. **BA Grade:** 40. **Risk:** High.

Born: June 2, 1999. **B-T:** L-R. **HT:** 5-10. **WT:** 195. **Drafted:** Arkansas State, 2021 (9th round). **Signed by:** Dustin Smith.
TRACK RECORD: Hicks' road to pro ball was long and winding. The Canadian-born backstop spent the first two years of this college career at Mineral State (Mo.) JC before transferring to Arkansas State for his junior and senior seasons. The Rangers took him in the ninth round of the 2021 draft and signed him for $30,000. Since then, he's done nothing but hit. He reached Double-A in 2023, then posted a standout stint in the Arizona Fall League that included the league's first six-hit game since 2009.
SCOUTING REPORT: Hicks' road to the big leagues will come through the batter's box, where the lefty hitter has shown outstanding bat-to-ball skills that included above-average rates of whiff and chase. Now, he needs to put some more impact behind his contact. His average and 90th percentile exit velocities were well below-average and he homered just four times while playing home games at two hitter-friendly atmospheres. Defensively, Hicks is a hard worker who will have to continue those efforts to get to even below-average. His arm strength grades as a 40 but plays down because of slow transfers and footwork. He got some time at first base as well. He'd be an adequate defender there but a move would put immense pressure on his bat to develop the power to profile at the position.
THE FUTURE: Hicks will spend his 2024 season at the upper levels of the minor leagues. If he can get stronger and produce more power, he could be a backup catcher whose value would come through his offense.

Year	Age	Club (League)	Level	AVG	G	AB	R	H	2B	3B	HR	RBI	BB	SO	SB	OBP	SLG
2023	24	Hickory (SAL)	A+	.311	15	45	5	14	1	0	1	5	10	11	3	.446	.400
2023	24	Frisco (TL)	AA	.269	77	253	30	68	14	1	3	40	49	52	4	.408	.368
Minor League Totals				.284	152	472	64	134	24	2	7	79	102	89	12	.426	.388

23 ALEJANDRO ROSARIO, RHP

FB: 60. **SL:** 55. **CHG:** 50. **CUT:** 40. **CTL:** 40. **BA Grade:** 40. **Risk:** High.

Born: January 6, 2002. **B-T:** R-R. **HT:** 6-1. **WT:** 182. **Drafted:** Miami, 2023 (5th round). **Signed by:** Tommy Dueñas.
TRACK RECORD: Rosario pitched three seasons at Miami with middling or worse results, including ERAs north of 7.00 in his final two years. He mixed in a brief, dominant stint in the Cape Cod League as well, and the Rangers took a flier on him in the fifth round in 2023 and signed him for $437,900.
SCOUTING REPORT: Despite a checkered career at Miami, the Rangers were intrigued by what Rosario's pitch mix might look like with a few tweaks. Specifically, they want him to establish his mid-90s sinker down in the zone early before moving up the ladder with the four-seamer for whiffs. He buttresses the fastball with a slurvy slider between 81-85 mph with Frisbee action and a split-grip changeup that was shelved during his time at Miami. To stick as a starter, he'll need to improve his control and command as well. He walked 9.8% of hitters over his career at Miami, including an 11.8% rate during his draft year.
THE FUTURE: Rosario will likely begin his career as a starter at Low-A Down East. If he shifts to the bullpen, he could quickly through the system and fit in the bullpen in short order.

Year	Age	Club (League)	Level	W	L	ERA	G	GS	IP	H	HR	BB	SO	BB%	SO%	WHIP	AVG
2023	21	Did not play															

24 JOSH STEPHAN RHP

FB: 40. **SL:** 60. **CHG:** 40. **CUT:** 40. **CTL:** 55. **BA Grade:** 40. **Risk:** High.

Born: November 1, 2001. **B-T:** R-R. **HT:** 6-3. **WT:** 185. **Drafted:** HS—Grand Prairie, TX, 2020 (NDFA).
Signed by: Josh Simpson.
TRACK RECORD: The Rangers cleaned up in the five-round 2020 draft, then put the icing on the cake in the undrafted free agent market. Stephan was one of a host of intriguing talents the Rangers added to their system post draft, and he experienced a bit of a breakthrough in 2023, when he reached Double-A for the first time. Stephan suffered a back injury at midseason and did not pitch after July 4. He was limited to just 66.1 innings all season.
SCOUTING REPORT: Stephan was able to dominate the lower levels with the help of a nasty slider that he threw nearly half the time. He used it to hitters of both hands and in any count, and could throw it for both called strikes and chases. He throws both two- and four-seam fastballs, each of which average around 92 mph. He uses the two-seamer more frequently, and it pairs nicely with his slider to give him an east-west approach that allows him to induce plenty of grounders. He also has a changeup that needs further development and a cutter that he introduced this season to help combat a weakness against lefthanded

hitters. His next steps involve learning to pitch more off his fastball and to be more unpredictable in general. He throws plenty of strikes and should have at least above-average command at peak.

THE FUTURE: Stephan finished the year healthy in Arizona. He needs to vary his arsenal and get one of his offspeed pitches to take steps forward to reach his ceiling in the back of a rotation.

Year	Age	Club (League)	Level	W	L	ERA	G	GS	IP	H	HR	BB	SO	BB%	SO%	WHIP	AVG
2023	21	Hickory (SAL)	A+	6	3	2.17	12	11	62	38	8	12	73	5.1	31.2	0.80	.175
2023	21	Frisco (TL)	AA	0	0	4.15	1	1	4	5	0	1	5	5.3	26.3	1.38	.294
Minor League Totals				14	10	3.26	44	40	210	162	26	60	243	7.1	28.7	1.06	.211

25 SKYLAR HALES, RHP
FB: 60. **SL:** 55. **CTL:** 45. **BA Grade:** 40. **Risk:** High.

Born: October 24, 2001. **B-T:** R-R. **HT:** 6-4. **WT:** 220. **Drafted:** Santa Clara, 2023 (4th round). **Signed by:** Gabe Sandy.

TRACK RECORD: Hales spent three seasons at Santa Clara. He was a near-exclusive reliever in his freshman and junior years but made 12 starts in his sophomore season. The Rangers liked his power mix, popped him in the fourth round and signed him for $565,000. He reached Low-A Down East in his pro debut and made a cameo during High-A Hickory's postseason run.

SCOUTING REPORT: Hales is a surefire reliever as a pro but could move quite quickly in that role. He works with a two-pitch mix of a mid-90s fastball and mid-80s slider. The fastball touched 100 mph as an amateur and has above-average life through the zone while occasionally showing sink and tail toward the bottom. The slider appears like a hybrid between a true slider and a cutter and should help him induce both whiffs and weak contact. Hales has a chiseled build at 6-foot-4, 220 pounds that has earned him the nickname Superman. His funky delivery, which features a low slot and an abbreviated arm stroke in the back, adds deception.

THE FUTURE: Hales' powerful mix should overwhelm hitters at the lowest levels of the minor leagues. If he can sharpen his command, he could reach the big leagues quickly and fit into a late-inning role.

Year	Age	Club (League)	Level	W	L	ERA	G	GS	IP	H	HR	BB	SO	BB%	SO%	WHIP	AVG
2023	21	ACL Rangers	Rk	0	0	11.57	2	0	2	4	2	0	4	0.0	36.4	1.71	.364
2023	21	Down East (CAR)	A	0	1	2.16	5	0	8	2	1	2	7	7.1	25.0	0.48	.077
Minor League Totals				0	1	4.50	7	0	11	6	3	2	11	5.1	28.2	0.80	.162

26 ZAK KENT, RHP
FB: 50. **SL:** 60. **CHG:** 45. **CTL:** 45. **BA Grade:** 40. **Risk:** High.

Born: February 24, 1998. **B-T:** R-R. **HT:** 6-3. **WT:** 208. **Drafted:** Virginia Military Institute, 2019 (9th round). **Signed by:** Brian Matthews.

TRACK RECORD: Kent was the Rangers' ninth-round pick in 2019 out of Virginia Military Institute. He reached Triple-A in 2022 and was rewarded with a spot on the team's 40-man roster before that year's Rule 5 draft. His 2023 season was limited to just 40.2 innings in the regular season thanks to an injury before six weeks in the Arizona Fall League to make up for lost time.

SCOUTING REPORT: Kent works with a three-pitch mix of a four-seam fastball, slider and changeup, though the first two pitches are the dominant parts of his arsenal. The four-seamer with natural cutting action sits in the low 90s with high spin but the velocity needs to come up a couple of notches before it looks as good as it did in 2021, his last healthy season. The slider, thrown around 85 mph, is his best offspeed pitch with traditional three-quarters break. If he were to use only the fastball and slider, he'd be a plug-and-play reliever. To seize a spot in a rotation, he needs to bring his mid-80s changeup forward and start using it more often. The pitch is thrown with a split-finger grip and was a dominant offering the last time he pitched a full season.

THE FUTURE: The biggest goal for Kent in 2024 will be a return to health. Two injury-filled seasons have dimmed his rotation chances, but if his velocity comes back he could fit in a bullpen.

Year	Age	Club (League)	Level	W	L	ERA	G	GS	IP	H	HR	BB	SO	BB%	SO%	WHIP	AVG
2023	25	ACL Rangers	Rk	0	0	9.45	3	3	7	8	3	3	9	9.7	29.0	1.65	.296
2023	25	Round Rock (PCL)	AAA	0	1	3.97	10	10	34	26	4	10	34	7.1	24.3	1.06	.205
Minor League Totals				9	12	4.07	68	59	259	239	36	87	288	8.0	26.4	1.26	.241

27 CADEN SCARBOROUGH, RHP

FB: 55. **CB:** 50. **CTL:** 40. **BA Grade:** 45. **Risk:** Extreme.

Born: April 1, 2005. **B-T:** R-R. **HT:** 6-5. **WT:** 185. **Drafted:** HS—Harmony, FL, 2023 (6th round).
Signed by: John Wiedenbauer.

TRACK RECORD: Scarborough was a helium prospect in the 2023 draft cycle thanks to a projectable frame and a fastball that ticked up a few notches from the previous season, when he didn't pitch at many of the highest profile summer showcase events. The Rangers, who have struck gold with low-profile signings of late, believed in Scarborough's athleticism and remaining growth and drafted him in the sixth round. His $515,000 signing bonus was the second-highest in the round.

SCOUTING REPORT: Scarborough is long, lanky and has the potential to pack much more muscle onto his frame. Currently, his fastball sits between 89-91 and is paired with a high-spin downer curveball in the low 70s. Normally, that's not the kind of mix that jumps off the page. Scarborough's nearly 7 feet of extension and low release height each help the pitch play up, and should amplify his mix as he fills out his body. He needs to add a third pitch and improve his control and command.

THE FUTURE: Scarborough is a long-term play, who, if he reaches his ceiling, will stand as another in the line of the Rangers' successful spelunking expeditions from the amateur ranks.

Year	Age	Club (League)	Level	W	L	ERA	G	GS	IP	H	HR	BB	SO	BB%	SO%	WHIP	AVG
2023	18	Did not play															

28 MITCH BRATT, LHP

FB: 40. **SL:** 50. **SPLIT:** 40. **CTL:** 50. **BA Grade:** 40. **Risk:** High.

Born: July 3, 2003. **B-T:** L-L. **HT:** 6-1. **WT:** 190. **Drafted:** HS—Statesboro, GA, 2021 (5th round).
Signed by: Takeshi Sakurayama.

TRACK RECORD: Bratt was born in Canada but moved to Georgia during the pandemic in order to get more exposure to scouts. He was drafted in the fifth round in 2021 and has advanced a level a year in his first two full pro seasons. He started a game against Team USA in the World Baseball Classic and was roughed up by a lineup chock full of all-stars. He missed roughly half the season with a lat injury and made up for lost time in the Arizona Fall League.

SCOUTING REPORT: As an amateur, a great deal of Bratt's value came from his remaining projection. Two years later, he still needs to add strength to bring his stuff up a few ticks. His arsenal was reconstructed during the season, and the lefty now works with a mix of four-seamer, splitter and sweeping slider. His fastball velocity is well below-average at 88-91 mph but might play up a tick due to a low release height that creates tough angles when the pitch is located at the top of the zone. Neither of his offspeeds is a knockout, though scouts were encouraged by Bratt's ability to move his mix around the zone.

THE FUTURE: Bratt has solid pitchability, but he needs to get stronger. If he does he could be a No. 5 starter or a bulk reliever.

Year	Age	Club (League)	Level	W	L	ERA	G	GS	IP	H	HR	BB	SO	BB%	SO%	WHIP	AVG
2023	19	Hickory (SAL)	A+	2	3	3.54	16	16	61	60	6	17	73	6.4	27.7	1.26	.244
Minor League Totals				7	8	2.80	39	34	148	130	10	45	185	7.2	29.6	1.19	.227

29 JOSEPH MONTALVO, RHP

FB: 55. **SL:** 40. **CHG:** 60. **CTL:** 50. **BA Grade:** 40. **Risk:** High.

Born: May 4, 2002. **B-T:** B-R. **HT:** 6-2. **WT:** 185. **Drafted:** HS—Kissimmee, FL, 2021 (20th round).
Signed by: Brett Campbell.

TRACK RECORD: Montalvo was the Rangers' final pick in the 2021 draft. He's a native Puerto Rican who went to high school in Florida and was committed to Eastern Florida State JC before Texas signed him for $125,000. He advanced a level per year and spent all of 2023 in Low-A Down East, where he struck out 107 hitters in 95.1 innings. He's a converted shortstop who in 2023 was in just his second year as a pitcher.

SCOUTING REPORT: Montalvo works with a three-pitch mix fronted by a low-90s four-seam fastball with above-average spin and horizontal movement as well as a low vertical approach angle that amplifies the pitch. He backs the fastball with a low-80s slider with high spin and a decent amount of sweep that projects to be below-average. His changeup, thrown in the mid 80s, is a potential plus pitch with decent fade and drop away from lefthanders at its best. His delivery is inconsistent, which is understandable considering how raw he is on the mound. If he can repeat more often, he could get to average control.

THE FUTURE: Montalvo will advance to High-A Hickory in 2023, when he'll work to develop his slider and streamline his delivery to the point that he can be a No. 5 starter. If not, he might fit as a bulk reliever.

Year	Age	Club (League)	Level	W	L	ERA	G	GS	IP	H	HR	BB	SO	BB%	SO%	WHIP	AVG
2023	21	Down East (CAR)	A	7	2	2.83	22	17	95	74	9	39	107	9.8	27.0	1.19	.211
Minor League Totals				11	2	2.75	32	18	119	96	10	42	143	8.5	29.0	1.17	.217

30 JONATHAN ORNELAS, SS/OF

HIT: 40. **POW:** 45. **RUN:** 40. **FLD:** 45. **ARM:** 60. **BA Grade:** 40. **Risk:** High.

Born: May 26, 2000. **B-T:** R-R. **HT:** 6-1. **WT:** 195. **Drafted:** HS—Glendale, AZ, 2018 (3rd round). **Signed by:** Levi Lacey.

TRACK RECORD: Ornelas was the Rangers' third-round pick in the 2018 draft and has moved slowly through the system. He had a breakout year at the upper levels in 2022 but stalled somewhat in 2023. Nonetheless, his defensive versatility earned him a big league cameo in August. He got into seven games and recorded his first MLB hit.

SCOUTING REPORT: Ornelas' value lies in his versatility. He can capably play on both the dirt and the grass, though he'll never be a standout at either spot. Scouts have long been skeptical of whether his aggressive approach would play long term. Those concerns showed up in 2023, when he hit for neither average nor power at Triple-A Round Rock. Scouts also noticed that he was having particular issues covering the outer half of the plate. Ornelas was also in worse shape than in past seasons, which showed up in diminished range at shortstop. His swing got a bit out of whack as well, and the team invited him to its fall instructional league camp to work out the kinks.

THE FUTURE: Ornelas will return to Triple-A in 2024 for more seasoning. If he can show something closer to his 2022 form, he fits as a versatile bench player.

Year	Age	Club (League)	Level	AVG	G	AB	R	H	2B	3B	HR	RBI	BB	SO	SB	OBP	SLG
2023	23	Round Rock (PCL)	AAA	.253	114	434	78	110	18	2	8	52	74	121	15	.368	.359
2023	23	Texas (AL)	MLB	.143	8	7	2	1	0	0	0	0	0	4	0	.250	.143
Minor League Totals				.272	492	1920	328	523	90	15	39	220	207	473	66	.350	.396
Major League Totals				.143	8	7	2	1	0	0	0	0	0	4	0	.250	.143

Nate Pearson

Toronto Blue Jays

BY GEOFF PONTES

Bad luck was abundant in Toronto in 2023 as the Blue Jays under-delivered on expectations.

The season was not a total loss. Toronto finished 89-73 and in third place in a competitive American League East, securing the final AL wild card on the penultimate day of the season.

In the Wild Card Series, the Blue Jays were swept by the Twins in two games as they were held to one total run.

On the bright side, the Blue Jays return most of their core in 2024. Gone are third baseman Matt Chapman and second baseman Whit Merrifield to free agency.

The 2023 Blue Jays were able to scratch out a playoff berth despite down seasons from Vladimir Guerrero Jr. and Bo Bichette. Kevin Gausman continued to pitch like an ace and finished third in Cy Young Award voting. George Springer stayed healthy for the entire season, playing in 154 games, his most since 2016.

On the downside, righthander Alek Manoah came undone and made just 19 starts. He spent long stints on the development list as he built himself back up in the minor leagues, going all the way down to the Florida Complex League for one start.

Prized trade acquisition Daulton Varsho underperformed by producing just a .674 OPS and spending most of his time in left field. The success of the two players traded for Varsho to the D-backs didn't help.

Catcher Gabriel Moreno played a pivotal role for Arizona on their World Series run and won the National League Gold Glove in his first full season. Veteran Lourdes Gurriel Jr. held down left field for the D-backs all season before reaching free agency.

It was a difficult season on the farm. Top prospect Ricky Tiedemann spent most of the year on the injured list with a left biceps strain. To add insult to injury, many of the players in the Blue Jays cachet of first- and second-round picks under-

PROJECTED 2027 LINEUP

Catcher	Alejandro Kirk	28
First Base	Vladimir Guerrero Jr.	28
Second Base	Orelvis Martinez	25
Third Base	Arjun Nimmala	21
Shortstop	Bo Bichette	29
Left Field	Alan Roden	27
Center Field	Daulton Varsho	30
Right Field	Addison Barger	27
Designated Hitter	Davis Schneider	28
No. 1 Starter	Kevin Gausman	36
No. 2 Starter	Ricky Tiedemann	24
No. 3 Starter	Jose Berrios	33
No. 4 Starter	Alek Manoah	29
No. 5 Starter	Brandon Barriera	23
Closer	Jordan Romano	34

performed or dealt with injuries.

First-round prep lefty Brandon Barriera spent the season on and off Low-A Dunedin's IL, while supplemental first-rounder Cade Doughty and supplemental second-rounder Tucker Toman woefully underperformed.

The minor leagues were not without bright spots however. Touted shortstop prospect Orelvis Martinez put 2022 in the rearview mirror as he showed a more refined approach throughout the season and reached Triple-A. Righthander Chad Dallas had a breakout season, while several of the Blue Jays' relief prospects took steps forward.

July's draft offered reprieve from the struggles of the 2022 class. The Blue Jays landed highly touted prep talents in first-round pick Arjun Nimmala and third-round pick Landen Maroudis. Both rank highly headed into 2024.

The Blue Jays need to continue to be active in free agency and trades as they look to find reinforcements for the final two years of club control they hold on Bichette and Guerrero.

In other words, it's make or break time in Toronto.

The Blue Jays find themselves at a crossroads. They must win with what they have or can acquire in trades or free agency—because they have little in the way of impact players coming up through the system. ∎

TORONTO BLUE JAYS

TOP 2024 CONTRIBUTORS	RANK
1. Ricky Tiedemann, LHP	1
2. Orelvis Martinez, SS/3B	2
3. Davis Schneider, 2B	8

BREAKOUT PROSPECTS	RANK
1. Enmanuel Bonilla, OF	11
2. Landon Maroudis, RHP	17
3. Sam Shaw, 2B	29

SOURCE OF TOP 30 TALENT

Homegrown	29	Acquired	1
College	11	Trade	1
Junior college	2	Rule 5 draft	0
High school	9	Independent league	0
Nondrafted free agent	0	Free agent/waivers	0
International	7		

LF
Alan Roden (9)
Gabriel Martinez
Will Robertson

CF
Enmanuel Bonilla (11)
Dasan Brown
Cam Eden

RF
Jace Bohrofen (19)
Sebastian Espino
Garret Spain

3B
Damiano Palmegiani (18)
Tucker Toman (29)
Alex De Jesus

SS
Orelvis Martinez (2)
Arjun Nimmala (3)
Addison Barger (5)
Leo Jimenez (7)
Josh Kasevich (15)
Nick Goodwin
Manuel Beltre

2B
Davis Schneider (8)
Sam Shaw (28)
Miguel Hiraldo

1B
Spencer Horwitz (21)
Rainer Nunez
Peyton Williams

C
Phil Clarke
Payton Henry
Zach Britton

LHP

LHSP	LHRP
Ricky Tiedemann (1)	Mason Fluharty (26)
Brandon Barriera (4)	Brendon Little
Kendry Rojas (6)	
Adam Macko (16)	
Jimmy Robbins	
Connor O'Halloran	

RHP

RHSP	RHRP
Landen Maroudis (13)	Connor Cooke (10)
Chad Dallas (14)	Yosver Zulueta (12)
Juaron Watts-Brown (17)	Hagen Danner (22)
Dahian Santos (20)	T.J. Brock (24)
Fernando Perez (23)	Hayden Juenger (27)
Nolan Perry (25)	
C.J. Van Eyk	
Trent Palmer	

1 RICKY TIEDEMANN, LHP

Born: August 18, 2002. **B-T:** L-L. **HT:** 6-4. **WT:** 220.
Drafted: Golden West (CA) JC, 2021 (3rd round).
Signed by: Joey Aversa.

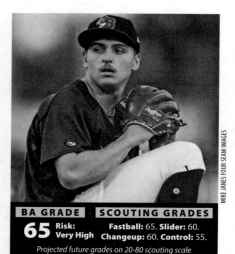

MIKE JANES FOUR SEAM IMAGES

BA GRADE	SCOUTING GRADES
65 Risk: Very High	Fastball: 65. Slider: 60. Changeup: 60. Control: 55.

Projected future grades on 20-80 scouting scale

TRACK RECORD: Teams likely regret passing on Tiedemann out of Lakewood (Calif.) High in the five-round 2020 draft. In pro ball, the lefthander has quickly developed one of the highest ceilings among pitching prospects. Tiedemann showed progress at Golden West (Calif.) JC in 2021, prompting the Blue Jays to draft him in the third round and sign him for a below-slot $644,800. He debuted with Low-A Dunedin in 2022, showing a jump in velocity and stuff across his arsenal. On the back of his elite stuff and strong performance, he climbed to Double-A that August. Tiedemann entered 2023 spring training with an opportunity to pitch his way to Toronto. He instead was shut down with left shoulder soreness and got a late start to his season. After four dominant but truncated Double-A starts, Tiedemann returned to the injured list with a left biceps sprain on May 5. He did not return to Double-A New Hampshire until Aug. 11. He made seven appearances there and one for Triple-A Buffalo before finishing with four starts in the Arizona Fall League, where he was league pitcher of the year. More critically, Tiedemann exceeded 70 pitches and five innings three times in the AFL, something he had not done since July 1, 2022.

SCOUTING REPORT: Tiedemann is a tall, strong-bodied lefthander with the build prototypical of workhorse starters. Despite his physical appearance, his health and durability have been major question marks. When healthy, Tiedemann has an outlier combination of velocity, movement and deception, delivering the ball from a low three-quarters slot. His fastball sits 94-97 mph and touches 98 mph. He generates below-average ride but heavy armside run that plays up due to his low slot and ability to hide the ball. While Tiedemann's best pitch historically has been his changeup, that pitch backed up in 2023 as concerns about the difference in release height and arm slot compared with his fastball became a larger issue. His changeup features heavy tumble and fade as he kills lift and generates a heavy dose of armside run. His slider became his primary secondary in 2023. It's a low-80s pitch with sweep and ride. Tiedemann shows an uncanny ability to manipulate his slider and land it in the zone. The pitch generated whiffs at a rate of 39%

BEST TOOLS

BATTING
Best Hitter for Average	Alan Roden
Best Power Hitter	Orelvis Martinez
Best Strike-Zone Discipline	Leo Jimenez
Fastest Baserunner	Cam Eden
Best Athlete	Dasan Brown

PITCHING
Best Fastball	Ricky Tiedemann
Best Curveball	Adam Macko
Best Slider	Connor Cooke
Best Changeup	Rafael Sanchez (splitter)
Best Control	Fernando Perez

FIELDING
Best Defensive Catcher	Phil Clarke
Best Defensive Infielder	Josh Kasevich
Best Infield Arm	Addison Barger
Best Defensive Outfielder	Cam Eden
Best Outfield Arm	Garrett Spain

in-zone in 2023 as well as a 49% rate of called-plus-swinging strikes. As the Blue Jays continue to refine Tiedemann's arsenal it should continue to improve, giving him three plus or better pitches, including one secondary pitch to neutralize hitters of either handedness. Tiedemann's command can come and go, but it's reasonable to think a large chunk of the season was impacted by injury.

THE FUTURE: No one questions that Tiedemann has the tools and attributes to develop into a No. 2 or 3 starter. It's only a matter of whether his body will cooperate. A strong season at Triple-A in 2024 will land him in Toronto. ∎

Year	Age	Club (League)	Level	W	L	ERA	G	GS	IP	H	HR	BB	SO	BB%	SO%	WHIP	AVG
2023	20	FCL Blue Jays	Rk	0	0	0.00	1	1	2	0	0	0	3	0.0	50.0	0.00	.000
2023	20	Dunedin (FSL)	A	0	0	0.00	2	2	6	1	0	1	15	5.0	75.0	0.33	.053
2023	20	New Hampshire (EL)	AA	0	5	5.06	11	11	32	28	1	20	58	13.7	39.7	1.50	.235
2023	20	Buffalo (IL)	AAA	0	0	0.00	1	1	4	2	0	2	6	14.3	42.9	1.00	.167
Minor League Totals				5	9	2.71	33	33	123	70	4	52	199	10.7	40.9	0.99	.165

2 ORELVIS MARTINEZ, SS/3B

HIT: 45. **POW:** 60. **RUN:** 45. **FLD:** 45. **ARM:** 60. **BA Grade:** 55. **Risk:** High.

Born: November 19, 2001. **B-T:** R-R. **HT:** 6-1. **WT:** 190.
Signed: Dominican Republic, 2018. **Signed by:** Alexis de la Cruz/Sandy Rosario.
TRACK RECORD: Martinez signed out of the Dominican Republic for $3.51 million in 2018. He skipped the Dominican Summer League and made his pro debut in the Rookie-level Gulf Coast League in 2019, hitting .275/.352/.549 in 40 games as a 17-year-old. Martinez moved quickly following the pandemic-lost 2020 season, seeing both levels of Class A in 2021 and spending all of 2022 at Double-A New Hampshire. After an uneven showing as a 20-year-old at Double-A, Martinez returned to the level in 2023. After a slow start, he hit .268/.390/.557 from May 1 through the end of the first half. He was promoted to Triple-A Buffalo on July 18 and spent the winter with Licey of the Dominican League.
SCOUTING REPORT: Martinez entered 2023 trending toward a power-over-everything hitter with major questions around his bat-to-ball skills and swing decisions. Instead, he showed a more refined and patient approach without sacrificing his aggressiveness. Martinez showed a willingness to make pitchers work and in turn saw better pitches in the zone. He made the most of those opportunities as his simple, powerful swing easily backspins his best contact to his pull side. Martinez has always had strong hands and the ability to get to plus power in games. His improvements in approach and contact have allowed him to project to get to his power against more advanced pitchers. Martinez is a fringe-average runner who will turn in an average run time on occasion. He's not rangy afield but shows the ability to play multiple infield positions. He has focused on shortstop and third base in pro ball, but his best long-term position is likely second base, where he has enough range and his plus arm would be an asset.
THE FUTURE: Martinez is a bat-first second baseman with the ability to hit 30-plus home runs at peak.

Year	Age	Club (League)	Level	AVG	G	AB	R	H	2B	3B	HR	RBI	BB	SO	SB	OBP	SLG
2023	21	New Hampshire (EL)	AA	.226	70	239	33	54	9	1	17	46	41	60	0	.339	.485
2023	21	Buffalo (IL)	AAA	.263	55	209	37	55	16	1	11	48	26	66	2	.340	.507
Minor League Totals				.239	381	1418	213	339	74	9	93	289	164	408	14	.326	.501

3 ARJUN NIMMALA, SS

HIT: 50. **POW:** 55. **RUN:** 50. **FLD:** 55. **ARM:** 55. **BA Grade:** 55. **Risk:** Extreme.

Born: October 16, 2005. **B-T:** R-R. **HT:** 6-1. **WT:** 170.
Drafted: HS—Dover, FL, 2023 (1st round). **Signed by:** Brandon Bishoff.
TRACK RECORD: Nimmala became the highest drafted first-generation Indian player when the Blue Jays selected him with the 20th overall pick in 2023. They signed him for $3 million, or about 80% of slot value for the pick. As a youth, Nimmala played primarily cricket before converting to the baseball diamond. During his senior season at Strawberry Crest High outside Tampa, Nimmala was selected Gatorade Player of the Year for the state of Florida and won the Wade Boggs Award as the best player in Hillsborough County. Nimmala made his pro debut in August in the Florida Complex League, playing in nine games and walking 14 times with eight strikeouts.
SCOUTING REPORT: Nimmala is a young, projectable infielder with plenty of tools to still develop. He has an average build that projects to add strength in the coming years. He shows at least average bat-to-ball skills with a simple righthanded swing that has a steeper path optimized for power. After often expanding the zone at a high rate as an amateur, Nimmala showed a more refined approach in his brief pro debut. He has natural loft in his swing that allows him to make his best contact in the air consistently. Nimmala possesses plus bat speed and his body should continue to get stronger in the coming years. He's an average runner, but his quick footwork allows him to cover ground at shortstop, where his hands and actions are above-average. His above-average arm strength should be the final ingredient that allows him to stick at shortstop.
THE FUTURE: Nimmala has plenty of tools and showed more refinement at the plate in his brief pro time. He projects as a power-hitting shortstop with above-average defensive ability who, if he develops, could hold down the position in Toronto for an extended spell.

Year	Age	Club (League)	Level	AVG	G	AB	R	H	2B	3B	HR	RBI	BB	SO	SB	OBP	SLG
2023	17	FCL Blue Jays	Rk	.200	9	25	7	5	1	1	0	3	14	8	1	.500	.320
Minor League Totals				.200	9	25	7	5	1	1	0	3	14	8	1	.500	.320

4 BRANDON BARRIERA, LHP

FB: 55. **CB:** 45. **SL:** 65. **CHG:** 45. **CTL:** 50 **BA Grade:** 55. **Risk:** Extreme.

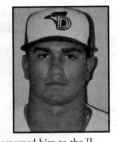

Born: March 4, 2004. **B-T:** L-L. **HT:** 6-2. **WT:** 180.
Drafted: HS—Plantation, FL, 2022 (1st round). **Signed by:** Adrian Casanova.
TRACK RECORD: Barriera went 5-0 with a 2.27 ERA in eight starts as a senior for American Heritage High in South Florida before deciding to sit out the remainder of the 2022 season to prepare for the draft. The Blue Jays selected him with the 23rd pick and signed him for just under $3.6 million. He made his pro debut in May 2023 after dealing with a shoulder issue in spring training. Barriera made four starts before heading to the injured list with an elbow sprain. He returned in mid July, then made three starts before biceps soreness returned him to the IL.
SCOUTING REPORT: Since his time as an amateur, Barriera has added mass at the expense of his athleticism. He returned looking noticeably larger than his listed 180 pounds. The added strength didn't translate to conditioning, and Barriera dealt with a trio of injuries. His fastball sits 92-94 mph with heavy cut, and he showed the ability to command his fastball at an average level to set up his slider. His slider is a plus bordering on double-plus sweeper that sits 82-84 mph with nearly a foot of horizontal break on average. He generated a high rates of swings-and-misses against the pitch and flashed the ability to dominate with the pitch in the zone. He showed a mid-to-high-80s changeup with parachuting drop. He threw his changeup just 14 times across all of his appearances. He also flashed a curveball with two-plane break in the upper 70s but it was thrown only a few times this season. His command of his slider and fastball are average, and that pair of pitches accounts for a majority of his usage.
THE FUTURE: Barriera is a risky prospect with a wide range of outcomes. He will need to improve his conditioning, add velocity and develop a third pitch to stay in the rotation. Otherwise he has the signature pitch to make it as a high-leverage reliever.

Year	Age	Club (League)	Level	W	L	ERA	G	GS	IP	H	HR	BB	SO	BB%	SO%	WHIP	AVG
2023	19	FCL Blue Jays	Rk	0	0	0.00	1	1	2	0	0	1	2	14.3	28.6	0.50	.000
2023	19	Dunedin (FSL)	A	0	2	4.42	6	6	18	10	0	8	23	11.0	31.5	0.98	.164
Minor League Totals				0	2	4.05	7	7	20	10	0	9	25	11.3	31.3	0.95	.149

5 ADDISON BARGER, 3B/SS

HIT: 50. **POW:** 55. **RUN:** 45. **FLD:** 45. **ARM:** 60. **BA Grade:** 50. **Risk:** High.

Born: November 12, 1999. **B-T:** L-R. **HT:** 6-0. **WT:** 175.
Drafted: HS—Tampa, 2018 (6th round). **Signed by:** Matt Bishoff.
TRACK RECORD: Drafted in 2018, Barger spent most of 2019 on the restricted list before emerging with added power from the 2020 pandemic shutdown. He had a strong season in 2021 with Low-A Dunedin before breaking out in 2022 by hitting .308/.378/.555 across three levels and reaching Triple-A. Barger returned to Buffalo in 2023 and struggled initially before an April 28 trip to the injured list with elbow pain. After an examination found no structural damage, Barger returned to Buffalo on June 21 and hit .254/.358/.424 over the final 68 games. He showed improved plate discipline upon his return via rates of 19% strikeouts and nearly 14% walks.
SCOUTING REPORT: After showing a more aggressive approach and more in-game power in 2021 and 2022, Barger showed more patience in 2023 and a toned-down launch angle. This in turn produced a more consistent bat path, and he showed improvements in contact, in-zone contact and swing decisions. Barger traded some fly balls for line drives and ground balls, but he closed some of the holes in his swing. While he hit for less power in 2023, his underlying exit velocity data improved across the board, with his average exit velocity jumping more than 3 mph and his 90th percentile EV increasing by 2 mph to 106 mph. Barger is a fringe-average runner and not a threat to steal bases. In the field, he is unlikely to stick at shortstop full time, and he saw time in right field and at third base and second base in 2023. He has a plus arm that could work at a variety of positions, but it's a matter of cleaning up some of his actions and footwork.
THE FUTURE: Barger is a versatile lefthanded hitter who has improved his hit tool while learning to play right field. He is a super-utility type with above-average hitting ability.

Year	Age	Club (League)	Level	AVG	G	AB	R	H	2B	3B	HR	RBI	BB	SO	SB	OBP	SLG
2023	23	FCL Blue Jays	Rk	.000	3	6	0	0	0	0	0	0	0	2	1	0	.250	.000
2023	23	Dunedin (FSL)	A	.273	3	11	3	3	0	0	0	1	3	3	0	.429	.273
2023	23	Buffalo (IL)	AAA	.250	88	340	53	85	25	0	9	46	52	86	5	.353	.403
Minor League Totals				.261	376	1401	231	366	92	6	58	246	171	401	21	.350	.460

6 KENDRY ROJAS, LHP

FB: 50. **SL:** 55. **CHG:** 45. **CTL:** 50. **BA Grade:** 55. **Risk:** Extreme.

Born: November 26, 2002. **B-T:** L-L. **HT:** 6-2. **WT:** 190.
Signed: Cuba, 2020. **Signed by:** Erick Ramirez/Luis Natera.
TRACK RECORD: Rojas signed for $215,000 out of Cuba in October 2020 and debuted the following summer in the Florida Complex League. He began 2022 at Low-A Dunedin making eight appearances before a lat injury put him on the injured list for a large chunk of the season. Rojas returned to Dunedin in 2023 and made 15 starts as part of 20 total appearances. He pitched 84 innings in total. Rojas ranked among the Florida State League leaders in several categories as he finished the season with a 3.75 ERA, a 23.4% strikeout rate and a 9.4% walk rate as a 20-year-old.

SCOUTING REPORT: Rojas has a whippy arm action with good arm speed and delivers the ball from a low three-quarters slot. He mixes a trio of pitches in his four-seam fastball, slider and changeup. Rojas' fastball sits 92-93 mph and touches 94-95 at peak with above-average ride and cut. He commands the pitch at a fringe-average level, with intermittent bouts of wildness. Rojas' primary secondary pitch is a mid-80s slider with some cut that he shows advanced feel to throw. It generated whiffs in and out of the zone in 2023. His changeup is a mid-to-high-80s pitch without heavy tumble or fade. Still, it was an effective chase pitch in 2023 and drove whiffs out of the zone. Rojas can frequently get out of sync mechanically, spinning off his plant foot at release. As he refines his mechanics, he should find greater consistency with his strike-throwing. Rojas has a projectable arsenal of pitches with command that should improve with time.

THE FUTURE: Rojas is a projectable lefthander who projects as a No. 4 starter. He is ready for an assignment to High-A Vancouver in 2024.

Year	Age	Club (League)	Level	W	L	ERA	G	GS	IP	H	HR	BB	SO	BB%	SO%	WHIP	AVG
2023	20	Dunedin (FSL)	A	4	6	3.75	20	15	84	71	8	33	82	9.4	23.4	1.24	.226
Minor League Totals				6	8	3.59	41	30	148	121	10	57	167	9.3	27.2	1.20	.220

7 LEO JIMENEZ, SS/2B

HIT: 55. **POW:** 40. **RUN:** 45. **FLD:** 55. **ARM:** 50. **BA Grade:** 45. **Risk:** High.

Born: May 17, 2001. **B-T:** R-R. **HT:** 6-0. **WT:** 195.
Signed: Panama, 2017. **Signed by:** Alex Zapata/Sandy Rosario.
TRACK RECORD: Jimenez was considered one of the top players to come out of Panama in the last decade when he signed for $825,000 in 2017. He endured two injury-shortened seasons in 2021 and 2022, missing time with shoulder and hand injuries. Jimenez began 2023 with Double-A New Hampshire, making 76 starts for the Fisher Cats primarily at shortstop and hitting .287/.372/.436 with a 15.9% strikeout rate. He earned a promotion to Triple-A Buffalo in late August.

SCOUTING REPORT: Jimenez does not wow with loud tools or flashy play, but he's an instinctual, disciplined ballplayer. He employs a simple swing with a direct path and average bat speed. He shows an ability to adjust his hands and make a high rate of contact. Jimenez rarely swings and misses in the strike zone and shows advanced swing decisions. He's patient but not passive, regularly attacking strikes. Jimenez shows sneaky power, but it's mostly in the form of line drives. He began to show the ability to pull the ball in the air without forcing it, hinting at untapped power. His underlying exit velocity data is above-average for his age, with a 88.5 mph average and a 90th percentile EV of 104.2. He's a fringe-average runner capable of clocking an average run time on a hustle play down the line. He's not a basestealing threat but has a quick first step and good infield instincts. He shows an average arm at shortstop, but his quick release and good internal clock allow him to make a majority of plays. Jimenez may end up at second base due to the limitations of his arm.

THE FUTURE: Jimenez is a solid all-around player who will likely break-in as a utilityman but should develop into a second-division regular over time.

Year	Age	Club (League)	Level	AVG	G	AB	R	H	2B	3B	HR	RBI	BB	SO	SB	OBP	SLG
2023	22	New Hampshire (EL)	AA	.287	76	289	54	83	15	2	8	44	32	53	8	.372	.436
2023	22	Buffalo (IL)	AAA	.190	18	63	8	12	3	0	0	3	9	15	0	.338	.238
Minor League Totals				.272	317	1130	195	307	63	9	15	149	159	223	22	.388	.383

8 DAVIS SCHNEIDER, 2B/OF

HIT: 50. **POW:** 55. **RUN:** 45. **FLD:** 30. **ARM:** 40. **BA Grade:** 40. **Risk:** Medium.

Born: January 26, 1999. **B-T:** R-R. **HT:** 5-10. **WT:** 190.
Drafted: HS—Voorhees, NJ, 2017 (28th round). **Signed by:** Mike Alberts.
TRACK RECORD: Signed in the 28th round for $50,000 in 2017, Schneider has been one of the best underdog stories in recent memory. The Blue Jays left him exposed to the Rule 5 draft after the 2021 and 2022 seasons despite above-average offensive performances in consecutive seasons. He began 2023 at Triple-A Buffalo, where he hit .275/.416/.553 with 21 home runs in 87 games. He earned a callup to Toronto on Aug. 4 and hit a home run off James Paxton in his first major league at-bat. Schneider hit .276/.404/.603 with eight home runs in 35 games. He made Toronto's postseason roster but did not appear in a game.
SCOUTING REPORT: Undersized and somewhat positionless, Schneider is a bat-first player with an advanced plate approach. His bat-to-ball skills are fringy due to a longer swing with a steeper bat path. His advanced approach at the plate and ability to discern balls from strikes limits his exposure to pitches outside the zone. Schneider struggles with offspeed pitches and curveballs but does damage against fastballs and different slider types. He has above-average power potential despite just average exit velocities due to his excellent launch angles that allow him to get the most out of his power. He showed the ability to get to his power consistently in his brief MLB debut. Schneider is a fringe-average runner who isn't much of a threat to steal a base. In the field, Schneider is a well below-average defender at second base with a below-average arm. He saw some time in left field, but Schneider's best long-term position is DH.
THE FUTURE: Schneider is an above-average hitter with a three-true-outcomes profile. He can carve out a role as a bat-driven second-division regular.

Year	Age	Club (League)	Level	AVG	G	AB	R	H	2B	3B	HR	RBI	BB	SO	SB	OBP	SLG
2023	24	Buffalo (IL)	AAA	.275	87	309	61	85	21	1	21	64	72	86	9	.416	.553
2023	24	Toronto (AL)	MLB	.276	35	116	23	32	12	1	8	20	21	43	1	.404	.603
Minor League Totals				.253	394	1332	230	337	86	8	59	218	245	404	33	.372	.462
Major League Totals				.276	35	116	23	32	12	1	8	20	21	43	1	.404	.603

9 ALAN RODEN, OF

HIT: 55. **POW:** 45. **RUN:** 50. **FLD:** 50. **ARM:** 55. **BA Grade:** 45 **Risk:** High.

Born: December 12, 1999. **B-T:** L-R. **HT:** 5-11. **WT:** 215.
Drafted: Creighton, 2022 (3rd round). **Signed by:** Wes Penick.
TRACK RECORD: Roden maintained freshman eligibility into his third season at Creighton after redshirting in 2019 and seeing just three games of action during the shortened 2020 season. He spurned draft interest following his 2021 freshman campaign in order to complete his physics degree. The Blue Jays drafted Roden in the third round in 2022 and signed him for an under-slot $497,500. Assigned to High-A Vancouver in 2023, he hit his way to Double-A New Hampshire on July 19 and batted .310/.421/.460 in 46 games at the higher level.
SCOUTING REPORT: Roden has always shown elite bat-to-ball skills and approach. He has a stockier build with broad shoulders but is a better athlete than he appears. Roden has an unusual setup and swing, as he sets up with his hands high above his head in a similar fashion to Angels first baseman Nolan Schanuel. This is an alteration from Roden's setup during college, when his bat rested on his shoulder in a deep crouch. Roden is now more upright and his front leg drift has been replaced by a more traditional leg kick. Despite the unusual setup and mechanics, Roden is able to control his barrel with high accuracy, rarely swinging and missing. He shows fringe-average game power, but it's not a matter of hard contact. It's a lack of lift in his bat path. Most of Roden's hardest-hit balls in play are line drives. He's an average runner underway, which allows him to play an average to perhaps a touch better defense in the corner outfield. Roden has an above-average arm that plays well in the corners.
THE FUTURE: Roden has a hit tool-driven profile with limited power upside due to his unusual swing and setup. He can be a solid second-division regular with the ability to play an outfield corner and provide high batting averages and on-base ability.

Year	Age	Club (League)	Level	AVG	G	AB	R	H	2B	3B	HR	RBI	BB	SO	SB	OBP	SLG
2023	23	Vancouver (NWL)	A+	.321	69	268	57	86	23	1	4	41	42	32	15	.437	.459
2023	23	New Hampshire (EL)	AA	.310	46	174	35	54	6	1	6	27	26	32	9	.421	.460
Minor League Totals				.303	140	532	109	161	33	2	11	77	85	77	29	.420	.434

10 CONNOR COOKE, RHP

FB: 60. **SL:** 55. **CHG:** 45. **CTL:** 45. **BA Grade:** 45. **Risk:** High.

Born: November 2, 1999. **B-T:** R-R. **HT:** 6-1. **WT:** 203.
Drafted: Louisiana-Lafayette, 2021 (10th round). **Signed by:** Chris Curtis.
TRACK RECORD: After coming out of the bullpen for two seasons at
Louisiana-Lafayette, Cooke made the jump to the rotation in his third season.
He went 7-3 with a 2.03 ERA with 90 strikeouts and 37 walks in 79.2 innings
as a starter in 2021, prompting the Blue Jays to draft him in the 10th round
and sign him for $141,900. After breaking camp with Low-A Dunedin in
2022, Cooke worked as a multi-innings piggyback starter. He was promoted
to High-A Vancouver on Aug. 2 and has been exclusively a reliever since. He broke camp with Vancouver
in 2023 and made nine appearances before he was promoted to Double-A New Hampshire. He spent a
majority of his season at Double-A before earning a late-August promotion to Buffalo.
SCOUTING REPORT: One of the best athletes in the Blue Jays organization, Cooke saw a giant leap in
stuff in 2023. He mixes three pitches, all of which can flash above-average. He has a unique ability to
ride a fastball, spin a breaking ball and turn over a changeup. Cooke's fastball sits 95-96 mph and touches
97-98 at peak, with ride, run and a difficult angle for hitters to get on plane. He spins his sweeper slider at
2,800-3,000 rpm with nearly a foot and a half of sweep on average. His slider sits 83-85 mph. He shows
average command of his fastball and slider and fringe-average command of his changeup. His offspeed is
infrequently used but shows heavy tumble and fade when he lands it. Overall, Cooke shows high-leverage
stuff and intensity.
THE FUTURE: Cooke is a high-powered reliever who has refined his arsenal with a potential high-leverage
relief future. His 40.6% strikeout rate ranked third among minor league relievers with at least 30 appearances in 2023 and he is in line to make his major league debut in 2024.

Year	Age	Club (League)	Level	W	L	ERA	G	GS	IP	H	HR	BB	SO	BB%	SO%	WHIP	AVG
2023	23	Vancouver (NWL)	A+	0	0	2.89	9	0	9	7	1	3	19	7.7	48.7	1.07	.194
2023	23	New Hampshire (EL)	AA	1	2	4.38	20	0	25	29	3	7	46	6.3	41.1	1.46	.282
2023	23	Buffalo (IL)	AAA	2	0	4.35	9	0	10	6	1	9	15	19.6	32.6	1.45	.182
Minor League Totals				6	9	4.58	68	8	106	99	11	37	163	8.1	35.6	1.28	.245

11 ENMANUEL BONILLA, OF

HIT: 50. **POW:** 55. **RUN:** 45. **FLD:** 50. **ARM:** 55. **BA Grade:** 50. **Risk:** Extreme.

Born: January 26, 2006. **B-T:** R-R. **HT:** 6-1. **WT:** 180. **Signed:** Dominican Republic, 2023. **Signed by:** Alexis De La Cruz.
TRACK RECORD: Bonilla garnered the largest bonus in franchise history for an international amateur
when he signed for $4.1 million. His was the fourth-highest bonus for any international signee in
2023. Highly regarded for his combination of hitting ability and present power, Bonilla debuted in the
Dominican Summer League and hit .307/.407/.429 in 50 games. Bonilla is likely to make his U.S. debut
in 2024 in the Florida Complex League.
SCOUTING REPORT: Bonilla was touted as one of the most advanced hitters in the 2023 international
class. He shows present strength and feel to hit with a good balance of aggression and patience. Bonilla is
still learning to hit spin and can be beaten by good breaking balls in the zone. He shows good adjustability
in his hands, but his lower half and upper halves can often get out of sync, leading to some inconsistent
swings. Bonilla has above-average raw power, and showed it in games with a max exit velocity of 108 mph.
His ability to hit the ball at good angles and elevate to his pull side portends well for future power gains.
Bonilla is an average runner, likely to slow down as he grows into his body. With potential for diminishing
speed, he is likely to move off center field to a corner, where he could grow into an average fielder. Bonilla's
arm is above-average and will play in all three outfield spots.
THE FUTURE: Bonilla is an exciting young outfielder with potential for an above-average hit and power
combination.

Year	Age	Club (League)	Level	AVG	G	AB	R	H	2B	3B	HR	RBI	BB	SO	SB	OBP	SLG
2023	17	DSL Blue Jays	Rk	.307	50	189	41	58	8	3	3	22	27	55	5	.407	.429
Minor League Totals				.307	50	189	41	58	8	3	3	22	27	55	5	.407	.429

12 YOSVER ZULUETA, RHP

FB: 55. **CB:** 50. **SL:** 65. **CHG:** 40. **CTL:** 40. **BA Grade:** 50. **Risk:** Extreme.

Born: January 23, 1998. **B-T:** R-R. **HT:** 6-1. **WT:** 190. **Signed:** Cuba, 2019. **Signed by:** Andrew Tinnish.

TRACK RECORD: Signed out of Cuba during the 2019 international signing period for $1 million, Zulueta had Tommy John surgery shortly after signing. Upon returning in 2021, Zulueta tore his anterior cruciate ligament in his right knee covering first base in his first game and missed the remainder of the season. Zulueta returned in 2022, moving up four levels and reaching Triple-A. He returned to Triple-A Buffalo for 2023 and made 45 appearances, primarily as a reliever.

SCOUTING REPORT: Zulueta is a true power pitcher who transitioned to a relief role full time in 2023. He mixes four pitches in a sinker, slider, curveball and changeup. Zulueta's sinker sits 95-96 mph and touches 100 with sink and heavy armside run. Despite the excellent velocity, Zulueta fails to miss many bats with the pitch, in large part due to his below-average command. His slider is plus and sits 83-85 mph with moderate sweep and slight depth. When he commands the pitch, it is rarely barreled and drives a high rate of chase swings. Against lefthanded hitters, Zulueta mixes in his low-80s curveball and a firm upper-80s changeup he rarely lands in the zone. He has premium stuff but his below-average command limits his overall profile. Zulueta showed hints of turning the corner over his final three months of 2023, posting a 2.88 ERA with 29 strikeouts to 12 walks over 25 innings with Buffalo to finish the season.

THE FUTURE: Zulueta is a ready-made relief option for the Blue Jays in 2024, with high-leverage upside if his command continues to improve.

Year	Age	Club (League)	Level	W	L	ERA	G	GS	IP	H	HR	BB	SO	BB%	SO%	WHIP	AVG
2023	25	Buffalo (IL)	AAA	4	4	4.08	45	7	64	53	1	45	73	15.7	25.4	1.53	.230
Minor League Totals				6	9	3.93	67	20	120	93	3	77	157	14.4	29.3	1.43	.215

13 LANDEN MAROUDIS, RHP

FB: 55. **CB:** 45. **SL:** 50. **CHG:** 60. **CTL:** 50. **BA Grade:** 50. **Risk:** Extreme.

Born: December 16, 2004. **B-T:** R-R. **HT:** 6-3. **WT:** 195. **Drafted:** HS—Clearwater, FL, 2023 (4th round). **Signed by:** Brandon Bishoff.

TRACK RECORD: Maroudis was a two-way standout for Florida high school powerhouse Cavalry Christian who started at shortstop on days he didn't pitch. He ranked as the 82nd overall prospect for the the 2023 draft and was viewed as one of the top high school talents in the state of Florida. The Blue Jays selected Maroudis in the fourth round and signed him for $1.5 million, their second-highest bonus in the class. He did not pitch following the draft.

SCOUTING REPORT: Maroudis is an athletic righthander with a tall, projectable build. He delivers the ball from a low three-quarters arm slot with some violence in his delivery at release, including a head whack and wicked recoil. Maroudis' stuff steadily grew over his time in high school. He mixes four pitches: a four-seam fastball, slider, curveball and changeup. His fastball sits 90-93 mph and touches 96 with above-average ride and good plane. Maroudis' primary secondary is a low-80s changeup with good velocity and vertical separation off his fastball. Maroudis mixes two breaking balls in a low-80s slider and a curveball in the mid 70s. The slider is a newer addition to his repertoire but has overtaken the curveball in effectiveness. Maroudis shows average command of his secondaries.

THE FUTURE: Maroudis is an exciting high school righthander with starter traits and the makings of an average or better three-pitch mix.

Year	Age	Club (League)	Level	W	L	ERA	G	GS	IP	H	HR	BB	SO	BB%	SO%	WHIP	AVG
2023	18	Did not play															

14 CHAD DALLAS, RHP

FB: 50. **CB:** 45. **SL:** 60. **CHG:** 30. **CUT:** 50 **CTL:** 50. **BA Grade:** 45. **Risk:** High.

Born: January 26, 2000. **B-T:** R-R. **HT:** 5-11. **WT:** 206. **Drafted:** Tennessee, 2021 (4th round). **Signed by:** Nate Murrie.

TRACK RECORD: Dallas spent his freshman season at Panola (Texas) JC, before transferring to Tennessee. He enjoyed success over two seasons with the Volunteers, striking out 143 batters and walking just 26 in 124.1 innings. Dallas was selected by the Blue Jays in the fourth round of the 2021 draft but didn't debut until the following spring. He spent all of his 2022 season at High-A Vancouver and returned there to begin 2023, but his improved physique and stuff saw him earn promotion to Double-A New Hampshire after five starts.

SCOUTING REPORT: Dallas mixes a four-seam fastball, slider, curveball, cutter and a changeup. His primary pitch is his mid-80s slider, which sees heavier usage than his fastball. Dallas' slider is a true sweeper that sits 84-85 mph with 13-14 inches of horizontal break, and he shows easy plus command of the pitch. His fastball sits 92-94 mph with average ride and cut. Dallas generates lots of bad contact against his fastball but does not generate many whiffs. He mixes a curveball at 81-82 mph with two-plane break and a cutter sitting 89-91 mph. Dallas' firm upper-80s changeup is thrown just a few times a game and isn't a major part of his repertoire. He shows average command of his pitch mix, with a knack for consistently landing his slider in the zone.

THE FUTURE: Dallas is an undersized starter with a shot at a back-of-the-rotation role.

Year	Age	Club (League)	Level	W	L	ERA	G	GS	IP	H	HR	BB	SO	BB%	SO%	WHIP	AVG
2023	23	Vancouver (NWL)	A+	2	0	2.03	5	5	27	13	1	12	37	11.8	36.3	0.94	.146
2023	23	New Hampshire (EL)	AA	7	3	4.10	18	18	97	85	15	37	107	8.9	25.8	1.26	.234
Minor League Totals				10	10	4.05	44	44	211	183	29	100	230	10.9	25.0	1.34	.229

15 JOSH KASEVICH, SS

HIT: 60. **POW:** 30. **RUN:** 45. **FLD:** 55. **ARM:** 45. **BA Grade:** 45. **Risk:** High.

Born: January 17, 2001. **B-T:** R-R. **HT:** 6-1. **WT:** 200. **Drafted:** Oregon, 2022 (2nd round). **Signed by:** Ryan Fox.

TRACK RECORD: Kasevich spent three seasons at Oregon earning all-Pacific-12 Conference honors as a junior. The Blue Jays drafted Kasevich in the second round in 2022. He debuted after the draft with Low-A Dunedin, hitting .262/.344/.336 across 25 games. Kasevich was assigned to High-A Vancouver out of spring training 2023 and stayed there all season.

SCOUTING REPORT: A highly skilled and polished player, Kasevich has made his bones on the strength of his plate skills. He is rarely fooled and his linear, contact-focused approach yields high rates of balls in play. He's adept at hitting velocity and spin but rarely with impact. Kasevich shows an advanced approach and keeps a tidy zone. He has the profile to hit for a high average against more advanced pitching but likely with very little impact. Kasevich's raw power is below-average with very little high-end power and flatter angles in his best contact. A fringe-average runner, Kasevich is a smart baserunner but not a major basestealing threat. He is a skilled infielder with strong hands, actions and instincts in the field. He saw a majority of his time at shortstop but likely lacks the range and arm strength to plate there everyday.

THE FUTURE: Kasevich fits as a utility infielder with quality bat-to-ball skills, approach and the ability to handle multiple positions.

Year	Age	Club (League)	Level	AVG	G	AB	R	H	2B	3B	HR	RBI	BB	SO	SB	OBP	SLG
2023	22	Vancouver (NWL)	A+	.284	94	334	46	95	15	0	4	50	38	41	11	.363	.365
Minor League Totals				.279	119	441	64	123	23	0	4	57	49	50	11	.358	.358

16 ADAM MACKO, LHP

FB: 55. **CB:** 50. **SL:** 50. **CHG:** 40. **CUT:** 30. **CTL:** 55. **BA Grade:** 45. **Risk:** High.

Born: December 30, 2000. **B-T:** L-L. **HT:** 6-0. **WT:** 170. **Drafted:** HS—Vauxhall, AB, 2019 (7th round). **Signed by:** Les McTavish/Alex Ross (Mariners).

TRACK RECORD: A native of Slovakia, Macko was introduced to baseball in grade school and learned to pitch by watching YouTube videos of MLB pitchers. His family moved to Ireland and then Canada, where Macko entered more formal baseball training and blossomed into a legitimate draft prospect. The Mariners drafted Macko in the seventh round in 2019. Macko was traded to the Blue Jays for Teoscar Hernandez after the 2022 season. He spent all of 2023 in his native Canada, making 20 starts for High-A Vancouver. Macko was added to the 40-man roster following the season.

SCOUTING REPORT: Macko is an undersized lefthander with a deep repertoire of pitches. He mixes five different pitches in his four-seam fastball, slider, curveball, changeup and cutter. Macko's fastball sits 93-95 mph with heavy ride and run, and the pitch is commanded well to both sides of the plate. He mixes two different breaking balls in a slider sitting 82-84 mph with moderate sweep and an upper-70s curveball with a big two-plane break. Macko's mid-80s changeup has good shape and is effective when he lands it, but he struggles to get in the strike zone. Macko's cutter sits 87-88 mph and was used sparingly. Overall, Macko shows above-average command of his three primary pitches.

THE FUTURE: Macko has multiple average or better pitches and improving command of his arsenal, giving him a chance as a back-of-the-rotation starter.

Year	Age	Club (League)	Level	W	L	ERA	G	GS	IP	H	HR	BB	SO	BB%	SO%	WHIP	AVG
2023	22	Vancouver (NWL)	A+	5	5	4.81	20	20	86	76	7	40	106	10.8	28.5	1.35	.239
Minor League Totals				7	12	4.38	46	39	181	157	13	93	254	11.7	31.9	1.38	.229

17 JUARON WATTS-BROWN, RHP

FB: 50. **CB:** 45. **SL:** 55. **CHG:** 30. **CTL:** 45. **BA Grade:** 45. **Risk:** High.

Born: February 23, 2002. **B-T:** R-R. **HT:** 6-3. **WT:** 190. **Drafted:** Oklahoma State, 2023 (3rd round).
Signed by: Max Semler.

TRACK RECORD: A shoulder injury sustained while playing high school football forced Watts-Brown to redshirt at Long Beach State in 2021. He returned fully healthy in 2022 and broke out, earning second-team Freshman All-America honors. Watts-Brown transferred to Oklahoma State for 2023. Over 15 starts with the Cowboys, he struggled with his command, walking 48 batters in 84.1 innings and finishing the season with a 5.03 ERA. Despite his poor performance, teams still liked his projectable frame and pitch mix. The Blue Jays drafted Watts-Brown in the third round and signed him for an above-slot bonus of $1 million.

SCOUTING REPORT: Watts-Brown has a prototypical tall pitcher's frame, with a smooth rhythmic operation on the mound and a high three-quarters slot. He mixes four pitches in his four-seam fastball, slider, curveball and an infrequently used changeup. Watts-Brown's fastball sits 90-93 mph with above-average ride and run, but the pitch lacks velocity and deception and rarely misses bats. His slider is the crown jewel of his arsenal. It's a mid-80s gyro slider with late bite, and it's equally effective against righthanded and lefthanded hitters. Watts-Brown mixes a curveball as his third pitch. It sits 80-82 mph with depth. He rarely throws his changeup, a mid-80s offspeed pitch he pockets in most starts. Watts-Brown has below-average command at present but could evolve to fringe-average with time and pro instruction.

THE FUTURE: A projectable righthander with command concerns, Watts-Brown could develop into a back-of-the-rotation starter.

Year	Age	Club (League)	Level	W	L	ERA	G	GS	IP	H	HR	BB	SO	BB%	SO%	WHIP	AVG
2023	21	Did not play															

18 DAHIAN SANTOS, RHP

FB: 50. **SL:** 60. **CHG:** 50. **CTL:** 40. **BA Grade:** 50. **Risk:** Extreme.

Born: February 26, 2003. **B-T:** R-R. **HT:** 5-11. **WT:** 160. **Signed:** Venezuela, 2019.
Signed by: Francisco Plasencia/Jose Contreras.

TRACK RECORD: Santos signed for $150,000 in 2019 and has impressed over the course of his young professional career. After a standout season at Low-A Dunedin in 2022, Santos saw a late-season promotion to High-A Vancouver. He returned to Vancouver to begin 2023 and pitched well over a dozen starts before he was shut down with an elbow strain. While with Vancouver, Santos struck out 27.2% of batters while holding opposing hitters to a .173 average.

SCOUTING REPORT: Santos is an undersized righthander with a low arm slot and a three-pitch mix. He mixes a low-90s two-seam fastball with heavy armside run that generates weak contact. Santos' most-used secondary—and best pitch—is his sweeper slider in the low 80s with 16 to 18 inches of horizontal break. He generates high rates of swings-and-misses in and out of the zone with his slider. It is an effective chase pitch. Santos' mid-80s changeup shows nearly reverse movement of his sweeper, running heavily off the plate with tumble. While Santos has three pitches with good shape and average or better projection, his lack of command and strike-throwing limit his upside and potential role.

THE FUTURE: Santos has the tools to start, but his undersized frame and lack of command will likely push him to a relief role long term.

Year	Age	Club (League)	Level	W	L	ERA	G	GS	IP	H	HR	BB	SO	BB%	SO%	WHIP	AVG
2023	20	Vancouver (NWL)	A+	3	3	3.54	12	12	48	30	5	27	56	13.1	27.2	1.18	.173
Minor League Totals				8	14	4.50	47	39	175	132	22	87	256	11.6	34.1	1.26	.207

19 DAMIANO PALMEGIANI, 3B

HIT: 45. **POW:** 55. **RUN:** 40. **FLD:** 40. **ARM:** 45. **BA Grade:** 45. **Risk:** High.

Born: January 26, 2000. **B-T:** R-R. **HT:** 6-1. **WT:** 195. **Drafted:** Southern Nevada JC, 2021 (14th round).
Signed by: Joey Aversa.

TRACK RECORD: Born in Venezuela, Palmegiani immigrated to British Columbia as a youth and grew up in Canada rooting for the Blue Jays. He was twice drafted by Toronto, first out of high school in the 35th round in 2018 and again in the 14th round in 2021. He got an opportunity to represent Canada in the 2023 World Baseball Classic and carried that momentum into the minor league season. Palmegiani has quickly ascended through the Blue Jays system, reaching Triple-A Buffalo by the end of 2023. Following the season he participated in the Arizona Fall League.

SCOUTING REPORT: Palmegiani is a bat-driven infielder with a balance of skills. He's a fringe-average contact hitter, adept at doing damage to pitches located middle-in. His stiff swing path lacks adjustability, and he can be beaten by good spin. Where Palmegiani excels is his approach. He rarely expands the zone and shows a good, balanced approach. His raw power is above-average and he gets to it in games. He shows the ability to backspin balls to his pull side with consistency. Palmegiani is a below-average runner and not a basestealing threat.vHe's below-average at third base and shows particular difficulty going back on shallow fly balls. His arm is average but lacks accuracy. Palmegiani might move to first base.
THE FUTURE: Palmegiani is the type of bat-first prospect the Blue Jays have had success with. He has a second-division regular upside.

Year	Age	Club (League)	Level	AVG	G	AB	R	H	2B	3B	HR	RBI	BB	SO	SB	OBP	SLG
2023	23	New Hampshire (EL)	AA	.249	108	393	57	98	25	1	19	71	58	125	6	.351	.463
2023	23	Buffalo (IL)	AAA	.284	20	74	13	21	8	0	4	22	15	28	1	.427	.554
Minor League Totals				.251	263	929	155	233	60	2	49	185	134	269	13	.358	.478

20 JACE BOHROFEN, OF

HIT: 40. **POW:** 55. **RUN:** 40. **FLD:** 45. **ARM:** 50. **BA Grade:** 45. **Risk:** High.

Born: October 19, 2001. **B-T:** L-R. **HT:** 6-2. **WT:** 205. **Drafted:** Arkansas, 2023 (6th round). **Signed by:** Max Semler.
TRACK RECORD: A highly touted prep player out of the state of Oklahoma, Bohrofen ranked 141st in the 2020 draft class. He honored his commitment to Oklahoma, lasting one season with the Sooners before transferring to Arkansas. He spent two seasons with the Razorbacks. After a down year in 2022, Bohrofen roared back in 2023 by hitting .318/.436/.612 with 16 home runs. The Blue Jays drafted him in the sixth round and signed him to a near-slot bonus of $302,000. In his pro debut, Bohrofen played in 17 games with Low-A Dunedin hitting .307/.442/.677 with six home runs.
SCOUTING REPORT: A powerful lefthanded hitter with a smooth swing, Bohrofen is a power-over-hit prospect with solid on-base skills. He is an excellent fastball hitter and does most of his damage there. He struggles against good spin, but his strong swing decisions limit some of his exposure. Bohrofen has strong on-base skills to go along with above-average game power. He makes consistent hard contact at positive angles and shows the ability to drive the ball to his pull side. Bohrofen is a fringe-average runner now who likely slows down. He has enough range to handle an outfield corner with an average throwing arm.
THE FUTURE: Bohrofen fits the profile of the modern slugger. How much contact he makes as he moves up will dictate whether or not he reaches everyday regular status.

Year	Age	Club (League)	Level	AVG	G	AB	R	H	2B	3B	HR	RBI	BB	SO	SB	OBP	SLG
2023	21	FCL Blue Jays	Rk	.267	7	15	3	4	0	0	1	2	4	6	1	.450	.467
2023	21	Dunedin (FSL)	A	.306	17	62	17	19	5	0	6	16	15	18	0	.442	.677
Minor League Totals				.299	24	77	20	23	5	0	7	18	19	24	1	.443	.636

21 SPENCER HORWITZ, 1B

HIT: 55. **POW:** 45. **RUN:** 40. **FLD:** 40. **ARM:** 50. **BA Grade:** 40. **Risk:** Medium.

Born: November 14, 1997. **B-T:** L-R. **HT:** 6-0. **WT:** 190. **Drafted:** Radford, 2019 (24th round).
Signed by: Coulson Barbiche.
TRACK RECORD: Horwitz has been one of the Blue Jays' most productive minor leaguers over the last three seasons. After hitting .290/.390/.453 in 2022 across Double-A and Triple-A, Horwitz was added to Toronto's 40-man roster. He returned to Triple-A Buffalo to begin 2023 and earned his first big league callup on June 16. He played in three games before being optioned back to Buffalo. Horwitz returned to Toronto in early September and appeared in 12 games. Horwitz, the grandson of Mets media relations director Jay Horwitz, was a member of Team Israel in the 2023 World Baseball Classic.
SCOUTING REPORT: Horwitz is a classic bat-first prospect, with major league-caliber hitting skills but a lack of defensive value. He is an above-average contact hitter with advanced approach and on-base skills. He has good adjustability in his barrel and hits a variety of pitch types. Horwitz possesses average raw power, but his lack of elevation on contact limits his home run production. Horwitz is a 30-grade runner who is station-to-station on the bases. He's below-average at first base and has an average arm.
THE FUTURE: Horwitz is a ready-made bench bat with a chance to be a second-division regular.

Year	Age	Club (League)	Level	AVG	G	AB	R	H	2B	3B	HR	RBI	BB	SO	SB	OBP	SLG
2023	25	Buffalo (IL)	AAA	.337	107	392	61	132	30	1	10	72	78	72	9	.450	.495
2023	25	Toronto (AL)	MLB	.256	15	39	5	10	2	0	1	7	4	12	0	.341	.385
Minor League Totals				.302	390	1448	243	438	112	4	38	241	245	265	25	.407	.464
Major League Totals				.256	15	39	5	10	2	0	1	7	4	12	0	.341	.385

22 HAGEN DANNER, RHP

FB: 55. **CB:** 40. **SL:** 60. **CTL:** 50. **BA Grade:** 40. **Risk:** Medium.

Born: September 30, 1999. **B-T:** R-R. **HT:** 6-2. **WT:** 210. **Drafted:** HS—Huntington Beach, CA, 2017 (2nd round).
Signed by: Joey Aversa.

TRACK RECORD: A standout two-way player in high school, Danner was drafted and developed as catcher over his first few professional seasons. He committed to pitching prior to the 2020 pandemic and has climbed the rungs of the Blue Jays system in the three years since. Danner spent a majority of 2023 with Triple-A Buffalo before earning his first big league callup. Danner pitched one inning for the Blue Jays before injuring his oblique and spending the final six weeks on the injured list. He has a long history of injuries and missed time.

SCOUTING REPORT: Danner is a flame-throwing reliever with major question marks about his durability. He mixes a trio of pitches in his four-seam fastball, slider and curveball. Danner's fastball sits 96-97 mph and touches 98-99 with good ride and armside run. It's not a bat-misser, but sets up his slider well. Danner's slider is his primary secondary. It sits 87-88 mph with heavy cut. The slider is Danner's best pitch and it misses bats in and out of the strike zone. He throws an upper-70s curveball with heavy two-plane break but struggles to land it. Danner's command is average overall, and he throws strikes with his fastball and slider.

THE FUTURE: Danner is a one-inning reliever with the stuff to cut it as a high-leverage arm.

Year	Age	Club (League)	Level	W	L	ERA	G	GS	IP	H	HR	BB	SO	BB%	SO%	WHIP	AVG
2023	24	Dunedin (FSL)	A	0	0	4.50	2	0	2	1	0	2	5	22.2	55.6	1.50	.143
2023	24	New Hampshire (EL)	AA	1	1	3.00	8	0	9	9	0	2	16	5.4	43.2	1.22	.257
2023	24	Buffalo (IL)	AAA	0	1	3.81	23	1	28	20	8	7	35	6.3	31.5	0.95	.192
2023	24	Toronto (AL)	MLB	0	0	0.00	1	0	0	0	0	0	0	0.0	0.0	0.00	.000
Minor League Totals				3	3	2.97	62	1	79	56	10	26	99	8.2	31.0	1.04	.193
Major League Totals				0	0	0.00	1	0	0	0	0	0	0	0.0	0.0	0.00	.000

23 FERNANDO PEREZ, RHP

FB: 50. **SL:** 50. **CHG:** 45. **CTL:** 55. **BA Grade:** 45. **Risk:** Extreme.

Born: February 12, 2004. **B-T:** R-R. **HT:** 6-3. **WT:** 170. **Signed:** Nicaragua, 2022. **Signed by:** Daniel Sotelo.

TRACK RECORD: Perez signed in January 2022 as an under-the-radar target. He grew up in a remote area of Nicaragua and was not considered a notable signing. Perez debuted in the Dominican Summer League in 2022, making 12 starts and showcasing advanced command. He made 10 starts in the Florida Complex League in 2023 and impressed over 49.2 innings. The most memorable moment of Perez's season came on Aug. 7 when he tossed seven no-hit innings to combine with two relievers to complete a no-hitter.

SCOUTING REPORT: A tall, projectable righthander, Perez has made his name early on the quality of his command. He mixes three pitches in his four-seam fastball, slider and changeup. Perez's fastball sits 92-93 mph and touches 94 at peak with ride and run. He shows good command for the pitch and consistently lands it in the zone. His most frequently thrown secondary is a low-80s gyro slider with some cut. He shows tremendous feel for the pitch. Perez's changeup sits 82-83 mph with nice tumble and fade, and he commands it. His control and command are above-average and he projects to remain a starter long term.

THE FUTURE: Perez is a talented strike-thrower with a projectable mix and body who should grow into a back-end starter.

Year	Age	Club (League)	Level	W	L	ERA	G	GS	IP	H	HR	BB	SO	BB%	SO%	WHIP	AVG
2023	19	FCL Blue Jays	Rk	2	2	2.72	11	10	50	35	1	12	57	6.2	29.2	0.95	.198
Minor League Totals				3	6	3.58	23	22	93	85	5	17	105	4.4	27.1	1.10	.236

24 T.J. BROCK, RHP

FB: 55. **SL:** 60. **CTL:** 45. **BA Grade:** 40. **Risk:** High.

Born: August 10, 1999. **B-T:** R-R. **HT:** 6-1. **WT:** 200. **Drafted:** Ohio State, 2022 (6th round). **Signed by:** Tom Burns.

TRACK RECORD: Brock spent four years in Ohio State's bullpen, impressing in consecutive summers in the Cape Cod League. The Blue Jays drafted Brock in the sixth round in 2022 and signed him for a below-slot bonus of $72,500. He debuted with Low-A Dunedin and earned a promotion to High-A Vancouver after one appearance. Brock returned to Vancouver to begin 2023. He earned promotion to Double-A New Hampshire in late May and made 32 appearances for the Fisher Cats.

SCOUTING REPORT: Brock is a high-powered reliever with a bulldog attitude on the mound. He mixes two pitches primarily in his four-seam fastball and slider. Brock's fastball sits 95-97 mph and will touch 100. The pitch features pedestrian movement and release traits and doesn't miss many bats. Brock's slider is his primary pitch and it drives excellent results, with high whiff rates in and out of the zone and poor-quality contact against. Brock's slider sits 88-90 mph with tight gyro shape, and he shows the ability to command it. Brock shows fringe-average command of his powerful two-pitch mix.

THE FUTURE: Brock is a two-pitch reliever with power stuff and the ability to move quickly.

Year	Age	Club (League)	Level	W	L	ERA	G	GS	IP	H	HR	BB	SO	BB%	SO%	WHIP	AVG
2023	23	Vancouver (NWL)	A+	4	0	1.77	15	0	20	8	1	9	31	11.4	39.2	0.84	.119
2023	23	New Hampshire (EL)	AA	2	1	6.68	32	0	32	38	7	14	56	9.1	36.4	1.61	.281
Minor League Totals				7	1	4.85	57	0	65	59	9	29	109	10.0	37.7	1.35	.236

25 NOLAN PERRY, RHP

FB: 50. **CB:** 45. **SL:** 50. **CHG:** 30. **CTL:** 45. **BA Grade:** 45. **Risk:** Extreme.

Born: September 2, 2003. **B-T:** R-R. **HT:** 6-2. **WT:** 195. **Drafted:** HS—Carlsbad, NM, 2022 (12th round).
Signed by: Adam Arnold.

TRACK RECORD: As a senior at Carlsbad High in New Mexico, Perry won a state title as a two-way standout serving the role of ace pitcher and starting shortstop. Ranked as the top player in the state, he slipped under the draft radar and the Blue Jays selected him in the 12th round in 2022. They signed him for $200,000. Perry debuted in the Florida Complex League in 2023.

SCOUTING REPORT: Perry is a projectable young righthander with a feel for spin. He mixes four pitches: a four-seam fastball, slider, curveball and changeup. His four-seam fastball sits 92-93 mph and touches 95 with heavy bore. Perry's slider is his most-used secondary. It sits 81-83 mph with cut. He uses his curveball at a similar rate to his slider, Perry's curveball sits 79-81 mph with two-plane break and heavier sweep than his slider. Perry is still developing feel for his changeup, and it was infrequently thrown in 2023. Perry shows fringe-average command of his secondaries.

THE FUTURE: Perry is a young projectable pitcher with starter traits and an opportunity to develop into a back-of-the-rotation starter.

Year	Age	Club (League)	Level	W	L	ERA	G	GS	IP	H	HR	BB	SO	BB%	SO%	WHIP	AVG
2023	19	FCL Blue Jays	Rk	2	3	7.28	9	4	38	46	4	16	51	8.9	28.3	1.62	.286
Minor League Totals				2	3	7.34	9	4	38	46	4	16	51	8.9	28.3	1.63	.286

26 MASON FLUHARTY, LHP

FB: 30. **SL:** 60. **CUT:** 50. **CTL:** 55. **BA Grade:** 40. **Risk:** High.

Born: August 13, 2001. **B-T:** R-L. **HT:** 6-2. **WT:** 215. **Drafted:** Liberty, 2022 (5th round). **Signed by:** Coulson Barbiche

TRACK RECORD: Fluharty spent three seasons in Liberty's bullpen, steadily improving with each season. He made the third most appearances in the Atlantic Sun Conference in 2022 and was drafted by the Blue Jays in the fifth round that year. Fluharty debuted with High-A Vancouver post-draft and made 10 appearances. He returned to Vancouver to begin 2023 and earned a promotion to Double-A New Hampshire on May 23. Fluharty make 36 appearances for the Fisher Cats, recording four saves.

SCOUTING REPORT: Fluharty did not start a game in college and is locked into a relief role in pro ball. He mixes three pitches. Fluharty's primary pitch is a nasty mid-80s sweeper with ride and on average a foot of sweep. He shows excellent command of the pitch and drives a high rate of swings-and-misses. Fluharty's second pitch is a cutter at 89-91 mph that functions like a fastball. With good command of the pitch, he misses bats in and out of the zone. He throws a four-seam fastball that sits 90-92 mph, but it's a clear third pitch. Fluharty is a funky relief prospect with good command of his arsenal.

THE FUTURE: Fluharty is a slider-first reliever who could handle middle-inning relief or situational usage.

Year	Age	Club (League)	Level	W	L	ERA	G	GS	IP	H	HR	BB	SO	BB%	SO%	WHIP	AVG
2023	21	Vancouver (NWL)	A+	1	0	0.59	12	0	15	7	1	5	21	8.6	36.2	0.78	.132
2023	21	New Hampshire (EL)	AA	2	5	4.25	36	0	42	49	6	18	54	9.3	28.0	1.58	.290
Minor League Totals				4	6	3.33	58	0	73	71	9	30	96	9.5	30.4	1.38	.255

27 HAYDEN JUENGER, RHP

FB: 55. **SL:** 45. **CHG:** 55. **CTL:** 40. **BA Grade:** 40. **Risk:** High.

Born: August 9, 2000. **B-T:** R-R. **HT:** 610. **WT:** 180. **Drafted:** Missouri State, 2021 (6th round). **Signed by:** Matt Huck.

TRACK RECORD: The Blue Jays drafted Juenger in the sixth round in 2021 out of Missouri State. He pitched mostly relief in college, but Toronto pushed him to Double-A New Hampshire to open 2022 and he worked primarily as a starter. After a late-season promotion to Triple-A Buffalo, Juenger returned to Triple-A to begin 2023. He spent the entire season with the Bisons working as a reliever.

SCOUTING REPORT: An undersized righthander whose arsenal plays up due to his unique release traits, Juenger mixes three pitches in a four-seam fastball, slider and changeup. His fastball sits 93-94 mph and touches 95-96, with an outlier approach angle. Juenger's most-thrown secondary is a changeup that he throws to both lefthanded and righthanded hitters, but it is nearly one-to-one with his fastball versus lefties. Juenger's changeup sits 83-85 mph with heavy fade. His slider is his primary secondary against righties and has undergone shape changes in the last year. It's now an upper-80s cutter-like slider. Juenger's command is below-average. He often leaves his fastball and slider in parts of the strike zone that result in trouble.

THE FUTURE: Juenger is a potential low-leverage reliever capable of going multiple innings, with a chance to debut in 2024.

Year	Age	Club (League)	Level	W	L	ERA	G	GS	IP	H	HR	BB	SO	BB%	SO%	WHIP	AVG
2023	22	Buffalo (IL)	AAA	5	2	6.33	54	5	75	86	11	39	92	11.2	26.4	1.66	.285
Minor League Totals				10	9	4.70	103	24	184	160	29	80	226	10.2	28.9	1.30	.231

28 SAM SHAW, 2B

HIT: 55. **POW:** 30. **RUN:** 50. **FLD:** 50. **ARM:** 45. **BA Grade:** 45. **Risk:** Extreme.

Born: February 26, 2005. **B-T:** L-R. **HT:** 5-10. **WT:** 180. **Drafted:** HS—Victoria, BC, 2023 (12 round).
Signed by: Pat Griffin.

TRACK RECORD: Shaw was a draft find for the Blue Jays in their own backyard. He was a well-known Canadian amateur who attended high school in the United States before moving back to Canada. The Blue Jays drafted Shaw in the 12th round in 2023, signing him for an above-slot bonus of $282,500. He debuted in the Florida Complex League playing in nine games.

SCOUTING REPORT: Shaw is a hit-over-everything second baseman with an advanced knowledge of the strike zone and excellent barrel control. His carrying tool is hitting, with a swing designed for a high rate of line drives and balls to the gaps. He is rarely fooled and shows the ability to spit on breaking stuff on the black. Shaw should hit for high averages while running near equal strikeout and walk totals. His power is below-average and his best-struck balls come in the form of line drives. Due to his build, he's unlikely to push below-average power totals. He's an average runner whose stride is limited by his diminutive frame. He shows average fielding skills at second base and a fringe-average arm.

THE FUTURE: Shaw is a young, bat-first second baseman with outlier contact and approach for his age and experience.

Year	Age	Club (League)	Level	AVG	G	AB	R	H	2B	3B	HR	RBI	BB	SO	SB	OBP	SLG
2023	18	FCL Blue Jays	Rk	.207	9	29	4	6	2	0	0	0	10	6	0	.425	.276
Minor League Totals				.207	9	29	4	6	2	0	0	0	10	6	0	.425	.276

29 TUCKER TOMAN, 3B

HIT: 30. **POW:** 45. **RUN:** 45. **FLD:** 50. **ARM:** 55. **BA Grade:** 45. **Risk:** Extreme.

Born: November 12, 2003. **B-T:** B-R. **HT:** 6-1. **WT:** 190. **Drafted:** HS—Columbia, SC (2nd round supplemental).
Signed by: Mike Tidick.

TRACK RECORD: Toman was a celebrated South Carolina prep hitter from a well-known baseball family when the Blue Jays drafted him in the supplemental second round in 2022. He signed for an above-slot $2 million and debuted following the draft in the Florida Complex League. Toman spent his first full professional season with Low-A Dunedin, hitting .208/.320/.313 with five home runs in 114 games.

SCOUTING REPORT: Toman was once viewed as an advanced switch-hitter with developing power, but his hit tool has taken a sizable step backward as a professional. His lefthanded swing has long been ahead of his righthanded swing. Toman struggled throughout the season with all pitch types but was particularly exposed by breaking balls. He did show an average approach at the plate, doing a solid job of discerning balls from strikes. Toman's raw power showed as just fringe-average and his lack of barrel control limited impact on his best-struck drives. Toman is currently an average runner who should slow down. He played predominantly third base in 2023, seeing some time at shortstop as well. Toman is an average defender at third with an above-average arm.

THE FUTURE: Toman will need to recapture his hitting ability from his amateur days in order to fulfill his second-division regular ceiling.

Year	Age	Club (League)	Level	AVG	G	AB	R	H	2B	3B	HR	RBI	BB	SO	SB	OBP	SLG
2023	19	Dunedin (FSL)	A	.208	114	428	59	89	24	3	5	51	63	135	7	.320	.313
Minor League Totals				.215	125	466	63	100	27	3	5	56	70	147	7	.326	.318

30 CADE DOUGHTY, 2B

HIT: 40. **POW:** 30. **RUN:** 45. **FLD:** 40. **ARM:** 50. **BA Grade:** 40. **Risk:** High.

Born: March 26, 2001. **B-T:** R-R. **HT:** 6-1. **WT:** 195. **Drafted:** Louisiana State, 2022 (2nd round supplemental).
Signed by: Chris Curtis.

TRACK RECORD: Louisiana State baseball is a family tradition for the Doughtys. Cade followed his father Richard and brother Braden to LSU after he spurned draft interest in 2019 and honored his commitment. Over his decorated college career, Cade was a three-year starter and hit .301 with 30 home runs and a .921 OPS. The Blue Jays drafted him in the supplemental second round in 2022 and assigned him to Low-A Dunedin out of the draft. Doughty spent all of 2023 with High-A Vancouver, hitting .264/.342/.459 with 18 home runs.

SCOUTING REPORT: A polished college player, Doughty was lauded for his balance of hitting, power and approach as an amateur, but that bottomed out in 2023. While Doughty's surface-level stats are solid, his underlying data showcases how poor his plate skills were in 2023. He swung and missed at a high rate in and out of the zone and showed a fringy approach. Doughty gets the most out of his power due to good angles at contact, but his raw power is well below-average. Doughty spent 2023 alternating between second base and third base. A fringe-average runner, he has limited range and an average arm.

THE FUTURE: Doughty will look to recapture his bat-to-ball skills but is trending toward an up-and down replacement role.

Year	Age	Club (League)	Level	AVG	G	AB	R	H	2B	3B	HR	RBI	BB	SO	SB	OBP	SLG
2023	22	Vancouver (NWL)	A+	.264	102	375	61	99	19	0	18	68	35	126	4	.342	.459
Minor League Totals				.266	128	478	82	127	24	0	24	92	45	155	7	.348	.467

Washington Nationals

BY SAVANNAH McCANN

A farm system overhaul is underway in Washington.

Buoyed by the selection of Dylan Crews second overall in the 2023 draft, the Nationals added more elite talent during the year. Crews immediately slotted in among the best prospects in the game and joined fellow minor leaguers in outfielder James Wood and third baseman Brady House as Top 100 Prospects.

The Nationals went 71-91 in 2023, finishing last for the fourth consecutive year in the National League East. But the season actually represented something of a step forward. Washington finished with its best winning percentage (.438) since 2019, when it won the World Series.

Now, the challenge is ensuring steps forward continue throughout the organization.

Washington's High-A and Double-A affiliates both ranked last in their respective leagues in home runs and slugging, even despite several of their top prospects spending ample time at those two levels. The Nationals felt something had to change and significantly changed their player development staff following the season.

The Nationals fired farm director De Jon Watson. International scouting director Johnny DiPuglia resigned, and scouting director Kris Kline was moved into a special assistant role.

The organization made several coaching changes as well. It let go of minor league hitting coordinator Joe Dillon and in addition to multiple other minor league hitting coaches.

These changes, along with their respective replacements, signify a new-look Nationals PD staff. Longtime general manager Mike Rizzo agreed to a multi-year extension at the end of the 2023 season, with the promise that the organization will move forward and improve.

"I think the change is good," Rizzo said at the GM meetings in November. "I think that we needed a refresh to a lot of parts of our baseball operations department."

The revamp of the PD staff includes promoting longtime front office member Eddie Longosz to vice president and assistant GM of player development. He's been with the organization since 2010. Reed Dunn returned to the organization as assistant director and national crosschecker of amateur scouting.

The Nationals hired Danny Haas from the D-backs as vice president of amateur scouting and Brad Ciolek from the Orioles as senior director of amateur scouting.

While prospects such as Crews, Wood and House enjoyed strong seasons, the Nationals need

The Nationals' rookie class of 2023 was thin. Jake Irvin made 24 starts and posted a 4.61 ERA.

PROJECTED 2027 LINEUP

Catcher	Keibert Ruiz	28
First Base	Yohandy Morales	25
Second Base	Luis Garcia	27
Third Base	Brady House	24
Shortstop	CJ Abrams	26
Left Field	Dylan Crews	24
Center Field	Elijah Green	23
Right Field	James Wood	24
Designated Hitter	Lane Thomas	31
No. 1 Starter	Josiah Gray	29
No. 2 Starter	MacKenzie Gore	28
No. 3 Starter	Cade Cavalli	28
No. 4 Starter	Jackson Rutledge	28
No. 5 Starter	Jake Irvin	29
Closer	Jarlin Susana	23

to develop more success stories. First-rounder Elijah Green and trade pickup Robert Hassell III, both outfielders, are two notable examples. Green, the fifth overall pick in 2022, hits the ball as hard as anyone but also struck out nearly 42% of the time at Low-A in 2023.

Other prospects like Jacob Young, Drew Millas and Darren Baker are on track to help in Washington this season. Getting more out of similar player types will show the organization is capable at developing talent beyond the first round.

The Nationals showed in the offseason they're willing to make significant changes to win. Now, the challenge is to prove they can do it in 2024. ∎

DEPTH CHART

WASHINGTON NATIONALS

TOP 2024 CONTRIBUTORS   **RANK**
1. Jackson Rutledge, RHP   6
2. Jacob Young, OF   17

BREAKOUT PROSPECTS
1. Daylen Lile, OF   11
2. DJ Herz, LHP   14
3. Israel Pineda, C   20

SOURCE OF TOP 30 TALENT

Homegrown	24	Acquired	6
College	10	Trade	6
Junior college	2	Rule 5 draft	0
High school	5	Independent league	0
Nondrafted free agent	1	Free agent/waivers	0
International	6		

LF
Robert Hassell III (7)
Andrew Pinckney (18)

CF
Dylan Crews (1)
Cristhian Vaquero (8)
Elijah Green (9)
Jacob Young (17)

RF
James Wood (2)
Daylen Lile (11)
Jeremy De La Rosa (24)

3B
Brady House (3)
Trey Lipscomb (15)

SS
Nasim Nunez (16)
Kevin Made (23)
Armando Cruz (25)
Jorgelys Mota

2B
Darren Baker (26)
JT Arruda
Sammy Infante

1B
Yohandy Morales (5)
TJ White (27)
Roismar Quintana
Will Frizzell
Branden Boissiere

C
Israel Pineda (20)
Drew Millas (21)
Matt Suggs
Onix Vega

LHP

LHSP	LHRP
Jake Bennett (12)	DJ Herz (14)
Andrew Alvarez (29)	Mitchell Parker (28)
Dustin Saenz	Tim Cate
	Evan Lee

RHP

RHSP	RHRP
Cade Cavelli (4)	Jarlin Susana (10)
Jackson Rutledge (6)	Zach Brzykcy (19)
Travis Sykora (13)	
Cole Henry (22)	
Andry Lara (30)	
Kyle Luckham	
Aldo Ramirez	

1 DYLAN CREWS, OF

Born: February 26, 2002. **B-T:** R-R. **HT:** 6-0. **WT:** 205.
Drafted: Louisiana State, 2023 (1st round).
Signed by: Kevin Ham

TRACK RECORD: Despite being a highly touted prospect out of Lake Mary (Fla.) High, Crews decided to withdraw his name from the 2020 draft and instead took his talents to Baton Rouge. During his time with Louisiana State, he became one of the top players in college baseball. In 2021, Crews set an LSU freshman record with 18 home runs. The next year, he was named a Golden Spikes semifinalist before ultimately winning the award a year later. He was named Southeastern Conference player of the year in both 2022 and 2023. As a junior, he put up massive offensive numbers, hitting .426/.567/.713 with 18 home runs, 16 doubles, a 13.4% strikeout rate and a 20.6% walk rate. Crews was integral to LSU winning its first College World Series championship since 2009 and its seventh overall. He made history with teammate Paul Skenes, who was drafted No. 1 overall by the Pirates, as the first pair of teammates selected with the first two picks of the draft. The Nationals took Crews second overall and signed him for $9 million, which is the second-highest bonus in draft history. After a brief appearance in the Florida Complex League, he was promoted to Low-A Fredericksburg for 14 games, proving more than capable at the plate. Crews ended the season playing 20 games for Double-A Harrisburg. While he hit just .208 in the Eastern League, Crews finished his pro debut with a .292/.377/.467 line that included five home runs in 35 games.

SCOUTING REPORT: Crews ranked as the top prospect for the 2023 draft because of his well-rounded game that included plus hitting and on-base ability with power to match. While he is not physically imposing at 6 feet, 205 pounds, Crews boasts proven, above-average tools across the board. He has also shown the ability to make adjustments at the plate. Crews faced some swing-and-miss concerns before the draft, and he showed slightly elevated in-zone miss in his pro debut. He balances that by rarely going outside the zone and has strong plate discipline. Crews knows when to take his pitches and when he can be aggressive—hammering velocity when given the chance. Crews is a plus runner who projects to stick in center field. He is a solid defender and good route-runner. He has good instincts and makes routine plays look easy.

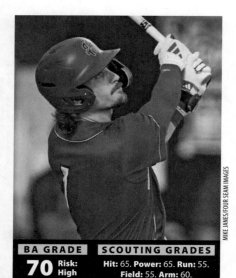

MIKE JANES/FOUR SEAM IMAGES

BA GRADE	SCOUTING GRADES
70 Risk: High	Hit: 65. Power: 65. Run: 55. Field: 55. Arm: 60.

Projected future grades on 20-80 scouting scale

BEST TOOLS

BATTING

Best Hitter for Average	Dylan Crews
Best Power Hitter	James Wood
Best Strike-Zone Discipline	Jack Dunn
Fastest Baserunner	Johnathon Thomas
Best Athlete	Elijah Green

PITCHING

Best Fastball	Jarlin Susana
Best Curveball	Cade Cavalli
Best Slider	Jarlin Susana
Best Changeup	DJ Herz
Best Control	Jake Bennett

FIELDING

Best Defensive Catcher	Israel Pineda
Best Defensive Infielder	Nasim Nunez
Best Infield Arm	Brady House
Best Defensive Outfielder	James Wood
Best Outfield Arm	Elijah Green

Due to the depth in the Nationals system, Crews could face a move to an outfield corner, where his plus arm profiles.

THE FUTURE: The Nationals believe that Crews could be their next homegrown franchise position player, joining the ranks of Bryce Harper, Anthony Rendon and Juan Soto before him. He has perennial all-star upside potential and has already proven himself on a large stage. He has a chance to reach Washington sometime during the 2024 season and should be a mainstay in the lineup for years to come. ∎

Year	Age	Club (League)	Level	AVG	G	AB	R	H	2B	3B	HR	RBI	BB	SO	SB	OBP	SLG
2023	21	FCL Nationals	Rk	1.000	1	3	3	3	1	0	0	0	0	0	0	1.000	1.333
2023	21	Fredericksburg (CAR)	A	.355	14	62	16	22	3	0	5	24	6	19	1	.423	.645
2023	21	Harrisburg (EL)	AA	.208	20	72	7	15	5	0	0	5	8	19	3	.318	.278
Minor League Totals				.292	35	137	26	40	9	0	5	29	14	38	4	.377	.467

2 JAMES WOOD, OF

HIT: 50. **POW:** 65. **RUN:** 55. **FLD:** 50. **ARM:** 55. **BA Grade:** 65. **Risk:** High.

Born: September 17, 2002. **B-T:** L-R. **HT:** 6-6. **WT:** 240.
Drafted: HS—Bradenton, FL, 2021 (2nd round). **Signed by:** John Martin (Padres).

TRACK RECORD: Wood's large stature made him easy to spot on the summer circuit, but that physicality made him one of the most impressive players in the 2021 draft class. The Padres selected him 62nd overall in the second round and went over slot to sign him for $2.6 million. Wood got off to a hot start in the Rookie-level Arizona Complex League in 2021 and continued the success during his first full season with Low-A Lake Elsinore. The Nationals acquired Wood, along with four other young talents, at the 2022 trade deadline in a blockbuster trade for Juan Soto. In 2023, Wood split time between High-A Wilmington and Double-A Harrisburg, where he continued to showcase his power with 26 home runs. He earned a Futures Game nod before finishing strong with an .881 OPS and 10 homers in August and September.

SCOUTING REPORT: There is no doubting Wood's plus-plus raw power. He crushes the ball to all fields and does a good job resisting pitches off the plate. Power hitters tend to have higher strikeout rates, which is the case with Wood at nearly 32%. He has more difficulty seeing spin well and will need to adjust. Wood adjusted his batting stance to keep his arms closer to his body to have a shorter swing he can manipulate better. He has a chance to stick in center field and is an above-average runner, but he will likely move to a corner as his body matures. His above-average arm will play there. Wood has above-average speed and was successful on 18 of 21 stolen base attempts in 2023.

THE FUTURE: Wood will add a massive power bat to the Nationals' lineup for many years to come. If he can lower his strikeout rate, he has the upside to hit 30-35 home runs. Nationals fans should start getting looks at Wood in Washington in 2024.

Year	Age	Club (League)	Level	AVG	G	AB	R	H	2B	3B	HR	RBI	BB	SO	SB	OBP	SLG
2023	20	Wilmington (SAL)	A+	.293	42	150	32	44	9	5	8	36	26	49	8	.392	.580
2023	20	Harrisburg (EL)	AA	.248	87	323	48	80	19	3	18	55	39	124	10	.334	.492
Minor League Totals				.291	231	850	168	247	60	9	41	175	128	280	48	.388	.527

3 BRADY HOUSE, 3B

HIT: 50. **POW:** 60. **RUN:** 50. **FLD:** 55. **ARM:** 60. **BA Grade:** 55. **Risk:** High.

Born: June 4, 2003. **B-T:** R-R. **HT:** 6-4. **WT:** 215.
Drafted: HS—Winder, GA, 2021 (1st round). **Signed by:** Eric Robinson.

TRACK RECORD: House was one of four premium high school shortstops at the top of the 2021 draft class, alongside Jordan Lawlar, Marcelo Mayer and Kahlil Watson. The Nationals drafted House 11th overall and signed him for $5 million, which was about 10% over slot. In his pro debut he displayed his double-plus power at the Florida Complex League, but his 2022 followup was compromised with a back injury and he was shut down in early June. The lack of power led to questions about his future projections. Those questions subsided when House hit .312/.365/.497 in 2023 and reached Double-A Harrisburg on July 18.

SCOUTING REPORT: Easy plus raw power and loud offensive tools are House's calling card. He hit a ball as hard as 113 mph in 2023 and averaged 91 overall. He makes a lot of hard contact at productive angles. House has shown ability to hit to all fields and has improved at hitting velocity—something he struggled with since his debut. But he chases pitches off the plate frequently and swings and misses enough to introduce hittability questions. House needs to work on patience at the plate and drawing walks, but he no longer faces questions about impact potential that arose after his flat 2022 season. The Nationals moved House from shortstop to third base, where his range is a better fit and his plus arm plays well. House stayed off the injured list in 2023 but appeared in just 88 games as the Nationals tightly managed his workload.

THE FUTURE: The further he gets from his back injury, the more House looks like the player the Nationals drafted. He should be Washington's answer at third base but won't see the major leagues for another full season. He should start the year at Double-A and reach Triple-A by the end of 2024.

Year	Age	Club (League)	Level	AVG	G	AB	R	H	2B	3B	HR	RBI	BB	SO	SB	OBP	SLG
2023	20	Fredericksburg (CAR)	A	.297	36	138	22	41	8	1	6	22	16	34	5	.369	.500
2023	20	Wilmington (SAL)	A+	.317	16	63	11	20	5	0	3	13	3	13	3	.368	.540
2023	20	Harrisburg (EL)	AA	.324	36	139	19	45	8	2	3	12	7	42	1	.358	.475
Minor League Totals				.303	149	575	90	174	32	3	19	90	45	161	10	.365	.468

4 CADE CAVALLI, RHP

FB: 70. **CB:** 65. **SL:** 55. **CHG:** 55. **CTL:** 50. **BA Grade:** 55. **Risk:** Very High.

Born: August 14, 1998. **B-T:** R-R. **HT:** 6-4. **WT:** 226.
Drafted: Oklahoma, 2020 (1st round). **Signed by:** Jerad Head.

TRACK RECORD: The Nationals drafted Cavalli 22nd overall in the five-round 2020 draft. Making his pro debut in 2021, he led the minor leagues with 175 strikeouts. He spent the first five months of 2022 at Triple-A Rochester and made his MLB debut on Aug. 26. He struck out six in 4.1 innings but was shut down after that lone start with right shoulder inflammation. Cavalli returned in 2023 ready to earn a spot in the Opening Day rotation, but during his third spring training appearance he left the game after feeling something behind his elbow. An MRI showed a Grade 3 sprain of his UCL and required Tommy John surgery. Cavalli missed the entire 2023 season.

SCOUTING REPORT: Cavalli's fastball is one of the best in the Nationals' system. His four-seamer tops out at 99-100 mph but sits closer to 96. His go-to breaking pitch is a mid-80s curveball that has a harsh downward break. His above-average slider adds to his repertoire, but he relies much more on the curve to get outs. Cavalli's changeup has been a work in progress. The Nationals wanted him to refine the pitch before making his MLB debut, and he saw improvements, especially when facing lefthanded hitters. Cavalli struggled with command for most of 2022, though he was trending in the right direction before the injury.

THE FUTURE: Washington believes that Cavalli is a future piece of its rotation and expects him to play a large role during the back half of the 2024 season. He has no definitive return date, but the organization is targeting June, about 15 months after surgery. Cavalli checked off an important milestone when he played catch in September 2023.

Year	Age	Club (League)	Level	W	L	ERA	G	GS	IP	H	HR	BB	SO	BB%	SO%	WHIP	AVG
2023	24	Did not play—Injured															
Minor League Totals				13	13	3.76	44	44	220	171	8	99	279	10.7	30.2	1.23	.214
Major League Totals				0	1	14.54	1	1	4	6	0	2	6	8.7	26.1	1.85	.333

5 YOHANDY MORALES, 3B

HIT: 45. **POW:** 55. **RUN:** 45. **FLD:** 50. **ARM:** 60. **BA Grade:** 55. **Risk:** Very High.

Born: October 9, 2001. **B-T:** R-R. **HT:** 6-4. **WT:** 225. **Drafted:** Miami, 2023 (2nd round).
Signed by: Alex Morales.

TRACK RECORD: Morales ranked No. 77 in the 2020 draft class but made it to Miami out of high school. As a freshman, he stepped into the Hurricanes' lineup and added pop at the plate and a steady arm at third base. His sophomore season was more of the same. He led the team in doubles, home runs, slugging and RBIs. Morales played for USA Baseball's Collegiate National Team in 2022 and led Team USA in most offensive numbers. This power and production led to the Nationals to draft him 40th overall in 2023 and sign him for an above-slot $2.6 million. Morales appeared in 42 games in his pro debut, mostly at Low-A and High-A, but when the Class A seasons finished, he moved to Double-A Harrisburg for the final four games.

SCOUTING REPORT: Morales, who also goes by "Yoyo," already has strength on his 6-foot-4, 250-pound frame. He inherits some of his athleticism from father Andy, who defected from Cuba and spent 2001 and 2002 as a minor leaguer with Yankees and Red Sox. Morales' swing generates a ton of damage on contact with an average exit velocity of nearly 91 mph during his pro debut. He has a longer swing and locks out his front arm, which could be adding to some of his swing-and-miss issues. Defensively, Morales has flashed solid tools, but he struggles to throw on the run. He is an average runner, which is surprising given his athleticism. If he added even more strength, it is likely that he will slow even more. A move to first base could be in Morales' future.

THE FUTURE: Morales has good bat-to-ball skills for a power hitter but could use more repetition to make more contact. He will likely start the season with Double-A and focus on defensive reps before he advances.

Year	Age	Club (League)	Level	AVG	G	AB	R	H	2B	3B	HR	RBI	BB	SO	SB	OBP	SLG
2023	21	FCL Nationals	Rk	.400	2	5	0	2	0	0	0	1	0	0	0	.400	.400
2023	21	Fredericksburg (CAR)	A	.390	18	77	18	30	10	2	0	17	8	18	1	.448	.571
2023	21	Wilmington (SAL)	A+	.314	18	70	12	22	5	2	0	14	8	16	0	.400	.443
2023	21	Harrisburg (EL)	AA	.286	4	14	0	4	1	0	0	0	3	2	0	.412	.357
Minor League Totals				.349	42	166	30	58	16	4	0	32	19	36	1	.423	.494

6 JACKSON RUTLEDGE, RHP

FB: 60. **CB:** 50. **SL:** 60. **CHG:** 50. **CTL:** 50. **BA Grade:** 50. **Risk:** High.

Born: April 1, 1999. **B-T:** R-R. **HT:** 6-8. **WT:** 250.
Drafted: San Jacinto (Texas) JC, 2019 (1st round). **Signed by:** Brandon Larson.

TRACK RECORD: The Nationals drafted Rutledge 17th overall in 2019, but his progression has been anything but smooth. He reached Low-A in his first pro summer before spending time at the alternate training site in 2020. In 2021, Rutledge dealt with a shoulder injury that sidelined him for a month, and when he returned he posted a 7.68 ERA in 36.1 innings. He responded with a breakout 2022 campaign in which he started 20 games and helped lead Low-A Fredericksburg to the Carolina League semifinals. The 2023 season was another step in the right direction for Rutledge, who pitched to a 3.71 ERA in 23 starts at Double-A and Triple-A before making his MLB debut on Sept. 13.

SCOUTING REPORT: At 6-foot-8, Rutledge is an imposing figure on the mound. Both his four-seam and two-seam fastballs touch the upper 90s but sit closer to 95 mph. He gets good ride on his four-seamer up, but his command results in more of an above-average pitch. Rutledge's low-80s slider is his go-to secondary pitch and generates the most swing-and-miss. He throws an average changeup that sits in the upper 80s but has touched 91 mph. One of the biggest changes Rutledge made to his approach was that he lengthened the arm action in his delivery. The automated ball-strike system and its tight strike zone at Triple-A elevated Rutledge's walk rate to 13%. It was about half that in MLB.

THE FUTURE: Rutledge has shown that he is willing to work and improve. The Nationals have been very impressed with how he has handled injuries and struggles throughout his career. He projects as a back-of-the-rotation starter and can impact the Nationals starting in 2024.

Year	Age	Club (League)	Level	W	L	ERA	G	GS	IP	H	HR	BB	SO	BB%	SO%	WHIP	AVG
2023	24	Harrisburg (EL)	AA	6	1	3.16	12	12	68	50	5	25	62	9.2	22.8	1.10	.209
2023	24	Rochester (IL)	AAA	2	3	4.44	11	11	51	46	7	30	44	13.3	19.6	1.50	.250
2023	24	Washington (NL)	MLB	1	1	6.75	4	4	20	24	4	6	12	6.8	13.6	1.50	.304
Minor League Totals				19	16	4.53	66	66	290	264	23	119	285	9.6	23.0	1.32	.241
Major League Totals				1	1	6.75	4	4	20	24	4	6	12	6.8	13.6	1.50	.304

7 ROBERT HASSELL III, OF

HIT: 50. **POW:** 40. **RUN:** 55. **FLD:** 55. **ARM:** 55. **BA Grade:** 50. **Risk:** Very High.

Born: August 15, 2001. **B-T:** L-L. **HT:** 6-2. **WT:** 195.
Drafted: HS—Thompson's Station, TN, 2020 (1st rd). **Signed by:** Tyler Stubblefield (Padres).

TRACK RECORD: The Padres signed Hassell for a below-slot $4.3 million with the eighth overall pick in 2020. He reached High-A in his 2021 pro debut and began 2022 at that level. At that year's trade deadline, he was one of the key pieces—along with CJ Abrams, MacKenzie Gore, James Wood and Jarlin Susana—the Padres sent to the Nationals for Juan Soto. Hassell finished that year with Double-A Harrisburg and joined the Nationals' contingent at the Arizona Fall League, but he broke the hamate bone in his right hand after just two games. He spent the beginning of 2023 rehabbing before making his season debut at Double-A in May. Hassell again struggled at the plate and again was assigned to the AFL, where the Nationals hope he taps into some power and regains a feel at the plate.

SCOUTING REPORT: Hassell was dubbed one of the best pure hitters in his draft class. He has a contact-based approach, but he adjusted his bat path at the end of the 2022 season and it has caused some issues. Some evaluators believe that the lefthanded-hitting Hassell could project for fringe-average power, but he has yet to tap into it in games. He finds a way to get on base and has above-average speed, which makes him a basestealing threat. His above-average arm combined with that speed gives him the ability to play any outfield position. Unless his bat takes a step forward, Hassell may slide into more of a fourth outfielder type of role.

THE FUTURE: Hassell did not reach Washington in September, as many expected before the season. The lack of offensive production raises concern, but the Nationals hope it was due to a longer recovery from the wrist injury rather than something mechanical.

Year	Age	Club (League)	Level	AVG	G	AB	R	H	2B	3B	HR	RBI	BB	SO	SB	OBP	SLG
2023	21	Fredericksburg (CAR)	A	.189	15	53	12	10	1	1	1	4	16	9	2	.377	.302
2023	21	Harrisburg (EL)	AA	.225	106	414	54	93	15	1	8	37	52	152	13	.316	.324
Minor League Totals				.265	343	1360	220	360	74	7	31	187	191	373	73	.358	.398

8 CRISTHIAN VAQUERO, OF

HIT: 50. **POW:** 55. **RUN:** 70. **FLD:** 50. **ARM:** 60. **BA Grade:** 55. **Risk:** Extreme.

Born: September 13, 2004. **B-T:** B-R. **HT:** 6-3. **WT:** 180.
Signed: Cuba, 2022. **Signed by:** Johnny DiPuglia.

TRACK RECORD: The Nationals signed Vaquero with the highest signing bonus—$4.925 million—in the international signing period which opened on Jan. 15, 2021. Despite signing at 17 years old, Vaquero was regarded by the organization as having talent and maturity well beyond his years. He began his pro career in the Dominican Summer League in 2022 and made his U.S. debut in 2023 in the Florida Complex League, where he hit .279/.410/.393 with one home run and 15 stolen bases in 23 attempts. His walk rate bordered on 16% and ranked 14th in the FCL among qualified hitters. The Nationals promoted him to Low-A Fredericksburg on Aug. 22. He hit consistently throughout the season but struggled to find power.

SCOUTING REPORT: Vaquero settled in this season and was less aggressive at that plate, which was a reputation he had in Cuba. He has a solid approach, with a big leg kick and open upright stance that requires him to be on time or he risks putting the ball right into the dirt. Vaquero is a natural lefthanded hitter who taught himself to hit from the right side before signing with the Nationals. His swing from the right side looks natural and sometimes better than his natural one. Vaquero has a lean, athletic frame and double-plus speed and plus arm strength. He covers a lot of ground in center field and looks more comfortable there than in either corner. Vaquero will need to put on muscle and tap into the power potential to unlock his high ceiling.

THE FUTURE: Though he is years away from seeing the big leagues, Vaquero has impressed the Nationals with his development. He will start the season at Low-A and should benefit from additional strength and conditioning.

Year	Age	Club (League)	Level	AVG	G	AB	R	H	2B	3B	HR	RBI	BB	SO	SB	OBP	SLG
2023	18	FCL Nationals	Rk	.279	42	140	34	39	9	2	1	16	29	35	15	.410	.393
2023	18	Fredericksburg (CAR)	A	.197	16	66	10	13	1	1	1	9	12	18	7	.321	.288
Minor League Totals				.254	113	382	77	97	14	7	3	47	74	91	39	.381	.351

9 ELIJAH GREEN, OF

HIT: 30. **POW:** 60. **RUN:** 70. **FLD:** 55. **ARM:** 60. **BA Grade:** 50. **Risk:** Extreme.

Born: December 4, 2003. **B-T:** R-R. **HT:** 6-3. **WT:** 225.
Drafted: HS—Bradenton, FL, 2022 (1st round). **Signed by:** Alex Morales.

TRACK RECORD: Washington drafted Green fifth overall in 2022, signing one of the most dynamic prospects scouts had seen in years for the slot value of $6.5 million. He put up a .939 OPS in the Florida Complex League during his pro debut but also struck out 40% of the time. Green regressed in nearly every offensive category in 2023 at Low-A Fredericksburg, but few players make such authoritative contact when they do connect. The Nationals don't view Green's 2023 as a step backward, but they acknowledge that in order for him to reach his potential, he needs to make better swing decisions and put more balls in play.

SCOUTING REPORT: Green's athleticism speaks loudly, and he has plus-plus raw power and has shown the ability to hit to all fields. Swing-and-miss is the major concern with his game after he struck out nearly 42% of the time in 2023 and whiffed at nearly 38% of pitches in the zone. Green is aggressive at the plate, so when he makes contact, it is loud. He hit a ball as hard as 117 mph, while his 90th percentile exit velocity of 110 mph was one of the very best in the minors. Green's swing does not look natural yet, but the Nationals are working on smoothing out his bat path. He has flashed elite speed and could stick in center field. His strong arm would play in right field if he gets pushed out of center by superior defenders.

THE FUTURE: Green is a physical player with loud tools but is still very raw at the plate. He hits the ball harder than anyone, but he needs to do it more frequently. If he is successful in fine-tuning his swing in the seasons ahead, he has impact potential. Green's development may be the toughest challenge facing Nationals player development.

Year	Age	Club (League)	Level	AVG	G	AB	R	H	2B	3B	HR	RBI	BB	SO	SB	OBP	SLG
2023	19	FCL Nationals	Rk	.318	8	22	9	7	1	1	1	3	7	11	1	.483	.591
2023	19	Fredericksburg (CAR)	A	.210	75	281	36	59	13	1	4	36	45	139	30	.323	.306
Minor League Totals				.228	95	346	54	79	18	2	7	48	58	171	32	.345	.353

10 JARLIN SUSANA, RHP

FB: 60. **CB:** 45. **SL:** 60. **CHG:** 50. **CTL:** 40. **BA Grade:** 50. **Risk:** Extreme.

Born: March 23, 2004. **B-T:** R-R. **HT:** 6-6. **WT:** 235.
Signed: Dominican Republic, 2022. **Signed by:** Trevor Schumm/Chris Kemp (Padres).
TRACK RECORD: Despite being eligible to be signed as an international free agent in 2021, Susana waited a year and signed with the Padres on Jan. 15, 2022. After just eight appearances in the Arizona Complex League, the hulking power pitcher was a key piece in San Diego's trade for Juan Soto. The Padres sent Susana and four other young players to the Nationals to acquire Soto at the 2022 trade deadline. Washington promoted Susana to Low-A Fredericksburg after acquiring him, and he touched 103 mph that August. Susana spent the entire 2023 season with Fredericksburg, where he pitched to a 5.14 ERA over 17 starts. While he impressed from a power standpoint, Susana still needs to work to find consistency.
SCOUTING REPORT: Susana is a flame-throwing righthander, with lots of power coming from his 6-foot-6 235-pound frame. His fastball sits 98-99 mph and has touched 103 more than once. The pitch generates strikes, but more control would go a long way in making this a no-doubt strikeout pitch. Also in Susana's arsenal is a high-80s power slider that projects to be nearly as effective as his fastball. He also throws a changeup that sits 89-91 mph, which is up nearly 2 mph since last season. Susana's changeup has touched 96 mph, however the pitch lacks the control it needs as velocity is added. He is working on improving his curveball, but that is the weakest of his pitches. While Susana is still working as a starter, a move to the bullpen is likely.
THE FUTURE: Susana has proven that he has rare power behind his pitches. However, he will need to dial in on his command to have any hope to start. He has multiple plus pitches in his arsenal and could develop into a first-division closer.

Year	Age	Club (League)	Level	W	L	ERA	G	GS	IP	H	HR	BB	SO	BB%	SO%	WHIP	AVG
2023	19	Fredericksburg (CAR)	A	1	6	5.14	17	17	63	56	3	40	62	14.1	21.8	1.52	.241
Minor League Totals				1	6	4.00	30	29	108	84	5	60	128	13.0	27.6	1.33	.216

11 DAYLEN LILE, OF

HIT: 55. **POW:** 45. **RUN:** 60. **FLD:** 50. **ARM:** 45. **BA Grade:** 45. **Risk:** High.

Born: November 30, 2002. **B-T:** L-R. **HT:** 5-11. **WT:** 195. **Drafted:** HS—Louisville, 2021 (2nd round).
Signed by: Brian Cleary
TRACK RECORD: Lile signed an over-slot $1.75 million bonus in the second round of the 2021 draft. His pro debut at the Florida Complex League left much to be desired and he missed the 2022 season recovering from Tommy John surgery. Lile redeemed himself in 2023, slashing .291/.381/.510 at Low-A Fredericksburg to earn a promotion to High-A Wilmington in mid July. He continued to impress in his first healthy season.
SCOUTING REPORT: Known as a pure hitter in high school, Lile lived up to that billing in 2023. He has a clean, simple swing and an innate ability to adjust pitch-to-pitch during an at-bat. Lile's adjustability allows him to get to pitches in all four quadrants of the strike zone. The question is whether he'll make enough impact when he connects. He posted a below-average .123 isolated slugging percentage in 40 games at High-A, and opposing scouts wonder if he'll ever develop more than below-average game power. He's a plus runner who split time between center and left field in Wilmington, but his defensive skills and arm may be best suited for left field, which would put even more pressure on his power to develop.
THE FUTURE: Lile played in 106 games in 2023, and the Nationals hope increased durability continues in 2024. He could elevate his stock quickly if he starts to tap into more power.

Year	Age	Club (League)	Level	AVG	G	AB	R	H	2B	3B	HR	RBI	BB	SO	SB	OBP	SLG
2023	20	Fredericksburg (CAR)	A	.291	66	251	49	73	20	7	7	48	36	58	21	.381	.510
2023	20	Wilmington (SAL)	A+	.234	40	154	16	36	7	3	2	18	16	41	2	.310	.357
Minor League Totals				.262	125	469	81	123	29	10	9	76	67	119	25	.356	.424

12 JAKE BENNETT, LHP

FB: 55. **SL:** 50 **CHG:** 60 **CTL:** 55. **BA Grade:** 45. **Risk:** High.

Born: December 2, 2000. **B-T:** L-L. **HT:** 6-6. **WT:** 234. **Drafted:** Oklahoma, 2022 (2nd round). **Signed by:** Cody Staab.
TRACK RECORD: Bennett's development path is eerily similar to fellow Nationals pitching prospect Cade Cavalli. Both are Tulsa natives who went on to pitch for Oklahoma. Bennett again followed Cavalli into the Nationals farm system when the organization selected him in the second round of the 2022 draft.

Bennett had a successful pro debut in 2023, owning a 3.14 ERA across the Nationals' two Class A affiliates. Unfortunately for the Nationals, the similarities between the two Oklahoma pitchers continued when Bennett was shut down in August and had Tommy John surgery in mid September.

SCOUTING REPORT: Bennett primarily attacks hitters with his fastball, which he threw more than 60% of the time in 2023. He relies on a low-90s two-seamer that has nearly 14 inches of horizontal break and projects as an above-average pitch. He became more comfortable deploying and commanding his secondaries throughout the season. Bennett's go-to secondary is a plus changeup that he consistently throws for strikes and is effective against both righties and lefties. He rounds out his arsenal with an average slider that lacks consistency. Bennett's command improved throughout the 2023 season, though he has a slight head whack in his delivery that he needs to iron out. Despite his considerable frame, Bennett struggled to hold his velocity deeper into outings.

THE FUTURE: The southpaw is sidelined for the entirety of the 2024 campaign. Bennett projects as a back-of-the-rotation starter, barring any setbacks with his recovery.

Year	Age	Club (League)	Level	W	L	ERA	G	GS	IP	H	HR	BB	SO	BB%	SO%	WHIP	AVG
2023	22	Fredericksburg (CAR)	A	1	3	1.93	9	9	42	34	2	8	54	4.9	32.9	1.00	.222
2023	22	Wilmington (SAL)	A+	0	3	5.57	6	6	21	26	2	8	19	8.5	20.2	1.62	.313
Minor League Totals				1	6	3.14	15	15	63	60	4	16	73	6.2	28.3	1.21	.254

13 TRAVIS SYKORA, RHP

FB: 70. **SL:** 50. **CHG:** 55. **CTL:** 50 **BA Grade:** 55. **Risk:** Extreme.

Born: April 28, 2004. **B-T:** R-R. **HT:** 6-6. **WT:** 220. **Drafted:** HS—Round Rock, TX, 2023 (3rd round).
Signed by: Kevin Ham.

TRACK RECORD: Sykora ranked as the No. 36 player in the 2023 draft class and owned the hardest-thrown fastball in the class by a high school pitcher. The Nationals managed to land Sykora No. 71 overall and signed him to a $2.6 million bonus, more than double the slot value at that pick, to pry him from a Texas commitment. He did not make his professional debut in 2023.

SCOUTING REPORT: At 6-foot-6, 220 pounds, Sykora is an athletic mover on the mound. His electric fastball sits in the upper 90s and has touched triple digits. His fastball, just based on velocity alone, seems to overwhelm hitters, though it is not always consistent. Sykora's secondaries both need significant development, but his mid-80s slider and mid-80s split-changeup have both flashed average or better at points. His slider doesn't have elite spin or movement, but the sheer velocity allows the pitch to generate swings and misses. The Nationals—under their old player development staff—said the righty will likely scrap his split-changeup and move toward a more traditional changeup. Sykora's biggest challenge will be working on control and learning to be more precise with his power.

THE FUTURE: Sykora, who turns 20 in late April, is ready for his pro debut. He has a long road of development ahead, but also a rather high ceiling. He will likely begin the season at the Florida Complex League and could earn a promotion to Low-A in relatively short order.

Year	Age	Club (League)	Level	W	L	ERA	G	GS	IP	H	HR	BB	SO	BB%	SO%	WHIP	AVG
2023	19	Did not play															

14 DJ HERZ, LHP

FB: 55. **CB:** 50. **CHG:** 65. **CTL:** 35. **BA Grade:** 45. **Risk:** High.

Born: January 4, 2001. **B-T:** R-L. **HT:** 6-2. **WT:** 175. **Drafted:** HS—Fayetteville, NC, 2019 (8th round).
Signed by: Billy Swoope (Cubs).

TRACK RECORD: A Cubs eighth-round pick in 2019, Herz quickly impressed in his first full season coming out of the lost 2020. He led all Cubs minor leaguers in with 272 strikeouts during the 2021 and 2022 seasons. The issue? He also led all Cubs farmhands with 114 walks over that same time frame. Herz struggled in Double-A to start 2023, and the Cubs traded him to the Nationals for third baseman Jeimer Candelario at the trade deadline. Herz pitched well in eight games for the Nationals' Double-A Harrisburg affiliate and earned an all-star nod in the Arizona Fall League.

SCOUTING REPORT: Herz's fastball is deceptive, which helped him rack up a third straight season of more than 130 strikeouts. Hitters note that Herz's fastball jumps on them much quicker than perceived despite its 91-94 mph velocity. However, his bread-and-butter is his changeup. The nearly double-plus pitch sits 80-84 mph and is easily the best in the Nationals' system. Herz rounds out his repertoire with an average, tight, vertical curveball in the upper 70s. Herz struggles with control, owning a walk rate near 14%—when league average is closer to 9.5%.

THE FUTURE: The Nationals were enthused by Herz's performance in the AFL. Because of the lack of lefthanded starting pitching depth, the Nationals want to develop Herz as a starter. If his control does not dramatically improve, a move to the bullpen is likely. He could be a candidate to help Washington as a reliever sooner rather than later.

Year	Age	Club (League)	Level	W	L	ERA	G	GS	IP	H	HR	BB	SO	BB%	SO%	WHIP	AVG
2023	22	Tennessee (SL)	AA	1	1	3.97	14	14	59	47	4	37	80	14.0	30.3	1.42	.216
2023	22	Harrisburg (EL)	AA	2	2	2.55	8	8	35	20	1	20	53	13.6	36.1	1.13	.161
Minor League Totals				10	14	3.64	74	74	282	176	20	179	413	14.9	34.3	1.26	.176
Minor League Totals				25	19	4.45	172	19	352	333	43	136	379	8.9	24.9	1.33	.247

15 TREY LIPSCOMB, 3B

HIT: 45. **POW:** 55. **RUN:** 45. **FLD:** 50. **ARM:** 55. **BA Grade:** 40. **Risk:** Medium.

Born: June 14, 2000. **B-T:** R-R. **HT:** 6-1. **WT:** 200. **Drafted:** Tennessee, 2022 (3rd round). **Signed by:** Brian Cleary.
TRACK RECORD: The Nationals felt Lipscomb flashed enough in his senior season at Tennessee to warrant a full-slot $758,900 bonus in the third round of the 2022 draft. He made a good first impression in 23 games with Low-A in 2022. He opened the 2023 season with High-A Wilmington and hit .251/.311/.387 in 49 games before being promoted to Double-A, where he hit .284/.310/.438 line in 80 games.
SCOUTING REPORT: Lipscomb is a versatile infielder who has shown some feel to hit, though it's unclear exactly where he ultimately ends up defensively. He has a relaxed setup in the box, stands at the plate with good posture and swings with conviction. His longer, flatter bat path leaves the barrel in the zone a touch longer than average. He showed good adjustability in 2023 upon arriving in the upper minors. There's work to be done with his approach. Lipscomb is an aggressive hitter who chased out of the zone frequently and walked just 27 times in 129 games. Lipscomb is an athletic defender with a slightly above-average arm who played every infield position. The Nationals believe he's good enough to slot in at any of them.
THE FUTURE: If Lipscomb can work more walks and tap into a bit more power, the Nationals believe he can be a multi-positional semi-regular. He could reach the majors at some point in 2024, though Washington's projected future infield mix includes Brady House at third base and CJ Abrams at shortstop and possibly Luis Garcia at second base.

Year	Age	Club (League)	Level	AVG	G	AB	R	H	2B	3B	HR	RBI	BB	SO	SB	OBP	SLG
2023	23	Wilmington (SAL)	A+	.251	49	191	19	48	14	0	4	27	15	42	6	.311	.387
2023	23	Harrisburg (EL)	AA	.284	80	320	40	91	15	2	10	45	12	61	4	.310	.438
Minor League Totals				.276	152	608	74	168	33	3	15	85	31	122	22	.313	.415

16 NASIM NUNEZ, SS

HIT: 45. **POW:** 30. **RUN:** 70. **FLD:** 70. **ARM:** 70. **BA Grade:** 45. **Risk:** High.

Born: August 18, 2000. **B-T:** B-R. **HT:** 5-9. **WT:** 168. **Drafted:** HS—Suwanee, GA, 2019 (2nd round).
Signed by: Christian Castorri (Marlins).
TRACK RECORD: During an excellent career at Collins Hill High in suburban Atlanta, Nunez was considered the best high school defender in his class. The Marlins drafted him 46th overall in 2019 and signed him for an over-slot $2.2 million. He has gradually progressed through the professional ranks and in 2023 had a quality first full season at Double-A Pensacola. The athletic Nunez slashed .225/.341/.286 and set a new career high with five home runs while also swiping 52 bases. He also represented the Marlins in the Futures Game and won its MVP award. The Marlins left him off their 40-man roster and the Nationals swooped in to select him in the 2023 Rule 5 draft.
SCOUTING REPORT: Nunez is small in stature at 5-foot-9 but has plus bat-to-ball skills and an outstanding feel for the strike zone. The switch-hitter has a simple setup with low, loose hands and a compact, direct swing. Nunez has looser, whippier hands from the left side, which is also where he produces most of his power. He is a hit-over-power profile with strong feel for the barrel and all-fields approach. Nunez has strong on-base skills with a career .359 OBP in the Marlins' pitcher-friendly home parks. He walked nearly 15% of the time at Double-A in 2023 and is a tough at-bat for opposing pitchers. Nunez's calling card is his outstanding defense. He is a double-plus defender at shortstop with a nearly double-plus arm. He is comfortable throwing from any arm slot and does an excellent job coming in on the baseball and moving laterally. He is a double-plus runner who has been successful on 84% of his stolen base attempts.
THE FUTURE: Nunez will hit for little power, but his defense, speed and overall approach will allow him to impact the game. He will serve as a utility infielder if he makes the team as a Rule 5 pick.

Year	Age	Club (League)	Level	AVG	G	AB	R	H	2B	3B	HR	RBI	BB	SO	SB	OBP	SLG
2023	22	Pensacola (SL)	AA	.224	125	490	84	110	11	2	5	43	87	107	52	.341	.286
Minor League Totals				.233	351	1306	230	304	35	7	7	106	252	340	183	.358	.286

17 JACOB YOUNG, OF

HIT: 40. **POW:** 40. **RUN:** 80. **FLD:** 50. **ARM:** 50. **BA Grade:** 40. **Risk:** Medium.

Born: July 27, 1999. **B-T:** R-R. **HT:** 5-11. **WT:** 180. **Drafted:** Florida, 2021 (7th round). **Signed by:** Tommy Jackson.

TRACK RECORD: Young ranked as the No. 356 prospect in the 2021 draft and signed for $275,000 with the Nationals that year in the seventh round. Despite never receiving much in the way of attention, he has always impressed within the organization. Young was one of just two minor league players to score at least 100 runs and steal at least 50 bases in 2022. He carried that momentum into 2023 and, despite starting the year in High-A, ultimately made his big league debut in Washington, hitting .252 with 13 steals in 33 games.

SCOUTING REPORT: Speed is Young's calling card. He stole 39 bases in the minors in 2023 and was not caught stealing in his 13 attempts in the majors. Some scouts remark that he's among the best baserunners they've ever seen and he posted a 98th percentile sprint speed in the big leagues. Young could compete for stolen base titles in a full-time role, but it's an open question whether he'll hit enough to command such an opportunity on a major league roster. Young makes plenty of contact, especially on pitches in the zone, but he struggles to hit for much power. Young primarily played center field upon arriving in Washington but is capable at all three outfield spots. He showed slightly above-average range and arm strength in his limited big league time.

THE FUTURE: While he's likely more of a fourth outfielder because of his limited power output, Young has played his way into the Nationals' outfield mix and could even push Victor Robles for the starting role in center in 2024.

Year	Age	Club (League)	Level	AVG	G	AB	R	H	2B	3B	HR	RBI	BB	SO	SB	OBP	SLG
2023	23	Wilmington (SAL)	A+	.307	56	212	28	65	10	2	2	28	25	31	22	.383	.401
2023	23	Harrisburg (EL)	AA	.304	52	204	30	62	11	3	3	28	17	37	17	.374	.431
2023	23	Rochester (IL)	AAA	.294	4	17	2	5	0	0	1	2	0	2	0	.294	.471
2023	23	Washington (NL)	MLB	.252	33	107	9	27	7	1	0	12	10	22	13	.322	.336
Minor League Totals				.275	253	999	194	275	37	13	8	109	111	169	104	.359	.362
Major League Totals				.252	33	107	9	27	7	1	0	12	10	22	13	.322	.336

18 ANDREW PINCKNEY, OF

HIT: 45 **POW:** 55 **RUN:** 60 **FLD:** 50 **ARM:** 55. **BA Grade:** 45. **Risk:** High.

Born: December 7, 2000. **B-T:** R-R. **HT:** 6-3. **WT:** 215. **Drafted:** Alabama, 2023 (4th round). **Signed by:** Tommy Jackson.

TRACK RECORD: Pinckney enjoyed a career year for Alabama in 2023, hitting .338/.442/.645 with 18 homers in the Southeastern Conference despite a 32% miss rate. The Nationals signed him to a below-slot $500,000 bonus in the fourth round of the 2023 draft. He split time between both Class A affiliates and ended the season with a brief cameo for Double-A Harrisburg, hitting .321/.415/.457 in 41 games overall.

SCOUTING REPORT: Pinckney's above-average bat speed translates to hard-hit balls—that is, when he makes contact. He has faced swing-and-miss concerns against all pitches, especially breaking balls, dating back to his amateur days. His chase, in-zone whiff and overall miss rates were far more manageable in his limited pro debut, but it's something that will need consistent maintenance. Pinckney will also need to improve his pitch recognition, especially against upper-level pitchers. He showed overall improvements each year offensively at Alabama. Pinckney is a good runner and likes to steal bases. He stole 11 bases on 14 attempts during his pro debut. He has an above-average arm that should play at any spot in the outfield. He played all three positions upon turning pro but mostly settled into right field.

THE FUTURE: The Nationals have a ton of organizational outfield depth, but Pinckney could move relatively quickly after already reaching the upper minors to end 2023.

Year	Age	Club (League)	Level	AVG	G	AB	R	H	2B	3B	HR	RBI	BB	SO	SB	OBP	SLG
2023	22	FCL Nationals	Rk	.500	2	4	2	2	1	0	0	1	2	0	1	.667	.750
2023	22	Fredericksburg (CAR)	A	.329	17	73	21	24	6	0	3	15	4	16	6	.402	.534
2023	22	Wilmington (SAL)	A+	.324	18	68	13	22	1	1	1	4	13	18	3	.446	.412
2023	22	Harrisburg (EL)	AA	.235	4	17	3	4	0	0	0	0	0	4	1	.235	.235
Minor League Totals				.321	41	162	39	52	8	1	4	20	19	38	11	.415	.457

19 ZACH BRZYKCY, RHP

FB: 65. **CB:** 55. **CHG:** 45. **CTL:** 50. **BA Grade:** 45. **Risk:** Very High.

Born: July 12, 1999. **B-T:** R-R. **HT:** 6-2. **WT:** 230. **Signed:** Virginia Tech, 2020 (NDFA). **Signed by:** Bobby Myrick.

TRACK RECORD: As a rising junior, Brzykcy was named the Cape Cod League reliever of the year. He tried to use that momentum throughout his senior season at Virginia Tech, but he struggled in seven appearances before the pandemic shutdown in 2020. He signed with the Nationals as a nondrafted free agent for $20,000. Brzykcy broke out in 2022, jumping three levels and ending the year in Triple-A. He pitched to a 8-2 record with 14 saves, owning just a 1.76 ERA in 51 appearances out of the bullpen. The righthander was well on his way to earning a spot in the 2023 Nationals' bullpen before having Tommy John surgery in April. He missed the entire season.

SCOUTING REPORT: Brzykcy's go-to pitch is an explosive fastball with excellent carry. The pitch sits 95-98 mph and is effective at getting hitters out. Prior to the injury, the righthander released the ball at a higher angle, which allowed him to attack the top of the zone. Rounding out his arsenal is an above-average curveball and a split-changeup that has some sink to it. Brzykcy isn't afraid to use his secondary pitches and has the makeup of a big league reliever.

THE FUTURE: Brzykcy is expected to return during the 2024 campaign. The Nationals view him as a key member of their future bullpen and shielded him from Rule 5 eligibility by adding him to the 40-man roster in November. As long as he can return to form after his injury, expect to see him in Washington soon.

Year	Age	Club (League)	Level	W	L	ERA	G	GS	IP	H	HR	BB	SO	BB%	SO%	WHIP	AVG
2023	23	Did not play—Injured															
Minor League Totals				14	6	3.49	79	1	124	88	13	54	181	10.5	35.3	1.15	.199

20 ISRAEL PINEDA, C

HIT: 30. **POW:** 50. **RUN:** 40. **FLD:** 55 **ARM:** 60. **BA Grade:** 40. **Risk:** High.

Born: April 3, 2000. **B-T:** R-R. **HT:** 5-11. **WT:** 190. **Signed:** Venezuela, 2016. **Signed By:** German Robles.

TRACK RECORD: Pineda's career has been up and down since the Nationals signed him out of Venezuela in 2016. He began to show more power in 2021, hitting 14 homers in 77 games with High-A Wilmington, then showed the same amount of power with better on-base ability in a breakout 2022 season that ultimately led to a brief big league debut. Injuries set him back almost immediately in 2023. He missed time in spring training with a pinky injury on his throwing hand and then strained his left oblique in July. Pineda spent the bulk of the year in Double-A, where he hit .153 with 34 strikeouts in 28 games.

SCOUTING REPORT: Pineda never found a rhythm at the plate in 2023. At his best, he has a quick swing and above-average power potential that helps him punish fastballs. Pineda's approach and strike-zone discipline has wavered throughout his development. That was again the case in limited action in 2023. He chased more than a third of the time and posted a 6.5% walk rate in 107 Double-A plate appearances. Defensively, Pineda's framing remains a work in progress, but his hands are improving. He added quickness and improved his mechanics at full strength in 2022. Now, the question is whether he can get back to that point.

THE FUTURE: The Nationals still view Pineda as a viable backup catcher option, though he has Keibert Ruiz and Riley Adams clearly ahead of him on the MLB depth chart entering 2024.

Year	Age	Club (League)	Level	AVG	G	AB	R	H	2B	3B	HR	RBI	BB	SO	SB	OBP	SLG
2023	23	FCL Nationals	Rk	.400	2	5	3	2	0	0	1	1	1	1	0	.500	1.000
2023	23	Wilmington (SAL)	A+	.205	11	39	3	8	1	0	1	4	1	10	0	.225	.308
2023	23	Harrisburg (EL)	AA	.153	28	98	6	15	3	0	1	9	7	34	0	.215	.214
Minor League Totals				.231	381	1393	179	322	59	4	44	204	109	373	4	.291	.374
Major League Totals				.077	4	13	1	1	0	0	0	0	1	7	0	.143	.077

21 DREW MILLAS, C

HIT: 45. **POW:** 30. **RUN:** 50. **FLD:** 50. **ARM:** 60. **BA Grade:** 40. **Risk:** High.

Born: January 15, 1998. **B-T:** B-R. **HT:** 6-2. **WT:** 205. **Drafted:** Missouri State, 2019 (7th round). **Signed by:** Steve Abney (Athletics).

TRACK RECORD: The Athletics drafted Millas in the seventh round of the 2019 draft, but a UCL injury in his throwing elbow and a blood-clotting issue, plus the coronavirus shutdown, delayed his pro debut to 2021. The Nationals acquired Millas that season in a deal that sent Yan Gomes and Josh Harrison to Oakland. He made a strong impression in the 2022 Arizona Fall League and then hit .291 in 83 games in the upper levels in 2023, earning a big league callup at the end of the year.

SCOUTING REPORT: Millas' offensive game took a step forward in 2023. He showed strong bat-to-ball skills, feel for the barrel and strike-zone awareness. Millas rarely missed on pitches in the strike zone, posting one of the better in-zone whiff rates of any Nationals minor leaguer in 2023. He also walked nearly as often as he struck out in the upper minors. His offense is limited by below-average power and he's never hit more than seven homers in a season. He's a good athlete—Millas clocked an 80th percentile sprint speed in his brief MLB debut—and threw out 28% of basestealers in the upper minors. Millas has average defensive skills but can make mistakes when he gets too overeager, and he also needs to work on his pitch framing.

THE FUTURE: Millas profiles as a solid backup catcher option and could be in line for a big league role out of spring training, depending on the health of Riley Adams and Israel Pineda.

Year	Age	Club (League)	Level	AVG	G	AB	R	H	2B	3B	HR	RBI	BB	SO	SB	OBP	SLG
2023	25	Harrisburg (EL)	AA	.341	25	82	14	28	4	0	4	19	16	16	2	.455	.537
2023	25	Rochester (IL)	AAA	.270	58	196	26	53	11	3	3	24	26	33	4	.362	.403
2023	25	Washington (NL)	MLB	.286	11	28	1	8	2	0	1	6	4	5	0	.375	.464
Minor League Totals				.260	257	889	129	231	45	6	16	127	147	188	29	.368	.378

22 COLE HENRY, RHP

FB: 55. **SL:** 55. **CHG:** 55. **CUT:** 40. **CTL:** 50. **BA Grade:** 45. **Risk:** Extreme.

Born: July 15, 1999. **B-T:** R-R. **HT:** 6-4. **WT:** 214. **Drafted:** Louisiana State, 2020 (2nd round).
Signed by: Brandon Larson.
TRACK RECORD: Henry has struggled to stay healthy since the Nationals selected him out of Louisiana State in the second round of the 2020 draft. He missed three months with elbow soreness in 2021 and had season-ending thoracic outlet syndrome surgery in August 2022. Henry returned to the mound in May 2023 but was limited to just 33.1 innings in 14 outings and has thrown just 112 innings in his career.
SCOUTING REPORT: Henry has a three-pitch mix, but the whole may end up being greater than the sum of the parts. Henry primarily relies on a mid-90s two-seam fastball that doesn't miss a ton of bats but is effective in manufacturing outs. He backs the fastball with a pair of offspeed pitches that could each be above-average. His slicing slider the better of the two and could play even better as he gets further from surgery. Henry rounds out the mix with a changeup that looked to be roughly above-average but got more consistent as the year progressed. He also throws a below-average cutter and has roughly average control.
THE FUTURE: Simply returning to the mound from TOS was a massive step in Henry's development. He could soon be knocking on the door of the big leagues, though his injury history and competitive mindset may ultimately land him in a multi-inning relief role.

Year	Age	Club (League)	Level	W	L	ERA	G	GS	IP	H	HR	BB	SO	BB%	SO%	WHIP	AVG
2023	23	Fredericksburg (CAR)	A	0	0	0.00	2	2	7	4	0	0	11	0.0	42.3	0.57	.167
2023	23	Wilmington (SAL)	A+	0	1	2.25	2	2	8	6	1	3	5	9.7	16.1	1.13	.214
2023	23	Harrisburg (EL)	AA	0	2	10.31	10	6	18	23	5	13	21	14.3	23.1	1.96	.311
Minor League Totals				4	8	3.29	34	29	112	75	11	39	141	8.7	31.3	1.02	.188

23 KEVIN MADE, SS

HIT: 40. **POW:** 40. **RUN:** 50. **FLD:** 65. **ARM:** 70. **BA Grade:** 40. **Risk:** High.

Born: September 10, 2002. **B-T:** R-R. **HT:** 5-9. **WT:** 160. **Signed:** Dominican Republic, 2019.
Signed by: Louis Elijaua/Jose Serra/Gian Guzman (Cubs).
TRACK RECORD: The Cubs signed Made out of the Dominican Republic for $1.5 million in 2019 and he debuted at 18 years old two years later with Low-A Myrtle Beach. He has yet to play his way to the upper levels of the minors. Made hit .241/.328/.355 in 70 games with High-A South Bend before Chicago dealt him to the Nationals in the Jeimer Candelario trade at the 2023 deadline. Made hit just .137 in 22 games with High-A Wilmington.
SCOUTING REPORT: Made showed signs of more power and patience in 2022, but it didn't translate as frequently a year later in a difficult Midwest League hitting environment. He isn't especially toolsy, but the ingredients are there for a solid future. Made's sound swing and barrel control allow him to make a considerable amount of contact on pitches in the zone. He has yet to tap into much power, especially when he gets overaggressive and expands the zone. Made's defense is ahead of his bat. He's a nearly double-plus defender at shortstop with a strong throwing arm. The Nationals believe he'll stick there, especially as his actions improve with more repetitions.
THE FUTURE: Made's defensive skills provide a solid foundation, but the clock is ticking on his bat to make up ground.

Year	Age	Club (League)	Level	AVG	G	AB	R	H	2B	3B	HR	RBI	BB	SO	SB	OBP	SLG
2023	20	South Bend (MWL)	A+	.240	70	262	39	63	17	2	3	25	30	54	3	.328	.355
2023	20	Wilmington (SAL)	A+	.137	22	73	5	10	4	0	0	5	9	18	1	.232	.192
Minor League Totals				.235	244	922	118	217	54	6	14	94	91	209	9	.310	.352

24 JEREMY DE LA ROSA, OF

HIT: 45. **POW:** 55. **RUN:** 50. **FLD:** 55. **ARM:** 45. **BA Grade:** 45. **Risk:** Extreme.

Born: January 16, 2002. **B-T:** L-L. **HT:** 5-11. **WT:** 215. **Signed:** Dominican Republic, 2018. **Signed by:** Modesto Ulloa.

TRACK RECORD: De La Rosa signed with the Nationals for $300,000 when the 2018 international signing period opened. He impressed the organization initially but struggled during his first full-season campaign in 2021. De La Rosa broke out in 2022, hitting .280/.358/.436 in 101 games while reaching High-A Wilmington before a hamate bone injury ended his season. He never quite found his footing 2023, striking out 129 times in 93 games with Wilmington, and an August injury again ended his season early. After the season, the Nationals removed De La Rosa from the 40-man roster.

SCOUTING REPORT: De La Rosa impressed the Nationals in 2022 with his work ethic and resilience after a slow start to his career. He added 15 pounds of muscle entering 2023, but the added strength took a toll on his athleticism. His power output took a noticeable dip and he managed just 25 extra-base hits. He struck out more in 2023 and whiffed nearly 39% of the time, showing an inconsistent approach and feel to hit. De La Rosa's average exit velocity and 90th percentile EV were on par with some of the better power hitters in the system, but he needs to get to it more frequently. De La Rosa was once an above-average runner, but the additional mass seemed to impact his speed and range defensively as well.

THE FUTURE: The Nationals hope De La Rosa can return to form after a frustrating season. The organization has added outfield depth ahead of him, but De La Rosa has the upside of a fourth outfielder if he can make better contact.

Year	Age	Club (League)	Level	AVG	G	AB	R	H	2B	3B	HR	RBI	BB	SO	SB	OBP	SLG
2023	21	Wilmington (SAL)	A+	.240	93	338	44	81	16	2	7	42	41	129	13	.324	.361
Minor League Totals				.244	307	1143	158	279	52	11	25	141	131	395	62	.325	.374

25 ARMANDO CRUZ, SS

HIT: 40. **POW:** 30 **RUN:** 55 **FLD:** 65 **ARM:** 60. **BA Grade:** 45. **Risk:** Extreme.

Born: January 16, 2004. **B-T:** R-R. **HT:** 5-10. **WT:** 160. **Signed:** Dominican Republic, 2021. **Signed By:** Modesto Ulloa/Ricky Vasquez.

TRACK RECORD: Cruz set a Nationals international bonus record when he signed for $3.9 million in January 2021. The glove-first shortstop showed promise during his first full season in 2022 in the Florida Complex League and briefly reached Low-A Fredericksburg at the end of the season. He returned to Low-A to start 2023, hoping to take another step forward at the plate. But Cruz hit .190/.266/.251 in 90 games.

SCOUTING REPORT: Cruz's glovework was renowned as a 16-year-old prospect in the Dominican Republic, to the point where clips of him taking infield during showcases were well-trafficked on social media even before he signed. Defense remains Cruz's calling card as a professional. He has a plus throwing arm and Gold Glove-caliber potential. The Nationals knew Cruz's hitting would need to improve—and that it may take time—but so far it's been a slow burn. He has quick hands at the plate and natural bat-to-ball skills, but his lack of strength leads to minimal impact and he also needs to dial in his approach.

THE FUTURE: Cruz still has the potential to be one of the best defensive shortstops in baseball, but his offensive game remains very raw.

Year	Age	Club (League)	Level	AVG	G	AB	R	H	2B	3B	HR	RBI	BB	SO	SB	OBP	SLG
2023	19	Fredericksburg (CAR)	A	.190	90	331	44	63	9	1	3	33	31	67	7	.266	.251
Minor League Totals				.226	193	730	110	165	26	4	6	72	60	135	24	.289	.297

26 DARREN BAKER, 2B

HIT: 50. **POW:** 30. **RUN:** 55. **FLD:** 45. **ARM:** 40. **BA Grade:** 40. **Risk:** High.

Born: February 11, 1999. **B-T:** L-R. **HT:** 5-10. **WT:** 180. **Drafted:** California, 2021 (10th round). **Signed by:** Bryan Byrne.

TRACK RECORD: Baker grew up around baseball as the son of future Hall of Fame manager Dusty Baker. The Nationals drafted Darren out of high school in the 27th round in 2017 while his father Dusty was their manager, but he opted to attend college. Washington again selected Baker in the 10th round of the 2021 draft out of California. Baker has been a solid producer in pro ball and reached Triple-A Rochester in 2023, hitting .273/.338/.340 with 19 steals in 99 games.

SCOUTING REPORT: Baker sprays the ball all over the field and has strong contact ability thanks to great barrel accuracy. He's tough to beat in the strike zone, whiffing on pitches in the zone roughly 10% of the time in 2023. The tradeoff is that Baker is very dependent on those balls in play dropping for hits. He rarely makes very strong contact and doesn't project for much more power, hitting just six homers over three minor league seasons. Baker is an above-average runner. He primarily plays second base, where his below-average arm fits best, but he did play left field for the first time as a professional in 2023.

THE FUTURE: Baker is on the cusp of the big leagues, but he's likely limited to a reserve role given his general lack of power.

Year	Age	Club (League)	Level	AVG	G	AB	R	H	2B	3B	HR	RBI	BB	SO	SB	OBP	SLG
2023	24	FCL Nationals	Rk	.444	3	9	0	4	1	0	0	2	0	1	0	.444	.556
2023	24	Wilmington (SAL)	A+	.444	5	18	1	8	0	0	0	1	4	2	2	.545	.444
2023	24	Rochester (IL)	AAA	.273	99	403	49	110	10	4	3	41	39	76	19	.338	.340
Minor League Totals				.286	234	925	121	265	39	6	6	89	89	171	38	.349	.361

27 TJ WHITE, 1B

HIT: 40. **POW:** 60. **RUN:** 40 **FLD:** 40 **ARM:** 45. **BA Grade:** 45. **Risk:** Extreme.

Born: July 23, 2003. **B-T:** B-R. **HT:** 6-2. **WT:** 210. **Drafted:** HS—Roebuck, SC, 2021 (5th round).
Signed by: Eric Robinson.
TRACK RECORD: White was one of the youngest players in the 2021 draft when the Nationals selected him in the fifth round. He impressed in the Florida Complex League that year and hit 11 homers in 92 games in 2022 as an 18-year-old with Low-A Fredericksburg. With plenty of outfield depth ahead of White, the Nationals moved him to first base in 2023 with the hope he could move quickly. Instead, he took a major step backward. White hit .170/.227/.279 and stuck out more than 36% of the time with High-A Wilmington. He was placed on the development list and missed the last three weeks of the season.
SCOUTING REPORT: At his best, White is a powerful switch-hitter. Evaluators rarely saw him at his best in 2023. White still showed a decent ability to parse through balls and strikes, but he posted a miss rate of nearly 40%. He was frequently beaten by premium velocity in the zone, and opposing scouts noticed that his swing had gotten longer. White was a solid runner as an amateur but added weight to his lower half and could continue to slow down as he fills out. He will need to continue to develop at first base.
THE FUTURE: White's contact woes were alarming, especially considering his profile. He'll need to put the ball in play more to work toward his ceiling as a slugging first baseman.

Year	Age	Club (League)	Level	AVG	G	AB	R	H	2B	3B	HR	RBI	BB	SO	SB	OBP	SLG
2023	19	Wilmington (SAL)	A+	.170	77	247	23	42	5	2	6	25	35	104	0	.277	.279
Minor League Totals				.226	184	629	89	142	27	4	21	89	84	222	9	.323	.382

28 MITCHELL PARKER, LHP

FB: 55. **CB:** 50. **SL:** 50. **CHG:** 45. **CTL:** 40. **BA Grade:** 40. **Risk:** Very High.

Born: September 27, 1999. **B-T:** L-L. **HT:** 6-4. **WT:** 195. **Drafted:** San Jacinto (TX) JC, 2020 (5th round).
Signed by: Jimmy Gonzales.
TRACK RECORD: Parker signed with the Nationals as a fifth-round pick in 2020. He broke out in 2022, posting a 2.88 ERA and a near 27% strikeout rate at High-A Wilmington. Parker did not create the same amount of buzz in his first taste of the upper minors in 2023. He spent most of the season with Double-A Harrisburg, where he pitched to a 4.20 ERA. He joined the Triple-A Rochester for three starts at the end of the year and gave up 12 runs in 10.1 innings.
SCOUTING REPORT: Parker has intriguing fastball characteristics. The lefthander throws a 92-93 mph four-seam fastball from a high slot that has roughly 20 inches of induced vertical break and cutting action. He pairs it with two distinct breaking balls. His downer low-80s curveball is his best secondary and was a major focus last offseason. He also throws a tight low-80s slider that batters missed roughly a third of the time. Parker has searched for a consistent feel on both a changeup and slider. He misses a lot of bats but also needs to tighten his control after he walked 11% of batters in Double-A.
THE FUTURE: The organization still believes Parker has the upside of a No. 5 starter. However, if he is unable to rein in his walk rate, a move to the bullpen is likely.

Year	Age	Club (League)	Level	W	L	ERA	G	GS	IP	H	HR	BB	SO	BB%	SO%	WHIP	AVG
2023	23	Harrisburg (EL)	AA	9	6	4.20	25	23	114	100	10	54	132	11.1	27.2	1.35	.235
2023	23	Rochester (IL)	AAA	0	1	10.45	3	3	10	15	3	7	18	13.2	34.0	2.13	.326
Minor League Totals				19	23	4.21	75	71	326	294	28	166	411	11.6	28.8	1.42	.237

29 ANDREW ALVAREZ, LHP

FB: 45. **CB:** 50. **CHG:** 50. **CTL:** 45. **BA Grade:** 40. **Risk:** Very High.

Born: June 13, 1999. **B-T:** L-L. **HT:** 6-3. **WT:** 215. **Drafted:** Cal Poly, 2021 (12th round). **Signed by:** Bryan Byrne.

TRACK RECORD: The Nationals selected Alvarez in the 12th round of the 2021 draft after the lefty had a breakout campaign as the member of Cal Poly's weekend rotation. In his first full season in 2022, Alvarez struggled across both Low-A and High-A, pitching to a 5.00 ERA. However, his 2023 season was reminiscent of his senior season. He led the Nationals' system with a 2.99 ERA and 129.1 innings while finishing second with 116 strikeouts. It was the first time since 2019 that a qualifying Nationals pitcher recorded a sub-3.00 ERA in a full-season minor league.

SCOUTING REPORT: Alvarez uses a funky lefthanded motion to deliver his 91 mph four-seam fastball. The pitch has below-average velocity but some slight cutting action to evade barrels. His two-seamer has some late sink and some armside life. Alvarez has a polished look and good feel for his arsenal, which includes an average curveball and a changeup that could develop into an average pitch. However, he is very much a "what you see is what you get" pitcher who does not project to develop more athleticism.

THE FUTURE: Alvarez was not added to the Nationals' 40-man roster and went unselected in the Rule 5 draft. The lack of velocity is the biggest question mark in his game. If he can add some strength and velo, the Nationals could have a depth lefthander capable of long relief or spot starts.

Year	Age	Club (League)	Level	W	L	ERA	G	GS	IP	H	HR	BB	SO	BB%	SO%	WHIP	AVG
2023	24	Wilmington (SAL)	A+	7	4	2.61	21	18	103	88	4	32	96	7.7	23.1	1.16	.235
2023	24	Harrisburg (EL)	AA	0	3	4.50	5	4	26	20	5	11	20	9.9	18.0	1.19	.206
Minor League Totals				12	14	3.67	61	31	223	204	13	81	231	8.5	24.3	1.28	.239

30 ANDRY LARA, RHP

FB: 45. **SL:** 50. **CHG:** 40. **CTL:** 50. **BA Grade:** 40. **Risk:** Extreme.

Born: January 6, 2003. **B-T:** R-R. **HT:** 6-5. **WT:** 235. **Signed:** Venezuela, 2019. **Signed by:** Ronald Morillo.

TRACK RECORD: Lara was the Nationals' top international target in 2019 and signed as a 16-year-old for $1.25 million. He spent the following year at the team's facility in Florida during baseball's shutdown. His pro debut in 2021 was promising, but he struggled in 2022 with Low-A Fredericksburg as the youngest player on the roster. He spent all of 2023 with High-A Wilmington in his age-20 season, posting a 4.58 ERA and 66 strikeouts in 98.1 innings. The Nationals did not protect him ahead of the 2023 Rule 5 draft in December and he was not selected.

SCOUTING REPORT: Lara has traditionally shown above-average velocity, touching 98 mph at his peak, but his fastball velocity backed up a bit in 2023 as it settled into the 92-93 mph range and touched 95. He threw his two-seamer nearly 60% of the time, but it does not have great bat-missing characteristics and was hit hard. Lara's best pitch is his mid-80s slider that has plus shape and misses bats. His upper-80s changeup continues to flash good sinking action, but he has yet to develop much feel for it. A lack of a true third pitch has heightened relief concerns for Lara, despite a decent track record of strike-throwing from a relatively simple delivery.

THE FUTURE: While Lara has flashed intriguing upside, the Nationals have yet to unlock either consistency or a reliable third pitch. He'll need to show improvement in both areas to remain on a starter track.

Year	Age	Club (League)	Level	W	L	ERA	G	GS	IP	H	HR	BB	SO	BB%	SO%	WHIP	AVG
2023	20	Wilmington (SAL)	A+	6	8	4.58	23	23	98	90	11	34	66	8.2	15.9	1.26	.241
Minor League Totals				12	19	4.97	57	55	248	234	28	99	223	9.2	20.8	1.34	.245

Beginning with the 2017 Collective Bargaining Agreement, international players who seek to sign with MLB organizations were sorted into two groups: amateurs subject to the bonus pool system or "foreign professionals," who are essentially major league free agents.

The latter group is defined by MLB as players who are at least 25 years of age and have played as a professional in a foreign league—typically in Japan, Korea or Cuba—for a minimum of six seasons.

New this year, Baseball America no longer considers foreign professionals to be prospects, even though they will be eligible for Rookie of the Year awards in 2024. We will still cover these players as rookies, and we will continue to provide you with the most accurate scouting reports. What we won't do is rank foreign professionals in organizational Top 30 Prospects or among the Top 100 Prospects.

Kyle Glaser reported and wrote about the top foreign professionals eligible to come to MLB in 2024.

YOSHINOBU YAMAMOTO, RHP

FB: 60. **CB:** 60. **SL:** 55. **SPLIT:** 60. **CTL:** 60. **BA Grade:** 70. **Risk:** Medium.

Born: August 17, 1998. **B-T:** R-R. **HT:** 5-10. **WT:** 176.

TRACK RECORD: In the long history of successful Japanese pitchers, none has been as decorated as Yamamoto. A former infielder who began focusing on pitching in high school, Yamamoto made his Nippon Professional Baseball debut at 18 years old in 2017 and quickly blossomed into Japan's premier pitcher. He posted a 1.82 ERA over seven seasons as Orix's ace and put together arguably the greatest three-year stretch by a pitcher in NPB history from 2021 to 2023. He won three straight Sawamura Awards, the Japanese equivalent of the Cy Young Award, and three straight Pacific League MVP Awards, the first player to do that since Ichiro Suzuki. He showed his stuff played against MLB hitters during standout showings at the Tokyo Olympics and 2023 World Baseball Classic, helping Japan win gold medals at both, and became the first pitcher in Japanese history to throw a no-hitter in consecutive seasons. Yamamoto fittingly finished his NPB career in record-breaking fashion in the Japan Series. Pitching in Game 6 with Orix facing elimination, Yamamoto pitched a complete game with 14 strikeouts, breaking the series strikeout record held by Yu Darvish.

SCOUTING REPORT: Yamamoto is undersized at 5-foot-10, 176 pounds, but he's strong in his frame and possesses a powerful arsenal he holds deep into games. His fastball sits 94-96 mph and touches 99 with little effort out of a clean, athletic delivery. He has a fast arm and commands his fastball in all quadrants of the strike zone. Yamamoto's most-used secondary pitch is a plus 88-91 mph splitter with huge depth that induces weak grounders and empty swings. He commands his splitter exceptionally well and has a good feel for when to use it. Yamamoto's tight-spinning 76-78 mph rainbow curveball is another plus pitch that freezes both lefthanded and righthanded hitters. He didn't throw it much in Japan, but it projects to be a larger part of his repertoire in MLB. He rounds out his arsenal with an above-average low-90s cutter/short slider that stays off of barrels. Yamamoto ties his stuff together with plus control and an aggressive, attacking mentality. He pitches with a chip on his shoulder and challenges hitters in the strike zone with no fear. He has exceptional feel for mixing his pitches and has the aptitude to make quick in-game adjustments. Yamamoto's size yields concerns about his durability, but he's pitched at least 170 innings each of the last three seasons and has a clean health record. He threw 138 pitches in his final start in the Japan Series and reached 98 mph in the ninth inning.

THE FUTURE: Yamamoto will have to adjust from pitching once a week in Japan to every five days in MLB, but like Darvish, Masahiro Tanaka, Daisuke Matsuzaka and Hideo Nomo before him, he has the stuff and aptitude to successfully make that transition. He projects to be a No. 2 starter and has a chance to contend for Cy Young Awards.

Year	Age	Club (League)	Level	W	L	ERA	G	GS	IP	H	HR	BB	SO	BB%	SO%	WHIP	AVG
2023	24	Orix (PL)	NPB	16	6	1.21	23	—	164	117	2	28	169	4.4	26.6	0.89	—
Japanese Major League Totals				70	29	1.82	172	—	897	633	36	206	922	5.9	26.4	0.94	—

Yoshinobu
Yamamoto

JUNG HOO LEE, OF

HIT: 60. **POW:** 45. **RUN:** 55. **FLD:** 50. **ARM:** 45. **BA Grade:** 55. **Risk:** High.

Born: August 20, 1998. **B-T:** L-R. **HT:** 6-1. **WT:**189.

TRACK RECORD: Lee is the son of Korean baseball icon and former Korea Baseball Organization MVP Jong-Beom Lee, who was nicknamed "Son of the Wind" for his legendary speed. The younger Lee emerged early as a baseball prodigy and skipped the Korean minor leagues to jump straight from high school to the KBO. He set a KBO rookie record for hits as an 18-year-old in 2017, won the rookie of the year award, and blossomed into a superstar in his 20s. Lee hit .340 over six seasons with the Kiwoom franchise, starred for Korea at the Tokyo Olympics and 2023 World Baseball Classic and won the KBO MVP award in 2022 after batting .349 with a career-high 23 home runs and 113 RBIs. He played just 86 games in 2023 after he suffered a fractured left ankle in July and had season-ending surgery.

YUICHI YAMAZAKI/AFP

SCOUTING REPORT: Lee is an exemplary hitter with a fast lefthanded swing and elite-hand eye coordination. He identifies pitches quickly and consistently gets the barrel to the ball, driving hittable pitches on a line to all fields. He controls the strike zone with a mature, patient approach, hits both lefties and righties and makes consistent contact against both fastballs and breaking balls. He has the athleticism and bat speed to adjust to higher velocities in MLB and projects to be an above-average and possibly plus hitter once he settles in. Lee doesn't hit the ball overly hard, but he has enough strength to yank balls over the fence to his pull side. He projects to rack up doubles while hitting 10-15 home runs per season. Nicknamed "Grandson of the Wind" in homage to his father, Lee is more of an above-average runner than true burner. He has solid instincts and runs good routes in center field, but his range is a tick short, particularly on balls over his head. He has reliable hands and projects to be an average defender in center field, though he may have trouble in more expansive outfields. He has fringy arm strength that will force him to left field if he has to move.

THE FUTURE: Lee projects to be a leadoff-hitting outfielder who hits for a high average and gets on base. He'll be 25 for most of the 2024 season and still has his prime years ahead of him.

Year	Age	Club	Level	AVG	G	AB	R	H	2B	3B	HR	RBI	BB	SO	SB	OBP	SLG
2023	24	Kiwoom	KBO	.318	86	330	50	105	23	2	6	45	49	23	6	.406	.455
Korean Major League Totals				.340	884	3476	581	1181	244	43	65	515	383	304	69	.407	.491

SHOTA IMANAGA, LHP

FB: 50. **CB:** 40. **SL:** 45. **SPLIT:** 55. **CTL:** 55. **BA Grade:** 50. **Risk:** Medium.

Born: September 1, 1993. **B-T:** L-L. **HT:** 5-10. **WT:** 190.

TRACK RECORD: Imanaga starred as one of Japan's top college pitchers at Komazawa University and was drafted by Yokohama in the first round in 2015. He made his NPB debut one year later and quickly emerged as one of Japan's preeminent lefthanders. He posted a 3.18 ERA over eight seasons with the BayStars, threw a no-hitter in 2022 and led the Central League with 174 strikeouts in 2023. He started for Japan against Team USA in the gold-medal game of the 2023 World Baseball Classic and pitched two innings to earn the win while striking out Paul Goldschmidt and Cedric Mullins.

SCOUTING REPORT: Imanaga is a crafty lefthander with a good feel for pitching. His fastball sits 88-92 mph with solid riding life as a starter and touches 94-95 in short bursts. His main secondary pitch is an above-average 84-85 mph splitter with late cut that induces grounders. Imanaga's success in MLB will hinge largely on the development of his slider. It's currently a fringy offering at 80-85 mph that stays on one plane and gets barreled in the strike zone. He's flashed the ability to throw it firmer and get chase swings, but it needs improvement. He also has a below-average 71-74 mph curveball he'll throw as a change-of-pace offering. Imanaga mostly throws to his glove side and can get one-sided in his repertoire, but he mixes and matches well to keep opponents off-balance. He has above-average control and keeps everything around the plate.

THE FUTURE: Imanaga's feel for pitching gives him a chance to be a No. 4 or 5 starter. He may fit best as a swingman or bulk reliever.

Year	Age	Club (League)	Level	W	L	ERA	G	GS	IP	H	HR	BB	SO	BB%	SO%	WHIP	AVG
2023	29	Yokohama (CL)	NPB	7	4	2.80	22	—	148	132	17	24	174	4.0	29.2	1.05	—
Japanese Major League Totals				64	50	3.18	165	—	1003	841	114	280	1021	6.9	25.0	1.12	—

YARIEL RODRIGUEZ, RHP

FB: 60. **CB:** 40. **SL:** 55. **SPLIT:** 45. **CTL:** 45. **BA Grade:** 45. **Risk:** Medium.

Born: March 10, 1997. **B-T:** R-R. **HT:** 6-1. **WT:** 214.

TRACK RECORD: Rodriguez was a soft-tossing starter with an 87-90 mph fastball in Cuba's Serie Nacional before blossoming with a move to Japan. His stuff increased markedly over three seasons with Chunichi and he emerged as one of NPB's top setup men, with a 1.15 ERA in 56 appearances in 2022. He returned to starting for Cuba in the 2023 World Baseball Classic and delivered a pair of solid outings to raise his profile as a potential rotation piece. He opted not to return to Chunichi for the 2023 season and spent the year training in preparation for a move to MLB.

SCOUTING REPORT: Rodriguez is an aggressive power pitcher whose stuff and performance keep improving. His four-seam fastball is now a plus pitch that sits 94-98 mph with natural cut and gets swings and misses in the strike zone. He also has a 93-96 mph two-seamer with hard armside run. Rodriguez's main secondary pitch is an above-average 83-86 mph slider with vertical bite and solid depth. He primarily throws his fastball and slider and is able to dominate with them. Rodriguez lacks touch on his softer offerings. He has inconsistent feel for his fringy splitter and below-average curveball and rarely throws them. He is a volatile, highly emotional pitcher prone to overthrowing and struggles to throttle down. He has an effortful delivery and fringy control overall.

THE FUTURE: Rodriguez will get the chance to start, but his arsenal and demeanor project best in relief. He has a chance to be a hard-throwing No. 5 starter or setup man.

Year	Age	Club (League)	Level	W	L	ERA	G	GS	IP	H	HR	BB	SO	BB%	SO%	WHIP	AVG
2023	26	Did not play															
Japanese Major League Totals				10	10	3.03	79	—	175	138	12	77	188	10.4	25.4	1.23	—

YUKI MATSUI, LHP

FB: 45. **CB:** 45. **SL:** 55. **SPLIT:** 55. **CTL:** 40. **BA Grade:** 40. **Risk:** Medium.

Born: October 30, 1995. **B-T:** L-L. **HT:** 5-8. **WT:** 163.

TRACK RECORD: Matsui first rose to prominence in high school when he set a Koshien tournament record with 22 strikeouts in a game. He was selected in the first round of the NPB draft the following year and debuted in NPB at 18 in 2014. After beginning his career as a starter, Matsui shifted to relief and became one of Japan's most decorated closers. He recorded 236 saves in nine seasons with Rakuten, led the Pacific League in saves three times and won a gold medal with Japan at the 2023 World Baseball Classic.

SCOUTING REPORT: Matsui is undersized at 5-foot-8, 163 pounds and throws with maximum effort in short stints. His average fastball sits 91-93 mph and touches 95 with riding life up in the zone. His diving 87-90 mph splitter is an above-average pitch that gets grounders from both lefthanded and righthanded hitters. Matsui mostly throws those two pitches, but he also has an above-average, sharp mid-80s slider that plays against hitters on both sides of the plate. He also has a fringy 75-78 mph curveball. Matsui struggles to control his effort at times and is prone to sailing fastballs. He posted a career-low walk rate in

2023 but has demonstrated below-average control over his career.

THE FUTURE: Matsui projects to be a low-to-mid-leverage reliever who handles both lefties and righties. He's ready to join a big league bullpen on Opening Day.

Year	Age	Club (League)	Level	W	L	ERA	G	GS	IP	H	HR	BB	SO	BB%	SO%	WHIP	AVG
2023	27	Rakuten (PL)	NPB	2	3	1.57	59	—	57	38	3	13	72	5.9	32.4	0.89	—
Japanese Major League Totals				25	46	2.40	501	—	660	436	31	295	860	10.9	31.9	1.11	—

NAOYUKI UWASAWA, RHP

FB: 40. **CB:** 40. **SL:** 45. **CUT:** 40. **SPLIT:** 50. **CHG:** 45. **CTL:** 55. **BA Grade:** 40. **Risk:** Medium.

Born: February 6, 1994. **B-T:** R-R. **HT:** 6-2. **WT:** 194.

TRACK RECORD: Uwasawa began his career as a rotation-mate of Shohei Ohtani with the Nippon Ham Fighters and emerged as their top starter after Ohtani departed for MLB. Despite a lack of big stuff, Uwasawa blossomed into a three-time all-star atop the Fighters' rotation and had one of his best seasons in 2023. He went 9-9, 2.96 in a career-high 170 innings and was posted after the season.

SCOUTING REPORT: Uwasawa is a finesse righthander who relies on command and changing speeds. His fastball sits 89-91 mph and tops out at 93, but he locates it on the edges of the strike zone to avoid hard contact. His most-used secondary is a fringy, vertical 80-82 mph slider with decent depth, while his mid-80s splitter with diving action is an average pitch he leans on to get outs. He also mixes in a looping, below-average mid-70s curveball, below-average 85-88 mph cutter and fringy 80-82 mph changeup to keep batters guessing. Uwasawa mostly relies on keeping hitters off-balance and inducing soft contact. He doesn't miss many bats and averaged just 6.6 strikeouts per nine innings last season. He is a good athlete with a fluid delivery and clean arm action and has above-average control.

THE FUTURE: Uwasawa's lack of stuff will be tested in MLB. He projects to be a low-end No. 5 or depth starter who relies on hitting his spots to be effective.

Year	Age	Club (League)	Level	W	L	ERA	G	GS	IP	H	HR	BB	SO	BB%	SO%	WHIP	AVG
2023	29	Nippon Ham (PL)	NPB	9	9	2.96	24	—	170	152	14	41	124	5.9	17.8	1.14	—
Japanese Major League Totals				70	62	3.19	173	—	1118	972	94	349	913	7.5	19.7	1.18	—

WOO SUK GO, RHP

FB: 55. **CB:** 45. **CUT:** 40. **CTL:** 45. **BA Grade:** 40. **Risk:** High.

Born: August 6, 1998. **B-T:** R-R. **HT:** 6-0. **WT:** 198.

TRACK RECORD: Go debuted in the Korea Baseball Organization as a teenager and quickly emerged as a top closer with premium velocity for the league. He recorded 139 saves in five seasons for the LG Twins after becoming their closer, including a league-leading 42 saves in 2022, and represented Korea at the Tokyo Olympics. Go missed the 2023 World Baseball Classic with shoulder and neck stiffness and missed a month during the regular season with a lower back injury, but he returned to help lead the Twins to their first Korean Series championship in 29 years. He closed out the title with a perfect ninth inning in the clincher.

SCOUTING REPORT: Go is a strong, physical righthander with power stuff. His fastball sits 93-95 mph and touches 98 with late movement at its best. He lacks deception in his delivery and his fastball flattens out at times, but he is still able beat hitters with his pure power. Go's best secondary pitch is a 79-83 mph downer curveball that flashes average with late bite, but it's inconsistent. He also has a below-average, low-90s cutter that works as a chase pitch but gets hit hard in the zone. Go is an aggressive competitor and goes after hitters with his fastball, but he tends to spray it and has fringy control overall. He is married to star outfielder Jung Hoo Lee's younger sister and decided to come to MLB in conjunction with his brother-in-law.

THE FUTURE: Go's fastball gives him a chance to be a low-leverage reliever, but he needs to sharpen his secondaries to be more. He'll be 25 for most of the 2024 season and still has room for growth.

Year	Age	Club (League)	Level	W	L	ERA	G	GS	IP	H	HR	BB	SO	BB%	SO%	WHIP	AVG
2023	24	LG	KBO	3	8	3.68	44	0	44	38	2	22	59	11.6	31.1	1.36	—
Korean Major League Totals				19	26	3.18	354	0	368	305	29	163	401	10.4	25.5	1.27	—

The major league phase of the Rule 5 draft occurred on Dec. 6, 2023. A few of these players rank in their new organizations' Top 30 Prospects, but since all 10 will be in big league spring training camp in 2024, we provide thumbnail scouting reports for all of them in this space.

Pick	Drafting Team	Player	Pos	2023 Org	BA Grade/Risk
1.	Athletics	Mitch Spence	RHP	Yankees	40/High

See full report on Page 336.

| 2. | Royals | Matt Sauer | RHP | Yankees | 40/Medium |

See full report on Page 206.

| 3. | Rockies | Anthony Molina | RHP | Rays | 40/High |

See full report on Page 158.

| 4. | White Sox | Shane Drohan | LHP | Red Sox | 45/High |

See full report on Page 111.

| 5. | Nationals | Nasim Nunez | SS | Marlins | 45/High |

See full report on Page 491.

| 6. | Cardinals | Ryan Fernandez | RHP | Red Sox | 40/High |

See full report on Page 384.

| 7. | Red Sox | Justin Slaten | RHP | Rangers | 40/Medium |

See full report on Page 80.

Note: Slaten was drafted by the Mets and traded to the Red Sox for lefthander Ryan Ammons and cash.

| 8. | Guardians | Deyvison De Los Santos | 3B/1B | D-backs | 50/Very High |

See full report on Page 138.

| 9. | Padres | Stephen Kolek | RHP | Mariners | 40/Medium |

Kolek made 44 appearances at Triple-A in 2023 and mixes a sinker at 94-95 mph with heavy armside run, a four-seamer at 95-96, a sweeper at 83-85 mph and a rarely used changeup. His two-seamer does an excellent job of generating weak groundball contact, while his slider misses bats. Kolek has a chance to stick with the Padres.

| 10. | Rangers | Carson Coleman | RHP | Yankees | 40/High |

Coleman had elbow surgery and missed the 2023 season, but when healthy the reliever sat 94-96 mph and touched 98 from a flat vertical approach angle with heavy armside run. His main secondary is his low-80s sweeper, a pitch synonymous with Yankees prospects. He'll flash a firm changeup at 89-90 mph but it's rarely used.

The top two picks in the Rule 5 draft were Yankees righthanders Mitch Spence (left) and Matt Sauer.

MIKE JANES/FOUR SEAM IMAGES (SPENCE); TOM PRIDDY/FOUR SEAM IMAGES (SAUER)

PROSPECT GRADUATION GRADES

Each fall, Baseball America develops its Top 30 Prospects rankings for the Prospect Handbook.

Now we have added a new wrinkle. We evaluated and ranked the top overall graduated prospects from last year's Prospect Handbook. The goal is to give prospects-turned-big leaguers their due before we say farewell and turn our attention to the next wave of talent working its way up the minor league ladder.

Each graduated prospect is listed here with his preseason BA Grade and then his updated BA Grade based on what happened in 2023. Players are ranked by updated end-of-season BA Grade, which gauges each player's realistic upside on the 20-80 scouting scale. A Risk assessment deducts points—10 for High, five for Medium and none for Low—to determine each prospect's Tier.

Each player's listed age is his baseball age in 2024.

Rk	Name	Pos	Team	Age	Preseason Grade/Risk	Updated Grade/Risk	Tier	Upside Role
1.	Corbin Carroll	RF	D-backs	23	65/Medium	70/Medium	65	Franchise OF
2.	Gunnar Henderson	SS	Orioles	23	70/Medium	70/Medium	65	Franchise SS
3.	Elly De La Cruz	SS	Reds	22	70/High	70/High	60	Franchise SS
4.	Eury Perez	RHP	Marlins	21	70/High	70/High	60	No. 2 starter
5.	Grayson Rodriguez	RHP	Orioles	24	70/High	70/High	60	No. 2 starter
6.	Bobby Miller	RHP	Dodgers	25	65/High	65/Medium	60	No. 2 or 3 starter
7.	Kodai Senga	RHP	Mets	31	55/High	60/Low	60	No. 3 starter
8.	Gabriel Moreno	C	D-backs	24	65/Medium	60/Medium	55	All-star C
9.	Francisco Alvarez	C	Mets	22	65/Medium	60/Medium	55	All-star C
10.	Jordan Walker	RF	Cardinals	22	70/High	65/High	55	All-star bat
11.	Royce Lewis	3B	Twins	24	60/High	65/High	55	All-star 3B
12.	Triston Casas	1B	Red Sox	24	60/Medium	60/Medium	55	All-star 1B
13.	Gavin Williams	RHP	Guardians	24	65/High	65/High	55	No. 2 or 3 starter
14.	Tanner Bibee	RHP	Guardians	25	55/High	60/Medium	55	No. 3 starter
15.	Josh Jung	3B	Rangers	26	55/High	60/Medium	55	All-star 3B
16.	Zack Gelof	2B	Athletics	24	50/High	55/Medium	50	First-division 2B
17.	Matt McLain	2B	Reds	24	45/Medium	55/Medium	50	First-division 2B
18.	Nolan Jones	RF	Rockies	26	40/Medium	55/Medium	50	First-division RF
19.	Brandon Pfaadt	RHP	D-backs	25	55/Medium	55/Medium	50	No. 3 or 4 starter
20.	Emmet Sheehan	RHP	Dodgers	24	50/High	55/Medium	50	No. 3 or 4 starter
21.	Luis Campusano	C	Padres	25	50/Medium	55/Medium	50	First-division C
22.	Ryan Pepiot	RHP	Dodgers	26	55/Medium	55/Medium	50	No. 3 or 4 starter
23.	Anthony Volpe	SS	Yankees	23	65/High	55/High	45	First-division SS
24.	Zach Neto	SS	Angels	23	55/High	55/High	45	First-division SS
25.	Yainer Diaz	C	Astros	25	50/Medium	50/Medium	45	Regular C
26.	Bryce Miller	RHP	Mariners	25	55/High	55/High	45	No. 3 or 4 starter
27.	Miguel Vargas	2B	Dodgers	24	60/Medium	55/High	45	Regular 2B or OF
28.	Ezequiel Tovar	SS	Rockies	22	65/High	50/Medium	45	Regular C
29.	Sal Frelick	CF	Brewers	24	55/Medium	50/Medium	45	Regular CF
30.	Christian Encarnacion-Strand	1B	Reds	24	55/V High	55/High	45	Regular 1B
31.	Endy Rodriguez	C	Pirates	24	65/High	55/High	45	Regular C
32.	Henry Davis	RF	Pirates	24	55/High	55/High	45	Regular RF
33.	Hunter Brown	RHP	Astros	25	65/High	55/High	45	No. 3 or 4 starter
34.	Cole Ragans	LHP	Royals	26	40/Medium	55/High	45	No. 3 or 4 starter
35.	Logan O'Hoppe	C	Angels	24	55/Medium	55/High	45	Regular C
36.	Brett Baty	3B	Mets	24	55/Medium	50/Medium	45	Regular 3B
37.	Jordan Westburg	2B	Orioles	25	50/Medium	50/Medium	45	Regular 2B or 3B
38.	Andrew Abbott	LHP	Reds	25	45/Medium	50/Medium	45	No. 4 starter
39.	Patrick Bailey	C	Giants	25	40/High	50/Medium	45	Regular C
40.	James Outman	CF	Dodgers	27	45/Medium	50/Medium	45	Regular CF
41.	Taj Bradley	RHP	Rays	23	55/Medium	55/High	45	No. 3 or 4 starter
42.	Bryan Woo	RHP	Mariners	24	50/High	55/High	45	No. 3 or 4 starter
43.	Edouard Julien	2B	Twins	25	55/High	50/Medium	45	Regular 1B
44.	Spencer Steer	1B/LF	Reds	26	45/Medium	50/Medium	45	Super utility
45.	Yennier Cano	RP	Orioles	30	Not ranked	50/Medium	45	Closer
46.	Johan Rojas	CF	Phillies	23	50/High	50/Medium	45	Regular CF
47.	Bo Naylor	C	Guardians	24	55/High	50/Medium	45	Regular C
48.	Masataka Yoshida	LF	Red Sox	30	50/Medium	50/Medium	45	Regular LF
49.	Matt Wallner	RF	Twins	26	50/High	50/Medium	45	Regular RF
50.	Chase Silseth	RHP	Angels	24	50/Medium	50/Medium	45	No. 4 starter

SIGNING BONUSES

2023 DRAFT

TOP THREE ROUNDS

FIRST ROUND

No. Team: Player, Pos.	Bonus
1. Pirates: Paul Skenes, RHP	$9,200,000
2. Nationals: Dylan Crews, OF	$9,000,000
3. Tigers: Max Clark, OF	$7,697,500
4. Rangers: Wyatt Langford, OF	$8,000,000
5. Twins: Walker Jenkins, OF	$7,144,200
6. Athletics: Jacob Wilson, SS	$5,500,000
7. Reds: Rhett Lowder, RHP	$5,700,000
8. Royals: Blake Mitchell, C	$4,897,500
9. Rockies: Chase Dollander, RHP	$5,716,900
10. Marlins: Noble Meyer, RHP	$4,500,000
11. Angels: Nolan Schanuel, 1B	$5,253,000
12. D-backs: Tommy Troy, SS	$4,400,000
13. Cubs: Matt Shaw, SS	$4,848,500
14. Red Sox: Kyle Teel, C	$4,000,000
15. White Sox: Jacob Gonzalez, SS	$3,900,000
16. Giants: Bryce Eldridge, OF/RHP	$3,997,500
17. Orioles: Enrique Bradfield Jr., OF	$4,169,700
18. Brewers: Brock Wilken, 3B	$3,150,000
19. Rays: Brayden Taylor, SS	$3,877,600
20. Blue Jays: Arjun Nimmala, SS	$3,000,000
21. Cardinals: Chase Davis, OF	$3,618,200
22. Mariners: Colt Emerson, SS	$3,800,000
23. Guardians: Ralphy Velazquez, C	$2,500,000
24. Braves: Hurston Waldrep, RHP	$2,997,500
25. Padres: Dillon Head, OF	$2,800,000
26. Yankees: George Lombard Jr., SS	$3,300,000
27. Phillies: Aidan Miller, SS	$3,100,000
28. Astros: Brice Matthews, SS	$2,478,200
29. Mariners: Jonny Farmelo, OF	$3,200,000

SUPPLEMENTAL FIRST ROUND

No. Team: Player, Pos.	Bonus
30. Mariners: Tai Peete, SS	$2,500,000
31. Rays: Adrian Santana, SS	$2,002,950
32. Mets: Colin Houck, SS	$2,750,000
33. Brewers: Josh Knoth, RHP	$2,000,000
34. Twins: Charlee Soto, RHP	$2,481,400
35. Marlins: Thomas White, LHP	$4,100,000
36. Dodgers: Kendall George, OF	$1,847,500
37. Tigers: Kevin McGonigle, SS	$2,847,500
38. Reds: Ty Floyd, RHP	$2,097,500
39. Athletics: Myles Naylor, 3B	$2,202,500

SECOND ROUND

No. Team: Player, Pos.	Bonus
40. Nationals: Yohandy Morales, 3B	$2,600,000
41. Athletics: Ryan Lasko, OF	$1,700,000
42. Pirates: Mitch Jebb, SS	$1,647,500
43. Reds: Sammy Stafura, SS	$2,497,500
44. Royals: Blake Wolters, RHP	$2,800,000
45. Tigers: Max Anderson, 2B	$1,429,650
46. Rockies: Sean Sullivan, LHP	$1,700,000
47. Marlins: Kemp Alderman, OF	$1,400,000
48. Diamondbacks: Gino Groover, 3B	$1,783,000
49. Twins: Luke Keaschall, 2B	$1,500,000

No. Team: Player, Pos.	Bonus
50. Red Sox: Nazzan Zanetello, SS	$3,000,000
51. White Sox: Grant Taylor, RHP	$1,659,800
52. Giants: Walker Martin, SS	$2,997,500
53. Orioles: Mac Horvath, OF	$1,400,000
54. Brewers: Mike Boeve, 3B	$1,250,000
55. Rays: Colton Ledbetter, OF	$1,297,500
56. Mets: Brandon Sproat, RHP	$1,474,500
57. Mariners: Ben Williamson, 3B	$600,000
58. Guardians: Alex Clemmey, LHP	$2,300,000
59. Braves: Drue Hackenberg, RHP	$1,997,500
60. Dodgers: Jake Gelof, 3B	$1,334,400
61. Astros: Alonzo Tredwell, RHP	$1,497,500

SUPPLEMENTAL SECOND ROUND

No. Team: Player, Pos.	Bonus
62. Guardians: Andrew Walters, RHP	$955,275
63. Orioles: Jackson Baumeister, RHP	$1,605,100
64. Diamondbacks: Caden Grice, LHP	$1,250,000
65. Rockies: Cole Carrigg, C	$1,300,000
66. Royals: Carson Roccaforte, OF	$897,500
67. Pirates: Zander Mueth, RHP	$1,797,500
68. Cubs: Jaxon Wiggins, RHP	$1,401,500
69. Giants: Joe Whitman, LHP	$805,575
70. Braves: Cade Kuehler, RHP	$1,045,000

THIRD ROUND

No. Team: Player, Pos.	Bonus
71. Nationals: Travis Sykora, RHP	$2,600,000
72. Athletics: Steven Echavarria, RHP	$3,000,000
73. Pirates: Garret Forrester, 3B	$772,500
74. Reds: Hunter Hollan, LHP	$597,500
75. Royals: Hiro Wyatt, RHP	$1,497,500
76. Tigers: Paul Wilson, LHP	$1,697,500
77. Rockies: Jack Mahoney, RHP	$925,000
78. Marlins: Brock Vradenburg, 1B	$916,000
79. Angels: Alberto Rios, 3B	$847,500
80. Diamondbacks: Jack Hurley, OF	$887,000
81. Cubs: Josh Rivera, SS	$725,000
82. Twins: Brandon Winokur, OF	$1,500,000
83. Red Sox: Antonio Anderson, SS	$1,500,000
84. White Sox: Seth Keener, RHP	$800,000
85. Giants: Cole Foster, SS	$747,500
86. Orioles: Kiefer Lord, RHP	$760,000
87. Brewers: Eric Bitonti, SS	$1,750,000
88. Rays: Tre' Morgan, 1B	$781,300
89. Blue Jays: Juaron Watts-Brown, RHP	$1,002,785
90. Cardinals: Travis Honeyman, OF	$700,000
91. Mets: Nolan McLean, RHP/OF	$747,600
92. Mariners: Teddy McGraw, RHP	$600,000
93. Guardians: C.J. Kayfus, OF	$700,000
94. Braves: Sabin Ceballos, SS	$597,500
95. Dodgers: Brady Smith, RHP	$703,000
96. Padres: J.D. Gonzalez, C	$550,000
97. Yankees: Kyle Carr, LHP	$692,000
98. Phillies: Devin Saltiban, SS	$602,500
99. Astros: Jake Bloss, RHP	$497,500
100. Orioles: Tavian Josenberger, OF	$603,000
101. Mets: Kade Morris, RHP	$666,500

2022 DRAFT

TOP THREE ROUNDS

FIRST ROUND

No. Team: Player, Pos.	Bonus
1. Orioles: Jackson Holliday, SS	$8,190,000
2. D-backs: Druw Jones, OF	$8,189,400
3. Rangers: Kumar Rocker, RHP	$5,200,000
4. Pirates: Termarr Johnson, SS	$7,219,000
5. Nationals: Elijah Green, OF	$6,500,000
6. Marlins: Jacob Berry, 3B	$6,000,000
7. Cubs: Cade Horton, RHP	$4,450,000
8. Twins: Brooks Lee, SS	$5,675,000
9. Royals: Gavin Cross, OF	$5,200,400
10. Rockies: Gabriel Hughes, RHP	$4,000,000
11. Mets: Kevin Parada, C	$5,019,735
12. Tigers: Jace Jung, 2B	$4,590,300
13. Angels: Zach Neto, SS	$3,500,000
14. Mets: Jett Williams, SS	$3,900,000
15. Padres: Dylan Lesko, RHP	$3,900,000
16. Guardians: Chase DeLauter, OF	$3,750,000
17. Phillies: Justin Crawford, OF	$3,894,000
18. Reds: Cam Collier, 3B	$5,000,000
19. Athletics: Daniel Susac, C	$3,531,200
20. Braves: Owen Murphy, RHP	$2,556,900
21. Mariners: Cole Young, SS	$3,300,000
22. Cardinals: Cooper Hjerpe, LHP	$3,182,200
23. Blue Jays: Brandon Barriera, LHP	$3,597,500
24. Red Sox: Mikey Romero, SS	$2,300,000
25. Yankees: Spencer Jones, OF	$2,880,800
26. White Sox: Noah Schultz, LHP	$2,800,000
27. Brewers: Eric Brown, SS	$2,050,000
28. Astros: Drew Gilbert, OF	$2,497,500
29. Rays: Xavier Isaac, 1B	$2,548,900
30. Giants: Reggie Crawford, LHP/1B	$2,297,500
31. Rockies: Sterlin Thompson, OF	$2,430,500
32. Reds: Sal Stewart, 3B	$2,100,000

SUPPLEMENTAL FIRST ROUND

No. Team: Player, Pos.	Bonus
33. Orioles: Dylan Beavers, OF	$2,200,000
34. D-backs: Landon Sims, RHP	$2,347,050
35. Braves: JR Ritchie, RHP	$2,397,500
36. Pirates: Thomas Harrington, RHP	$2,047,500
37. Guardians: Justin Campbell, RHP	$1,700,000
38. Rockies: Jordan Beck, OF	$2,200,000
39. Padres: Robby Snelling, LHP	$3,000,000

SECOND ROUND

No. Team: Player, Pos.	Bonus
40. Dodgers: Dalton Rushing, C	$1,956,890
41. Red Sox: Cutter Coffey, SS	$1,847,500
42. Orioles: Max Wagner, 3B	$1,900,000
43. D-backs: Ivan Melendez, 1B	$1,400,000
44. Pirates: Hunter Barco, LHP	$1,525,000
45. Nationals: Jake Bennett, LHP	$1,734,800
46. Marlins: Jacob Miller, RHP	$1,697,900
47. Cubs: Jackson Ferris, LHP	$3,005,000
48. Twins: Connor Prielipp, LHP	$1,825,000
49. Royals: Cayden Wallace, 3B	$1,697,500
50. Rockies: Jackson Cox, RHP	$1,850,000
51. Tigers: Peyton Graham, SS	$1,800,000

No. Team: Player, Pos.	Bonus
52. Mets: Blade Tidwell, RHP	$1,850,000
53. Padres: Adam Mazur, RHP	$1,250,000
54. Guardians: Parker Messick, LHP	$1,300,000
55. Reds: Logan Tanner, C	$1,030,500
56. Athletics: Henry Bolte, OF	$2,000,000
57. Braves: Cole Phillips, RHP	$1,497,500
58. Mariners: Tyler Locklear, 3B	$1,276,500
59. Cardinals: Brycen Mautz, LHP	$1,100,000
60. Blue Jays: Josh Kasevich, SS	$997,500
61. Yankees: Drew Thorpe, RHP	$1,187,600
62. White Sox: Peyton Pallette, RHP	$1,500,000
63. Brewers: Jacob Misiorowski, RHP	$2,350,000
64. Astros: Jacob Melton, OF	$1,000,000
65. Rays: Brock Jones, OF	$1,077,600
66. Giants: Carson Whisenhunt, LHP	$1,866,220

SUPPLEMENTAL SECOND ROUND

No. Team: Player, Pos.	Bonus
67. Orioles: Jud Fabian, OF	$1,026,800
68. Twins: Tanner Schobel, SS	$1,002,000
69. Athletics: Clark Elliott, OF	$900,000
70. Rays: Chandler Simpson, SS	$747,500
71. Rays: Ryan Cermak, OF	$747,500
72. Brewers: Robert Moore, SS	$800,000
73. Reds: Justin Boyd, OF	$847,500
74. Mariners: Walter Ford, RHP	$1,250,000
75. Mets: Nick Morabito, OF	$1,000,000
76. Braves: Blake Burkhalter, RHP	$647,500
77. Blue Jays: Tucker Toman, SS	$2,000,000
78. Blue Jays: Cade Doughty, 2B	$831,100
79. Red Sox: Roman Anthony, OF	$2,500,000
80. Astros: Andrew Taylor, RHP	$804,700

THIRD ROUND

No. Team: Player, Pos.	Bonus
81. Orioles: Nolan McLean, RHP	Did not sign
82. D-backs: Nate Savino, LHP	$700,000
83. Pirates: Jack Brannigan, 3B/RHP	$770,700
84. Nationals: Trey Lipscomb, 3B	$758,900
85. Marlins: Karson Milbrandt, RHP	$1,497,500
86. Cubs: Christopher Paciolla, SS	$900,000
87. Royals: Mason Barnett, RHP	$697,500
88. Rockies: Carson Palmquist, LHP	$775,000
89. Angels: Ben Joyce, RHP	$997,500
90. Mets: Brandon Sproat, RHP	Did not sign
91. Padres: Henry Williams, RHP	$800,000
92. Guardians: Joe Lampe, OF	$800,000
93. Phillies: Gabriel Rincones, OF	$627,500
94. Reds: Bryce Hubbart, LHP	$522,500
95. Athletics: Colby Thomas, OF	$750,000
96. Braves: Drake Baldwin, C	$633,300
97. Cardinals: Pete Hansen, LHP	$629,800
98. Blue Jays: Alan Roden, OF	$497,500
99. Red Sox: Dalton Rogers, LHP	$447,500
100. Yankees: Trystan Vrieling, RHP	$608,900
101. White Sox: Jonathan Cannon, RHP	$925,000
102. Brewers: Dylan O'Rae, SS	$597,500
103. Astros: Michael Knorr, RHP	$487,500
104. Rays: Trevor Martin, RHP	$586,200
105. Dodgers: Alex Freeland, SS	$580,200
106. Giants: William Kempner, RHP	$522,500

SIGNING BONUSES

2021 DRAFT

TOP THREE ROUNDS

FIRST ROUND

No. Team: Player, Pos.	Bonus
1. Pirates: Henry Davis, C	$6,500,000
2. Rangers: Jack Leiter, RHP	$7,922,000
3. Tigers: Jackson Jobe, RHP	$6,900,000
4. Red Sox: Marcelo Mayer, SS	$6,664,000
5. Orioles: Colton Cowser, OF	$4,900,000
6. D-backs: Jordan Lawlar, SS	$6,713,300
7. Royals: Frank Mozzicato, LHP	$3,547,500
8. Rockies: Benny Montgomery, OF	$5,000,000
9. Angels: Sam Bachman, RHP	$3,847,500
10. Mets: Kumar Rocker, RHP	Did not sign
11. Nationals: Brady House, SS	$5,000,000
12. Mariners: Harry Ford, C	$4,366,400
13. Phillies: Andrew Painter, RHP	$3,900,000
14. Giants: Will Bednar, RHP	$3,647,500
15. Brewers: Sal Frelick, OF	$4,000,000
16. Marlins: Kahlil Watson, SS	$4,540,790
17. Reds: Matt McLain, SS	$4,625,000
18. Cardinals: Michael McGreevy, RHP	$2,750,000
19. Blue Jays: Gunnar Hoglund, RHP	$3,247,500
20. Yankees: Trey Sweeney, SS	$3,000,000
21. Cubs: Jordan Wicks, LHP	$3,132,300
22. White Sox: Colson Montgomery, SS	$3,027,000
23. Guardians: Gavin Williams, RHP	$2,250,000
24. Braves: Ryan Cusick, RHP	$2,700,000
25. Athletics: Max Muncy, SS	$2,850,000
26. Twins: Chase Petty, RHP	$2,500,000
27. Padres: Jackson Merrill, SS	$1,800,000
28. Rays: Carson Williams, SS	$2,347,500
29. Dodgers: Maddux Bruns, LHP	$2,197,500
30. Reds: Jay Allen, OF	$2,397,500

SUPPLEMENTAL FIRST ROUND

No. Team: Player, Pos.	Bonus
31. Marlins: Joe Mack, C	$2,500,000
32. Tigers: Ty Madden, RHP	$2,500,000
33. Brewers: Tyler Black, 2B	$2,200,000
34. Rays: Cooper Kinney, 2B	$2,145,600
35. Reds: Mat Nelson, C	$2,093,300
36. Twins: Noah Miller, SS	$1,700,000

SECOND ROUND

No. Team: Player, Pos.	Bonus
37. Pirates: Anthony Solometo, LHP	$2,797,500
38. Rangers: Aaron Zavala, OF	$830,000
39. Tigers: Izaac Pacheco, SS	$2,750,000
40. Red Sox: Jud Fabian, OF	Did not sign
41. Orioles: Connor Norby, 2B	$1,700,000
42. D-backs: Ryan Bliss, SS	$1,250,000
43. Royals: Ben Kudrna, RHP	$2,997,500
44. Rockies: Jaden Hill, RHP	$1,689,500
45. Angels: Ky Bush, LHP	$1,747,500
46. Mets: Calvin Ziegler, RHP	$910,000
47. Nationals: Daylen Lile, OF	$1,750,000
48. Mariners: Edwin Arroyo, SS	$1,650,000
49. Phillies: Ethan Wilson, OF	$1,507,600
50. Giants: Matt Mikulski, LHP	$1,197,500

No. Team: Player, Pos.	Bonus
51. Brewers: Russell Smith, LHP	$1,000,000
52. Marlins: Cody Morissette, SS	$1,403,200
53. Reds: Andrew Abbott, LHP	$1,300,000
54. Cardinals: Joshua Baez, OF	$2,250,000
55. Yankees: Brendan Beck, RHP	$1,050,000
56. Cubs: James Triantos, 3B	$2,100,000
57. White Sox: Wes Kath, 3B	$1,800,000
58. Guardians: Doug Nikhazy, LHP	$1,200,000
59. Braves: Spencer Schwellenbach, RHP	$997,500
60. Athletics: Zack Gelof, 3B	$1,157,400
61. Twins: Steve Hajjar, LHP	$1,129,700
62. Padres: James Wood, OF	$2,600,000
63. Rays: Kyle Manzardo, 1B	$747,500

SUPPLEMENTAL SECOND ROUND

No. Team: Player, Pos.	Bonus
64. Pirates: Lonnie White Jr., OF	$1,500,000
65. Orioles: Reed Trimble, OF	$800,000
66. Royals: Peyton Wilson, 2B	$1,000,800
67. D-backs: Adrian Del Castillo, C	$1,000,000
68. Rockies: Joe Rock, LHP	$953,100
69. Guardians: Tommy Mace, RHP	$1,100,000
70. Cardinals: Ryan Holgate, OF	$875,000
71. Padres: Robert Gasser, LHP	$884,200

THIRD ROUND

No. Team: Player, Pos.	Bonus
72. Pirates: Bubba Chandler, RHP	$3,000,000
73. Rangers: Cameron Cauley, SS	$1,000,000
74. Tigers: Dylan Smith, RHP	$1,115,000
75. Red Sox: Tyler McDonough, 2B	$828,600
76. Orioles: John Rhodes, OF	$1,375,000
77. D-backs: Jacob Steinmetz, RHP	$500,000
78. Royals: Carter Jensen, C	$1,097,500
79. Rockies: McCade Brown, RHP	$780,400
80. Angels: Landon Marceaux, RHP	$765,300
81. Mets: Dominic Hamel, RHP	$755,300
82. Nationals: Branden Boissiere, OF	$600,000
83. Mariners: Michael Morales, RHP	$1,500,000
84. Phillies: Jordan Viars, OF	$747,500
85. Giants: Mason Black, RHP	$708,200
86. Brewers: Alex Binelas, 3B	$700,000
87. Astros: Tyler Whitaker, OF	$1,500,000
88. Marlins: Jordan McCants, SS	$800,000
89. Reds: Jose Torres, SS	$622,500
90. Cardinals: Austin Love, RHP	$600,000
91. Blue Jays: Ricky Tiedemann, LHP	$644,800
92. Yankees: Brock Selvidge, LHP	$1,500,000
93. Cubs: Drew Gray, LHP	$900,000
94. White Sox: Sean Burke, RHP	$900,000
95. Guardians: Jake Fox, SS	$850,000
96. Braves: Dylan Dodd, LHP	$122,500
97. Athletics: Mason Miller, RHP	$599,100
98. Twins: Cade Povich, LHP	$500,000
99. Padres: Kevin Kopps, RHP	$300,000
100. Rays: Ryan Spikes, SS	$1,097,500
101. Dodgers: Peter Heubeck, RHP	$1,269,500

INDEX

A

Abel, Mick (Phillies) 341
Abreu, Wilyer (Red Sox) 71
Acosta, Adrian (Angels) 223
Acosta, Victor (Reds) 124
Acuña, Luisangel (Mets) 294
Adams, Jordyn (Angels) 222
Adams, Luke (Brewers) 266
Aguiar, Julian (Reds) 122
Ahuna, Maui (Giants) 412
Albright, Mason (Rockies) 160
Alcantara, Kevin (Cubs) 87
Aldegheri, Samuel (Phillies) 347
Alderman, Kemp (Marlins) 252
Alejandro, Jerson (Yankees) 319
Alexander, Blaze (D-backs) 25
Aliendo, Pablo (Cubs) 93
Almeyda, Luis (Orioles) 61
Almonte, Ariel (Reds) 127
Alvarez, Andrew (Nationals) 497
Alvarez, Ignacio (Braves) 40
Amador, Adael (Rockies) 148
Amaya, Jacob (Marlins) 249
Anderson, Antonio (Red Sox) 78
Anderson, Max (Tigers) 172
Anthony, Roman (Red Sox) 69
Areinamo, Jadher (Brewers) 269
Arias, Franklin (Red Sox) 78
Arias, Michael (Cubs) 92
Arias, Rayner (Giants) 407
Arias, Roderick (Yankees) 310
Armbruester, Justin (Orioles) 63
Arrighetti, Spencer (Astros) 181
Arroyo, Edwin (Reds) 118
Arroyo, Michael (Mariners) 424
Arteaga, Aeverson (Giants) 411
Ashcraft, Braxton (Pirates) 361
Auer, Mason (Rays) 447

B

Bachman, Sam (Angels) 214
Baez, Jesus (Mets) 299
Baez, Josh (Cardinals) 385
Baez, Juan (Brewers) 270
Baez, Luis (Astros) 181
Baker, Andrew (Phillies) 351
Baker, Darren (Nationals) 495
Baker, Dru (Rays) 448
Baker, Luken (Cardinals) 383
Balazovic, Jordan (Twins) 287
Balcazar, Leo (Reds) 120
Baldwin, Drake (Braves) 39
Ballesteros, Moises (Cubs) 86
Banfield, Will (Marlins) 251
Barber, Colin (Astros) 192
Barco, Hunter (Pirates) 364
Barger, Addison (Blue Jays) 470
Barnett, Mason (Royals) 199
Baro, Boston (Mets) 302
Barriera, Brandon (Blue Jays) 470
Barrios, Gregory (Brewers) 273
Barrosa, Jorge (D-backs) 29
Basabe, Osleivis (Rays) 439
Basallo, Samuel (Orioles) 53
Basso, Brady (Athletics) 334
Bastardo, Angel (Red Sox) 79
Baumann, Garrett (Braves) 44

Baumeister, Jackson (Orioles) 58
Baz, Shane (Rays) 438
Beavers, Dylan (Orioles) 58
Beck, Jordan (Rockies) 150
Beeter, Clayton (Yankees) 315
Belgrave, Nigel (Marlins) 256
Bencosme, Frederick (Orioles) 64
Benitez, Diego (Braves) 47
Bennett, Jake (Nationals) 489
Bergert, Ryan (Padres) 394
Bergolla Jr., William (Phillies) 344
Bernabel, Warming (Rockies) 159
Bernal, Leonardo (Cardinals) 377
Bernard, Derek (Rockies) 160
Berroa, Prelander (Mariners) 426
Berry, Jacob (Marlins) 248
Bidois, Brandon (Pirates) 368
Bigbie, Justice (Tigers) 169
Birchard, Ryan (Brewers) 271
Birdsell, Brandon (Cubs) 95
Birdsong, Hayden (Giants) 407
Bitonti, Eric (Brewers) 265
Black, Mason (Giants) 408
Black, Tyler (Brewers) 262
Blakely, Werner (Angels) 222
Blalock, Bradley (Brewers) 268
Blanco Jr., Tony (Pirates) 369
Bleis, Miguel (Red Sox) 70
Bliss, Ryan (Mariners) 428
Bloss, Jake (Astros) 185
Blubaugh, AJ (Astros) 186
Boeve, Mike (Brewers) 267
Bohrofen, Jace (Blue Jays) 477
Bolte, Henry (Athletics) 330
Bonilla, Enmanuel (Blue Jays) 473
Bouchard, Sean (Rockies) 156
Bowen, Darren (Mariners) 430
Bowen, Jase (Pirates) 367
Bowlan, Jonathan (Royals) 204
Bowman, Cooper (Athletics) 333
Boyd, Emaarion (Phillies) 350
Boyle, Joe (Athletics) 328
Bradfield Jr., Enrique (Orioles) 56
Brannigan, Jack (Pirates) 362
Brannon, Brooks (Red Sox) 80
Bratt, Mitchell (Rangers) 464
Braun, Lucas (Braves) 43
Briceño, Josue (Tigers) 172
Bright, Trace (Orioles) 62
Brito, Juan (Guardians) 134
Brock, T.J. (Blue Jays) 478
Brown, Ben (Cubs) 88
Brown, Cam (Phillies) 352
Brown, Vaun (Giants) 409
Brown Jr., Eric (Brewers) 270
Bruns, Maddux (Dodgers) 233
Brzykcy, Zach (Nationals) 492
Burke, Jacob (White Sox) 109
Burke, Sean (White Sox) 106
Burkhalter, Blake (Braves) 47
Burns, Connor (Reds) 129
Burrowes, Ryan (White Sox) 109
Burrows, Michael (Pirates) 362
Busch, Michael (Dodgers) 228
Bush, Ky (White Sox) 105
Bush Jr., Homer (Padres) 395
Butler, Lawrence (Athletics) 327
Butto, Jose (Mets) 301
Buxton, Ike (Marlins) 255

C

Caba, Starlyn (Phillies) 342
Cabrera, Ricardo (Reds) 122
Caceres, Kelvin (Angels) 220
Caissie, Owen (Cubs) 86
Calabrese, David (Angels) 224
Calaz, Robert (Rockies) 153
Callihan, Tyler (Reds) 128
Camargo, Jair (Twins) 287
Cameron, Noah (Royals) 206
Caminero, Junior (Rays) 436
Campbell, Justin (Guardians) 144
Canario, Alexander (Cubs) 89
Cannon, Jonathan (White Sox) 104
Canterino, Matt (Twins) 279
Cantillo, Joey (Guardians) 137
Cappe, Yiddi (Marlins) 247
Carela, Juan (White Sox) 113
Carr, Kyle (Yankees) 313
Carreras, Julio (Rockies) 157
Carrigg, Cole (Rockies) 153
Cartaya, Diego (Dodgers) 232
Carter, Evan (Rangers) 452
Casparius, Ben (Dodgers) 238
Castañon, Marcos (Padres) 399
Castro, Allan (Red Sox) 76
Catuy, Pedro (D-backs) 30
Cauley, Cameron (Rangers) 456
Cavalli, Cade (Nationals) 486
Ceballos, Sabin (Braves) 46
Cecconi, Slade (D-backs) 27
Celesten, Felnin (Mariners) 423
Cerantola, Eric (Royals) 208
Cerda, Christian (D-backs) 31
Cespedes, Yoeilin (Red Sox) 73
Champlain, Chandler (Royals) 199
Chandler, Bubba (Pirates) 357
Charles, Austin (Royals) 202
Cheng, Tsung-Che (Pirates) 359
Chivilli, Angel (Rockies) 158
Cho, Won-Bin (Cardinals) 378
Chourio, Jackson (Brewers) 260
Chourio, Jaison (Guardians) 136
Clark, Max (Tigers) 164
Clarke, Denzel (Athletics) 326
Clarke, Wes (Brewers) 267
Clase, Jonatan (Mariners) 425
Clemmey, Alex (Guardians) 137
Clifford, Ryan (Mets) 294
Cole, Zachary (Astros) 183
Coley, Mark (Marlins) 255
Collier, Cam (Reds) 121
Cooke, Connor (Blue Jays) 473
Corniell, Jose (Rangers) 460
Corona, Kenedy (Astros) 184
Cossetti, Andrew (Twins) 287
Costeiu, Ryan (Angels) 220
Cowser, Colton (Orioles) 54
Cox, Jackson (Rockies) 156
Cox, Jonah (Athletics) 336
Crawford, Justin (Phillies) 341
Crawford, Reggie (Giants) 408
Crews, Dylan (Nationals) 484
Crooks, Jimmy (Cardinals) 379
Cross, Gavin (Royals) 200
Crow-Armstrong, Pete (Cubs) 84
Cruz, Armando (Nationals) 495
Cruz, John (Yankees) 318

Cruz, Jose (Giants)	416
Culpepper, CJ (Twins)	280
Curet, Yoniel (Rays)	441
Curry, Aidan (Rangers)	458
Cusick, Ryan (Athletics)	335

D

Dallas, Chad (Blue Jays)	474
Dana, Caden (Angels)	213
Danner, Hagen (Blue Jays)	478
Davis, Brennen (Cubs)	97
Davis, Chase (Cardinals)	375
De Andrade, Danny (Twins)	281
De Avila, Luis (Braves)	46
De La Cruz, Carlos (Phillies)	346
De La Cruz, Juan (Marlins)	255
De La Rosa, Jeremy (Nationals)	495
De Leon, Luis (Orioles)	59
De Los Santos, Deyvison (Guardians)	138
De Oleo, Branny (Mets)	302
De Paula, Josue (Dodgers)	231
Del Castillo, Adrian (D-backs)	32
DeLauter, Chase (Guardians)	132
Delgado, Keiner (Yankees)	317
DeLoach, Zach (Mariners)	426
Deluca, Jonny (Dodgers)	234
Dettmer, Nathan (Athletics)	334
Devers, Jose (Guardians)	141
DeVos, Nolan (Astros)	189
Dezenzo, Zach (Astros)	182
Di Turi, Filippo (Brewers)	272
Diaz, Camilo (Astros)	191
Diaz, Joel (Mets)	304
Diaz, Yilber (D-backs)	26
Dickerson, Blake (Padres)	397
Dingler, Dillon (Tigers)	168
Dirden, Justin (Astros)	193
Dobbins, Hunter (Red Sox)	79
Dodd, Dylan (Braves)	41
Dollander, Chase (Rockies)	149
Dollard, Taylor (Mariners)	427
Dombroski, Trey (Astros)	189
Dominguez, Jasson (Yankees)	308
Doughty, Cade (Blue Jays)	481
Drake, Isaiah (Braves)	45
Drohan, Shane (White Sox)	111
Dunn, Blake (Reds)	122
Dunn, Oliver (Brewers)	268
Duno, Alfredo (Reds)	120

E

Echavarria, Steven (Athletics)	329
Eddington, Jacob (Phillies)	352
Eder, Jake (White Sox)	103
Edwards, Xavier (Marlins)	246
Eldridge, Bryce (Giants)	405
Emerson, Colt (Mariners)	421
Espino, Daniel (Guardians)	133
Estes, Joey (Athletics)	331

F

Fabian, Jud (Orioles)	59
Farmelo, Jonny (Mariners)	424
Fernandez, Ryan (Cardinals)	384
Fernandez, Yanquiel (Rockies)	149
Fernandez, Yeiner (Dodgers)	237
Ferris, Jackson (Cubs)	89
Festa, David (Twins)	278
Figuereo, Gleider (Rangers)	460
Fisher, Cam (Astros)	190
Fitts, Richard (Red Sox)	73

Fletcher, Dominic (D-backs)	29
Fleury, Jose (Astros)	187
Flores, Juan (Angels)	219
Flores, Rafael (Yankees)	321
Flores, Wilmer (Tigers)	171
Floyd, Ty (Reds)	121
Fluharty, Mason (Blue Jays)	479
Ford, Harry (Mariners)	421
Ford, Walter (Mariners)	429
Forrester, Garret (Pirates)	367
Foscue, Justin (Rangers)	454
Foster, Cole (Giants)	414
Fox, Jake (Guardians)	142
Francisca, Welbyn (Guardians)	138
Franklin, Jesse (Braves)	43
Frasso, Nick (Dodgers)	230
Freeland, Alex (Dodgers)	239
Frias, Dayan (Guardians)	140
Fulton, Dax (Marlins)	248
Funderburk, Kody (Twins)	286

G

Garcia, Johanfran (Red Sox)	74
Garcia, Saul (Mets)	305
Gasser, Robert (Brewers)	262
Gauthier, Austin (Dodgers)	237
Gelof, Jake (Dodgers)	239
Genao, Angel (Guardians)	139
Gentry, Tyler (Royals)	201
George, Kendall (Dodgers)	235
Gerardo, Jose (Marlins)	253
Gil, Luis (Yankees)	316
Gil, Samuel (Tigers)	176
Gilbert, Drew (Mets)	293
Gillies, Keagan (Orioles)	65
Gipson-Long, Sawyer (Tigers)	172
Glod, Douglas (Braves)	48
Gomez, Raimon (Mets)	304
Gomez, Yoendrys (Yankees)	316
Gonzales, Nick (Pirates)	360
Gonzalez, Cesar (Athletics)	335
Gonzalez, Gabriel (Mariners)	422
Gonzalez, J.D. (Padres)	394
Gonzalez, Jacob (White Sox)	103
Gonzalez, Tres (Pirates)	368
Gonzalez, Wikelman (Red Sox)	71
Goodman, Hunter (Rockies)	154
Gordon, Colton (Astros)	188
Gorski, Matt (Pirates)	363
Graceffo, Gordon (Cardinals)	376
Graham, Peyton (Tigers)	175
Gray, Drew (Cubs)	93
Green, Elijah (Nationals)	488
Grice, Caden (D-backs)	26
Groover, Gino (D-backs)	22
Guanipa, Luis (Braves)	44
Guerrero, Brailer (Rays)	445
Guerrero, Tyson (Royals)	208
Guilarte, Daniel (Brewers)	270
Gutierrez, Anthony (Rangers)	457
Guzman, Denzer (Angels)	216

H

Hackenberg, Drue (Braves)	40
Hales, Skylar (Rangers)	463
Hall, DL (Orioles)	55
Halpin, Petey (Guardians)	138
Hamel, Dominic (Mets)	298
Hamilton, David (Red Sox)	77
Hampton, Chase (Yankees)	311
Hancock, Emerson (Mariners)	425
Hansen, Pete (Cardinals)	384

Harrington, Thomas (Pirates)	359
Harris, Brett (Athletics)	332
Harris, Dustin (Rangers)	455
Harris, Hayden (Braves)	45
Harrison, Kyle (Giants)	404
Haskin, Hudson (Orioles)	63
Hassell III, Robert (Nationals)	487
Hawkins, Garrett (Padres)	401
Haynes, Jagger (Padres)	400
Head, Dillon (Padres)	391
Headrick, Brent (Twins)	289
Helman, Michael (Twins)	289
Hence, Tink (Cardinals)	374
Henderson, Logan (Brewers)	268
Henry, Cole (Nationals)	494
Heredia, Raylin (Phillies)	349
Hernaiz, Darell (Athletics)	327
Hernandez, Alberto (Astros)	193
Hernandez, Cristian (Cubs)	94
Hernandez, Ronald (Mets)	303
Herrera, Ivan (Cardinals)	375
Herrin, Tim (Guardians)	145
Herz, DJ (Nationals)	490
Hettiger, Kehden (Phillies)	349
Heubeck, Peter (Dodgers)	240
Hickey, Nathan (Red Sox)	75
Hicks, Liam (Rangers)	462
Hinds, Rece (Reds)	125
Hitt, Grayson (D-backs)	28
Hjerpe, Cooper (Cardinals)	376
Hodge, Porter (Cubs)	93
Hollan, Hunter (Reds)	128
Holliday, Jackson (Orioles)	52
Honeyman, Travis (Cardinals)	379
Horn, Bailey (Cubs)	96
Horton, Cade (Cubs)	85
Horvath, Mac (Orioles)	61
Horwitz, Spencer (Blue Jays)	477
Houck, Colin (Mets)	296
House, Brady (Nationals)	485
Hughes, Gabriel (Rockies)	155
Humphries, Jackson (Guardians)	139
Hurley, Jack (D-backs)	25
Hurt, Kyle (Dodgers)	231
Hurtado, Joel (Angels)	221
Hurter, Brant (Tigers)	170
Hurtubise, Jacob (Reds)	126

I

Ibarguen, Pedro (Brewers)	271
Iriarte, Jairo (Padres)	392
Isaac, Xavier (Rays)	438

J

Jacob, Alek (Padres)	399
Jarvis, Bryce (D-backs)	31
Jebb, Mitch (Pirates)	361
Jenkins, Walker (Twins)	276
Jensen, Carter (Royals)	201
Jimenez, Enrique (Tigers)	175
Jimenez, Leo (Blue Jays)	471
Jobe, Jackson (Tigers)	165
Johnson, Marcus (Rays)	442
Johnson, Seth (Orioles)	57
Johnson, Termarr (Pirates)	358
Johnston, Troy (Marlins)	252
Jones, Druw (D-backs)	21
Jones, Jared (Pirates)	357
Jones, Spencer (Yankees)	309
Jordan, Blaze (Red Sox)	77
Jordan, Rowdey (Mets)	305
Jorge, Carlos (Reds)	119

Jorge, Dyan (Rockies) 151
Joyce, Ben (Angels) 215
Joyce, Jimmy (Mariners) 431
Juarez, Victor (Rockies) 159
Juenger, Hayden (Blue Jays) 479
Jung, Jace (Tigers) 166

K

Kasevich, Josh (Blue Jays) 475
Keaschall, Luke (Twins) 281
Keegan, Dominic (Rays) 440
Keener, Seth (White Sox) 108
Keirsey Jr., DaShawn (Twins) 285
Keith, Colt (Tigers) 165
Kemp, Kannon (Padres) 398
Kempner, William (Giants) 415
Kennedy, Michael (Pirates) 365
Kent, Barrett (Angels) 215
Kent, Zak (Rangers) 463
Kerkering, Orion (Phillies) 343
Kerr, Ray (Padres) 398
Kessinger, Grae (Astros) 189
Kilian, Caleb (Cubs) 95
Kinney, Cooper (Rays) 449
Kjerstad, Heston (Orioles) 54
Klassen, George (Phillies) 351
Klein, Will (Royals) 204
Kloffenstein, Adam (Cardinals) 384
Knack, Landon (Dodgers) 233
Knorr, Michael (Astros) 186
Knoth, Josh (Brewers) 265
Kochanowicz, Jack (Angels) 216
Kopp, Ronan (Dodgers) 235
Kouba, Rhett (Astros) 188
Krob, Austin (Padres) 401
Kudrna, Ben (Royals) 201
Kuehler, Cade (Braves) 41

L

LaCombe, Mathias (White Sox) 111
Lagrange, Carlos (Yankees) 314
Lalane, Henry (Yankees) 311
Langford, Wyatt (Rangers) 453
Lara, Andry (Nationals) 497
Lara, Erick (Rays) 449
Lara, Jhancarlos (Braves) 42
Lara, Luis (Brewers) 263
Lasko, Ryan (Athletics) 332
Laverde, Dario (Angels) 218
Lawlar, Jordan (D-backs) 20
Leasure, Jordan (White Sox) 106
Ledbetter, Colton (Rays) 441
Lee, Brooks (Twins) 277
Lee, Hao-Yu (Tigers) 170
Leiter, Jack (Rangers) 458
Leonard, Eddys (Tigers) 176
Lesko, Dylan (Padres) 390
Letson, Bishop (Brewers) 272
Levenson, Zach (Cardinals) 380
Lewis, Cory (Twins) 284
Lile, Daylen (Nationals) 489
Lin, Sheng-En (Reds) 128
Lin, Yu-Min (D-backs) 23
Lipcius, Andre (Tigers) 177
Lipscomb, Trey (Nationals) 491
Liranzo, Thayron (Dodgers) 234
Little, Luke (Cubs) 90
Lizarraga, Victor (Padres) 396
Locklear, Tyler (Mariners) 423
Loftin, Nick (Royals) 197
Lombard Jr., George (Yankees) 312
Loperfido, Joey (Astros) 183

Lopez, Fabian (Marlins) 250
Lopez, Jacob (Rays) 447
Lord, Kiefer (Orioles) 65
Lowder, Rhett (Reds) 117
Lowe, Isaiah (Padres) 397
Luciano, Marco (Giants) 405
Luis, Jansel (D-backs) 23

M

Mack, Joe (Marlins) 254
Macko, Adam (Blue Jays) 475
Madden, Ty (Tigers) 166
Made, Kevin (Nationals) 494
Maldonado, Anthony (Marlins) 253
Maldonado, Gerelmi (Giants) 416
Malloy, Justyn-Henry (Tigers) 167
Manzardo, Kyle (Guardians) 134
Marcheco, Jorge (Angels) 225
Maroudis, Landen (Blue Jays) 474
Marsee, Jakob (Padres) 393
Marte, Noelvi (Reds) 116
Martin, Austin (Twins) 280
Martin, Payton (Dodgers) 236
Martin, Walker (Giants) 406
Martinez, Angel (Guardians) 135
Martinez, Jeter (Mariners) 433
Martinez, Orelvis (Blue Jays) 469
Martorella, Nathan (Padres) 396
Mata, Bryan (Red Sox) 81
Mathews, Quinn (Cardinals) 382
Matthews, Brice (Astros) 182
Matthews, Zebby (Twins) 282
Mattison, Tyler (Tigers) 174
Mauricio, Ronny (Mets) 293
Mautz, Brycen (Cardinals) 381
Maxwell, Zach (Reds) 127
Mayea, Brando (Yankees) 313
Mayer, Marcelo (Red Sox) 68
Mayo, Coby (Orioles) 53
Mazur, Adam (Padres) 392
McCabe, David (Braves) 39
McCollum, Tommy (Phillies) 352
McCray, Grant (Giants) 409
McCullough, Brody (Cubs) 96
McDermott, Chayce (Orioles) 57
McDonald, Trevor (Giants) 412
McDougal, Tanner (White Sox) 107
McFarlane, Alex (Phillies) 348
McGarry, Griff (Phillies) 345
McGeary, Haydn (Cubs) 95
McGonigle, Kevin (Tigers) 168
McGowan, Christian (Phillies) 347
McGraw, Teddy (Mariners) 428
McGreevy, Michael (Cardinals) 378
McLean, Nolan (Mets) 298
McMillon, John (Royals) 203
Meachem, Xavier (Marlins) 256
Mead, Curtis (Rays) 437
Meadows, Parker (Tigers) 167
Meckler, Wade (Giants) 411
Mederos, Victor (Angels) 217
Meidroth, Chase (Red Sox) 74
Mejia, Ian (Braves) 48
Mejia, Juan (Rockies) 158
Melendez, Ivan (D-backs) 22
Melton, Jacob (Astros) 180
Melton, Troy (Tigers) 169
Mena, Cristian (White Sox) 104
Mendez, Hendry (Phillies) 350
Mendoza, Jordarlin (Yankees) 318
Mercedes, Yasser (Twins) 284
Merrill, Jackson (Padres) 389
Mervis, Matt (Cubs) 90

Mesa Jr., Victor (Marlins) 246
Messick, Parker (Guardians) 143
Meyer, Max (Marlins) 245
Meyer, Noble (Marlins) 244
Millas, Drew (Nationals) 493
Milbrandt, Karson (Marlins) 247
Miller, Aidan (Phillies) 342
Miller, Cole (Athletics) 333
Miller, Jacob (Marlins) 249
Miller, Mason (Athletics) 324
Miller, Noah (Twins) 286
Milligan, Cody (Braves) 47
Minacci, Camden (Angels) 221
Misiorowski, Jacob (Brewers) 261
Misner, Kameron (Rays) 447
Mitchell, Blake (Royals) 196
Mitchell, Garrett (Brewers) 263
Mogollon, Javier (White Sox) 110
Molina, Anthony (Rockies) 158
Monegro, Yordanny (Red Sox) 76
Montalvo, Joseph (Rangers) 464
Montero, Keider (Tigers) 170
Montes, Lazaro (Mariners) 422
Monteverde, Patrick (Marlins) 254
Montgomery, Benny (Rockies) 153
Montgomery, Colson (White Sox) 100
Montgomery, Mason (Rays) 443
Montgomery, Torin (Marlins) 257
Morales, Luis (Athletics) 326
Morales, Michael (Mariners) 430
Morales, Yohandy (Nationals) 486
Morel, Braylin (Rangers) 460
Morgan, Tre' (Rays) 446
Morris, Cody (Guardians) 144
Morris, Kade (Mets) 301
Morrobel, Felix (Angels) 219
Morrobel, Yeison (Rangers) 461
Mozzicato, Frank (Royals) 197
Mueth, Zander (Pirates) 363
Muncy, Max (Athletics) 328
Muñoz, Samuel (Dodgers) 240
Murphy, Chris (Red Sox) 78
Murphy, Owen (Braves) 38
Murphy, Ryan (Giants) 415
Murray, B.J. (Cubs) 92
Muzziotti, Simon (Phillies) 350
Myers, Dane (Marlins) 250

N

Nastrini, Nick (White Sox) 101
Naylor, Myles (Athletics) 330
Neely, Jack (Yankees) 320
Nett, Braden (Padres) 397
Newell, Chris (Dodgers) 241
Nicolas, Kyle (Pirates) 362
Nimmala, Arjun (Blue Jays) 469
Noel, Jhonkensy (Guardians) 144
Norby, Connor (Orioles) 56
Nuñez, Edwin (Cardinals) 381
Nunez, Nasim (Nationals) 491
Nuñez, Juan (Orioles) 62

O

O'Rae, Dylan (Brewers) 269
Ochoa Jr., Nehomar (Astros) 191
Ogans, Keshawn (Braves) 49
Olson, Emmett (Marlins) 257
Oppor, Christian (White Sox) 112
Ornelas, Jonathan (Rangers) 465
Ortiz, Abimelec (Rangers) 459
Ortiz, Capri (Angels) 224
Ortiz, Joey (Orioles) 55
Owens, Tyler (Braves) 45

P

Pacheco, Izaac (Tigers)	174
Packard, Spencer (Mariners)	430
Pages, Andy (Dodgers)	230
Pages, Pedro (Cardinals)	380
Painter, Andrew (Phillies)	340
Palencia, Daniel (Cubs)	91
Pallette, Peyton (White Sox)	105
Palmegiani, Damiano (Blue Jays)	476
Palmquist, Carson (Rockies)	154
Pan, Wen-Hui (Phillies)	348
Parada, Kevin (Mets)	297
Paris, Kyren (Angels)	214
Parker, Mitchell (Nationals)	496
Pauley, Graham (Padres)	393
Paulino, Eddinson (Red Sox)	76
Peete, Tai (Mariners)	426
Pena, Dameury (Twins)	288
Peoples, Ben (Rays)	448
Perales, Luis (Red Sox)	72
Pereira, Everson (Yankees)	309
Perez, Fernando (Blue Jays)	478
Perez, Onil (Giants)	412
Perez, Wenceel (Tigers)	173
Perkins, Jack (Athletics)	331
Perry, Nolan (Blue Jays)	479
Petty, Chase (Reds)	118
Pham, Alex (Orioles)	64
Phillips, Connor (Reds)	117
Pinckney, Andrew (Nationals)	492
Pineda, Israel (Nationals)	493
Placencia, Adrian (Angels)	218
Porter, Brock (Rangers)	455
Povich, Cade (Orioles)	57
Pratt, Cooper (Brewers)	266
Prielipp, Connor (Twins)	283
Priester, Quinn (Pirates)	360
Prieto, Cesar (Cardinals)	380
Prosecky, Michael (Rockies)	157

Q

Quero, Edgar (White Sox)	102
Quero, Jeferson (Brewers)	261

R

Rada, Nelson (Angels)	213
Rafaela, Ceddanne (Red Sox)	70
Rajcic, Max (Cardinals)	377
Ramirez, Agustin (Yankees)	316
Ramirez, Alex (Mets)	298
Ramirez, Pedro (Cubs)	97
Ramirez, Ramon (Royals)	205
Ramirez Jr., Rafael (Guardians)	140
Ramos, Bryan (White Sox)	102
Ramos, Heliot (Giants)	415
Ramos, Jose (Dodgers)	239
Ray, Dylan (D-backs)	24
Raya, Marco (Twins)	278
Redfield Jr., Joe (Angels)	224
Reed, Carlson (Pirates)	367
Reimer, Jacob (Mets)	299
Restituyo, Bladimir (Rockies)	161
Rhodes, John (Orioles)	64
Rice, Ben (Yankees)	313
Richardson, Lyon (Reds)	123
Ricketts, Caleb (Phillies)	348
Riggio, Roc (Yankees)	319
Rincon, Bryan (Phillies)	343
Rincones Jr., Gabriel (Phillies)	345
Rios, Alberto (Angels)	217

Ritchie, J.R. (Braves)	37
Ritter, Ryan (Rockies)	156
Roa, Christian (Reds)	126
Robberse, Sam (Cardinals)	377
Roberts, Caleb (D-backs)	30
Robertson, Nick (Cardinals)	382
Robinson, Kristian (D-backs)	32
Roby, Tekoah (Cardinals)	373
Roccaforte, Carson (Royals)	202
Rocchio, Brayan (Guardians)	133
Rock, Joe (Rockies)	159
Rocker, Kumar (Rangers)	456
Rodden, Brock (Mariners)	431
Roden, Alan (Blue Jays)	472
Rodriguez, Alberto (Mariners)	429
Rodriguez, Carlos (Brewers)	264
Rodriguez, Emmanuel (Twins)	277
Rodriguez, Hector (Reds)	124
Rodriguez, Jeremy (Mets)	300
Rodriguez, Jose (Twins)	285
Rodriguez, Johnathan (Guardians)	142
Rodriguez, Jose (White Sox)	110
Rodriguez, Yophery (Brewers)	265
Rodriguez-Cruz, Elmer (Red Sox)	80
Rojas, Jefferson (Cubs)	88
Rojas, Kendry (Blue Jays)	471
Rom, Drew (Cardinals)	383
Romero, Mikey (Red Sox)	75
Romo, Drew (Rockies)	152
Rooney, John (Dodgers)	241
Rosario, Alejandro (Rangers)	462
Rosario, Eguy (Padres)	395
Rosario, Kala'i (Twins)	282
Roupp, Landen (Giants)	410
Rucker, Carson (Tigers)	174
Rudick, Matt (Mets)	303
Ruiz, Jorge (Angels)	222
Rumfield, TJ (Yankees)	320
Rushing, Dalton (Dodgers)	229
Rutledge, Jackson (Nationals)	487
Ryan, River (Dodgers)	232

S

Saalfrank, Andrew (D-backs)	33
Saggese, Thomas (Cardinals)	374
Salas, Ethan (Padres)	388
Salinas, Royber (Athletics)	330
Saltiban, Devin (Phillies)	346
Sanchez, Jadiel (Angels)	220
Sandlin, David (Royals)	204
Sanoja, Javier (Marlins)	251
Santa, Alimber (Astros)	192
Santana, Adrian (Rays)	440
Santana, Cristian (Tigers)	176
Santana, Ruben (D-backs)	24
Santos, Dahian (Blue Jays)	476
Sasaki, Shane (Rays)	445
Sauer, Matt (Royals)	206
Scarborough, Caden (Rangers)	464
Schanuel, Nolan (Angels)	212
Schneider, Davis (Blue Jays)	472
Schobel, Tanner (Twins)	279
Schoenwetter, Cole (Reds)	125
Schultz, Noah (White Sox)	101
Schweitzer, Tyler (White Sox)	113
Schwellenbach, Spencer (Braves)	38
Scott, Christian (Mets)	295
Scott II, Victor (Cardinals)	373
Scull, Anthony (Angels)	223
Segura, Enrique (Phillies)	353
Selby, Colin (Pirates)	369
Selvidge, Brock (Yankees)	314
Serna, Jared (Yankees)	317

Serwinowski, Adam (Reds)	126
Severino, Yunior (Twins)	284
Seymour, Carson (Giants)	413
Seymour, Ian (Rays)	443
Shaw, Matt (Cubs)	85
Shaw, Sam (Blue Jays)	480
Shenton, Austin (Rays)	444
Shewmake, Braden (White Sox)	112
Shim, Jun-Seok (Pirates)	365
Showalter, Zack (Cardinals)	382
Silva, Eric (Giants)	413
Simon, Liam (Giants)	417
Simpson, Chandler (Rays)	444
Simpson, Will (Athletics)	337
Sims, Landon (D-backs)	29
Skenes, Paul (Pirates)	356
Slaten, Justin (Red Sox)	80
Smith, Aidan (Mariners)	428
Smith, Cade (Guardians)	143
Smith, Dylan (Tigers)	173
Smith-Shawver, AJ (Braves)	36
Snelling, Robby (Padres)	389
Soderstrom, Tyler (Athletics)	325
Soler, Yassel (D-backs)	28
Solometo, Anthony (Pirates)	358
Soto, Charlee (Twins)	281
Spence, Mitch (Athletics)	336
Spiers, Carson (Reds)	124
Sproat, Brandon (Mets)	297
Stafura, Sammy (Reds)	123
Stephan, Josh (Rangers)	462
Stewart, Sal (Reds)	119
Stone, Gavin (Dodgers)	229
Stowers, Kyle (Orioles)	60
Stuart, Tyler (Mets)	302
Suarez, Santiago (Rays)	442
Suero, Estuar (Pirates)	366
Sugastey, Adrian (Giants)	414
Sullivan, Sean (Rockies)	155
Susac, Daniel (Athletics)	329
Susana, Jarlin (Nationals)	489
Sweeney, Trey (Yankees)	315
Sykora, Travis (Nationals)	490

T

Tait, Eduardo (Phillies)	344
Tarnok, Freddy (Athletics)	335
Tatum, Terrell (White Sox)	109
Tavarez, Ambioris (Braves)	49
Tavera, Braylin (Orioles)	61
Taylor, Andrew (Astros)	185
Taylor, Brayden (Rays)	439
Taylor, Grant (White Sox)	108
Taylor, Troy (Mariners)	432
Teel, Kyle (Red Sox)	69
Tejeda, Enmanuel (Yankees)	319
Tena, Jose (Guardians)	142
Teodo, Emiliano (Rangers)	458
Thomas, Colby (Athletics)	333
Thompson, Matthew (White Sox)	112
Thompson, Sterlin (Rockies)	150
Thorpe, Drew (Padres)	390
Tidwell, Blade (Mets)	295
Tiedemann, Ricky (Blue Jays)	468
Tiger, Izack (Rangers)	461
Toman, Tucker (Blue Jays)	480
Torin, Cristofer (D-backs)	27
Tredwell, Alonzo (Astros)	184
Triantos, James (Cubs)	90
Troy, Tommy (D-backs)	21

U

Ullola, Miguel (Astros)	186
Urbina, Jose (Rays)	442
Urena, Walbert (Angels)	218
Ureña, Engelth (Yankees)	318

V

Valenzuela, Brandon (Padres)	400
Valera, George (Guardians)	135
Valor, Andres (Marlins)	249
VanScoter, Reid (Mariners)	432
Vaquero, Cristhian (Nationals)	488
Vargas, Echedry (Rangers)	459
Vargas, Joendry (Dodgers)	237
Vargas, Jordy (Rockies)	152
Vargas, Marco (Mets)	300
Varland, Gus (Dodgers)	238
Vasil, Mike (Mets)	296
Vasquez, Randy (Padres)	394
Vasquez, Willy (Rays)	446
Vaz, Javier (Royals)	203
Vazquez, Daniel (Royals)	205
Vazquez, Luis (Cubs)	91
Veen, Zac (Rockies)	151
Velasquez, Diego (Giants)	414
Velazquez, Ralphy (Guardians)	136
Veneziano, Anthony (Royals)	198
Veras, Wilfred (White Sox)	107
Vines, Darius (Braves)	42
Vivas, Jorbit (Dodgers)	236
Vradenburg, Brock (Marlins)	252
Vukovich, AJ (D-backs)	27

W

Wagner, Max (Orioles)	60
Wagner, Will (Astros)	187
Walcott, Sebastian (Rangers)	453
Waldrep, Hurston (Braves)	37
Waldron, Matt (Padres)	399
Wallace, Cayden (Royals)	198
Walston, Blake (D-backs)	25
Walters, Andrew (Guardians)	140
Walton, TJayy (Phillies)	346
Warren, Will (Yankees)	312
Watson, Kahlil (Guardians)	141
Watters, Jacob (Athletics)	337
Watts-Brown, Juaron (Blue Jays)	475
Wells, Austin (Yankees)	310
Werner, Trevor (Royals)	209
Whisenhunt, Carson (Giants)	406
Whitcomb, Shay (Astros)	190
White, Owen (Rangers)	454
White, Thomas (Marlins)	245
White, TJ (Nationals)	496
White Jr., Lonnie (Pirates)	364
Whitley, Forrest (Astros)	192
Whitman, Joe (Giants)	410
Wicks, Jordan (Cubs)	87
Wiggins, Jaxon (Cubs)	94
Wilcox, Cole (Rays)	445
Wilken, Brock (Brewers)	264
Williams, Alika (Pirates)	366
Williams, Carson (Rays)	437
Williams, Henry (Royals)	208
Williams, Jett (Mets)	292
Williamson, Ben (Mariners)	427

Wilson, Jacob (Athletics)	325
Wilson, Paul (Tigers)	171
Wilson, Peyton (Royals)	207
Winans, Allan (Braves)	43
Windish, Hogan (Mariners)	432
Winn, Keaton (Giants)	410
Winn, Masyn (Cardinals)	372
Winokur, Brandon (Twins)	283
Wolf, Jackson (Pirates)	365
Wolkow, George (White Sox)	106
Wolters, Blake (Royals)	200
Wood, James (Nationals)	485
Wood, Matt (Brewers)	272
Woods Richardson, Simeon (Twins)	288
Wrobleski, Justin (Dodgers)	234
Wyatt, Hiro (Royals)	206

Y

Yorke, Nick (Red Sox)	72
Young, Cole (Mariners)	420
Young, Jacob (Nationals)	492

Z

Zanetello, Nazzan (Red Sox)	73
Zapata, Gian (D-backs)	31
Zavala, Aaron (Rangers)	457
Zavala, Samuel (Padres)	391
Ziegler, Calvin (Mets)	304
Zobac, Steven (Royals)	207
Zulueta, Yosver (Blue Jays)	473